COMPANY LAW

AUSTRALIA
Law Book Co.
Sydney

CANADA and USA
Carswell
Toronto

HONG KONG
Sweet & Maxwell Asia

NEW ZEALAND
Brookers
Wellington

SINGAPORE and MALAYSIA
Sweet & Maxwell Asia
Singapore and Kuala Lumpur

Company Law

Michael Forde

B.A. (Mod.) and LL.B (Dublin),
LL.M (Brussels)
Ph.D. (Cantab.)
of King's Inns and Middle Temple
Senior Counsel

and

Hugh Kennedy

A.B. (Princeton)
of King's Inns
Barrister-at-Law

THOMSON ROUND HALL
2008

Published in 2008 by
Thomson Round Hall
43 Fitzwilliam Place
Dublin 2
Ireland

Typeset by
Datapage International Limited, Dublin

Printed by
MPG Books, Cornwall

ISBN 978-1-85800-461-7

A catalogue record for this book
is available from the British Library

FOREWORD TO THE FIRST EDITION

The economic, industrial and commercial development of this country has had many consequences. One of these is the ever increasing volume of cases relating to Company Law being decided by the Irish Courts.

Company Law is a vast and complex subject. Legal practitioners, accountants, bankers and businessmen are constantly confronted with problems in solving the different aspects of this subject. Consequently there has been an ever growing need and demand for an Irish treatise on the subject.

In this book *Company Law* Dr Forde has met that need. His book is a scholarly and comprehensive account of this important topic and is written with commendable accuracy and clarity.

In addition to dealing with the provisions of the Companies Act 1963 and the Companies (Amendment) Act 1983 and the volume of case law arising therefrom, this book deals with and draws our attention to particularly significant developments in other jurisdictions, particularly in British Commonwealth countries and the United States of America; it explains the impact of membership of the European Community on the law and highlights the relevance of the Stock Exchange Regulations to the legal practitioners.

This book is an outstanding contribution to Irish legal scholarship, will be of invaluable assistance to those concerned with the subject, and the author is entitled to the congratulations, thanks and support of all interested therein.

Liam Hamilton
President of the High Court

To the Memory of
Pat Murphy (M.F.)
&
David O'Callaghan (H.K.)

PREFACE

Company Law has very significantly expanded since the previous edition, some eight years ago. Seven major Companies Acts have been passed—two in 1999 (dealing mainly with stabilising activities, and with examinership and audit exemptions, respectively); one in 2001 (dealing mainly with aspects of enforcement); one in 2003 (dealing mainly with auditing and accounting); one in 2005 (dealing mainly with prospectuses, and with insider and other securities markets abuses); one in 2006 (dealing mainly with transparency in trading on regulated markets and takeovers); and one in late 2007 (the "MiFI" regime). Several extremely important EC Directives on securities markets behaviour were implemented between 2005 and 2007. The volume of case law continues to grow at a great rate, especially in England (see the Butterworths Company Law Cases, or B.C.L.C.s), where in many respects, the statutory provisions, common law and equitable principles are identical to those in Ireland (at least in theory).

For this 4th edition, we have decided on two versions. Last June there was published a compact version for students, covering all core aspects of the subject. This full or practitioners' version covers (hopefully) every conceivable aspect of the law, and should meet the needs of specialist commercial lawyers, accountants, company secretaries and tax advisors. So that the book is not too unwieldy, a separate volume on insolvency and liquidation is at an advanced stage of preparation. The law is stated as of the end of December 2007.

We perhaps could have covered in greater detail the restriction and disqualification of company directors. But most of the cases in this area turn on their own facts, and the overarching approaches to many issues remain to be laid down by the Supreme Court. It is an area that remains in flux and is more than adequately covered in our colleague Nessa Cahill's very recent *Company Law Compliance and Enforcement* (Haywards Heath: Tottel Publishing, 2008), Chs D and E. Too late for inclusion is the important judgment in *Re Tralee Beef and Lamb Ltd* [2008] I.E.S.C. 1, February 1, 2008, a rare and welcome appeal against a restriction declaration. In allowing the appeal, Hardiman J. described the law governing restriction as "draconian", especially the reverse onus of proof, and castigated the "Delphic posture" of the ODCE in refusing without reason to accede to the liquidator's request for relief from the obligation to seek a restriction there. He says it is unclear how the ODCE could disagree with the liquidator's professional judgment that the director in question had acted honestly and responsibly when the liquidator had the opportunity to question the directors of the company on the affairs of the business. He described as "extraordinary" a law that forces liquidators to spend a company's money bringing restriction applications instead of paying off its creditors. The time may have come for the entire restriction regime (unique to

Ireland) to be revisited by the Oireachtas and perhaps even abolished – an ideal opportunity to do so arises with the long-promised Companies Consolidation and Reform Act.

MF once more thanks Catherine, Patrick, Peter and Sinead for their support while endeavouring to finish the work. HK would like to thank in particular Declan Murphy B.L., Paul Coughlan B.L., Lyndon MacCann S.C. and Brian P. Dempsey S.C. for sharing their expertise and time, as well as his colleagues who have brought to his attention various novel points and unanswered questions of Irish company law. HK has told Kyoko that he won't be doing another project like this for a long time, but for some reason she doesn't believe him. We both wish to express our gratitude to Marie Armah Kwantreng, who worked wonders with the manuscript and kept everyone on the same page, and to the hardworking staff at Round Hall, in particular Stephen Lucek, Maura Smyth and Frieda Donohue. Sadly, the author of the foreword, the Hon. Mr. Justice Liam Hamilton, died in 2000, shortly after he retired as Chief Justice of Ireland.

St. Valentine's Day, 2008

Michael Forde,   Hugh Kennedy,
Mountain View Road,   Law Library,
Dublin 6.   Four Courts,
                                                                  Dublin 7.

TABLE OF CONTENTS

TABLE OF CASES

Irish Cases

English Cases

Scottish Cases

Northern Irish Cases

European Court of Justice Cases

Australian Cases

New Zealand Cases

United States of America Cases

Canadian Cases

French Cases

Indian Cases

International Court of Justice Cases

European Court of Human Rights Cases

European Commission of Human Rights Cases

TABLE OF LEGISLATION

The Irish Constitution

Irish Statutes

Irish Statutory Instruments

English Statutes

Scottish Statutes

European Directives

European Regulations

EC Treaty

European Convention on Human Rights

Australian Statutes

Canadian Statutes

New Zealand Statutes

US Statutes

CHAPTER 1

INTRODUCTORY

1–01 A company is an association of persons constituted for some purpose, generally to carry on a business. It can be an informal arrangement between persons, or it can take the form of a joint venture or a partnership. Where the objective is *not* to make a profit for distribution among the members, a company can take the form of an unincorporated association, a friendly society, a credit union or indeed a trade union. A registered company is an artificial legal device by which rights, powers, privileges and liabilities may be attributed to a fictional entity, equated for many purposes to a natural person. This entity acquires rights and liabilities through the acts of those who control it, its directors and its ultimate controllers, its members or shareholders.[1] Most companies are bodies registered under the Companies Acts 1963–2006[2] and, since 1994, may comprise a single member. Many are established to engage in some industrial or commercial enterprise and are run to make profits for their members. But some are established for non-profit objectives. For corporation-tax purposes, a company includes any corporate body, trustee savings bank, European economic interest group, local authority, vocational education committee and committee of agriculture.[3] There are almost 160,000 companies registered in Ireland, and approximately 300 new companies are registered every week.[4] Since 2007, it has become possible to register an entirely new form of limited company, the *Societas Europoea*.[5]

1–02 There are three main types of registered company. By far the most common is the company formed by a person or a small group of individuals to carry on a business: the "one-person" or "micro" company, or "family" company or "quasi-partnership". These are often referred to as "close companies".[6] A particular type of close company is one set up entirely to hold assets or contracts for tax-planning purposes. Then there are companies formed to enable members of the public to invest in an enterprise known as a public limited company or Plc; many are well-known corporate names and have their shares traded on

---

[1] J. Micklethwait and A. Wooldridge, *The Company: A Short History of a Revolutionary Idea* (London: Phoenix, 2005).

[2] Unofficially consolidated and annotated in L. McCann and T.B. Courtney, *Companies Acts 1963–2006* (Haywards Heath: Tottel Publishing, 2007).

[3] Taxes Consolidation Act, 1997, s.4(1).

[4] Many of these companies are simply members of groups controlled by holding companies.

[5] See para.21–55.

[6] See Ch.13.

the Irish Stock Exchange.[7] Finally, there is the non-profit company, which is established for social or charitable purposes.[8]

ATTRACTIONS OF THE REGISTERED COMPANY

1–03   Individuals may choose to conduct their businesses either in their own names as "sole traders" or under the aegis of registered companies, in which they own all or virtually all the shares. Where a number of persons wish to engage in a business in common, they have the choice principally of either forming a partnership or forming a registered company. If a considerable number of persons are involved, the partnership option is not always available to them. Among the principal advantages of the sole trader and the partnership forms are that they do not need any special formalities or expenditures to be established. One becomes a sole trader simply by virtue of trading on one's own behalf, while the mere fact of doing business in common with others with a view to making some profit constitutes a partnership.

1–04   There are a number of distinct advantages in running a business under the registered company form,[9] arising principally from the company's separate legal personality. A registered company has a legal identity that is entirely distinct from that of its owners. A sole trader's business is part of his own property, and its obligations and debts are also that trader's own personal liabilities. A partnership is merely an association of the individual partners; its assets and liabilities are in law those of its members.[10] By contrast, a registered company exists in law entirely separately from its members or shareholders; company assets belong to it, not to the shareholders, and the shareholders are not directly answerable for the company's liabilities. Legal proceedings are brought by or against the company in its own name. The separate legal personality of companies, therefore, enables business persons to segregate their own private affairs from their business, and also to segregate the affairs of their various businesses that are conducted under the aegis of different companies.

Entity Shielding

1–05   The most distinctive feature of the registered company is that it secures what may be described as entity shielding or affirmative asset partitioning.[11] Incorporation insulates entirely claims by creditors of any of its members or shareholders against the assets of the company. Its property and business is thus not radically affected as a matter of law by the insolvency of one or more of its owners. Their own creditors' redress is only against their personal assets.

---

[7]   See Ch.15.

[8]   See para.16–02.

[9]   *cf.* Freedman, "Small Businesses and the Corporate Form: Burden or Privilege?" 57 *Mod. L. Rev.* 555 (1994).

[10]   R.C. l'Anson Banks (ed.), *Lindley and Banks on Partnership,* 18th edn (London: Sweet & Maxwell, 2002).

[11]   See generally, Hansman & Kraakman, "The Essential Role of Organisation Law" 10 *Yale L.J.* 387 (2000).

Those creditors have no redress whatsoever against the company's assets, although the insolvent member's shares in the company may be a realisable asset of his if they are easily transferable.[12]

Owner Shielding

1–06 For most companies, that aspect is complemented by what may be described as owner shielding or negative asset partitioning, in the form of limited liability.[13] "Limited liability" means that the liability of a company's owners (i.e. the shareholders or members) for debts incurred by their company is subject to a limit or ceiling: those owners cannot be held personally responsible for its debts beyond that limit. This limit is one the owners agreed to when establishing the company or when acquiring shares in it. If the company's shares are fully paid up, shareholders cannot then be held personally responsible for any of its debts; in companies limited by shares, shareholders' liability is limited to the amount remaining unpaid on their shares. Thus, where Paddy owns €1 fully paid-up share in Craggy Co. Ltd, if the company is wound up as insolvent, its creditors cannot claim against him for any of the company's unpaid debts. But if only 60c was paid up on those €1 shares, then his liability to the company, and through it to its creditors, is the 40c outstanding on every share that he holds.

1–07 This method of separating business persons' and investors' personal wealth from the fortunes of their enterprises is designed to encourage them to take business risks, without which a capitalist economy and society would stagnate. Limited liability sees to it that if the particular enterprise fails, its owners' other wealth is not called upon to satisfy unpaid business creditors. The privilege of limited liability gained by forming a company is not a fundamental constitutional or human right, but is a right granted to save members from having to seek limitation of liability by more rudimentary methods under contract law. The following justifications have been given for having limited liability[14]:

> "(i) Limited liability decreases the need for shareholders to monitor those who direct companies in which they invest because the financial consequences of company failure are limited. Shareholders may have neither the incentive (particularly if they have only a small shareholding) nor the expertise to monitor the actions of managers. The potential costs of operating companies are reduced because limited liability makes shareholder diversification and passivity a more rational strategy.
>
> (ii) Limited liability provides incentives to managers to act efficiently and in the interests of shareholders by promoting the free transfer of

---

[12] See para.9–53.

[13] See generally, Easterbrook and Fischel, "Limited Liability and the Corporation" 52 *U. Chicago L. Rev.* 89 (1985) and B. Cheffins, *Company Law: Theory, Structure and Operation* (Oxford: Clarendon Press, 1997), p.497 *et seq.*

[14] Ramsay, "Allocating Liability in Corporate Groups: An Australian Perspective" 13 *Conn. J. Int'l L.* 329 (1999) at 341.

shares. This argument has two parts to it. First, the free transfer of shares is promoted by limited liability because under this principle, the wealth of other shareholders is irrelevant. If a principle of unlimited liability applied, the value of shares would be determined partly by the wealth of shareholders. In other words, the price at which an individual shareholder might purchase a share would be determined in liability. The second part of the argument is derived from the fact that if a company is being managed inefficiently, shareholders can be expected to be selling their shares at a discount to the price which would exist if the company were being managed efficiently. This creates the possibility of a takeover of the company and the replacement of the incumbent management.

(iii) Limited liability assists the efficient operation of the securities markets because, as was observed in (ii), the prices at which shares trade does not depend upon an evaluation of the wealth of individual shareholders.

(iv) Limited liability permits efficient diversification by shareholders which in turn allows shareholders to reduce their individual risk. If a principle of unlimited liability applied and a shareholder could lose his or her entire wealth by reason of the failure of one company, shareholders would have an incentive to minimise the number of shares held in different companies and insist on a higher return from their investment because of the higher risk they would face. Consequently, limited liability not only allows diversification but permits companies to raise capital at lower costs because of the reduced risk faced by shareholders.

(v) Limited liability facilitates optimal investment decisions by managers. As we have seen, limited liability provides incentives to shareholders to hold diversified portfolios. Under such circumstances, managers should invest in projects with positive net present values and can do so without exposing each shareholder to the loss of his or her personal wealth. However, if a principle of unlimited liability applied, managers might reject some investments with positive present values on the basis that the risk to shareholders was thereby reduced. By definition this would be a social loss, because projects with a positive net present value are beneficial uses of capital."

1–08 A major concern of company law is to prevent limited liability from being abused. It is an offence for a person or a body other than a registered limited company to carry on business with the words "limited" or "ltd", or their Irish equivalent in its name.[15]

Transferable Interest

1–09 A registered company is comprised of members, who usually are shareholders.[16] All that shareholders who wish to liquidate their investment in

---

[15] Section 381 of the 1963 Act.

[16] There are companies which have members who are not shareholders; they are one category of guarantee company—see below, para.16–06.

their company need do is to sell their shares. This transaction can be effected quite simply; it does not require the assistance of a lawyer and causes no legal disruption to the running of the business. A sole trader who wishes to dispose of his business must execute conveyances and other elaborate contracts. As a general rule, a partnership must come to an end whenever any one partner retires.[17] The transferable share in a registered company is an administratively simple way of attracting further investment in the company. All the company seeking more capital needs to do is allot additional shares in return for cash or other assets to those willing to invest in it.[18] Where a company's shares are quoted on a stock exchange, its shareholders are guaranteed liquidity.[19] However, the transferability of shares in many private companies is severely restricted by those companies' own regulations.[20] Companies may be used as structures for collective investment schemes, to which investors are invited to subscribe by taking up shares. Such investment companies attract special regulation over and above that of other companies.[21]

Continuous Existence

1–10 When a sole trader dies, his business comes to an end. It may be sold off to satisfy claims by the estate or it may be transferred under the deceased's will. On the death of any partner, generally the partnership is automatically dissolved.[22] By contrast, a company never dies but continues in existence until it is wound up. Therefore, the business is not disrupted to any like extent when the principal or even the sole shareholder dies as when the sole trader or a partner dies. In the case of a registered company, the actual business continues to remain in the same ownership and it is only the company's shares that change hands following the death. Some companies are formed to act as trustees. A trustee in corporate form obviates the inconvenience of having to appoint new trustees when human trustees die or become unable to act.

The Floating Charge

1–11 There is one important method of securing borrowing, thereby financing the business, which in practice is available only to registered companies—the floating charge.[23] A fixed or specific charge involves giving fixed assets of a business (i.e. land, buildings and the like) as security for loans. In contrast, a floating charge involves providing the debtor's floating assets as security, i.e. assets acquired to be used up in various ways in the business and that ultimately may be disposed of in the course of the business. Some businesses may

---

[17] R.C. l'Anson Banks (ed.), *Lindley and Banks on Partnership*, 18th edn (London: Sweet & Maxwell, 2002), Ch.24.

[18] See para.8–21 *et seq.*

[19] From June 18, 2007, the Irish Stock Exchange has implemented a "free-float" based methodology when calculating indices: see www.ise.ie.

[20] See para.9–55 *et seq.*

[21] See para.20–57 *et seq.*

[22] R.C. l'Anson Banks (ed.), *Lindley & Banks on Partnership*, 18th edn (London: Sweet & Maxwell, 2002), Ch.24.

[23] See para.16–29 *et seq.*

have a high proportion of floating assets, and so giving a floating charge is a most attractive way to finance their activities. On account of provisions of the Bills of Sale Acts and, until 1988, the Bankruptcy Acts, it is very difficult for sole traders and partnerships to resort to this method of secured financing.[24]

Regulated Industries

1–12   To participate in some commercial activities, it may be necessary to be a registered company, e.g. to obtain Central Bank approval to operate a stock exchange.[25] In practical terms, it may be impossible to carry on certain businesses in regulated environments other than through such companies. On the other hand, some professions are not allowed to be practised by registered companies, for instance that of auditors and solicitors.

Co-Enjoyment of Property

1–13   A company may provide a suitable structure for co-ownership of property. In recent times, arrangements for giving individual ownership of apartments and flats in multi-unit complexes, and the right to enjoy common areas in such structures, has in Ireland taken the form of the company. The memorandum and articles of association of such companies allocate individual rights over a given property by attaching rights to a particular class of shares identified with the property. It is hoped that in future legislation will provide better, specially designed vehicles, as part of the law of property, to serve the needs of apartment-owners.[26]

Fiscal Considerations

1–14   Company incomes and chargeable gains are subject to corporation tax, rather than to income tax and capital gains tax.[27] The company mode of doing business, as opposed to the sole trader or the partnership, may have certain advantages from a taxation point of view.[28] Over the years, taxation has played a major role in the choice of a company as a vehicle to either carry on a trade or receive income. At different points along the way the divergence between corporate rates and personal tax rates has been substantial. In the mid-1970s corporation tax rates varied between 40 per cent and 50 per cent, while personal tax rates were as high as 80 per cent. In those circumstances the ability to shelter income in a corporate, rather than personal, capacity was a major tax planning point. The ratio between corporate and personal rates has since then varied. At present, the standard corporate rate is 12.5 per cent while top personal rates are 42 per cent plus various

---

[24]   See M. Forde, *Commercial Law*, 3rd edn (Haywards Heath: Tottel Publishing, 2005), pp.211–215.

[25]   European Communities (Markets in Financial Instruments) Regulations 2007 (SI 2007/60) reg.48(a).

[26]   See *Consultation Paper on Multi-Unit Developments* (Law Reform Commission, 2006).

[27]   See generally M. Feeney, *The Taxation of Companies* (Haywards Heath: Tottel Publishing, 2006).

[28]   *cf.* Chittenden & Sloan, "Quantifying Inequity in the Taxation of Individuals and Small Firms" [2007] *Brit. Tax Rev.* 58.

levies, which is a substantial differential. A director must take sufficient income from the company to meet his normal living expenses and on those drawings he will pay a personal tax rate. Income over and above that level can be sheltered at the lower rates. There is a higher rate of 25 per cent for certain types of corporate income and for profits from dealing in development land, working minerals and petroleum activities.[29] In the case of close companies, certain expenses and interest paid to participators, and loans granted to them are treated as their income.[30] Any undistributed income of close "service companies" and also undistributed investment income of close companies are subject to surcharges.[31]

1–15   Several tax incentives are available only to companies or in respect of them; most notably manufacturing relief and the Business Expansion Scheme.[32] Taxation rules governing pension contributions are more generous for company directors than they are for self-employed persons. In addition, it is much easier to offer incentive schemes in a tax-efficient manner to employees of companies than to employees in a sole business or a partnership. These can vary from bonus payments to share incentive schemes. From a capital tax point of view, there are major benefits in trading as a company. It is easier to move small elements of the enterprise where one is dealing with a company; it suffices to earmark an appropriate number of shares and have them transferred. The ability to transfer equity or value of a company while retaining control through voting shares, which otherwise carry little or no value, has been a major feature of capital tax arrangements for decades.

Disadvantages

1–16   There also are certain drawbacks in doing business or conducting other activities in the form of a registered company. A company's managers are subject to extensive regulation under the Companies Acts in the manner in which decisions are to be taken, relations with outsiders and, where applicable, costly compliance with notification, auditing and accounting requirements. If the business gets into financial difficulties, its directors are legally obliged to take due account of the creditors' interests. If the business happens to fail, the directors are subject to the rigours of the formal winding-up process, and they may be made subject to restriction and disqualification orders, and criminal charges.

ALTERNATIVE STRUCTURES

1–17   Where those who associate for the purpose of carrying on some business and to profit thereby do not organise their affairs in the form of a registered

---

[29]   Feeney, above, fn.27, p.45 *et seq.*
[30]   Feeney, above, fn.27, p.1236 *et seq.*
[31]   Feeney, above, fn.27, p.1254 *et seq.*
[32]   Feeney, above, fn.27, p.746 *et seq.*

company, alternative structures exist that may suffice in their circumstances. For the purpose of the Competition Acts 2002–2006, companies and most other types of business organisation are "undertakings".

Partnership

1–18   What in law constitutes a partnership is defined broadly in s.1(1) of the Partnership Act 1890 as "the relation which subsists between persons carrying on a business in common with a view to profit".[33] The mere existence of such a relationship is sufficient to create a partnership[34] and there is no necessity to have any formal agreement or deed of partnership—although some formality in this regard is desirable to avoid future disputes. Partners may be individuals or incorporated bodies, or a combination of them. Except on questions where the partners have otherwise agreed, the incidents of their relationship are governed by the provisions of the 1890 Act.

1–19   Ever since incorporation of a business by registration became possible in 1844, the law has discouraged over-large partnerships.[35] Their size is restricted, in that an association of persons in excess of the prescribed number may only carry on their business as a registered company or under some other statutory regime, such as an industrial or provident society.[36] The numerical limit laid down is 20 partners, an exception being made for a banking business. Further exceptions were made for accountants and for solicitors, and the Minister is empowered to exempt other types of business as well.[37] In 2004, the Minister declared that s.376 would not apply to limited partnerships with not more than 50 partners providing investment and loan finance services to persons engaged in industrial or commercial activities.[38]

1–20   Partnerships do not have a legal personality separate from that of their members, so partnership property is not owned by the association as such but by its members collectively, who are obliged to use it for the purpose of their common enterprise. In general, each partner is an agent for the others in concluding contracts on behalf of their enterprise. Partnership incomes and chargeable gains are governed by income tax and capital gains tax rules, not corporation tax.[39] A distinctive feature of partnerships, which explains why risk-taking ventures usually do not adopt this form, is unlimited liability: if the common business becomes insolvent, then each partner is liable for its entire unpaid

---

[33]   R.C. l'Anson Banks (ed.), *Lindley & Banks on Partnership*, 18th edn (London: Sweet & Maxwell, 2002) M. Blachett-Ord, *Partnership – The Modern Law of Partnership and Limited Liability Partnership*, 2nd edn (London: Butterworths, 2002; reprinted Haywards Heath: Tottel Publishing, 2007) and M. Twomey, *Partnership Law* (Dublin: Butterworths, 2000).

[34]   e.g. *M. Young Legal Associates Ltd v Zahid Solicitors* [2006] 1 W.L.R. 2562.

[35]   The policy gave outsiders dealing with them the benefit of disclosures to regulatory authorities that are required of a company and other artificial entities: *Smith v Anderson* (1880) 15 Ch. D 247 at 273.

[36]   1963 Act, s.376.

[37]   1982 Act, 5.13.

[38]   Companies (Amendment) Act 1982 (Section 13(2)) Order 2004 (SI 2004/506).

[39]   Taxes Consolidation Act 1997, Pt 43 (ss.1007–1013).

debts. Such assets as the insolvent partnership has are applied first to meet the claims of the partnership creditors; where those assets are insufficient, each partner becomes personally liable, without limit. Nor do partnerships enjoy full entity shielding. Where individual partners become insolvent, their personal assets are applied first to meet their own debts but, where those are insufficient, the partner's creditors have recourse to the entire partnership assets.

1–21 Unlimited liability of partners can be avoided under the Limited Partnership Act 1907, which allows what may be described as "sleeping partners" to limit their liability, i.e. partners who do not take any active part in running the business. All limited partnerships must register with the Registrar of Companies, to whom various details of charges on partnership assets must be forwarded.

1–22 The Investment Limited Partnership Act 1994 was enacted principally to enable collective investment fund managers in the State to offer collective investment opportunities to US-based investors in an attractive and convenient form. Bodies may be established under this Act if authorised by the Central Bank, which under the auspices of the Irish Financial Services Regulatory Authority supervises their activities.

1–23 Certain partnerships have been made subject to some provisions of the Companies Acts in respect of accounts and audit. Those are partnerships comprised of companies limited by shares or by guarantee, where any other members are limited partners.[40]

Joint Venture

1–24 Although many joint ventures are structured in the form of registered companies and most others are partnerships, it is possible to have such an arrangement that is not incorporated and that falls outside the partnership definition. The term "joint venture" may have different meanings, but generally indicates several persons participating in a single project rather than an ongoing business. An example of this would be unincorporated mining joint ventures in Australia, where the common activity falls short of realising the product of the participants' common venture.[41] An attraction of this arrangement is that each party is treated as an independent taxpayer and also none of the parties is deemed to be an agent capable of binding the others. Cross-border joint ventures within the EC can take the form of a European economic interest grouping, which is a corporate entity but without limited liability.

Industrial and Provident Society

1–25 Some major businesses, especially in the food sector, are not registered companies but, instead, come under the Industrial and Provident Societies Acts

---

[40] European Communities (Accounts) Regulations 1993 (SI 1993/396).
[41] See generally, Merralls, "Mining and Petroleum Joint Ventures in Australia—Some Basic Legal Concepts" 62 *Australian L.J.* 907 (1988).

1893–1978.[42] Several of the large UK-based "mutual" insurers also take this form. In recent years, however, the trend has been towards these shedding that legal status and becoming registered companies, or putting their main businesses into registered companies.

1–26 Industrial and provident societies are essentially cooperatives, although the rules of some of them diverge significantly from the cooperative or mutual ideal. As originally envisaged, these were "industrial", in the sense that they made profits by the mutual exertion of their members, and they were "provident", in that they provided for their members' futures. Often trading would be restricted to the society's own members—for instance the many dairy cooperatives that were scattered around the country. Usually shareholdings were limited in size and dividends were calculated not on a percentage of shareholding but on the amount of business each member had done with the society in the relevant period. Moreover, since the society traded mainly with its members, the objective was not to charge the optimum price to earn large profits for distribution. Often prices were kept lower than the maximum obtainable in the market and the members-customers gained in that way, rather than through payment of dividends. Usually share capital was readily withdrawable, so that the paid-up capital fluctuated from time to time. The "fundamental nature" of these bodies was described by McCarthy J. in *Kerry Co-Operative Creameries Ltd v An Bord Bainne Co-Operative Ltd* as:

> "contrast[ing] with a company of limited liability in that its shareholders invest their efforts in the betterment of activity with each other being persons of a like interest, rather than their seeking a return on investment capital, which is the role of the investor in a company of limited liability; the latter is indifferent to the operation of the company so long as he is assured of an adequate return on his investment. The development of industrial and provident societies, including agricultural co-operatives, is one of the happier features of the Victorian age."[43]

1–27 Although these societies tend to be confined to certain sectors, they can exist in all parts of the economy. The 1893 Act allows persons who are "carrying on any industries, businesses or trades specified in or authorised by [their] rules, whether wholesale or retail, and including dealings of any description with lands" to register under its provisions.[44] Every society has to register its own rules, the contents of which are summarised in the Second Schedule to that Act. These resemble the memorandum and articles of association of registered companies. No individual member is permitted to have more than €150,000 of the share capital or an amount equal to one per cent of the total assets of the society, whichever is the greater,[45] but the rules of a society may reduce this ceiling on shareholdings. Like in most registered companies, the members of these societies enjoy limited liability and, once it is duly registered, every society acquires

---

[42] See generally, I. Snaith, *The Law of Cooperatives* (London: Waterlow, 1984).
[43] [1991] I.L.R.M. 851 (S.C.) at 863.
[44] Section 4.
[45] Section 85 of the Investment Funds, Companies and Miscellaneous Provisions Act 2005.

corporate personality, with perpetual succession, its own seal and power to sue and capacity to be sued in its own name. The registering authority for these bodies is the Registrar of Friendly Societies.

1–28 For over 100 years, it has been possible to wind up industrial and provident societies through the machinery of the Companies Acts.[46] Numerous other provisions of these Acts have been applied to such societies.[47] These bodies, by special resolution, may convert into registered companies; also companies may convert into industrial and provident societies.[48]

Building Society

1–29 In the nineteenth century, numerous societies were formed as self-help mutual funds for their members. Many of these registered under the Friendly Societies Acts, often as loan fund societies, collecting societies and building societies. With the advent of social insurance in 1911, the role for such societies significantly diminished, leading to the dissolution of several.[49] But one category of society continues to play an important role in the economy, the building society. The regime governing these was radically overhauled in the Building Societies Acts 1989–2006, which subject societies to extensive regulation by the Irish Financial Services Regulatory Authority and to rules often identical to those in the Companies Acts.[50] Building societies can be wound up under these Acts.[51] They may convert into public limited companies.[52]

Trust

1–30 An enterprise involving the contribution of capital by two or more persons can be structured as a trust.[53] Such arrangements are most unusual outside non-profit activities (e.g. private hospitals, the GAA and the IRFU, and political parties) and also the financial services sector, where there are trustee savings banks,[54] pensions trusts,[55] unit trusts[56] and trust-like entities such as common contractual funds[57] and undertakings for collective investment in

---

[46] *Re Independent Protestant Loan Fund Soc.* [1895] 1 I.R. 1; *cf. Re Devon and Somerset Farmers Ltd* [1994] 1 B.C.L.C. 99.

[47] e.g. Companies Act 1990, ss.159 (disqualification) and 182 (audit).

[48] 1893 Act, ss.54 and 55.

[49] e.g. *Tierney v Tough* [1914] 1 I.R. 142.

[50] See generally, T. Lloyd et al, *Wurtzburg & Mills: Building Society Law*, 15th edn (London: Sweet & Maxwell, 1989).

[51] 1989 Act, s.109.

[52] Pt XII (ss.100–108) of the 1989 Act, as amended in 2006.

[53] See generally, G. Thomas et al, *The Law of Trusts* (Oxford: Oxford U.P., 2004) Chs 53–55 and M. Graziadei, *Commercial Trusts in European Private Law* (Cambridge: Cambridge U.P., 2005).

[54] Trustee Savings Banks Acts 1989–2001.

[55] Pt VI (ss.59–64) of the Pensions Act 1990.

[56] Unit Trusts Act 1990.

[57] Pt 2 (ss.6–21) of the Investment Funds, Companies and Miscellaneous Provisions Act 2005.

transferable securities.[58] In recent years trading trusts as a form of business organisation have attained some prominence in Australia[59]; in the US they are known as "Massachusetts trusts".[60] A commercial trust resembles the private family trust, where the participants' assets are vested in a trustee, who manages the enterprise on their behalf and subject to their wishes. If, however, the trust instrument gives the beneficiaries extensive authority to direct the trustee, the relationship between them becomes one of agency, as well as beneficiary-*cestui*, thereby exposing the participants to unlimited liability. Usually the trustee in commercial trusts is a registered company.

Statutory Corporation

1–31   Several state-owned and managed businesses are statutory corporations, established under their own constitutive statutes, for instance the Electricity Supply Board and the Voluntary Health Insurance Board.

THE PATH TO THE MODERN COMPANY

1–32   The registered company as we know it came into existence in 1844. In 1855, companies were first permitted to register with limited liability. Prior to then,[61] the principal institution through which persons pooled capital and other factors for the purpose of doing business was the partnership and its derivative, the deed of settlement company. There were other legal forms within which persons could do business, most notably the chartered company and the statutory company; but those were available only to the very wealthy and privileged. One variant of the statutory company that became comparatively common by the middle of the nineteenth century was the public utility company, such as railways and waterworks companies, established under the Companies Clauses Acts.[62]

Corporations Sole

1–33   Mention should be made of the corporation sole, meaning certain offices that are legally distinct from the persons who occupy them from time to time. Traditionally, bishops and other occupants of important religious offices had this status, and the property in their name, in this capacity, was not

---

[58] European Communities (Undertakings for Collective Investment in Transferable Securities) Regulations 2003 (SI 2003/211).

[59] See Ford and Hardingham, "Trading Trusts: Rights and Liabilities of Beneficiaries" in *Equity and Commercial Relationships* (P.D. Finn (ed.), Law Book Company of Australasia, 1987), Ch.3; Ford, "Trading Trusts and Creditors' Rights" 13 *Melbourne U.L. Rev.* 1 (1981); and McPherson, "The Insolvent Trading Trust" in *Essays in Equity* (P.D. Finn (ed.), Law Book Company of Australasia, 1985), Ch.8.

[60] Discussed in *Inside Scoop Inc v Curry* 755 F. Supp. 426 (D.D.C., 1989).

[61] An excellent account is contained in P.L. Davies, *Gower and Davies' Principles of Modern Company Law*, 7th edn (London: Sweet & Maxwell, 2003). See also B.C. Hunt, *The Development of the Business Corporation in England, 1800–1867* (Cambridge, Mass.: Harvard U.P., 1936) and Horwitz, "Historical Development of Company Law" 62 *L.Q.R.* 375 (1946).

[62] Acts of 1845 (8 and 9 Vic. c. 16, 17, 18 and 20) and of 1847 (10 and 11 Vic. c. 15, 17 and 27).

theirs beneficially; on their being succeeded in the office, the property would vest in their successors. In the United Kingdom, the monarch is a corporation sole. Under the Ministers and Secretaries Act 1924, every Government Minister is a corporation sole. Holders of numerous other public offices are designated as corporations sole, for instance the Director of Corporate Enforcement.[63]

Chartered Corporations

1–34 In the past, one way of obtaining legal autonomy for an enterprise was by having it constituted by a royal charter; the charter would establish an incorporated body that was legally distinct from its members. In *Re Commercial Buildings Co. of Dublin*[64] Johnston J. described how the former Commercial Buildings Company, which was located in Dublin's Dame Street where the Central Bank now stands, obtained its charter:

> "In 1797 a number of business men in the City of Dublin formed themselves into a voluntary society for the purpose of 'the founding of buildings to be appropriated to 'the convenience of commercial dealing and intercourse within the City of Dublin.' These gentlemen bore names which are to this day well known and honoured in commercial and professional circles in this city names such as Nathaniel Hone, Randal MacDonnell, Joshua Pim, Richard Verschoyle, George Maquay and others – and on their application it was referred by Lord Camden, the Lord Lieutenant of the day, to the Attorney-General and Solicitor-General to inquire whether a royal charter ought to be granted. The Attorney-General of the day was none other than Arthur Wolfe, who subsequently became the ill-fated Lord Kilwarden, whilst the Solicitor-General was none other than John Toler, who later was raised to the peerage as Lord Norbury, and became known to fame as 'the hanging judge'. These gentlemen reported in favour of the scheme, and a royal charter was granted on January 1st 1798, erecting a corporation under the name of 'The Commercial Buildings Company of Dublin', with very extensive powers, including that of making bye-laws. The first of these byelaws ordained that the common seal of the company should be 'kept in an iron repository at the office of the said company, to which there shall be three good locks, each of which shall be materially different in its internal construction from the others', and the keepers of the keys should be three directors of the company, each being responsible for one key.
>
> The commercial building, as we all know, was built on a plot of ground on the North side of Dame Street, ground granted to the Company by the commissioners of Wide Streets, a statutory body which did so much in the eighteenth century to make Dublin the beautiful city that it is today."[65]

---

[63] Section 7(4) of the Company Law Enforcement Act 2001 says that "[t]he Director [of Corporate Enforcement] shall be a corporation sole and, notwithstanding any casual vacancy in the office from time to time, shall have perpetual succession and shall be capable in his or her corporate name of holding and disposing of real or personal property and of suing and being sued."

[64] [1938] I.R. 477.

[65] [1938] I.R. 477 at 480.

1–35   The great majority of existing chartered bodies were established for other than business purposes. An example of a chartered non-profit corporation is the Law Society of Ireland; it was founded for "facilitating the acquisition of legal knowledge, and for the better and more conveniently discharging of [solicitors'] professional duties".[66] Other such bodies include Dublin University[67] and the Royal College of Surgeons.[68] No new chartered corporations were established after the State was founded in 1922, but Acts of the Oireachtas have been passed on several occasions amending the terms of existing charters.[69]

1–36   The Bank of Ireland is perhaps the most prominent of those bodies in private ownership, tracing its origin to the Act for Establishing the Bank of Ireland of 1781–1782,[70] and a charter issued under the terms of that Act.[71] Several amendments have since been made to the Bank's charter, all by way of legislation. Private Acts of the Oireachtas were passed in 1929 and in 1935[72] which altered the charter so as to prevent the Bank from being taken over without the Minister of Finance's consent and also introducing limited liability for the Bank's shareholders. Further changes to the charter were made by the Central Bank Acts, including removing the restriction on a takeover.

1–37   Before the "Glorious" Revolution of 1688, it was the Crown that issued charters, so that entrepreneurs would have had to exercise considerable political influence in order to get their enterprises constituted in this manner. Subsequently, Parliament sought to control the issuing of charters, and it established the practice of passing special legislation authorising the Crown to charter a particular body. By the nineteenth century it was almost unheard of for commercial undertakings to be chartered, which heightened the demand for some other form of company. In the 1830s legislation was enacted authorising the Crown by letters patent to confer the privileges of incorporation in place of a full-blown charter.[73] For a time, a major method of establishing commercial companies was by letters patent and it still remains the predominant mode in some Canadian provinces.[74] Several provisions of the Companies Acts apply to chartered companies established under a private Act, other than those with non-profit objectives and those exempted by the Minister.[75] Bodies have been found to be incorporated by prescription, by a royal charter that has been lost, if for a long enough time they have been treated as though they were incorporated.[76]

---

[66]   Society's Charter of 1852.
[67]   cf. *Trinity College Dublin v Commissioners for Valuation* [1919] 2 I.R. 493.
[68]   cf. *Miley v Attorney-General* [1918] 1 I.R. 455.
[69]   e.g. Universities Act 1997.
[70]   21 & 22 Geo. III, c. 16.
[71]   Charter issued on May 10, 1783 and enrolled in the Court of Chancery of Ireland on May 15, 1783.
[72]   Bank of Ireland Acts of 1929 (No. 4, private) and 1935 (No. 1, private).
[73]   Trading Companies Act 1834 (4 & 5 Will. IV, c. 94).
[74]   See B. Welling, *Corporate Law in Canada: The Governing Principles*, 3rd edn (Australia: Scribblers Publishing, 2006), Ch.2.
[75]   1963 Act, s.377.
[76]   *Re Company or Fraternity of Free Fishermen of Faversham* (1887) 36 Ch.D. 329.

Statutory Corporations

1–38 Statutory corporations are companies established by special legislation other than under the Companies Acts 1963–2006 and their predecessors. A little-known example is the proprietor of the Mount Jerome cemetery in Dublin, which was established by a private Act of Parliament in 1834[77] and was the subject of a private Act of the Oireachtas, the Dublin General Cemetery Company's Act 1933.

1–39 Most statutory corporations today that engage in commercial or industrial activity are state-owned or public corporations like the Central Bank,[78] the Electricity Supply Board,[79] the Irish Gas Board,[80] Radio Telefís Éireann,[81] Coras Iompair Éireann[82] and the Voluntary Health Insurance Board.[83] However, not all state-owned public utilities and business ventures are established in this manner.[84] Many are companies registered under the Companies Acts but whose internal regulations contain various provisions specified in the legislation which authorised registration of the company in question.[85] For instance, under the Postal and Telecommunications Services Act 1983, the Minister was required to arrange for two limited companies, named An Post (or the Post Office) and Bord Telecom Éireann (or The Irish Telecommunications Board) to be formed and registered under the Companies Acts. That Act then went on to set out in considerable detail the principal features of these two companies, their authorised share capital, their principal objects, the contents of their articles of association, the issue of and subscription for shares in them. In 1999 its telecommunications business was privatised.[86] Several provisions of the Companies Acts apply to statutory corporations established by a private Act, other than those with non-profit objectives and those exempted by the Minister.[87]

1–40 In the past, special Acts of Parliament were enacted to establish public utilities which, subject to numerous restrictions, were run as private enterprises. Eventually, rather than pass separate statutes constituting each individual utility being set up, Acts known as Companies Clauses Acts[88] were enacted. These established common rules for the various categories of utilities, and they were supplemented by Acts establishing common rules unique to particular utilities, such as the Lands Clauses Consolidation Act of 1845,[89] the

---

[77] 4 & 5 Will. c. 65.
[78] Central Bank Acts 1942–2004, esp. 1942 Act, s.5 and 1971 Act, s.51.
[79] Electricity (Supply) Acts 1927–2001, esp. 1927 Act, s.2.
[80] Gas Acts 1976–1998, esp. 1976 Act, s.7.
[81] Broadcasting Authority Acts 1960–2007, esp. 1960 Act, s.3.
[82] Transport Acts 1950–1987, esp. 1950 Act, s.5.
[83] Voluntary Health Insurance Act 1957, esp. s.3.
[84] See Goulding, "The Juristic Basis of Irish State Enterprise" 13 *Ir. Jur.* 302 (1978).
[85] See para.16–34 *et seq*.
[86] Postal and Telecommunications Services (Amendment) Act 1999.
[87] 1963 Act, s.377.
[88] *cf.* Companies Clauses Consolidation Act 1845, 8 & 9 Vict., c. 16.
[89] 8 & 9 Vict., c. 18; consolidated again by 32 & 33 Vict., c. 8. 1869.

Railway Clauses Consolidation Act of 1846[90] and the numerous Gasworks
Clauses Acts.[91] Under the Gas Regulation Act 1982, any private organisation
which supplies gas is empowered to adopt a memorandum and articles of association and, thereby, several of the main provisions of the Companies Acts then
apply to those bodies. This was enacted principally to facilitate the re-organi-
sation of the Alliance and Dublin Gas Consumers Company, which was a deed
of settlement company.[92]

Deed of Settlement Companies

1–41   In 1720, the "Bubble Act" of the British Parliament[93] sought to regulate the growing phenomenon of entrepreneurs purporting to establish incorporated trading associations, the shares of which were freely transferable and
some of which even claimed limited liability. It was a somewhat clumsily
drafted measure and precisely what it sought to achieve is far from clear. Its
central thrust appears to have been to forbid the establishment of incorporated
trading associations, i.e. joint business enterprises where it was sought to segregate the assets and liabilities of the businesses from those of their owners. Its
enactment undermined public confidence in many companies, led to extensive
litigation aimed at having the charters of numerous existing companies forfeited, all of which caused a collapse in share prices and a long business reces-
sion. Thereafter it became increasingly difficult for entrepreneurs to obtain
royal charters or legislative backing for incorporating their undertakings; the
letters patent system was not introduced until the 1830s. Business venturers
and their legal advisers, accordingly, began to experiment with a new form of
business organisation.

1–42   The deed of settlement company is a hybrid of a partnership and a trust.
Entrepreneurs would associate for some common business objective but,
instead of drafting up articles of partnership to govern their relationship, they
would have drawn up something more akin to a trust deed. Unlike the registered company or the chartered or statutory company, however, the deed of settlement company was not completely segregated from its owners. That
company could neither sue nor be sued in its own name; save in exceptional
circumstances, suit had to be brought in the name of or against all the company's members, which became virtually impossible where there was a large
number of members whose identity changed frequently. Nor could members of
a deed of settlement company limit their liability in respect of its debts,
although the constituting instruments of many such companies used to
stipulate that their members' liability was limited.

1–43   While this form of doing business is virtually extinct today,[94] it has
had a profound influence on the development of our company law by placing

---

[90]   8 & 9 Vict., c. 20.
[91]   e.g. 10 & 11 Vict., c. 15, 1847 and 34 & 34 Vict., c. 41, 1871.
[92]   10 & 11 Vict., c. xiii, 1847, and 29 & 30 Vict., c. ccv, 1866. 2 5. 6 Geo. I, c. 18.
[93]   6 Geo. I, c. 18.
[94]   A variant, however, is vigorous in Australia; see para.1–30.

emphasis on the inherently contractual nature of registered companies. Thus, in one of the 1963 Act's central provisions, it is stated that a company's constitution (its memorandum and articles of association) shall "bind the company and the members thereof to the same extent as if they respectively had been signed and sealed by each member, and contained covenants by each member to observe all the provisions of the memorandum and of the articles".[95]

1–44 Perhaps the principal difference between Irish and English company law, on the one hand, and that of the United States, is that the American law originally developed in a society where the essentially contractual form of constituting companies had not taken root. As the late Professor Gower explained:

> "In England ... incorporation with limited liability by a simple process of registration is only one hundred years old, having attained its centenary (in 1955). Considering the transcendent role played by England in the mercantile community during the nineteenth and early twentieth centuries this is difficult to credit—but so it is. The explanation is that joint-stock enterprise had flourished considerably earlier but had operated principally in the guise of an unincorporated company or partnership under a deed of settlement. It was this familiar form of organisation which the legislation of 1844 and 1855 adopted, successively conferring on it the boons of corporate personality and limited liability. Hence the modern English business corporation has evolved from the unincorporated partnership, based on mutual agreement, rather than from the corporation, based on a grant from the state, and owes more to partnership principles than rules based on corporate personality. Thus we in England still do not talk about business corporations or about corporation law, but about companies and company law.
>
> In America, on the other hand, the Bubble Act seems, wisely, to have been ignored despite the fact that it had been extended to the colonies by statute in 1741. After the Declaration of Independence, incorporation by special acts of the state legislature was granted far more readily than in England, and the unincorporated joint-stock company, though not unknown, was correspondingly less important. In a number of industrially important states incorporation by registration under a general act came earlier than in England—33 years earlier in New York—and when it came, the model which the legislative draftsmen had in mind was the statutory or chartered corporation rather than the unincorporated company or partnership. Hence modern American corporation law owes less to partnership and contractual principles than does the British. This tends to make it less flexible than the English mode."[96]

---

[95] 1963 Act, s.25.

[96] "Some Contrasts Between British and American Corporation Law" 69 *Harv. L. Rev.* 1369 (1956) at 1371–1372. For most of the nineteenth century the principal book on the subject was Lindley's *Treatise on the Law of Partnership and its Application to Companies* (1860), 2 Vols.

Incorporation by Registration

1–45   In 1844, the administratively convenient method of establishing companies by registration with a public official was adopted, and ten years later the members of these companies were permitted to have limited liability. The history of company law from that period onwards is, briefly, as follows.

1–46   The Joint Stock Companies Act 1844[97] was the first law which gave the privilege of incorporation by registration and without a royal charter or a special Act of Parliament. Under this Act, partnerships in which the capital was divided into freely transferable shares, partnerships in which there were more than 25 members and assurance companies were all required to register in a registry of companies. On registration and on filing a deed of settlement, these associations became incorporated and acquired a separate legal existence distinct from that of their members. Thus, for the first time, it became possible for an enterprise to become incorporated as of right by fulfilling prescribed conditions. The deed of settlement corresponded broadly to the modern memorandum and articles of association. However, every member could be made liable for the company's debts as if it had not been incorporated. But a creditor of the company could not sue a member for a debt due by the company without first trying to levy execution against the property of the company as such.

1–47   In 1852, a Commission to consider whether any alteration should be made to partnership law, so as to give limited liability to partners, reported that limiting liability would not be beneficial. Nevertheless, in the following year the House of Commons passed a resolution as a result of which the Limited Liability Act 1855[98] was passed. This amended the 1844 Act and made it possible for registered companies to limit the liability of all their members to the amounts due on their shares provided that certain conditions were observed.

1–48   Many of the essential features of modern company law are contained in the Joint Stock Companies Act 1856,[99] which consolidated the 1844 and the 1855 Acts. Any seven or more persons were entitled to register a company with limited liability. An annual return had to be filed giving information about the capital of the company and its shareholders, but filing a balance sheet with the auditors' report attached (which had been made compulsory in 1844) became no longer necessary. The Companies Act 1862,[100] which consolidated existing legislation regarding joint stock, banking and assurance companies, also made provision for companies limited by guarantee. It required the objects of the company to be stated and absolutely prohibited their alteration, thus introducing the doctrine of *ultra vires*.

1–49   Although the advantages of companies with limited liability are considerable, in its early form the system offered opportunities for fraudulent

---

[97] 7 & 8 Vict., c. 110.
[98] 18 & 19 Vict., c. 133.
[99] 19 & 20 Vict., c. 47.
[100] 25 & 26 Vict., c. 89.

enrichment to company promoters, as numerous leading cases decided around the end of the nineteenth century testify to. A number of Acts dealing with specific reforms in company law were passed between 1862 and 1900. In 1895, a Committee under the chairmanship of Lord Davey recommended further legislative amendments.[101] The collapse which had followed the over-optimism of the railway boom had caused many public companies to fail, and in some of those the promoters and the directors had made substantial illicit profits. The Companies Act 1900[102] made provision for a number of matters which had to be stated in every prospectus and imposed new obligations and liabilities on directors of companies. It also re-introduced the compulsory audit of a company's accounts.

1–50 In 1905, a Committee under the chairmanship of Sir Robert Reid (subsequently Lord Loreburn, L.C.) was set up to enquire into what additional amendments were necessary to the companies legislation.[103] It recommended that every company should be obliged each year to file a balance sheet, which would be available for inspection by every member of the public. It also made recommendations in relation to accepting the special position of "family" companies. It had been held by the House of Lords in *Salomon v Salomon & Co.*[104] that there was nothing in the Companies Acts which prohibited the registration of a company with seven members, six of whom held a small number of shares on behalf of the seventh, who owned the rest of the shares. The Companies Act 1907[105] provided that a private or "family" company could be registered with two members only and that it should be exempt from the obligation to file a balance sheet for public inspection. A private company was defined as a company in which restrictions were imposed by the articles of association on the transfer of shares, in which the number of members of the company did not exceed 50 and in which the shares and debentures of the company could not be offered to the public. Many of the smaller limited companies previously incorporated availed of this legislation by converting themselves into private companies. Another significant development was the emergence of the "holding company" as distinct from the operating company. The holding company was, in the main, the child of the operations of financiers interested in the development of the diamond fields in South Africa before and after the Boer War.[106]

1–51 All the legislation from 1862 to 1907 was consolidated by the Companies (Consolidation) Act 1908.[107] This Act was amended and added to in minor details by the Companies Act 1913,[108] the Companies (Foreign Interests) Act 1917,[109]

---

[101] C. 7779.
[102] 63 & 64 Vict., c. 48.
[103] Cd. 3052 (1906).
[104] [1897] A.C. 22; see below, para.3–52 *et seq.*
[105] 7 Ed. VII, c. 50.
[106] See generally, N. Horn and J. Kocka (eds), *Law and the Formation of the Big Enterprises in the 19th and Early 20th Centuries* (Gottingen, 1979).
[107] 8 Ed. VII, c. 69.
[108] 3 & 4 Geo. V, c. 25.
[109] 7 & 8 Geo. V, c. 18.

the Companies (Particulars of Directors) Act 1917,[110] and the Companies (Reconstitution of Records) Act 1924,[111] which was the first company law statute passed by the Oireachtas. This latter Act dealt with the reconstitution of records consequent on the destruction of the Companies Registration Office when the Custom House in Dublin was burned in 1922, during the Civil War. For the next quarter of a century, there were no significant legislative developments of company law in the State.

1–52   In 1925 in Britain a Committee was set up to consider and report on what amendments were desirable in the law, chaired by Mr Wilfrid Greene K.C. (subsequently Lord Greene M.R.). Most of the recommendations in its report (frequently referred to as "the Greene Report")[112] were embodied in the Companies Act 1928.[113] The existing law and the changes made by that Act were consolidated in the Companies Act 1929.[114] Later, Parliament there passed the Prevention of Fraud (Investments) Act 1939,[115] the main objects of which were regulating the business of dealing in securities and preventing fraud in connection with dealings in investments.

1–53   In 1943, a Committee in Britain chaired by Mr Justice Cohen (subsequently Lord Cohen) was set up to consider and report on what major amendments were desirable, in particular to review the requirements in relation to the formation and affairs of companies, and the safeguards afforded for investors and for the public interest. Its report (usually referred to as "the Cohen Report")[116] recommended a number of major alterations but some of these were not accepted and did not appear in the Companies Act 1947.[117] The law there was then consolidated in the Companies Act 1948.[118]

The Companies Acts 1963–2006

1–54   In 1958, the Company Law Reform Committee, chaired by Arthur Cox, a prominent solicitor, whose secretary was Kenny J., reported to Andreas O'Keeffe, the then Attorney General.[119] Its remit was to recommend what amendments should be made to the Companies (Consolidation) Act 1908, which at that time was the principal companies legislation in force in the State. Effect was given to some of this committee's principal recommendations in the Companies Act of 1959. Four years later, what remains the cornerstone of our present company law was enacted, the Companies Act 1963, which replaced the

---

[110] 7 & 8 Geo. V, c. 28.
[111] No. 21 of 1924.
[112] Cmd. 2657 (1926).
[113] 18 & 19 Geo. V, c. 45.
[114] 19 & 20 Geo. V, c. 23.
[115] 2 & 3 Geo. VI, c. 16, replaced by an Act of the same name in 1958 and presently part of the Financial Services and Markets Act 2000.
[116] Cmd. 6659.
[117] 10 & 11 Geo. VI, c. 47.
[118] 11 & 12 Geo. VI, c. 38.
[119] Pr. 4523.

Act of 1908 and incorporated the 1959 Act and most other recommendations made by the Cox Committee.

1–55 There were few developments of great significance in Irish company legislation between 1963 and 1990. The Stock Transfer Act 1963 and the Companies (Amendment) Act 1977 introduced administrative reforms to facilitate the transfer of shares. New winding-up rules were adopted in 1966; and the Companies (Amendment) Act 1982 altered the 1963 Act in several respects. Other initiatives in this field were mainly the result of Ireland's accession to the European Communities (EC) in 1973. To bring domestic law in line with the EC's requirements, SI 163 of 1973, SI 282 of 1984 and the Companies (Amendment) Acts of 1983 and 1986 were enacted. Much of the Act of 1983 deals with the capital of limited companies to ensure that they are adequately capitalised[120]; the Act of 1986 is concerned with the format and content of company accounts.[121]

1–56 Perhaps the most significant of all the legislative changes since 1963 are those contained in the Companies Act 1990,[122] which had a long gestation period. Numerous major areas are affected by this measure, which re-cast the system for conducting investigations into companies' affairs and disclosing beneficial interests in shareholdings; placed additional restrictions on transactions between companies and their own directors; introduced a system of banning certain persons from acting as directors or restricting their doing so; extended the safeguards against insider trading; eased some of the restrictions against companies buying or taking some financial interest in their own shares; tightened up rules regarding accounts and auditing; and introduced various changes in the regime governing corporate insolvency. Another measure adopted in 1990, the Companies (Amendment) Act 1990, provided for the protection of companies in serious financial difficulties, and the appointment of an examiner to assess their underlying viability and seek to establish a compromise with the bulk of the creditors.

1–57 These in turn were succeeded by two amending Acts of 1999, the second of which made it more difficult to appoint examiners and also exempted some companies from having to audit their accounts. A radical initiative was adopted in the Company Law Enforcement Act 2001, which provided for regulatory oversight of the entire company law field by the Director of Corporate Enforcement, who was given extensive powers to ensure high standards of governance in registered companies.[123] The Companies (Auditing and Accounting) Act 2003 provided for another regulatory agency to supervise the

---

[120] See generally, M. Forde, "The Companies (Amendment) Act 1983" 18 *Ir. Jur.* 289 (1983).

[121] See generally, S. Kelleher, *Companies (Amendment) Act 1986: a guide to the accounting, reporting and filing requirements* (Dublin: Institute of Chartered Accountants in Ireland, 1987).

[122] See generally, M. Forde, D. Hogan, B. O'Neill and F. Brennan, *The New Companies Law* (conference papers, 1991) and G. McCormack, *The New Companies Legislation* (Dublin: Round Hall, 1991).

[123] See www.odce.ie.

activities of auditors, the Irish Auditing and Accounting Supervisory Authority.[124] The main focus of the Investment Funds, Companies and Miscellaneous Provisions Act 2005 is to regulate public offers of securities in companies and to suppress abuses in the securities market, for instance insider trading; in doing so, it complements EC Directives of 2003 on these topics. The Investment Funds, Companies and Miscellaneous Provisions Act 2006 provides for a large increase in company audit exemption thresholds, but in the main deals with the transposition into Irish law of the EC Transparency Directive.

1–58   A Company Law Review Group was established under Pt 7 (ss.67–71) of the 2001 Act.[125] It is charged with monitoring and advising the Minister on major aspects of company law, the objective being to "provide enterprise, facilitate commerce, simplify the operation of the Companies Acts, enhance corporate governance and encourage commercial probity". One of the tasks it has assumed is to draw up consolidating legislation for the area of company law, which ought to be published by 2008.[126]

---

[124] See www.iaasa.ie.
[125] See www.clrg.org.
[126] *cf.* P. Egan, "In good company", *Law Society Gazette* (May 2007), p.36.

CHAPTER 2

REGULATION OF COMPANIES

2–01 The affairs of registered companies, their officers, promoters, members, creditors and employees are regulated by the State in a variety of ways. Conditions for forming, operating and winding up companies are prescribed by the Oireachtas. All such companies must register with the Registrar of Companies and make numerous returns to the Companies Registration Office (the CRO), including an annual return. Where companies are wound up, the High Court exercises an extensive supervisory function. A major innovation came about in 2001, with the establishment of the office of the Director of Corporate Enforcement (the DCE). In addition to company law rules as such, and general legislation on questions of employment, environment and taxation, public companies (Plcs) are affected by rules concerning the capital and securities markets. Companies in the financial services sector are subject to additional detailed regulation under the supervision of the Irish Financial Services Regulatory Authority.

OBJECTIVES OF REGULATION

2–02 According to the authors of *The Anatomy of Corporate Law*[1]:

> "As a normative matter, the overall objective of corporate law—as of any branch of law—is presumably to serve the interests of society as a whole. More particularly, the appropriate goal of corporate law is to advance the aggregate welfare of a firm's shareholders, employees, suppliers, and customers without undue sacrifice—and, if possible, with benefit—to third parties such as local communities and beneficiaries of the natural environment. This is what economists would characterize as the pursuit of overall social efficiency.
>
> It is sometimes said that the goals of corporate law should be narrower. In particular, it is sometimes said that the appropriate role of corporate law is simply to assure that the corporation serves the best interests of its shareholders or, more specifically, to maximize financial returns to shareholders or, more specifically still, to maximize the market price of corporate shares. Such claims can be viewed in two ways.
>
> First, these claims can be taken at face value, in which case they neither describe corporate law as we see it, nor do they offer a normatively appealing aspiration for that body of law. There would be little to recommend a

---

[1] R. Kraakman et al, *The Anatomy of Corporate Law: A Comparative and Functional Approach* (Oxford: OUP, 2004), pp.18–19.

body of law that, for example, permits corporate shareholders to enrich themselves through transactions that make creditors or employees worse off by $2 for every $1 that the shareholders gain.

Second, such claims can be understood as saying, more modestly, that focusing principally on the maximization of shareholder returns is, in general, the best means by which corporate law can serve the broader goal of advancing overall social Welfare. In general, creditors, workers, and customers will consent to deal with a corporation only if they expect to be better off themselves as a result. Consequently, the corporation—and, in particular, its shareholders—has a direct pecuniary interest in making sure that corporate transactions are beneficial, not just to the shareholders, but to all parties who deal with the firm. We believe that this second view is—and surely ought to be—the appropriate interpretation of statements by legal scholars and economists asserting that shareholder value is the proper object of corporate law.

Whether, in fact, the pursuit of shareholder value is generally an effective means of advancing social welfare is an empirical question on which reasonable minds can differ.

To say that the pursuit of aggregate social welfare is the appropriate goal of corporate law is not to say, of course, that the law always serves that goal. Legislatures and courts are sometimes less attentive to overall social welfare than to the particular interests of some influential constituency, such as corporate managers, controlling shareholders, or organized workers. Moreover, corporate law everywhere continues to bear the imprint of the historical path through which it has evolved, and reflects as well various non-efficiency-oriented intellectual ideological currents that have sometimes influenced its formation."

2–03 To secure these objectives, company law makes available to persons a structure through which they can carry on a business in a manner that limits their liability to the enterprise's creditors in the event of insolvency. The law seeks to provide a variety of safeguards for the interests principally of minority shareholders in the business and of its creditors, while allowing the shareholders a considerable latitude as to how management is to function and be supervised. The more extensive such safeguards are for minorities and creditors, the less flexibility is allowed to those controlling the company in arranging governance and management structures. In the case of companies with securities that are listed on a stock exchange, the law also seeks to protect investors in the market from sharp practices, such as deceptive prospectuses, insider trading and other market abuses.

SOURCES OF REGULATION

2–04 The legal regime governing registered companies is derived from different sources. What can make company law difficult to grasp is that the legal position can be contained in an amalgam of contractual clauses in the company's own regulations, common law rules, equitable principles, statutory provisions, the rules of stock exchanges and standards imposed by the accountancy profession. As the French comparative lawyer, Professor André Tunc, observed "a piece of legislation is sometimes superimposed over an unfortunate judicial rule. But the statute does not eliminate the rule. On the contrary, it takes it for granted and eliminates or alleviates only some of its results .... Because the ... legislator has such a respect for the common law background that it practically never dares to prepare a *tabula rasa* in order to build a new law, its interventions may have the result of increasing the complexities of the law."[2]

The Company's Own Regulations

2–05 Subject to peremptory rules in the Companies Acts 1963–2006, the principal source of company law is each company's own regulations, which comprises the memorandum and the articles of association that it registers with the Registrar of Companies. Many aspects of how the affairs of companies should be conducted are determined by their own members or shareholders, in the form of the memorandum and articles of association. These are the very constitution of the company and take precedence except where mandatory law requires otherwise. Major aspects of how a company should conduct its affairs are contained in these and, by virtue of s.25 of the 1963 Act, they have contractual force between the company and its members, and also between its members *inter se*. In close companies, these documents are often supplemented by a separate shareholders' agreement, which is a contract between all the members of the company about how its affairs, or certain aspects of its affairs, should be conducted.

Legislation

2–06 A registered company, as an artificial person separate from its members, exists only by virtue of the Companies Acts under which it was incorporated.[3] The principal statutes that affect registered companies are the Companies Acts 1963–2006, together with the Stock Transfer Act of 1963; and indirectly, the legislation on taxation,[4] on bankruptcy,[5] on restrictive practices, monopolies and mergers.[6] The 2003 Act authorises the Minister to regulate numerous matters by way of statutory instrument[7] and several other provisions also give him regulatory authority for particular purposes. Rules regarding issuing and the content of prospectuses may be made by the Irish Financial Services Regulatory Authority, and rules regarding takeovers and mergers of listed companies may be made by the Irish Takeover Panel. Although much of the legislation is similar to that in Britain, there are important differences of detail that can easily go unnoticed between the Irish Acts and parallel British provisions. In 2006 the law in Britain radically changed,[8] and it is likely that

---

2   "A French Lawyer Looks at British Company Law" 45 *Mod. L. Rev.* 1 (1982) at 6–7.
3   "These companies are the creature of statute", *per* Lord Macnaghten in *Welton* v *Saffery* [1897] A.C. 299 at 324.
4   See generally M. Feeney, *The Taxation of Companies* (Haywards Heath: Tottel Publishing, 2006).
5   See generally, M. Forde, *Bankruptcy Law in Ireland* (Cork: The Mercier Press, 1990).
6   See generally, A. McCarthy & V. Power, *Irish Competition Law: The Competition Act 2002* (Haywards Heath: Tottel Publishing, 2003).
7   Sections 48–50.
8   With the Companies Act 2006, which received Royal Assent on November 8, 2006, and all parts of which will be commenced by October 2008. It is the most extensive revision of British company law since 1856.

similar changes will be adopted by the Oireachtas in years to come. In July 2007 the Cabinet approved publication of a Company Law Consolidation Bill, which it was intended to bring before the Dáil later in the year.[9]

2–07   The Companies Acts 1963–2006, are comprised of the following primary legislation:[10]

> Companies Act 1963
> Companies (Amendment) Act 1977
> Companies (Amendment) Act 1982
> Companies (Amendment) Act 1983
> Companies (Amendment) Act 1986
> Companies Act 1990
> Companies (Amendment) Act 1990
> Companies (Amendment) Act 1999
> Companies (Amendment) (No. 2) Act 1999
> Company Law Enforcement Act 2001
> Companies (Auditing and Accounting) Act 2003
> Investment Funds, Companies and Miscellaneous Provisions Act 2005
> Investment Funds, Companies and Miscellaneous Provisions Act 2006

There is also the Stock Transfer Act 1963, the Irish Takeover Panel Act 1997 and the Markets in Financial Instruments and Miscellaneous Provisions Act 2007.

2–08   The following are the principal statutory instruments that affect company law:[11]

> Companies (Recognition of Countries) Order 1964 (SI 1964/42)
> European Communities (Companies) Regulations 1973 (SI 1973/163)
> European Communities (Mergers and Divisions of Companies) Regulations 1987 (SI 1987/137)
> European Communities (Companies: Group Accounts) Regulations 1992 (SI 1992/201)
> European Communities (Transferable Securities and Stock Exchange) Regulations 1992 (SI 1992/202)
> Companies Act 1990 (Auditors) Regulations 1992 (SI 1992/259)
> European Communities (Credit Institutions: Accounts) Regulations 1992 (SI 1992/294)
> European Communities (Branch Disclosures) Regulations 1993 (SI 1993/395)
> European Communities (Accounts) Regulations 1993 (SI 1993/396)
> European Communities (Single-Member Private Limited Companies) Regulations 1994 (SI 1994/275)
> European Communities (Insurance Undertakings: Accounts) Regulations 1996 (SI 1996/23)
> Companies Act 1990 (Uncertified Securities) Regulations 1996 (SI 1996/68)

---

[9]   See www.clrg.org.
[10] See Consolidated Company Legislation service from Thomson Round Hall, now available on www.westlaw.ie.
[11] *ibid.*

European Communities (Public Limited Companies Subsidiaries) Regulations 1997 (SI 1997/67)

Companies Act 1963 (Section 377(1)) Order 1999 (SI 1999/64)

European Communities (Corporate Insolvency) Regulations 2002 (SI 2002/333)

Companies Act 1990 (Form and Content of Documents Delivered to Registrar) Regulations 2002 (SI 2002/39)

Company Law Enforcement Act 2001 (Section 56) Regulations 2002 (SI 2002/324)

European Communities (Corporate Insolvency) Regulations 2002 (SI 2002/333)

European Communities (Reorganisation and Winding-up of Insurance Undertakings) Regulations 2003 (SI 2003/168)

European Communities (Credit Institutions) (Fair Value Accounting) Regulations 2004 (SI 2004/720)

European Communities (Credit Institutions) (Fair Value Accounting) Regulations 2004 (SI 2004/765)

Companies Communities (Companies) Regulations 2004 (SI 2004/839)

European Communities (International Financial Reporting Standards and Miscellaneous Amendments) Regulations 2005 (SI 2005/116)

Prospectus (Directive 2003/71/EC) Regulations 2005 (SI 2005/324)

Market Abuse (Directive 2003/6/EC) Regulations 2005 (SI 2005/342)

European Communities (Takeover Bids (Directive 2004/25/EC)) Regulations 2006 (SI 2006/255)

European Communities (Companies) (Amendment) Regulations 2007 (SI 2007/49)

European Communities (Admission to Listing and Miscellaneous Provisions) Regulations 2007 (SI 2007/286)

European Communities (Markets in Financial Instruments) Regulations 2007 (SI 2007/60)

Mandatory and Optional Rules

2–09 A general feature of company legislation that cannot be over-emphasised is the distinction between mandatory (or peremptory) and optional (or permissive or default) provisions.[12] The former are rules that apply irrespective of the wishes of those to whom they are addressed, whereas the latter are rules that persons affected may agree shall not apply to dealings between themselves. For instance, taxation, environmental protection rules and much of what may be called individual protective employment legislation are mandatory, whereas the Sale of Goods Act 1893 is a classic optional measure. Many provisions of the Companies Acts are mandatory; often, violation of their requirements are criminal offences and other rules stipulate that the obligation

---

[12] See generally, B. Cheffins, *Company Law: Theory, Structure and Operation* (Oxford: Clarendon Press, 1997), Ch.3 on "classification of company law rules"; Contractual Freedom in Corporate Law 89 *Columbia L. Rev.* (Vol.7) 1395 (1989); and Ramsay, "Models of Corporate Regulation: the Mandatory/Enabling Debate" in *Corporate Personality in the 20th Century* (Grantham, Ross and Rickett, Charles (eds), Oxford: Hart, 1998), Ch.12.

being imposed may not be set aside by agreement between the parties, not even by any provision in a company's own regulations. Thus, ss.133 and 137 of the 1963 Act, which concern minimum periods of notice for calling general meetings and demanding polls at those meetings, state that any provision to the contrary in the company's articles of association shall be void. It has been held that companies cannot contract with their creditors that some basic principles of bankruptcy law shall not apply in the event of liquidation.[13]

2–10 However, the Companies Acts also contain numerous optional rules—the most common form being that the statutory requirement in question applies unless the company's own regulations (i.e. memorandum or articles of association) provide otherwise. A recent innovation is the "break through" provision in regulations governing takeovers and mergers, whereby quoted companies can "opt in" to part of the prescribed regime.[14] Additionally, under what is known as the *Re Duomatic* principle,[15] where all members of a company agree informally on a course of conduct, this displaces any contrary provision in the company's own regulations, other than a stipulation that is mandatory under the Companies Acts.

Interpretation

2–11 There are two principal contrasting methods of interpreting statutes: these may be called the "mischief" and the "literal" approaches. Under the former, the judge is concerned primarily with ascertaining the policy or goals which the provision in question was adopted to promote, and the rules will be applied in the light of that purpose. The other approach focuses entirely on the section's very terms and the judge will give effect to its literal meaning even if that be inconsistent with what it is thought the legislature was trying to achieve. In favour of this latter approach, it can be said that, even though occasionally it may give rise to a nonsense, it nevertheless is preferable because it provides greater certainty than what often amounts to guessing what objective the legislature had in mind when it adopted some provision. Where the provision in question is obscure or ambiguous, or where a literal application would be absurd or would not reflect the plain intention of the Oireachtas, the court is now directed to consider the Act as a whole in order to ascertain the true meaning of the words used. Subject to this, it appears that the literal or plain meaning approach is endorsed in s.5(1) of the Interpretation Act 2005.

2–12 In the British courts, there has been a tendency to interpret legislative provisions that impose detailed restrictions on directors' and shareholders' freedom of action in an exceptionally literal and limited manner, somewhat in the same way as tax laws were construed until recently there.[16] That is to say, courts have upheld transactions and arrangements that arguably contravened the spirit of the provision in question but were not caught by the section's very

---

[13] *Ex p. Mackay* (1873) 8 Ch. App. 643.
[14] See para.15–136.
[15] See para.5–66 *et seq.*
[16] i.e. until *Furniss v Dawson* [1984] A.C. 474.

terms.[17] Indeed, what perhaps was the most important company law case of all time, *Salomon v Salomon & Co.*,[18] concerning the separate legal personality of companies and the extent to which proprietors of "one-person" companies can insulate their personal financial situations from that of their companies, reads as an exercise in ultra-literalism. It was contended there, and accepted by a unanimous Court of Appeal[19] that, in exceptional circumstances, debts owed by an insolvent company to its general creditors should be paid off before satisfying secured debts owed by the company to its own shareholders. This view was rejected by a unanimous House of Lords, because, in Lord Halsbury L.C.'s words, "I can only find the true intent and meaning of the Act from the Act itself, and the Act appears to me to give a company a legal existence with . . . rights and liabilities of its own, whatever may have been the ideas or schemes of those who brought it into existence".[20]

2–13 A contrary phenomenon, however, and one which may partly explain the literal construction approach to the Companies Acts, is that there are some provisions in those Acts that give the courts remarkably extensive discretions. One of these, s.205 of the 1963 Act, sweeps so widely that it could almost be said that many aspects of company law are governed by two separate standards—the "ordinary" rules based on the one hand on the Acts, the memorandum and articles of association and the common law and, on the other hand, the section 205 "discretionary" standard. It establishes a broad and amorphous criterion of "oppression" for inter-shareholder, company-shareholder and director-shareholder relations; and empowers the court to take appropriate measures whenever the company's or the directors' powers are being exercised "oppressive[ly]" or "in disregard of the interests [of any] member".[21] A somewhat similar and related provision is s.213(f) of the 1963 Act, which empowers the court to order that a company be wound up on "just and equitable grounds".[22] Virtually all the Companies Acts' provisions for drastically altering a company's structure, such as reducing its capital, changing the objects and making schemes of arrangement, either require prior approval by the court or empower the court on the application of dissident members to veto changes; in each instance the governing criterion is some vague standard of justice or fairness.[23]

Common Law and Equity

2–14 "Common law" and "equity" mean rules and principles which, it has been concluded by courts, have the force of law. Much of these judge-made rules concerning companies are the product of equity as distinct from the common law, in

---

[17] Perhaps the best example is *Bushell v Faith* [1970] A.C. 1099; to a lesser extent, *Russell v Northern Bank Development Corp.* [1992] 1 W.L.R. 588.

[18] [1897] A.C. 22.

[19] *Broderip v Salomon* [1895] 2 Ch. 323.

[20] [1897] A.C. 22 at 31.

[21] See below, para.10–71 *et seq.*

[22] See below, para.10–109 *et seq.*

[23] See below, Ch.11.

that most company cases were heard by the Court of Chancery,[24] where tradition-ally disputes concerning trusts were determined and the estates of deceased per-sons were administered. Many doctrines of equity have been applied in relation to companies, especially the application of fiduciary principles to directors and other officers. Common law and equity have been merged since the Judicature Act of 1877, although for purely administrative purposes the bulk of company lit-igation still takes place on the Chancery side of the High Court and, since 2004, in what is known as the Commercial Court.[25]

2–15 Some central principles governing the structure and operation of compa-nies were devised by the judges and not the legislature, many of these being incorporated subsequently into the Companies Acts. Thus, in a series of cases, of which *Ooregum Gold Mining Co v Roper*,[26] *Trevor v Whitworth*[27] and *Flitcroft's Case*[28] are the best known, the courts laid down a broad principle of capital integ-rity: in limited companies, shares must not be issued for a price lower than their par value, the company may not purchase its own shares and dividends may not be paid out of capital. This principle and these rules, coupled with analogous rules but subject to some exceptions, are now contained in the 1963 Act (ss.60 and 72), and are the main subjects of the 1983 Act. In *Ashbury Railway Carriage Co. v Riche*[29] it was held that contracts entered into by a company but which are for purposes other than any of those set out in its objects clause are *ultra vires*, void and unenforceable. However, the hardship that unsuspecting outsiders doing business with companies suffered on account of this rule led to its virtual repeal by s.8(1) of the 1963 Act. The conclusions reached in these cases are pre-sented as if they were the automatic consequences of the rules contained in the Companies Acts of the time. Given that observers of the business scene then must have been shocked by the implications of *Salomon & Co.* and *Ashbury Railway*, it may have been felt necessary to give the separate legal personality and the *ultra vires* principles unquestionable legitimacy by claiming that they arose from the very terms of the Companies Act as a matter of inexorable logic.

2–16 In recent years, some decisions of the Supreme Court in the company law field have raised the question of whether Ireland is developing, perhaps unwittingly, its own distinct jurisprudence with regard to companies, because it significantly departs from the approach adopted in other common law jurisdic-tions. Perhaps the most striking example is *Re Wogans (Drogheda) Ltd*,[30] con-cerning whether a certain form of charge granted over a company's book debts was a fixed or a floating charge; it was held unanimously to be fixed. However,

---

[24] See generally, B. Cheffins, *Company Law: Theory, Structure and Operation* (Oxford: Clarendon Press, 1997), Ch.7 and Milman, "The Courts and the Companies Acts: The Judicial Contribution to Company Law" [1990] *Lloyd's Maritime and Commercial Law Quarterly* 401.

[25] See generally, S. Dowling, *The Commercial Court* (Dublin: Thomson Round Hall, 2007).

[26] [1892] A.C. 125.

[27] (1887) 12 App. Cas. 409.

[28] (1882) 21 Ch.D. 519.

[29] (1875) L.R. 7 H.L. 653.

[30] [1993] I.R. 157.

when a similar question came before the Privy Council and later before the House of Lords in the *Agnew* case[31] and in *Re Spectrum Plus Ltd*,[32] both tribunals, relying on the very same authorities and principles, unanimously concluded that the charges were floating.[33] Had the court in *Wogans* explicitly departed from the criteria that obtain elsewhere in the common law world, explaining why and stating the case for a different analysis, it could then be said that an indigenous coherent approach to these and other questions is under way. If the court was not being so adventurous but was endeavouring to apply long-established principles and authorities, the analysis in *Agnew* and in *Spectrum* is far more persuasive than that in *Wogans*. As is explained later,[34] the outcome endorsed there would appear to be unworkable, from any practical point of view, which perhaps explains why it was subsequently "distinguished" on grounds that are difficult to understand, if taken at their face value. At least two other decisions of the court fall into this category,[35] in that courts in other comparable jurisdictions most likely would not have reached the same conclusions in the light of the relevant principles and authorities that were applicable.

EC Measures

2–17 A number of significant measures bearing directly on company law have been adopted by the European Communities (EC).[36] There also are numerous EC Directives aimed at regulating the securities market that profoundly affect public companies, their officers and shareholders. Additionally, after almost 40 years of gestation, in 2001 the Council adopted Reg.2157/2001 on the Statute for a European Company,[37] which is supplemented by Directive 2001/86 concerning employee involvement in such bodies.[38] This permits a new pan-European form of company (a "*Societas Europaea*") to be established.[39] Companies are also affected by developments in the more general area of European law concerning freedom of movement and of establishment.[40]

2–18 To facilitate companies being able to freely establish themselves in the various EC Member States, Art.44(2)(g) of the EC Treaty authorises Directives

---

[31] [2001] 2 A.C. 710.

[32] [2005] 2 A.C. 680.

[33] See J. Breslin, and K. Smith, "The House of Lords decision in Spectrum Plus—the implications for Irish banking law" 12(9) *Commercial Law Practitioner* 228 (2005).

[34] See para.20–77.

[35] *Re Frederick Inns Ltd* [1994] 1 I.L.R.M. 387, discussed at para.18–28 *et seq* and *Re Greendale Developments Ltd (No. 2)* [1998] 1 I.R. 8, discussed at para.3–48 *et seq.*

[36] See generally, V. Edwards, *E.C. Company Law* (Oxford: Clarendon Press, 1999), J. Dine, *Gore–Browne on EU Company Law* (Bristol: Jordans, looseleaf) and K. Hopt & E. Wymeersch, *European Company and Financial Law, Text and leading Cases*, 4th edn (Oxford, OUP, 2007). See also the bi-monthly journal, *European Company Law* (Kluwer) and at www.KluwerLawOnline.com.

[37] Implemented by the European Communities (European Public Limited-Liability Company) Regulations 2007 (SI 2007/21).

[38] [2001] OJ L294/1, implemented by the European Communities (European Public Limited Liability Company) (Employee Involvement) Regulations 2006 (SI 2006/623).

[39] See para.21–55 *et seq.*

[40] See para.21–59 *et seq.*

for "coordinating to the necessary extent the safeguards which, for the protection of the interests of members and others, are required by Member States of companies or firms ... with a view to making such safeguards equivalent throughout the Community." All of the earlier Directives in the company law field were adopted under this rubric, and most EC measures squarely within the company law field are identified for convenience by reference to numbers—the First, Second, etc. Directives. At present there are no plans for a uniform company law in Europe; Art.44(2)(g) requires laws to be made "equivalent", not "uniform".

2–19 When measures giving effect to various Directives are being considered, in interpreting the Act or statutory instrument in question the court should have regard to the very terms of the relevant Directive.[41] In a case involving the "nullity" of companies, the European Court of Justice has ruled that, when interpreting any provision of national law, irrespective of whether it was passed before or after a Directive was adopted, the national court must look to the relevant Directive when applying national law.[42] In Britain courts have even looked behind the Directives themselves to the national legislation in France and Germany which inspired adoption of a particular measure.[43] It remains to be seen whether Irish courts will resort to comparative law techniques when confronted with such questions.

2–20 *First Directive—68/151*: The First Company Law Directive[44] deals mainly with the relations between companies and persons seeking to enter into transactions with them; its primary objective was to remove several legal "traps" in the way of dealing with companies, notably the pre-incorporation contract rule, the *ultra vires* rule and the rule that companies' articles of association could restrict the contracting authority of directors and other agents. In fact, the first two of these had been removed by ss.37(2) and 8(1) of the 1963 Act, in terms almost identical to those contained in the Directive; the other trap was substantially removed by the European Communities (Companies) Regulations 1973.[45]

2–21 *Second Directive—77/91*: This deals mainly with the protection of companies' paid-up capital.[46] It aims to ensure that companies obtain reasonably equivalent consideration for shares they issue and that contributed capital is not improperly repaid or dissipated among the shareholders. Its provisions were implemented by the Companies (Amendment) Act 1983; some of them do not apply to private companies.

---

[41] See generally, T.C. Hartley, *The Foundations of European Communities Law*, 5th edn (Oxford: OUP, 2003), p.219 *et seq.*

[42] *Marleasing SA v La Comercial International de Alimentation* (C–106/89) [1990] E.C.R. 4135.

[43] *Phonogram Ltd v Lane* [1982] Q.B. 938.

[44] [1968] O.J. L65/8 (special edn).

[45] SI 1973/163, amended in 2007 in response to Directive 2003/58 by SI 2007/49.

[46] [1977] O.J. L26/1. This has been amended by Directive 2006/68 [2006] O.J. L264/32 in respect of Plcs, and must be implemented by April 15, 2008.

2–22   *Third and Sixth Directives—78/855 and 82/89*: These have little practical impact on companies.[47] They deal with a form of merger and of division
of a company that is most uncommon in this country. Effect was given to them
by the European Communities (Mergers and Division of Companies) Regulations 1987,[48] which apply only to public limited companies.

2–23   *Fourth Directive—78/660*: This sets out various rules regarding limited companies' accounts, formats for those accounts, and the contents of
reports that must accompany accounts.[49] It also deals with the annual return of
information to the Registrar of Companies. Its provisions were implemented
by the Companies (Amendment) Act 1986.[50]

2–24   *Seventh Directive—83/349*: This sets out rules regarding the annual
accounts of groups of companies, including the contents and formats of those
accounts.[51] It complements the Fourth Directive, which deals with the accounts of
single companies. The measure acknowledges that many businesses are conducted through groups of companies and that, to fully comprehend the financial
circumstances of the business, there must be consolidated or group accounts. This
was implemented by the European Communities (Accounts) Regulations 1993.[52]

2–25   *Eighth Directive—84/253*: This sets out minimum standards of education and competency that persons must possess before they can be entitled to
act as a company's auditors.[53] Because the standards being applied in Ireland
were at least as stringent as those set out in the Directive, implementation of
this measure did not demand extensive legislative changes in Pt X (ss.182–205)
of the 1990 Act.[54] It has now been replaced by Directive 2006/43,[55] which is
due to be implemented by June 29, 2008.

2–26   *Tenth Directive—2005/56*: This facilitates mergers of companies
across frontiers[56] and requires implementation before the end of 2007.

2–27   *Eleventh Directive—89/666*: This requires companies which have a
branch in one EC state but which are registered elsewhere to disclose various
matters in the state where the branch is located, including the company's own
annual report.[57] It has been implemented by the European Communities
(Branch Disclosures) Regulations 1993.[58]

---

[47] [1978] O.J. L295/36 and [1982] O.J. L378/47.
[48] SI 1987/137.
[49] [1978] O.J. L222/11.
[50] It has been significantly amended; see paras 2–30 and 2–31.
[51] [1984] O.J. L126/28.
[52] SI 1993/396, which has been significantly amended; see paras 2–30 and 2–31.
[53] [1983] O.J. L193/1.
[54] As amended by S.I. 1992/259.
[55] [2006] O.J. L157/87.
[56] [2005] O.J. L310/1.
[57] [1989] O.J. L395/36.
[58] SI 1993/395.

2–28   *Twelfth Directive—89/667*: This made it possible to have private limited companies with a single member only.[59] Several EC states' laws already provided for the true "one person" company. In practice there were one-person companies in this country and in Britain; the owner of the company would hold all the issued shares but one, and that one share would be held by someone else in trust for the owner. This Directive was implemented by the European Communities (Single Member Private Limited Companies) Regulations 1994.[60]

2–29   *Thirteenth Directive—2004/25*: This deals principally with takeovers of Plcs, with the goal of providing greater legal certainty for European companies facing takeover bids, while protecting the interests of shareholders (particularly minority shareholders), employees and other interested parties.[61] It was finally adopted in April 2004, and implemented by the European Communities (Takeover Bids (Directive 2004/25/EC)) Regulations 2006.[62]

2–30   *Company Accounts*: In addition to the Fourth Directive on companies' individual accounts and the Seventh Directive on group accounts, Directives 86/635[63] and 89/117[64] were implemented by the European Communities (Credit Institutions: Accounts) Regulations 1992[65] and Directive 91/674[66] was implemented by the European Communities (Insurance Undertakings: Accounts) Regulations 1996,[67] each of which modify parts of the 1986 Act with regard to the accounts of banks and other credit institutions, and insurers respectively. To prevent the requirements of all of these directives being evaded by interposing an unlimited entity between an operating company and its owners, Directives 90/604 and 605[68] were adopted, which were implemented by the European Communities (Accounts) Regulations 1993.[69]

2–31   These in turn have been amended by what are referred to as the Fair Value Directive 2001/65[70] concerning certain valuation rules and the Modernisation Directive 2003/51.[71] The former was implemented by the European Communities (Fair Value Accounting) Regulations 2004[72] and the European Communities (Credit Institutions) (Fair Value Accounting)

---

[59]   [1989] O.J. L395/40.
[60]   SI 1994/275.
[61]   [2004] O.J. L142/12.
[62]   SI 2006/255.
[63]   [1986] O.J. L372/1.
[64]   [1989] O.J. L44/40.
[65]   SI 1992/294.
[66]   [1991] O.J. L374/7.
[67]   SI 1995/23.
[68]   [1990] O.J. L317/57 and /60.
[69]   SI 1993/396.
[70]   [2001] O.J. L283/28.
[71]   [2003] O.J. L178/16.
[72]   SI 2004/765.

Regulations 2004.[73] What is known as the International Accounting Standards (or IAS) Regulation 1606/2002[74] applies directly to the group accounts of companies and other entities, whose securities have a listing on a stock exchange in the EC. It and also the Modernisation Directive were implemented by the European Communities (International Financial Reporting Standards and Miscellaneous Amendments) Regulations 2005,[75] which made significant changes to, *inter alia*, the 1986 Act.

2–32 *Securities Regulation*: In addition to its endeavours to harmonise company law rules as such, measures adopted by the EC for regulating financial markets profoundly affect companies with securities that are listed or are about to be listed on a stock exchange.[76] Because these measures apply not alone to companies but to other types of securities issued to the public, such as by governments and public authorities, they do not feature in the numbered series of EC Directives above. They deal principally with requirements for obtaining a listing for securities on a stock exchange, issuing prospectuses and offering securities to the public, insider trading and other market abuses, continuous disclosure of information about companies and disclosure to companies and to stock exchanges of major shareholdings acquired in listed companies. The principal EC measures in the area of securities regulation include the Market Abuse Directive 2003/6,[77] the Prospectus Directive 2003/71[78] and the Transparency Directive 2004/109[79], which were implemented principally by Pts 4 (ss.29–37) and 5 (ss.38–55) of the Investment Funds, Companies and Miscellaneous Provisions Act 2005 and by Pt 3 (ss.19–24) of the Investment Funds, Companies and Miscellaneous Provisions Act 2006. The major Shareholdings Directive 88/627[80] (replaced by the Transparency Directive) was implemented by ss.89–96 of the 1990 Act.

2–33 *Other Measures*: The financial services sector has been subjected to intense EC regulation, especially in the areas of banking and insurance, and special provision has been made for certain company law rules for these, most notably their accounting regime.[81] Jurisdiction over cross-border disputes concerning most company law issues, within the EC, is subject to Regulation 44/2001 on Jurisdiction and the Recognition and Enforcement of Judgements in Civil and Commercial Matters[82] or, if the company is insolvent, the Insolvency Regulation 1346/2000,[83] which also determines the principal applicable substantive rules and is directly applicable. It and

---

[73] SI 2004/720.
[74] [2002] O.J. L 243/1.
[75] SI 2005/116.
[76] See generally, N. Moloney, *EC Securities Regulation* (Oxford: OUP, 2002).
[77] [2003] O.J. L96/16.
[78] [2003] O.J. L345/64.
[79] [2004] O.J. L390/38.
[80] [1988] O.J. L348/62.
[81] See paras 2–30 and 2–31.
[82] [2002] O.J. L12/1.
[83] [2002] O.J. L160/1.

Directive 2001/17[84] on insolvent insurers have been implemented by the European Communities (Corporate Insolvency) Regulations 2002[85] and by the European Communities (Reorganisation and Winding Up of Insurance Undertakings) Regulations 2003[86] respectively.

2–34   Direct taxes do not ordinarily fall within the EC's competence. Provided they are exercising a genuine economic activity, Member States may not impede companies from setting up subsidiaries in other such states, where the objective is to avail of a more favourable tax regime in the latter.[87] But the EC has adopted several Directives concerning corporate taxation. The one per cent stamp duty that is charged when Irish registered companies issue shares, regulated by Pt 8 (ss.114–122) of the Stamp Duty Consolidation Act 1999, derives from EC Directive 1969/335.[88] The tax treatment of mergers, divisions, transfers of assets and exchanges of shares concerning companies in several EC Member States, regulated by Pt 21 (ss.630–638) of the Taxes Consolidation Act 1997, derives from EC Directive 90/434.[89] The tax treatment of distributions by non-resident Irish companies based in another EC Member State to their Irish-resident parents, regulated by s.831 of that 1997 Act, derives from EC Directive 1990/435, as amended in 2003.[90]

2–35   *Proposed Directives*: Several draft Directives were considered by the EC institutions, most notably the draft Fifth on company structures,[91] concerning principally two-tier boards of directors and the involvement of employees in decision-making at board level; the draft Ninth on groups of companies[92]; and the draft Fourteenth on transfers of companies' registered offices across frontiers.[93] It has proved impossible to achieve consensus on the draft Fifth and Ninth because they advocate predominantly German models for corporate governance that are not acceptable to some Member States, in particular the United Kingdom, which has a far less interventionist approach to the matters which are the subjects of these drafts. To an extent, differences about these two proposals stopped the momentum for further harmonisation of company law. Several of the earlier Directives that were adopted also have been criticised for being over-prescriptive, in particular the Second on companies' capital. In 2003,

---

84   [2001] O.J. L110/28.
85   SI 2002/333.
86   SI 2003/168.
87   *Cadbury Schweppes Plc v Revenue Commissioners* (Case 196/04) [2007] Q.B. 30.
88   [1969] O.J. L249/25.
89   [1990] O.J. L225/1.
90   [1990] O.J. L225/6.
91   See generally, du Plessis & Dine, "The Fate of the Draft Fifth Directive on Company Law: Accommodation Instead of Harmonisation" [1997] *J. Bus. L.* 23.
92   See generally, D. Sugarman & G. Teubner (eds), *Regulating Corporate Groups in Europe* (Baaden-Baaden: Nomos, 1990).
93   *Comm. Doc. xv/6002/97 – EN.*

the EC Commission published an action plan for its initiatives in this general area.[94]

Stock Exchange Requirements

2–36 To secure or to retain a quotation for their securities on a stock exchange, so that those securities may be traded on that exchange, companies must comply with the exchange's own rules. In Ireland and in the U.K., these are known as the Listing Rules (L.R.). In 2007, there were 62 companies listed on the Irish Stock Exchange, including most of the major enterprises like Allied Irish Banks, the Bank of Ireland and CRH. But there are some large indigenous concerns that have not gone public in this manner, for instance the Dunnes Stores chain and Clerys in O'Connell Street, Dublin, and others that were quoted for many years have "gone private", such as Arnotts. Some even went private for a while and then returned to the Exchange, for instance Eircom Plc.

2–37 Under the European Communities (Markets in Financial Instruments) Regulations 2007,[95] which is to replace the Stock Exchange Act 1995, the Central Bank and the Minister for Finance were given extensive regulatory powers over the Irish Stock Exchange and any other such exchange as may be established in the State. Takeovers of listed companies are also subject to the Irish Takeover Panel Act 1997, and to the Takeover Rules issued by the Panel established under this Act. If the Minister so prescribes, these Rules may be made applicable to Plcs generally or to particular categories of Plcs.

Precedents

2–38 While they may not be a source of law in the narrow sense, established precedents and their accepted meaning in the legal profession are an important feature of company law. Perhaps the most widely used and influential sets of precedents are those collected in *Palmer's Company Precedents* and *Butterworth's Company Precedents*. Of the former it was observed that "[t]he views of a draftsman of precedents, however eminent, cannot of course override the provisions of a statute; but in construing a statutory provision which seems to be devoid of any direct authority on the point, I think I am entitled to pay some regard to a book of precedents of high repute which must have provided a foundation for a very large number of sets of articles [of association] now in use".[96] An excellent addition to these is Volume 1 of Thomson Sweet & Maxwell's *Practical Commercial Precedents*, as is *Smith's Company Procedures Precedents* (both looseleaf). For Irish practitioners, *Jordan's Irish Company*

---

[94] Modernising Company Law and Enhancing Corporate Governance in the European Union—A Plan to Move Forward, COM (2003) 284. See generally, Winter, "EU Company Law on the Move", 31 *Legal Issues of European Interpretation* 97 (2004).

[95] SI 2007/60. and see para.15–48.

[96] *Gaiman v National Association for Mental Health* [1971] 1 Ch. 317 at 328; see also FitzGibbon J. in *Cork Electric Supply Co. v Concannon* [1932] I.R. 314 at 333.

Secretarial Precedents[97] and BCM Hanby Wallace—Thomson Round Hall's *Irish Commercial Precedents Service* (looseleaf) are invaluable.

The Constitution and the European Convention on Human Rights

2–39 There is no express reference to registered companies in the Constitution.[98] To the extent to which they are necessary for "promot[ing] the welfare of the whole people" and to which they enhance "private initiative in industry and commerce",[99] the policy of the Constitution is to support companies. Registered companies have been accepted as proper plaintiffs in actions to declare legislation unconstitutional.[100]

2–40 There have been no major decisions undermining the constitutionality of key provisions in the Companies Acts. A constitutional challenge to the 1963 Act's provisions on fraudulent trading (s.297) was rejected; it was held that imposing unlimited liability for an insolvent company's debts did not in substance create a criminal offence.[101] A related provision imposing liability for reckless trading (1963 Act, s.297A) was held not to have retrospective effect because, if it did, that would contravene the prohibition against retrospective laws that "declare acts to be infringements of the law."[102] Relying on a liquidator's certificate to prove insolvency in restrictions proceedings was upheld; such certificates do not create an irrebuttable presumption of insolvency.[103] An instance where a provision of those Acts was struck down was in *Desmond v Glackin (No. 2)*,[104] which concerned s.10(5) of the 1990 Act regarding penalising persons who refused to cooperate with inspectors appointed under Pt II (ss.7–24) of that Act. The inspectors were authorised to certify to such non-cooperation, which would then be investigated by the court and, if the facts warranted it, the person would be punished in the same way as if he had committed contempt of court. As such a sanction could involve a very substantial fine or indeed imprisonment, and since s.10(5) did not provide that the matter should be determined by way of a jury trial, the subsection was held to be invalid. Section 19 of the 1990 Act, again concerning inspectors, was declared invalid by Kearns J. in one of the *Dunnes Stores* cases because it infringed the principle against compelled self-incrimination.[105] It has been amended. However, because ss.10 and 18 of that Act did not provide automatic sanctions for recalcitrant interviewees, they withstood a similar challenge in *Re National Irish Bank (No. 1)*.[106] Whether the system of court-appointed company

---

[97] 3rd edn (2004).

[98] See generally, A. O'Neill, *The Constitutional Rights of the Company* (Dublin: Thomson Round Hall, 2007).

[99] Article 45(1), (3).

[100] *Iarnród Éireann Teo v Ireland* [1996] 3 I.R. 321.

[101] *O'Keeffe v Ferris* [1997] 3 I.R. 463.

[102] *Re Hefferon Kearns Ltd (No. 1)* [1993] 3 I.R. 177.

[103] *Carway v Attorney-General* [1996] 3 I.R. 300.

[104] [1993] 3 I.R. 67.

[105] *Dunnes Stores (Ireland) Co. v Ryan* [2002] 2 I.R. 60.

[106] [1999] 3 I.R. 145; [1999] 1 I.L.R.M. 321.

inspectors in Pt II of the 1990 Act would withstand a constitutional challenge on separation of powers grounds is debatable[107]; as is s.22(a) of that Act, purporting to render admissible in evidence the contents of an inspector's report, which could not be cross-examined.[108]

2–41 A provision that could possibly be struck down, though it is unlikely, is s.201 of the 1963 Act, which permits a three-quarters majority of shareholders and creditors to impose settlements on the remaining members of their classes. What should save this from invalidity is that the extensive confiscatory power it confers is subject to review by the High Court on broad fairness grounds. The same applies to the "cram down" provisions of the Companies (Amendment) Act 1990, where dissenting members and creditors can be compelled to accept settlements agreed to by specified majorities.[109]

2–42 Some of the above matters were touched on by the European Commission of Human Rights in *Bramelid and Malmstrom v Sweden*[110] which concerned a provision in Swedish law that is very similar to the "take out merger" powers in s.204 of the 1963 Act. If, in trying to take over a company, the "bidder" acquires more than 90 per cent of the shares in the "target", the bidder could obtain a court order that the remaining shareholders in the target must sell their shares to the bidder at an independently fixed price. An order was made under this law against the applicants, who held a small stake in a company that was taken over. They contended that the order contravened, *inter alia*, the European Convention's private property guarantee, on the grounds that they had been compelled to surrender their property for less than its true value. According to the Commission on Human Rights, the applicants' shares were in principle protected by the Convention's property right. Furthermore, the "take out merger" power could not be justified on the usual grounds of public interest because the Swedish "legislature is pursuing the general aim of reaching a system of regulation favourable to those [private] interests which it regards as most worthy of protection, something which however has nothing to do with the notion of "the public interest" as commonly understood in the field of expropriation."[111] Nevertheless, the "take-out" in these circumstances could not be regarded as a violation of the right to enjoy property. In the first place, provision was made to compensate shareholders whose shares were taken from them. As well as that, compulsory transfers of property between individuals is a central feature of the laws of all state parties to the Convention, for instance the division of property on succession, the winding up of certain matrimonial settlements, and seizing and selling goods in the course of execution proceedings. In the Commission's view, "the right of everyone to the peaceful enjoyment of his possessions cannot form the basis for challenging

---

[107] *cf. Gould v Brown* (1998) 72 A.L.J.L.R. 375.

[108] *cf. County Glen Plc v Carway* [1998] 2 I.R. 540 and *Re Employment Equality Bill 1996* [1997] 2 I.R. 321 at 382–383.

[109] *cf. Louisville Joint Stock Land Bank v Radford* 195 U.S. 555 (1935).

[110] (1983) 5 E.H.R.R. 249.

[111] *ibid.* at 256.

the right of the legislature to amend, when and how it considers desirable, the rule of private law which can have some effect on the property of individuals, subject of course to the principle of balance [i.e. that] the legislature does not create an imbalance between [individuals] which would result in one person arbitrarily and unjustly being deprived of his goods for the benefit of another."[112] Relying, *inter alia,* on this reasoning, in *Moran v Valentia Telecommunications Ltd*[113] s. 204 of the 1963 Act, the "take out merger" provision, was upheld by Smyth J.

2–43   A question that has been largely unexplored is the Constitution's impact on relations between individuals, as contrasted with state impositions of burdens on individuals[114]—what may be described as the impact of the Constitution on private law, known in Germany as the *drittwirkung* question.[115] In what circumstances do shareholders, creditors, employees or directors have constitutionally guaranteed rights vis-à-vis the other shareholders or against the company, over and above those rights under the Companies Acts and the general law? It is questionable whether attempting to "constitutionalise" problems of this nature greatly assists their proper resolution; the law of contract and of tort, the principles of equity and the extensive provisions of the Companies Acts would seem to adequately protect legitimate shareholders' and others' grievances.[116] In *Glover v BLN Ltd,*[117] which concerned the legality of a managing director's dismissal, it was held that, in not telling the plaintiff the charges against him and not giving him some opportunity to rebut them before deciding to dismiss him, the company broke an implied term of the employment contract that the dismissal procedure should be fair. This therefore suggests that some company decisions that affect persons' vital interests may be subject to quasi-constitutional procedural standards.[118]

IMPLEMENTATION AND ENFORCEMENT

2–44   Legal rules governing companies are implemented and enforced in different ways, the methods of securing compliance running from civil actions and public and private administrative processes, to prosecutions and social sanctions. For most practical purposes, prior to 1990, persons aggrieved by *prima facie* violations of company law had one mode of redress: civil proceedings in the High Court. If the company in question was being wound up and there were sufficient funds in the liquidation, aggrieved parties could look to the liquidator to safeguard their interests. Prosecutions for

---

[112] *ibid.* at 256 and 257.

[113] [2002] I.E.H.C. 159; unreported, Smyth J., January 21, 2002.

[114] See generally, M. Forde, *Constitutional Law*, 2nd edn (Dublin: First Law, 2004).

[115] See generally, B. Markesinis, *The German Law of Obligations*, 3rd edn (Oxford: Clarendon Press, 1997), Vol.2, pp.352–376; and C. von Bar, *The Common European Law of Torts* (Oxford: Clarendon Press, 1998), Vol.1, pp.569–620.

[116] *cf. Crindle Investments v Wymes* [1998] 4 I.R. 567.

[117] [1973] I.R. 388.

[118] *cf. Gaiman v National Association of Mental Health* [1971] 1 Ch. 317.

breach of the Companies Acts were extremely rare.[119] The introduction in 1990 of procedures for either restricting or entirely disqualifying company officers has brought about a sea change in attitudes towards compliance. What did not exist in Ireland until 2001 was a public administrative body charged with the special duty of ensuring that company law is respected, such as the United States' Securities and Exchanges Commission[120] and the Australian Securities and Investments Commission[121]; we now have the office of the Director of Corporate Enforcement.

The Minister

2–45 The Companies Acts assign various functions to the Minister for Enterprise, Trade and Employment. For example, the Minister may make regulations governing any matter that is required to be prescribed or to give effect to the Companies Acts.[122] The Minister appoints the Director of Corporate Enforcement and also the Registrar of Companies, and can remove both from office[123]; is responsible for maintaining and administering the Companies Registration Office[124]; decides which accounting bodies shall be recognised for the purposes of auditors' qualifications[125]; and can appoint an auditor where the shareholders have not appointed one.[126] Powers to impose several sanctions that were vested in the Minister have been transferred to the DCE and others to the Registrar of Companies.[127] Within seven months of the end of each year, the Minister must report to the Oireachtas on issues arising under the Companies Acts.[128] These reports are most informative about many aspects of the company law regime.[129]

The Director of Corporate Enforcement

2–46 An administrative agency designed to secure compliance with numerous aspects of company law was established by the Company Law Enforcement Act 2001, the Director of Corporate Enforcement ("the DCE").[130] He is a corporation sole who is "independent in the performance of his functions".[131] He is appointed by the Minister,[132] who may remove

---

[119] "Since such prosecutions are about as common as the Irish elk, this provision [s.184 of the 1963 Act] is not in practice much used": P. Ussher, *Company Law in Ireland* (London: Sweet & Maxwell, 1986), p.80.

[120] See generally, J. Seligman, *The Transformation of Wall Street—A History of the Securities and Exchange Commission and Model Corporate Finance*, 3rd edn (Aspen Publishers, 2003).

[121] See generally, H. Ford et al, *Ford's Principles of Corporations Law*, 13th edn (Sydney, Australia: LexisNexis Butterworths, 2007).

[122] Many of which are enumerated in ss.48–50 of the 2003 Act.

[123] Sections 7 and 10 of the 2001 Act; s.368(2) of the 1963 Act.

[124] Section 36(1) of the 1963 Act.

[125] Section 187(1)(a) of the 1990 Act, as amended by s.35 of the 2003 Act.

[126] Section 160(4) of the 1963 Act.

[127] Under the 2001 Act.

[128] Section 392 of the 1963 Act.

[129] The most recent are available at www.entemp.ie.

[130] See www.odce.ie.

[131] 2001 Act, s.12(5).

[132] 2001 Act, s.7(2).

him from office for "stated reasons", a statement of which has been laid
before each House of the Oireachtas.[133] He is charged with enforcing and
encouraging compliance with the Companies Acts, supervising the activities of liquidators and receivers, investigating instances of suspected
wrongdoing and, where he deems it appropriate, referring cases to the
Director of Public Prosecutions to be prosecuted on indictment.[134] Many
supervisory functions previously exercised by the Minister were transferred to the DCE.[135] Within three months of the end of each year, he must
report to the Minister on the performance of his functions and other activities.[136]

2–47 On the DCE's request, a company is obliged to disclose to him the
contents of minutes of general meetings, and of meetings of directors and
directors' committees, and to facilitate him making copies of them.[137] Where
he reasonably is of the opinion that certain wrongdoing has taken place in
respect of a company, he may demand that he be given such books and documents as he specifies.[138] Where, in order to implement company law, the
DCE's functions, or in the public interest, he requires information regarding
the ownership of a company's securities, he may require any person who he
believes to have that information to furnish it to him.[139] Where he deems it
necessary for those purposes, he may appoint inspectors to investigate the
company's ownership.[140] To investigate concerns about wrongdoing or
where a company's members have not been given adequate information
about its affairs, he may apply to the High Court to appoint inspectors.[141] On
application to the District Court, he may obtain a warrant to search any
premises, including a dwelling, and to search for and seize any material
information that may be there.[142] He may apply to have directors of insolvent
companies restricted or banned from managing companies.[143] He may apply
to the High Court for an order restraining any directors or company officers
from leaving the country,[144] or that such persons shall not reduce their assets
in the State.[145] Where a company is insolvent but not in liquidation, he may
invoke a variety of remedies that ordinarily are available to a liquidator.[146]
Where he believes that a person has committed an offence under the Companies Acts that can be prosecuted summarily, he may notify the person or

---

[133] 2001 Act, s.10.
[134] 2001 Act, s.12.
[135] 2001 Act, s.14.
[136] 2001 Act, s.16.
[137] 1963 Act, s.145(3A).
[138] 1990 Act, s.19.
[139] 1990 Act, s.15.
[140] 1990 Act, s.14.
[141] 1990 Act, s.8.
[142] 1990 Act, s.20.
[143] 1990 Act, ss.150(4A)–(4B) and 160(6A).
[144] 1963 Act, s.282D.
[145] 2001 Act, s.55; *cf.* O'Reilly, "Freezing Orders Under Section 55 of the Company Law
     Enforcement Act 2001" 9 *Commercial Law Practitioner* 109 (2002).
[146] 1990 Act, s.251(2A).

company in question and nominate a sum to be paid to the DCE in lieu of his bringing a prosecution.[147] Where a company or any of its officers fails to make good a default in complying with the Companies Acts, he may apply for a court order compelling compliance.[148] He has been entrusted with extensive powers to monitor the activities of liquidators and receivers of insolvent companies, and also with regard to companies in liquidation.

The Registrar of Companies

2–48 The Registrar of Companies is a statutory office-holder, appointed by the Minister, who can remove him from office.[149] His functions may be performed by an assistant registrar.[150] The registrar is responsible for administering the Registry of Companies, which is located in Parnell Square, Dublin.[151] Before a registered company can be formed, the registrar must be satisfied that all of the statutory prerequisites have been met; he will then issue the certificate of incorporation.[152] Up-to-date details concerning every company's directors must be filed with him, within 14 days of the relevant occurrence.[153] Copies of special resolutions and the like must be registered within 15 days of being decided,[154] and every company must deliver to the registrar each year an annual return.[155] Where a company is in receivership or in examinership, or is being wound up, prescribed information must be filed with him by the receiver, examiner or liquidator, as the case may be. He can strike off the register companies that are no longer carrying on business or that fail to make returns.[156] He has authority to institute prosecutions for breaches of numerous provisions of the Companies Acts, such as those concerning the annual accounts and returns, and liquidations and receiverships.[157] Although he can be compelled by court order to discharge his statutory functions and he is subject to the same general principles of public law as are other public agencies, he is not subject to any more extensive supervisory jurisdiction of the courts. For instance, except where the Act or regulations so provide, he cannot be compelled to rectify any of his records in respect of which his certificate is conclusive evidence of their correctness.[158] Where a company is no longer carrying on business or where it has failed to file annual returns, the registrar may strike it off the Register of Companies, with the effect that legally it no

---

[147] 2001 Act, s.109, framed in identical terms as s.66 of the 2001 Act, which enables the Registrar to give notice of failure to comply with filing requirements under the Acts.
[148] 1963 Act, s.371.
[149] 1963 Act, s.386(2).
[150] 1999 Act (No. 2), s.52.
[151] See www.cro.ie. While the CRO's public office remains in Parnell Square, in 2007 some administrative functions were decentralised to an office on O'Brien Road, Carlow.
[152] 1963 Act, s.18. On the conclusiveness of this certificate, see 1983 Act, s.5(4).
[153] 1963 Act, s.195(6)–(7) and Form B10.
[154] 1963 Act, s.143(1).
[155] 1963 Act, ss.125–129 and Form B1.
[156] 1982 Act, ss.11 and 12 (as amended by 1990 Act, s.245).
[157] 1982 Act, s.16.
[158] *Re A Company (No. 007466 of 2003)* [2004] 1 W.L.R. 1357.

longer exists.[159] But application can be made to have the company restored to the register.[160]

2–49 Documents sent to the registrar must be in legible form and comply with any regulations concerning their format.[161] They may be filed electronically, in accordance with regulations made for that purpose.[162] For the purpose of signing documents and delivering them to the registrar electronically, a company may appoint electronic filing agents.[163] Where the requisite information has not been supplied to the registrar or where what is submitted does not comply with the prescribed format, he may send to the relevant responsible person a notice of default or of non-compliance, and stipulate a sum to be paid by that person in lieu of the registrar bringing a prosecution.[164] Failure thereafter to pay and comply is an offence. Where a company or any of its officers fail to make good any default, the registrar (and also the DCE) may apply to the court for an order compelling compliance.[165]

2–50 On payment of the appropriate fee, any person is entitled to inspect the documents kept at the Registry of Companies and to have certified copies made of them.[166] To avoid the registrar being compelled to come to court to prove documents that he has received, he may certify an extract from his records which are admissible in evidence as if it was an original. Until the contrary is shown, his certificate as to the contents of his records is admissible without further proof as evidence of the facts stated therein.[167]

2–51 Certain information concerning companies must be published in a journal maintained by the registrar, the *Companies Registration Office Gazette* ("the *Gazette*"). Previously, this information was published in the *Iris Oifigiúil*.[168]

The Irish Auditing & Accounting Supervisory Authority

2–52 A regulatory agency for overseeing the accountancy and auditing profession was established by Pt 2 (ss.4–33) of the Companies (Auditing and Accounting) Act 2003, the Irish Auditing and Accounting Supervisory Authority.[169] It is a company limited by guarantee, the incorporation of which was procured by the Minister, and the memorandum and articles of association of which may not be amended without his consent. Its membership comprises representatives of many

---

[159] 1963 Act, s.311 and 1982 Act, ss.12 and 12A.
[160] 1963 Act, s.11A and 1982 Act, s.12C.
[161] 1990 Act, s.248 and Companies Act 1990 (Form and Content of Documents Delivered to the Registrar) Regulations 2002 (SI 2002/39).
[162] 1990 Act, s.249.
[163] 2001 Act, ss.57 and 58.
[164] 1990 Act, s.249A and 2001 Act, s.66.
[165] 1963 Act, s.371.
[166] 1963 Act, s.370.
[167] 1963 Act, s.370(3) and (4).
[168] The European Communities (Companies) Regulations 2004 (SI 2004/839). The *Gazette* is to be kept solely in electronic form, and can be found on www.cro.ie.
[169] See www.iaasa.ie.

of the bodies and institutions involved in auditing and accountancy, and the financial services sector, as well as the DCE and the Irish Congress of Trade Unions. Its functions include recognising accountancy bodies, investigating those bodies and intervening in their disciplinary proceedings.

The Revenue Commissioners

2–53 The Revenue Commissioners play largely an indirect role in ensuring that the laws regarding companies are complied with. If, for example, a company's accounts do not satisfy the statutory requirements, it is likely that they will not be accepted for the purposes of determining how much corporation tax it must pay. Provision is made for the Minister to consult with the Commissioners in connection with bonds given where none of a company's directors reside in the State and also for a statement to be given to the Commissioners in connection with that.[170] Provision also exists for the Commissioners to notify the Registrar of Companies that a company has not furnished them with a particular statement required by tax law, which can lead to the company's name being struck off the Register of Companies.[171] An informal practice has arisen at the Companies Registration Office, whereby interested parties such as the Commissioners can request that an "enforcement block" be put in place, staying the dissolution of a "strike-off listed" company pending the bringing of proceedings or other action against the company by the interested party. Before a company that has been struck off the register for failing to file its annual return may be restored to the register, it requires the Revenue's consent,[172] which will not be forthcoming if the company's tax affairs are not in order.

The Central Bank and the Irish Financial Services Regulatory Authority

2–54 Many aspects of dealings in the shares of companies that are traded on the Irish Stock Exchange are supervised by the Central Bank and the Irish Financial Services Regulatory Authority,[173] which has extensive regulatory authority and power to impose drastic sanctions and administrative penalties.

The Takeover Panel

2–55 Takeovers of and mergers with companies traded on the Irish Stock Exchange are supervised by the Irish Takeover Panel,[174] which has extensive rule-making authority and powers to ensure compliance with its rules on takeovers and on substantial acquisitions.

The Irish Stock Exchange

2–56 There is only one official securities exchange in the State, the Irish Stock Exchange, with an address at 28 Angelsea St, Dublin 2. This Exchange

---

[170] 1999 Act No. 2, ss.43–46.
[171] 1982 Act, s.12A.
[172] 1982 Act, s.12C.
[173] Established on May 1, 2003; see www.ifsra.ie.
[174] Irish Takeover Panel Act 1997 and see www.irishtakeoverpanel.ie.

has been designated a competent authority for the purpose of several EC Directives.[175] In order to get and maintain a listing of securities with the Exchange, the company must satisfy, *inter alia,* its Listing Rules.[176]

Inspectors

2–57 The system of Minister-appointed (and more recently DCE-appointed) inspectors, whereby the running of a company may be thoroughly investigated, has been in existence since 1862.[177] Court-appointed inspectors with equivalent functions and powers are the product of Pt II (ss.7–24) of the 1990 Act, under which the Minister's separate power to appoint inspectors has been transferred to the DCE. Inspection systems are designed to ensure that the full facts relating to allegations of mismanagement and the like are brought to light and disclosed in an official report. That information may then be used either in a civil claim by aggrieved shareholders or creditors, or in proceedings to have directors restricted or disqualified,[178] or in criminal prosecutions. Even where the information unearthed is not so used, its publication in a report and any criticisms made therein may have a very considerable impact on the future management of the company and on those persons whose activities have been the subject of comment. Reports of this nature also give the general public a revealing insight into how some companies' affairs are actually conducted. Powers of inspectors to compel disclosure of confidential information have withstood challenges maintaining that they contravene the constitutional guarantees of private property and of privacy,[179] and the privilege against self-incrimination.[180] Where persons are likely to be criticised in an inspector's report, they are entitled to be given copies of the intended criticism, so that they can comment on it before the report is published.[181]

Prosecution

2–58 Breach of the Companies Acts is a criminal offence where the provision in question so stipulates. Where some form of non-custodial sanction is stipulated without reference to being "guilty" or there being an "offence", it would appear that the breach in question is not a crime; instead, the offending party is rendered liable to a civil penalty.[182] Authority to institute summary proceedings for the offence may be vested in the Registrar of Companies or in the DCE, as the case may be. Subject to some exceptions, only the Director of Public Prosecutions may prosecute on indictment. Where

---

[175] European Communities (Stock Exchange) Regulations 1984 (SI 1984/282).

[176] See www.ise.ie.

[177] Companies Act 1862, ss.56 and 57.

[178] *cf. DCE v Curran*, unreported, Murphy J., May 23, 2007; *DCE v D'Arcy* [2006] 2 I.R. 163.

[179] *Chestvale Properties Ltd & Hoddle Investments Ltd v Glackin* [1993] 3 I.R. 35 and *Desmond v Glackin (No. 2)* [1993] 3 I.R. 67.

[180] *Re National Irish Bank (No. 1)* [1999] 3 I.R. 145.

[181] *Maxwell v Department of Trade and Industry* [1974] Q.B. 523.

[182] If it is not a civil penalty, the provision in question may be unconstitutional: *Murphy v GM* [2001] 4 I.R. 113.

a company is so prosecuted, it may appear and speak at all stages through a representative.[183] Frequently, it is company officers who are prosecuted for being "in default" of their obligations, either for authorising the breach in question or, in breach of duty, permitting the default.[184] There is a statutory rebuttable presumption that the accused officer permitted the default in question. Where a person has been notified by the Registrar of Companies or by the DCE of some default but has not paid the designated civil penalty or has not complied with the requirement in question, he can be prosecuted.[185]

2–59 Proof that a person did not furnish certain items to one of the regulatory authorities, or that he did or did not receive certain notices from one of them, or that a document was duly filed or registered with one of them, can be done by way of certificate, in the absence of evidence to the contrary.[186] Copies or extracts from documents held by regulatory authorities are rendered admissible in evidence and are deemed to be valid. In the absence of evidence to the contrary, a document that purports to have been created by any person is presumed to have been created by him. The maximum fine that can be imposed under the Companies Acts is €10 million (for insider trading and other market abuses); the maximum period of imprisonment is ten years.

2–60 Often, it is only when a company is being wound up that crimes committed by its directors or officers are unearthed. A liquidator who, in the course of the winding up, comes across evidence of offences having been committed, is required to make a report on the matter to the Director of Public Prosecutions; where the court comes across such evidence it may direct the liquidator to refer the matter to the DPP.[187] Company receivers are under a similar duty,[188] as are auditors.[189] During a winding-up, the court has extensive power to call before it any company officer or any person suspected of having property belonging to the company, to examine them on oath, and require them to produce any books and papers they may possess relating to the company.[190] Although all questions put by the court must be answered, it is provided that any incriminating answers may not be used against the person who gave them in any other civil or criminal proceedings, apart from prosecution for perjury in respect of their answers.[191] It was held in *Re Aluminium Fabricators Ltd*[192] that such answers may be used for the purposes of any

---

[183] 1963 Act, s.382.

[184] 1963 Act, s.382.

[185] 2001 Act, ss.66 and 109.

[186] 2001 Act, s.110A.

[187] 1963 Act, s.299.

[188] 1990 Act, s.179.

[189] 2001 Act, s.74; *cf.* E. Scully, "Accounting for Crime" (April 2003) *Law Society Gazette* 24.

[190] 1963 Act, s.245 (as amended by the 1990 Act, s.126).

[191] Section 245(6); contrast the 1990 Act, s.18 regarding investigations into companies, providing that answers given by a person may be used in evidence against him.

[192] [1984] I.L.R.M. 399.

application to the court in the context of the winding-up proceedings, as under s.297 of the 1963 Act on fraudulent and reckless trading and s.298 of that Act on misfeasance, for example.

Civil Action

2–61   Depending on the nature of the complaint, there are various civil remedies available to persons aggrieved by company law violations. Thus, companies may sue directors for negligence and for breach of their fiduciary duties to the company; shareholders may sue their company, or its controllers, for breach of the contract contained in the memorandum and articles of association, and for breach of numerous provisions of the Companies Acts. Some of their most significant provisions explicitly provide for a civil remedy against violations. Additionally, either by virtue of express stipulation or the general law, transactions entered into in breach of one or other provision may be unenforceable, as being either void or voidable. Where a company is in liquidation, certain claims may be brought by the liquidator for the benefit of aggrieved creditors or, at times, members.

2–62   Where a statute imposes some obligation on individuals but does not say that persons who suffer financial loss on account of its requirements being violated are entitled to compensation or to an injunction, it depends very much on the circumstances whether those persons possess a right of action. In the leading case dealing with the question of when a private right of action exists under regulatory legislation, it was said that:

> "the answer must depend on a consideration of the whole Act and the circumstances, including the pre-existing law, in which it was enacted ... For instance, if a statutory duty is prescribed but no remedy by way of penalty or otherwise for breach is imposed, it can be assumed that a right of civil action accrues ... But this general rule is subject to exceptions. It may be that, though a specific remedy is provided by the Act, yet the person injured has a personal right of action in addition."[193]

In one instance, however, which concerned an unsuccessful attempt to prohibit a building society from doing business on the grounds that it had been improperly registered under the Building Societies Acts, Barrington J. suggested that constitutional law considerations may dictate deviation from these principles governing the availability of a civil remedy.[194]

2–63   These principles may be summed up as follows[195]:

• Where the statute establishes some special technique for obtaining the benefit arising from its requirements, then almost invariably it does not create a private or civil right of action.

---

[193] *Cutler v Wandsworth Stadium Ltd* [1949] A.C. 389 at 407.
[194] *Irish Permanent Building Society v Cauldwell* [1981] I.L.R.M. 245 at 254.
[195] See generally, Buckley, "Liability in Tort for Breach of Statutory Duty" 100 *L.Q.R.* 204 (1984).

- Where the obligation imposed is coupled with a criminal sanction, then, as a general rule, there is no civil remedy; there can be situations where persons who stand to lose because of a proposed violation can obtain an injunction, although they may not be entitled to damages if the offence has been committed.

- Even where the provision neither provides for a special remedy nor for prosecution, a court may nonetheless treat its breach as a "mere irregularity" and as not entitling persons in the class intended to have the provision's protection to a personal right of action.

2–64 American developments in securities law in this regard are instructive. In the past the trend was in favour of implying private remedies out of regulatory statutes, but this has been significantly reversed in recent years.[196] There is much to be said for the view that, apart from where it is expressly provided for, the Companies Acts do not grant a civil remedy, or at least a remedy in damages, on the grounds that expressly granting that remedy in various provisions of those Acts implies an intention to exclude it elsewhere.

2–65 One of the few modern cases that addresses this matter directly in the context of company law comes from Australia, *Castlereagh Motels Ltd v Davies-Roe Motel,*[197] where a company sued its director for, *inter alia*, breach of what is s.194 of our 1963 Act. Under this section, any director who has a financial interest in a contract that the company proposes to enter into must disclose the nature of that interest at the first board meeting at which the contract is considered; the defendant there had not done so in this case. After analysing the major authorities on liability in damages for breach of statutory duty and the relevant section in its context, the court concluded that it could not detect a legislative intendment that a company should have a private right of action for alleged loss sustained in consequence of a director violating the section. Rather, the general intendment was to ensure that a company's affairs are better administered by preventing directors from possibly abusing their positions.[198]

2–66 Even though shareholders' rights in their companies have been treated as property rights entitled to constitutional protection, it is almost inconceivable that the Civil Legal Aid Board would provide legal aid or assistance for shareholders' suits that do not arise in the context of family disputes. However, it is possible in certain cases for the plaintiff at the outset to obtain an indemnity against costs from the company.[199]

2–67 A somewhat unusual feature of the Companies Acts is that they contain provisions empowering the court to exonerate persons from civil liability for

---

[196] Compare *JJ Case Co. v Borak*, 377 U.S. 426 (1964) with *Transamerica Mortgage Advisors Inc v Lewis* 444 U.S. 11 (1979).

[197] [1966] 2 N.S.W.L.R. 79.

[198] *cf.* Lord Gough in *Guinness Plc v Saunders* [1990] 2 A.C. 663. See also *Conway v Petronius Clothing Co.* [1978] 1 All E.R. 185 and *IRC v Goldblatt* [1972] Ch. 498.

[199] *Wallersteiner v Moir* (No.2) [1975] Q.B. 373.

having committed breaches of the law: a kind of pardoning power. The most far-reaching of these is s.391 of the 1963 Act, which deals with where a company director or other officer is found to have contravened a duty owed to the company.[200] If it is determined that he acted "honestly and reasonably", and that in the light of all the circumstances he "ought fairly to be excused" from liability, the court may exonerate him wholly or partly on such terms as it thinks fit. A somewhat similar provision is s.34 of the 1983 Act, which enables the court to exempt persons from liability to the company in respect of payments made in violation of some of that Act's capital integrity requirements. Those exemptions may be granted where it is "just and equitable" to do so, and the section sets out a number of matters that ought to be taken into account by the court in reaching that decision.

Civil Penalties

2–68 In between being prosecuted and convicted of an offence and, on the other hand, in a civil action being ordered to pay compensation to a person who suffered loss in consequence of breach of the relevant legislation or being enjoined to do something or not to do it, there are several civil penalties that may be imposed, principally on defaulting officers of a company. One is to render them liable without limit for the unpaid debts of their insolvent company; for instance, where they did not keep proper books of account.[201] Another is to either restrict or to entirely prohibit them from acting as company directors. Part VII (ss.149–168) of the Companies Act 1990 provides for placing restrictions on directors of companies that were wound up and found to be insolvent; those even can extend to the outright banning of persons' involvement in any way in the management of companies for a prescribed period. Apart from grounds of fraud and the like, disqualification can be imposed for persistent default in complying with the requirements of the Companies Acts.[202]

2–69 A recent innovation has been to empower the Registrar of Companies or the DCE to nominate a sum, in lieu of a fine, to be paid where there has been non-compliance with the requisite duty. By paying that sum and complying with the obligation in question, the person can avoid being prosecuted.[203] Another innovation, in respect of companies that seek or that have a stock exchange quotation, is to empower the Central Bank to impose what are characterised as administrative sanctions, *inter alia,* disqualifying persons from being involved in the financial services sector and also imposing penalties of up to €2.5 million.[204]

2–70 For the purpose of the rule against "double jeopardy", which prohibits persons being prosecuted twice in respect of the same offence, in *Registrar of*

---

[200] See para.7–145 *et seq.*
[201] 1990 Act, s.204.
[202] 1990 Act, s.160(2)(f).
[203] 2001 Act, ss.66 and 109.
[204] See para.15–78, 15–113 and 15–123.

Companies v Anderson[205] it was held that having paid an administrative penalty of this nature is not a bar to the person being then prosecuted in respect of the underlying wrongdoing. Company directors who had failed to file their company's annual returns on time were obliged to pay late filing fees of €1,200 and €379. They were then prosecuted for not having filed those returns within time. But the District Judge struck out the prosecution, on the grounds of double jeopardy. Because these fees were an "administrative sanction" and not "punishment", the Supreme Court held that the double jeopardy rule had no application here. Those fees were not a criminal sanction because, as explained by Murray C.J., "the liability to pay higher fees is an automatic consequence of the objective fact of a certain statutory deadline having passed. The amount or amounts are fixed and there is no discretion. It is a foreseeable, objective and automatic consequence for lateness in filing an annual return by any company. It is clearly designed to encourage timely filing and discourage the dilatory; that is something which is clearly in the interest of good and efficient administration."[206]

Voiding Transactions

2–71   Where a transaction is carried on that does not comply with some regulatory requirement, it depends on all the circumstances whether what was done is void or is voidable, or is notwithstanding an effective transaction.[207] Sometimes there is express provision as to the status of non-compliant transactions.

---

[205] [2005] 1 I.R. 21.
[206] *ibid.* at 25.
[207] e.g. *Chase Manhattan Equities Ltd v Goodman* [1991] B.C.L.C. 897 (insider trading).

CHAPTER 3

CORPORATE PERSONALITY

3–01   The principal attraction the registered company offers over many other legal forms of business organisation is that the company has a separate legal personality from that of its owners.[1] Saying that an individual or thing possesses legal personality means that he, she or it enjoys rights and is subject to duties under a given legal system.[2] He, she or it has a distinctive legal identity and autonomy, can acquire rights and/or incur liabilities in respect of themselves or itself, and not merely vicariously on behalf of others: "the individual members of a corporation are quite as distinct from the metaphysical body called 'the corporation', as any others of his Majesty's subjects are."[3] Neither trees nor dogs possess legal personality, although the law lays down certain rights and obligations that individuals possess and are subject to regarding trees and dogs. The laws of some societies confer separate legal personality on certain things, like a religious idol in a famous case concerning Hindu law.[4] In many slave-owning societies, slaves are regarded as not possessing any legal personality.[5] Prior to the Married Women's Property Act 1957, married women did not have quite the same legal personality to act as their spouses had. It has been a matter of considerable political as well as legal controversy whether the human foetus has legal personality. Adult citizens of sound mind, by contrast, possess as complete a legal personality as can exist in Irish law. Some of the general principles that are dealt with in this chapter, like *ultra vires*, piercing the corporate veil and limited liability, recur throughout company law.

WHAT IS MEANT BY CORPORATE PERSONALITY?

3–02   To determine the nature and extent of registered companies' legal personality, one must start with some inescapable facts. A company is an association of at least two or more persons (except for "one-person" companies) who themselves each possess a separate legal personality of their own, so that

---

[1]   See generally, *Corporate Personality in the Twentieth Century* (R. Grantham, and C. Rickett (eds), Oxford: Hart, 1998).

[2]   See generally, Naffine, "Who Are Law's Persons? From Cheshire Cats to Responsible Subjects" *Mod. L. Rev.* 346 (2003). The concept of non-human legal entities goes back to at least the Roman times: P. W. Duff, *Personality in Roman Private Law* (New York: Kelley, 1971).

[3]   *Bligh v Brent* (1837) 2 Y. & C. Ex. 268.

[4]   *Pramatha Nath Mullick v Pradyumna Kumar Mullick* (1925) L.R. 52 Ind. App. 245; see brief account of this case by Duff, "The Personality of an Idol" 3 *Cam. L. J.* 42 (1927). See also *Bumper Development Corp. v Commissioner of Police* [1991] 1 W.L.R. 1362.

[5]   *cf. Dred Scott v Sandford* 60 U.S. 393 (1857).

there is nothing inconsistent with attributing to companies many of the legal characteristics of those individuals who constitute them. Indeed, the Constitution's guarantee of the "liberty for the exercise of the ... right ... to form associations" may mean that, subject to public order and morality, associations and companies may be formed that possess a legal autonomy and capacities not that fundamentally different from individuals.[6] On the other hand, there are human characteristics that associations and companies are incapable of possessing. For instance, they have no distinctive sexual identity, so that they cannot marry; and since they have "no soul to be damned, and no body to be kicked",[7] they cannot be subjected to the penalties of excommunication, imprisonment or corporal punishment. Associations and companies are dependent on human beings to act for them; without human intervention, a company as such cannot conclude contracts or inflict the kinds of physical or economic damage that form the basis for tortious and criminal liability.

3–03 In contrast with the position in continental Europe,[8] the separate legal personality of associations and companies has not attracted much abstract speculation among lawyers in Ireland or Britain. Our inherited legal tradition has been to segregate group institutions into two principal legal types, corporations and unincorporated bodies. Blackstone, writing in the 1780s,[9] described corporations as possessing five characteristics "inseparably incident" to their status, namely:

> "(a) To have perpetual succession until they are formally dissolved. They are but one person in law, a person that never dies: in like manner as the river Thames is still the same river, though the parts which compose it are changing every instant.
> (b) To be capable of suing and being sued in their own name.
> (c) Subject to the purposes for which they were created, to be capable of holding in their own right and disposing of property[10] and to perform such other acts as human persons may (subject to obvious limitations).
> (d) To have a common seal through which they act and speak.
> (e) To have internal regulations that bind their members."

---

[6] *cf.* Decision of French Conseil Constitutionnel, July 16, 1971, J.O. July 18, 1971.

[7] Attributed to Baron Thurlow (1731–1806); *cf.* C.M.V. Clarkson "Kicking Corporate Bodies and Damning their Souls" 59 *Mod. L. Rev.* 557 (1996).

[8] See, e.g. J. P. Gastaud, *Personnalité Morale et Droit Subjectif* (Paris : Librairie Générale de Droit et de Jurisprudence, 1977); and S. Bastid et al (eds), *La Personnalité Morale et ses Limites* (Paris : Librairie Générale de Droit et de Jurisprudence, 1960).

[9] W. Blackstone, *Commentaries on the Laws of England* (1765) Vol.1, Ch.18, 475. See too, S. Kyd, *A Treatise on the Law of Corporations* (London: J. Butterworth, 1793–1794, Reprinted 2006 by the Lawbook Exchange, Ltd, NJ); J. Grant, *A Practical Treatise on the Law of Corporations in General, as well Sole as Aggregate* (London: Butterworths, 1850); and Mark, "The Personification of the Business Corporation in American Law" 54 U.*Chicago L.Rev.* 1441 (1987).

[10] *cf. Kathleen Investments (Australia) Ltd v Australia Atomic Energy Commission* 139 C.L.R. 117 (1977).

Many of the modern enactments which create statutory corporations reiterate this catalogue of the incidents of corporate status. Thus, s.2(2) of the Electricity (Supply) Act 1927 stipulates that the Electricity Supply Board "shall be a body corporate having perpetual succession and may sue and be sued under its said style and name." Under s.3(2) of the Broadcasting Authority Act 1960, which establishes the Radio Telefís Éireann Authority, it is provided that the Authority "shall be a body corporate with perpetual succession and power to sue and be sued in its corporate name and to acquire, hold and dispose of land."

3–04 In the past, it was not easy for an enterprise to acquire the status of a corporation. As has been explained, only Parliament or the king by charter or by letters patent could create such entities. Why this should have been so is a difficult question to answer. Presumably there was some reluctance to facilitate the creation of private power centres with a legal autonomy of their own and that were not regulated by the State. Taxation may have had a bearing on the matter, since a major source of revenue was the passing of property on death, marriage and the like. Because corporations have a potentially limitless lifespan and they never marry, those taxes could not be imposed directly on them.[11] Enactment of the Joint Stock Companies Act 1844,[12] and the Limited Liability Act 1855,[13] enabled persons by registration to form corporations with limited liability. The central provision of those Acts is now contained in the 1963 Act, which states that "the subscribers of the memorandum, together with such other persons as may from time to time become members of the company, shall be a body corporate ... capable forthwith of exercising all the functions of an incorporated company ... but with such liability on the part of the members to contribute to the assets of the company in the event of its being wound up as is mentioned in this Act."[14]

3–05 Although the general legal implications of being an incorporated body were established by the middle of the 19th century, numerous unresolved questions remained. For instance, were registered companies capable of legally effective action beyond the objects for which they were established? Could they be held responsible for committing crimes that required *mens rea?* To what extent did they possess rights and were they subject to obligations arising from statute or from the Constitution? Could sole traders acquire the shield of limited liability merely by incorporating their business under the Companies Acts?

THE SCOPE OF CORPORATE LEGAL CAPACITY

3–06 Subject to whatever restrictions are contained in the Companies Acts and in their instruments of incorporation (i.e. the *ultra vires* principle), and to obvious limitations as arise from the fact that ultimately they are mere legal constructs, registered companies have almost as complete a legal personality as natural persons and possess the additional attribute of perpetual succession.

---

[11] *cf.* Mortmain (Repeal of Enactments) Act 1954.
[12] 7 & 8 Vic. c. 110.
[13] 18 & 19 Vic. c. 133.
[14] 1963 Act, s.18(2).

Perpetual succession

3–07 Perhaps the most remarkable feature of their legal personality is that companies continue in existence until they are formally wound up. Shareholders and directors may come and go and, indeed, all of them may die at the same time. But their company remains in existence until its name has been removed from the Register of Companies through the appropriate procedure.[15] Failure to keep proper or any books of account or to submit annual returns to the Registrar of Companies does not put an end to the corporate existence, although it may prompt the taking of steps to have it struck off. A great advantage of doing business in the corporate form, therefore, is that the incorporated business is not in a legal sense fundamentally affected by the death or retirement of its proprietors. All that happens is that the company's shares change hands. In contrast, on the death of a sole trader, his executor or the administrator of the estate must sell off the business to complete the succession, which can involve expensive conveyancing charges. A sole trader who wishes to retire and dispose of his business will be confronted with those same charges and, moreover, certain contractual rights and obligations may not be capable of assignment, like rights of a personal nature.[16] Where a partner retires or dies, in principle the partnership is dissolved, although the inconvenience of such a state of affairs can be avoided by an appropriate provision in the partnership agreement.

Holding and disposing of property

3–08 An unincorporated association cannot actually own property; any property which in a colloquial sense belongs to the association will be vested in its trustees[17] or in its management committee, or in its members, as the case may be. Enactments establishing statutory companies usually stipulate that the body in question is authorised to "acquire, hold and dispose of land".[18] In the case of registered companies, the objects clause in their memorandum of association usually empowers them to own land. Even where there is no express provision to that effect, if land-owning is a reasonable incident to their general objects, they are empowered to own land for those purposes. In the past there was a "mortmain" restriction on making gifts of land to corporations, but it was repealed in 1954.[19] A company can be a member of another company or of a partnership.[20]

Suing and being sued

3–09 An unincorporated association cannot sue or be sued in its own name and, in the absence of special statutory provision on the question, considerable

---

[15] Either after being wound up or by being de-registered under s.12 of the 1982 Act (as amended by s.245 of the 1990 Act).

[16] e.g. *Griffith v Tower Publishing Co.* [1897] 1 Ch. 21.

[17] e.g. trade unions; *cf.* Trade Union Act 1871, s.8.

[18] See *Kathleen Investments Ltd v Australian Atomic Energy Commission* 139 C.L.R. 117 (1977).

[19] Mortmain (Repeal of Enactments) Act 1954.

[20] *cf.* R.C. l'Anson Banks (eds), *Lindley and Banks on Partnership*, 18th edn (London: Sweet & Maxwell, 2002) Ch.11.

difficulties therefore can arise when associations wish to bring suit or someone wishes to sue them.[21] On occasions, their officers may be entitled to sue or may be liable personally, or the requirements for bringing a representative action may be satisfied. Legislation enabling some of the principal kinds of unincorporated association to be established or registered, like trade unions and friendly societies, provides that actions may be brought by and against the association's trustees or, sometimes, its officers. Thus, according to s.94(1) of the Friendly Societies Act 1896: "The trustees of a registered society ... or any other officers authorised by the rules thereof, may bring or defend, or cause to be brought or defended, any action or other legal proceeding ... touching or concerning any property, right or claim of the society ... and may sue and be sued in their proper names, without other description other than the titles of their office."[22]

3–10   One of the classic characteristics of incorporated bodies is the capacity to sue and be sued in their own names. Service of documents, including notice of proceedings, is effected by leaving them at or sending them to the company's registered office. Whereas in civil actions an individual can appear in court on his own behalf, a registered company must be represented by counsel or a solicitor; generally, none of its officers will be permitted to appear as an advocate on its behalf.[23] When a company is charged with an indictable offence, a duly authorised representative may appear for it at all stages of the proceedings, answer any questions put, exercise any right of objection or election conferred on accused persons by an enactment and enter any plea to charges against the company.[24] Where the plaintiff is a limited company, the court in an appropriate case may require that security be given by that company for the defendant's costs.[25]

Legal rights and duties

3–11   Registered companies enjoy broadly the same legal rights and are subject to broadly the same legal duties as adult individuals. In the case of duties, the separate question of attribution of liability to companies has to be considered, i.e. the circumstances where certain acts purportedly done on behalf of the company or in the course of its business are deemed to be the acts of the company for the purpose of attracting civil or criminal liability.[26] There also is a separate question of the extent to which a company's directors and other officers are personally liable for wrongs committed on behalf of the company, in which they are directly or indirectly implicated.[27]

---

[21] See generally, D. Lloyd, *The Law of Unincorporated Associations* (London, Sweet & Maxwell, 1938).
[22] Similarly, Trade Union Act 1871, s.9.
[23] *Battle v Irish Art Promotion Centre Ltd* [1968] I.R. 252 and para.22–45.
[24] 1963 Act, s.382 and para.22–35.
[25] 1963 Act, s.390 and para.22–15 *et seq.*
[26] See para.18–72 *et seq.*
[27] See para.7–157 *et seq.*

Contract

3–12 Except where the Companies Acts or the company's own memorandum or articles of association otherwise provide, companies have the same contractual capacity as individuals.[28] Even where a contract is entered into on behalf of a company in a manner or for a purpose that is not permissible under its own memorandum and articles of association, and thereby *ultra vires* the company or beyond the authority of those purporting to act on its behalf, by virtue of s.8(1) of the 1963 Act[29] the company may nonetheless be bound by the contract or, in the case of exceeded authority, what is referred to as the "rule in *Turquand's* case".[30]

Tort

3–13 Companies are protected by and are subject to the law of tort just as much as partners and sole traders are.[31] A company may sue in defamation; even if it has never traded, it may in the circumstances of the case succeed in a claim for defamation.[32] On account of their very nature, companies may not possess some of what are described as rights of personality, like certain aspects of the right of privacy.[33] Companies are entitled to invoke the plea of self-incrimination, i.e. to refuse to give evidence on the grounds that the answers would incriminate them.[34] However, it has been held by the European Court of Justice that, in the course of investigations by EC enforcement agencies, companies are not protected by fundamental rights, like the right to silence and the inviolability of their premises.[35] Since members of a company cannot owe a duty of care in respect of the company's acts, as the company is a separate person, the members cannot be liable in tort for its acts.[36] A company cannot have hurt feelings or suffer distress, and so cannot in principle be awarded aggravated damages.[37]

---

[28] See generally, P. A. McDermott, *Contract Law* (Dublin: Butterworths, 2001), p.912 *et seq.*

[29] See para.18–21 *et seq.*

[30] See para.18–55 *et seq.*

[31] See generally, B. McMahon & W. Binchy, *Irish Law of Torts*, 3rd edn (Dublin: Butterworths, 2000).

[32] *Scott v Fourth Estate Newspaper Ltd* [1986] 1 N.Z.L.R. 336; *Jameel v Wall Street Journal Europe Sprl* [2007] 1 A.C. 359; *cf.* G. Gibbons, "Corporate defamation: Increased clarity and law reform" 13 *Commercial Law Practitioner* 284 (2006).

[33] See generally, J.G. Fleming, *The Law of Torts*, 9th edn (Sydney: L.B.C. Information Services, 1998), Ch.26.

[34] *New Zealand Apple and Pear Marketing Board v Master & Sons Ltd* [1986] 1 N.Z.L.R. 191; *cf.* A. O'Neill "The Right to Silence and the Company" 39 *Ir. Jur.* 111 (2004).

[35] *Orkem v EC Commission* (Case 374/87) [1989] E.C.R. 3283.

[36] Thus, a shareholder who controls the appointment of a company's director owes no duty to a company's creditors to ensure that the director discharges his duties with diligence and competence: *Kuwait Asia Bank EC v National Mutual Life Nominees Ltd* [1991] 1 A.C. 187.

[37] *Collins Stewart Ltd v Financial Times Ltd* [2005] E.W.H.C. 262 (Q.B.); *Lewis v Daily Telegraph* [1964] A.C. 234 at 262; and *Thomas Management Ltd v Alberta*, 276 D.L.R. (4th) 430 (2006).

Statute

3–14   Some statutes make it clear that their provisions either apply or do not apply to registered companies. Apart from what companies by their very nature cannot do, there are certain rights which they could exercise but are not permitted by law to, for instance to vote in elections for the major public offices. But express provision is made for bodies corporate being represented and voting at general meetings of registered companies.[38] By law, several of the major professions may not be practised by companies or on their behalf. Under the Companies Acts themselves, for instance, a body corporate is not permitted to be either a company's director, examiner, receiver, liquidator or auditor.[39] Corporate bodies are forbidden from providing services as solicitors,[40] as dentists,[41] or as veterinary surgeons,[42] and special provision is made for companies acting as pharmacists.[43] Certificates of fitness to operate bookmaking premises may not be granted to corporate bodies,[44] although an individual may hold such a certificate as agent for a company.[45]

3–15   Where the position of companies is unclear under the legislation in question, the issue is often resolved by the Interpretation Act 2005, which generally includes companies within the word "person". According to s.18(c) and (j) of this Act, "[t]he word 'person' shall, unless the contrary intention appears, be construed as importing a body corporate ... as well as an individual"; and "[r]eference to a person in relation to an offence ... shall, unless the contrary intention appears, be construed as including references to a body corporate". Thus in *Lawler v P & H Egan Ltd*,[46] it was held that a prohibition against "any person" other than a pharmaceutical chemist selling poison applied as much to registered companies as to individuals. In 2001, the privilege against self-incrimination that was afforded to "persons" who give evidence to company inspectors was restricted to "individuals",[47] and the term "individual" has been used when it is intended to exclude companies.[48] Although the Interpretation Act 2005 provides that "[a] word importing the singular shall be read as also importing the plural, and a word importing the plural shall be read as also importing the singular",[49] a "company" has been held to mean just one "person" or one "occupier".[50]

---

[38]   1963 Act, s.139.
[39]   1963 Act, ss.176, 314, 300, and 1990 Act, s.187(2)(g).
[40]   Solicitors Act 1954, s.64.
[41]   Dentists Act 1985, s.52; *cf. O'Duffy v Jaffe* [1904] 2 I.R. 27 and *Attorney-General (O'Duffy) v Middletons* [1907] 1 I.R. 471.
[42]   Veterinary Surgeons Act 1931, s.47.
[43]   Pharmacy Act 1962, s.2(1)(c); *cf. Pharmaceutical Society of Ireland v Boyd & Co.* [1899] 2 I.R. 133.
[44]   Betting Act 1931, s.4(1).
[45]   *McDonnell v Reid* [1987] I.R. 51.
[46]   [1901] 2 I.R. 589.
[47]   1990 Act, s.18(1).
[48]   *Per* Viscount Cave L.C. in *Whitney v Commissioners of Inland Revenue* [1926] A.C. 37 at 43.
[49]   Section 18(a).
[50]   *Prior v Sovereign Chicken Ltd* [1984] 1 W.L.R. 921.

3–16   If it is still not clear whether or not a provision applies to companies, in resolving the issue the courts will consider the general background and context of the measure in question. Thus, in *King (Cottingham) v Cork Justices*,[51] the issue was whether a liquor licence could be granted to a company. On the grounds that one of the prerequisites for getting a licence was that the applicant be of "good character", it was argued that mere legal entities cannot possess any character and, accordingly, can never qualify for a licence. That view was rejected by Palles C.B., in the light of the history of the Licensing Acts and the purpose of their good character requirement:

> "I cannot see why a public company cannot have a character. No doubt it has no soul; but it can act by others, and through others do acts which in the case of a natural person would affect conscience, and be the foundation of that reputation which the law knows as 'character', be it good or bad. It can be guilty of fraud, of malice, and of various criminal offences, some of commission, others of omission ... 'Character' as used in the section means reputation. Reputation is acquired by conduct. The conduct of the authorised agents of a company is its conduct. Why should not that conduct give rise to a reputation as to its character, good, bad or indifferent?"[52]

Although registered companies did not exist at the time it was enacted, it has been held that the Fraudulent Conveyances Act 1634[53] applies to transactions entered into by companies.[54] Although companies are prohibited from being company directors,[55] it has been held that a company may be found to be a "shadow director" of another company.[56]

3–17   In England it was held that the Sunday Observance Act 1677 did not bind companies because they are incapable of performing that Act's declared objective, of "repairing to church and being pious and religious" on one day every week.[57] Similarly, the Protection from Harassment Act 1997 has been held not to afford protection to companies[58] but, on the other hand, companies can be made vicariously liable under that Act for harassment carried out on their behalf.[59] In another instance, reference to "a person" in a liquor licensing Act was held to apply only to individuals who sold liquor in an off-licence and not to a company which is their employer but not the licensee.[60] Reference in

---

[51]   [1906] 2 I.R. 415.

[52]   [1906] 2 I.R. 415 at 422–423, applied in *McMahon v Murtagh Properties Ltd* [1982] I.L.R.M. 342. on other aspects of company ownership of liquor licences, see *state (Hennessy) v Commons* [1976] I.R. 238 and *DPP v Roberts* [1987] I.R. 268.

[53]   10 Car. I. sess. 2, c. 3.

[54]   *Re Kill Inn Motel Ltd*, unreported, Murphy J., September 16, 1987. See also *Lawler v Egan Ltd* [1901] 2 I.R. 589.

[55]   1963 Act, s.176.

[56]   *Re Worldport Ireland Ltd* [2005] I.E.H.C. 467, unreported, O'Leary J., February 16, 2005; *Fyffes Plc v DCC Plc* [2005] I.E.H.C. 477, unreported, Laffoy J., December 21, 2005.

[57]   *Rolloswin Investments Ltd v Chromolit etc. SARL* [1970] 1 W.L.R. 912.

[58]   *Dzivrzynski v Dakchi* [2004] 1 W.L.R. 1503.

[59]   *Majrowski v Guys & St Thomas NHS* [2005] Q.B. 848.

[60]   *Haringay LBC v Marks & Spencer Plc* [2005] 1 W.L.R. 1742.

the Rating Acts to the "persons" occupying premises and to the "occupiers" of a premises was held to connote plural occupation and, accordingly, did not apply where the occupier was a company.[61]

Constitution

3–18   Are registered companies "persons" in the constitutional law sense and, in particular, in what circumstances are they entitled to the fundamental rights guaranteed in Arts 40–44 of the Constitution to "persons" and "citizens"?[62] In some countries, "moral persons" and corporations enjoy the protection of constitutional human rights provisions. A matter of controversy in the US has been the scope of companies' First Amendment free speech rights.[63] In France the provision of a law on audio-visual communications that excluded profit-orientated companies from the statutory right of response was struck down as violating the principle of equality before the law.[64] Guarantees under the European Convention on Human Rights can be invoked by companies, for instance that of privacy.[65] But the Canadian courts have shown considerable reluctance to apply to companies several rights guaranteed in the Charter.[66] There are a number of instances in Ireland of incorporated plaintiffs obtaining judgments that their constitutional rights had been violated.[67] In *Quinn's Supermarket Ltd v Attorney-General*,[68] where the central issue was whether regulations concerning the sale of kosher meat contravened the guarantee against religious discrimination, no objection was taken to the fact that the first plaintiff was a company.

3–19   Due to their very nature, certain fundamental rights guarantees can have no direct application to companies. It is highly unlikely that companies have legally enforceable claims under Art.41 on the family; indeed, that Article has been held not even to extend to extra-marital families.[69] On a number of occasions, however, guarantees that by their general nature are capable of being enjoyed by companies were held not to extend to them on account of the very terms in which those guarantees are formulated. On account of Art.40.1's reference to "all citizens ... as human persons" being equal before the law, in

---

[61] *Prior v Sovereign Chicken Ltd* [1984] 1 W.L.R. 921; similarly *Real Estate House (Broadtop) Ltd v Real Estate Agents Licensing Board* [1987] 2 N.Z.L.R. 593.

[62] See generally, A. O'Neill, *The Constitutional Rights of the Company* (Dublin: Thomson Round Hall, 2007) and M. Emberland, *The Human Rights of Companies: Exploring the Structure of ECHR Protection* (Oxford: OUP, 2006).

[63] *First National Bank of Boston v Bellotti*, 435 U.S. 765 (1978). See generally, "Constitutional Rights of the Corporate Person" 91 *Yale L.J.* 1641 (1982); "Developments in the Law—Corporations and Society", 117 *Harv. L. Rev.* 2169 (2004) 2272 *et seq.* and A. O'Neill, "Corporate Freedom of Expression" 27 *D.U.L.J.* 184 (2005).

[64] Decision of July 27, 1982, Conseil Constitutionel.

[65] *R. (Ex p. British Broadcasting Corp.) v Broadcasting Standards Comm.* [2001] 1 B.C.L.C. 244.

[66] See generally, P. Hogg, *Constitutional Law of Canada* (student edn, Toronto: Carswell, 2002), pp.81–82.

[67] *cf. National Union of Railwaymen v Sullivan* [1947] I.R. 77.

[68] [1972] I.R. 1.

[69] *State (Nicolaou) v An Bord Uchtála* [1966] I.R. 567.

Quinn's Supermarket it was held that companies had no rights under that Article because "under no possible construction of [this] guarantee [can] a body corporate or any entity but a human being be considered to be a human person for the purpose of this provision."[70] Yet there are numerous American cases where claims by companies under the equal protection clause of the Fourteenth Amendment were upheld.[71]

3–20 On account of the way in which property rights are formulated in Art.43 of the Constitution, there was some authority for the proposition that companies did not enjoy the guarantee in it and in Art.40.1.3°.[72] The practice grew up of the shareholders in a plaintiff company being made co-plaintiffs in cases where it was sought to vindicate corporate property claims under the Constitution. However, in *Iarnród Éireann v Ireland*,[73] where the state-owned railway company challenged the constitutionality of part of the Civil Liability Act 1961, that theory was rejected and it was held that companies have *locus standi* to challenge the constitutionality of an Act of the Oireachtas as contravening those Articles. As Keane J. observed:

> "[t]here ... would be a spectacular deficiency in the guarantee to every citizen that his or her property rights would be protected against 'unjust attack', if such bodies were incapable in law of being regarded as 'citizens' at least for the purpose of this Article, and if it was essential for shareholders to abandon the protection of limited liability to which they are entitled by law in order to protect, not merely their own rights as shareholders but also the property rights of the corporate entity itself, which are in law distinct from the rights of its members."[74]

Whether this logic would similarly apply to challenges based on the equality guarantee is debatable because its scope has been narrowly confined by the courts.[75]

3–21 The fact that they are not human beings does not debar companies from initiating claims under the European Convention on Human Rights and Fundamental Freedoms.[76] The European Court of Justice in Luxembourg does not extend to companies all the fundamental rights which it recognises individuals as possessing, like the right to silence and to inviolability of their premises.[77] In Britain, the common law privilege against self-incrimination can be invoked by companies.[78] Whether, under the

---

[70] [1972] I.R. 1 at 14, per Walsh J.

[71] e.g. *Santa Clara Co. v Southern Pacific Railway Co.* (1886) 118 U.S. 394 and *Weeling Steel Corp. v Glander* (1949) 337 U.S. 562.

[72] *Private Motorists Protection Society v Attorney-General* [1983] I.R. 339.

[73] [1996] 3 I.R. 321.

[74] *ibid.* at 345.

[75] On account of the reference in Art.40.1 to "human persons".

[76] e.g. *Sunday Times* case, Series A, No.30, 2 E.H.R.R. 245 [1979–1980].

[77] *Orkem v EC Commission* (Case 374/87) [1989] E.C.R. 3283.

[78] *Rio Tinto Zinc Corp. v Westinghouse Electric Corp.* [1978] A.C. 547; *cf. Re Atrium Trading Ltd* (Manx Court of Appeal, September 19, 2003), noted in 120 *L.Q.R.* 378 (2004).

Constitution or the European Convention, companies can be deprived of this right by legislation is questionable.[79]

3–22 Many countries with constitutions like that of Ireland tend to confine constitutional obligations to the state and to other public authorities, and not subject private individuals and organisations to those duties.[80] Under the US Constitution, most of the Bill of Rights' guarantees obtain against "state action" only. In what circumstances companies are bound by specific guarantees in the Constitution remains to be determined. In a case concerning the dismissal of a managing director for alleged misconduct, it was held that he should have been afforded an opportunity to meet the charges against him before a final decision to dismiss him was taken.[81] Although Walsh J. there referred to the constitutional guarantee of fair procedures,[82] the decision was based on there being an implied term in the employment contract that he would be afforded some kind of hearing in those circumstances. Since a term to this effect is implied by the common law in comparable situations, it would be wrong to regard this case as an authority for the general proposition being considered here.

3–23 In *Attorney-General (SPUC) v Open Door Counselling Ltd,*[83] the plaintiff sought an injunction against two registered companies giving abortion-related advice to pregnant women, on the grounds that this activity contravened the right to life guarantee in Art.40.3.3°. According to this, "[t]he State acknowledges the right to life of the unborn ... and guarantees in its laws to respect" that right. Since neither of the defendants were agents or instrumentalities of the State, one might have thought that the constitutional provision had no direct application to them; that it instead called on the State, in particular through its legislative organ, to adopt appropriate measures for preventing abortion. But it was held by Hamilton P. that, for the purposes of this guarantee, the courts are as much a part of the State as are the legislature and the executive. Consequently, the courts are constitutionally obliged to combat abortion whenever cases involving that question come before them. According to the learned President:

> "Under the Constitution .... the State's powers of government are exercised in their respective spheres by the legislature, executive and judicial organs established under the Constitution and the courts will act to protect and enforce the rights of individuals and the provisions of the Constitution. ... Consequently, the judicial organ of government is obliged to lend its support to the enforcement of the right to life of the unborn, to defend and vindicate that right and, if there is a threat to that right from any source, to protect that right from such threat, if its support is sought."[84]

---

[79] See generally, O'Neill, "The Right to Silence and the Company" *Irish Jurist* 111 (2005).
[80] See generally, Forde, "Non-Governmental Interference With Human Rights" 56 *Brit. Y. Bk. Int'l L.* 253 (1986).
[81] *Glover v BLN Ltd* [1973] I.R. 388.
[82] *ibid.* at 425.
[83] [1988] I.R. 593.
[84] *ibid.* at 599.

It would seem that the force of this reasoning was so compelling that the defendants chose not to argue this point on appeal before the Supreme Court.

EC Law

3–24 For the purpose of freedom of establishment under the EC Treaty, companies formed in accordance with the law of any Member State "shall ... be treated in the same way as natural persons who are nationals of Member States."[85]

Crime

3–25 Irish and English law appear to differ as to whether a company can possess *locus standi* to institute a private prosecution.[86] Where the only penalty is imprisonment or corporal punishment, this question hardly arises because, as has been observed already, a company has "no body to be kicked", nor can it be incarcerated in a prison.[87] However, companies can be fined, and the prospect of being convicted on criminal charges and suffering large fines is a potent deterrent against offences being committed in the course of a company's activities. Applying the criminal law to companies has given rise to two related questions: whether there are some offences which never can be attributed to them, and the agency issue, i.e. when are acts done on a company's behalf attributable to it so as to attract criminal liability?[88]

3–26 There are certain offences which a company cannot be held guilty of committing. A company has never been convicted of murder, although manslaughter convictions have been recorded.[89] It has been suggested that companies can never be guilty of perjury[90]; another such possibility is treason.[91] In a Scottish case,[92] it was held that a company could not be convicted on a charge of conducting itself in a "shameless indecent manner" by selling pornographic materials to young persons. This was because many states of mind have been attributed to companies, through their directors, like malice and an intent to deceive, but a "sense of shame" would not be so attributed; shame was "something which is defined by reference to a type of behaviour of which human beings alone are capable".[93]

3–27 It was held in 1955[94] that a district judge could not return a company for trial for an indictable offence because witnesses had to be examined in

---

[85] EC Treaty, Art.48; see para.21–62.

[86] See para.22–26.

[87] See fn.7 above.

[88] See para.18–82 *et seq.*

[89] *R. v Murray Wright Ltd* [1970] N.Z.L.R. 476. See generally, Law Reform Commission, *Report on Corporate Killing* (LRC 77–2005).

[90] *Dean v John Menzies (Holdings) Ltd* (1981) Justiciary Cases (Scotland) 23 at 35.

[91] Constitution, Art.39.

[92] *Dean v John Menzies (Holdings) Ltd* (1981) Justiciary Cases (Scotland) 23.

[93] *ibid.* at 38. Similarly, *Rolloswin Investments Ltd v Chromolit Portugal S.A.* [1970] 1 W.L.R. 912.

[94] *State (Batchelor & Co.) Ireland Ltd v Ó'Leannáin* [1957] I.R. 1.

the presence of the accused but, under the then rules, there was no provision enabling a company to be present at the examination. According to Murnaghan J., referring to s.17 of the Indictable Offences (Ireland) Act 1849, he could not "construe the word 'person', where it therein appears as including a body corporate" and it was "impossible to construe this section so as to deal with anything but the case of an individual".[95] This anomaly is now rectified by authorising a company to appear at all stages of the proceedings by means of a representative, who may answer questions for the company.[96] If no such representative appears, the judge is authorised to take the depositions and to return the company for trial. A company's representative for these purposes is also authorised to enter any plea and to exercise any right of objection or of election on its behalf. In England it was held that a company had a sufficient interest in the matter to be entitled to lay an information for the purpose of prosecuting a shareholder who allegedly assaulted its chief executive by kneeing him in the groin at the annual general meeting.[97]

THE CONCEPT OF *ULTRA VIRES*

3–28   *Ultra vires* means an act performed in excess of the authority conferred by law on the actor and which is therefore invalid. The inherent capacity of incorporated bodies to make contracts and to enter into various engagements is subject to a number of qualifications. In the first place, a distinction has been drawn between what are called "common law" corporations, i.e. corporations created by charter or by letter patent, and "statutory" corporations, i.e. corporations created by or that owe their origin to statute. The former possess the legal capacity to do anything other than what they cannot do by virtue of their artificial being (e.g. marry, beget, etc.).[98] The latter are subject to the *ultra vires* principle: they can do only what their constituting documents empower them to do and any transaction they purport to enter into beyond those powers (subject to s.8(1) of the 1963 Act) does not bind them.[99]

3–29   For example, the Loan Fund Act 1843[100] enabled loan fund societies to be formed in any district to make loans to the "industrious classes resident therein". In *Enniskillen Loan Fund Society v Green*,[101] the plaintiff sought to recover money it had lent to the defendant, who did not live in the Enniskillen district. It was held that, in the light of the 1843 Act's terms, the loan agreement

---

[95]   *ibid.* at 17.

[96]   1963 Act, s.382.

[97]   *R. (Gladstone Plc) v Manchester Magistrates (Guiver, interested party)* [2005] 1 W.L.R. 1987.

[98]   *Case of Sutton's Hospital* (1610) 10 Co. Rep. la, 23a; *cf. Pharmaceutical Society v Dickson* [1970] A.C. 403.

[99]   *Attorney-General v Great Eastern Railway* (1880) 5 App. Cas. 473; *cf. Credit Suisse v Allerdale Borough Council* [1997] Q.B. 306 at 336–340, which describes the evolution of the law on *ultra vires*.

[100] 6 & 7 Vic. c.71.

[101] [1898] 2 I.R. 103.

was *ultra vires* and therefore invalid.[102] As is explained below, the *ultra vires* rule can operate most unfairly, especially against persons dealing with a company who do not know that it is acting in breach of its own regulations. Its scope was considerably narrowed in the 1963 Act (s.8(1)) but other countries have gone further and abolished it entirely, for instance Australia and Canada, most states in the US, and in 2006 the UK.[103] Eighty years ago, a leading US commentator described the rule as unsound doctrine, arguing that a company's "objects and purposes clause ... should operate simply like bye-laws or articles of partnership, as limitations on the actual authority of the directors and officers to bind the corporation, but not upon their ostensible or apparent authority, unless reasonably to be inferred or actually known".[104]

Invalidity of *ultra vires* acts by companies

3–30 When it became easy after 1844 to incorporate any kind of lawful business, one burning issue was whether registered companies should be treated in the same way as common law or as statutory corporations: could they only do what their constituting statute empowers them to do or were they in a class all of their own? It was not seriously doubted that transactions contravening the very terms of peremptory rules in the Companies Act were illegal and *ultra vires*, such as repaying a company's capital to its shareholders otherwise than by the authorised method,[105] or without their consent attempting to increase the liability of shareholders beyond the amount remaining unpaid on their shares.[106]

3–31 Every registered company's memorandum of association is required to state "the objects of the company".[107] In 1862, companies' objects clauses became immutable.[108] What, therefore, was the status of engagements that were entered into and beyond those objects? In *Ashbury Railways Carriage Co. v Riche,*[109] the company purchased a concession to build and operate a railway line in Belgium, and the defendant contracted with it to finance the construction work. After he had done some of that work, the company repudiated the contract, on the grounds that it was *ultra vires*. The defendant's claim for damages against the company for breach of contract was rejected on the grounds that, being *ultra vires*, the contract was void. A unanimous House of Lords came down in favour of the statutory analogy, depicting it as the inexorable consequence of the Companies Act's provisions. Lord Cairns L.C. reasoned that the 1862 Act:

---

[102] A recent celebrated example of this principle is the "interest swaps" case, *Hazell v Hammersmith & Fulham LBC* [1992] 2 A.C. 1 and the numerous cases this decision gave rise to, e.g. the *Credit Suisse* case [1997] Q.B. 306, mentioned at n.98 above.

[103] Companies Act 2006. The Company Law Review Group has proposed its abolition here too: see www.clrg.org.

[104] Ballantine, "Proposed Revision of the Ultra Vires Doctrine" 12 *Cornell L.Q.* 453 (1927), at 455.

[105] e.g. *Trevor v Whitworth* (1887) 12 App. Cas. 409.

[106] e.g. *Bisgood v Henderson's Transvaal Estates Co.* [1908] 1 Ch. 743.

[107] 1963 Act, s.6.

[108] Companies Act 1862, 25 & 26 Vic. c.89, s.12.

[109] (1875) L.R. 7 H.L. 653.

"does not speak of that incorporation as the creation of a corporation with inherent common law rights ... but it speaks of the company being incorporated with reference to a memorandum of association ... .

[T]he memorandum which the persons are to sign as a preliminary to the incorporation [is] to state 'the objects for which the proposed company is to be established'; and the existence, the coming into existence, of the company is to be an existence and to be a coming into existence for those objects and for those objects alone ...

[I]f that is so—if that is the condition upon which the corporation is established—it is a mode of incorporation which contains in it both that which is affirmative and that which is negative. It states affirmatively the ambit and extent of vitality and power which by law are given to the corporation, and ... negatively, that nothing shall be done beyond that ambit, that no attempt shall be made to use the corporate life for any other purpose than that which is so specified ...

[E]very court ... is bound to treat the contract ... I will not say as illegal but as *extra vires*, and wholly null and void, and to hold also that a contract wholly void cannot be ratified."[110]

In other words, because the memorandum of association is a public document, all persons are deemed to know its contents, i.e. they have "constructive notice" of what it contains. Accordingly, an *ultra vires* transaction with an outsider was void and could not be enforced against registered companies.

3–32 It was further held there that an *ultra vires* transaction could not be rendered effective by all the company's members attempting to ratify it, by extending the company's objects with retroactive effect. As explained by Lord Cairns L.C., "it would be perfectly fatal to the whole scheme of legislation ... if directors might do that which even the whole company could not do, and that then, the shareholders finding out what had been done, could sanction, subsequently, what they could not antecedently have authorised."[111] Prior to 1963, there was a clear basis for this principle, because at that time objects could never be altered and, after 1890, companies could not change their objects without the prior sanction of the court. But the logic in continuing it since s.10 of the 1963 Act was passed is questionable,[112] especially in view of the emphasis in *Ashbury Railways* on the objects being unalterable in any circumstances—the position before 1890 only.

3–33 It was to remedy injustices that can arise from the above state of affairs that s.8(1) of the 1963 Act was enacted, under which *ultra vires* acts are made legally enforceable unless, at the time, the person dealing with the company was "actually aware" that the company was acting beyond its powers.[113] However, s.8(1) by no means renders the *ultra vires* principle redundant, for any shareholder or debenture-holder may apply to the court to restrain a company from

---

[110] *ibid.* at 668–670 and 673.
[111] *ibid.* at 673.
[112] *Northern Bank Finance Corp. v Quinn* [1979] I.L.R.M. 221 at 230.
[113] See para.18–21 *et seq.*

attempting to act beyond its stated objects.[114] Accordingly, the contents and meaning of the objects clause remain vital matters in the running of a company.

How are objects clauses to be construed?

3–34 Most reported cases where the construction of an objects clause is the central issue concern a contract between the company and some outside body, which one party seeks to have declared void on the grounds that it is *ultra vires* the company. In the past, the tendency was to read a company's objects in a restrictive if not an excessively narrow fashion, as incorporation of a business by registration was regarded as a special privilege and, like statutory corporations, registered companies should be allowed to do only what they had clear authority for. Thus, in the *fons et origo* of the *ultra vires* principle, the *Ashbury Railways* case,[115] the company, which had agreed to purchase a concession for constructing a railway in Belgium, claimed that it was not bound by that agreement. Its objects clause suggested that it was principally in the rolling stock business, although one of those objects was stated as "to carry on the business of mechanical engineers and general contractors". It was held that the term "general contractors" could not be read so extensively as to cover, and render effective, acquiring the concession contract with Riche to finance building the railway because, "according to the principles of construction, the term 'general contractors' would be referred to that which goes immediately before, and would indicate the making generally of contracts connected with the business of mechanical engineers—such contracts as mechanical engineers are in the habit of making ..."[116]

3–35 This tendency to "read down" the scope of a particular object in the light of its context among other objects of the company is now usually prevented by inserting what are referred to as "independent objects" clauses into the memorandum, i.e. by stipulating that each and every one of the enumerated objects is independent of all the others and stands on their own. In recent years, a more generous approach to construction has been adopted. For instance, objects "to carry on business as financiers, exporters and importers ... and merchants generally" were read as extending to all purely commercial occupations, such as running a petrol service station.[117]

3–36 Yet loosely worded and ambiguous objects can be a trap for the unwary, as *Northern Bank Finance Corp. v Quinn*[118] demonstrates. The company, which was the first defendant's unlimited investment vehicle, guaranteed a bank loan made to him. When the bank called in the guarantee, the company pleaded *ultra vires*. One of its relevant objects was "to raise or borrow or

---

[114] 1963 Act, s.8(2).
[115] (1875) L.R. 7 H.L. 653.
[116] *ibid.* at 665.
[117] *Re New Finance & Mortgage Co.* [1975] Ch. 420; *cf. Halifax Building Society v Meridian Housing Association Ltd* [1994] 2 B.C.L.C. 540.
[118] [1979] I.L.R.M. 221.

secure the payment of money". Keane J. had no hesitation in concluding that the guarantee provided by the company fell outside this object, since:

> "[t]he wording used plainly indicates that it was essentially intended to confer a power of borrowing on the company. Viewed in this context, the words 'secure the payment of money' could not reasonably be read ... as conferring a power to execute guarantees. Th[ose] words ... are used disjunctively in opposition to 'raise' and 'borrow', clearly indicating that it was intended to confer on the company a power of obtaining money for its own purposes and not a power to guarantee advances made to other persons".[119]

It may well be that in practice, some account is taken of the commercial nature of the transaction and of who the other party is, so that if it can reasonably be expected that the other party will employ legal expertise to vet the proposed arrangement, the objects clause will be interpreted in a more legalistic manner.

Subjectively worded clauses ("Bell Houses" clauses)

3–37   It has become common for companies' objects to be drafted in discretionary and subjective terms, such as providing that the company may "carry on any other trade or business whatsoever which can, in the opinion of the board of directors, be advantageously carried on by the company in connection with or ancillary" to its other objects.[120] Among the questions that such provisions give rise to are whether the board's conclusion that a particular line of business is ancillary and would be advantageous can be contested successfully, and whether it is necessary that the transaction embarked upon is of some economic benefit to the company (other than when it is a "not-for-profit" undertaking).

3–38   The only Irish case on the ancillary-advantageous evaluation stresses that the decision must be reached "reasonably", whereas what is demanded in Britain is that it was reached in good faith and honestly; but this difference may be more one of terminology than of substance. In *Northern Bank Finance Corp. v Quinn*,[121] another clause within which it was sought to bring the contested guarantee discussed above was one enabling the company to act in the manner just described. But Keane J. concluded that executing the guarantee "could not reasonably be regarded as" and "could not properly be regarded as being fairly" ancillary to the main objects, in that only the bank and Mr Quinn could possibly derive any benefit from the guarantee from the transaction there.[122]

3–39   In *Bell Houses Ltd v City Wall Properties Ltd*,[123] a construction company, which had an objects clause in the form quoted above, became involved in money-broking for small building companies. The contention that the criterion

---

[119] *ibid.* at 226.
[120] From *Bell Houses Ltd v City Wall Properties Ltd* [1966] 2 Q.B. 656.
[121] [1979] I.L.R.M. 221.
[122] *ibid.* at 226.
[123] [1966] 2 Q.B. 656.

of what was ancillary and advantageous to its main objects was the "bona fide, but also objective", opinion of the board was rejected. All that was necessary was "the opinion of the directors, if bona fide"; "a clause on the lines of [the above] is able to make the bona fide opinion of the directors sufficient to decide whether an activity of the company is *intra vires*".[124] Nor is it necessary that there be a formal board resolution as to the bona fide opinion of the directors. It neverthe-less was suggested that transactions involving company "insiders" might not be treated as generously. In one instance following *Bell Houses,* a test of the "objec-tive view" and "reasonable[ness]" of the board's bona fide opinion was used, but that part of the judgment was largely *obiter*, and it was held that the contract there easily satisfied even this more stringent test.[125]

Difference between a company's objects and powers

3–40   There is a vital distinction between a company's objects, meaning what it was founded for, its *raison d'être*, and its powers, meaning the vari-ous ways it can go about achieving those objects. Companies possess the power to do everything that is reasonably necessary and incidental to advancing their objects,[126] each case turning on the terms of the particular objects clause and the surrounding circumstances. For instance, a company has implied power to borrow and to give security for loans obtained to finance its *intra vires* business.[127] But a power cannot be converted into an object simply by the memorandum of association saying so. Whether a stip-ulation in the memorandum is an object or is only a power turns on whether, by its very nature, it is capable of standing alone as an independent object. Thus borrowing and giving security can be objects for banks and other finan-cial companies but may not be for specialised trading companies. In one instance, the contrast was made between advertising which, apart from in advertising agencies, can only be an ancillary power, and granting pensions to ex-directors and ex-employees which, it was held, was capable of being an object in its own right.[128] Yet paying pensions surely is just as much one method by which a trading company achieves its underlying commercial purposes as are borrowing and advertising?

3–41   A transaction that falls within the terms of a mere power but is entered into for a purpose other than those set out in the objects is void and unenforce-able.[129] Even before 1963, such a transaction might have conferred rights on a third party who dealt with the company in good faith and for valuable consid-eration, and who did not have notice of the fact that the transaction, while ostensibly within the company's powers, was entered into for an *ultra vires*

---

[124] *ibid.* at 683 and 688. Similarly, *American Home Assurance Co. v Timond Properties Ltd* [1984] 2 N.Z.L.R. 452.

[125] *Charterbridge Corporation v Lloyds Bank* [1970] Ch. 62.

[126] *Attorney General v Great Eastern Railway Co.* (1880) 5 App. Cas. 473.

[127] *General Auction Estate & Monetary Co. v Smith* [1891] 3 Ch. 432.

[128] *Re Horsley & Weight Ltd* [1982] 1 Ch. 442. Similarly, *Simmonds v Heffer* [1983] B.C.L.C. 298.

[129] 1963 Act, s.8(1) aside.

purpose. Take, for example, *Re Introductions Ltd*,[130] where the company's objects clause stated one kind of business (entertaining foreign visitors) but the company embarked on (what would seem to be) a wholly different venture (pig breeding). On the strength of one of its independent objects clauses, which read "to borrow or raise money", a bank lent the company money. This loan received and the security provided by the company were held to be *ultra vires* the company because "a power or an object conferred on a company to borrow cannot mean something in the air: borrowing is not an end in itself and must be for some object of the company; and since this borrowing was for an *ultra vires* object, that is the end of the matter".[131] If the bank had given the loan to enable the company to carry on its entertainment business but, unknown to the bank, the money was spent on pig breeding, the money would have been recoverable by the bank. However, because the bank knew that the loan was to be spent by the company on pig breeding, it had notice of the fact that it was being used for an *ultra vires* object and, accordingly, did not fall within the above exception.[132] As is explained later, whether the bank there would now be protected by s.8(1) of the 1963 Act is debateable—was it "actually aware" that the company had been acting *ultra vires*?

3–42 A particularly vexed case is one that combines what arguably is a power in the guise of an object, that "object" being expressed in subjective terms and where the transaction in question is of no economic benefit to the company. In *Rolled Steel Products (Holdings) Ltd v British Steel Corp.*,[133] the plaintiff company provided security for loans made to another company that was owned by the plaintiff's controlling shareholder, and paid off some debts this associated company owed. Reliance was placed on the following "objects" clause to support these transactions: "to lend and advance money or give credit to such persons, firms or companies and on such terms as may seem expedient and ... to give guarantees or become security for any such persons, firms or companies." Note that the central criterion is expediency and not some assessment of benefit to the company. It was held, on appeal, that the impugned transactions were "well capable of" falling within those objects.[134]

3–43 Having conducted an extensive review of the cases on the subject, Slade L.J. summarised the governing principles regarding *ultra vires* as follows:

> "(1) The basic rule is that a company incorporated under the Companies Acts only has the capacity to do those acts which fall within its objects as set out in its memorandum of association or are reasonably incidental to the attainment or pursuit of those objects. Ultimately, therefore, the question whether a particular transaction is

---

[130] [1970] Ch. 199.
[131] *ibid.* at 210.
[132] Similarly, *Re Jon Beauforte (London) Ltd* [1953] Ch. 131.
[133] [1986] Ch. 246.
[134] In *Re PMPA Garage (Longmile) Ltd* [1992] 1 I.R. 315 at 321–325, Murphy J. upheld guarantees given by companies in respect of the debts of their associated companies.

within or outside its capacity must depend on the true construction of the memorandum.

(2) Nevertheless, if a particular act (such as each of the transactions ... in the present case) is of a category which, on the true construction of the company's memorandum, is capable of being performed as reasonably incidental to the attainment or pursuit of its objects, it will not be rendered *ultra vires* the company merely because in a particular instance its directors, in performing the act in its name, are in truth doing so for purposes other than those set out in its memorandum. Subject to any express restrictions on the relevant power which may be contained in the memorandum, the state of mind or knowledge of the persons managing the company's affairs or of the persons dealing with it is irrelevant in considering questions of corporate capacity.

(3) While due regard must be paid to any express conditions attached to or limitations on powers contained in a company's memorandum (e.g., a power to borrow only up to a specified amount), the court will not ordinarily construe a statement in a memorandum that a particular power is exercisable 'for the purposes of the company' as a condition limiting the company's corporate capacity to exercise the power; it will regard it as simply imposing a limit on the authority of the directors. ...

(6) If, however, a person dealing with a company is on notice that the directors are exercising the relevant power for purposes other than the purposes of the company, he cannot rely on the ostensible authority of the directors and, on ordinary agency principles, cannot hold the company to the transaction."[135]

Gratuitous transactions

3–44 A gratuitous transaction is an arrangement or act that is of no tangible economic benefit to a company. Generally, benevolence that is not authorised by the very terms of the objects clause is nonetheless within a company's powers where it is "reasonably incidental to the carrying on of the [authorised] business" and is dispensed "for the benefit and to promote the prosperity of the company".[136] Gifts to charities and to educational institutions by companies have been upheld on these grounds,[137] and presumably modest political donations would similarly be upheld.[138] Much depends on the particular facts of the case. Although there is extensive literature on what is commonly referred to as corporate social responsibility, meaning the extent to which companies should engage in activities that are not of immediate economic benefit to their shareholders,[139] apart from some leading US

---

[135] [1986] Ch. 246 at 295.
[136] *Re Lee Behrens & Co.* [1932] 2 Ch. 46 at 51.
[137] e.g. *Evans v Brunner Mond & Co.* [1921] 1 Ch. 359.
[138] See generally, Ewing "Company Political Donations and the Ultra Vires Rule" 47 *Mod. L. Rev.* 57 (1984).
[139] Or alternatively, the responsibility of companies for their effect on the societies in which they operate.

cases,[140] there are no significant modern authorities on the issue. The question of gifts in the form of fees, pensions and "golden handshakes" for directors and their dependents is regulated in some detail in the legislation and is considered separately below.[141]

3–45   A classic instance of benevolence is *Parke v Daily News Ltd*,[142] where a newspaper company that was making losses on its publications sold the copyrights of its papers, its plant and premises for a substantial sum. Rather than sink the proceeds into other ventures or repay it to the shareholders, the board decided to distribute the bulk of it to the company's employees as compensation for making them redundant, and sought general meeting approval for the scheme. The company was under no legal obligation whatsoever to give its employees these sums; the proposed payments were being made entirely as a favour. While it appears that the vast majority of the shareholders would have voted for the payments, one shareholder sought a declaration that the proposals were *ultra vires* and illegal, and an injunction stopping the distribution. He succeeded on the grounds that:

> "[T]he decision to distribute this enormous sum of money was [not] taken simply in the interests of the company as it would remain after the transfer of the newspaper enterprise … [T]he decision … was motivated by other considerations. Predominant among such other considerations was … the desire to treat the employees generously, beyond all entitlement, and to appear to have done so … [T]he defendants were prompted by motives which, however laudable, and however enlightened from the point of view of industrial relations, … is an application of the company's funds which the law … will not allow [and] which a majority of the shareholders is not entitled to ratify."[143]

The test of *ultra vires* in the classic sense, however, is whether the proposal is incapable of ratification by the entire membership of the company. If the proposed payment there would stand had all the shareholders supported it (the judgment is silent on this), then the true basis for the decision in *Parke* was "fraud on a minority".[144] Another possible basis might be that the scheme amounted to a distribution of paid up capital other than through the statutory means for doing so.[145]

3–46   Gratuitous transactions that fall four-square within the terms of a particular object are not *ultra vires* the company. In *Charterbridge Corp. v Lloyds Bank*,[146] a mortgage granted by an associated company, to secure loans made

---

[140] The most prominent perhaps being *AP Smith Mfg Co. v Barlows* (1953) 13 N.J. 145, an action by minority shareholders opposing their company's intended gift to Princeton University.
[141] See para.6–95 *et seq.*
[142] [1962] Ch. 927.
[143] *ibid.* at 962 and 963.
[144] See below, para.10–45 *et seq.*
[145] 1963 Act, s.72.
[146] [1970] Ch. 62.

to the central company in the group, was held not to be *ultra vires* the associated company because its objects clearly envisaged those transactions. Therefore, any question of economic benefit to it was "irrelevant upon this issue". The principle is that:

> "[W]here a company is carrying on the purposes expressed in its memorandum, and does an act within the scope of a power expressed in its memorandum, that act is an act within the powers of the company. The memorandum of a company sets out its objects and proclaims them to persons dealing with the company and it would be contrary to the whole function of a memorandum that objects unequivocally set out in it should be subject to some implied limitation by reference to the state of mind of the parties concerned."[147]

3–47   This analysis was endorsed in *Re Horsley & Weight Ltd*,[148] which concerned an objects clause that authorised paying pensions to directors and employees. According to Oliver J.:

> "The objects of a company do not need to be commercial, they can be charitable or philanthropic; indeed, they can be whatever the original incorporators wish, provided that they are legal. Nor is there any reason why a company should not part with its funds gratuitously or for non-commercial reasons if to do so is within its declared objects … Of course if the memorandum of association expressly or by implication provides that an express object only extends to acts which benefit or promote the prosperity of the company, regard must be paid to that limitation; but where there is no such express or implied limitation, the question whether an act done within the terms of an express object of the company will benefit or promote the prosperity of the company or of its business is … irrelevant."[149]

Greendale

3–48   *Re Greendale Developments Ltd (No. 2)*[150] concerned whether it was *ultra vires* and unlawful for a solvent company with negligible subscribed capital to give over substantial assets to one or more of its members when, at the time, all of its members were agreeable to that being done. Approximately £450,000 was paid from time to time to one of its directors/one third shareholder; the cheques were countersigned by the other director/one third shareholder and the remaining shareholder, who was the recipient's wife, assented to those payments being made and benefited from many of them.[151] The company's memorandum of association contained in the

---

[147] *ibid.* at 69.

[148] [1982] 1 Ch. 442.

[149] *ibid.* at 450, 452.

[150] [1998] 1 I.R. 8. MF was the defendants' counsel in the appeal, which may colour the views expressed here. For a contrary account of the case from the former Chief Justice (as he was subsequently), who gave the judgment for the Supreme Court, see R. Keane, *Company Law*, 4th edn (Haywards Heath: Tottel Publishing, 2007), pp.70–71.

[151] The company's entire activities were directly funded by both of them informally.

objects clauses provisions that the company could "grant ... gratuities, bonuses or other payments to the officers ... or the dependents or connections of such persons", and also that the company could "distribute among the members in specie or otherwise as may be resolved, any assets of the company ... ". Its articles of association contained, *inter alia*, clauses 116 and 118 of Table A, and a stipulation that a resolution in writing, signed by all of the members, shall be deemed to be a valid and effective resolution of the company as if a members' meeting had been duly convened and the proposal had been passed at it.

3–49 If the company had been insolvent when the money was paid over to the director/one third shareholder, undoubtedly the transactions would have been *ultra vires*.[152] If any one of the members were not in agreement with the company's assets being dealt with in that manner, there would have been a fraud on the minority and again undoubtedly the transfer of assets would have been unlawful.[153] Such reported authority as there was on the point suggested that all of a company's members are entitled to sanction a very substantial gratuitous disposition of its assets to one or more of them, provided the company was solvent at that time and was not thereby rendered insolvent[154] or that any of the paid-up capital was not being returned to the members.

3–50 The question posed above had not been considered in any detail by the trial judge (Costello J.).[155] The Supreme Court determined the question *de novo* and concluded that transactions of this nature are *ultra vires* and unlawful, and that the assets disposed of in the circumstances were recoverable by the company through its liquidator. This decision would seem to be wrong, being not compatible with the existing case law, and the court did not purport to create any "new law" on the question.[156] The authorities relied on by Keane J. (for the court) to support the conclusion were cases where either a minority shareholder was contesting a gratuitous disposition,[157] or the company was insolvent[158] or it was a non-profit company.[159] It had never previously been held that all of the members of a solvent "for profit" company cannot make a distribution of assets

---

[152] *Re George Newman & Co.* [1895] 1 Ch. 674 and *Re Frederick Inns Ltd* [1994] 1 I.L.R.M. 387.

[153] *Cook v Deeks* [1916] A.C. 554 and *Re Newbridge Sanitary Steam Laundry Co.* [1917] 1 I.R. 67.

[154] *Re SM Barker Ltd* [1950] I.R. 123. Also supportive are *Re Wellington Publishing Co.* [1973] 1 N.Z.L.R. 133, and *Multinational Gas & Chemical Co. v Multinational Gas & Petrochemical Services Ltd* [1983] 1 Ch. 25.

[155] Unreported, March 12, 1996.

[156] See discussion para.13–16 *et seq.*

[157] *Hutton v West Cork Railway Co.* [1883] 23 Ch. D 654 and *Parke v Daily News Ltd* [1962] Ch. 927; see observations in: P. Davies, *Gower and Davies' Principles of Modern Company Law*, 7th edn (London: Sweet & Maxwell 2003), pp.133–134 and para.13–16 *et seq.*

[158] *Re Lee Behrens & Co.* [1932] Ch. 46, see observations at para.6–118.

[159] *Roper v Ward* [1981] I.L.R.M. 408, which concerned how the assets of the Dublin Gas Company Employees' Social and Sports Club Limited should be distributed in the course of its liquidation; moreover, not all the company's members had supported the impugned mode of distribution.

to such one or more of them as they choose. In the US, unanimous shareholder approval has always been a bar to *ultra vires* invalidity unless the creditors were prejudiced by the impugned transaction.[160] A decision by the English Court of Appeal in 2000[161] is predicated on such distributions being *intra vires*, except where prohibited by statutory provision or expressly by the memorandum of association. If *Greendale* is correct, then as a matter of logic it would seem that, unless expressly allowed by the memorandum of association, all dividend payments are *ultra vires*, since there is no reciprocal benefit for the company. Or does it matter that the dividend is quite big rather than comparatively small and, if yes, how is "quite big" to be measured?[162]

SEGREGATION FROM OWNERS

3–51 A distinctive feature of corporate status is that a registered company's legal rights and obligations are wholly separate from its owners' own entitlements and duties. In law, the company and its owners are entirely distinct entities, whereby there is, *inter alia*, affirmative and negative asset-partitioning. Creditors of the owners have no claims against the company's assets; property acquired by the company belongs to it and not to its members. Debts and obligations incurred by the company are its own liabilities and not liabilities of the members.

3–52 This principle was endorsed emphatically in the leading case of *Salomon v Salomon & Co. Ltd.*[163] The plaintiff, who sued in *forma pauperis*, had owned a moderately successful boot manufacturing business which he decided to incorporate, i.e. to convert into a limited liability company. To do this, he formed the defendant company, in which he held all the shares (2,001) except for a share each held by his wife and five children. He then transferred to the company his business at an apparent valuation of £30,000, the consideration being 20,000 fully paid shares of £1 in the company and 100 debentures of £100 issued by the company to him. These debentures were acknowledgements by the company of its indebtedness to him to the amount of £10,000, that debt being secured by a floating charge on the company's assets. But the business failed and the company was put into an insolvent liquidation. The net question was whether Salomon's secured debt of £10,000 should be paid by the company in priority to debts amounting to about £7,500 owing to the company's unsecured creditors. It was contended that, in the circumstances, the latter should have priority because the entire arrangement "was a mere scheme to enable [Salomon] to carry on business in the name of the company with limited liability contrary to the true intent and meaning of the Companies Act ... and further to enable him to obtain a preference over

---

[160] See generally Note at 83 *U. Pennsylvania L. Rev.* 479 (1935), 488–492.

[161] *MacPherson v European Strategic Bureau Ltd* [2000] 2 B.C.L.C. 683.

[162] For a more detailed and contemporaneous critique of the judgment in *Greendale*, see the 1999 edition of this work.

[163] [1897] A.C. 22. For information on the general background to the case, see Rubin, "Aaron Salomon and his Circle" in *Essays for Clive Schmitthoff* (J. Adams (ed.), Oxford: Professional Books, 1983).

other creditors of the company by procuring a first charge on [its] assets ...".[164] In other words, in reality Salomon owed himself £10,000, which is a logical impossibility. Therefore, in this instance his "loan" ought to rank in priority behind sums borrowed from the trade creditors to finance his business.

3–53 A unanimous House of Lords decided that, since legally a company is wholly distinct from its shareholders, priority must be accorded to Salomon's debenture. Referring to what is now s.18(2) of the 1963 Act, Lord Macnaghten remarked that:

> "When the memorandum is duly signed and registered, ... the sub-scribers are a body corporate 'capable forthwith ... of exercising all the functions of an incorporated company.' Those are strong words. The company attains maturity on its birth ... I cannot understand how a body corporate thus made 'capable' by statute can lose its individuality by issuing the bulk of its capital to one person ... The company is at law a different person altogether from [its shareholders]; and ... the company is not in law the agent of the [shareholders] or trustee for them. Nor are the [shareholders] as members liable, in any shape or form, except to the extent and in the manner provided by the Act."[165]

> "The argument that it was not intended that the Companies Acts should be used to enable a person to incorporate any business in order merely to obtain the advantage of limited liability was rejected, with the observation that it is not 'possible to contend that the motive of becoming shareholders or of making [persons] shareholders is a field of inquiry which the statute itself recognises as legitimate'."[166]

3–54 The contention that there ought not be a complete segregation between a company and its members, when the latter are essentially one person, was answered by again referring to the Companies Act: it "enacts nothing as to the extent or degree of interest which may be held by each of the [subscribers] or as to the proportion of interest or influence possessed by one or the majority of the shareholders over the others".[167] Thus, once the statutory formalities for registration are complied with, a wholly distinct legal entity comes into being. A logical consequence of this is that companies can be created simply to evade legal obligations and indeed to be engines of fraud. To prevent such outcomes, the courts and the legislature have grafted exceptions to *Salomon & Co.*'s "segregation" principle.[168]

---

[164] [1897] A.C. 22 at 26, summarising judgment of the Court of Appeal [1895] 2 Ch. 323.
[165] *ibid.* at 51.
[166] *ibid.* at 30.
[167] *ibid.*
[168] *cf.* M. Pickering, "The Company as a Separate Legal Entity" 31 *Mod. L. Rev.* 481 (1968).

Consequences of segregation

3–55 The mere fact that, by incorporating their business, persons obtain some legal privilege that would be beyond their reach without incorporation, or they escape some statutory obligation that otherwise would fall on them, is not in itself reason for disregarding incorporation. In *Irish Permanent Building Society v Cauldwell*,[169] the registration under the Building Societies Act of a building society was challenged on the grounds that the society was not an association of 10 or more persons, as required by that Act, but was merely the instrument of a large financial institution. Most of the society's founders were employees of that institution, and it was contended that they had acted as agents for it and not as independent individuals. Relying extensively on the *Salomon & Co.* case, Barrington J. rejected this argument "as being based on too fine and metaphysical a distinction to be useful in dealing with practical affairs".[170]

3–56 The leading Irish authority on persons being allowed to use the company form to avoid legal consequences they otherwise would face is *Roundabout Ltd v Beirne*,[171] which concerned a picket by bar workers who had been dismissed for joining a trade union. Their employer was a company but, following a dispute about unionisation, its directors formed a new company, the plaintiff, and leased the business to it with an option to purchase the entire premises. It was argued that, although for conveyancing and title purposes the plaintiff might be a distinct entity, the reality was that the ownership of the business had not changed, the plaintiff being dominated by the same persons as owned the other company. Accordingly, it was said, the purported lease was a "sham transaction" merely entered into to extinguish the original trade dispute with the employees. Dixon J. agreed that "there is considerable substance in that view". But speculating that this was not "the sole, or possibly even the primary" purpose of what had happened (most implausible), the new company was held to be a distinct legal entity from the other company and, therefore, was not the barmen's employer, thus stymieing the trade union for the purposes of the Trade Disputes Act 1906.[172]

3–57 In England, it was held that a landlord can avoid being made subject to the obligations under the Rent Acts to a "statutory tenant" by letting the premises to an "off-the-shelf company", which a person owns and controls, even though that person then goes into occupation of the premises.[173]

3–58 Nor does the fact that the company is a "one-person" company, with every share held by its creator and driving force, make any difference in

---

[169] [1981] I.L.R.M. 242.
[170] *ibid.* at 264.
[171] [1959] I.R. 423.
[172] A similar instance is *Dimbleby & Sons Ltd v National Union of Journalists* [1984] 1 W.L.R. 427. Compare *Canada Safeway Ltd v Local* 373 46 D.L.R. (3d) 113 (1974).
[173] *Hilton v Plustitle Ltd* [1989] 1 W.L.R. 149.

principle, as is demonstrated by *Lee v Lee's Air Farming Ltd.*[174] Some social welfare benefits are available only to employees as distinct from the self-employed.[175] It was held in *Lee* that entrepreneurs can enjoy such benefits by incorporating their business and then becoming employees of their own company. The plaintiff's deceased husband held all but one of the defendant company's shares; he was its governing director for life; under its articles of association he was authorised to exercise all the company's powers; and the articles designated him a salaried employee of the company. He was killed while carrying out the company's work. His widow's claim for workmen's compensation on his behalf was resisted by social welfare authorities on the grounds that in reality he was not an employee; that although a company director is capable of being the company's employee, a "governing director in whom was vested the full government and control of the company, ... could not also be a servant of the company".[176] The Privy Council would not accept this argument. According to it, the criterion of employee status is whether the employer possesses the right of control; following *Salomon & Co.*, "one person may function in dual capacities" and the broad power the deceased possessed over the company did "not alter the fact that the company and [he] were two separate and distinct legal persons"; the mere fact that control was exercised by the deceased in effect giving orders to himself "would not affect or diminish the right to its exercise".[177] What would create a *res judicata* or an issue estoppel between a party and two or more others does not do so as between that party and a company which those others own entirely and of which they are the sole directors.[178] Whether this would invariably be the case with a truly "one-person" company can be debated. A principal director of and major shareholder in a company may not avail of the double jeopardy defence on the grounds that it was previously prosecuted for the same offence.[179]

Unfavourable consequences

3–59   That the legal segregation of a registered company from its owners is not invariably a boon to them is borne out by *Macaura v Northern Assurance Co.*[180] The plaintiff transferred his business to a company he controlled but inadvertently allowed the insurance policy on the company's stock to remain in his own name. The stock subsequently having been destroyed in a fire, it was held that he could not claim on the insurance policy because he did not possess the requisite insurable interest in that stock; the stock belonged to his company and not to him. In contrast, in Canada, where the courts are not as

---

[174] [1961] A.C. 12.

[175] Social Welfare (Consolidation) Act 1993.

[176] [1961] A.C. 12 at 24, quoting from the New Zealand Court of Appeal [1959] N.Z.L.R. 393.

[177] [1961] A.C. 12 at 26–27; *cf. Buchan v Secretary of State* [1997] I.R.L.R. 80.

[178] *Belton v Carlow CC* [1997] 1 I.R. 172 and *Baracot Ltd v Epiette Ltd* [1998] 1 B.C.L.C. 283.

[179] *Spencer v Wellington District Court* [2000] 3 N.Z.L.R. 102; *cf.* A. O'Neill, "The rule against double jeopardy and the company—Some thoughts on interpretive seepage" 15 *Irish Criminal Law Journal* 16 (2005).

[180] [1925] A.C. 619.

solicitous of insurers' interests, it was held that a sole shareholder in and director of a company carrying on a leather goods business had a sufficient residual interest in its assets as to be insurable.[181] The fact that a company's directors and shareholders may themselves have the requisite "sufficient interest" to challenge a grant of planning permission by way of judicial review does not confer such interest on their company. Thus, in *Ballintubber Heights Ltd v Cork Corp.*,[182] a husband and wife who lived alongside a property in respect of which planning permission was granted, incorporated a company in order to launch a legal challenge to the grant. O'Caoimh J. held that the company did not possess the requisite *locus standi* as it, *inter alia*, did not own any of the adjoining property.

3–60 In *Tunstall v Steigman*,[183] it was held that a tenant had no claim to the renewal of a lease for carrying on a business in the premises when, in fact, the business was done in the name of a company controlled and virtually wholly owned by the tenant.[184] As one judge there observed, a tenant "cannot say that in a case of this kind she is entitled to take the benefit of any advantages that the formation of a company gave her, without at the same time accepting the liabilities arising therefrom".[185]

3–61 A person in total control of a company by reason of owning all but one of its shares and controlling the directors can nevertheless be found guilty of stealing the company's property.[186] In *MacLeod v R.*,[187] where the director and sole shareholder in a film production company was convicted of defrauding it of AUS$2 million, it was held that his consent to what he had done did not constitute consent by his company, because it was "self-interested" consent in furtherance of a crime. It was held by the Supreme Court in *Taylor v Smyth*[188] that the owner and controller of a company can be held liable for engaging in an unlawful conspiracy with it; in this case to deprive the plaintiff of his title to a hotel. McCarthy J. saw "no reason why the mere fact that one individual controls the company of limited liability, should give immunity from suit to both that company and that individual in the case of an established arrangement for the benefit of both company and individual to the detriment of others".[189] Those were civil proceedings, and it is questionable whether this applies in a

---

[181] In *Constitution Insurance Co. of Canada v Kosmopoulos* (1983) 304 D.L.R. 4d 208, the Supreme Court of Canada declined to follow the reasoning in *Macaura*, preferring American decisions which hold that having a substantial shareholding in a company can amount to having an insurable interest in its assets. In any event, a shareholder can always insure against the loss or diminution in value of his shares; *cf. Verderame v Commercial Union Assurance Co.* [1992] B.C.L.C. 793, where directors-cum-shareholders were held not to have any claim against the company's negligent insurance broker.

[182] [2002] I.E.H.C. 19, unreported, O'Caoimh J., June 21, 2002.

[183] [1962] 2 Q.B. 593.

[184] This is no longer so by virtue of the Landlord and Tenant (Amendment) Act 1980, s.5(3).

[185] [1962] 2 Q.B. 601.

[186] *Attorney-General's Reference (No. 2 of 1982)* [1984] 2 W.L.R. 447.

[187] 197 A.L.J.L.R. 333 (2003).

[188] [1991] I.R. 142.

[189] *ibid.* at 12. Compare *R. v McDonnell* [1966] 1 Q.B. 233.

prosecution where the object of the conspiracy is to benefit the company only and not the owner personally, and where liability is predicated on the coming together of two or more distinct minds.

3–62   A striking example of just how far courts will allow the legal distinction between a company and its shareholders to be stretched is *Northern Counties Securities Ltd v Jackson & Steeple Ltd.*[190] One step in an agreed merger between two companies was that the defendant would issue to the plaintiff shares, for which there was a stock exchange quotation. In proceedings to enforce that agreement, the defendant was ordered to use its best endeavours to see that a resolution was passed in general meeting authorising the share issue. Because by then the company would have made a relative loss if the agreed merger went through, and in light of an opinion obtained from leading counsel, the defendant's directors in effect invited the shareholders to reject the proposed resolution. The contention that the company would contravene the court order if the resolution was not passed was rejected on the grounds that it is the shareholders who determine the outcomes of general meetings, and shareholders and their companies are entirely separate legal entities. A shareholder "who casts his vote … is not casting it as an agent of the company in any shape or form. His act, therefore, in voting as he pleases, cannot in any way be regarded as an act of the company".[191]

Reflective Loss

3–63   Where both the company and also any one or more of its shareholders have a similar claim, the question arises of what is described as "reflective loss", *viz.* whether both claims can proceed, or whether one takes precedence over the other, or whether what has or can be received in one can be set off in some fashion against the other.[192] This was considered in *Johnson v Gore Wood & Co.,*[193] where a firm of solicitors had failed to properly serve a notice to exercise an option over land on behalf of their client company. In addition to their duty to the company to serve that notice efficaciously, the solicitors had given a direct undertaking to its principal shareholder that they would do so. When the company was in the process of settling its claim against them, that shareholder notified the solicitors that he would be suing them on foot of their undertaking to him personally. Because such financial loss as he had suffered from their breach of duty was indirect, via the loss the company had suffered, it was held that his action should not be allowed to proceed. According to Lord Millett, where there are overlapping duties of this nature:

> "[t]he shareholder's loss, in so far as this is measured by the diminution in value of his shareholding or the loss of dividends, merely reflects the loss suffered by the company in respect of which the company has its own cause of action. If the shareholder is allowed to recover in respect of such

---

[190] [1974] 1 W.L.R. 1133.
[191] *ibid.* at 1144. See also *Re Parnell GAA Club Ltd* [1984] I.L.R.M. 246.
[192] See para.22–47 *et seq.* and *cf.* D. Ahern, "The Rule against Shareholders' Recovery of Reflective Loss" 12(6) *Commercial Law Practitioner* 163 (2005).
[193] [2002] 2 A.C. 1.

loss, then either there will be double recovery at the expense of the defendant or the shareholder will recover aT the expense of the company and its creditors and other shareholders. Neither course can be permitted. This is a matter of principle; there is no discretion involved."[194]

3–64   This decision goes much further than did the Supreme Court in the somewhat similar *O'Neill v Ryan*,[195] where the plaintiff, a (former) shareholder in and managing director of Ryanair, sued Aer Lingus and other outside defendants for damages for breach of the EC's competition rules. He alleged that they conspired to cause loss to the company and thereby caused him financial loss in his capacity as officer and shareholder. The short answer (apart from the problem that he had already disposed of his shares) would appear to be that liability under the competition rules was to the parties who are the direct targets of the unlawful activity and who suffer direct losses. Those who suffer entirely incidentally did not have a cause of action, as otherwise every supplier, customer, creditor and employee of the target enterprise could sue for damages.[196] Invoking what is known as the rule in *Foss v Harbottle*,[197] the plaintiff's claim was struck out on the basis of reasoning similar to that in the *Johnson* case.

3–65   The scope of the principle has been summarised as follows:

> "(1) a loss claimed by a shareholder which is merely reflective of a loss suffered by the company—*i.e.* a loss which would be made good if the company had enforced in full its rights against the defendant wrongdoer—is not recoverable by the shareholder [*save in a case where, by reason of the wrong done to it, is unable to pursue its claim against the wrongdoer*];
> (2) where there is no reasonable doubt that that is the case, the court can properly act, in advance of trial, to strike out the offending heads of claim;
> (3) the irrevocable loss (being merely reflective of the company's loss) is not confined to the individual claimant's loss dividends on his shares or diminution in the value of his shareholding in the company but extends ... to 'all other payments which the shareholder might have obtained from the company if it had not been deprived of its funds' and also ... 'to other payments which the company would have made if it had had the necessary funds even if the plaintiff would have received them qua employee and not qua shareholder' [*save that this does not apply to the loss of future benefits to which the claimant had an expectation but no contractual entitlement*];
> (4) the principle is not rooted simply in the avoidance of double recovery in fact; it extends to heads of loss which the company has settled for less than it might ...;
> (5) provided the loss claimed by the shareholder is merely reflective of the company's loss and provided the defendant wrongdoer owed

---

[194] *ibid.* at 62, adopted in *Madden v Anglo Irish Bank Corporation Plc* [2005] 1 I.L.R.M. 294.
[195] [1990] 2 I.R. 200; (H.C.); [1993] I.L.R.M. 557 (S.C.).
[196] Yet they may have *locus standi* under the Competition Acts 2002–06; see para.22–49.
[197] (1843) 2 Hare 461.

duties both to the company and to the shareholder, it is irrelevant that the duties so owed may be different in content."[198]

Groups

3–66 On account of the several advantages arising from incorporation, companies often establish wholly owned subsidiary and sub-subsidiary companies, all of which are legally distinct entities.[199] *State (McInerney) Ltd v Dublin County Council*[200] concerned rights in respect of planning permission within a closely integrated group of companies. The applicant company agreed to buy the land in question but, at its direction, the land was conveyed to one of its wholly owned subsidiaries. In the interval between the agreement and the conveyance, the applicant applied for planning permission, which in the event was refused. The applicant then sought to have that refusal set aside on several grounds. Under the planning legislation, it was the "owner" of land who was entitled to permission.[201] The County Council contended that, because the applicant did not own the land, it had no *locus standi* to challenge the decision refusing permission. Carroll J. would not accept the applicant's claim that it and its wholly owned subsidiary should be treated as one body for the purposes of the case, observing that instances where the English courts treated wholly owned subsidiary companies as agents of their parent company, involved "entirely different considerations".[202] Here, there had been some legal and presumably fiscal advantages in organising the applicant's business under the aegis of numerous subsidiary companies, and the courts should not readily set aside this segregation at the request of a company which usually takes advantage of distinct corporate structures. According to the judge:

> "the corporate veil is not a device to be raised or lowered at the option of the parent company or group. The arm which lifts the corporate veil must always be that of justice. If justice requires … the courts will not be slow to treat a group of subsidiary companies and their company as one … It is not for a corporate group to claim that the veil should be lifted to illuminate one aspect of its business while it should be left in situ to isolate the individual actions of its subsidiaries in other respects."[203]

3–67 The same conclusion was reached in *Stewarts Supermarkets Ltd v Secretary of State*,[204] which concerned compensation under the Northern Ireland scheme for criminal injuries to property. The plaintiff was a wholly owned subsidiary of a major British supermarket chain, and its constant practice had been to transfer any surplus cash it had to the parent holding company. This subsidiary owned a business premises which was destroyed in a terrorist attack. The

---

[198] *Giles v Rhind* [2001] 2 B.C.L.C. 582 at 594. However, the *application* of these principles in the case was reversed on appeal: [2003] Ch. 618.
[199] Post Ch. 14, for a fuller account of the issues being considered here.
[200] [1985] I.R. 1.
[201] See generally, S. Dodd, *Planning Regulations* (Dublin: Thomson Round Hall, 2005).
[202] *ibid.* p.7.
[203] [1985] I.R. 1 at 7, 8.
[204] [1982] N.I. 286.

holding company spent funds on restoring the premises, and compensation was claimed in respect of the interest which could have been earned on that money if it did not have to be spent on rebuilding. Since it was the holding company which was being deprived of the opportunity to earn interest and not the plaintiff, Hutton J. had no hesitation in rejecting the claim. The fact that the parent had complete control of the subsidiary was not sufficient reason, in the circumstances, for piercing the corporate veil and treating both entities as one.[205]

3-68 EC competition law often treats parent and subsidiary group companies as economic units or unitary undertakings.[206] However, as a group of companies possesses no legal personality of its own, one company within the group must be selected as the addressee of any competition law decision, and be made liable for the payment of any penalty.[207]

Piercing the corporate veil

3-69 The term "corporate veil" simply means the legal segregation that exists between the interests of a company and the private interests of its owners. Where the legislature decrees or a court decides to identify the company with its owners, it is said that the law "pierces the corporate veil".[208] Although the *Salomon & Co.* case lays down a broad principle of segregation of the company from its owners, there are statutory and other qualifications, especially in regard to wholly owned subsidiaries. Indeed, the further one moves from 1896 (the year of the *Salomon & Co.* case) the less reluctant courts are becoming to take account of economic realities behind corporate facades. Hard and fast rules for this purpose have not been laid down and perhaps are incapable of being developed. Courts exercising equitable jurisdiction tend to rely on the amorphous criterion of "justice" to determine whether the corporate veil should be lifted in particular instances. Thus, in *Power Supermarkets Ltd v Crumlin Investments Ltd,*[209] where it was sought to identify a wholly owned subsidiary with its holding company and where the evidence indicated that both companies were merely instruments for carrying out the wishes of their controlling family, Costello J. concluded that:

---

[205] Following principally *Woolfson v Strathclyde Regional Council* (1979) 38 P. & C.R. 521 (H. L.); see generally, F.G. Rixon, "Lifting the Veil Between Holding and Subsidiary Companies" 102 *L.Q.R.* 415 (1986); and G. Dee, "Lifting the Veil in Ulster" 7 *Company Lawyer* 248 (1986).

[206] e.g. *Shell International Chemical Co. Ltd v Commission* (1992/C 187/10).

[207] e.g. *Provimi Ltd v Roche Products Ltd* [2003] 2 All E.R. (Comm.) 683.

[208] See generally, Pickering, "The Company as a Separate Legal Entity" 31 *Mod. L. Rev.* 481 (1968); Ottolenghi, "From Peeping Behind the Corporative Veil to Ignoring it Completely" 53 *Mod. L. Rev.* 338 (1990); Gallagher & Zegler, "Lifting the Corporate Veil in the Pursuit of Justice" (1990) *J. Bus. L.* 292; Payne, "Lifting the Corporate Veil: A Reassessments of the Fraud Exception" 56 *Cam. L. J.* 284 (1997); Moore, "A Temple Built on Faulty Foundations: Piercing the Corporate Veil and the Legacy of Salomon v. Salomon" (2003) *J. Bus. L.* 180 and Gallagher, "A Company's Seperate Legal Personality—Lifting the Corporate Veil" 23 *Irish Law Times* 167 (2005).

[209] [1981] I.E.H.C. 137, unreported, Costello J., June 22, 1981.

"[A] court may, if the justice so requires, treat two or more related companies as a single entity ... if this conforms to the economic and commercial realities of the situation. It would [moreover] be very hard to find a clearer case than the present one for the application of this principle. [In the circumstances here,] to treat the two companies as a single economic entity ... accord[s] fully with the realities of the situation. Not to do so could involve considerable injustice to the plaintiffs as their right under [contract] might be defeated by the mere technical device of the creation of a company with a £2 issued capital which had no real independent life of its own."[210]

3–70   There are several types of circumstances where the legislature or the courts take full account of who actually owns and controls a company. One is where it is necessary to determine if it falls into a particular category or classification, such as where it "does business" or where it "resides" for tax and other purposes,[211] or whether it is an "enemy alien",[212] or whether it is bound by some particular requirement. Another is to impose on the company's owners responsibility for its actions, including unlimited liability for its unpaid debts. Closely related to this is establishing those owners' direct interest in the company's assets.

Piercing the corporate veil through statutory authority

3–71   There are numerous statutes under which controllers or dominant shareholders are expressly made personally accountable for certain activities of their companies. In the 1963 Act itself, *inter alia*, there is s.297A concerning "fraudulent trading", s.149 requiring public companies to consolidate their accounts with those of their subsidiaries and s.32 prohibiting a subsidiary from becoming a member of its holding company. Closely related companies may be required in certain cases to contribute towards payment of each others' debts when one of them is being wound up, and the court may direct that their assets be pooled where several related companies are being wound up (1990 Act ss.140 and 141). The Tax Acts contain numerous instances where companies and their owners are treated as one and the same, most notably transactions with "participators" in "close companies".[213] Under the Landlord and Tenant (Amendment) Act 1980, a tenant of a business premises is entitled to obtain a renewal of the lease where he occupies the premises and also where it is being occupied by his private company, or by its holding company or fellow subsidiary company, for business purposes.[214] Particular significance is given in several regulatory regimes to who owns and controls a company that seeks an authorisation or licence to engage in business in the sector in question.

---

[210] *ibid.* at pp. 8 and 9; *cf. Re Polly Peck International Plc (No. 3)* [1996] 1 B.C.L.C. 428.

[211] e.g. *Apthorpe v Peter Schoenhofen Brewing Co.* 4 T.C. (Reports of the United States Tax Court) 41 (1899) but contrast *Gramophone & Typewriter Co. v Stanley* [1908] 2 K.B. 89.

[212] e.g. *Daimler Co. v Continental Type & Rubber Co.* [1916] 2 A.C. 307. See generally, Foxton, "Corporate Personality in the Great War" 118 *L.Q.R.* 428 (2002).

[213] See generally, M. Feeney, *The Taxation of Companies* (Dublin: Tottel Publishing, 2006), p.1236 *et seq.*

[214] Section 5, reversing *Tunstall v Steigman* [1962] 2 Q.B. 593.

There are certain exceptional circumstances where the courts permit a holding company to assert statutory rights strictly belonging to its wholly owned subsidiary.[215] The other side of this coin is that, exceptionally, a subsidiary and its parent company will be treated as one for the purpose of complying with statutory obligations and incurring liability under them.[216] For the purpose of EC competition law, highly integrated companies in a group are treated as a single entity.[217]

3–72   In *Fyffes Plc v DCC Plc*,[218] it was held that where a public company might avoid civil liability under provisions in the Companies Acts concerning "insider trading", by routing transactions through wholly owned subsidiaries that have no economic activities of their own, the company and its subsidiaries could be treated as a single entity for those purposes. A substantial shareholding in the plaintiff was held in the names of the first defendant, DCC, and of one of its wholly owned subsidiaries, beneficially for one of the defendant's wholly owned sub-subsidiaries that was resident abroad for tax purposes. In February 2000, when those shares had reached an unprecedented high price on the stock market, they were sold. Given that up to that time DCC's chief executive was a director of the plaintiff and had certain significant information concerning its business, proceedings were brought against him and the defendant companies for insider trading.[219] One of the defences advanced was that, because the foreign resident company had not "dealt" in those shares and the two companies that did deal with them obtained no profit from the transaction (not being beneficial owners of the shares), they avoided liability under the statutory prohibition. On account of the relationship between DCC and that sub-subsidiary, the method by which the latter was controlled by the former, and the manner in which the entire transaction was carried out, Laffoy J. held that they should be treated as a single entity as regards the sale of those shares and the generation of profits therefrom. Otherwise, the statutory remedy for insider trading could be avoided, thereby causing injustice to injured parties.[220]

Discretionary powers of the court to lift the corporate veil

3–73   Courts exercising broad discretionary powers given by the Companies Acts and by other legislation often take full account of the fact that the company in question is owned by particular individuals or groups, and treat the company as if it were its actual owner or owners. Thus, in four major instances where majority shareholders, acting within the literal terms of the 1963 Act's provisions were seeking to "squeeze out" a minority, but where the schemes in question needed court approval before they could become effective, critical

---

[215] See para.14–21 and 14–22.
[216] See para.14–23 *et seq.*
[217] *Viho Europe BV v EC Commission* (Case 73/95) [1997] I.C.R. 130.
[218] [2005] I.E.H.C. 477, unreported, Laffoy J., December 21, 2005.
[219] See para.15–106 *et seq.*
[220] Considered in detail at para.14–28 *et seq.*; *cf.* S. Dowling, "Fyffes v DCC—Analysis and Implications" 13(2) *Commercial Law Practitioner* 27 (2006).

inferences were drawn from the actual identity of the majority shareholders: *Re Holders Investment Trust Ltd*,[221] which concerned a s.72 capital reduction; *Re Bugle Press Ltd*,[222] involving a s.204 "take-out"; *Re Hellenic & General Trust Ltd*,[223] arising out of a s.201 "scheme of arrangement"; and *Scottish Co-op. v Meyer*,[224] concerning "oppression" under s.205.

Companies formed or used for fraudulent purposes

3–74 Judges have stressed continuously that they would disregard the legal segregation of a company and its shareholders where the company was a "sham or a mere simulacrum", or a "facade concealing the real facts". As observed by Meredith M.R. in 1911, "the Companies ... Act ... embodies a code framed (*inter alia*) for the purpose of preserving and enforcing commercial morality, and it would be strange indeed if that code could be turned into an engine for the destruction of legal obligations, and the overthrow of legitimate and enforceable claims."[225] In *Salomon & Co.* emphasis was laid on the fact that there were no fraudulent intentions underlying the creation of the company there. But it is legitimate to form or use a company so as not to become subject to several legal obligations. Thus the difficult question, of what exactly constitutes fraud for these purposes: of what kinds of obligations—avoidance by resorting to the corporate device are permissible and are not permitted.

3–75 One category of case is where there is outright criminality taking place, in which the company is a central vehicle. Thus in *Re H (Restraint Order: Realisable Property)*,[226] where two family companies were used in a massive excise duty fraud, it was held that their assets could be treated as the property of their owners and controllers. In order to freeze those companies' assets, it was sufficient that their owners were charged with the relevant offences and no useful purpose would have been served by separately charging the company. Similarly, in *Official Assignee v 15 Insoll Ave Ltd*,[227] an accountant who had a history of convictions for fraud set up a company, which purchased a property. Its original directors were fictitious persons; he arranged for shares to be issued to his minor children but they were completely unaware that they were shareholders; he also arranged for shares to be issued to his girlfriend, which he then had transferred to his wife without her authority or approval; he had subsequent directors and a secretary sign documents, the contents of which they were not aware; his child maintenance commitments were paid from the company's account. Four years later he was adjudicated bankrupt. It was held that the company was a sham, manipulated by him in complete disregard of the legal requirements for his own benefit and not for its shareholders.

---

[221] [1971] 1 W.L.R. 583.
[222] [1961] 1 Ch. 270.
[223] [1976] 1 W.L.R. 123.
[224] [1959] A.C. 324.
[225] *Cummings v Stewart* [1911] 1 I.R. 236 at 240.
[226] [1996] 2 B.C.L.C. 500.
[227] [2001] 2 N.Z.L.R. 492.

3–76   Another category of case is where a company is formed solely to ena-ble its controllers to avoid their ongoing contractual obligations. In *Cummings v Stewart*,[228] under a patent licence agreement involving a system of reinforced concrete construction, the defendant acquired the licence and agreed that he "may ... transfer the said licence to any limited liability company he may form to carry on his business or the business connected with or arising out of said patents and this license." He transferred the licence to a company that was not formed for any of those purposes. Describing this as a "trick by which the defendant endeavoured to evade his legal obligations", he was held to be in breach of contract. This view was more recently reiterated in *Mastertrade (Exports) Ltd v Phelan*,[229] where it was held that for the courts to disregard the separate legal personality of a company on this ground, there must be actual evidence of the use of the company primarily for the purpose of circumventing legal obligations.

3–77   In *Gilford Motor Co. v Horne*,[230] the individual defendant was bound by a restrictive covenant under which he could not compete in business against his ex-employer, a garage in a certain area. To get around this restriction, he formed a car sales company which he controlled. As, in the circumstances, the company was "a mere cloak or sham", the court restrained him and his com-pany from competing against the plaintiff. However, it may not have been nec-essary to approach the case as one requiring piercing the veil, because it would appear that the company could have been made liable for unlawful interference with contractual relations.

3–78   Similarly, it was held that a person could not escape his obligation of specific performance under an agreement to sell property by incorporating a company or acquiring one "off the shelf" and then conveying the property to it. In *Jones v Lipman*,[231] where this was attempted, the court said that the com-pany "was a creature" of its owner and was "a device and a sham, a mask which he holds before his face in an attempt to avoid recognition by the eye of equity" and that the "equitable remedy is rightly to be granted directly against the creature in such circumstances".[232] Again, it may not have been necessary to resort to veil-piercing analysis there, because the company would have acquired the property with notice of the contract and, accordingly, would be deemed to hold it as a constructive trustee for the intending purchaser.

3–79   The principle in these cases was extended somewhat in *Kensington International Ltd v Republic of the Congo*,[233] where to avoid enforcement of judgments obtained against it, the defendant arranged to establish several com-panies through which fictitious sales and purchases of oil were channelled.

---

[228] [1911] 1 I.R. 236.
[229] [2001] I.E.H.C. 171, unreported, R. Murphy J., December 4, 2001.
[230] [1933] Ch. 935.
[231] [1962] 1 W.L.R. 832.
[232] *ibid.* at 836.
[233] [2006] 2 B.C.L.C. 296.

Because those were dishonestly structured artificial transactions between supposedly independent companies, it was held that the judgments against the defendant could be enforced against those companies' assets. Even if there is no evidence of fraud, where a *Mareva*-type injunction is granted against someone who owns and controls a company and there are grounds for believing that its assets belong to him, that order will also be made against the company as a co-defendant.[234]

3–80   To avoid future potential liabilities, generally it is permissible to arrange one's affairs through one or more companies.[235] Where assets are transferred out of a company, with the result that it cannot honour a liability it incurred, generally the courts did not pierce the veil and treat the transferee as if it were that company; in so far as the transfer may have been unlawful, the appropriate remedy is to wind up the company and the liquidator would take such steps as are necessary.[236] In *Rohani v Rohani*,[237] in divorce proceedings brought by the wife, the court refused to treat the husband's company, into which he had transferred substantial assets, as if it were the husband. That was because those transfers had occurred before the couple split up, the company had served legitimate business and tax planning purposes, and during the marriage the wife had received benefits as a result of its incorporation. According to Mackenzie J., "the wife, having received the benefits of incorporation, should not be allowed to escape the burden of its existence by looking directly to its assets as if they were the personal assets of the husband".[238] That the husband had irregularly used company funds for personal expenses was not a sufficient reason to treat him and the company as one.[239]

3–81   An instance where the court intervened by piercing the veil, *Creasey v Breachwood Motors Ltd*,[240] has since been disapproved of in England.[241] Almost as soon as one company was served with the plaintiff's writ for wrongful dismissal, it ceased trading, transferred its business and assets to two related companies, and then paid off all its existing creditors. Apparently on account of the plaintiff's impecuniosity, which would have rendered the winding-up option practically impossible, it was held that those transferees could be substituted for the company as defendants in his claim.

---

[234] See generally, Devonshire, "Pre-Emptive Orders Against Evasive Dealings: An Assessment of Recent Trends" [2004] *J. Bus. L.* 357, 362 *et seq.*

[235] *Adams v Cape Industries Plc* [1990] Ch. 433, where the company was formed to confine future or contingent liabilities within limits.

[236] Under s.251 of the 1990 Act, however, liquidation may not be necessary and, further, the Director of Corporate Enforcement now has power to intervene: see para.20–16 *et seq.*

[237] 247 D.L.R. (4th) 17 (2005).

[238] *ibid.* at 26.

[239] However, see *Wildman v Wildman* 273 D.L.R. (4th) 37 (2006), which distinguished *Rohani* on the facts, and *Mubarak v Mubarak* [2001] 1 F.L.R.673.

[240] [1993] B.C.L.C. 480 and in similar vein, *Aveling Barford Ltd v Perion Ltd* [1989] B.C.L.C. 626; *cf. Yukong Line Ltd v Rendsburg Investment Corp.* [1998] 1 W.L.R. 294.

[241] *Ord v Belhaven Pubs Ltd* [1998] 2 B.C.L.C. 447; *cf.* D. Bromilow, "*Creasey v Breachwood Motors*: Mistaken Identity Leads to Untimely Death" 19 *Company Lawyer* 198 (1998).

3–82 Where the owner-controller leads a person to believe that he is dealing with him and not the company, the question of veil-piercing simply does not arise; he is liable as a principal or as an undisclosed principal. Nor, ordinarily, does the question arise where a company acquires property that its owner and controller unlawfully obtained, in particular where he was a director of another company and obtained the asset in breach of his fiduciary duty to it. Liability arises from knowing receipt or receipt in circumstances where the company ought to have known the property's provenance. But veil-piercing analysis was adopted in *Trustor AB v Smallbone (No. 2)*[242] where, in breach of fiduciary duty, a company director transferred substantial sums belonging to it to another company that he owned and controlled. It was held that the latter company was accountable for those funds, it having been used to conceal the true facts and to avoid personal liability.

Company formed as agent or **alter ego** *of its controllers*

3–83 Instances of the separate existence of companies being ignored because they are mere "shams" and "facades" have also been explained as *alter ego* situations: in the circumstances, the company is merely the agent or instrument of its controllers, so that in justice they should be held directly responsible for its actions. Sometimes the company will have acted as an outright agent for its controllers, or vice versa, or a trustee-*cestui* relationship will have existed between them.

3–84 Where an express agency agreement exists, the question of piercing the corporate veil does not arise because liability will be based on ordinary agency principles. Thus, an incorporated club which purchased beer as agent for its members was able to surmount licensing provisions that otherwise would have prevented it from selling beer on its premises[243]; and a foreign company was able to carry on business in England through the agency of its UK-registered subsidiary to obtain a tax advantage there.[244] However, an agency or a trust will not be inferred from the mere fact of ownership or control of a company[245]; additional factors must exist which point compellingly to such a legal relationship between the company and its controllers.[246] In *Fyffes Plc v DCC Plc*,[247] it also was contended that, in dealing with the plaintiff's shares and taking the profit from them, a principal–agency relationship existed between the defendant group companies. But Laffoy J. refused to accept that either the sub-subsidiary acted in the transaction as agent for its parent companies or that those companies acted as agent for the sub-subsidiary. On each occasion that they dealt in the shares, they dealt as principals.

---

[242] [2001] 3 All E.R. 987.
[243] *Re Parnell GAA Club Ltd* [1984] I.L.R.M. 246.
[244] *Firestone Tyre & Rubber Co. v Llewellin* [1957] 1 W.L.R. 464.
[245] *JJ Harrison (Properties) Ltd v Harrison* [2002] 1 B.C.L.C. 162.
[246] *The Maritime Trader* [1981] 2 Lloyd's Rep. 153.
[247] [2005] I.E.H.C. 477, unreported, Laffoy J., December 21, 2005.

3–85   *Power Supermarkets Ltd v Crumlin Investments Ltd*[248] provides an
excellent demonstration of the *alter ego* principle being applied in the context
of groups of companies. An agreement was made by a wholly owned subsidiary of the Dunnes Stores Group, which had leased part of a shopping centre,
not to "grant a lease for, or to sell or permit or suffer the sale by any of its tenants" of groceries in a particular manner. Subsequently, that subsidiary conveyed the fee simple interest in that part of the shopping centre to its parent
company, which then traded in the manner the lease had sought to prevent.
Fraud on the contract in the sense described above was not contended, but the
evidence disclosed that the subsidiary was never treated as if it were an auton-
omous legal and economic entity. Costello J. concluded that the two companies were merely vehicles for carrying out the wishes of the Dunne family and
that, in the circumstances, justice required that their separate existence be disregarded.[249]

Fraud on a Minority

3–86   Where some wrong has been done to the company, under the "reflective loss" principle it is for the company itself and not its shareholders to bring
suit against the wrongdoers, since the members' own legal rights have not been
infringed. Where, however, the wrong is done by those who control the company, the majority shareholders, and it amounts to fraud in a loose equitable
sense, the individual shareholder may be permitted to bring suit in the company's name against the wrongdoer. This complex aspect of company law is
often referred to as the rule in *Foss v Harbottle*.[250]

Limited liability and lifting the corporate veil

3–87   It would seem that limited liability was not a necessary attribute of chartered business corporations, although there does not appear to be any authoritative statement that members of a corporation are personally liable for its debts
unless the grant of incorporation includes some express limitation on their liability. In 1935 limited liability was conferred by statute on shareholders in the Bank
of Ireland.[251] Where an entity is created by statute and thereby possesses its own
legal personality, but no provision is made regarding its members' liability for its
unpaid debts, it was held that they cannot be rendered so liable.[252] Under the
Joint Stock Companies Act 1844,[253] it was stipulated that a registered company's
members were liable for its unpaid debts, in much the same way as if it were a
partnership, and that remained the position until the Limited Liability Act of
1855.[254] The immediate significance of *Salomon & Co.*[255] was that it entrenched
the principle that shareholders can entirely insulate their own financial positions

---

[248] [1981] I.E.H.C. 137, unreported, Costello J., June 22, 1981.
[249] *cf. Adams v Cape Industries Plc* [1990] Ch. 433.
[250] (1843) 2 Hare 461 and see post 10–45 *et seq.*
[251] Bank of Ireland Act 1935, s.2.
[252] *J. H. Rayner (Mincing Lane) Ltd v Dept of Trade & Industry* [1990] 2 A.C. 418.
[253] 7 & 8 Vic. c.110.
[254] 18 & 19 Vic. c.133.
[255] [1897] A.C. 22.

from that of their company, in that they themselves are not in jeopardy of being bankrupted if the company is wound up without being able to pay its debts. In the absence of any agreement to the contrary or such exceptional circumstances as are indicated below, shareholders in a limited company are liable to it only in respect of the amounts remaining unpaid on their shares.[256] A number of rules and doctrines exist, however, under which the plight of the limited company's unpaid creditors may be alleviated.

Fraud

3–88 As has been indicated above, in appropriate circumstances the courts will pierce the corporate veil on the grounds that the company is a mere puppet of its controllers, especially where it is being used for fraudulent purposes. This approach is given a degree of statutory expression in s.297A of the 1963 Act on "fraudulent trading". Persons managing a company can be made personally liable for its entire debts if it is shown that "any business of the company has been carried on with intent to defraud creditors ... or for any fraudulent purpose ...".[257] Company controllers who, in effect, give themselves presents of company assets, with the consequence that the company is unable to pay its debts, can be compelled to disgorge those sums to the company's creditors. In *Re George Newman & Co.*,[258] it was pointed out that "to make presents out of profits is one thing [but] to make them out of capital or out of money borrowed by the company is a very different matter. Such money cannot be lawfully divided among the shareholders themselves, nor can it be given away by them for nothing to their directors so as to bind the company in its corporate capacity".[259] That is to say, such payments are *ultra vires* the company. Where capital is repaid to any member other than by the method set out in s.72 of the 1963 Act or an otherwise authorised mode, the funds must be repaid if the member knew or ought to have known that it was a prohibited "distribution". Where a party represents that a company has sufficient assets to meet a commitment, when it does not, he is directly liable for fraud.

Under-capitalisation

3–89 The core contention in *Salomon & Co.* was not that the unsecured creditors should have a direct claim against Mr Salomon, but merely that whatever claims he had against the company should be postponed, or subordinated, until other creditors' claims were satisfied first. In support of this, it was argued that he had established an insufficiently capitalised entity and that, accordingly, he should suffer the adverse consequences of its overtrading, especially when he exercised complete control over the company and stood to benefit virtually exclusively from any profits it made. More particularly, it was said that, in return for securities in it, the company had acquired assets from him at a considerable overvaluation, that in consequence the actual capital possessed by

---

[256] 1963 Act, ss.27 and 207(1)(d).
[257] See para.24–97.
[258] [1895] 1 Ch. 674.
[259] *ibid.* at 686.

the company was seriously overstated and, therefore, it was unfair for unse-cured creditors to bear the entire loss when they may have believed they were doing business with a much more substantial entity. This line of argument foundered on one of the House of Lords' leading cases on promoters' liabil-ity.[260] It established that, where the price paid by a company for a business is exorbitant but all of its shareholders are perfectly cognisant of the conditions under which the company was formed and the circumstances of that purchase, it is impossible to contend that the company is being defrauded.[261] It further-more was said of the unpaid creditors that "if they had thought fit to avail them-selves of the means of protecting their interests which the Act provides, [they] could have informed themselves of the terms of the purchase" and that "the law does not lay any obligations … to warn those members of the public who deal with [a company] on credit that they run the risk of not being paid".[262]

3–90   It nevertheless is conceivable that in exceptional circumstances, the controlling shareholders might be held liable for the debts of their inade-quately capitalised companies—as where the creditor is of the "involuntary" category, or where there was some misrepresentation about the company's true worth, or the shareholder had "milked" the company of substance.[263] Such an outcome is especially likely where the company is a wholly owned subsidiary being operated in fact as an integral part of the parent's busi-ness.[264] Section 140 of the 1990 Act empowers a court to order that a com-pany contribute towards paying the debts of its insolvent related company.

Involuntary creditors

3–91   In *Salomon & Co.* the argument that, in the circumstances, it would be unjust to give Salomon priority over the company's unsecured creditors was also met with the answer that they "may be entitled to sympathy, but they have only themselves to blame for their misfortunes. [For] they had full notice that they were no longer dealing with an individual, and they must be taken to have been cognizant of the memorandum and of the articles of association".[265] How-ever, what is the position of what is called the involuntary creditor, for example the pedestrian who is injured by a company-owned vehicle and has a right of action in negligence against the company as a consequence?[266] The victim does not choose to be struck by a vehicle owned by a limited company as opposed to

---

[260] *Erlanger v New Sombrero Phosphate Co.* (1878) 3 App. Cas. 1218.

[261] [1897] A.C. 22 at 33.

[262] *ibid.* at 40. See also, *Henry Brown & Sons Ltd v Smith* [1964] 2 Lloyd's List Law Reports 476.

[263] See generally, Hackney & Benson, "Shareholder Liability for Inadequate Capital" 43 *U. Pittsburgh L. Rev.* 837 (1982) and Halpern et al., "An Economic Analysis of Limited Liability in Corporation Law" 30 *U. Toronto L.J.* 117 (1980).

[264] Lifting the corporate veil in group of company situations is discussed at para.14–23 *et seq.*

[265] [1897] A.C.22 at 53. Similarly, *Henry Brown & Sons Ltd v Smith* [1964] 2 Lloyd's List Law Reports 476.

[266] e.g. *Walkovszky v Carlton*, 223 N.E. 2d. 6 (1966), extracts reproduced in Eisenberg, *Cases and Materials on Corporations and Other Business Organizations*, 9th edn (New York: Foundation Press, 2005), p.169.

being owned by an individual trader or partnership. Under the bankruptcy rules, which also apply to winding up,[267] the position was that claims for damages in tort were not provable debts against the insolvent tortfeasor.[268] At common law, such claims simply could not be asserted at all against the company, thereby precluding any argument that the company's shareholders should be rendered responsible for those debts because of the very special circumstances of the case. This rule, embodied in the bankruptcy legislation,[269] was abolished by s.61 of the Civil Liability Act 1961, according to which: "[n]ot withstanding any other enactment or any rule of law, a claim for damages or contribution in respect of a wrong shall be provable in bankruptcy where the wrong out of which the liability to damages or the right to contribution arose was committed before the time of the bankruptcy".[270] Consequently, involuntary creditors are now entitled to maintain claims against insolvent companies, thereby making it at least possible to argue that the company's shareholders should be held responsible to them because of the special circumstances of the case.

3–92   There would be no great difficulty in distinguishing *Salomon & Co*. To do so, the argument could be made that the public policy supporting limited liability must be reconciled with, if not forced to make way for, the broad principle that persons who, through no fault whatsoever of their own, suffer damage as a result of another's fault, ought not to go uncompensated.[271] It may even be possible to demonstrate that the economic and social goals that limited liability was intended to achieve are not unduly compromised by allowing recourse in this context against the shareholders, who in any event stand to benefit from the company's risky activities.[272] An inevitable problem with any involuntary creditor doctrine is separating the voluntarily assumed legal relationships from those imposed by events. Take a Canadian case concerning against whom costs should be awarded when a "one-person" company loses a wholly unmeritorious legal claim brought by it, and is then discovered to be insolvent.[273] In *Sweeney v Duggan*,[274] it was contended that the plaintiff, a former employee of an insolvent company who was injured at work, fell into the "involuntary" category and that *Salomon & Co*. did not protect the "one man" owner of the company, who (along with his wife) was its director and who managed its business. However, the Supreme Court declined to comment on the proposition, finding against the plaintiff on other grounds.[275]

---

[267] 1963 Act, s.283.

[268] See generally, M. Forde, *Bankruptcy Law in Ireland* (Cork: Mercier Press, 1990), p.139.

[269] Section 30(1) of the 1914 Act.

[270] See Bankruptcy Act 1988, s.75(1).

[271] *Kirby v Burke* [1944] I.R. 207.

[272] The argument for imposing liability is made in Hansmann and Kraakman, "Towards Unlimited Shareholder Liability for Corporate Torts" 100 *Yale L.J.* 1879 (1991).

[273] *Rockwell Developments Ltd v Newtonbrook Plaza Ltd* (1972) 30 O.R. (2d.) 199.

[274] [1997] 2 I.R. 531.

[275] *cf. Berger v Willowdale AMC*, 145 D.L.R. (3d.) 247 (1983).

CHAPTER 4

COMPANY FORMATION

4–01　The most convenient way to set up business as a registered company is to buy an already formed company from a specialist in selling companies "off-the-shelf". The purchasers then make whatever alterations to that company they deem necessary, like changing its name, the address of its registered office, directors, capital structure, memorandum and articles of association. Alternatively, one may decide to form a new company, which in any event is not a particularly onerous or complex task. All that is needed is one or two founders and a signed memorandum and articles of association; these documents must be accompanied by a statutory declaration and a cheque for capital tax, and be registered with the Registrar of Companies. A number of additional formalities must be complied with before Plcs can commence doing business—these are most helpfully set out on the Companies Registration Office website (www.cro.ie).

THE PRINCIPAL TYPES OF REGISTERED COMPANY

4–02　There is an infinite variety of registered companies: there are large and small companies, companies with closely held and with widely dispersed shareholdings, profit-orientated and non-profit companies, indigenous and transnational companies. Registered companies fall into a number of distinct legal categories: principally, limited or unlimited companies; private or public companies; one-person companies; public limited companies; and guarantee companies.

Limited Company

4–03　A company may be registered either with limited liability or with unlimited liability.[1] One of the main reasons why persons choose to do business through the vehicle of registered companies is to obtain the privilege of limited liability. By this is meant that, if the business fails, the owners of the limited company are not personally responsible for all of its unpaid liabilities. Their obligations in respect of the company's debts are measured by how much, if anything, remains unpaid or outstanding on the shares they own.[2] An alternative method of limiting liability, which in practice is confined to "non-profit" companies, is by guarantee: the company's members undertake to contribute

---

[1]　1963 Act, ss.5(2)(a), 207(1)(d).
[2]　1963 Act, s.207(1)(d).

towards its liabilities up to a stated or guaranteed amount in the event of it being wound up.[3]

4–04 No company, whether limited or unlimited, may increase in any way its members' liability to it or otherwise oblige them to pay it money, unless the member has consented in writing to do so.[4] Nor may a company reduce in any way its members' liability on their shareholding or guarantees, other than by way of a court-approved capital reorganisation.[5]

Unlimited Company

4–05 There are comparatively few unlimited companies, since the members can be held liable without limit for their company's debts. There nevertheless are some advantages in having the unlimited form.[6] These companies are exempted from many of the Companies Acts' disclosure requirements, notably from disclosing financial information that the Companies (Amendment) Act 1986 requires to be contained in the annual return to the Registrar of Companies.[7] Accordingly, unlimited companies provide their individual members with greater secrecy about their affairs; in many respects they are *sociétés anonymes*.[8] Many of the Companies Acts' rules on capital integrity do not apply to unlimited companies, so that it is relatively easy for them to return contributed capital to their members. Tax avoidance schemes often make use of unlimited companies, again because it is relatively easy for them to return contributed capital to their members. There is a numerical ceiling on the size of partnerships other than of accountants or solicitors[9]; an unlimited company, therefore, is used where more than 20 persons, or more than 10 in the case of bankers, wish to engage in business in common but for one reason or another desire unlimited liability. Unlimited companies do not have to pay *ad valorem* stamp duty on being registered,[10] and they enjoy certain other fiscal advantages.[11] As they possess separate legal personality, unlimited companies are fundamentally different from partnerships, with the consequence that company creditors have no direct claim against company members. Instead, those creditors must secure the company's winding-up and the liquidator will then attempt to recover outstanding amounts from those members.[12] The 1963 Act allows for limited companies where the liability of the directors, or of the

---

[3] 1963 Act, ss.5(2)(b) and 207(1)(e) and (3).

[4] 1963 Act, s.27.

[5] 1963 Act, s.72.

[6] See generally, Rice, "The Unlimited Company—An Anachronism or a Modern Opportunity" 27 *Conv.* 442 (1963); and Grossman, "The Market for Shares of Companies with Unlimited Liability: The Case of American Express" 24 *J. Legal Stud.* 63 (1995).

[7] 1983 Act, s.1(1).

[8] In France, the name of a public company (*société anonyme*) ends with 'SA' while a private company (*société à responsabilité limitée*) ends 'Sàrl'.

[9] 1963 Act, ss.372 and 376 (as amended by 1982 Act, s.13). See generally, Calvert "The Prohibition of Large Associations" 26 *Conv.* 253 (1962).

[10] Finance Act 1973, ss.67–68.

[11] *cf.* Corporation Tax Act 1976, Pt IX.

[12] 1963 Act, s.207(1).

managing director, is unlimited.[13] Any shareholder who knows that the company is carrying on business for more than six months with less than the statutory minimum membership becomes severally liable for company debts contracted during that time.[14]

Private Company

4–06   A company may be registered as either a private or a public company.[15] The paradigmatic private company is the one-person or small family trading concern, or "quasi-partnership". Some major firms are private too, however, and the portfolios of very rich persons tend to be held by their private companies, which usually have unlimited liability as well. The principal advantage of being private is that, provided the company is small or medium-sized, a comparatively restricted amount of information about the company's financial and trading position need be disclosed to the public via the registry of companies.[16] Also, many of the rules that derive from EC Directives apply only to public limited companies. The securities of a private company cannot be listed on the Irish Stock Exchange. In some Commonwealth countries, private companies are called "proprietary" companies and their names end with the abbreviation "Pty".

4–07   The Investment Funds, Companies and Miscellaneous Provisions Act 2006 redefines what a "private company" is for the purposes of the Companies Acts. It is a company that, under its articles of association, contains three requirements, *viz.* its membership is restricted to 99 persons at most (excluding employees), freedom to transfer its shares is restricted and, subject to qualifications, it may not invite the public to subscribe for any of its shares, debentures or other securities.[17]

4–08   Unless its articles otherwise proscribe, however, a private company may offer shares to qualified investors, or to 99 or fewer persons, or to both qualified investors and 99 or fewer persons. "Qualified investors" include entities authorised to operate in the financial markets, large businesses and national governments, entities of a certain size and individuals who meet requirements regarding transactions, portfolio size and professional experience.[18] In the case of small and medium-sized enterprises and individuals, Member States have the option to establish a register of such entities and persons. Ireland has availed of this option.[19] The only qualification for SMEs for inclusion on the register is that they come within certain financial thresholds and they have their registered office in Ireland. The criteria for individuals are quite complex, broadly requiring two of the three following criteria: frequent

---

[13] Sections 197, 198, 207(2).
[14] 1963 Act, s.36.
[15] 1963 Act, s.5(1).
[16] 1963 Act, s.128(6) and 1986 Act, ss.10–12.
[17] 1963 Act, s.33, as substituted by the 2006 Act, s.7.
[18] *cf.* Art.2(1)(e) of the Prospectus Directive 2003/71/EC.
[19] IFSRA maintains a Qualified Investors Register, under r.10 of its *Prospectus Rules*, issued pursuant to the 2005 Act, s.51.

transactions of size in the markets; an investment portfolio of over €500,000; and/or having worked in the financial sector in a professional position requiring knowledge of securities investment.

4–09 Further, unless its articles otherwise proscribes, a private company may offer debentures to qualified investors, or to less then 100 persons other than them, or may offer debentures where the minimum separate consideration is €50,000 or where they are denominated in units of at least €50,000, or where the total sum on offer does not exceed €100,000, or offer securities that are normally traded and have a maturity date of less than 12 months.

4–10 This amended definition primarily facilitates the investment funds industry, as its special purpose vehicles previously had to incorporate as Plcs, due to the 1963 Act's definition of a private company and the broad definition of "offer to the public" contained in the Prospectus Regulations. Certain investment funds vehicles can now operate as private companies and this is expected to reduce the cost of many securities transactions. The minimum capital requirement of approximately €40,000 which must be satisfied to establish a Plc can now also be avoided, and incorporating a private company is often quicker than a Plc. Most existing private companies' articles of association contain the old numeric limit of 50 members, so it will be necessary that most amend their articles of association before increasing their membership to 99.

4–11 Part II of Table A, which is in the first schedule to the 1963 Act, contains model articles of association for private companies. When valuing shares for capital acquisitions tax purposes, there is a special definition of a private company.[20]

4–12 Where a private company contravenes any of those requirements that its articles must contain about maximum membership, share transfers and public offers, it does not thereby lose its private status. Instead, it becomes no longer entitled to several of the legal privileges of this status.[21] However, on application, the court is empowered to permit it to retain these privileges where the breach of the articles was accidental or happened through inadvertence or some other sufficient cause, or where it is "just and equitable" to do so.[22] Where a private company offers its shares or debentures to the public, or agrees to allot its securities to members of the public, the company and its responsible officers commit an offence.[23] This does not apply to the categories of public offers permitted by s.33(5) and (6), nor to any allotment or agreement to allot securities made under such offers. Notwithstanding this prohibition, an allotment of securities in contravention of it is not thereby invalid (s. 21(4)). A private company

---

[20] Capital Acquisitions Tax Act 1976, s.16(2).
[21] 1963 Act, s.34(1).
[22] 1963 Act, s.34(2).
[23] 1983 Act, s.21.

becomes a public company when any of the above-mentioned three requirements are removed from its articles of association.[24]

4–13 Since 1994, when the EC Council Directive of 1989 on single-member
companies was implemented,[25] it has been possible to form a private company
with just one member. Further, a private company with two or more members
can convert itself into a single-member company.[26]

Public Limited Company—"Plc"

4–14 A new kind of company, the public limited company, or "Plc" for short,
was inaugurated by the 1983 Act. This was passed principally to give effect to
the EC Second Directive on Company Law,[27] which expresses itself as applying to the public company limited by shares or limited by guarantee and possessing a share capital. Had this new entity, the Plc, not been created, many
small firms that were not private companies would have been made subject to
various onerous obligations deriving from that Directive.

4–15 In the past, the law made no distinction, apart from the very obvious
one, between public companies with and without limited liability. But since
1983, to be a public company with limited liability (Plc), a number of requirements, designed principally to protect creditors from being victims of under-
capitalisation and overtrading, must be satisfied.[28] The company must have a
minimum authorised share capital of at least €38,092[29]; at least one quarter of
the nominal amount must have been paid up on its issued share capital,
together with any premium on its shares[30]; it must not have allotted any shares
it offered for subscription when the offer was undersubscribed[31]; it must not
have allotted shares in return for service contracts[32] or for contracts that can be
performed more than five years from the allotment date[33]; an independent valuation must have been made of non-cash consideration transferred to acquire
shares in it[34] and also of major transactions between it and its first members
during its first two years' commercial existence[35]; shares taken by its subscribers must have been paid for in cash[36]; any lien or other charge on its own shares
is void[37]; and it may not pay a dividend if it is insolvent in the sense of its net

---

[24] 1963 Act, s.35.
[25] European Communities (Single Member Private Limited Companies) Regulations 1994
      (SI 1994/275).
[26] 1963 Act, s.35.
[27] O.J.L26/1 (1977).
[28] 1983 Act ss.22, 26(2), 28–33, 35, 44 and 46.
[29] 1983 Act, ss.5(2), 19(1), 17(1).
[30] 1983 Act, s.28.
[31] 1983 Act, s.22.
[32] 1983 Act, s.26(2).
[33] 1983 Act, s.29.
[34] 1983 Act, ss.30, 31
[35] 1983 Act, ss.32, 33.
[36] 1983 Act, s.35.
[37] 1983 Act, s.44.

assets being less than its called-up share capital and its undistributable reserves.[38] A company that is limited by guarantee and having a share capital cannot become a Plc.[39] For the purpose of the restriction on holding more than 25 directorships, Plcs are not included in calculating the number of companies involved.[40]

Guarantee Company

4–16   In most limited companies, the members of the company will own shares in them and the limit of their liability for the company's unpaid debts will be defined by reference to the amount unpaid on those shares. However, it is possible to be a member of a company without holding any transferable shares in it; companies can have a form of personal membership. A guarantee company falls into this category. It has members who are not shareholders but have undertaken or guaranteed to be responsible for its unpaid debts up to a prescribed amount.[41] The extent of their liability to the company is defined by the terms of their guarantees. Since 1994, it has been possible to have single-member companies limited by guarantee as well as by shares.[42] Guarantee companies almost invariably are established for reasons other than engaging in commercial activities, such as for sporting, cultural, philanthropic and other non-profit objectives. The Irish Auditing and Accounting Supervisory Authority and the Irish Takeover Panel are guarantee companies.

4–17   There also is a hybrid form of guarantee company; it has shareholders who also have guaranteed to pay the company's liabilities up to a specified amount. Companies of this hybrid nature cannot become Plcs[43]; but such companies which existed when the 1983 Act came into force are not affected by this prohibition.[44]

Societas Europoea

4–18   Since 2007, it has been possible to register with the CRO a European company, known as a *Societas Europoea*. These have a minimum subscribed share capital of €120,000 and their shareholders enjoy limited liability.[45] Subject to such modifications as are necessary, the regime for registering these companies and the functions of the CRO are the same as under the Companies Acts.[46]

---

[38]   1983 Act, s.46.
[39]   1983 Act, s.7.
[40]   1999 Act No. 2, s.45(3)(a).
[41]   1963 Act, s.5(2)(b).
[42]   See para.4–13.
[43]   1983 Act, s.7.
[44]   1983 Act, Sch.2, Pt II.
[45]   See para.21–55 *et seq.*
[46]   European Communities (European Public Limited Liability Company) Regulations 2007 (SI 2007/21), reg.10.

MEMORANDUM OF ASSOCIATION

4–19   Every registered company must have a memorandum of association.[47] The 1963 Act's first schedule and the 1983 Act's second schedule set out the forms that the memoranda for different kinds of company should take, notably as companies limited by shares (Table B), unlimited companies (Table E), guarantee companies (Tables C and D), Plcs limited by shares (1983 Act) and Plcs limited by guarantee (1983 Act). Books containing company precedents have a variety of model memoranda, for instance for private companies, for Plcs, for dwellingholders' guarantee companies, for property management companies, for guarantee members' clubs, for guarantee charities and for unlimited companies.[48] The memorandum must be printed, be duly stamped for the capital duty and be signed by each founder (or "subscriber"), which signature must be witnessed and attested.[49] This document is the company's fundamental law and may be amended only in the circumstances and in the manner as provided by the Companies Acts.[50] The memorandum and articles of association are commonly referred to as the company's own regulations or its constitution.

Name

4–20   The memorandum must state the company's name.[51] If it is a limited company, then the name must include that term or its abbreviation "Ltd"— or the Irish equivalent, teoranta or "teo".[52] If it is a public limited company, this must be stated in the name or with the abbreviation "Plc", or with the Irish equivalent.[53] A limited company that is a "non-profit" organisation, in the sense that it has the prescribed non-profit objects, its income must be devoted to those objects, and it may not pay any dividends or distribute any assets to its members, may, once the requisite statutory declaration has been made, be authorised by the Registrar of Companies to omit the term "Ltd" from its name.[54] It is an offence for a person to carry on business under any name or title of which "limited" or "teoranta" or any contraction or imitation of either is the last word, unless that person has been incorporated with limited liability.[55]

4–21   The Registrar of Companies may refuse to register a company possessing a name that is deemed inappropriate[56]; any name which in his opinion is undesirable will not be accepted. Among such names, presumably, are those that suggest that the company is something fundamentally different from what

---

47   1963 Act, ss.5–16.
48   See para.2–38.
49   1963 Act, s.7.
50   *cf. Wilson v Dunnes Stores (Cork) Ltd* [1982] I.L.R.M. 444.
51   1963 Act, s.6(1)(a).
52   1963 Act, ss.6(2)–(3), 22.
53   1983 Act, s.4(1).
54   1963 Act, s.24 and para.16–07.
55   1963 Act, s.381.
56   1963 Act, s.21.

it purports to be, or suggest close association with the State, or which may lead to it being mistaken for another established company.[57] His discretion in this regard is not absolute; there is a right of appeal to the High Court against rejection of a name, although the grounds on which an appeal may succeed are not indicated. There do not appear to be any reported decisions that deal with this matter.[58] Where the name the company does business under is one other than its own, then that must be registered with the Registrar of Companies as a business name under the Registration of Business Names Act 1963.[59]

4–22 A particular name may be reserved in connection with a company it is proposed to form. Unless the Registrar is of the view that the intended name is undesirable, he may specify a period during which it will be reserved, which shall not exceed 28 days, but which may be extended on application to him.[60]

4–23 To change its name, a special resolution to that effect must be passed and the Registrar of Companies must be notified[61] and give approval for the new name.[62] He also must be notified of any change of a business name[63] and give approval for the new name; and of ceasing to carry on a business under such a name.[64] Any rights or obligations of the company or legal proceedings by or against it are not adversely affected merely by it changing its name.[65] Where a name that is too similar to the name of an existing company is registered, the Registrar is empowered to require that it be altered.[66] However, the court has no jurisdiction to direct the Registrar to change a company's registered name, without the company passing the requisite resolution.[67]

Authorised Capital

4–24 In Ireland and most European countries, shares are required to have a fixed "par" or "nominal" value, i.e. shares must be designated by the company with a particular value. Almost invariably, a share's actual worth will vary with the company's own fortunes. For instance, in a company with shares of €1 par that is earning considerable profits, those shares quite easily might be changing hands in the market at €3 or more. A share's par value has very little bearing on its actual worth. Companies are not allowed to have shares of "no par"

---

[57] Use of a name very similar to another company's name could give rise to liability for passing off or, exceptionally, for breach of trade mark; see generally, M. Forde, *Commercial Law*, 3rd edn (Haywards Heath: Tottel Publishing, 2005), pp.344 *et seq.*

[58] *cf. Unity Insurance Brokers (Windsor) Ltd v Unity Realty & insurance Inc.* 251 D.L.R. (4th) 268 (2005). In *The King (Rowell) v Registrar of Companies* [1904] 2 I.R. 634, the CRO's decision to refuse registration for a misleading name was upheld.

[59] 1963 Act, s.22 and Form RBNIB; *cf. Re Griffin* (1935) 65 I.L.T.R. 106.

[60] 2005 Act, ss.59 and 60.

[61] Form G1Q.

[62] 1963 Act, s.23.

[63] Form RBN2B.

[64] Form RBN3.

[65] 1963 Act, s.23(4); *cf. Singh v Atombrook Ltd* [1989] 1 W.L.R. 810.

[66] 1963 Act, s.23(2).

[67] *Halifax Plc v Halifax Repossessions Ltd* [2004] 2 B.C.L.C. 455.

value—a practice that is permitted in the US.[68] Authorised capital is the aggregate par value of the shares that a company has authority to issue to its members; it is a kind of theoretical maximum capital.

4–25 Where, as is usually the case, the company is one with a share capital, the memorandum must state the amount of the authorised capital and how it is to be divided into shares.[69] Plcs must have a minimum authorised capital of €38,092.[70] Provided that some of its share capital is denoted in euros, it would seem that a company can be registered with a multi-currency authorised capital, i.e. capital denoted in several currencies.[71] The Companies Acts say that the capital must be expressed as a "fixed amount", which it has been held to mean a monetary amount—as distinguished from an amount of gold or some other metal or commodity.[72] The nominal value of a share may be an amount which cannot be paid in legal tender, such as a fraction of a cent.[73]

4–26 Non-controversial alterations to the memorandum's authorised capital clause may be effected in general meeting, provided the articles of association authorise the change in question.[74] The procedure for reducing the capital is far more elaborate; those articles must authorise the reduction, it must be approved by a special resolution of the members and by the creditors, and be sanctioned by the court.[75] Court sanction is not required where the company purchases its own shares in the manner authorised by Pt XI (ss.206–234) of the Companies Act 1990.

Objects

4–27 The memorandum of association must state what it is intended that the company shall do, or what are its "objects".[76] Since 2001, these can be contained in a standard form text, given to the Registrar, which the memorandum states it incorporates.[77] As any shareholder or debenture-holder may apply to have a transaction that is *ultra vires* the company's objects restrained,[78] and because outsiders generally will not knowingly enter into engagements that are not contemplated by a company's objects, promoters frequently give companies a multitude of objects or have the objects expressed in broad and general terms. On the other hand, some intending shareholders may insist on the

---

[68] See Reports of "Gedge Committee", Cmd. 9112 (1954), and of "Cox Committee", Pr.4523, paras 63–72.

[69] 1963 Act, s.6(4)(a).

[70] 1983 Act, s.5(2).

[71] According to Harman J., "[t]he proposition that the share capital of an English company may be denominated in US dollars is now I think a common place." *Re Anglo-American Insurance Co. Ltd* [1991] B.C.L.C. 564.

[72] *Re Scandinavian Bank Group Plc* [1988] 1 Ch. 87.

[73] *Re Australian Pacific Technology Ltd* [1995] 1 V.R. 457.

[74] 1963 Act, ss.68–70.

[75] 1963 Act, ss.72–77.

[76] 1963 Act, s.6(1)(b).

[77] 2001 Act, ss.80–83.

[78] 1963 Act, s.8(2).

objects being drafted in as restrictive a fashion as possible, to protect their investment from being put at risk in *"ultra-vires*-the-company" ventures. A company's stated objects must not be inconsistent with the Companies Acts or with the general law.[79] In a tax case, the House of Lords accepted virtually unlimited objects: "[conducting] all kinds of operations".[80] Having virtually limitless objects cannot be impeached once the company is registered because the certificate of incorporation is "conclusive evidence" that all the Act's requirements regarding registration were complied with.[81]

4–28 At one time, companies could never change their objects, and then for a time it was necessary to get the prior sanction of the High Court, but this is no longer so. A special resolution is required to change the company's objects,[82] but dissenting members and certain debenture-holders may apply to the High Court to veto the proposed alteration.[83]

Limited Liability

4–29 If the liability of the members for the debts of their company is to be limited, that fact must be stated in the memorandum of association.[84] Procedures exist whereby limited companies can change their status to unlimited companies, and where unlimited companies can convert into having limited liability.[85]

Subscribers

4–30 For a private company, at least one person, and for a public company, at least seven persons, must subscribe to the memorandum, i.e. agree to take at least one share each in the company when formed and sign the memorandum opposite the number of shares they are to take.[86] The Companies Acts contain no restrictions on who can be subscribers. Thus, non-nationals,[87] bankrupts, minors,[88] lunatics and organisations with a legal personality of their own can subscribe; although a minor on attaining full age may repudiate the contract arising from his signature.[89] There must be at least one (or seven) subscribers, who become the company's members,[90] but one (or six) of them may be mere agents of the person who in fact is founding the company; they may even hold their shares as trustees for the founder.[91] On the

---

[79] 1963 Act, s.5(1).
[80] *Newstead v Frost* [1980] 1 W.L.R. 135.
[81] 1983 Act, s.5(4).
[82] 1963 Act, s.10.
[83] 1963 Act, s.10.
[84] 1963 Act, s.6(2)(a).
[85] See paras.11–90 and 91.
[86] 1963 Act, ss.5(1) and 6(4)(b) and (c) (as amended by SI 1994/275).
[87] *Princess of Reuss v Bos* (1871) L.R. 5 H.L. 176.
[88] Signature of a memorandum by a minor is valid unless the minor has repudiated the signature before registration: see *Re Nassau Phosphate Co.* (1876) 2 Ch D 610 and *Re Laxon and Co. (No. 2)* [1892] 3 Ch. 555.
[89] *Re Blakeley Ordinance Co., Lumley's Case* (1868) 4 Ch. App. 31.
[90] 1963 Act, s.31(1).
[91] *cf. Irish Permanent Building Society v Cauldwell* [1981] I.L.R.M. 242.

company being registered, these subscribers are deemed to be its members, and their names should then be entered in the register of members as such.[92]

ARTICLES OF ASSOCIATION

4–31 The second major document needed to form a registered company is the articles of association,[93] which may be regarded as the company's by-laws: the rules that set down in detail how the company is to be governed and managed.[94] The constitution of a company is considered to comprise both the memorandum and articles of association.[95] Since 2001, these can be contained in a standard form text, given to the Registrar of Companies, which the articles state are incorporated in them.[96] Articles of association must be printed, divided into paragraphs that are numbered consecutively, stamped in the same way as a deed and signed by each subscriber to the memorandum.[97] The Companies Acts do not stipulate what the articles must contain other than that certain information must be provided in the case of unlimited companies and companies limited by guarantee,[98] and that certain major changes in a company's structure may be made only where there are provisions to that effect in the articles. Articles of companies that are listed on the Irish Stock Exchange are required by the Listing Rules to contain provisions on matters such as transfers of securities, share certificates, dividends, directors, accounts, rights, notices, redeemable shares, capital structure, voting entitlements and proxies.[99] Most company law precedent books contain several model sets of articles for different types of company.

"Table A" Model Articles

4–32 The 1963 Act's first schedule contains a model set of articles of association, called "Table A".[100] Most companies adopt these as their own, either in their entirety or subject to some alterations. Where no separate articles are registered, the Table A model automatically becomes the company's articles. Any special articles that are registered are supplemented by the provisions of Table A except to the extent that the model clauses are expressly excluded or modified by the registered articles.[101] The 1963 Act's first schedule contains model articles of association for guarantee companies (Tables C and D) and for unlimited companies (Table E). Previous Companies Acts contained earlier

---

[92] 1963 Act, s.31(1).
[93] 1982 Act, s.2.
[94] *Guinness v Land Corporation of Ireland* (1883) 22 Ch D 349.
[95] *Wilson v Dunnes Stores (Cork) Ltd* [1982] I.L.R.M. 444.
[96] 2001 Act, ss.80–83.
[97] 1963 Act, s.14.
[98] 1963 Act, s.12.
[99] *cf.* Rule Book of the Irish Stock Exchange.
[100] As amended by 1983 Act, Sch.1, para.24. A very extensive commentary on the case law under these articles is contained in *Palmer's Company Precedents*, 17th edn (London: Stevens, 1956), Ch.10 and also in *Buckley on the Companies Acts*, 14th edn (London: Butterworths, 1981), pp.908–1055.
[101] 1963 Act, s.13 and 1982 Act, s.14.

versions of Table A and companies which were registered before 1963, without adopting special articles of association, would still be subject to the model articles in force at the time of their registration. Thus, if the company was registered some time between 1908 and 1963, it is the model articles in the Companies (Consolidation) Act 1908 which apply to it. Earlier versions still of the model articles are contained in the Companies Act 1862 and in the Joint Stock Companies Act, 1856. Company precedent books contain model articles for different varieties of company and for particular needs of some companies. As Table A is regarded as showing the legislature's view of what articles of association ideally should contain, no article that is substantially similar to any of those in Table A will be held to be *ultra vires* the company.[102]

4–33 Although the contents of the memorandum of association take precedence over those of the articles,[103] the latter may be considered to clarify ambiguities in the memorandum.[104] Except for restrictions in the general law or in the Companies Acts or the company's own memorandum of association, there are no limits on what may be included in its articles. That particular articles are most unusual or extraordinary does not mean that a company cannot adopt them. Given the relative ease with which the articles can be amended later by special resolution, it is not uncommon for provisions that could be included in them instead to be entrenched, against alteration, in the memorandum of association.[105]

4–34 While the memorandum and articles are defined by s.25 of the 1963 Act as a contract between the company and its shareholders, and between the shareholders *inter se*, there are certain kinds of articles of association the breach of which does not give rise to a civil right of action between the company and the member or between the members *inter se*.[106] Depending on the circumstances, however, provisions in the articles of association may be incorporated by implication into contracts between the company and its directors or other officers. An area of some complexity is where contracts are entered into on behalf of the company in a manner not envisaged by its articles.

4–35 When interpreting a company's articles, courts may infer a term into them. But no term will be implied from external circumstances, such as the actions and beliefs of the members at the time they incorporated their company. It appears that courts will not rectify the terms of articles of association that do not accord with the members' intentions when they were being adopted.[107] This is because the articles are given statutory force by s.25 and are open to inspection by anyone considering dealing with the company or taking shares in it.[108] On the other hand, where the articles have been amended, it is

---

[102] *New Balkis Eersteling Ltd v Randt Gold Mining Co.* [1904] A.C. 165.

[103] *Guinness v Land Corporation of Ireland* (1883) 22 Ch D 349.

[104] *Roper v Ward* [1981] I.L.R.M. 408; *Angostura Bitters Ltd v Kerr* [1933] A.C. 550; *Re Bansha Woollen Mills Co.* 21 L.R. Ir. 181 (1887).

[105] 1963 Act, s.28.

[106] See para.10–14 *et seq.*

[107] *Scott v F. Scott (London) Ltd* [1940] Ch. 794.

[108] *Brattan Seymour Services Co. v Oxborough* [1992] B.C.L.C. 693.

permissible to take account of their earlier versions in the construction of their present provisions.

THE PROCESS OF COMPANY REGISTRATION

4–36   To constitute themselves as a company, the subscribers must deliver to the Registrar of Companies the signed memorandum and articles of association, together with some other documents and a cheque for capital duty.[109] In *Arab Monetary Fund v Hashim (No. 3)*, Lord Templeman said: "When the promoters of a company enter into an agreement to incorporate a company and the agreement takes the form of a memorandum and articles of association of the company, that agreement does not create a corporation. When the memorandum and articles are registered under the Companies Act ... that registration does not recognise a corporation but creates a corporation."[110]

The requirements for existing companies re-registering under some other form are considered separately below.

Formalities

4–37   All applications to the CRO for registration as a company must be accompanied by the following:

• Unless the articles of association are Table A, a signed articles document, which may disapply all or part of those model articles.[111]

• A statement naming the intended first directors and secretary, and indicating where the company's registered office is to be.[112] This statement must give that office's address and such particulars regarding the company's intended officers as are required to be disclosed and to be kept in each company's register of directors and secretaries.[113] As regards directors, these are their names and any former names, usual residential address, nationality if not Irish, business occupation, if any, particulars of other directorships of Irish companies and details of any disqualification in another country[114]; as regards the secretaries, their names and any former names, and their usual or registered addresses. This statement must be signed by or on behalf of the subscribers to the memorandum of association and it must be accompanied by signed consents of the persons named as officers to act as such. Where the memorandum is being delivered to the Registrar of Companies by the subscribers' agent, that fact must be indicated and the agent's name and address stated.

---

[109] 1963 Act, s.5(1).
[110] [1991] 2 A.C. 114 at 160.
[111] 1963 Act s.11.
[112] 1982 Act, s.3 and Form A1.
[113] See para.6–91.
[114] 1982 Act s.3 and 1963 Act s.195.

- Under the Stamp Duties Consolidation Act 1999,[115] if the company's registered office or its "effective centre of management" is in the State, a statement of its assets, liabilities and expenses for the purpose of reckoning the amount of stamp duty to be charged on its formation. This duty is €1 for every €100 of the company's net assets, i.e. assets to be contributed by the members less liabilities attaching to them and any expenses incurred in the formation; but where this amount is less than the nominal value of shares allotted to members immediately after registration, the charge is on the latter amount instead. Assets contributed by prospective shareholders with unlimited liability are excluded from this calculation. There is no stamp duty charged on forming certain non-profit companies.

4–38 There must be a signed memorandum of association and a statutory declaration[116] by either a solicitor involved in forming the company or by a person designated as first director or secretary of the company, to the effect that all the prerequisites for registration were complied with.[117] A company will be registered only when the Registrar is satisfied that all these requirements have been complied with.[118] Registration cannot be refused once all those formalities have been met. But it will be refused where the objects are unlawful,[119] as happened in *R. v Registrar of Joint Stock Companies, Ex p. More*,[120] where it was held that a company being formed in England to deal in Irish hospital sweepstake tickets could not be registered there because those activities constituted an illegal lottery in England. Dentists and several other professionals (e.g. doctors and lawyers) are prohibited from practising their profession through registered companies and, when the Registrar of Companies refused to register a company with the name "S.G. Rowell (Dentist) Ltd", the High Court on appeal declined to direct that it be so registered.[121] That was because persons might be deceived and believe that the company had been duly registered to practise dentistry. In 1980, an English court quashed the registration of a company called Lindi St Claire (Personal Services) Ltd, which was engaged in prostitution, on the grounds that its registration was against public policy and was illegal.[122]

4–39 Registration also will be refused where it appears to the Registrar of Companies that the company will not carry on an activity in the State, being an activity mentioned in its memorandum of association.[123] The Registrar may accept a statutory declaration form as proof that such an activity will be carried on in the State.[124]

---

[115] Sections 114–122.

[116] *cf.* 2006 Act, s.6, concerning statutory declarations sworn outside the State for the purposes of the Companies Acts.

[117] 1983 Act, s.5 (replacing 1963 Act, s.19(2)).

[118] 1983 Act, s.5(1); *cf. R. v Registrar of Companies, Ex p. Bowen* [1914] 3 K.B. 1161.

[119] 1983 Act, s.5(1).

[120] [1931] 2 K.B. 197.

[121] *R. (Rowell) v Registrar of Companies* [1904] 2 I.R. 634.

[122] *R. v Registrar of Companies, Ex p. Attorney-General* [1991] B.C.L.C. 476.

[123] 1999 (No.2) Act, s.42.

[124] Companies (Forms) No. 2 order 2004 (SI 2004/824), Form AI.

4–40   When the certificate of incorporation has been granted, a notice to that effect must be published in the *Gazette*.[125] Similar notices must be published in the *Gazette* of any alteration in the company's memorandum or articles of association.

Consequences of Registration

4–41   A certificate of incorporation issued by the Registrar of Companies is conclusive evidence that the statutory requirements have been complied with and that the company was duly registered.[126] This gives shareholders and outsiders dealing with registered companies legal security, in that it precludes re-opening matters that occurred prior to or contemporaneously[127] with registration[128]; no evidence that might show that the company was irregularly incorporated will be admitted. Irish law, therefore, is not bedevilled with problems of defectively formed companies and the nullity of companies.[129] However, the certificate of incorporation does not render lawful a company's objects that otherwise would be unlawful. If a company is registered with such objects, it would appear that the Attorney-General can proceed to have it de-registered.[130] From the time of incorporation, the registered company acquires a legal personality of its own and unrelated to that of its members,[131] with all the significant consequences resulting from being a distinct legal entity, without any further formalities and regardless of whether it undertakes any business. There is no need for a meeting of members or directors to ratify incorporation.

Re-Registration

4–42   Provided they satisfy the various prescribed requirements, companies which register under one form can re-register under a different form.[132] For instance, a private company can go public, a public company can go private, an unlimited company can acquire limited liability. Where companies have been struck off the register, frequently for not filing annual returns, endeavours may be made to have them re-registered, often not by their shareholders but by creditors or persons seeking to sue the company.[133] An entity already completely constituted as a partnership or a corporation under another legal system

---

[125] Available at www.cro.ie.

[126] 1983 Act, s.5(4).

[127] A company is a body corporate from the date of incorporation on the certificate, which means from the first moment of that day: see *Jubilee Cotton Mills Ltd v Lewis* [1924] A.C. 958.

[128] *cf. Cotman v Brougham* [1918] A.C. 514.

[129] *cf.* EC First Directive on Company Law [1968] OJ L65/41, Arts 10–12, restricting the doctrine of the nullity of companies, *Ubbink Isolatie BV v Dak-en Wantechniek BV* (Case 136/87) [1990] 1 C.M.L.R. 262 and *Marleasing SA v La Commercial Internacional de Alimentacion SA* (Case 106/89) [1990] E.C.R. 4135. See generally, Drury, "Nullity of Companies in English Law" 48 *Mod. L. Rev.* 644 (1985).

[130] *cf. Bowman v Secular Society* [1917] A.C. 406.

[131] 1963 Act, s.18(2).

[132] See para.11–85 *et seq.*

[133] See para.23–104.

cannot be re-registered as a company under the Companies Acts.[134] In Australia, there has been some debate over whether a court-sanctioned arrangement with members can be used to effect a change of status for which there is no specific statutory procedure.[135]

Judicial Review

4–43 A refusal by the Registrar to register a company is subject to judicial review.[136] It is important for persons who deal with a company to be confident that the company's existence cannot easily be challenged, and so a positive decision by the Registrar to register a company is less amenable to judicial review than a refusal to register, as an applicant would have to present evidence to the court that the provisions in respect of registration had not been complied with, whereas the certificate of incorporation is conclusive evidence that they have been complied with.[137]

REGISTERED OFFICE

4–44 Every Irish-registered company must have a registered office in the State, to which all communications and notices relating to the company must be addressed, and some of the company's principal records must be kept at that office.[138] Its location must be given in the statement that is delivered to the Registrar of Companies prior to incorporation.[139] The company's name must be displayed outside this office conspicuously and legibly.[140] Where documents, for instance legal proceedings, must be served on a company, that may be done by leaving them at or posting them to its registered office.[141]

4–45 Any change in the office's location must be notified to the Registrar of Companies within 14 days.[142] Since neither the Companies Acts nor the model Table A articles of association stipulate the procedure for changing the office, any such change would seem to be a matter for determination in general meeting unless the company's own regulations provide otherwise. A notice of the change in the registered office must be published in the *Gazette* within six weeks of it occurring.[143] A company that does not cause such a notice to be published is estopped from relying, as against others, on the new registered address.[144]

---

[134] *Bulkeley v Schutz* (1871) L.R. 3 P.C. 764; *Bateman v Service* (1881) 6 App. Cas. 386.

[135] *cf. Windsor v National Mutual Life Association of Australasia* (1992) 106 A.L.R. 282 and *Australian Securities Commission v Marlborough Gold Mines Ltd* (1993) 177 C.L.R. 485.

[136] *R. v Registrar of Joint Stock Companies, Ex p. Moore* [1931] 2 K.B. 197.

[137] 1983 Act, s.5(4).

[138] 1982 Act, s.4.

[139] Companies (Forms) No. 2 order 2004 (SI 2004/824), Form AI.

[140] 1963 Act, s.114(a).

[141] 1963 Act, s.379.

[142] 1982 Act, s.4(3) and Form B2.

[143] SI 1973/163.

[144] SI 1973/163, reg.10.

COMMENCING BUSINESS

4–46   Once it is registered, a private company is legally free to commence doing business and to borrow. Public limited companies (Plcs), by contrast, must comply with a number of formalities before they can do so. An originally incorporated Plc that has not re-registered may do business and borrow only after the Registrar of Companies has issued a "trading certificate" stating that the nominal value of the shares that the company has allotted is not less than €38,092 and that there has been delivered to the registry a statutory declaration concerning capital integrity.[145] This declaration, which one of the company's directors or secretaries has to sign, must state that the nominal value of the allotted share capital does not fall below the above sum; the amount actually paid up on those shares; the amount or estimated amount of the company's preliminary expenses, and the person who has paid or will pay these; and any amount or benefit paid to or given to, or intended to be paid to or given to any promoter, and the consideration therefor. Transactions entered into by a Plc that did not satisfy these requirements are not thereby invalid.[146] Rather, a Plc that contravenes this requirement commits an offence, as do any of its officers who are in default.

4–47   Most company law precedent books contain model notices, resolutions and other documents for formalising the company getting up and going,[147] for instance the minutes of the first board meeting, at which the original directors may be replaced, the registered office may be changed, auditors are appointed, the financial year's date is fixed and a transfer of shares in the company is recorded.

4–48   Every company must have its own seal,[148] as certain types of corporate transactions may only be effected by seal.[149]

4–49   Every limited company must state the following on all its letter heads and order forms[150]:

(a)   its name and legal form;
(b)   its place of registration and the number with which it is registered;
(c)   the address of its registered office;
(d)   if it has been exempted from having the words "ltd" or "teo" in its name, the fact that it is a limited company;
(e)   any reference to share capital should be to subscribed and paid-up capital;
(f)   if it is being wound up, that fact.

If the company has a website, this information should be described in a prominent and easily accessible place on the site.[151]

---

[145] 1983 Act, s.6 and Form 70.
[146] 1983 Act, s.6(8).
[147] See para.2–38.
[148] 1963 Act, s.114(1)(b).
[149] See para.18–06.
[150] European Communities (Companies) Regulations 1973 (SI 1973/163), reg.9.
[151] European Communities (Companies) (Amendment) Regulations 2007 (SI 2007/49).

4–50 Whenever a company commences its trade, business or profession, it must notify the Revenue Commissioners within 30 days of that time of the following[152]:

(a) the name of the company;
(b) the address of its registered office; if it is a foreign company, the address of its principal place of business in the State;
(c) the name of its secretary; if a non-resident company, the name and address of its agent, manager or other representative in the State;
(d) the date it commenced its economic activity; if a non-resident company, the date it commenced that activity in the State;
(e) the nature of its trade, profession or business;
(f) the date up to which its accounts are made up.

4–51 On its being incorporated, a company often acquires a business, frequently from its own shareholders; their very purpose may have been to incorporate their business. Alternatively, a newly formed company may acquire a business from a third party; its very purpose may have been to constitute a vehicle for acquiring that business. Most company precedents books contain model documentation for achieving either of these purposes.

4–52 A question that often arises shortly after a company is incorporated is the extent to which it is bound by or may take advantage of contracts entered into on its behalf before it was incorporated. It can assume liability for them and take advantage of them by ratifying the contracts.[153]

4–53 Another issue that often arises is the rights and duties of promoters.[154] These are persons who were active in forming the company and getting it up and going, the classic definitions being "anyone who undertakes to form a company with reference to a given project and to get it going and … takes the necessary steps to accomplish that purpose".[155] Promoters are subject to fiduciary duties similar to those applicable to company directors and, accordingly, are not entitled to make any profit from their endeavours unless there was full disclosure by them to the members or an independent board of directors, who assented to that profit. In the case of Plcs, where the company has agreed to acquire a substantial asset from any of its first members, that property must be independently valued and the transaction must be approved in general meeting.[156] Where persons have been duped by promoter fraud to invest in companies, they have a variety of remedies.

---

[152] Taxes Consolidation Act 1997, s.882. See generally, M. Feeney, *The Taxation of Companies* (Dublin, Tottel Publishing, 2006), pp.2023–2025.
[153] 1963 Act, s.37(1); see para.18–12 *et seq.*
[154] See para.8–57 *et seq.*
[155] *Twycross v Grant* (1877) 2 C.P.D. 469 at 541.
[156] 1983 Act, ss.32 and 33.

CHAPTER 5

GOVERNANCE—THE MEMBERS

5–01 In the context of company law, the term "governance" means the way in which companies as organisations are run by those who own and control them. It can be contrasted with management, which signifies how a company's ordinary business affairs are conducted, although the line between overall governance and day-to-day management is not always clearly defined. Different companies possess different methods of governance, which differ depending on the size of their membership and the scale and complexity of the business that they conduct. In one-person or quasi-partnership companies, generally a very simple system will suffice. In contrast, large public companies involved in several businesses and with numerous subsidiaries will need more elaborate systems.

5–02 Company law in this regard is predominantly optional or facilitative.[1] The Companies Acts lay down certain grounds rules for meetings and resolutions but many of these may be disapplied, either by a company's articles of association or by the unanimous agreement of its members. What is not optional is that ultimate control over companies' destinies is consigned to their members or shareholders. Members' meetings must be convened at least once a year and a significant minority of the membership may call meetings at any time. Various matters concerning the company must be decided at those meetings. But it is for companies themselves to determine how votes are to be allocated among their members and what particular powers should be entrusted to the directors. Companies can change their own regulations provided sufficient members support the proposed change. In many small private companies, especially where they are in the nature of joint ventures, their governance may also be regulated by separate shareholders' agreements that purport to override any contrary provisions in their articles of association.[2] Irish company law does not require representation of other constituencies, involved in the conduct of a company's affairs, in its governance structures—for instance, employees, creditors, suppliers and customers.

5–03 Legal responsibility for managing a company's business is conferred on the directors. In companies with a few members, all or most of the directors may also be the members and, in a practical sense, there may be little difference

---

[1] See generally, Nolan, "The Continuing Evolution of Shareholder Governance" 65 *Cam. L.J.* 92 (2006).

[2] See para.13–25 *et seq.*

between members' meetings and directors' meetings. Except that they must have two directors, usually no distinction at all exists in the case of single-member companies. At the other end of the scale, many of the directors of publicly quoted companies may own very few of the company's shares and owe their positions to managerial skills identified by some of the major shareholders, who often may be institutional investors. As usually most shareholders in such companies are geographically dispersed and often have comparatively small stakes in their company, there is a tendency for management to acquire extensive *de facto* control over issues of governance and, to an extent, become their own governors. What to some extent counteracts this tendency is that institutional investors—such as banks, insurance companies, investment companies and pension funds, who own substantial stakes in the company—monitor more closely what management is doing or is seeking to do.

DIVISION OF POWERS BETWEEN MEMBERS AND DIRECTORS

5–04 Before examining how each of a company's principal organs—the members and the directors respectively—are required to conduct their separate affairs, their interrelationship calls for consideration. The Companies Acts require that some major and mainly constitutive decisions be taken by the members in general meeting; for instance, authorising the issue of additional shares and waiver of pre-emption rights to new shares, where applicable. Otherwise, the allocation of particular powers in any company is a matter for the company's own regulations to determine. Where authority over some matter is not delegated to the directors or otherwise, it falls to be decided by the general meeting.

Allocating Particular Powers

5–05 As well as authorising them to manage the company's business generally (art.80), the Table A model articles empower the directors, for instance, to allot unissued shares, within the overall authorisation given by the general meeting[3]; to make calls on shares from time to time[4]; to borrow money and give security on behalf of the company[5]; to determine the managing director's remuneration[6]; to recommend a dividend[7]; and to carry forward undistributed profits and place them in reserve.[8] In private companies it is usual to give the directors a discretion to refuse to register any transfer of shares.[9] Except perhaps for the general managing power, any or all of these powers could be reserved by the articles of association to the general meeting. Under Table A, although the board recommends the dividend, it is for the general meeting to decide whether

---

[3] Article 5.
[4] Article 119.
[5] Article 79.
[6] Article 111.
[7] Article 116.
[8] Article 119.
[9] Article 3 of Pt II.

one should be paid,[10] and the board may not borrow more than the nominal amount of the issued share capital without the general meeting's consent.[11]

5–06 Where any particular power is given to the directors, how they are to exercise it in any instance cannot be dictated by the shareholders. Neither a bare majority nor a 75 per cent majority, nor possibly all but one of the entire body of members, can lawfully compel the directors to carry out a specific mandate, such as to recommend a dividend[12] or make calls on shares.[13] For so long as there is a validly constituted and effective board of directors, none of those specific powers can be exercised by the members as such. Of course, the members always have the choice of altering the articles of association and withdraw the power in question from the directors. Conversely, the directors can always ratify action which the members took without authority but which could only have been taken by the directors.

5–07 The articles of association may even confer powers on certain shareholders or even on outsiders, provided these powers are not reserved by the Companies Acts to the general meeting. Examples include a case[14] where the articles empowered each of two director-shareholders to veto any proposal by the board to buy or sell property; in another case the plaintiff was empowered under the articles to nominate two persons of its choice to the board.[15] Often special allocations of powers in the articles are the subject of parallel contractual provisions.

"Manage the Business"

5–08 Article 80 of Table A, which empowers the board to "manage [the] business of the company", raises a number of important questions to which there are few categorical answers.[16] Stripped of some of the excessive verbiage, it stipulates that "[t]he business of company shall be managed by the directors, who ... may exercise all such powers of the company as are not, by the Act or by these [articles], required to be exercised by the company in general meeting, subject, nevertheless, to any of these [articles], to the provisions of the Act and to such directions, being not inconsistent with the aforesaid [articles] or provisions, as may be given by the company in general meeting ..." The conventional interpretation is that this gives the directors managerial autonomy, in the sense that the general meeting cannot interfere with the board's functions except by altering the articles or, indirectly, by removing the existing directors.[17] But some of the cases do not squarely support this view and, more importantly, the very

---

[10] Article 116.

[11] Article 79.

[12] *Scott v Scott* [1943] 1 All E.R. 582.

[13] *Re Coachman Tavern (1985) Ltd* [1988] 2 N.Z.L.R. 635.

[14] *Salmon v Quin & Axtens Ltd* [1909] 1 Ch. 311.

[15] *British Murac Syndicate Ltd v Alperton Rubber Co.* [1915] 2 Ch.186.

[16] See generally, Sullivan, "The Relationship Between the Board of Directors and the General Meeting in Limited Companies" 93 *L.Q.R.* 569 (1977).

[17] Endorsed in *Massey v Wales* (2003) 47 Australian Corporations and Securities Reports 1, noted in R. Grantham, "The Reserve Powers of Company Shareholders" 1 *Cam. L.J.* 36 (2004).

structure and terms of the article suggest that the general meeting may by ordinary resolution "give ... directions" to the board. Additionally, the 1963 formulation of art.80 is not identical to that contained in the British 1948 version nor in the 1908 version, on which many of the cases were decided. Instead of "regulations ... prescribed", "directions ... given" is used, and a court might fasten on this difference in terminology to distinguish the decided cases. Three major categories of decision ought to be considered separately.

Everyday Affairs

5–09 It would be most impractical if the general meeting could interfere with the board in a company's day-to-day management, like selecting suppliers, determining the terms for which products are to be sold, or hiring and firing. For this reason, it is likely that art.80 would be construed to prevent the general meeting from issuing instructions on these matters or from vetoing board decisions regarding them. In *Scott v Scott*,[18] an attempt by the general meeting to dictate dividend policy to the board was held to be ineffective because it concerned "an ordinary financial matter" and was "purely a matter of the management of the business". The judge deemed the case to be "such an easy one" that it was not necessary for him to consider in detail the authorities.

Strategic Decisions

5–10 "Strategic" decisions are those major management choices that will have a significant and long-lasting effect on a company's development, such as substantial expansions or contractions of capacity, the purchase and sale of major assets, takeovers, etc. They are to be contrasted, on the one hand, with everyday business affairs as just described and, on the other, with what may be termed fundamental changes, such as altering the objects clause, repaying capital and otherwise drastically re-arranging the company's capital structure. Structural changes require at the minimum the shareholders' overwhelming approval; also such changes that obtain the requisite support can nevertheless be vetoed by the court.[19]

5–11 How decision-making power over strategic matters is allocated in companies with regulations along the lines of art.80 of Table A is an open question. A case could be made that it is more practical for the board to have only initiating power in relation to them. But the argument against the general meeting having a veto over them is less convincing. Managements can engage in takeovers, for example, principally to enhance their own prestige and power rather than for the benefit of the company. The leading case on the question is *Automatic Self-Cleansing Filter Syndicate Co. v Cunninghame*[20] where, by an ordinary resolution, the shareholders sought to instruct the board to sell the company's undertaking. Whether they lawfully could do so, the court stressed, depended on the construction of the articles. In the event, it was concluded that

---

[18] [1943] 1 All E.R. 582. See also *Re Olderfleet Shipbuilding Co.* [1922] 1 I.R. 26 at 31–33.
[19] See Ch. 11.
[20] [1906] 2 Ch. 34.

those instructions could not be given there. The case, however, is more important for its affirmation of what may be called a presumption of board autonomy: that in the absence of unambiguous indications to the contrary, "it is not
competent for the majority of the shareholders at a [general] meeting to affect
or alter the mandate originally given to the directors, by the articles ..."[21] This
arises from the fact that, at least in the Table A scheme, the board are representatives of the entire company and not just the agents of the majority or of a
special majority of the shareholders. As explained by Collins M.R.:

> "No doubt for some purposes directors are agents. For whom are they
> agents? You have, no doubt, in theory and law one entity, the company,
> which might be a principal, but you have to go behind that when you look
> to the particular position of directors. It is by the consensus of all the indi-
> viduals in the company that these directors become agents and hold their
> rights as agents. It is not fair to say that a majority at a meeting is for the
> purposes of this case the principal so as to alter the mandate of the agent.
> The minority also must be taken into account. There are provisions by
> which the minority may be over-borne, but that can only be done by spe-
> cial machinery in the shape of special resolutions. Short of that the man-
> date which must be obeyed is not that of the majority—it is that of the
> whole entity made up of all the shareholders. If the mandate of the direc-
> tors is to be altered, it can only be under the machinery of the memoran-
> dum and articles themselves."[22]

5–12   This case could be distinguished on the grounds that it did not deal with
art.80 of Table A, not even with the then British version of that article. For
under the company's own regulations there, the board's general powers of
management were subject only to the Companies Acts, the articles themselves
and any special resolution; and the board's specific power there to sell property
was unqualified. Nevertheless, its underlying pro-board autonomy sentiments
would most likely be followed today even under art.80. It is possible, on the
other hand, that a general meeting veto on a "strategic" decision would be sustained here.[23] However extensive a managerial monopoly it may confer on the
directors, it does not extend beyond questions of the company's business and
management. Thus, unless duly authorised to do so by the articles of association, directors have no authority to resolve that their company should be
wound up.[24]

5–13   Where the company has securities listed on the Irish Stock Exchange,
what are called "class one" "significant transactions" must be notified to the
Exchange authorities, be explained in a circular sent to the shareholders and
require the shareholders' prior approval before they can be conducted.[25] These
transactions are principally those valued in excess of 25 per cent of the company,

---

[21]   *ibid.* at 42.
[22]   *ibid.* at 42–43; see also *Re Gramophone & Typewriter Ltd v Stanley* [1908] 2 K.B. 89.
[23]   *Cf. Dowse v Marks* (1913) 13 S.R. (N.S.W.) 332, upholding a veto power.
[24]   *Re Emmadart Ltd* [1979] Ch. 540.
[25]   Listing Rule 7.5.

measured by reference to the consideration involved, and the company's gross capital, gross assets and profits, as well as certain reverse takeovers.

Litigation

5–14 Where the articles of association do not refer expressly to the matter, the question of who has the power to sue in the company's name is somewhat complex. Where some loss or damage has been caused to a company, the proper plaintiff is the company itself and not any of its members or directors, no matter how large a shareholding they may have.[26] But where the majority shareholders commit what is termed a "fraud on the minority", then the minority may sue them in the company's name—in what is called the "derivative" suit.[27] Apart from that, the case law is somewhat inconclusive. In one instance it was held that, once the majority shareholders commence an action in the company's name to vindicate its property rights, then the directors cannot intervene to have the action struck out.[28] But the grounds on which *Automatic Self-Cleansing* was distinguished there are far from convincing, and the judge indicated that he was not bound by *dicta* in that case affirming the principle of board autonomy. Another case is often cited in support of the view that, once the board commences an action in the company's name, the shareholders cannot intervene to stop the action.[29] But one judge there dissented and the judgments of the other two do not rest on art.80. When subsequently the matter was raised, it was said that "there are deep waters here", and it was found unnecessary in the circumstances to reconcile whatever conflict exists between the authorities.[30]

5–15 This uncertainty was resolved in *Breckland Group Holdings Ltd v London & Suffolk Properties Ltd*,[31] where the company had articles similar to art.80. Proceedings were commenced in its name by its majority shareholder, without any reference to the directors, and the question to be determined was whether the action had been properly commenced. Relying on the pro-board autonomy decisions, Harman J. concluded that only the directors could commence proceedings in the company's name. The principle is that "where matters are confided by articles such as art.80 to the conduct of the business by the directors, it is not a matter where the general meeting can intervene ... [T]he action was wrongly brought [and i]f the board do not adopt it, a general meeting would have no power whatever to override that decision of the board and to adopt it for itself".[32] It furthermore has been held that no individual director, not even a managing director, may authorise bringing proceedings in the company's name unless the directors delegated such

---

[26] *Stein v Blake (No. 2)* [1998] 1 B.C.L.C. 573.

[27] See para.10–47 *et seq.*

[28] *Marshall's Valve Gear Co. v Manning Wardle & Co.* [1909] 1 Ch. 267; *cf. Paramount Acceptance Ltd v Souster* [1981] 2 N.Z.L.R. 38.

[29] *John Shaw & Sons (Salford) Ltd v Shaw* [1935] 2 K.B. 113.

[30] *Re Argentum Reductions Ltd* [1975] 1 W.L.R. 186 and *Paramount* case, above, fn.28.

[31] [1989] B.C.L.C. 100.

[32] *ibid.* at 106.

authority to him,[33] although the unauthorised commencement of proceedings is something that the directors may subsequently ratify.

5–16   The directors cannot prevent a true "derivative" claim being brought by one or more members, because what is involved there is not merely management of the business; the allegation is that the directors abused and exceeded whatever powers of management they possessed. But it would seem that a claim of that nature may be prevented by a decision of a majority of the members not directly involved in the dispute.[34]

Deadlock

5–17   Where for one reason or another the board is deadlocked and cannot reach a decision on a matter ordinarily within its competence, then it falls to the shareholders in general meeting to resolve the question. In one instance where there were but two directors and one of them refused absolutely to discuss company business, it was held that there was "power in the company to do itself that which under other circumstances would be otherwise done".[35] Acts can be done on behalf of a company possessing no directors, which can be ratified subsequently by the shareholders.[36]

5–18   However, an Australian court has rejected the thesis that there is some "reserve power" in the general meeting, holding that the only way to resolve deadlock in the board is for the members to alter its composition.[37] In a recent English case,[38] described by the judge as "bizarre", one group of shareholders were entitled to appoint two of the directors and another shareholder was entitled to appoint the other two. There was no provision for chairing the company's board or for a casting vote. Without any board resolution being passed authorising commencing proceedings, solicitors for the company instituted proceedings in its name against that other shareholder, to prevent a receiver being appointed over the company's assets by that shareholder. But he challenged the authority to bring those proceedings without any authorisation. Because blocking the action would have caused serious damage to the company, it was held that the defendant's appointees would be in breach of their fiduciary duty to the company by endeavouring to block its "defensive" proceedings.

MEMBERS' MEETINGS AND RESOLUTIONS

5–19   A company's primary organ is its members in general meeting. Decisions reached at these meetings take the form of resolutions. In the case of

---

[33]   *Mitchell & Hobbs (UK) Ltd v Mill* [1996] 2 B.C.L.C. 102.

[34]   See para.10–63 *et seq.*

[35]   *Barron v Potter* [1914] 1 Ch. 895 at 903.

[36]   *Alexander Ward & Co. v Samyang Navigation Co.* [1975] 1 W.L.R. 673.

[37]   *Massey v Wales* (2003) 47 A.C.S.R. 1.

[38]   *Fusion Interactive Communications Solutions Ltd v Venture Investment Placement Ltd* [2005] 2 B.C.L.C. 250; *Fusion etc. No. 2* [2005] 2 B.C.L.C. 571.

single-member companies registered as such, as provided for in the regulations on those companies, the position as described here is subject to the very obvious qualification: the one member only will comprise the meeting in question. The conduct of company meetings is regulated by the Companies Acts, and by each company's own regulations and resolutions it has adopted, supplemented by the general common law on meetings.[39]

Meetings

5–20 A company must hold an annual general meeting ("AGM") every year and not more than 15 months may elapse between these meetings.[40] In companies with Table A, the principal business to be transacted at AGMs is consideration of the company's audited accounts and of the directors' and the auditors' reports, filling vacancies on the board, appointing auditors and fixing their remuneration, and declaring a dividend.[41]

5–21 There are also "extraordinary" general meetings ("EGMs"), which usually are convened when matters of some urgency or of very considerable significance must be considered by the members.[42]

5–22 Meetings of particular classes of the membership are called "class" meetings.[43]

Convening Meetings

5–23 Ordinarily, it is the directors who convene general meetings.[44] Where the board convenes a meeting in some manner inconsistent with the company's own regulations, this may be a "mere irregularity" that does not nullify the outcome of the shareholders' deliberations. It depends on the circumstances and on the nature of the regulation in question whether or not contravening it is fatal to the meeting. For instance, in *Browne v La Trinidad*,[45] where directors other than the plaintiff met and issued notices of a general meeting to consider, *inter alia*, whether the plaintiff should be removed from the board, it was held that not notifying him of that board meeting was insufficient reason to stop the ensuing general meeting from taking place. In another instance, where the number of directors fell below the quorum for board meetings but they nevertheless acted as a board and convened a shareholders' meeting, it was held that resolutions passed at the general meeting were not thereby invalid.[46]

---

[39] See generally, M. Cordes, *Shackleton on the Law and Practice of Meetings*, 10th edn (London: Sweet & Maxwell, 2006) and D. Impey et al, *The Modern Law of Meetings*, 25th edn (Bristol: Jordans Publishing, 2005).

[40] 1963 Act, s.13(1) and Table A, Art.48. See *Smith's Precedents*, Pt 4.

[41] Article 53.

[42] 1963 Act, s.132. See *Smith's Precedents*, Pt 5.

[43] See *Smith's Precedents*, Pt 6.

[44] 1963 Act, s.132.

[45] (1887) 37 Ch D 1.

[46] *Boschoek Pty v Fuke* [1906] 1 Ch. 148.

5–24 On the other hand, a notice convening a meeting issued, for example, by the company's secretary and without the board's consent is ineffective.[47] A properly constituted board must meet as such before calling a shareholders' meeting to deal with "matters of such vital moment" as winding up the company or appointing a liquidator[48] or petitioning for the appointment of an examiner.[49]

Notices

5–25 Company law precedent books contain model notices and related documentation.[50] Periods of notice needed for convening general meetings are usually fixed in the articles of association. The very minimum period for AGMs is 21 days; for EGMs it is 14 days but only seven days for EGMs of private or unlimited companies.[51] Where the purpose is to pass a special resolution, it is 21 days.[52]

5–26 Provision, however, is made for shorter notice periods. Any general meeting may be called within whatever period the auditors and all the members entitled to attend and to vote agree upon.[53] Except for "extended notice" resolutions, less than 21 days' notice of a special resolution may be given where that is agreed to by enough members as hold 90 per cent of the nominal value of the shares entitling them to attend and vote.[54]

5–27 Although notices of meetings "shall be served on every member",[55] this is made subject to any contrary provision in the articles of association. Under Table A notices must be sent to such persons as are entitled under the company's own regulations to receive them.[56] These model articles, moreover, state that the proceedings of a meeting shall not be invalid because of the non-receipt of a notice or the accidental omission to give notice.[57] An injunction was once given against holding a meeting because some notices were posted to the shareholders during a postal strike.[58] Even though the company's articles of association expressly deemed the posting of notices as good service, it was held that the distinct likelihood of some shareholders not being notified in time, thereby being deprived of the opportunity to vote on a proposed transaction, warranted deferring the meeting until an application would be made to the court to discharge the injunction. A notice sent by fax has been held to be sufficient for these purposes.[59]

---

[47] *Re State of Wyoming Syndicate Co.* [1901] 2 Ch. 431.
[48] *Re Haycraft Gold Reduction & Mining Co.* [1900] 2 Ch. 230.
[49] *Re Aston Colour Print Ltd* [2005] 3 I.R. 609.
[50] See *BCM's Precedents* Part H.
[51] 1963 Act, s.133.
[52] 1963 Act, s.141.
[53] 1963 Act, s.133(3).
[54] 1963 Act, s.141(2).
[55] 1963 Act, s.134(a).
[56] Article 51 and Pt II, art.4.
[57] Article 52.
[58] *Bradman v Trinity Estates Ltd* [1989] B.C.L.C. 757.
[59] *PNC Telecom Plc v Thomas* [2004] 1 B.C.L.C. 88.

5–28 Apart from some special kinds of notices, the Companies Acts do not indicate what notices of meetings generally must contain. According to Table A, they must state the place and time of the meeting and, in the case of special business "the general nature of that business …"[60]

Location

5–29 Every AGM must be held in the State, except where the articles of association do not require meetings to be held in Ireland and, additionally, all the members agree that they should meet abroad or it was resolved at the preceding AGM to hold the next meeting outside the State.[61] Any business transacted at a meeting held in contravention of this requirement is void. There are no statutory restrictions on where EGMs can be held; the matter can be determined by the articles of association. Table A requires that all general meetings of the company be held in the State.[62] Arguably this does not apply to general meetings of particular classes of shareholders. Table A does not indicate where within Ireland the meetings must be held, except that any notice must specify, *inter alia*, the "place" of the meeting.[63]

Timing

5–30 In exercising their power to convene general meetings, directors will not be permitted to call one at an unusually early date to prevent a recent purchaser of shares from voting against the board.[64] In *Kinsella v Alliance & Dublin Consumers Gas Co.*,[65] in an attempt to wrest control from the existing board, the plaintiff and those who supported him bought a considerable number of shares in the company. As many of those share transfers were not yet registered, their anti-directors' motions at an EGM were defeated. Barron J. confirmed that persons who buy shares have no right to vote until they are registered as members. The argument was made that the outcome of the meeting should nonetheless be declared invalid because the plaintiff's transfers were not registered as a result of a conscious decision by the incumbent directors to thwart his designs. It was concluded, however, that no such decision had been established in evidence and indeed all the indications were that the best reasonable efforts had been made to register those transfers in time. In any event, it was pointed out that there was nothing to prevent the plaintiff calling another EGM once his transfers were registered.

Default Powers

5–31 Default powers exist where the board either refuses or is unable to convene a general meeting. In the case of the AGM, any member may apply to the DCE, who may direct that the meeting be called and give such

---

[60] Article 51 and Pt II, art.4.
[61] 1963 Act, s.140.
[62] Article 47.
[63] Article 51 and Pt II, art.4.
[64] *Cannon v Trask* (1875) L.R. 20 Eq. 669.
[65] [1982] I.E.H.C. 195, unreported, Barron J., October 5, 1982.

ancillary directions as are deemed appropriate.[66] In the case of EGMs, members representing at least one tenth of the paid-up capital carrying voting rights may request the board to call a meeting. If the directors do not do so within 21 days, the meeting may be convened by at least half of those requisitionists.[67] Any reasonable costs those requisitionists thereby incur can be recovered from the company, which in turn can deduct the equivalent from the defaulting directors' remuneration.

5–32 The possibility of the directors undermining these provisions, by convening a meeting but to be held in the very distant future, does not exist because it must be convened for not later than two months after receiving the members' requisition.[68] In England, where there is no set deadline for actually holding the meeting, it was held that convening one for a distant date can amount to oppression under the equivalent of s.205 of the 1963 Act.[69]

Court-Ordered Meetings

5–33 Where for any reason it is "impractical" to call or to conduct a meeting in the normal manner, the court may intervene.[70] Either on the application of a director or of a voting member, or of its own motion, the court may order that a meeting be held and may give such ancillary directions as it deems appropriate.[71] In many of the cases here, there is deadlock in the company because one or more members refuse to attend meetings, preventing a quorum from existing. A well-known Australian case where this power was exercised concerned a company, of which a husband and wife were the only shareholders and directors, who were killed together in a car crash.[72] The court directed that a meeting be held and that the personal representatives of the deceased should be treated as shareholders entitled to attend and to vote.

5–34 The power is not restricted to extreme situations, nor to where there is no shareholder opposition to a meeting being held[73]; it is of "a necessarily wide scope" and, in considering applications, the court should consider the practicalities of the situation. Meetings are often ordered where it has proved impossible to make up a quorum.[74] Even though the articles of association of a company did not provide for voting by ballot, an application for an order that a meeting be held to vote by ballot succeeded, on account of the very considerable disruption that had previously occurred when a minority of the members

---

66 1963 Act, s.131.
67 1963 Act, s.132.
68 1963 Act, s.132(3).
69 *McGuinness v Bremner Plc* [1988] B.C.L.C. 673.
70 See generally, Gertz "Court Ordered Company Meetings" 3 *Conv.* 399 (1969).
71 1963 Act, s.135.
72 *Re Noel Tedman Holdings Pty* [1967] Qd. R. 561.
73 *Re El Sombrero Ltd* [1958] Ch. 900 and *Re Opera Photographic Ltd* [1989] 1 W.L.R. 634.
74 e.g. *Re Woven Rugs Ltd* [2002] 1 B.C.L.C. 324 and *Vectone v South Entertainment Ltd* [2004] 2 B.C.L.C. 224.

attended at the general meeting.[75] That one or more of the shareholders have sued for "oppression" under s.205 of the 1963 Act has been held not to be a reason for not directing a general meeting to be held, although it is a factor the court will take into account when exercising its discretion.[76] But if the applicants have a sufficient majority under the default system to call for a meeting to be convened and the directors have not declined to do so, the remedy is not applying to the court under s.135.[77] If the reason for seeking an order is that, as presently constituted the chair of the meeting would have a conflict of interests, that is not a sufficient ground for exercising the discretion.[78]

5–35 The court is not empowered to make orders that would decisively shape the outcome of any meeting it directs to convene; in particular, in order to resolve a deadlock between members. Thus in *Ross v Telford*,[79] where the two equal shareholders and the directors of the company were a husband and wife who had gone through a bitter divorce, and the ex-wife declined to attend meetings convened by him, the court refused to direct that a representative of his solicitors could attend the meeting as an additional member. The jurisdiction was described as "procedural … not designated to affect substantive voting rights or to shift the balance of power between shareholders in a case where they have agreed that power should be shared equally and where the potential deadlock is something which must be taken to have been agreed on with the consent and for the protection of each of them".[80] Similarly, in *Harman v BML Group Ltd*[81] where the company had two classes of shareholding ("A" and "B" shares) and there was a shareholders' agreement that a representative of the B shareholders must be present at all general meetings, the court refused to direct a meeting to be held without such representative being present. Their agreement conferred a "class right" to have some B shareholders present and the court has no authority to override class rights. However, a provision in a company's articles of association or in a separate shareholders' agreement providing for a quorum, which cannot be met because one some of the members refuse to attend, resulting in a deadlock, is not regarded as a class right for these purposes.[82] Courts will not readily infer, from a course of conduct, the existence of a contract elevating a quorum into a class right.

Resolutions

5–37 There are two principal kinds of resolution, ordinary and special resolutions.[83] In the absence of provision to the contrary in legislation or in the

---

[75] *Re British Union for the Abolition of Vivisection* [1995] 2 B.C.L.C. 1.

[76] *Re Sticky Fingers Restaurant Ltd* [1992] B.C.L.C. 84 and *Re Whitechurch Insurance Consultants Ltd* [1993] B.C.L.C. 1359.

[77] *Angelis v Algemene Bank Nederland (Irl.) Ltd* [1974] I.E.H.C. 33, unreported, Kenny J., July 4, 1974.

[78] *ibid.*

[79] [1998] 1 B.C.L.C. 82.

[80] *ibid.* at 87.

[81] [1994] 1 W.L.R. 893.

[82] *Union Music Ltd v Watson* [2003] 1 B.C.L.C. 455.

[83] See *Smith's Precedents*, Pt 10.

company's own regulations, the general meeting acts by a simple majority of those voting. Within 15 days of it being passed, a printed copy of every special or equivalent resolution must be given to the Registrar of Companies.[84] Where the company has securities listed on the Irish Stock Exchange, notice must be given to the Exchange authorities of all resolutions passed by the members other than those relating to ordinary business passed at the AGM.[85]

Ordinary Resolution

5–38   "Ordinary" resolutions are not expressly mentioned in the Companies Acts and, although referred to in several parts of Table A, are not defined there. An ordinary resolution is understood as meaning one that needs a simple majority of the votes cast.[86]

Special Resolution

5–39   A "special" resolution—previously known as an "extraordinary" resolution[87]—is one passed by a majority of at least three quarters of the votes cast, at a meeting of which at least 21 days' notice was given.[88] If however, a numerical majority of members entitled to vote, who hold more than 90 per cent in value of the voting shares agree, a special resolution may be passed on shorter notice.[89] Special business is defined in Table A as all business transacted at EGMs and at AGMs other than the principal AGM business referred to above. It seems that a special resolution is not necessary to determine matters that are "special" in this sense.

Extended Notice Resolution

5–40   A variant of these, the "extended notice" resolution, is necessary for certain kinds of drastic decisions, like removing a director from the board or replacing the incumbent auditors.[90] Except where such a resolution is submitted by the board, those moving it must notify the company not less than 28 days before the meeting; the company must then notify the members in the same way as notice of the meeting was given. Where it is "not practicable" to do this, within 21 days of the meeting, the company must either give notice by advertisement in a newspaper that circulates in the district where the registered office is located or notify the members in such other mode as the articles allow for.

Notices of Proposed Resolutions

5–41   One of the fundamental principles of company law is that notices of ordinary and of special resolutions must sufficiently describe what is being

---

[84]   1963 Act, s.143(1) and Form G1.
[85]   Listing Rule 6.6.18.
[86]   *Bushell v Faith* [1970] A.C. 1099.
[87]   The only difference between a special and an extraordinary resolution is that normally, the notice of intention to propose a special resolution must be given at least 21 days before the meeting.
[88]   1963 Act, s.141.
[89]   1963 Act, s.141(2).
[90]   1963 Act, s.142.

proposed, so as to permit shareholders to form a reasoned judgment. In particular, notices must not be misleading. For instance, in *Kaye v Croydon Tramways Co. Ltd* [91] notices convening a general meeting stated that the purpose was to approve the sale of the company's undertaking for a specified sum but did not indicate that, as an additional part of the consideration, the buyer was to pay the directors "golden handshakes". On the grounds that, although they did not contain untruths, the notices were "playing with words" and were "tricky", and "most artfully framed to mislead the shareholders", it was held that the ensuing resolution endorsing the sale did not bind absent and dissenting shareholders. As it was put in a later similar case: "[i]f any attempt is to be made by the directors to get the sanction of the shareholders it must be made on a fair and reasonably full statement of the facts upon which the directors are asking the shareholders to vote ... [S]pecial resolutions obtained by means of a notice which did not substantially put the shareholders in the position to know what they were voting about cannot be supported, and in so far as ... resolutions were passed on the faith and footing of such a notice the [company and directors] cannot act upon them".[92] Whether a particular notice is misleading or does not provide enough information is essentially a factual matter and depends on the circumstances of each case.[93] If the effect of any resolution is that the directors will obtain some material benefit, to which they otherwise would not be entitled, this fact must be disclosed.[94]

5–42 It is not necessary to give the actual text of a proposed special resolution. But clear and precise indications of its entire substance must be provided, because "all the situations in which special resolutions are required are special situations, where the resolutions in question are by their very nature likely either to affect the company's constitution or to have an important effect on its future".[95] Therefore, it is imperative that each shareholder be fully appraised, "so that he may decide whether he should attend the meeting or is content to absent himself and leave the decision to those who do".[96]

5–43 The resolution ultimately passed must not depart in its substance from the one notified, not even *de minimus*, although minor variations of mere form may be tolerated. In *Re Moorgate Mercantile Holdings Ltd,*[97] the requirement of "absolute identity at least in substance" was perhaps carried to an extreme. Notices were issued of a proposed resolution that the share premium account, standing at £1,356,900, be cancelled on the grounds that the entire amount had been lost. Due to an oversight, the proposer did not make provision for a premium of £321 obtained shortly before then when the minority interests had

---

[91] [1898] 1 Ch. 358.
[92] *Baille v Oriental Telephone & Electric Co.* [1915] 1 Ch. 503 at 514–515.
[93] See, e.g. *Jackson v Munster Bank Ltd* (1884) 13 L.R. Ir. 118, *Tiessen v Henderson* [1999] 1 Ch. 861, *Re Dorman Long & Co.* [1934] Ch. 635 and *Rose v McGovern* [1998] 2 B.C.L.C. 593 at 600–603.
[94] *Normandy v Ind Coope & Co.* [1908] 1 Ch. 84.
[95] *Re Moorgate Mercantile Holdings Ltd* [1980] 1 W.L.R. 277 at 283.
[96] *ibid.*
[97] [1980] 1 W.L.R. 277.

been bought out. On discovering this, the chairman proposed to amend the proposal to one reducing the share premium account from £1,356,900 to £321, which was carried. Even this small variation rendered the resolution invalid.[98]

5–44 To have a resolution set aside on the grounds that misleading or inadequate information was circulated to the members, it does not have to be shown that it was the misrepresentation that induced members to vote for the resolution.[99] Where, however, the transaction that was approved has been executed, it may be too late to have the resolution set aside, even where the transaction involved "insiders". In that leading case on minority shareholders' rights, *Prudential Assurance Co. v Newman Industries Ltd (No. 2)*,[100] it was held that individual shareholders have no "personal" right of action in damages against directors who, by tricky and misleading notices, deliberately caused the company to suffer a loss by buying assets at overvalued prices.

Conduct of Meetings

5–45 All that the Companies Acts say about the conduct of general meetings is that, unless the articles of association provide otherwise, the quorum for a private company (other than a one-person company) is two and for a public company is three members present in person[101]; the members present can elect anyone of their number to the chair[102]; corporate members can be represented in such manner as their own directors or governing bodies determine[103]; and a company's articles of association cannot unduly restrict a member's right to demand a poll.[104] Articles 53–62 of Table A sets out the "proceedings at general meetings". These are supplemented by special articles, where they exist.

Place

5–46 On account of modern audio-visual techniques, it has been held that a meeting does not have to take place in any single room or hall. According to Browne Wilkinson V.C. in *Byng v London Life Association Ltd*:

> "The rationale behind the requirement for meetings in the [Companies] Act is that members shall be able to attend in person so as to debate and vote on matters affecting the company. Until recently, this could only be achieved by everyone being physically present in the same room face to face. Given modern technological advances, the same result can now be achieved [otherwise].... [I]n cases where the original venue proves inadequate to accommodate all those wishing to attend, valid general meetings of a company can be properly held using overflow rooms provided, first, that all due steps are taken to direct to the overflow rooms those

---

[98] *cf. Re Willaire Systems Plc* [1987] B.C.L.C. 67.
[99] *Bulfin v Bebarfalds Ltd* (1938) 38 S.R. (N.S.W.) 423.
[100] [1982] 1 Ch. 204 and para.10–61.
[101] 1963 Act, s.134(c).
[102] 1963 Act, s.134(d).
[103] 1963 Act, s.139.
[104] 1963 Act, s.137.

unable to get into the main meeting and, second, that there are adequate audio-visual links to enable those in all the rooms to see and hear what is going on in the other rooms."[105]

Quorum

5–47 The 1963 Act and Table A fix the quorum at three members in the case of a public company and two where the company is private (other than a "one-person" company).[106] But a higher quorum may be fixed by the articles of association. The members must be present in person when the meeting commences. In a private company which has Table A, the meeting can continue provided that at least one member remains present.[107] No company business can be transacted where these requirements are not satisfied. If within a half an hour of a meeting being convened a quorum is not present, the meeting stands adjourned for a full week or to such other time and place as the directors determine; in such cases the meeting is dissolved if it was one that the members had requisitioned.[108] Where all of a company's members are present then it is probable that the quorum is filled even where the regulations stipulate for a higher number. It is not settled whether one member only can constitute a meeting, other than in a duly registered one-person company. Neither personal representatives of deceased members nor official assignees of bankrupt members who have not themselves been entered on the register in respect of the deceased's shares may be counted in the quorum.[109]

5–48 If it is "impracticable" to make the quorum, any director or member with voting rights may apply to the court, to order that a meeting be held and conducted, and to make any necessary ancillary directions.[110] Thus, in *Re Opera Photographic Ltd*[111] there were two shareholders and directors of a company, one holding 51 per cent of the shares. He wanted to remove the other from the board of directors but that other would not attend at general meetings, where a resolution for his removal could be considered and voted on. The court decided to resolve the deadlock by directing that a meeting attended by the majority shareholder, for the purpose of removing the other from the board, would be an effective meeting of the company.

Chair

5–49 The chair of the meeting regulates its proceedings. Who occupies the chair and the extent of the chair's powers is determined primarily by the articles of association. Under Table A, general meetings should be chaired by the chair of the board of directors[112]; failing that, the directors present can choose one of their number to take the chair and, if they do not do so, the members

---

[105] [1990] 1 Ch. 170 at 183.
[106] Section 134(c) and art.54.
[107] *Re Hartley Baird Ltd* [1955] Ch. 143; *cf. Re London Flats Ltd* [1969] 1 W.L.R. 711.
[108] Art.55.
[109] *Arulchelvan v Wright* [1996] I.E.H.C. 5, unreported, Carroll J., February 7, 1996.
[110] 1963 Act, s.135.
[111] [1989] 1 W.L.R. 634.
[112] Article 56.

present at the meeting decide who chairs it. Table A gives the chair a casting vote where there is an equality of votes.[113]

5–50   A chair's powers and responsibilities derive partly from the common law regarding meetings generally as well as from provisions in the articles. In *Byng v London Life Association Ltd*[114] it was held that decisions taken by the chair, even within the general terms of those he undoubtedly possesses, might be set aside if, in the circumstances, he failed to take account of relevant factors or he acted unreasonably. At common law, he has no general right to adjourn a meeting for his own convenience but he can adjourn where unruly behaviour impedes the conduct of the meeting. Table A empowers him to adjourn the meeting with its consent. Where in the circumstances it is possible to ascertain the meeting's view on the matter, he should not adjourn without its consent.[115] Table A requires him to adjourn where the meeting so directs. No entirely new business may be transacted at an adjourned meeting.

5–51   The chair should ensure that the business before the meeting is properly conducted. His rulings on points of order and related matters are deemed *prima facie* to be correct.[116] Those members present must be afforded a reasonable opportunity to debate the proposed resolutions and all views on them must be adequately aired. But the chair may stop discussions when enough has been said and, provided minority views get a fair hearing, must do so when so directed by the meeting.[117] One of the chair's most delicate tasks is in deciding whether to allow an amendment to a proposed resolution to be moved. Any amendment must remain within the scope of the notice which was given. In the case of "special" business, proposals may be amended only in form and not in substance.[118]

Voting

5–52   There are two major aspects to voting in general meetings. One, which is considered fully later, is the very entitlement of shareholders to vote and restrictions on any franchise they possess.[119] The other is the process by which they cast such votes as they have. Votes may be cast by members who are present at the meeting, or through their proxies who attend. The right of every enfranchised member to have his vote recorded was proclaimed in most emphatic terms in *Pender v Lushington*,[120] where it was held that the plaintiff was "a member of the company, and whether he votes with the majority or the

---

[113] Article 61.
[114] [1990] 1 Ch. 170.
[115] Article 58.
[116] *cf. John v Rees* [1970] Ch. 345.
[117] *Wall v London & Northern Assets Corp.* [1898] 2 Ch. 469.
[118] *Re Moorgate Mercantile Holdings Ltd* [1980] 1 W.L.R. 277.
[119] See para.9–33 *et seq.*
[120] (1877) 6 Ch D 70.

minority he is entitled to have his vote recorded—an individual right in respect of which he has a right to sue".[121]

5-53 *Right to Vote:* Assuming that the category of shares in question carry a vote, a precondition of being entitled to vote at a general meeting is registration as a member in the company's register of members.[122] The chair of the meeting has an extensive power to determine who shall vote.[123] No objection to the qualification of any voter may be raised except at the meeting. The chair's decision on the matter is "final and conclusive" and any vote not disallowed is declared "valid for all purposes". In one instance it was said that there was much to commend a regulation that promotes finality in this way.[124]

5-54 Persons who sell their shares and execute the relevant transfer documents remain entitled to notices of general meetings and to vote as they please at them until the purchaser pays for the shares and is duly registered as a member.[125] But a vendor of shares who has received the full purchase price is a trustee for his purchaser and must vote in the interests of the *cestui* or as the *cestui* directs.[126] Similarly, a mortgagor of shares or a bankrupt whose name remains on the share register must vote as the mortgagee or the official assignee, respectively, directs.[127]

5-55 Subject to what is said below about class and minority rights, shareholders may exercise their voting rights for the most selfish reasons, disregarding what other persons may consider are the interests of the company at large.[128] It even has been held that they may vote against a resolution that the court has ordered the company to adopt and implement.[129]

5-56 *Show of Hands:* Voting can be done by way of a show of hands or a poll. Usually the question will first be put to a show of hands of the members present.[130] Then one or more members may demand a poll, in which case they can cast whatever number of votes are attached to their respective shareholdings. Where there was no poll, the chairman determines whether or not a proposed resolution was carried on a show of hands; that decision is "conclusive evidence" of the fact.[131]

---

[121] *ibid.* at 81.
[122] See para.9–07 *et seq.*
[123] Table of Art.67.
[124] *Marx v Estates & General Investments Ltd* [1975] 3 All E.R. 1064.
[125] *Musselwhite v CH Musselwhite & Son Ltd* [1962] Ch. 964.
[126] *Lyle & Scott Ltd v Scott's Trustee* [1959] A.C. 763 and *Re Piccadilly Radio Plc* [1989] B.C.L.C. 683.
[127] *Wise v Landsell* [1921] 1 Ch. 420 and *Morgan v Gray* [1953] Ch. 83.
[128] *North West Transportation Co. v Beatty* (1887) 12 App. Cas. 589.
[129] *Northern Counties Securities Ltd v Jackson & Steeple Ltd* [1974] 1 W.L.R. 1133.
[130] *Duggan v Bank of Ireland* [1998] I.E.H.C. 124, unreported, McCracken J., July 29, 1998.
[131] 1963 Act, s.141(3).

5–57 *Poll:* At common law, every member is entitled to demand a poll in the general meeting. This right could be qualified or excluded by express terms in the articles of association but the scope of any exclusionary provision is now drastically restricted. The right to demand a poll may be excluded only in respect of electing the chairman and decisions about adjournments.[132] Furthermore, the articles of association may not "mak[e] ineffective" any demand for a poll by either not less than five members with voting rights or by a member representing not less than one-tenth of the total voting rights.[133] On a resolution authorising an "off market" purchase by a company of its own shares, every member may demand a poll.[134] Under Table A, a member is entitled to demand a poll provided he has the support of two other members present at the meeting or he (and his supporters) hold at least 10 per cent of the voting shares.[135] Apart from motions for selecting who chairs the meeting and for an adjournment, the chairman determines at what stage of the meeting a poll demanded on any question shall be held.[136] He also decides the manner in which any poll is to be taken.[137] Members are not obliged to cast all their votes in the same way.[138]

5–58 *Proxy Votes:* Proxy voting is the dominant mode of decision-making in public companies with widely diffused shareholdings. In the US, in disputes between shareholders or between them and management, often each side engages the services of professional proxy solicitors. One of their functions is to identify beneficial owners of the company's shares, being held by banks or brokers as nominees, as well as mailing the proxy material and following it up with phone calls or further mailings.

5–59 Members of corporations have no right at common law to vote by proxy.[139] At one time, to be able to vote, a shareholder had to attend the general meeting in person unless the articles of association allowed for proxy voting. Today, any shareholder who is entitled to attend and vote at a meeting of the company, be it a general meeting or a class meeting, may appoint someone else as their proxy to speak and to vote for them.[140] The proxy may vote either in a poll or on a show of hands. Unless the articles of association provide otherwise, a member may appoint more than one proxy. But entitlement to vote by proxy is not made compulsory for guarantee companies which have no share capital.

5–60 Every notice calling a meeting of a company possessing share capital must make it clear that members entitled to attend and vote may appoint a

---

[132] 1963 Act, s.137(1).
[133] 1963 Act, s.137(1)
[134] 1990 Act, s.213(4).
[135] Article 59.
[136] Article 62.
[137] Article 60.
[138] 1963 Act, s.138.
[139] *Harben v Phillips* (1883) 23 Ch D 114.
[140] 1963 Act, s.136.

proxy, who need not be a member of the company. A company may not require that the instrument that evidences the appointment of a proxy be deposited with the company more than 48 hours before the meeting. Under Table A (arts 68–73), the instrument of appointment, which must approximate to a particular form, must be signed by the shareholder or his duly authorised agent. It must be deposited at the company's registered office or such other specified place not less than 48 hours before the meeting. A person who is both a member and a proxy can vote only once on a show of hands; the chair cannot be expected to ascertain how many votes a hand is intended to convey.[141] A duly appointed proxy is entitled to demand a poll. Unless the company has received prior intimation of the fact, any vote cast by proxy is valid notwithstanding the shareholder's death, insanity or revocation of the proxy.[142] Absent agreement to the contrary, it would appear that a proxy is not obliged to cast the votes with which he was entrusted. But company directors who are appointed proxies may not refrain from casting those votes.

5–61 In *Re Abbey National Plc*,[143] where the meeting was considering a scheme of arrangement under the equivalent of s.201 of the 1963 Act, one of the objectors applied for an adjournment. A substantial number of proxy votes, given by institutional investors, were held by the chair. On the adjournment proposal, he voted the proxies that favoured the scheme in support and the proxies objecting to the scheme against, thereby carrying the proposal. It was held that the chair had acted reasonably, by casting the votes in that manner. It was contended that he did not have the authority of the institutions to do so but it was held that "the institution will have the authority of the beneficial owner, the investor in the institution, to vote as the institution thinks appropriate ..."[144]

5–62 There is a danger of directors manipulating proxies in order to entrench their positions and to resist shareholder pressure against them. Typically, a resolution critical of the board or its policies will be tabled for a general meeting. In response to those criticisms, the directors will send the shareholders a glowing account of their own accomplishments, and will ask shareholders either to vote against the resolution or to give their proxy to someone (usually one of the directors) who will vote against it. It has been held that the expenses of distributing such circulars and proxy forms may be paid from the company's funds[145] and that it is not necessary for the directors to state the views of their opponents.[146] But directors must not circulate misleading information with proxy forms.[147] The costs of distribution may not be charged to the company where the board policy that is being challenged is one that advances the directors' personal interests.[148] Additionally, where proxies are being solicited

---

[141] *cf. McGrattan v McGrattan* [1985] N.I. 28.
[142] Article 73.
[143] [2005] 2 B.C.L.C. 15.
[144] *ibid.* at 20.
[145] *Peel v North West London Railway Co.* [1907] 1 Ch. 5.
[146] *Campbell v Australia Mutual Provident Soc.* (1908) 24 T.L.R. 623.
[147] e.g. *Jackson v Munster Bank Ltd* (1884) 13 L.R. Ir. 118.
[148] e.g. *Peel*, above, fn.144.

at the company's expense, every member entitled to a notice of the meeting and to vote must be sent a copy of the invitation.[149] The board, therefore, cannot invite only those from whom they expect a favourable response; and opponents of the board may learn the grounds on which votes are being sought. Under the Rules of the Irish Stock Exchange, every quoted company's articles of association must allow for the "two way" form of proxy, i.e. forms by which the shareholder can direct the proxy to vote either for or against the resolutions.[150]

Minute Book

5–63   Every company must keep a minute book of the proceedings at its general meetings.[151] Where they are signed by the person who chaired the meeting in question or the very next meeting, the minutes are *prima facie* evidence of what took place. Until the contrary is proved, all proceedings at the meeting and all appointments of directors or of liquidators made at it are deemed to be valid. Every member is entitled to inspect these minutes and to have copies made from them.[152]

Registering Resolutions

5–64   Printed copies of various kinds of most resolutions must be sent to the Registry of Companies within 15 days of their being passed.[153] These are: special resolutions; decisions made by all the members that have the effect of special resolutions; decisions made by all the members of a particular class that are equivalent to special resolutions of that class; resolutions increasing the company's share capital; resolutions that the company be wound up voluntarily by reason of its liabilities or because the time for which it was incorporated has expired, or the task for which it was incorporated has been achieved; resolutions attaching rights or restrictions to any share or varying any such incidents of the share; resolutions converting shares of one class into shares of another; resolutions classifying any unclassified share. Failure to comply with this requirement is an offence, and renders the company and every officer in default liable to a fine. A copy of these resolutions must be forwarded to every member on request. At one time outsiders dealing with a company were deemed to have notice of the contents of any special resolution recorded in the registry of companies but that is no longer entirely the case.[154] However, failing to duly register a resolution does not affect the validity of that resolution, which will nonetheless have full force and effect, although authority on this point is scant.

---

[149] 1963 Act, s.136(5); *cf. Wilson v London Midland & Scottish Rly Co.* [1940] 1 Ch. 169.
[150] Listing Rules 9.9.26, 13.28, 13.29.
[151] 1963 Act, s.145.
[152] 1963 Act, s.146.
[153] 1963 Act, s.143.
[154] See para.18–53 *et seq.*

Irregular Meetings

5–65 Regardless of company size, there is always the danger of irregularities occurring in general meetings. The public law distinction between "mandatory" and merely "directory" rules,[155] and the uncertainty as to where exactly the line between them should be drawn, applies also to the law of company meetings. Some rules on the conduct of meetings are regarded as so vital that any member may sue to enjoin their violation or have declared invalid the purported outcome of a violation; for instance, the right to have one's votes counted and that notices of resolutions should not be misleading. But breaches of other rules are regarded as mere irregularities that can be "cured" by an ordinary resolution and, therefore, may not be the subject of a shareholder suit.[156] The question of the basis on which these categories can, or ought to be, distinguished is dealt with below in relation to minority shareholders' rights.[157] Also considered separately is the extent to which outsiders dealing with companies are adversely affected by irregularities that can take place in general meetings.[158]

INFORMAL UNANIMITY

5–66 Especially in small companies, general meetings may take place in a most informal manner. A written agreement signed by all the shareholders will be treated as a special resolution, provided that the company's articles of association so authorise it.[159] It must be clear from the document that it is to have the effect of a special resolution, although it probably is not necessary for it to proclaim itself formally as a resolution. All the signatures must be of persons entitled to attend the general meeting and to vote on the subject. Any purported resolution meeting these requirements will be deemed to have been passed at the time it was signed by the last member to sign it. In the case of private companies, Pt II of Table A provides that a purported resolution in writing that is signed by all the members entitled to vote on it in general meeting, is deemed a "valid and effective" resolution, as if it had been passed at a duly convened and conducted general meeting.[160]

5–67 The logic underlying this principle, that a resolution will be deemed to have been passed where it is shown that the proposal had the unanimous support of the members entitled to vote, was anticipated in *Buchanan v McVey*[161] and held to apply to companies generally, in the absence of any contrary provision in their own regulations. According to Kingsmill Moore J., "[i]f all the corporators agree to a certain course then, however informal the manner of their agreement, it is an act of the company and binds the company subject only

---

[155] See generally, G. Hogan & D. Morgan, *Administrative Law*, 3rd edn (Dublin: Round Hall, 1998), p.440 *et seq.*
[156] e.g. *McDougall v Gardiner* [1875] 1 Ch D 13.
[157] See para.10–14 *et seq.*
[158] See para.18–55 *et seq.*
[159] 1963 Act, s.141(8).
[160] Article 6.
[161] [1954] I.R. 89.

to two prerequisites [namely] 1, that the transaction to which the corporators agree should be *intra vires* the company; [and] 2, that the transaction be honest".[162] Payments made to the defendant by way of cheques drawn by him on the company's bank account, were held to have been sanctioned by a resolution of all the members, because it was clear that those members had informally agreed to those payments being made. However, because they were part of an elaborate scheme devised to avoid paying taxes to a foreign revenue authority, leaving the company insolvent, the purported resolution was declared invalid on the grounds of dishonesty.

5–68   The principle, commonly associated with the case *Re Duomatic Ltd*,[163] was stated as follows: "where it can be shown that all shareholders who have a right to attend and vote at a general meeting of the company assent to some matter which a general meeting ... could carry into effect, that assent is as binding as a resolution in general meeting would be".[164] A more recent formulation is:

> "where the articles of a company require a course to be approved by a group of shareholders at a general meeting, that requirement can be avoided if all members of the group, being aware of the relevant facts, either give their approval to that course or so conduct themselves as to make it inequitable to deny that they have given their approval. Whether the approval is given in advance or after the event, whether it is characterised as agreement, ratification, waiver or estoppel, and whether members of the group give their consent in different ways and at different times, does not matter".[165]

Provided the procedures that have been bypassed were for the benefit of those who declined to comply with them, it does not matter whether those procedures are statutory, in the company's articles of association or in a separate shareholders' agreement.[166] The principle here also applies to informal unanimity among a class of shareholders.[167]

5–69   Unanimous assent of the beneficial owners of the shares does not suffice for this purpose; the principle only applies to consensus among those members entitled to attend and vote at general meetings.[168] In one instance where, due to an irregularity, a person continued to be a shareholder but all others involved had assumed that his membership had ceased, it was held that they were estopped from denying his membership for the purpose of the principle here.[169]

---

[162] *ibid.* at 96.
[163] [1969] 2 Ch. 365. See generally, Grantham, "The Unanimous Consent Rule in Company Law" 52 *Cam. L.J.* 245 (1993) and "Commentary" [2004] *J. Bus. L.* 121.
[164] *Re Duomatic Ltd* [1969] 2 Ch. 365 at 373.
[165] *EIC Services Ltd v Phipps* [2004] 2 B.C.L.C. 584 at 621, overturned by C.A. on other grounds at 650 *et seq.*
[166] *Re Torvale Group Ltd* [1999] 2 B.C.L.C. 605.
[167] *ibid.*
[168] *Domaney v Godinho* [2004] 2 B.C.L.C. 15.
[169] *Pena v Dale* [2004] 2 B.C.L.C. 508.

5–70 In *Cane v Jones,*[170] the principle was held to apply to unanimous decisions to alter the articles of association. All the shareholders of a family company, the shares in which were split evenly between two camps, at one stage agreed in writing that the chairman should no longer have a casting vote. It was argued that, for effect to be given to this agreement, at the least an actual meeting must have taken place between the members and the agreement reached must have purported explicitly to alter the articles of association. But it was held that the English equivalent of s.15 of the 1963 Act "is merely laying down a procedure whereby some only of the shareholders can validly alter the articles: and if … all the corporators, acting together, can do anything which is *intra vires* the company, then [there is] nothing in [section 15] to undermine this principle".[171] Support for the view that the articles of association could be changed in this manner was derived from the equivalent of s.143(4)(c) of the 1963 Act, concerning the compulsory registration of *de facto* special resolutions. In *Re Home Treat Ltd,*[172] the informal unanimity principle was held to apply to the *ultra vires* rule, in that where all of a company's members have agreed to a particular course of conduct, it will be deemed to be *intra vires* the company. The silence of one of the company's members on the matter in question was held, in the circumstances, to constitute acquiescence by him in what was being done by the others.

5–71 For this principle to apply, all the shareholders must have sufficiently full knowledge of what is involved and that they are actually assenting to the transaction.[173] Further, it has no application where what is involved is specifically forbidden or is dishonest, or where in consequence the creditors would be jeopardised by rendering the company insolvent.[174] Where the Companies Acts lay down certain steps that must be taken before a resolution is effective and those steps are more than formalities (e.g. pre-1963, obtaining court approval for a proposed change of objects), the informal unanimity principle may not apply. It depends on the nature and purpose of that statutory requirement whether it is peremptory or not in this context. Where the procedure is designed to safeguard creditors' or other third party interests, then generally it must be followed.[175] Where on the other hand, its objective is to ensure full and informed consent by the shareholders, generally their unanimous informal asset suffices.[176] Accordingly, the *ultra vires* qualification referred to in *Buchanan v McVey* may only signify something that is prohibited by the Companies Acts or

---

[170] [1980] 1 W.L.R. 1451.

[171] *ibid.* at 1459.

[172] [1991] B.C.L.C. 1105.

[173] *EIC* case (see fn.164 above), *Re Ravenhart Service (Holdings) Ltd* [2004] 2 B.C.L.C. 376 and *Queensway Systems Ltd v Walker* [2007] 2 B.C.L.C. 577.

[174] *MacPherson v European Strategic Bureau Ltd* [2000] 2 B.C.L.C. 683 and *Bowthorpe Holdings Ltd v Hills* [2003] 1 B.C.L.C. 226.

[175] e.g. *Precision Dippings Ltd v Precision Dippings Marketing Ltd* [1986] 1 Ch. 447 and *Re RW Peak (Kings Lynn) Ltd* [1998] 1 B.C.L.C. 193.

[176] e.g. *Wright v Atlas Wright (Europe) Ltd* [1999] 2 B.C.L.C. 301, *Euro Brokers Holdings Ltd v Monecor (London) Ltd* [2003] 1 B.C.L.C. 506 and *NBH Ltd v Hoare* [2006] 2 B.C.L.C. 649.

by some other law, or by the memorandum of association, and not merely something honestly done outside the company's objects clause. A resolution to remove any of the company's directors or to remove its auditors, or to have the company wound up, ordinarily cannot be passed in this manner.

5–72   Because of the express requirement that, in order to be effective, a purported resolution in this form should be permitted by the articles of association, it may very well be that an Irish court would not follow *Cane v Jones*, absent such a provision in the company's articles—for instance, a company which has adopted Table A but not Pt II.

CONTROL

5–73   There are a variety of circumstances where the question arises of who controls a company.[177] What constitutes control can vary, depending on the context. Those holding a 50 per cent of the voting shares control a company, in that they are entitled to remove any or all of the directors; those holding 75 per cent of the voting shares control it, in that they are entitled to amend the articles of association, subject to some qualifications. For the purpose of the regime governing takeovers of listed securities, control means holding directly or indirectly securities in the company that confer in aggregate no less than 30 per cent of the voting rights on it.[178] What is meant by such indirect control is not defined. There is a more extensive definition of control of listed companies for the purpose of financial reporting and other disclosures.[179] Where for the purposes of the tax regime a company is "connected with" another person or company, or is a close company, there are elaborate definitions of the concept.[180] Under the Companies Acts, the concept is relevant to whether a company is another's subsidiary or is its "controlled undertaking", to whether it is a person "connected" with a director in the context of rules regarding him being interested in any contract with company, and to the requirement that a director notifies a company of transactions in any securities in it in which he has an interest. A company is another's subsidiary if the former, *inter alia*, is a member of it and controls the composition of its board of directors.[181] By this is meant that, without the agreement of anyone else, the former can appoint or remove at least a majority of the latter's directors. By entitlement to appoint a director here is meant that either the appointment cannot be made unless the former exercises his power to do so or that appointment follows automatically from the person being made a director of the former.[182]

---

[177] See generally, Hornsey, "Some Aspects of the Law Relating to Company Control" 13 *Mod. L. Rev.* 470 (1950).

[178] Irish Takeover Panel Act 1997, s.1(1).

[179] Transparency (Directive 2004/109/EC) Regulations 2007, SI 2007/277, reg.2(1).

[180] See generally, M. Feeney, *The Taxation of Companies 2006* (Dublin: Tottel Publishing, 2006), p.23 *et seq.*

[181] 1963 Act, s.155 and see para.14–04.

[182] 1963 Act, s.155(2).

5–74 A body is controlled by a company's director and thereby a "connected person" if he, either alone or with any other director of the company, or with any person connected with him or any of those other directors, is "interested in" more than one half of that body's "equity share capital" or, alternatively, is, either alone or along with those others, entitled to exercise or control the exercise of at least half of the voting power cast at that body's general meeting.[183]

5–75 For the purpose of a director notifying the company of any interest he acquires or disposes of in its securities, he is so interested if, *inter alia*, a company has the requisite interest and either it or its directors are accustomed to act in accordance with his directions or instructions (i.e. he is a "shadow director"), or else he can exercise or controls the exercise of at least one third of the voting power at general meetings.[184] This also is the case where he can exercise or control the exercise of at least one third of the voting power at general meetings in another company, which can exercise that same influence over the company in question.

---

[183] 1990 Act, s.26.
[184] 1990 Act, s.54(5) and (6).

CHAPTER 6

MANAGEMENT—THE OFFICERS

6–01 How a company's business affairs are managed is determined in the main by its articles of association and any other internal regulations. The Companies Acts do not insist on any particular organisational structure other than that every company must have two directors[1] and a secretary,[2] and various duties regarding the company's affairs are imposed on these officers. In many small family companies and quasi-partnerships, the shareholders and the directors may be one and the same person and, in one-person companies, the shareholder almost invariably will be one of the directors. In a typical medium-sized company, there will be a board of directors comprised of a managing director, salaried executive directors who work full time for the company, and some non-executive directors, who have significant interests elsewhere as well. Especially in large companies, various managerial functions will be assigned to management committees. Occasionally, companies delegate the running of their business to outsiders through what are known as management contracts. Ordinarily, it is the shareholders who select the directors, and they can be removed by a simple majority vote. Directors must not be negligent in exercising their functions, and they owe their company extensive fiduciary and other duties. The Companies Acts have established an elaborate set of rules governing directors' remuneration, their dealings with their companies in which they have a significant conflict of interest, and on disclosing information about their affairs to the shareholders and to the general public. Several of the statutory duties and liabilities apply to other officers involved in a company's affairs, such as promoters, auditors, receivers, examiners and even liquidators.

COMPANY OFFICERS

Board of Directors

6–02 In the model articles of association, Table A, the board of directors as a collectivity is given a wide power to "manage ... the business of the company",[3] together with a number of particular powers, the most important of which are dealt with separately. However, a company's regulations could just as easily restrict drastically the directors' powers in ways not envisaged by Table A, such as by insisting that borrowing must first be approved by a resolution of the

---

[1] 1963 Act, s.174.
[2] 1963 Act., s.175; *cf. Levin v Clarke* [1962] N.S.W.L.R. 686.
[3] Article 80.

members or that certain managerial decisions shall be taken by named share-holders or be subject to their veto. Unless the regulations stipulate otherwise, the board itself must exercise the specific powers conferred on it and must determine general policies about running the company's business affairs.[4]

Delegation of Directors' Powers

6–03   Often a board will delegate some of its powers.[5] How far directors may validly delegate their powers has not been authoritatively established.[6] As they are exercising fiduciary powers, important discretions cannot be delegated without there being express authority to do so in the legislation or in the company's articles of association.[7] Under the Table A scheme, the board can delegate any of its powers to committees comprising at least one director, which may even be one-person committees.[8] It is not clear how far these committees may sub-delegate policy-making power. Table A also authorises the board to appoint attorneys for such purposes and with such powers as the directors may think fit, which includes the power to sub-delegate.[9]

Managing Director

6–04   The everyday business affairs of most substantial commercial companies are run by managing directors. Under the Table A scheme, the board can appoint a managing director from one of its members and determine his terms of service[10]; the retirement from the board by rota system does not apply to him,[11] and he may be entrusted with any of the board's powers, either exclusively or collaterally, and subject to such terms and qualifications as the board deems fit.[12] Table A suggests that it is possible for the board provisionally to divest itself of all its powers and transfer them to a managing director. Whether this can lawfully be done has not been determined. The precise scope of a managing director's authority and entitlements depends on the actual terms of his appointment; some are given very extensive powers, others are subject to various constraints. What is said below about directors' status, remuneration and duties applies to managing directors too.

6–05   Although their "ostensible" or "usual" authority to enter into contracts that bind the company is most extensive,[13] in *Battle v Irish Art Promotion Centre Ltd*[14] it was held that a managing director, who was also a major shareholder in the company, had no inherent authority to represent it in civil

---

[4]   *Re Haycroft Gold Reduction & Mining Co.* [1900] 2 Ch. 230.
[5]   See *Smith's Precedents*, Pt 3.
[6]   See, however, *Guinness Plc v Saunders* [1990] 2 A.C. 663.
[7]   *Re Leeds Banking Co.* (1866) 1 Ch. App. 561.
[8]   Articles 105–107.
[9]   Article 81.
[10]   Articles 110–112; *cf. Runciman v Walter Runciman Plc* [1992] B.C.L.C. 1084.
[11]   Article 110.
[12]   Article 112.
[13]   See para.18–42 *et seq.*
[14]   [1968] I.R. 252.

proceedings. One consequence of a company's separate legal personality is that it cannot attend court and argue its case personally; its right of audience is confined to counsel or a solicitor instructed on its behalf. In exceptional circumstances, however, the court may permit a director to represent his company.[15]

Chair of the Board

6–06 Many directors choose a person to chair their meetings. Under the Table A scheme, where that person does not attend any particular board meeting, the directors may choose another chair in his place.[16] Generally, the chair has no authority other than to preside at directors' meetings and, if the company's articles so provide, vote, including casting a tie-breaking vote. Often, however, the chair has considerable moral influence over his colleagues. He also can have some ostensible authority to enter into contracts that bind the company.[17]

Governing Director

6–07 In some companies, the articles of association may confer very extensive authority on one director in particular; this is especially the case in small enterprises where the person who founded and built up the business wants to retain full control over most of its affairs.[18] As the 1963 Act requires at least two directors, it is questionable whether all of the directors' powers and discretions can, notwithstanding, be vested in the one person.

Executive Directors

6–08 Executive directors are directors who are employed by the company and are remunerated for their services to it as employees, as well as being office holders.[19] They are to be contrasted with non-executive directors,[20] whose legal relationship with the company is predominantly if not exclusively as office holders. Aspects of executive directors' rights and responsibilities are affected by employment law.[21]

Alternate Directors

6–09 An alternate director is someone who stands in for a duly appointed director in his absence. Although the office of a director cannot be assigned, if the articles of association so permit, a person can be appointed as an alternate.

---

15 See para.22–46.
16 Article 104.
17 See para.18–42 *et seq.*
18 e.g. *Lee v Lee's Air Farming Ltd* [1961] A.C. 12.
19 See generally, B. Cheffins, *Company Law: Theory, Structuring and Operation* (Oxford: Clarendon Press, 1997), Ch.13.
20 See generally, M. Sweeney-Baird, "The Role of the Non Executive Director in Modern Corporate Governance" 27 *Co. Law* 67 (2006).
21 See generally M.Forde, *Employment Law*, 2nd edn (Dublin: Round Hall, 2001), Ch.12.

A provision to that effect is contained in Pt II of Table A; the alternate there must first be approved by a majority of the directors and also by a special resolution.[22] While holding that position, the alternate is entitled to notice of all directors' meetings and to attend and vote at them.

De Facto **Directors**

6–10 Frequently, persons act as directors without having been properly appointed to or being eligible for the office; they are only *de facto* directors. For many purposes, however, these are deemed to be directors of the company. The 1963 Act's general definition of a director merely speaks of anyone "occupying the position of director".[23] It does not appear to have been decided that a person who is acting as a director, without being duly appointed to the office, is subject to all the duties of a director under the Companies Acts. Some of these Acts' provisions simply refer to persons who are "carrying on the [company's] business", like s.297A on fraudulent trading; others speak merely of company "officers", like s.298A on the misfeasance summons. A *de facto* director is a director for the purposes of the general duty of care and fiduciary duties, and for the rules regarding restriction and disqualification orders. Whether a person is a *de facto* director depends on all the circumstances of the case.[24] Relevant considerations include the company's size, its internal practices and whether the person in question was perceived by outsiders as being involved in the company's management at the highest level. In *Re First Class Toy Traders Ltd*,[25] Finlay-Geoghegan J. adopted the question asked by Jacob J. in *Secretary for State and Industry v Tjolle*[26] when examining if a person may be considered a de facto director: "Was this individual part of the corporate governing structure?"

6–11 It was to protect persons dealing with companies from adverse consequences of internal management irregularities that s.178 of the 1963 Act was enacted. According to this, "[t]he act of a director shall be valid notwithstanding any defect which may afterwards be discovered in his appointment or qualification".[27] Thus, in the absence of notice to the contrary, persons dealing with companies either as shareholders or as outsiders are entitled to assume that those who the company treats as directors were properly appointed, and that they accordingly act as the board. In the leading case, *Morris v Kanssen*,[28] s.178's potentially extensive sweep was significantly restricted. The objective underlying the equivalent English section was described as "to avoid questions being raised as to the validity of transactions where there has been a slip in the appointment of a director"; it was not intended to be "utilised for the purpose of ignoring or overriding the substantive provisions relating to such appointment"

---

22 Article 9.
23 1963 Act, s.2(1). See generally, de Lacy, "The Concept of a Company Director: Time for a New Expanded and Unified Concept" [2006] *J. Bus. L.* 267.
24 e.g. *Re Lo Line Electric Motors Ltd* [1988] Ch. 477, *Secretary of State v Tjolle* [1998] 1 B.C.L.C. 333 and *Primlake Ltd v Mathews* [2007] 1 B.C.L.C. 666.
25 [2004] I.E.H.C. 289, unreported, Finlay Geoghegan J., July 9, 2004, *ex tempore*.
26 [1998] 1 B.C.L.C. 333.
27 Similarly Table A, art.108.
28 [1946] A.C. 459.

or to give efficacy to "a total absence of appointment, and still less to a fraudulent usurpation of authority".[29] This analysis does not indicate where the line is to be drawn between "slips or irregularities" and breaches of "substantive provisions". The "vital" distinction is between "an appointment in which there is a defect" and "no appointment at all".[30] Yet the argument could be made that, once a defect exists, then the appointment has not been made; that there can be no such thing as a "defective appointment". Although it was not an issue in that case, it was also said that s.178 does not apply where the term of office of a director has expired but he nevertheless continues to act as a director.[31]

6–12   Despite the above qualifications, however, a company may be bound by the acts of *de facto* directors who are usurpers or who overstay their term of office, where they were "held out" by the company as being authorised to act for it and the other party has no notice of the irregularity surrounding their position.[32]

Shadow Directors

6–13   A shadow director is someone who is not appointed to the board of directors or is not manifestly involved in running the business, but who nevertheless has a decisive say in managing the company from a distance.[33] As the actual directors do his bidding, there is no necessity for him to be appointed a director; in that way he would hope to escape many of the liabilities which the law imposes on directors. He is defined as "a person in accordance with whose directions or instructions the directors of the company are accustomed to act ..."[34] There is a similar definition in the Competition Act, 2002.[35] Accordingly, it must be shown that there is a well-established practice or pattern of the company's directors carrying out someone's directions before he can be regarded as their shadow director.[36] Although a company or other body corporate cannot be a director, it can be a shadow director in appropriate circumstances.[37] But the individual members of the board of a parent company are not also shadow directors of its subsidiary.[38] Nor do directors' professional advisors ordinarily fall into this category. In one case[39] it was suggested that, in certain circumstances, even banks could be shadow directors, where many features of the company's business are being run

---

[29]   *ibid.* at 472.

[30]   *ibid.* at 472.

[31]   *ibid.* at 471, e.g. *Re New Cedos Engineering Co.* [1994] 1 B.C.L.C. 797. Compare *Clark v Libra Developments Ltd* [2007] 2 N.Z.L.R. 709 (director a bankrupt).

[32]   See para.18–45 *et seq.*

[33]   See generally, Norman & Watson, "The Nature of Shadow Directorship: Ad hoc Statutory Intervention or Core Company Law Principle?" [2006] *J. Bus. L.* 763.

[34]   1990 Act, s.27(1).

[35]   Section 3(1).

[36]   *Secretary of State v Laing* [1996] 2 B.C.L.C. 324.

[37]   *Re Worldport Ireland Ltd* [2005] I.E.H.C. 467, O'Leary J., February 16, 2005 (currently under appeal) and *Fyffes Plc v DCC Plc* [2005] I.E.H.C. 477; unreported, Laffoy J., December 21, 2005.

[38]   *Re Hydrodam (Corby) Ltd* [1994] 2 B.C.L.C. 180.

[39]   *Re Tasbian Ltd (No.3)* [1991] B.C.L.C. 792.

on their instructions; for instance, where the debenture sets out in detail how the business is to be conducted.

6–14 In *Secretary of State v Deverell*,[40] which was an application to disqualify directors, the following general observations were made by Morritt L.J.:

> "[T]he use of epithets or descriptions in place of the statutory definition of a shadow director ... may be very effective in graphically conveying the effect of the definition in the light of the facts of that case, as shown by their frequent use in the reported cases ... But they may be misleading when transposed to the facts of other cases. Thus to describe the board as the cat's paw, puppet or dancer to the tune of the shadow director implies a degree of control both of quality and extent over the corporate field in excess of what the statutory definition requires. What is needed is that the board is accustomed to act on the directions or instructions of the shadow directors. [S]uch directions and instructions do not have to extend over all or most of the corporate activities of the company; nor is it necessary to demonstrate a degree of compulsion in excess of that implicit in the fact that the board are accustomed to act in accordance with them. Further ... it is not necessary to the recognition of a shadow director that he should lurk in the shadows, though frequently he may, for example, in the case of a person resident abroad who owns all the shares in a company but chooses to operate it through a local board of directors. From time to time the owner, to the knowledge of all to whom it may be of concern, gives directions to the local board what to do but takes no part in the management of the company himself. [S]uch an owner may be a shadow director notwithstanding that he takes no steps to hide the part he plays in the affairs of the company. Lurking in the shadows may occur but is not an essential ingredient to the recognition of the shadow director."[41]

Elaborating on the terse statutory definition of "shadow director", the judge stated:

> "(1) The definition of a shadow director is to be construed in the normal way to give effect to the parliamentary intention ascertainable from the mischief to be dealt with and the words used. In particular, as the purpose of the act is the protection of the public and as the definition is used in other legislative contexts, it should not be strictly construed because it also has quasi-penal consequences in the context of ... directors' disqualification ...
>
> (2) The purpose of the legislation is to identify those, other than professional advisers, with real influence in corporate affairs of the company. But it is not necessary that such influence should be exercised over the whole field of its corporate activities ...
>
> (3) Whether any particular communication from the alleged shadow director, whether by words or conduct, is to be classified as a direction or instruction must be objectively ascertained by the court in

---

[40] [2001] Ch. 340 (C.A.).
[41] *ibid.* at 354–355.

the light of all the evidence. [I]t is [not] necessary to prove the understanding or expectation of either giver or receiver. In many, if not most, cases it will suffice to prove the communication and its consequence. Evidence of such understanding or expectation may be relevant but it cannot be conclusive. Certainly the label attached by either or both parties then or thereafter cannot be more than a factor in considering whether the communication came within the statutory description of direction or instruction.

(4) Non-professional advice may come within that statutory description. The proviso excepting advice given in a professional capacity appears to assume that advice generally is or may be included. Moreover the concept of "direction" and "instruction" do not exclude the concept of "advice" for all three share the common feature of "guidance".

(5) It will, no doubt, be sufficient to show that in the face of "directions or instructions" from the alleged shadow director the properly appointed directors or some of them cast themselves in a subservient role or surrendered their respective discretions. But I do not consider that it is necessary to do so in all cases. Such a requirement could be to put a gloss on the statutory requirement that the board are "accustomed to act" "in accordance with" such directions or instructions ...".[42]

6–15 On the question of when does advice constitute the requisite "directions or instructions", in *Fyffes Plc v DCC*[43] Laffoy J. observed that:

"It is implicit ... that the directions or instructions emanating from the alleged shadow director must have an imperative quality. It may be that advice, in a given factual context, will have an imperative quality. If that is the case, it would explain the apparent oddity ... why the legislature thought it necessary to exclude advice given in a professional capacity, if advice does not come within the expression 'directions or instructions'. Therefore, for a communication of any type to constitute a direction or instruction, it must have an imperative quality. Secondly, just because there is consideration by the board interposed between the direction, instruction or imperative advice does not mean that the act of the board is not to be taken into account in applying s. 27, if the board acts in accordance with the direction, instruction or imperative advice. If it were otherwise, the effect of s. 27 could be seriously diluted, particularly because of the difficulty inherent in making an objective assessment as to why the board acted in the manner it did. Thirdly, s. 27 does not require that the board should always act on the directions and instructions if a shadow directorship is to exist. That is indicated by a requirement that the board should be accustomed so to act."[44]

---

[42] *ibid.* at 354.
[43] [2005] I.E.H.C. 477, unreported, Laffoy J., December 21, 2005; [2007] I.E.S.C. 36, unreported.
[44] [2005] I.E.H.C. 477 at 534.

6–16 One of the issues in this insider trading case was whether the parent company (DCC), as well as its managing director, were shadow directors of its foreign resident sub-subsidiary, which beneficially owned the shares in the plaintiff that were sold, making a large profit. It had been argued by the defendants that, although the sub-subsidiary may have dealt in those shares, no liability could accrue to it because it did not have the requisite price sensitive information. But that would not be the case if DCC or its chief executive were its shadow directors. Although he was responsible for many of the sub-subsidiary's major decisions and he "totally controlled" the process by which the shares were sold, to the extent that the sub-subsidiary's involvement was a "mere formality", the judge held that there was insufficient evidence of "real influence on an on-going basis to render him a shadow director". On the other hand, because DCC appointed its chief financial officer to be an "A" director of the sub-subsidiary, who was entitled to veto any board decision and thereby "exercise a level of real influence over the corporate affairs of [that company] on an ongoing basis", she held that DCC was a shadow director.

6–17 Before it was amended, a handful of provisions of the 1963 Act applied to shadow directors as well as to directors proper. The 1990 Act very significantly extends these obligations, notably in respect of restrictions on acting and disqualifications from acting as a director, fraudulent and reckless trading, and disclosure of any financial interest in a contract with the company. Unless the contrary is indicated, statutory reference to directors does not include their "shadows". The question of whether shadow directors are subject to the office-holder's usual fiduciary duties does not appear to have been determined, but it would appear that any profit or gain that a shadow director may make arising from breaches of those duties can be recovered from him. Because *de facto* directors are subject to these duties, it would be incongruous if they did not apply to shadows

Nominee Directors

6–18 There is no discrete legal category of nominee directors, who are persons appointed to the board on behalf of some identified party and who have extraneous loyalty to that or to some other party that may not always converge with the interests of the company as a whole. These directors can cause particular problems with conflicts of interest and other fiduciary duties. Nominees of certain financial institutions or of venture capital companies may be exempted from the restriction regime for directors of insolvent companies.[45]

The Secretary

6–19 Every company must have a secretary, who may be one of its directors.[46] Neither the Companies Acts nor Table A set down qualifications for holding this office. The directors of a Plc are obliged to ensure that the secretary

---

[45] 1990 Act, ss. 150 (2) (b) and (c).
[46] 1963 Act, s.175. See generally, C. Doyle, *The Company Secretary*, 2nd edn (Dublin: Round Hall, 2002).

is a person who appears to have "the requisite knowledge and experience to discharge the functions of secretary".[47] Thus, if the secretary of a Plc is a person who is demonstrably incapable of doing that job properly, the directors who hired him would be held responsible for any losses the company suffers through his actions or inactivity. Additionally, the secretary of a Plc must be someone who either was the secretary of a company during three of the five years before his appointment, or is a member of a body recognised by the Minister for these purposes, for instance, the major accountancy organisations and the Chartered Institute of Secretaries, or appears "capable of discharging his functions" by virtue of his membership of any body or his previous work.[48] Those who were secretaries of Plcs before the 1990 Act came into force can continue in that position. What is said below about persons convicted of an offence involving fraud, undischarged bankrupts and former directors of insolvent companies being restricted from again being company directors[49] also applies to their becoming company secretaries.

6–20   A company's first secretary or secretaries are appointed in the same way as its initial directors, i.e. by designation in the statement delivered to the Registrar of Companies along with the memorandum of association.[50] Subject to this, the company's own regulations determine his status. Under Table A, the directors are empowered to appoint and remove secretaries, and to determine their terms and conditions of employment.[51] The secretary may also be one of the directors; where this is the case, any provision authorising or permitting anything to be done by a director and secretary acting in tandem is not satisfied where it is done by the one person holding both offices.[52] Certain details about the secretary and his beneficial shareholdings in the company must be kept available for inspection at the company's registered office.[53] Although the secretary's role is primarily administrative, in some companies the secretary is allowed to participate in broader policy and managerial decisions. In recent years, courts have come to accept that the secretary has a somewhat extensive "ostensible" or "usual" authority to bind the company in contract.[54]

6–21   The Companies Acts do not define the secretary's function but it is regarded as principally to ensure that the company's affairs are conducted in accordance with the law and its own regulations.[55] Among the statutory duties that fall on the secretary are to sign the annual return that is made to the Registrar of Companies; to issue share and debenture certificates; to deliver to the Registrar of Companies a return of allotments; to keep and make available for inspection the minutes of general meetings and the various registers

---

[47]   1990 Act, s.236.
[48]   1990 Act, s.236.
[49]   See para.6–38 *et seq.*
[50]   1982 Act, s.3 and Form A1.
[51]   Article 113.
[52]   1963 Act, ss.175 and 177.
[53]   1963 Act, s.195 and 1990 Act, s.59.
[54]   See para.18–42 *et seq.*
[55]   1963 Act, s.383(3).

concerning shareholders, debenture-holders, charges, directors and secretaries; to send out copies of the balance sheet and the auditors' and directors' reports; to ensure that the company's name is published on its business letters and the like, and outside all of its places of business. He is required to verify the statement of affairs filed in court in a compulsory winding up[56] and also must verify the statement of affairs given to a receiver who is appointed by debenture-holders who have a floating charge.[57] The secretary is liable to a fine where there is default by the company in complying with these requirements unless he has some special defence.[58] As well as the company, the secretary can be penalised under Pt XIV (ss.141–154) of the Corporation Tax Act 1976 for failure to supply specified information or make returns to the Revenue Commissioners.[59] Under the VAT legislation, the secretary is answerable for performing all acts required of the company with regard to that tax.[60]

6–22   It may be negligent for a secretary who knows that the company is in serious financial difficulties not to warn the directors that it is insolvent. But the mere fact of being secretary of a company and knowing that it is insolvent does not render him liable for fraudulent trading.[61] While there is little authority on the point,[62] company secretaries are subject to the same general fiduciary principles as are company directors, being to use their powers for a proper purpose and the benefit of the company, and not to become involved in undue conflicts of interests.

Officer

6–23   Several requirements in the Companies Acts apply to "officers" of the company, who the 1963 Act defines for some purposes as including the directors and secretary,[63] leaving the ambit of the requirement in question uncertain.[64] For many purposes, however, such as for enforcing the various duties contained in the 1963 Act, they are defined as including "a director, a shadow director, an officer, a promoter, a receiver, a liquidator or an auditor ..."[65] For the purpose of assisting the statutory audit, an officer includes an employee.[66] Whether an examiner appointed under the 1990 Amendment Act is an officer is debatable; in any event (like court-appointed receivers and liquidators), he is an officer of the court. Where outside the Companies Acts context, something is required to be done by an "officer" of the company, it may suffice that

---

[56] 1963 Act, s.224.
[57] 1963 Act, s.320.
[58] 1963 Act, s.371.
[59] Taxes Consolidation Act 1997, ss.1052 and 1054.
[60] Value Added Tax Act 1972, s.33.
[61] 1963 Act, s.297A.
[62] *New Zealand Netherlands Society "Oranje" Inc. v Kuys* [1973] 2 All E.R. 1222.
[63] Section 2(1).
[64] *cf. Re A Company* [1980] 2 W.L.R. 241.
[65] Section 371(4).
[66] 1990 Act, s.193(3).

the person in question has been authorised by the company's directors to perform that act, for instance presenting a bankruptcy petition.[67]

Officers' Families

6–24 One of the distinctive features of the 1990 Act is that several of its key requirements apply as much to immediate members of directors' families as they apply to the directors themselves. One of the most important of these deals with so-called "connected persons" in Pt III (ss.25–52) of that Act, which concerns making loans to directors and entering into several other kinds of contracts with them. Many of these rules apply to contracts and arrangements with companies that the director controls and also with his spouse, parent, brother, sister or child, the trustee of a trust for any of them and the director's partner. In Pt IV (ss.53–106) of that Act, which requires directors and company secretaries to disclose to the company any beneficial interest they have acquired in the company's shares, an interest for these purposes includes one acquired by their spouse or minor children. Where persons are disqualified from having certain positions in respect of the company, for instance, from being its auditor or liquidator, by virtue of being an officer of the company, the disqualification extends to any parent, spouse, brother, sister or child of a company officer.

Managers

6–25 Some statutory obligations are imposed on "managers" in companies. Under the Market Abuse Regulations that apply to companies whose securities are listed on a stock exchange, "persons discharging managerial responsibilities" within the company are required to notify the Central Bank of specified transactions in the company's securities.[68] Where a company is being wound up, liability can be imposed on any "knowing … party to carrying on of any business of the company with intent to defraud" for fraudulent trading.[69] However, to be held liable for reckless trading, the defendant must be an "officer" of the company. Directors subject to disqualification orders under s.160 of the 1990 Act are prohibited from being concerned with or taking part in, *inter alia,* the management of a company.[70]

Registrars

6–26 Companies with securities listed on a stock exchange often entrust to specialist registrars responsibility for maintaining their registers of members and of debenture holders, and for processing transfers in the company's securities.[71]

---

[67] *Re HJ Tomkins & Son Ltd* [1990] B.C.L.C. 76.
[68] Regulation 12.
[69] 1963 Act, s.297.
[70] *cf. R. v Campbell* (1984) 78 Cr. App. R. 95; *Commissioner of Corporate Affairs v Bracht* [1989] V.R. 821.
[71] *cf. IRC v Brander & Cruickshank* [1971] 1 W.L.R. 212.

Close Companies

6–27 For tax purposes, a close company's director includes a shadow director, a person concerned in managing the company's trade or business and also a person who directly or indirectly owns 20 per cent or more of its ordinary share capital.[72]

DIRECTORS' APPOINTMENT AND TENURE

6–28 A company director must be properly appointed to the office. That a person's name may be registered as a director does not determine conclusively whether he holds or has held the office.[73]

Office-Holder/Employee Distinction

6–29 Traditionally, office-holders[74] possess some degree of autonomy as to how they accomplish the duties accompanying their office; they also have extensive procedural rights if it is sought to remove them. Employees, on the other hand, enjoy the protection of modern labour legislation, some of which does not extend to office holders. It is common for executive directors, especially managing directors, to hold their appointments under service contracts with their companies. In those circumstances, it was held in *Glover v BLN Ltd*,[75] which concerned the dismissal of a managing director, that the relevant common law rules of contract are not affected by the person's legal status as an office-holder. According to Walsh J., "once the matter is governed by the terms of a contract between the parties, it is immaterial whether the employee concerned is deemed to be a servant or an officer in so far as the distinction may be of relevance depending on whether the contract is a contract for services or a contract of service".[76]

6–30 Whether or not a director is an employee of the company as well as an office holder depends on the circumstances.[77] The relevant criteria were elaborated on in the *Ready Mixed Concrete* case.[78] The general tendency was against regarding directors, even executive ones, as employees, but this is not a hard and fast rule. In *Stakelum v Canning*,[79] Kenny J. found that a salaried full-time executive director was an employee. He said that when a person who is a director but is not a managing director is working whole-time with the company, "the inference that he was a ... salaried employee seems ... to be justified unless there is evidence that he was a whole-time director only and was paid as such".[80] In other words, unless the circumstances strongly suggest

---

[72] Taxes Consolidation Act 1997, s.433(4).
[73] *POW Services Ltd v Clare* [1995] 2 B.C.L.C. 435.
[74] *cf. Edwards v Clinch* [1982] A.C. 845.
[75] [1973] I.R. 388.
[76] *ibid.* at 427.
[77] See generally, Rubin, "The Director as Employee of a Company" [1978] *J. Bus. L.* 328.
[78] *Ready Mixed Concrete (South East) Ltd v Minister of Pensions* [1968] 2 Q.B. 497.
[79] [1976] I.R. 314.
[80] *ibid.* at 316.

that he was not engaged as an employee, the inference is that he is employed by the company.[81]

Appointment

6–31   The Companies Acts do not lay down any set method for appointing directors except for a company's first directors. Before registering a company, the subscribers to the memorandum of association must select at least two persons to be its directors.[82] These must sign consents to act as such and a statement, containing their personal particulars together with those consents, must be delivered to the Registrar of Companies. Once it is incorporated, they are deemed to be the company's directors.

6–32   Where directors are appointed by the general meeting, any motion to appoint must refer to only one proposed director at a time.[83] This prohibition on such "composite" motions is to ensure that an unpopular candidate is not elected on the back of a very strong candidate. However, this can be circumvented where the meeting resolves separately to proceed by the composite method. Otherwise, companies can appoint their directors by whatever way they choose[84]; there is no legal obligation to select directors in general meeting, although that is the appropriate method where the articles of association do not stipulate otherwise. Thus, companies may in their own regulations designate persons by name as directors[85]; or those regulations may empower a shareholder, or even a complete outsider, to appoint one or more of the directors.[86] Power of appointment may even be the subject of contractual arrangements between the shareholders, but those agreements cannot prevent the articles of association from being altered.[87]

6–33   In companies which have adopted Table A, the size of the board is fixed by the general meeting, which may increase or reduce the number of directors and also fix how they are to retire by rotation.[88] The first directors are chosen by the subscribers to the memorandum of association.[89] No shareholding qualification is required, i.e. the appointees are not required to hold shares in the company, but the general meeting may lay down a share-owning qualification of that nature.[90] Where it is intended to appoint any new director, notice of more than three but less than 21 days must be given to the company of the intention to propose that person and also his written assent to serve, if

---

[81]   *cf. Lee v Lee's Air Farming Ltd* [1961] A.C. 12; and *Buchan v Secretary of State for Employment* [1997] I.R.L.R. 80.
[82]   1983 Act, s.3.
[83]   1963 Act, s.181.
[84]   See *Smith's Precedents,* Pt 6.
[85]   e.g. *Punt v Symons & Co.* [1903] 2 Ch. 506.
[86]   e.g. *British Murac Syndicate v Alperton Rubber Co.* [1915] 2 Ch. 186.
[87]   1963 Act, s.15.
[88]   Article 97.
[89]   Article 75.
[90]   Article 77.

elected.[91] This notification does not apply to a candidate who is recommended by the existing directors or to a director who is retiring by rotation and is seeking re-election. Directors who are retiring by rotation and offer to serve again are deemed to have been re-elected, unless the general meeting resolves either not to fill their vacancy or not to re-appoint them.[92] Casual vacancies can be filled by the directors themselves and the person so chosen serves until the next AGM; he is then eligible for re-election but is not treated as a director retiring by rotation.[93] In the case of companies with securities listed on the Irish Stock Exchange, not more than one third of the directors may be co-opted to the board.[94]

6–34 If AGMs are not held for a period, there is a risk that all of the directors will be deemed to have retired by rotation and none of them will have been replaced.[95] Whether failure to hold AGMs has this effect depends on the terms of the relevant article of association. In *Phoenix Shannon Plc v Purkey,*[96] which concerned the status of persons who were purportedly co-opted as directors after the AGM for 1996 was not held, Costello J. declined to imply into that company's articles of association a term that the offices should then be deemed vacated. The article there provided that at the next AGM, those directors "shall retire" but, until an AGM actually took place, it was held that they remained in office.[97]

6–35 Where the full quota of directorships is not filled, under Table A the directors can fill any vacancy temporarily until the next AGM.[98] The members too are empowered to fill any vacancies.[99] In private companies that are subject to Pt II of Table A, with the approval of a majority of the board, any director may appoint an alternate or substitute who is acceptable to a majority of his fellow directors.[100]

6–36 Whenever there is a change of directors or secretary, or in any of their relevant particulars, notice of it must be sent to the Registrar of Companies within 14 days.[101] If there is a new appointment, that notice must be accompanied by the person's written consent to so act.

Qualifying Shares

6–37 The only other statutory rules on appointing directors is that "qualifying shares", where required, must be taken up within two months by newly

---

[91] Article 96.
[92] Article 95.
[93] Article 98.
[94] Listing Rule 6.10.
[95] e.g. in *Re New Cedos Engineering Co.* [1994] 1 B.C.L.C. 797.
[96] [1998] 4 I.R. 597.
[97] Distinguishing *Re New Cedos Engineering Co.* [1994] 1 B.C.L.C. 797.
[98] Article 98.
[99] Article 100.
[100] Article 9.
[101] 1963 Act, s.195(6)–(7) and Form B10.

appointed directors.[102] By qualifying shares is meant the number of shares that a company's articles of association specifies each director must acquire in order to hold the office. Their rationale is that directors with a direct financial stake in their company are more likely to manage it better than non-investor managers. Qualifying shares are not required by Table A but the general meeting may still lay down such a requirement.[103] Any director who, within two months of being appointed or such shorter time as is stated in the articles, does not take up any requisite "qualifying shares" automatically vacates the office and cannot be re-appointed until he acquires those shares.[104]

Restraints on Appointment as Director

6–38   There are no set age or other qualifications for being a company director. Infants,[105] the senile,[106] the illiterate and innumerate[107] are all legally eligible to be elected to company boards. It even has been said that there is nothing shareholders can do against the majority placing on the board a bunch of "amiable lunatics",[108] although that probably exaggerates the present legal position. However, a body corporate is not allowed to become a company director,[109] nor is a partnership.[110] Various grounds of disqualification are contained in the Companies Acts and others may be set out in the company's own regulations; for instance, Table A prohibits, *inter alia,* bankrupts and persons of unsound mind.[111] Under the regulatory regime for the financial services sector, directors may be required to meet prescribed standards of ability and integrity. Any prohibition in the articles against persons resident in the State becoming a director is void.[112] It is an open question whether exclusion on grounds such as race, sex, religion, political affiliation and the like are unconstitutional.

Bankrupts

6–39   An undischarged bankrupt commits an offence if he acts as a director or as any other officer of a company or, indeed, in any other way "directly or indirectly" takes part in or is concerned in the management of a company.[113] However, the court has a discretion in an appropriate case to permit a bankrupt to so act. This prohibition extends to persons who are declared bankrupt by the court of any competent foreign jurisdiction and who have not obtained a discharge from bankruptcy there. It is an offence involving strict liability, in the sense that

---

[102] 1963 Act, s.180.
[103] Article 77.
[104] 1963 Act, s.180.
[105] *cf. Re Cardiff Savings Bank (Marquis of Bute's Case)* [1892] 2 Ch.100.
[106] *cf. Re Brazilian Rubber Estates & Plantations Ltd* [1911] 1 Ch. 425.
[107] *cf. Re Denham & Co.* (1884) 25 Ch D 752.
[108] *Turquand v Marshall* (1886) L.R. 6 Eq. 112.
[109] 1963 Act, s.176.
[110] *Commercial Management Ltd v Registrar of Companies* [1987] 1 N.Z.L.R. 744.
[111] Article 91.
[112] 1999 (No.2) Act, s.43(12).
[113] 1963 Act, s.183.

mens rea is not required.[114] That the person's adjudication as a bankrupt was subsequently annulled is no defence to a prosecution for this offence.[115]

6–40 Where a bankrupt was involved in running a company's business, it was held that contracts negotiated by him on behalf of the company can nonetheless be enforced by the company. In *Hill v Secretary of State*,[116] an undischarged bankrupt transferred most of his business assets to a company, of which his wife owned all the shares and was the sole director. His role was that of farm manager. He negotiated two contracts with a government agency, which refused to honour them on discovering his background. Because the company was not a complete "sham" to conceal his ownership and control of the business, the contracts were held to enforceable by the company.

6–41 Where the Director of Corporate Enforcement has reason to believe that a director is an undischarged bankrupt, he may require that person to give him a sworn statement setting out the relevant facts, especially those as may have a bearing on the bankruptcy.[117] That person may be required by court order to be questioned on oath regarding that statement.[118]

Non-Residents

6–42 At least one director is required to be resident in the State, unless a bond for €25,395 is posted or else the company has been issued by the Registrar of Companies with a certificate that it has "a real and continuous link with one or more economic activities that are being carried on in the State".[119] Principally it is the Revenue Commissioners who decide whether the requisite economic link exists.[120] If the only director of a company who resides in the State ceases to hold the office, he is required to notify the Registrar of Companies of that fact and append to that notice a copy of the bond, if one was furnished by the company; failure to do so renders him personally liable for any fine or penalty in respect of which the company is liable under the bond. Having an Irish-resident alternate director does not suffice for these purposes. Where the Registrar of Companies is of the opinion that the requisite economic link to the State has ceased, he must revoke the certificate. A company that does not comply with the residency rule is on risk of being struck off the Registrar of Companies; additionally, the company and every officer in default commits an offence.

Maximum Number of Directorships

6–43 A person may not be a director or shadow director of more than 25 companies at any one time.[121] This does not apply, however, to directorships

---

[114] *R. v Doring* [2003] 1 Cr. App. R 143 and *R. v Brockley* [1994] 1 B.C.L.C. 606.
[115] *IRC v McEntaggart* [2006] 1 B.C.L.C. 476.
[116] [2006] 1 B.C.L.C. 601. See too *Clark v Libra Developments Ltd* [2007] 2 N.Z.L.R. 709 at 736.
[117] 1963 Act, s.183A.
[118] 1963 Act, s.183A(2).
[119] 1999 (No.2) Act, ss.43 and 44.
[120] 1999 (No.2) Act, s.44(8)–(10).
[121] 1999 (No.2) Act, s.45.

of Plcs, or one of a company in respect of which the Registrar of Companies has issued a certificate that it has the requisite economic link with the State, as described above. Also excluded are companies listed in the second schedule of the 1999 (No. 2) Act (that need not have audited accounts) where either the Registrar of Companies or the Minister has certified that the company comes within this category, or the Minister directs that it is not to be reckoned for this purpose. Directorships of a holding company and of other companies in a group are counted as one for these purposes. An appointment that contravenes these provisions is void and the person who acts in breach of them commits an offence.

Disqualification

6–44   One of the objectives of the 1990 Act was to strike at so-called "rogue directors", meaning persons who had been involved in company frauds or who had committed other wrongs when managing a company. This replaced the civil penalty regime under s.184 of the 1963 Act, by which persons are disqualified for prolonged periods from holding several offices in any company— director, auditor or other officer, receiver, examiner or liquidator—or being "in any way whether directly or indirectly, concerned or take part in the promotion, formation or management of any company ..."[122] A person can be the subject of a disqualification order by a court, prohibiting him from acting as a company director or being otherwise involved in the management of a company's business.[123] That the basis for disqualifying a person also would constitute a criminal offence is not a bar to making the order.[124] A register of disqualified persons is kept at the registry of companies.[125]

6–45   *Grounds for Disqualifying*: A person who is convicted of contravening a s.150 "restriction order", as described below, is automatically deemed to be subject to a disqualification order.[126] On application by the DCE, the court may disqualify an undischarged bankrupt.[127] Where a person is convicted on indictment of any indictable offence either in relation to a company, or involving fraud or dishonesty, the court may order that he be so disqualified for five years, or for a longer period if the prosecutor so requests.[128]

6–46   In certain circumstances, application may be made to the court for such an order by either the DCE or the Director of Public Prosecutions, or by any

---

[122] 1990 Act, s.159. These are not criminal proceedings for the purposes of Art.6(1) of the European Convention on Human Rights: *Storbraten v Norway*, 44 E.H.R.R., SE24(2007).

[123] 1990 Act, s.160. See generally, A. Walters & M. Davis-White, *Directors' Disqualification and Bankruptcy Restrictions* (London: Sweet & Maxwell, 2005).

[124] 1990 Act, s.161(1).

[125] 1990 Act, s.168.

[126] 1990 Act, s.161(2).

[127] 1963 Act, s.183A(3).

[128] The longest period of disqualification imposed to date is 12 years: see "Three directors disqualified by High Court", *Irish Times*, February 20, 2007. A period of 10 years was imposed in *DCE v D'Arcy* [2006] 2. I.R. 163; nine years in *DCE v Collery* [2006] I.E.H.C. 67.

member, officer, employee, creditor, receiver, liquidator or examiner of the company in question, or in the case of "persistent default", by the Registrar of Companies.[129] If the court is then satisfied of the following, it may make the order and indeed may do so of its own motion: that, while an "officer" of the company, the person committed a fraud in relation to it, its members or creditors, or was in breach of any of the duties attaching to his office, or was held to have committed fraudulent trading or reckless trading, or whose conduct as such officer made him "unfit to be concerned in the management of a company", or who was "persistently in default" of his obligations under the Companies Acts, or who has been convicted at least twice for not keeping proper books of account for a company, or who was a director of a company that was struck off after receiving a notification letter from the DCE; or who has been disqualified as a director under the law of any foreign state in circumstances similar to those that would merit disqualification in the State.

6–47   In a "struck off" case, jurisdiction to disqualify exists once the company has been sent the usual "warning letter" by the DCE and has subsequently been stuck off, and the person was a director of the company in that period. But an order will not be made in such cases where the company had no liabilities when it was struck off or such liabilities as existed were discharged before the strike off was sought. It was held by Finlay Geoghegan J. in the aptly named *Cautious Trading* case[130] that the onus is on the respondent director to show that there were no unpaid debts or to adduce other evidence why the sanction should not apply to him.

6–48   Where a company is being wound up and one of its directors is either subject to a current section 150 "restriction order" or he had been so restricted and the winding-up commenced within five years of the previous liquidation beginning, the liquidator must report the matter to the court if it appears that the company is insolvent. In such circumstances the court may order that he be disqualified.[131]

6–49   Whenever a person who has been disqualified in a foreign state from acting as a director is appointed to a directorship, notice of that fact must be given to the Registrar of Companies, along with particulars of the country in question, the date of the order and its duration. If notice to this effect is not given or the notice is false in any material particular, the person becomes automatically disqualified for the unexpired period of that order.[132]

6–50   *Sanctions*: Breach of a disqualification order is an offence, which also can result in that disqualification being extended for a period of 10 years without the possibility of relief, and can render the person personally liable without

---

[129] 1990 Act, s.160 and see para.22–62 *et seq.* on procedural aspects.
[130] *Re Cautious Trading Ltd (orse Director of Corporate Enforcement v McDonnell)* [2005] 1 I.R. 503.
[131] 1990 Act, s.161(5).
[132] 1990 Act, s.160(1A) and 1982 Act, s.3A.

limitation for the unpaid debts of the company.[133] Additionally, any payment made or other consideration given by a company for the services of a person who is disqualified may be recovered from him by the company or its liquidator. Any company director or other officer who acts on the directions or instructions of a disqualified person commits an offence and, if convicted, can be rendered liable for the company's unpaid debts incurred in the period when he so acted.[134]

6–51   *Relief*: A person who is disqualified under s.160 may apply to the court for relief from the order, either entirely or in part—such application must be made within one year of the declaration of disqualification. No criteria are prescribed for determining these applications other than what the court deems to be "just and equitable".[135] As yet, no formal application for relief from a disqualification or a deemed disqualification declaration has been brought before the courts.

Restriction

6–52   Another objective of the 1990 Act was to deal with the so-called "phoenix syndrome", where directors liquidate one company, leaving substantial unpaid debts behind, and then go on to set up a new company, often in the very same or a similar business. It was felt that certain restrictions should be placed on former directors of insolvent companies. Unless permitted to do so by the court, s.150 of that Act prohibits every director of a company which is wound up and is found to be insolvent from being a director, for a period of five years, of a company that does not meet certain minimum capital requirements.[136] Those are that in the case of a Plc, the nominal value of its allotted share capital must be at least €317,440 and in the case of other companies, at least €63,487. These amounts must be fully paid up in cash in respect of the allotted shares and any premium on them. Additionally, the company is not allowed to avail of a procedure which permits it to lend money or otherwise assist persons to purchase the company's own shares or those of its holding company to meet the minimum capital amounts.[137] Also, the company must comply with the requirements in ss.32–36 of the 1983 Act, regarding having certain acquisitions of substantial assets by the company subjected to independent valuation, as if it were a Plc. An allottee of shares in a Plc or a private company which are not fully paid up in cash, as required above, remains liable for the outstanding sum. A register of restricted persons is kept at the registry of companies.[138]

6–53   *Grounds for Restriction*: Restriction orders will be made unless the court is satisfied that the person "has acted honestly and responsibly in relation to the conduct of the affairs of the company and there is no other reason why

---

[133] 1990 Act, s.163.
[134] 1990 Act, ss.164 and 165.
[135] 1990 Act, s.160(8).
[136] 1990 Act, s.150 and see para.22–62 *et seq.* on procedural aspects.
[137] 1963 Act, s.60(2)–(11).
[138] 1990 Act, s.153.

it would be just and equitable that he should be … restrict[ed] …"[139] Although the main focus of enquiry is events within the 12 months before the winding up commenced, it would appear that the court is not confined to examining that period.[140]

6–54 Dishonesty for those purposes was described by Peart J. in *Re USIT World Plc*[141] as "something akin to improper dealing with money or other assets belonging to the company or some form of fraudulent trading. In an extreme case this would involve a director depleting the assets of the company directly for his own benefit, rather than settling his creditors, thereby leading to the collapse of the company; or obtaining funds from others with a fraudulent intent".

6–55 Irresponsibility for these purposes is more difficult to pin down and is compounded by the danger of being wise after the event. There are parallels here with the law on directors' liability for negligence[142] but it has not been determined whether the standard for a restriction order is more or is less onerous. It was held in *Re Squash (Ireland) Ltd*[143] that the same general criteria for disqualification under s.160 also apply here; what principally is relevant is the extent to which the director complied with his statutory obligations, his general competence and commercial probity, and the extent to which he was responsible for the insolvency. Other judges have formulated comparable broad criteria,[144] but, as Peart J. observed in *Re USIT World Plc*,[145] each case turns on its own particular facts. Some leniency will be shown to non-executive directors, who generally are entitled to rely on their fellow executive directors to get information about the company and to carry out normal management functions in it.[146]

6–56 Four main issues arise. First is whether the company kept adequate books and records and, if not, the extent of that deficiency and whether the director should bear responsibility for it. Second is whether subordinates in the company were adequately supervised if the insolvency was largely their doing. Third is the question of bad business decisions: was the decision so appallingly bad that no responsible director would ever have taken it? Most important of all perhaps is what was done when it should have become clear that the company was in financial difficulty and insolvency was a realistic prospect. There are parallels here with directors' liability for misfeasance and for wrongful trading

---

[139] 1990 Act, s.150(2)(a).

[140] *Re Squash (Ireland) Ltd* [2001] 3 I.R. 35.

[141] [2005] I.E.H.C. 285 unreported, August 10, 2005.

[142] See para.7–07 *et seq.*

[143] [2001] 3 I.R. 35.

[144] See judgment of Clarke J. in *Re Swanpool Ltd* [2005] I.E.H.C. 341, unreported, November 4, 2005.

[145] [2005] I.E.H.C. 285, unreported, August 10, 2005.

[146] However, this is not always so—see judgments of Finlay Geoghegan J. in *Re SPH Ltd* [2005] I.E.H.C. 152, unreported, May 25, 2005 and *Re Tralee Beef and Lamb Ltd* [2004] I.E.H.C. 139, unreported, July 20, 2004.

but, again, it has not been determined whether the standard for restrictions is more or is less onerous.

6–57   Nor has it been determined what kind of "other reason" would warrant a restriction order where the director was honest and reasonable, apart from culpable failure to cooperate with the liquidator.[147]

6–58   There is a substantial body of case law dealing with the circumstances where disqualification and restriction orders will be made, much of it unreported. In *Re Squash (Ireland) Ltd*[148] (a section 150 case), the Supreme Court endorsed the observation of Browne Wilkinson V.C., that "the primary purpose of the[se] section[s] is not to punish the individual but to protect the public against the future conduct of companies by persons whose past record as directors of insolvent companies have shown them to be a danger to creditors and others ... Ordinary commercial misjudgement is not sufficient to justify disqualification. In the normal case, the conduct complained of must display a lack of commercial probity, although ... in an extreme case of gross negligence or total incompetence disqualification could be appropriate".[149]

6–59   *Sanction*: Any person who contravenes a restriction order commits an offence[150] and, additionally, is deemed to be subject to a "disqualification order" for five years.[151] If at that time he was subject to a disqualification order, then the period of the order is extended by an additional ten years and he may not apply to the court to have that order relaxed or lifted. Any payment made or other consideration given by a company for the services of a person who is restricted from being involved in its management may be recovered from him.[152] Moreover, the court is empowered to impose unlimited liability on him in respect of any debts incurred by the company during the period he acted as its director or officer, if the company was not adequately capitalised, subject to the restriction.[153]

6–60   *Relief*: Within one year of the court declaring the restriction applicable, a person who is restricted may apply to the court for relief from the order, either entirely or in part.[154] Notice of any such application must be given to the company's liquidator, who is obliged to then notify the company's creditors and contributories. No criteria are prescribed for determining such applications other than what the court deems to be "just and equitable". In *Re X-Net Information Services Ltd*,[155] O'Neill J. stated that the court's primary concern when

---

[147] *Re CMC (Ireland) Ltd* [2005] I.E.H.C. 59, unreported, Clarke J., March 4, 2005.
[148] [2001] 3 I.R. 35.
[149] *Re Lo Line Electric Motors Ltd* [1988] Ch. 477 at 486.
[150] *DCE v Colin and Mandy Sullivan* (Drogheda District Court, March 3, 2006), where Judge Brennan imposed a six-month suspended sentence on a couple who had continued to act as directors of an insufficiently – capitalised company after being restricted.
[151] 1990 Act, s.161.
[152] 1990 Act, s.163(2).
[153] 1990 Act, s.163.
[154] 1990 Act, s.152.
[155] [2006] I.E.H.C. 289, unreported, October 10, 2006.

considering an application for relief was "the protection of the public", and that the court must also have regard to factors such as the past and present conduct of the applicant. In that case, relief was granted in the form of a reduction in the level of capitalisation required of any company of which the applicant became a director or secretary or in which he took up any position, from the statutory threshold of €63,487 to a level more affordable for the applicant, namely €7,500. Furthermore, the court refused to accede to demands from the DCE for the imposition of additional, onerous conditions on the applicant in the event that he acted as a director of such a company.[156]

Directors' Service Contracts

6–61 Not all directors have service contracts with their company but many full-time executive directors have contracts, as may some non-executive directors.[157] The various incidents of directors' service contracts raise mainly questions of employment law, for instance, the scope of the work obligation, times of work and absences from work, sick pay, holidays, non-disclosure of confidential information, restraints on employment when they cease to be directors, occupational pension schemes, stock options and income taxation. As is explained below, the Companies Acts lay down certain requirements regarding the dismissal of directors and also directors' remuneration and expenses.

Authority to Conclude Directors' Service Contracts

6–62 Questions of remuneration aside, the Companies Acts do not lay down who is entitled to conclude directors' service contracts for the company. At times, that power is exercised by a special committee of the board of directors established to deal with these matters. Where a committee of this nature exists, ordinarily it will be comprised entirely or mainly of non-executive directors. Table A does not deal with authority to conclude service contracts as such but provides that the directors' "remuneration", in the sense of fees, is to be fixed by the general meeting.[158] However, the managing director's and executive directors' remuneration, in the sense of salary, other terms and conditions and pensions, may be fixed by the board of directors.[159]

"Golden Umbrellas"

6–63 A golden umbrella is a phrase used to describe a service contract of very long duration. The gilded element is that if the employer wants to terminate the contract, he must pay the equivalent of the remuneration which would have been earned during the remainder of the contract period. Thus, the longer the duration the higher the price to be paid to rid the company of the director. In *Re Hafner*,[160] it was disclosed that one of the directors had a 20-year service

---

[156] See generally, Kennedy, "Can't Get No Relief?" *Accountancy Ireland* 39(2), April 2007, p. 52; and Buckley, "Back to the Boardroom—Relief from Directors' Restriction Orders", 13(10) *Comm. L.P.* 258 (2006).

[157] See sample agreement in *Smith's Precedents*, P618.

[158] Article 76.

[159] Article 85.

[160] [1943] I.R. 426.

contract. A device used at times to discourage takeover bids is to give the directors golden umbrellas; if an intending bidder then wants to take over the company, it will have to pay large sums of compensation to any of the directors it wants to replace. Companies with securities listed on the Irish Stock Exchange may not resort to such devices.[161]

6–64   The conclusion of such contracts with a duration longer than five years is prohibited without the prior approval of an ordinary resolution of the company's members.[162] That approval is required whether the contract is one of service or for services, i.e. whether under the contract the director is an employee or is to be treated as self-employed. Approval must be obtained for any service contract which the company is not completely free to terminate lawfully within five years of the service commencing. In the case of a director of one or more companies within a group of companies, approval must come from the members of the holding company. Before any approval can be given to these contracts, a written memorandum of the proposed terms must be available for inspection for at least fifteen days prior to the general meeting taking place; that memorandum must also be available at the meeting. The term of any service contract which contravenes these requirements is void and can be determined by the company at any time on giving reasonable notice of dismissal. It has been held that the informal approval or acquiescence by all the company's members suffices for these purposes.[163]

Inspecting Directors' Service Contracts

6–65   Every shareholder is entitled to inspect a copy or a memorandum of the terms of directors' service contracts, regardless of who is entitled to appoint directors or determine their remuneration.[164] The right here applies to all contracts with an unexpired duration of three years or more. A copy or memorandum of the contract must be kept at either the registered office, the principal place of business or where the register of members is kept. This information must be open for inspection during business hours by any member, without charge. Similar information regarding directors of subsidiaries must be kept by their holding company. In the case of directors who work "wholly or mainly outside" the State, only the name of the director and the duration of the contract need be disclosed in this manner.[165]

Vacating the Office

6–66   Subject to the members' statutory removal power,[166] persons can be appointed to directorships even for the duration of their lives. Most articles of association, however, provide for periodic retirements. Under Table A, all the

---

[161] See para.15–133 *et seq.*
[162] 1990 Act, s.28. See *Smith's Precedents*, P606C.
[163] *Wright v Atlas Wright (Europe) Ltd* [1999] 2 B.C.L.C. 301.
[164] 1990 Act, s.50.
[165] 1990 Act, s.50(5).
[166] 1963 Act, s.182. See also art.99 of Table A.

directors are required to retire at the first AGM[167]; following that, one third of the board must retire every year on a rota basis.[168] Also, the office is deemed vacated when the director, *inter alia,* is adjudged bankrupt, makes an arrangement or composition with his creditors generally, becomes of unsound mind so found, is convicted of an indictable offence (unless the other directors decide that he should stay on) or is absent for more than six months from board meetings without the board's consent.[169]

Resignation

6–67   Except where a company's own regulations provide otherwise, a director may resign at any time and for any reason, and such action is effective notwithstanding that the company does not accept his resignation.[170] Whether he can freely resign in circumstances where the company is left with one director only or indeed no director at all is debatable. Where he is required to give a stipulated period of notice before resigning, the company may agree to him resigning before that period expires. If he has a service contract, he may be liable in damages if he resigns in a manner not compatible with his obligations under the contract.

6–68   An intention to resign does not become effective until, at minimum, the company has been notified of the fact and a recipient of the letter or other notice would not be left in reasonable doubt as to what was intended. In one instance involving proceedings for wrongfully exploiting a "corporate opportunity", the defendants had been directors of two related companies.[171] When it became clear that the companies were in financial difficulties, the defendants wrote to the board of one of them, at what was thought to be its registered address, giving notice of termination of "directorship of your Company". This was held to be an effective resignation from only that company.

Removal

6–69   Although the Companies Acts do not set down grounds for removing directors from office, a simple majority of the members who vote is empowered to remove any or all the directors for any reason whatsoever.[172] Whether an executive director was in fact removed from office depends on the circumstances of each case, the question being whether the company's conduct amounted to a repudiation of the service agreement.

Right to Dismiss Directors

6–70   It used to be the case that, in the absence of express provision to the contrary in the company's own regulations or in a service contract, shareholders

---

[167] Article 92.
[168] Article 93.
[169] Article 91.
[170] 1963 Act, s.195(11A)–(11E) sets out the procedure to be followed. See sample severance agreement in *Smith's Precedents*, P618.
[171] *Quarter Master UK Ltd v Pyke* [2005] 1 B.C.L.C. 245.
[172] 1963 Act, s.182.

did not possess the "inherent" power to remove directors appointed for a definite period until that time had expired. Shareholders are now entitled, by passing an ordinary resolution, to remove any or all of the directors from the board before their periods of office expire.[173] That is to say, a simple majority of the members voting may immediately sack any director and even the entire board. Extended notice[174] must be given of an intention to propose such a resolution[175] and a copy of it must be forwarded by the company to the director in advance. Ordinarily, he is entitled to have written representations circulated to the shareholders and to speak at the general meeting on the resolution. A director of a private company who, under the articles of association, holds office for life is excepted from this rule.[176] Table A does not make any provision for life directors.

6–71   Consequently, the ultimate control over running companies lies with whoever owns or has influence over 50 per cent of the voting shares. Although the board itself may be legally free to ignore instructions given to it by a resolution of the general meeting,[177] the fact that a bare majority of the voting members can oust the board means that the directors will pay particular attention to the majority's wishes. Persons seeking to take over a company may be satisfied with a 51 per cent stake, in that this brings them control of the management; although more often they may prefer at least a 75 per cent stake, so that they are in a position to alter the articles of association.

6–72   To entrench the principle of simple majority rule here, the power to remove by ordinary resolution cannot be excluded by anything in the articles of association or in any agreement between the company and the director.[178] But this does not prohibit a contrary provision in the memorandum of association. Nor does it prohibit separate agreements between shareholders, or between shareholders and directors, not to exercise their statutory removal power. In *Bushell v Faith*,[179] it was held that effectively perpetuating directors' positions by giving them weighted votes on the very issue of their removal from office was permissible. The company had three shareholders, each with an equal number of shares. According to its regulations, on any resolution to remove a director, that director should have three votes for every share he owned. A and B with 100 shares each cast 200 votes to remove C; but C, although he held only 100 shares, under that regulation cast 300 votes and defeated that proposal. It was contended that if such a scheme were sustained it would "make a mockery of the law", in that if "writ large it would set out a director is not to be removed against his will and that in order to achieve this and to thwart the express provision of [s.183], the voting power of any director threatened with removal is to be deemed to be greater than it actually is".[180]

---

[173] 1963 Act, s.182.

[174] 1963 Act, s.142.

[175] *cf. Currie v Cowdenbeath FC* [1992] B.C.L.C. 1029.

[176] 1963 Act, s.182(1). Cf. *Bersel Manufacturing Co. Ltd v Berry* [1968] 3 All E.R. 552.

[177] See para.5–08 *et seq.*

[178] 1963 Act, s.182(1).

[179] [1970] A.C. 1099.

[180] *ibid.* at 1106, Lord Morris dissenting.

6–73 In answer, a majority fastened on the requirement of an ordinary resolution, which means a majority of the votes cast, and the fact that the legislature "has never sought to fetter the right of the company (set out in art. 2 of Table A) to issue a share with such [voting] rights and restrictions it may think fit".[181] Classes of shares with different voting weights have always been allowed, whether the weighing is for all questions or for particular issues only;[182] there is nothing in the Companies Acts to suggest that the freedom companies have to devise their internal power structures in this way was abrogated. It did not matter that the actual device used here was inconsistent with what it was hoped that s.182 would achieve. This decision is perhaps the most extreme example of literal construction in modern company law.[183]

6–74 Entitlement to dismiss and the grounds for dismissal may also be contained in the company's own regulations. The right of removal may be conferred on, for example, the other directors or one of them, or on one or more of the shareholders, or on some complete outsider. Table A provides that any or all of the directors can be removed by an ordinary resolution of the members.[184] Resolutions to remove often are framed to take effect only on the election of a successor. It has been held that where, under such a regulation, directors resolve to remove one of their number but that resolution is unlawful, in the sense that the directors were pursuing extraneous objectives and were not acting for the company's benefit, the resolution nevertheless is legally effective.[185] This result is justified by the need to give "business sense" to the regulation in question and to prevent paralysis of the company's management pending the outcome of any dispute about the removal from office of a director.

Oppression and Inequity

6–75 In exceptional circumstances, removal of a director from the board can amount to "oppression" under s.205 of the 1963 Act[186] or be grounds for winding up the company on "just and equitable" grounds.[187] For these purposes, the director must also be a member of the company and must show that, in the circumstances, he had a very compelling "legitimate expectation" to remain in office against the wishes of the majority of members. An example might be where the company is what is termed a quasi-partnership and was established on the clear understanding that he would always have a full say in managing the business. If however, the director had misconducted himself in some manner and his removal was to safeguard the company's wellbeing or its assets, generally that will not constitute oppression.

---

[181] *ibid.* at 1109.
[182] See para.9–33 *et seq.*
[183] P.V.B's note in 86 *L.Q.R.* 155 (1970).
[184] Article 99.
[185] *Lee v Chou Wen Hsien* [1984] 1 W.L.R. 1202.
[186] See para.10–71 *et seq.*
[187] See para.10–109 *et seq.*

6–76   Where the likelihood of oppression is shown to be the case, a court may grant an injunction restraining the general meeting from considering a proposed resolution that the director/shareholder should be removed from office. In *Feighery v Feighery*,[188] which did not involve a "quasi partnership" and where there was little evidence to support a strong "legitimate expectation", Laffoy J. refused to make such an order on account of the importance of the shareholders' statutory right. Even if passing such a resolution would amount to oppression, the shareholders were entitled to so act, albeit the aggrieved member may then become entitled to appropriate redress under s.205. In *McGilligan v O'Grady*,[189] however, the Supreme Court distinguished that case and made an interlocutory order restraining the plaintiff's removal from the board, holding that the normal principles applicable to interlocutory relief apply here, *viz.* an arguable case, damages not being an adequate remedy and the balance of convenience.

Damages

6–77   A director, especially an executive director, may hold office under a contract that runs for a set period or until terminated on expressly stated or impliedly provided-for grounds. The 1963 Act and also Table A stipulate that the power to remove them by ordinary resolution shall not deprive the directors of any entitlement to damages or compensation they otherwise may possess. A director may lawfully be removed from office only in accordance with any service contract's provisions regarding notice and procedures, except where he has broken a major term of the contract, in which case he may be summarily dismissed once he has been afforded fair procedures.

6–78   Whether a director was in fact removed from office depends on the circumstances of each case, the question being whether the company's conduct amounted to a repudiation of the service agreement. For instance, in *Harold Holdsworth & Co. (Wakefield) Ltd v Caddies*,[190] the plaintiff was appointed director of a company for a five-year period, his function being defined as running the company and its associated companies in such manner as may from time to time be assigned to or vested in him by the board. Following differences that arose between them, the board resolved that he should confine his attentions to just one company in the group. It was held that this was not a breach of the service agreement because, under its terms, the board reserved the power to limit his responsibilities as it saw fit. The mere appointment out of court by creditors of a receiver and manager to act for the company does not *ipso facto* amount to a repudiation of the service contract with its managing director.[191]

6–79   In *Glover v BLN Ltd*,[192] the plaintiff's contract as managing director provided that he could be removed without compensation for serious misconduct,

---

[188] [1999] 1 I.R. 321.
[189] [1999] 1 I.R. 346.
[190] [1955] 1 W.L.R. 352.
[191] *Griffiths v Secretary of State for Social Services* [1974] 1 Q.B. 468.
[192] [1973] I.R. 388.

serious neglect of duties, wilful disobedience of reasonable orders and the like. One issue before the court was whether, when dismissing him, the defendant's board possessed sufficient evidence of serious misconduct and neglect. It was held that only one of the many allegations made against him could have provided grounds for summary dismissal.

6–80 At times, the director's required standard of performance must be implied from the surrounding circumstances. A director whose conduct repudiates the service agreement can be removed almost instantaneously. In *Carvill v Irish Industrial Bank Ltd*,[193] what, to use a neutral term, was unwise conduct on the part of a small bank's managing director, was held by Kenny J. to warrant immediate dismissal. But the Supreme Court concluded that, in the circumstances, his indiscretion was not sufficiently repudiatory for that purpose.

6–81 Unless the contract provides for a fixed term of service or for dismissal only on stated grounds, a director may lawfully be removed for any reason whatsoever if given proper notice. Proper notice means the period stipulated in the contract or, where the contract is silent, a "reasonable" period. In *Carvill,* for example, it was found that twelve months was a reasonable period.

Procedure

6–82 Natural justice and fair procedures must be complied with before the members can pass a resolution to remove a director. The proposed resolution must follow the 1963 Act's (s.142) extended notice procedure, and a copy of it must be forwarded by the company to the director. Ordinarily, the director is entitled to have written representations circulated to the shareholders and to speak at the general meeting on the resolution to remove him.

6–83 It was held in the *Glover* case that, additionally, it is an implied term of a director's service contract, especially one that lays down grounds for removal from the board, that the removal procedures be fair. For example, if the grounds stated for dismissal are misconduct or neglect of duty, then the director must be "told of the charges against him [and be] allow[ed] to meet the charges ... and afford[ed] an adequate opportunity of answering them ..." It is of no relevance that the director is an employee and not an office holder. Refusal to accord these procedural rights is a breach of contract regardless of how guilty the director may have been.

The Articles of Association and the Directors' Service Contract

6–84 There remains the question of the relationship between directors' tenure under a service contract and removal provisions contained in the articles of association. Provisions in the articles are not automatically incorporated in the contract but they may be incorporated by either express provision to that effect by way of implication.[194]

---

[193] [1968] I.R. 325.
[194] e.g. *Globalink Telecommunications Ltd v Wilmbury Ltd* [2003] 1 B.C.L.C. 145.

6–85 In the first place, a company may alter its articles of association by special resolution,[195] which could enable it to remove any director. Thus, in *Shuttleworth v Cox Brothers & Co.*,[196] the plaintiff was designated in the articles of association as a permanent director entitled to hold office for as long as he lived. Those articles were later amended to add a new ground for disqualifying a director: a request in writing by all his co-directors that he should resign. Such a request to resign was then made of the plaintiff, and thereafter he was treated as no longer holding office. As, in the circumstances, there was no evidence of bad faith or discriminatory motives in changing the articles of association, it was held that the alteration and, accordingly, his removal under the new article, were effective.

6–86 A company cannot waive its power to alter its own regulations,[197] not even by express stipulation in a separate contract.[198] There is some authority to the effect that a court will prohibit a company from altering its articles where doing so would contravene an earlier contractual obligation undertaken by it.[199] But it most likely would not be followed today, at least in this context. Nevertheless, to act on such an alteration by removing a director may be a breach of contract, if doing so is contrary to a term in a contract entered into before the alteration. In *Southern Foundries (1926) Ltd v Shirlaw*,[200] where the plaintiff had a 10-year service contract as a managing director, the company's articles of association were changed so as to empower the parent company to remove him from office. While the alteration itself could not be impeached, it did not follow that the company was free to act on the new article by dismissing him in breach of contract.

6–87 Table A stipulates that a managing director's appointment shall be automatically determined if he "ceases from any cause to be a director"[201]; it also empowers the general meeting to remove any director before their period of office expires "notwithstanding anything in ... any agreement".[202] The question has arisen whether a company may lawfully dismiss its managing director through the simple expedient of removing him from the board. Is the managing director's service contract subject to an implied power by the company, under Table A, to terminate it in this manner? The answer is generally "no" because of the principle against self-induced frustration of contracts: that "if a party enters into an arrangement which can only take effect by the continuance of a certain existing state of circumstances, there is an implied engagement on his part that he shall do nothing of his own motion to put an end to that state of circumstances, under which alone the arrangement can be operative".[203]

---

[195] 1963 Act, s.15.
[196] [1927] 2 K.B. 9.
[197] See para.11–10 *et seq.*
[198] *Russell v Northern Bank Development Corp.* [1992] 1 W.L.R. 588.
[199] *British Murac Syndicate Ltd v Alperton Rubber Co.* [1915] 2 Ch. 186.
[200] [1940] A.C. 701.
[201] Article 110.
[202] Article 99.
[203] *Stirling v Maitland* (1864) 5 B & S 840 at 852.

6–88 Thus, in *Shindler v Northern Raincoat Co.,*[204] the plaintiff was appointed managing director of the defendant under a 10-year service contract. Following a subsequent takeover of the company and disagreements between him and the new controllers, resolutions were passed removing him from office and terminating the service agreement in so far as it might still be subsisting. The company's regulations included clauses along the lines of Table A. The contention that he could be removed under these articles was flatly rejected on the grounds that: "[a]pplying the [self-induced frustration] principle to the present case, there is an implied engagement on the part of the defendant company that it will do nothing of its own motion to put an end to the state of circumstances which enables the plaintiff to continue as managing director. That is to say, there is an implied undertaking that it will not revoke his appointment as a director, and will not resolve that his tenure of office be determined."[205]

6–89 One line of defence in the earlier *Southern Foundries* case was that, since the power under the articles of association to remove from office was in effect vested in the defendant's parent company, the defendant fell outside the self-induced frustration principle. But it was held that the defendant there was "sufficiently involved in the removal process to be caught by that principle; "if a wrong ... if done by [the defendant] it surely must be a wrong ... if done by [the parent] who derives [its] power to do the act from [the defendant] only".[206]

6–90 It nevertheless can happen that the service contract by implication authorises the company without "cause" to terminate the agreement before its normal expiry date; although there would need to be very persuasive circumstances to raise such an implication when the contract states that it is for a fixed term. In one instance where the contract was for an indeterminate period, *Read v Astoria Garage (Streatham) Ltd,*[207] it was held that, although the board would have to give proper notice in order lawfully to remove the plaintiff, under Table A he could be removed without notice by a general meeting resolution. However, in *Shindler* this case was said to have been wrongly decided.

Formalities

6–91 Every company must keep a register of its directors and secretaries, containing specified details. Every such officer is obliged to keep the company informed of those matters.[208] Whenever a company is being incorporated, the Registrar of Companies must be supplied with details of its intended first directors and secretaries, together with their signed consents to so act.[209] If any of those persons are disqualified under the law of another State, the Registrar must be notified as to the state in question, the date the person was disqualified

---

[204] [1960] 1 W.L.R. 1038.
[205] *ibid.* at 1043.
[206] [1940] A.C. 701 at 718.
[207] [1952] Ch. 637.
[208] 1963 Act, s.195.
[209] 1982 Act, s.3 and Form A1.

and the period of disqualification.[210] Whenever there is a change in the holders
of these offices or in their relevant particulars, the company must notify the
CRO within 14 days of its occurrence, along with written consent to act in the
case of a new appointment.[211] Any person may notify the Registrar of Companies of a director's death.[212] Where the company has securities listed on the
Irish Stock Exchange, specified details concerning its directors and board
changes must be notified to the Exchange authorities.[213]

6–92   Where a company fails to notify the Registrar that a person has ceased
being a director for any reason, that person may notify the company, requesting
it to forthwith notify the CRO or, failing that, he will so notify the company
and every one of its officers of the fact. If the company does not do that, then
he may notify the Registrar and any other such person of the fact, furnishing
the CRO such additional information as may be prescribed.[214]

6–93   Whenever, following notification of ceasing to hold office, no person
is recorded in the CRO as being a director, that can be sufficient grounds for
the Registrar believing that the company is no longer carrying on business. He
may thereupon set about having it struck off the register.[215]

DIRECTORS' REMUNERATION

6–94   The question of directors' remuneration[216] is a sensitive matter in many
companies.[217] In closely held companies, tax considerations bear heavily on
whether the directors are to be rewarded by emoluments that are subject to
Schedule E or by generous expenses, both of which are deductible from the
company's own tax bill; or else by way of dividends or, indeed, loans to directors.[218] At times, there may be concern that majority shareholders will occupy
all the seats on the board, pay themselves handsome directors' fees and leave
little or nothing for distribution to members by way of dividends. In large companies with many shareholders, the dilemma may be whether the directors are
being adequately rewarded to ensure that they will give of their best in advancing the company's interests.[219] To this end, part of their remuneration may be
options on the company's shares. On the other hand, there may be concerns
that the directors are being extravagantly over-remunerated and numerous
shareholders may feel powerless to do anything about it. "Golden handshakes"

---

[210] 1982 Act, s.3A and Form B74.
[211] 1963 Act, s.195(6)–(7) and Form B10.
[212] 1963 Act, s.195(11E) and Form B70, along with official copy of death certificate.
[213] Listing Rule 6.6.11.
[214] 1963 Act, s.195(11A)–(11B) and Form B69.
[215] 1999 No. 2 Act, s.48.
[216] See L. MacCann, "Directors' Remuneration and Loans Part I" 9 *I.L.T.* 250 (1991).
[217] See generally, B. Cheffins, *Company Law: Theory, Structure and Operation* (Oxford: Clarendon Press, 1997), Ch.14.
[218] *cf. James v Garnett* [2007] 1 W.L.R. 2030 on anti-avoidance provisions in the UK.
[219] See generally, L. Bebchuk and J. Fried, *Pay Without Performance: The Unfulfilled Prom-ise of Executive Compensation* (Cambridge, Mass.: Harvard University Press, 2004).

paid to retiring directors can give rise to concern among shareholders about for whose benefit the company in fact was being run, either for the professional directors or for the shareholders. Another area of some concern is separate but lucrative "consultancy" contracts with one or some of the directors, or with a firm they control.

Ultra Vires

6–95 In *Re Horsley & Weight Ltd*,[220] it was held that a provision in a company's objects clause authorising it to pay pensions was a substantive object of the company and not just an ancillary power. Accordingly, such payments could not be set aside as being *ultra vires* simply because they were gratuitous and brought no benefit whatsoever to the company. It remains to be seen whether this reasoning finds favour in Ireland and whether it will be extended to "golden handshakes" and loans to directors. However, a payment that is *intra vires* on this basis is nonetheless unlawful and *ultra vires* where it amounts to an unauthorised repayment of the company's subscribed capital.

6–96 Where, as usually is the case, the company's objects do not deal with it but the articles of association set down the procedure for determining directors' remuneration, it would appear that payment of remuneration cannot then be impeached on *ultra vires* grounds, in the sense of being outside the company's very capacity. In *Re Halt Garage (1964) Ltd*,[221] which concerned a company with Table A as its articles of association, it was held that remuneration paid for a director's services, even if the rate was excessive, could not be struck down. It may be that the memorandum or articles of non-profit companies must stipulate remuneration for directors before those payments can be *intra vires*.[222] As is explained below, there are several cases on pensions for directors' widows which were held to be *ultra vires* but which might not be followed today, at least on that ground. None of the cases appear to have considered the relevance of taxation principles to this enquiry, i.e. the view that if the payment would not be allowed as an expense in computing the company's tax bill then it is not a genuine fee or salary.

Fees and Salaries

6–97 The Companies Acts do not state who shall determine whether or how much any or all of the directors should be paid in fees and/or salaries, other than that no such payment may be made free of income tax.[223] The right to inspect directors' service contracts with a duration of three years or more enables every shareholder to ascertain exactly how much they are being paid, in what manner and for what services.[224] Every set of annual accounts must contain or be accompanied by a statement showing the aggregate of, *inter alia*,

---

[220] [1982] 1 Ch. 442.

[221] [1982] 3 All E.R. 1016.

[222] *cf. Cyclists' Touring Club v Hopkinson* [1910] 1 Ch. 179.

[223] 1963 Act, s.185.

[224] 1990 Act, s.50.

directors' "emoluments" or the returns arising from office or employment, usually in the form of compensation or perquisites.[225] Although not expressly referred to, stock and share options would appear to come within this category, on account of the definition being inclusive.

Authorised Remuneration

6–98 A distinction must be drawn between fees for non-executive directors and salaries paid to executive directors who have service contracts with the company. In the case of the former, there must be express authority in the memorandum or articles of association to pay them any fee or salary.[226] Table A authorises the general meeting to determine directors' "remuneration",[227] although this term is not defined. Where all the directors are also the entirety of the shareholders, then their approval of accounts that include amounts drawn by them during the year as remuneration is equivalent to them sanctioning the payments in general meeting.[228]

6–99 Even though a company is implicitly empowered to do everything incidental to securing its business objects, like paying reasonable salaries, it has been held that directors may not appoint any one of their number to a salaried office in the company without having express power to do so.[229] Under Table A, the board can appoint any director as managing director or to any other office or "place of profit" in the company, and determine the terms on which these positions are to be held, including the remuneration.[230] Although in principle the director in question may not vote on the matter of his own appointment to such a position or even be counted in the quorum for this purpose, this rule is modified by Table A, which includes that director in the quorum.[231] In companies that have adopted Pt II of the model regulations, that director is even allowed to vote on this very matter.[232]

6–100 A distinction must be drawn between where remuneration is set by the board and, as is more often the case, by the general meeting or is ratified by it. The board's determination is subject to the general fiduciary standards that bind directors: they must act bona fide and for the company's benefit.[233] Violation of this duty does not render the payment *ultra vires* but payment may be unenforceable, as being beyond the board's authority. Further, the company, and possibly minority shareholders in a derivative action, may have a case against the directors for breaking their obligations to the company. Where the determination is made by the general meeting but in reality amounts to defrauding the company

---

[225] 1963 Act, s.191.
[226] *Re George Newman Co.* [1895] 1 Ch. 674 and *Boschoek Property Co. v Fuke* [1906] 1 Ch. 148.
[227] Article 76.
[228] *Re Duomatic Ltd* [1969] 2 Ch. 365.
[229] *Boschoek Propriety Co. v Fuke* [1906] 1 Ch. 148.
[230] Article 85.
[231] Article 86.
[232] Article 7.
[233] See para.7–91 *et seq.*

for the benefit of the majority shareholders, it may be impeached at the instigation of any shareholder as a "fraud on the minority".[234] However, this too does not render the payment *ultra vires*, because "the test of bona fides and benefit to the company [is] appropriate, and really only appropriate, to the question of the propriety of an exercise of a power rather than the capacity to exercise it".[235]

6–101   The only qualification to any express power in a company's articles of association to pay remuneration is that its capital must not be repaid: "a gratuitous payment out of the company's capital to a member, qua member, is unlawful and cannot stand, even if authorised by all the shareholders".[236] That is to say, remuneration may be paid on any scale provided there are profits available for distribution and the company is solvent. Where, however, there are no such profits and the money in fact is coming from contributed capital, the payment is unlawful if it is shown that the transaction in question is not a "genuine exercise of the power" to remunerate but instead is "a cloak for making payments out of capital to the shareholders as such".[237]

6–102   Apart from these circumstances, the size of the remuneration, "whether it be mean or generous, must be a matter of management for the company to determine in accordance with its constitution which expressly authorises payment for directors' services. Shareholders are required to be honest but … there is no requirement that they must be wise and it is not for the court to manage the company".[238]

6–103   Application of the principles stated here can be demonstrated by several cases. In *Taupo Totara Timber Co. v Rowe*,[239] which concerned a combination of a director's salary with a "golden handshake" agreement, the contention that a lavish arrangement with an "outsider" or non-member managing director was beyond the directors' powers and even the company's powers was rejected on the grounds that:

> "[t]here is no question as to the bona fides of the directors in entering into this particular agreement. It was shown that similar agreements had been entered into with other employees, and that to do so had been the company's policy for several years. The view that inclusion of a provision giving protection in the event of a take-over was in the interests of the company, was clearly one that reasonable and honest directors might take. In its absence, the staff might be likely to go elsewhere".[240]

6–104   In *Re Halt Garage (1964) Ltd*,[241] the first defendant acquired a shelf company and thereafter carried on a garage business through the company.

---

[234] See para.10–22 *et seq.*
[235] *Re Halt Garage (1964) Ltd* [1982] 3 All E.R. 1016 at 1034.
[236] *ibid.* at 1038; see also *Re Horsley & Weight Ltd* [1982] 1 Ch. 442.
[237] *ibid.* at 1039.
[238] *ibid.*
[239] [1978] A.C. 537.
[240] *ibid.* at 546.
[241] [1982] 3 All E.R. 1016.

He and his wife owned the only issued share capital in the company and were its only directors. Its articles of association incorporated Table A, which gave the company an express power to remunerate a director, the amount to be determined in general meeting; they also included an express power for the company to determine and pay directors remuneration for the mere assumption of the post of director. They both built up the company and drew weekly sums from the business as remuneration. Then the wife became ill. She remained a director, but soon afterwards it became apparent that she would not be active again in the business. The husband continued to work virtually full-time in the business for several years, apart from two periods of three and six months when he was away because of his wife's illness and because of an accident he sustained. At the start the business was making a substantial trading profit, but from then on the profits began to decline and, despite an increase in turnover, the company became insolvent and was wound up. Throughout the entire period the husband and wife drew directors' remuneration. The liquidator brought proceedings against both of them, seeking to recover the whole of the remuneration drawn by the wife from the very beginning and such part of the husband's remuneration as exceeded the market value of his services to the company, on the grounds that they were guilty of misfeasance and breach of trust in making the drawings. The liquidator submitted that although the amounts drawn were either formally determined by the company in general meeting as directors' remuneration or were otherwise sanctioned as such by the company, and although they were made in good faith, nevertheless they were *ultra vires* as being gratuitous payments made out of capital otherwise than for consideration unless it could be shown that they were made for the benefit of the company and to promote its prosperity. He further submitted that, having regard to the amount of the drawings, they could not have been made for the company's benefit when it was suffering a loss and the money was needed for the business.

6–105   Regarding the husband's drawings, it was held that there was no evidence that, in the light of the company's turnover, those payments were patently excessive or unreasonable as director's remuneration, or that they were disguised gifts of capital rather than genuine remuneration. Accordingly, the court would not inquire into whether it would have been more beneficial to the company to have paid him less as that was a matter for the company alone to determine. As for the wife's drawings, it was held that although the company's articles included power to award remuneration for the mere assumption of the office of director, even where the director was not active in the conduct of the business, the mere fact that the label of directors' remuneration was attached to her drawings did not preclude the court from examining their true nature. Having regard to her inactivity during the period in question, it could not be said that the whole of the amounts drawn by her in that period were genuine remuneration for holding office as a director. That part of her drawings in excess of what would have been a reasonable award of remuneration amounted to a disguised gift of capital or payment of dividends in recognition of her co-proprietorship of the business; it therefore was *ultra vires* the company and repayable to the liquidator.

6–106 In *MacPherson v European Strategic Bureau Ltd,*[242] the two plaintiffs incorporated a partnership they had with L; each of the plaintiffs held 25 per cent of the shares, L holding the remainder, and he along with one of the plaintiffs were the directors. In its first year of trading, revenue was not sufficient to meet outgoings and the business was kept afloat by the three of them foregoing any remuneration and by loans from the plaintiffs. Following disagreements, the plaintiffs decided to leave the company, on terms contained in an agreement. Under this, the plaintiffs would transfer their shares to L; the plaintiff director would resign his office immediately but would remain as a consultant for six months; expenses incurred by all of them in setting up the company were to be treated as loans to it; all payments that the company would receive under certain contracts it had would be applied in paying accrued liabilities, then the loans made by the parties and the remainder to them as "payment for consultancy services provided by them" to the company, in amounts proportionate to their original shareholdings in the company. But there would be nothing left for any other creditors the company had. At that time the company was insolvent. Subsequently, however, the company received a substantial payment in respect of a contract it had, causing the plaintiffs to sue it for their remuneration under that agreement.

6–107 It was accepted that the agreement provided for paying remuneration, was supported by consideration and was not a sham; although one of the judges was of the view that the remuneration was for services that had been provided gratuitously at the time and, therefore, could not support a contractual obligation to pay for them. In any event, the agreement was held to be unlawful because, in substance, it provided for a distribution on winding up the company without making any provision for the residual creditors. The parties' intention "was to effect an informal winding up of the business" and their overriding objective was "to achieve a distribution of assets as if on a winding up, but without making any proper provision for creditors", which was *ultra vires* the company. Had the company been solvent throughout, the position would be different.

6–108 *Guinness Plc v Saunders*[243] concerned a very large "success fee" which the plaintiff company paid to one of its directors for services he had provided the company in connection with a takeover bid. The company sought to recover the money on the grounds that its payment had not been properly authorised. A sub-committee of the directors had been established to implement the bid, which the board had decided to make; the payee of the fee was a member of that committee. It was held that the authority delegated by the board to the committee did not extend to approving payments of that nature. Under the company's articles of association, it was for the board of directors to determine the directors' remuneration and, since the board itself had not given its approval for the large fee, it had not been properly authorised.

---

[242] [2000] 2 B.C.L.C. 683.
[243] [1990] 2 A.C. 664.

Referring to the article which enabled the board to decide its own members' remuneration, Lord Templeman observed that:

> "The shareholders ... run the risk that the board may be too generous to an individual director at the expense of the shareholders but the shareholders have ... chosen to run this risk and can protect themselves by the number, quality and impartiality of the members of the board who will consider whether an individual director deserves special reward. Under [that] article the shareholders ... do not run the risk that a committee [of the directors] may value its own work and the contribution of its own members ... A committee, which may consist of only two or ... three members, however honest and conscientious, cannot assess impartially the value of its work or the value of the contribution of its individual members."[244]

6–109   Several other provisions in the articles of association of the company which might be regarded as authorising the committee to sanction the payment—like establishing local committees and boards with extensive authority and also permitting directors to be paid for services rendered to the company in a "professional capacity"—were held not to have that effect. As the power to fix remuneration was conferred on the board of directors themselves, they could not, even if they wanted to, delegate that sensitive matter entirely to one of its committees.

6–110   But if all the members who are entitled to vote at general meetings are aware of that power being delegated and acquiesce, the payments are lawful unless there is something express in the company's memorandum of association prohibiting them.[245]

6–111   Where remuneration has been paid to a director without due authorisation being given under the company's own regulations, the transaction is entirely void, not just voidable. Accordingly, an equivalent sum can be recovered either for him or from a third party who is not a bona fide purchaser for value without notice. Thus in *Clark v Cutland*,[246] where substantial unauthorised payments were made on behalf of a director to a pension fund, it was held that the fund's trustees were obliged to reimburse the company.

Obligation to Remunerate Directors

6–112   In the absence of an agreement to the contrary, directors have no right against the company to be paid for their services; any remuneration paid to them is in the nature of a gratuity or honorarium. Where under a company's articles of association the remuneration is to be determined by a general meeting,[247] no binding obligation to pay arises until the members have so agreed or

---

[244] *ibid.* at 686.
[245] *Re Ravenhart Service (Holdings) Ltd* [2004] 2 B.C.L.C. 376.
[246] [2003] 4 All E.R. 733.
[247] e.g. Table A, art.76.

they have ratified a salary arrangement made on behalf of the company.[248] A company may be obliged on the basis of *quantum meruit* to pay a reasonable remuneration for services in fact rendered to it.[249] Where, however, the articles stipulate a mechanism for determining remuneration, which is not followed, then a *quantum meruit* claim will not usually be recognised.[250]

Share Options

6–113 A common component of executive directors' remuneration in companies whose shares are traded on a stock exchange is options to acquire the company's shares. There are a variety of such schemes, which involve entitling the directors to acquire at some future date or dates, shares in the company at a price below their then anticipated market price. The theory is that the directors' endeavours will cause the company's business to become more profitable, thereby resulting in an increase in its share price, and they then will reap some of the benefit for enhanced corporate performance. Tax considerations often play a significant role in devising particular schemes. Part 17 (ss.509–519) of the Taxes Consolidation Act 1997 confers certain tax advantages on employee share ownership trusts, savings-related option schemes and approved share option schemes, in which directors who are not employees may participate. Option schemes for employees, that are exempted from the statutory pre-emption requirements,[251] include schemes for directors holding a salaried position in the company or in any of its subsidiaries. An issue that arises from time to time where a director has been removed from office is the exact status of share option arrangements he had.[252]

Insurance

6–114 Directors' remuneration often includes contributions towards insurance against personal contingencies, such as company health, disability and life plans. Tax considerations can play a significant role here. Formerly, there was uncertainty about whether or in what circumstances, or under what procedures, it was permissible for companies to pay for insurance in respect of any liability their directors may incur to the company. Companies may now purchase and maintain such insurance for any officer of the company, including its auditors.[253] Additionally, any director may count in the quorum and may vote on any resolution in connection with his own insurance.

Pensions

6–115 As average life expectancy is significantly increasing, pensions are forming a greater role in corporate remuneration packages. Another possible contribution to this trend is that such details of directors' pension arrangements

---

[248] *Knopp v Thane Investments Ltd* [2003] 1 B.C.L.C. 380.
[249] *Craven Ellis v Canons Ltd* [1936] 2 K.B. 403.
[250] *Re Richmond Gate Property Co.* [1965] 1 W.L.R. 335.
[251] 1983 Act, s.23.
[252] See para.19–13 *et seq.*
[253] 1963 Act, s.200.

as can be ascertained by the members often do not disclose the true cost of the company's commitment.

6–116 A pension is a form of deferred salary that an employer is obliged by contract to pay or that may be paid as a gratuity. It depends on the circumstances whether a sum paid to a retiring or retired director is a pension or more in the nature of a "golden handshake". For the purpose of disclosure in the company's accounts, there are elaborate definitions of each of these terms.[254] The same general principles explained above that apply to fees and salaries govern pensions.

6–117 All that the Companies Acts require is that directors' pensions may not be paid free of income tax[255] and the aggregate amount of pensions must be shown in a company's annual accounts.[256] Companies in business have implied power to agree to pay pensions to executive directors and, after those directors have died, may agree to pay pensions to their dependents.[257] Even in the absence of any express authority in the articles of association, it has been said that "it is within the power of the [directors] of a trading company ... to grant a pension to a retiring officer or servant, and to do that with or without any reasonable terms which may be bargained for or imposed".[258] It has also been said, however, that, where the articles are silent, the directors cannot make "a gift or reward ... out of the company's assets ... to one of their own body ... unless authorised ... by the shareholders at a properly convened meeting ..."[259] The matter may turn on the size of the payment in question and the extent to which it can be justified by the directors' past services. Boards of companies subject to Table A are authorised to pay pensions to directors who worked for the company in any capacity under a service contract, and to their dependents.[260]

6–118 There are two reported instances of agreements to pay pensions to directors' widows being struck down at the instigation of liquidators. In *Re Lee Behrens & Co.*,[261] three years before the company was wound up, the board agreed to pay a £500 per annum pension for life to the long-deceased managing director's widow. It was argued that the agreement was in effect a gratuitous distribution from the company's capital, but there was no evidence to support this. It then appears to have been assumed that, since the company derived no perceptible advantage from its generosity, the payment was *ultra vires* unless expressly authorised by the memorandum of association. In fact, the memorandum there empowered the company to pay pensions and the like to "persons in [its] employment". It was held that the agreement fell outside these terms

---

[254] 1963 Act, ss.191(3) and (4).
[255] 1963 Act, s.185.
[256] 1963 Act, s.191(1)(b) and (3).
[257] *Henderson v Bank of Australia* (1888) 40 Ch D 170.
[258] *Normandy v Ind. Coope & Co. Ltd* [1908] 1 Ch. 84.
[259] *Re Lee Behrens & Co.* [1932] 2 Ch. 46 at 53.
[260] Article 90.
[261] [1932] 2 Ch. 46.

because it was made by the directors and had never been ratified by the company in general meeting; additionally, the managing director was not an employee. Two of the three criteria announced there for determining the capacity of companies to make such payments (bona fide and to promote the company's prosperity) have since been held relevant only to questions of directors' powers and minority shareholders' rights, and not to *ultra vires* as it is understood today.[262] Despite this criticism, it could be argued that, even by today's standards, in the circumstances of that case the pension was *ultra vires* as a "gratuitous" transaction falling outside any of the company's express or implied powers, because the agreement took no account of the company's solvency. However, the widow might now be able to enforce the agreement against the company if she was not "actually aware" of this defect.[263]

6–119 In the other case, *Re W. & M. Roith Ltd*,[264] a director who also was general manager of a company and its controlling shareholder, but had no service agreement with it, became anxious about providing for his dependents should he die. Acting on legal advice, the memorandum and the articles of association were changed to authorise the board to pay pensions to, *inter alia*, directors' widows. Then an agreement was made appointing him full-time general manager for life and providing for payment of a substantial widow's pension. In fact, he was in poor health at the time and died within a year. Following *Lee Behrens*, the pension provision was struck down because, in the circumstances, the entire agreement was neither reasonably incidental to the company's business nor made bona fide to promote its prosperity. Rather, "the whole object of the plan of campaign was to benefit not the company but [the widow]".[265] While these considerations have a bearing on whether the board's decision was a breach of its fiduciary duties or was a "fraud on a minority", in light of the power inserted in the company's own regulations they are irrelevant to the question of *vires*. The only way the agreement there could be set aside now, in Ireland, is if it were shown that its true purpose was to return contributed capital to the shareholders or that it was a gift by the board to one of themselves in breach of their fiduciary duties and which the majority could not ratify in general meeting.

6–120 In *Clark v Cutland*,[266] where the company made substantial pension contributions to a fund on behalf of one of its directors, without complying with the procedure for approval contained in Table A, it was held that those sums could be recovered by the company from the fund, which had not given any value for them. Had the fund's trustees known that the contributions had been paid without the company's authority, they would be personally liable to it as constructive trustees.

---

[262] *Charterbridge Corp. v Lloyds Bank* [1970] Ch. 62.
[263] 1963 Act, s.8(1).
[264] [1967] 1 W.L.R. 432.
[265] *ibid.* at 439.
[266] [2003] 4 All E.R. 733.

"Golden Handshakes"

6–121 The term "golden handshake" signifies sizeable payments made to company directors on their retirement other than by way of ordinary pensions; these are called "compensation for loss of office or as consideration for or in connection with retirement from office".[267] These may be either the estimated cost of removing a director from office prematurely or may be more in the nature of a gratuity. These usually used to be made in lump sums, but tax considerations now compel companies to space them out over a number of years.[268]

6–122 These payments must not be made income tax-free[269] and the aggregate amount of them in any year must be disclosed in or along with the annual accounts.[270] Over and above any questions of *ultra vires* and bona fides, to be valid the particulars, including the amount of any proposed payment connected with retirement from the position of a *de facto* or a *de jure* director, must be disclosed to the company's members, who must give their approval in general meeting.[271] Disclosure must be made while the payment is still only a proposal[272] and must be made to all the company's members, even to those who do not have full voting rights in general meeting,[273] like many preference shareholders. Parallel provisions exist for such payments intended to be made in the context of full or partial takeovers and purchases of sizeable assets from the company in question.[274] A person who does not observe these parallel provisions must disgorge the payment. It is not stipulated that "ordinary" golden handshakes are recoverable but, since unauthorised payments are declared not lawful, they can be recovered by the company from the directors who were responsible for making them.

6–123 The prerequisite of prior general meeting approval does not apply to "any bona fide payment by way of damages for breach of contract or by way of pension in respect of past services ...".[275] How an arrangement such as that in the *Taupo Totara Timber Co.* case[276] would fare under this exemption is debatable. The plaintiff had been employed as the defendant company's managing director for a five-year period. In the service contract it was provided that, in the event of the company being taken over at any time during that period, he could resign and would thereupon become entitled to a sum equivalent to five times his annual salary. The contention that the New Zealand versions of ss.186 and 189 of the 1963 Act required prior disclosure to and approval by the shareholders of the resignation terms was rejected, because

---

[267] 1963 Act, ss.186–189.
[268] See *Smith's Precedents*, P606A and 606B.
[269] 1963 Act, s.185.
[270] 1963 Act, s.191(1)(c) and (4); *cf. Mercer v Heart of Midlothian Plc* (2001) S.L.T. 945.
[271] 1963 Act, s.186.
[272] *Kaye v Croydon Tramways Co. Ltd* [1898] 1 Ch. 358.
[273] *Re Duomatic Ltd* [1969] 1 All E.R. 161; *cf. Re Greenore Trading Ltd* [1980] I.L.R.M. 94.
[274] 1963 Act, ss.187(2) and 188(2).
[275] 1963 Act, s.189(3).
[276] [1978] A.C. 537.

those provisions dealt with "uncovenanted payments", as contrasted with payments which the company is legally obliged to make.[277] That is to say, if, under a separate contract, the company is required to pay sums to a retiring director, then the arrangement is not caught by those sections. Otherwise, it was said, any service agreement with a managing director that provided for a special payment on relinquishing the job would have to be approved in advance in general meeting, which could be very impracticable. Nevertheless, a strong argument could be made that s.186 of the 1963 Act applies to a payment of the kind made in *Taupo Totara,* as the New Zealand version did not contain an express exclusion of bona fide damages and pensions. Also an understanding reached at the outset to pay the equivalent of five years' salary in the event of a takeover could not be regarded as damages. There is no compelling reason why the general meeting should be kept in the dark about such unusual, and at times very expensive, compensation terms. Furthermore, if all sums due under contract fell outside the requirement, it would take little legal ingenuity to devise golden handshake packages that did not have to be disclosed to and approved by the shareholders.

6–124 It is only in the most exceptional circumstances that golden handshakes endorsed in general meeting would be held unlawful, the classic instance being *Hutton v West Cork Railway Co.*[278] The general meeting of a company that was in the process of going into liquidation voted to pay large sums to the directors for their unremunerated past services. That decision was challenged by a dissenting shareholder/debenture holder. It was held that, while it would be permissible to make payments "reasonably measured by the services they have rendered in winding up this company and in connection with the completion of the dissolution",[279] because the business by then was defunct, paying remuneration in respect of past services could not conceivably be for the company's benefit and could not be authorised by a majority of the shareholders; it was the company's and not the majority's money. In any event, special statutory provisions governing the closedown and transfer of that company's business[280] did not permit payments of this nature. Authority in the memorandum of association to pay golden handshakes would dispose of any *ultra vires* challenge if such a clause is treated as a substantive object and not an ancillary power. If it is a power, or where authority for such payments is contained in the articles of association, then the criterion of legality is the *Re Halt Garage*[281] one, of disguised repayment of capital. Even if it is *intra vires*, the handshake may nevertheless constitute a "fraud on a minority" or "oppression" within s.205 of the 1963 Act.

---

[277] *ibid.* at 546.

[278] (1883) 23 Ch D 654.

[279] (1883) 23 Ch D 654 at 677.

[280] Section 12 of 42 & 43 Vict. c. clxxxvii, Cork & Kinsale Junction etc. Railway Act 1879 (private).

[281] [1982] 3 All E.R. 1016.

Expenses

6–125 Companies doing business have an implied power to pay directors' expenses. Table A authorises paying all expenses properly incurred in connection with the company's business.[282] As is explained below, loans and a variety of related payments to directors are prohibited but an exception is made for any arrangement whereby vouched expenses properly incurred by a director in the course of his duties will be met by the company.[283] However, where the company incurs a liability that would have been caught by the prohibition against loans and the like but for the exception here for expenses, that liability must be discharged within six months of the date it was incurred.[284]

DIRECTORS' POWERS AND RIGHTS

6–126 The question of what powers and rights company directors possess raises two separate issues. One is the extent of their authority and entitlements as a collectivity—as the board of management of the company. The other concerns their positions as individuals. These may be dealt with in the articles of association and also in separate contracts. Their power to manage the company's business without interference from the shareholders has already been considered. Important powers like issuing additional shares in the company, vetoing share transfers and recommending dividends are dealt with separately.

Directors' Meetings

6–127 Directors' collective powers are exercised by way of resolutions passed at their meetings.[285] Articles of association will stipulate how those should be held. According to Table A, it is for the directors to determine "as they think fit" how board meetings are to be conducted, subject to the following qualifications.[286] Any director may at any time summon a board meeting. It is implied that reasonable notice must be given to all directors.[287] But the directors may resolve that any director resident in Ireland but temporarily abroad need not be notified. It is not necessary to give notice of the actual business to be transacted.[288] The quorum is set at two, neither of whom may have a financial interest in the resolution under consideration.[289] But if the number of directors falls below the quorum, the remaining board member, or members, are empowered to fill vacancies or summon a general meeting.[290]

---

[282] Article 76.

[283] 1990 Act, s.36.

[284] 1990 Act, s.36(2).

[285] See generally, P. Loose, *Company Director: Powers, Duties and Liabilities*, 9th edn (Bristol: Jordan Publishing, 2007), and M. Cordes, *Shackleton on the Law and Practice of Meetings*, 9th edn (London, Sweet & Maxwell, 2006).

[286] Article 101.

[287] *Holland v McGill* [1990] I.E.H.C. 64, Murphy J., unreported, March 16, 1990.

[288] *ibid.*

[289] Article 102 and *Re Greymouth-Point Elizabeth Railway* [1904] 1 Ch. 32; but *cf.* Table A, Pt III, art.7 and below, para.7–60 *et seq.*

[290] Article 103.

6–128   Decisions are taken by majority vote of those present.[291] In the event of a tie the chair, who may be elected by the directors or chosen by those attending the meeting, has a casting vote.[292] The casting vote of a chair who was invalidly appointed is void.[293]

6–129   Where the board of directors is improperly constituted because not all of its members have been notified of the meeting, or those in attendance fall below the quorum, or it comprises wholly or partly of *de facto* directors, it depends on the circumstances whether or not deviation from the company's regulations renders the outcome of its deliberations legally ineffective.[294] There are instances of breach of the articles of association governing these matters being deemed to be "mere irregularities".[295]

Minutes

6–130   Every company must keep a minute book of the proceedings of its board meetings and of meetings of committees of directors.[296] When signed by the chair, these are *prima facie* evidence of what took place at those meetings.

Informality

6–131   That board meetings may be informal is acknowledged by Table A, where it is provided that a written resolution signed by all of those entitled to notice of board meetings shall be as valid as if it had been passed at a properly constituted meeting.[297] A meeting of the entire board can take place without the directors being assembled in the one place at the one time.[298] Once it is shown that those "whose concurrence is necessary to give validity to the act did so concur, with full knowledge of all that they were doing", that suffices.[299] Moreover, where one director makes an agreement on behalf of the company and all the other directors informally acquiesced to it, that agreement binds the company.[300]

6–132   But where issues affecting the very survival of the company are being considered, some formality is required so that there can be no doubt that a fully informed decision was taken: for instance, to wind up the company or to petition for an examiner to be appointed. In *Re Aston Colour Print Ltd*,[301] a meeting which decided to petition for an examiner was attended by two directors who

---

[291] Article 101.

[292] Article 101.

[293] *Clark v Workman* [1920] 1 I.R. 107.

[294] *Colin Gwyer & Associates Ltd v London Wharf (Limehouse) Ltd* [2003] 2 B.C.L.C. 153 at 175.

[295] e.g. *Browne v La Trinidad* (1887) 37 Ch D 1.

[296] 1963 Act, s.145.

[297] Article 109 and *Hood Sailmakers Ltd v Axford* [1997] 1 W.L.R. 625.

[298] *Parker & Cooper Ltd v Reading* [1926] Ch. 975.

[299] *Hunter v Senate Support Services Ltd* [2005] 1 B.C.L.C. 175 at 208.

[300] e.g. *Runciman v Walter Runciman Plc* [1992] B.C.L.C. 1084.

[301] [2005] 3 I.R. 609.

were shareholders and the company's financial controller. Meetings of that nature occurred weekly, were known as executive management meetings, and discussed the day-to-day running of the company. No notices were issued convening the meeting in question, nor was any vote taken on the question of an examiner. In the absence of formality, Kelly J. held that the decision taken there to petition for such appointment could not be treated as a decision of the directors.

6–133　Nor will casual communications or encounters between directors be treated as duly convened meetings over the objection of any director entitled to attend. Thus, in *Barron v Potter*,[302] following discussions that took place on the platform at Paddington Railway Station between the only two directors of a company, it was argued by one of them that they had resolved effectively to fill a vacancy on the board. But the other had constantly maintained that he would not attend a board meeting of the company. It was held that, in those circumstances, no such resolution had been passed as no board meeting at all had taken place because, although "if directors are willing to hold a meeting they may do so under any circumstances, ... one of them cannot be made to attend the board or to convert a casual meeting into a board meeting ..."[303]

Individual Directors' Rights

6–134　Apart from their tenure and agreed remuneration, the rights of individual directors *per se* are surprisingly limited. For instance, unless he is duly authorised to do so under the articles of association or by the board, no single director (not even managing director) is entitled to sanction the bringing of legal proceedings on behalf of the company.[304]

Participation in Board Meetings

6–135　Every director is entitled to be notified of and to participate in board meetings; the court will restrain directors from excluding some duly appointed director from their proceedings. Thus, in *Coubrough v James Panton & Co.*,[305] the court ordered that the plaintiff-director ought not be prevented from participating in board meetings. Budd J. rejected the contention that an injunction should not be granted because the shareholders no longer wished the plaintiff to be a director, pointing to the possibility of him being held responsible for decisions made by the board in his absence; to the fact that *qua* shareholder he had a substantial interest in knowing what occurred at board meetings; and the possibility of directors' resolutions being invalid because one of their number was excluded improperly. Where, however, there is strong shareholder resistance against a person attending board meetings and his title to act as a director cannot easily be resolved, the courts tend to hold the matter over to be decided in general meeting.[306]

---

[302] [1914] 1 Ch. 895.
[303] *ibid.* at 901.
[304] *Mitchell & Hobbs (UK) Ltd v Mill* [1996] 2 B.C.L.C. 102.
[305] [1965] I.R. 272.
[306] e.g. *Harben v Phillips* (1883) 23 Ch D 14; *cf. Lee v Chou Wen Hsien* [1984] 1 W.L.R. 1202 and *Moylan v Irish Whiting Manufacturers Ltd* [1980] I.E.H.C. 97, Hamilton J., unreported, April 14, 1980.

Inspect all Books and Records

6–136   Every director is entitled to inspect the company's books of account regarding income and expenditure, sales and purchases, and assets and liabilities.[307] In *Healy v Healy Homes Ltd*,[308] it was held that a director is entitled to make copies of these accounts and to be accompanied by an accountant when making the inspection. Furthermore, an accountant may inspect alone the books of account if so authorised by a director. In those circumstances, the accountant may be required to give a written undertaking that any information thereby acquired will be used only to advise the director in relation to the matter for which the accountant was retained. It was held in England that the statutory right to inspect the company's books could not be enforced in a civil action because the sanction provided for violation of the right was prosecution, but that nevertheless a director has a common law right to inspect those books to enable him to fulfil his duties as a director.[309]

Indemnity

6–137   Trustees have an extensive right of indemnity from the trust fund for costs incurred in litigation and other forms of proceedings taken against them. Table A confers an equivalent indemnity on every director, managing director, agent, auditor, secretary and other officer for the time being of the company. It is against the costs incurred in defending any prosecution or civil proceedings against him, concerning his actions in the office, provided he has been acquitted or he succeeded in the action. This also applies to successful applications for exoneration under s.391 of the 1963 Act. Companies may purchase indemnity insurance against any liability they may incur in this regard.[310]

Rights under the Articles

6–138   The company's memorandum and articles of association may purport to confer additional rights on a director. But when it comes to enforcing those rights, the conventional view is that rights so conferred *qua* director are different from rights *qua* shareholder. While the courts will enforce rights conferred by the articles on the director *qua* shareholder, rights conferred on him only in his capacity as director ordinarily will not be enforced. In other words, the articles of association are a contract between the company and the shareholders, but third parties, even if they are named in the articles, cannot sue to enforce them; they are third party beneficiaries of a contract. This is so even if they happen to be members of the company if they are seeking to enforce rights other than those of a member—for instance, to hold office in the company.[311] At times the distinction between rights *qua* member and *qua* director is not an easy one to draw. Although the point does not appear to have receive judicial consideration, most likely a director can enforce his right to expenses and to

---

[307] 1990 Act s.202(8).
[308] [1973] I.R. 309.
[309] *Conway v Petronius Clothing Co.* [1978] 1 All E.R. 185.
[310] 1963 Act, s.200.
[311] *cf. Eley v Positive Government Security Life Assurance Co.* (1876) 1 Ex.D. 21.

indemnity conferred by Table A.[312] Where the director has a service contract, there can be implied into that contract rights which the articles of association purport to give him *qua* director connected with discharging his office.

RECORDS REGARDING OFFICERS

6–139   Companies are required to keep certain records concerning their officers and their activities. Every company must keep a register of its directors and secretaries, which is to contain specified personal information concerning them that they are obliged to supply to the company and keep up to date.[313] For at least two hours during business hours, it must be open for inspection by every member, and also by any other person on payment of a small fee. Anyone can require the company to furnish him with a copy of this register or part of it, on payment of a small fee. If inspection or copying is refused, it may be ordered by the court. Companies that process data relating to shareholders, directors or other officers in compliance with the Companies Acts are exempt from the requirement to register as data controllers/processors with the Data Protection Commissioner.[314]

6–140   Every company must keep minutes of all meetings of its directors or their committees, which when signed constitute evidence of what occurred.[315] These are not open to inspection by the members, let alone by outsiders, but the DCE is entitled to inspect them and to be facilitated in making copies of them.[316]

6–141   Every company must keep a record of every declaration made or notice given to its directors of any interest in a contract or proposed contract with the company.[317] It must be available for inspection by any director, secretary, auditor or member of the company, without charge. It must be produced at every general meeting and also at any board meeting if any director so requests. If inspection or production is refused, it may be ordered by the court.

6–142   Every company must keep a record of the nature and extent of any "interest" in its securities held by any of its directors and secretaries, or persons connected with them, including shadow directors.[318] For at least two hours during business hours, it must be open for inspection by any member of the company without charge and by anyone else for a small fee. Anyone can require the company to furnish him with a copy of it or part of it, on payment of a small fee. It is also meant to be open and accessible to any person attending the AGM. If inspection or production is refused, it may be ordered by the court. A person's name may be removed from this register only where no entry has been made in respect of it in the preceding six years.[319]

---

[312] Articles 76 and 138.
[313] 1963 Act, s.195.
[314] Data Protection (Amendment) Act 2003 s.16, commenced on October 1, 2007 by the Data Protection (Amendment) Act 2003 (Commencement) Order 2007 (SI 2007/656).
[315] 1963 Act, s.145.
[316] 1963 Act, s.145(3A).
[317] 1963 Act, s.194(5).
[318] 1990 Act, ss.59–60.
[319] 1990 Act, ss.61 and 62.

CHAPTER 7

DIRECTORS' DUTIES AND LIABILITIES

7–01 Directors owe their company a general duty to manage its affairs with reasonable care and skill. They must not unjustly enrich themselves at their company's expense, nor put themselves in a situation where there is a serious conflict or potential conflict between their individual interests and those of their company. Discretionary powers must be exercised bona fide in what they consider to be in the interests of their company, and any particular power conferred on them must not be used for some extraneous purpose. While *de facto* directors too are subject to these duties, whether or to what extent they apply to shadow directors remains to be clarified. These duties do not invariably come to an end immediately on the person ceasing to be a director. The Companies Acts place numerous obligations on directors, including "to ensure that the requirements of the Companies Acts are complied with by the company".[1] Many of these duties are supported by penal sanctions, which can be imposed on the director who authorised the default or who, in breach of his duties, permitted the default.[2] Several of these also apply to shadow directors. Additional duties may be laid down in other legislation and in every company's own regulations, and further obligations may be imposed in service contracts. In the case of companies with securities that are listed on the Irish Stock Exchange, their directors and senior management are required to "collectively have appropriate expertise and experience for the management of the group's business".[3] Additionally, they must be "free of conflicts between duties to the company and private interests and other duties", unless adequate avoidance measures have been adopted.[4]

7–02 Ordinarily, it is to the company only, not to its shareholders nor its creditors as individuals, that directors' legal duties are owed, no matter how large the shareholding or the liability may be; directors are officers and agents of the company, not of its individual members or creditors. But for a variety of reasons, directors rarely arrange for their company to sue one or more of their fellow members, especially for negligence.[5] In several of the leading cases

---

[1] 1963 Act, s.383(3).
[2] 1963 Act, s.383(1).
[3] Listing Rule 3.4.3.
[4] Listing Rule 3.4.4.
[5] See generally, Hirt, "The Company's Decision to Litigate Against its Directors: Legal Strategies to Deal with the Board of Directors' Conflict of Interest" [2005] *J. Bus. L.* 159.

where directors were sued by their company, control of it had changed hands since the wrongdoing occurred. In several more of those cases, the plaintiff was a minority shareholder bringing "derivative" proceedings, on the company's behalf, because its controllers declined to pursue the errant directors.[6] Certain breaches of directors' duties that the company does not act against can constitute "oppression" for the purposes of s.205 of the 1963 Act.[7] It has been held by the High Court that directors of insolvent companies owe a fiduciary duty to the creditors but it is debatable whether this is good law.[8] If, however, a director enters into direct dealings with a shareholder, supplier or creditor, those arrangements are subject to the general law of contract.

CARE AND SKILL

7–03 To intentionally cause others financial loss is often an actionable wrong. Those circumstances in which negligently inflicted financial loss is actionable are problematic,[9] especially the category of persons to whom a duty of care is owed. Anyone who works for another is obliged to perform that work with reasonable care and skill. Company directors, be they executive or non-executive, paid or unpaid, are liable to their company for any foreseeable loss to the company that results from their own negligence.[10] This duty of care arises at common law and in equity,[11] and also under their service contracts if they are executive directors.

7–04 It is only in the most exceptional circumstances, however, that companies sue directors who have shown ineptitude in managing the business; what reported decisions as exist mainly concern failure by directors of banks and other financial institutions to detect frauds. More often than not, all that happens is that negligent directors are asked either to resign from the board or not to seek re-election.[12] If the company in question has a widely dispersed shareholding, bad business decisions may render it prey to takeover bidders, who most likely would remove the incompetent directors. Where the company's performance is so bad that it is forced into liquidation, the liquidator might bring misfeasance proceedings against the directors if their negligence was compounded by impropriety. As is explained below, subject to certain requirements and limits, a company can exonerate directors from liability for negligence, either by way of an ordinary resolution or a provision to that effect in its articles of association.

---

[6] See para.10–47 *et seq.*

[7] See para.10–71 *et seq.*

[8] *Jones v Gunn* [1997] 3 I.R. 1 and see para.20–13.

[9] See generally, P. Cane, *Tort Law and Economic Interests*, 2nd edn (Oxford: Clarendon Press, 1996).

[10] See generally, Reed, "Company Directors: Collective or Functional Responsibility", 27 *Co. Law.* 170 (2006) and Riley, "The Company Director's Duty of Care and Skill: The Case for an Onerous but Subjective Standard" 62 *Mod. L. Rev.* 697 (1999).

[11] *Base Metal Trading Ltd v Shamurin* [2005] 2 B.C.L.C. 171.

[12] But see Keay, "Company Directors Behaving Poorly: Disciplinary Options for Shareholders", [2007] *J. Bus. L.* 656.

A Duty to Whom?

7–05 The general principle, that directors' duties of care are owed only to the company and not to its members, is subject to one important statutory qualification. Ever since 1890,[13] where a company issues a prospectus soliciting investment in its securities, the directors are personally liable to persons who subscribed for shares on foot of the prospectus where it contained some inaccurate material statement.[14] There are certain defences to such claims.

7–06 In very exceptional circumstances, directors may owe a directly enforceable duty of care to one or more of a company's creditors.[15] But ordinarily, where directors are neglectful of creditors' interests, the latter's remedy is through the winding-up process and the various modes of redress available to liquidators, which are designed principally to safeguard creditors. Creditors may be able to secure indirect redress through the offices of the DCE.[16]

The Standard of Care

7–07 Unlike trustees, whose duty is to invest the trust assets in a prudent manner, directors of most companies are expected to make reasonable profits with the corporate assets, which of necessity will involve some risk-taking, which is the very rationale for conferring limited liability on the shareholders. While the same general principles of liability apply to executive and to non-executive directors, their application to the latter usually differs to some extent. Formerly, in the absence of special circumstances, non-executives could rely on the other directors or officers in the company performing their duties, but this is no longer the case.[17] While the same principles also apply to small and closely held companies, and to companies whose shares are traded on a stock exchange, their application to these also can differ. In the former case, most directors will be involved in the day-to-day running of the company and many of them may have comparatively limited business experience or familiarity with the law. In the latter case, most directors will have considerable business and legal acumen, but they will have little if any involvement in the company's day-to-day business, as their function is mainly to advise the chief executive officer, to review broad policy and strategic questions, and to deal with such emergency situations as may arise. Because the directors of close companies are almost invariably their majority shareholders too, often liability tends only to be established where a minority shareholder brings derivative proceedings. In such cases, the actual relevant standard is the level of ineptitude required to succeed in a derivative claim.

7–08 The scope of a director's duty of care was summarised as follows 80 years ago in *Re City Equitable Fire Insurance Co.*[18]:

---

[13] Directors Liability Act 1890 (53 & 54 Vict., c. 64).
[14] Now contained in the 2005 Act, ss.42 and 43 and see para.15–82 *et seq.*
[15] See para.20–14.
[16] See para.20–16 *et seq.*
[17] *Equitable Life Assurance Society v Bowley* [2004] 1 B.C.L.C. 180 at 189.
[18] [1925] Ch. 407.

"In ascertaining the duties of a director of a company, it is necessary to consider the nature of the company's business and the manner in which the work of the company is, reasonably in the circumstances and consistently with the articles of association, distributed between the directors and the other officials of the company.

In discharging those duties, a director (a) must act honestly, and (b) must exercise such degree of skill and diligence as would amount to the reasonable care which an ordinary man might be expected to take, in the circumstances, on his own behalf. But, (c) he need not exhibit in the performance of his duties a greater degree of skill than may reasonably be expected from a person of his knowledge and experience; in other words, he is not liable for mere errors of judgment; (d) he is not bound to give continuous attention to the affairs of his company; his duties are of an intermittent nature to be performed at periodical board meetings, and at meetings of any committee to which he is appointed, and though not bound to attend them he ought to attend when reasonably able to do so."[19]

7–09 More recently in *Re Barings Plc*,[20] a leading case on disqualifying directors, the authorities were summarised in these terms:

"(i) Directors have, both collectively and individually, a continuing duty to acquire and maintain a sufficient knowledge and understanding of the company's business to enable them properly to discharge their duties as directors.

(ii) Whilst directors are entitled (subject to the articles of association of the company) to delegate particular functions to those below them in the management chain, and to trust their competence and integrity to a reasonable extent, the exercise of the power of delegation does not absolve a director from the duty to supervise the discharge of the delegated functions.

(iii) No rule of universal application can be formulated as to the duty referred in (ii) above. The extent of the duty, and the question whether it has been discharged, must depend on the facts of each particular case, including the director's role in the management of the company."[21]

7–10 There is no fixed minimum standard of care for all directors; the standard is what one can reasonably expect of that person with his own background and experience. In other words, what may be negligent for an accountant-director may not render a dilettante or a "country gentleman" liable.[22] For instance, in one of the very few modern reported cases on damages claims for directors' negligence, the court took account of the fact that two of them were chartered accountants and that the third director had considerable accountancy experience.[23] When the position of directors of that or comparable calibre is being determined, the general principles governing professional negligence would apply.

---

[19] From case headnote.
[20] [1999] 1 B.C.L.C. 433.
[21] *ibid.* at 484; *cf. Cohen v Selby* [2001] 1 B.C.L.C. 176.
[22] *Re Denham & Co.* (1884) 25 Ch. D 752.
[23] *Dorchester Finance Co. v Stebbings* [1989] B.C.L.C. 498.

7–11 There are four main categories of case. One is what may be described as what in hindsight was a downright bad business decision. Company directors, especially those in industrial and trading companies, are expected to demonstrate entrepreneurial skills that involve risk-taking. From this arises what Americans call the "business judgment" defence to negligence claims. That is to say, if at the critical time it was not patently unreasonable to take a particular business decision, like investing in some enterprise or disinvesting, the director will not be held responsible because that transpired to be the wrong decision. There must be some scope for reasonable business error. How extensive that scope is depends on variables like the director's own background and experience, and the information reasonably available at the time when the wrong decision was taken. There do not appear to be any modern reported cases that illustrate the range within directors are legally free to run commercial risks. It is likely that directors of trust companies, insurers, banks and other firms charged with looking after other peoples' money would be held to a somewhat exacting standard.

7–12 Another category and the commonest to feature in the law reports is failure to become in any way seriously involved in the role of director, such as not attending meetings, not learning basic facts about the company's business and taking no action when alerted to the need for some intervention. Directors do not have to attend each and every board meeting, although they ought to attend when they reasonably can. Absence from a meeting at which a negligent decision was taken may be a defense to a damages claim. In one notorious instance,[24] the president of a trustee savings bank was exonerated from liability for irregularities in the way the bank was run because he had attended only one board meeting in 38 years. On the other hand, it is no answer for directors in attendance to say that they were not paying attention. As one judge put it: "It is their duty to be awake, and their being asleep would not exempt them from the consequences of not attending to the business of the company".[25]

7–13 Today, a professional director probably would be held responsible for major miscalculations made at board meetings which he consistently declined to attend. Indeed, it is possible that the titled gentleman and absentee president of the Cardiff Savings Bank for nearly four decades might not be exonerated if his case were heard today. A difficulty with holding an absentee liable in damages is, since his fellow directors were fully aware of the absences but did not make an issue of the matter, could the company not be regarded as condoning those absences? Additionally, under Table A, a director's office becomes vacated if he is absent from meetings for more than six months continuously without the other directors' permission.[26] There also is the problem of causation. For instance, could it be said that the 38-year absence of the president of that bank actually caused the losses it incurred? As was said in a leading

---

[24] *Re Cardiff Savings Bank (Marquis of Bute's Case)* [1892] 2 Ch. 100.
[25] *Land Credit Co. of Ireland v Lord Fermoy* (1870) L.R. 5 Ch. App. 763 at 770.
[26] Article 91(g).

American case, "when a business fails from general mismanagement... how is it possible to say that a single director could have made the company success-ful, or how much in [money] he could have saved?"[27]

7–14 These difficulties were overcome in *Dorchester Finance Co. Ltd v Stebbing*,[28] where two defendants, who each had considerable accounting experience, were non-executive directors of a company. They visited the company's office infrequently, left the management of its affairs to a third director and often signed blank cheques to be counter-signed by that other director at a later date. But he grossly mismanaged the company's affairs, which caused it to suffer a very large loss. Those defendants were held responsible for failing to exhibit the necessary care and skill, and failing to perform any duty as directors.[29]

7–15 In contrast, in *Jackson v Munster Bank*,[30] in breach of its own regula-tions, most of the plaintiff bank's directors had authorised making loans to themselves without providing adequate security, which the court described as a "nefarious system" and a "systematic fraudulent misappropriation" of the bank's funds. A director not involved in these transactions, who did nothing to investigate them after some shareholders had made allegations to him about them, was held to have been negligent in not looking into the matter fully and raising it at the general meeting. He was based in Dublin and his principal job was to look after the bank's Dublin business, but all the misappropriations were taking place in Cork, where the bank had its headquarters. Had he not been appraised of the shareholders' concerns and there was no other special reason why he should have known about what was occurring in Cork, he would not have been held liable in negligence to the company.

7–16 A third category is failure to ensure that proper systems of management and control are established in their company, of which *Dorchester Finance*[31] also is an example. In what for many years was the leading case, *Re City Equi-table*,[32] where a major insurance company was rendered insolvent on account of management fraud, its directors were held liable for permitting a managing director to control large sums of the company's money, without any supervi-sion at all; the money was lost. In *Re Queens Moat Houses Plc (No. 2)*,[33] a disqualification case involving a quoted company that had excessively exag-gerated its profits and assets in its accounts, the chairman was held not entitled to deny responsibility because he relied on the finance director to prepare the accounts and they had been certified by the auditors. Although he lacked accountancy qualifications and expertise, the duty to prepare proper accounts

---

27 *Barnes v Andrews*, 298 F. 614 (SDNY 1924).
28 [1989] B.C.L.C. 498.
29 Contrast *Norman v Theodore Goddard* [1991] B.C.L.C. 1028; *cf. Re Barings Plc (No. 5)* [1999] 1 B.C.L.C. 433.
30 (1885) 15 L.R. Ir. 356.
31 [1989] B.C.L.C. 498.
32 *Re City Equitable Fire Insurance. Co.* [1925] Ch. 407.
33 [2005] 1 B.C.L.C. 136.

applies to all directors. While he may be excused for not querying certain aspects of the accounts, there were other features of them that should have attracted his attention and which he ought to have pursued. It was accepted there that the auditors had been negligent in giving their certificate to the accounts.

7–17   An aspect of this category is the statutory duty to keep proper accounts, breach of which can result in the directors being held liable, without limit, for the company's unpaid debts.[34] Large private companies as well as Plcs are required to have audit committees, with responsibility for overseeing accounts and record-keeping.[35] As state regulation of commercial activities continues to expand, either under the Companies Acts or by way of other legislation (e.g. political contributions, competition, environmental, bribery and money laundering), large companies are beginning to adopt their own legal monitoring systems, to avoid incurring substantial liabilities. A requirement that large private companies as well as Plcs file annual "directors' compliance statements", showing the extent to which there has been compliance with company and tax law and other materially applicable regimes, remains to be implemented, and indeed may never be activated.[36]

7–18   Where tasks are delegated to a suitable person then, unless there are reasons to be suspicious, a director is entitled to assume that the delegate will perform those tasks honestly and diligently. But there remains a residual duty of supervision and control of delegates, the extent of which depends on the circumstances of each case. In *Land Credit Co. of Ireland v Lord Fermoy*,[37] an executive sub-committee of the board lent two associates money to buy the company's own shares, thereby enhancing its image in the stock market. The board approved the loans on being satisfied of the borrowers' creditworthiness but without being told why the funds were being lent. It was held that "it would be carrying the doctrine of liability too far to say that the directors are liable for negligence ... because they did not enquire what [the borrowers] were going to do with the money".[38]

7–19   A final category of uncertain scope is what may be described as commercially unsound decisions which are easily explicable as arising from some conflict of interest, but it cannot be proven that the conflict existed or was the motivating factor. A recent example in the United States is the $140 million settlement agreement entered into by the Walt Disney Co. on terminating the employment contract it had concluded with a new company president a year earlier.[39] That company's CEO and that president had been close friends for many years, the latter had very limited management experience, the agreed

---

[34]   1990 Act, s.202.
[35]   1990 Act, s.205B.
[36]   1990 Act, s.205E.
[37]   (1870) L.R. 5 Ch. App. 763.
[38]   *ibid.* at 772; see also *Dovey v Carey* [1901] A.C. 477.
[39]   *Re Walt Disney Co. Derivative Litigation*, 825 A.2d. 275 (Delaware Chancery Court 2003). See generally. J. Stewart, *Disney War* (New York: Simon & Schuster, 2005).

remuneration was exceptionally high and the directors appear to have endorsed the contract without adequate deliberation and consideration. Where it can be shown that a director's actions are the result of a conflict between his personal interests and that of the company, ordinarily he will have contravened his fiduciary duty to it.

Remedies

7–20   The company is entitled to be fully compensated by a director for foreseeable losses caused by his negligence. In so far as they diverge, it has not been determined whether the criteria for measuring those losses are those for tort or for equity, or in the case of executive directors, for breach of contract. Except where the negligence is tainted with impropriety, it cannot be the subject of misfeasance proceedings brought by a liquidator.[40] Where the director in question happened to profit from his negligence but the company declines to sue him, a minority shareholder may be entitled to bring a derivative claim on its behalf.[41]

FIDUCIARY OBLIGATIONS

7–21   What are called fiduciary duties and disabilities are imposed by principles of equity on trustees and others who hold similar positions,[42] most notably on executors with reference to their beneficiaries, on solicitors with reference to their clients, on agents with reference to their principals and on partners to each other.[43] Many of these duties have a common thread and can be classified under a logically coherent set of principles. As the function of directors is similar to that of trustees, executors and business agents—to manage other persons' property on their behalf—they are also regarded as falling within the general principles of fiduciary obligation. The precise extent of this duty varies somewhat from one category of fiduciary to another. Requirements that trustees do not make any profit from their office without their *cestuis'* consent and that they avoid situations where a significant conflict may arise apply also to company directors, the company being their *cestui*. Fiduciary obligation has become a residual concept, is applied to novel fact situations and continues to evolve. Some of the instances that constantly recur are dealt with in most companies' articles of association and also in the Companies Acts, most notably, contracts with their company in which directors have

---

[40]   *Re Mount Clare Hotels Ltd* [1986] I.E.H.C. 200 unreported, Costello J., December 2, 1986.

[41]   e.g. *Extrasure Travel Insurances Ltd v Scattergood* [2003] 1 B.C.L.C. 598.

[42]   See generally, P. Finn, *Fiduciary Obligations* (Sydney: Law Book Co., 1977); H. Delany, *Equity and the Law of Trusts*, 4th edn (Dublin: Round Hall, 2007), p.419 *et seq.;* M. Conaglen, "The Nature and Function of Fiduciary Loyalty", 121 *L.Q.R.* 453 (2005); J. Shepherd, "Towards a Unified Concept of Fiduciary Relationships" 97 *L.Q.R.* 50 (1981); R. Flannigan, "The Adulteration of Fiduciary Doctrine in Corporate Law" 122 *L.Q.R.* 459 (2006) and "Fiduciary Duties of Shareholders and Directors" (2004) *J. Bus. L.* 277.

[43]   *cf. Halton Int'l Inc. v Guernoy Ltd* [2006] 1 B.C.L.C. 78 on whether a shareholders' voting agreement give rise to fiduciary duties.

some financial interest, loans they obtain from the company, sales by them to or acquisitions by them from the company of valuable property, and dealings in their company's securities.

7–22 In recent years, some English judges have concluded that, in addition to the duty to act or not to act in a variety of ways, directors have an overriding duty to disclose their own misconduct to the company.[44] That a person has ceased being a director does not automatically liberate him from his duties to the company in this regard; there are circumstances where, following dismissal or resignation, he still has fiduciary obligations to it not to profit at its expense.[45] As is explained below, subject to certain requirements and limits, the company can exonerate directors for breach of many of these duties, either by way of an ordinary resolution or a provision to that effect in the articles of association.[46]

A Duty to Whom?

7–23 Ordinarily, fiduciary duties are owed to the company, not to any of its individual members.[47] In exceptional circumstances, where the transaction is vitally important to the company but its full implications have not been explained to a major shareholder, he may be entitled to insist on being given additional information about it.[48] Furthermore, where the directors–shareholders relationship is particularly close, directors may have a duty to disclose to them special information acquired by virtue of their position in the company.[49] As was explained in a case[50] involving demutualisation of a non-profit company and then the sale of its individual businesses:

> "fiduciary duties owed to the shareholders ... are dependent on establishing a special factual relationship between the directors and the shareholders in the particular case. Events may take place which may bring [them] into direct and close contact ... in a manner capable of generating fiduciary obligations, such as a duty of disclosure of material facts..., or of an obligation to use confidential information or valuable commercial or financial opportunities, which have been acquired by the directors in that office, for the benefit of the shareholders, and not to prefer or promote their own interests at the expense of the shareholders".[51]

7–24 In *Crindle Investments v Wymes*,[52] the Bula companies, which owned a large ore body near Navan, had brought proceedings against, *inter alia*, a neighbouring mine-owner, Tara, and banks that had appointed receivers over

---

[44] See generally, Ho and Lee "A Director's Duty to Confess: A Matter of Good Faith?" 66 *Cam.L.J.* 348 (2007).
[45] See generally, P. Koh, "Once a Director, Always a Fiduciary?" 62 *Cam. L.J.* 403 (2003).
[46] See para.7–136 *et seq.*
[47] *Crindle Investments v Wymes* [1998] 4 I.R. 567.
[48] *Re Clubman Shirts Ltd* [1983] I.L.R.M. 323 and *Securities Trust Ltd v Associated Properties Ltd* [1980] I.E.H.C. 128 unreported, McWilliam J., November 19, 1980.
[49] *Coleman v Myers* [1977] 2 N.Z.L.R. 225.
[50] *Peskin v Anderson* [2001] 1 B.C.L.C. 372.
[51] *ibid.* at 378.
[52] [1998] 4 I.R. 567.

those companies. Bula's majority shareholders/directors also brought personal claims against those defendants. Offers of settlement were made by the defendants, which were rejected both by Bula and its controllers personally. It was contended by the plaintiffs in *Crindle*, who held 40 per cent of the shares in Bula, that by refusing to cooperate with the company in seeking to settle those actions, Bula's controllers were in breach of a fiduciary duty to the plaintiffs. On account of the circumstances in which Bula was formed and managed for some time, they argued that the case fell into that narrow category where a direct fiduciary obligation to shareholders exists. Murphy J. was of the view that Bula's controllers' refusal to cooperate in reaching a composite settlement "amounts to folly in the extreme and a course which ... they will have every reason to regret".[53] Notwithstanding, he held that their fiduciary duties were owed only to the companies. According to the judge:

> "Whilst I recognise that the original enterprise and perhaps even the litigation following upon it, was something in the nature of a joint enterprise, that undertaking was conceived and consciously promoted in the form of a company incorporated under the Companies Act, 1963, and it was the requirements of that legislation which governed the relationship between the parties ... I accept that duties may be imposed or accepted by parties above and beyond those derived from particular offices or status [but] that the presumption must be that parties who elect to have their relationship governed by corporate structures rather than, say, a partnership, intend their duties—and where appropriate their rights and remedies—to be governed by the legal provisions relating to such structures and not otherwise. It would require ... reasonably clear evidence to impose obligations on directors or shareholders above and beyond those prescribed by legislation or identified by long established legal principles ... [T]he requisite evidence is not forthcoming in the present case ... and accordingly the claim under this heading must be dismissed."[54]

Self-Enrichment

7–25   On account of his overriding duty of good faith, a trustee must not profit from the trust except where his *cestui* or the trust instrument permits self-enrichment. Directors are subject to an identical equitable duty.[55] Additionally, certain forms of self-enrichment are criminal offences, *inter alia*, fraud and insider trading, and can be actionable conspiracies.[56] In some exceptional circumstances, where directors' self-enrichment was not at their company's expense, they may be permitted to retain their profit. But, generally, the company is entitled to recover from them any profit that they made by virtue of their position as directors. Additionally, the company may be entitled to trace property into the hands of third parties and, on the basis that they are "constructive trustees", it may be entitled to recover from them any profit they made in consequence of the director's breach of duty.

---

[53]   *ibid.* at 578.

[54]   *ibid.* at 576.

[55]   See generally, P. Finn, *Fiduciary Obligations* (Sydney: Law Book Co., 1977), Pt I.

[56]   e.g. *Adams v R.* [1995] 1 W.L.R. 572 and *Simtel Communications Ltd v Rebak* [2006] 2 B.C.L.C. 571.

Company "Property"

7–26 A director may not, without the shareholders' consent, take or use for his own benefit what belongs to the company. Such financial rewards as he derives from his office must be provided for in his agreed remuneration package, and he may not unilaterally appropriate any additional benefits for himself or his associates. In *Cockburn v Newbridge Sanitary Steam Laundry Co.,*[57] for instance, the managing director of a laundry company entered into a substantial contract in his own name to do work for one customer, the military authorities based in the Curragh. Under an arrangement he made with the other directors, the actual work was done by the company, but he would get £3,000 on the contract and £1,000 of that was paid over to the company. Most of the difference apparently was paid in bribes to get the work. It was held that he had to account to the company for that difference.

7–27 Similarly, where one of the sons of the late Robert Maxwell was party to a transfer of shares, held by a company of which he was a director, as trustee for its pensioners, to a company controlled by his father and for no consideration whatsoever, the son was held liable.[58] Where a director transferred substantial sums to his pension fund without that remuneration being duly authorised, it was held that the company could recover that sum from the fund's trustees.[59] Where one of the two directors of a company (the other being his wife) procured the transfer of a valuable shareholding it had to another company he owned, and did nothing in his capacity as director to block that transfer, he was held liable.[60] Where a majority shareholder and director of a company that had sold its business diverted half the consideration to a partnership he owned, he was held liable.[61] Where a director permitted a trade mark for a product the company produced to be registered in his own name, he too was held liable.[62] Where a director arranged to pay off a substantial inter-company debt, which was to be used to pay off an underwriting liability of its related company, which shortly afterwards became insolvent, the transaction was held to be unlawful because it was not concluded in the best interests of the company.[63] Where company funds were used to purchase a house in the name of its chairman's and majority shareholder's wife, it was held that those monies were recoverable from her.[64]

7–28 Where the "taking" is done bilaterally, by way of an agreement with the company that takes unfair advantage of it, there are special rules in the Companies Acts and in most companies' articles of association, requiring full

---

[57] [1915] 1 I.R. 429.
[58] *Bishopgate Investment Management Ltd v Maxwell (No. 2)* [1993] B.C.L.C. 1282.
[59] *Clark v Cutland* [2004] 1 W.L.R. 783.
[60] *Gardner v Parker* [2004] 2 B.C.L.C. 554.
[61] *Re MDA Investment Management Ltd* [2004] 1 B.C.L.C. 217.
[62] *Ball v Eden Project Ltd* [2002] 1 B.C.L.C. 313.
[63] *Extrasure Travel Insurance Ltd v Scattergood* [2003] 1 B.C.L.C. 598.
[64] *Bracken Partners Ltd v Gutteridge* [2004] 1 B.C.L.C. 377.

disclosure.[65] The premise for these provisions is that the requisite disclosure will prevent unfair transactions being authorised.

7–29   There is no exhaustive definition of what constitutes company property for these purposes. Does it extend to using the company yacht for an entire month or occupying the corporate box for a whole season, when those facilities could have been rented out for a substantial sum?[66] At times confidential information will be treated as property, the governing principle being that "a person who had obtained information in confidence is not allowed to use it as a springboard for activities detrimental to the person who made the confidential communication, and springboard it remains when all the features have been published or can be ascertained by actual inspection by any member of the public".[67] But not every single piece of information acquired by a director in the course of his duty must *ipso facto* be regarded as received in confidence and remaining confidential.

7–30   Company property that has been misappropriated by a director is subject to a trust for the company.[68] It can be made the subject of a tracing order, even where it goes into the possession of a party who did not owe any fiduciary duty to the company, other than a bona fide purchaser for value without notice.[69]

"Corporate Opportunities"

7–31   Corporate opportunity means the chance for a company to become involved in some business project that could yield it a sizeable profit.[70] These opportunities are not strictly company property because the company has no legal right to prevent them being taken up and exploited by outsiders, even shareholders. But fiduciaries may not intercept, for their own personal gain, opportunities through which the *cestui* stood to derive a substantial gain. A classic instance is *Cook v Deeks*,[71] which concerned a major construction company that had prospered from contracts it carried out for a railway enterprise. When a new railway construction contract was being negotiated, the defendants, who were some of the company's directors, succeeded in having the contract eventually awarded to themselves rather than to the company. They never gave the company an opportunity of obtaining the contract and they concealed from their co-directors all the circumstances regarding the negotiations; in

---

[65] See para.7–60 *et seq.*

[66] See for example, "O'Brien questions expenses Independent pays O'Reilly" *Irish Times,* June 9, 2007, p.1.

[67] *Cranleigh Precision Engineering Co. v Bryant* [1965] 1 W.L.R. 1293 at 1318.

[68] *Clark v Cutland* [2004] 1 W.L.R. 783.

[69] *Bracken Partners Ltd v Gutteridge* [2004] 1 B.C.L.C. 377.

[70] See generally, Kershaw, "Does it Matter How the Law Thinks About Corporate Opportunities?" 25 *Leg.Stud.* 533 (2005); Lowry & Edmunds, "The Corporate Opportunity Doctrine: The Shifting of the Duty and its Remedies" 61 *Mod. L.Rev.* 515 (1998), and Brudney & Clark, "A New Look at Corporate Opportunities" 94 *Harv. L. Rev.* 997 (1981).

[71] [1916] A.C. 554.

other words, "while entrusted with the conduct of the affairs of the company they deliberately designed to exclude, and used their influence and position to exclude, the company whose interest it was their first duty to protect".[72] The Privy Council had no hesitation in concluding that they violated their fiduciary duties, observing that persons "who assume the complete control of a company's business must remember that they are not at liberty to sacrifice the interests which they are bound to protect, and, while ostensibly acting for the company, divert in their own favour business which should properly belong to the company they represent".[73] Even if they were not the controlling shareholders, they would have been in breach of their fiduciary duties.[74]

7–32 What exactly comprises a corporate opportunity has not been comprehensively defined and, given the potentially wide range of circumstances in which the question can arise, the concept may defy precise definition. Difficulties arise where it cannot be said that the director was acting in bad faith; or where the board fully considered the opportunity and rejected it; or where, from lack of resources or other reasons, the company could never have availed of the opportunity. In some of these situations, moreover, the company may have been taken over in the meantime and it could be argued that the new owners obtain an unfair windfall when they act against ex-directors who, in good faith, availed of a corporate opportunity. An argument can be made that, in applying the principle here, some flexibility should be shown where close companies are involved and that overall fairness considerations should apply in determining whether a director should be deprived of an opportunity that his company did not take up. There are no reported Irish cases on the topic. The underlying principle is that where one makes a personal profit, either as a result of one's position as a director or in any situation where there is a conflict or a potential conflict of one's duty to the company and one's personal interests, the company is entitled to recover that profit. This it appears is the case regardless of whether the director acted in good faith or whether the company rejected the opportunity, or in fact could not have earned the profit.[75] In other words, there is a strict rule against directors profiting from their office.

7–33 In *Regal (Hastings) Ltd v Gulliver*,[76] to enhance a cinema company's asset value, with a view to selling the entire business, the board decided to take a lease on an additional cinema. As the company did not have sufficient funds to provide the lessor with security, the directors came to its assistance by putting some of their own funds into a subsidiary, which then would take the lease. Subsequently, the company and its subsidiary were taken over at a price which earned those directors substantial profits from their investment. But the company, then under new management, claimed that those ex-directors had contravened their

---

[72] *ibid.* at 562.
[73] *ibid.* at 563. A similar case is *Canadian Aero Services Ltd v O'Malley* 40 D.L.R. (3d) 371 (1974), noted in (1974) 37 Mod. L. Rev. 464.
[74] e.g. *Item Software (UK) Ltd v Fassihi* [2005] 2 B.C.L.C. 91.
[75] *Phipps v Boardman* [1967] 2 A.C. 46; *cf. Holder v Holder* [1968] Ch. 353.
[76] [1967] 2 A.C. 134.

fiduciary duties. A unanimous House of Lords held that they must account for those profits regardless of the fact that they "acted with *bona fides*, intending to act in the interests of the company".[77] The governing rule, it was held, is "the rule of equity which insists on those, who by use of a fiduciary position make a profit, being liable to account for that profit, in no way depends on fraud, or absence of *bona fides*; or upon such questions or considerations as whether the profit would or should otherwise have gone to the plaintiff, or whether [the profiteer] was under a duty to obtain the source of the profit for the plaintiff, or whether he took a risk or acted as he did for the benefit of the plaintiff, or whether the plaintiff has in fact been damaged or benefited by his action".[78]

7–34 Application of the principle in the very situation as arose in *Regal (Hastings)* has been modified for most companies today. Directors of companies which have adopted Table A are exempted to some extent from liability: they are permitted to acquire shares in or become directors of a company that their company promotes or is interested in, and they are not accountable for any remuneration or benefits they thereby receive.[79] However, the company reserves the option of directing them to account for those benefits. This regulation has not yet been interpreted by the courts.

7–35 The principle here was held to apply even where an executive director comes across the opportunity entirely in a private capacity. In *Industrial Development Consultants Ltd v Cooley*,[80] the defendant, who was managing director of an engineering firm, was approached privately and offered a lucrative engineering contract which, under no circumstances, would have been offered to his company. He then resigned his position on the pretext of being ill and took up the contract for himself. It was held that he ought to account for the profit he made on the grounds that he allowed himself to be placed in a situation where his legal obligations and his personal interests conflicted and, additionally, he:

> "had not been wholly honest with the company. He had one capacity and one capacity only in which he was carrying on business at that time. That capacity was as managing director of the plaintiffs. Information which came to him while he was the managing director and which was of concern to the plaintiffs to know, was information which it was his duty to pass on to [them... Furthermore,] he embarked on a deliberate policy and course of conduct which put his personal interest as a potential contracting party... in direct conflict with his pre-existing and continuing duty as a managing director of the plaintiffs".[81]

7–36 Similarly, in *CMS Dolphin Ltd v Simonet*,[82] the defendant and another formed an advertising agency; he was to manage it and the other was to arrange

---

[77] *ibid.* at 143.
[78] *ibid.* at 144.
[79] Article 78.
[80] [1972] 1 W.L.R. 443.
[81] *ibid.* at 451. Contrast *Island Export Finance Ltd v Umunna* [1986] B.C.L.C. 460 and *Fromlington Group Plc v Andersen* [1995] 1 B.C.L.C. 475.
[82] [2001] 2 B.C.L.C. 704.

for its financing. But it was always underfunded and tensions grew between them. One day, the defendant resigned as director and employee, with immediate effect, and set up a rival business. He offered work to all the company's employees, who left it to join him. All of the principal clients he had introduced to the company also defected to him. It was held that he was liable to the company for the profits he made from his business, which originally was a partnership and later was incorporated by him.

7–37   On several occasions since, it has been held to be irrelevant whether or not the company would have availed of the opportunity, if offered to it; or was not in a position to avail of it; or that the potential business partner would not have dealt with the company[83]; or that such profit as accrued from the opportunity was entirely the product of the director's skill and knowledge.[84] His duty is to communicate to the company the existence of every commercial opportunity capable of being exploited in conjunction with its business.[85] Additionally, where he becomes aware that someone is unlawfully endeavouring to exploit an opportunity of this nature, he is obliged to disclose the fact to the company so that it can resort to such measures as may be appropriate to protect its interests.[86]

7–38   On the other hand, a director may resign and thereafter use his general fund of skill and knowledge in competing with the company, even if that involves diverting a lucrative opportunity that the company otherwise might have exploited. Prior to resigning, he is not prohibited from taking preliminary steps to investigate what opportunities may be open to him when he leaves the company and thereafter commences competing with it.[87]

7–39   In two Commonwealth cases it was held that directors,[88] even managing directors,[89] of small companies have a defence where full disclosure about the project is made to the board, which is given the opportunity to take it up but does not do so because the company lacks the necessary resources. Superficially, these decisions conflict with *Regal (Hastings)*[90] but it may be significant that the *Regal* directors did not offer the company's 15 independent shareholders the chance of investing in what was virtually guaranteed to be a very profitable enterprise. In the circumstances there, a gain of almost 300 per cent was made from a three weeks' investment carrying practically no risk

---

[83] *Gencor ACP Ltd v Dalby* [2000] 2 B.C.L.C. 734; *Bhullar v Bhullar* [2003] 2 B.C.L.C. 241; and *Crown Dilmun v Sutton* [2004] 1 B.C.L.C. 468. See generally, S. Scott, "The Corporate Opportunity Doctrine and Impossibility Arguments" 66 *Mod. L.Rev.* 852 (2003).

[84] *Crown Dilmun v Sutton* [2004] 1 B.C.L.C. 468.

[85] *CMS Dolphin Ltd v Simonet* [2001] 2 B.C.L.C. 704.

[86] *Item Software (UK) Ltd v Fassihi* [2005] 2 B.C.L.C. 91 and *British Midland Tool Ltd v Midland Int'l Tooling Ltd* [2003] 2 B.C.L.C. 523.

[87] *Island Export Finance Ltd v Umunna* [1986] B.C.L.C. 460 and *Balston Ltd v Headline Fillers Ltd* [1990] F.S.R. 385.

[88] *Peso Silver Mines v Cropper* 55 D.L.R. (2d) 1 (1966).

[89] *Queensland Mines v Hudson* 52 A.L.J.L.R. 399 (1978).

[90] [1967] 2 A.C. 134.

whatsoever. Whether those directors really did act entirely bona fide is debatable. The case can be contrasted with a leading trusts case[91] where trustees profited from an investment they made in a trust asset, in circumstances where their bona fides could not seriously be questioned. They nevertheless were compelled to hand over the profit they made on the basis of well-settled equitable principles.

7–40   What remains to be determined in this country is whether the full rigour of those principles always applies to corporate opportunities or whether, exceptionally, the deserving director, who revealed everything to his fellow directors and did his best in the circumstances, will be permitted to retain his profit. While those fellow directors ordinarily would have no authority to exonerate him from his breach of duty, it may be that in a special case full disclosure to them and unquestionable bona fides may provide a complete defence to an action for breach of fiduciary duty, especially where those directors have substantial shareholdings in the company.

7–41   Where there has been a breach of fiduciary duty, the director or former director is obliged to account for such profit as he made from it or else must pay damages, at the company's election. Liability to account for profits exists whether he exploited the opportunity personally, or through a partnership or a company he controlled. In one instance a director was held liable in conspiracy, on account of the manner in which he diverted the company's business.[92] Third parties who knowingly involved themselves in the breach or reaped its rewards also are liable; for instance if they were knowing directors of a company that exploited the opportunity.[93] Where that opportunity is a particular asset, such as commercial property, that is acquired by a company controlled by the errant director, that company can be held to be a trustee of that asset and be directed to transfer it to the other company.[94] Where the company through which the opportunity was exploited is wholly owned and controlled by the defaulting director, and is no more than a shell used for that purpose, it may be held directly liable as his *alter ego*.[95] A company that does not take steps to obtain redress against a defaulting director may commit "oppression" under s.205 of the 1963 Act.[96]

Competing Against the Company

7–42   It would seem that it is not always prohibited for a trustee to have a share in a business which competes with one belonging to the trust.[97] In the absence of an express prohibition or some exceptional circumstances, employees in their spare time may work for an enterprise that competes with their

---

[91] *Phipps v Boardman* [1967] 2 A.C. 46.
[92] *Simtel Communications Ltd v Rebak* [2006] 2 B.C.L.C. 571.
[93] *Crown Dilmun v Sutton* [2004] 1 B.C.L.C. 468.
[94] *Bhullar v Bhullar* [2003] 2 B.C.L.C. 241.
[95] *Gencor ACP Ltd v Dalby* [2000] 2 B.C.L.C. 734.
[96] *Clark v Cutland* [2004] 1 W.L.R. 1783.
[97] *Moore v McGlynn* [1894] 1 I.R. 74.

employer's.[98] A partner, on the other hand, is not permitted to compete against the partnership without the consent of the other partners.[99] In 1891[100] an application made to restrain one of the plaintiff's directors from becoming a director of a rival concern was rejected on the grounds that, since the company's regulations did not prohibit him from doing so and it was not established that confidential information acquired in the plaintiff's service would be passed on to the rival, the director was at liberty to join the rival's board. This decision was cited with approval in *Bell v Lever Bros Ltd*,[101] where it was added that "[w]hat he could do for the rival company, he could of course, do for himself".[102] It, therefore, would appear that, in the absence of any contractual prohibition, or of a strong likelihood of confidential information being passed on, management of a rival enterprise is not incompatible with a directorship.

7–43 Having reviewed what the various textbooks had to say on the subject and the case law since then,[103] Sedley J. in *In Plus Group Ltd v Pyke*[104] observed that those decisions were somewhat out of line with the very rationale for the fiduciary obligation, and that being involved in running a competing business would not ordinarily be permitted today. There, however, the defendant had been seriously ill for a period; on recovering, the company ceased paying him any remuneration and refused to give him information about its financial position, and he then refused to accede to a request that he should resign his directorship. For entirely unrelated reasons, a major customer of the company ceased to do business with it. When the defendant set up a rival business, that customer gave it sub-contract work. It was held that, in these circumstances, he had not contravened his fiduciary duty. Generally, it is not a breach of duty, while a director, to decide to compete against the company and to take certain preliminary steps to that end, provided that use is not made of company property or personnel for that purpose.[105]

7–44 There are significant restrictions on the extent to which an executive director may work for a rival and whatever freedom to do so as exists under the general law most likely would be the subject of an express or implied prohibition in the service contract. Where to that end, an executive director indirectly purchased equipment that the company did not want and involved some of its employees in the preparations he was making, it was held that he was in breach of his contract.[106] Depending on the circumstances, at some stage in the

---

[98] *Hivac v Park Royal Scientific Instrument Ltd* [1946] 1 Ch. 169.
[99] Partnership Act 1890, s.30.
[100] *London & Masheland Exploration Co. v New Masheland Exploration Co.* [1891] W.N. 165.
[101] [1932] A.C. 161.
[102] *ibid.* at 195.
[103] See generally, Christie, "The Director's Fiduciary Duty Not to Compete" 55 *Mod. L. Rev.* 506 (1992).
[104] [2002] 2 B.C.L.C. 201.
[105] *Coleman Taymar Ltd v Oakes* [2001] 2 B.C.L.C. 749 and *Quarter Master UK Ltd v Pyke* [2005] 1 B.C.L.C. 245.
[106] *Coleman*, see above, fn.105.

course of taking preliminary steps, a director may be obliged to inform the company of his decision to resign when he is about to commence a rival business. It is difficult to generalise here and much depends on the facts of each individual case.[107]

Insider Trading

7–45 Insider trading connotes a person buying or selling something in a marketplace who, by virtue of his unique position or other special circumstances, possesses information concerning that asset's value which is unknown to others in the market. What is objectionable about this practice is that the person with inside knowledge has an overwhelming advantage over others in the market and it can be unfair for him to exploit that advantage at the expense of those others. Although it arises in other contexts too,[108] insider trading is most often associated with takeovers and mergers. Armed with special knowledge of an expected bid, which he obtained by virtue of his position, the bidder's or the target company's director may buy, or may purchase options on, the target's shares. Once the bid is announced publicly, the value of those shares should rise significantly and that director would then sell out at a handsome profit. Or alternatively, the target's shares may be at a relatively high price due to a takeover bid that is rumoured or that has been announced. But with inside knowledge that the bid will fail, a director may sell, or take options to sell, the target's shares. When the failure becomes known generally, the share price would fall, with the director making a sizeable profit. A common reaction to such practices is one of condemnation because it offends against market egalitarianism, it involves use by the insiders of something that is not really theirs, and it smacks of persons getting something for nothing.

7–46 Insider trading was first made an offence in 1990.[109] An EC Directive which outlaws the practice was implemented by Pt 4 (ss.29–37) of the 2005 Act.[110] This applies to dealings in the securities of quoted companies, affects not only directors of the company in question but many others who have valuable inside information, makes the practice an actionable wrong as well as an offence, and also attracts swingeing administrative penalties. Several key features of Pt 4's predecessor (Pt V of the 1990 Act) were considered in *Fyffes Plc v DCC Plc*.[111]

7–47 *Fiduciary Obligation*: It was held in *Fyffes* that where a director makes a profit for himself by dealing in a company's shares with the aid of material inside information, he breaches his fiduciary duty and is liable to account to the

---

[107] Compare *Shepherds Investments Ltd v Walters* [2007] 2 B.C.L.C. 202 with *Foster Bryant Surveying Ltd v Bryant* [2007] 2 B.C.L.C. 239, where the authorities are analysed comprehensively.

[108] e.g. *Securities & Exchange Comm. v Texas Gulf Sulphur Co.* (1968) 401 F2d. 833. See para.15–96 *et seq.*

[109] 1990 Act, Pt V (ss.107–121).

[110] See para.15–96 *et seq.*

[111] [2005] I.E.H.C. 477, unreported, Laffoy J., December 21, 2005 and [2007] I.E.S.C. 36, unreported, July 27, 2007.

company for his profit on the transaction. If, instead of using the information for his own benefit, it is used by another company of which he too is a director, it is liable to account to the company for the profit it made where it either knew or ought to have known about the breach. Those liabilities were not imposed by the trial judge who held that the director in question did not possess the requisite price-sensitive information; this conclusion was overturned on appeal.

7–48 Most instances of insider trading concern securities in quoted companies, where often the insider will seek to conceal his identity by using nominees to buy or sell the securities or options in them. Where the securities involved are not listed, there can be practical obstacles to enforcing the fiduciary obligation. Because the company itself will not suffer any direct loss by virtue of one of its directors taking unfair advantage of one of its shareholders, it may choose not to bring proceedings against the director.

7–49 Outside the 2005 Act's regime, redress for the aggrieved party who either sold securities to, or bought them from, an insider may be blocked by *Percival v Wright*.[112] It was held there that directors ordinarily have no fiduciary duties to their company's shareholders; put the other way, the rights that shareholders possess under the articles of association do not extend to rights against the directors arising from the latter's dealings in the company's shares. Shareholders of a private company, the shares of which could not be transferred without the board's consent, offered to sell their shares at a stated price. The directors agreed to buy them, although at the time negotiations were under way with the board to take over the company at a much higher price per share. On discovering this, the plaintiffs sought to have the sale set aside, contending that the defendants should not have made the purchase without disclosing that "special information". Their claim was rejected on three grounds. The general principle that directors' duties are owed only to the company does not admit of an exception in these circumstances, because "a shareholder is fixed with knowledge of all the directors' powers, and has no more reason to assume that they are not negotiating a sale of the undertaking than to assume that they are not exercising any other power".[113] Nor was there any question of unfair dealing here; the approaches were made by the plaintiffs and it was they who named the price.[114] Finally, a general obligation of disclosure prior to directors purchasing shares would be most impracticable, in that it would "place directors in a most invidious position, as they could not buy or sell shares without disclosing negotiations, a premature disclosure of which might well be against the best interests of the company".[115]

7–50 This decision has been criticised as an insider dealers' charter and has been said to have been wrongly decided.[116] But some central matters of fact

---

[112] [1902] Ch. 421.
[113] *ibid.* at 462. Similarly, *Chase Manhattan Equities Ltd v Goodman* [1991] B.C.L.C. 897.
[114] Contrast *Allen v Hyatt*, 30 T.L.R. 444 (1914).
[115] [1902] 2 Ch. 421 at 426.
[116] Goddard, Note in 116 *L.Q.R.* 197 (2000).

were conceded by the plaintiffs there. One was that the directors would not have been obliged to disclose a large casual profit that was made on the discovery of a new deposit of ore. Another was that there was no unfair dealing or any purchase at an undervalue. Thus, the case is far from being authority for the proposition that insider trading can never give rise to liability to the shareholders. A selling or purchasing shareholder would succeed where the insider furnished him with misleading information to induce him to enter into the transaction.[117] And in some special circumstances the relationship between director and shareholder can be so intense that the former is subject to fiduciary constraints vis-à-vis the shareholder.[118]

7–51   *Safeguards and Prohibitions:* There are certain reporting and recording requirements aimed, *inter alia*, at deterring and detecting insider trading. Whenever a director, shadow director or secretary, or person or body appropriately connected with him, acquires or disposes of any interest in the company's securities, he or it is obliged to notify the company, so that the transaction can be duly recorded.[119] Companies are required to keep a register of all securities in the company held by its directors and secretary, and their immediate families, including shares held in trust for them or in which they have a beneficial interest.[120] This information must be disclosed in the directors' annual report or in the notes to its annual accounts.[121]

7–52   Where the securities involved are traded on a stock exchange, it is only in the most exceptional circumstances that an insider buyer or seller of them would incur fiduciary liability to his vendor or purchaser. On account of the enormous profits that can be made from insider trading in quoted securities, the practice was banned by the Oireachtas. In *Fyffes Plc v DCC Plc*,[122] it was held that the sale of a substantial stake in the plaintiff company was based on inside information and, accordingly, civil liability arose under (since replaced) s.109 of the 1990 Act.[123] As these provisions apply to a far wider category of insiders than company directors, they are best considered below in the discussion of public companies.[124]

7–53   Even where it cannot be shown that they actually abused their position by trading with relevant inside knowledge, dealings by directors in options in their companies' quoted securities are prohibited.[125] This applies to directors and shadow directors, and it is an offence for them to deal in "put" or "call" options on their own company's shares, and shares in its subsidiary or holding

---

[117] e.g. *Allen*, see above, fn.114.

[118] *Coleman v Myers* [1977] 2 N.Z.L.R. 225.

[119] 1990 Act, Pt V (ss.53–58). See para.17–101 *et seq.*

[120] 1990 Act, ss.59–62.

[121] 1990 Act, s.63.

[122] [2005] I.E.H.C. 477, unreported, Laffoy J., December 21, 2005 and [2007] I.E.S.C. 36, unreported, July 27, 2007.

[123] Equivalent to s.33 of the 2005 Act.

[124] See para.15–96 *et seq.*

[125] 1990 Act, s.30.

company, or in another subsidiary of that company, or to deal in options in debentures. It extends to persons who buy options for or at the instigation of a director. But it does not apply to buying an option to subscribe for securities or buying convertible debentures, or an acquisition pursuant to a scheme that has been approved by the Revenue.

7–54 As well as prohibiting insider trading in quoted securities, by way of rendering it a crime and imposing civil liability and administrative sanctions, the 2005 Market Abuse Regulations provide for monitoring and reporting suspected instances of the practice, under the supervision of the Central Bank and Financial Services Authority of Ireland.[126]

Conflict of Interest

7–55 The strict equitable rule against self-enrichment is reinforced by one that invalidates all transactions between directors and their company where a conflict of interest exists, regardless of whether or not the director profited from the transaction.[127] This is necessary because there always is a great danger of directors abusing their positions to make a profit for themselves when, directly or indirectly, they have dealings with their company. For instance, they might sell their own property or goods to the company at an excessive price, or they might buy something from it at a knock-down price; or they might borrow substantial sums from the company without providing adequate security or paying market rate interest. Accordingly, contracts with a company in which any of its directors possess any financial interest are subject to a number of restrictions, which fall into three tiers. In equity, those contracts may be avoided by the company unless full disclosure of the essential details about them is made to the general meeting, which then ratifies them.[128] However, this is not always a very effective deterrent against unjust enrichment; the transaction may be concluded in its entirety before the fact of a conflict comes to light,[129] or the interested directors may be the majority shareholders or otherwise control the general meeting.[130] On the other hand, especially in large companies with numbers of outside directors, serious administrative difficulties could arise if every contract in which a director had some financial interest had to be voted on in general meeting. As one judge put it, the shareholders "may think in ... matters of this description it is better to have directors who may advance the interest of the company by their connection, and by the part which they themselves take in large money dealings, than to have persons who would have no share in such transactions as those in which the company is concerned".[131]

---

[126] See para.15–113 *et seq.*
[127] See generally, R. Kraakman et al., *The Anatomy of Corporate Law: A Comparative and Functional Approach* (Oxford: Oxford University Press, 2004), Ch.5 on related party transactions; and P. Finn, *Fiduciary Obligations* (Sydney: Law Book Co., 1977), Ch.21.
[128] *Aberdeen Railway Co. v Blaikie Bros.* (1854) 1 Macq. 461.
[129] e.g. *Prudential Assurance Co. v Newman Industries Ltd (No. 2)* [1982] Ch. 204.
[130] *ibid.*
[131] *Imperial Mercantile Credit Association v Coleman* (1871) L.R. 6 Ch. App 558 at 568.

7–56 Almost invariably, the equitable rule is set aside by the articles of association in favour of, usually, a requirement that disclosure of any interest must be made to the board, coupled with certain other safeguards. There is now a minimum degree of disclosure that cannot be waived by the articles; the director must "declare the nature of his interest" to the board.[132] The 1990 Act introduced rigid safeguards aimed at preventing companies from entering into several kinds of potentially disadvantageous contracts with their directors, members of their families and certain other close associates. Where the company has securities listed on the Irish Stock Exchange, what are called "related party transactions" must be notified to the Exchange authorities, explained in a circular sent to the shareholders and be approved by them in advance, with that related party and his associates not voting on the resolution.[133] This does not apply where the transaction is small or it does not have unusual features.

7–57 Occasionally the equitable obligation of fidelity applies where the beneficiary of a company's bounty is not a director but his business partner or some person closely connected with him, such as a family member, or a company he controls. For the purpose of several legislative restrictions on dealings between companies and their directors, there is a defined category of "connected persons" who are caught in the statutory net.[134] In the case of listed companies, an "associate" of a "related party" includes a company in which the director exercises or controls the exercise of at least 30 per cent of the votes cast on all or substantially all matters at general meetings.[135]

Equity

7–58 In equity all contracts between a company and any of its directors or with one of their partners can be avoided by the company, should it choose to do so. As explained in *Aberdeen Railway Co. v Blaikie Brothers*[136]:

> "The directors are a body to whom is delegated the duty of managing the general affairs of the company. A corporate body can only act by agents, and it is of course the duty of those agents so to act as best to promote the interests of the corporation whose affairs they are conducting. Such agents have duties to discharge of a fiduciary nature towards their principal. And it is a rule of universal application, that no one, having such duties to discharge, shall be allowed to enter into engagements in which he has, or can have, a personal interest conflicting, or which possibly may conflict, with the interests of those whom he is bound to protect. So strictly is this principle adhered to, that no question is allowed to be raised as to the fairness or unfairness of a contract so entered into. It obviously is, or may be, impossible to demonstrate how far in any particular case the terms of such a contract have been the best for the interest of the *cestui que* trust, which it was possible to obtain. It may sometimes happen that the terms on which

---

[132] 1963 Act, s.194.
[133] Listing Rules, Ch.8.
[134] 1990 Act, s.26 and see para.7–130 *et seq.*
[135] Listing Rules, Appendix 1.
[136] (1854) 1 Macq. 461.

a trustee has dealt or attempted to deal with the estate or interests of those for whom he is a trustee, have been as good as could have been obtained from any other person—they may even at the time have been better."[137]

7–59 This principle applies even if it is shown that the company obtained good value or indeed more than full value from the transaction; "[s]o inflexible is the rule that no inquiry on the subject is permitted".[138] Today, however, the articles of association of most companies modify this principle in one way or another, the commonest requirement being that the director's financial interest in the transaction with the company be disclosed to an independent board of directors.

Declaration and Abstention

7–60 In companies which have adopted Table A, these are matters regulated by arts 83–86; only some of those requirements apply to companies with Pt II of Table A, i.e. to the great majority of private companies. Common to both types of company is the stipulation that contracts with the company in which the directors are "in any way interested" are not invariably voidable nor constitute breaches of fiduciary duty.[139] Although *Aberdeen Railway Co.*, therefore, does not apply, full disclosure is required of the director's interest to the board. A director "who is in any way, whether directly or indirectly, interested in a contract or a proposed contract with the company shall declare the nature of his interest at a meeting of the directors in accordance with section 194 of the Act".[140] This article does not refer to "shadow directors" but they are brought within s.194.[141] However, even though shadow directors who do not make due disclosure may contravene s.194, it does not follow that they have contravened the article. Informal disclosure to all the shareholders may suffice here but it would have to be complete disclosure of all relevant details.[142] Where a decision other than to conclude a contract is being taken and a significant conflict exists, it is debatable whether the requirement here applies by analogy.[143]

7–61 The director must be in some way or another, "whether directly or indirectly, interested" in the contract. Almost always this interest will be a financial one; what other kinds of interest are caught could be debated. A director would be directly interested where he or his partnership were one of the parties. It depends on all the circumstances of the case whether the director has an indirect financial interest. To an extent the burden is on him to show that he did not have an interest, when the matter is challenged.[144] An interest most likely would be found where the contracting party was the director's spouse or

---

[137] *ibid.* at 471–472.
[138] *ibid.* at 472.
[139] Article 85.
[140] Article 83.
[141] 1990 Act, s.273.
[142] *Gwembe Valley Development Co. v Koshy (No. 3)* [2004] 1 B.C.L.C. 131.
[143] *Hunter v Senate Support Services Ltd* [2005] 1 B.C.L.C. 175.
[144] *Lee Panavision Ltd v Lee Lighting Ltd* [1991] B.C.L.C. 575.

a company in which he had a substantial shareholding. How far the net should be cast among his relations and other companies in which he has some involvement depends on the nature of the contract in question and the extent of his relationship with his family and those companies.[145] The 1990 Act defines a category of "connected persons" for the purpose of its requirements regarding contracts with the company[146] and guidance may be obtained from that definition in an appropriate case. Even where the director holds shares in the other contracting company in trust, he still has a financial interest for these purposes. In one instance, a director held 1,000 shares in trust under his father-in-law's will and his wife was beneficially interested in 100 of them, subject to her mother's life interest.[147] Since 1990, loans and equivalent arrangements with connected persons are brought within s.194 of the 1963 Act and, most likely, within these articles. There is some authority which suggests that merely being a director of the other contracting company is not a sufficient interest.

7–62   Once the requisite interest exists, it must be disclosed to the board at the first meeting which considers entering into the contract. If the director only becomes interested in the contract at a later date, that interest must be declared at the very next board meeting. While making some formal declaration may be envisaged, it has been said that there is sufficient disclosure where there is genuine informal consent by all the directors.[148] However, informal disclosure made piecemeal or the fact that individual directors were aware of the transaction does not suffice[149]; disclosure must be such as enables them to give due consideration to what is involved. Consequently, it must be full disclosure of all material facts.[150] Thus, where a company agreed to sell property to one of its directors for £8,400, on the basis of a valuation in that sum, but he did not disclose that this valuation made no allowance for development potential or for a planning application he had made, it was held that the company was entitled to set the transaction aside, subject to any equitable defences or to other appropriate relief.[151] Where it is a shadow director who is involved, he must give written notice before the meeting that first considers the contract takes place.[152]

7–63   A director can declare his interest in all contracts with a particular company simply by giving a general notice which states his membership of that company, which is to be regarded as being interested in all contracts with it.[153]

[145] *cf. Re Dominion International Group Plc (No. 2)* [1996] 1 B.C.L.C. 572 at 579.
[146] See para.7–130 *et seq.*
[147] *Transvaal Lands Co. v New Belgium (Transvaal) Land & Development Co.* [1914] 2 Ch. 488; *cf. Wilson v London, Midland & Scotish Rly* [1940] 1 Ch. 169 and *Costa Rica Rly v Forwood* [1900] 1 Ch. 746.
[148] *Re Dominion Int'l Group Plc (No. 2)* [1996] 1 B.C.L.C. 572 and *Runciman v Walter Runciman Plc* [1992] B.C.L.C. 1084.
[149] *Hunter v Senate Support Services Ltd* [2005] 1 B.C.L.C. 175.
[150] *Gwembe Valley Development Co. v Koshy (No. 3)* [2004] 1 B.C.L.C. 131.
[151] *J.J. Harrison (Properties) Ltd v Harrison* [2002] 1 B.C.L.C. 162.
[152] 1990 Act, s.27(3).
[153] 1963 Act, s.194(3).

There is no similar notice procedure for where he is merely a director of the other company, although all other directorships they hold are one of the matters which directors must disclose to the company and have entered in the register of directors. Against all of this, Table A implies that being an officer of the other contracting company always constitutes a financial interest in contracts with that company.[154] This notice must be given either at a board meeting or else read at the next meeting after it was given to the company. The requirements in Table A private companies and public companies diverge. Where Pt II applies, nothing further is required; it permits the director to "vote in respect of any contract, appointment or arrangement in which he is interested, and he shall be counted in the quorum present at the meeting". If the director does not declare his interest but he votes for the contract—or he remains silent and, having made the quorum, leaves the meeting when it comes up for consideration, the contract can be avoided by the company and in many cases the director can be obliged to account to the company for whatever profit he made on the contract.[155]

7–64 Outside of Part II, the director cannot be counted in the quorum of the meeting which considered the contract, nor is he allowed to vote on the contract.[156]

7–65 These restrictions can be relaxed or waived at any time by the company in general meeting, presumably by way of an ordinary resolution. Additionally, under Table A there are four types of arrangement which are not caught by these quorum and voting restrictions.[157] One is where the director's interest is by virtue of being an officer of the other company or holding shares or other securities in it.[158] The others are where the contract is for him to subscribe for or underwrite securities in the company, or an arrangement to give any security or indemnity to him for liabilities he undertook for the company, or an arrangement to give any security or indemnity to a third party for certain liabilities he undertook on the company's behalf.[159] In *Cox v Dublin Distillery Co. (No. 2)*[160] the directors decided to issue debentures to several of their number as security for advances they had made to the company. It was held that those directors could not have made up the quorum and, accordingly, their debentures were held to have been invalidly given and therefore were worthless. An arrangement like that would now be protected by Table A.

7–66 While Table A modifies the *Aberdeen Railway Co.*[161] principle, if these requirements are not scrupulously complied with, that relaxation is lifted and the general equitable rule applies.[162] A further foundation for liability could be

---

[154] Article 84(d).
[155] e.g. *Gwembe Valley Development Co. v Koshy (No. 3)* [2004] 1 B.C.L.C. 131.
[156] Article 84.
[157] Article 84(a)–(d).
[158] e.g. *Movitex Ltd v Bulfield* [1988] B.C.L.C. 104.
[159] e.g. *Re Olderfleet Shipbuilding & Engineering Co.* [1922] 1 I.R. 26.
[160] [1915] 1 I.R. 345.
[161] (1854) 1 Macq. 472.
[162] *Gwembe Valley Development Co. v Koshy (No. 3)* [2004] 1 B.C.L.C. 131.

breach of the articles themselves. Where a director does not comply with the above requirements, the company is entitled to avoid the contract and either obtain damages or can recover any profit he made on it.[163]

7–67   Declarations of interests should be recorded in the minutes of the directors' meeting, although the absence of any such record does not preclude other proof that a declaration was duly made.[164] Furthermore, the company is required to keep a book which records every declaration of interest made by a director.[165]

Substantial Acquisitions/Dispositions

7–68   General meeting approval is required for substantial acquisitions or disposals of assets from or to a director, or person connected with him.[166] A director for these purposes includes a shadow director. The value of the asset in question must exceed either €63,486.90 or 10 per cent of the company's net assets, i.e. its total assets less its total liabilities together with provisions for liabilities and charges. For these purposes, it has been held that where the property in question is subject to a charge, the relevant value is the company's equity of redemption;[167] in the case of a lease, the relevant value is its capital value and not the periodic value of the right of occupation under it. What constitutes an acquisition here is widely defined.

7–69   Before the company enters into any arrangement for acquiring or for disposing of an asset of that value (other than cash) from a director or connected person, the proposal must have been sanctioned by a resolution of the general meeting. If the person is a director of the holding company, the resolution must be passed by its members. For these purposes, it has been held that unanimous informal shareholder approval suffices.[168]

7–70   These requirements do not apply to where the person gets property from the company "in his capacity as a member", for instance a distribution *in specie* to members as provided for in the articles of association. Nor do they apply where the company is being wound up, other than in a members' voluntary liquidation, nor to certain inter-group acquisitions and disposals.

7–71   Any arrangement which is not so approved is voidable at the company's instance, and the party to it is liable to account to the company for any resulting gain he made and to indemnify the company for any resulting loss or damage it suffered.[169] Any director of the company who authorised that arrangement is similarly obliged to account to the company and to indemnify

---

[163] e.g. *Coleman Taymar Ltd v Oakes* [2001] 2 B.C.L.C. 749 and *Re MDA Investment Management Ltd* [2004] 1 B.C.L.C. 217.

[164] *Neptune (Washing Vehicle Equipment) Ltd v Fitzgerald* [1996] Ch. 274.

[165] 1963 Act, s.194(5).

[166] 1990 Act, s.29.

[167] *Ultraframe (UK) Ltd v Fielding* [2005] All E.R. (D) 397.

[168] *NBH Ltd v Hoare* [2006] 2 B.C.L.C. 649.

[169] 1990 Act, s.29(3) and (4).

it. But there is no liability under these heads where the person took all reasonable steps to secure compliance with the requirement or he did not know the circumstances which constituted the breach.[170] An arrangement as described above is no longer voidable where, within a reasonable period, it was sanctioned in general meeting.[171] Nor is it voidable where the company is indemnified, as provided for above, for any loss it suffered, or restitution is no longer possible, or the rights acquired by third party bona fide purchasers without notice would be affected by the avoidance.[172]

Loans and Similar Arrangements

7–72   Loans to directors, especially at below-market interest rates, can be a convenient method of indirect remuneration. At one time, company controllers could pay themselves what in effect were tax-free dividends by having their company advance them loans that were never called in.[173] However, this method of turning the separate legal personality of the company to the shareholders' fiscal advantage has for long been forestalled.[174] Often executive share option schemes are accompanied by generous loan arrangements. Loans to what are known as "participators" in close companies are treated as dividends for income tax purposes.[175] Whether any particular payment or series of payments to a director is a loan, or was remuneration or otherwise, depends on all the circumstances of the case.[176]

7–73   Apart from any requirements in a company's articles of association and specific statutory provisions, loans to directors are not *per se* unlawful. Except for prohibiting companies from financing the purchase of their own shares[177] and requiring that the aggregate amount of loans to directors be disclosed in the annual accounts,[178] before 1990 the Companies Acts said nothing about a company lending money to its own directors or obtaining security for their borrowings. As was emphasised in *Re Ciro Citterio Menswear Ltd,*[179] "a loan to a director is not of itself the sort of transaction that is inevitably a misapplication of the company moneys. There is nothing inherently wrong with such a transaction in the abstract. It may or may not be a misapplication on any particular set of facts, but it is not, as such, a breach by a director of his trusteeship of company assets".[180]

---

[170] 1990 Act, s.29(5).
[171] 1990 Act, s.29(3)(c).
[172] 1990 Act, s.29(3).
[173] *IRC v Sansom* [1921] 2 K.B. 492.
[174] Taxes Consolidation Act 1997, ss.438 and 439.
[175] See generally, M. Feeney, *The Taxation of Companies* (Haywards Heath: Tottel Publishing, 2006), p.1241 *et seq.*
[176] *Currencies Direct Ltd v Ellis* [2002] 2 B.C.L.C. 482.
[177] See para.8–117 *et seq.*
[178] See para.17–79.
[179] [2002] 1 W.L.R. 2217.
[180] *ibid.* at 2231.

7–74 However, where a substantial loan was made to a foreign company that the lender company's director and controlling shareholder owned, and the proceeds were then used to repay debts to him, leaving the borrower insolvent, it was held that he had acted in breach of fiduciary duty and was obliged to reimburse the company.[181]

7–75 *The Articles:* Depending on the company's objects and the nature of the transaction, a loan made to one of the directors or security provided for such a loan may be *ultra vires*.[182] There is no express authority in Table A to make loans to the company's directors or members of their families, nor to provide security for their borrowings. Directors who are not parties to such transactions but who are or, in the circumstances, ought to be aware of them and who do not take appropriate action, are liable for breach of duty. The *causes célèbres* are the *Jackson v Munster Bank* cases,[183] where the bank's regulations forbade it from making loans to its directors, even on their personal guarantees, unless there was adequate security. Rumours began to spread that many of its directors were heavily indebted to it, without there being any or sufficient security for their liabilities. Following complaints made by numerous shareholders, an investigation into the matter was conducted and some members' meetings were held. Eventually, but at very short notice, the directors called a special general meeting to consider resolutions, *inter alia*, to alter the articles of association in a way that would facilitate granting loans to themselves; they also sought proxies in support of those proposed resolutions. But voting on them was enjoined because the information circulated with the proxy forms was misleading; it was "neither fair nor candid" because it "did not call the attention of the shareholders to the real operation that would be effected by such a change".[184] The Vice-Chancellor observed of the proposed amendment, which sought to allow a unanimous board to lend to any of its members on their personal guarantee: "Can anyone say that this would be for the benefit of the company, or that it would be a bona fide exercise of their powers by the directors for the benefit of the shareholders?"[185] In the following year, one of the directors who had not borrowed from the bank was held responsible in negligence for not taking steps to protect the bank from the "fraudulent misconduct of its directors".[186]

7–76 Where a director is interested in any way in a loan made by the company, he is subject to the statutory and Table A (where applicable) disclosing and abstention obligations described above. Thus, where insufficient disclosure was made when authorising a loan to a company that the director controlled, the company was held entitled to recover massive profits he made from investing in that other company.[187] These obligations have now been superseded by a comprehensive statutory regime.

---

[181] *Knight v Frost* [1999] 1 B.C.L.C. 364.
[182] *Northern Bank Finance Corp. v Quinn* [1979] I.L.R.M. 221.
[183] (1884) 13 L.R. Ir. 118 and (1885) 15 L.R. Ir. 356.
[184] (1884) 13 L.R. Ir. 118 at 135 and 137.
[185] *ibid.* at 136.
[186] (1885) 15 L.R. Ir. 356 at 361.
[187] *Gwembe Valley Development Co. v Koshy (No. 3)* [2004] 1 B.C.L.C. 131.

7–77 *Mandatory Minima*: Subject to some exceptions, Pt III (ss.25–52) of the 1990 Act introduced extensive restrictions on companies making substantial loans to their directors, shadow directors and "connected persons", and hit at a wide category of transactions akin to loans, whereby those parties obtain substantial credit at ultimately their company's expense. Unlike many other restrictions in that Act, those here are not conditional on the transaction getting prior or subsequent shareholder approval; they are absolute, contravention being an offence as well as a civil wrong.

7–78   Except as otherwise provided, a company shall not:

> "(a) make a loan or a quasi loan to a director of the company or of its holding company or to a person connected with such a director;
> (b) enter into a credit transaction as creditor for such a director or a person so connected;
> (c) enter into a guarantee or provide any security in connection with a loan, quasi loan or credit transaction made by any other person for such a director or a person so connected."[188]

Indirect ways of achieving the same result as that set out here are also prohibited. Additionally, information, concerning all loans and comparable arrangements with directors and connected persons, must be disclosed in the annual accounts.[189] Licensed banks are exempted from this disclosure[190] but they must disclose the aggregate amounts outstanding[191] and also must maintain a separate register containing a copy of every relevant transaction.[192]

7–79   To prevent evasion of these requirements, guarantees, other securities and what are called "quasi-loans" and "credit transactions" are also restricted.[193] A quasi-loan envisages arrangements where some third party is to pay money to, or to reimburse expenditure incurred by, the director or connected person, on the basis that he will be reimbursed by the company. A credit transaction envisages hire purchase and comparable arrangements, like conditional sale, leases and licences in return for periodic payments and any other transfer of land, goods or services on the understanding that payment will be deferred. A transaction or arrangement is "made for" a person when, *inter alia*, a loan or quasi-loan is made to him, property or services are transferred to him under a credit transaction, or a guarantee or security is given in connection with a loan, quasi-loan or credit transaction made to or for him.[194]

7–80   As well as outlawing a loan or similar arrangement with a director or connected person, or the company giving security for such a transaction, the prohibition extends to the company agreeing to assume, by way of assignment,

---

[188] 1990 Act, s.31(3).
[189] 1990 Act, ss.41–45.
[190] 1990 Act, ss.41(6) and 43(4).
[191] 1990 Act, s.43(5) and (6).
[192] 1990 Act, s.44.
[193] 1990 Act, s.25.
[194] 1990 Act, s.25(b).

credit obligations incurred by some party in favour of the director or connected person.[195] This covers, for example, where X Ltd guarantees a loan and the company arranges to take over the liability on that guarantee. Also prohibited is an arrangement whereby a third party will receive a benefit from the company, or another company in the group, for entering into a transaction which would be prohibited if the company itself had entered into it.[196] For instance, X Ltd is given a contract to supply the company with goods and services on the understanding that X Ltd will guarantee a loan to one of those persons.

7–81   To fall within the prohibitions here, the aggregate of loans or comparable transactions with all of those persons must exceed 10 per cent of the company's net assets.[197] In other words, the company must not have lent money or become party to other credit-type transactions which in sum exceed 10 per cent of net assets. For this calculation, the relevant accounts are those of the previous financial year.[198] If no accounts for that year were prepared or laid, then the maximum is 10 per cent of the company's called-up share capital. A formula is laid down for measuring the value of every loan and the like[199] but if, for some reason, a fixed value could not be put on any transaction, it is deemed to exceed €63,486.90.[200]

7–82   Circumstances can arise where the total loans, etc. to those persons did not exceed that figure but, because of a fall in value of the company's assets or high losses or some other reason, the 10 per cent is then exceeded. Where a fall in asset value occurs with that result and they learn or should have become aware of it, the company, the directors and the persons for whose benefit the credit arrangements were made are given two months to bring these loans, etc. within the 10 per cent ceiling.[201]

7–83   *Exceptions*: Some transactions are not caught by the above provisions. One is vouched expenses properly incurred in the course of the directors' duties, provided that any liability falling on the director is discharged within six months.[202]

7–84   Another is a transaction the company entered into in the ordinary course of its business and in respect of which the director was not treated any better than someone else of comparable standing.[203] This would cover, for example, a house purchase loan made to a bank's director on the usual commercial terms, or a hire purchase company selling a car to a director on the usual terms available to persons of his standing. It is unlikely that loans or

---

[195] 1990 Act, s.31(2).
[196] 1990 Act, s.31(3).
[197] 1990 Act, s.32.
[198] 1990 Act, s.29(2).
[199] 1990 Act, s.25(4).
[200] 1990 Act, s.25(5).
[201] 1990 Act, s.33.
[202] 1990 Act, s.36.
[203] 1990 Act, s.37.

comparable arrangements made in connection with share option schemes would be regarded as within the ordinary course of the company's business. Neither will a transaction be found to be in the ordinary course of business if the company has ceased trading.[204]

7–85   Yet another is a lease of land with a nominal annual rent of no more than €12.70, provided it is paid for in a manner that represents its open market value.[205] Certain transactions with the company's holding company and also within that group of companies are also exempted.[206]

7–86   There is a procedure which allows companies to guarantee or provide security for otherwise prohibited transactions, that does not prejudice solvency but could be challenged by dissenting shareholders.[207] For these purposes, there has to be a statutory declaration made by several of the directors containing various details of the proposed transaction and stating that the company will still be able to pay its debts in full. There also has to be a report by an independent person, who would be qualified to act as the company's auditor, that the directors' opinion about solvency is reasonable. Notice of a special resolution approving the transaction must be sent to the members, along with a copy of the directors' declaration. Unless all the members vote for this resolution, it cannot take effect until 30 days expire, during which time at least 10 per cent of the objecting shareholders may apply to court to have that resolution cancelled. Any guarantee or security authorised by the resolution must be given within 12 months of its being passed. Where it is proposed to enter into any of those permissible transactions, the director involved must notify his co-directors in advance, as described above.[208]

7–87   *Sanction:* A loan made in breach of these provisions is voidable at the instance of the company and, therefore, recoverable by it irrespective of the terms.[209] However, in the absence of special circumstances, obtaining the loan is not a breach of fiduciary duty and, consequently, the borrower is not invariably a constructive trustee of the money or property for the company.[210] It is not an offence on the part of the company itself to make a prohibited loan, but every company "officer" who authorised or permitted it to make a loan, and any other person who procures the company to make it, commits an offence.[211] If the company is wound up and insolvent, and one or more prohibited loans contributed materially to its insolvency, the borrower or person who benefited from the transaction can be declared personally liable for all or part of the company's debts.[212] Those persons can be made to account to the company for any

---

[204] *Re Ashmark Ltd (No. 2)* [1990] I.L.R.M. 455.
[205] 1990 Act, s.25(3A).
[206] 1990 Act, s.35.
[207] 1990 Act, s.34.
[208] 1990 Act, s.47.
[209] 1990 Act, s.38(1).
[210] *Ciro Citterio Menswear Plc v Thakrar* [2002] 1 W.L.R. 2217.
[211] 1990 Act, s.40.
[212] 1990 Act, s.39.

gain that resulted from the loan or transaction; they and any director who "authorised" it, or who failed to prevent an unauthorised loan,[213] can be made to indemnify the company for any loss or damage resulting therefrom.[214] Furthermore, to the extent that the company has obligations under any credit-related transaction, it can choose to avoid them.[215] However, that option is not open to the company where it is no longer possible to return the money or property in question, or the company has been indemnified for any loss it suffered, or the rights of any third party bona fide purchaser for value without notice would be prejudiced.[216]

Executive Directors

7–88 While executive and non-executive directors are subject to the same broad fiduciary duty to avoid conflicts, it may be somewhat more exacting of well-paid executives than of non-executives who are in receipt of a modest fee and have other business interests outside of the company. It was held in *Item Softwear (UK) Ltd v Fassihi*[217] that the duties of executive directors to their company are more exacting than those of employees, for directors are obliged always to act in good faith, in the best interests of their company. That employees generally are not obliged to disclose to their employer their own misconduct (unless required to do so under the express or implied terms of their contracts) does not exonerate an executive director from the fiduciary duty, which may involve disclosing his own wrongdoing. A managing director secretly approached a rival company, with a view to it taking on a contract that the company might have obtained. His defence to the plaintiff's claim was that he had been summarily dismissed and that, generally, it is a breach of contract to dismiss an employee for not disclosing his own wrongdoing. That was rejected, on the grounds that the fiduciary duty supersedes any implied contractual obligation.

Remedies

7–89 When considering what non-statutory remedies are available to a company, against breach of fiduciary duty, several distinctions arise. One is whether the remedy is proprietary or personal; the former entitles the company to recover property, of which it has been divested, the latter is a money claim against the wrongdoer. In the case of proprietary claims, the question arises of the extent to which the company may pursue particular properties into the hands of third parties—either of companies that the errant director controls or others with whom he is closely connected. There are two principal legal bases for liability here. One is the principles at common law and in equity that permit a party to "trace property" that falls into another's hands.[218] The other is the

---

[213] *Neville v Krikorian* [2007] 1 B.C.L.C. 1 and *Queensway Systems Ltd v Walker* [2007] 2 B.C.L.C. 577.

[214] 1990 Act, s.38(2).

[215] 1990 Act, s.38(1).

[216] *Ruby Property Co. Ltd v Kilty* [1999] I.E.H.C. 50, unreported, McCracken J., December 1, 1999.

[217] [2005] 2 B.C.L.C. 91.

[218] H. Delany, *Equity & the Law of Trusts,* 4th edn (Dublin: Thomson Round Hall, 2007), Ch.18.

principles governing the imposition of a "constructive trust" on a party, who assisted in the director's breach or who, with the requisite *scienter*, received the property subject to the trust in favour of the company.[219] In several respects the law here is far from crystal clear and some recent Irish decisions in this general area have attracted academic criticism.[220] Indeed, across the common law world, there is a significant lack of consistency in the approach to the constructive trust, due partly to the evolving legal regime for restitution.

7–90   In the case of personal claims, usually the director is liable not only for any loss that his wrongdoing caused the company but also he may be required to pay it any profit he made from the impugned transaction. The latter is fault-based, requiring dishonesty, and is personal and not proprietary; whether it is only compensatory and not restitutionary is debatable.

Abuse of Power: Interests of the Company and Proper Purpose

7–91   Whether the general obligation on directors to exercise their powers only for the purposes for which those powers were given and not to abuse their powers is strictly a fiduciary obligation is debatable. Being entrusted with power to act on behalf of others for certain purposes logically implies that those powers must not be exceeded. Modern judicial rhetoric categorises the overriding obligation that directors stay within their mandate and not abuse their powers as fiduciary.[221] In *Re Smith & Fawcett Ltd*,[222] this was formulated as follows: they must exercise their discretion "*bona fide* in what they consider ... is in the interests of the company, and not for any collateral purpose".[223] Since a company in fact is the generality of its members, what this really means is that directors must act for the advantage of the members as a whole and not serve their own selfish interests or other external interests, or the interests of a discrete section of the membership. Moreover, any powers that are conferred by a company's own regulations for a particular purpose must not be used for wholly extraneous reasons.

7–92   While it is easy to generalise and to apply the bona fide principal in the most egregious of cases, one runs into difficulty in trying to pin down more precisely what is envisaged by the interests of the company's membership as a whole. When dealing with publicly owned companies it may be possible to speculate on what is to the advantage of the average shareholder. But what approach can be taken to the closely held company where the membership is split into two distinct factions,[224] or into two or more distinct classes of shareholder?[225] At times, courts can avoid answering questions like these by reverting to a principle

---

[219] *ibid.* at 234 *et seq* and *Fyffes Plc v DCC Plc* [2005] I.E.H.C. 477, unreported, Laffoy J., December 21, 2005.
[220] H. Delany, *Equity & the Law of Trusts*, 4th edn (Dublin: Thomson Round Hall, 2007), p.257 *et seq.*
[221] See generally, P. Finn, *Fiduciary Obligations* (Sydney: Law Book Co., 1971), Pt I.
[222] [1942] Ch. 304.
[223] *ibid.* at 306.
[224] e.g. *Clemens v Clemens Bros Ltd* [1976] 2 All E.R. 268.
[225] e.g. *Mills v Mills* (1938) 60 C.L.R. 150.

somewhat similar to the business judgment standard in the law on directors' negligence. Where the power in question concerns a "matter of management", considerable deference will be paid to the directors' own judgment or assessment.

7–93 It is only where the directors are pursuing their very own interests, or are unashamedly pursuing some external interest, or are discriminating blatantly between groups of shareholders, or are acting in a wholly capricious manner, that the courts tend to intervene. The approach, as formulated by Lord Wilberforce, in *Howard Smith Ltd v Ampol Petroleum Ltd*,[226] is:

> "to start with a consideration of the power whose exercise is in question ... Having ascertained, on a fair view, the nature of this power, and having defined as can best be done in the light of modern conditions the, or some, limits within which it may be exercised, it is then necessary for the court, if a particular exercise of it is challenged, to examine the substantial purpose for which it was exercised, and to reach a conclusion whether that purpose was proper or not. In doing so it will necessarily give credit to the bona fide opinion of the directors, if such is found to exist, and will respect their judgment as to matters of management; having done this, the ultimate conclusion has to be as to the side of a fairly broad line on which the case falls."[227]

7–94 More recently, in *Peoples Dept Stores v Wise*,[228] the Supreme Court of Canada said that "the best interests of the corporation" is not confined to the interests of the shareholders as a collectivity or any one stakeholder's interests. Rather:

> "if they [the directors] observe a decent respect for other interests lying beyond those of the company's shareholders in the strict sense, that will not ... leave directors open to the charge that they have failed in their fiduciary duty to the company ...We accept as an accurate statement of law that in determining whether they are acting with a view to the best interests of the corporation of law that in determining whether they are acting with a view to the best interests of the corporation it may be legitimate, given all the circumstances of a given case, for the board of directors to consider, *inter alia*, the interests of the shareholders, employees, suppliers, creditors, consumers, governments and the environment ... At all times, directors and officers owe their fiduciary duties to the corporation. The interests of the corporation are not to be confused with the interests of the creditors or those of any other stakeholders."[229]

7–95 In 2006 in Britain, the obligation here was given statutory formulation for the first time:

> "A director of a company must act in a way that he considers, in good faith, would be likely to promote the success of a company for the benefit of its members as a whole, and in doing so have regard (amongst other matters) to –

---

[226] [1974] A.C. 821.
[227] *ibid.* at 835.
[228] 244 D.L.R. (4th) 564 (2004).
[229] *ibid.* at 580–582.

    (a) the likely consequences of any decision in the long term

    (b) the interests of the company's employees

    (c) the need to foster the company's business relationship with suppliers, customers and others

    (d) the impact of the company's operations on the community and the environment

    (e) the desirability of the company maintaining a reputation for high standards of business conduct, and

    (f) the need to act fairly between the members of the company."[230]

7–96 Exercise of certain powers tends to be more strictly policed than that of others; for instance, the power to issue additional shares is scrutinised far more carefully than the power which is often found in the regulations of private companies to veto share transfers. Different parts of this book deal with abuses of particular powers, such as those just mentioned, those regarding directors' remuneration, and the dividends-reserves option. Additionally, as was explained above, where directors in any way profit from their position or act in circumstances where their own interests and that of the company may significantly conflict, they automatically exceed their powers unless they were authorised by the company's own regulations or by the members to do so.

Furthering Own Interests

7–97 A fiduciary who uses his powers simply to further his own personal interests almost always contravenes his duties. A problem that arises frequently is proving that the powers in question were exercised in the interests of a director or of the directors in question in circumstances where he or they did not obtain any personal profit. Often their own personal interests and those of the company will coincide. If evidence can be adduced of self-serving motives, that should resolve the matter. But proof of that nature is often difficult to find; there are very few self-dealing directors who leave behind them a trail of incriminating documents.

7–98 As the cases on vetoing share transfers demonstrate, it is not enough to make allegations against the director and then not challenge his explanations for his conduct. For instance, in *Re Smith & Fawcett Ltd*,[231] where a director was accused of refusing to register a share transfer because he wanted those shares for himself, the plaintiff did not apply to cross-examine him on his affidavit. For that reason, the court declined to find that the defendant's inaction was for the wrong motives. However, if sufficient circumstantial evidence is assembled which strongly suggests self-dealing,[232] especially in connection with such vital matters as influencing control, the court will readily find wrong motives unless the directors can give a satisfactory explanation.

---

[230] Companies Act 2006, s.172(1). See generally, A. Keay, "Section 172(1) of the Companies Act 2006: An Interpretation and Assessment" 28 *Co. Law* 106 (2007).

[231] [1942] Ch. 304.

[232] e.g. *Re Hafner* [1943] I.R. 426.

Furthering Interests of Third Parties

7–99 The classic view of the company has been that of a closed community devoted to financial gain for its shareholders, and of the directors' role as essentially to manage the business so that it will earn profits for them. Absent express authority in the company's own regulations and distinct statutory duties, like those in the Companies Acts designed to protect creditors, directors must not exercise their powers principally to benefit persons other than the shareholders. They may not bestow lavish gifts on others, except where that largesse is designed to bring a substantial benefit to the company. Nor may directors bind themselves to otherwise advance the interests of third parties over those of the company as a whole, although the exact boundaries of this principle remain to be fixed.

7–100 Where the company is in financial difficulties, its directors are required to give due consideration to its creditors' interests.[233] Exactly when this duty first arises and the full extent of the obligation arising under it remain to be determined.

7–101 Formerly, it was a breach of directors' duty for them to use their powers in the exclusive interests of the company's employees, where the company would not receive any reciprocal advantage. For instance in *Parke v Daily News Ltd*,[234] which was an extreme case, the board of a newspaper company that had sold off its entire undertaking proposed to distribute the bulk of the proceeds of sale among its employees in the form of gratuitous compensation for being made redundant. That generosity was held to be beyond the directors' powers.[235] Nevertheless, boards of companies that envisage continuing in business are entitled to be benevolent on a relatively small scale, provided the company stands to benefit to some extent. It would appear that directors of one company in a "group" may take some account of the group's overall interests.[236]

7–102 Employees' interests are now a matter of legitimate concern for the directors. Among the matters they should "have regard [to] in the performance of their functions shall include the interests of the company's employees in general, as well as the interest of its members".[237] Therefore, what happened in the *Daily News* case might no longer be a breach of the directors' duties, although a minority shareholder in those very circumstances might still succeed in having a payment of that nature blocked on the grounds of "fraud on a minority" or "oppression" under s.205 of the 1963 Act. Although directors are now required to take account of the interests of the employees, that duty is

---

[233] See para.20–11.
[234] [1962] Ch. 927.
[235] Similarly, *Re Lee Behrens & Co.* [1932] 2 Ch. 46.
[236] See generally, Lee Pey Woan, "Servicing Two Masters—The Dual Loyalties of the Nominee Director in Corporate Groups" (2003) *J. Bus. L.* 449.
[237] 1990 Act, s.52(1).

owed only to the company and cannot be enforced by any or all of those employees.[238]

Mixed Motives

7–103   It sometimes happens that directors act both for genuinely proper as well as for improper purposes. For instance, the company may badly need additional capital but the minority shareholders are impecunious and, for the time being, cannot pay for additional shares they are offered, a fact that the majority well know and take advantage of. Or the inevitable, and for the directors happy, consequence of an allotment of shares may be to defeat a takeover bid that was poised to succeed. Reported cases on these questions should be treated with caution because the outcome in many of them turned on inferences the judges drew from evidence on affidavit, and appellate courts must accept the trial judge's findings of fact which are not patently erroneous. Most cases say that the best approach is to ascertain what the directors' principal or dominant purpose was. Yet this does not resolve the cases where the various purposes are somewhat evenly balanced.

7–104   There is authority to the effect that the judge should then fall back on the overriding criterion of what, in good faith, the directors consider to be the best interests of the company. If this approach were to be followed, it would leave the matter to be determined on the merits on a case-by-case basis. Some commentators urge that, while this may be acceptable as regards business decisions that do not fundamentally alter the power structure within companies, it is too lenient in the context of, for instance, allotting additional shares. The argument is made that, given the effect a share allotment can have on relative voting strengths within a company, an improper motive, whether primary or secondary, should render invalid an exercise of that power. In the *Lancegaye Glass* case,[239] Dixon J. appears to have endorsed this analysis. According to him "having the two-fold object ... is it of any avail to the defendant directors that they may have had the object, other things being equal, of benefiting the company ... Even if (this latter object) contributed to their decision ... that would not suffice to validate the resolutions if the motives were partly improper".[240]

Fettering Discretion

7–105   Fiduciaries must not unduly fetter their discretion, i.e. tie themselves down as to how in the future they will exercise their discretionary powers.[241] Without the company's consent, directors may not enter into agreements with outsiders or with a section of the members under which they undertake to vote in a particular way at board meetings. In *Clark v Workman*,[242] during negotiations in which an English-based syndicate sought to buy control of a Belfast

---

[238] 1990 Act, s.52(2).
[239] *Nash v Lancegaye Safety Glass (Ireland) Ltd* 92 I.L.T.R. 11 (1958).
[240] *ibid.* at 22.
[241] See generally, P. Finn, *Fiduciary Obligations* (Sydney: Law Book Co., 1977), Ch.7.
[242] [1920] 1 I.R. 107.

shipbuilding company that was owned by two families, the chairman of the board promised the syndicate that he would use his best endeavours to ensure that their bid would succeed. To that end, he exercised his casting vote to facilitate transfers of shares to them. It was held that his vote was invalid because "he had fettered himself by a promise ... and [thereby] had disqualified himself from acting *bona fide* in the interests of the company ..."[243] In one case[244] the analogy was drawn between a company director and a Member of Parliament, who equally would be acting unlawfully if, for payment from some outside body, he agreed to vote in a particular way.

7–106 Difficulties arise in determining what kinds of understandings between directors and others amount to fetters and in what circumstances they can be justifiable. Take, for example, the nominee director, i.e. one who is nominated by a large shareholder to represent his interests in the company. It has been said that there is nothing wrong with this "so long as the director is left free to exercise his best judgment in the interests of the company which he serves. But if he is put upon terms that he is bound to act in the affairs of the company in accordance with the directions of his patron, it is beyond doubt unlawful".[245] Somewhat general understandings existing between directors and outsiders should not automatically be assumed to constitute proscribed fetters; any such contract is to be construed "in the light of the presumption that the parties to it contemplate and intend performance in a lawful manner only".[246]

7–107 A distinction has been drawn between three types of voting agreements: those between directors and others, which are forbidden; those with or between the shareholders themselves, which are permissible; and agreements made in good faith between the company and some outside interest that envisages the directors exercising their powers in a specified manner. In one Australian case,[247] for example, in order to finance a project, a small property company agreed to allot shares to another company for cash and undertook, *inter alia*, to reorganise its capital structure, to pay dividends in a specified manner and to execute certain contracts and the like. Defending a claim for damages for wrongfully repudiating this agreement, it was contended that it was voidable as an undue fetter on the directors' discretion. This was rejected because, assuming the directors initially decided that it was in the company's interest to enter into the contract, it therefore could not be said that they had improperly fettered the exercise of their future discretion.

---

[243] *ibid.* at 117–118.
[244] *Boulting v Association of Cinematographic, Television & Allied Technicians* [1963] 2 Q.B. 606 at 627.
[245] *ibid.* at 627–628.
[246] *ibid.* at 649.
[247] *Thorby v Goldberg* 112 C.L.R. 597 (1965).

7–108 In *Fulham FC v Cabra Estates Plc*,[248] the company held a lease of land from a subsidiary of the defendant. As part of a very large transaction, where the company got £11 million, its directors gave the defendant a letter of undertaking that they "individually but not jointly" would use their powers as directors and members to support any planning application the defendant may make in respect of the leased property. When later they were called on to give that support but had a "change of heart", claiming that there had been a radical change of circumstances, it was held that their undertaking was not an unlawful fetter and they were obliged to give that support. Where at the time all of the directors concerned are also members of the company or where the "fetter" in question has been assented to by all of its members, it is legally effective and enforceable. It was left open what the position would be if their undertaking was solely in their capacity as directors.

7–109 On the other hand, in *Lee Panavision Ltd v Lee Lighting Ltd*,[249] as part of a share option agreement, the company concluded a management agreement with the plaintiff, whereby the latter would run its business. When it became clear that the option would not be exercised, the company's controlling shareholders indicated an intention to serve notice to terminate the management agreement. But its directors then resolved to grant the plaintiff a new agreement. Because the effect of this was to prevent their majority in the company from determining how its affairs should be managed, it was held that the resolution was invalid.

Influencing Control

7–110 Depending on the circumstances, actions by directors that significantly affect overall control of their company can be a breach of their fiduciary duties.[250] Their power to affect control by allotting unissued shares has been the subject of considerable litigation. Frequently, it is alleged that their objective was not to raise additional capital but was for some improper purpose, such as to alter a delicate balance of voting power in the company or to ward off a takeover bid which, if successful, could lead to them being replaced. Most articles of association give the board the exclusive power and a wide discretion over allotting further shares. Under Table A, for instance, "the shares shall be at the disposal of the directors, and they may ... dispose of them to such persons, on such terms and conditions and at such times as they may consider to be in the best interests of the company and its shareholders".[251] Before there was statutory intervention on this question, it was held that existing shareholders are not always entitled to be given the opportunity to subscribe for additional shares in the company before they are offered to others. Except as is otherwise provided for in legislation[252] or in the company's own regulations,

---

[248] [1994] 1 B.C.L.C. 363.
[249] [1992] B.C.L.C. 22.
[250] *cf. Pilmer v Duke Group Ltd* [2001] 2 B.C.L.C. 773 (High Court of Australia).
[251] Article 5.
[252] e.g. 1983 Act, ss.20–23.

no shareholder had any right "to expect that his fractional interest in the company will remain for ever constant".[253]

7–111 One kind of case may be described as the corporate *coup d'état,* where the directors, who own or control a minority of shares, allot additional shares to themselves or their associates to secure overall control of the company. The classic instance is *Piercy v S. Mills & Co.,*[254] where a proposed share allotment was enjoined because its "purpose [was] converting a minority into a majority, and… defeating the wishes of the existing majority …"[255] A similar instance is *Nash v Lancegaye Safety Glass (Ireland) Ltd,*[256] where the personal defendant and his supporters held about 49 per cent of the voting shares and dominated the board, whereas the plaintiff and the proxies he had obtained controlled about 51 per cent. Major differences about policy arose between them, which led to the plaintiff requisitioning an EGM at which he would propose to increase the size of the board and to appoint new directors. In the meantime, the board decided to issue £16,000 of unissued voting shares, £5,000 of which were to be allotted to the defendant and the remaining to be allotted to the existing members on a *pro rata* basis. Two reasons were given for allotting the £5,000 shares to the defendant: much of the company's commercial success was a result of his endeavours and the board wished to reward him for past services or to meet some supposed claim on moral grounds for compensation. It also was said that new capital was needed. But Dixon J. found that, while" [t]here can be a legitimate difference of opinion as to whether fresh capital was necessary", it was "hard, however, to see how the [share] issue could reasonably be regarded as an urgent necessity"; he considered that "the suggestion of urgency [was] wholly unconvincing and quite inadequate to explain the somewhat indecent haste with which the matter was put through".[257] Therefore, that decision to issue additional shares was not made "in good faith in what [was] believed to be in the interests of the company", but was "primarily inspired by the dual desire to confer a privilege or benefit on [the defendant] and to increase the voting strength of [his] interests".[258] This was sufficient to warrant a declaration of invalidity.

7–112 A number of the leading cases concern takeover bids, where additional shares in the "target" company were allotted either to ward off a bid or to favour one bidder over another. For instance, in *Hogg v Cramphorn Ltd,*[259] the board decided to resist a bid in the firm belief, which was not contested, that leaving themselves, the existing board, to manage the company's affairs would be more advantageous to the shareholders, the company's staff and its customers. To this end, a trust for the employees was established, which was under the directors' control, and the company lent it money to enable it to

---

[253] *Mutual Life Insurance Co. v The Rank Organisation Ltd* [1985] B.C.L.C. 11 at 24.
[254] [1920] 1 Ch. 77.
[255] *ibid.* at 85.
[256] 92 I.L.T.R. 11 (1958).
[257] *ibid.* at 22.
[258] *ibid.* at 23.
[259] [1967] Ch. 254.

purchase a block of shares that the company would allot to it. With their own shares and those of their supporters, and being in a position to determine how the employees' trust shares would be voted, the directors could then defeat the bid. It was held that the allotment and the loan in the circumstances were made for an improper motive, *viz.* "the primary object ... was to deprive those members who were not recognised supporters of the board of their position as a majority in the company".[260] In *Howard Smith Ltd v Ampol Petroleum Ltd,*[261] a company that was short of funds was the subject of a takeover bid from its principal shareholder. To prevent that bid from succeeding and, as well, to raise further capital, new shares were issued to another company, which then was to launch a takeover bid. It was held that, since the substantial purpose of that share issue was "simply and solely to dilute the majority voting power held by the first bidders so as to enable a then minority of the shareholders to sell their shares more advantageously",[262] the board acted improperly. The governing principle is that "it must be unconstitutional for directors to use their fiduciary powers over shares ... purely for the purpose of destroying an existing majority, or creating a new majority that did not previously exist. To do so is to interfere with that element of the company's constitution which is separate from and set against their powers".[263]

7–113 It remains to be determined in what circumstances directors may resort to what are termed "poison pills" to ward off a takeover of their company.[264]

STATUTORY DUTIES

7–114 Over and above those provisions that closely relate to the fiduciary duties, considered above, other statutory duties are imposed on directors. Many of these are supported by penal sanctions. Under some of them, the primary obligation is imposed on the company and a director's liability only arises where he has been "in default", in not ensuring that the company did what is required of it.

Disclosing Information

7–115 Every company must keep a registrar of directors and secretaries that contains prescribed details about them: for directors, their present and any former names, date of birth, nationality, occupation, usual address and particulars of other directorships held by them.[265] A married woman director does

---

[260] *ibid.* at 271.
[261] [1974] A.C. 821.
[262] *ibid.* at 837.
[263] *ibid.* at 837. See too, *Whitehouse v Carlton Hotel Property Ltd,* 61 A.L.J.L.R. 216 (1987). Compare *CAS (Nominees) Ltd v Nottingham Forest F.C. Plc* [2002] 1 B.C.L.C. 613 and see para.9–47.
[264] See para.12–28.
[265] 1963 Act, s.195.

not have to give any different name she had before she married, nor need a person give a former name that has not been used in the previous 20 years. Whenever there is any change in these details, or the person ceases to hold office, the company must notify the Registrar of Companies within 14 days, enclosing a consent if there is a change.[266] To enable the company to comply with those obligations, every director and secretary must keep it informed in writing as soon as any relevant circumstances arise.[267]

7–116 If a director who is resident in the State ceases to hold office and knows that the company has no other Irish-resident director, he must so inform the CRO within 14 days.[268] Failure to do so renders him liable, along with the company, for such fine or penalty as may be imposed.

7–117 Every company must keep a register of "interests" in its securities held by its directors and secretaries, and by parties connected with them, details of which must be disclosed in the company's annual accounts.[269] For so long as any director and secretary (including any shadow director) has such an interest, he must notify the company in writing promptly of its existence and specified details.[270] Companies with securities that are listed on the Irish Stock Exchange are required to send this information to the regulatory authorities.[271]

7–118 Every company must keep a book that records every contract it has entered into in which any of its directors has a financial interest, whether direct or indirect, which must be produced at every general meeting.[272] Whenever a director becomes in any way so interested in a contract or proposed contract, he must declare the nature of that interest at the first directors' meeting at which the contract comes up for consideration.[273]

7–119 Where certain kinds of takeover offers are made for the company's shares and some payment is to be made to a director by way of a "golden handshake", particulars of the payment must be included in any notice of the bidder's offer that is sent to the shareholders.[274] That director must take all reasonable steps to ensure that such disclosure is made.

7–120 To facilitate an audit of a company's accounts, every officer is obliged to cooperate with the auditors by furnishing such information and explanations as they have or can obtain, as the auditors deem necessary to discharge their duties.[275]

---

[266] Form B10.
[267] 1963 Act, s.195(11).
[268] 1999 No. 2 Act, s.43(9)–(11).
[269] 1990 Act, ss.59 and 60.
[270] 1990 Act, ss.53 and 56–58.
[271] Listing Rule 6.11.
[272] 1963 Act, s.194(5) and 1990 Act, s.47.
[273] 1963 Act, s.194(1)–(4).
[274] 1963 Act, s.188.
[275] 1990 Act, s.193(3).

7–121 Whenever civil or criminal proceedings are pending against a director, alleging fraud or dishonesty, the court may require him to lodge with it the names of companies of which he is or was a director in the preceding 12 months, and details of any disqualification order made against him.[276]

7–122 To facilitate the work of any inspector appointed, examiner or liquidator, every director must furnish such relevant information as may be required, subject to certain caveats.

Keeping Proper Books of Account

7–123 Companies must keep proper books of account, most of which must comply with the 1986 Act and give a "true and fair view" of the company's financial position.[277] Any director who either fails to take all reasonable steps to secure compliance or who, by his own wilful act, causes the company to contravene these requirements, commits an offence.[278] If the company is wound up and is found to be insolvent, any director who was in breach may be fastened with unlimited liability for all or part of the company's debts, where that breach either contributed to the insolvency or resulted in substantial uncertainty regarding the company's assets or liabilities, or otherwise impeded an orderly liquidation. Such liability was imposed in *Re Rayhill Property Co. Ltd,*[279] where the records kept were spasmodic and infrequent, and were muddled with the affairs of other companies and businesses. In the circumstances, it was held that there was a causative connection between the deficient bookkeeping and the company's inability to pay its debts.[280]

Prohibited Distributions and Share Purchases

7–124 Dividends can only be paid by solvent companies and from distributable profits.[281] Any director responsible for paying an unauthorised dividend can be held personally liable for the amount to the company. [282]

7–125 Where a company acquires shares in its holding company but, within six months, is wound up and is found to be insolvent, the directors are jointly and severally liable to repay the company the price it paid for those shares.[283] However, the court has a discretion to relieve one or more of them from this liability.

---

[276] 1990 Act, s.166.
[277] 1990 Act, s.202.
[278] 1990 Act, s.203.
[279] [2003] 3 I.R. 588.
[280] *cf. Mehigan v Duignan* [1997] 1 I.R. 340.
[281] 1983 Act, ss.45 and 46.
[282] 1983 Act, s.50 and *It's a Wrap (UK) Ltd v Gula* [2006] 2 B.C.L.C. 634.
[283] 1990 Act, s.225.

Securities Transactions

7–126 Where a prospectus issued by or on behalf of a company in respect of securities that are or are to be quoted on a stock exchange contains any false or misleading information, and a person acquires shares on foot of the prospectus, every director (and others) are liable to him for any loss he suffered thereby, subject to certain defences.[284]

7–127 Where prohibited "insider trading" in quoted securities is attributable to a director (or to others), he incurs a potential double liability. One is to the company for such profit he made from the transaction. Insofar as the other party to that transaction can be located, he must be compensated for any loss that he suffered arising from it.[285]

7–128 Directors (and persons acting at their instigation) may not deal at all in certain options in the quoted securities of their company or any related company, other than under share option schemes that possess Revenue approval.[286]

Disqualification and Restriction

7–129 Where a person, who is subject to a disqualification order or restriction under ss.160 or 150 of the 1990 Act, acts as a director or otherwise takes part in the management of a company—or of a company that does not satisfy the capitalisation requirements for s.150—in a winding-up, he is at risk of being made personally liable for all the company's unpaid debts.[287]

CONNECTED PERSONS

7–130 Obligations imposed on directors or with reference to them often extend to what are described as "connected persons" or to persons or bodies with which they are associated. These are, principally, business partners and close relatives of the director, companies that he controls to a significant extent and trusts in respect of which he or one of those other parties is a substantial beneficiary. The concept of a director being identified with others arises principally with reference to transactions that the company enters into, from which he may benefit indirectly,[288] and being obliged to disclose to the company shareholdings in it in which he is indirectly interested.[289] It also arises in the context of the taxation of close companies, where the key concept is an "associate", which means the person's partner, "relative", the trustee(s) of a settlement in which he or a close relative was a settlor and certain circumstances where he is interested in shares that are being held in trust.

---

[284] 2001 Act, s.41.
[285] 2005 Act, s.33.
[286] 1990 Act, s.30.
[287] 1990 Act, s.163(3).
[288] See para.7–60 *et seq.*
[289] See para.17–100 *et seq.*

7–131 There are a variety of prerequisites for, or restrictions on, a director becoming a party, directly or indirectly, to contracts with the company. This indirect interest exists if the contract is with a "connected person".[290] These are his business partners, spouse, parent, brother, sister or child, or any body that he controls. These, additionally, are a trust of which the principal beneficiaries are that director, his spouse, any company that he controls.

7–132 For these purposes, he controls another body if, alone or along with any other director or directors of the company, or with any of the above-mentioned parties with which he or any of these directors are connected, he has a significant influence in the body. The nature of this influence is being entitled to exercise at least one half of the voting power in its general meeting, or controlling the exercise of those votes, including doing so via another body that he controls. Alternatively, it is being "interested" in at least one half of the body's equity share capital, meaning shares in respect of which there is no cap on the amount of dividends that may be paid on them *and* on the amount that may be repaid to the members on a winding-up.[291] What constitutes an interest in such shares is extensively defined[292] and includes: having entered into a contract to purchase the shares; being entitled to exercise that right; having a "call" option on the shares or having some other right to acquire an interest in them, or being obliged to take an interest in them, whether conditionally or absolutely; or apart from any of the above, being a beneficiary of a trust that has an interest in the shares.

7–133 A director or directors are also deemed to be interested in a contract, as envisaged above, where he or they control a company that is so interested. By control here is meant that he or they are its "shadow directors" or are entitled to exercise at least one half of the voting power at general meetings, or control its exercise. Control here includes where some other company has this kind of influence over the votes at general meetings and the director, or he and any of his co-directors, is/are entitled to exercise one half of the votes at that meeting or to control their exercise.

7–134 Certain interests in shares are excluded for these purposes: most notably, being appointed a proxy to vote at a specified meeting; being appointed to represent a company at meetings; where the director's or co-director's interest in shares held in trust is as a bare trustee, or a discretionary interest, or an interest in reversion or remainder.

7–135 Where a director, a shadow director or secretary acquires or disposes of an interest in shares or debentures in a company, or in its subsidiary, or in its holding company or in another a subsidiary of it, he is obliged to notify relevant details to the company.[293] Being interested in those securities has the same meaning as it

---

[290] 1990 Act, s.26.
[291] 1963 Act, s.155(5).
[292] 1990 Act, ss.54 and 55.
[293] 1990 Act, s.53.

has for the purpose of determining whether a contracting party is a "connected person", with one main exception. Apart from being a shadow director, the indirect interest through another body requires only being entitled to exercise at least one third of the votes cast at general meetings, or to control their exercise.

RELIEVING LIABILITY

7–136   There are circumstances where directors may be exonerated from liability for breaking, or indeed may be authorised to break, what ordinarily would be their duties to the company. In the absence of explicit authority in the company's own regulations to do so, the board itself does not possess any power to relieve individual directors from such liability. Any effective exemption must arise either from those regulations, or be given by the shareholders in general meeting or by the court.

Exemption Clauses

7–137   The extent to which a clause in a trust deed may exempt trustees from liability for what ordinarily would be a breach of trust has been the subject of controversy in England in recent years.[294] It is accepted that liability for fraud or dishonesty cannot be exonerated in this manner, and the controversy mainly concerns the degree of negligence or recklessness that may be excused.

7–138   In the past, sweeping exemption clauses in articles of association were a common phenomenon; they could exonerate directors from liability in negligence and for breach of several other duties, even from losses resulting from *ultra vires* actions, provided the directors were not acting dishonestly. In support of these, an eminent judge once observed that:

> "It is not for me to say which was the wiser or better course nor do I think that this Court professes to lay down rules for the guidance of men who are adult, and can manage and deal with their own interests. It would be a violent assumption if any thing of that kind were attempted. It must be left to such persons to form their own contracts and engagements, and this Court has only to sit here and construe them, and also to lay down certain general rules for the protection of persons who may not have been aware of what the consequences would be of entrusting their property to the management of others where nothing is expressed as to the implied arrangement …"[295]

7–139   This absolute *laissez-faire* philosophy suggests that, in so far as the shareholders are concerned, company directors can be permitted to engage in all kinds of skulduggery once there is clear authority to do so in the company's own regulations. They have been held to exonerate liability for *ultra vires* acts in which a director innocently participated. But it has always been the position

---

[294] *Armitage v Nurse* [1998] Ch. 241 and *Walker v Stones* [2001] Q.B. 902.

[295] *Imperial Mercantile Credit Association v Coleman* (1871) L.R. 6 Ch. 558 at 568 per Lord Hatherley, L.C. (overruled on appeal, (1873) L.R. 6 H.L. 184). See too *Costa Rica Railway v Forwood* [1900] 1 Ch. 746.

that company officers may not be exempted in this way from liability for their own dishonesty.[296]

7–140 Companies are now prohibited from having any provision in their own regulations or in some other contract "exempting any officer ... from, or indemnifying him against, any liability which by virtue of any rule of law would otherwise attach to him in respect of any negligence, default, breach of duty or breach of trust of which he may be guilty in relation to the company ..."[297] The *City Equitable* case[298] on directors' and auditors' negligence was fresh in the legislature's mind when this equivalent provision was first adopted in England. There the directors, who were found to have managed the company negligently, were held nevertheless not to be accountable to it because of an exclusion clause in the company's articles of association. The statutory prohibition has generated academic comment[299] but has been the subject of little authoritative interpretation by the courts.

7–141 What is envisaged is a clause purporting to exempt an officer or to indemnify him against liability under any "rule of law". That "rule" may be in the company's articles, in any contract with it or arising "otherwise": Whether the prohibition extends to a clause in a memorandum of association is debatable. That liability-imposing "rule" must be in respect of "any negligence, default, breach of duty or breach of trust". Exception is made for an indemnity against costs incurred in successfully defending civil or criminal proceedings[300] and for officers' liability insurance purchased by the company.[301]

7–142 Especially in view of its *City Equitable* provenance, liability for negligence of any kind cannot be exempted in this manner. The reference to "default" would appear to mean breach of any requirement in the Companies Acts.

7–143 Breach of "duty", however, cannot refer to the entirety of fiduciary obligations because several aspects of the no-conflict principle are the subject of exoneration clauses in Table A.[302] Does it then mean all fiduciary obligations other than those ameliorated by Table A? One view is that, provided the director is not enriched at the company's expense and provided he exercises such powers as he has under its constitution for the benefit of the company, he can be exempted from the more general requirement not to put himself in a position where his own and the company's interests may conflict. As was suggested in *Movitex Ltd v Bulfield*[303]:

---

[296] *Re City Equitable Fire Insurance Co.* [1925] Ch. 407.
[297] 1963 Act, s.200(1).
[298] [1925] Ch. 407.
[299] See generally, Birds, "The Permissible Scope of Articles Excluding the Duties of Company Directors" 39 *Mod. L. Rev.* 394 (1976) and Gregory, "The Scope of the Companies Act 1948 Section 205" 98 *L.Q.R.* 413 (1982).
[300] 1963 Act, s.200(1)(b).
[301] 1963 Act, s.200(2)–(4).
[302] Articles 78, 85 and 86.
[303] [1988] B.C.L.C. 104.

"the true principle is that if a director places himself in a position in which his duty to the company conflicts with his personal interest or his duty to another, the court will intervene to set aside the transaction without inquiring whether there was any breach of the director's duty to the company. That is an over-riding principle of equity. The shareholders of the company, in formulating the articles, can exclude or modify the application of this principle. In doing so they do not exempt the director from or from the consequences of a breach of a duty owed to the company."[304]

It was held that a provision that went somewhat further than art.78 of Table A did not fall foul of the prohibition. Strictly, there is no "rule" as such against avoiding conflicts; provided there is no unjust enrichment or abuse of particular powers, what potential conflicts are permissible is entirely a matter for each company's own regulations.

7–144 The reference to "breach of trust" here would seem to be redundant, as it is difficult to envisage something that is not a breach of a fiduciary obligation but nonetheless is a breach of trust in favour of the company.

Court Exoneration

7–145 The court has been given some discretion to exonerate any officer of a company, be he director or auditor, from liability for breach of a duty owed to the company. Relief will be granted provided three conditions are satisfied, *viz.* that the officer acted "honestly", that he acted "reasonably" and that "having regard to all the circumstances of the case he ought fairly to be excused".[305] Relief granted may be in whole or in part.[306] It is not necessary in advance to plead this section; it can be raised at the trial for the first time.[307] This power is most extensive, in that the court can even exonerate from liability for *ultra vires* acts.[308] But it does not apply to claims being made by third parties that do not directly involve the director's duties to his company; for instance, it has been held not to apply to claims by the Revenue against directors to recover unpaid taxes of various kinds.[309] Nor does it apply to certain proceedings being brought by a liquidator, that are predicated on a director's wrongdoing, as for fraudulent or reckless trading,[310] nor to penal proceedings to enforce the Companies Acts.[311]

7–146 Any dishonesty or unreasonableness prevents the officer from even being considered for relief. For these purposes, honesty is judged subjectively and reasonableness is judged objectively. Thus, where the directors of a public

---

[304] *ibid.* at 120.
[305] 1963 Act, s.391. See generally, Edmunds & Lowry, "The Continuing Value of Relief for Directors' Breach of Duty" 66 *Mod. L. Rev.* 195 (2003).
[306] e.g. *Re D'Jan of London Ltd* [1994] 1 B.C.L.C. 561.
[307] *Re Kirby's Coaches Ltd* [1991] B.C.L.C. 414.
[308] *Re Claridge's Patent Asphalte Co.* [1921] 1 Ch. 543.
[309] *Customs & Excise Cmrs v Henden Alpha Ltd* [1981] 1 Q.B. 818 and *IRC v McEntaggart* [2006] 1 B.C.L.C. 476.
[310] *Re Produce Marketing Consortium Ltd* [1989] 1 W.L.R. 745.
[311] *IRC v McEntaggart* [2006] 1 B.C.L.C. 476.

company had published over-inflated profits, in order to boost its share price in the market, the court declined to consider their claim for exoneration against having to repay dividends that should never have been declared.[312] Where a director of a company that was closing down negotiated with its landlord to take over its leases, without any reference to his fellow directors, it was held that he had not acted reasonably.[313] Where a director obtains any material personal benefit from his breach of duty, it is only in the most exceptional circumstances that the court will grant exoneration.[314] Engaging in somewhat complex transactions, without seeking legal advice, has been held to be unreasonable.[315] So too has declaring a dividend on the assumption that a roll-over from a tax-driven strategy would be effective, when patently the underlying transaction made no commercial sense and was entirely a tax-avoidance measure, which did not succeed.[316] In one instance, the court rejected the director's application because he declined to give evidence and submit himself to cross-examination, which it held was necessary for him to discharge the onus of proving that he acted honestly and reasonably.[317]

7–147 But having taken certain action on foot of counsel's opinion has been held to indicate reasonableness,[318] as has acting consistently with past practice.[319]

Ratification by Members

7–148 There are numerous instances where the courts have upheld general meeting resolutions that ratified, after the event, breaches of various directors' duties, such as allotting additional shares to forestall a takeover and voting for a contract with the company in which the director had a financial interest. But there are other kinds of breaches of duty that cannot be ratified, at least over the objections of a minority of the members. Much confusion exists about what wrongs are capable of ratification and the legal consequences of shareholders' approval for directors' wrongs. Certain elementary principles and distinctions are often overlooked when considering this subject.[320]

7–149 Many of the cases do not involve the company suing the errant director but are proceedings being brought, on the company's behalf, by aggrieved minority shareholders. In those instances, the issue then is when does general meeting approval or "ratification" of the breach of duty prevent those proceedings being heard. The question of when majority approval for what was done

---

[312] *Bairstow v Queens Moat Houses Plc* [2001] 2 B.C.L.C. 531.

[313] *Coleman Taymar Ltd v Oakes* [2001] 2 B.C.L.C. 531.

[314] *Re In A Flap Envelope Co.* [2004] 1 B.C.L.C. 64 and *Re Duckwari Plc* [1997] 2 W.L.R. 48.

[315] *Re Duomatic Ltd* [1969] 2 Ch. 365.

[316] *Re Loquitur Ltd* [2003] 2 B.C.L.C. 442.

[317] *Re In A Flap Envelope Co.* [2004] 1 B.C.L.C. 64.

[318] *Re Claridge's Patent Asphalte Co.* [1921] 1 Ch. 543.

[319] *Re Duomatic Ltd* [1969] 2 Ch. 365.

[320] See generally, Partridge, "Ratifications and Release of Directors From Personal Liability" 46 *Cam. L.J.* 122 (1987) and Whincop, 'Of Fault and Default: Contractarianism as a Theory of Anglo-Australian Corporate Law' 21 *Melbourne U.L. Rev.* 187 (1997).

bars shareholders' claims, requires analysis of the "derivative" claim and of the principles and exceptions associated with the early Victorian case, *Foss v Harbottle*.[321] However, the fact that majority approval blocks a derivative action does not mean that the company may not at some later stage change its mind and itself sue those directors for their wrongs. It would be different if the company and the directors reached an enforceable agreement putting an end to all claims between them. But a mere "ratifying" resolution, which can have the effect of rendering binding otherwise voidable contracts or deficient decisions of the directors, is not an enforceable agreement to waive all claims. For there has been no consideration given. Nor normally would that resolution operate as an effective estoppel against the company subsequently bringing proceedings. For practical purposes, however, provided control of the company has not changed, it is unlikely that, having passed a resolution exonerating the directors, the company will later turn around and bring proceedings against them.

7–150   If, at the general meeting's behest, a contract under seal was made with the directors exonerating them, the question then arises whether the company is legally capable of making such an agreement. On the basis of the *Re Duomatic Ltd*[322] principle, that agreement would be effective if it had the backing of all the shareholders, provided it is not *ultra vires* the company. But where it has the support of a majority only, it would be set aside if it fell within the circumstances where aggrieved minority shareholders' claims would succeed. These same considerations apply to *ex ante* exonerations. If, before the wrong was done or at the very time it was done, the shareholders signified their approval, that would amount to a waiver of the directors' duty to the company. As the duty would not then exist, the directors could not then be in breach of duty. As with the sealed contract not to sue, however, an *ex ante* waiver is only fully effective if it was in respect of a matter which would not give rise to an aggrieved minority shareholders' claim. If the matter did not indeed fall within the so-called exceptions to *Foss v Harbottle,* the purported waiver would be a "fraud on the minority" and not binding on the company.

7–151   Accordingly, the question of the legal enforceability of directors' duties is closely related to the issue of minority shareholder protection. This is particularly so in companies with relatively few members—the great majority of registered companies—where the directors usually hold a majority of the shares as well. Where the directors as a group or a majority of them are negligent or otherwise in breach of duty, if they also are the controlling shareholders there is little real prospect of the company suing them for breach of duty. In those companies, therefore, for practical purposes the directors' wrongs which can be redressed in court are the breaches of duty which also are a basis for a minority shareholders' action, namely most breaches of the memorandum and articles of association and what falls under the rubric "unfair discrimination" and "fraud on the company". Another mode of redress against errant directors

---

[321] (1843) 2 Hare 461.
[322] [1969] 2 Ch. 365 and see para.5–67 *et seq.*

is an action under s.205 of the 1963 Act for "oppression" or to have the company wound up on "just and equitable grounds" under s.213 of that Act.

LIABILITY TO THIRD PARTIES

7–152 Unless the memorandum of association so provides,[323] directors are not liable for their company's unpaid debts, either under contract, in tort or otherwise. But their breach of several provisions in the Companies Acts can result in their being made liable for its debts without limit.[324] Further, if the company is wound up, they may be pursued by the liquidator in respect of their wrongdoings, such as in proceedings for fraudulent trading, reckless trading and misfeasance.[325] Additionally, where a director is in some way implicated in a wrong done by the company to a third party, the question of his personal liability to that person arises. Depending on the circumstances and the nature of the particular wrong, that liability may be exclusive or it may be jointly with the company. Especially where the company becomes insolvent, rather than await liquidation or incur the expense of putting it into liquidation, the injured party may seek redress through the DCE.[326]

Contract/Agency

7–153 A company's liability for any contract one of its directors enters into on its behalf turns principally on whether he had the requisite authority to bind the company.[327] If he represented that he has been authorised to enter into a contract on its behalf, but that is not the case, he will be liable for breach of warranty of authority.

7–154 At times those negotiating a contract may intend it to be with the director, as principal, and not with the company. Even where that the company is involved in the contracting process, it may be acting as the director's agent, either openly or on the basis of the doctrine of an "undisclosed principal". This question arose in the *Yukong Line Ltd* case,[328] a dispute concerning a charterparty which had been signed on behalf of the first defendant by one of its directors, who was the beneficial owner of that defendant and who also controlled the ship brokers. It was held that, in all the circumstances, the contract was not intended to be with that director personally.

7–155 Where a lessee company committed waste, the director who directed or procured the wrongful action was held also liable to the landlord.[329]

---

[323] 1963 Act, s.197.
[324] e.g. for not keeping proper books of account; see para.7–123.
[325] See para.24–97 *et seq.*
[326] See para.20–16 *et seq.*
[327] See para.18–36 *et seq.*
[328] *Yukong Line Ltd of Korea v Rendsburg Investments Corp. of Liberia (No. 2)* [1998] 1 W.L.R. 294.
[329] *Mancetter Developments Ltd v Garmanson Ltd* [1986] 1 Q.B. 1212.

7–156   Whenever a company issues a bill of exchange, order, business letter, notice, invoice or receipt, the company's name must be mentioned on the document in legible characters.[330] Where a director or other "officer" of the company causes a bill of exchange or cheque, or an order for money or goods, to be issued, but which does not adequately identify the company, he can be made personally liable for the amount on that bill or order. For instance, in *Rafsanjan Pistachio Producers Co-Op v Reiss*,[331] the plaintiffs obtained a default judgment against the company but then settled the dispute, whereby the company gave them several post-dated cheques. These were dishonoured. Because the cheques did not have the company's full name (although they bore its bank account number), the plaintiffs sued the director who had signed them. It was held that he was personally liable and that, in the circumstances, the plaintiffs were not estopped from relying on the requirement. Even where the company's name is mentioned but not the entire name, or the words "limited" or "ltd" are omitted, liability can arise. But a misspelling of the company's name on the cheque, that does not mislead parties about the company they are dealing with, does not incur liability on the part of the directors.

Extra-Contractual Liability

7–157   Unless it is expressly so provided by statute, the mere fact that the company has committed a tort does not make its directors personally responsible[332]; something more is required before individual directors can be rendered accountable. Personal liability will not arise where a director does no more than carry out his constitutional role in the governance of the company, by voting at board meetings.[333] The relevant enquiry is "whether he has been personally involved in the commission of the tort to an extent sufficiently to render him liable as a joint tortfeasor ... [His] liability ... is not founded on any concept of vicarious responsibility".[334] How heavily involved he must be in the wrongdoing to attract personal liability depends on the nature of the tort. In proceedings relating to intellectual property, the standard is whether he "intends and procures and shares in a common design that the infringement takes place".[335] In *House of Spring Gardens v Point Blank Ltd*[336] where the first defendant company was held liable for, *inter alia*, breach of copyright, its directors were held personally liable for having "authorised" those breaches, contrary to s.7(3) of the Copyright Act 1963.

---

[330] 1963 Act, s.114.

[331] [1990] B.C.L.C. 352.

[332] See generally, Flannigan, "The Personal Tort Liability of Directors" 81 *Can. Bar. J.* 247 (2002), Campbell & Armour, "Demystifying the Civil Liability of Corporate Agents" 62 *Cam. L.J.* 290 (2003) and Grantham, "The Limited Liability of Company Directors," [2007] *Lloyds Mar. & Comm. L.Q.* 365.

[333] *MCA Records Inc. v Charly Records Ltd* [2003] 1 B.C.L.C. 93 at 116.

[334] *ibid.* at 111.

[335] *ibid.* at 117. See too *Koninklijke Phillips Electronics NV v Princo Digital Disk Gmbh* [2004] 2 B.C.L.C. 50.

[336] [1984] I.R. 612.

7–158 Liability for fraud arises where the director made or authorised making a fraudulent representation. As Lord Rodger observed in *Standard Chartered Bank v Pakistan National Shipping Corp. (No. 2)*,[337] where a managing director had signed a letter falsely stating that all the documents required under a letter of credit were present, "no man can escape the clutches of the criminal law by the simple device of showing that he had carried out his frauds in his capacity as a director of a company in circumstances where his acts were to be attributed to the company".[338]

7–159 Where a director is being sued for inducing breach of contract or otherwise interfering with contractual relations in the course of the company's business, he may in the circumstances have a defence of justification.[339]

7–160 With regard to liability in negligence, the central issue is whether a duty of care exists in the circumstances; company law considerations as such have little or anything to do with the issue. In *Shinkwin v Quin-Con Ltd*[340] the Supreme Court held that a director, who had full control of his company's factory, owed a personal duty of care to the plaintiff employee, who was injured there; in the circumstances, there was a sufficient nexus of "proximity" between them. On the other hand, in *Sweeney v Duggan*[341] that court held that a director, who was the designated manager of his company's quarry, did not have a duty to the plaintiff, who was injured there, to ensure that there was employers' liability insurance to cover the plaintiff's claim for damages against the company. Courts more readily find a duty of care where the claim is one in respect of personal injury than for exclusively financial loss; any such *Skinkwin*-type claim that the plaintiff had in *Sweeney* was statute-barred.

7–161 For a director to be held liable in negligence for a representation made for the benefit of a company, it must be shown that he was assuming a personal responsibility to the plaintiff, who relied on what was said[342]; that the requisite relationship of "proximity" exists between the plaintiff and the company is not sufficient. As was summed up by Lord Steyn in *Williams v Natural Life Ltd*[343]:

> "[w]hether the principal is a company or a natural person, someone acting on his behalf may incur general liability in tort as well as imposing vicarious or attributed liability on his principal. But in order to establish personal liability under the principle of *Hedley Byrne*, which requires the existence of a special relationship between the plaintiff and tortfeasor, it is not sufficient that there should have been a special relationship with the principal. There must have been an assumption of responsibility such as to create a special relationship with the director himself".[344]

---

[337] [2003] 1 A.C. 959.
[338] *ibid.* at 973.
[339] *Said v Butt* [1920] 3 K.B. 497 and *369413 Alberta Ltd v Pocklington*, 194 D.L.R. (4th) 109 (2000).
[340] [2001] 1 I.R. 514. In *Fay v Tegral Pipes Ltd* [2005] 2 I.R. 261, proximity was not pleaded.
[341] [1997] 2 I.R. 531.
[342] *Partco Group Ltd v Wragg* [2002] B.C.L.C. 323 and *Noel v Pollard* [2001] 2 B.C.L.C. 695.
[343] [1998] 1 W.L.R. 830.
[344] [1998] 1 W.L.R. 830 at 835.

7–162 In one instance where a chief executive and a finance director were sued because profit projections they gave to a "friendly" takeover bidder proved to be over-optimistic, the court refused to strike out the bidder's claim as not disclosing any cause of action. It was stated that "the potential liability of directors in a situation of this kind has still to be regarded as a developing jurisprudence, or at least one which is uncertain in its application."[345]

7–163 A director who dishonestly assists or procures his company to commit a breach of a trust for the benefit of a third party, is also liable to the beneficiary.[346] In Britain, directors who knew or ought to have known that their company had not paid social welfare contributions that were due, have a statutory liability to pay them to the authorities.[347]

Statute

7–164 Where specific statutory duties are imposed on a company, generally its directors will not be held liable to outsiders for non-compliance with them. In *Dun Laoghaire Corp. v Parkhill Developments Ltd*,[348] the plaintiff obtained a statutory injunction against a property development company for contravening the planning legislation. But Hamilton P. refused to make any such order against the company's managing director and effective controller because there was no evidence of impropriety on his part. The position could be different if the company was disabled from carrying out its statutory responsibilities on account of the director siphoning off money from the company or other fraud on his part. In *Wicklow County Council v Fenton (No. 2)*,[349] when making an order against a company under the "polluter pays" principle, O'Sullivan J. made a "fall-back" order against "individual directors and/or shareholders" if the company could not comply with the order against it.[350] The extent to which directors may be held personally liable under the Competition Act 2002 remains to be clarified.

Contempt

7–165 Where the company broke a court order, none of its directors are personally liable for contempt merely by virtue of their office, even if they knew of the making of that order.[351] But if any of them committed some act of omission which caused the company's contempt or showed wilful disregard of what was going on, he then could be held in contempt.[352]

---

[345] *Partco Group Ltd v Wragg* [2002] 2 B.C.L.C. 323 at 363. See also *Noel v Pollard* [2001] 2 B.C.L.C. 695 and *New Zealand Guardian Trust Co. v Brooks* [1995] 1 W.L.R. 96.
[346] *Royal Brunei Airlines v Tan* [1995] 2 A.C. 378.
[347] *Dept of Health & Social Security v Evans* [1984] 1 Ch. 317.
[348] [1989] I.R. 447.
[349] [2002] 4 I.R. 44.
[350] Similarly, *Laois County Council v Scully* [2006] 2 I.R. 292.
[351] See generally, C.J. Miller, *Contempt of Court* (Oxford, OUP, 2000), p.670 *et seq.*
[352] *ibid.* p.674.

Costs

7–166   To date, the Irish courts do not appear to have determined whether or in what circumstances a director may be required to pay the costs of proceedings brought by or against the company, in which it was unsuccessful.[353]

Indemnity

7–167   It is questionable whether or in what circumstances a company could indemnify its directors, or pay for directors' liability insurance, in respect of their own liabilities to third parties. Since 2003, companies have been permitted to pay for their officers' and auditors' liability insurance against costs incurred in successfully defending civil or criminal proceedings.[354]

CRIMINAL RESPONSIBILITY

7–168   Before a company can be convicted of a crime, the wrongdoing must be attributed to it through the appropriate "organs".[355] But it does not follow that if a company is criminally responsible its directors are similarly accountable, unless there is express provision to that effect. Several provisions in the Companies Acts set out circumstances in which directors can be convicted of an offence where the company has contravened a penal section of those Acts. Whenever one of these provisions renders an officer who is in default liable to a fine, the defaulting officer is the one who either authorised the default or, in breach of duty, permitted it to occur.[356] For these purposes, the officer is presumed to have permitted the default unless he can show that he took all reasonable steps to prevent it or that he could not do so because of circumstances beyond his control.

7–169   There are numerous other statutory provisions that impose criminal liability provided, however, the director knew about and condoned the wrongdoing in question. Perhaps the most elaborate of these is s.8(6)–(8) of the Competition Act 2002, concerning the offences of anti-competitive arrangement and abuse of dominant position, contrary to ss.6 and 7 of that Act:

> "(6) Where an offence under section 6 or 7 has been committed by an undertaking and the doing of the acts that constitute the offence has been authorised, or consented to, by a person, being a director, manager or other similar officer of the undertaking, or a person who purports to act in any such capacity, that person as well as the undertaking shall be guilty of an offence and shall be liable to be proceeded against and punished as if he or she were guilty of the first-mentioned offence.
>
> (7) Where a person is proceeded against as aforesaid for such an offence and it is proved that, at the material time, he or she was a director of the undertaking concerned or a person employed by it whose duties

---

[353] See paras.22–24 and 22–34.
[354] 1963 Act, s.200(2).
[355] See para.18–80 *et seq.*
[356] 1963 Act, s.383.

included making decisions that, to a significant extent, could have affected the management of the undertaking, or a person who purported to act in any such capacity, it shall be presumed, until the contrary is proved, that that person consented to the doing of the acts by the undertaking which constituted the commission by it of the offence concerned under section 6 or 7.

(8) Where the affairs of a body corporate are managed by its members, subsections (6) and (7) shall apply in relation to the acts or defaults of a member in connection with his or her functions of management as if he or she were a director of the body corporate."

Section 80 of the Safety, Health and Welfare at Work Act, 2005, is to the same effect with regard to breaches of that Act or of regulations made under it.[357]

Sub s.(6) above is replicated in the European Communities (Markets in Financial Instruments) Regulations 2007.[358]

7–170   Where directors act dishonestly or illegally in relation to their company, but in their defence claim consent, knowledge by them of their own wrongdoing will not normally be imputed to the company; this principle applies in the criminal law just as much as in civil law.

---

[357] See Guidance for Directors and Senior Managers on their Responsibilities for Workplace Safety: www.hsa.ie. *Cf.* Social Welfare Consolidation Act, 2005, s.251(7).
[358] SI 2007/60, reg.189(1).

CHAPTER 8

SHARE CAPITAL

8–01 To engage in any significant business activity, a company needs finance, which in most companies primarily takes the form of contributed share capital. Every company's memorandum of association must stipulate what its authorised share capital is.[1] Rules governing companies' capital focus on three main issues. One is to ensure that persons are not duped into subscribing for shares that are worthless or are worth far less than their issue price. This objective is secured by a combination of contract and tort law, supplemented by equitable principles. In the case of share offers to the investing public, these are supplemented principally by Pt 5 (ss.38–55) of the 2005 Act and the Prospectus Regulations 2005, which gave effect to the EC Prospectus Directive of 2003. Another is a variety of rules aimed at ensuring that companies obtain adequate consideration for shares that they issue and that protect subscribed capital from being improperly depleted, to the prejudice of, *inter alia*, the company's creditors. A third is to ensure that existing shareholders have some opportunity to take up any new shares that the company intends to issue, thereby retaining their proportionate stake in the company.[2]

8–02 A fundamental doctrine of company law is that of capital integrity, which has spawned a number of sub-principles and sub-rules.[3] Many of these were "discovered" by judges between 1880 and 1900, the evidence for their existence being the underlying scheme of the Companies Acts. Their principal objective is to provide company creditors with a degree of security. As Jessel M.R. explained: "[t]he creditor has no debtor but that impalpable thing the corporation, which has no property except the assets of the business. The creditor, therefore … gives credit to that capital, gives credit to the company on the faith of the representation that the capital shall be applied only for the purpose of the business …"[4] That is to say, the law enables persons to do business under the aegis of registered companies which are legally segregated from their owners and almost invariably have limited liability. Accordingly, all that persons dealing with limited companies can look to for satisfaction of obligations owing to them is the company's own assets. However, there is always a danger of the shareholders withdrawing funds from the company in the shape of dividends

---

[1] 1963 Act, s.6(4).
[2] See para. 9–44 *et seq*.
[3] See generally, Armour, "Share Capital and Creditor Protection: Efficient Rules for a Modern Company Law" 63 *Mod. L. Rev.* 355 (2000).
[4] *Flitcroft's Case, Re Exchange Banking Co.* (1882) 21 Ch D 519 at 533.

or otherwise, with the resultant diminution of the amount creditors can claim against. It, therefore, is necessary to provide that the subscribed capital be protected against the depredations of shareholders and to the detriment of creditors, and indeed of minority shareholders as well.

8–03 The rules regarding capital integrity have been extended significantly by the 1983 Act, which was adopted in response to the EC Second Directive on Company Law,[5] it being based on features of French and German law. This Directive's central objective is summed up in its preamble, "[w]hereas Community provisions should be adopted for maintaining the capital, which constitutes the creditors' security, in particular by prohibiting any reduction thereof by distribution to shareholders where the latter are not entitled to it and by imposing limits on the company's rights to acquire its own shares". Some of this Directive's requirements were already incorporated in the 1963 Act, such as the restrictions on companies buying or financing the purchase of their own shares. Other parts of that Act had to be drastically amended, notably in respect of paying dividends from capital, requiring that Plcs have a minimum capital and that consideration paid for shares in Plcs must be shown to be adequate.

SOURCES OF FUNDS FOR COMPANIES

8–04 One of the first things that must be determined when embarking on a business venture is how to finance it. Various options present themselves, like equity investment by shareholders, long-term and short-term borrowings, grants of various kinds that can be obtained from the State, and financing expansion from profits generated by the business.[6] If a company seeks to raise additional share capital it must choose whether first to approach its existing shareholders for funds or to offer its shares to others, even to the general public. It is most unusual today for newly formed companies to approach the investing public immediately for funds.

Shareholders

8–05 To begin with, how much should be invested in the business as risk capital?[7] Whatever sum that is will be represented by shares subscribed for. For instance, if €50,000 is needed initially as risk capital, those starting the business will take up shares in the company representing that sum by exchanging cash or other assets for those shares. Thus, if the shares are to be fully paid up and have a nominal value of €1 each, 50,000 shares of €1 will be allotted in return for the company obtaining consideration worth at least €50,000. Share capital is commonly referred to as equity.[8] At some stage, most very large

---

5   Directive 77/91 [1977] OJ L26/1.
6   See generally, T. Power et al, *Financial Management: An Irish Text*, 2nd edn (Dublin: Gill & Macmillan, 2005) and G. Arnold, *Handbook of Corporate Finance* (London: Financial Times Prentice Hall, 2004) (hereafter *Power* and *Arnold* respectively).
7   See generally *Power*, Ch.11 and *Arnold*, Ch.17.
8   *cf.* Companies (Amendment) Act 1983, s.23(13).

businesses will obtain a quotation for their shares on a stock exchange, which ensures liquidity for their shareholders and also facilitates raising share capital from the investing public. A prerequisite for listing on the Irish Stock Exchange is that the aggregate market value of the company's shares exceeds €1 million.[9]

8–06 A number of general points should be made at this stage about share capital. In most Western European countries, shares are required to have some fixed *nominal* or "par" value, i.e. be assigned a specific theoretical value, be it €1, 20 cent, £200 or whatever. Although persuasive reasons can be advanced for permitting companies to issue shares without having to assign them some par value, as occurs in the US, there would appear to be little demand for such innovation.

8–07 A company's *authorised* capital (sometimes called nominal capital) is the aggregate par value of the shares that its memorandum of association permits it to issue: its theoretical maximum capital. Its *issued* capital means the aggregate par value of the shares that have been issued to subscribers: the total par value of the shares that have been acquired by its members. *Allotted* capital means the same as *issued* capital. The Companies Acts generally speak of allotting rather than of issuing shares; allotting is the technical term for appropriating to a person a certain number of shares. Usually, companies will not issue all of their authorised capital but will retain some of it unissued.

8–08 *Paid-up* capital means the amount in money or money's worth that has been paid to a company in return for shares allotted by it. The laws in most Western European countries prohibit allotting shares at a discount, i.e. at the very least, their par value must be paid up on shares in the event of insolvency. Frequently, shares are allotted for more than their par value, i.e. at a premium; where this happens, the paid-up capital is the aggregate par value of the shares that have been allotted together with the total premia paid on them. Where a company does not require to be paid to it immediately the entire par value and any premium on shares it allots, it will require its shareholders to pay part of the amount due and may call up part or all of the remainder at some later stage. The amount that it requires to be paid over to it is the *called-up* capital; the remainder is the *uncalled* capital.

8–09 Subject to what may be stipulated in a company's own regulations, the principal contractual rights of shareholders are to be given certain information concerning how the business is faring, to attend and vote at general meetings, to be paid a dividend when one has been declared and to transfer their shares to others.[10] Especially in companies whose shares are not traded on a stock exchange or secondary market, atypical arrangements may exist in respect of some or all of those matters. For instance, under the articles of association shareholders may be entitled to get more than the statutory

---

[9] Listing Rules 3.2.7.
[10] See Ch.9.

minimum financial information; different categories of shares may have different voting rights and different dividends entitlements; freedom to transfer the shares may be severely restricted. Except for "preference" shares, entitling their holders to be paid dividends before any dividend may be paid to the other shareholders, in most publicly quoted companies all shareholders have the same entitlements in respect of obtaining financial information and voting. A prerequisite for obtaining a quotation is that those shares are freely transferable.

Debt Finance

8–10 How much the company should borrow depends on circumstances like the nature of its business, how much funds its shareholders themselves possess to invest in risk capital, what security it can offer, its creditworthiness and the like. It is trite to say that a company should not borrow more than it comfortably can repay.

8–11 Borrowing can take various forms.[11] It can be mainly from the company's own shareholders, or from personal investors who do not wish to be exposed unduly to risk, or from financial institutions such as banks and insurance companies, who usually will require security. Institutions offer a wide variety of borrowing facilities, like overdrafts, term loans, factoring, accepting bills of exchange and furnishing guarantees. A method of financing that has become popular due to taxation considerations is equipment leasing. Borrowing may even be the consequences of the company's cash flow. That is to say, if the company can get paid for the goods or services it produces before it is required to pay for its principal inputs, the suppliers of those inputs in fact finance much of its business. A dangerous and potentially unlawful variant of this is relying on employees' social insurance contributions, sums deducted for PAYE purposes and VAT collected, that have not yet been paid over to the State.[12] In much the same way as companies may raise share capital from the investing public, they may obtain debt finance in that manner, principally by issuing debentures or bonds. Where a company issues its lenders documents evidencing the liability, those are called debentures.[13] Although transferable debentures can resemble shares in various respects, they are fundamentally different.

8–12 A power to borrow for the purposes of the company's business is usually included in the memorandum of association's objects clause; where no such power is expressly given, borrowing for business purposes would usually be *intra vires* a registered company as an implied power. Borrowing or providing security for loans that are of no economic benefit to the company can be *ultra vires* unless they are expressly authorised by the memorandum, as *Northern Bank Finance Corp. v Quinn*[14] demonstrates. But *ultra vires*

---

[11] See generally *Power*, Chs 15 and 21, and *Arnold*, Chs 15 and 16.
[12] Reliance on this can lead it to directors being restricted or even disqualified.
[13] See para.20–19 *et seq.*
[14] [1989] I.L.R.M. 221.

borrowing may be rendered legally effective by virtue of s.8(1) of the 1963 Act.[15] How a company's borrowing powers are to be exercised is almost invariably determined by its articles of association. Table A, under which the "business of the company shall be managed by the directors",[16] empowers the board to borrow for business purposes. An express power to borrow usually will be accompanied by a power to give security; where borrowing falls within a company's implied powers, almost invariably the company will have an implied power to give security. Ordinarily, the articles of association will set out how the power to grant security is to be exercised.

Gearing

8–13   The term "financial gearing", or leverage, means the ratio between a company's share capital and its borrowings—between its equity and its debt.[17] A company that has borrowed heavily in comparison with its share capital is said to be highly geared. The main attraction of high gearing is that, if the business is very successful, the shareholders will get a much higher return on their investment. Take a business that needs €50,000 in capital and that is being inaugurated by three persons, each with €8,300 to invest in it (i.e. €25,000 in aggregate); assume that it would earn €10,000 in each year. If the remaining €25,000 could be borrowed at say 10 per cent per annum, this would require €2,500 per annum to service, leaving a surplus of €7,500 at the end of the year to be divided among the three shareholders— or €2,500 each. If, however, instead of borrowing they bring in other shareholders who invest €25,000, at the end of the year the original three will be entitled, between themselves, at most to only half of the €10,000 annual profits—or €1,666 each.

8–14   These figures demonstrate the principal argument for borrowing substantially in order to finance a business. Another attraction of high gearing is taxation; interest on loans is a business cost and can be deducted from the trading surplus, leaving even more to be distributed as dividends. The main argument against high gearing is that if the business runs into difficulties, it may not be possible to meet the interest charges, which could easily result in the company being put into receivership or into liquidation. Moreover, companies that are highly geared may experience some difficulties in attracting further equity investment, on account of there being prior charges on earnings and also because of lenders' tendency to close down businesses in bad times.

Hybrids

8–15   There are various intermediate solutions to resolving the debt-equity dilemma. One is that the company borrows from its own shareholders, assuming they have the funds to lend. In this way there is less likelihood of

---

[15] See para.18–21 *et seq.*
[16] Article 80.
[17] See generally *Power,* Ch.8 and *Arnold,* Ch.18.

finance creditors shutting the business down as soon as it encounters temporary difficulties. Sometimes shareholders-lenders will have agreed to subordinate their claims to be repaid, i.e. accept that, in an insolvency, all other creditors must be paid before their own entitlements arise.

8–16 A "convertible" security is a liability of the company that, on or after some specified time or event, either can be converted or must be converted into a claim of another kind.[18] The commonest form is the convertible debenture, i.e. a loan to the company that it, at some stage, can convert into equity. A major attraction of this form of security is that it enables a company to obtain investment at a time when persons are reluctant to acquire shares in it and, should the company prosper, to convert those borrowings into share capital.

8–17 Another option is the "preference" share, which in fact though not in law, is a hybrid of debt and equity.[19] This is a special class of share the owners of which have prior claims against the company over the "ordinary" shareholders. A common form of preference share is one the holders of which, if profits are earned and dividends are declared, are entitled to be paid a fixed dividend before any dividend can be paid to the other shareholders. These shares usually carry a prior claim over other shares to the return of their capital, in the event of the company being wound up. With preference shares, therefore, the company enjoys some advantages of high gearing without the main disadvantage.

8–18 It is not uncommon in small companies, whose owners and managers are not legally sophisticated, for them to place their own money or other property at their company's disposal, without any formal arrangement being made about the basis on which the company is to have those assets. Depending on the circumstances, they are a loan to the company or they may be an outright gift to it. Exceptionally, those assets are characterised by the company as a "capital contribution", without shares being duly issued in respect of them. In such circumstances, those assets might be treated as a contingent payment on calls it is anticipated will be made when new shares are issued. In one instance, notwithstanding such characterisation, those assets were treated as the equivalent of a gift.[20]

Retained Earnings

8–19 Next is the question of self-financing; how much should the company rely on profits generated by the business to finance its expansion?[21] Among the advantages of what is referred to as "ploughing back" profits is that the immediate dependence on banks and other lending institutions is greatly reduced, and there is less need to go to the existing shareholders or to outsiders for further equity. Indeed, few businesses prosper and endure without retaining an appreciable proportion of their earnings in good trading years. Especially in

---

[18] See para.20–31.
[19] See para.9–118 *et seq.*
[20] *Kellar v Williams* [2000] 2 B.C.L.C. 390.
[21] See generally *Power,* Ch.12 and *Arnold,* Ch.14.

"close" companies, taxation is an important consideration influencing the pay-or-not-pay-a-dividend decision.

State Grants and Aids

8–20   Another source of company finance is the grant and aid schemes offered by various public bodies, especially by Enterprise Ireland.[22] Assistance can take the form of outright cash grants, loans, the purchase of shares in the company and several other methods. How much and what types of aid a company can obtain will depend on its bargaining power, such as how risky its business is, the likelihood of it expanding, its contribution to exports and to import-substitution and, perhaps of greatest importance, its geographical location and how many persons it will employ.

ISSUING SHARES

8–21   On it being registered, those persons who subscribe to a company's memorandum of association become its first shareholders. Subsequent shareholders are either persons to whom the company allots shares, i.e. who put cash or other assets into the company in return for shares, and those persons' successors-in-title.

Application and Allotment

8–22   Occasionally investors will search for a company into which they can put funds at their disposal. More often it is the company, or its shareholders or directors, or persons promoting the company, who will seek out potential investors. The formalities are that the investor applies to the company to subscribe for its shares, i.e. offers to acquire its shares in return for some consideration. At least 5 per cent of a share's nominal value must be paid on application[23]; in the case of Plcs, at least 25 per cent must be paid then, along with any premium on the shares.[24]

8–23   If the offer is accepted, the company will allot the requisite number of shares to that person and enter his name on its register of members.[25] "Allotted" is defined as "when a person acquires the unconditional right to be included in the company's register of members in respect of those shares".[26] The term "issue" with regard to shares has slightly different meanings according to the context.[27] The general principles of contract law govern the offer and acceptance here, such as informal and conditional offers; acceptance within a reasonable time, by post or otherwise; notification of acceptance; revocation of the offer or acceptance; mistake,[28] etc. For tax purposes, shares

---

[22]   See www.enterprise-ireland.com.
[23]   1963 Act, s.53(1).
[24]   1983 Act, s.28.
[25]   See *BCM's Precedents* part C, containing model subscription and related agreements.
[26]   1983 Act, s.2(2).
[27]   *National Westminster Bank v Inland Revenue* [1995] 1 A.C. 119.
[28]   e.g. *EIC Services Ltd v Phipps* [2005] 1 W.L.R. 1377.

are treated as having been issued under a letter of allotment unless the right to them remains provisional until acceptance and there has been no accept-ance.[29] Within one month of making the allotment, a return must be sent by the company to the Registrar of Companies containing specified details of the transaction.[30]

Minimum Amounts

8–24 A major cause of company failure is under-capitalisation, by which is meant having a volume of turnover and of debtors that is far in excess of what the firm's contributed capital can sustain. It, therefore, is often argued that companies should not be permitted to trade unless the subscribers and members put a minimum amount of capital into them. Persons who decry the ease with which the corporate entity can be availed of to avoid, if not evade, legal obligations also look to a peremptory minimum capital as the panacea.

8–25 Under the 1963 Act, there was no specific legal duty to ensure that a company had sufficient capital to finance the business embarked upon, other than that a company might not allot shares to the public for the first time until it has raised the "minimum amount"[31] (5 per cent of the nominal share capital) and that corporate officers become personally liable for the company's debts where they permit it to trade when there is no reasonable prospect of its debts being paid.[32] In many continental European countries, by contrast, to do business as any of the more important categories of com-pany, it has been necessary to have a sizeable minimum authorised capital and a minimum paid-up capital; and where a company's capital is seriously depleted, a general meeting must be convened to consider what should be done.

8–26 Requirements along these lines were adopted in 1983, principally for Plcs,[33] which must have a minimum authorised capital of €38,092.41 and, when allotting shares, at least one quarter of their nominal value must be paid up, together with the full amount of any premium payable on them.

Consideration

8–27 While companies usually prefer to allot their shares for the highest premium over their nominal value that can be obtained, occasions can arise where, without any suggestion of fraud, shares can be allotted only at a discount, i.e. for less than their nominal or par value. The company's business, for instance, may have been doing so badly that its €1 shares now stand at 40 cent in the market; if it wishes to raise further capital by issuing additional

---

[29] Taxes Consolidation Act 1997, s.5(1).
[30] 1963 Act, s.58 and Form B5.
[31] 1963 Act, s.53.
[32] 1963 Act, s.297.
[33] See para.15–15 *et seq.*

shares of that class, it will not attract subscribers if it fixes the subscription price at more than what those shares can be obtained for in the market. However, in *Ooregum Gold Mining Co. v Roper*[34] it was held that it was implicit in the very structure of the Companies Acts that limited companies may not allot their shares for less than par. As Lord Macnaghten explained, the Acts: "proceed on the footing of recognising and maintaining the liability of the individual members to the company until the prescribed limit is reached. [Accordingly,] the liability of a member continues so long as anything remains unpaid upon his shares. Nothing but payment, and payment in full, can put an end to the liability".[35] An exception to this principle was allowed in special circumstances, with the court's approval,[36] but it was rarely availed of and was repealed.

Allotment at a Discount

8–28 Regardless of whether a company is limited or unlimited, its "shares … shall not be allotted at a discount".[37] This iron rule admits of no exceptions or qualification other than certain brokerage and commissions and, possibly, where the company was formed with the express object of acquiring a particular asset by allotting its shares to the vendor. This situation arose in *Re Leinster Contract Corp.*,[38] where the company was incorporated to acquire certain patent rights in return for its shares, but the patents proved to be valueless. It was held that, as there was no fraud there, the allotment to the vendor could not be set aside. Since the shares were issued as fully paid, the allotment was not regarded as *ultra vires* because the entire transaction "was not only contemplated, but imperatively required by the very constitution of the company".[39] However, this decision may not represent the law today since it did not deal with an explicit statutory prohibition. It was held in the *Ooregum Gold Mining* case[40] that the original allottees who hold shares that were allotted at a discount are liable to pay the company the difference between their issue price and the par value. Under the 1983 Act, the allottees of such shares are liable in the same way, as are subsequent holders in the extended sense unless they satisfy the defence for *bona fide* purchasers for value without notice,[41] as described below.

"Watering" Shares

8–29 Watering shares means a company allotting its shares for a consideration that is worth less than their issue price and, in particular, less than their par value. The objection to that practice is that it gives a wholly misleading picture

---

[34] [1892] A.C. 125.
[35] *ibid.* at 144 and 145.
[36] 1963 Act, s.63.
[37] 1983 Act, s.27.
[38] [1902] 1 I.R. 349.
[39] *ibid.* at 359; *cf. Re British Seamless Paper Box Co.* (1881) 17 Ch D 467.
[40] [1892] A.C. 125.
[41] Section 26(4).

of a company's true worth, and can be a device for defrauding shareholders and creditors. To ensure some equivalence between the face value of shares allotted to subscribers and the consideration that the company receives from them in return, the 1963 Act prohibited issuing shares at a discount and struck at transactions where the discrepancy in value was patent or there was fraud. These standards are now supplemented by exacting provisions of the 1983 Act for Plcs,[42] the thrust of which is to prohibit them from allotting shares for consideration of dubious value and to ensure a degree of equality in exchange in transactions between Plcs and their initial members.

8–30   Subject to the conditions and exceptions outlined below, private companies may allot their shares for a consideration other than cash, for instance, in return for property or for some service that someone has undertaken to perform for the company. This principle is now endorsed by statute, that "shares allotted by a company and any premium payable on them may be paid up in money or money's worth (including goodwill and expertise)".[43] When any private company proposes to allot shares in return for some consideration other than cash, it is for the company itself to determine what that consideration is worth. In companies subject to Table A, this discretion is consigned to the board of directors, who can allot shares "on such terms and conditions ... as they may consider to be in the best interests of the company and its shareholders".[44] But this state of affairs can make it relatively easy for companies to evade the proscription against allotting shares at a discount; acquiring property at a greatly overvalued price in consideration for its shares is no different in substance from allotting those shares for less than their par value.

8–31   *Registering the Contracts*: Where any limited company allots shares for a non-cash consideration, within one month, it must deliver to the Registrar of Companies the relevant stamped contracts and returns.[45] These are the written contract constituting the allottee's title to the shares in question; the contract for the consideration obtained, be it property or goods or services, or of other consideration; a return stating the number and nominal amount of the shares allotted, the extent to which they are treated as paid up and the consideration for them. If any of these contracts is not written, then a duly stamped statement of its particulars must be registered. In this way, shareholders and the public generally can be informed of precisely what consideration shares have been allotted for.

8–32   However, these requirements do not apply where the company already owes money to the allottee and it simply sets off that sum against the price of the shares. For a cash payment has traditionally been regarded as including the exercise of a right of set-off.[46] Where there are mutual debts between the

---

[42]   See para.15–18 *et seq.*
[43]   1983 Act, s.26(1).
[44]   Article 5.
[45]   1963 Act, s.58 and Form 52.
[46]   *cf.* 1983 Act, s.2(3)(a).

company and an applicant for its shares, it is "not necessary that the parties should go through the form of handing the money over and receiving it back or giving crossed cheques".[47] Accordingly, registration of the contract can be avoided by the company first issuing the shares for cash, the allottee then selling assets to the company for cash and the company then setting these debts off against each other.

8–33 *Bona Fides and Honesty*: In determining the value of property or some other advantage that the company will acquire on allotting its shares, the directors must not violate their general duties of acting with due care and skill, nor abuse their powers or put themselves in a situation where conflicts of interests arise. However, these duties are owed to the company, not to its shareholders and creditors. So far as the company itself is concerned, it has an extensive discretion to place a value on the consideration it will accept for its shares. As it was put in *Re Wragg Ltd*,[48] where the previous authorities on this question were reviewed:

> "the obligation of every shareholder in a limited company to pay the company the nominal amount of his shares [can] be satisfied by a transaction which amount[s] to accord and satisfaction as distinguished from payment in cash. As regards the value of the property which a company can take from a shareholder ... unless the agreement [can] be impeached for fraud, the value of the property or the services [can] not be inquired into. In other words, the value at which the company is content to accept the property must be treated as its value as between itself and the shareholder whose liability is charged by its means.
>
> It has ... never been decided that a limited company cannot buy property or pay for services at any price it thinks proper, and pay for them in fully paid up shares. Provided a limited company does so honestly and not colourably, and provided that it has not been so imposed upon as to be entitled to be relieved from its bargains [such] agreements are valid and binding on the company and their creditors."[49]

8–34 There are three circumstances where the courts will set aside the valuation placed by a company on non-cash consideration received for its shares. One is where fraud has been established; yet fraud is notoriously difficult to prove. Another is where the consideration given is wholly "illusory".[50] The third is where it is patently obvious from the very terms of the contract that the property is worth less than the nominal value of the shares being allotted and any premium, if there is one.[51] Sometimes schemes of arrangement or other

---

[47] *North Sydney Investment Co. v Higgins* [1899] A.C. 263 at 273.

[48] [1897] 1 Ch. 796.

[49] *ibid.* at 826, 827 and 830; applied in *Park Business Interiors Ltd v Park* [1992] B.C.L.C. 1034. For a critique of *Wragg*, see Guigni, "Consideration for Shares Issues: Price or Value?" 65 *Australian L.J.* 379 (1991).

[50] e.g. *Re Eddystone Marine Ins. Co.* [1893] 3 Ch.9; compare *Re Theatrical Trust Ltd* [1951] 1 Ch. 771 and *Re Leinster Contract Corp.* [1902] 1 I.R. 349.

[51] e.g. *Re White Star Line Ltd* [1938] Ch. 458 and *Mosely v Koffyfontein Mines Ltd* [1904] 2 Ch. 108.

measures for reorganising companies' capital structure can fall foul of the anti-watering rule.

8–35 Apart from such instances, the court will not inquire into the value of the consideration; the general principle is that it is for the contracting parties alone to judge the adequacy of consideration being exchanged. The *Salomon & Co.* case,[52] which was decided in the same year as *Re Wragg Ltd*, is a licence for over-optimism in valuing assets that are acquired in return for shares. Lord Macnaghten described the price of £39,000, at which Mr Salomon valued his business when he transferred it to his company in exchange for its shares and debentures, as an "extravagant" price, "a sum which represented the sanguine expectations of a fond owner rather than anything that can be called a businesslike or reasonable estimate of value".[53] But fraud was not alleged, the consideration given was not entirely illusory and the value placed on his business was not demonstrably insufficient on the face of the contract. This case was decided at a time when there was no express statutory prohibition against allotting shares at a discount. It is possible that the approach adopted there no longer fully reflects the law; that where the evidence points persuasively to a substantial overvaluation of assets, the burden then falls on the allottee to demonstrate that there was no hidden discount.

Liability

8–36 In the light of *Ooregum Gold Mining*[54] it would appear that where, to the knowledge of the board and the allottees, overvalued consideration is exchanged for shares, the company may recover any deficiency from the allottees, at least where they still own the shares. The issue that arose in *Pilmer v Duke Group Ltd*[55] was the liability of financial advisers where, in a takeover bid, the bidder issued shares in exchange for the target's shares but the latter proved to be worth far less than they were believed to be worth at the time. Presumably because dishonesty was not involved and the discrepancy in values was not patent, the target company was not sued. While the defendant was held to be subject to a duty of care to the bidder and was negligent in the valuations he had made of the target's shares, it was held that no damages were recoverable for the curious reason that the bidder had lost nothing sufficiently tangible to justify awarding compensation.

8–37 Persons who have acquired shares in respect of which the original allottees are liable to pay sums to the company under the requirements regarding minimum amounts and allotting shares at a discount or for a non-cash consideration, are protected.[56] This applies where the holder of the shares was a purchaser for value of them and at the time he bought them had no

---

"actual notice" of the violation, or he derived title to the shares from a person who had acquired them and was not so liable. Notice here is "of the facts which constitute the contravention. It does not require the offending [persons] to be learned in the law".[57] A holder of shares in this context has an extended meaning, including as well as transferees who are registered members, persons who are unconditionally entitled to be but are not so registered, and also persons unconditionally entitled to have an instrument of transfer executed in their favour. Additionally, the court may declare valid any issue of shares which is invalid.[58]

Share Premia

8–38 It is common in successful companies to issue shares at a premium, i.e. at a price above their nominal or par value, e.g. €1 shares at €1.60. The excess over par is the share premium. Under Table A, it is for the directors to decide whether to issue shares at a premium and the size of any premium.[59] Although the courts hesitate to interfere with essentially business decisions, like the issue price for shares (provided it is above par), flagrant abuse by the directors of the share-issuing power for discriminatory or self-serving reasons would be a breach of fiduciary duties and, in appropriate circumstances, might provide the basis of "oppression" under s.205 of the 1963 Act. A very low issue price could call for justification in that, apart from any impact the share issue may have on relative voting strengths within the company, the exceptionally favourable issue terms prevent the company from raising more funds than it otherwise could have done, and give the new shareholders an extremely lucrative investment opportunity. But there is no overriding duty to allot shares for as high a premium as can be obtained in the market. Nor is it *per se* wrong to allot shares at par even though other investors are prepared to pay a substantial premium for them. In *Hilder v Dexter*[60] to raise working capital, a company issued shares at par and gave options to take further shares at par at some later stage. When the price of its shares rose significantly in the market, the holders of those options sought to exercise them. It was held that there is no "law" which obliged a company to issue its shares above par because they are saleable at a premium in the market.[61]

8–39 The aggregate amount or value of any premium received must be placed in a share premium account, which is treated mostly in the same way as contributed capital.[62] It can only be repaid to the shareholders through the capital reduction mechanism set out in ss.72–77.[63] This sum may be used either to finance the issue to existing members of fully paid-up "bonus" shares, or to defray the company's preliminary expenses, or the cost of issuing shares

---

[57] *System Control Plc v Munro Corporate Plc* [1990] B.C.L.C. 659 at 663.
[58] 1963 Act, s.89.
[59] Article 5.
[60] [1902] A.C. 474.
[61] *ibid.* at 480.
[62] 1963 Act, s.62.
[63] See para.11–35 *et seq.*

or debentures in the company, or to pay any commission or discount on such an issue.

Calls

8–40   When a company allots shares, it does not invariably insist on the full amount due on them being paid up there and then. Instead, the shares may be only partly paid up and further payments are deferred until shareholders are called upon to pay up. Often questions about the accuracy of statements contained in a prospectus, and about ownership of and title to shares, arise in the context of disputes about liability for calls. A member who disposes of his shares is no longer liable for calls on them.[64] Where a shareholder petitions for an arrangement with his creditors and subsequently the company makes calls on those shares, the call is not a debt provable in the arrangement.[65]

8–41   Companies whose articles of association so provide, may differentiate between shareholders in the amounts of and times for paying calls, and may accept payments of unpaid amounts although they have not been called up.[66] Provisions to this effect are contained in Table A[67] which, *inter alia*, permit the company to pay not more than 5 per cent interest on uncalled amounts that have been paid up. Directors from time to time may make calls on unpaid amounts on shares, provided that no call shall exceed a quarter of the share's nominal value or be payable within a month of the time when the last preceding call should have been paid.[68]

8–42   While the courts will not interfere with most determinations regarding calls, on the grounds that they are primarily matters of business policy to be decided by the board, on a number of occasions calls have been set aside on the grounds that they were unfairly discriminatory. In *Galloway v Halle Concerts Society*,[69] the plaintiffs had been in dispute with the directors, had been slow in paying up calls in the past and had not paid anything on a third call. Because of this, the directors resolved to call up all outstanding amounts on their shares. It was held that these circumstances did not furnish sufficient justification for treating the plaintiffs so differently from other shareholders—for violating the "implied condition of equality between shareholders in a company".[70] Not alone will a court declare void and enjoin a call made in those circumstances, but it was held in *Alexander v Automatic Telephone Co.*[71] that shareholders who had paid up over half the nominal amount on their shares could sue directors who, without disclosing it to the plaintiffs, allotted a considerable number of the company's shares to themselves and made no calls

[64]   *Re Discoverers' Finance Corp., Lindlar's* [1910] 1 Ch. 312.
[65]   *Re Ligoniel Spinning Co., Ex p. Bank of Ireland* [1900] 1 I.R. 250.
[66]   1963 Act, s.66.
[67]   Articles 20 and 21.
[68]   Article 15.
[69]   [1915] 2 Ch. 233.
[70]   *ibid.* at 239.
[71]   [1900] 2 Ch. 56.

whatsoever on them. Procedural irregularities in the way directors make calls can render them invalid, like where directors were not properly appointed, where there was no quorum when they met and where the number of members fell below what the articles required; but not every procedural slip-up is fatal to a call.

Issuing Additional Shares

8–43 Virtually every business that is growing will need to raise further capital at one or more stages of its existence; it is rarely that a firm can expand entirely on the strength of retained earnings or borrowings. Companies have a broad discretion to increase their share capital, if their articles of association so provide.[72] But exercise of this power can in effect be blocked by appropriate provisions in a shareholders' agreement.[73] Power to issue additional shares is usually conferred by the articles, either on the members in general meeting or on the directors. Under Table A, the general meeting is empowered to issue new shares, be they identical to those already issued or some entirely new class of shares.[74] Between 1862 and 1963, Table A gave existing shareholders a right of pre-emption. In the ensuing 20 years, the board had a wide discretion about to whom and on what terms unissued shares should be allotted.[75] As was explained when considering directors' duties,[76] the directors could improperly seek to change the balance of power within the company by allotting additional shares to themselves or to their favourites. The courts intervened on occasion to prevent the share allotment power from being so abused.

8–44 One of the EC Second Directive's main objectives is their "equal treatment of the shareholders in the same position" and, to that end, it requires measures restricting the freedom that company boards and even shareholders had in respect of issuing additional shares. The two most important of these are the requirements of specific shareholder authority and compulsory pre-emption.

Authority

8–45 A company's directors shall not allot additional shares unless they are authorised to do so as follows.[77] Such authority must be contained either in an ordinary resolution of the general meeting[78] or in the articles of association, and must state the maximum amount of shares that may be allotted. This authority may be particular or general, conditional or unconditional; that is to say, it can leave it entirely to the directors to determine to whom and on what terms the shares may be allotted, or it may set out who the allottees are or what the terms of allotment are to be. Any authority, moreover, must state how long

---

[72] 1963 Act, s.68(1)(a).
[73] See para.13–28.
[74] Articles 2 and 4.
[75] Article 5.
[76] See para.7–110 *et seq.*
[77] 1983 Act, s.20.
[78] Subject to s.143 of the 1963 Act.

it is to last, which period cannot exceed five years, although it may be renewed for a further five–year period at most. The general meeting retains the power by ordinary resolution to vary or revoke any such authority. But an allotment not so authorised is not thereby invalid.[79] These requirements do not apply to an allotment made in pursuance of an employees' share scheme.[80] Nor do these affect a right to subscribe for or to convert into shares other than those being allotted, but they apply to the grant of such a right.

Rights Issue/Pre-emption

8–46   Having decided to raise further capital by issuing additional shares, the question that then confronts the company is to whom should it look for the funds. Should it ask its existing shareholders to subscribe for the additional equity, or should the shares be offered to outsiders, even to the general public? Usually in the case of small companies and often with big companies, the new shares are offered initially to the existing shareholders before being offered to outsiders. This is called a "rights" issue; the existing shareholders are given a prior right to subscribe for the new shares. Where the company's shares are quoted on a stock exchange, it is common to offer such rights at a price substantially below the market value of the already issued shares, and to make the rights renounceable in favour of anybody. For instance, a company with 100,000 issued shares of €1 par value, that are worth €1.90, may decide to offer an additional 50,000 shares of €1 par to its shareholders on a *pro rata* basis at, say, €1.20 a share. The relative attractiveness of this price and the desire to maintain their proportionate stake in the company will induce many of those shareholders to take up their rights by applying for the new shares. Some, however, may not wish to do this and, if the rights are fully renounceable, they can sell them to outsiders wishing to invest in the company. Depending on the demand, it may be possible to sell the rights at an appreciable profit. For instance, investors may be prepared to pay 40 cent a share for the right to acquire shares in the above company at €1.20 each. A listed company's offer relating to a rights issue must remain open for acceptance for at least 21 days and, where existing holders do not take up their rights, the company must ensure that any premium obtained for their shares goes to them.[81]

8–47   Pre-emption in this context means compulsory rights issues, i.e. obliging companies when they issue new equity to do so by giving their shareholders a first option on those shares in proportion to their existing holdings. Shareholders value pre-emption because it enables them to protect their stake in the company from dilution. They can retain what proportionate voting strength they possess and, if the company becomes progressively more profitable, they have an exceptionally favourable outlet for funds at their disposal.

---

[79]   1983 Act, s.20(8).
[80]   See para.19–11.
[81]   Listing Rules 6.5.4–6.5.6.

8–48 Before 1983 there was no general principle that gave existing share-holders a pre-emptive right to any new shares being issued.[82] In *Mutual Life Insurance Co. of New York v Rank Organisation Ltd*,[83] it was said that, in the absence of a contrary stipulation in a company's own regulations, "no shareholder ... has any right ... to expect that his fractional interest in the company would remain for ever constant".[84] The defendant proposed to issue further shares without giving all of its shareholders a first option on them. Principally to avoid having to comply with onerous US securities regulations, it proposed to offer the new shares to all its members except its American share-holders. This was challenged as being unfairly discriminatory. But it was upheld on the grounds that company law does not invariably require identity of treatment and there was no evidence, nor indeed any allegation, that the decision there was prompted by some improper motive. A court might possibly prohibit directors offering further shares to all members on a *pro rata* basis where the directors knew that a minority shareholder, who would dearly like to take up his proportion of shares, is temporarily short of funds. Such action was held to be unlawful in the special circumstances of one English unreported case.[85] Yet in an American case, decided in a state where pre-emption was compulsory, it was said that directors are "not to blame for a shareholder's failure to obtain the money necessary for him to avail himself of his pre-emption rights".[86] Subject to several exceptions, pre-emption has been made compulsory for all companies.[87]

"Bonus" Shares

8–49 Except where the articles of association provide otherwise, or the company is insolvent or its accumulated losses exceed retained earnings, prof-its earned in the past and that were placed in reserve may be drawn upon in order to pay dividends. Often, however, sizeable sums that build up in the profit and loss account or the reserves are capitalised. That is to say, those funds are used to finance a further issue of the company's shares, which are distributed free to the existing members. By free here means that the reserves are used to pay for those shares, either entirely or in part. For example, say over €30,000 has accumulated in the profit and loss account and it is decided that this entire sum should be capitalised; and say the company's issued share cap-ital is 25,000 shares of €1 each. Capitalisation would mean every shareholder being given one and one fifth shares for each share that he owns. A similar method can be used to pay up as calls unpaid amounts outstanding on shares. Take the same figures as above but say that only 10 cents has been paid up on

---

[82] See generally, Macneil, "Shareholders' Pre-Emptive Rights", [2002] *J. Bus. L.* 78.

[83] [1985] B.C.L.C. 11.

[84] *ibid.* at 24; *cf. Kerry Co-Op Creameries Ltd v An Bord Bainne* [1991] I.L.R.M. 851 applying this principle to industrial and provident societies.

[85] *Pennell v Venida Investments Ltd* (July 25, 1984, Templeman J.), discussed in Burridge, "Wrongful Rights Issues" 44 *Mod. L. Rev.* 40 (1981).

[86] *Hyman v Velsical Corp.* (1951) 342 111; App. 489, 97 N.R. (2d) 122.

[87] 1983 Act, s.23. See para.9–44 *et seq.*

the €1 shares. In a capitalisation, there is no reason in principle why bonus shares cannot be issued nil paid.

8–50 Companies capitalise retained earnings principally to prevent their balance sheets from being misleading, so that the figure representing capital in those accounts corresponds more closely to the amounts originally invested and what has been ploughed back into the business. Some shareholders, more-over, may be pleased with their apparent windfall, and the more impecunious of them may be tempted to sell off what they obtain as a bonus. Another motive for capitalising is to deter takeover bidders with their eyes on the company's bank balances, in that capitalised reserves can only be paid out *in specie* to the shareholders under the elaborate ss.72–77 capital reduction procedure[88] or through the special procedures for companies purchasing or redeeming their own shares.[89]

8–51 Table A empowers the general meeting, on the directors' recommenda-tion, to capitalise reserves and other amounts that are available for distribution as dividends[90] and gives the directors authority to take various measures to give effect to a resolution to capitalise.[91] Sums that are capitalised in this way must be "applied on behalf of the members who would have been entitled to receive the same if the same had been distributed by way of dividend and in the same proportions ..." In other words, the amounts of the bonus shares allotted, or amounts paid on shares that were not fully paid up, are to be in the same proportion as shareholders are entitled to on distributions of dividends. Capitalisation of retained earnings, which on account of the 1983 Act's rules against paying dividends from capital are not available for distribution, can be done only by way of financing an allotment of fully paid bonus shares.[92] Where bonus shares were issued on the erroneous assumption that there were distributable profits to cover all or even part of the issue, it was been held that there was a common mistake, rendering the entire issue void.[93] A similar con-clusion was reached when the requisite ordinary resolution approving a bonus issue had not been passed and, further, other requirements in the company's articles governing the issue of bonus shares had not been satisfied, in particular that the issue should be *pro rata* with the fully paid-up shares in the company.[94]

Validation

8–52 On account of the complexity of the regime governing the issue of shares, the court is empowered to declare valid certain transactions that strictly would be invalid. If the court deems it "just and equitable" to do so, it may declare valid the creation or issue of any shares, or their repurchase or

---

[88] See para.11–35 *et seq.*
[89] See para.8–102 *et seq.*
[90] Article 130.
[91] Article 131.
[92] Article 130A.
[93] *Re Cleveland Trust Plc* [1991] B.C.L.C. 424.
[94] *EIC Services Ltd v Phipps* [2005] 1 W.L.R. 1377.

redemption.[95] This power does not exist if the share acquisition was not funded from distributable profits or from the proceeds of a fresh share issue, or were not authorised by the company's articles of association. In *Re Sugar Distribution Ltd*,[96] Keane J. described the object of the power here as, where "the validity of the transaction is in question, persons who had innocently subscribed or paid for the share could find that they had spent their money for no return, because of a defect ... of which they had no knowledge and could not be expected to have any knowledge".[97] Accordingly, the possible hardship involved can "be avoided if it could be done in a manner which would not be unjust or unequitable having regard to the interests of any other persons who were or might be affected by the transaction in question."[98] But he refused to validate an irregular issue of redeemable preference shares there because, it being an inter-group transaction, the professed objective could have been achieved by other means within the group. More importantly, the real objective was to enable the ostensible holder of those shares and its associated company to gain a substantial tax advantage by validating "seriously irregular transactions". The court was being "asked to subscribe to the fiction that meetings took place with never took place and that resolutions were passed which were never passed",[99] so that the applicants could reap a tax windfall. Keane J. emphasised that he was expressing no view on the findings of inspectors that the share issue there was effected to deceive and defraud the Revenue.

INVESTOR PROTECTION

8–53 One of the earliest major concerns of company law, which was the focus of many of the leading cases around the end of the nineteenth century, was to protect investors against being duped into putting their money into financially unsound companies. Before the Companies Acts addressed this issue, there were two governing principles. Where the investor acquires securities from an existing shareholder or holder of debentures, the maxim *caveat emptor* applies[100]: a purchaser buys at his own risk and there is no legal obligation on the seller to disclose material information that might influence the decision to buy. But a seller who provided inaccurate information in order to make the sale might in the circumstances be liable in tort for deceit or for negligent misrepresentation, or for breach of a stipulation regarding disclosure in the sale contract.

8–54 Where, on the other hand, the shares are acquired directly from the company in question, by way of application and allotment, or from some intermediary who is disposing of them on the company's behalf, the company or

---

[95] 1963 Act, s.89.
[96] [1995] 2 I.R. 194.
[97] *ibid.* at 207.
[98] *ibid.* at 207.
[99] *ibid.* at 210.
[100] *Seddon v North Eastern Salt Co.* [1905] 1 Ch. 326.

intermediary not only must not make material misrepresentations, but are under a duty to disclose relevant material information to the prospective investor. As Palles C.B. explained in *Components Tube Co. v Naylor*,[101] there is a:

> "distinction between an ordinary purchase [of shares] and the purchase from a company of some of its shares. It is utterly immaterial to an ordinary purchaser to know what the vendor will do with the purchase money when he gets it. The purchaser has no further interest in it. But an applicant for shares in a company is in a totally different position. His money becomes part of the capital of the company, and to him it is all important to know what sort of persons are to have control of his money when he has paid it, and how that money is to be applied, whether upon the enterprise itself or in remunerating, perhaps with lavish extravagance, those who have brought the company into existence."[102]

8–55 As FitzGibbon L.J put it in *Aaron's Reefs Ltd v Twiss*, "[t]hough *uberrima fidei*, *i.e.* the obligation to disclose everything known that could influence an intending subscriber, is not demanded of the authors of a prospectus, no case has, as yet, applied the rule of *caveat emptor* to an invitation to the public to take shares".[103] While strictly speaking agreements to allot shares are not *uberrimae fidei*, they are so in practice because non-disclosure by or on behalf of a company that solicits investment in itself is sufficient basis for the court to set aside the allotment where rescission remains possible.

8–56 Beginning with the provisions of the Companies Act 1845 on prospectuses[104] and those of the Directors' Liability Act 1890[105] on personal liability in damages, the common law rules and equity principles were supplemented by a detailed code governing offers of shares to the investing public. It is now contained in the Prospectus (Directive 2003/71/EC) Regulations 2005 and Pt 5 (ss. 38–55) of the 2005 Act. This complex regime for public securities regulation is discussed separately below.[106] Many of the early cases on the non-statutory regime for investing in unquoted securities, considered here, concerned public offers.

Promoters

8–57 A company promoter is someone who plays an instrumental role in forming a company and getting it going. Sometimes promoters are professionals, like merchant banks and investment houses that specialise in establishing companies and getting the public to invest in them. But a sole trader who, like Mr Salomon in the *Salomon & Co.* case[107] takes steps to convert a business into a registered company, is just as much a promoter. In the past the duties and

---

[101] [1900] 2 I.R. 1.
[102] *ibid.* at 51, referring to *Twycross v Grant* (1877) 2 C.P.D. 469 at 483.
[103] [1895] 2 I.R. 207 at 269; aff'd [1896] A.C. 273.
[104] 8 & 9 Vic. c.16.
[105] 53 & 54 Vic. c.64.
[106] See para.15–63 *et seq.*
[107] [1897] A.C. 22.

responsibilities of company promoters generated a sizeable quantity of litigation. Many of those cases concerned schemes devised by fraudsters to persuade individuals to invest in worthless enterprises. In the popular mind, the word promoter had connotations of a high-living financier who prospered from complex schemes of questionable financial merit. The classic definition is anyone who "undertakes to form a company with reference to a given project, and to get it going and ... takes the necessary steps to accomplish that purpose".[108] Whether a person is a promoter, and when a promotion begins and ends, are questions of fact, although there are numerous authorities indicating where the lines have been drawn.[109]

Remuneration

8–58 Professional promoters especially require remuneration for their services to the company in getting it going. Their payment can take various forms; for instance, a fixed sum of money, an option on the company's shares, or a commission or a direct profit on sales of property to the company. The *Salomon & Co*-type promoter may look to some paper profit by transferring his business to the new company at a favourable price. Any contract for either reimbursing promotion expenses or for remuneration, made on the company's behalf before it was incorporated, will not bind the company unless it is subsequently ratified. It would appear that any contract for services must be made before those services were rendered, because past services are not consideration[110]; although the promoter may be entitled to some payment on a *quantum meruit* basis. Table A authorises the directors to pay the expenses incurred in promoting and registering the company.[111]

Duties to the Company

8–59 On account of the tremendous influence over embryo and infant companies that promoters possess, there are significant opportunities for them to make a profit for themselves at the company's or the investors' expense. The commonest promoters' fraud, perhaps, is the sale by them to the company of their own property at inflated prices. Promoters are subject to the same general fiduciary standards as apply to company directors. They are not permitted to make secret profits from their activities; in view of their situation of at least potential conflict of interests, they must disclose all matters to the company relevant to how they may be remunerated, either directly or indirectly.

8–60 As promoters frequently are a company's first shareholders and directors, a particularly vexed question has been in what circumstances

---

[108] *Twycross v Grant* (1877) 2 C.P.D. 469 at 541.
[109] e.g. *Gluckstein v Barnes* [1900] A.C. 240.
[110] *Re Eddystone Marine Insurance Co.* [1893] 3 Ch. 9.
[111] Article 80.

disclosure to the company constitutes disclosure to themselves only and, accordingly, is not effective disclosure. The rule is that it is "incumbent upon the promoters to take care that in forming the company they provide it with an executive, i.e. with a board of directors, who shall both be aware that the property which they are asked to buy is the property of the promoters, and who shall be competent and impartial judges as to whether the purchase ought or ought not to be made".[112] In one case, a promoter-director's contention that the company had been informed of all the profits he had made was rejected as absurd, because disclosure "[i]s not the most appropriate word to use when a person who plays many parts announces to himself in one character what he has done and is doing in another".[113] In the *Salomon & Co.* case,[114] it was held that informing all the initial shareholders, even though they are dominated by the promoters, satisfies the disclosure rule where the shares have not changed hands afterwards and new shares are not issued to outsiders.[115] The plaintiff had promoted a company that acquired his boot-manufacturing business at what may have been an excessive price. Assuming that the price was exorbitant, it was said that "when all the shareholders are perfectly cognizant of the conditions under which the company is formed and the conditions of the purchase, it is impossible to contend that the company is being defrauded".[116] In stressing that the disclosure rule is satisfied where approval for an acquisition from promoters is given "by all the shareholders who ever were, or were likely to be, members of the company",[117] Lord Watson intimated that disclosure of a promoter's profit to all the then shareholders does not discharge the fiduciary responsibility where it is envisaged, for instance, that the promoters will dispose of their shares in the company in the not-too-distant future.[118]

8–61   To protect Plcs from the kind of promoter fraud that *Salomon & Co* might render permissible, independent valuation and reporting requirements were introduced for where any subscriber to a Plc's memorandum of association, within two years of the company becoming entitled to do business, sells it some non-cash asset in return for a consideration worth at least one-tenth of the company's issued share capital.[119]

The Company's Remedies

8–62   A company's principal remedies for breach of promoters' duties are rescission of any contract with them and disgorgement of their profits.[120] In

---

[112] *Erlanger v New Sombrero Phosphate Co.* (1878) 3 App. Cas. 1218 at 1236.
[113] *Gluckstein v Barnes* [1900] A.C. 240 at 249.
[114] [1897] A.C. 22.
[115] *ibid.* at 33.
[116] *ibid.* at 37.
[117] Compare *Old Dominion Copper Mining & Smelting Co. v Lewisohn* 210 US 2006 (1907) with *Old Dominion Copper Mining & Smelting Co. v Bigelow*, 89 NE 193 (1909), aff'd 225 US 111 (1912).
[118] [1897] A.C. at 37–38.
[119] See para.15–11 *et seq.*
[120] See generally, J. Cartwright, *Misrepresentation, Mistake and Non-Disclosure*, 2nd edn (London: Sweet & Maxwell, 2007).

Lagunas Nitrate Co. v Lagunas Syndicate,[121] promoters made a sizeable profit in forming a company, of which they became the directors and original share-holders, and then issued a prospectus, on foot of which many investors acquired shares in it. Subsequently, the company sued its promoters to recover their profit on the grounds that full disclosure had not been made to the share-holders. Lindley M.R. drew attention to one remarkable aspect of the case: that not one individual who had subscribed for shares had brought a claim against the company or the promoters. Since, in principle, a company is legally sepa-rate from its shareholders and since the real complaint in cases like this is that investors have been duped into buying the company's shares, one might have expected that the action by the company itself would be struck out on the basis of reverse "reflective loss".[122] It, however, was concluded that:

> "it does not follow that the ... company, in its corporate capacity, may not prove a case entitling it to relief. It may prove such concealment of material facts or such misrepresentations as to entitle it to repudiate the contracts [with its promoters] unless [they] can show that the members of the company knew the real truth, and were not, therefore, imposed upon [because] [t]he ... company, although, in one sense formed when registered, was not completely formed as contemplated by the promoters, until a prospectus had been issued and a huge capital had been subscribed. The issue of the prospectus was the last act of promotion."[123]

8–63 One of the best-known instances is *Gluckstein v Barnes*,[124] where the defendant was a member of a syndicate that bought the London Olympia exhi-bition hall for £140,000, then formed a company and sold it the hall for £180,000, disclosing a profit of £40,000. But there was no mention of an addi-tional profit of £20,000 he made by previously having bought up various charges on the property. In an action brought by the company's liquidator, it was held that an impermissible secret profit had been made and that an equivalent amount had to be returned to the company.

8–64 Provided it acts promptly after discovering their secret profit and that *restitutio in integrum* remains possible, the company can have the contract to purchase property from promoters rescinded and set aside. For instance, in *Erlanger v New Sombrero Phosphate Co.*[125] a syndicate bought leases on mines and later formed a company with "dummy" directors, which acquired those leases at an inflated price. The directors then offered shares in the company to the general public, without the full history of the leases being disclosed. When the new shareholders discovered the truth, they had the original directors removed and replaced by independent directors, who then sought to have the contract to acquire those leases set aside. Rescission was

---

[121] [1899] 2 Ch. 392.

[122] See para.22–47 *et seq.*

[123] [1899] 2 Ch. 392 at 428, 429.

[124] [1900] A.C. 240.

[125] (1878) 3 App. Cas. 1218.

ordered, one Law Lord observing that "those who deal inequitably with a company know that it must necessarily be slow in its proceedings, and are not entitled to complain that time elapes ... unless the delay is excessive".[126] By contrast, in the *Lagunas* case,[127] which was identical in most respects except that all allegations of fraud against the defendants were withdrawn, the court declined to order rescission because the assets acquired from the promoters had been transformed so much in the meantime that it was impossible to restore the parties to their original positions.

8–65   Secret profits made on property the promoter owned before the promotion actually commenced are not recoverable by the company; in such a case the only remedy is rescission provided that *restitutio in integrum* is still possible.[128] Where, however, this principle would lead to injustice, there is a tendency to hold that the promotion in fact commenced before the property was bought[129] or that the promoters committed deceit or "equitable fraud" and, therefore, are liable in damages or for equitable compensation.[130]

Shareholders' Remedies

8–66   Where persons have been unlawfully induced to subscribe for shares, their potential remedies are rescission of the contract to acquire those shares or to recover compensation for misrepresentation or for breach of the subscription contract. In the case of shares in a company that are or are about to be quoted on the Irish Stock Exchange, the Prospectus (Directive 2003/71/EC) Regulations and the 2005 Act (ss.41–43) impose a regime of virtual *caveat vendor*, in respect of which the company and its directors, as well as promoters and others, may be held liable in damages for losses incurred and also be subjected to substantial criminal penalties.[131] For investors outside this regime, damages cannot be recovered from the company and recovering damages from its directors requires proving deceit or establishing the requisite duty of care and surmounting the standard for liability.

Rescission

8–67   Rescission is one of the principal remedies where parties have contracted under some material mistake.[132] The main advantage of this remedy is that it can be obtained against the company itself and it is not dependent on proving fraud. It involves having the entire transaction cancelled and any purchase money refunded, together with interest and expenses, which in this context usually means obliging the company to repay the investment and having that shareholder's name removed from the register of members. One

---

[126] *ibid.* at 1282.
[127] [1899] 2 Ch. 392.
[128] *Re Cape Breton Co.* (1885) 29 Ch D 795.
[129] e.g. *Gluckstein v Barnes* [1900] A.C. 240 at 252.
[130] *cf. Re Leeds & Hanley Theatre of Varieties Ltd* [1902] 2 Ch. 809.
[131] See para.15–76 *et seq.*
[132] See para.8–62 *et seq.*

rationale for this remedy here is that, since an innocent principal is not always liable in damages for the fraud of an agent who exceeds the scope of his authority, and since a shareholder cannot recover damages against the company in respect of the shares,[133] "in relation to retaining a benefit obtained through the fraud [the company] cannot be in a better position than the fraudulent agent himself".[134] Rescission may be awarded even in the absence of any fraud; "a contract to [subscribe for] shares may be rescinded if it has been induced by a material allegation which was not true, even if there was no fraud in the matter".[135] It is often sought by investors seeking to disclaim liability for calls, on the grounds that they were unlawfully induced to subscribe for shares, *Aaron's Reefs Ltd v Twiss*[136] and *Components Tube Co. v Naylor*[137] being the leading Irish examples. A person who is entitled to rescind against the company can apply to have the register of members rectified.[138]

8–68   To succeed in a claim for rescission, the following conditions must be satisfied. The defendant's representation of fact must have been addressed to the plaintiff or it must have been known that the plaintiff's application for the securities was based on it. The inaccuracy must have been material or must have induced the plaintiff to acquire the securities. While as a general rule mere non-disclosure of some fact exclusively within a seller's knowledge is not a sufficient basis for rescission, this is not so where suppression of certain facts distorts the meaning of information that is volunteered[139]; nor is it so where the representation is a continuing one that, although originally correct, later becomes untrue.[140]

8–69   If an undue amount of time elapses before an investor looks for rescission or he deals with the securities in a manner that suggests affirmation of the purchase (such as attempts to sell them, acceptance of dividends, participating in general meetings etc.), the right to rescind is lost. In the *Aaron's Reefs* case the rule about delay and its rationale were stated as follows:

> "Lapse of time without rescinding will furnish evidence of an intention to affirm the contract. But the cogency of this evidence depends upon the particular circumstances of the case and the nature of the contract in question. Where a person has contracted to take shares in a company and his name has been placed on the register, it has always been held that he must exercise his right of repudiation with extreme promptness after the discovery of the fraud or misrepresentation for this reason: the presence of his name on the register may have induced other persons to give credit to the company or to become members of it."[141]

---

[133] See para.8–72.

[134] *Components Tube Co. v Naylor* [1900] 2 I.R. 1 at 37.

[135] *ibid.* at 26.

[136] [1896] A.C. 273, which affirmed [1895] 2 I.R. 207.

[137] [1900] 2 I.R. 1.

[138] 1963 Act, s.122.

[139] e.g. *Aaron's Reef v Twiss* [1896] A.C. 273, which affirmed [1895] 2 I.R. 207.

[140] e.g. *Briess v Woolley* [1954] A.C. 337.

[141] [1896] A.C. 273 at 294, affirming [1895] 2 I.R. 207.

There, a prospectus was issued in February 1890 offering shares in a company that had acquired a gold mine of doubtful value in Venezuela. It was promised in so many words that dividends of 100 per cent per annum would be paid once work on the mine got under way. The defendant subscribed for 100 shares, initially paying one shilling per £1 share. When, a year later, a call of four shillings per share was made, he refused to pay it, which led to his shares being forfeited. The company then sued him for the unpaid calls, to which he entered the defence that the prospectus was untrue in material respects. The fraud practised on him was unearthed only at the trial of the action, which was lengthy. It was held that he had not lost his right to rescind, since where there is fraud or breach of fiduciary duty time begins to run from when the truth is discovered. But in the case of innocent misrepresentation, it would appear that the right to rescind is barred by mere lapse of time, i.e. of such time as would enable a reasonably diligent person to discover the truth.[142]

8–70 Nor will rescission be ordered where *restitutio in integrum* becomes impossible or would disrupt third party rights.[143] But a change in the value of shares is no bar to rescission.[144] It was held in *Oakes v Turquand*[145] that rescission will not be ordered once proceedings have commenced to wind up a company, because third parties may have been dealing with the company on the basis that the person now claiming rescission was a shareholder. Whether *Oakes* was correctly decided has been doubted.[146]

Compensation

8–71 By compensation is meant financial recompense for loss suffered, this being principally in the nature of damages either for breach of contract, in tort or for breach of statutory duty;[147] it also includes indemnity and equitable compensation. A person who succeeds in obtaining rescission will also be entitled to an indemnity against liabilities incurred by having made the investment; such as where the shares acquired carried unlimited liability. The court's equitable jurisdiction includes the power to award compensation, as distinct from damages, where fiduciaries misapply property or otherwise violate their duties of good faith, and also where misrepresentations were made by persons other than strict fiduciaries[148]; though much of this latter area is now occupied by common law damages.

8–72 *No Damages against the Company*: Except where the shares are listed on a stock exchange, the investor who was defrauded or otherwise misled into subscribing for shares cannot obtain damages against the company itself.

---

[142] *cf. Leaf v International Galleries Ltd* [1950] 2 K.B. 86.

[143] *Northern Bank Finance Corp. v Charlton* [1979] I.R. 149.

[144] *Armstrong v Jackson* [1917] 2 K.B. 822.

[145] (1867) L.R. 2 H.L. 325; *cf. Tennant v City of Glasgow Bank* (1879) 4 App. Cas. 615.

[146] See generally, Wotherspoon, "Property by Any Other Name: The Trouble with Shareholder Claims in Australia" 81 *Australian L.J.* 75 (2007).

[147] See generally, H. McGregor, *Damages*, 17th edn (London: Sweet & Maxwell, 2003).

[148] *cf. Newbiggin v Adam* (1886) 34 Ch D 582.

Accordingly, his remedy is against the promoters, directors or whoever wrong-fully induced him to buy the shares. This somewhat anomalous rule was laid down in *Houldsworth v City of Glasgow Bank*,[149] where the plaintiff claimed damages against a company because its directors fraudulently induced him to subscribe for shares in it. A bank which failed, leaving enormous debts, and whose shares carried unlimited liability, was being wound up when the plain-tiff shareholder commenced his claim for damages (rescission then being impossible). Even though the purchaser of a chattel who is defrauded is allowed to retain it and sue for damages,[150] it was held that this option is not open to those who obtain shares by subscription. The reasons were that to award damages here would be "[i]nconsistent with the contract [with the company] into which [the member] has entered, and by which he wishes to abide"[151]; for a member to claim damages here "[I]n truth ... is trying to rec-oncile two inconsistent positions, mainly, that of shareholder and that of cred-itor of the whole body of shareholders including himself".[152] This rule runs against the fundamental principle of the company's separate legal personality. Its justification would appear to be that rescission and indemnity will not be ordered because that would unduly prejudice outsiders. Awarding damages against the company would have a similar effect, in that those sums would deplete whatever fund the company has for paying its third party creditors. For the company to pay damages to disappointed subscribers for its shares would be the equivalent of it repaying its capital in a manner not authorised by the Companies Acts. Another justification is the principle that the fraud of an agent acting outside the scope of his authority does not bind the innocent prin-cipal and the view that, in situations like that in *Houldsworth*, where directors fraudulently induced the parties to acquire the bulk of a company's shares, those directors should in this context be treated as acting beyond their author-ity.[153] Whether *Houldsworth* was correctly decided has also been doubted.[154]

8–73 It is possible that damages would be awarded against the company where the duped shareholders are only a minority and paying the award would not prejudice the company's creditors.[155] Further, where the shares have been purchased from a third party, as contrasted with being subscribed for, the *Houldsworth* principle does not preclude a right of action in damages nor sub-ordinate any claim against the company. It no longer applies where the shares have been acquired on foot of an offer for subscription by the public.[156] The following are the principal heads under which damages may be claimed

---

[149] (1880) 5 App. Cas. 317.
[150] Sale of Goods Act 1893, s.53.
[151] (1880) 5 App. Cas. 317 at 325.
[152] *ibid.* at 333.
[153] *cf.* Lord Blackburn in *Houldsworth* case (1880) 5 App. Cas. 317 at 338–341, discussing *Barwick v English Joint Stock Bank* (1867) L.R. 2 Exch. 259. The *Houldsworth* case was decided before *Barwick* was overruled in *Lloyd v Grace Smith & Co.* [1912] A.C. 716.
[154] *Sons of Gwalia Ltd v Margaretic* 81 A.L.J.L.R. 525 (2007) and see also fn.146.
[155] See comments by Hornby and also by Gower in 19 *Mod. L. Rev.* 54 and 185 (1956).
[156] 2005 Act, s.41.

against those other than the company and, subject to *Houldsworth*, perhaps against the company too.

8–74   *Deceit/Fraud:* Persons who acquire securities in consequence of some fraudulent misrepresentation made to them have a cause of action in damages for deceit against that representor. In one of the early Irish examples, *Jury v Stoker*,[157] the plaintiff acquired shares in the newly formed Cork Milling Co. on foot of a prospectus which stated, wrongly, that the vendor from whom the company purchased its mills would be investing £7,500 in the company. Subsequently, it was wound up and the plaintiff lost his entire investment. It was held that the directors responsible for the prospectus were liable for his entire loss because they had deliberately misled him.

8–75   The tort of deceit is somewhat narrowly defined. It must be shown that the defendant made, or authorised the making of, a false statement of fact, so as to induce the plaintiff to acquire the securities in question, and that the inducement worked. In *Derry v Peek*,[158] it was held that the misleading statement must have been made knowing it to be false or recklessly as to its truth or falsity. While mere omission to state some material fact,[159] or even gross negligence on the maker's part,[160] is not enough to establish deceit, non-disclosure in particular circumstances can be fraudulent. The governing principles were summed up as follows:

> "many facts and circumstances may be lawfully omitted, although some subscribers might be of opinion that these would have been of materiality as influencing the exercise of their judgment. But the statement of a portion of the truth, accompanied by suggestions and inferences which would be possible and credible if it contained the whole truth, but became neither possible nor credible whenever the whole truth is divulged, is … a false statement.
>
> [T]he true test [is], taking the whole thing together, was there a false representation? [It does not matter] by what means it is conveyed—by what trick or device or ambiguous language … If by a number of statements you intentionally give a false impression and induce a person to act upon it, it is not the less false although if one takes each statement by itself there may be a difficulty in showing that any specific statement is untrue."[161]

As regards causation, a person who reads a glowing prospectus and thereupon subscribes for shares in the company is not "bound to be able to explain with exact precision what was the mental process by which he was induced to act".[162]

8–76   The measure of damages for deceit is the difference between what was paid for the securities in question and their true value at the time they were

---

[157] (1882) 9 L.R. 385.
[158] (1889) 14 App. Cas. 337.
[159] *Peek v Gurney* (1873) L.R. 6 H.L. 377.
[160] *Derry v Peek* (1889) 14 App. Cas. 337.
[161] *Aaron's Reefs v Twiss* [1896] A.C. 273 at 287 and 281. A more recent example is *Smith New Court Securities Ltd v Scrimgeour Vickers (Asset Management) Ltd* [1997] A.C. 254.
[162] [1896] A.C. 273 at 280.

bought.[163] But the actual market price will not invariably be used to fix the latter sum; account will be taken of subsequent events because they may well show that the shares in fact were worth far less than they appeared to be.[164] On the other hand, if the enterprise proves to be a failure for reasons entirely extrinsic to the deceit or misrepresentation, a purchaser of its securities is not entitled to be compensated for losses arising from this fact.[165] But in practice it is difficult to distinguish between the causes of failure that were due to and that were wholly extrinsic to the wrong. Although the amount recoverable in damages is subject to the usual principles regarding causation, remoteness and mitigation, the victim of a fraud is entitled to be compensated for all loss directly flowing from the deceptive transaction, including consequential loss, and not merely loss that was reasonably foreseeable.[166] Where the deceptive statement is a term of the contract to buy the securities, then the damages will cover any loss of expected profit.[167] Recently there has been movement toward giving some compensation in tort for loss of the bargain.

8–77 Negligent Misrepresentation: Many of the authorities on the liability of those who sell securities to investors were decided long before *Donoghue v Stevenson*[168] established a general obligation not to act in a manner that foreseeably may damage another, and before *Hedley Byrne & Co. v Heller & Partners Ltd*[169] confirmed that this duty of care applies to economic or financial loss, as well as to physical damage caused by another's negligence. A company offering shares for subscription, or a promoter who is seeking to induce another to buy shares in a company, must not through carelessness and possibly inadvertence give misleading relevant information. This duty may extend in special circumstances to one of taking reasonable steps to ensure that only correct information is given. In what particular circumstances liability under this head will arise depends on the nature of the relationship that exists between the purchaser and the defendant.[170] The same principles govern the measure of damages here as in deceit.

8–78 In *Securities Trust Ltd v Hugh Moore & Alexander Ltd*,[171] a shareholder applied for and obtained from his company a copy of its memorandum and articles of association. He held his shares as trustee for the plaintiff. His application for those documents was in his own name and the company was unaware that he held his shares in trust. The copy supplied to him contained an error which suggested that, on a winding-up of the company, both its ordinary and

---

[163] *McConnell v Wright* [1903] 1 Ch. 546.

[164] *Potts v Miller* 64 C.L.R. 282 (1940).

[165] *ibid.*

[166] *Smith New Court* case [1997] A.C. 254.

[167] *cf. Archer v Brown* [1985] Q.B. 401.

[168] [1932] A.C. 562.

[169] [1964] A.C. 465.

[170] *cf. Bank of Scotland v 3i Plc* [1993] B.C.L.C. 968. Where shares were brought on the stock market, compare *Al-Nakib Investments (Jersey) Ltd v Longcroft* [1990] 1 W.L.R. 1390 with *Possfund Custodian Trustee Ltd v Diamond* [1996] 1 W.L.R. 1351.

[171] [1964] I.R. 417.

its preference shareholders would participate in a distribution of surplus assets. On the faith of this, the plaintiff made several purchases of preference shares at prices in excess of their true value. Subsequently, the error was discovered by the company and it notified the shareholder of the error in the copy of the articles supplied to him. On the company's winding-up, the plaintiff claimed to be entitled to participate in the distribution of surplus assets in respect of those shares, which was rejected by the liquidator. Proceedings for damages for negligent misrepresentation were dismissed on the grounds that the requisite degree of proximity, or relationship, between the plaintiff and the company did not exist. Davitt P.'s judgment hints obliquely that the liability-triggering relationship would have existed had the actual purchaser of shares and plaintiff been the shareholder who was given a copy of the articles, especially in the light of the statutory obligation to provide all company members with copies of the memorandum and articles.[172] But even if this were so and causation was established, it still would have to be shown that the defendant was negligent or did not adopt such precautionary measures as were reasonably necessary.

8–79 *Innocent Misrepresentation:* As a general rule, a person who by a material misrepresentation, made innocently and not negligently, induces another to acquire shares is not thereby liable in damages. If, however, the misrepresentation amounts to a warranty, then the party making it can be made liable in damages for breach of contract.[173] Liability for simple misrepresentation can arise where some exceptional relationship exists between the parties.

Criminal Penalties

8–80 In addition to or apart from penalties under the Prospectus Regulations,[174] defrauding investors may constitute the offence of making a gain or causing loss by the deception,[175] or criminal conspiracy.

PAYMENTS FROM CAPITAL

8–81 Once contributed, a limited company's capital must be "maintained" in the company and not be redistributed to its shareholders, except in the manner provided for in the Companies Acts. That dividends must not be paid out of subscribed capital, but only from profits, gained general recognition in *Flitcroft's Case*.[176] Given the special statutory procedures for effecting a capital reduction, it was said, "a company cannot reduce its capital except in the manner and with the safeguards provided by statute, and looking at the Act … it clearly is against the intention of the legislature that any portion of the capital should be returned to the shareholders without the statutory conditions being complied with".[177] This conclusion was reinforced by the requirement that

---

[172] *cf. New Zealand Motor Bodies Ltd v Emslie* [1985] 2 N.Z.L.R. 569.

[173] *Bank of Ireland v Smith* [1966] I.R. 646.

[174] See para.15–76 *et seq.*

[175] Criminal Justice (Theft and Fraud Offences) Act, 2001, s.6.

[176] *Re Exchange Banking Co.* (1882) 21 Ch D 519.

[177] *ibid.* at 533.

every company must have an objects clause, "which is a statement that the capital shall be applied for the purposes of the business, and on the faith of that statement, which is sometimes said to be an implied contract with creditors, people dealing with the company give it credit".[178] The related rule, that companies may not purchase their own shares, was first proclaimed in *Trevor v Whitworth*.[179] Its existence too was inferred from the procedures for returning capital to shareholders, "the effect of [which] is to prohibit every transaction between a company and a shareholder, by means of which the money already paid to the company in respect of his shares is returned to him, unless the court has sanctioned the transaction".[180] These two rules were incorporated into the 1963 Act, which also prohibits companies from financing the purchase of their own shares,[181] and they have been extended and amended in places by the 1983 Act and by Pt XI of the 1990 Act.

8–82 Of course a company cannot maintain its capital in an absolute sense in that if, for example, it commences trading with a capital of say €50,000 but incurs losses of €5,000 each year for its first three years doing business, then its capital in fact is depleted by €15,000 and stands at €35,000. The law does not strictly require companies to preserve their contributed capital intact against trading losses. Thus in *Re Horsley & Weight Ltd*[182], where it was contended, unsuccessfully, that pension arrangements made by the company were *ultra vires*, it was argued as well that, in the circumstances, those payments contravened the requirement that companies must maintain their capital. This was rejected because:

> "[it] is a misapprehension to suppose that the directors of a company owe a duty to the company's creditors to keep the contributed capital of the company intact. The company's creditors are entitled to assume that the company will not in any way repay any paid up share capital to the shareholders except by means of a duly authorised reduction of capital … On the other hand, a company and its directors acting on its behalf, can quite properly expend contributed capital for any purpose which is *intra vires* the company".[183]

Pre-1983 Position

8–83 Occasionally, companies have good reasons for repaying part of their capital. For instance, large profits may have been made on the sale of a major asset and there may be no commercial justification in re-investing them in the existing business, so that the shareholders may prefer to have part of their investment returned to them. Or one or more shareholders may want to realise their investment but there is no market for the shares and the company may have plenty of funds. The 1963 Act sets out a formal procedure under which, with

---

[178] *ibid.*
[179] (1887) 12 App. Cas. 409.
[180] *ibid.* at 423.
[181] Section 60.
[182] [1982] 1 Ch. 442.
[183] *ibid.* at 455–454. See too *Dale v Martin* (1882) 2 L.R. Ir. 498.

court approval, capital may be repaid.[184] A limited company may not "reduce its capital in any way" other than through this procedure or, since 1991, by purchasing or redeeming its own shares under Pt XI of the 1990 Act (ss.206–234).

8–84   An example of the breadth of this prohibition is *Jenkins v Harbour View Courts Ltd*,[185] which concerned a condominium organised in the form of a limited company, under which a holder of a certain number of the company's shares was entitled to live in any one of its apartments. It was proposed that the company should grant the holders of the relevant number of shares 99-year leases on their apartments, the rent to be fixed annually by the directors at an amount no greater than what was needed to meet outgoings and place something in reserve. An objection to this proposal was upheld, on the grounds that in substance it amounted to an unauthorised return of capital to the members. In *Re Halt Garage (1964) Ltd*,[186] the payments made by an insolvent company to one of the two shareholders-directors, who was suffering from a long-term illness, were characterised not as remuneration but as repayments of capital; the recipient was obliged to reimburse the company. In *MacPherson v European Strategic Bureau Ltd*,[187] where three members of a loss-making company entered into a shareholders' agreement for its winding down, involving payment to them for "consultancy services" previously provided gratuitously, it was held to be unenforceable because it was entered into when the company was insolvent and it sought to achieve a winding-up without making proper provision for the creditors. Similarly, in the "asset stripping" case, *Aveling Barford Ltd v Perion Ltd*,[188] the company, which was insolvent and had no profits from which it could have paid any dividends, sold a property for far less than its market value; both the company and the purchaser were controlled by the one individual. The sale was held to be *ultra vires*, as an unlawful return of capital to the company's owner, and in substance a fraud on its creditors. And in *Barclay's Bank v British & Commonwealth Holdings Plc*,[189] covenants the company had with the plaintiff and other banks to maintain certain asset ratios, as security for completing a capital restructuring, were held to contravene the principle against paying dividends from capital. Furthermore, this principle applies even if the recipient of the distribution is not a member of the company who takes the money or assets in that capacity.

8–85   Its classic formulation was that limited companies may not pay dividends from capital and that dividends may not be paid if, in consequence, the company would be rendered insolvent. As they were applied, however, these gave somewhat inadequate protection to creditors. The approach to what amounted to capital, and accordingly was undistributable, was the *res*

---

[184] Sections 72–77. See para.11–35 *et seq.*
[185] [1966] N.Z.L.R. 1.
[186] [1982] 3 All E.R. 1016.
[187] [2000] 2 B.C.L.C. 683.
[188] [1989] B.C.L.C. 626.
[189] [1996] 1 B.C.L.C. 1.

theory.[190] By this is meant that capital was identified, not by the monetary quantum stated in the memorandum of association and balance sheet, but connoted the assets contributed by the shareholders in exchange for their shares, or assets into which those original assets had been converted. Consequently, it was concluded, there was no obligation to make up for fixed capital that had depreciated or was lost in trading.[191] The criterion of solvency was not that of assets exceeding liabilities but that of cash flow, i.e. whether the company could pay its debts as they fell due.[192] In the cases where some of the ground rules were laid down, it was emphasised that many aspects of dividend policy were more matters of good business or accounting practice than of law, and that the Companies Acts themselves allowed companies an extensive discretion as regards paying dividends.

Restricted Distributions

8–86 Major changes in the requirements, initiated by the EC Second Directive,[193] are incorporated in Pt IV (ss.45–51) of the 1983 Act. For all companies, the fund from which dividends can be paid has become the aggregate net earned surplus, i.e. current profits and any profits carried forward, less current losses and any losses carried forward. For Plcs, the test of solvency has become one of balance sheet surplus, i.e. the company's net assets must not be less than the subscribed capital together with any undistributable reserves. There are variations on these rules for investment companies and for industrial and life assurance companies.[194]

"Distribution"

8–87 Instead of the term dividend, which has a somewhat narrow connotation, the 1983 Act uses the word "distribution". For tax purposes, this concept has a lengthy and complex definition.[195] For present purposes, it is defined as "every description of distribution of a company's assets to members of the company, whether in cash or otherwise, except [certain itemised] distributions".[196] It involves any transfer of money or property to a company's member in his capacity as such, but not otherwise, such as a genuine arms-length transaction for valuable consideration. The proposed leases of flats in the *Harbour View Courts* case[197] would be a distribution. It could be argued that the payment to the director/shareholder in the *Halt Garage* case[198] and the asset

---

[190] See generally, Gold, "Fixed and Circulating Capital in the English Law of Dividends" 6 *U. Toronto L.J.* 14 (1945) and Yaney, "Aspects of the Law Relating to Company Dividends" 4 *Mod. L. Rev.* 273 (1941).

[191] *Verner v General & Commercial Investment Trust* [1894] 2 Ch. 239 and *Kehoe v Waterford & Limerick Railway Co.* (1888) 21 L.R. Ir. 221.

[192] *Re Castleisland Railway Co.* [1896] 2 I.R. 661 and *Peter Buchanan Ltd v McVey* [1954] I.R. 89.

[193] Directive 77/91, [1977] O.J. L26/1.

[194] See para.16–26 *et seq.*

[195] *cf. Federal Commissioner of Taxation v Sun Alliance Investments Pty Ltd* 80 A.L.J.L.R. 202 (2005).

[196] Section 51(2). *Re DML Resources Ltd* [2004] 3 N.Z.L.R. 490.

[197] [1966] N.Z.L.R. 1.

[198] [1982] 3 All E.R. 1016.

disposal in the *Aveling Barford* case[199] are not distributions as defined here, because they were made to one member only and not to "members". It was emphasised in the *British & Commonwealth Holdings* case[200] that what matters is the substance and economic effect of the transaction in question, not its technical form. However, the complex reconstruction of capital, which was in dispute there, was held not to contravene the statutory prohibition because it had previously obtained court approval. Those distributions that are excepted are the issue of bonus shares as fully or partly paid; the purchase or redemption of shares under Pt XI of the 1990 Act; reduction of capital within ss.72–77 of the 1963 Act; and distributions to members on a winding-up.

Solvency

8–88   Companies other than Plcs remain subject to the cash flow, or equitable, test of solvency, i.e. that they manage to pay their debts as they fall due.[201] This may not adequately safeguard creditors' interests, in that firms whose liabilities exceed their assets are nevertheless permitted to pay dividends if they succeed in meeting their debts as they fall due. For Plcs, however, the criterion is balance sheet surplus.[202]

Available Profits

8–89   It used to be said that, since "the word 'profits' is by no means free from ambiguity, [the law is] more accurately expressed by saying that dividends cannot be paid out of capital, than by saying that they can only be paid out of profits".[203] This is no longer the case. The governing principle is that a company "shall not make a distribution except out of profits available for the purpose".[204] Available profits for distribution are defined as a company's "accumulated, realised profits, so far as not previously utilised by distribution or capitalisation, less its accumulated, realised losses, so far as not previously written-off in a reduction or reorganisation of capital duly made".[205] An end, therefore, has been put to the system under which "nimble dividends" could be paid, i.e. although the company had sizeable accumulated losses, if it made a profit in any one year it could pay a dividend from those profits. In other words, even though it made a large loss in any one or more years, it still could pay a dividend out of profits it previously or subsequently had earned but never distributed. Any current profits and distributable reserves carried forward must now exceed aggregate present and past losses that have not been written off in a capital reduction or reorganisation. Thus, the revenue account is treated as

---

[199] [1989] B.C.L.C. 626.

[200] [1996] 1 B.C.L.C 1.

[201] e.g. *Re Bryant Investment Co.* [1924] 1 W.L.R. 826 and *Re Capital Annuities Ltd* [1979] 1 W.L.R. 170.

[202] See para.15–27.

[203] *Verner v General & Commercial Investment Trust* [1894] 2 Ch. 239 at 266 and *Bond v Barrow Haematite Steel Co.* [1902] 1 Ch. 353.

[204] 1963 Act, s.45(1).

[205] 1963 Act, s.45(2).

one continuous stream, and dividends cannot be paid until all deficits have been eliminated, which is the normal accounting practice.

8–90   It is realised profits and losses that are relevant to this calculation, i.e. profits that in fact are earned and actual losses incurred.[206] Moreover, unrealised profits may not be used to pay up debentures or any amounts unpaid on issued shares,[207] but this does not preclude using unrealised profits to pay up allotments of fully or partly paid bonus shares. Except for a number of particular contexts, the Act does not differentiate in principle between revenue and capital profits and losses.[208]

Accounting Rules

8–91   Three categories of accounting rules govern determinations of whether a company has profits available or is solvent as described above.

8–92   *Relevant Accounts*: First, there are the relevant accounts.[209] Normally, these are the properly-prepared last annual accounts about which the auditors made a report and a copy of which was laid before a general meeting. Where that report was qualified, the auditors must have stated their opinion whether the matter giving rise to the qualification was relevant to the legality of the distribution in question. If those accounts would cause a distribution to contravene the Act, reliance may be placed on properly-prepared more recent interim accounts, provided a copy of them was delivered to the Registrar of Companies. If it is proposed to make the distribution in the company's first financial year, then properly-prepared initial accounts suffice, provided that certain safeguards are complied with. Any accounts being relied on for these purposes must not only comply with the strict accounting standards in the Companies Acts but must also give a "true and fair view" of the company's trading or capital position, as the case may be.

8–93   That strict compliance with these accounting rules will be insisted on is demonstrated by the *Precision Dippings Ltd* case,[210] where the accounts indicated that there were sufficient funds from which a dividend could be paid. However, those accounts were qualified and the auditors had not provided the statement required, as above. It was held that the company's liquidator was entitled to recover the dividend paid on foot of those accounts.[211] Moreover, even though the auditors subsequently gave the requisite statement and the members passed a resolution purporting to ratify the dividend payment, the breach was not thereby cured. Because these rules are designed to protect creditors, shareholders cannot waive any breach of the safeguards.

---

[206] *Re Cleveland Trust Plc* [1991] B.C.L.C. 424.
[207] But see 1963 Act, s.51(1).
[208] cf. *Lubbock v British Bank of South America* [1892] 2 Ch. 198.
[209] 1963 Act, s.49.
[210] *Precision Dippings Ltd v Precision Dippings (Marketing) Ltd* [1986] Ch. 447.
[211] Similarly, *BDG Roof Bond Ltd v Douglas* [2000] 1 B.C.L.C. 401 and *Bairstow v Queens Moat Houses Plc* [2001] 2 B.C.L.C. 531.

8–94   *Difficulties in Determination*: Then there are rules for where it is not possible to say whether a profit or loss was made, or whether some profit or loss was realised.[212] Where no record exists or can be traced of a particular asset's original cost, it is deemed to be worth the amount which was first entered into the company's books. Where the directors cannot determine whether a profit made or a loss incurred before the appointed day is realised or unrealised, they are permitted to treat the profit as realised and the loss as unrealised.[213] There is a special rule of thumb for determining when surpluses and deficits constitute realised profits and losses in the case of companies carrying on industrial or life assurance business, or both.[214]

8–95   *Depreciation*: Finally, there are the vexed questions of depreciation and other changes in the values of fixed assets. While the law does not strictly require companies to make provision for depreciation or for contingent liabilities, any such provision made must now be treated as a realised loss, with the exception of a provision made in consequence of a decline in value discovered in the course of revaluing all the fixed assets.[215] Because the relevant accounts must give a "true and fair view" and failure to provide for depreciation might very well distort that view, for practical purposes appropriate provision should be made for writing down the values of depreciating assets. The extent of that write-down would depend on normal accountancy practice. The rule that an unrealised surplus arising in a revaluation of fixed assets may not be distributed as dividends,[216] is now subject to a qualification. A company may treat as a realised profit any difference between the sum set aside for depreciation of a fixed asset which has been revalued and the amount of the unrealised profit thereby discovered.[217]

Enforcement

8–96 In *Flitcroft's Case*,[218] it was held that the company or its liquidator can recover any unauthorised distribution from those directors responsible for making it. In *Bairstow v Queens Moat Houses Plc*,[219] where the directors had authorised dividend payments when they knew that the accounts greatly exaggerated the company's financial position, it was held that they were personally liable to the full amount of what had been paid. The contention that their liability should not exceed the difference between the dividends that they could have authorised, based on the company's actual financial situation then, and what was paid, was rejected on the grounds that directors are in a position analogous to trustees. That going against the directors, but not against the shareholders who had obtained the unlawful payments, would result in some double recovery, was held to be unfortunate but unavoidable. In this instance,

[212] 1963 Act, s.45(7).
[213] 1963 Act, s.45(8).
[214] 1963 Act, s.48.
[215] 1963 Act, s.45(4).
[216] 1963 Act, s.149(6)(a).
[217] 1963 Act, s.45(6).
[218] *Re Exchange Banking Co.* (1882) 21 Ch D 519.
[219] [2001] 2 B.C.L.C. 531.

the company had been quoted on the London Stock Exchange and a considerable number of the shares would have changed hands in the meantime. Even if the company had been solvent when it made those payments, the legal position was held to be the same.[220]

8–97   It is not a defence that the shareholder(s) had no knowledge of what the legal requirements here are. In *It's a Wrap (UK) Ltd v Gula*,[221] a husband and wife ran a small gift card shop business. On being advised that it was more tax-efficient, rather than pay them salaries, the company paid them dividends in lieu of salary. It never made a profit and was wound up as insolvent. It was held that it is no answer that they were not aware of the prohibition; it is sufficient to trigger liability that they knew that the business was not earning profits. It would appear that there was a right of recovery against shareholders who knowingly accepted such distributions.[222] It is now stipulated that a member who, knowing or with reasonable grounds for believing that it is unlawful, receives a distribution that contravenes the 1983 Act, is liable to the company for that amount.[223]

ACQUIRING OWN SHARES

8–98   Before 1990, limited companies were not permitted to purchase their own shares. Among the objections to this practice, first announced in *Trevor v Whitworth*,[224] are that it endangers creditors' security, since it is a disguised way of returning capital to the shareholders; it also enables company controllers to manipulate its share price; and it makes it easier for controllers to entrench their positions of power in a company. Yet there are arguments in favour of allowing companies to buy back their own shares, subject to sufficient safeguards for creditors and against abuse of power by controllers. Tax considerations aside, it is a much simpler method of returning capital to some shareholders than the procedure under ss.72–77 of the 1963 Act. Individual shareholders may wish to liquidate their investment but there may be no ready market for it; or the management may wish to reduce the number of shareholders below a certain figure, for instance, to under 100 to "go private"; or a majority may wish to be in a position where they can resolve deadlock and expel particularly troublesome members, by the company repurchasing their shares. This method can be used to prevent a stake in a company from going outside a family or some other narrowly defined group; in *Trevor v Whitworth*, for instance, the reason the company sought to buy its own shares was to keep it a family concern. Some of the justifications advanced for quoted companies being able to acquire their own shares should be viewed with scepticism.

---

[220] Similarly, *Inn Spirit Ltd v Burns* [2002] 2 B.C.L.C. 780.
[221] [2006] 2 B.C.L.C. 634.
[222] *Welton v Saffery* [1897] A.C. 299; *cf.* Thom, "Unjust Enrichment and Unlawful Dividends: A Step Too Far?" 64 *Cam. L.J.* 177 (2005).
[223] Section 50(1).
[224] (1887) 12 App. Cas. 409.

The Prohibition

8–99 Subject to the exceptions and qualifications set out below, any limited company having a share capital may not "acquire its own shares (whether by purchase, subscription or otherwise)", including redemption.[225] Additional requirements and also other exceptions exist for Plcs.[226] *Vision Express (UK) Ltd v Wilson*[227] vividly demonstrates the thrust of this prohibition. A dispute between the company and a senior employee concerning his alleged fraud was settled on terms that, *inter alia*, the company would purchase shares he held in and options he had on shares in the company; the terms of settlement were annexed to what is known as a "Tomlin order". It was held that this part of the settlement could not be enforced because it involved a breach of the prohibition and did not fall within any of the stipulated exceptions. Where a company issues its own shares to its nominee or where that nominee acquires partly paid shares in it from some third party, provision is made to ensure that the company recovers any sums due to it on those shares.[228] There are special rules for cross-shareholdings between parent and subsidiary companies. Subject to these, the prohibition does not preclude a company from acquiring shares in another company even where that acquired company's sole asset is shares in the acquiring company.[229]

8–100 But a limited company may acquire its own fully paid shares "otherwise than for valuable consideration"[230]; in other words, by way of gift and the like. But this exemption would not seem to cover the situation that arose in *Re Irish Provident Assurance Co.*,[231] which was one of a series of cases concerning the transformation of a friendly society into an insurance company. The central issue concerned a compromise made of various claims between the company and its former managing director, which was ratified in general meeting. One of the terms was that he would transfer without payment all his shares in the company to such person as the company should direct, and that the company would pay him a lump sum. It was held that this agreement was void in that "the real transaction, notwithstanding the conveyancing effort to conceal its true nature, included a sale to the company of the shares, not a gift of them".[232]

Charge and Lien on Own Shares

8–101 On the authority of a case that afterwards was overruled,[233] it was held in *Re Balgooley Distillery Co.*,[234] that a limited company could accept its own

---

[225] 1983 Act, s.4(1).
[226] See para.15–28 *et seq.*
[227] [1995] 2 B.C.L.C. 419.
[228] 1983 Act, s.42(2).
[229] *Acatos & Hutchinson Plc v Watson* [1995] 1 B.C.L.C. 218.
[230] 1983 Act, s.41(2).
[231] [1913] 1 I.R. 352.
[232] *ibid.* at 369.
[233] *Re Dronfield Silkstone Coal Co.* (1880) 17 Ch D 76.
[234] (1886) 17 L.R. Ir. 239.

fully paid-up shares as security for an ordinary business transaction, and later enforce that security by cancelling those shares. Stating that, under the *stare decisis* system, he had no choice but to uphold the transaction, FitzGibbon L.J. expressed the view that an absolute prohibition against all dealings by companies in their own shares would be preferable. There was "no satisfactory ground for determining the validity of a purchase of its own shares by a company on considerations of motive or intention"; and he "fail[ed] to see any satisfactory distinction between 'trafficking in shares' as it is called ... and acquiring them for valuable consideration for other motives".[235] Acceptance by a company of its own shares as security for a debt owed to it is not a violation of the prohibition against companies "purchas[ing]" their own shares or otherwise reducing their share capital.[236] Whether it amounts to "acquir[ing]" their own shares[237] is arguable since the word acquiring is not defined. But the position as regards Plcs is made clear in that, subject to one main exception, they are not allowed to have a lien or any other charge over their own shares, regardless of how that security interest may arise.[238] Table A allows companies a lien over their partly paid shares in respect of sums payable on those shares.[239] Especially in light of that provision, the validity of articles purporting to grant a lien over the company's fully paid shares in respect of all kinds of debts to the company must be doubted, especially where there is no ready market for those shares.

Permitted Acquisitions

8–102 Exception is made for the acquisition of any shares in a court-approved reduction of capital; the purchase of shares under a court order approving a change of objects or in "oppression" proceedings; where a Plc is "going private"; or where under the company's own regulations shares are forfeited or are surrendered in lieu, for failure to pay calls.[240]

8–103 Part XI (ss.206–234) of the 1990 Act permits limited companies to purchase or otherwise acquire their own shares, or shares in their holding company, subject to the conditions laid down.[241] Changes in the tax rules to make buy-backs of shares a fiscally realistic option for companies and their members were adopted in 1991.[242] In addition to the straightforward share re-purchase by the company, companies may issue redeemable shares of any class.[243] They may even convert their normally irredeemable shares into redeemable ones. Companies also may acquire shares in their own holding company, subject to the safeguards.[244] Where a company or its nominee holds

---

[235] *ibid.* at 264.

[236] 1963 Act, s.72.

[237] 1983 Act, s.41(1).

[238] 1983 Act, s.44.

[239] Article 11 and 1983 Act, s.44(2)(a).

[240] 1983 Act, s.41(3).

[241] See *BCM's Precedents* parts H47 *et seq.*

[242] See generally, M.Feeney, *The Taxation of Companies* (Haywards Heath: Tottel Publishing, 2006), p.1403 *et seq.*

[243] 1990 Act, s.207.

[244] 1990 Act, s.224.

its shares or an interest in them, these may not be shown in the balance sheet as an asset, but their cost and nominal value must be disclosed in the notes to the accounts.[245]

8–104 Certain common prerequisites for each of these kind of share acquisitions are laid down.[246] The company's articles of association must permit it to make the kind of acquisition envisaged. The shares being acquired must be fully paid. Generally, the funds used to pay for those shares must come from profits which the company is free to distribute by way of dividend; the same applies to any premium being paid on the shares. The "accounting rules" referred to above are also applicable here. Accordingly, in *BDG Roof Bond Ltd v Douglas*,[247] even though at the time the company's auditors believed it had the requisite funds, because the relevant accounts were qualified but no statement that this qualification was not material was laid before the EGM that approved the transaction, the buy-back was held to be invalid. But where the company proposes to then cancel the shares, their repurchase may instead be funded from a fresh issue of shares made for that very purpose. Not more than 10 per cent of the company's shares may be acquired within these terms. Any payment by a company for its shares, otherwise than as provided for here, is unlawful.[248] Payment does not always have to be made in cash; it also may take the form of a set-off and even of a transfer by the company of some other asset in exchange for the shares. The mere fact that a quoted company purchased its own shares is not deemed to be prohibited "insider trading".[249] Special rules are laid down for acquisitions by investment companies.[250]

8–105 Where a company acquires its own shares in the manner provided for here, ordinarily it has an option. It may cancel them; in that event, the share capital is deemed to have been accordingly reduced.[251] Alternatively, it may retain them as what are called "treasury" shares[252]—terminology borrowed from the US. Throughout the period while the company holds its shares in this form, they are virtually frozen, in the sense that the votes attaching to them cannot be exercised and no dividend or other distribution may be made in respect of them.[253] If those shares could be voted on, the company's management might thereby obtain too influential a say in its affairs, and there is little point in the company paying itself a dividend. When desirable circumstances arise, treasury shares can be re-issued by the company. A return must be made to the Registrar of Companies of all repurchase transactions.[254]

---

[245] 1983 Act, s.43A.
[246] 1990 Act, s.207.
[247] [2000] 1 B.C.L.C. 401.
[248] 1990 Act, s.218.
[249] 1990 Act, s.223.
[250] 1990 Act, ss.254 and 255.
[251] 1990 Act, s.208.
[252] 1990 Act, s.209.
[253] 1990 Act, s.209(3).
[254] 1990 Act, s.226 and Form H5.

Purchases

8–106 The maximum number of shares which can be purchased by a company in this manner is measured by reference to any redeemable shares it may have in its share capital. Share buy-backs must not reach the state that the nominal value of the company's irredeemable shares falls below 10 per cent of the total issued share capital.[255] The common conditions set out above must be met, regarding authority in the articles, the shares being fully paid and the purchase money usually coming from distributable profits; additional conditions may be laid down in the company's articles.[256] Where it is proposed to cancel the shares, their purchase may be financed by a fresh issue of shares made for this very purpose and also by drawing from the share premium account.[257] What authority is needed to go ahead with a proposed re-purchase depends on whether or not the shares are being traded on a stock market; a distinction is drawn between "market" purchases and "off market" purchases. The Minister is authorised to prescribe additional conditions in regulations regarding, for example, the kinds of shares which may or may not be purchased, prices, timing, methods and the volume of trading companies may carry out in their shares.[258]

8–107 *Authority*: What are called "off market" purchases are purchases other than stock-market transactions.[259] Because it is far more difficult to ascertain a fair price for unlisted than for listed shares, each off-market purchase contract must have been authorised in advance by a special resolution.[260] A copy of that contract or a memorandum of its terms must have been available for inspection by the members for at least 21 days before the meeting which considers it. If it relates to any present shareholder, he must be identified if his name does not appear on the contract. The intending seller is not permitted to vote his own shares on the resolution in that, if the proposal would only be carried by virtue of his votes, they will not count. Notwithstanding anything in the company's articles of association, any member can demand a poll on these proposals. In the case of "market purchases", an ordinary resolution is sufficient authority, which must specify the maximum number of shares that may be bought and the maximum and minimum prices that may be paid.[261] This authority lapses after 18 months.[262]

8–108 *The Contract*: A contract with a company whereby it may purchase its own shares is not assignable.[263] Even though it may have been fully authorised to do so, a company will not be held liable in damages for breach of a contract to purchase its own shares.[264] However, that does not prejudice any other

---

[255] 1990 Act, s.211(3).
[256] 1990 Act, s.207.
[257] 1990 Act, s.208(b)(ii).
[258] 1990 Act, s.228.
[259] 1990 Act, s.212(1)(a).
[260] 1990 Act, s.213.
[261] 1990 Act, s.215.
[262] 1990 Act, s.216.
[263] 1990 Act, s.217.
[264] 1990 Act, s.219.

rights the contracting party may have against the company, notably an action for rescission. Moreover, a court may award specific performance of the contract, but will not do so if the company does not possess sufficient available profits to cover the purchase price. In the event of the company being wound up, its liability under a contract to purchase its own shares ranks after all debts and liabilities to non-members and any claims by preference shareholders.[265]

8–109 *Cancelling shares*: Where the company decides to cancel its shares it has acquired, the issued share capital is deemed to have been duly reduced.[266] Where the purchase was funded entirely from distributable profits, an amount equivalent to the nominal value of the shares purchased must be credited to a capital reserve fund; that fund will be treated as if it were fully paid-up capital in the company.[267] Accordingly, in an accounting sense, the company's aggregate capital was never diminished. Where, on the other hand, a fresh issue of shares funded the buy-back, either entirely or in part, then the difference between the nominal value of the shares purchased and the proceeds of the fresh issue must be credited to a capital reserve account. This reserve can be used to finance an issue of fully paid bonus shares.

8–110 *Treasury shares*: Where the company decides to hold the shares it has acquired as treasury shares, no more than 10 per cent of its issued shares may be held by it at any time in this form.[268] For the purpose of calculating this ratio, shares which its subsidiary holds in the company and also shares held by someone else acting on the company's behalf are included with the treasury shares. These shares cannot be voted, nor can any dividend or any other payment be made by the company in respect of them.[269] At some later stage the company may decide to cancel all or some of them; in that event the rules for cancellation apply.[270]

8–111 Alternatively, the company may decide to re-issue all or some of its treasury shares.[271] In that case, the normal rules for issuing additional shares apply, for instance, regarding prior authority and pre-emption.[272] Where they are being re-issued on a stock market, no special procedure is laid down for fixing the issue price. But in the case of a non-market re-issue, the issue price range must be stipulated in the special resolution which authorised the purchase of those shares at the outset, passed within the preceding 18 months.[273] The price fixed there can always be varied and the time can be extended by a special resolution.

---

[265] 1990 Act, s.219(6).
[266] 1990 Act, s.208.
[267] 1990 Act, s.208(b).
[268] 1990 Act, s.209.
[269] 1990 Act, s.209(3)
[270] 1990 Act, s.208.
[271] 1990 Act, s.209(5) and (6).
[272] See paras.8–45 and 9–44 *et seq*.
[273] 1990 Act, s.209(6)(e).

8–112 *Enforcement*: It was not necessary in *Trevor v Whitworth*[274] to determine the consequences of a limited company owning its own shares because the transaction there was inchoate. Nor did the 1963 Act deal directly with this matter. But it stipulates that any unauthorised allotment or transfer of shares in a holding company to its subsidiary is void.[275] Acquisitions by a company of its own shares, that contravene the 1983 Act, are rendered void,[276] as are any liens or charges taken by a Plc on its own shares that are not permitted.[277] Where, in breach of that Act, a company's shares are issued to its nominees, or they are called upon to pay up any outstanding amounts on them but fail to do so within 21 days, then the company's other subscribers or other directors, as the case may be, become jointly and severally liable to pay those amounts.[278]

8–113 *Validation*: The jurisdiction conferred on the court to validate irregular issues of shares, on "just and equitable" grounds,[279] excludes the irregular purchase or redemption of its own shares.[280] But this does not apply where the company acquired those shares other than out of distributable profits or the proceeds of a fresh share issue, as the case may be, or otherwise in a manner incompatible with its articles of association. The court may direct that any such exemption shall relieve the company or any of its officers of criminal liability for contravening the general prohibition against unauthorised share buy-backs.

Redeemable Shares

8–114 Formerly, companies could issue only redeemable preference shares.[281] They now may issue redeemable shares of any class, provided that at least one tenth of their share capital is comprised of non-redeemable shares.[282] The general conditions described above for purchasing own shares[283] also apply to redeeming them; additional requirements may be laid down in the articles of association. Once redeemed, the shares may be cancelled or, instead, held as treasury shares. Where they are subsequently reissued off the stock market, the issue price range must be fixed in advance by a special resolution.

8–115 Instead of purchasing non-redeemable shares, a company also may convert its own shares into redeemable shares, and then go on and redeem them as provided for above.[284] But conversion cannot be forced on any member. Where the articles of association enable a conversion of this nature to be

---

[274] (1887) 12 App. Cas. 409.
[275] Section 32(1).
[276] Section 41(3).
[277] Section 44(1).
[278] Section 42(2).
[279] See para.8–52.
[280] 1963 Act, s.89 (initially Companies Act 1959, s.2).
[281] 1963 Act, s.64.
[282] 1990, s.207.
[283] See para.8–104.
[284] 1990 Act, s.210.

made, it is subject to such "class rights" as may exist, i.e. special rights which attach to any distinctive classes of shares. A member who objects to having his shares being made redeemable must notify the company before the date fixed for any conversion to take place. Additional requirements may be laid down in the articles of association. What is said above regarding cancelling the shares or holding them as treasury shares also applies here.

FINANCING THE PURCHASE OF OWN SHARES

8–116   Ordinarily a company may not lend money or guarantee a loan to enable the borrower to purchase shares in that company. In *Re MJ Cummins Ltd,*[285] the shareholders wanted to sell their company but the intended purchaser was not in funds at the time. So the local bank manager devised an "ingenious plan" whereby the bank would advance a substantial sum to the company, which in turn would lend that money to the purchaser, with which he could then buy the shares. Johnston J. held that the bank could not recover that loan as it was *ultra vires* the company. The position there would not have been affected by s.8(1) of the 1963 Act (if in force at the time) because the bank would have been "actually aware" of the improper application of its loan. Transactions of the kind entered into in that case are now expressly prohibited and constitute an offence.[286] But for this prohibition, the restrictions on companies purchasing their own shares could be avoided very easily. The arguments against financial assistance in this context are the same as those against a company acquiring its own shares. Some situations where such assistance can be beneficial are covered by exceptions. Where part of a contract consists of an agreement to provide the proscribed assistance, it may be possible to "sever" that offending part and enforce the remainder of the contract.[287]

The Prohibition

8–117   Any registered company, whether or not limited, may not "give, whether directly or indirectly, and whether by means of a loan, guarantee, the provision of security or otherwise, any financial assistance for the purpose of or in connection with a purchase or subscription made or to be made by any person of or for any shares in the company …".[288] Although this was aimed principally at preventing persons from taking over companies, by using those companies' very own resources for that purpose, the net is cast much wider. If this were always to be given a purely literal interpretation, it would condemn some arrangements which actually benefit the company and its members, and do not jeopardise the creditors' interests. The view that the very broad scope of this section should be narrowed in the light of the mischief it seeks to remedy has received some judicial support in New Zealand[289] and in 2005 led to modifications.[290] The regime here was described as "riddled with costly uncertainty

---

[285] [1939] I.R. 60.
[286] 1963 Act, s.60.
[287] *Carney v Herbert* [1985] A.C. 301.
[288] 1963 Act, s.60(1) (initially Companies Act 1959, s.3).
[289] *Re Wellington Publishing Co.* [1973] 1 N.Z.L.R. 133.
[290] 2005 Act, s.56 (amending s.60(12) and (13)).

which results in the corporate sector spending a huge amount each year for legal advice on financial assistance".[291] Especially because a criminal provision which casts its net almost indiscriminately widely might be unconstitutional, a purposive and narrow construction most likely should be adopted, with the overriding test being the commercial substance of the transaction.

8–118 What is prohibited is a company financing the acquisition of its own shares or of shares in its holding company,[292] either by way of subscription or purchase, and whether done before or after the actual assistance was provided. Assistance rendered must be financial. But it does not matter whether it is given gratuitously or on commercial terms; transactions entirely at arm's length can be caught. It was held that the payment by a subsidiary company of its holding company's debt was not excluded from the prohibition.[293] There is no requirement about the form the assistance must take; it may be a loan, a guarantee or other kind of security, or some other method of putting the purchaser of the shares in funds, like buying assets from him. Assistance may be indirect as well as direct, i.e. the initial recipient of the funds or whatever need not be the person who acquired the shares. It was held to include payment of a professional fee to carry out a due diligence exercise and certain other inducements aimed at acquiring the company's shares.[294] As one judge put it, the prohibition "is directed to financial assistance to whomsoever given, provided that it be for the purpose of ... or in connection with a purchase of shares".[295] In a notorious case that involved circular cheques, strings of puppet companies and other stratagems, Lord Denning M.R. recommended that the corporate veil be cast aside and you "look to the company's money and see what has become of it. You look to the company's shares and see into whose hands they have got. You will soon see if the company's money has been used to finance the purchase".[296] Actual detriment to the company is not required, nor does it matter that the directors acted bona fide in the company's interests.

8–119 It is in determining the precise scope of the *scienter* requirement that the greatest difficulties arise, which are compounded by the fact that companies have no minds of their own, the beneficiaries of their subsidising share-buying are often their own directors, contravention of the section is a criminal offence, as well as a civil wrong, and there are complications about the appropriate civil sanction. A breach occurs where the impugned transaction's sole or primary objective is to finance an acquisition of the company's or its holding company's shares. But it depends very much on the inferences drawn from the established facts whether that very purpose can be shown.[297]

---

[291] Ferran, "Corporate Transactions and Financial Assistance: Shifting Policy Perceptions But Static Law" 63 *Cam. L.J.* 225 (2004).

[292] But not of a foreign-registered subsidiary: *Arab Bank Plc v Mercantile Holdings Ltd* [1994] Ch. 71.

[293] *Armour Hick Northern Ltd v Whitehouse* [1994] Ch. 71.

[294] *Chatson v SWP Group Plc* [2003] 1 B.C.L.C. 675.

[295] *EH Dey Pty Ltd v Dey* [1966] V.R. 464 at 470.

[296] *Wallersteiner v Moir* [1974] 3 All E.R. 217 at 238; *cf. Mercato Holdings Ltd v Crown Corp.* [1989] 3 N.Z.L.R. 704.

[297] e.g. not shown in *Dyment v Boyden* [2005] 1 B.C.L.C. 163.

8–120   *Re CH (Ireland) Inc.*[298] concerned a complex series of transactions involving a Swiss bank and its Canadian subsidiary, a Montreal-based finance company and its New Brunswick subsidiary. £18.8 million was deposited in Switzerland by an Irish company and, in due course, the financier's subsidiary subscribed for shares in the company, paying that amount. McCracken J. concluded that the only or main purpose of the company making that deposit was to assist in its shares being acquired in that manner and, accordingly, the deposit and the payment obligation arising from it were unlawful. On the other hand, he found that a guarantee given by the financier's subsidiary was not made principally for that purpose, as it was one of several guarantees given by all the subsidiaries at the time when the group was in serious financial difficulty. The judge declined to declare that other steps in the circular scheme were unlawful, because the only "transactions" that were condemned were those directly involving the company in question; further, some of the parties to them were not involved in the proceedings brought by the company's liquidator.

8–121   In determining whether there has been a breach, McCracken J. endorsed the following statement of principle:

> "There is no definition of giving financial assistance in the section, although some examples are given. The words have no technical meaning and their frame of reference is in my judgement the language of ordinary commerce. One must examine the commercial realities of the transaction and decide whether it can properly be described as the giving of financial assistance by the company, bearing in mind that the section is a penal one and should not be strained to cover transactions which are not fairly within it.
>
> [T]he sale of an asset by a company at a fair value can properly be described as giving financial assistance if the effect is to provide the purchaser of its shares with the cash needed to pay for them. It does not matter that the company's balance sheet is undisturbed in the sense that the cash paid out is replaced by an asset of equal value. In the case of a loan by a company to a credit worthy purchaser of its shares, the balance sheet is equally undisturbed but the loan plainly constitutes giving financial assistance. It follows that if the only or main purpose of such a transaction is to enable the purchaser to buy the shares, the section is contravened."[299]

8–122   In most of the cases here it is the buyer of the shares, or someone facilitating their purchase, who gets the assistance. Occasionally, the alleged assistance is given to the seller. Whether surrendering tax losses can constitute the prohibited financial assistance arose in *Charterhouse Investment Trust Ltd v Tempest Diesels Ltd*.[300] A management buy-out from the parent company of a company in financial difficulties involved the parent conferring several financial advantages on the subsidiary, notably, injecting around £750,000 in cash into the company, converting considerable outstanding indebtedness into an interest-free loan repayable on advantageous terms, not charging any interest, and paying

---

[298] [1999] 4 I.R. 542.
[299] From *Charterhouse Invesment Trust Ltd v Tempest Diesels Ltd* [1986] B.C.L.C. 1 at 10.
[300] [1986] B.C.L.C. 1.

redundancy compensation to its managing director. In return, the subsidiary agreed, *inter alia*, to surrender its tax losses to the parent company. At the time, those losses were of little benefit to the subsidiary because of its unpromising financial situation. But the subsidiary became a commercial success and its losses would have been quite valuable if it had retained them. Hoffman J. rejected the contention that the surrender of those losses was unlawful, holding that the transaction should not be looked at in isolation; it was part of a scheme in which, if anything, the subsidiary received considerable financial assistance rather than gave any such assistance. He counselled a pragmatic approach, observing that: "[t]he need to look at the commercial realities means that one cannot consider the surrender [here] in isolation ... It was in truth part of a composite transaction under which [the subsidiary] both received benefits and assumed burdens. It is necessary to look at the transaction as a whole and decide whether it constituted the giving of financial assistance".[301] The subsidiary did not pay over any cash to facilitated the transfer of its shares and the balance of advantages in the entire arrangement was predominantly in the subsidiary's favour.[302]

Permitted Transactions

8–123 The following financing arrangements are permitted.[303] Where two of these involve a Plc, the assistance may be given only where the "net assets" are not thereby reduced or, if reduced, the assistance comes from profits that are available for distribution by way of dividend.[304] By net assets here is meant the company's aggregate assets, less its aggregate liabilities.

Lawful Distributions

8–124 The prohibition does not apply to paying a dividend or making any other distribution from the company's distributable profits.[305]

Discharging Liabilities

8–125 Nor does it apply to "the discharge ... of a liability lawfully incurred by" the company.[306] By "lawfully incurred" here means presumably where the liability was not assumed for the purpose of enabling the prohibited share purchase to be funded. In *Belmont Finance Corp. v Williams Furniture Ltd (No. 2)*,[307] it was held that it was unlawful for a company to acquire an asset at a fair price from a third party so as to enable him to acquire its shares. Funding the purchase of its shares was the sole purpose of the transaction there; emphasis was placed on the fact that the company had no genuine need for what it bought and had entered into the transaction without regard to its own commercial interests. The court

---

[301] *ibid.* at 11.
[302] *Barclays Bank Plc v British & Commonwealth Holdings Plc* [1996] 1 B.C.L.C. 1 and *Parlett v Guppys (Bridport) Ltd* [1996] 2 B.C.L.C. 34 are in similar vein.
[303] See *Smith's Precedents* part 34.
[304] 1963 Act, s.60(13).
[305] 1963 Act, s.60(12)(a).
[306] 1963 Act, s.60(12)(b).
[307] [1980] 1 All E.R. 393.

there declined to rule on the position where "the transaction is of a kind which A Ltd could in its own commercial interests legitimately enter into, and ... is genuinely entered into ... in its own commercial interests and not merely as a means of assisting B financially to buy shares of A Ltd, the circumstances that A Ltd enters into the transaction with B partly with the object of putting B in funds or with the knowledge of B's intended use of the proceeds of the sale ..."[308]

Loans by Financial Institutions

8–126   Another exception is "where the lending of money is part of the ordinary business of the company, the lending of money ... in the ordinary course of its business".[309] This envisages ordinary bank loans and the like; it depends on the circumstances whether the loan in question can fairly be described as being made in the ordinary course of the company's business.

Employees' Shares

8–127   A company may assist its employees to acquire its shares or shares in its subsidiary, either individually or under the aegis of some employees' share scheme.[310]

Quoted Companies

8–128   Applying the "mischief" and "commercial substance" approach, it was held in *Chaston v SWP Group*[311] that it was unlawful for a company to pay for a "due diligence" report being carried out on its business, in anticipation of a takeover bid being made for its shares. That was held to be the case even though no detriment was caused to the company being acquired, the assistance was given before and not during the takeover and the payment had no impact on the share price. In response to this, several amendments were adopted in 2005 to take a variety of activities, mainly involving takeovers of quoted companies, out from the prohibition.[312]

Private Companies

8–129   A "whitewash" mechanism exists under which private companies may subsidise purchases of their own shares, provided there is shareholder approval for the proposal and creditors will not be jeopardised.[313] In brief, the directors must make a statutory declaration concerning the proposed payment and the company must pass a special resolution approving the proposal; dissident shareholders may apply to the court to have the proposal vetoed. The statutory declaration must be made by the directors within 24 days before the shareholders' meeting; it must specify the form, the beneficiaries and the purposes of the assistance, and that the declarants after making due inquiry believe that the proposal

---

[308] *ibid.* at 402.
[309] 1963 Act, s.60(12)(d).
[310] 1963 Act, s.60(12)(e), (f) and (n). See para.19–108 *et seq.*
[311] [2003] 1 B.C.L.C. 675.
[312] Section 60(12)(g)–(m).
[313] Section 60(2)–(11). See *BCM's Precedents* part H 61 *et seq.*

will not affect the company's ability to meet its debts as they fall due.[314] It is not sufficient to make the declaration without carrying out enquiries and being duly satisfied, as provided.[315] Copies must be sent to every member and to the Registrar of Companies. In determining whether the declaration is fully compliant, it should be looked at as a whole, and minor errors of fact on it will not invalidate it.[316] Every shareholder is entitled to notice of and to attend the meeting in question. But it is not essential that a meeting as such takes place; the somewhat informal procedure for recording assent to resolutions suffices.[317] Unless it gets unanimous support from those members who are entitled to vote, the proposal cannot be put into effect until at least 30 days have elapsed. In the meantime objecting members, who comprise at least 10 per cent of the issued shares' nominal value or of any class, may apply to the court and the proposal fails except to the extent that it is confirmed by the court.

8–130 *Lombard & Ulster Banking Ltd v Bank of Ireland*[318] is the first major case on compliance with those procedures and the consequences of non-compliance. A company owned valuable property, on which it ran a private school. An arrangement was made whereby several individuals, through a trust company, would acquire the bulk of its shares. Since the prospective purchasers did not have sufficient funds, it was agreed that they should borrow from the plaintiff bank and that the company would guarantee the loan, giving a charge over its property as security. Because this was a classic instance of the company financing the purchase of its own shares, it was necessary to follow the procedures for the transaction to be fully effective. Two major issues arose, namely, was there compliance with these procedures and what are the legal consequences of non-compliance? One of the company's shareholders swore an affidavit that he never attended a shareholders' meeting, at which it was claimed that the proposed transaction had been sanctioned. The company had not kept minute books of those meetings, nor of the directors' meetings. The company's file at Dublin Castle was produced but the documents in it were not proof of their contents; in particular, they were not proof that the requisite resolution had been passed. Indeed, those documents said that the shareholders' resolution had been passed on May 21 and the statutory declaration was made on May 22, which, if correct, was wholly improper. Because of this and other circumstantial evidence, Costello J. concluded that no statutory declaration was made on or before May 21 and no special resolution had been passed subsequently approving the transaction. The judge stressed that the court requires strict compliance with the procedures; that if exemption is claimed, "then strict compliance with the procedures is necessary ... If the procedural requirements were not adopted the transaction is an illegal one ...".[319] The procedures were not satisfied where

---

[314] *cf. Re SH & Co. (Realisations) 1990 Ltd* [1993] B.C.L.C. 1309 and *Re NL Electrical Ltd* [1994] 1 B.C.L.C. 22 on requiring strict compliance.

[315] *Re In a Flap Envelope Co.* [2004] 1 B.C.L.C. 64.

[316] *Re Hill & Tyler Ltd* [2005] 1 B.C.L.C. 41.

[317] 1963 Act, s.141(8).

[318] [1987] I.E.H.C. 154, Costello J., unreported, June 2, 1987.

[319] *ibid.* at 9–10 of the judgment.

all of the shareholders authorised an agent, such as their solicitor, to look after all the formalities and subsequently they ratified what had been done.

8–131   In *Re Northside Motor Co. Ltd*,[320] with the full knowledge of its bankers, a company guaranteed a bank loan for the purpose of assisting the purchase of its own shares. Some time later the bank realised that the procedures had not been followed and, accordingly, prevailed on the company to make a statutory declaration and pass a special resolution approving the guarantee. But since these steps must be taken before the actual assistance is given, there was no compliance and, consequently, the guarantee was ineffective because the bank had actual notice of all the circumstances. Additionally, the special resolution passed was inaccurate and misleading and, for that reason also, failed to comply.

Enforcement

8–132   The appropriate civil consequences of contravening the rule against financing the purchase of a company's own or its holding company's shares has been a source of controversy in practically every common law jurisdiction. Generally, the transaction by which the assistance is, or is to be, given is void and unenforceable. Thus, for instance, in *Heald v O'Connor*,[321] where the plaintiff agreed to sell a company's shares to the defendant and to lend him the money to make the purchase, which loan was guaranteed by a charge on that company's assets, it was held that the charge and guarantee could not be enforced. The principle of consequent invalidity is qualified by the 1963 Act, under which " [a]ny transaction in breach of this section shall be voidable at the instance of the company against any person (whether a party to the transaction or not) who had notice of the facts which constituted such breach".[322]

8–133   Although it is not stipulated expressly, the implication is that the company cannot avoid the transaction where the other party did not have the requisite notice. That interpretation was accepted in *Bank of Ireland v Rockfield Ltd*.[323] The bank had agreed to advance money to two individuals to enable them to buy a certain piece of land, an equitable mortgage of the certificate of title being intended to be the security. In the event, the money was advanced to the order of the defendant company, the land was in its name and it deposited the certificate of title with the bank. Those individuals then used the money to acquire control of the company. It not being contested that this was unlawful, the issue was whether the company could avoid its agreement to secure the bank loans. The Supreme Court concluded that the bank did not have sufficient actual knowledge of how the money was to be used. It held that notice in this context means actual knowledge and not the equitable "constructive notice". It is not necessary that the person must be aware of the prohibition or that the transition is in breach of it.

---

[320] [1985] I.E.H.C. 42, Costello J., unreported, July 24, 1985.
[321] [1971] 1 W.L.R. 497.
[322] Section 60(14).
[323] [1979] I.R. 21.

8–134   This issue arose again in *Lombard & Ulster Banking Ltd v Bank of Ireland*,[324] which concerned an agreement whereby control could be acquired of a private school that owned valuable land, but the procedures under which private companies are permitted to finance the purchase of their own shares had not been followed there. The question then was the effect of non-compliance. Costello J. construed s.60(14) as "mean[ing] (a) that although a transaction in breach of the section is illegal it is only voidable, not void, and (b) it is only voidable against a person who had notice of the facts which constituted the breach".[325] In other words, the company cannot avoid the transaction unless the other party to the transaction had the requisite notice. Where no attempt was made to go through the prescribed procedures, the notice means actual notice that the prohibition had been contravened, i.e. knowledge of facts which clearly point to the conclusion that it was breached. Where it was sought to have the transaction sanctioned by the shareholders but their approval was not given in the manner prescribed, the transaction can be avoided by the company only where it is shown that the other party had actual notice that the statutory procedures had not been followed to the letter. As Costello J. put it:

> "it is not sufficient ... to show that if [the other party] had made proper inquiries that they would have ascertained that the company had failed to comply with the sub-sections. It must be shown that [the party] had actual notice of the facts which constituted the breach, that is (a) that they or their officials actually knew that the required procedures were not adopted or that they knew facts from which they must have inferred that the company had failed to adopt the required procedures, or (b) that an agent of theirs actually knew of the failure or knew facts from which he must have inferred that a failure had occurred".[326]

It was found that, in the circumstances, the plaintiff bank did not have that kind of notice.

8–135   Where the company itself seeks to sue on the transaction, such as to recover money lent for the proscribed purpose, the courts tend to grant enforcement because the prohibition was enacted for its benefit. Especially when the beneficiaries of its assistance happen to be its own directors acting improperly, it is not in *pari delicto* and, accordingly, should be allowed to recover.[327] While this trend is not universal,[328] some countries have amended their companies legislation to incorporate it.[329] It is not settled whether the agreement itself to acquire the shares is tainted with the illegality.[330] Directors who are responsible for a company becoming a party to a proscribed transaction are liable to it for consequent losses that the company may incur.[331] Additionally, anyone

---

[324] [1987] I.E.H.C. 154, Costello J., unreported, June 2, 1987.
[325] *ibid.* at 10 of the judgment.
[326] *ibid.* at 11 of the judgment.
[327] e.g. *Wallersteiner v Moir* (No. 2) [1975] Q.B. 373.
[328] e.g. *Central & Eastern Trust Co. v Irving Oil Ltd* 110 D.L.R. (3d) 257 (1980).
[329] e.g. Canada Business Corporation Act, s.42(3).
[330] cf. *South West Mineral Water Co. v Ashmore* [1967] 1 W.L.R. 110.
[331] e.g. *Belmont Finance Co. v William Furniture Ltd (No. 2)* [1980] 1 All E.R. 393.

who receives a company's funds that are so misapplied and has knowledge of the breach will be liable to the company as a constructive trustee.[332] In appropriate circumstances, the responsible directors and those who receive the assistance may be liable for the tort of conspiracy.[333]

8–136   Breach of the prohibition here also can amount to "oppression" under s.205 of the 1963 Act in appropriate circumstances. That was held to be the case in *Re Greenore Trading Co.*,[334] where a majority shareholder bought out one of the other shareholders. But the cheque paying for those shares was drawn on the company's own bank account. Because relationships between the petitioner and the majority holder had broken down, because the petitioner had not been told that company funds would be used for that purchase, and on account of the general circumstances in the company, Keane J. held that making the payment constituted oppression.

<h3 align="center">Capital Haemorrhage</h3>

8–137   At times a company may start out with adequate funds but may find that years of unprofitable trading erode its capital base. The directors of every limited company, who find that its financial position has deteriorated to the extent that net assets (i.e. aggregate assets minus total liabilities) are worth not more than half of its called-up share capital, are obliged to convene an EGM.[335] This must be done within 28 days of a director learning of the deficiency and the meeting must be convened for not later than 56 days from that same day. The matter for deliberation at that meeting is "whether any, and if so, what measures be taken to deal with the situation". A director who "knowingly and wilfully" does not convene a shareholders' meeting to consider the capital haemorrhage is guilty of an offence. Every auditors' report on a company's accounts must state an opinion whether the company is in a "section 40" situation.[336]

---

[332] *ibid.*
[333] *ibid.*
[334] [1980] I.L.R.M. 94.
[335] 1983 Act, s.40.
[336] 1990 Act, s.193(4c)(ii).

CHAPTER 9

MEMBERS' RIGHTS

9–01   The rights and obligations of company members (usually shareholders) are defined principally by their company's memorandum and articles of association, supplemented by the Companies Acts. Occasionally the terms on which the shares were issued have a bearing. Where there is a separate shareholders' agreement, in practical terms that may have precedence over the company's own regulations. Particular classes of members may be given preferential rights with regard to some questions. The process of becoming a member, title to shares and other proprietary interests in them, requires consideration of shares as items of personal property. Members of companies limited by guarantee usually do not hold shares in them and much of the discussion below accordingly is not applicable to those persons.

THE NATURE OF SHARES

9–02   The 1963 Act (s.79) defines the "nature of shares" as personal property which are inherently transferable: "shares or other interest of any member in a company shall be personal estate, transferable in manner provided by the articles of the company, and shall not be of the nature of real estate". A share is a legal chose in action. It is not a "good" within the meaning of the Sale of Goods Acts.

9–03   Membership of a company, by holding one or more shares in it, represents a complex web of liability to and interests in the company.[1] The classic definition of a share is "the interest of a shareholder in the company measured by a sum of money, for the purpose of liability in the first place, and of interest in the second, but also consisting of a series of mutual covenants entered into by all the shareholders *inter se* in accordance with [s.25 of the 1963 Act]. The contract contained in the articles of association is one of the original incidents of the share".[2] Kenny J. adopted and amplified this definition in a case concerning the valuation of shares for tax purposes:

> "No shareholder has a right to any specific portion of the company's property, and save by, and to the extent of, his voting power at a general meeting of the Company, cannot curtail the free and proper disposition of it.

---

[1]   See generally, Rice, "The Legal Nature of a Share" 21 *Conv.* 443 (1957) and Grantham, "The Doctrinal Basis of the Rights of Company Shareholders" 57 *Cam. L.J.* 554 (1998).

[2]   *Borland's Trustees v Steel Bros* [1901] 1 Ch. 279 at 288.

He is entitled to a share of the Company's capital and profits, the former ... being measured by a sum of money which is taken as the standard for the ascertainment of his share of the profits. If the Company disposes of its assets, or if the latter be realised in a liquidation, he has a right to a proportion of the amount received after the discharge of the Company's debts and liabilities. In acquiring these rights——that is, in becoming a member of the Company—he is deemed to have simultaneously entered into a contract under seal to conform to the regulations contained in the articles of association... Whatever obligations are contained in those articles, he accepts the ownership of the shares and the position of a member of the Company, bound and controlled by them. He cannot divorce his money interest, whatever it may amount to, from these obligations. They are inseparable incidents attached to his rights, and the idea of a share cannot, in my judgment, be complete without their inclusion."[3]

9–04   As well as having various entitlements under their company's own regulations, shareholders enjoy an extensive range of rights under the Companies Acts (e.g. to be given copies of the annual reports, to be notified of all proposed general resolutions, to demand a poll at general meetings and to pre-emption in certain circumstances) and they have a general right not to be subjected to "oppression". In *Jones v Garnett*,[4] another tax case, the intrinsic nature of the ordinary shares there were held to be "not wholly or even substantially a right to income. It was an ordinary share conferring a right to vote, to participate in the distribution of assets on a winding up, to block a special resolution, to complain under s.[205] of the Companies Act. These are rights over and above the right to income."[5]

9–05   The precise extent of shareholders' interest in their company is usually determined by the par value of their shares and the number of shares they possess. Occasionally, the amount actually paid up on them may be determinative.

9–06   Ownership of one or more shares does not give the member any proprietary rights in the underlying assets of the company. By virtue of the separate legal personality principle, even the sole beneficial shareholder of a "one person" company does not even have an insurable interest in the assets of his company.[6] Such rights as a shareholder has against his company, as opposed to anyone else, are personal.

REGISTER OF MEMBERS

9–07   Every company must keep a register of its members.[7] Ordinarily it must be kept at the registered office. But it may be kept elsewhere in the State, such

---

[3] *Attorney-General v Jameson* [1904] 2 I.R. 644 at 669–670; *cf. Pilmer v Duke Group Ltd* [2001] 2 B.C.L.C. 773 (High Court of Australia).

[4] [2007] 1 W.L.R. 2030.

[5] *ibid.* at 2038.

[6] *Macaura v Northern Assurance Co.* [1925] A.C. 619.

[7] 1963 Act, ss.116–124.

as where someone has agreed to maintain it for the company (e.g. professional registrars), in which event its location should be notified to the Registrar of Companies.[8] It may be closed for not more than 30 days in a year.[9]

9–08   There are three ways in which a person can become a member of a company or, for short, a shareholder. The original subscribers to the memorandum of association are deemed to be shareholders as soon as the company is registered.[10] Persons who agree to subscribe for shares that are allotted to them and whose names are then registered as such also become shareholders.[11] Thirdly, as is explained below, the successors in title of the original members and of those to whom shares were allotted and registered as members become shareholders on their being duly registered as such,[12] i.e. persons who agreed to acquire the subscribers' or the allottees' shares, and persons to whom those shares passed by operation of law, like personal representatives on death, trustees in bankruptcy, etc. Except where the general law so requires or its own regulations authorise it to do so, a company cannot refuse to register a person who has properly acquired shares in it.[13]

Contents

9–09   The register of members must contain every member's name, address, the amount and the numbers of shares held, the amounts paid up on the shares, and the date on which each became and ceased to be a member.[14] These details must be entered within 28 days of the person agreeing either to become a subscriber or a member. Its contents are not conclusive; they are only prima facie evidence of what it states.[15] Depending on the circumstances, however, a company may be estopped from disputing the accuracy of its contents and may even be liable for negligent misstatement for errors it contains. A company which has more than 50 members must keep a separate index of their names.[16]

9–10   A company with a stock exchange listing which has chosen to participate in the CREST electronic transfer of title system must enter on the register of members the number of shares that each member holds in uncertificated form and in certificated form, respectively.[17]

9–11   A Plc that has issued share warrants in respect of its bearer shares must enter on the register the fact that the warrants were issued, a statement of the shares included in them and the dates of issue.[18]

---

[8]   1963 Act, ss.116(5) and 120.
[9]   1963 Act, s.121.
[10] 1963 Act, s.31(1); *Evan's Case* (1867) L.R. 2 Ch. 427.
[11] 1963 Act, s.31(2).
[12] 1963 Act, s.31(2).
[13] *Tagney v Clarence Hotels Ltd* [1933] I.R. 51.
[14] 1963 Act, s.116.
[15] 1963 Act, s.124.
[16] 1963 Act, s.117.
[17] See para.15–87 *et seq.*
[18] 1963 Act, s.118(1).

Nominee Holdings

9–12   Often the real or beneficial ownership of shares is disguised by having them registered in the name of nominees—frequently in the name of special nominee companies that financial institutions establish for this purpose. Table A authorises the company to require that information be furnished to it as to the beneficial ownership of shares in it.[19] Previously there was no requirement to record separately the names of those who hold substantial interests in a company's voting shares, or for ascertaining who in fact owns or has material interests in shares that are registered in the names of others. These matters are now dealt with in Pt IV (ss.53–106), of the 1990 Act, headed "Disclosure of Interests in Shares".[20]

Inspection

9–13   Not alone is every member of a company entitled to inspect its members' register but, on payment of a small charge, so too may any stranger.[21] On payment of a small charge, the company must give them a copy of the register or any part of it. If the company refuses to do so, the court may order immediate inspection and copying. In exceptional circumstances, an order of this nature will be refused or will be granted subject to appropriate undertakings being given.[22]

Rectification

9–14   Companies may alter the contents of their register of members but any such change does not prejudice any affected member unless he has consented to it.[23] In the case of shares that are transferred electronically, the company cannot alter those contents, except where the operator of the CREST system consents or where the court has so ordered.[24]

9–15   Where a dispute arises about ownership of shares, persons may wish to have names removed from the register or to have it otherwise altered. For instance, they are no longer members or they never agreed to take shares in the company, or the subscription or purchase agreement they made was void (e.g. for misrepresentation). To that end, they may apply to have the register rectified.[25] On such an application, the court is empowered to decide issues concerning title to the shares in question and also to award compensation for any loss sustained by a party. However, where resolving a dispute about ownership would require oral evidence and cross-examination, this summary rectification procedure will not be adopted.[26] Depending on the circumstances, delay may be fatal to an application for rectification on the grounds of misrepresentation.

---

[19]   Article 7.
[20]   See para.17–100 *et seq.*
[21]   1963 Act, s.110.
[22]   *Pelling v Families Need Fathers Ltd* [2002] 1 B.C.L.C. 645.
[23]   1963 Act, s.122(5).
[24]   See para.15–92.
[25]   1963 Act, s.122.
[26]   *Re Hoicrest Ltd* [2000] 1 B.C.L.C. 194.

INCIDENTS OF MEMBERSHIP

9–16 Members have a general right against those who control their company to have it run in accordance with its own regulations and the Companies Acts; also that majorities do not unfairly discriminate against minorities and that the majority do not "defraud" the company. Members ordinarily have six vital specific rights against their company, namely, to certain information concerning its affairs, to vote at general meetings, to a dividend if declared, to statutory pre-emption, to transfer their shares and to a return of capital and of any surplus if the company is wound up. A company's own regulations may give particular classes of shareholders, such as those with preference shares or indeed named individuals, "class" or "special personal" rights. A recent example in New Zealand is redeemable preference shares entitling their holders to membership of a golf club.[27]

Memorandum and Articles

9–17 In determining an individual member's rights and obligations *vis-à-vis* the company under its own regulations, the following principles apply, although on occasion these are subject to certain qualifications and exceptions.

9–18 The nature and extent of a member's or class of members' rights and obligations are primarily a question of the interpretation of the company's memorandum and articles of association, any resolutions passed under the articles and the terms on which the shares in question were issued. Members' rights "must depend on the terms of the instrument which contains the bargain that they have made with the company and each other".[28] That the answer to most disputes about shareholders' rights is to be found in the correct construction of the company's own regulations was emphasised in *Cork Electric Supply Co. v Concannon*,[29] where Kennedy C.J. warned against relying too much on reported decisions on similar questions. One set of articles "cannot [be] construe[d] by the construction applied by some court to another set of articles (save, or course, as to any principle or rule of construction of general application authoritatively declared for the purpose of such construction)".[30] However, FitzGibbon J. observed that: "If a particular article, clause, or expression has received a judicial interpretation, and has been subsequently adopted as precedent in the formation of other companies, it is better, in a doubtful question of construction, to adhere to previous decisions rather than upon a nice balance of opinion to disaffirm a construction in reliance upon which large amounts of capital may have been invested".[31]

9–19 The general principles regarding the construction of commercial documents apply to interpreting companies' memoranda and articles of

---

[27] *Gulf Harbour Development Ltd v CIR* [2004] 2 N.Z.L.R. 768.
[28] *Scottish Ins Corp. v Wilson & Clyde Coal Co.* [1949] A.C. 462 at 488.
[29] [1932] I.R. 314.
[30] *ibid.* at 328.
[31] *ibid.* at 333.

association. Where Table A is not adopted, the articles or at least some of them are often taken from off-the-shelf precedents rather than being the outcome of individual negotiation. Courts may infer a term into them by way of purely constructional implication.[32] However, no term will be implied from existing circumstances, such as the actions and beliefs of the members at the time they incorporated their company. This is because the documents are given statutory force and are open to inspection by anyone considering dealing with the company or taking shares in it. On the other hand, where they have been amended, it is permissible to take account of their earlier versions in the construction of their present provisions.[33] It appears that courts will not rectify the terms of articles of association that do not accord with the members' intentions when they were being adopted.[34]

9–20   Although the memorandum of association is the dominant instrument and must prevail where there is any conflict, reference may be made to the articles to explain ambiguities in the memorandum or to supplement it on matters about which it is silent.[35] Where there is inconsistency between provisions in the articles, the following two principles of interpretation were stated by Gavan Duffy J. in *Re Imperial Hotel (Cork) Ltd.*[36] Where an "earlier clause is followed by a later clause which destroys altogether the obligation created by the earlier clause, the later clause is to be rejected as repugnant and the earlier clause prevails".[37] And a "clause embodying a declaration of rights for a class of preferred members must, on a conflict of language, prevail … over administrative provisions of an intrinsically ancillary and subordinate character".[38]

9–21   Whatever provisions are contained in the company's own regulations regarding a particular kind of right are deemed to be exhaustive, i.e. as regards any one of the major rights that are defined in those regulations, shareholders are entitled to nothing more than what is expressly provided for. For instance, where one class of shares is described as being entitled to a 10 per cent dividend, their holders have no right to be paid dividends over and above that amount.

9–22   Where, however, the regulations are silent as to any of the usual rights, then all shareholders possess those rights in an equal measure. Thus, where nothing is said about voting or about dividend entitlements, every shareholder has the same rights to vote and to dividends.

9–23   Finally, there is the nominalist principle, by which is meant that, in the absence of some contrary provision in the regulations, for most purposes the measure of members' rights is the nominal value of their shares, not the

[32] *Bratton Seymour Service Co. v Oxborough* [1992] B.C.L.C. 693.
[33] *Folkes Group Plc v Alexander* [2002] 2 B.C.L.C. 254.
[34] *Scott v F Scott (London) Ltd* [1940] Ch. 794.
[35] *Re Bansha Woollen Mills Co.* (1887) 21 L.R. Ir. 181.
[36] [1950] I.R. 115.
[37] *ibid.* at 119.
[38] *ibid.*

amount paid up on them or the price paid for them. Thus, where the right to dividends is stated in percentage terms (e.g. dividend of 12 per cent), this means 12 per cent of the share's nominal or par value.[39] Similarly, the measure of the member's right to share in a surplus that is left over in a winding-up, after all debts have been paid and provision is made to repay the subscribed capital, is the share's nominal value[40]; although unpaid amounts may have to be paid up before holders of partly paid shares can participate in the surplus.[41]

Evidence of Rights

9–24 Since the memorandum and articles of association and any amendments made to them, and all special resolutions, must be registered in the registry of companies, the incidents of membership as recorded in them are matters of public record. However, incidents can be attached to shares by virtue of an ordinary resolution of the company or otherwise. Every company must forward to the Registrar of Companies all resolutions relating to any rights or restrictions attaching to their shares within 15 days of their being passed.[42] Where shares are allotted with rights attaching to them that are not stated in the company's own regulations or in a resolution that must be registered, particulars of those rights must be delivered to the CRO within one month of the allotment.[43] Particulars of any variation of those rights must be registered and, as well, particulars of any name or designation assigned to the shares. The articles of association of listed companies must state how their various classes of shares rank for distribution; any non-voting or limited or restrictive voting shares must be described in the articles as such. Any change in the rights attaching to those shares must be promptly disclosed to the public.[44]

Restrictions on Rights

9–25 Shareholders' rights are sterilised in several respects to encourage disclosure of who their beneficial owner is. Where an official enquiry or inspection is being carried out into the affairs of a company or into the ownership of its securities, the DCE may by notice impose restrictions on its shares. While these are in force, no dividend may be paid or repayment of capital may be made in respect of the shares, their voting rights may not be exercised and any transfer of or agreement to transfer them is void.[45] On application to the court, it may permit the shares to be sold, but it may decline to do so until all relevant information about their ownership is disclosed. For instance, where shares were in the name of a Swiss bank and its nominee company, who contended that under bank confidentiality rules they could not disclose the identity of the shares' owner, the court refused to authorise their sale on the stock market.[46]

---

[39] *Oakbank Oil Co. v Crum* (1882) 8 App. Cas. 65. But *cf.* Table A, art.120.
[40] *Birch v Cropper* (1889) 14 App. Cas. 525.
[41] *Re Newtownards Gas Co.* (1885) 15 L.R. Ir. 51.
[42] 1963 Act, s.143(4) (f) and (g).
[43] 1983 Act, s.39.
[44] Transparency (Directive 2004/109/EC) Regulations, 2007 (SI 2007/277), reg.26(1).
[45] 1990 Act, s.16.
[46] *Re Geers Gross Plc* [1987] 1 W.L.R. 1649.

9–26   Where a director or secretary does not make the requisite disclosure to the company of the interest he has in its securities or the interests of a "connected person", "no right or interest of any kind whatsoever" in respect of them is enforceable by him, "directly or indirectly, by action or legal proceedings".[47] The shares of any person who fails to give any of the notices required by the provisions on "individual and group acquisitions" in the 1990 Act, or who knowingly or recklessly makes a false statement to the company concerning such agreements, suffer a similar fate.[48]

9–27   Where a Plc seeks to ascertain the beneficial ownership of its shares but is not being provided with the requisite information, it may apply to the court for an order freezing the rights to them to the same effect.[49] Any such order must freeze all of the rights in question; there is no jurisdiction to exempt some of the parties who would be affected from the order, notwithstanding that they are entirely innocent.[50]

9–28   Where a private company obtains a disclosure order, with a view to ascertaining the beneficial ownership of some of its shares, that has not been complied with, the person to whom it is directed is barred from taking legal proceedings to enforce any right in respect of those shares.[51]

9–29   Votes attaching to "treasury shares" cannot be exercised and no distribution can be made in respect of them.[52]

INFORMATION

9–30   All members are entitled to be given extensive information concerning their company's affairs.

- They have the right to inspect, free of charge, the various registers that companies are obliged to maintain—registers of members, of debenture-holders, of charges, of directors' interests in the company's shares, of contracts in which directors have interests.

- Notices of general meetings and of resolutions it is proposed to consider at such meetings must be sent to them.[53]

- They must be supplied with copies of their company's annual accounts, together with its auditors' and its directors' annual reports.[54]

- One of the grounds on which inspectors may be appointed to investigate the affairs of a company is where "its members have not been given all the information concerning its affairs which they might reasonably expect".[55]

---

[47] 1990 Act, s.58(3).
[48] 1990 Act, s.79(3).
[49] 1990 Act, s.85.
[50] *Re Lonrho Plc (No. 2)* [1990] 1 Ch. 695.
[51] 1990 Act, s.101(4).
[52] 1990 Act, s.209(3).
[53] 1963 Act, s.133.
[54] 1963 Act, s.159.
[55] 1990 Act, s.8(1)(c).

Companies with securities quoted on a stock exchange must make extensive disclosure not only to their members but also to the exchange's regulatory authorities and to the general public.

9–31 Table A is undemanding in this regard. Its only purely informational requirements are circulating notices of general meetings and of proposed resolutions to be considered at them, and circulating, to those entitled to receive them, copies of the annual accounts and the directors' and the auditors' annual reports.[56] It authorises the directors to determine the circumstances under which members may inspect the company's books and records but adds that members shall have no right to inspect those documents "except as conferred by statute or authorised by the directors or by the company in general meeting".[57] However, there exists a very general power for the court, upon the application by, *inter alia,* a member, to compel a company or any officer of a company to make good its or his "default in complying with *any* provision of the [Companies Acts]" within a specified time, and to make the company or officer responsible bear the costs of the application to the court.[58]

9–32 Exceptionally, the failure to provide information over and above that required in the company's articles or in the legislation may amount to "oppression" under s.205 of the 1963 Act. In *Re Clubman Shirts Ltd,*[59] where the company was in serious financial difficulties and was threatened with receivership and liquidation, the directors transferred its business to another company under a scheme whereby the transferor's shareholders received no payment. For a number of years the directors refused to hold annual general meetings or to present annual accounts or file an annual return. Nor would they give the petitioner, who held 20 per cent of the equity, details about the transfer of the undertaking. O'Hanlon J. characterised most of their conduct as "negligence, carelessness [and] irregularity" rather than oppression. But he found that, despite the position in "strict law", a minority shareholder ought ordinarily to be provided with adequate information about such a vital matter as disposal of the undertaking and that, accordingly, the petitioner had been a victim of oppression. It was held in England that minority shareholders were wrongfully oppressed where the company had not filed annual accounts for several years and no general meeting had been held for years.[60] They were thereby deprived of "their right to know and consider the state of the company and its directorships and to ask questions of its directors ..."[61]

---

[56] Articles 51, 52 and 129.

[57] Article 127.

[58] 1963 Act, s.371. *Cf. Airscape Ltd v Powertech Logistics Ltd* [2007] I.E.H.C. 43, Laffoy J., unreported, February 5, 2007; *Brosnan v Sommerville* [2006] I.E.H.C. 329, Smyth J., unreported, October 3, 2006.

[59] [1983] I.L.R.M. 323.

[60] *Re A Company, Ex p. Shooter* [1990] B.C.L.C. 384.

[61] *ibid.* at 393.

VOTE

9–33   Members generally are entitled to vote in general meetings. Except for imposing a degree of voting equality in exceptional circumstances, however, the legislation does not determine which shareholders have a vote or the extent of their voting powers; the Companies Acts are mainly concerned with the actual conduct of meetings, the machinery for passing resolutions and proxies. In the past, the presumption was that every shareholder had one vote regardless of the number of shares they held.[62] Unless the company's own regulations provide otherwise, one vote attaches to every share or to each €12.69 of stock.[63]

9–34   Table A provides that every member at the general meeting has one vote on a show of hands and, when a poll is taken, one vote per share; but this is subject to any special voting rights or restrictions attached to any class or classes of shares that were issued.[64] In the absence of some contrary stipulation, the amount paid up on or paid for shares does not affect the value of the vote they carry.[65]

Inequalities

9–35   Where it is sought to allocate control in a company in a way other than that reflected by the actual amounts shareholders have invested in it, i.e. other than the "one share one vote" system, a device commonly used is to create different kinds of voting shares. Table A empowers companies subject to it to issue shares "with such preferred, deferred or other special rights or restrictions ... in regard to ... voting ... as the company may from time to time by ordinary resolution determine".[66] For instance, the shares may be divided into separate classes, like "ordinary" and "deferred" shares, or "A" and "B" shares, with one category carrying greater voting rights per share than the other. Alternatively, on certain issues, such as the removal of directors, one group of shares may carry more votes than the others. Or there may be a basic "one share one vote" system but with no individual shareholder entitled to cast more than a specified number of votes regardless of how many shares they possess; which is the system of voting in Alliance & Dublin Consumers Gas Co.,[67] said to have been introduced at the instigation of its founder, Daniel O'Connell, to ensure that the company would not be taken over by large financial interests. There are companies with some classes of shares that have no voting rights whatsoever. Non-voting shares are discouraged by the Irish Stock Exchange.

9–36   The freedom of companies to devise whatever voting scheme suits them best was affirmed in *Bushell v Faith*.[68] The articles of association

---

[62] The E.C.'s Voting Rights Directive of 2007 (Directive 2007/36 [2007] O.J. L184/17), for listed companies, must be implemented by August 3, 2009.

[63] 1963 Act, s.134(e). See para.5–52 *et seq.*

[64] Article 63.

[65] *Re Wakefield Rolling Stock Co.* [1892] 3 Ch D 165.

[66] Article 2.

[67] *cf. Kinsella v Alliance & Dublin Consumers Gas Co.* [1982] I.E.H.C. 195, Barron J., unreported, October 5, 1982.

[68] [1970] A.C. 1099.

provided that, on any proposal to remove him from office, a director would have three votes for each share that he held. It was argued that this contravened the equivalent of the 1963 Act, under which any director can be removed from office by ordinary resolution "notwithstanding anything in the articles ..."[69] But that contention was rejected on the grounds that the legislature "has never sought to fetter the right of the company to issue a share with such [voting] rights or restrictions as it may think fit. There is no fetter which compels the company to make the voting rights or restrictions of general application and ... such rights or restrictions can be attached to special circumstances and to particular types of resolution".[70]

Imposed Equalities

9–37   In certain circumstances, voting inequalities in a company's own regulations will be overridden by legislation. Where it is proposed to make an arrangement or reconstruction under s.201 of the 1963 Act, the matter cannot be resolved in accordance with any special voting system the company adopted. Instead, the proposal must have been accepted by at least 75 per cent in nominal value of the class or classes affected and who vote before it can become binding on that class and the company.[71] Similarly, for a "take-out merger" to take place, the acquiring company must have bought at least 80 per cent (or 90 per cent in the case of a listed company) in value of the shares affected.[72] And rights given to minority shareholders to apply to the court to veto certain fundamental structural changes in the company are expressed in terms of a minority who hold a stipulated percentage in value of the issued share capital, and not in terms of a percentage of votes.[73]

DIVIDEND

9–38   Where a company's business is profitable, the shareholders will expect to be rewarded by being paid dividends. Except for prohibiting paying dividends from capital, the legislation is virtually silent in this regard. Unless expressly excluded, income tax under Schedule F is chargeable on all dividends paid and other distributions made by a company resident in the State.[74]

9–39   Table A envisages all shareholders having the same dividend entitlements, with the decision to declare a dividend being split between the directors and the members in general meeting. Before any dividend can be declared, it must be recommended by the board.[75] But it is for the general meeting to decide whether any dividend should be paid, provided that the amount

---

[69]   Section 182.
[70]   [1970] A.C. 1099 at 1109.
[71]   See para.11–67.
[72]   See paras.12–43 and 15–141.
[73]   See para.11–15.
[74]   Taxes Consolidation Act 1997, s.21 and see generally M.Feeney, *The Taxation of Companies* (Haywards Heath: Tottel Publishing, 2006), Ch.11.
[75]   Article 116.

does not exceed that recommended by the board.[76] Special classes of shareholders, like those owning preference shares, may be entitled to be paid in priority to other classes.[77] Although the presumption is that dividend rights are based on the nominal amounts as opposed to the amounts called up or in fact paid up on shares, Table A provides that dividends are to be calculated on the amounts paid up or credited as paid up.[78] The directors have authority to pay such interim dividends "as appear to [them] to be justified by" the company's profits.[79] They, moreover, are given a wide discretion to carry forward any profits "which they think it prudent not to divide"; and they are empowered "as they think proper" to place profits in reserve and either to invest those funds or use them in the company's business.[80]

Declining to Declare a Dividend

9–40   Several variables go into the decision whether the company should pay a dividend in any particular year and, if so, the size of that payment.[81] Much depends on the extent of the company's profitability, its investment intentions, its liabilities and also taxation considerations. In the case of large companies with many shareholders and where the directors tend to have a considerable degree of autonomy, the likelihood of their control over dividends being abused must be set alongside economic considerations that deter abuse. For instance, a takeover bid can be a response to a pattern of either unduly miserly or excessively generous distributions. But where small companies are concerned, it is not unusual for the majority shareholders to occupy all the seats on the board, to pay themselves lavish directors' fees and never to recommend a dividend; in consequence the minority shareholders may be discriminated against in fact. While such conduct might be a breach of directors' fiduciary duties, in the absence of other aggravating factors it is unlikely to amount to an unlawful interference with minority shareholders' rights. What tends to prevent the courts from intervening here is that a decision against the company may in effect require the judge to determine its dividend policy, a task which the court would be reluctant, and may be ill-equipped, to undertake.

9–41   Exceptionally, however, the failure to declare dividends where there are more than ample funds to cover any distribution may constitute "oppression" under s.205 of the 1963 Act.[82] For instance, in *Re Sam Weller & Sons Ltd*,[83] the company was a prosperous family business, in which the two petitioners held about 15 per cent of the shares in it but then inherited shares, taking their

---

[76] Article 116. See *Scott v Scott* [1943] 1 All E.R. 582.
[77] See para.9–122 *et seq.*
[78] Article 120.
[79] Article 117.
[80] Article 119.
[81] See generally, T. Power et al, *Financial Management: An Irish Text*, 2nd edn (Dublin: Gill & Macmillan, 2005), Ch.12 and G. Arnold, *Handbook of Corporate Finance: A Business Companion to Financial Markets, Decisions & Techniques* (Harlow: Financial Times Prentice Hall, 2005), Ch.14.
[82] See para.10–91.
[83] [1990] 1 Ch. 683.

stake up to 42.5 per cent. The company's net assets were worth approximately £500,000, half of that being in cash. For the previous 37 years the company always paid the same dividend, which at the relevant time was covered 14 times by earned profits. There was no indication that dividends would be increased. The proceedings were an application to strike out the petition for oppression, on the grounds that, on the evidence, the case could not possibly succeed. But it was held that there can exist circumstances, where no dividend or a derisory dividend has been paid for a long period, without any reasonable business justification, where a court would be justified in making an order under s.205. Whether those circumstances existed in this case was to be determined at the trial of the action. There is a famous American case of 90 years ago involving the Ford Motor Co.,[84] where minority shareholders, the Dodge brothers, obtained an order from a Michigan court that the company pay $19m in dividends. Non-payment of dividends in exceptional circumstances might even justify winding up the company on just and equitable grounds.

Debt

9–42   Unless there is a stipulation to the contrary in the company's own regulations, dividends must be paid in cash.[85] Table A authorises their payment by cheque.[86] It was held in *Re Drogheda Steampacket Co.*[87] that a duly declared dividend is a speciality debt and therefore may be recovered from the company after more than six years have elapsed. This was reiterated by Kenny J. in *Re Belfast Empire Theatre of Varieties*,[88] where it was held that the appropriate period under the Statute of Limitations 1957, in which dividends declared can be recovered from the company, is 12 years. However, the English Chancery Division has concluded that a debt of this nature is a simple contract debt and, therefore, becomes statute-barred after six years.[89] Table A empowers the company to deduct from the dividends payable any sums immediately due to it in respect of the share, such as unpaid calls.[90]

In Specie

9–43   Table A also permits distributions *in specie* by way of dividend, in particular, paid-up shares and debentures of any other company.[91] The reference there to "specific assets" and to securities of "any other" company means that the article does not authorise a company to distribute its own shares by way of dividend—what are called "scrip" or "stock" dividends. Yet some companies have special articles giving themselves such authority, which often take the form of giving the shareholders an option of taking their dividends either in money or in additional equity in the company. Many US corporations

---

[84]   *Dodge v Ford Motor Co.* 170 N.W. 668 (1919).
[85]   *Wood v Odessa Waterworks Co.* (1889) 42 Ch D 636.
[86]   Article 123.
[87]   [1903] 1 I.R. 512.
[88]   [1963] I.R. 41.
[89]   *Re Compania de Electricidad de Buenos Aires Ltd* [1980] Ch. 146.
[90]   Article 121.
[91]   Article 122.

offer "dividend reinvestment plans" to their shareholders, whereby dividends are used to purchase further stock in the corporation.

PRE-EMPTION

9–44 Pre-emption in this context means compulsory "rights issues", i.e. companies being obliged when they issue new equity to do so by giving their shareholders a first option on those shares in proportion to their existing holdings.[92] Shareholders value pre-emption because it enables them to protect their stake in the company from dilution. They can retain what proportionate voting strength they possess and, if the company becomes progressively more profitable, they have an exceptionally favourable outlet for funds at their disposal.

9–45 Pre-emption is compulsory for every company: "a company proposing to allot any equity securities shall not allot any of those securities on any terms to any person unless it has made an offer to each person who holds relevant shares … to allot to him on the same or more favourable terms a proportion of those securities which is as nearly as practicable equal to the proportion in nominal value held by him of the aggregate of relevant shares …"[93] Thus, for example, in a situation like that in the *Rank Organisation* case,[94] the American shareholders would now be entitled to a first option on the new shares being issued there. The offer need not be a mathematically exact *pro rata* one; a proportion that is "as nearly as practicable" equal suffices. An offer must remain open for at least 21 days.[95] Any shareholder may renounce his pre-emption rights in favour of somebody else.[96] The statutory regime here is replicated in the Irish Stock Exchange's Listing Rules.[97] However, statutory pre-emption does not apply, or applies only partly, in the following circumstances.

9–46 A private company by its memorandum or articles of association may exclude or vary the right; any provisions in a private company's own regulations that are inconsistent with the right take precedence over it.[98] Some would argue that private companies should not be allowed to contract out of the statutory requirement so easily.

9–47 Where authority exists to make a share allotment, the articles of association or the general meeting by special resolution may waive, either wholly or partly, the pre-emption requirement.[99] For such a waiver to be effective, the authority to make the allotment must be in force; the waiver must have been recommended by the directors; and the notice proposing the special resolution

---

[92] See generally, MacNeil, "Shareholders' Pre-emptive Rights" [2002] *J.BUS.L.* 78.
[93] 1983 Act, s.23(1)(a).
[94] *Mutual Life Insurance Co. of New York v Rank Organisation Ltd* [1985] B.C.L.C. 11.
[95] *cf. Re Thundercrest Ltd* [1995] 1 B.C.L.C. 117.
[96] Subject of course to any restrictions in the company's own regulations regarding the admission of new members, e.g. those considered at para.9–55 *et seq.*
[97] Listing Rules 6.3.11/12.
[98] 1983 Act, s.23(10).
[99] 1983 Act, s.24.

must be accompanied by the directors' written statement, giving reasons for waiving the right, stating the price to be paid for the shares in question and "justify[ing]" that amount. In one instance, where a company obtained a substantial outside investment but as a direct consequence its minority shareholders lost the capacity to veto a new share issue, it was held that in all the circumstances they had not been unlawfully oppressed.[100]

9–48   The right does not apply to shares that are being allotted for a consideration wholly or partly other than cash.[101] This leaves companies relatively free to acquire property and other non-cash assets in return for their shares. But it also presents opportunities for easily evading what the entitlement broadly seeks to achieve.

9–49   Only "equity securities" carry the right of pre-emption. By these are meant shares that are not subject to any ceiling on the amounts that may be distributed to their holders by way of dividends and capital, and rights to subscribe for or to convert into such shares.[102] Equity securities, therefore, are principally "ordinary" shares and "preference" shares where the preference is only in respect of dividends or capital.

9–50   There is a special provision for equity securities of a particular class where the company's own regulations give their holders a pre-emptive right in any further issues of those shares. Where the company offers any additional shares in the class to the class members on a *pro rata* basis and the offer is accepted, or alternatively the offeree renounces his right to them, there is no general obligation to offer those shares to all equity shareholders proportionately.[103]

9–51   Special provision also is made for shares held under an employees' share scheme, i.e. a scheme designed to encourage or facilitate a company's employees to acquire its shares.[104] Holders of those shares must be offered a proportionate amount of any further equity that is being issued. However, where it is proposed to allot shares under such a scheme, there is no obligation to offer them to the other shareholders on a *pro rata* basis.[105] In *Hogg v Cramphorn Ltd*,[106] it was held that it was a breach of their fiduciary duties for directors, in an attempt to defeat a takeover bid, to establish an employees' share scheme of which they themselves were the trustees, and arrange for the company to lend money to the scheme so that it could subscribe for a large block of shares in the company.

9–52   A company that contravenes the statutory pre-emption requirements and every officer knowingly involved in the breach is liable jointly or severally

---

[100] *CAS (Nominees) Ltd v Nottingham Forest FC Plc* [2002] 1 B.C.L.C. 613.
[101] 1983 Act, s.23(4); *cf. Siemens AG v Nold* (Case C 42/95) [1997] 1 B.C.L.C. 291.
[102] 1983 Act, s.23(13).
[103] 1983 Act, s.23(2) and (3).
[104] See para.19–08 *et seq.*
[105] 1983 Act, s.23(6).
[106] [1967] Ch. 254.

to compensate shareholders for all loss, damages and expenses arising therefrom, which right of action is subject to a two-year limitation period.[107] However, this does not preclude having the register of members rectified in an appropriate case where, under the pre-emption rules, the shares in question should have been allotted to the plaintiff rather than to the persons in whose name they stand registered.[108]

TRANSFER OF SHARES

9–53   The inherent transferability of shares is proclaimed in the 1963 Act, as being "transferable in the manner provided by the articles of the company …"[109] A condition for obtaining a stock exchange quotation for a company's shares is that they are freely transferable.[110] Transfers of shares often have certain tax consequences; generally, stamp duty is payable on the transaction and often it results in liability for capital gains tax or capital acquisitions tax.

9–54   How far-reaching this right to transfer is can be gathered from *Re Discoverers Finance Corp.*[111] Fearing that the company was in difficulties and that he might be obliged to pay further calls on his partly paid shares, the owner of 2,000 shares of £1 par, on which 30 pence each had been paid up, sold them for £5 in all to a journeyman tanner from Germany. The consideration was never paid nor even asked for. It was held that, provided the company's own regulations did not place a restriction on the free transferability of the shares and that the sale in fact was genuine, the seller ceased to be a member of the company once his transfer was registered. He, therefore, was no longer liable for calls on those shares. The fundamental principle is that:

> "in the absence of restrictions in the articles the shareholder had by virtue of [s.79 of the 1963 Act] the right to transfer his shares without the consent of any body to any transferee, even though he be a man of straw, provided it is a bona fide transaction in the sense that it is an out-and-out disposal of the property without retaining any interest in the shares—that the transferor bona fide divests himself of all benefits … .

> "It was the policy of the [Companies Acts] to give a right of free disposition, leaving it to the regulations of the company to impose such restrictions upon its exercise as might be desired. In the absence of restrictions it is competent to a transferor, notwithstanding that the company is in extremes, to compel registration of a transfer to a transferee notwithstanding that the latter is a person not competent to meet the unpaid liability upon the shares. Even if the transfer be executed for the express purpose of relieving the transferor from liability, the directors cannot upon that ground refuse to register it …"[112]

---

[107] 1983 Act, s.23(11).
[108] *Re Thundercrest Ltd* [1995] 1 B.C.L.C. 117.
[109] Section 79.
[110] Listing Rule 3.2.4.
[111] [1910] 1 Ch. 312.
[112] *ibid.* at 316, 317.

The mechanisms by which shares may be transferred and questions of title to shares that are transferable are considered separately below.

Restrictions on Transfers

9–55 For practical purposes, the principal legal difference between private companies and public companies relates to the freedom to transfer shares in them. Freedom to transfer may be restricted or conditioned by the company's own regulations; every private company's regulations are required to impose some constraint on their transferability.[113] At times, freedom to transfer shares is prohibited or restricted in contractual arrangements between a company and some outside body; it also can be in the terms of authorisations given to a company, for instance as a condition for holding a licence.[114]

9–56 As shares are inherently transferable property rights, provisions in articles will not be interpreted so as to cut down that freedom, unless that is a fair construction of them. An absolute prohibition on transferring would be invalid.[115] An argument could be made that, in the light of the Constitution's protection for private property, a restriction on the right to transfer shares must not be unreasonable; notably that transferees should not be excluded from membership on grounds of their sex, race or religious beliefs. In the US all restrictions on the transferability of shares are required to be reasonable because they are restraints on the alienation of property rights.

9–57 There is a great variety of possible restrictions. One is that the transferee must be an existing member of the company or that he must be a close relative of the transferor. A common form is a pre-emption requirement, explained below: that existing members, or sometimes directors, be given the right of first refusal to purchase them before the shares are otherwise disposed of. Table A empowers the directors to block the transfer of partly paid shares to any person they "do not approve" of,[116] the most obvious example being someone not able to pay up the calls when made on the shares. The directors are also empowered to block a transfer of shares over which the company has a lien, or where the transfer would prejudice the company's status in the State, or where it would imperil any tax concession or rebate coming to the company or, fourthly, where the transfer would require the company to pay any additional stamp or other duty on a conveyance of property to the company.[117] The form of restriction contained in Pt II of Table A is perhaps as extensive as could be formulated. According to it "the directors may, in their absolute discretion, and without assigning any reason therefor, decline to register any transfer of any share, whether or not it is a fully paid share".[118] It, accompanied by a pre-emption requirement, often features in the articles of private companies.

---

[113] 1963 Act, s.33(1)(a).
[114] e.g. *Re Piccadilly Radio Plc* [1989] B.C.L.C. 683.
[115] *Re Hafner* [1943] I.R. 426 at 448.
[116] Article 24.
[117] Article 24.
[118] Article 3.

Construction of Clauses

9–58   The principles applied when construing clauses restricting share transfers may be summarised as follows. A formal decision to refuse registration must be made. If the transferee is not notified of the refusal after a reasonable time has passed then, unless there are special circumstances, the right of veto will be deemed to have lapsed.[119] Ordinarily, two months will be regarded as a reasonable time because transferees must be informed within that time that their applications have been refused.[120] Special circumstances may warrant either extending or contracting this period. Where the board members are deadlocked, it cannot resolve to refuse registration, and the transfer accordingly can go ahead. But that is not the case where the articles state that the shares shall not be transferable except with the approval of the directors, the members or whoever. Whether the "reasonable time" rule referred to above applies in these latter circumstances has not been determined, but the usual rationale for that rule would not seem to have any application here, i.e. that the inherent right to transfer can be blocked by the directors' power of veto but all powers lapse after a reasonable time.

9–59   Where the clause in question possesses more than one potential meaning, then the narrowest construction will be adopted.[121] For instance, in *Tangney v Clarence Hotels Co.*,[122] the clause empowered the directors to refuse to register a transfer to any person who, in their opinion, was not desirable to admit into membership. Johnston J. held that they had no power to refuse registration where the transferee already held some shares in the company. However, the courts will not indulge in excesses of literalism to defeat the obvious purpose behind a clause. In *Re Dublin North City Milling Co.*,[123] where the transferee had to be "approved of by the board", Meredith M.R. held that the mere fact that he was already a member of the company did not oblige the directors to approve the transfer to him.[124]

Discretionary Veto

9–60   Where the directors possess a discretion to veto a transfer, they must exercise it as fiduciaries. The governing principles were stated in *Re Smith & Fawcett Ltd*[125]:

> "they must exercise their discretion *bona fide* in what they consider—not what a court may consider—is in the interests of the company, and not for any collateral purpose. They must have regard to those considerations, and those considerations only, which the articles on their true

[119] *Re Swaledale Cleaners* [1968] 1 W.L.R. 432, *Re New Cedos Engineering Co.* [1994] 1 B.C.L.C. 797 and *Popely v Planarrive Ltd* [1997] 1 B.C.L.C. 8.
[120] 1963 Act, s.84.
[121] *Stothers v William Stewart (Holdings) Ltd* [1994] 2 B.C.L.C. 266.
[122] [1933] I.R. 51.
[123] [1909] 1 I.R. 79.
[124] cf. *Re Bede Steam Shipping Co.* [1917] Ch. 123.
[125] [1942] 1 Ch. 304.

construction permit them to take into consideration ... Where articles are framed with some ... limitation on the discretionary power of refusal ... if the directors go outside the matters which the articles say are to be the matters and the only matters to which they are to have regard, [they] will have exceeded their powers."[126]

In practice, it is difficult to have set aside an exercise of the directors' veto as they are not obliged to give reasons and a plaintiff may not simply allege but must show that the directors were acting for an improper purpose.[127]

9–61 As was explained in *Re Dublin North City Milling Co.*,[128] the disappointed transferee "must allege and prove some indirect motive on the part of the directors in refusing his application [and] the law allows the directors to hold their tongues. It allows them to say that everything was done honestly and bona fide in the interests of their company; [the court has] no power to make them say more".[129] This leads to the situation where, as Black J. put it in *Re Hafner*,[130] "[h]edged round with the privilege of remaining mute and the prima facie presumption of rectitude, the astutely silent director who wishes to exercise this power illegitimately may well consider himself all but invulnerable. No need to speak and no unfavourable inference from reticence—that is the settled rule".[131] In *Re Smith & Fawcett Ltd*,[132] the company was founded by two persons on a 50/50 basis and, when one of them died, he bequeathed his shares to his two children. The directors refused to register those transfers, although the survivor shareholder offered to register half of them if he were allowed to purchase the other half at a price to be fixed by himself. It was argued that the true reason for not registering the transfers was so that the surviving member could acquire those shares for himself at an undervalue. It was held that insufficient evidence had been brought forward to show that the directors had abused their power of veto.

9–62 Where, however, it is demonstrated that the directors acted for some improper motive, then the court will inquire carefully into the real reasons. *Re Hafner*[133] is an excellent example of the mute directors' defence of presumed rectitude being overcome. It concerned a very profitable family company, the regulations of which contained a clause similar to Pt II of Table A.[134] The plaintiff inherited some shares in the company, but the directors refused to register him as a member, without assigning any reasons. However, it was shown in evidence that, by 1939 standards, one director was to be paid the "exorbitant" sum of £7,000 a year, another was given the

---

[126] *ibid.* at 306, 307.
[127] *Charles Forte Investments Ltd v Amanda* [1964] 1 Ch. 240 and *Popely v Planarrive Ltd* [1997] 1 B.C.L.C. 8.
[128] [1909] I.R. 179.
[129] *ibid.* at 183, 184.
[130] [1943] I.R. 426.
[131] *ibid.* at 440.
[132] [1942] 1 Ch. 304.
[133] [1943] I.R. 426.
[134] Article 3.

"commercially fantastic" service contract of £3,000 a year for a term of 20 years and, if the company was wound up before that term expired, he was to be entitled to half that sum for the unexpired residue of the term. In the light of these facts, Black J. felt constrained to conclude that the reason for refusing to admit the plaintiff into membership was to prevent those payments from being questioned and challenged in court Accordingly, "[o]nce an illegitimate motive for such a decision is [shown], the normal legal presumption that they acted legitimately must go by the board and [the court] is no longer bound to ignore their silence, or to refuse to draw any inference from it".[135] He found that in the circumstances the directors had acted improperly in excluding the plaintiff. A similar conclusion was reached by Laffoy J. in *Banfi Ltd v Moran*,[136] where the plantiff was seeking to bring "oppression" proceedings against a company, in which he was the beneficial owner of shares and had sought to have those shares registered in his own name. In evidence, explaining why the company rejected his application, it was said that he had refused to respond to certain questions put to him. It was held that, in the circumstances, that explanation was entirely implausible and that the most likely reason was to enable his s.205 case to be struck out on account of his lacking *locus standi*.

9–63   It is only persons who have been registered as members of the company who can commence proceedings for oppression under s.205 of the 1963 Act. Accordingly, the transferee of shares whose registration is being blocked cannot avail of this mode of redress. An exception is made for a deceased member's personal representative or any person beneficially interested in his shares by virtue of his will or intestacy.[137] Where the transferor of shares is alive and the company refuses to register his transferee, the oppression remedy is open to the transferor. It remains to be seen whether, when a veto is challenged in such proceedings, the courts will be less indulgent of the directors' standing on their privilege of mute presumed rectitude. Additionally, as *Banfi Ltd v Moran* illustrates, circumstances can arise where the beneficial owner of shares, who wishes to bring "oppression" proceedings, can compel registration of his shares in the teeth of the directors' virtually unfettered discretion to refuse registration.

Pre-emption

9–64   In their articles of association many private companies also stipulate for some kind of pre-emption arrangement before shares can be transferred, especially where the proposed transferee is a complete outsider. Equivalent stipulations often are contained in shareholders' agreements. The form of pre-emption used can vary enormously.[138] Most often it is provided that, where a member wishes to transfer his shares, he should thereupon notify the company secretary, who will notify the directors or the other members, as the case may be. Any of these who wishes to purchase the shares should so notify

---

[135] [1943] I.R. 426 at 444.
[136] [2006] I.E.H.C. 257, unreported, Laffoy J., July 20, 2006.
[137] 1963 Act, s.205(6).
[138] e.g. *BCM's Precedents*, A 126.

the secretary, who then will arrange for the shares to be valued in accordance with a prescribed formula, or by an arbitrator or a valuer, or in some other manner as provided for. The intending transferor may then either be obliged to sell the shares at that price or remain a member.

9–65   There is a presumption in favour of the shares being freely transferable, so that the circumstances must come four-square within the pre-emption requirements for them to bite.[139] Against this, however, because the objective of pre-emption is to keep the shares within a defined category of member, it should not be rendered ineffective by over-technicality. These clauses should be construed in the same way as any other commercial document and circumstances can warrant implying terms into them to render them effective.[140] In construing them, context is everything. Thus, references in them to a "transfer" of shares can mean one of several things, depending on the context, *viz.* an agreement to transfer, the execution of a transfer instrument or registration of a transfer. Mere change of trustees holding shares may in some circumstances trigger pre-emption.[141] Ordinarily, a reference to a transfer of shares does not mean their transmission by operation of law, such as when the shareholder dies.[142] Where what is required by the relevant articles is notification of an intention to transfer the shares, ordinarily it is not sufficient that there is a conditional intent to do so. The question is whether there is an intention to do so in a manner not compatible with the pre-emption process.[143] Where the rules are clear, it is no objection that they operate most unfairly on the member in question;[144] although some rules may be so oppressive as to contravene public policy, such as a condition about an intended transferee's sex, age, race or religion. Compliance with pre-emption can be enforced with an injunction, and transfers that occurred in breach of pre-emption may be undone by having the register of members rectified.

9–66   A common formula in these clauses is where a shareholder intends to transfer all or part of his shares, he must notify the company of that intent. Ordinarily, this requires a decision by the member to dispose of his shares. In *Re Claygreen Ltd,*[145] where a letter was sent on behalf of a shareholder to the company saying that she had agreed to sell all her shares to F and seeking clarification that any transfer to him would be registered, it was held that this was not sufficient to trigger pre-emption. That was because, in all the circumstances, the true nature of her enquiry was to ascertain whether, if she did transfer the shares to F, he would be duly registered; she had not yet formed the definite intent to transfer her shares. Often the notice required to be given to the company must designate the price being sought for the shares. In such an instance, where the price was stipulated by reference to a formula the operation

---

[139] *Greenhalgh v Mallard* [1943] 2 All E.R. 234.
[140] *Tett v Phoenix Property & Investments Co.* [1986] B.C.L.C. 149.
[141] *Ord v Calan Healthcare Properties Ltd* [2005] 2 N.Z.L.R. 96.
[142] *Stothers v William Stewart (Holdings) Ltd* [1994] 2 B.C.L.C. 266.
[143] *Re Sedgefield Steeplechase Co. (1927) Ltd* [2000] 2 B.C.L.C. 211.
[144] *Holt v Faulks* [2000] 2 B.C.L.C. 816.
[145] [2006] 1 B.C.L.C. 715.

of which depended on future events and for which there was no completion date, it was held that the process had not been triggered.[146]

9–67 Pre-emption under such clauses becomes operative where the shareholder has concluded an unconditional agreement with another to transfer his shares. For this involves more than giving that other some beneficial interest in the shares, such as a charge; it is an agreement to vest the very legal interest in them. Pre-emption under such a clause was held to apply where the shareholder executed a transfer of shares by way of gift to her nephew, in circumstances that gave him equitable title to those shares.[147] To hold otherwise would deprive the word "transfer" in the clause of its business meaning.

9–68 On the other hand, subjecting someone to certain obligations with reference to the shares may not be sufficient to trigger pre-emption. In *Safeguard Industrial Investments Ltd v National West Minister Bank Ltd*,[148] a bank held the deceased's shares as executor under his will. Because the bank's interest operated by way of transmission, it was accepted that pre-emption did not apply at that stage. However, it was contended that, because the beneficiaries were then entitled to compel the bank to transfer the shares into their names, they came within the pre-emption net. The bank had informed the company that it was holding the shares in trust for those beneficiaries absolutely and they had made it clear to the bank that they did not want it to transfer the shares to them. It was held that the bank did not fit the description of a "proposing transferor" in the article. Those words were apt to describe a person who had voluntarily undertaken to transfer the shares but not someone who could be obliged to do so.

9–69 Even giving an outsider extensive rights with reference to the shares, against an overall objective of assisting him to acquire them, may not be sufficient for pre-emption to bite,[149] unless of course the article in question squarely covers the state of affairs. As stated by Lord Hoffman in *Re Sedgefield Steeplechase Co. (1927) Ltd*,[150] if the arrangements made by the shareholder show a definite intention not to activate pre-emption, then it does not do so; "a shareholder who has done nothing inconsistent with an intention to comply, at the appropriate moment, with the subsisting provisions [on pre-emption] cannot be required to serve a transfer notice at an earlier stage".[151] He is only obliged to do so where, as in a sale by him or granting an option, he can be compelled to execute and deliver a share transfer, in contravention of pre-emption. In the course of a takeover, shareholders agreed to sell their equitable interest to the bidder but stipulated that he did not have any authority to transfer his interest in the shares in a manner that would contravene pre-emption; further, they agreed

---

[146] *BWE International Ltd v Jones* [2004] 1 B.C.L.C. 406.
[147] *Hurst v Crampton Bros (Coopers) Ltd* [2003] 1 B.C.L.C. 304.
[148] [1982] 1 W.L.R. 589.
[149] *Theakston v London Trust Plc* [1984] B.C.L.C. 390.
[150] [2000] 2 B.C.L.C. 211.
[151] *ibid.* at 221.

that they would use their best endeavours at general meeting to delete that clause. Because this did not impose any obligation to do something that was incompatible with the clause, it was held that it had not been triggered. So far as the other shareholders were concerned, all that matters was that there was an intention to comply with the existing pre-emption arrangements and no intention of infringing any of their rights as defined therein.

9–70   Once the requirements for triggering pre-emption have occurred, it becomes operative notwithstanding how unfair that may be. Where under the company's articles, if a director ceased to hold office "for any reason" his shares come into pre-emption, it was held that this applies even if his dismissal was unlawful.[152] That the price to be paid for getting shares under pre-emption is significantly below their market price would appear not to render the process invalid.[153]

9–71   Except where the article clearly states otherwise, the initial notification of an intention to transfer is construed as a notice to treat and not an offer for sale.[154] Therefore, if a would-be purchaser wants to buy the shares, he must make an offer for them. Where this is the case, the proposing vendor can change his mind, for instance, because he is dissatisfied with the price at which the shares were valued. The extent to which any value reached for the shares can be challenged in court depends on the mode of valuation used. Most often, that is by the company's auditors acting as experts and not as arbitrators.[155]

9–72   Where pre-emption exists, its requirements must be complied with before the member becomes free to transfer his shares. In *Re Hafner*,[156] the company's articles provided for pre-emption as well as a discretionary veto on share transfers. The defendants there also contended that, because the deceased's shares had not been put into pre-emption, the plaintiff could not be registered as a member. Even though they had improperly blocked registration of a transfer of the shares to him, they sought to prevent him from becoming a member simply by claiming his shares under the pre-emption clause. According to the articles there, no member could dispose of his shares "without first offering them to the directors ... who shall have the first option of purchasing same ..." But the Supreme Court held that, having attempted to block the transfer under the discretionary clause, the directors had thereby waived their rights to pre-emption.

9–73   Where pre-emption has not been complied with, the purported transferee cannot compel the company to put his name on the register of members.[157] Any shareholder who has been denied pre-emption because

---

[152] *Holt v Faulks* [2000] 2 B.C.L.C. 816.
[153] *Castello v London General Omnibus Co.*, 107 Lt 576 (1912).
[154] *Tett v Phoenix Property & Investments Co.* [1986] B.C.L.C. 149.
[155] cf. *Burgess v Purchase & Sons (Farms) Ltd* [1983] Ch. 216.
[156] [1943] I.R. 426.
[157] [1943] I.R. 426 at 453.

there has not been substantial compliance with the prescribed process is entitled to an injunction restraining the registration of a purported transferee.[158] Where a person acquired shares under pre-emption but it transpires that the process was never applicable, ordinarily the person whose shares he acquired is entitled to have the register of members duly rectified and his name re-entered in it.[159] Where, conversely, shares are registered in the name of a party who was not entitled to them under the process, rectification also can be obtained. But rectification is a discretionary remedy and circumstances may warrant refusing it. In one instance, where the applicant's objective was not really to have his name substituted for the person on the register, rectification was refused.[160]

CAPITAL AND SURPLUS

9–74 Where a company is being wound up and all its creditors are paid off, the shareholders become entitled to be repaid their investment from the remaining assets.[161] The claims of shareholders *inter se* to priority in return of capital on a winding-up have been the subject of little litigation, presumably because this matter tends to be provided for unambiguously in companies' own regulations. Where no express provision is made, application of the "equality" and "nominalist" principles does not give rise to serious difficulties.

9–75 However, division of the surplus left over after all the claims against the company are satisfied is the subject of extensive case law involving preference shares.[162] A cause of particular difficulty with the surplus is the relevance of how it could have been disposed of prior to liquidation. Assume that there are just ordinary and preference shares, and that all outstanding preference dividends have been paid. Before liquidation, what can be done with any surplus? Unless there are regulations to the contrary, the ordinary shareholders may pay themselves a dividend out of it. Therefore, the argument goes, where this is the case the equality principle should not apply in a liquidation to deprive the ordinary shareholders of what hitherto was theirs, albeit contingently. If, on the other hand, the surplus was capitalised, in the sense of not being available for paying dividends, then the ordinary shareholders no longer have a special claim on it and, therefore, it is said, the equality principle should come into play in the liquidation. Two complications cloud this argument. Often it can be difficult to determine whether funds were capitalised and, even where the intention to capitalise is uncontrovertible, the funds may not have been spent on capital items when the company goes into liquidation. Furthermore, since the matter ultimately is one of construction, meaning must be given to stipulations in the regulations that deal with these matters, though these be in ambiguous terms.

---

[158] *Curtis v JJ Curtis & Co.* [1986] B.C.L.C. 87.
[159] *Re Claygreen Ltd* [2006] 1 B.C.L.C. 715.
[160] *Re Piccadilly Radio Plc* [1989] B.C.L.C. 683.
[161] 1963 Act, s.275(1)(b).
[162] See para.9–126 *et seq.*

PROPERTY RIGHTS IN SHARES

9–76   Being often extremely valuable assets, it is vital that the rules governing the ownership of shares and transferring title to them are clear and easily operable. In the common law system, achieving this goal can be difficult because it does not provide for the *rei vindicati*, i.e. a proceeding that results in the absolute determination of who has title to a particular asset. Instead, the outcome of title disputes only determines the position as between the parties to the proceedings.

9–77   There are two principal methods by which ownership of property is normally determined. One is by having possession of the item in question; in the case of securities, this would be possessing the document of title to them. The other is by way of registration of title; ownership is signified by having one's name entered in the relevant register for the asset in question, which in the case of shares is the company's share register. But such registration is never absolutely conclusive as to who has good title to the shares; it is only *prima facie* evidence of ownership.[163] Questions about acquiring and disposing of ownership in or other proprietary interests in shares are governed by the law of personal property[164]: by the regime for interests in choses in action, being an amalgam of contractual stipulations, common law rules and equitable doctrines, supplemented by some statutory provisions.

Acquiring Ownership

9–78   Except for bearer shares, a person becomes a member of or shareholder in a company when his name is entered as such in the register of members. Insofar as the company is concerned, it should deal with that person alone with regard to supplying information, paying dividends, voting and other matters. Where shares are registered in two or more names, it depends on the circumstances whether those persons hold them as joint tenants or tenants in common.[165]

9–79   Ownership changes hands by the shares either being transferred under a proper instrument of transfer or electronically, or by them vesting in another person by operation of law. Subject to any restrictions in the company's own regulations,[166] shareholders have a statutory right to transfer their shares.[167] Unless they fall within any such restrictions, transferees under a valid instrument are entitled to be registered as members. But to acquire a valid title, the transferor must have had a good title to give: unless

---

[163] 1963 Act, s.124.

[164] See generally, A. Bell, *Modern Law of Personal Property in England and Ireland* (London: Butterworths, 1989) and S. Worthington, *Personal Property Law: Text, Cases and Materials* (Oxford: Hart, 2000).

[165] *O'Connell v Harrison* [1927] I.R. 330.

[166] e.g. Table A, art.24 and Pt II, art. 3.

[167] 1963 Act, s.79.

they are bearer shares, their ownership is subject to the fundamental rule of *nemo dat quod non habet.*[168]

Contracting to Transfer

9–80   The process of agreeing to transfer ownership of shares is governed by general contract law principles, as to offer and acceptance, conditions and warranties, mistake and the like. Where all the shares in a company or a substantial stake in it is being bought, usually the intending purchaser will require extensive disclosure about the company's assets, liabilities and business. Accountants involved directly and sometimes indirectly in the "due diligence" process may incur liability in negligence, where there was a material oversight.[169] Precedent books contain a variety of contract documents for this purpose,[170] *inter alia,* disclosure letters and short, medium and long form contracts. At times the transaction is a "put" or "call" option on shares, or a purchase/sale with an option to sell/buy back,[171] rather than an outright disposal of them. Often provision is made for independent determination of the price in the event of a dispute.[172] Once the contract to transfer is entered into, the transferor holds the shares as trustee for the transferee.[173]

9–81   *Implying terms:* In addition to it being an implied term of the contract that the vendor can give good title to the shares, in the absence of any stipulation to the contrary, he impliedly undertakes to do nothing to prevent or delay registration of the transferee as a member. But there is no implied term that the transferee will be registered. Thus, in *Casey v Bentley,*[174] the plaintiff executed a transfer of his shares to the defendant. It was held that, since purchasers who are refused registration as members cannot rescind their contracts,[175] neither could the vendor there rescind.

9–82   *Enforcement:* Except for shares that are listed on a stock exchange, share sale agreements can be enforced by way of an order for specific performance.[176] It is possible that a contract for the sale of listed shares can be so enforced in special market situations.

9–83   *Breach of Pre-emption:* Where a contract to transfer shares has been made that contravenes a company's pre-emption regime, the directors must refuse to register the transfer. If inadvertently it has been registered, a party entitled to

---

[168] See generally, M. Forde, *Commercial Law,* 3rd edn. (Haywards Health: Tottel Publishing, 2005), p.105 *et seq.*

[169] *cf. Infiniteland Ltd v Artisan Contracting Ltd* [2006] 1 B.C.L.C. 632.

[170] *BCM's Precedents* part B; *Practical Commercial Precedents* Vol.1 part D. See generally, Sinclair, *Warranties and Indemnities and Share and Asset Sales,* 6th edn (London: Thomson Sweet & Maxwell, 2005).

[171] e.g. *Gloyne v Richardson* [2001] 2 B.C.L.C. 669.

[172] e.g. *Hillsbridge Investments Ltd v Moresfield Ltd* [2002] 2 B.C.L.C. 241.

[173] See paras.9–102 and 9–103.

[174] [1902] 1 I.R. 376; *cf. Rackham v Peek Foods Ltd* [1990] B.C.L.C. 895.

[175] *London Founders Association v Clarke* (1888) 20 Q.B.D 576.

[176] *Keisner v Terrus Group Ltd* [2007] 1 B.C.L.C. 303.

avail of pre-emption may obtain an order rectifying the register of members, although special circumstances may justify the court in refusing to so order. Whether or to what extent the "transferee" who has not been registered as a member has some equitable title to those shares is a vexed question, about which different views have been expressed.[177] These were addressed in some detail by Black J. in *Re Hafner*,[178] who suggested that some equitable interest did pass but, as he did not have to decide the point, left it for consideration at some other time. The question arises in two principal contexts, *viz.* as between the transferor and transferee, and as between the transferor and the one or more parties who are entitled to avail of the pre-emption. With regard to the former, Black J.'s view was endorsed at first instance in *Tett v Phoenix Property & Investment Co Ltd*.[179] However, the point was not considered when that case went on appeal and the correctness of the proposition has been doubted. It also was held at first instance there that the effect of executing a transfer in breach of the pre-emption regime is to create an interest equivalent to an option on the beneficiaries of that regime. On account of the principle *nemo dat quod non habet*, any interest a "transferee" of such shares obtains, especially where he knows that pre-emption is being breached, is a somewhat weak equity.

9–83a According to the Supreme Court in *Walls v P.J. Walls Holdings Ltd*,[180] the "transferee" under a contract that contravenes pre-emption acquires the "beneficial ownership" of those shares. But if this were entirely correct, that transferee would be entitled to an order that he shall be registered as a member, which cannot be the case. The two authorities relied on by the Court for its conclusion[181] do not support it, as they go no further than saying that a party who, in breach of pre-emption, has contracted to acquire shares for consideration, has some equity in them. But they do not hold that this interest is as extensive as the "beneficial ownership" of the shares. None of the detailed submissions made and authorities relied on by the losing side there, on this point, are recorded, let alone addressed in the judgment. In the leading English case,[182] where a transfer of shares to a bank as security was actually entered in the members' register, notwithstanding that it contravened the pre-emption clause, Lord Atkin expressed the view that no member could enter into a binding contract for the sale of his shares capable of conferring any legal or equitable interest in their purchaser until such time as the pre-emption regime was satisfied. Several of his fellow judges did not go quite that far, holding that, depending

---

[177] See generally, Borrowdale, "The Effect of Breach of Share Transfer Restrictions" [1988] *J. Bus. L.* 307 and Luxton, "Share Transfer Restrictions and the Relative Nature of Property Rights" [1989] *J. Bus. L.* 14.

[178] [1943] I.R. 426 at 453 *et seq.*

[179] [1984] B.C.L.C. 599.

[180] [2008] 1 I.L.R.M. 1.

[181] *Re Hafner* [1943] I.R. 426 and *Hawks v McArthur* [1951] 1 All E.R. 22.

[182] *Hunter v Hunter* [1936] A.C. 222, not referred to in the judgment, where the share transfer to the creditor bank's nominees was actually entered in the members' register, as was a subsequent transfer of those shares to other nominees of the same bank. Nor was any reference made, in the judgment, to the debate between Borrowdale and Luxton, f'n above, nor to the detailed analysis in the *Tett* case [1984] B.C.L.C. at 615 *et seq.*

on the context, some equity could be asserted by the "purchaser". For instance, he may not have known of the pre-emption requirement or may have reasonably believed that it had been complied with, or as in *Hawks v McArthur*,[183] have acquired the shares intending that they would be put into pre-emption if any other member wanted to buy them. According to Finnegan J., for an unanimous Court, *Egan Wholesale Ltd*[184] shows that, notwithstanding pre-emption, a shareholder may enter a "binding and enforceable contract for the sale of his shares". This is correct, except that the remedy there is damages or, if the vendor is somehow in a position to secure compliance with pre-emption, an order that he shall do so. But such equity as the transferee obtains is not permitted to encroach on pre-emption entitlements. The Court also asserted that, if there is a conflict between the articles of association and the 1963 Act, the latter takes precedence – in this instance, the s.204 "take-out" provision. But there was no conflict. By virtue of the pre-emption clause and on the basis of all existing authority, the "transferees" of those shares never acquired "beneficial ownership" of them; at most, they got some equity in them, which, at times, could be relied on, and that was an extremely weak equity because they would have know throughout that the "transfers" to them contravened the company's articles of association.

9–84　　In the *Egan (Wholesale) Ltd* cases,[185] the company's articles of association gave existing members a pre-emptive right to buy shares which any other member sought to sell. The co-defendant, who was the company's principal shareholder, agreed in substance to sell all the company's issued shares to the plaintiff, although he did not have the other shareholders' authority to do this. Kenny J. held that he could be enjoined to take such steps as were possible to ensure that the shares he owned were transferred to the plaintiff. Additionally, damages were payable where the articles' pre-emption clause prevented that transfer from taking place. It was held, furthermore, that it would be an unlawful abuse of power for him to use his 75 per cent shareholding to amend or rescind the articles' pre-emption requirement. Damages were also awarded for breach of the agreement to transfer what were the other members' shares. In the *Walls Holdings Ltd* case,[186] it was held that entering into a

---

[183] [1951] 1 All E.R. 22. All that this *ex tempore* first instance judgment decided was that, in those circumstance, the plaintiff creditor of the "transferror" cannot enforce a judgment subsequently obtained against him, by way of a charging order on those shares. Because his "transferees" obtained the shares, having agreed with the company to make them available for pre-emption, if requested, they had an equity in those shares that deserved to be protected, notwithstanding that the plaintiff did not and could not know that the shares had been "transferred" to them. In substance, the "transfers" there did not contravene the other members' pre-emption entitlements, should they choose to exercise them; that gave the "transferees" "some rights" (at 27H) in them, which the "transferor's" later judgment creditor should not be permitted to defeat. Because the plaintiff was not responsible for the "muddle" that led to this litigation, he was not ordered to pay the successful "transferees" costs.

[184] *Lee & Co. (Dublin) Ltd v Egan (Wholesale) Ltd*, High Court, Kenny J., unreported, April 27, 1978; May 23, 1978; December 18, 1979.

[185] *ibid.*

[186] [2008] 1 I.L.R.M. 1.

contract to acquire over 80 per cent of the shares in a company conferred sufficient interest in them as to trigger the "take out" mechanism in the 1963 Act, overriding the remaining shareholders' pre-emption rights. The requisite interest for this purpose is "beneficial ownership" of the shares.

Gifts

9–85 Where a person intends to make a gift of shares, it is legally effective once he has done everything required of him to effect the transfer, which in the circumstances may involve signing the share transfer form and giving it to the donee to be countersigned. A valid equitable transfer can occur by simply signing the transfer form.[187]

Transmission of Title

9–86 By transmission of title to shares is meant their ownership changing hands by operation of law, as by vesting in a deceased member's personal representative or, if a bankrupt member, in the Official Assignee or his trustee in bankruptcy. A personal representative or the assignee or trustee may be registered as a member, without an instrument of transfer being executed.[188] But the company will satisfy itself of their right to be entered on the register.[189] Under Table A, that person may elect to be registered as a member in respect of those shares or may designate a nominee to be so registered, subject to any restrictions on transfers in the company's articles.[190] Even if there is no such election, that person is entitled to receive dividends from and to enjoy other advantages in the company, other than in respect of meetings.[191] But if the directors call on him to elect and he does not do so within 90 days, those various benefits can be withheld. It is not necessary for a personal representative to so elect in order to transfer title to the shares.[192]

The Transfer Mechanism

9–87 Where a member has contracted to transfer or has decided to make a gift of shares, ownership of them will not pass until the contract has been performed or the gift is completed. This is done by having the transferee's name entered in the register of members. An application to transfer shares may be made to the company by the transferor or the transferee.[193] On it receiving a proper instrument of share transfer, the company may register the transfer of the relevant shares.[194]

---

[187] *Pennington v Waine* [2002] 1 W.L.R. 2075.

[188] 1963 Act, s.81(2).

[189] See generally, C. Doyle, *The Company Secretary*, 2nd edn (Dublin: Round Hall, 2002), pp.182–185.

[190] Articles 30 and 31.

[191] Article 32.

[192] 1963 Act, s.82.

[193] 1963 Act, s.83.

[194] 1963 Act, s.81.

9–88   The standard form for transferring fully paid-up registered shares is set out in the First Schedule to the Stock Transfer Act 1963.[195] This must be executed by the transferor but need not be attested. It must show particulars of the consideration, the description and number or amount of the shares, the transferor's full name, and the transferee's name and address. The company may accept transfers in another form if it was common or usual before 1963 and it is a form that the company has authorised, provided that it is executed by the transferor and contains the above-mentioned information. Although not obliged to maintain one, many companies keep a separate register of transfers, in which the principal details of these transactions are recorded.

9–89   In the case of a full transfer, it will be executed by the transferor and, where required, also by the transferee; the transferor will have given it to the transferee, along with his share certificate, who usually forwards it to the company for registration. Where necessary, the instrument will have been lodged with the Revenue Commissioners to determine how much stamp duty is to be charged on the transaction. Table A entitles the directors to require that evidence be given to them showing the transferor's entitlement to transfer the shares[196] and also to charge a small fee. Generally, it is the company secretary who will ensure that all the necessary formalities have been complied with, and who will duly register the transferee and forward him a share certificate. At times, as a precaution against fraud, the transferor is notified of the transaction and given a short period within which he may object to it. Ordinarily, details of the transaction are submitted to the company's directors for their approval. If they refuse to approve it, they should so notify the transferee within two months of having received the instrument.[197]

9–90   Where it is a partial transfer of the member's holding or there are several transferees, some additional steps are required, *inter alia,* "certification". This involves the transferor first sending the share certificate and transfer instrument[s] to the company, to have certified on the instrument[s] the fact that the transferor has good title. The instrument[s] will then be returned to the transferor, along with a "balance receipt" representing any shares that are not being transferred. On receiving the duly executed transfer instrument[s], the company will issue a receipt[s] for it/them, stating that a share certificate will be sent to the transferee. He will then be sent a new certificate and a new one also will be sent to the transferor for such balance of shares that he retained.

9–91   To facilitate the transfer of shares in quoted companies, a broker's transfer form for stock exchange transactions that involve transfers to a number of transferees is set out in the Stock Transfer Act 1963's second schedule. Transactions on the Irish and the London Stock Exchanges are now carried out by computer, through what is known as the CREST system. It was to accommodate this and equivalent systems that regulations were adopted,

---

[195] And the various Stock Transfer (Forms) Regulations 1980–2000.
[196] Article 25(b).
[197] 1963 Act, s.84 and Table A, art.26.

making it possible to transfer title to shares electronically, without any need for the usual written instrument: the Companies Act 1990 (Uncertified Securities) Regulations 1996.[198] Table A makes no provision for shares being transferred in this manner.

9–92   Forged transfers are always a risk for companies; they are void and do not confer title. A company is obliged to compensate the innocent party for any loss that he suffered thereby. Where the fraudulent transfer request has been made to the company by a broker or other party acting for the purported trans-feror or the transferee, ordinarily the company will be entitled to an indemnity from that third party.[199] By resolution, a company may create its own indem-nity fund to cover any such losses. Many companies insure against them.

Title Documentation

9–93   Companies issue share certificates and also certifications of transfers that acknowledge ownership of the shares named in them. Exceptionally, Plcs issue share warrants and shares in listed companies are held in uncertified form.[200]

Share Certificates

9–94   Apart from CREST transactions, within two months of being notified of a share transfer, a company must issue a sealed certificate to the transferee, which states how many shares he has registered in his name and how much is paid up on them.[201] Although share certificates are not documents of title, often a company is estopped from denying the correctness of statements made in them to any person who has altered his position in reliance of them. As Lord Herschell L.C. explained in *Balkis Consolidated Co. v Tomkinson*[202]:

> "an estoppel might arise where a certificate was issued stating that the person named on it was the registered holder of certain shares in the company ... [T]he giving of the certificate amount[s] to a statement by the company, intended by them to be acted upon by the purchasers of shares in the market, that the persons certified as the holders were enti-tled to the shares; and that the purchasers having acted on that statement by the company, they were estopped from denying its truth and liable to pay as damages the value of the shares ... [I]f the company have been deceived and the statement is not true, they may have been guilty of neg-ligence, but they and no one else had power to inquire into the matter."[203]

9–95   Without their owner's authority, the company was deceived into registering a transfer of his shares and issued a new share certificate to the purported transferee. When the full facts came to light, by virtue of the *nemo*

---

[198] SI 1996/68; see para.15–86 *et seq.*
[199] *Yeung v Hong Kong & Shanghai Banking Corp.* [1981] A.C. 787.
[200] See para.15–95.
[201] 1963 Act, s.86 and art.8 of Table A.
[202] [1893] A.C. 396.
[203] *ibid.* at 403–404.

dat quod non habet principle, that "transferee" never acquired title to those shares. It was held that nevertheless, on the basis of estoppel, he was entitled to be compensated by the company for the loss he thereby suffered.[204] This principle can also apply to statements on share certificates about how much has been paid up on those shares.[205] Circumstances can arise where estoppel will not operate.

9–96   In *Ruben v Great Fingall Consolidated*,[206] it was held that a company is never estopped by its forged certificate, i.e. one issued without the company's authority. In the light of subsequent developments in the law of agency, however, the fact that an instrument issued in a company's name is a forgery does not always deprive it of legal effect.[207]

Certification of Transfers

9–97   Certifying transfers is the practice that arises where, say, A sells 100 shares, which are the subject of the one share certificate; B buys, say, 60 of them; and C buys the remainder. As A's certificate cannot be given to both buyers, the practice is for it to be sent to the company, which then certifies that it has been received; the buyers then pay against delivery of the certified transfers. Certification is a representation to anyone acting on the faith of it that the transferor has a prima facie title to the shares in question.[208] A certification given by a duly authorised officer of the company estops it from denying the truth of the essential facts stated in it and the company may be held liable for false statements that were negligently made in it.

Shares Held in Trust

9–98   When someone other than the true or beneficial owner of shares is registered as a member, he holds them as trustee for their owner. That owner may be the *cestui* under a formal trust or someone who put the shares in the name of a bare nominee; or he may be someone who has agreed to buy and has paid for the shares, or who has not yet paid for them, or a transferor of the shares who has not yet been paid for them, or a person in whose favour the shares have been charged. The reciprocal rights and duties of the registered owner and the beneficial owner are governed by the law of trusts.[209] A registered owner must comply with the terms of whatever arrangement under which he holds the shares for another and must not exercise his membership rights, such as to vote, for his own personal gain to the detriment of the beneficial owner. Ordinarily, he is entitled to an indemnity from his *cestui* in respect of his liability for calls on unpaid shares.[210]

---

[204] See too *Dixon v Kennaway & Co.* [1900] 1 Ch. 833.
[205] *Bloomenthal v Ford* [1897] A.C. 156.
[206] [1906] A.C. 439.
[207] See para.18–50.
[208] 1963 Act, s.85.
[209] See generally, H. Delany, *Equity and the Law of Trusts*, 4th edn (Dublin: Thomson Round Hall, 2007).
[210] *Hardoon v Belilios* [1901] A.C. 118.

Notice of Trusts

9–99 Normally, the company itself will not be party to any trust arrangement affecting its shares. Company law attempts to insulate the company from those arrangements so that, insofar as the company itself is concerned, the registered owner and nobody else has all the rights attaching to the shares. No notice of any trust may be entered in the register of members or be receivable by the company,[211] so that a beneficiary who is not registered as the holder of shares has no direct connection with, or rights in, the company itself. Table A goes further by providing first that, except where required by law, no person shall be recognised by the company as holding any share on trust and, second, that the company shall not be bound by any equitable or analogous interest in its shares.[212] The purpose behind these provisions was explained as being to:

> "spare the company of the responsibility of attending to any trusts or equities whatever attached to their shares, so that they might safely and securely deal with the person who is registered owner, and with him alone, recognising no other person and no different right; freeing them … from all embarrassing enquiries into conflicting claims as to shares, transfers, calls, dividends, right to vote, and the like; and enabling them to treat the registered shareholder as owner of the shares for all purposes, without regard to contract as between himself and third persons."[213]

9–100 Some potentially drastic implications of those two provisions were rejected in *Rearden v Provincial Bank*,[214] where it was held that, if a company's duly authorised agent actually knows of some equitable interest held in its shares, then it is not always exonerated from liability it otherwise might incur for ignoring facts of which it was aware. The trustee of shares in a bank was registered as their owner and the bank knew that he held those shares in trust. When he failed to pay his own debts to the bank, it claimed a lien over those shares, contending that the articles' lien clause entitled it to override the *cestui's* interest in shares. This view was rejected on the grounds that "[t]he mere fact of notice does not convert the company into trustees for the persons of whose beneficial interest they have notice; but if, having that notice, they advance money to the trustee on the security of the trust property, their conduct is not protected by [s.123] and they participate in a breach of trust."[215] As for the common form article, it "applies to the company qua company, in respect of matters arising between the company and its members, as such; [but] it has no application to the acts of the company in its trading character, such as lending money upon security, [and] as a lender of money, upon the security of its own shares, the company is bound by the same equities as if it were advancing money upon the security of the shares of any other company."[216] Similarly,

---

[211] 1963 Act, s.123 and the Companies Act, 1990 (Uncertified Securities) Regulations, 1996 (SI 1996/68), reg.10(6).
[212] Article 77.
[213] *Rearden v Provincial Bank of Ireland* [1896] 1 I.R. 532 at 567.
[214] [1896] 1 I.R. 532.
[215] *ibid.* at 578, following *Bradford Banking Co. v Briggs* (1886) 12 App. Cas. 29.
[216] [1896] 1 I.R. 532 at 583.

when the chargee of shares notified the company of its security interest in them, that was held to be sufficient to give it priority over a lien that subsequently arose in favour of the company over those same shares.[217]

Voting

9–101   A bare nominee must always vote in accordance with the absolute beneficial owner's directions. A trustee must exercise his vote in accordance with the best interests of the trust, subject of course to any stipulation in the trust deed.

9–102   To protect his interest in shares, a beneficial owner can obtain orders against the trustee and indeed against the company where that interest may be prejudiced. The effect of Table A is not that the company shall never be affected by a trust or that no trust shall be created in any share, but that the company is not to be affected by any notice of a trust. Thus, in *McGrattan v McGrattan*,[218] in breach of trust the registered owner of shares voted for a members' resolution that seriously prejudiced their beneficial owner. The votes attaching to those shares were decisive in carrying the resolution. It was held that the resolution was thereby invalid.

9–103   Where there is an agreement to sell shares but the vendor has not yet been paid, he remains free to exercise his voting rights in the company whatever way he wishes and regardless of the intending purchaser's wishes, except perhaps where voting a particular way would damage the very subject-matter of the purchase.[219] Even then, while the intending vendor may be restrained by an injunction or have damages awarded against him, it would seem that the court will not direct him to vote in accordance with the purchaser's desires.[220]

9–104   There exists a mechanism for those claiming beneficial interests in stock to protect their interests in them, whereby the beneficiary may serve a "stop notice" on the company to notify it of his interest.[221] Upon receipt of a "stop notice", the company is not permitted to transfer the stock specified in the notice or to pay dividends on it, for so long as the notice remains operative. If the company then receives a request from the person in whose name the stock in question is standing, to permit a transfer or to pay dividends thereon, the company cannot refuse to accede to the request for more than eight days following the request, unless the court orders otherwise. Any other person claiming to be interested in the stock affected by the "stop notice" can apply to the court to cease its operation.[222]

---

[217] *Champagne Perrier-Jouet SA v HH Finch Ltd* [1982] 1 W.L.R. 1359 and *JRRT (Investments) Ltd v Haycraft* [1993] B.C.L.C. 401.

[218] [1965] N.I. 28.

[219] *Musselwhite v CH Musselwhite & Son Ltd* [1962] Ch. 964 and *JRRT (Investments) Ltd v Haycraft* [1993] B.C.L.C. 401.

[220] *Michaels v Harley House (Marylebone) Ltd* [1997] 2 B.C.L.C. 166.

[221] Rules of the Superior Courts, 1986, Order 46, Rules 5–13.

[222] For example, see *Lee v Buckle* [2004] 3 I.R. 544.

Dividend

9–105   Dividends paid to a trustee are prima facie deemed to be income and not capital, other than on a reduction of capital, payment in a winding-up, or where they are used to fund the allotment of new shares. However, this is not so where the distribution would produce a result that is manifestly incompatible with the proposed intention of the settlor or testator. Thus, when a listed company "demerged" by transferring some of its business to another company and the shares in the latter were distributed to the former's shareholders by way of dividend, it was held that those should be treated as capital.[223]

Trust for the Company

9–106   The prohibition against companies purchasing their own shares is not a bar to its own shares being held in trust for the company. Where a company is the recipient of a gift of its own shares, it should direct that they be held in name of a nominee, beneficially for the company.[224] Provisions in the articles of association restricting freedom to transfer the shares can cause difficulties in choosing who shall be a nominee for these purposes.

9–107   Where shares are issued to a company's nominees or it otherwise acquires them as partly paid up, they are deemed to belong beneficially to the nominee and not to the company, and it has no liability to pay any sums due on those shares.[225] This does not apply to shares in a Plc acquired, other than by subscription, with financial assistance given by the company.

Charge on Shares

9–108   Shares are often given by their owners as security for obligations they have assumed.[226] A legal mortgage of registered shares involves the mortgagee's name being entered in the register as a member of the company in respect of those shares. The mortgagor's right to redeem would then be contained in a separate document. On default, the mortgagee has an implied power to sell the shares. A disadvantage for the creditor with a legal mortgage is that he can be made liable for any unpaid calls on his shares.

9–109   Assignments of registered shares as security usually take the form of an equitable charge, such as an express agreement to mortgage the shares, a deposit of the share certificate, a purported transfer which is not in a registrable form or a registrable transfer which was never registered. By far the commonest form of security is the deposit of the share certificate with the creditor. In the past, those

---

[223] *Sinclair v Lee* [1993] Ch. 497; *cf. Manukau City Council v Lawson* [2001] 1 N.Z.L.R. 599.

[224] *Re Castiglione's Will Trusts* [1958] 1 Ch. 549.

[225] 1983 Act, s.42.

[226] See generally, J. Breslin (with K. Smith), *Banking Law*, 2nd edn (Dublin: Thomson Round Hall, 2007), pp.433–434, T. Parsons, *Lingard's Bank Security Documents*, 4th edn (London: Lexis Nexis, 2006) Ch.15 and R. Goode, *Legal Problems of Credit and Security*, 3rd edn (London: Sweet & Maxwell, 2003), Ch.6.

transactions were regarded as pledges, not mortgages.[227] This led to debtors also depositing a written memorandum declaring that the deposit was by way of a mortgage. Eventually it was decided that where a share certificate is deposited as security, but without any transfer form or memorandum, an equitable mortgage is created and, on default, the creditor then holding the certificate is entitled to foreclose.[228] Later, in similar circumstances, it was held that the depositee of the shares has an implied power of sale; that the deposit is "a transaction of mortgage and not ... of pledge" and, where no express power to sell was given, the law "implies a right in the mortgagee to sell after giving reasonable notice".[229]

9–110 A disadvantage for the creditor with an equitable charge is that the shares are subject to any right of lien or forfeiture that the company has in respect of them, and to any restrictions on their transferability under its articles of association. Also, the chargeor may fraudulently obtain a duplicate share certificate from the company and then sell the shares to a bona fide purchaser for value. Also, unknown to the creditor, bonus shares may be issued to the chargeor, thereby diluting the value of the security. All communications from the company are sent to the chargeor only. While in principle any prior equity will take precedence over the secured creditor's interest, this is not the case where, when it took the charge or performed the act which is being secured, it is a bona fide purchaser for value without notice. To exercise the right of sale on default, if the creditor does not have a signed transfer form, he requires a court order to that effect. If the shares can only be transferred by way of deed under seal, the creditor will require a power of attorney (or court order) to realise his security.

9–111 In the case of dematerialised listed shares that are transferable under the CREST system, equitable charges are facilitated by way of special escrow accounts operated by CRESTCo. The chargeor (CREST member acting for him) will transfer the charged shares into his escrow account, to which the creditor (or member acting for him) has access and is entitled to veto any transfer of those shares until the liability to him has been discharged.

Lien on Shares

9–112 A lien is a security interest that a person in possession of something of value has over the thing, in respect of obligations owed by its owner, whereby he is entitled to retain possession of that thing until the owner's obligation has been discharged. A company has no inherent lien over its own shares.[230] However, most articles of association grant companies that right in particular circumstances. Private companies, by their own regulations, may give themselves a lien over their own shares, whether partly paid or fully paid, in respect of any sums owed to them by their shareholders. It would seem that any such lien is effective where the shareholder becomes a bankrupt. But any

---

[227] *Re Butler* [1900] 2 I.R. 153.
[228] *Harrold v Plenty* [1901] 2 Ch. 314.
[229] *Stubbs v Slater* [1910] 1 Ch. 632 at 639.
[230] *Re Kingston Yacht Club* (1888) 21 L.R. Ir. 199.

lien or charge held by a Plc over its own shares is void except for a charge on partly paid shares for amounts payable on them, or a charge that existed when the company re-registered as a Plc, or a charge by a money-lending company arising out of its ordinary business transactions.[231]

9–113 Table A gives a company a "first and paramount" lien on every share that is not fully paid in respect of sums due on those shares and in respect of all other debts owed to the company by any shareholder or his estate.[232] This extends to dividends payable on the shares. The directors may exempt any shareholder from this lien. They have a power of sale under the lien, which may be exercised provided that the shareholder in default is given at least 14 days' notice of the fact. Where the articles impose restrictions on the transferability of the company's shares, these equally apply where it is the company that seeks to enforce its lien in this manner, in the absence of any contrary provision.[233] Where the shares have been charged to a third party, who gives notice to the company of his security interest, it appears that it has priority over any lien that the company acquires over those shares subsequent to that date.[234]

9–114 In *Allen v Gold Reefs of West Africa Ltd*,[235] where the broad equitable criterion of "good faith" was articulated, it was held that a company may alter its articles to acquire for itself a lien over its own shares, even if they are fully paid, together with the right to forfeit them. However, it is not permissible to alter the articles to give a company a lien and entitlement to forfeit the shares in respect of pre-existing debts to the company, arising other than as a shareholder.[236] That is an unlawful reduction of capital.

Forfeiture of Shares

9–115 Forfeiture means exercising a right to deprive a person of ownership of something; the person entitled to forfeit becomes its owner instead. As with liens, companies have no inherent right to forfeit their own shares. Any provision in the articles of association giving such a right must not offend against the Companies Acts or public policy. A provision for forfeiture where a shareholder directly or indirectly commences or threatens proceedings against the company was held to be invalid.[237]

9–116 Table A authorises the directors to forfeit and sell shares for non-payment of calls on them.[238] Before they can do this, the directors must notify the shareholder in question,[239] requiring payment of the amount due and

---

[231] 1983 Act, s.44.
[232] Article 11.
[233] *Champagne Perrier-Jouet SA v HH Finch Ltd* [1982] 1 W.L.R.
[234] *ibid.*
[235] [1900] 1 Ch. 656.
[236] *Hopkinson v Mortimer Harley & Co.* [1917] 1 Ch. 646.
[237] *Hope v International Financial Society* (1876) 4 Ch.D. 327.
[238] Articles 33–39.
[239] cf. *Parkstone Ltd v Gulf Guarantee Bank* [1990] B.C.L.C. 850.

stating that, if it is not paid, the shares are liable to be forfeited. Because of its drastic implications, the courts construe this power strictly.[240] Not alone must every prescribed detail be followed scrupulously, but *mala fides* or abusive exercise by the directors of their fiduciary power will cause a forfeiture to be struck down. Provided, however, that the power was properly exercised, a court will not award relief against forfeiture.

9–117   In *Hunter v Senate Support Services Ltd*,[241] when calls were made on the plaintiff's shares that he did not meet, the directors purported to forfeit them for non-payment. His contentions that his shares were to be deemed fully paid, that the decision to forfeit could not be made at informal board meetings, that those directors had conflicted their interests in making the decision and that he was never properly notified of the calls were all rejected. But it was held that the decision was unlawful because it had been made on the assumption that the only means available to the company to obtain what was due to it was forfeiture, when at least one other means was available—in the circumstances, excluding the plaintiff from any future dividends. Thus, the directors' decision was flawed for "neglecting to take into account matters which they ought to have taken into account" in all the circumstances.[242]

9–118   Once the power to forfeit is exercised, the shareholder ceases to be a member of the company and prima facie any liability by him to the company on the shares is extinguished. However, the ex-member remains liable for all unpaid amounts on those shares due to the company at the date the forfeiture took place[243]; this liability ceases when those sums are paid up either by him or by whoever the shares were re-issued to. A right of forfeiture that was exercised in fact to relieve a shareholder of liability to the company is ineffective.[244] A statutory declaration about a forfeiture enables the company to give whoever the shares are re-issued to a good title that cannot be impeached because the process was irregular.[245]

PREFERENCE SHARES

9–119   Preference shares carry prior or preferential rights over other shares.[246] These rights are usually as regards dividends and return of capital, i.e. the preference shareholders must be paid a dividend or repaid their investment, or both as the case may be, before any such payment can be made to the other shareholders. For tax purposes, "ordinary" (as compared with preference) shares are defined as "all the issued share capital (by whatever name

[240] *Ward v Dublin North City Milling Co.* [1919] 1 I.R. 5.
[241] [2005] 1 B.C.L.C. 176.
[242] *ibid.* at 231.
[243] Article 37.
[244] *Re London & County Assur. Co., Ex p. Jones* (1858) 27 L.J. Ch. 666.
[245] Article 38.
[246] See generally, Pickering, "The Problem of the Preference Share" 26 *Mod. L. Rev.* 499 (1963) and Rice, "Capital Rights of Preference Shares" 26 *Conv.* 115 (1962).

called) … other than capital the holders of which have a right to a dividend at a fixed rate, but have no other right to share in the profits of the company."[247]

9–120   In the past, preference shares were popular with investors because they guaranteed a degree of income and capital security but in the 1970s and 1980s inflation eroded their value. Although they are equity and not debt, companies tend to regard preference shares as a form of borrowing, in that they provide a source of capital on which the company is expected to pay a fixed percentage dividend every year. The advantage to a company of these shares is that they enable it more easily to gear its capital structure. Usually, there is no absolute obligation to pay a dividend on them every year or to repay them by a fixed date, nor is there any question of the company putting up security to obtain the funds. Nevertheless, dividends cannot be set off against profits for taxation purposes.

9–121   The exact rights and liabilities of preference shareholders are set out in the memorandum and articles of association, resolutions passed and the terms on which the shares were issued. Although Table A envisages creating a class of share with certain preferential rights, it does not contain provisions dealing specifically with them. A preference shareholder's liability is simply to pay any unpaid amounts on his shares when called upon to do so. It is almost unheard of for companies' own regulations to contain special provisions about the transferability of their preference shares.

Vote

9–122   Companies' own regulations usually give preference shareholders a vote in general meeting only when their dividends are in arrears or where it is proposed to alter their rights as a class.[248] Often their entitlement is confined to simply attending and speaking at general meetings.[249] In contrast, the preference shareholders in *Re Williams Group Tullamore Ltd*[250] had the sole right to attend and vote at general meetings, as well as non-cumulative dividend rights and priority when repaying capital in liquidation.

Dividend

9–123   Where the company's own regulations give one class of shares preferential rights regarding dividends, then those are their entire income rights; there is "something so definitely pointed to as to suggest that it contains the whole of what [they are] to look to from the company".[251] They have no entitlement to participate any further in the profits unless expressly enabled to do so. Any claim they may have to equal participation with the other members is derogated from by the exhaustive statement of their entitlement to the company's

---

[247] Taxes Consolidation Act 1997, s.2(1).
[248] e.g. *Re Bradford Investments Ltd* [1991] B.C.L.C. 224.
[249] e.g. *Young v Pearce* [1996] S.T.C. 743.
[250] [1985] I.R. 613.
[251] *Will v United Lankat Plantation Co.* [1914] A.C. 11 at 17, 18.

profits.[252] For tax purposes, a preference dividend is defined as "a dividend paid on a prescribed share … at a fixed rate per cent or, where a dividend is paid on a preferred share … partly at a fixed rate per cent and partly at a variable rate, such part of that dividend as is payable at a fixed rate per cent."[253]

Participation

9–124   Occasionally, preference shares carry participating dividend rights. That is to say, over and above their basic (usually fixed) dividend entitlement, they may be given some right to participate with other shareholders in the remaining profits for distribution. At times, companies' own regulations stipulate that their preference shareholders' dividend rights are not just cumulative, in the sense described below, but that a dividend shall be payable on those shares every year, or perhaps every year in which profits are earned, or every year when there are profits available for distribution.[254] Any such obligation must be clearly provided for in the regulations; ambiguities tend to be read in favour of the directors' and members' discretion as to what should be done with the profits.[255] In *Re Lafayette Ltd,*[256] the company's regulations stated that the preference shareholders were entitled to a six per cent "cumulative preferential dividend for each year … out of the subsequent profits of the company". Kingsmill Moore J. held that the preference shareholders, therefore, became entitled to a dividend in every year in which there were "business profits" and that this was not contingent on any dividend being declared; the articles give them "a right to their dividend, irrespective of any declaration, and, again without any declaration, automatically charge arrears of preference dividend on any future profits".[257]

Cumulation

9–125   As entitlement to a dividend is usually contingent on one being declared, the "exhaustiveness" principle has been qualified somewhat in respect of preferential dividend rights. Unless the company's own regulations provide otherwise, preference shareholders have no right to be paid a dividend in any one year. It has been said that if it were otherwise it "might enable the preference shareholders to ruin the company, and would certainly lead to great inconvenience in enabling them to compel the payment out of the last penny without carrying forward any balance".[258] Yet this state of affairs can work unfairly against preference shareholders, who most likely acquire their shares in anticipation of receiving dividends at least in years when the company is making good profits; for over a number of years the company could retain all profits earned and then in one year declare a single (usually fixed) preference dividend together with a

---

[252] *ibid.*

[253] Taxes Consolidation Act 1997, s.4(1).

[254] e.g. *Staples v Eastman Photographic Materials Co.* [1896] 2 Ch.303 and *Evling v Israel & Oppenheimer* [1918] 1 Ch. 101. *Re Bradford Investments Ltd* [1991] B.C.L.C. 224: articles deemed dividend payable even if no available profits.

[255] *Re Buck (deceased)* [1964] V.R. 284.

[256] [1950] I.R. 100.

[257] *ibid.* at 112.

[258] *Bond v Barrow Haematite Steel Co.* [1902] 1 Ch. 353 at 362.

bumper dividend for the ordinary shareholders. On account of this, preference dividends tend to be presumed to be cumulative, i.e. in the absence of contrary provision, where a preference dividend has not been declared in any year or years, then all arrears of undeclared preference dividends for those years must be paid before any other class of shareholder may get a dividend.

9–126   The presumption that preference dividends are cumulative is traced to *Webb v Earle*.[259] Ordinary shareholders sought a declaration of invalidity against decisions by directors, in years where no dividends were paid, to place in a special reserve sums representing preference dividends to be paid when the funds became available. It was held that "there is nothing to prevent [the directors] from going to the profits of a subsequent period when they are sufficient to make up" preference dividends that had not been paid.[260] The case does not say in so many words that preference dividends are presumed to be cumulative but, if that were not so, the directors would not have the power to set sums by in order to pay arrears of dividends on them. However, authority supporting presumed cumulation is not very weighty.[261]

Winding Up

9–127   Where a company has not paid a preference dividend for a number of years and then goes into liquidation, the question arises of whether the preference shareholders have a claim for those dividends it passed or could not have paid. Generally, once a winding-up commences no claim to undeclared dividends can arise.[262] But where, as in *Re Lafayette Ltd*,[263] the company's own regulations treat dividend expectations as if they were declared, they then become a debt of the company from the time they were deemed to have been declared. Those sums are in the understandably "peculiar position of not being payable *pari passu* with the liabilities generally, because [they are] a deferred debt, not payable in competition with those of creditors who are not members of the company ...".[264] The English courts have tended to strain the meaning of companies' regulations in order to conclude that preference shareholders were granted a right in a winding-up to have arrears of dividends paid to them.[265]

Capital and the Surplus

9–128   It is usual when issuing preference shares to attach to them priority in respect of repayment of capital but to exclude them from participating in any surplus that may remain in a winding-up after all classes of shareholders are paid off. Whatever the company's own regulations say about preference shareholders' right to a return of capital is a complete statement of their rights in these regards. Where those regulations do not deal with these

---

[259] (1875) L.R. 20 Eq. 556.
[260] *ibid.* at 561.
[261] *JJ Thorneycroft & Co. v Thorneycroft*, 44 TLR 9 (1927) and cases referred to there.
[262] *Re Crichton's Oil Co.* [1901] 2 Ch. 184.
[263] [1950] I.R. 100.
[264] *Re Imperial Hotel (Cork) Ltd* [1950] I.R. 115 at 119.
[265] e.g. *Re F de Jong & Co.* [1946] 1 Ch. 211 and *Re EW Savory Ltd* [1951] 3 All E.R. 1036.

matters then the ordinary and preference shareholders have equal rights to a repayment and to share in any surplus. And where preference shares participate in the surplus, the measure of their rights is their nominal amounts and not the amounts paid up on them.[266] Beyond this, the legal positions in Ireland and in the UK are radically different.

9-129   *The Surplus:* The area of greatest controversy has been preference shareholders' claims to participate in a surplus where the regulations do not address the question directly. At one time it was accepted that, by virtue of a combination of the exhaustiveness and the equality principles, those members were entitled to participate rateably in the surplus. This view was endorsed in 1932 in *Cork Electric Supply Co. v Concannon*[267] and also in 1946 by the Canadian Supreme Court in *International Power Co. v McMaster University.*[268] However, when in 1949 the matter came before the Law Lords in *Scottish Insurance Corp. v Wilsons & Clyde Coal Co.,*[269] by a majority they reached the contrary conclusion. There are weighty logical and practical arguments for both points of view.

9-130   In the *Wilsons & Clyde Coal Co.* case, a large capital profit was made by the company when its major assets, coal mines, were nationalised in return for cash. It then proposed to repay its preference shareholders following which it intended to distribute the sizeable surplus to its ordinary shareholders. Predictably, the preference shareholders opposed this scheme on the grounds, *inter alia,* that they had a legal right to a share in the surplus. Under the company's regulations, the preference shareholders had priority as to repayment of capital in a winding-up but nothing at all was said about who was to get any surplus or whether it should be shared. Other regulations deemed relevant were to the effect that the board could create a reserve fund for repaying the preference shares; also that the company might convert any surplus funds it had into capital and distribute it among the ordinary shareholders, for instance by issuing bonus shares. The dissenting minority of the court emphasised the underlying equality principle; the company's regulations contained "not a word which raises the implication that [the preference holders] are to be excluded from the ordinary right, as corporators, to share equally with other corporators in a winding up on this portion of the property of the company"; "the considerations affecting capital and dividend are entirely different"; the minority concluded that the case law as it stood indicated that the surplus had to be shared between the two classes.[270]

9-131   The kernel of the successful contrary argument was that a surplus represents retained profits that the ordinary shareholders, had they chosen to do so, could have appropriated to themselves in the form of dividends or bonus shares. It therefore would be unjust and indeed illogical if the claims they had

---

[266] *Birch v Cropper* (1889) 14 App. Cas. 525.
[267] [1932] I.R. 314.
[268] 2 D.L.R. 81 (1946).
[269] [1949] A.C. 462.
[270] *ibid.* at 501, 506.

over those funds were defeated by the event of a liquidation. Repayment of capital and participation in any surplus are not distinct; the central question is what rights to "company property" arise in a winding-up. If a company's regulations are silent on any aspect of this matter, then the equality principle comes into play. But where the regulations address either repayment of capital or the surplus, or both, those provisions are an exhaustive recitation of the preference shareholders' entitlement to both.[271] This, it was said, is consistent with the business world's perception of the preference shareholder's position.

9–132   In the earlier *Cork Electric Co.* case,[272] which arose out of similar facts, a unanimous Supreme Court adopted the same reasoning as in that House of Lords dissent. A company that ran trains in Cork and supplied the city with electricity was expropriated under the Electricity Supply Act 1927. The central issue was how the compensation paid for the undertaking should be divided among the ordinary and the preference shareholders. Under the company's regulations, the latter were entitled to a five per cent cumulative preference dividend per annum and, in a winding-up, "to priority in payment of the capital over the ordinary shares". According to Kennedy C.J.:

> "Preference shareholders are holders of shares in the capital of a company in the same way as ordinary shareholders are holders of shares in its capital. Both classes of shareholders are equally members of the Company. Their respective positions are differentiated only to the extent to which the rights and privileges attaching to their respective shares are qualified contractually by the Memorandum and Articles of Association of the Company. I turn, therefore, to the Memorandum and Articles of Association of the plaintiff company to ascertain whether the right of the preference shareholder to participate in surplus assets on a winding up of the company has been abrogated, cut down, or qualified in any way. There is no such specific provision, and we have to look for a limitation by implication. Upon the construction of the Articles of Association before us it is to be observed that, while as regards participation in profits, the words of exclusion "but to no further dividend" were carefully inserted, no such limitation was added to the immediately following clause as to priority in payment of capital. Moreover, I can find no grounds for cutting down the word 'shareholders'… or the words 'member of the Company for the time being' in [the articles] to ordinary shareholders only … I must say that there is not, so far as I know, any rule of law or construction requiring a Court of construction to find a logical consistency between the rights of preference shareholders while a company is a going concern and their rights on a winding-up. It is difficult to know what is meant precisely by 'logical consistency' in this connection, but, as I understand it, it is quite foreign to the great diversity of bargains which may lawfully be made in these business contracts."[273]

---

[271] *cf. Re Isle of Thanet Electricity Supply Co.* [1950] Ch. 161.
[272] [1932] I.R. 314.
[273] *ibid.* at 327, 329.

That the numerous Companies Acts passed since this case was decided never sought to interfere with the principle as stated here suggests that it would still be followed today.

9–133   *Sharing the Surplus*: Where both ordinary and preference sharehold-ers are entitled to share in the surplus, the question then arises of whether a dis-tinction should be drawn between the part of the surplus that remains or was available for distribution as dividends and that which has been capitalised. Where the company's own regulations are silent, the practice would appear to be that all classes share in the capitalised amounts but only the ordinary share-holders are entitled to participate in the sums that were not capitalised. For example, in *Re Marshall Bros, Belfast, Ltd*[274] the surplus comprised, *inter alia,* a profit on the sale of the undertaking, which was treated as a capitalised amount, and tax refunds held in "special reserve", which was treated as uncapitalised. The former was divided among all the shareholders whereas the latter went to the ordinary shareholders only. Yet difficulties can arise in deter-mining whether particular reserves were, or were intended to be, capitalised; art. 119 of Table A does not differentiate between the two kinds of reserves. In the *Wilsons & Clyde Coal Co.* case, reference was made to the unlikelihood of investors "intend[ing] a bargain which would involve an investigation of an artificial and elaborate character into the nature and origin of surplus assets".[275]

9–134   Where it is expressly provided that the two or more classes are to share in the surplus, how exactly this is to be distributed turns on how the regulations in their entirety are construed. It would appear that there is no pre-sumption against the parties having intended to distinguish between capitalised and uncapitalised funds. In *Dimbula Valley (Ceylon) Tea Co. v Laurie,*[276] pref-erence shareholders were entitled to a cumulative preference dividend, to pri-ority in the return of capital and any arrears of dividend, and to participate in "any further surplus assets" rateably with other shareholders. The company's regulations stated that, subject to any preferential rights, profits remaining after placing sums in reserve "shall be divisible among the members"; and the com-pany could capitalise sums standing in any "reserve fund" and any "undivided profits". One question was whether the preference shareholders could partici-pate rateably in the entire surplus or only in such part of it as could not have been paid as dividends on the ordinary shares. Buckley J. acknowledged the ordinary shareholders' power to defeat any preference shareholders' expecta-tion of sharing in undistributed profits by, on the one hand, declaring a dividend from the profits and, on the other, where profits could not be so distributed, to capitalise them and issue the ordinary shareholders with further equity repre-senting the capitalised amount. This, however, it was said, is not inconsistent with the preference shareholders on a winding-up having a right to participate in retained earnings. It was concluded that, in the absence of clear contrary indications, "the right of the ordinary shareholders to the exclusive enjoyment

---

[274] [1956] N.I. 78.
[275] *Scottish Insurance Corp. Ltd v Wilsons & Clyde Coal Co Ltd* [1949] A.C. 462 at 489.
[276] [1961] Ch. 353.

of accumulated profits … depends on appropriate resolutions being passed before liquidation begins, and that in default of appropriate resolutions such accumulated profits will form part of the fund of assets distributable" between all members rateably on a winding-up. To reach this conclusion and to distinguish pre-1900 authority[277] on the point, the judge fastened on the terminology of the company's dividends regulation, where it was said that profits were "divisible among" the members once preference dividends were met and subject to sums being placed in reserve. This, it was said, meant not that those profits "belonged to" the ordinary shareholders, but merely that such profits could be divided among them by a decision of the general meeting before a winding-up commenced. Yet an Irish court might choose to follow *Re Bridgewater Navigation Co.*,[278] where 70 years earlier the English Court of Appeal reached the opposite conclusion when construing somewhat similar articles.

---

[277] *Re Bridgewater Navigation Co.* [1891] 2 Ch. 326.
[278] *ibid.*

CHAPTER 10

MINORITY PROTECTION

10–01 Often differences will arise between shareholders about their company's affairs. One of the fundamental principles of company law is majority rule: that it is for the majority of members with voting rights to decide most questions concerning their company and that only certain fundamental issues should be resolved by super-majorities (usually either a special resolution or a decision of three quarters in value of the shareholders). Consequently, the dissatisfied shareholders who cannot persuade the majority to come around to their point of view will often have to choose between having their preferences ignored or disposing of their shares. Minority interests in some companies are safeguarded to an extent by them being given a right to representation on the board of directors, or by a limit existing on the number of votes that holders of large blocks of shares may cast. Transactions involving controlling shareholders have become the subject of considerable regulation. In companies whose shares are quoted on a stock exchange, the threat by disgruntled members to sell off a large block of shares may persuade the majority to make their peace with the minority. Additionally, the Listing Rules and the Transparency Directive ensure a degree of protection, by guaranteeing "equality of treatment" for shareholders "in the same position" and that the company's business is "capable at all times of carrying on ... independently of a controlling shareholder".[1] In private companies, on the other hand, restrictions in the articles of association on the transferability of shares may render a minority stake virtually unsaleable. Most minority shareholder disputes litigation concerns private companies.

10–02 Judges have always been hesitant about adjudicating on inter-shareholder disputes.[2] Many of the matters that give rise to conflict between shareholders concern essentially business judgments, like hiring and firing employees, expanding or contracting particular lines of activity, paying dividends or placing profits in reserve. If those choices were readily reviewable

---

[1] Listing Rules 3.4.5 and 6.3.1 and the Transparency (Directive 2004/109/EC) Regulations 2007 (SI 2007/277), reg.25(3).

[2] See generally, R. Kraakman et al, *The Anatomy of Corporate Law: A Comparative and Functional Approach* (Oxford: Oxford University Press, 2004), para.3.2; V. Joffe, *Minority Shareholders: Law, Practice and Procedure*, 2nd edn (London: LexisNexis, 2004); R. Hollington, *Shareholders' Rights*, 4th edn (London: Sweet & Maxwell, 2004); A.J. Boyle, *Minority Shareholders' Remedies* (Cambridge: Cambridge University Press, 2002).

by the courts, then the spectre of judges "taking on the management of every playhouse and brewhouse" in the country[3] would be realised. Lawyers do not possess any special competence in business affairs, and legal procedures are far too expensive and cumbersome processes for resolving differences of policy between shareholders. There nevertheless are several grounds on which the courts will intervene on the minority shareholder's behalf and, since the jurisdiction was given to rectify "oppression", the basis for judicial intervention and the remedies available have been radically expanded. Articles of association of private companies, or separate shareholders' agreements, often contain arbitration clauses for resolving issues of this nature.

10–03   The law here is often analysed and explained with reference to a case decided some 160 years ago, *Foss v Harbottle*.[4] It stands for the proposition that, if some wrong has been committed in the course of a company's affairs, it is the company in its corporate capacity which should seek redress, and not any of its shareholders. The acknowledged "exceptions", where a shareholder rather than the company is permitted to bring proceedings, are usually classified under four heads:[5]

(1) where the act complained of is illegal or *ultra vires*;
(2) where the requirement of a "special majority" procedure has been ignored;
(3) where the plaintiff's own "personal and individual" rights have been invaded;
(4) where those who control the company committed a "fraud on the minority".

To those grounds must now be added statutory "oppression" and also the petition to have the company wound up on "just and equitable" grounds.[6]

10–04   Where some shareholders' interests stand to be prejudiced in major capital reorganisations and in takeovers, the legislature has provided for additional safeguards.[7] Other remedies are applying to the High Court or to the DCE to appoint inspectors, to investigate aspects of the company's affairs, and for the DCE to otherwise intervene. Additionally, a shareholder may have a direct remedy against one or more of the company's directors, either where one is provided in the Companies Acts or in those exceptional circumstances where the director owes a duty of care or a fiduciary duty to that member. A member's interests also can be safeguarded in an appropriately drafted separate shareholders' agreement.

---

[3] *Carlen v Drury* (1812) 1 V & B 154 at 158.
[4] (1843) 2 Hare 461. See generally, Wedderburn, "Shareholders' Rights and the Rule in *Foss v Harbottle*" [1958] *Cam. L.J.* 93.
[5] *Edwards v Halliwell* [1952] 2 All E.R. 1064 at 1067 (summarised).
[6] 1963 Act, ss.205 and 213(f) respectively.
[7] Considered in Ch.11.

10–05 The hands-off stance taken by courts in the past to many inter-shareholder disputes is founded on three broad doctrines, each of which is a manifestation of the underlying majority rule principle.

Injury to the Corporation

10–06 Where it suffers a loss as a consequence of some unlawful act, it is for the company itself and not individual shareholders to sue the wrongdoer, because in law it is a separate legal person. In *Foss v Harbottle,* a group of shareholders sued promoters and directors alleging fraud: that the defendants had arranged to sell their own properties to the company at exorbitant prices. It was held that the immediate victim of the alleged wrong was the corporation and "[I]t [is] not ... a matter of course for any individual members of a corporation ... to assume to themselves the right of suing in the name of the corporation".[8] What those plaintiffs ought to have done was call an extraordinary general meeting, at which the majority could have voted to avoid those contracts or take other appropriate action.

Mere Irregularity

10–07 Next there is what may be termed the mere irregularity principle: that if the company or those acting for it do something which, though unlawful, could be "cured" and rendered lawful by the shareholders ratifying it in general meeting, then the illegal act is a mere irregularity in respect of which aggrieved individual shareholders do not have a right of action. The most far-reaching example is *McDougall v Gardiner,*[9] where the plaintiff, who suspected that the defendant directors were implicated in fraudulent transactions involving the company's property, convened a general meeting to consider the matter, and obtained proxies representing almost half of the company's voting capital. But the directors and their supporters, including the chairman, prevented a poll from taking place.[10] A claim against the directors brought in the name of the plaintiff, the company and all the shareholders other than the directors, was rejected on the grounds that what was alleged was a mere irregularity which was within the power of the majority shareholders to ratify; therefore, any legal claim against those responsible for the alleged fraud ought to be brought by the company rather than by individual shareholders. Mellish L.J., whose judgment is generally referred to, stated that, since it is common for irregularities to occur in companies, if there were no principle deterring resultant shareholder suits, the courts would be flooded by actions brought by one or other "cantankerous member" or "member who loves litigation". Accordingly, a shareholder has no personal right of action:

---

[8] (1843) 2 Hare at 490. Followed more recently in *Stein v Blake (No. 2)* [1998] 1 B.C.L.C. 573 and *Crindle Investments v Wymes* [1998] 4 I.R. 567.

[9] (1875) 1 Ch D 13.

[10] This would not be possible today: 1963 Act, s.137.

"if the thing complained of is a thing which in substance the majority of the company are entitled to do, or if something has been done irregularly which the majority of the company are entitled to do regularly, or if something has been done illegally which the majority of the company are entitled to do legally... If the matter is of that nature, the majority are the only persons who can complain that a thing which they are entitled to do has been done irregularly".[11]

Voting Property

10–08   Thirdly, there is what may be referred to as the voting property principle: that, save in exceptional circumstances, a shareholder's vote in general meeting cannot be impeached merely because he voted for self-serving reasons. This "novel" point was decided in *North-West Transportation Co. v Beatty*,[12] where minority shareholders sued their company and five ex-directors in an action to have set aside the sale to the company of a substantial asset by one of those directors, who also was its largest shareholder. It was contended that the common law rule, under which contracts with directors are rendered enforceable when ratified by the company in general meeting, ought not apply where the director, who makes the contract, votes his own shares and that vote is decisive in carrying the ratifying resolution. In the interests of legal certainty, the Privy Council rejected the view that the validity of resolutions might turn on the motives or circumstances of individuals voting for them. Instead, in questions such as this "a pure question of policy ... the voice of the majority ought to prevail; [and] to reject the votes of the [majority] would be to give effect to the views of the minority, and to disregard those of the majority".[13]

Ratifying Officers' Wrongs

10–09   Many of the instances where minority shareholders seek redress involve breaches of directors' duties which, where those directors and their allies own a majority of the voting shares, are most unlikely to result in a claim by the company against them. If their wrong is to be remedied, that can only be done by permitting individual shareholders to bring a claim. Especially in "close companies", for practical purposes the whole question of enforcing the directors' duties of care and fiduciary duties is inextricable from the rights of minority shareholders under the "exceptions" to *Foss v Harbottle*.[14] A general resolution purporting to ratify a breach of directors' duty does not legally prevent the company from later claiming damages from the errant director, because any effective release of the director's liability must be supported by consideration. But there are certain kinds of officers' wrongs which are

---

[11]   (1875) 1 Ch D 13 at 25.

[12]   (1887) 12 App. Cas. 589.

[13]   *ibid.* at 601. See too *Burland v Earle* [1902] A.C. 83 and an extreme example, *Northern Counties Securities Ltd v Jackson & Steeple Ltd* [1974] 1 W.L.R. 1133.

[14]   See generally, Worthington, "Corporate Governance: Remedying and Ratifying Directors' Breaches" 116 *L.Q.R.* 638 (2000); Hannigan, "Limitation on a Shareholder's Right to Vote—Effective Ratification Revisited" [2000] *J. Bus. L.* 493 and Partridge, "Ratification and Release of Directors from Personal Liability" 46 *Cam. L.J.* 122 (1987).

capable of being ratified by a majority of the members. In those conflict of interest situations, where the mode of redress is for the company to avoid contractual obligations, a members' resolution adopting the contract may debar the company from later seeking to rescind the contract. Similarly, where some of the directors' powers are used for an improper purpose; at least as regards "insiders", the company is not bound by what the directors have done. But a members' resolution approving what the directors did may operate to bind the company. Where, however, the directors acted unlawfully, contravened the memorandum or articles of association, discriminated unfairly against the minority or defrauded the company in an equitable sense, the purported ratification of their wrong will be ineffective unless perhaps done by the entire membership of the company.

ILLEGALITY

10–10 Where the company or its directors have contravened a provision of the Companies Acts, the section in question may give the aggrieved shareholder a right to civil redress; for instance, to inspect the register of members, to be given a copy of the annual accounts, to requisition EGMs and (subject to what the articles of association may provide) to vote at AGMs and EGMs, and to transfer shares. If the breach in question is an offence, then it depends on the nature of the legislative requirement and the surrounding circumstances whether a civil right of action also arises.[15] Many transactions entered into by a company which contravene these Acts are deemed to be *ultra vires* and, accordingly, unenforceable.[16]

10–11 A rare example of unlawful activities outside of the Companies Acts giving rise to questions of shareholders' rights is *Cockburn v Newbridge Sanitary Steam Laundry Co.*[17] The company had a contract to do certain work for the armed forces for £3,000 but payment was made to the defendant director, who handed only £1,000 over to the company. When the plaintiff sued in his own and other shareholders' names against that director and the company, to recover the difference, the first and unsuccessful line of defence was the *Foss v Harbottle*[18] injury-to-the-corporation principle, i.e. since it was the company that was wronged, they had no cause of action. Another defence was that much of the missing £2,000 had been paid in bribes, with the tacit consent of the shareholders. Even if this was so, it was held that the company would still have been acting illegally (breaking the Prevention of Corruption Acts) and consequently *ultra vires*; that the:

> "whole matter is tainted with criminality. The real agreement which it is suggested the directors did make in this case would have been an agreement, if made, so tainted with crime and so subversive of public policy as to be illegal in itself. It would, accordingly, have been quite beyond

---

[15] *Cutler v Wandsworth Stadium Ltd* [1949] A.C. 389.
[16] e.g. paying dividends from capital.
[17] [1915] 1 I.R. 237.
[18] (1843) 2 Hare 461.

the powers of the company to have entered into it, nor could any memorandum or articles have given it power; it would be equally wrong for the company to ratify it."[19]

10–12 However, not every unlawful act done by a company is *ultra vires* in the sense that any shareholder is entitled to have its continuation enjoined. As was said in the *Newbridge Laundry* case, "[I]llegality and *ultra vires* are not interchangeable terms", although it was added that "it is difficult, if not impossible, to conceive a case in which a company can do an illegal act, the illegality arising from public policy, and act within its powers".[20]

BREACH OF MEMORANDUM OR ARTICLES

10–13 Any member (or debenture-holder) may bring an action to prevent a company from "doing any act or thing which [it] has no power to do"[21]; in other words, from acting *ultra vires*. The core meaning of *ultra vires* is acting contrary to or beyond the company's objects or legal capacity.

10–14 The memorandum and articles of association are deemed to be a sealed contract between the company and its members, and also between the membership *inter se*. This contract "binds the company and the members thereof to the same extent as if they respectively had been signed and sealed by each member, and contained covenants by each member to observe all the provisions of the memorandum and of the articles".[22] Many shareholder–company and inter-shareholder claims, therefore, are for breach of what is referred to as the s.25 contract, i.e. the contract contained in its own regulations.[23] As the cases on pre-emption clauses demonstrate,[24] individual members can sue other members for breach of any obligation the members assumed to each other in this contract. The company can enforce some provisions of this contract against individual members.[25] Subject to some exceptions, any member can require the company to abide by the terms of this contract and seek redress for it not having done so. Generally, the remedy is a declaration of invalidity and/or an injunction. It is questionable whether a shareholder can recover damages from the company for breaches of this nature.

Allocation of Powers

10–15 Where the directors act within their exclusive competence, as defined in the company's own regulations, then the general meeting is not entitled to issue legally binding instructions to them.[26] Whether or in what circumstances

---

[19] [1915] 1 I.R. 237 at 255.
[20] *ibid.* at 254.
[21] 1963 Act, s.8(2).
[22] 1963 Act, s.25.
[23] See generally, Drury, "The Relative Nature of a Shareholder's Rights to Enforce the Company Contract" 45 *Cam. L.J.* 219 (1986).
[24] e.g. *Rayfield v Hands* [1960] 1 Ch. 1.
[25] e.g. *Peninsular Co. v Fleming* (1872) 27 L.T. 93.
[26] *Automatic Self-Cleansing Filter Syndicate Co.* v *Cunninghame* [1906] 2 Ch. 4.

the general meeting is entitled to veto board decisions is not entirely clear, in particular board decisions made under the broad authority in Table A to "manage ... [t]he business of the company"[27] and that concern strategic matters that will have a major impact on the company's development. But where decision-making power over certain matters is allocated by those regulations to a named shareholder or narrow group of shareholders, the member or members in question may prevent the company's other organs from acting contrary to his or their properly expressed decisions. In *Quin & Axtens Ltd v Salmon*,[28] the articles gave each of two named managing directors, who as well were the company's principal shareholders, what in effect was a veto over major property transactions envisaged by the company. Against the objections of one of them, the board and then the general meeting resolved to enter into such a transaction. It was held that the company should be enjoined from acting on that resolution because it in effect sought to alter the articles without going through the requisite procedures. Those resolutions were "absolutely inconsistent with [the] article[s]; in truth this is an attempt to alter the terms of the [section 25] contract between the parties by a simple resolution instead of by a special resolution".[29] If a company's regulations purported to authorise a particular shareholder to issue instructions to the board or the general meeting, the court presumably would compel the organ in question to act in accordance with those instructions, or would at least declare invalid resolutions that are inconsistent with them.

Procedures

10–16   Where a company's own regulations set down procedures to be followed in order to pass an ordinary or a special resolution, as a general rule any shareholder can enjoin the majority from acting on a decision reached that is not consistent with those procedures.[30] A shareholder may stop the holding of a general meeting called at great haste so as to prevent him from voting at it.[31] There are numerous reported instances of resolutions being held invalid because the shareholders were given misleading or inadequate information about what it was they were being asked to vote on.[32] Although, in *McDougall v Gardiner*[33] the court refused to intervene against a breach of the company's regulations about calling a poll, that decision must be regarded as very exceptional and may be explained by the particular facts of the case.

10–17   There are also numerous reported instances that deal with what procedures should be followed at company board meetings, but few of these are actions brought by minority shareholders as such against the company or its directors. Often contravention of board procedures is

---

[27]   Art.80.
[28]   [1909] 1 Ch. 311, aff'd [1909] A.C. 442.
[29]   [1909] 1 Ch. 311 at 319.
[30]   e.g. *Pender v Lushington* (1877) 6 Ch D 70.
[31]   e.g. *Cannon v Trask* (1875) L.R. 20 Eq. 669.
[32]   e.g. *Kaye v Croydon Tramways Co.* [1896] 1 Ch. 358.
[33]   (1875) 1 Ch D 13. See generally, Baxter, "The Role of the Judge in the Enforcing Shareholders' Rights" 42 *Cam. L.J.* 96 (1983).

pleaded by a shareholder as a defence to an action by the company for forfeiture of his shares, or is pleaded by the company itself (usually unsuccessfully) in order to disclaim liability on a contract supposedly made by the board. In *Browne v La Trinidad*,[34] it was held that a shareholder ordinarily has no cause of action merely because there was a breach of the procedures for board meetings. The plaintiff shareholder and director sought to restrain the holding of a general meeting, which was to consider a resolution proposing that he be removed from the board, on the grounds that the board meeting that purported to convene the general meeting had not been properly constituted; inadequate notice of it had been given to him. Accepting for the purpose of the argument that the board meeting had been improperly held and, strictly speaking, was incompetent to act, the court concluded that the notice of the general meeting nevertheless was legally effective. This was because "if there was an irregularity at the board meeting it was not such an irregularity as to vitiate the action of the board, and even if there had been an irregularity in the constitution of the board, it would not have deprived the general body of shareholders of the power of acting, when the notice was issued by the directors as such, and was signed in the usual way ... as required in the articles ..."[35]

10–18 The difficult question, of course, is how one is to determine which board improprieties are and are not ratifiable by a simple majority of the shareholders who vote. In the *Browne* case, it was emphasised that the plaintiff, who was aware of the irregularity, did not protest to his fellow directors until the very last minute, and that to uphold his application in those circumstances "[w]ould be paralysing the whole course of business of these companies".[36] This suggests that the outcome depends on the circumstances of each case, especially whether the plaintiff stands to suffer irreparable harm if the court does not rule in his favour. Many of the cases in this area are applications for interlocutory injunctions, where the balance of convenience is always an important consideration, and undertakings are often extracted from the defendants to preserve the *status quo*.[37]

Substantive Entitlements

10–19 Many actions brought by shareholders against their companies are to recover something of tangible economic benefit, to which they claim to be entitled under the memorandum or articles. That claim may be to be furnished with certain information concerning the company, to have one's vote recorded in general meetings, to be paid a dividend that has been declared,[38] to have one's transfer of shares in the company registered, to acquire shares in the company where they are being disposed if there is a pre-emption clause,[39] to a

---

[34] (1887) 37 Ch D 1.
[35] *ibid.* at 10. See too *Bentley Stevens v Jones* [1974] 1 W.L.R. 638.
[36] (1887) 37 Ch D 1 at 17.
[37] e.g. *Harben v Phillips* (1883) 23 Ch D 14 at 42.
[38] *Re Drogheda Steampacket Co.* [1903] 1 I.R. 512.
[39] *Rayfield v Hands* [1960] 1 Ch. 1.

share in any surplus where certain classes of shares are being repaid or redeemed and also in a winding-up.

10–20 A source of dispute has been what may be called the individualised substantive right, i.e. where a named shareholder is described in the company's own regulations as being entitled to something of value from it. For instance, that Ms X shall be the company's advertising manager at a certain remuneration, or shall be paid a special dividend each year in recognition of unique services to the company, or shall be entitled to buy a fixed proportion of the company's output at a favourable price. The conventional wisdom is that these rights will not be enforced against companies. Nevertheless, it has never been satisfactorily explained why this should be so. In some of the authorities relied on to support non-enforceability, the article relied on by its very terms did not purport to confer the right being claimed.[40] In others, such as in *Eley v Positive Government Security Life Assurance Co.*,[41] the plaintiff was not an original party to the statutory contract. One provision in the articles of a newly formed company was that he should be its solicitor for life. On a case stated by the arbitrator, the court held, for reasons that are far from clear, that he was not entitled to enforce that clause. Although he had not been a subscriber to the memorandum, he acquired shares in the company not long after it was incorporated. Whether this analysis would be applied to clauses designating a member to be a director of the company on certain terms is questionable, especially where he was appointed to the office and the company then seeks to contravene the articles.

10–21 The most recent exposition of the so-called outsider rights controversy is *Beattie v Beattie*,[42] where it was held that only those provisions in a company's regulations "as apply to the relationship of the members in their capacity as members" are rendered enforceable. One of the company's regulations provided that, whenever "any ... dispute shall arise between any members of the company, or between the company or any member or members", it shall be referred to arbitration. The plaintiff sought to bring a derivative suit (i.e. to sue on the company's behalf) against the company's chairman and managing director, who was also a shareholder, for breach of the fiduciary duty not to enrich himself unjustly at the company's expense. The central issue was whether that regulation amounted to a contract between the parties to submit their dispute to arbitration. Accepting the members'/outsiders' rights dichotomy, it was concluded that there was no binding agreement to arbitrate this dispute, because s.25 of the 1963 Act does not give contractual force to an article as between the company and its directors as such.

---

[40] e.g. *Pritchard's Case* (1873) 8 Ch. App. 956.

[41] (1876) 1 Ex. D. 88.

[42] [1938] 1 Ch. 708, considered in *Read v Astoria Garage (Streatham) Ltd* [1952] Ch. 637. See too, *Hickman v Kent or Romney Marsh Sheep Breeders Association* [1915] 1 Ch. 881.

FRAUD ON MINORITY

10–22 The concept "fraud on a minority" subsumes two completely distinct situations. One is where the majority shareholders directly discriminate against the minority in a wholly unacceptable matter; the other, defrauding the company, is considered separately below. As shareholders generally make their decisions by way of resolutions, almost all of the cases here concern challenges to special or to ordinary resolutions.

10–23 The common law tradition has been one that regards rights, especially property rights, in absolute terms. That is to say, if a person has a right to something, he may exercise that right regardless of whether he is being inspired by selfish, petty, spiteful or anti-social motives.[43] Because a share in a company is a property right, the view used to be that every shareholder could exercise his right to vote those shares for any reason whatsoever. But the common law does not adopt an unqualifiedly absolutist stance to legal rights[44] and equity is far from being absolutist. Some of the most important rights that shareholders possess arise from the memorandum and articles of association. But it is now accepted that rights arising out of contracts that form the basis of a continuing and active relationship are subject to a good faith qualification.[45] Put negatively, those rights must not be exercised in bad faith. Other shareholder rights are founded on statute, like the right by special resolution to alter the articles of association. However, discretions conferred by statute on subordinate representative bodies must not be exercised unreasonably or for an improper purpose.[46]

10–24 Differences, however, arise in formulating precisely the criteria against which shareholders' resolutions should be judged. Australian courts have made the analogy with the equitable doctrine of fraud on a power; that powers may not be used for purposes other than what they are designed to serve.[47] However, by what criteria is it to be determined whether any particular power has been used "fraudulently"?

Benefiting the Company as a Whole

10–25 In *Allen v Gold Reefs of West Africa*,[48] where the company's articles were amended to enable it to forfeit the plaintiff's shares for non-payment of calls, it was held that the right by special resolution to alter the memorandum or articles is subject to a criterion of good faith. Not alone must the requisite majority give its approval, but the alteration must be adopted "*bona fide* for the benefit of the company as a whole".[49] Accordingly, amendments to the memorandum or articles made simply to give the majority a significant advantage over the minority will be set aside. Precise criteria for ascertaining what is for

---

[43] *Bradford Corp. v Pickles* [1895] A.C. 589.
[44] *Quinn v Leatham* [1901] A.C. 495.
[45] *cf.* Goetz & Scott, "Principles of Relational Contracts" 67 *Virginia L. Rev.* 1089 (1981).
[46] *Listowel UDC v McDonagh* [1968] I.R. 312.
[47] *Mills v Mills* (1938) 60 C.L.R. 150.
[48] [1901] 1 Ch. 656.
[49] *ibid.* at 671.

the benefit of the company have not been articulated by the courts, other than that the company in this context "does not ... mean the company as a commercial entity, distinct from the corporators: it means the corporators as a general body. That is to say, the case may be taken of an individual hypothetical member and it may be asked whether what is proposed is, in the honest opinion of those who voted in its favour, for that person's benefit".[50]

10–25a Ordinarily, it is not for the court to decide whether, in its view, the alteration advantages the company; instead, it is to determine whether sufficient basis exists for a member reasonably concluding that it would be so advantageous. Except where what is involved is something in which the company as a corporate entity has no interest or in some expropriation cases, the role of the court is equivalent to that where the verdict of a jury is being challenged, i.e. the alteration must stand unless there was no reasonable basis for it or complete lack of *bona fides* has been established. It is not for the court to decide what benefits the company as a matter of business policy. That what was decided on benefits a particular shareholder or group of shareholders is no reason for the court overriding the decision, even where that member or group voted for the proposal. That ordinarily the court should not endeavour to be the arbiter of what is beneficial for the company was stressed by the Privy Council in *Citi Banking Corp NV v Pusser's Ltd*,[51] where a company's articles were amended to give one of its major shareholders substantially enhanced voting rights. He held 28 per cent of the issued shares and had advanced substantial sums to the company. He then arranged a private placing for a block of the company's shares and also a line of credit with a bank, which was made conditional on him taking control of the company and personally guaranteeing repayment of all advances to it. In consequence, in a proposed amendment to its articles, the company decided to create a new category of shares, each carrying 50 votes per share, and that his 200,000 single vote shares would be converted into those new shares. Objection was raised by another bank, that held 13 per cent of the company's shares, on the grounds that it was not in the company's interest to come under the sole control of a single member for his life, who could not be removed by other shareholders if they lost confidence in his management of the business. The proposal was carried by an overwhelming majority and would indeed have been carried even if he did not vote his own shares. Because there was no evidence to suggest dishonesty here and the proposal was not manifestly unreasonable, it was held that it should not be impeached. Lord Hoffman accepted that this non-interventionist stance would not be adopted in cases involving the distribution of dividends or of capital, or involving the power to dispose of shares, but declined to say whether "expropriation" cases would also be treated differently.

10–26 In instances such as these, a number of difficulties arise with this standard for judging the acceptability of special resolutions. Its application often depends on the individual judge's intuition: what the judge believes the

---

[50] *Greenhalgh v Arderne Cinema Ltd* [1951] 1 Ch. 286 at 291.
[51] [2007] Bus. L.R. 960.

hypothetical member would have voted for. If it were applied literally, this test would impose an unduly high standard on shareholders: that they must never canvass their own individual interests or, at least, an individual interest not shared by the other members. Furthermore, in companies that are comprised of rival shareholders or factions, ascertaining what in the hypothetical member's view would be in the company's interest is virtually an impossible task. While in companies with diverse groups of shareholders (such as pensioners, financial institutions, private speculators, professional managers, the firm's major suppliers or customers, perhaps competing enterprises), determining what is the company's own interests becomes almost as difficult as discovering the national interest. The entire question becomes even more confusing if majorities must take some account of employee interests and the interests of creditors. Additionally, even if some agreement can be reached on what in fact "benefit[s] the company as a whole", ascertaining what motivated a collective decision (be it legislation or a local government regulation, or a resolution passed by shareholders in general meeting) is no easy task. One approach to determining this question is the rule that the burden of proof is upon the person who challenges the validity of the amendment.[52] Another consideration is whether the shareholders who stood to benefit from the proposed change, as against the other shareholders, voted for the proposal and it was their votes which carried it.[53]

Non-Discrimination

10–27   An alternative criterion, therefore, has been suggested, that of non-discrimination.[54] It was held in *Greenhalgh v Arderne Cinemas Ltd,*[55] that a majority decision "would be liable to be impeached if the effect of it were to discriminate between the majority shareholders and the minority shareholders, so as to give the former an advantage of which the latter were deprived …"[56] In favour of this test, it is said, that it is "not necessary to require that persons … should, so to speak, dissociate themselves altogether from their own prospects and consider whether what is thought to be for the benefit of the company as a going concern".[57] Equality, or non-discrimination, is a fundamental principle of most modern systems of public law and, given the similarities between public law and this part of company law, non-discrimination has much to recommend it as the appropriate standard here. It is incorporated into the EC Second Directive, where it is stipulated that "[f]or the purposes of the implementation of this Directive, the laws of the Member States shall ensure equal treatment to all shareholders who are in the same position".[58] Perhaps the reason why non-discrimination did not take hold in English company law is that, until recently, English public law eschewed equality as a basic norm.[59]

---

[52] [2007] 2 Bus L.R. 960. See *Peters' American Delicacy Co Ltd v Heath* (1939) 61 C.L.R. 457.
[53] *Rights & Issues Investment Trust Ltd v Stylo Shoes Ltd* [1965] Ch. 250.
[54] See generally, B. Cheffins, *Company Law: Theory, Structuring and Operation* (Oxford: Clarendon Press, 1997), pp.472–495.
[55] [1951] 1 Ch. 286.
[56] *ibid.* at 291.
[57] *ibid.* at 291.
[58] Article 42.
[59] e.g. *Theodore v Duncan* [1919] A.C. 696 and *Short v Poole Corp.* [1926] Ch. 66.

Nevertheless, it has since been adopted as a central requirement under the Irish Stock Exchange's Listing Rules and in the Takeover Panel's rules.

10–28 This criterion does not require identical treatment for all shareholders of the same class in every conceivable circumstance; such a requirement would paralyse the flexibility needed in the governance of companies, just as much as it would frustrate sensible public administration. Where, however, a shareholders' resolution would adversely affect a minority to a significant extent, it should be evaluated carefully in order to see if indeed it is unfairly discriminatory. If the contested decision is aimed at a single member, then it is the equivalent of a Bill of Attainder and would be struck down unless there are overwhelming justifications for it. If the impugned decision does not simply degrade the economic value of a minority's shares but encroaches directly on some fundamental interest of the shareholder, such as to vote in general meeting or to veto vital decisions, or to designate certain persons as directors, it would require weighty justifications to be upheld. Where the decision does not directly take away or cut down a shareholder's right but only adversely affects it by impact, it is easier to justify than direct discrimination.

10–29 In *Greenhalgh*,[60] it was held that, in the circumstances, the plaintiff had not established discrimination. This case was part of a series of litigation between persons with interests in a private company the regulations of which restricted the transferability of its shares in one of the usual ways. No shares could be transferred to outsiders unless they were first offered to and refused by existing members, and the directors could decline to register any share transfer. Principally, to enable a controlling director to sell his shares to an outsider, the company resolved to alter these provisions by adding that, with the sanction of an ordinary resolution, any member could transfer his shares to any named outsider. This amendment was contested by a minority shareholder. The governing principle, said the Court of Appeal, is that a shareholder has no right to expect that a company's articles will remain unaltered, provided that any alteration is passed bona fide or does not unfairly discriminate. The court accepted that the amendment in question would work very much to the majority's advantage; if they found an outsider buyer they had it in their hands to ensure that their shares could be transferred. Whereas a minority holder would be faced with both losing in general meeting any proposal to transfer his stake and, additionally, having any purported transfer blocked by the board. Because, however, the alteration was merely a relaxation of the very stringent restrictions on transferring shares, and the directors in any event could always refuse to register his transfer, it was held that the plaintiff was not unlawfully discriminated against.[61]

---

[60] [1951] 1 Ch. 286.
[61] *cf. Lee & Co. (Dublin) Ltd v Egan (Wholesale) Ltd* [1979] I.E.H.C. 131, Kenny J., May 23, 1979.

10–30 Some commentators have criticised this conclusion, contending that it is difficult to conceive of a clearer case of discrimination. The late Professor Gower asked "if discrimination is the true test, why was [this] resolution upheld ...?"[62] The result of the resolution was that a majority would always be in a position to sell to an outsider whereas the minority would not. Is this not discrimination? But the test propounded was not the simple but impractical one of non-discrimination *per se*. Rather, it was "discrimination as falls within the scope of the principle as [was] stated", namely, that shareholders should not be treated differently in a way that "give[s] the [majority] an advantage of which the [minority] were deprived".[63] Could it be said that the advantage taken by the majority in *Greenhalgh* was acquired unfairly at the plaintiff's expense? Granted, the minority there lost a right to acquire shares in the company before they could be transferred to an outsider, but the resolution deprived every shareholder of that right. In the jargon of US company law, the impugned transaction did not cause the minority to be "frozen in" to the company; they were always frozen in until the directors consented to their disposing of their shares, and the proposed resolution did not alter that fact.

Ordinary Resolutions

10–31 Will ordinary resolutions passed in general meeting be set aside on similar grounds? Most commentators contend that they will not; that the majority rule principle applies without qualification to ordinary resolutions. The cases, however, suggest otherwise and support the proposition that, in exceptional circumstances, the court will intervene against ordinary resolutions that discriminate unfairly against the minority. As is explained below, because of the special character of closely held companies, or "quasi-partnerships" as they are often called, a court will much more readily block discriminatory action by majorities in such companies than it would in the case of companies with numerous members and the shares of which have a ready market.

10–32 The principle considered below, of "fraud on the company" (that serious breaches of directors' duties may not be ratified by those directors voting *qua* shareholders in general meeting), could be regarded as an illustration of an overriding standard of non-discrimination against minorities. An example is *Alexander v Automatic Telephone Co.*,[64] where minority shareholders sued the majority and the directors for having allotted shares to themselves, without any calls being made on them, while the plaintiffs had to pay up nearly two thirds of the nominal amounts of their own shares. In other words, the directors practically bootstrapped themselves into control of the company without paying. Even though it was stipulated in the company's articles that the directors

---

[62] *Principles of Modern Company Law*, 4th edn (London: Stevens, 1979), p.627.
[63] [1951] 1 Ch. at 292, 291; *cf.* analysis in *Redwood Master Fund Ltd v TD Bank Europe Ltd* [2006] 1 B.C.L.C. 149 at 172 *et seq.*
[64] [1900] 2 Ch. 56.

may differentiate between shareholders as regards the amounts and the times of calls,[65] it was held that the directors/shareholders had acted wrongfully here. Stress was placed on the fact that the company was newly formed and the defendants were all subscribers to its memorandum of association; that they had allotted to themselves about two thirds of the issued shares and, in not making calls on themselves, they paid nothing in respect of their own shares. Most significant of all, the minority had not been fully appraised of the fact that the defendants "had so managed matters as to place themselves in a better position as regards payment than the other shareholders ..."[66] The defendants, "threw upon other shareholders a burden which they did not share themselves", and the relevant article of association did not "justify them in making a difference in their own favour without disclosing the fact to the [others] and obtaining their consent ..."[67] In other words, the defendants acquired for themselves full control of a potentially profitable concern without paying hardly a penny for it. To compound this, they hid from the plaintiffs the fact that they had obtained their shares in that manner, while at the same time the plaintiffs' funds were being used to finance the entire undertaking. Furthermore, the defendants could have paid to themselves the bulk of the company's profits by way of dividends, thereby possibly financing the calls that ultimately would be made on them, because dividend rights, as a general rule, are based on the nominal value of the shares.[68]

Expropriation

10–33 Perhaps the most acute inter-shareholder controversy is an attempt by the majority to expropriate other members' shares; in other words, to expel individuals from the company. For instance, members may owe money to the company, and it may claim a lien on their shares and seek to forfeit them[69] rather than go through the more cumbersome processes for recovering the amount due. Or members may be acting so much against the company's interests that most other shareholders may desire to exclude them entirely from the company. An example might be a company that prospers on a reputation for being anti-alcohol or anti-tobacco, but one of its prominent shareholders becomes addicted to the bottle or the pipe and, if this became public knowledge, the business would be adversely affected. One case on this question involved the National Association for Mental Health, a non-profit company limited by guarantee and without a share capital, that sought to expel Scientologists from its ranks.[70] Or the company may be about to become far more profitable, perhaps on account of connections with other businesses owned by the majority, who may then want an even larger stake in the company.

---

[65] e.g. Table A, art.20.
[66] [1900] 2 Ch. 56 at 64.
[67] *ibid.* at 66.
[68] *Oakbank Oil Co. v Crum* (1882) 8 App. Cas. 65. Of course the articles of association may provide for paying dividends on the called up share capital only or otherwise, e.g. art.120 of Table A.
[69] Table A, art.35, e.g. *Hunter v Senate Support Services Ltd* [2005] 1 B.C.L.C. 175 at 223.
[70] *Gaiman v National Association for Mental Health* [1971] Ch. 317.

10–34   The commonest method of excluding unwanted members is by way of a resolution under an expulsion power contained in the articles of association; that result also may be achieved through more complex takeover and capital reorganisation techniques. The circumstances in which it is permissible to alter the articles of association to incorporate an expulsion or expropriation power in them was considered by the Australian High Court in *Gambotto v WCP Ltd.*[71] A company passed a special resolution to the amend its articles, to enable a shareholder holding 90 per cent or more of the issued shares to acquire compulsorily shares held by others for a stipulated price per share. The notice of meeting was accompanied by a valuation prepared by a firm of accountants and the price exceeded the net asset value of share as so valued. Two minority shareholders applied for a declaration that the amendment was invalid. The majority shareholders, who were related, held about 99.7 per cent of the issued capital. But they or companies associated with them could not have acquired the plaintiff shareholders' shares compulsorily under takeover "take out" powers (similar to s.204 of the 1963 Act). The plaintiffs conceded that the valuation was independent and fair. There would have been considerable tax advantages and administrative benefits for the company if it had become a wholly owned subsidiary of the majority shareholder's holding company. They did not vote on the resolution, which was passed on the votes of minority shareholders other than the plaintiffs.

10–35   As shares are a valuable property right and not merely a partially guaranteed stream of income, the court rejected the criterion of "*bona fide* for the benefit of the company as a whole". Such test may suffice for amendments that can be squared with the broad objectives of the company, but removing one or more of its members cannot ordinarily be part of those objects. Expropriation is only justified where "it is reasonably apprehended that the continued shareholding of the minority is detrimental to the company, its undertaking or the conduct of its affairs—resulting in detriment to the existing shareholders generally—and expropriation is a reasonable means of eliminating or mitigating that detriment".[72]

10–36   An example of where an expropriation power might be permissible is where the shareholder is competing with the company, especially where he may have access to information that facilitates his competition. In *Sidebottom v Kershaw, Leese & Co,*[73] a private company passed a special resolution introducing a new article, under which the directors were empowered to compel any member, who carried on a business that competed directly with the company to transfer his shares to another member for a fair price. It was said that the test of validity—whether the clause was adopted bona fide for the company's

---

[71]   (1994) 182 C.L.R. 432. See generally, Hannigan, "Altering the Articles to Allow for Compulsory Transfer – Dragging Minority Shareholders to a Reluctant Exit," [2007] *J. Bus. L.* 471.

[72]   *ibid.* at 445. However, note *obiter* comments of Privy Council about *Gambotto* in *Citco Banking Corp. Nv v Pusser's Ltd* [2007] Bus L.R. 960.

[73]   [1920] 1 Ch. 154.

benefit—ultimately comes down to a narrow question of fact. The court found that an objectively reasonable view might be taken that it could be very much in the interests of a company to expel members that compete with it. Emphasis was placed on the shareholder's position as an insider to obtain behind-the-scenes information about the company's activities; though one doubts whether minority shareholders could get their hands on vital information about the company's trading plans, especially in those pre-Fourth Directive days. An important aspect of the case was that it was admitted that what induced the company there to adopt the expulsion power was that one member, not the plaintiff, was known to the directors to be in a competing business. This, it was held, did not invalidate the resolution.

10–37   Another suggested example of a permissible expropriation power is where it is necessary to ensure that the company could continue to comply with a regulatory regime governing its principal business; for instance, if the company's business was licensed broadcasting and, under that regime, its shareholders had to have certain characteristics, which one or more of them did not possess. If nonetheless that minority refused to sell their shares, a resolution to allow for expropriation may be valid.

10–38   On the other hand, adopting an expropriation power in order to secure for the majority the benefit of a corporate structure that can derive some new commercial advantage is not permissible, even if the generality of the remaining members stand to substantially benefit thereby. An extreme example is *Brown v British Abrasive Wheel Co.*[74] where the 90 per cent majority failed to persuade the minority to sell out to them at par, so they amended the articles by introducing an expulsion power. The majority wished to put additional capital into the company but did not want to share with the minority the benefits that might flow from the company's finances improving. It was held that expelling shareholders in those circumstances could not be for the company's benefit; it was merely a device enabling a majority "on failing to purchase the shares of a minority by agreement, [to] take power to do so compulsorily".[75]

10–39   A less extreme example is *Gambotto*,[76] where the apparent objective of the contemplated expropriation was to secure substantial tax advantages for the company's business, when the ownership structure is altered following the expropriation. It was held that this was not a sufficient justification; that the expropriation "being fair will advance the interest of the company as a legal and commercial entity or those of the majority, albeit the great majority, of corporations". That those proposing the resolution there did not vote for it was not sufficient to save it from invalidity.

10–40   Nor may a wholly discretionary authority to expropriate, somewhat along the lines of that in Pt II of Table A restricting the transferability of

---

[74] [1919] 1 Ch. 290.
[75] *ibid.* at 295–296.
[76] (1994) 182 C.L.R. 432.

shares at the directors' absolute discretion, be introduced into the articles. In *Dafen Tinplate Co. v Llanelly Steel Co.*,[77] a company was formed by a number of manufacturers to supply them with steel bars. An understanding existed, though without legal obligation, that each member would take its supplies of steel from the company. Having done that for a number of years, the plaintiff transferred its custom to a subsidiary it set up. This caused the others to amend the company's articles by including a power enabling a majority of shareholders to resolve that any member's shares be transferred to another at a fair price. It was held that the virtually unbounded discretion this power purported to give was fatal to its validity; by its terms, it went further than striking at members who reneged on the original and perhaps vital understanding, and purported to authorise expulsion of any shareholder at the majority's will and pleasure.

10–41 Even where the purpose of the proposed amendment comes within the narrowly permissible grounds, it was stated in *Gambotto* that certain procedural safeguards are required. All relevant information leading to the proposed expulsion power must be disclosed by the majority shareholders. Ordinarily the shares must be independently valued. Where the envisaged expropriation price is less than market value, the resolution is very likely to be held unfair. The court declined to rule on whether the majority may vote on a proposed resolution of this nature.

10–42 Another category of case here is where the amendment would enable some valuable rights of shareholders to be taken away without them being fully compensated; for example, diminishing rights to dividends and/or return of capital, disenfranchisement or qualification of a right to vote. Such reported cases as address this question relate to "class rights variations" in the context of capital reorganisations, where court approval usually is required. Outside of that context, it would seem that the *Gambotto* approach would be followed.[78]

Diluting Shareholdings

10–43 Instead of seeking to entirely or partly expropriate shareholders, the majority may seek to significantly dilute one or more member's shareholding in the company by issuing additional shares to the majority or their supporters. It is a breach of fiduciary duty for directors to issue shares in the company for an improper purpose, in particular where the object is to convert an existing majority stake in the company into a minority holding or to thwart the present majority from accepting a takeover bid about to be made for the company.[79] Exercises of the power to issue new shares is now considerably curtailed by a prior authority requirement and a pre-emption regime.[80] Where the share issue

---

[77] [1920] 2 Ch. 124.

[78] e.g. *Peters' American Delicacy Co. Ltd v Heath*, 61 C.L.R. 457 (1939), involving a radical diminution of dividend rights.

[79] See para.7–110 *et seq.*

[80] See paras.8–45 and 9–44 *et seq.*

is approved by a majority of the members, circumstances can arise where it would be declared invalid on the grounds that it unfairly discriminated against a shareholder.

10–44   *Clemens v Clemens Brothers Ltd*[81] concerned a small family company, with only two shareholders: the plaintiff, who held 45 per cent of the voting shares, and her aunt who held the remaining 55 per cent. Resolutions were passed in general meeting to issue additional shares to the aunt and her associates. The effect of implementing these would have been to dilute the plaintiff's stake to just less than 25 per cent of the voting shares, and thereby deprive her of the power to block alterations to the company's regulations. The plaintiff was not a director whereas the aunt and her associates were on the board for some years; no dividends were paid; directors' generous emoluments exceeded the substantial profits the company made; the company did not obviously need further capital; and the aunt declined to give any evidence. Emphasising the difficulty of formulating hard-and-fast rules for such cases, Foster J. concluded by saying that "it would be unwise to try to produce a principle, since the circumstances of each case are infinitely varied", other than that majority shareholders' rights are "subject to equitable considerations which may make it unjust ... to exercise [them] in a particular way".[82] The outcome can be explained under the non-discrimination principle in that the impugned resolutions did not merely degrade the value of the plaintiff's holding but directly deprived her of a fundamental interest, namely, her power to veto any proposed alterations to the company's regulations. This right is so fundamental that its violation by the directors cannot ordinarily be rectified by a majority of the shareholders approving what was done.

FRAUD ON COMPANY

10–45   The true exception to what was decided in *Foss v Harbottle*[83] is that part of the "fraud on a minority" rubric which involves the majority shareholders directly damaging the company itself and thereby indirectly prejudicing the minority; as contrasted with directly disadvantaging the minority shareholders. Several of the circumstances where fraud could easily arise are now the subject of specific legal measures and also the Listing Rules on transactions with related parties. In *Foss*, the complaint was that the directors and promoters practically "looted" the company by causing it to buy property from them at extravagant prices. As that loss fell directly on the company and only indirectly on the plaintiff shareholder, it was held that the company was the proper plaintiff.

10–46   In *O'Neill v Ryan*,[84] where several of the defendants had proceedings being brought against them struck out, the plaintiff claimed that they had

---

[81]   [1976] 2 All E.R. 268.
[82]   *ibid.* at 282.
[83]   (1843) 2 Hare 490.
[84]   [1990] 2 I.R. 200.

unlawfully conspired to damage Ryanair, a company of which he had been managing director and a shareholder. As any direct damage would have been done by them to the company and not to him, and such loss as he would have suffered would have been entirely "reflective" of that caused to the company, he was not allowed to continue the action. The company itself was free to sue those defendants, and what it would recover would be reflected in the increased value of his shares. Similarly, in *Gardner v Parker*,[85] where the claimant owned 15 per cent of the shares in company B and the defendant, who managed it, owned the other 85 per cent. The defendant also managed and owned 91 per cent of the shares in company S. B's principal assets were the remaining 9 per cent of the shares in S and a debt due from S of £799,000. S's principal asset were shares in a third company, which were valued in S's accounts at approximately 5m. The defendant caused S to sell those shares for £400,000, payment to be deferred. Shortly afterwards, S became insolvent and receivers were appointed over its assets. In consequence, B was not able to recover the £799,000 owed to it and, assuming that the shares were sold by S at a significant undervalue, B also lost a valuable investment through its 9 per cent of S. It was not disputed that, in permitting S to sell its shares for so low a price, the defendant not alone breached his fiduciary duty to S but also to B. It was held that the plaintiff's claim could not be prosecuted, because S's receivers had already sued that defendant for the very same alleged wrongdoing, which eventually was settled for £350,000. If the plaintiff's action were to succeed, it was held that there would be "double recovery", which should not be allowed.[86]

Derivative Claim

10–47 Where, however, those who control the company inflict losses on it but, because of their control, the company will not or cannot act against them, then the courts may permit an individual shareholder to bring proceedings on behalf of himself and of the company.[87] If that were not allowed, there would be no effective mechanism for protecting the company from the depredations of its controllers. Thus the term "fraud on a minority"; in this context it forms the basis for giving *locus standi* to aggrieved minority shareholders. Proceedings under this heading are often described as "derivative" claims; the plaintiff derives his entitlement to sue from the virtual helplessness of the company to protect itself against its controllers. If the claim succeeds, judgment will be given in favour of the company. For this reason, before the action is heard, the court may direct that, in the event of the plaintiff losing, the company should pay the costs of the proceedings.[88] Many of the major minority shareholder disputes in the US take the derivative form and there are special procedures there and also in Canada for how such actions should proceed. In 1999, rules

---

[85] [2004] 2 B.C.L.C. 554.

[86] See para.22–50 *et seq.*

[87] See generally, Wedderburn, "Shareholders" Rights and the Rule in *Foss v Harbottle* II" 18 *Cam. L.J.* 93 (1958); and Sullivan, "Restating the Scope of the Derivative Suit" 44 *Cam. L.J.* 236 (1985).

[88] *Wallersteiner v Moir (No. 2)* [1975] Q.B. 373.

of court were adopted in Britain[89] for such actions, and in 2006 they were placed on a statutory footing.[90] There are no special rules of any kind in Ireland applicable to them.

10–48 In a derivative claim, the plaintiff must establish that the company has been defrauded and that those who control it unjustifiably failed to take appropriate action against the wrongdoers—frequently those controllers and/or their associates. Whether such a claim would succeed outside these broad parameters, simply on the basis of some underlying injustice, remains to be determined. In *Crindle Investments v Wymes*,[91] Keane J. referred to the "less solidly based fifth exception [to the 'rule' in *Foss*] which suggests that the rule may be relaxed where the interests of justice so require."[92] An "exception" along these lines has been rejected in England but has obtained some acceptance in Australia.[93] Before a full trial is allowed to proceed, the court may require the plaintiff to make out a *prima facie* case that the defendants controlled the company and defrauded it or, if there is a fifth exception, that justice warrants him going ahead. If allowing the action to proceed would be damaging to the company, which would be far better off if the action were stopped, the court may not permit it to proceed.

Locus Standi

10–49 Company creditors, employees, suppliers or customers may not pursue a derivative claim. Once a company goes into liquidation, a claim of this nature can no longer lie. But such a claim can be brought by a shareholder in respect of wrongs done before he became a member.[94] If after commencing a claim he ceases to be a member, it would seem that he can still maintain his claim, although it is hard to see what his incentive would be. One possibility could be where a purchaser of his shares would be statute-barred if he commenced a fresh action. In *O'Neill v Ryan*,[95] some emphasis was put on the plaintiff there having agreed to sell his shares but the law report does not indicate if that happened before he commenced those proceedings. In any event, those were not in the derivative form. It would seem that an equitable interest in shares does not confer *locus standi*.

10–50 The court will not entertain a claim of this nature where it is being prosecuted for some ulterior motive, especially where there is an alternative remedy.[96]

---

[89] R.S.C., Ord.15 r.12A.
[90] Companies Act 2006, Pt 11, Ch.1.
[91] [1998] 4 I.R. 567.
[92] *ibid.* at 592.
[93] *Biala Pty Ltd v Mallina Holdings (No. 2)* 11 A.C.L.C. 1082 (1993).
[94] *cf. Lloyd v Casey* [2002] 1 B.C.L.C. 454, a section 205 case.
[95] [1990] 2 I.R. 200.
[96] See generally, Payne, "'Clean Hands in Derivative Actions" 61 *Cam. L.J.* 76 (2002).

Fraud

10–51 What amounts to "fraud" for these purposes has never received a comprehensive judicial definition. With the trend towards higher standards of conduct in companies' affairs, the ambit of fraud here continues to expand. Megarry J. observed that "[I]t does not seem to have yet become very clear exactly what the word 'fraud' means in this context; but I think it is plainly wider than fraud at common law in the sense of *Derry v Peek* ... [It] seems to be being used as comprising... fraud in the wider equitable sense of that term, as in the equitable concept of fraud on a power".[97] A blatant example of fraud is the first reported derivative action, *Atwool v Merryweather*,[98] which concerned a sale by the defendants, promoters and directors, of overvalued property to their company.[99] When other shareholders discovered what had occurred they sought to sue, but their action was adjourned pending consideration of the matter in general meeting. At that meeting a motion to discontinue their action and instead to refer it to arbitration was carried by a narrow majority, the defendants voting for discontinuance with their own shares together with proxies that they controlled. On account of the nature of the impugned dealings and the way partial shareholder approval had been obtained, the court allowed the action to proceed.[100]

10–52 At the other end of the spectrum are instances such as "where the majority think that one of themselves is the best person to be managing director and proceed to appoint that person managing director at a remuneration [that is not] excessive or grossly unfair"; this is not "appropriat[ing] to themselves the assets of the company"[101] and cannot give rise to an action by a minority shareholder. In *Palvides v Jensen*,[102] where it was alleged that the board agreed to the sale of one of the company's properties for significantly less than its market value, it was held that an individual shareholder could not institute proceedings against the directors for being negligent.

10–53 As with the non-discrimination principle, the difficulty is drawing the boundary between what constitutes mere breach of directors' duties on the one hand and, on the other, improper conduct that entitles any individual shareholder to initiate derivative proceedings against the wrongdoers. In the past and perhaps even today the line was defined by reference to certain kinds of wrongs which are inherently ratifiable by a majority of the members, including the alleged wrongdoers. They could ratify directors' negligence and the making of "incidental" secret profits from their position, provided they acted bona fide. But misappropriation of the company's property and also mala

---

[97] *Eastmanco (Kilner House) Ltd v Greater London Council* [1982] 1 W.L.R. 2 at 12.
[98] (1868) L.R. 5 Eq. 464n.
[99] This state of affairs is now regulated by the 1983 Act, ss.30 and 32, and by the 1990 Act, s.29.
[100] See also, *Menier v Hooper's Telegraph Works* (1874) L.R. 9 Ch. App. 350.
[101] *Foster v Foster* [1916] 1 Ch. 532 at 549. See also, *Normandy v Ind. Coope & Co.* [1908] 1 Ch. 84.
[102] [1956] Ch. 565.

fides exercises of directors' powers could only be sanctioned by the votes of shareholders who were entirely independent of the wrongdoers.

10–54 *Corporate Opportunity*: Directors must not divert to their own ends business opportunities that could benefit their company. Depending on the circumstances, moreover, a company in general meeting cannot exonerate directors from this obligation. The classic instance is *Cook v Deeks*,[103] which concerned lucrative construction contracts that the defendant directors diverted to their own benefit. One of their defences was that the company in general meeting had passed resolutions renouncing any legal claims it might have had against them with regard to those contracts. But those were passed with the votes of the defendants *qua* shareholders. It was held that to allow them to retain the profits they had made in the circumstances "would be to allow a majority to oppress the minority". *North-West Transportation Co.*[104] was distinguished on the grounds that it concerned a sale of directors' (and majority shareholders') own property to the company and not, as in the instant case, taking property which "belonged in equity to the company".

10–55 Contrast with *Cook* the other leading case on this subject, *Regal (Hastings) Ltd v Gulliver*,[105] which concerned directors who put their own funds into their company's subsidiary, to enable it to acquire some cinemas. They made a sizeable profit on this investment when the entire group companies were taken over shortly afterwards. Even though they acted in good faith, they had broken their fiduciary duty to the company and, therefore, had to account for the profits they made. Unlike in *Cook*, the plaintiff was the company (under new control). But Lord Russell observed that the defendants there "could, had they wished, have protected themselves [from liability] by a resolution (either antecedent or subsequent) of the Regal shareholders in general meeting" ratifying the entire transaction.[106]

10–56 There are three grounds on which the outcome in *Cook* and this suggestion in *Regal* have been distinguished, *viz.* control, property and motive. Although it would appear that the defendant directors in *Regal* were also its controlling shareholders, Lord Russell may have been speaking as if they were not the controllers, or as if their action would most likely have obtained the support of the independent shareholders at the time the transaction was decided upon. Assuming that the defendants in *Regal* had control, it has been said that the construction contracts in *Cook* were company property whereas the investment opportunity in *Regal* was not its property. Thirdly, in *Cook* there was bad faith, which did not exist in *Regal*. The problem with the "property" explanation is that it can be used in virtually every case to rationalise why a party wins in one instance and loses in another: he wins because in that instance his property was being interfered with. The difficulty with motive is

---

[103] [1916] 1 A.C. 554.
[104] (1887) 12 App. Cas. 589.
[105] [1967] A.C. 134.
[106] *ibid.* at 150.

that often it is not easy to show that a group of persons, such as shareholders when voting, reached a decision for mala fide reasons.

10–57 *Interest in Contract*: *North-West Transportation Co. v Beatty*[107] is often cited in support of the proposition that, where a company enters into a contract in which a director has a financial interest, then provided the director complies with the letter of the articles of association and the Companies Acts, he may vote his shares on the proposed resolution to ratify the contract even where he is the majority shareholder. It nevertheless is significant that the Privy Council examined the details and circumstances of the contract there, and concluded that its terms were not unduly unfair on the company.[108] Additionally, the issue before the meeting there was whether to adopt the contract – not whether to bring proceedings against the controller to recover an excessive profit he made from it. It therefore would appear that where directors/controllers deal with their companies and thereby make an excessive profit for themselves, but the minority interests object and demand that the transaction be rescinded or the gain be repaid to the company, those directors may not vote *qua* shareholders, to block proposals made in general meeting that the company should sue them.

10–58 A more recent instance is *Daniels v Daniels*,[109] which was a strike out application. Minority shareholders sued a director and controlling shareholder who had bought property from the company for significantly less than its current value. Their statement of claim accused him of gross negligence and not fraud. The contention that, since fraud was not pleaded, there could be no cause of action was rejected on the grounds that:

> "if minority shareholders can sue if there is fraud, [there is] no reason why they cannot sue where the action of the majority and the directors, though without fraud, confers some benefit on those directors and majority shareholders themselves. It would seem to me quite monstrous, particularly as fraud is so hard to plead and difficult to prove, if the confines of the exception to *Foss v Harbottle* were drawn so narrowly that directors would make a profit out of their negligence".[110]

The full implications of this decision remain to be seen. At one extreme it could signify that a case should not be prevented from going to trial simply because it does not allege fraud or does not fall within one of the other established exceptions to *Foss v Harbottle*. At the other, it may mark a stage in the evolution of a rule that shareholders have a right of action in respect of all forms of self-dealing negligence on the part of the directors and majority shareholders, i.e. business judgments that nevertheless leave the majority financially better off to a significant extent. In *Crindle Investments v Wymes*, Keane J. remarked that it was "unnecessary to say whether [*Daniels*] states the law too widely." [111]

---

[107] (1887) 12 App. Cas. 589.
[108] See also *Burland v Earle* [1902] A.C. 83.
[109] [1978] Ch. 406.
[110] *ibid.* at 414.
[111] [1998] 4 I.R. 567 at 593.

10–59   *Crindle* is a variant of the interest-in-contract paradigm. It concerned endeavours to settle legal proceedings that companies had brought but which could not be consummated because the companies' controllers, also parties to those actions in their separate personal capacities, were not willing to settle their own claims. The background is complex, involving two earlier sets of proceedings. The first were actions brought by the Bula companies and also by Bula's majority shareholders and directors in their personal capacities, against, *inter alia*, a rival company, Tara, and banks which had appointed receivers over the companies' assets (the "actions"). The second were for statutory "oppression" brought by the minority shareholders in those companies against those majority shareholders ("the petition"). The defendants in the actions had made several offers to settle, which were rejected by the companies and by the personal plaintiffs. That caused the minority shareholders to petition for oppression, where it was held that the companies rejecting several of those settlement offers was oppression. In consequence, it was ordered that the minority shareholders should have control of further settlement negotiations with the companies, that they could settle those claims on broadly similar terms to what already had been offered, but any lesser offer could not be accepted unless it was agreed to by all the companies' members or else was approved by the court. An order sought in the petition, but refused, required, *inter alia,* the majority shareholders in their personal capacities to accept a settlement offer that had been made to them, if it remained available. Thereafter there was an impasse, because Tara and the banks would not settle with the companies unless the majority's personal claims against them also were settled.

10–60   With no immediate prospect of these claims being settled, the minority shareholders sued the majority, contending that they were acting unlawfully in not settling their personal claims, thereby preventing the companies from concluding settlement. The contention that the defendants owed the plaintiffs a fiduciary duty or a duty of care was rejected; to succeed, the plaintiffs would have to meet the requirements for bringing a derivative claim. It was held by the Supreme Court that they could not succeed because what in substance they sought was an order equivalent to what had been refused in the petition, i.e. compelling the defendants to settle. The cause of the plaintiff's grievance was the defendants failing to act reasonably in dealing with proposals to settle their personal claims. But that was remedied, so far as the law permitted, in the oppression petition. By holding out for better personal terms, the defendants were not acting negligently as directors, let alone fraudulently in a broad sense. According to Keane J.:

> "The plaintiffs cannot point to any conduct on the part of the[se] defendants which is causing, or will continue to cause unless restrained, damage to the company except their actions as controlling majority shareholders in failing to act reasonably in dealing with possible settlement proposals. They have, however, already been granted relief in respect of that conduct in the petition.
>
> Should there be no reasonable offer forthcoming and approval by the court, the maintenance by the defendants of their personal claims will not

constitute any form of wrongdoing *quoad* the company or any one else. If there were such an offer forthcoming and the defendants maintained their personal claims, no benefits would flow to the individual defendants – an essential constituent of the exceptions to the rule – since they would only derive such a benefit in the event of a victory in the Tara and bank proceedings or a compromise of both. In either event, far from any damage being caused to the company, benefits would accrue to it as a result of the persistence of the[se] defendants in maintaining their claims and declining to co-operate in any offers of settlement, however ill-judged that course of conduct might now appear to be. Thus even on the widest construction of the exceptions to the rule in *Foss v Harbottle* ... the maintenance of the personal claims does not come within them."[112]

10–61 **Act, Motive or Circumstance?**: The question has been posed whether the answer lies, not in classifying into fixed legal categories the kinds of wrongs majorities may and may not cure by ratification, but more in considering the circumstances in which and methods by which directors/controllers prevent their company from taking action against themselves in respect of their alleged wrongs. In determining whether to allow a derivative claim to succeed, it was remarked that "[t]he dividing line between what a majority can condone or ratify and what cannot be so condoned or ratified is a difficult one to draw and the many cases are not entirely easy to reconcile."[113] The traditional view has been that, although there is some uncertainty about precisely what amounts to defrauding the company, nevertheless the "fraud lies rather in the nature of the transaction than in the motives of the majority".[114] But this analysis is not universally accepted and was rejected by Vinelott J. in *Prudential Insurance Co. v Newman Industries Ltd (No.2)*.[115] The proper approach to such matters, he asserted, is that "fraud lies in [the majority's] use of their voting powers, not in the character of the act or transaction giving rise to the cause of action. [The question is not what is the] category of acts or transactions which are incapable of being authorised or ratified by the majority in general meeting".[116] In his view, the fraud exception to *Foss v Harbottle* applies even "where there is [no] conscious and deliberate wrongdoing on the part of the directors who are alleged to be liable to the company for breach of their fiduciary duty or improper retention or appropriation of property or advantages belonging to the company, [such as where] it is alleged that the directors though" acting in the belief that they are doing nothing wrong "are guilty of a breach of duty to the company (including their duty to exercise proper care) and as a result of that breach obtain some benefit".[117] The Court of Appeal declined to comment on this analysis other than to express dissatisfaction with a broad and "[im]practical"

---

[112] [1998] 4 I.R. 567 at 594.

[113] *Airey v Cordell* [2007] Bus. L.R. 391 at 403.

[114] Wedderburn, "Shareholders" Rights and the Rule in *Foss v Harbottle* II" 18 *Cam. L.J.* 93 (1958) at 96.

[115] [1981] 1 Ch. 257.

[116] *ibid.* at 307.

[117] *ibid.* at 312.

test, of "whenever the justice of the case so requires",[118] to determine when shareholders can bring suit.

10–62　According to Vinelott J., virtually every breach by controllers/directors of their fiduciary duties, other than ones from which they obtain no significant financial advantage at the company's expense, can be the subject of a derivative claim, unless it is shown that the independent shareholders, being properly informed, voted or would vote to ratify the breach of duty. This analysis has been criticised as conflicting with the understanding that a share is the property of its holder and can be voted as he wishes in general meeting.[119] But if a share is that kind of property, how is it that a special resolution will be struck down if it is shown that it was not passed for the benefit of the company as a whole? The principal criticism of this approach is its impracticability— that it would introduce" great confusion … into the affairs of joint stock companies …".[120] Against the objection, it is unjust if controllers/directors, acting in breach of their fiduciary duties, are allowed to make large profits for themselves and at their company's expense. This is especially so in companies whose shares cannot be transferred without the directors' consent (i.e. most private companies) or whose shares do not have a ready market, in that the minority do not even have the option of cutting their losses by selling off their somewhat devalued investment.

Court Authorisation

10–63　Even where the requisite elements of control and fraud exist, a derivative claim may be blocked if a sufficient number of entirely independent members of the company do not want the action to proceed or the court otherwise concludes that a reasonable board would be against it proceeding. In *Smith v Croft (No. 2)*[121] the plaintiffs, who held approximately 14.5 per cent of the company's capital, alleged fraud on the company on several grounds. The defendants, who held 62.5 per cent of the shares, were the executive director, chairman and non-executive director, and companies associated with them. A substantial shareholder, not directly involved in the dispute, was a trust, and the company chairman was the trust's nominee on the board. The allegations were that the executive directors were paid excessive remuneration, that they dishonestly caused the company to make substantial payments to other companies which they controlled, that they caused it to make payments of what were really gifts to themselves and that they used the company's money to enable another company to buy shares in it. However, the trust, which held 20 per cent of the shares, and a handful of other shareholders were opposed to pursuing the claim in the courts. The preliminary question of whether the action should be allowed to go ahead was argued for fifteen days before Knox J., who ordered that it should be struck out.

---

[118] [1982] 1 Ch. 204 at 221.
[119] Wedderburn, "Notes of Cases: Derivative Actions and *Foss v Harbottle*" (1981) 44
• 　*Mod. L. Rev.* 202 at 211.
[120] *North West Transportation Co.* (1877) 12 App. Cas. 589 at 600.
[121] [1988] 1 Ch. 114.

10–64   The net issue was had the plaintiffs "establish[ed] a *prima facie* case (i) that the company is entitled to the relief claimed and (ii) that the action falls within the proper boundaries of the exceptions to the rule in *Foss v Harbottle*".[122] It was found that a *prima facie* case had been made out only in respect of one head of the claim, namely, financing the purchase of the company's shares. While the various other payments that were challenged may have been an abuse of the directors' powers, they could not be regarded as *ultra vires* the company in the sense of beyond its corporate capacity. With regard to the claim of unlawfully financing the purchase of the company's own shares, which by definition is *ultra vires*,[123] it was held that the fact that the majority has caused the company to so act to its detriment does not invariably entitle any minority shareholder to bring proceedings to recover what the company may have lost. As was emphasised by the Court of Appeal in the *Newman Industries Ltd (No.2)* case,[124] the right to recover loss caused to the company is the company's right of action and not a right personal to any of its shareholders. But the "derivative" procedural device to assist the company does not entitle a shareholder to sue in all conceivable circumstances. If there is some persuasive reason why the company should not bring the claim, then the shareholder will not be permitted to sue on the company's behalf. One such reason is where a majority of the independent shareholders are opposed to the proceedings on the grounds that, in the end, a trial of the action may cause the company far more damage than good. This principle, it was held, applies as much to actions to recover loss resulting from *ultra vires* acts as it applies to other forms of "fraud" on the company.

10–65   In *Airey v Cordell*,[125] where the case law was reviewed in detail, it was held that the action should not be allowed to proceed where the court concluded that no reasonable board of directors would in all the circumstances pursue it. There were no independent shareholders whose views could be considered; there was just the minority shareholder and the alleged fraudsters. It involved alleged taking a corporate opportunity but, if the action had been allowed to proceed and was successful, it appeared unlikely that the opportunity could be exploited by the company due to difficulties in raising finance. The judge suggested a mechanism that, if acceptable to the parties, would preserve that opportunity's viability and adjourned the matter so that his proposal could be fully considered. If the issue in dispute is capable of resolution by some alternative means, the court is disinclined to sanction a derivative claim.

Personal Claims

10–66   Personal claims in the present context concern where those who control a company have damaged it but, in doing so, have also contravened a duty owed directly to a minority shareholder. For instance, the controller has

---

[122] Citing *Newman Industries Ltd* [1982] Ch. 204 at 221.
[123] *Re M.J. Cummins Ltd* [1939] I.R. 60.
[124] [1982] 1 Ch. 204.
[125] [2007] Bus. L.R. 391 at 403. See too *Konamanei v Rolls Royce Industrial Power (India) Ltd* [2002] 1 W.L.R. 1269 at 1277 *et seq.*

contravened a statutory requirement or something in the articles of association, or in a shareholders' agreement, or it is one of those exceptional circumstances where the controller owed a direct duty of care or fiduciary duty to a shareholder. *Crindle Investments* began as a claim of this nature and it was only after judgment had been given against the plaintiffs in the High Court that the Bula companies were added as defendants, causing Keane J. to describe the claim as "in substance, although not in form, what has been described as a 'derivative suit' ...".[126] But in the circumstances there, it was held that the defendants, majority shareholders in and directors of the companies, did not owe the minority plaintiffs any independent duty. It is not entirely clear whether in *O'Neill v Ryan*[127] the plaintiff's case was that Ryanair's competitors (who succeeded in having his claims against them struck out) did anything that was directly unlawful against him.

10–67 Notwithstanding that a minority shareholder plaintiff may have a good independent cause of action against a company's controllers, his personal claim against them will often founder on the "reflective loss" principle, as occurred for example in *Gardner v Parker*.[128] What in substance was alleged there was that the company's controller "looted" another company that he also controlled, which in consequence prevented the plaintiff's (15 per cent shareholding in) company from being repaid a substantial debt and deprived it of a valuable investment. In such circumstances, generally the company's potential claim against the wrongdoer "trumps" the shareholder's personal claim, on the grounds that if both claims were allowed to proceed, there would be "double recovery". To date, there does not appear to be any reported decision of the Irish courts addressing this general question in the present context, i.e. a minority suing a majority shareholder for unlawfully damaging the company in a manner that breaches a duty owed independently to that minority holder. In *Gardner*, the principle involved was described by the Court of Appeal as "a difficult and developing topic".

10–68 This principle has been held to be subject to at least one exception, *viz.* where the actions of the controllers disabled the company from suing them. In *Giles v Rhind*,[129] in breach of a shareholders' agreement, the company's controller diverted virtually all of its business to a new company that he set up. The company thereupon sued him for appropriating its business and opportunities. But he succeeded in blocking that action by obtaining an order for security for costs. Because he had thereby prevented the company from obtaining any redress against him, it was held that the plaintiff could prosecute his personal claim against him. It would seem that the reflective loss principle also does not apply where the company does not have a good cause of action against its controller, even though the minority shareholder's loss is entirely indirect, through the company. If it had been held in *Crindle Investments* that

---

[126] [1998] 4 I.R. 567 at 594.
[127] [1990] 2 I.R. 200.
[128] [2004] 2 B.C.L.C. 554.
[129] [2003] 1 B.C.L.C. 1.

the defendants there had been in breach of duties that they owed the plaintiffs directly, the question of double recovery would strictly not have arisen because the only reliefs being sought were injunctions.

Overlap With Oppression

10–69   There would seem to be no good reason in principle why a derivative claim and a petition for statutory oppression cannot be consolidated or tried at the same time, provided the parties and underlying issues are the same. Such a course was adopted in *Clark v Cutland*,[130] to recover substantial unauthorised contributions made, for the benefit of a 50 per cent shareholder and director, to his pension fund. As the scope of the statutory remedy is so ample, the question arises of the practical utility of even resorting to the derivative procedure at all. As *Bhullar v Bhullar*[131] demonstrates, what is remediable in such claims can also be remedied in the statutory mode; it concerned a director and 50 per cent shareholder who intercepted a corporate opportunity. It was held there that where oppression proceedings were a proxy for a derivative claim, the petitioner could obtain costs that would be awarded in such a claim.

10–70   In *O'Neill v Ryan*,[132] the plaintiff had previously brought oppression proceedings, which he settled, and only then commenced his derivative claim against *inter alia* entirely different defendants. In *Crindle Investments v Wymes*,[133] the plaintiffs had been partly successful in earlier oppression proceedings against the defendants and, at the time the case was before the Supreme Court, those plaintiffs had re-entered their s.205 petition and had also brought a fresh petition.

OPPRESSION AND DISREGARD OF INTERESTS

10–71   When the Companies Act, 1948, was being drawn up in Britain, it was felt that the law as it stood at the time did not afford minority shareholders adequate protection against abuse of power by majorities. The various grounds considered above (i.e. breach of contract, fraud and bad faith) were regarded as insufficiently demanding and, it should be remembered, the *Greenhalgh*[134] anti-discrimination principle had not yet been articulated by the courts. One remedy against certain abuses did exist, namely, having the company wound up on "just and equitable grounds".[135] However, few aggrieved shareholders would want to see their entire enterprise being brought to an end and sold off, and the courts were reluctant to invoke that drastic power against tyrannical majorities. This led to the enactment of a novel provision empowering the court, in instances where it found that a minority was "oppressed", to order that appropriate remedial measures be

---

[130] [2003] 2 B.C.L.C. 241.
[131] [2004] 1 W.L.R. 783.
[132] [1990] 2 I.R. 200.
[133] [1998] 4 I.R. 567.
[134] *Greenhalgh v Arderne Cinema Ltd* [1951] 1 Ch. 286.
[135] See para.10–109 *et seq.*

taken.[136] It is no exaggeration to say that this provision was revolutionary; it sat alongside the existing statutory and common law rules regarding inter-shareholder relations a new form of statutory equity jurisdiction based on the somewhat vague concept of oppressive conduct.[137] A close analogy is the Unfair Dismissals Act 1977, which complements much of traditional employment law with an overriding standard of "fairness in the circumstances." Perhaps because it could range so widely and in a sense wreak havoc on the established company law, the British courts used to interpret it in a very restrictive fashion.[138] Criticism of the excessive caution with which it was being applied there eventually led to its being replaced.[139]

10–72   Section 205 of the 1963 Act, which is very similar, authorises the court to intervene against the oppression of shareholders that:

> "[a]ny member of a company who complains that the affairs of the company are being conducted or that the powers of the directors of the company are being exercised in a manner oppressive to him or any of the members (including himself), or in disregard of his or their interests as members, may apply to the court for an order under this section".

Where the court is "of the opinion" that oppression as thus defined has taken place, it is empowered to make orders of various kinds. A shareholder may also apply to have the company wound up compulsorily because oppression, as so defined, has taken place.[140]

10–73   Although the overwhelming majority of oppression cases involve private companies, this remedy is applicable to quoted companies too.[141] However, because shareholders in such companies have a ready exit option, the onus of proving legitimate expectation over and above the company's own regulations would be greater.

10–74   Minority shareholder complaints tend more and more to be brought under s.205, its attractions being that the criteria to be applied are very broad, provision is made for hearing all or part of the proceedings *in camera* and the court has an extensive choice over which remedy should be granted. On the

---

[136] Companies Act 1948, s.210.

[137] The history is summarised in *Re BSB Holdings Ltd (No. 2)* [1996] 1 B.C.L.C. 155 at 234–250.

[138] See Rajak, "The Oppression of Minority Shareholders" 35 *Mod. L. Rev.* 156 (1972).

[139] See generally, V. Joffe, *Minority Shareholders: Law, Practice and Procedure*, 2nd edn (London: LexisNexis, 2004), Chs 5 and 6; R. Hollington, *Shareholders' Rights*, 4th edn (London: Sweet & Maxwell, 2004), Chs 7–9; Prentice, "The Theory of the Firm: Minority Shareholders' Oppression" 8 *Oxford J. Legal Studies* 55 (1988); Hannigan, "Section 459 of the Companies Act 1985—A Code of Conduct for Quasi-Partnerships" [1988] *Lloyds Maritime and Commercial Law Quarterly* 60; Paterson, "A Criticism of the Contractual Approach to Unfair Prejudice" 27 *Co. Law.* 204 (2006); and Payne, "Sections 459–461 Companies Act 1985 in Flux: The Future of Shareholder Protection" 64 *Cam. L.J.* 647 (2005).

[140] 1963 Act, s.213(g).

[141] *Latimer Holdings Ltd v SEA Holdings NZ Ltd* [2004] N.Z.C.A. 226.

other hand, the other modes of redress considered above may provide greater predictability of outcome, which in turn enhances the prospect of a satisfactory settlement before the costs and inconvenience of a trial are incurred. In *Re R. Ltd,*[142] the Supreme Court held that only in the most exceptional cases should the court agree to hear oppression proceedings *in camera.*[143] On account of the highly discretionary scope of this remedy, the question has arisen whether it should be subject to some form of pre-trial filtering mechanism as is adopted for derivative claims.[144] A common defensive strategy adopted in Britain is the motion to dismiss the proceedings at the very outset because they do not disclose a claim that is likely to succeed.

10–75   Applications under s.205 are sometimes used as leverage to obtain better bargaining positions and, unless carefully controlled, can themselves become a medium of oppression.[145] For the threat of such proceedings by a dissident shareholder in a small company can bring pressure on a majority to accept the price he demands for his shares. The burden of legal costs and expenditure of management time in defending these petitions can be crippling. Regardless of size, many companies would be concerned about confidential information about their affairs getting into the public domain. Where it can be shown that the purpose of the proceedings are designed to achieve some entirely collateral purpose, they will be dismissed; as for instance, where the petitioner was seeking to pressurise his company to pay a substantial debt to another company in which he was interested.

Alternative Remedy

10–76   Where the dispute results from a breakdown of relations between the shareholders, and it is better that one or some leave the company entirely, often the issue really is one about the price of buying them out. A strong case can be made that the statutory procedure should not be used where the company's own articles of association or a shareholders' agreement contains a fair mechanism for dealing with the sale of shares.[146] However, in *Re Murray Consultants Ltd,*[147] the Supreme Court refused to dismiss, as an abuse of the process, a s.205 claim where the respondents (majority shareholders) offered to buy out the petitioner's shares at a price to be determined independently. O'Flaherty J. dissented, observing that "while undoubtedly the citizen is entitled to full and free access to the courts, nonetheless, the courts have an obligation too, to provide for exit mechanisms from litigation so that people are not put to the burden of paying costs and expenses which are totally disproportionate to the end to be achieved".[148] Although Murphy J., for the majority, was sympathetic

---

[142] [1989] I.R. 126.

[143] Followed in *Irish Press Plc v Ingersoll Irish Publications Ltd (No 1)* [1994] 1 I.R. 176.

[144] See para.22–56.

[145] *cf.* remarks of Hoffman J. in *Re A Company* [1986] B.C.L.C. 362 at 367; English Law Commission's paper, *Shareholders' Remedies* (1996).

[146] See generally, Chio, "Contextualising Shareholders' Disputes—A Way to Reconceptualise Minority Shareholders' Remedies" [2006] *J. Bus. L.* 312.

[147] [1997] 3 I.R. 23.

[148] *ibid.* at 30.

to this view, he concluded that once a *prima facie* case of oppression is stated in the pleadings, the case should not be struck out, reflecting the greater reluctance of Irish courts generally to dismiss actions *in limine*. Where the central issue in the dispute is excluding the petitioner from any say in the running of the company's business, it has been suggested that ordinarily there is no oppression if the majority shareholders offer to buy his shares for fair value.[149]

10–77   At times, the issues in dispute may be subject to an arbitration clause. In England, where the courts have a discretion to stay proceedings in such circumstances, it depends on all the circumstances whether the court will insist on the matter being resolved by arbitration.[150] Because s.5 of the Arbitration Act, 1980, provides for mandatory stays, it was held by the Supreme Court in *Re Via Net Works Ireland Ltd*[151] that, in such circumstances, the parties must go to arbitration. As explained by Keane C.J., by "entering into the arbitration agreement, they were expressly waiving the right to have issues that arose between them … litigated in any form other than the arbitral tribunal"[152] and it was irrelevant that their right of action derived from the common law or from statute. But this may be too dogmatic a position, as there may be issues in dispute that are not proper to be determined in arbitration; also what may be the most suitable remedy may not be available to an arbitrator.

Locus Standi

10–78   Subject to the exceptions explained below, only a "member" can apply for an order under s.205 (or petition for a winding up order under s.213 (g) on the basis of oppression). Ordinarily, a majority shareholder cannot obtain relief because his control of the company should empower him to rectify whatever loss he may be suffering.[153] Nominee shareholders have *locus standi* even though the prejudice is being suffered by the shares' beneficial owners.[154] It was held in *Re Via Net Works (Ireland) Ltd*[155] that, where a person has agreed to sell his shares in a company but remains on the share register until the sale has been completed, he does not have *locus standi*. This was because, according to Keane C.J., "[he] had no doubt that, when the legislature enacted s. 205(1) it was not envisaged that persons without any interest in the company but who for whatever reason remained on the register as members would be entitled to present a petition grounded on alleged oppression of them as members".[156]

10–79   Former members of the company lack *locus standi*, even where they complain about what was done when they were members. But a member is not

---

[149] *O'Neill v Phillips* [1999] 1 W.L.R. 1092.

[150] *Exeter City FC v Football Conference Ltd* [2004] 1 W.L.R. 2910.

[151] [2002] 2 I.R. 47.

[152] *ibid.* at 57–58.

[153] *Re Baltic Estate Ltd (No. 2)* [1993] B.C.L.C. 503 and *Re Legal Costs Negotiators Ltd* [1999] 2 B.C.L.C. 171.

[154] *Atlasview Ltd v Brightview Ltd* [2004] 2 B.C.L.C. 191.

[155] [2002] 2 I.R. 47.

[156] *ibid.* at 56.

entirely debarred from complaining about events that occurred before his name was put on the register.[157] Where a member dies, an application for relief may be made by his personal representative and also by trustees of or any person beneficially interested in his shares under a will or intestacy.[158] Accordingly, persons like the plaintiff in *Re Hafner*[159] could complain that the refusal to register them as shareholders amounts to oppression. But this extended definition does not encompass the Official Assignee or a trustee in bankruptcy, or a receiver appointed over the shares.

Focus of Complaint

10–80   The potential focus of the complaint under s.205 is most extensive: either the exercise of the directors' powers or the conduct of the company's affairs. But if what is being complained of is the conduct of the majority's personal affairs, there cannot be oppression even if that adversely affects minority shareholders. In *Crindle Investments v Wymes*,[160] what prevented the company from settling claims it had brought against a competitor and certain banks was that its majority shareholders had brought similar claims in their own right but refused to entertain such settlement offers as had been made to them. It was held that, insofar as in their capacity as controlling members, they directly prevented the company from settling, they had acted oppressively. But by not being prepared to settle their own proceedings, this concerned how they conducted their own affairs and could not constitute oppression.[161] Similarly, the sale of a member's shares or his refusal to sell his shares ordinarily would fall outside the ambit of s.205.[162]

10–81   Additionally, the prejudice being complained of must be to the petitioner in his capacity of a member of the company rather than in an extraneous capacity. Thus, prejudice as a supplier to the company or as its customer, or as its employee or its creditor, generally is not caught by s.205.[163] Where parties formed a joint venture company on the understanding that it would be financed by loans that they would advance to it, refusal by the majority of them to make those loans can constitute oppression.[164]

10–82   Depending on the circumstances, even inaction by the majority can be so caught,[165] as can a single instance which prejudices the minority.[166] So too can past actions, even if they took place before the petitioner became a shareholder, as the effect of the prejudice then caused may still be being carried

---

[157] *Lloyd v Casey* [2002] 1 B.C.L.C. 454.
[158] 1963 Act, s.205(6).
[159] [1943] I.R. 426.
[160] [1998] 4 I.R. 567.
[161] *ibid.* at 581–584.
[162] *Re Legal Costs Negotiators Ltd* [1999] 2 B.C.L.C. 171.
[163] *Arrow Nominees Inc v Blackledge* [2000] 2 B.C.L.C. 167.
[164] *Gamlestaden Fastigheter AB v Baltic Partners Ltd* [2007] Bus. L.R. 1521.
[165] *Scottish Co-Op Wholesale Soc. v Meyer* [1959] A.C. 324.
[166] *Re Westwinds Holding Co.*, unreported, High Court, Kenny J., May 21, 1974.

through.[167] Depending on the circumstances, a company's affairs can include those of the subsidiary.[168]

Oppression or Disregarding Interests

10–83 What must be shown is that the directors' actions or the company's activities are either "oppressive to" the applicant(s) or "disregard … his or their interests" as members. The word oppression has been defined as "burdensome, harsh and wrongful"[169]; it is something akin to unconscionable. The alternative basis is not contravening "rights" of a member but impairing his "interests" as such, which broadens the inquiry considerably. What precisely is meant by an interest in this context has not been defined. A slightly different formulation is contained in the comparable UK legislation, that of conduct which is "unfairly prejudicial" to the interests of one or more of the members. But the courts in both countries adopt broadly similar approaches to what kind of conduct—or, at times, failure to act—warrants an appropriate remedy being afforded to aggrieved parties. A difficulty here, which arises in many other areas of law, is reconciling the need for predictability of outcome with the flexibility that is desirable to do justice in any particular instance. Without governing criteria with some degree of precision, the remedy may become a form of "palm tree" jurisdiction, with a myriad of single instances and no overriding coherent principles for its application. To date, the Irish courts have not opted for any overarching approach to these cases.

10–84 Many of them involve what are described as quasi-partnerships, i.e. a small number of persons who formed a company on the understanding that each of them would participate equally in most of its aspects. As described by Lord Millett,

> "[t]heir essential feature is that the legal, corporate and employment relationships do not tell the whole story; and that behind them there is a relationship of trust and confidence similar to that obtaining between partners which makes it unjust or inequitable for the majority to insist on its strict legal rights. The typical characteristics of such a company are that there should be (i) a business association formed or continued on the basis of a personal relationship of mutual trust and confidence, (ii) an understanding or agreement that all or some of the shareholders should participate in the management of the business and (iii) restrictions on the transfer of shares so that a member cannot realise his stake if he is excluded from the business. These elements are typical, but the list is not exhaustive."[170]

As most of the decisions here turn of their particular facts, care should be taken in treating them as precedents in somewhat similar instances.

---

[167] *Lloyd v Casey* [2002] 1 B.C.L.C. 454.
[168] See para.14–14 *et seq.*
[169] *Scottish Coop* [1959] A.C. 324 at 342.
[170] *CVC/Opportunity Equity Partners Ltd v Demario Almeida* [2002] 2 B.C.L.C. 108 at 117. See *Strahan v Wilcock* [2006] 2 B.C.L.C. 555.

10–85   In the leading English case, *O'Neill v Phillips*,[171] Lord Hoffman set out some general propositions regarding the jurisdiction. The overriding objective is to secure a degree of fairness for minority shareholders, who almost invariably cannot readily transfer their shares for fair value. But fairness here does not turn on any individual judge's instinct for what is just; it is founded on rational principles. First, where members have agreed, either formally or informally as to how a company's affairs are to be conducted, then generally those in control of a company will be held to the terms of that agreement. That what they agreed on is not a legally binding contract hardly matters. This resembles the "legitimate expectation" doctrine in public law and the equitable doctrine of estoppel. As articulated by a New York court, under equivalent legislation, oppression refers to "conduct that substantially defeats the reasonable expectations held by minority shareholders in committing their capital to the particular enterprise"; it arises "when the majority conduct substantially defeats expectations that, objectively viewed, were both reasonable under the circumstances and were central to the petitioner's decisions to join the venture", adding that much depends on the circumstances of the individual case.[172]

10–86   Second, circumstances can arise where those in control should not be permitted to insist on the strict literal terms of the law, the articles of association or a shareholders' agreement, but should be obliged to exercise powers conferred thereby in good faith. This resembles the doctrines of *bonne foi* and *gute sitten* in continental European law, and indeed the concept of abuse of right (or *abus de droit*) discussed above on the context of the "fraud on a minority" doctrine. In other words, it is exercising a particular entitlement in a manner that, had the matter been raised earlier, in all likelihood many of shareholders would not have agreed to that course of conduct. Accordingly, that what was done or is being proposed fully accords with the provisions of the Companies Act, the company's articles of association or a shareholders' agreement does not insulate it from being impugned under s.205.

10–87   To obtain a remedy here, it is not essential to show that the respondent was consciously seeking to disadvantage the petitioner or that there has been a lack of probity on the respondent's part. Although many instances of oppression consist of the minority being treated differently from the majority, circumstances can arise when the equal treatment of all the shareholders is nonetheless oppressive to a minority of them. Most important of all, fairness here will not be considered in a vacuum; context is everything, for instance, whether the company is public or private, is or is not a quasi-partnership, or is a family company. There are few hard and fast rules as to what amounts to oppression and a considerable amount of judicial discretion is involved.

---

[171] [1999] 1 W.L.R. 1092.
[172] *Re Kemp & Beatley Inc.*, 473 N.E. 2d 1173 (1984).

Exclusion from Management

10–88   Perhaps the paradigm case is where a small number of individuals establish a company where it is intended that each of them should have equivalent shareholdings, and should participate in its management and equally in its profits. But the majority of them then turn on the minority, and remove them from their position as directors and, possibly, as employees as well. Because the excluded member will have lost a significant return (status and income) from his investment and cannot readily recover that investment (by selling his shares), he generally will succeed in establishing what for convenience may be described as oppression. In the leading Irish case along these lines, *Re Murph's Restaurant Ltd*,[173] where two brothers and a third party set up a thriving restaurant business but the two then turned on the other, in the manner just described, Gannon J. ordered that the entire company should be wound up. *O'Neill v Phillips* is a variation of this paradigm, where the controller of a company gave his employee 25 per cent of its issued shares and appointed him as a director and, later, as managing director. Subsequently, bonus shares were issued to him and the controller waived part of his strict proportion in favour of that director/25 per cent shareholder. But when the company's business began to experience difficulties, the controller removed the other from being managing director, and the company paid the latter only his salary as employee and no more than 25 per cent of any dividends declared. Because the controller never promised the other that he would always be managing director and have 50 per cent of the profits, and because also the other remained a board member and employee, and he was paid a substantial dividend and a salary, it was held that there had not been unfair prejudice.

10–89   There are numerous other reported instances of minority shareholders, who lost their seats on the board or their jobs with the company, seeking a remedy for oppression, including the two reported Irish cases on whether an interlocutory injunction can be obtained to restrain consideration of a proposed EGM resolution that a minority shareholder/director should be removed from the board. In *Feighery v Feighery*,[174] one issue was whether the company was a quasi partnership, on the grounds that the shareholders had not come together on the understanding that they all would actively participate in running the company's affairs; that accordingly, the petitioner could not maintain that he had good grounds for believing that he was entitled to remain a director for so long as he chose. In the event, it was not necessary for Laffoy J. to decide this point. In *McGilligan v O'Grady*,[175] the company had entered an agreement with a bank, as nominee for its BES investors, that, *inter alia*, the petitioner would be a member of its board and would have full access to all financial information concerning the company. Because the object of that agreement was to protect those investors, it was held that its breach constituted a "strongly arguable case" that there had been oppression.

---

[173] [1979] I.L.R.M. 141.
[174] [1999] 1 I.R. 321.
[175] [1999] 1 I.R. 346.

10–90   Where the key issue in the dispute is excluding a party from a remunerated role in managing the business, it was said in *O'Neill v Phillips* that there will not have been oppression if a reasonable offer was made for his shares. As to what would be a reasonable offer here, Lord Hoffman listed five criteria: ordinarily, there should be no discount for it being a minority holding; where value is not agreed, it should be decided by a competent expert, with both sides sharing the cost; it is not necessary that this be done by way of formal arbitration; both sides should have equal right of access to such records as are needed to make a proper valuation; where there is a breakdown in relations, the majority should have reasonable time within which to make an offer and the minority should then have reasonable time to consider it, before commencing any proceedings. If an ostensibly capable valuation method is chosen, courts are reluctant to go behind the valuation arrived at.[176]

Remuneration/Dividends Imbalance

10–91   Another common case is where the company's business is very profitable and substantial remuneration is being paid to its directors, who are its majority shareholders, but no or a very small dividend is paid to the shareholders. Although courts are most reluctant to intervene in the choice between retaining profits and declaring dividends, circumstances can reach such an extreme as to constitute oppression for these purposes. In *Grace v Biagioli*,[177] the petitioner, a one-third shareholder and director, was removed from the company's board for serious misconduct. Additionally, the company refused to pay him a dividend it had declared and, instead, paid the equivalent of that sum to his co-members as management fees. While his removal was found in the circumstances to be justified, it was held that depriving him of dividends amounted to oppression.

10–92   *Re Sam Weller & Sons Ltd*[178] was an application to strike out a claim of oppression on the grounds that the facts alleged did not disclose any cause of action under this heading. The petitioners, who held a substantial minority stake in a prosperous family company, complained that for many years past a derisory dividend was paid, even though the company had abundant reserves and cash to pay much higher dividends. The company would not disclose what remuneration its directors were being paid and it refused to register transfers of shares which the petitioners had inherited, thereby locking them into the company. It was held that these facts could amount to oppression.[179]

Denying Access to Information

10–93   Persistent refusal to convene AGMs or to furnish shareholders with the annual accounts or with other financial information which, in all the circumstances they should get, almost invariably constitutes oppression, as the

---

[176] *Re Belfield Furnishing Ltd* [2006] 2 B.C.L.C. 705.
[177] [2006] 2 B.C.L.C. 70.
[178] [1990] 1 Ch. 683.
[179] Oppression was also established in *Irvine v Irvine (No. 1)* [2007] 1 B.C.L.C. 349.

McGilligan case indicates.[180] Even if there were no restrictions on how a minority shareholder could transfer his shares, being denied access to the profit and loss account and the balance sheet would seem to be so oppressive as to be inexcusable, save in perhaps the most exceptional of circumstances. It was held by O'Hanlon J. in *Re Clubman Shirts Ltd*[181] that, where a company is in the process of undergoing a radical transformation in its structures, a substantial minority shareholder should be furnished with information concerning what is going on, over and above his strict entitlements under the legislation.

Fraud on the Company

10–94 Some doubt has been expressed about whether, outside quasi partnerships, s.205 is the appropriate remedy for misappropriation of a company's assets by its directors/majority shareholders. In *Re Via Net Works (Ireland) Ltd*,[182] where the focus of the complaint was damage being done directly to the company, and thereby only indirectly to the shareholders, the Supreme Court suggested that no remedy exists under s. 205. Keane C.J. observed that "[t]here are undoubtedly well established exceptions to the [reflective loss] rule but it is clear that this case does not come within any of them."[183] The correctness of this conclusion is questionable. In England, the existence of an element of "reflective loss" is not regarded as a bar to oppression proceedings. In *Clark v Cutland*,[184] it was held that this statutory remedy could be deployed where the respondent, a majority shareholder, had misappropriated more than £500,000 from the company and, additionally, had taken from it large payments by way of salary and pension contributions that had never been authorised. The remedy granted there was that the company should be fully reimbursed for those sums.

Abuse of Powers

10–95 Even where self-enrichment by or condoned by the majority is not involved, in appropriate circumstances a remedy will be granted where particular powers in the company's own regulations or in the legislation, or in a shareholders' agreement, are abused; for instance, a decision to allot additional shares that significantly alters voting powers in a company in a particularly unfair manner.[185]

Other

10–96 Breaches of a company's articles of association or of the Companies Acts, if sufficiently serious, may amount to oppression, again depending on all

---

[180] *McGilligan v O'Grady* [1999] 1 I.R. 326. See too *Fisher v Cadman* [2006] 1 B.C.L.C. 499.

[181] [1983] I.L.R.M. 323.

[182] [2002] 2 I.R. 47.

[183] *ibid.* at 56.

[184] [2004] 1 W.L.R. 783 and see J. Payne, "Shareholders' Remedies Reassessed" 67 *Mod. L. Rev.* 500 (2004).

[185] Compare *Re Regional Airports Ltd* [1999] 2 B.C.L.C. 30 with *CAS Nominees Ltd v Nottingham Forest FC* [2002] 1 B.C.L.C. 613.

the surrounding circumstances; for instance, failure to hold shareholders' meetings and failure to make requisite disclosures concerning the company's affairs.

10–97 It is only in exceptional circumstances that what may be categorised as ordinary business decisions, in running a company, will be treated as unlawfully oppressive. Managerial errors of judgment and inefficiencies are no basis for a remedy here, at least in the absence of bad faith. If it can be shown that the shareholders had agreed that a business should be run in a particular manner but, instead, the majority ran it differently, that may constitute oppression, depending on all the surrounding circumstances.[186] Certain dealings with the affairs of a subsidiary company can constitute oppression of the parent company's majority shareholders, as well as of the minority in the subsidiary.[187]

10–98 That the minority have lost all confidence in the majority does not suffice to attract the statutory remedy, not even in quasi partnerships. There must be specific conduct by the latter that is oppressive to the former or that unlawfully disregards their interests. In one instance, where the relationship between two 50/50 quasi-partners had entirely broken down and one of them offered to resolve the deadlock through a sealed bid procedure for the other's shares, it was held not to constitute oppression for the latter to reject that proposal.[188] In another instance involving a 49/51 quasi-partnership, although the majority shareholder-director's breach of fiduciary duty did not cause any particular loss to the company, a serious breach of the nature involved there was found to be sufficiently prejudicial to the relationship to be oppression.[189]

10–99 Even if conduct that ordinarily amounts to oppression is established, circumstances may nevertheless justify the court refusing to remedy it, for instance, wrongdoing by the petitioner or acquiescence by him in the activity which is the subject of his complaint.[190] Where relations have broken down and the minority has been significantly prejudiced, there may nevertheless not be oppression if in all the circumstances the minority ought to leave the company and the majority has made a reasonable offer to buy his shares.[191]

10–100 The most far-reaching of the Irish cases is *Re Williams Group Tullamore Ltd*,[192] which demonstrates the liberal interpretation given to s.205. A very successful private company reorganised its share structure in the 1970s to take into account the different forms of family involvement in the business. Because only some members of the family took part in its management, it was decided to create and to issue to those members preference shares, which were

---

[186] *Re Guidezone Ltd* [2000] 2 B.C.L.C. 321.
[187] See para.14–18.
[188] *Re Jayflex Construction Ltd* [2004] 2 B.C.L.C. 145.
[189] *Re Baumler (UK) Ltd* [2005] 1 B.C.L.C. 92.
[190] *McKee v O'Reilly* [2004] 2 B.C.L.C. 145.
[191] *West v Blanchett* [2001] 1 B.C.L.C. 795.
[192] [1985] I.R. 613.

to carry non-cumulative dividend rights of eight per cent, be entitled to priority when repaying capital on a liquidation and, most significantly, carried the sole right to attend and to vote at general meetings. For as long as these shares were in existence, the ordinary shareholders could not participate in the company's general meetings. The focus of the petition was a decision by the company (in effect made by the preference shareholders only) to pay a very substantial dividend (£267,080 in aggregate) of £1 per share to every one of the company's shareholders. This course of conduct was adopted because it was felt that, on account of the huge inflation since the capital reorganisation, the preference shareholders, who had managed the company so successfully, ought to be paid something more than their fixed eight per cent per annum. Because almost certainly there would be considerable objection if all of the funds available for distribution were paid to the preference shareholders only, it was decided that the money should be paid to every shareholder on a *pro rata* basis. Some ordinary shareholders claimed that this disregarded their interests as members.

10–101 Barrington J. found that the share structure as established in the 1970s was one that contemplated "that the ordinary shareholders would take the greater risks and would, in the event of the company being successful, reap the greater rewards".[193] The money it was proposed to pay the preference shareholders could have been used, for example, to reduce borrowings or for some other purpose of which the ordinary shareholders approved. If the proposed distribution would give the company a distinct advantage, for instance regarding taxation, a court might take a different view of it. But it was held that the only real beneficiaries of the scheme proposed here were the preference shareholders. Consequently, it was "contrary to the interests of the ordinary shareholders", it disregarded their interests and, if the company persisted in implementing the scheme, it would be oppressive to them.

10–102 The argument does not seem to have been made that it was within the preference shareholders' power not to pay any dividends whatsoever to the ordinary shareholders and that the latter could not change the company's articles of association in order to deprive the former of that power—presumably because it is likely that such action of itself would be regarded as oppressive in the circumstances. The facts of the other leading Irish cases on this section, the *Murph's Restaurants* case,[194] the *Greenore Trading* case[195] and the *Clubman Shirts* case,[196] as well as seminal *Scottish Co-op* case,[197] are considered elsewhere.

Remedies

10–103 The remedies available for oppression are most extensive; they are "with a view to bringing an end to the matters complained of, [to] make such order as [the court] thinks fit, whether directing or prohibiting any act or cancelling or

---

[193] *ibid.* at 621.
[194] [1979] 1 I.L.R.M. 141. See para.10–117.
[195] [1980] I.L.R.M. 94 and see para.8–136.
[196] [1983] I.L.R.M. 323 and see para.9–32.
[197] [1959] A.C. 324 and see para.14–15.

varying any transaction or for regulating the conduct of the company's affairs in future, or for the purchase of the shares of any members ..."[198]

Range of Remedies

10–104 In many instances the court orders that the oppressed member's shares be bought out, either by the oppressors or by the company, at a fair price. At times, as in *Re Greenore Trading Co.*,[199] an element is built into the buying price to compensate for losses that the oppressed member previously suffered. The court could order the oppressors to sell their shares to those who were being oppressed but an order of this nature would be made only in very unusual circumstances. The court even has power to order a person who is no longer a member of the company to purchase the petitioner's shares. In *Clark v Cutland*,[200] where the majority shareholder/director had misappropriated over £500,000 from the company and had taken substantial remuneration and pension contributions, without being authorised, the court ordered that he repay the company the sums that he had obtained and, additionally, granted the company a charge over the pension fund's assets for a sum equivalent to what that fund had been paid, coupled with adjustment provisions to ensure that the company was fully reimbursed. Other remedies that it appears could be granted are orders directing the company to amend its own regulations in a particular manner, or requiring it to prosecute or defend or discontinue particular proceedings, or appointing provisional directors or receivers, or a receiver and manager over all or part of the company's assets. If some alteration to the company's own regulations is directed, those cannot be amended subsequently in any manner incompatible with the court's order.

10–105 It would appear that the court cannot make an award of damages as such or that, unless the application includes a petition to wind up the company, to direct its winding up. However, where a member seeks a winding up order on account of oppression, even though he establishes his case the court may dismiss that petition if it concludes that a remedy under s.205 is a more appropriate solution in the circumstances.[201]

Valuation

10–106 By far the commonest remedy is an order requiring the respondents to purchase the oppressed member's shares at fair value; exceptionally, the oppressors may be directed to sell their shares to the petitioner. Unless the parties agree on some mechanism for valuing the shares (e.g. appointing a valuer or an arbitrator) or the court directs some mechanism, the court will have to decide what they are worth.[202] This involves, firstly, deciding the time at which

---

[198] 1963 Act, s.205(3).
[199] [1983] I.L.R.M. 94.
[200] [2004] 1 W.L.R. 783.
[201] 1963 Act, s.213(g).
[202] See generally, T. Power et al, *Financial Management: An Irish Text*, 2nd edn (Dublin: Gill & Macmillan, 2005), Ch.6 and C. Glover, *The Valuation of Unquoted Companies*, 4th edn (London: Thomson GEE, 2002).

they should be valued: for instance, at the date the proceedings were commenced or at the date the court decided the dispute, or at the date when the oppression commenced. The individual circumstances of each case will determine the appropriate valuation date.

10–107   There then must be determined the basis of the valuation: is it the sum that would be distributed on an orderly winding up of the business, or should the shares be valued on a "going concern" basis, or by capitalising estimated future earnings at a rate appropriate to the type of business involved? As they do not confer control, minority shareholdings are usually valued at a discount from their *pro rata* value; for tax purposes, for instance, the standard discount is 25 per cent or higher in certain cases. It depends on the entire circumstances of a case whether or not the minority shareholding should be valued subject to a discount. In *Re Bird Precision Bellows Ltd*,[203] the court rejected the contention that, when the court orders the purchase of shares, the price must be the market price as determined by ordinary valuation principles. Generally, the innocent minority shareholder in a quasi partnership should not be penalised by either having his shares being bought out at a discount from their *pro rata* price, or by having to pay a premium where the remedy is for him to buy out the majority. This approach was endorsed by O'Hanlon J. in *Re Clubman Shirts Ltd*,[204] where the company's shares were first valued by an accountant who had been appointed by the court for that purpose.[205] To properly value the shares, discovery may be required, which could involve disclosing highly confidential information.

Interim Relief

10–108   Interlocutory injunctions preserving the *status quo* can be obtained in an appropriate case. However, it appears that a *Mareva*-type injunction will not normally be granted unless the evidence discloses a strong arguable case of conduct that would be the basis of a separate cause of action and not simply unfair prejudice to the applicant.[206]

WINDING UP ON JUST AND EQUITABLE GROUNDS

10–109   Until statutory oppression was introduced in 1963, the only remedy available to aggrieved minority shareholders against conduct that was not strictly unlawful, as described above, was to force the liquidation of their company. Ever since 1848, the courts have been empowered to order that a company be wound up on "just and equitable grounds".[207] For many years they adopted a restrictive interpretation of this jurisdiction. But in *Re Newbridge Steam Laundry Ltd*[208] it was held that the phrase "just and equitable" "ought

---

[203] [1986] 1 Ch. 68.
[204] [1991] I.L.R.M. 43.
[205] Compare *Irvine v Irvine (No. 2)* [2007] 1 B.C.L.C. 445, not involving a quasi-partnership.
[206] *Re Premier Electronics (GB) Ltd* [2002] 2 B.C.L.C. 634.
[207] Now, s.213(f) of the 1963 Act.
[208] [1917] 1 I.R. 67.

not to be narrowly construed in this way, but that in all cases which cannot be brought under the preceding clauses [of s. 213], but where, having regard to the established principles of courts of equity, justice and equity require a company to be wound up, an order for its winding up ought to be made".[209] That case was the sequel to the *Cockburn* case,[210] where it was held that the managing director of the company had acted unlawfully in taking £3,000 for laundry work done by the company for the military authorities on the Curragh but paying only £1,000 of that over to the company.

10–110   Although the court has a broad discretion to order that a company be wound up, it is far from completely free; its exercise must be founded on reasoning which can be examined and justified. The principal factor limiting the availability of this remedy is the existence of an alternative mode of liquidation, in the form of voluntary winding up.[211] Whether or not the company should go into liquidation has always been treated as a matter of domestic policy, which the members are entitled to determine, and it is not sufficient to show that a simple majority of members favour liquidation (unless the company is insolvent). A resolution for voluntary winding up must be passed by a majority of three quarters of those entitled to vote,[212] and it follows that an order for compulsory winding up will only be made where the circumstances are so exceptional as to justify the court in disregarding that statutory requirement. Analysis of the authorities suggests that there are five situations in which those circumstances exist:

(1)   where the company was fraudulent in its inception;
(2)   where it becomes impossible for the company to achieve what it was incorporated to do, as set out in its objects clause or under some other common understanding between the members;
(3)   where the company is unable to carry on business, for instance because there is complete deadlock between the members;
(4)   where control or management of the company's affairs is characterised by fraud, misconduct, or oppression; and
(5)   where the company is substantially a domestic company, in the nature of a partnership, whose members are unable to cooperate in the conduct of its affairs.

10–111   Due to its drastic consequences, a compulsory winding up is a significant deterrent against majorities overreaching themselves. Yet the winding up procedure itself is slow and expensive, and the aggrieved shareholder may ultimately get far less than his shares are really worth when the company's business is disposed of in a forced sale. If it is shown that the real purpose of a winding up petition is to bring pressure on the company or its controllers to yield to the petitioner's unreasonable demands, it will be rejected

---

[209] *ibid.* at 90.
[210] *Cockburn v Newbridge Steam Laundry Co.* [1915] 1 I.R. 237.
[211] See para.23–08.
[212] 1963 Act, s.251.

as an abuse of the legal process. Where the central point of a petitioner's complaint is that he has been excluded from the management of a quasi partnership, it was held that it would be an abuse for him to petition a winding up where an offer was made to buy his shares at a reasonable price, which normally would not involve their value being discounted because they are a minority stake.[213]

Fraud and Misconduct

10–112   That the winding up jurisdiction will be invoked against truly oppressive, as compared with manifestly unlawful, conduct was confirmed in *Loch v John Blackwood Ltd*,[214] concerning a private family company and its managing director holding the majority of the shares. The minority petitioned to have it wound up, claiming that the directors never held general meetings nor submitted annual accounts, that they never recommended dividends and, by keeping the petitioners in ignorance, hoped to acquire their shares for a small consideration. It was held that, if these claims could be substantiated, the court would have jurisdiction to order that the company be wound up. The basis of the law was summed by Lord Shaw:

> "It is undoubtedly true that at the foundation of applications for winding up on the 'just and equitable' rule, there must lie a justifiable lack of confidence in the conduct and management of the company's affairs. But this lack of confidence must be grounded on conduct of the directors, not in regard to their private life or affairs, but in regard to the company's business. Furthermore, the lack of confidence must spring not from dissatisfaction at being outvoted on the business affairs or on what is called the domestic policy, of the company. On the other hand, wherever the lack of confidence is rested on a lack of probity in the conduct of the company's affairs, then the former is justified by the latter and it is, under the statute, just and equitable that the company be wound up."[215]

10–113   The *Newbridge Laundry* case[216] was one of the earliest applications of this principle, involving breach of directors' duties and fraud on the company. But where the focus of dispute may be described as "domestic policy", it must be demonstrated that the directors' powers have been exercised in a flagrantly improper manner before winding up will be directed; for instance, in the matters concerning the registration of share transfers,[217] the declaration of dividends and placing profits in reserve. The precise boundaries of the "misconduct-oppression" heading remain to be determined.

---

[213] *CVC/Opportunity Equity Partners Ltd v Demarco Almeida* [2002] 2 B.C.L.C. 108, where in the circumstances it was held not to be an abuse.
[214] [1924] A.C. 783.
[215] *ibid.* at 788.
[216] [1917] 1 I.R. 67.
[217] *Charles Forte Investments Ltd v Amanda* [1964] Ch. 240.

Partnership Analogy

10–114   Special considerations arise where the company is a "quasi partner-ship".[218] Generally, a winding up order will be made if a shareholder demonstrates that the company has so utterly disregarded his rights and legitimate expectations, that there has been an irretrievable breakdown in relationships, even where it acts entirely consistently with the legislation and its own articles of association. In *Re Westbourne Galleries Ltd*,[219] the petitioner and his partner for many years incorporated their business, each holding equal shares, and both were executive directors. When the partner brought his son into the business, the petitioner became a minority shareholder. Substantial profits were earned, all of which were distributed by way of directors' remuneration; dividends were never paid. Having acted on that basis for ten years, a disagreement arose between the petitioner and the other two members and directors. As a result, they removed him from the company's board and dismissed him from its employment. It was held that he was entitled to an order that the company be wound up.

10–115   Three principles were laid down or confirmed there. The jurisdiction is not confined to circumstances that affect the petitioner *qua* member; while he must be a member, there "is no reason for preventing him from relying upon any circumstances of justice or equity which affect him in his relations with the company, or ... with the other shareholders".[220] Therefore, prejudicing the petitioner *qua* director or creditor, or employee, of the company is not by definition excluded from consideration. Secondly, the fact that what is being complained of is perfectly consistent with the company's own regulations does not invariably justify it: "[a]cts which, in law, are a valid exercise of powers conferred by the articles may nevertheless be entirely outside what can fairly by regarded as having been in the contemplation of the parties when they became members of the company; and in such cases the fact that what had been done is not in excess of powers will not necessarily be an answer to a claim for winding up".[221]

As for the governing criterion, Lord Wilberforce's words defy paraphrase:

> "The foundation ... lies in the words 'just and equitable'... [These] are a recognition of the fact that a limited company is more than a mere legal entity, with a personality in law of its own: that there is room in company law for recognition of the fact that behind it, or amongst it, there are individuals, with rights, expectations and obligations inter se which are not necessarily submerged in the company structure. That structure is defined by the Companies Act and by the articles of association by which shareholders agree to be bound. In most companies and in most contexts, this definition is sufficient and exhaustive, equally so whether the

---

[218] See generally, V. Joffe, *Minority Shareholders: Law, Practice and Procedure*, 2nd edn (London: LexisNexis, 2004), Ch.4; R. Hollington, *Shareholders' Rights*, 4th edn (London: Sweet & Maxwell, 2004), Ch.10; Prentice, "Winding Up and Just and Equitable Grounds: The Partnership Analogy" 89 *L.Q.R.* 107 (1973).
[219] [1973] A.C. 360.
[220] *ibid.* at 375.
[221] *ibid.* at 378.

company is large or small. The just and equitable provision does ... not entitle one party to disregard the obligation he assumed by entering a company, nor the court to dispense him from it. It does, as equity always does, enable the court to subject the exercise of legal rights to equitable considerations; considerations, that is, of a personal character arising between one individual and another, which may make it unjust, or inequitable, to insist on legal rights, or to exercise them in a particular way.

It would be impossible, and wholly undesirable, to define the circumstances in which these considerations may arise. Certainly the fact that a company is a small one, or a private company, is not enough. There are very many of these where the association is a purely commercial one, of which it can safely be said that the basis of association is adequately and exhaustively laid down in the articles. The superimposition of equitable considerations requires something more, which typically may include one, or probably more, of the following elements: (i) an association formed or continued on the basis of a personal relationship, involving mutual confidence—this element will often be found where a pre-existing partnership has been converted into a limited company; (ii) an agreement, or understanding, that all, or some (for there may be sleeping members), of the shareholders shall participate in the conduct of the business; (iii) restriction upon the transfer of the members' interest in the company—so that if confidence is lost, or one member is removed from management, he cannot take out his stake and go elsewhere."[222]

10–116   Accordingly, circumstances which would not justify winding up a non-"domestic" company may warrant intervention in the affairs of an incorporated partnership. Questions arising in companies with a significant number of members, which are subject to the majority rule principle, therefore assume a different aspect, where the aggrieved member cannot easily exit from the company, especially when he is dependent on it for his livelihood.[223]

10–117   An extreme example is *Re Murph's Restaurants Ltd,*[224] concerning a successful restaurant enterprise which had grown very rapidly and had three shareholders who also were its directors, BS, K and M. The latter two were brothers and had worked full-time for the company since its foundation in 1972, whereas BS, the petitioner, in 1977 gave up a promising career in the computer business to work for the company full-time. No annual meetings were ever held, no annual accounts were prepared and board meetings were most informal. Dividends and directors fees as such were never paid. Instead, drawings were made by the directors against projected earnings; there was an informal arrangement by which each could take about £200 a month "slush money" from cash, and on various occasions sums were transferred into accounts in building societies in the names of one or other of the directors. Special care was taken to ensure that each shared these disbursements equally.

---

[222] *ibid.* at 377.
[223] *Tay Bok Choon v Tahansan Sdn Bhd* [1987] 1 W.L.R. 413.
[224] [1979] 1 I.L.R.M. 141.

In 1977 they agreed to enter the property market and bid, unsuccessfully, for a hotel. But in the following year K and M bought that property on their own behalf. In the meantime, BS had gone to Cork to run the very successful branch there. In early 1979 K and M agreed that BS should be removed from the board and be no longer employed by the company. While BS's management of the Cork branch was criticised by K and M, it was the profits from it that, in the form of a loan from the company, financed K and M's hotel purchase; and BS did not agree with various aspects of the loan.

10–118   Gannon J. characterised the entire enterprise as one where BS, K and M "were equal partners in a joint venture, and the company was no more than a vehicle to secure a limited liability for possible losses and to provide a means of earning and distributing profits to their best advantage with minimum disclosure". The "strict equity" of their participation in the profits of a company that was run in such an informal and irregular nature "was achieved, and could be achieved, only by a relationship of mutual confidence and trust and active open participation in the management and conduct of the affairs of the company …". The evidence showed that "[w]hatever cause of complaint or fault K and M may have found in BS it did not relate to the talents or qualifications which he had shown, and must have been known to them to have had, at a time when he was induced to join with them in a venture of strictly drawn equality". Therefore, K and M's attempt to treat BS as a mere employee and to exclude him from further participation in the company, as well as being" entirely irregular", was "a deliberate and calculated repudiation by both of them of that relationship of equality, mutuality, trust and confidence between the three of them which constituted the very essence of the existence of the company". The action of K and M deprived BS of a livelihood, and not simply of an investment, which he was induced by their representations to take and in so doing to abandon to his irretrievable loss a [promising] career …" Not alone was the petitioner unlawfully oppressed but he was entitled to an order that the company be wound up.

Alternative Remedies

10–119   Exceptionally, some alternative remedy may exist that outweighs the reasons for having the company wound up. There is express acknowledgement that the existence of another remedy can justify the court refusing the order.[225] In view of what was said in *Re Via Net Works (Ireland) Ltd*,[226] it is conceivable that an arbitration clause could exclude entitlement to this remedy. However, such a clause can only cover disputes arising from contract, so that several circumstances that would warrant winding up would not come within it.[227] Even if notwithstanding such remedy winding up would be justified, the court may still dismiss the winding up petition if it is of the opinion that proceedings for oppression are "more appropriate".

---

[225] 1963 Act, s.213(g).

[226] [2002] 2 I.R. 47.

[227] In *Jenkins v Supscaf Ltd* [2006] 3 N.Z.L.R. 264 the court rejected the arbitration solution, as being unlikely to produce a satisfactory result.

CHAPTER 11

FUNDAMENTAL CHANGES

11–01 The system laid down in the Companies Acts for the governance of companies can be divided into four distinct tiers. The directors, who ordinarily run the business, are subject to the *de facto* control of a simple majority of the shareholders, who have the power to remove directors by an ordinary resolution.[1] Most provisions of a company's own regulations can be altered by special majorities of the members, in that the articles of association can be changed by special resolution.[2] Third, certain vital changes in the nature of companies cannot be made unless they are approved of by super-majorities of the members and either are not vetoed by or are endorsed by the court: notably, altering the objects clause, reducing or repaying capital, varying class rights and making certain "arrangements". In dealing with some of these issues, the Companies Acts override or modify any special voting rights or disabilities, that may exist under the company's own regulations, and wholly or partly enfranchise shareholders to the extent of their shares' nominal values. Thus, a section 201 arrangement must be approved by a majority representing 75 per cent in value of those members of each class affected by it who vote on the proposal.[3] Similarly, the holders of not less than 15 per cent in nominal value of the company's issued share capital or any class of shares or debentures may apply to the court to veto a change in the company's objects.[4] And the holders of not less than 10 per cent of the issued shares of the class in question can apply to the court to have an agreed variation of class rights blocked.[5] The Companies Acts also empower the court, when approving some of these changes, to order appraisal for dissenting shareholders, i.e. to order that their shares be bought out at an objectively determined price. The fourth tier in the statutory system of governance permits matters to be "entrenched" in the memorandum of association so that they can be altered only in some special way or, indeed, be unalterable.

ALTERING THE MEMORANDUM AND ARTICLES

11–02 A company's constitution or regulations, i.e. its memorandum and articles of association, may be altered by its members. The Companies Acts

---

[1] 1963 Act, s.182.
[2] 1963 Act, s.15.
[3] 1963 Act, s.201(3).
[4] 1963 Act, s.10(3).
[5] 1963 Act, s.78(1).

forbid inclusion of certain provisions in these regulations—such as clauses purporting to exonerate directors from liability for egregious breaches of duty to the company.[6] In addition, the power to alter the memorandum and articles of association is subject to a broad equitable constraint, that it must not be exercised mala fide or in an unfairly discriminatory manner. A copy of the amended full text must be delivered to the Registrar of Companies.[7]

Memorandum of Association

11–03 The memorandum of association can be changed. Power to amend it is put negatively: the memorandum "may not [be] alter[ed] ... except in the cases, in the mode and to the extent for which express provision is made" in the Acts.[8] Thus, in order to reduce authorised share capital in any way, the articles must permit this and there must be a special resolution authorising the reduction, which must be confirmed by the court.[9] The objects clause may be changed by special resolution but dissenters, if they make up at least 15 per cent of the shareholders or of any "class" of shareholder, or of debenture-holders, may apply to the court to have any such change cancelled.[10]

11–04 Where there is a provision in the memorandum that could lawfully be contained in the articles, it can be altered by special resolution in the absence of a stipulation there to the contrary or it involves interference with "class rights",[11] or it involves increasing a member's liability as a shareholder.[12] But an application can be made to the court to cancel any such change; the procedure for dealing with objections of this nature is the same as for contesting resolutions changing the objects clause.[13] Any proposed change of this nature in the memorandum is not permitted to take effect until it has been confirmed by the court.[14] Special provision is made for "entrenched" clauses and for "class rights" in the memorandum.

Articles of Association

11–05 Any clause that could lawfully have been contained in the original articles may subsequently be inserted in them by amendment. A company's power to change its articles by special resolution is stated in the most unequivocal terms.[15] The scope of this power is demonstrated by *Allen v Gold Reefs of West Africa Ltd*,[16] where the company sought to change its articles so as to

---

[6] 1963 Act, s.200.
[7] European Communities (Companies) Regulations 1973 (SI 1973/163), reg.5.
[8] 1963 Act, s.9.
[9] See para.11–35 *et seq.*
[10] See para.11–13 *et seq.*
[11] See para.11–20 *et seq.*
[12] 1963 Act, s.28(1) and (3).
[13] 1963 Act, s.28(3).
[14] 1963 Act, s.28(2).
[15] 1963 Act, s.15.
[16] [1900] Ch. 656.

enable it in effect to confiscate the shares of any member indebted to it. It was held that, once the requisite majority is not acting in bad faith, even an alteration as drastic as this is permissible.

11–06   Where the amendment sets up a conflict between the interests of the company as a commercial entity and the objecting shareholder, the primary test of validity is that used in the *Allen* case, i.e. whether it was adopted "bona fide for the benefit of the company as a whole".[17] It is for the objector to demonstrate that those who voted for the change were motivated by some improper purpose. Since, however, mala fides can be difficult to prove, in an appropriate case bad faith may be inferred from the nature of the change being made and the surrounding circumstances, as is exemplified in some of the "expulsion" cases.[18] As was observed in a case concerning altering a clause that affected the tenure of directors, "[t]he alteration may be so oppressive as to cast suspicion on the honesty of the persons responsible for it, or so extravagant that no reasonable man could really consider it for the benefit of the company".[19]

11–07   Where the change being made affects the rights and liabilities of the shareholders *inter se*, the primary test of validity is that of unfair discrimination articulated in *Greenhalgh v Arderne Cinemas Ltd*,[20] i.e. did it "discriminate between the majority shareholders and the minority shareholders, so as to give, to the former an advantage of which the latter were deprived?"[21] For instance, in one Australian case[22] a change which radically curtailed the dividend rights of one group of members was condemned on those grounds. More recently a change which would allow 90 per cent of the shareholders to forcibly buy out the minority was condemned on similar grounds.[23]

11–08   Where objectors seek to challenge an alteration claiming that it is "oppressive" under s.205 of the 1963 Act, presumably the same general approach would be followed as in *Allen* and in *Greenhalgh*. It is possible, however, that some changes which would pass the tests laid down in those cases might still be regarded as amounting to oppression, in light of a petitioner's exceptional circumstances. But it would not follow that the change is unlawful. If it was passed bona fide for the company's benefit and does not unfairly discriminate, most likely the new article would be allowed to stand, subject to special arrangements being made to redress any prejudice which would have fallen on the petitioner.

---

[17]   Also *Citco Banking Corp NV v Pusser's Ltd* [2007] 2 B.C.L.C. 483 and see para.10–25 *et seq.* See generally, Rixon, "Competing Interests and Conflicting Principles: An Examination of the Power of Alteration of Articles of Association" 49 *Mod. L. Rev.* 446 (1986).
[18]   See para.10–33 *et seq.*
[19]   *Shuttleworth v Cox Bros. & Co.* [1927] K.B. 9 at 18.
[20]   [1951] Ch. 286.
[21]   [1951] Ch. 286 at 291 and see para.10–27 *et seq.*
[22]   *Peters' American Delivery Co. v Heath* (1938–1939) 61 C.L.R. 512.
[23]   *Gambotto v WCP Ltd* (1994) 182 C.L.R. 432.

Entrenchment

11–09 Provisions in the regulations can be entrenched against alteration. The power to change the articles of association is "subject to… the conditions contained in the memorandum"[24] and, as has been pointed out, the memorandum itself may be altered only in the ways permitted by that Act.[25] In order to entrench some clause, all that is necessary is to put it into the memorandum with the stipulation that it may not be altered or may be altered only in some particular way. It would appear that the original memorandum, once registered, cannot subsequently be amended to entrench some clause; although a not implausible argument could be made against such a view. Some uncertainties about the impact of attempted entrenchments of "class rights" are resolved by the 1983 Act,[26] which are considered separately below.

Agreement Not to Alter the Regulations

11–10 Leaving aside where the change abrogates class rights, to what extent is a company's statutory discretion to amend its articles in any way mandatory and incapable of being contracted out of? A variant of this question called for decision in *Russell v Northern Bank Development Corp.*,[27] which concerned a decision to increase a company's capital in a manner envisaged by the articles of association. Following the reconstruction of their businesses, the four managers/shareholders of the company entered into a shareholders' agreement that forbade any increase in capital without the assent of all of them. When three of them, notwithstanding, proposed a resolution to have the capital increased, the plaintiff sought an injunction restraining them. Insofar as that agreement was a contract between those four individuals, it was held that it simply created personal obligations between them "dehors the … or collateral to" the company's articles, "neither in substitution for nor in conflict with" them.[28] Accordingly, any effort by some of them to increase the share capital would be a breach of contract on their part. The same logic would apply to a stipulation in a shareholders' agreement not to change the articles of association. It is debatable, however, whether the court would grant an injunction to prevent breach of a contract between the company itself and a third party not to effect such a change.[29] However, it has been held that damages can be awarded against a company which acts on such a change being made, contrary to what it had agreed with a third party.[30]

11–11 In the *Russell* case, somewhat unusually the company itself also was a party to the shareholders' agreement. Insofar as that agreement purported to prevent the company from exercising its statutory discretions, it was held that

---

[24] 1963 Act, s.9.
[25] 1963 Act, s.28(3).
[26] Sections 38 and 39.
[27] [1992] 1 W.L.R. 588.
[28] *ibid.* at 593.
[29] cf. *Punt v Seymour & Co.* [1903] 2 Ch. 506 and *British Murac Syndicate Ltd v Alperton Rubber Co.* [1915] 2 Ch. 186.
[30] *Southern Founderies (1926) Ltd v Shirlaw* [1940] A.C. 701.

"such an undertaking [was] as obnoxious as if it had been contained in the articles of association and therefore is unenforceable".[31] Whether this statement was part of the *ratio decidendi* or was *obiter* has been questioned[32] and the assertion that a stipulation of that nature is entirely void and without legal effect has been the subject of criticism.[33] It has been pointed out that the position is complex and depends, *inter alia*, on whether the stipulation in the contract had the assent of all the members at the time and what the company was to receive in return for it. The position regarding contracts of this nature was summarised as follows:

"Firstly ... a company cannot, by contract, deprive its members of their rights to alter the articles by special resolution.

Secondly, if a company does contract that its articles will not be altered, none the less its members are entitled to requisition a meeting and pass a special resolution altering the articles.

Thirdly, if the articles are validly altered, the company cannot be prevented from acting on the altered articles, even though so to act may involve it in breach of contract ... .

Fourthly, where a company has contracted that its articles will not be altered, [there is] no reason why it should not, in a suitable case, be injuncted from [itself] initiating the calling of a general meeting with a view to alteration of the articles".[34]

CHANGING THE NATURE OF THE BUSINESS

11–12   The management or the shareholders may wish to change the nature of their company's business or alter drastically the way it conducts its existing business. For instance, the proposal may be that a tailoring company becomes a candlestick-maker, that a construction firm goes into property development, that a trading concern should possess its own financial arm etc. Or it may be proposed that the company sell off a major asset; for example, that to raise funds, a retailing company sells the freehold of all its stores to some financial institution and then leases them back, or that the stores be sold off to the parent company's shareholders under the aegis of a separate company. Where a company's securities are listed on the Irish Stock Exchange and what is being proposed is a "class 1 transaction", it must be explained in a circular sent to the shareholders and their assent to the proposal is required.[35]

---

[31] [1992] 1 W.L.R. 588 at 594.
[32] Davenport, "What did *Russell v. Northern Bank Development Corp.* Decide?" 109 *L.Q.R.* 553 (1993).
[33] Ferran, "The Decision of the House of Lords in *Russell v. Northern Bank Development Corp.*" 53 *Cam. L.J.* 343 (1994).
[34] *Cumbrian Newspapers Group Ltd* v *Cumberland & Westmoreland Herald Newspaper & Printing* Co. [1987] Ch. 1 at 24.
[35] Listing Rule 7.

Altering the Objects

11–13 The change envisaged may be so drastic that it is necessary for the company to amend its objects clause. Between 1862 and 1890, companies' objects clauses were immutable.[36] It was to enable such changes to be made that the Companies (Memorandum of Association) Act 1890,[37] was enacted, which enumerated what kinds of alterations would be permissible and required confirmation by the courts of all proposed changes. The 1963 Act then removed almost all restrictions. Subject to various procedures being satisfied, a company by special resolution may "alter the provisions of its memorandum by abandoning, restricting or amending any existing object or by adopting a new object…".[38] A company, therefore, may take any object with which it originally could have been incorporated and may abandon all or any of its existing objects. The informal unanimous agreement by all of a company's members to a course of conduct that otherwise would be *ultra vires* can be equivalent to a special resolution sanctioning a change in the objects to permit that conduct.[39]

11–14 In *Northern Bank Finance Corp. v Quinn*,[40] it was held that the objects clause cannot be changed with retroactive effect. When the second defendant, a company, realised that the guarantee it had given for a bank loan to the first defendant might be *ultra vires,* it sought to alter its objects so as to enlarge its legal capacity retroactively. It was contended that, by providing that any duly made alteration of the objects "shall be as valid as if originally contained" in the memorandum of association, the 1963 Act[41] allows such changes to be made. Keane J., however, took the view that this meant only that it is not necessary to go through all the formalities of drawing up a new memorandum. He moreover pointed to "strange" consequences if companies could retrospectively deprive themselves of certain objects;[42] although this point is not convincing against retroactively extending objects, especially in the light of the procedure for dealing with objections to proposed changes.

11–15 Not alone must the alteration of the objects clause have been approved by a special resolution, but a minority consisting of 15 per cent in value of the shareholders, or of any class of shareholders, within 21 days may apply to the court to veto any such change. A similar application may be made by 15 per cent of the holders of debentures who are entitled to object to alterations.[43] The Act does not say by what criteria the court is to evaluate alterations and objections to them. Presumably, it would veto proposals that in the circumstances are oppressive or unduly discriminatory, or that go against some accommodation the shareholders previously had reached between themselves.

---

[36] *Ashbury Railway Carriage & Iron Co. v Riche* (1875) L.R. 7 H.L. 653.
[37] 53 & 54 Vict., c.62.
[38] 1963 Act, s.10. See *Smith's Precedents,* Pt 14.
[39] *Re Home Treat Ltd* [1991] B.C.L.C. 705.
[40] [1979] I.L.R.M. 221.
[41] Section 10.
[42] [1979] I.L.R.M. 221 at 230.
[43] 1963 Act, s.10(3)(b), (7).

It was suggested in *Re Munster & Leinster Bank Ltd*,[44] which was decided under the 1890 Act, that questions of general public interest ought not to be the court's concern in these applications. Some shareholders, who in fact were speaking for the Incorporated Law Society and the Southern Law Association, sought to prevent approval being given to a proposed change in the bank's objects that would allow it to act as a professional trustee. It was said that this would damage the solicitors' profession; that as a precedent this could lead to an undesirable concentration of trustee business in banks; that it was likely to lead to an interruption of the friendly relations existing between the legal profession and the court. It was held that these matters were not relevant to the question, which was whether the proposed change would benefit the bank and its shareholders; it was found that it would.[45]

11–16   That the court possesses a wide discretion in this area is underlined by the power it has to make appropriate orders, including appraisal. It may cancel the alteration or confirm it, or confirm it only, partly or on such terms as it thinks fit. One such term is that the dissidents' interests be bought out, and the court may give directions and make orders to render any such arrangement effective.

Strategic Matters—Expansion and Contraction

11–17   Even where the proposed change of direction or method of doing business does not require altering the objects clause, there are a number of ways in which the members can decisively influence the outcome. Where it is necessary to increase the authorised share capital to finance expansion, then the memorandum of association must be amended to permit the increase.[46] In companies with Table A, this requires only an ordinary resolution.[47] Where it is proposed to issue additional shares, then the 1983 Act's provisions on authority and pre-emption must be satisfied,[48] as must any special requirements in the company's own regulations regarding share issues.

11–18   Issuing a new class of shares carrying preferential rights in respect of dividends, capital or voting does not normally amount to a variation of existing shareholders' "class rights" and, therefore, does not require separate class approval. In *Andrews v Gas Meter Co.*,[49] previous authority to the contrary effect was rejected, on the grounds that companies' memoranda of association do not imply an overriding stipulation that all groups of shareholders be treated equally at all times. The governing principles have been expressed as follows:

> "While the memorandum must state the amount of capital, divided into shares of a certain fixed amount, provision as to the character of the shares

---

[44] [1907] 1 I.R. 237.
[45] See also *Re Ulster Marine Insurance Co.*, 27 L.R. Ir. 487 (1871), *Re Marcus Ward & Co.* [1897] 1 I.R. 435 and *Re Cork Employers' Federation* [1921] 1 I.R. 69.
[46] 1963 Act, s.68(1)(a).
[47] Article 44.
[48] Sections 21 and 23.
[49] [1897] Ch. 361.

and rights to be attached to them is more properly made by the articles of association, which may be altered from time to time by special resolution of the company. If equality of the shareholders is expressly provided in the memorandum, that cannot be modified by the articles of association. If nothing is said in the memorandum, the articles of association may provide for the issue of the authorised capital in the form of preference shares; if the articles do not so provide, or do provide for equality *inter socios*, the power to issue preference shares may be obtained by alteration of the articles. If the memorandum prescribes the classes of shares into which the capital is to be divided and the rights to be attached to such shares respectively, the company has no power to alter that provision by special resolution."[50]

These, however, must now be read in the light of developments in the law regarding minority shareholders' protection, most notably s.205 of the 1963 Act on "oppression".

11–19 How the directors take what may be called major strategic decisions, or indeed everyday business decisions, can always be regulated by an appropriate change in the articles of association. Whether the general meeting by ordinary resolution can veto strategic decisions remains an open question in companies with Table A. As has been pointed out above, *Automatic Self-Cleansing Filter Syndicate Co. v Cunninghame*[51] can be distinguished on a number of grounds and it did not deal with resolutions in the negative. It was held in *Re Clubman Shirts Ltd*[52] that refusal to divulge to a major minority shareholder details concerning drastic changes in the nature of the company, in appropriate circumstances, can amount to "oppression".

VARYING CLASS RIGHTS

11–20 Where there is more than one category of shares in a company, like ordinary and preference shares, it is said that there are different classes of shares. The special rights attaching to these are termed "class rights". Whereas a company may alter its articles of association by a special resolution, as a general rule class rights may be taken away or cut down only with the consent of that particular class.[53] Questions regarding class rights arise especially when a company is contemplating restructuring its capital, by raising further equity or debt, or repaying some categories of shares. If what is proposed is an infringement of one group's class rights—such as taking away the preference shareholders' voting rights entirely or in particular circumstances, or cutting their dividend entitlement, or depriving them of their claim to any surplus—then as a rule this proposal must obtain that class's approval before it can be put into effect.

---

[50] *Campbell v Rofe* [1933] A.C. 91 at 98.
[51] [1906] 2 Ch. 34.
[52] [1983] 1 I.L.R.M. 323.
[53] See generally, Baxt, "The Variation of Class Rights" 41 *Australian L.J.* 490 (1968) and Reynolds, "Shareholders' Class Rights: A New Approach" [1996] *J.Bus.L.* 554.

"Class Rights"

11–21   There is no comprehensive definition of what a class of shareholders is or of what class rights are. Generally, the absence of precision on these questions is of little practical consequence; it will be clear that in a particular company there are, say, ordinary, preference and deferred shares, i.e. three classes, and their respective rights regarding voting, dividends, repayment of capital and to any surplus would be class rights. Bowen L.J. once announced a somewhat vague definition of class, namely, "those persons whose rights are not so dissimilar as to make it impossible for them to consult together with a view to their common interest".[54] There are three possible answers to the question of what are class rights: (1) all rights that attach to a class of shares; (2) those rights that distinguish a class from other classes; or (3) those central and fundamental rights that attach to a class, such as to vote, to dividends and to repayment of capital and a share in any surplus, as opposed to more peripheral rights. Any right vis-à-vis the company given to a group of shareholders is most likely to be a class right if it is described in the company's own regulations as such. Rights of this nature contained in a separate shareholders' agreement and not in the memorandum or articles of association are also treated as class rights.[55]

11–22   It may be that the best approach is to focus on a particular right in the company's regulations and, if it can be regarded as a class right, then the shares to which it attaches are a class, at least for the purposes of that right. This analysis was adopted in one of the few decisions that addresses the question, *Greenhalgh v Arderne Cinemas Ltd.*[56] The company's share capital was comprised of ten shillings and two shillings ordinary shares that were identical in all respects except for their nominal values. It was proposed to sub-divide each ten shillings shares into five two shillings shares, the consequence of which would be to dilute considerably the existing two shillings shares' voting power. It was held that the two kinds of ordinary shares formed one class but, on any question which arose as to voting rights or anything of that kind, the ten shillings shares formed a different class from the two shillings shares.

11–23   This issue was considered again in *Cumbrian Newspapers Group Ltd v Cumberland & Westmoreland Herald Newspaper & Printing Co. Ltd.*[57] Two newspaper companies decided to forge closer links, in the course of which the plaintiff acquired slightly more than 10 per cent of the shares in the defendant company, which altered its articles of association in such a way as would enable the plaintiff to block any attempt to take it over. That article provided that the plaintiff had rights in respect of unissued shares of the defendant, rights to override the defendant's directors' veto on registering transfers of shares, rights of pre-emption over other shares and the right, so long as it held 10 per cent of the defendant's shares, to appoint a director to the company's board. The articles also contained a class rights variation clause along the lines of

---

[54]   *Sovereign Life Assurance Co. v Dodd* [1892] 2 Q.B. 573 at 583.
[55]   *Harman v BML Group Ltd* [1994] 2 B.C.L.C. 674.
[56]   [1945] 2 All E.R. 719, aff'd [1946] 1 All E.R. 512.
[57]   [1987] Ch. 1.

Table A.[58] The company now proposed to alter its articles once more so as to cancel all of the above special rights of the plaintiff. If those were indeed class rights then the proposed alteration could not be made without the plaintiff's consent, which was not forthcoming.

11–24 In reaching a conclusion, Scott J. found some guidance in the equivalent of s.38 of the 1983 Act, which he described as "intended to provide a comprehensive code setting out the manner in which" class rights may be varied. Those rights and benefits that articles of association may confer can be divided into three main categories. One is where the rights and benefits are annexed to particular shares only; they are class rights. However, the entitlements in this case were not attached to any specific share or shares held by the plaintiff; the articles simply described the plaintiff as having the above mentioned rights, which would enable it to block a takeover bid. The 1983 Act might seem not to catch entitlements of this nature, because it speaks of "rights attached to any class of shares" when the company's shares are divided into "different classes".[59] It was held, however, that these two phrases have the same meaning and cover entitlements as just described where they are conferred on a shareholder *qua* member of the company. According to Scott J:

> "if specific rights are given to certain members in their capacity as members or shareholders, then those members become a class. The shares those members hold for the time being, and without which they would not be members of the class, would represent... a 'class of shares'.... The share capital of a company is ... divided into shares of different classes, if shareholders, qua shareholders, enjoy different rights".[60]

Therefore, the special entitlements that the articles conferred on the plaintiff constituted it a class of shareholder for the purpose of those rights and, accordingly, they could not be changed without its consent. On the other hand, where the right in question was not conferred on the individual *qua* shareholder but in some other capacity, it is not a class right. It will depend on the entire circumstances of the case what capacity the articles purport to confer the right in question.

"Variation" or "Abrogation" of Rights

11–25 As a general rule, class rights may not be "varied or abrogated" without the consent of that class. In the interests of allowing companies a degree of freedom to alter their capital structures, the courts have adopted a narrow concept of what constitutes variation or abrogation in this context, so as to place many proposed increases in, and reductions of, capital outside the veto power of classes. In particular, where a company has excess funds and wishes to repay its preference shareholders, by way of reducing the preference capital, those members' class rights have not been varied or abrogated. Instead, their right to be repaid their capital in a winding up before any of the other

---

[58] Article 3.
[59] Section 38(1).
[60] [1987] Ch.1 at 22.

shareholders can get repaid has been given effect to.[61] But this is not the case where the articles provide otherwise,[62] nor where the preference shareholders are entitled to a share in any surplus which might arise in a winding up.[63] The view appears to be that, unless the proposal involves a literal and direct alteration of a class right, it does not constitute a "variation" of the right, even though in consequence the right is significantly diminished in its relative effect or value. What seems to matter is the form and not the substance of what is done. This approach has been criticised for being unduly narrow and legalistic. However, it may be virtually redundant today in the light of modern developments in minority shareholders' rights; changes which do not amount to varying class rights may still be set aside on the grounds of "oppression".

11–26   In *White v Bristol Aeroplane Ltd*,[64] for example, the company's capital was comprised of £600,000 preference shares and £3,000,000 ordinary shares. It was proposed to increase the capital by issuing £660,000 new cumulative preference shares and £1,000,000 new ordinary shares and, additionally, that the entirety of the new issues would be distributed among the existing ordinary shareholders. The actual impact of this scheme on the existing preference shareholders' voting strength would be significant; even within their own class they would become outnumbered by the existing ordinary shareholders who would get new preference shares. Yet it was held that their class rights were not varied. A distinction was drawn between "an affecting of the rights and an affecting of the enjoyment of the rights, or of the stockholders' capacity to turn them to account"[65]; between, for instance, a direct reduction in the actual weight of a share's vote or a deprivation of the vote over a particular issue, and something that indirectly dilutes the significance of the class' voting power. For there to be a variation, the right must be "varied as a matter of law" and not just "affected as a matter of business".[66] Thus, it is possible by "upstream conversion" to undermine a class's voting rights. The following are examples drawn from cases on voting and on dividend rights.

11–27   An almost identical earlier instance is the *Arderne Cinemas* case,[67] where the company had ten shillings and two shillings ordinary shares, and where it was proposed to sub-divide the ten shillings shares into five two shillings shares. The consequences of this would be to swamp the existing two shillings shares' voting power. Assuming that the voting rights there were class rights, it was held that those were not varied because "[t]he only right of voting which is attached ... to the [two shillings] shares ... is the right to have one vote per share *pari passu* with the other ordinary shares ... for the time being issued [and] that right has not been taken away".[68]

---

[61] *House of Fraser Plc v ACGE Investments Ltd* [1987] 2 W.L.R. 1083.
[62] *Re Northern Engineering Industries Plc* [1994] 2 B.C.L.C. 704.
[63] *Cork Electric Supply Co. v Colcannon* [1932] I.R. 314.
[64] [1953] 1 Ch. 65.
[65] *ibid.* at 74.
[66] *ibid.* at 80.
[67] See fn.56 *supra*.
[68] [1946] 1 All E.R. 512 at 516.

11–28 In *Re Mackenzie & Co.*,[69] the company had 5,000 £1 preference shares and 1,500 £1 ordinary shares. A scheme to reduce capital was drawn up, in which the par value of each share would be reduced by 25p, and a further 15p per share would be returned to each shareholder. The effect of this was to reduce significantly the existing preference shareholders' income per share, while making no difference to the ordinary shareholders' expectations about income. It was held that the former's right to dividends was not thereby varied, since they remained entitled to a four per cent cumulative preference dividend on the nominal amount of their shares. The "Australian Pound" cases[70] are striking examples of a dilution of a class's dividend expectations without it infringing their actual rights to a dividend.

Power to Vary or Abrogate

11–29 Most companies' own regulations contain authority to vary or abrogate class rights, usually contingent on the class giving its consent by a special resolution of the class. Table A has a class rights variation clause to this effect.[71] Table A furthermore stipulates that two major kinds of change in capital structure shall not *ipso facto* be deemed to vary class rights in the absence of some provision to the contrary. These are the issue of additional shares ranking *pari passu* with the existing ones,[72] and the issue of new shares carrying preferential rights as regards voting, dividend, return of capital "or otherwise".[73] A number of major questions regarding a company's power to vary class rights that were the subject of some controversy have been resolved by the 1983 Act,[74] although this does not define what precisely is meant by the central concern of that section, namely, "shares of different classes", "rights attached to a class of shares" and "variation of class rights". This applies only to companies with share capital, not to guarantee companies.

11–30 The basic rule is that if, as usually is the case, the class rights attach otherwise than by way of the memorandum of association (such as by the articles or by the shares' terms of issue), any variation procedure contained in the articles must be followed.[75] However, if the class rights attach by way of the memorandum, then they can only be varied either in accordance with a procedure set down in the memorandum itself or a procedure that was in the articles from the time the company was originally incorporated.[76] If there is neither procedure, then class rights set out in the memorandum may be varied only with the consent of every member.[77]

---

[69] [1916] 2 Ch. 450.
[70] Most notably *Adelaide Electric Supply Co.* v *Prudential Assurance Co.* [1934] A.C. 122.
[71] Article 3.
[72] Article 4.
[73] Article 2.
[74] Section 38.
[75] 1983 Act, s.38(4)(b).
[76] 1983 Act, s.38(4)(a).
[77] 1983 Act, s.38(5).

11–31   One matter of dispute was whether class rights could be varied where a company's own regulations contain no express authority to vary them. Where those rights attach otherwise than by the memorandum of association, they may be varied by way of a special resolution of the class meeting separately or by written consent of at least three quarters in nominal value of that class.[78]

11–32   Another disputed issue was whether a class rights variation clause in the articles of association could itself be altered by a special resolution of the company. The old cases suggest that the answer is yes. But if this were so, it would defeat the entire logic underlying special protection for class rights. It is now provided that any alteration of the variation clause shall be treated as if it too were a variation of class rights.[79]

11–33   There then was the question of authority to vary class rights in the course of court-approved capital reductions. In one case[80] it was said that a court may permit class rights to be varied in this way even though the requisite consents under the class rights variation clause in the articles were not obtained. Some argue that this analysis is wrong and is not consistent with prior authority. A provision in the articles of association may be construed as conferring a class right not to be repaid capital without the consent of the class.[81] It is now provided that the variation may take place only with the approval of three quarters in nominal value of the class or by a special resolution of the class and, moreover, any additional requirements that are contained in the company's own regulations must be complied with.[82] This is the case even if the variation of rights clause in the articles lays down less stringent requirements. A similar rule exists for variations that ensue from giving, changing, revoking or renewing authority for the directors to allot additional securities.

Contesting the Change

11–34   Where a proposed variation of class rights obtains the requisite approval of the class affected, under the rights variation clause, dissenting shareholders representing at least 10 per cent in value of the class may apply to the court to stop the proposal being put into effect.[83] The criterion against which the court will evaluate any such application is whether, "having regard to all the circumstances of the case … the variation would unfairly prejudice the shareholders of the class represented by" the objector. That the change prejudices only the minority who are objecting most likely is not enough to have it condemned under this procedure. There is no reason, however, why any member of

---

[78]   1983 Act, s.38(2).

[79]   1983 Act, s.38(7).

[80]   *Re Holders Investment Trust* [1971] 1 W.L.R. 583. See generally, Telfer & Mitchell, "Reduction of Capital and the Rights of Minority Shareholders" 55 *Australian L.J.* 249 (1981).

[81]   *Re Northern Engineering Industries Plc* [1994] 2 B.C.L.C. 704.

[82]   1983 Act, s.38(3).

[83]   1963 Act, s.78.

the company could not, under s.205 of the 1963 Act, challenge an agreed variation on the grounds that, in all the circumstances, he is being "oppressed".

CAPITAL REDUCTION

11–35   While it is a fundamental principle of company law that contributed capital must be "maintained" in all limited companies, sound business reasons may nevertheless exist for distributing part of the capital to the shareholders or otherwise reducing capital. For instance, the company may have far more funds in its coffers than it needs to finance its business and, therefore, may prefer that the money be returned to the shareholders. Or it may not need any additional capital and, accordingly, may wish to cancel the unpaid amounts on its shares. Or trading losses may have been incurred to such extent that the figure in the balance sheet for the capital no longer represents the true position and, therefore, it is sought to write off the losses. Or an individual member or group of members may want to realise their investment and the only practical way that this can be done is for the company to repay the capital that they contributed. Since 1983, a frequent reason is to enable a company, which has accumulated past losses, to pay dividends from current profits, because the company's capital and undistributable reserves is a factor in determining whether dividends may be paid. The Companies Act of 1867[84] first responded to these needs; the 1963 Act now set out the machinery whereby, subject to confirmation by the court, a limited company may reduce or repay its capital "in any way".[85] A Plc may not reduce its capital below the authorised minimum of €38,092.14.[86] Since 1991, capital also can be repaid by the company purchasing its own shares in accordance with Part XI of the 1990 Act.[87]

11–36   In a number of leading cases decided around the turn of the 20th century, emphasis was placed on the generality of the capital reduction power. Provided that the statutory procedures are satisfied, it is for the company itself "to determine the extent, the mode, and the incidence of the reduction, and the application or disposition of any capital moneys which the proposed reduction may set free".[88] It is "no part of the business of a court of justice to determine the wisdom of a course adopted by a company in the management of its own affairs"; restrictions will not readily be implied into the "perfectly general" power to reduce capital because that would "lead to inconvenience and expense and hamper and embarrass companies in the conduct of their domestic affairs".[89] While the court retains a discretion to veto any proposed capital reduction, "if the parties to the transaction come to the conclusion that the bargain is a fair one, why should the court say that there is a preference on the one side or on the other? If there is nothing unfair or inequitable in the transaction, ... there is [no]

---

[84]   30 & 31 Vict., c.131., s.9.
[85]   Sections 72–77.
[86]   1983 Act, s.17.
[87]   Sections 206–234.
[88]   *British & American Trustee & Finance Corp. v Couper* [1894] A.C. 399 at 411–412.
[89]   *Poole v National Bank of China* [1907] A.C. 229 at 236 and 237.

objection to allowing a company ... to extinguish some of its shares without dealing in the same manner with all other shares of the same class. There may be no real inequality in the treatment of a class of shareholders although they are not paid in the same coin or in coins of the same denomination".[90] Thus there is no absolute requirement of formal or even of substantive equality for shareholders of the same class on a partial distribution of capital.

11–37 Assuming that the proper procedures were followed and the creditors' interests are sufficiently safeguarded, there are four broad grounds on which the court will nevertheless refuse to sanction a proposed reduction, namely, infringements of class rights, discrimination, disproportionality and the public interest. Confirmation by the court may be granted "on such terms and conditions as it thinks fit".[91] In particular, the court may order the company to add the words "and reduced" to its name, and to publish the reasons for the reduction and such other relevant information as directed. Every reducing resolution must be registered with the Registrar of Companies before it can become effective.[92]

Procedure

11–38 There must be separate authority in the articles of association to make the kind of reduction in question. Table A gives extensive authority for this purpose.[93] The proposal to make the reduction must be approved by a special resolution of the company.[94] In England, an application to reduce capital was heard, which had the unanimous support of the shareholders but no special resolution as such was passed.[95] The judge there allowed the reduction, but ruled that thenceforth in all similar cases that might come before the court, the company in question must go through the formalities of passing a resolution for this purpose.

11–39 For nearly a hundred years the courts have adopted a markedly restrictive approach to what are "class rights" and what constitutes a "variation" of such rights, as is demonstrated in the context of capital reductions by *In re Mackenzie & Co.*[96] and the *Wilsons & Clyde Coal* case.[97] Even where a capital reduction did amount to a variation or abrogation of those rights, there was some authority that it was not essential to have separate class approval for the reduction to go ahead,[98] although opinions were divided on this matter.[99] Another source of confusion was the status of class rights in the absence of a

---

[90] *British & American Trustee & Finance Corp. v Couper* [1894] A.C. 399 at 415–416.
[91] 1963 Act, s.74(1).
[92] 1963 Act, s.75.
[93] Article 46.
[94] *cf. Re Meux's Brewery Co.* [1918] 1 Ch. 28 on disclosure in this context.
[95] *Re Barry Artist Ltd* [1985] 1 W.L.R. 1305.
[96] [1916] 2 Ch. 450.
[97] [1949] A.C. 462. See also *Re William James & Son Ltd* [1969] 1 W.L.R. 146.
[98] *Re Holders Investment Trust* [1971] 1 W.L.R. 583.
[99] See generally, Telfer & Mitchell, "Reduction of Capital and the Rights of Minority Shareholders" 55 *Australian L.J.* 249 (1981).

variation clause along the lines of Table A.[100] These questions are now resolved by the 1983 Act, whereby class rights may not be varied in a capital reduction without the requisite class approval.[101]

11–40 Where what is being proposed is to extinguish liability in respect of unpaid capital, or to actually refund capital, or whenever the court so directs, then every creditor is entitled to object. In these cases the proposal will not be sanctioned unless every creditor consents or is paid off, or their debts are adequately secured.[102] However, in "special circumstances" the court may waive this requirement as regards a class or classes of creditors.[103] Where the capital reduction is sought on the grounds that the company has suffered a serious loss of capital, the loss must be permanent and not temporary.[104] But the court has a discretion to order a duly sanctioned capital reduction where the loss may prove to be temporary, on condition that the company gives appropriate undertakings.[105]

Disclosure

11–41 Where the notice convening the meeting or any accompanying circular contains some inaccuracy, that often is fatal to the outcome. The question is whether the shareholders or creditors, as the case may be, have been given a fair warning of exactly what was to be considered at the meeting. Exceptionally, however, it may be established that an inaccuracy would not have influenced the minds of reasonable shareholders or creditors.[106] Even where the information provided to the members is correct at the time the notices were sent, but circumstances changed between then and when the meeting was held, that is often fatal. The principle is that "material representations must not only be accurate when made but must remain the whole story when they come to be acted upon".[107]

Court Approval

11–42 Any scheme that does not provide for uniform treatment of shareholders whose rights are similar will be carefully scrutinised by the court.

Discrimination

11–43 It is not forbidden to repay only one class of shareholders. That the class which it is intended to repay could not get as favourable a return on their

---

[100] Article 3.

[101] Section 39(3); *cf. Re Hunting Plc* [2005] 2 B.C.L.C. 211.

[102] 1963 Act, ss.73(2) and 74(1).

[103] 1963 Act, s.73(3); e.g. *Re Northern Bank Ltd* [1963] N.I. 90 and *Re Ransomes Plc* [1999] 2 B.C.L.C. 591.

[104] *Re Jupiter House Investments (Cambridge) Ltd* [1985] 1 W.L.R. 975 and *Re Grosvenor Press Plc* [1985] 1 W.L.R. 980.

[105] *ibid.*

[106] *Re European Home Products Plc* [1988] B.C.L.C. 690 and *Re Heron International NV* [1994] 1 B.C.L.C. 667.

[107] *Re Minister Assets Plc* [1985] B.C.L.C. 200 at 201. See also *Re Jessel Trust Plc* [1985] B.C.L.C. 119; *Re MB Group Plc* [1989] B.C.L.C. 672 and *Re Ransomes Plc* [1999] 2 B.C.L.C. 591.

funds if invested elsewhere does not *ipso facto* prevent a company from paying them off.[108] That one class has a prior right to be repaid its capital in a winding up does not of itself entitle that class to be paid off before other classes when the company proposes to repay part of the capital.[109] Nor is it forbidden to pay off a discrete group of shareholders in one class, or even one individual member. But where preference shareholders have priority as regards repayment of capital, then *prima facie* it is unfair to repay all, or a considerable proportion of, the ordinary shares without paying anything off on the preference shares.[110]

11–44   Where the entire membership of the class that votes for a reduction is split into factions, with one group in a position of significant conflict of interests, in that it uniquely suits them for other reasons that the reduction goes ahead, then the court would tend to refuse confirmation. There is a theoretical difficulty in that shares are property rights and the classic view has been that every member is entitled to canvass his own selfish interests when voting in general meeting. However, majorities are not permitted to discriminate unfairly against minorities; especially when making major decisions about the company's structure, members are required to cast their votes for the benefit of the company as a whole.[111] An alternative ground for refusing to sanction a proposed reduction that is tainted by a significant conflict of interests, is to conclude that it affects not just one but two classes of shareholders, namely, those in the position of conflict and the other shareholders, and if the latter have not given their approval the requisite authority of a class affected was not obtained.[112] In any event, the court's veto power here is entirely discretionary.

11–45   A classic example of unfair discrimination is *Re Holders Investment Trust Ltd.*[113] The company had an issued share capital comprised of ordinary shares and five per cent cumulative preference shares which were to be redeemed in 1971. It was proposed in 1970 that those preference shares should be repaid then, by their holders being allotted the same nominal amounts of six per cent unsecured loan stock for 1985–1990. This was approved by a special resolution of the company and by a special resolution of the preference shareholders meeting as a separate class. Of the latter, approximately three per cent did not vote and seven per cent opposed the proposal; but the remaining 90 per cent which voted for it were trustees who also held over 50 per cent of the equity. From the evidence it was clear that the trustees were influenced solely by the benefit of the trust as a whole, which in the circumstances meant what was most advantageous to the equity. According to Megarry J.:

> "the question [is] whether the supporting trustees voted for the reduction in the bona fide belief that they were acting in the interests of the general

---

[108] *Re Chatterly Whitfield Collieries Ltd* [1948] 2 All E.R. 593.

[109] *Re Ransomes Plc* [1999] 2 B.C.L.C. 591.

[110] *British & American Trustee* case [1894] A.C. 399 and *Re Thomas de la Rue & Co.* [1911] 2 Ch. 361.

[111] *British American Nickel Corp. v O'Brien Ltd* [1927] A.C. 369.

[112] *cf. Re Hellenic & General Trust Ltd* [1978] 1 W.L.R. 123.

[113] [1971] 1 W.L.R. 583.

body of members of [the preference shareholders. There is] no evidence that the trustees ever applied their minds to what, under company law, was the right question, or that they ever had the bona fide belief that is requisite for an effectual sanction of the reduction".[114]

Therefore, the necessary class approval was not given.

Fairness—Proportionality

11–46 The court attempts to ensure that the very terms of the proposed reduction are not unjust as between shareholders. To this end, it has been guided by two *prima facie* principles. Where there is no preference as to a return of capital in a winding up, a reduction should fall rateably on all classes of shares.[115] Where there is a preference as to capital, any losses should be borne by those who have a last claim on the assets in a winding up.[116] But the circumstances of the case may warrant departure from these guidelines. In the end, it is the broad criterion of "fairness, reasonableness and equity" that applies.[117] Confirmation will be refused where one class or group, or individual, is being asked to bear a disproportionate sacrifice in the light of what advantages others will derive from the reduction. The courts, nevertheless, have shown considerable reluctance to reject as unfair compromises that were reached by the requisite majority of the membership. As one judge explained, when proposed reductions have "been considered, first of all by a committee consisting of businessmen chosen by the shareholders themselves, and that they have subsequently been sanctioned by large majorities at the various meetings of shareholders which have been held, it would require a very strong case to induce [a] Court to interfere".[118] The perspective from which the court views such proposals is the "common sense man-of-the-world point of view".[119] An analysis of the cases led one commentator to conclude that "in practice the reduction will always be confirmed in the absence of the very strongest evidence that it is inequitable. So long as the petitioners can give some semblance of reasonableness to their argument, the presumption in their favour is almost irrebuttable".[120] Due to the discretionary nature of the jurisdiction, the cases cannot be treated as precedents on the matter, but the following themes can be derived from some of them.

11–47 There are numerous reported instances of preference shareholders as a class being repaid in cash. In the *Wilsons & Clyde Coal Co.* case[121] and its companion case, *Re Chatterley-Whitfield Collieries Ltd,*[122] it was contended that, even if the repayments there did not vary class rights, they nevertheless were unfair in the circumstances. In the *Chatterley-Whitfield* case, the court

---

[114] [1971] 1 W.L.R. 583 at 589.

[115] *Re Barrow Haematite Steel Co.* (1888) 39 Ch.D. 582.

[116] *Re Floating Dock Co. of St Thomas* [1895] 1 Ch. 691.

[117] *Wilsons & Clyde Coal* case [1949] A.C. 462 at 462. See, e.g. *Re Quebrada Rail etc. Co.* (1889) 40 Ch.D. 363 and *Re Showell's Brewery Co.* (1914) 30 T.L.R. 428.

[118] *Re Welsback Incandescent Gas Light Co.* [1904] 1 Ch. 87 at 101.

[119] *Re Old Silkstone Collieries Ltd* [1954] 1 Ch. 169 at 189.

[120] Rice, "Capital Reduction and its Effect on Class Rights" 23 *Conv.* 244 (1959) at 258.

[121] [1949] A.C. 462.

[122] [1948] 2 All E.R. 593.

sanctioned the repayment by a cash-bloated company of its six per cent preference shares, at a time when interest rates were at an historic low, because:

> "A company which has issued preference shares carrying a high rate of
> dividend and finds its business so curtailed that it has capital surplus to
> its requirements and sees the likelihood, or at any rate the possibility, that
> its preference capital will not ... earn its keep, would be guilty of finan-
> cial ineptitude if it did not take steps to reduce its capital by paying off
> preference capital so far as the law allowed it to do so. That is mere com-
> monplace in company finance ... . The position of the company itself as
> an economic entity must be considered, and nothing can be more destruc-
> tive of a company's financial equilibrium than to have to carry the burden
> of a high rate of dividend which it cannot earn. In a company so situated,
> the ordinary shareholders will be unfairly treated *vis-à-vis* the preference
> shareholders, and the company may well fall into the situation when its
> preference dividends will begin to fall into irretrievable arrears. It is a
> fallacy to suppose that because ordinary shareholders will benefit, the
> transaction ought to be vetoed as being unfair to the preference share-
> holders."[123]

11–48 In *Wilsons & Clyde Coal Co.* the preference shareholders emphasised that 45 per cent of their class actively opposed the proposed reduction;
that the ratio between ordinary and preference shares was 13–1; that unlike
in *Chatterley-Whitfield*, the company proposed to go into liquidation shortly
afterwards, so that there was no question of the business carrying a continuing burden of relatively high dividend payments; that the proposed repayment of preference shares was designed "not in the interests of the company
but "solely in order that the ordinary stockholders may eventually appropriate 13/13ths of the surplus assets instead of 12/13ths".[124] Perhaps acting on
the then prevailing public policy of post-war reconstruction, the Law Lords
held that the scheme was fair. Contrast a very similar case that was decided
four years later,[125] where confirmation was refused because the proposed
scheme was inconsistent with representations that had been made to the preference shareholders and that they had acted upon; the scheme "involve[d] a
volte-face of which these ... stockholders can legitimately complain as
amounting to a breach of faith".[126]

11–49 Where capital is being repaid otherwise than in cash, it is not essential
that there be an exact correspondence between the amount of capital paid off
and the value of the assets used to pay it off, because in many cases it is
impossible to make any exact valuation of such assets.[127] But in the face of
objections by shareholders, the court will attempt to ensure that the consideration is, at least, not disproportionately inadequate. To this end, account is taken

---

[123] [1948] 2 All E.R. 593 at 595–596. Similarly, *Re Hunting Plc* [2005] 2 B.C.L.C. 211.
[124] Lord Morton dissenting: [1949] A.C. 462 at 508.
[125] *Re Old Silkstone Collieries Ltd* [1954] 1 Ch. 169.
[126] *ibid.* at 199. See also, *Re W. Jones & Sons Ltd* [1969] 1 W.L.R. 146 and *Re Saltdean
   Estate Co.* [1968] 1 W.L.R. 188.
[127] *Ex p. Westburn Sugar Refineries Ltd* [1951] A.C. 625 at 632–633.

of the proportions of the group in question voting for and against the proposal, and also of valuers' evidence. Thus in a case arising out of a major capital reconstruction in the mid–1930s,[128] where, *inter alia*, deferred shareholders were repaid with four ordinary shares for every deferred share, and where only one of the deferred shareholders lodged objections, it was held that "interpreting the scheme in its business sense ... the fair equivalent" was given.[129] By contrast, in *Re Holders Investment Trust Ltd*, it was concluded that, in particular, the substitution of a one-point increase in guaranteed income for a twenty-years postponement of the repayment date in the circumstances fell "substantially below the threshold of anything that can justly be called fair".[130]

11–50   One instance where the public interest was raised, *Ex parte Westburn Sugar Refineries Ltd*,[131] concerned a scheme devised to evade a feared nationalisation of the company's principal assets, sugar refineries. The proposal, which had the shareholders' unanimous consent, was that the assets should be returned to the members *in specie*. It was held that the ulterior object was no reason for the court to block the scheme – that "the contingency of nationalisation has [no] relevance to the public policy that the [court] should support".[132]

Reducing the Share Premium Account

11–51   The procedure outlined above also applies where a company wants to reduce its share premium account in any manner other than most notably by funding an issue of bonus shares.[133] In the 1980s, there were numerous court applications to reduce share premiums, principally it would appear because of Statements of Standard Accounting Practice (S.S.A.P). No. 22's treatment of "goodwill". Goodwill can be written off over time against profits or, alternatively, against reserves in the premium account to create a capital reserve which, on consolidation into group accounts, can be used to eliminate so-called goodwill. The Irish courts do not appear to have adopted any set procedure for these applications, but the practice in England is as follows.

11–52   Normally, the special resolution would provide that the capital or share premium, as it stands when the resolution is passed, shall be reduced by the specified amount. However, it is permissible to resolve that capital will be reduced in some way after it has been increased, i.e. a resolution to take effect after the contingency of an increase in capital has occurred. Because the actual reduction of capital does not take effect until the resolution is duly registered, the court will confirm a contingent resolution in those terms, provided that contingency occurs before the date of the court hearing.[134] The criteria against

---

[128] *Carruth v Imperial Chemical Industries Ltd* [1933] A.C. 707.
[129] *ibid.* at 751.
[130] [1971] 1 W.L.R. 583 at 590.
[131] [1951] A.C. 625.
[132] *ibid.* at 635; *cf. Re Data Homes Property Ltd* [1972] 2 N.Z.W.L.R. 22, where a scheme devised for tax-avoidance purposes was rejected.
[133] 1963 Act, s.62.
[134] *Re Tip-Europe Ltd* [1988] B.C.L.C. 231.

which resolutions to reduce the share premium are judged are whether proposals were properly explained to the shareholders,[135] whether the creditors' position is adequately safeguarded, whether the shareholders are treated equitably and whether the reduction is for some discernible purpose.[136]

SCHEMES OF ARRANGEMENT

11–53 A mechanism for bringing about major changes in a company's capital structure or otherwise in its constitution, that is used sometimes in conjunction with a capital reduction as described above, is the formal scheme of arrangement that obtains court approval.[137] This procedure was first adopted in the Joint Stock Companies Arrangements Act, 1870,[138] for compromises with creditors only, and in 1900 it was made applicable where the company was not in liquidation. It can be used to achieve a variety of objectives and in several different ways. It has been adopted to effect a disposal of a substantial part of the company's undertaking, such as when the Royal Automobile Club demutualised and sold its motoring business in the late 1990s.[139] At times it is used to engineer take-over bids—even where the bidder could not succeed under the normal rules.[140] More often, the company may be in financial difficulties and seeks either to eliminate one or more category of preferred or deferred shares, that prevent it from raising further capital, or to persuade creditors to exchange some or all of their claims against the company for shares in it or for less demanding obligations.

11–54 This procedure confers on super majorities in companies one of the most extensive of powers to bind minorities, to the extent of expropriating shares or rights attached to them, or requiring creditors to accept less than what the company owes them. Whether in an appropriate case they permit creditors' claims to be substituted for shares in the company is questionable because, generally, persons cannot be compelled to become shareholders. But a scheme substituting debt for equity was held to be permissible where the creditors were not obliged to take the shares in exchange for their claims.[141] The potential breadth of this procedure would give rise to constitutional and European Convention difficulties but for the broad supervisory power exercised by the court. Bowen L.J. explained its outer limits as follows: "[t]he object ... is not confiscation. It is not that one person should be a victim, and that the rest of the body should feast upon his rights. Its object is to enable compromises to be made which are for the common benefit of the creditors as creditors [or shareholders as shareholders], or the common benefit of some class... as such".[142] This

---

[135] *Re European Home Products Plc* [1988] B.C.L.C. 690.
[136] *Re Thorn EMI Plc* [1989] B.C.L.C. 612; *Re Ratners Group Plc* [1988] B.C.L.C. 685.
[137] 1963 Act, ss.201–203.
[138] 33 & 34 Vict., c. 104.
[139] *Re RAC Motoring Services Ltd* [2000] 1 B.C.L.C. 307.
[140] See para.12–51 *et seq.*
[141] *Re Empire Mining Co.* (1890) 44 Ch.D. 402.
[142] *Re Alabama etc Railway Co.* [1891] 1 Ch. 213 at 243.

procedure has been held to be compatible with the property rights guarantee in the European Convention on Human Rights.[143]

11–55   The leading Irish case, *Re John Power & Sons Ltd*,[144] concerned a distillery company that was established in 1921 with a capital of 400,000 ordinary shares of £1 par and 400,000 preference shares of £1 par, which were entitled, *inter alia*, to a cumulative preference dividend of eight per cent per annum. The company's profits continually and drastically fell during its first ten years' existence, until the directors concluded that there was no prospect of it ever earning sufficient to meet the preference dividend each year and at the same time set aside sums for depreciation. They, therefore, proposed that the nominal value of the ordinary shares be reduced to 50 pence a share and that each preference share be exchanged for a redeemable loan carrying interest at five per cent per annum. In 1933 this scheme was approved by the Supreme Court.

11–56   Where the company is in such serious difficulties that it is insolvent or nearly is, it most likely will resort instead to the court protection and examination system under the Companies (Amendment) Act 1990.[145] But if there is no immediate danger of its creditors seeking to enforce their security or levy execution on its assets, or seek to have it wound up, a scheme of arrangement may be a preferable option. For this procedure will not give the impression that the company is in severe difficulties, it does not involve a third party coming in and examining the company's entire affairs and making a detailed report on them to the court, and there is not as much running back and forth to the court involved. It can be a much less expensive procedure for the company and its creditors. On the other hand, if there is one class of creditors who will not agree to a scheme or compromise, which is acceptable to all the others, this procedure may be impracticable because, for that scheme to be adopted, any dissenting class affected must be paid off in full.[146]

Ambit

11–57   An arrangement in this context is defined as including "a reorganisation of the share capital".[147] It has been held that the term "arrangement" is of very wide import and extends to practically anything that colloquially could be called an arrangement involving a company, other than something that is *ultra vires* the company or that must be done under other special statutory procedure.[148] At a time when companies' memoranda of association could not readily be changed, it was held that this procedure could be used to change rights attached to shares by the memorandum.[149] There is no requirement that

---

[143] *Re Waste Recycling Group Plc* [2004] 1 B.C.L.C. 352.
[144] [1934] I.R. 412. Another excellent example is *Re Van Dyk Models Ltd* (1966) 100 I.L.T.R. 177.
[145] See para.24–24 *et seq.*
[146] *Re Pye (Ireland) Ltd* [1984] I.E.H.C. 56, Costello J., unreported, March 11, 1985.
[147] 1963 Act, s.201(7).
[148] *Re Guardian Assurance Co.* [1917] 1 Ch. 431.
[149] *Re Schweppes Ltd* [1914] 1 Ch. 322 and *Re City Property Investment Trust Corp.* [1951] S.L.T. 371.

there must have been some pre-existing dispute or, in a scheme involving creditors, that the company is in financial difficulty. As was observed in *Re T & N Ltd (No. 3)*,[150] which concerned a complex scheme for paying several categories of creditors with asbestos-related claims against a group of companies,

> "it is not a necessary element of an arrangement ... that it should alter the rights existing between the company and the creditors or members with whom it is made. No doubt in most cases it will alter those rights. But, provided that the context and content of the scheme are such as properly to constitute an arrangement between the company and the members or creditors concerned, it will fall within [s. 201]. It is ... neither necessary nor desirable to attempt a definition of arrangement. The legislature has not done so. To insist on an alteration of rights, or a termination of rights as in the case of schemes to effect takeovers or mergers, is to impose a restriction which is neither warranted by the statutory language nor justified by the courts' approach over many years to give the term its widest meaning. Nor is an arrangement necessarily outside the section, because its effect is to alter the rights of creditors against another party or because such alternation could be achieved by a scheme of arrangement with that other party. These considerations ... do not fetter the discretion as to whether to sanction a scheme of arrangement. The looser the connection between the subject matter of the scheme and the relationship between the company and creditors concerned, the more substantial might be the court's objections on discretionary grounds to sanctioning the scheme."[151]

11–58   However, in *Re NFU Development Trust Ltd*,[152] the court refused to convene meetings to approve a proposed scheme on the grounds, *inter alia*, that it was not an arrangement as envisaged here. Under this scheme, most memberships of a company limited by guarantee would be cancelled because those members had no interest in the company's affairs, and there would be significant costs saved by removing them. It was held that for there to be an arrangement, there must be some element of "give and take"; here what was envisaged was outright expropriation without any compensation.

11–59   Where what is being proposed involves transferring assets or liabilities between two or more companies, there must be some significant degree of continuity between the owners of both companies. In *Re Mytravel Group Plc*,[153] where the company was heavily insolvent, a debt-equity swap was negotiated. Under this, the company's assets and only some of its liabilities would be transferred to new company, the existing shareholders were to get four per cent of the issued shares in that new company, with the major creditors being allotted the other 96 per cent of those shares. No provision whatsoever was made for the holders of subordinated bonds in the company. Relying principally on cases concerning what is a "reconstruction" for tax purposes, it was

---

[150] [2007] 1 B.C.L.C. 563.
[151] *ibid.* at 585.
[152] [1972] 1 W.L.R. 1548.
[153] [2005] 2 B.C.L.C. 123.

held that this scheme was outside the statutory procedure. What is required is a scheme that "involves treating the company for these purposes as the same as its corporators. The company is reconstructed when [they] are the same in both the old and the new companies ... The undertaking of the company is, for these purposes, different from the company itself".[154]

Procedure

11–60   If a compromise or arrangement between shareholders, or between the company and creditors, or with any class of them, is proposed, an application may be made to the court to stay or restrain any "proceedings" against the company.[155] A company in financial difficulties thereby can continue in business in the expectation that some arrangement will be made with its creditors.[156] The extent to which this applies to enforcing judgments obtained against the company remains to be clarified.[157]

11–61   When the scheme has been negotiated, an application will be made to the court to summon meetings of each class of shareholders and of any classes of creditors affected. If the terms proposed are such that they would not be sanctioned by the court, if eventually put before it, the court will not even take the first step of summoning class meetings.[158] Except where the class in question consists of one member only, a meeting of two or more of them must take place.[159]

11–62   To determine who the various classes of shareholders are, the classic definition of a class in this context is that of Bowen L.J., namely, "those persons whose rights are not so dissimilar as to make it impossible for them to consult together with a view to their common interests".[160] In other words, the classes depend on whether the rights of some persons are affected by a factor as renders it not possible for them to pursue their own interests and also the interests of the broader category into which they fall. This factor may exist prior to the scheme being canvassed or it may be a very component of the scheme.

11–63   When classifying creditors for these purposes, the following criteria were adopted by a Canadian court:

> "The principles to be considered by the court in determining whether creditors have a common interest are: (a) commonality of interest should be viewed based on the non-fragmentation test, not on an identity of interest test; (b) the interests to be considered are the legal interests of the creditor *qua* creditor toward the debtor corporation and not by their rights toward each other; (c) the commonality of interests should be viewed purposively, having regard to the fact that the object of the statute

---

[154] *ibid.* at 139.
[155] 1963 Act, s.201(2).
[156] *Re John Clarke & Co.* [1912] 1 I.R. 24.
[157] Contrast with the position in an examinership; see para.24–38.
[158] *Re My Travel Group Plc* [2005] 2 B.C.L.C. 123.
[159] *Re Altitude Scaffolding Ltd* [2007] 1 B.C.L.C. 199.
[160] *Sovereign Life Assurance Co. v Dodd* [1892] 2 Q.B. 573 at 583.

is to facilitate restructuring if possible; (d) the court should resist classifications that could potentially jeopardize workable plans; (e) absent bad faith, the creditors' motivations to approve or reject the plan are irrelevant; and (f) the classification should enable creditors to consult together regarding their legal entitlement as creditors."[161]

Many of the cases involving creditors concern reorganisation of insurers' business[162]; in recent years often as a result of liabilities arising from individuals' exposure to asbestos or other pollutants.[163]

11–64   The more classes that there are, the more difficult it can become to obtain the requisite approval for a scheme. Sometimes, what appears to be a class turns out to be two separate classes on account of conflicts of interest that arose at the meeting when considering the proposed scheme.

Disclosure

11–65   Details of the proposed arrangement and an adequate explanation of its effect must be circulated to all members of the classes who would be affected.[164] That information must include a statement of any material interest the directors possess, whether as directors or as creditors or otherwise, and of any material interest of the trustees for any debenture-holders.[165] Exactly what and how much information must be supplied depends on all the circumstances; the test being whether in the overall context sufficient has been provided to enable each class member make an intelligent business decision with reference to what is being proposed. The contents of the formal statement issued may be expanded on in an accompanying circular.[166] Where it alleged that some particular piece of information ought to have been disclosed to the members, the court asks itself whether those who voted for the proposal would have acted any differently if they had been informed about those facts.

11–66   At times, circumstances change following the dispatch of notices. Where the nature of any director's interest has changed, the court will not approve the scheme unless it is satisfied that no reasonable shareholder would have altered his decision as to how to act on the scheme if he had been aware of these new circumstances. Where the change occurred before the meetings were held, there is a particularly strong onus on those supporting the scheme to prove that "knowledge of the undisclosed change in the material interests of a director of the company could not have influenced the minds of reasonable

---

[161] *Re Stelco Inc.*, 261 D.L.R. (4th) 368 at 364 (2005) (from headnote). See too *Re Telewest Communications Plc (No. 1)* [2005] 1 B.C.L.C. 752.

[162] e.g. *Re Colonia Insurance (Ireland) Ltd* [2005] 1 I.R. 497.

[163] e.g. *Re T & N Ltd* [2006] 2 B.C.L.C. 374; *Re T&N Ltd (No. 3)* [2007] 1 B.C.L.C. 563, and *Re British Aviation Insurance Co.* [2006] 1 B.C.L.C. 665 and *Re Cape Plc* [2007] 2 B.C.L.C. 546.

[164] 1963 Act, s.202.

[165] *Noakes* v *Doncaster Amalg. Colleries Co.* [1940] A.C. 1014.

[166] *Re RAC Motoring Services Ltd* [2000] 1 B.C.L.C. 307.

shareholders …"[167] In *Re Allied Domecq Plc*,[168] where the company devised a scheme whereby it would sell part of its business to one company, another company then put in a higher bid for the business, which caused the first company to resile from the proposal. Approval was then given for the sale to the second company. It was held that the scheme should not be rejected because there was no mention of the second company in the information that had been circulated. Under the terms of the scheme, as explained in the documentation, it was implicit that the mechanics for selling that part of the business were to be established, even if a sale to the first company did not go ahead. As in reductions of capital, inaccurate information supplied to the class meetings usually will cause the scheme to be rejected by the court.

Court Approval

11–67 To obtain sanction from the court, at the meetings that were summoned the scheme must be supported by at least three quarters *in value* of each class affected by it who vote, either in person or by proxy.[169] Unlike in capital reductions, therefore, a special resolution of the company as a whole or a special resolution of those in each class who vote is not enough. Approval will be refused where the proposals adopted cannot fairly be described as a scheme as envisaged by the Act. Where in reality there is no *quid pro quo* worth speaking of, then the proposal does not even qualify as a scheme, because a member "whose rights are expropriated without any compensating advantage is not … having his rights rearranged in any legitimate sense of that expression".[170] Approval also will be refused where there was not sufficient disclosure.

11–68 At times, it is only at the stage when the class meeting is held that sufficient disparity of interests comes to light, which warrants concluding that there are two or more discrete classes, at least one of whom has not given the requisite approval. In *Re Hellenic & General Trust Ltd*,[171] an arrangement was proposed whereby all of the company's existing shares would be cancelled, new shares in it would be issued to a merchant bank that owned the company's 53 per cent majority shareholder (MIT), and the remaining shareholders would be paid off in cash. The proposal was approved by 84 per cent of the members in value; one member, a foreign bank with 14 per cent of the shares, voted against. That bank contended that the requisite class majority had not been obtained because MIT had a major conflict of interests, in that the object of the scheme was that its parent company should acquire all the shares in the investment trust. It was held that in the circumstances there were two classes—MIT and the other shareholders—and, since three quarters of the latter did not endorse the scheme, it could not go ahead. According to Templeman J., the merchant bank "are purchasers making an offer. When the vendors meet to discuss and vote whether or not to accept the offer, it is incongruous that the loudest voice in theory and the most significant

---

[167] *Re Jessell Trust Ltd* [1985] B.C.L.C.119 at 126.
[168] [2000] 1 B.C.L.C. 134.
[169] 1963 Act, s.201(3).
[170] *Re NFU Development Trust Ltd* [1972] 1 W.L.R. 1548 at 1555.
[171] [1976] 1 W.L.R. 123.

vote in practice should come from the wholly owned subsidiary of the purchaser. No one can be both a vendor and a purchaser and ... for the purpose of the class meeting [here], MIT were in the camp of the purchaser".[172]

11–69   In much the same way as it deals with reductions of capital, the court will not sanction an arrangement where the terms are unfair or disproportionate. The court will satisfy itself that "the proposal is such that an intelligent and honest man, a member of the class concerned and acting in respect of his interest, might reasonably approve".[173] On numerous occasions the following summary of its approach has been adopted:

> "In exercising its powers of sanction the court will see, first, that the provisions of the statute have been complied with, second, that the class was fairly represented by those who attended the meeting and that the statutory majority are acting *bona fide* and are not coercing the minority in order to promote interests adverse to those of the class whom they purport to represent, and thirdly that the arrangement is such as an intelligent and honest man, a member of the class concerned and acting in respect of this interest might reasonably approve.
>
> The court does not sit merely to see that the majority are acting *bona fide* and thereupon to register the decision of the meeting, but at the same time, the court will be slow to differ from the meeting, unless either the class has not been properly consulted, or the meeting has not considered the matter with a view to the interests of the class which it is empowered to bind, or some blot is found in the scheme."[174]

11–70   Another statement of the governing principle is that of Bowen L.J., that

> "a compromise or arrangement which has to be sanctioned by the court must be reasonable, and no arrangement or compromise can be said to be reasonable in which you can get nothing and give up everything. A reasonable compromise must be a compromise which can, by reasonable people conversant with the subject, be regarded as beneficial to those on both sides who are making it. Now, I have no doubt at all that it would be improper for the Court to allow an arrangement to be forced on any class.., if the arrangement cannot reasonably be supposed by sensible business people to be for the benefit of that class as such ..."[175]

11–71   Whether or not an exchange of old for new interests in, or claims against, the company is adequate turns on the circumstances of the case, account being taken of objective valuations, of the proportions of the class concerned that voted in support of and against the proposal, and any sizeable though not fatal conflict of interests in the class. In *Re John Power & Sons*

---

[172] *ibid.* at 136.
[173] *Re Dorman Long & Co.* [1934] 1 Ch. 635 at 657.
[174] *Buckley on the Companies Acts*, 14th edn (London: Butterworths, 1981), pp.473–474.
[175] *Re Alabama etc. Railway Co.* [1891] 1 Ch. 213 at 243.

Ltd,[176] for instance, the proposal to replace eight per cent cumulative preference shares with an equal amount of five per cent redeemable debentures had the support of nine tenths of the preference shareholders and three quarters of them did not own ordinary shares. The court rejected the suggestion that debt ought never to be simply substituted for equity in these schemes; it accepted that, in the circumstances, the proposed scheme there was fair. That the scheme permits future variation of some of its substantive provisions regarding creditors is not a reason for rejecting it, where there is a clear need for it and the creditors' interests are sufficiently safeguarded.[177]

11–72   Although in the past courts have leaned in favour of sanctioning any compromise where adequate information was provided and where there was no unacceptable conflict of interests, on the grounds that the statutory majorities are themselves the best judges of whether a scheme is a reasonable one for their class, there are indications that judges today assess these schemes more critically.[178] In *Re British Aviation Insurance Co.*,[179] which involved an insurer against which claims had been made arising from exposure to asbestos and other pollutants, Lewison J. observed that no case in the UK courts had been found "in which the court, having decided that it had jurisdiction to sanction a scheme, nevertheless refused as a matter of discretion to do so".[180] But the scheme there was rejected because of the manner in which some of the insurers' claims were valued, which affected voting strengths; an excessively wide discretion the scheme would confer on the company; and the effect of the scheme was to unfairly transfer the risk of exposure to claims back to the insured parties.

11–73   Once the requisite majority of each class votes for a scheme, which obtains court approval, it binds all the members of that class and the company.[181] The court, however, is empowered to order that provision be made for persons who dissent from what their class agreed to.[182] The scheme takes effect once a copy of the court's sanction is delivered to the Registrar of Companies.[183]

Facilitating the Scheme

11–74   Where the scheme sanctioned is for a "reconstruction" of one or more companies or an "amalgamation" of two or more companies, and involves the transfer of property or of the undertaking between companies, the court possesses extensive powers to make orders that facilitate making the scheme effective.[184] These orders include the transfer of the transferor company's assets or liabilities, allocating shares or debentures in the transferee company,

---

[176] [1934] I.R. 412.
[177] *Re Cape Plc* [2007] 2 B.C.L.C. 546.
[178] e.g. *El Pollo NZ Ltd* [1990] 1 N.Z L.R. 356 and *Re National Dairy Association of New Zealand Ltd* [1987] 2 N.Z.L.R. 607.
[179] [2006] 1 B.C.L.C. 665.
[180] *ibid.* at 685.
[181] 1963 Act, s.201(3).
[182] 1963 Act, s.203(1)(e).
[183] 1963 Act, s.201(5).
[184] 1963 Act, s.203.

and dissolving a transferor company without winding it up. Property in this context is defined as including "property, rights and powers of every description", and liabilities as including duties. But the court does not have the power to order the transfer of rights and duties under an employment contract.[185]

LIQUIDATION MERGER/RESTRUCTURING

11–75   A method of bringing about major changes in a company's capital structure or constitution, that has existed since 1862, is what may be called a merger/restructuring that involves liquidating the company.[186] There is no definition of the kinds of schemes that fall within this procedure. It can be used, for example, to bring about a straightforward merger, to segregate liquid assets from the rest of the business or for other purposes. However, something that is *ultra vires* the company or that must be done under some special statutory procedure cannot be accomplished in this way. Nor can class rights be varied without the requisite class approval.[187] Nor can creditors' rights be adversely affected.[188] The principal advantage for companies in proceeding in this way is that a mere special resolution of the company as a whole suffices to initiate the scheme and there is no requirement of court approval.[189] On the other hand, the procedure requires that dissenters be bought off in cash and that the company be wound up.

Procedure

11–76   A company's liquidator is empowered to sell its assets, usually for cash. But where by way of special resolution the members so agree, he may sell those assets for securities of one kind or another, and then distribute these securities among the members. This procedure can be used to change a company's constitution or rearrange its capital structure. First, a new company, which need not be registered under the 1963–2006 Acts, is created with the desired regulations or structure. The old company then, having resolved to be wound up voluntarily, authorises its liquidator to transfer its undertaking to the new company in return for stock, shares, debentures or other interests in the new company. These securities are then distributed to the old company's shareholders in accordance with their capital rights in it. It then goes into liquidation. Thus, when the smoke clears the old company has been transformed into one with a different constitution or capital structure. Where a company is already in voluntary liquidation, these transactions can be carried out at any time.

Dissent

11–77   Shareholders who dissent from the special resolution adopting such a scheme are entitled to be bought out for cash if the liquidator decides to go

---

[185] *Noakes* v *Doncaster Amalgamated Collieries Co.* [1940] A.C. 1014.
[186] 1963 Act, s.260.
[187] *Griffith* v *Paget* (1877) 5 Ch. D 894 and *Re Sandwell Park Colliery Co.* [1914] 1 Ch. 584.
[188] If the company is insolvent, the committee of inspection or the court must consent.
[189] But *cf.* 1963 Act, s.260(7).

ahead with it.[190] Notice of such dissent must be left with the liquidator within seven days of the special resolution being passed.[191] Where the securities being received are not traded on a stock exchange, valuation can be difficult. It has been held that a dissenter is not entitled to examine the company's books or the directors in an attempt to show the value of the shares[192]; although these decisions might now fall foul of the Constitution. Where the price cannot be agreed upon, it must be fixed by independent arbitration.[193] An alternative for an objector is to apply to the court to have the company compulsorily wound up. If the court so orders, then the entire transaction will require its approval and, unless so approved, the assets must be sold for cash.[194]

11–78   A device once used to deprive dissident shareholders of their full right of appraisal—having a provision in the company's own regulations whereby it was sought to contract out of the statutory mechanism—was permitted in some circumstances until it was condemned in a number of cases, culminating in *Bisgood v Henderson's Transvaal Estates Ltd*.[195] One of the company's objects was said to be to sell all its property or the undertaking and to distribute the proceeds among the shareholders *in specie*. It was resolved that the entire undertaking be sold to a new company, that the first company be wound up and that the partly paid shares received in the sale be distributed among its members on a *pro rata* basis. But instead of being paid cash immediately, dissenters were to receive the proceeds from the sale of those shares in the new company that they would not take up. It was contended that this was merely carrying out one of the company's objects. Buckley L.J., however, held that any such object was invalid because objects under the Companies Acts can have "no relation to acts to be done after the corporate life has come to an end" and cannot "define... the distribution of the assets after the corporate life is over".[196] Although a company's own regulations may within limits provide how its assets are to be dealt with following liquidation, they cannot provide that a shareholder "shall not enjoy the rights and immunities which the statute gives him",[197] such as to appraisal. Furthermore, the proposals contravened the equivalent of s.27 of the 1963 Act because they sought to "impose upon [each] member the alternative of accepting liability for a larger sum or of being dispossessed of his status as a shareholder upon terms which he is not bound to accept ..."[198]

REMOVAL OF SHAREHOLDERS

11–79   There are a variety of ways in which shareholders can cease to be members of a company, either voluntarily or against their wishes. Except where

---

[190] 1963 Act, s.260(3).

[191] *cf. Braily v Rhodesia Consolidated* [1910] 2 Ch. 95.

[192] *Re British Building Stone Co.* [1908] 2 Ch. 450.

[193] 1963 Act, s.260(6), which incorporated the arbitration procedure under the Companies Clauses Consolidation (Scotland) Act 1845.

[194] *Re Consolidated South Rand Mines Deep Ltd* [1909] 1 Ch. 491.

[195] [1908] Ch. 743.

[196] *ibid.* at 757–758.

[197] *ibid.* at 758.

[198] *ibid.* at 759.

restricted by provisions in the articles of association, they are free to transfer their shares to whoever is willing to take their place.[199] Where the requirements of Pt XI of the 1990 Act[200] are satisfied, they may even sell their shares to the company or to its holding company, or have their shares redeemed by the company.

11–80 Compulsory acquisitions of a member's shares and thereby his expulsion from the company may be effected in several ways where such a power is conferred in the articles of association. Where a company seeks to amend its articles of association to give itself such a power, against the objections of one or more members, the wider the power being sought, the stronger the justification that will be required.[201] Comparison can be made between, on the one hand, a power to expropriate to pay for debts due by a member to the company and, on the other, an almost unbounded discretion to expropriate, which only in the most exceptional circumstances would withstand a court challenge to the special resolution.

11–81   At times, a member's loss of his shareholding will be automatic on the occurrence of an event specified in the articles; for instance where he is removed from office as director or he ceases employment with the company or with a group company.[202] Table A grants companies a lien over their shares in respect of members' liabilities to them, which may be exercised by the directors transferring those shares to a purchaser and the company recouping itself from the proceeds.[203]

11–82 As compared with the question of the directors refusing to register transfers of shares, there is scant authority on companies invoking expulsion powers contained in their articles. Where that power is conferred on the directors, they must exercise it in accordance with the fiduciary standards of bona fides and proper purpose. But where the power is formulated in wholly discretionary terms, it has not been settled on what grounds exercises of it will be impeached. In the only reported Irish case on the matter, *Walsh v Cassidy*,[204] the "family" company's regulations authorised directors to expropriate any member who is "employed in the company in any capacity [and who] ceases to be so employed by [it]". It is implicit in Kingsmill Moore J.'s judgment that such a power should be construed as narrowly as is reasonably possible. He suggested that the clause there might not authorise expelling a member who acquired shares for full value and who subsequently took up some employment in the company. But he emphasised that an expulsion falling four square within the clause's terms would not be set aside merely because it would result in considerable hardship. On the other hand, "fraudulent" exercises of the power would be restrained.

11–83   Exercise of an expulsion power by the members in general meeting was considered in *Phillips v. Manufacturers' Securities Ltd*,[205] which

---

[199] 1963 Act, s.79.
[200] Sections 206–234.
[201] See para.10–33 *et seq.*
[202] e.g. *Holt v Faulks* [2000] 2 B.C.L.C. 816.
[203] Articles 11–14.
[204] [1951] Ir. Jur. Rep. 47.
[205] (1917) 116 L.T. 290.

concerned a non-profit federation of manufacturers. In a move to assert its authority and even though its shares were worth around £1.00 each, it was resolved to transfer the plaintiff's shares to other members on a *pro rata* basis for one shilling per share. There was a power in the articles whereby the members "may, by resolution … determine that the shares of any member shall… be offered for sale … to the other members" at a price of not less than one shilling. There was no evidence supporting an allegation of fraud, and the contention that the resolution should be struck down because it was motivated by "malicious intention" was rejected with a reference to *Bradford Corp. v Pickles*.[206] The matter was treated as essentially one of construction of the articles; what happened there fell squarely within their terms, and the evidence indicated that the majority reasonably believed that the resolution was in furtherance of the objects of the company and therefore for its benefit.

11–84   As is explained above, there are two statutory procedures under which members may be deprived of their shares. In the case of court-approved capital reductions and schemes of arrangement, super majorities of each class affected is required and court approval will be refused if there is something intrinsically unfair in the proposal. Where a company is being wound up, an inevitable consequence is that membership of it must cease. But if the liquidator disposes of its assets for shares in another company, those shares may be substituted for shares in the liquidating company. Where a company is the subject of a successful takeover bid, with the bidder acquiring over 80 per cent of its equity (or 90 per cent if shares are listed on the Stock Exchange), he may compulsorily buy out those who refused to accept the bid.[207]

RE-REGISTRATION

11–85   Occasionally it is sought to transform a private company into a public company, or a public company into a private one, or that a limited company become unlimited, or *vice versa*. Certain companies that were not formed under the Companies Acts may register as companies under these Acts.

Going Public

11–86   The public limited company, or Plc, was inaugurated by the 1983 Act. Public companies[208] that existed then and had limited liability were required to become Plcs or else to re-register under some other form.[209]

11–87   For a private limited company to become a Plc, a special resolution to this effect, appropriately altering the company's memorandum and articles of association, must be passed and a statutory declaration, together with various documents (such as the amended regulations, a balance sheet, an auditors' statement and report), must be delivered to the Registrar of Companies.[210] The

---

[206] [1895] A.C. 587.
[207] See para.12–42 *et seq.*
[208] i.e. whose articles did not satisfy s.33 of the 1963 Act.
[209] 1983 Act, ss.12 and 13.
[210] 1983 Act, s.9 and Forms 71 and 72.

company must be financially healthy, in that its net assets must exceed the aggregate of its called up share capital and its undistributed reserves.[211] There must be a written statement from the company's auditors to this effect, supported by a balance sheet dated within seven months of the application to re-register and an unqualified report of the auditors in relation to the balance sheet. In the meantime, the net assets must have not fallen below the called up capital and undistributable reserves. The statutory declaration must state that the allotted share capital is not less than €38,092; that a quarter of the nominal amount, together with any premium, was paid up on those shares; where the consideration for any shares allotted was performing work or services, that due performance was already made; where such consideration was some other undertaking, that it either has been discharged or that there is a contract to have it performed within five years.

11–88   In the case of private unlimited companies seeking transformation, the procedure just described for becoming Plcs must be followed, but the special resolution to change the company's share capital will be that the members' liability is limited by shares, and to make other appropriate changes to the company's own regulations.[212]

Going Private

11–89   A private company is one the regulations of which place a ceiling of 99 on its membership, which restricts the right to transfer its shares and which forbids invitations to the public to subscribe for its securities.[213] For Plcs to "go private", a special resolution must be passed taking all reference to being a Plc out of the memorandum of association and altering the articles so as to bring in these prohibitions; an application to re-register, together with a copy of the company's amended regulations, must be delivered to the Registrar of Companies.[214] Shareholders who object to this change of status can apply to the court to cancel or vary the special resolution.[215] The court has an extensive discretion in dealing with such applications and may make such relevant orders as it thinks fit, including appraisal of dissident members' shares.

Going Limited

11–90   Machinery to enable unlimited companies to transform themselves into organisations with limited liability was first introduced following the celebrated City of Glasgow bank crash,[216] and shortly afterwards was availed of by many banks to protect their shareholders from financial disaster. To avail of limited liability, a special resolution must be passed, altering the company's own regulations in the appropriate places, and an application to re-register, together with a copy of the amended regulations, must be made to the Registrar

---

[211] 1983 Act, s.9(3)(b) and (e)(ii).
[212] 1983 Act, s.11 and Forms 71 and 72.
[213] 1963 Act, s.33.
[214] 1983 Act, s.14 and Form 76. See *Smith's Precedents*, Pts 15 and 17.
[215] 1983 Act, s.15.
[216] *cf. Houldsworth v City of Glasgow Bank* (1880) 3 App. Cas. 317.

of Companies.[217] If, however, the company is wound up within three years of its going unlimited, any past member who was a member when it re-registered can be held liable to contribute to the company's assets in respect of obligations incurred before that time.[218]

Going Unlimited

11–91   There are certain advantages that accrue from unlimited liability status.[219] For limited companies to go unlimited, every member of the company must agree to this change of status and there must be delivered to the Registrar of Companies the prescribed form of assent by or on their behalf, a statutory declaration that they assented, and a copy of the appropriately changed memorandum and articles of association.[220]

Unregistered Companies

11–92   Certain companies that are not registered under the Companies Acts of 1862, of 1908 or of 1963 may register under the 1963–2006 Acts.[221] These are companies with seven or more members, with a registered office or principal place of business in the State and either are joint stock companies in existence since November 1862 or were formed since then under some other private Act or under letters patent, or are otherwise duly constituted by law. However, if the company's members' liability is limited by statute or the letters patent, it cannot avail of this procedure. For joint stock companies, the requisite majority to authorise registration is a majority in general meeting; for companies constituted by an Act or by letters patent, it is three quarters of the members voting in general meeting. Relevant details regarding the company must be given to the Registrar of Companies and verified by a statutory declaration.[222] A joint stock company may register as a Plc by delivering to the Registrar a copy resolution approving that change of status, certain reports regarding the company's financial status and the prescribed statutory declaration.[223]

11–93   On being re-registered as a Plc or otherwise, all provisions regulating the company contained in the constituting Act or instrument shall be treated as if contained in its memorandum and articles of association. But the company cannot alter any of these provisions unless that constituting measure permitted such alteration.[224] On being registered, all obligations, contracts and debts of the old entity bind the company, and all actions and legal proceedings by or against it continue with the company.[225]

---

[217] 1983 Act, s.53 and Form 86. See *Smith's Precedents*, Pts 17 and 18.
[218] 1983 Act, s.53(7).
[219] See para.16–13 *et seq.*
[220] 1983 Act, s.52 and Form D.6. See *Smith's Precedents*, Pt 19.
[221] Pt IX (ss.328–343) of the 1963 Act.
[222] 1963 Act, ss.330–333.
[223] 1983 Act, s.18 and Forms 78 and 79.
[224] 1963 Act, s.340.
[225] 1963 Act, ss.338 and 339.

CHAPTER 12

TAKEOVERS AND MERGERS

12–01 By takeovers and mergers[1] is meant where a company (or exceptionally an individual) acquires control of another company, or where two or more companies amalgamate. There are no general definitions for these terms in the Companies Acts.[2] For the purposes of the Irish Takeover Panel Act 1997, which regulates takeovers of and by companies listed on the Irish Stock Exchange, a takeover is defined as:

> "(a) any agreement or transaction (including a merger) whereby or in consequence of which control of a relevant company is or may be acquired; or
> (b) any invitation, offer or proposal made, or intended or required to be made, with a view to concluding or bringing about such an agreement or transaction."[3]

12–02 Transactions of this nature can be brought about in significantly different ways. For instance, one company may simply sell its entire undertaking to another—either for cash or for securities in that other company.[4] A common method is where one company simply acquires most or all of the shares in another company, so that the latter becomes a subsidiary of the former.[5] Under this, where B Co. (call it the "bidder") wishes to take over or merge with T Co. (call it the "target"), B Co. will make an offer to T Co.'s shareholders to buy their shares in T. The consideration offered may be cash or a new issue of B Co.'s own shares, or some combination of B Co.'s own shares, cash and debt. Where all or most of the consideration being offered is shares in the bidder, then the target's shareholders are being asked to exchange their shares in T Co. for those in B Co.; if they accept and depending on the relative sizes of the companies, they may end up owning a significant stake in B Co. It is usual where the target's shares are widely dispersed to make the offer conditional on a certain proportion of its shareholders accepting—either 50 or 75

---

[1] See generally, B. Clarke, *Takeovers and Mergers Law in Ireland* (Dublin: Round Hall Sweet & Maxwell, 1999); G. Eaborn, *Butterworth's Takeovers: Law and Practice* (London: Lexis Nexis, 2005); Weinberg and Blank, *Takeovers and Mergers*, 5th edn (London: Sweet & Maxwell, 1989); R. Kraakman et al, *The Anatomy of Corporate Law: A Comparative and Functional Approach* (Oxford: Oxford University Press, 2006), Ch.2.

[2] *cf.* 1983 Act, s.30(4).

[3] s.1(1).

[4] *cf. BCM Precedents* part B 127 *et seq.*

[5] *cf. BCM Precedents* part B 1 *et seq.*

or 80 or 90 per cent. The bidder, therefore, does not have to acquire any of those shares unless there were sufficient acceptances as will guarantee the degree of control he wants. A mechanism exists where it is sought to sell the undertaking for shares in the acquiring company and then distribute those securities to the seller's own shareholders.[6] The procedure for court-authorised arrangements[7] can be used to take over or merge with another company.

12–03 At times these transactions are structured through subsidiary companies, specially incorporated for the purpose. Sometimes takeovers are instigated by the company's existing management, who believe that they can run its business even more efficiently: what are described as "management buy-outs". In the case of publicly quoted companies, a takeover may involve it "going private", by the acquirer getting all or most of the voting shares and then de-listing the company. In the case of private companies, takeovers of one kind or another may be motivated principally by tax considerations. Takeovers almost invariably involve major changes in the acquired company and often in the buyer itself and, accordingly, may be resisted strenuously by some shareholders in those companies. At times, shareholders and managements can make sizeable profits out of these transactions. Takeover bids for companies whose shares are traded on a stock exchange occasionally become bitter battles between rival managements and even attract extensive press coverage.[8]

12–04 All that the Companies Acts dictate about takeovers generally is the requirement that directors of companies being taken over disclose any special compensation arrangements they may have with the acquiring parties and, secondly, granting the power to expropriate the shares of a small minority who have refused to accept a bid. The E.C.'s Tenth Company Law Directive on cross-border mergers[9] is due to be implemented by December 13, 2007. Additional rules affecting takeovers of listed companies, in particular the activities of the Irish Takeover Panel and the regime under the European Communities (Takeover Bids Directive 2004/25/EC) Regulations 2006,[10] are considered separately in the discussion of public companies. Although the Irish Stock Exchange's requirements concerning takeovers may not strictly be "law", from time to time courts take account of them when determining the legal position in respect of unquoted companies.[11] Takeovers and mergers involving large firms, whether or not they are quoted on a stock exchange, are also subject to Pt 3 (ss.16–28) of the Competition Act 2002, which is designed to prevent the undue concentration of economic power by way of monopoly and the like.[12] Where the transaction has an intra-EC element, it also is subject to Regulation

---

[6] 1963 Act, s.260

[7] 1963 Act, s.201.

[8] e.g. "Hedge funds hold power in battle for Irish Continental Group", *Sunday Times*, June 24, 2007, p.3,

[9] Directive 2005/56, [2005] O.J.L.142/12.

[10] SI 2006/255.

[11] e.g. *Fiske Nominees Ltd v Dwyka Diamonds Ltd* [2002] 2 B.C.L.C. 123.

[12] See generally, A. McCarthy & V. Power, *Irish Competition Law: the Competition Act, 2002* (Haywards Heath: Tottel Publishing, 2007).

139/2004 on the control of concentration between undertakings.[13] Special provisions exist to facilitate completion of takeovers and acquisitions of banks and insurers,[14] building societies[15] and industrial and provident societies.[16]

AUTHORITY AND DISCLOSURE

12–05   Where a company is required to alter its objects clause in order lawfully to engage in some new form of activity, it must also extend those objects where it intends to merge completely with another concern that is already empowered to engage in that activity. In *Hennessy v National Agricultural & Industrial Development Association*,[17] an agreed amalgamation between two non-profit companies was held to be invalid because, *inter alia*, their combined activities would be *ultra vires* one of them. Presumably, if a company acquired all or virtually all the shares in another that carried on a completely different business, the newly acquired business would have to fall within the purchaser's objects. But it is not clear whether acquisition of, say, 50 per cent or 75 per cent of the shares in another company would be treated as carrying on that company's business for the purpose of vires considerations.

12–06   Where all or some of the consideration being offered by the bidder is its own shares, the requirement of shareholders' prior authority to issue them has to be satisfied.[18] Where the transaction takes the form of the company issuing its shares to the bidder, in return for cash or other assets it will put into the business, the statutory pre-emption regime also must be complied with.[19] *CAS Nominees Ltd v Nottingham Forest FC Plc*[20] concerned a football club in the English Premier Division that was facing relegation to a lower division, where its business would be far less profitable. To turn around its fortunes, it needed substantial investment. Eventually the directors found an investor but he would only get involved if he were to obtain full control of the club. The company that owned the club was a wholly owned subsidiary of the defendant, a listed company. But because members who were strongly opposed to the investment controlled about 25 per cent of its issued shares, a special resolution to bypass the pre-emption requirement[21] would not have passed. Instead, it was decided that the investor would be issued new shares in the subsidiary, sufficient to give him control of it and, as the company's directors had full control of the subsidiary, pre-emption would not then present a difficulty. In a petition for "oppression", the objectors contended that this was a breach of the directors' duty, which deprived them of the substance

---

[13]   [2004] OJ L 24/1; see generally, E. Navarro *et al, Merger Control in the EU: Law, Economics and Practice*, 2nd edn (Oxford: Oxford University Press, 2005).
[14]   See para.16–24 and 16–27.
[15]   Building Societies Act 1989, Pt X, ss.95–99.
[16]   *cf. Stansell Ltd v Co-operative Group (Cons) Ltd* [2006] 1 W.L.R. 1704.
[17]   [1947] I.R. 159.
[18]   1983 Act, s.20.
[19]   1983 Act, s.23.
[20]   [2002] 1 B.C.L.C. 613.
[21]   1983 Act, s.24.

of their pre-emption entitlements. But it was held that, in all the circumstances, the directors were seeking to achieve a proper purpose and that "the accident that the business activities were carried on in the wholly owned subsidiary, the club, opened the way to the solution that was adopted, [which] achieved the same economic effect as an injection of capital at the level of the company would have achieved, and avoided the obstacle of a special resolution".[22] The contention that there was some understanding between all the shareholders that pre-emption rights would not be bypassed in this manner was rejected, as was the contention that those rights were subject to some overall anti-avoidance requirement which was not expressed in the statute.

12–07 An argument can be made that a majority of the shareholders in a company with regulations along the lines of Table A, art.80, are entitled, by ordinary resolution, to veto a "strategic" decision by the directors to take over or merge with another company. *Automatic Self-Cleansing Filter Syndicate v Cunninghame*[23] does not preclude this view and there are weighty practical arguments in its favour. Where a takeover requires alteration of the bidder's objects clause or is carried out under ss.260 or 201 of the 1963 Act, then the requisite shareholder approval must be obtained. Such approval is also required for substantial takeovers being made by companies with securities listed on the Irish Stock Exchange.[24]

12–08 Details of "golden handshakes" given in the context of takeovers and mergers must be disclosed to the shareholders.[25] Additionally, the courts have always insisted that information provided by directors to shareholders, with a view to obtaining the latter's approval for a takeover or merger, or their consent to measures taken to resist a bid, should not be misleading. Resolutions passed on foot of misleading information will be declared invalid, as may agreements entered into that were connected with such resolutions. For instance, in *Kaye v Croydon Tramways Co.*,[26] where payments made by the acquiring company to the defendant's directors were not disclosed, the agreement to sell the defendant's undertaking and the special resolution purporting to authorise that sale were held to be void and unenforceable, resulting in an injunction restraining the agreement from being carried out.

12–09 If some material misrepresentation is made to the target company's shareholders and they act on it to their detriment, they may have a claim for deceit or for negligent misrepresentation under the general law of contract and tort.[27] Not infrequently where successful bidders discover that they have acquired a "pig in a poke", they sue either valuers they have engaged to perform

---

[22] [2002] 1 B.C.L.C. 613 at 630.
[23] [1906] 2 Ch. 34.
[24] See para.15–131.
[25] See para.12–36 *et seq.*
[26] [1896] 1 Ch. 358.
[27] e.g. *Northern Bank Finance Corp. v Charleton* [1979] I.R. 149 (deceit), *Securities Trust v Hugh Moore & Alexander Ltd* [1964] I.R. 417 and *Partco Group Ltd v Wragg* [2002] 2 B.C.L.C. 323 (negligence).

"due diligence" or the target company's auditors, seeking damages for negligence.[28] It was held in *Pilmer v Duke Group Ltd*[29] that, where new shares are issued and allotted to pay for the target company's shares, the successful bidder cannot recover damages if it transpires that the target had been substantially over valued. Relying on valuations made by the defendant accountants, the plaintiff took over a company, the consideration being cash and 67.9 million fully paid AUS $1 shares. Shortly afterwards, there was a dramatic fall in stock prices on exchanges around the world. It was held that the defendant owed the plaintiff a duty of care and also that it had been negligent in overvaluing the target. Had the plaintiff paid cash entirely for the target or had it furnished consideration other than its own shares, it would have recovered damages. But because the principal consideration was its own shares, it had not lost anything, as it could not have lawfully traded in its own shares. In other words, in calculating what damages may be payable, the basis for valuation was the price of its shares in the market. But because companies are not permitted to trade in their own shares, the plaintiff could not have realised that value for the shares it had issued. Granted, the plaintiffs' shareholders were substantial losers but they were not parties to the action. It remains to be seen how proceedings they might have brought would have fared under the "reflective loss" principle.[30]

12–10   While directors owe a fiduciary duty to their company, ordinarily they have no such duty to the company's shareholders, even when a takeover is taking place. Their position vis-à-vis the members in this context has been summed up as follows–there is:

> "no good reason why it should be supposed that directors are, in general, under a fiduciary duty to shareholders, and in particular current shareholders with respect to the disposal of their shares in the most advantageous way … If on the other hand directors take it on themselves to give advice to current shareholders, … they have a duty to advise in good faith and not fraudulently, and not to mislead, whether deliberately or carelessly. [This is] a potential liability arising out of their words or actions which can be based on ordinary principles of law".[31]

12–11   However, there can be a fiduciary duty to minority shareholders in exceptional circumstances, for instance where they are being "frozen out" by the management who also are majority shareholders. In *Coleman v Myers*,[32] the target's managing director, who was also the purchaser of its shares, was held responsible in damages to the sellers for not disclosing the extent of the profit he stood to make from the acquisition. The plaintiffs, who had been minority shareholders in a "close" company, sold their shares to the defendant, its managing director, which enabled him to secure control of the company. He knew that the company's assets were worth far more than their stated value in

---

[28] See para.17–34 *et seq.*
[29] [2001] 2 B.C.L.C. 773.
[30] See para.22–47 *et seq.*
[31] *Dawson International Plc v Coats Patons Plc* [1989] B.C.L.C. 233 at 243–244.
[32] [1977] 2 N.Z.L.R. 225.

the accounts and, on buying the shares, he had some of those assets sold off and the proceeds distributed as dividends (going principally to himself). It was concluded that he owed a duty of the utmost good faith not alone to the company but to the shareholders in the special circumstances of the case— which were the closely held nature of the company, the degree of confidence that existed between the parties and the extent to which the plaintiffs depended on him for information, the extent of his personal interest in the transaction and its very significance. Analogy was drawn with contract cases where bargains made are stuck down on account of undue influence and inequality of bargaining power.[33] Although there is nothing inherently wrong in directors making a profit when dealing directly with shareholders,[34] where their relations with shareholders are sufficiently intense to assume a fiduciary character the directors must "disclose material matters [of] which [they] know or have reason to believe that the shareholders whom they are trying to persuade to sell are or may be inadequately informed".[35] The defendant had not done this and, in any event, it was found that he had been guilty of fraud in having deliberately misrepresented his intentions and the value of the company's assets. As for the appropriate remedy, one judge favoured rescission in the form of an order that a fairer transaction be renegotiated. But the majority opted for damages (and not just equitable compensation) on the grounds that rescission was not commercially practicable there.

12–12 *Coleman* was distinguished in *Peskin v Anderson*,[36] which concerned the demutualisation and sale of the Royal Automobile Club's business in the late 1990s, effected by way of a scheme of arrangement. The plaintiffs had been members of the club, a non-profit company, until shortly before those proposals were mooted and, accordingly, they did not share in the proceeds of the sale. It was contended that, in the special circumstances, the directors owed them a fiduciary duty to advise them that a likely sale was imminent. But it was held that there was nothing particular in the factual relationship between them and the directors as to give rise to that duty. There were no relevant dealings, negotiations or other contacts directly between them, nor did any of the directors' actions cause the plaintiffs to retire when they did, nor at that time was there any sufficiently concrete proposal in existence or in contemplation that might have warranted disclosure.

FINANCING

12–13 Where the acquisition (be it of shares in the target or the target's assets) is for cash, then if the acquiring company does not possess sufficient funds it must borrow the money or else raise further capital by issuing additional shares. Where the bidder issues shares to pay for the target and the

---

[33] *Lloyds Bank v Bundy* [1975] Q.B. 326.
[34] *Percival v Wright* [1902] 2 Ch. 421.
[35] [1977] 2 N.Z.L.R. 225 at 333. See *Chez Nico Restaurants Ltd* [1992] B.C.L.C. 192 at 208.
[36] [2001] 1 B.C.L.C. 372.

value of what is acquired exceeds those shares' nominal value, the shares have been issued at a premium.[37] That premium must be placed in the share premium account and used only in the manner permitted.[38]

12–14   One aspect of financing takeovers that gives rise to considerable difficulties is when an acquirer, with little resources of its own, believes or knows that the company being bought is worth considerably more than the asking price. To make the acquisition, the buyer may through the acquiring company borrow the necessary funds and, when the takeover has been completed, assets in the acquired company may be sold off at a high profit and the proceeds of the sale then used to pay off the acquiring company's borrowings. Self-financing mergers of this variety may fall foul of the prohibition against companies financing the acquisition of their own shares.[39] For instance, in *Heald v O'Connor*,[40] the plaintiff agreed to sell to the defendant all the shares in a company and, as well, to lend him the money to make the purchase. Since the defendant could not provide adequate security of his own for the loan, it was agreed that the loan should be secured by a charge on the company's assets. This was held to fall within the prohibition, and the charge and the personal guarantee given on it by the defendant were held to be void and unenforceable.[41] In *Chaston v SWP Group Plc*,[42] it was held that paying a firm of accountants to carry out a due diligence exercise on a takeover target came within the prohibition, where the payment was made by a subsidiary of the target. But the effect of this decision has been largely set aside, where the expense in question was incurred on terms approved by the Irish Takeover Panel.[43]

12–15   Not every "self-financing" merger is caught by the prohibition, however; much depends on the circumstances of each case. In *Re Wellington Publishing Co.*,[44] a company obtained approximately NZ$3,000,000 bridging finance to take over another. Once the merger was completed, the acquired company's assets were revalued and were shown to be worth far more than their stated value. In anticipation of the profit that would be made when those assets were realised, a dividend of about NZ$3,000,000 was declared.[45] It was held that the potentially expansive scope of the prohibition must be confined by its *raison d'être*, which it was said was to protect creditors and minority shareholders. Since, in the circumstances, the creditors' interests were not jeopardised by the transaction and there were no minority shareholders (all the acquired company's members having accepted the offer), the dividend was held not to constitute financial assistance within the prohibition. While it may be debated whether an Irish court would follow this functional approach, the

---

[37]   *Henry Head & Co. v Ropner Holdings Ltd* [1952] Ch. 124.
[38]   1963 Act, s.62.
[39]   1963 Act, s.60.
[40]   [1971] 1 W.L.R. 497.
[41]   cf. *McCormick v Cameo Investments Ltd* [1978] I.L.R.M. 191.
[42]   [2003] 1 B.C.L.C. 675.
[43]   2005 Act, s.60(12)(k) and (l).
[44]   [1973] 1 N.Z.L.R. 133.
[45]   It is now not permissible to pay a dividend from unrealised profits: see para.8–90.

prohibition does not apply to the payment of a dividend "properly declared" by the company.[46] It is most likely that properly declared here means declared in compliance with the procedures set down in the articles of association and the statutory provisions on capital maintenance. As *Coleman v Myers*[47] demonstrates, in exceptional circumstances "self-financing" takeovers can fall foul of general equitable principles.

DEFENCES

12–16 In the usual takeover bid, by offering to buy the target company's shares, it is for the target's shareholders to decide for themselves whether or not to accept the bid. That they may make handsome profits if they accept, or that all or some of them may incur significant losses if the bid does not succeed, ordinarily has no legal bearing on their decision. But it is common for directors to resist bids being made for their companies and to encourage the shareholders to resist. Opposition may be based simply on the threat to the directors' own positions on the target's board. Or they may believe that the price being offered is too low and that resistance is in the shareholders' interest, in that the bidder will be induced to offer more, or indeed that other more generous bidders may be attracted. Or the directors may be of the view that the bidder would damage the company because it has no experience or has a bad record in that business, or that it is an "asset stripper". Or they may prefer that, if control is to pass out of the existing shareholders' hands, it should go to one favoured company (a "White Knight") and not to another.

12–17 Where there is opposition to a bid, various defensive strategies present themselves, which fall into two categories. Before a bid is made or is imminent, voting agreements may be concluded between shareholders; interlocking shareholdings may be established between a number of companies; the company's capital structure may be altered by introducing weighted or non-voting shares, or a category of shares entitled to acquire additional equity; the company may dispose of a key asset that is attracting bidders; a block of shares may be issued to some outsider who would favour the status quo; or a defensive merger may be concluded with some "White Knight". Measures that may be adopted against a particular bid include refusal by the board to register transfers of the company's shares; purchases in the market of the company's shares by the directors and their associates; increasing the dividend; a "bonus" share issue or a reconstruction of capital to improve gearing; disclosure of favourable information about the company's prospects or of unfavourable information about the bidder. In the case of companies with securities listed on the Irish Stock Exchange, the scope of defensive measures is significantly restricted.[48]

---

[46] Compare *MT Realisations Ltd v Digital Equipment Co.* [2002] 2 B.C.L.C. 688, holding that the arrangements there did not constitute financial assistance; doubted in *Chatson* case: above n.42.

[47] [1973] 1 N.Z.L.R. 133.

[48] See para.15–133 *et seq.*

Fiduciary Principles and Minority Protection

12–18   The directors' ability to oppose takeover bids is constrained by their fiduciary duties to their company. In determining the legality of defensive measures, the approach is as set out by Lord Wilberforce in the *Ampol Petroleum Ltd* case, namely:

> "to start with a consideration of the power whose exercise is in question
> … Having ascertained, on a fair view, the nature of this power, and having
> defined as can best be done in the light of modern conditions the, or some,
> limits within which it may be exercised, it is then necessary for the court,
> if a particular exercise of it is challenged, to examine the substantial
> purpose for which it is exercised, and to reach a conclusion whether that
> purpose was proper or not. In doing so it will necessarily give credit to the
> bona fide opinion of the directors, if such is found to exist, and will respect
> their judgment as to matters of management; having done this, the
> ultimate conclusion has to be as to the side of a fairly broad line on which
> the case falls."[49]

12–19   Assuming that by adopting certain defensive measures the directors break their fiduciary duties, an individual shareholder in some circumstances can have those measures enjoined.[50] But in the principal authorities where such shareholder claims (either "personal" or "derivative") succeeded, the defendant directors who controlled the companies' boards held only a minority of the shares. This was so even in *Clark v Workman*,[51] where, on the casting vote of the chairman who had promised full support for the bidders, the board resolved that any transfers of shares to the bidding syndicate should be registered. Although part of Ross J.'s judgment suggests that defensive action by directors who were also the majority shareholders would be enjoined,[52] any such injunction would be futile because, if the majority resist the bid, then there is no way in which it can succeed. In *Bamford v Bamford*,[53] which concerned a "wrongful rights issue", it was held that at least some unlawful defensive measures by directors could be cured by ratification in general meeting. It would seem that this curing power may be exercised *ex ante*, i.e. before the breaches of duty actually take place.[54]

Refusal to Register Transfers

12–20   Whether directors exceed or abuse powers they possess over registering transfers of shares depends on the circumstances of the case and on the very nature and scope of the power in question. In the *Alliance & Dublin Consumers Gas Co.* case,[55] it was intimated that directors must not obstruct

---

[49] *Howard Smith Ltd v Ampol Petroleum Ltd* [1974] A.C. 821 at 835.
[50] *ibid.* and e.g. *Hogg v Cramphorn* [1967] Ch. 254.
[51] [1920] 1 I.R. 108.
[52] *ibid.* at 112–113.
[53] [1970] Ch. 212.
[54] *Winthrop Investments Ltd v Winns* [1975] 2 N.S.W.L.R. 666.
[55] *Kinsella v Alliance & Dublin Consumers Gas Co.* [1982] I.E.H.C. 195, Barron J., unreported, October 5, 1982.

registration of transfers with a view to influencing shareholders' decisions on an offer for the company or for its shares.[56] On the other hand, it would appear that directors of private companies have almost an "absolute discretion" to decline to register transfers when the articles of association incorporate cl.3 of Pt II of Table A.

Issuing Additional Shares

12–21   Use by directors of their power to issue and allot additional shares in the company in an attempt to defeat a takeover bid may, in the circumstances, amount to a breach of their fiduciary duties. Examples include *Hogg v Cramphorn Ltd*,[57] where the "primary object" of creating a trust for the company's employees and lending it money, so that it could subscribe for a large block of shares in the company, was to resist a bid; and *Howard Smith Ltd v Ampol Petroleum Ltd*,[58] where the "substantial purpose" of allotting further equity to a "White Knight" company was to prevent the plaintiff's bid from succeeding. Such steps have become rare since the 1983 Act's authority and pre-emption provisions. The board's authority to allot shares may be general and may last for up to five years. The pre-emption requirement does not apply to, *inter alia,* private companies whose own regulations exclude it; also, where the consideration for the shares is wholly or partly otherwise than in cash or where the issue is in pursuance of an employees' share scheme.[59]

12–22   It may be that a major, but not the only, reason for issuing the shares was other than to thwart the wishes of a majority by blocking a bid. For instance, the target company may genuinely need additional capital or a particular asset, or the services of another company, while the directors at the same time may desire to defeat a bid being made for their company. In the *Ampol Petroleum Ltd* case, it was emphasised that the courts will not become entangled in the commercial merits of those decisions; that "such a matter as the raising of finance is one of management within the responsibility of the directors [and] it would be wrong for the court to substitute its opinion for that of the management, or indeed to question the correctness of the management's decision, on such a question, if bona fide arrived at".[60] The legal position where it is established that a significant though not the "primary purpose" was to prevent a bid from succeeding is subject to conflicting authority.

12–23   In *Nash v Lancegaye Safety Glass (Ireland) Ltd*,[61] which was not a takeover case but concerned an attempt by those who controlled 49 per cent of the shares to acquire overall control of the company, Dixon J. held that the existence of an improper motive was fatal to the allotment. However, in an

---

[56] See too *Australian Metropolitan Life Assurance Co. v Ure*, 33 C.L.R. 199 (1923).
[57] [1967] Ch. 254.
[58] [1974] A.C. 821.
[59] 1983 Act, s.23.
[60] [1974] A.C. 821 at 832.
[61] 92 I.L.T.R. 11 (1958).

Australian case[62] where the contested allotment did not turn a minority into a majority, but diluted a 19 per cent stake in the company that otherwise would have prevented the bid from succeeding, it was said that the criterion of validity is the "but for" test: would the allotment not have been made but for the improper purpose? Whereas in another Australian case[63] and in a Canadian case,[64] and more recently in England,[65] it was said that, if the allotment is made to raise funds or to acquire some other business advantage, and at the same time the directors would like to see a takeover bid defeated or one bidder succeed rather than another, the net question becomes whether in fact the directors acted to promote the company's interests. According to the Australian High Court in the *Harlowe's Nominees* case,[66] in those circumstance the ultimate question must always be "whether in truth the [new] issue was made honestly in the interests of the company. Directors ... may be concerned with a wide range of practical considerations, and their judgment, if exercised in good faith and not for irrelevant purposes, is not open to review in the court".[67] But this formula virtually denies the existence of an irrelevant purpose, which is the cause of the entire difficulty. Furthermore, if the test is the directors' bona fide belief then, in the absence of damning evidence and assuming that the directors are convincing witnesses, it would be virtually impossible to prevent, under some plausible pretext, an allotment being made to advance the directors' own interests.

12–24   *Teck Corp Ltd v Millar*[68] concerned a small mining company with several properties that were ripe for development. Its directors were convinced that the business would be best served if a long-term development contract was concluded with one major mining group. In the meantime the plaintiff had been buying shares in the company on the stock market, with a view to a takeover, and had secured just over a 50 per cent stake in it. Fully conscious of this, its directors concluded a development contract with the other company, part of which involved allotting shares to it, the consequence of which was to dilute the plaintiff's stake in Teck. It was held that, just as directors today are no longer absolutely prohibited from taking some account of employees' interests or of the consequence of the company's actions in the general community, so too they might concern themselves with the company being infiltrated by persons or groups who they bona fide consider not to be desirable in the best interests of the company. It was concluded that the directors were not seeking merely to retain control for themselves, that throughout they believed that the development contract was in the company's best interests, and that the mines would not be developed efficiently and profitably for

[62]   *Winthrop Investments Ltd v Winns* [1975] 2 N.S.W.L.R. 666.
[63]   *Harlowe's Nominees Ltd v Woodside (Lakes Entrance) Oil Co.*, 121 C.L.R. 483 (1968).
[64]   *Teck Corp Ltd v Millar*, 33 D.L.R. (3d) 288 (1972).
[65]   *CAS (Nominees) Ltd v Nottingham Forest FC Plc* [2002] 1 B.C.L.C. 613.
[66]   121 C.L.R. 483 (1968).
[67]   *ibid.* at 493.
[68]   33 D.L.R. (3d) 288 (1972).

the benefit of the shareholders if the plaintiff had obtained control. The share allotment therefore was upheld.

Lock-Out

12–25 A lock-out is some understanding or agreement between the target company or its directors and a bidder that the latter will be favourably treated if there are competing bids. Where such an arrangement has been made without the approval of the shareholders, the question arises whether the directors have unlawfully fettered their discretion. That was answered in the affirmative in *Clark v Workman*,[69] where the chairman of a shipbuilding company had promised the chairman of a syndicate that he would use his best endeavours to see that they would get control of the company. A board resolution to approve all share transfers that might be made to that consortium, passed with his casting vote, was held to be invalid because he had "fettered himself ... and had disqualified himself from acting bona fide in the interests of the company he was leaving".[70]

12–26 The issue in *Dawson International Ltd v Coats Paton Plc*[71] was whether fiduciary principles provided a defence to a claim for damages for breach of a lock-out arrangement. There had been negotiations about the plaintiff company taking over the defendant and both made a joint press announcement that the defendant's directors would recommend the bid. It was contended that, in addition, both companies had agreed that the defendant would not cooperate with any rival bidder. When the plaintiff's bid did not succeed, it claimed damages for breach of contract. An application was made to have the action dismissed *in limine* as disclosing no cause of action. The plaintiff conceded that such contract as it may have had with the target company was subject to fiduciary principles in that, if circumstances altered materially, the target's directors were entitled to put their shareholders' interests foremost and refuse to implement the agreement. It was held that there was a stateable case on the pleadings of breach of contract but there seems to be no reported decision on the ultimate outcome. In an earlier similar instance,[72] the disappointed bidder's claim was dismissed because, in the circumstances, the directors properly recommended a rival's bid, notwithstanding previous undertakings they had given to the plaintiff.

12–27 A variant of the lock-out is where the directors themselves own the majority of the company's shares and they side with one rather than with another bidder. While the directors *qua* shareholders would then be in a position to give their preferred bidder voting control of the company, that bidder most likely will want to acquire almost all if not all of the issued shares, to avoid possible difficulties with minority shareholders. That was the position in

---

[69] [1920] 1 I.R. 108.
[70] *ibid.* at 117–118.
[71] [1989] B.C.L.C. 233, aff'd [1990] B.C.L.C. 560.
[72] *John Crowther Group Plc v Carpets Int'l Plc* [1990] B.C.L.C. 460.

Re a Company[73] where the bidder for a private company, which was preferred by the directors, was another company that they controlled. However, a rival bidder offered a better price. The issue was whether the directors acted properly in sending a circular to the shareholders advising them, notwithstanding, to accept their own company's bid and not that of the rival, because its bid could not possibly succeed in the circumstances, since the directors would never accept its offer. It was held that, providing the circular was not misleading, no breach of fiduciary duty would be committed.[74]

Poison Pills

12–28 "Poison pills" are arrangements that are deliberately disadvantageous to the company, adopted to ward off a bid or bids. For instance in *Criterion Properties Ltd v Stratford UK Properties LLC*,[75] two companies established a limited partnership to develop properties. They later amended the partnership agreement to provide that, if any person gains control of the smaller 15 per cent partner, the other and bigger partner could require it to buy out its 85 per cent interest at market value plus 25 per cent per annum on the invested capital, to be compounded monthly. This was agreed in order to prevent a takeover of that company by a certain third party, who was perceived to the disreputable, and the parties' bona fides in that regard was not disputed. However, on account of the manner in which the case had been conducted, the House of Lords declined to rule on the propriety of the arrangement, remitting the case for a full trial. The Court of Appeal had held the arrangement to be unlawful because, as drafted, it applied to a takeover by any person and not just the "hostile predator".[76] An even stricter attitude was adopted by the High Court, concluding that since the agreement was designed to severely impoverish the company in the event of a takeover, it was inevitably an abuse of power notwithstanding the directors' good faith.[77]

Pre-emption Requirements

12–29 A major obstacle to a successful takeover of a private company is the existence of pre-emption rights in its articles of association or in a shareholders' agreement, whereby any intending transferor of shares must first offer them for sale to a category of "insiders" before they may be transferred to the outsider bidder.[78] An insider who is opposed to the bid and who has sufficient resources to acquire the shares being sought by the bidder can block it entirely, at least until such time as the articles of association are amended to remove pre-emption.

---

[73] [1986] B.C.L.C. 382.
[74] A more complex variant, involving a listed company, is *Heron Int'l Ltd v Grade* [1983] B.C.L.C. 382.
[75] [2004] 1 W.L.R. 1846.
[76] [2003] 2 B.C.L.C. 129.
[77] [2002] 2 B.C.L.C. 151.
[78] e.g. *Lyle Scott Ltd v Scott's Trustees* [1959] A.C. 763.

12–30 Depending on the terms of the particular pre-emption clause, it may be possible for the bidder to at least partly overcome the difficulties that it presents. The commonest of these clauses is that, where a shareholder decides to transfer his shares, he must first offer them for sale to the designated insiders—usually to be acquired at a fair valuation. However, concluding an agreement that envisages a share transfer at some future stage is not always caught by provisions of this nature.[79] Thus, in *Re A Company, Ex p. Schwarcz (No. 2),*[80] where the applicants held 5.5 per cent of the company's issued share capital, the holder of 80 per cent of its shares, a public company, entered into an agreement with an outsider concerning their possible disposal. Under it, the outsider undertook to make an offer for the shares if, *inter alia,* the members passed resolutions deleting the existing pre-emption clause and for the company to re-register as a private company. It was held that this arrangement did not trigger pre-emption because, under it, no interest in the shares had so far been disposed of and any obligation to sell them could not arise until several conditions were satisfied. For the standard pre-emption clause to bite, the member must have a present and unequivocal intention to dispose of his shares. It was not contended that the special resolution passed to so amend the articles, by all the other shareholders, was unlawful. In answer to the contention that it nonetheless amounted to "oppression", it was held that the circumstances fully justified the company taking that step and, since the petitioners would be paid the same price for their shares as under the agreement would be paid to the parent company, they would not be unfairly discriminated against.

12–31 This was followed by *Re Sedgefield Steeplechase Co. (1927) Ltd,*[81] where the applicant, holding 21.3 per cent of the company's shares, contended that an arrangement made between other shareholders and a potential bidder contravened her pre-emption rights. Those shareholders agreed to sell their equitable interests in their shares; that as trustee for them, the bidder had no authority to transfer the shares in a way that would contravene pre-emption rights in the articles; that they would use their best endeavours to amend the articles and remove those rights. While the sale of beneficial ownership of shares ordinarily is enough to bring them within pre-emption, it was held that the beneficial interest transferred here did not entitle the bidder to do anything inconsistent with the pre-emption regime and, consequently, this arrangement did nothing that violated the plaintiff's rights under it. An agreement to vote in favour of the proposed change in the articles did not do so.

12–32 The pre-emption formula in *Theakston v London Trust Plc,*[82] was somewhat different from the standard. The directors were obliged to register a share transfer "to any other member of the company"; except in such cases, any proposed share transfer was subject to pre-emption. The plaintiff held 48 per cent of the company's shares, Paul held 11 per cent and M the remaining

---

[79] See para.9–68 *et seq.*
[80] [1989] B.C.L.C. 427.
[81] [2000] 2 B.C.L.C. 211.
[82] [1984] B.C.L.C. 390.

9 per cent. The plaintiff wished to sell its shares but Paul and M disagreed about which of two non-members should purchase them. The plaintiff there-fore agreed to transfer its shares to Paul for £1.42 million and, at the same time Paul agreed as follows with an outsider, Brown. The share purchase would be financed by Brown; the shares were charged to Brown; Paul would endeavour to have his shares transferred to Brown; Paul would vote as Brown directed and would account to Brown in respect of any distribution made on the shares; the loan was interest-free and was not repayable until such time as Brown had acquired the shares himself or Paul sold them on his directions; Paul would endeavour to have the shares transferred to him, would accept any offer made by him and seek to have the shares registered in his name; where Paul served a notice to transfer the shares and an existing member offered to buy them, Paul would withdraw the notice and submit a fresh one. It was held that this was a share transfer to Paul, not to Brown, and accordingly the directors were obliged to register it. Notwithstanding the extent to which Brown was involved in the whole transaction and that it was devised to assist him in his endeavours to acquire the shares. Paul did not hold them in trust for him. For if Paul became bankrupt, the shares would not then vest in Brown but would vest in the Official Assignee. Brown's interest in them was as a mortgagee, with several additional entitlements but, on account of the pre-emption regimes, legal title could not be transferred to Brown over the objections of M.

PROFITING

12–33 Management and shareholders engaged in takeovers and mergers almost invariably to make a profit. In the typical takeover of a public company, the buyer will believe that it can run the company more efficiently than it is being managed at present and that its real worth is not fully reflected in its existing share price. At the same time its shareholders will be tempted to sell out because the price being offered exceeds the then going rate for their shares. Both companies' management may also stand to gain; for instance, positions in a merged and much larger entity may carry greater prestige and be more lucrative. Moreover, some directors may be tempted to chase quick profits by "insider trading" before the envisaged merger becomes public knowledge. Also, the target's directors may negotiate "golden handshakes" and "golden umbrellas" for themselves. The Takeover Panel's principles and the Irish Stock Exchange's Listing Rules, which apply to quoted companies, subject profiting by the target's shareholders in takeovers to the equality principle and, addition-ally, either forbid or require extensive prior disclosure of profiting by direc-tors.[83] Subject to a number of exceptions, however, the general law tolerates profiting by sections of the shareholders and the management.

Fiduciary Principles and Minority Protection

12–34 Not alone must company directors not enrich themselves at their company's expense but they must not place themselves in a position where their

---

[83] See para.15–138 *et seq.*

own private interests and those of the company conflict. It will depend on the circumstances of each case whether or not these duties were complied with. Is it permissible, for example, for directors to recommend acceptance of a takeover bid in the knowledge, not disclosed to shareholders, that the acquiring company will give them places on its board, or that they will be allowed to retain their seats on the target company's board? Assuming that this is a breach of fiduciary duty, what is the appropriate remedy: resignation from the directorship or handing up the directors' fees? There are no authorities squarely on those questions.

12–35 The fact that directors' duties are owed to their companies rather than to the shareholders individually gives rise to an anomalous situation where the target company's officers made a profit from their position. Those with the greatest reason to feel aggrieved are the target's old shareholders; they may feel that they were, so to speak, sold down the river so that the directors could make large profits for themselves. In very exceptional circumstances, like in *Coleman v Myers*,[84] the directors will be fiduciaries for those shareholders as well, who therefore may have a remedy. Usually, however, fiduciary duties are owed to the company only but, when the bid succeeds, the company would have new owners who may have collaborated with the errant directors, and the company may choose not to pursue the matter.[85] This dilemma cannot be resolved satisfactorily by placing profiteering by directors on the same level as "defrauding" the company, because any redress obtained in a derivative action would be in favour of the target and not necessarily its aggrieved shareholders. Additionally, most if not all of those aggrieved would have disposed of their shares, so that they would not possess the standing to institute a derivative suit or to make an application under s.205 of the 1963 Act for "oppression".

"Golden Handshakes" and "Golden Umbrellas"

12–36 A company that acquires control of another may wish to remove all or some of the latter's directors. Assuming that the acquirer controls at least 50 per cent of the voting shares, it can remove the directors by an ordinary resolution, subject to whatever rights to compensation as exist under their service contracts.[86] Often, however, the acquirer may choose to pay those directors *ex gratia* sums on their retirement, for instance, to win their support for a takeover bid or simply to avoid the embarrassment of having to put down removal resolutions for the general meeting. Where a "golden handshake" of this nature has a bearing on any resolution being proposed in general meeting, full disclosure must be made to the shareholders[87]; a resolution passed without such disclosure being made is invalid. The details of any payment made to directors and *de facto* directors by way of compensation for loss of office, or as consideration for or in connection with retirement from office, as

---

[84] [1977] 2 N.Z.L.R. 225.
[85] The converse occurred in *Royal (Hastings) Ltd v Gulliver* [1967] 2 A.C. 134.
[86] 1963 Act, s.182.
[87] *Kaye v Croydon Tramways Co.* [1898] 1 Ch. 358.

defined, must be disclosed to the members and approved by them in general meeting.[88]

12–37   This disclosure and shareholder approval rule applies to two kinds of takeover or merger. One is where the payment is made in connection with the transfer of all or part of the company's undertaking to another.[89] Any such payment that is not approved in general meeting is deemed to be received by the director in trust for the company. The other concerns with the usual kind of takeover: where an offer to buy their shares is made to all the shareholders, or an offer is made with a view to the target becoming a subsidiary company, or with a view to the offeror obtaining control of at least one third of the voting rights, or an offer that is conditional on acceptance to a given extent.[90] Particulars of a payment proposed to be made to a director in any of these circumstances must accompany the notice of the offer sent to the shareholders, who must approve of the payment in a meeting summoned for that purpose. Otherwise, the director is deemed to have received the funds in trust for those who sold their shares in consequence of the offer.

12–38   These requirements do not apply to any bona fide payment by way of damages for breach of contract or by way of pension in respect of past services Although the compensation paid to the retiring managing director in *Taupo Totara Timber Co. v Rowe*[91] was held to fall outside of the New Zealand version of these rules, most likely those payments come within the 1963 Act's requirements. These are supplemented by general fiduciary standards; they do not prejudice the operation of any rule of law concerning disclosure or accountability.[92] These, moreover, are supplemented by a number of deeming provisions designed to prevent their evasion. Two kinds of payment are treated as subject to the disclosure and shareholder approval rule. One is the difference between the price paid to a director for shares in the company and the amount that other like shareholders could have obtained at the same time, or any valuable consideration given to such director in connection with the transfer of assets or of shares.[93] Unless the contrary is shown, another is a payment made in pursuance of any "arrangement" that was made within one year before or two years after the time of the offer, or where the transferee was privy to that arrangement.[94]

12–39   The term "golden umbrella" signifies service contracts made with company directors where the remuneration is significantly high and the contracts are for a long duration. Often those arrangements serve the purpose of deterring shareholders from removing directors, in that the amount of damages payable for breach of contract would be prohibitively high. Such

---

[88]   1963 Act, s.186.
[89]   1963 Act, s.187.
[90]   1963 Act, s.188.
[91]   [1978] A.C. 527.
[92]   1963 Act, s.198(4).
[93]   1963 Act, s.189(2).
[94]   1963 Act, s.189(1).

contracts are entered into especially with a view to the existing membership changing in a takeover. Service contracts of longer than five years' duration must be approved by the shareholders.[95] Assuming the company's own regulations permit the board to decide on service contracts for less than that duration, the question will be whether the directors used these powers for an extraneous purpose. Assuming that directors break their fiduciary duties in entering into "golden umbrella" contracts, it would appear that any damages paid subsequently for breach of those contracts must be disclosed as a "golden handshake", on the grounds that it is not a "bona fide payment by way of damages".[96]

Price Discrimination

12–40 "Price discrimination" means charging different prices for what is essentially the same product or service. As far as the general law is concerned and so long as there are no exceptional circumstances,[97] every shareholder is entitled to have the best price that he can get for his shares. In particular, a person with a controlling or a key block of shares may accept more than what the others obtained for their shares. Although majorities in companies must not discriminate unfairly at the expense of minorities, it would appear that it is permissible to obtain a premium for selling controlling shares. Unless they retain their office as directors of the company, any premium obtained by directors for their shares in the context of a takeover must be disclosed to and approved by the shareholders.[98] But in the case of takeovers by acquiring shares that are listed on the Irish Stock Exchange, holders of each class of shares must be paid the same price.[99]

Insider Trading

12–41 Insider trading or dealing is a notorious source of easy profits when a takeover bid is being mounted. Before Pt V of the 1990 Act and several other provisions of that Act came into force, the legal remedies against that practice were very deficient. The matter is now governed principally by Pt IV (ss.29–37) of the 2005 Act and the Market Abuse (Directive 2003/6/EC) Regulations 2005.[100]

REMOVING DISSIDENTS

12–42 A company that is seeking to take over another may succeed in acquiring the vast majority of the shares in the target but there may remain a

---

[95] 1990 Act, s.28.
[96] 1963 Act, s.189(13).
[97] *Heron Int'l Ltd v Grade* [1983] B.C.L.C. 244. See generally, A. Boyle, "The Sale of Controlling Shares" 13 *I.&C.L.Q.* 185 (1964).
[98] 1963 Act, ss.186 and 187.
[99] Takeover Panel Rules, s.14.
[100] SI 2005/342 and see para.15–96 *et seq.*

minority who refuse to sell out their shares at the price being offered; indeed that minority may be so opposed to the bid that they refuse to sell out at almost any price. A "take-out merger" power exists to enable bidders who acquire the bulk of the target's shares to compel the remaining shareholders to sell out to them. It also enables a minority that originally refused to accept the bid to change their minds and insist that the partially successful bidder buys them out. Where a bidder does not satisfy the requirements for take-outs, it may nevertheless in exceptional circumstance be permitted to achieve the same result through the statutory mechanisms for "arrangements" or for "restructuring".

"Take-Out"

12–43   Subject to what is said below, where at least 80 per cent of the target's shareholders accept a full takeover bid, the bidder may expropriate the remaining 20 per cent or less on the same terms as the others got.[101] Where the shares are listed on the Irish Stock Exchange, the relevant proportion to instigate a take-out is 90 per cent.[102] This power is strictly construed by the courts. In *Bramelid and Malmstrom v Sweden*,[103] the European Commission of Human Rights ruled that a similar provision in Swedish law did not contravene the property rights guaranteed in the First Protocol of the European Convention on Human Rights. An equivalent constitutional challenge was rejected in *Moran v Valentia Communications Ltd*,[104] which concerned the takeover and eventual privatisation of Telecom Eireann Plc. The applicant there owned a miniscule stake in the company and the vast majority of its shareholders accepted the bid that was made. On account of the public interest in facilitating takeovers, because the wishes of an overwhelming majority should not be frustrated by a tiny minority, as the price being paid for the shares appeared to be fair and since there was a statutory procedure for challenging any intended take-out, it was held that the guarantee of private property had not been infringed.

Procedure

12–44   For a bidder to be entitled to expropriate dissident shareholders in non-listed companies, the following must be satisfied. There must be a "scheme, contract or offer" made by one company to acquire ownership of all the shares in another. In England it was held that an offer to treat, as compared with an offer to acquire, shares, does not come within this procedure.[105] But the formulation in the 1963 Act is different in this respect. An offer is not invalid merely because the actual offer documents were not sent to each and every member of the company, wherever in the world they may reside. The documentation must contain sufficient information to enable members to take a properly informed decision; typically this would include details of the

---

[101] 1963 Act, s.204. (initially Companies Act 1959, s.8).
[102] See para.15–141.
[103] 5 E.H.R.R. 249 (1982).
[104] [2002] I.E.H.C. 159, Smyth J., unreported, January 21, 2002.
[105] *Re Joseph Holt Plc* [2001] 2 B.C.L.C. 604.

offeror, its most recent profit and loss accounts and balance sheet, and an auditors' or accountants' report, as well as such interest or other connection if any that the bidder has with the company.[106] Shareholders must be given sufficient time to make a decision and the company must have an opportunity to obtain independent advice on the proposals and communicate that to its members. At least 80 per cent *in value* of the latter's shareholders must have accepted or endorsed this offer. Where, however, at the outset the bidder was the beneficial owner of at least 20 per cent in value of the target's shares, the offer or arrangement must be accepted by holders of four fifths in value and also three quarters in number of those other shareholders. Shares held beneficially by a subsidiary of the bidder are treated as being held by it for these purposes. Accordingly, the greater the stake that the bidder already has in the target, the larger the proportion of acceptances are required before it can avail of this mechanism. But this qualification does not apply where the bidder, together with one or more of its own shareholders, hold at least 20 per cent of those shares. An argument to the contrary was rejected by the Supreme Court in *Duggan v Stoneworth Investment Ltd,*[107] which concerned a bid made for the shares in Fitzwilton Plc and where the two individuals who owned and controlled the bidder already held 27.6 per cent of the shares in the target. In the absence of exceptional circumstances, the court will not identify the bidder with its actual owners for this purpose. Where the offer is being made for a particular class or classes of shares, then these requirements apply to each class in question.

12–45 Within six months of the bid being published, the bidder may notify the dissenting minority of its intention to acquire their shares. When one month of giving that notice expires, provided that the court does not intervene, the bidder becomes entitled to acquire those shares on the same terms as it offered the accepting shareholders.[108] The bidder may then send the target company instruments of transfer, together with payment for those shares, and the target is obliged to register the shares in the name of whoever is designated as transferee. Any sums that the target company receives in payment for the dissidents' shares must be held in a separate bank account in trust for them.

Challenging the Take-Out

12–46 Any dissenting shareholder who is notified of the intention to expropriate in this manner may apply to the court, which "if it thinks fit [may] order otherwise".[109] This gives the court a discretion to veto a take-out when in the circumstances it is particularly unjust, even if all the procedural requirements have been satisfied. Where the entire transaction is at arm's length, the burden of proof is on the dissident. It is a heavy burden to overcome, where those who held the bulk of the shares have accepted the bid; for the court starts with the assumption that the other shareholders are likely to know

[106] *Fiske Nominees Ltd v Dwyka Diamonds Ltd* [2002] 2 B.C.L.C. 123.
[107] [2000] 2 I.R. 563.
[108] *Re Simo Securities Trust Ltd* [1971] 1 W.L.R. 1455.
[109] 1963 Act, s.204(1).

where their own interests lie as well as the objector does. In an appropriate case, however, for instance where the directors advised acceptance of the bid on the strength of advice they got from independent experts, the court will order discovery of documents in the possession of either or both companies.[110] Circumstances can arise where the dissidents have been left in the dark about major features of the bid, that the target's own directors are obliged to provide them with "full particulars of the transaction, its purpose, the method of carrying it out and its consequences".[111]

12–47   If the transaction is not at arm's length, as where the bidder already has a large stake in the target's shares, then the burden of proof is reversed. In those circumstances, it is for the bidder to satisfy the court that the price being offered is fair.[112] This may require the bidder to disclose information about valuations and related matters to the dissidents. In *Re Chez Nico Restaurants Ltd,*[113] although the power here was held not to apply, because the offer made was one to receive offers of shares rather than of acceptance (i.e. a notice to treat), it was stated that court approval would not have been given if the matter had come within the statutory power. This was because those seeking control were directors of and substantial shareholders in the "target" company, which was quoted, but all the information that the City Code required to disclose was not made available to the other shareholders. Since the transaction there was covered by the Code, Browne Wilkinson V.C. found it unnecessary to decide whether, under the general law, directors seeking to acquire control of a company must make full disclosure of all relevant facts to the other shareholders.

12–48   Several objections to the proposed take-out were rejected in *Walls v Walls Holdings Ltd,*[114] which concerned family-owned property development companies. The Supreme Court rejected the contention that the shareholders in the bidder must be entirely independent of the target companies, that the price being paid and the payment arrangements were inadequate, that there had been insufficient disclosure of relevant information and that the time period allowed to accept the offer was too short. The Court also rejected the argument that pre-emption provisions in the companies' articles of association were an obstacle to the expropriation, on the grounds that the acquiring party obtains "beneficial ownership" of the shares, notwithstanding others' pre-emption entitlement to them, and consequently the statutory provisions take precedence over the articles. In the *Duggan* case[115] objections to the price being paid for the shares were rejected; there was overwhelming evidence that, in the circumstances, the price was fair.

12–49   Even where exception cannot be taken to the price, the court may veto the take-out where the expropriation power is being abused; for

---

[110] *Re Lifecare Int'l Ltd* [1990] B.C.L.C. 222.
[111] *Securities Trust Ltd v Associated Properties Ltd* [1980] I.E.H.C. 128, unreported, McWilliam J., November 19, 1980.
[112] *Re Bugle Press Ltd* [1961] 1 Ch. 270.
[113] [1992] B.C.L.C. 192.
[114] [2008] 1 I.L.R.M. 1 and see para.9–83.
[115] [2000] 2 I.R. 563.

instance, where the target's directors had misled some of its shareholders into accepting the offer[116] or where a majority in the target are merely seeking to expel unwanted shareholders from the company. Thus in *Re Bugle Press Ltd*,[117] two shareholders tried to use this machinery to rid themselves of the remaining shareholder and thereby acquire complete control of the company. The two, who held 4,500 shares each, formed the bidder company and it then made an offer for all the shares in the target. Predictably, this was accepted by the two but was rejected by the third shareholder, who held 1,000 shares. Since its offer had secured 90 per cent acceptance, the bidder sought to acquire those 1,000 shares under the British equivalent (which does not have the proviso about acceptance by three quarters in number in these circumstances). Given the actual background to the bid, the court enjoined the "barefaced attempt simply to expel a shareholder from the company", stating that

> "the section has been used not for the purpose of any scheme or contract properly so called or contemplated by the section but for the quite different purpose of enabling majority shareholders to expropriate or evict the minority and that ... is something for the purposes of which prima facie the court ought not to allow the section to be invoked – unless at any rate it were shown that there was some good reason in the interests of the company for so doing, for example, that the minority shareholder was in some way acting in a manner destructive or highly damaging to the interests of the company from some motives entirely of his own".[118]

Sell-Out

12–50 When a bidder acquires 80 per cent of the non-listed target's shares in the manner described above but chooses to leave the minority hold on to their shares, there is an equivalent appraisal machinery whereby the minority can change their minds and insist on the bidder buying them out on the same terms as were offered to the accepting shareholders.[119]

"Arrangement"

12–51 Provided that 75 per cent *in value* of each class affected, who vote, agree and that the court consents, companies may bring about drastic changes in their constitutions or capital structures by way of statutory schemes of arrangement.[120] While this procedure is usually resorted to so that companies in financial difficulties can reorganise their balance sheets, it also can be used to arrange the takeover of another company.[121] Before any such scheme can take effect, it must be one to which the company is a party.[122]

---

[116] *Gething v Kilner* [1972] 1 W.L.R. 337.
[117] [1961] 1 Ch. 270.
[118] [1961] 1 Ch. 270 at 287.
[119] 1963 Act, s.204(4).
[120] 1963 Act, ss.201–204.
[121] e.g. *Re RAC Motoring Services Ltd* [2000] 1 B.C.L.C. 307.
[122] *Re Savoy Hotel Ltd* [1981] 1 Ch. 351.

12–52   On one occasion of significance in Irish financial history, a scheme of arrangement was permitted to be used to remove dissident shareholders who objected to a takeover bid and who most likely could not have been taken out under the English equivalent of 1963 Act's procedure.[123] This was in *Re National Bank Ltd*,[124] concerning the former National Bank, a mainly Irish bank that was founded by Daniel O'Connell but was registered as a company in England, and had its headquarters and some other offices there. An elaborate scheme was devised to enable the Bank of Ireland and a Scottish bank to take it over. In brief, National's Irish business was to be transferred to a company, NBI, in return for shares in it; those shares would then be sold to the Bank of Ireland in return for cash and renounceable loan stock, which would be distributed pro rata to National's members once the scheme was approved of by special resolution.[125] Although the scheme was supported by a 90 per cent majority at a general meeting held in London, this represented only 61 per cent of National's entire shareholders. Since 72 per cent of its shareholders had Irish addresses, many of them being small shareholders living in rural Ireland, and because opposition to the entire arrangement appears to have been badly organised, it could be argued that approximately 35 per cent of National's shareholders did not support the proposals.

12–53   Two grounds were put forward in opposing the petition requesting that the court sanction the scheme. It was said that National's secret reserves should have been disclosed to the members, the implication being that those reserves were worth a considerable amount and therefore the purchase price being paid for National's shares was insufficient. But accountants' reports approved the price; in any event, it was held, the Companies Acts did not (then) oblige banks to disclose "secret" reserves.[126] The second objection was that use should not be made the arrangement procedure to acquire full control of another company by way of takeover in circumstances where the bidder could not otherwise take out dissidents. Plowman J.'s somewhat cryptic answer was that:

> "It seems to me to involve imposing a limitation or qualification either on the generality of the word "arrangement" in [s.201] or else on the discretion of the court under that section. The legislature has not seen fit to impose any such limitation in terms and I see no reason for implying any. Moreover, the two sections, [s.201 and s.204], involve quite different considerations and different approaches. Under [s.201] an arrangement can only be sanctioned if the question of its fairness has first of all been submitted to the court. Under [s.204] on the other hand, the matter may never come to the court at all. If it does come to the court then the onus is cast on the dissenting minority to demonstrate the unfairness of the scheme. There are, therefore, good reasons for requiring a smaller

---

[123] Section 204.
[124] [1966] 1 W.L.R. 819.
[125] *cf.* National Bank Transfer Act 1966.
[126] Due to the 1963 Act, Sch.6, Pt III, this is no longer possible.

majority in favour of a scheme under [s.201] than the majority which is required under [s.204] if the minority is to be expropriated."[127]

12–54　In the subsequent and similar *Re Hellenic & General Investment Trust* case,[128] which involved the most blatant conflict of interests and some unfairness, although the price paid was not objectionable, undercutting the take-out protections was one of the reasons why the court refused approval for the arrangement there that envisaged expelling the minority.

Restructuring

12–55　An alternative strategy for removing dissidents in a takeover is for the majority to get the company to sell its undertaking or principal assets to themselves; they then put the company into liquidation, in which they recover much of the purchase price they paid. It is highly unlikely that the court would give its consent a change of objects that is designed to facilitate such a manoeuvre. However, the 1963 Act provides a mechanism whereby the company can sell the undertaking without running into this obstacle.[129] The company can resolve to go into voluntary liquidation; then require the liquidator to transfer the undertaking to another company in return for cash and securities in the transferee, which will then be distributed among the transferee's members; the transferor will be wound up.

12–56　A rare reported instance of this procedure being used to remove dissidents arose out of measures adopted to reorganise privately-owned public transport in London early in the last century. In *Castello v London General Omnibus Co.*,[130] 95 per cent of a company's equity was owned by the defendant, which sought to acquire the remaining five per cent. To this end, a scheme was drawn up under which the defendant would form a new company, the first company would then be put into liquidation and the new company would buy the entire undertaking in return for paying off debentures, repaying the preference shareholders and paying enough cash to distribute £275 per share among the former's £100 ordinary shareholders. Once approved by a special resolution, such a scheme is binding on the company's members; members who dissent are entitled to have their shares bought out for cash at a price fixed by arbitration. The minority sought an injunction against implementing these proposals, contending that they were entitled to continue to participate in the company's prosperity, such as by coming into the new company on a pro rata basis, and that it was improper for the purchaser to in effect set the price for the exchange. Since "there [was] no pretence of fraud [or] bad faith" and the price was shown to be fair, the court declined to intervene. The court conceded that "it may well be that the [majority] will get an advantage from the opportunity to invest in the new company which possibly the plaintiff … will not

---

[127] [1966] 1 W.L.R. 819 at 829–830.
[128] [1976] 1 W.L.R. 123.
[129] s.260.
[130] (1912) 107 L.T. 576.

have".[131] This outcome, however, was justified on the grounds that it "is not an inequality produced by these resolutions. As to the effect of these resolutions it appears ... to be an effect produced by the [parties] unequal position"[132]; and in any event, it was concluded, the majority acted not in bad faith but merely in their own interests. It is doubtful if a court today would make the same decision, which may very well constitute "oppression".

12–57   In *Rock Nominees Ltd v RCO (Holding) Plc*,[133] a bidder succeeded in acquiring 96.26 per cent of the shares in the target. But the minority share-holder refused to sell; instead he offered to buy the majority stake at a lower price. Because in the circumstances the bidder was short by 0.8 per cent of the shares it needed to "take out" the minority, it devised the following strategy. Its directors agreed to sell the company's operating subsidiary and to then liquidate the company. This deprived the minority of the kind of bargaining position they might have had to obtain a significantly higher price for their shares. However, because the minority's objective had been to extract a ransom price and also because the operating subsidiary was sold at fair market value, it was held that there had not been "oppression".

---

[131] *ibid.* at 581.
[132] *ibid.* at 581.
[133] [2004] 1 B.C.L.C. 439.

CHAPTER 13

CLOSELY-HELD COMPANIES

13–01 A "closely held", or "close", company is a company the shares of which are owned by one person or by a closely-knit group, like the members of a family or a few partners. The vast majority of registered companies that are not part of a "group" are closely held in this sense, being either so-called "one-person" companies, family firms or "quasi partnerships". Although most of these are small concerns, some of Ireland's largest enterprises remain closely held.

13–02 In many continental European countries there are separate legislative provisions for close companies, which in France are known as SARLs *(Société à responsabilité limitée)* and in Germany as GMbHs *(Gessellschaft mit beschrankter Haftung)*. Various American states have included in their companies statutes special chapters on close corporations. Apart from issues of taxation, there is no special regime governing this type of company yet in Ireland. Part 13 (ss.430–441) of the Taxes Consolidation Act 1997, concerns expenses incurred by and loans made to participators in such companies, and surcharges for undistributed investment income and income from service companies.[1] The EC Twelfth Directive 89/667 on one-person companies was implemented by the European Communities (Single Member Private Limited Companies) Regulations 1994,[2] but these have not made any profound changes to the existing system. A close company will almost invariably be registered as a private company, principally so that it does not have to disclose to the public extensive information about its financial affairs.

MINIMUM NUMBERS

13–03 Until the "single-member" company was made possible in 1994, every private company had to have at least two members.[3] Prior to 1994, in "one-person" companies, one individual would hold all but one of the issued shares and the remaining share would be held by a "dummy" shareholder—who might be the principal shareholder's spouse, child, solicitor or accountant.

---

[1] See generally, M. Feeney, *The Taxation of Companies* (Haywards Heath: Tottel Publishing, 2006), Ch.10.
[2] O.J. L395/40 (1989) and SI 1994/275.
[3] 1963 Act, s.36.

This, of course, still remains the case unless the company is actually incorporated or re-registers as a single-member company.

13–04　Every company is still required to have at least two directors.[4] The Companies Acts do not say what happens when there is only one or no director. Where a company's membership falls below the legal minimum, the court will entertain a petition to have it wound up compulsorily.[5] If a private company with only one member (other than a duly registered "single member" company) continues doing business for more than six months, that member becomes personally liable for all debts that the company incurred during that time.[6]

INTERNAL REGULATIONS AND GOVERNANCE

13–05　A close company's articles of association will usually include Pt II of Table A, which contains rules on such matters as refusal to register transfers of shares in the company, calling general meetings at short notice, a low quorum for general meetings, informally adopted resolutions, and directors voting on matters in which they have a financial interest. These regulations may contain special clauses that deal with particular concerns of the members; some of these clauses may even be entrenched in the memorandum of association.[7] Perhaps the commonest special clause is a pre-emption provision, whereby existing members or directors are given a first option on shares in the company which any member wishes to dispose of.[8] Examples of special clauses from the leading cases include where the directors were given weighted votes on any proposed resolution to remove them, thereby rendering them virtually irremovable[9]; where each of two joint managing directors was given a veto over major transactions in property by the company[10]; where the principal shareholder was designated the company's governing director for life with authority to do everything that is not by law required to be done in general meeting[11]; where it was provided that all internal disputes should be submitted to arbitration.[12] Often, however, instead of putting special clauses in the articles of association, they will form part of a collateral shareholders' agreement, which takes precedence over the articles.

13–06　Closely-held companies are frequently run on a very informal basis. Under Pt II of Table A, the quorum for general meetings (other than for "one-person" companies within the 1994 Regulations) is two members present

---

[4]　1963 Act, s.174.
[5]　1963 Act, s.213(d).
[6]　1963 Act, s.36.
[7]　1963 Act, s.28.
[8]　See para.9–64 *et seq.*
[9]　*Bushells v Faith* [1970] A.C. 1099.
[10]　*Quin & Axtens Ltd v Salomon* [1909] A.C. 442.
[11]　*Lee v Lee's Air Farming Ltd* [1961] A.C. 12.
[12]　*Beattie v Beattie & Co.* [1938] Ch. 708.

either in person or by proxy when the meeting "proceeds to business".[13] It is not necessary to actually hold formal general meetings to pass resolutions; a resolution in writing signed by all the members entitled to attend the meeting and vote is "valid and effective for all purposes" as a duly passed resolution, provided that due notice was given.[14] *Cane v Jones*[15] goes even further and makes fully effective any unanimous agreement of all the members who, acting together, can do anything which is *intra vires* the company, such as alter the articles of association. Where all of the members assent to a course of conduct that would be *ultra vires* in the conventional sense, that conduct will be regarded as *intra vires*.[16]

13–07 Complex voting systems occur principally in closely-held companies; their function is to ensure that a majority of the members do not out-vote a minority on all questions or on certain issues that are of particular concern to the minority. Thus, the regulations may adopt the common law rule of "one member, one vote"; or the shares may be divided into two or more classes, with different voting strengths; or some members may be given weighted votes on particular issues. There may even be entirely separate agreements between them in which shareholders undertake either to vote or not to vote, or not to vote in a particular way.

13–08 On account of their small membership and especially where they are owned by two individuals or two families, or where some shareholders possess extensive veto powers, close companies are often deadlocked. Sometimes the company's own regulations will contain a mechanism for untying deadlocks; for instance, that the matter in dispute be referred to arbitration or that the dissenting members shall be bought out under certain conditions. The court has power to order that a general meeting be held and in the manner directed by it[17] also authorises the court to direct that one member present, either in person or by proxy, shall constitute the meeting.[18] Where deadlock persists, the court may order that the company be wound up on just and equitable grounds.[19]

MANAGEMENT

13–09 A closely-held company's most distinctive feature is the overlap between its membership and its management; usually the company's principal shareholders are also its directors. Moreover, these companies often possess other devices that give groups of shareholders or individuals extensive control over the board of directors. Part II of Table A allows any director, with the board's approval, to appoint an alternate or substitute, who shall be entitled to

---

13 Article 5.
14 1963 Act, s.141.
15 [1980] 1 W.L.R. 1451.
16 *Re Home Treat Ltd* [1991] B.C.L.C. 705.
17 1963 Act, s.135.
18 *cf. Noel Tedman Holdings Pty Ltd* [1967] Qd. R. 561.
19 1963 Act, s.213(f).

notices of board meetings and to attend and vote at them.[20] The informal way that many close companies are run is also reflected in their management, where persons may be acting as directors, or as the managing director, without ever having formally been appointed to those offices. A company will be held to contracts made by a *de facto* board of directors or by a *de facto* managing director. Many of the Companies Acts' provisions imposing duties on directors extend to *de facto* directors.

Fiduciary Duties

13–10   There is some support for the view that the rules regarding fiduciaries' conflicts of interests and abuse of powers should be relaxed somewhat in the case of those who direct close companies. Many of those directors are not full-time executives and may have other commercial interests, even in related businesses, so that a company may frequently have to enter into contracts in which its directors have a personal interest. It is for this reason that Pt II of Table A allows directors to vote in respect of such contracts, and to be counted in the quorum present at the board meeting.[21] They nevertheless must declare their interests and satisfy the requirement to maintain the interests-in-contracts book. Part II allows directors to secure some personal advantage from their position where the company owns some shares in another, by permitting them to exercise the votes on those shares "in such manner and in all respects as they think fit" and, in particular, for resolutions appointing them or any of them to remunerated offices in that other company.[22]

13–11   The British courts have taken a categorical approach to corporate opportunities,[23] in that directors are not allowed to exploit opportunities for themselves, even where that action would enure to the company's advantage or where the company could not have exploited the opportunity itself. This approach may be unrealistic and inefficient when applied to close companies. It may ignore a tacit understanding between those involved in such companies that the directors should have some freedom to engage in other businesses; and prohibiting part-time directors from getting personally involved in projects that the company itself cannot finance or otherwise cannot exploit might result in that project never getting under way or a valuable director resigning. Against that, if the company's incapacity to exploit an opportunity is permitted to be a defence, this could easily induce self-serving directors not to try their best for the company.

13–12   In *Queensland Mines Ltd v Hudson*,[24] the Privy Council upheld the incapacity defence in the special circumstances of that case. The company was formed to exploit mining licences that it expected to obtain. It had two

---

[20]   Article 9.

[21]   Article 7.

[22]   Article 8.

[23]   See para.7–31 *et seq.*

[24]   52 A.L.J.L.R. 399 (1978), noted in 42 *Mod. L. Rev.* 711 (1979).

shareholders, F with 51 per cent of the shares, who was to finance the undertaking, and A, who possessed the "know how". When the company's managing director was engaged in difficult negotiations to obtain the licences, F was forced into liquidation, which then left the company without working capital. The managing director took the licence in his own name, resigned from office (but not from the board), formed a company to exploit the properties and, after years of strenuous endeavour, made a sizeable profit from them. Shortly after he obtained the licence, he provided the board with a full account of what he had done and, having considered the matter, the board agreed that he should be permitted to "go it alone". It was held that, having obtained the board's informed consent, he need not reimburse the company for the profits he had made.

Remuneration

13–13   There are several instances of generous directors' remuneration paid to company controllers or their dependents being held invalid as *ultra vires*. In *Re Halt Garage (1964) Ltd*,[25] where the insolvent company's only two share-holders and directors were C and his wife, and the articles of association empowered the general meeting to pay directors' remuneration, the test of *vires* propounded was twofold. One is the financial state of the company at the time: were the payments made from earned or retained profits, or did they come from contributed capital? If they came from capital, there then arises the motive for payment: were the payments really directors' remuneration or were they gratuitous distributions to a shareholder out of capital, dressed up as remuneration? In the event, it was concluded that the payments made to C were valid but that part of the sums paid to his since-deceased wife were *ultra vires* on the above test.

13–14   The facts as stated in that much-criticised case dealing with pensions for ex-directors' dependents, *Re Lee, Behrens & Co.*,[26] do not tell us who held the shares in the company at the time the impugned covenant for a £500 per annum annuity was entered into in favour of the ex-managing director's widow. It would appear that she was an outsider, i.e. did not possess a signifi-cant or possibly any shareholding in the company. In any event, the issue there was not *ultra vires* in the sense presently understood, being beyond the very capacity of the company. Because the company's shareholders there never gave their approval for the covenant entered into by their board, the issue was simply whether that contract exceeded the directors' powers. In *Re W & M Roith Ltd*,[27] the pension in dispute was agreed between the company and its ailing managing director, who owned two thirds of the shares, many of the other shares being held by his relatives. Because, however, the articles of association there expressly authorised paying pensions to directors' widows, the tests of reasonably incidental to carrying on the company's business and

---

[25]   [1982] 3 All E.R. 1016.
[26]   [1932] 2 Ch. 46.
[27]   [1967] 1 W.L.R. 432.

bona fides and to promote the prosperity of the company were of no relevance to the question of *ultra vires*. In so far as the pension there may have been *ultra vires*, the proper test should have been the disguised repayment of capital criterion applied in the *Halt Garage* case.

DISTRIBUTIONS

13–15 In the case of solvent companies, any substantial distribution of surplus assets to some of their members is unlawful where one or more of the members object to such unnecessary benevolence; it constitutes a "fraud on a minority" or "oppression".[28] Where the company is insolvent, then any such distribution would contravene the 1983 Act's provisions against paying dividends from capital[29] and in any event is conventionally *ultra vires*.[30]

13–16 Where, however, the company is solvent and all of the members assent to the distribution, which does not involve repaying capital, the legal position is unclear in view of the Supreme Court's decision in *Re Greendale Developments Ltd (No. 2)*,[31] where most of the relevant points and authorities are not addressed in the judgment. The case concerned a small property development company which had a paid-up share capital of £18 and three shareholders, two of whom were also its directors and one of whom informally financed all of the company's activities. Substantial payments were made by the company to that director, the cheques were countersigned by the other director and the third shareholder (the recipient's wife) assented to the money being so paid. Following a dispute between the directors, on the recipient's petition the company was wound up on "just and equitable" grounds. At the time these payments were made the company was solvent and there was no suggestion that they were for some unlawful purpose, such as tax evasion. No consideration appears to have been given by the court to whether the contents of the company's memorandum or articles of association were relevant to the issue[32] of whether those payments were *ultra vires*.

13–17 Giving judgment, Keane J. said that the payments were *ultra vires*, relying principally on the dictum of Bowen L.J. in the *West Cork Railway* case.[33] But the benevolence at issue there was a directors' proposal to pay themselves gratuities, which was being challenged by a minority shareholder[34]; similarly with the *Daily News* case,[35] which was cited "to the same

---

[28] *Cook v Deeks* [1916] 1 A.C. 554.

[29] *Aveling Barford Ltd v Perion Ltd* [1989] B.C.L.C. 626.

[30] *Re George Newman & Co.* [1985] 1 Ch. 174.

[31] [1998] 1 I.R. 8. M.F. was the defendants' counsel in the appeal, which may colour the views expressed here.

[32] The payments would appear to have been permissible under these.

[33] *Hutton v West Cork Railway Co.* (1883) 23 Ch D 654. at 672–673 and see para. 19–07.

[34] At first instance Fry J. emphasised that the issue was whether it was "a matter in which the majority can bind a minority" (*Hutton v West Cork Railway Co.* (1883) 23 Ch D 654 at 658) and not conventional *ultra vires*.

[35] *Parke v Daily New Ltd* [1962] Ch. 927.

effect". Further, in both of those cases, the payments were intended to be made at a time when the companies had ceased trading entirely and all that was left was to wind them up. Keane J. cited "to the same effect" the *Lee Behrens* case.[36] But the issue there concerned the powers of the directors only, and also the company was insolvent at the time. Keane J. finally cited "to the same effect" *Roper v Ward*,[37] although the issue in that case has no bearing whatsoever on the matter in dispute in *Greendale*, involving as it did a non-profit company.

13–18 Keane J. distinguished *Re S M Barker Ltd*[38] on the grounds that the shareholders' assent given there was encapsulated in a formal resolution, whereas the assent of all the members in *Greendale* had been informal. But if a formal resolution could have validated the payments, then logically they could not have been *ultra vires* the company. In the somewhat similar *Buchanan* case,[39] involving substantial distributions of surplus assets in order to avoid paying tax in Scotland, the informality of the members' assent was not considered fatal by Kingsmill Moore J.; what was decisive there was that the purpose of those distributions was unlawful and, as well, they left the company spectacularly insolvent. Why the formality of passing a resolution would have made any difference in *Greendale* is not explained. Keane J. described the *Barker* case as authority for the proposition that "shareholders in a company cannot be made amenable under misfeasance proceedings for profits made by them, not in their capacity as directors of the company, but as shareholders."[40] What exactly is contemplated by these two "capacities" is not elaborated on; in the *Buchanan* case, no such distinction was drawn. Once all of the shareholders have approved the transaction in question and the company is solvent, there does not seem to be any practical grounds for differentiating between those capacities, assuming such difference indeed exists. Further, it was held in the *Home Treat* case[41] that, where a company does something that would be *ultra vires,* as not being within its objects, it is not to be treated as *ultra vires* where all of its members informally assented to it. Keane J. makes no reference to the *Rolled Steel Products* case,[42] which is the leading modern authority on the entire law of *ultra vires.* That case emphasises the distinction between the intrinsic capacity of a company and abuse of the directors' or the majority shareholder's powers that for-profit companies possess, such as to make distributions of surplus assets to their members in such manner as they choose.

13–19 The facts in *Greendale* resemble those in *Peter Buchanan Ltd v McVey*, except that in the latter the £300,000 which was distributed (in 1943) to the company's principal shareholder was to evade tax and rendered the company insolvent. With £100 paid capital, the company made enormous

---

[36] [1932] 2 Ch. 46.
[37] [1981] I.L.R.M. 408.
[38] [1950] I.R. 123.
[39] *Peter Buchanan Ltd v McVey* [1954] I.R. 89.
[40] [1998] 1 I.R. 8 at 24.
[41] [1991] B.C.L.C. 705.
[42] *Rolled Steel Products (Holdings) Ltd v British Steel Corp* [1986] Ch. 46.

profits in whiskey-dealing during World War II. When punitive taxes were imposed on those transactions, the owner of all but one of its shares decided to take almost all of those profits out of the company and transfer the money to Ireland, in the belief that the Scottish Revenue could not then recover what was due to them. He kept the Scottish Revenue in the dark about disposals of the company's stocks and, when most of them were sold, drew a cheque for £200,000 on the company's account, payable to another bank but for his own benefit. When all of the stocks were sold, his co-shareholder and director filled in several signed blank cheques for about £100,000, payable to a man in Dublin, who was a nominee of the defendant. When the company was wound up, the liquidator brought proceedings to have those disbursements recovered, arguing that they were *ultra vires*. He succeeded on that point, not because the payments had never been sanctioned by a formal resolution, nor because the recipient got the money *qua* shareholder rather than *qua* director, but because the underlying purpose was fraudulent and the transaction left the company unable to pay off its only creditor, a tax assessment for £370,000.

MINORITY PROTECTION

13–20 For practical and legal considerations, a court is more likely to intervene against majority action that approximates to fraud on the company by its controllers or unfair discrimination against the minority where the company concerned is closely held. If its shares are traded on a stock exchange, the view may be taken that in the marginal case the aggrieved shareholder should look to the exchange's own disciplinary mechanisms for redress; the outcome in the *Newman Industries Ltd (No.2)* case[43] would seem to support this analysis. Where the company's shares are freely transferable, especially if they have a ready market, the view may be taken that in the marginal case the dissatisfied shareholder always has the option of selling out, thereby cutting his losses. It may also be the case that there is far less likelihood of shareholders in widely-held companies forming grand coalitions with a view to unfairly discriminating against a minority. And where those coalitions are formed, there probably would be unambiguous evidence of their true objectives.

13–21 In contrast, majorities in close companies cannot be disciplined by the capital markets. On account of restrictions on the transferability of shares, often along the lines of Pt II of Table A,[44] aggrieved minorities in close companies may not be able to avail of the exit option. Where this is so, their funds would then be locked into a company, the governance of which they are profoundly dissatisfied with. Moreover, coalitions against minorities can be formed relatively easily and without formalities, so that it may be difficult to prove the majority's actual improper motives. In *Clemens v Clemens*

---

[43] [1982] 1 Ch. 204.
[44] Article 3, see para.9–60 *et seq.*

Bros Ltd,[45] there were only two shareholders in the company and the majority shareholder declined to testify at the trial. That close companies have a greater propensity to treat minority shareholders in unacceptably unfair ways is borne out by the reported cases on "oppression" and on winding up on "just and equitable grounds", virtually all of which involve such companies.[46]

13–22   It was stressed, however, in *Re Westbourne Galleries Ltd*[47] that the fact that a company is a small private company is not enough to warrant judicial intervention on behalf of a dissatisfied minority. The House of Lords there also cautioned against undue emphasis on the analogy with partnership law; saying that:

> "To refer, as so many of the cases do, to 'quasi-partnerships' or 'in substance partnerships' may be convenient but may also be confusing. It may be convenient because it is the law of partnership which has developed the conceptions of probity, good faith and mutual confidence, and the remedies where these are absent, which become relevant once [certain other] factors are found to exist ... And in many, but not necessarily all, cases there has been a pre-existing partnership the obligations of which it is reasonable to suppose continue to underlie the new company structure. But the expressions may be confusing if they obscure, or deny, the fact that the parties (possibly former partners) are now co-members in a company, who have accepted, in law, new obligations. A company, however small, however domestic, is a company not a partnership or even a quasi-partnership and it is through the just and equitable clause that obligations, common to partnership relations, may come in."[48]

13–23   While these remarks were addressed to petitions for winding up on "just and equitable" grounds, they are also relevant where "oppression" is alleged and ought to be taken into account in the personal action claiming unfair discrimination. Notable examples of this latter category of case include *Clemens Bros Ltd*,[49] which concerned a blatant "freeze in". Another is *Coleman v Meyers*,[50] a blatant "squeeze out", where the managing director and chairman used inside information about the company's affairs to buy out the minority shareholders for much less than their shares were really worth. It was held that, in the light of the family character of the company and the way the defendant went about the takeover and persuaded the plaintiffs to sell him their shares, he owed a fiduciary duty not alone to the company but to the minority shareholders as well.

13–24   This is not to say that all action taken by majorities in close companies that disadvantages the minority will be held to be unlawful. The classic instance of somewhat unfair action by the majority being upheld is *Greenhalgh v Arderne Cinemas Ltd*,[51] where the gravamen of the plaintiff's case was that he had been "frozen in" to the company.

---

[45] [1976] 2 All E.R. 268.
[46] *cf.* English Law Commission's *Shareholders' Remedies* (Report No. 246, October 1997).
[47] [1973] A.C. 360.
[48] *ibid.* at 379–380.
[49] [1976] 2 All E.R. 268.
[50] [1977] 2 N.Z.L.R. 255.
[51] [1951] Ch. 286.

SHAREHOLDERS' AGREEMENTS

13–25 Members of close companies at times conclude agreements between themselves, which are entirely separate from the memorandum and articles of association, but which purport to regulate in some detail how aspects of their company's affairs are to be run. One rarely encounters agreements of this nature where a company has many members because multiplicity of parties can make them cumbersome. Shareholders' agreements are often made at the time when the company is set up and are designed to ensure, from the very outset, that the various understandings reached by the individuals concerned are fully implemented, thereby avoiding disputes and divisions. Company law precedent books contain draft shareholders' agreements.[52] Unlike the articles of association, these agreements need not be disclosed to the public through the Registry of Companies. Although not strictly part of the company's constitution, disputes arising from these agreements are treated as if they were for the purpose of trans-national jurisdiction.[53]

13–26 A common form is a voting or "pooling" agreement, whereby the members agree either to vote or not to vote in a particular way or under particular circumstances.[54] But these agreements may range far wider and deal with matters like issuing new shares, declaring dividends, borrowing, disposal or acquisition of major assets, composition of the board and the remuneration of directors, transfers of shares and pre-emption rights.[55] These often provide for the resolution of inter-shareholder disputes by way of arbitration or some other means. Where the matter in dispute is covered by an arbitration clause, "oppression" proceedings in respect of it will be stayed.[56]

13–27 The Companies Acts do not expressly recognise these agreements. At one time voting agreements were regarded as contrary to public policy and not enforceable, but that is no longer the case. However, they are strictly interpreted, with the presumption favouring freedom to vote. There also were reservations about agreements that operated to fetter the discretion of the directors. But provided that all the present members of a company are party to them, those are not fundamentally objectionable.[57] Reservations also existed about agreements that purported to prevent the company in question (and not just its directors) from exercising a discretion which the Companies Acts granted the company as such, for instance, to amend the articles of association or to increase the share capital. Those doubts were laid to rest in 1992, at least in so far as rights and obligations between the members *inter se* are concerned.

---

[52] See *BCM's Precedents* part A99 & A113 and *Practical Commercial Precedents* parts B8 and 8A. See generally, R.K. Thomas & C. Ryan, *The Law and Practice of Shareholders' Agreements*, 2nd edn (London: Butterworths, 2007).

[53] *Speed Investments Ltd v Formula One Holdings Ltd (No. 2)* [2005] 1 W.L.R. 1936.

[54] e.g. *Halton Int'l (Holdings) SARL v Guernoy Ltd* [2006] 1 B.C.L.C. 78.

[55] e.g. *Holt v Faulks* [2000] 2 B.C.L.C. 80.

[56] *Re Via Net Works (Ireland) Ltd* [2002] 2 I.R. 47.

[57] *Fulham FC Ltd v Cabra Estates Ltd* [1994] 1 B.C.L.C. 363.

13–28   In *Russell v Northern Bank Development Corp.*,[58] the four founding members of a company had separately agreed between themselves that no additional shares would be issued without all of them consenting. This was held to be a valid and enforceable contract, even though its effect was to veto the statutory discretion to issue shares[59]; the agreement was "purely personal to the shareholders who executed it and [did] not purport to bind future share-holders".[60] The company itself also was a party to that agreement. It was held that, *qua* the company, the agreement was void and created no legally binding obligations. There is speculation that this finding is *obiter* because it is not fully consistent with earlier cases.[61] The court there "severed" this part from the remainder of the agreement, which it enforced by giving a declaration that any attempt to issue additional shares would be a breach of the inter-share-holder part of the agreement. It remains debatable whether any such attempted breach would be enjoined or whether, in view of the discretionary authority, the breach would be remediable only in damages.

13–29   Where the focus of a claim for breach of a shareholders' agreement is damage done directly to the company, thereby diminishing the value of the aggrieved party's investment, that generally operates as a bar against his claim, under the reflective loss principle. Where, however, the alleged wrongdoers' actions disable the company from suing them to recover the loss and damage that they have caused, this principle no longer applies.[62]

CREDITOR PROTECTION

13–30   That a company is owned almost entirely by one individual does not warrant the court disregarding its incorporation, whether it be to hold the owner liable for the company's obligations or to confer on the owner or his creditors rights accruing to the company (i.e. disregarding owner shielding and entity shielding). Instances like the *Salomon & Co.* case[63] and *Macaura v Northern Assurance Co.*[64] demonstrate the legal significance of individuals running their businesses as registered companies. Indeed, those individuals can be convicted of stealing from their own "one-person" companies.[65] Courts nevertheless disregard the incorporation of one kind of closely-held company, the wholly-owned subsidiary, where it is merely its parent's *alter ego*.[66]

13–31   Where a limited company is wound up and cannot pay its creditors in full, then various kinds of fraud affecting the company raise special problems

---

[58]   [1992] 1 W.L.R. 588.
[59]   1963 Act, s.68(1)(a).
[60]   [1992] 1 I.R. at 594.
[61]   See para.11–11.
[62]   *Perry v Day* [2005] 2 B.C.L.C. 405.
[63]   [1897] A.C. 22.
[64]   [1925] A.C. 619.
[65]   *Attorney General's Reference (No. 2) of 1982* [1984] 2 W.L.R. 453.
[66]   See para.3–83 *et seq.*

for the liquidator by virtue of the company's closely-held nature. If the company was managed negligently and, consequently, would have a right of action against its directors, that right is lost if its shareholders assented to or ratified those negligent acts. In the *Multinational Gas* case,[67] which concerned a company that was owned by three giant oil companies, at those shareholders' behest the nominee directors made some financially disastrous and negligent decisions. The company was wound up insolvent, owing enormous debts, and the liquidator sought to have its three owners made responsible for those debts. His claim was rejected on the grounds that the company was a separate legal entity; that it was not its owners' agent; that its owners owed it no duty of care and owed no such duty to its creditors. Whatever claim the company might have had against its directors for negligence was lost because they were carrying out its owners' wishes. One judge, however, suggested that the result would be different if the enormous damage to the company was plain before its owners endorsed the directors' wrongs.[68] Another judge suggested that the owners would be held liable if the directors' wrongs constituted statutory misfeasance.[69] According to the dissenting judge, the company had a cause of action in negligence against its directors and this was an asset that could only be gratuitously released for the company's benefit.[70] An argument that does not appear to have been made is that the justifications for limited liability in the *Salomon & Co.* situation does not obtain here because the owners of this insolvent company were organisations that themselves possessed limited liability; that the company's real owners were seeking to shield themselves from personal liability by an elaborate tier of limited companies.

13–32   Where the wrong done to the company is an unratifiable fraud on the company then, by definition, the liquidator can press the company's claim against the fraudsters. But the authorities (apart from *Greendale*), most of which are cited in *Multinational Gas* (not referred to in *Greendale*), tell us that the shareholders of a solvent company, acting unanimously, can do anything that is not *ultra vires* the company. Since 1963, all the shareholders are able to alter the objects clause without the need for court approval.[71] It, therefore, would seem to follow that, unless the company is rendered insolvent or there is some separate illegality, all of the shareholders can ratify frauds on the company that are not ratifiable by a simple majority. This happens frequently in "one-person" companies; the owners take or, as is sometime said, give themselves presents of, company property. But according to Gavan Duffy P. in *Re S. M. Barker Ltd*,[72] it is not officer misfeasance where the directors, who are also all of the shareholders, help themselves to company property, so long as the company is not thereby rendered insolvent. This state of affairs,

---

[67] *Multinational Gas & Petrochemical Co. Multinational Gas & Services Ltd* [1983] 1 Ch. 258.
[68] *ibid.* at 269 (Lawton L.J.).
[69] *ibid.* at 291 (Dillon L.J.).
[70] *ibid.* at 282 (May L.J.).
[71] See para.11–13 *et seq.*
[72] [1950] I.R. 123.

however, does not leave creditors of companies that were looted by their owners without redress.

13–33 To begin with, there is the *ultra vires* principle, which will catch straightforward fraud; owners who were aware of the fraud would not be protected by s.8(1) of the 1963 Act. However, some forms of what might be regarded as looting may be expressly authorised by the company's own regulations, like paying lavish directors' remuneration or even appropriating company property for its owners' benefit, i.e. distributions of surplus assets to them. Secondly, in *Re George Newman & Co.*,[73] it was said that insolvent companies have no right to give their directors presents out of their capital or borrowings. Indeed, Lawton L.J. in *Multinational Gas* ventured that, if it becomes clear that the directors' negligence will bankrupt the company, then the shareholders, even acting unanimously, cannot exonerate those directors from liability by ratifying their wrongs.[74] Thirdly, as *Re Halt Garages (1964) Ltd*[75] demonstrates, there is the principle against repaying shareholders their capital and such payments will not be permitted even if they are disguised as directors' remuneration. Fourthly, if the looting takes the form of repaying money lent to the company by its owners, this might constitute a fraudulent preference.[76] Fifthly, if the owners extract assets from the company to prevent it from paying a particular debt, the creditor may have a direct right of action against them for the tort of inducing breach of contract.[77]

ONE-PERSON COMPANIES

13–34 Since 1994 it has been possible to incorporate a company with a single member only, or to change status from a multi-member to a single-member company.[78] Such companies may be limited by shares or by guarantee. Subject to "any necessary modifications", the Companies Acts apply to these except where otherwise provided.[79] Such provisions exist for holding general meetings and for concluding contracts with the sole member,[80] and certain consequences of the membership falling below two are disapplied.[81]

13–35 All powers that are exercisable by a company at general meeting may be exercised by the sole member without holding such meeting, including removing the auditors.[82] Requirements for holding a meeting or having a

---

[73] [1895] 1 Ch. 674.
[74] [1983] 1 Ch. 258 at 280.
[75] [1982] 3 All E.R. 1016.
[76] 1963 Act, s.286.
[77] *Einhorn v Westmount Investments Ltd* 6 D.L.R. (3d) 71 (1969), aff'd 11 D.L.R. (3d) 509 (1970).
[78] European Communities (Single-Member Private Limited Companies) Regulations 1994 (SI 1994/275), giving effect to EC Directive 89/667, [1989] O.J. L395/40.
[79] Regulation 3.
[80] Regulation 13 and see para.18–12.
[81] Regulations 7 and 11 (1963 Act, ss.36, 213(d) and 215(a)(i)).
[82] Regulation 9.

resolution of the company are deemed to be satisfied in that manner. But where that member decides something that ordinarily could only be done at a general meeting, he must furnish the company with a written note of the decision. If the matter is one that should be notified to the Registrar of Companies, notice must be given within 15 days. Notwithstanding what the company's articles may state, the quorum for meetings of such companies is one.[83]

13–36   From year to year, the sole member may dispense with holding an AGM.[84] In any year where no decision to this effect was made, either the sole member or the auditors may require an AGM to be held. Where the AGM has been dispensed with, requirements to present reports and accounts to the AGM are deemed to be satisfied by having them sent to the sole member. Requirements to submit an annual return within 60 days of the AGM, that the accounts be made up to a time not earlier than nine months before the AGM and that there shall be a list of members drawn up 14 days after the AGM are adopted where a decision is made to dispense with an AGM.

---

[83]   Regulation 10.
[84]   Regulation 8.

CHAPTER 14

GROUP ENTERPRISES

14–01   Many businesses are run in the form of groups of companies. At the centre, typically, is the parent or controlling company. If the parent is a private company it may be registered without limited liability, either for reasons of taxation or to avoid having to make certain disclosures to the public about its affairs. Various parts of the business may be operated by subsidiary companies, the shares in which are owned either entirely or mainly by the parent company. Other aspects of the business may be run by affiliate companies in which wholly separate interests have a sizeable stake. If the business extends to different parts of the world, it may be described as a multinational enterprise.

14–02   The Companies Acts contain a number of rules for group enterprises[1]; a prominent feature of many parts of the 1990 Act is the extent to which it provides for group transactions and relationships. Thus, the prohibition on loans and comparable arrangements to directors or connected persons, on acquiring substantial assets from them, on directors dealing in options in their company's securities, as well as the requirement to disclose any of these transactions, apply vis-à-vis holding and subsidiary companies. So too does the right to inspect directors' service contracts and the prohibition on such contracts in excess of five years. Most Plcs with subsidiaries must present group accounts at their AGMs. The Taxes Consolidation Act 1997 (ss.410–429) provides for "group" tax reliefs for associated companies within groups[2] and group circumstances are also taken into account for the purposes of stamp duty and for VAT.[3] Work has been done by the EC Commission on a proposed Directive for corporate groups, that is stalled due to a lack of consensus about the appropriate approach.[4]

---

[1]   See generally, J. Dine, *The Governance of Corporate Groups* (Cambridge: Cambridge University Press, 2000); C.M. Schmitthoff and F. Wooldridge, *Groups of Companies* (Sweet & Maxwell: Centre for Commercial Law Studies, 1991); Austin, "Corporate Groups" in *Corporate Personality in the 20th Century* (C. Rickett and R. Grantham (eds), (Oxford: Hart, 1998); *cf.* P. Blumberg *et al*, *Blumberg on Corporate Groups*, 2nd edn (Maryland: Aspen Publishers, five vols, 2004), on the US law and practice.

[2]   See generally, M. Feeney, *The Taxation of Companies* (Dublin: Tottel Publishing, 2006), Ch.8.

[3]   *cf. State (Melbarian) v Revenue Commissioners* [1986] I.L.R.M. 476.

[4]   See generally, Derum, "The E.E.C. Approach to Groups of Companies" 16 *Virginia J. Int'l L.* 565 (1976).

SUBSIDIARY, RELATED AND ASSOCIATED COMPANIES

14–03 The principal legal relationship within a group of companies is that between the holding or parent company and its subsidiary company or companies. Most of the rules considered here were adopted with this relationship in mind. But there are certain rules which cast the net far wider and bring in other companies with some lesser connection with the company in question. Enterprises can be connected in a variety of ways, ranging from wholly-owned subsidiary at one end to a significant trading relationship at the other extreme.

"Holding"/"Subsidiary" Company

14–04 A company is another's (i.e. holding company's or parent company's) subsidiary for the purposes of the Companies Acts if it satisfies any of three criteria[5]:

• One is based on owning a majority of the company's shares: where one company or its nominee holds more than half in nominal value of the other's voting shares or, alternatively, more than half in nominal value of the other's "equity share capital". Preference shares do not count as "equity" here where their preference is in respect of dividends or return of capital that are capped at a particular amount. Shares held in a fiduciary capacity, shares held as security under the provisions of a debenture and shares held by a money-lending company as security for loans made in the ordinary course of business are excluded for the purposes of this computation.[6]

• Another criterion is based on ability to control the company's directors: where one company is a member of the other and controls the composition of the latter's board. Control means where one company has the unrestricted power to appoint or remove all or at least a majority of the other's directors.

• Thirdly, a holding company-subsidiary relationship arises where one company is a subsidiary of the other's subsidiary.

However, arrangements can easily be made whereby one company effectively owns and controls another without there being a holding company-subsidiary relationship as therein defined.[7]

14–05 In certain contexts there is a more expansive definition. Thus for the regime on purchasing shares in its holding company, a subsidiary of a Plc includes where the Plc is one of its shareholders or members and, by agreement with its other members, controls a majority of the voting rights.[8] In determining whether consolidated group accounts must be prepared, a company is also

---

[5] 1963 Act, s.155 (initially Companies Act 1959, s.5).

[6] *cf. Michaels v Harley House Ltd* [2000] Ch. 104 concerning a slightly different definition.

[7] See generally, Pickering, "Shareholders' Voting Rights and Company Control" 81 *L.Q.R.* (1965) 248 at 263–267.

[8] European Communities (Public Limited Companies Subsidiaries) Regulations 1997 (SI 1997/670), reg.4(1).

another's subsidiary if it can control a majority of the voting rights, alone or pursuant to an agreement with other shareholders;[9] also, where that other has a right to exercise or exercises, or has the power to exercise, a "dominant influence" or control over the company; also, where both are managed on a unified basis. A company does not have a right to exercise a dominant influence over another unless it is entitled to give directions to the other's directors regarding its operating and financial policies, with which they are obliged to comply. It depends on the circumstances of the particular case whether a company actually exercises a dominant influence over another or whether they are being managed on a unified basis. For tax purposes, there is still a more elaborate definition of subsidiary and a distinction is made between 51 per cent, 75 per cent, 90 per cent and wholly-owned subsidiaries.[10]

Related, Associated and Connected Companies

14–06 Several company law provisions are made with reference to what are called "related companies", notably, the extension of an inspection under Pt II of the 1990 Act to such companies,[11] the extension of an examination under the Companies (Amendment) Act 1990, to such companies,[12] the obligation to contribute towards the liabilities of an insolvent company,[13] and the pooling of assets of those companies when insolvent.[14]

14–07 "Related" here means,[15] in addition to parent and subsidiary companies:

- where more than half the nominal value of the company's equity share capital is held by the other company and by companies related to that other company (whether directly or indirectly, but not in a fiduciary capacity); or

- where more than half of the nominal value of the equity share capital of each of them is held by members of the other (whether directly or indirectly, other than in a fiduciary capacity); or

- where that other company or a company or companies related to that other company, or that other company together with a company or companies related to it, are entitled to exercise or control the exercise of more than one half of the voting power at any general meeting of the company; or

- where the businesses of the companies have been so carried on that the separate business of each company, or a substantial part thereof, is not readily identifiable; or

- where there is another company to which both companies are so related[16]; or

---

9 European Communities (Companies: Group Accounts) Regulations 1992 (SI 1992/201), reg.4.
10 Taxes Consolidation Act 1997, s.9.
11 Section 2.
12 Section 4.
13 1990 Act, s.140.
14 1990 Act, s.141.
15 1990 Act, s.140.
16 1990 Act, s.140(5).

• for the purposes of extending inspections, where goods or services are sold or given by one company to the other.[17]

A different definition is used for determining if companies are related for the purpose of disclosure in the annual accounts. Companies are there presumed to be related where one holds more than 20 per cent of the voting shares in the other.[18]

14–08 The Companies Acts occasionally use the terms "affiliate" or "associate" company, which means a company in which another has a sizeable equity stake, whether directly or indirectly, but not a subsidiary within the definition explained above. Thus, for purpose of the annual accounts, holding 20 per cent of the voting shares or of the allotted shares renders one company another's "associated company".[19] For the purpose of group accounts and credit institutions' accounts, an "associated undertaking" means a company in which another holds a participating interest on a long-term basis and where that other exercises a significant influence over its operating and financial policy.[20] For the purposes of the Redundancy Payments Act 1967, concerning the re-engagement of an employee by an "associate company",[21] this term signifies holding and subsidiary companies, as defined by the 1963 Act, and also two or more companies which are subsidiaries of a third company.

14–09 This concept also appears in regulatory and tax legislation, for instance in the Central Bank Acts, which enable persons authorised by the Central Bank to inspect all books and records of an "associated enterprise", i.e. a business which is associated with a licensed bank in the manner defined there. A similar provision exists in the Insurance Act 1989,[22] for what is described as any "connected body". For several tax purposes, companies are "connected" if the same person or persons connected with him have control of both.[23] There is a category of "related undertakings" in the Stock Exchange Act 1995, which includes related companies under the Companies Acts and two other types of link between undertakings.[24] For the purposes of close company taxation,[25] an "associated company" is defined as any company which controls or is under the control of another, or companies under the control of the same person; what constitutes "control" for this and other purposes is defined extensively.[26]

---

[17] 1990 Act, s.9(2).
[18] 1986 Act, Schedule, para.73.
[19] 1986 Act, s.18(1)(b).
[20] See fn.9, regs 34 and 35; there is a different definition for insurers' accounts.
[21] Section 16.
[22] Section 16.
[23] Taxes Consolidation Act 1997, s 10(6).
[24] *ibid.* s.3(1).
[25] *ibid.* s.432.
[26] *ibid.* ss.11 and 432(2)–(6).

HOLDING SHARES IN PARENT COMPANY

14–10   Generally a subsidiary may not acquire or hold shares in its own holding company.[27] Any such purported shareholding is void. Where a subsidiary acquired shares in its holding company other than in a manner authorised and, within six months of that time the company is unable to pay its debts, the directors are on risk of being made liable to repay whatever sum was paid for those shares.[28]

14–11   The above prohibition does not apply where the subsidiary's holding in its parent preceded May 5, 1959. Nor does it apply where, before it became a subsidiary, that company already held shares in what was to become its parent company; for instance, it had investments and was then taken over by one of the companies in which it held shares. Another exception is where the subsidiary itself is a member of an approved stock exchange and a professional dealer in securities, and it acquires the shares in its holding company in the ordinary course of its business.[29] Another still is where the interest of the subsidiary in the shares is as a personal representative or as trustee, unless either company is beneficially interested under the trust (other than as security for money lent in the ordinary course of business). A subsidiary may vote the shares it holds in this fiduciary capacity. A subsidiary with shares may accept and hold further shares in its parent company allotted in a capitalisation, provided the subsidiary is under no obligation to make any payment or give other consideration in respect of them.[30]

14–12   A subsidiary may acquire and hold shares in its holding company, subject to safeguards.[31] Before that acquisition can be made, the relevant contracts must have been authorised in advance by resolutions of both the subsidiary and the holding company. The same general principles apply to these resolutions as apply where the company wishes to purchase its own shares.[32] For instance, if it is an "off market" purchase, there must be a special resolution authorising the transaction and the parent company's votes must not have been the decisive ones in carrying that proposal. And a copy of the proposed contract must have been available for inspection by the members for at least three weeks before the resolution was passed. The consideration for this acquisition must come from profits of the subsidiary which are available for distribution. Provision was made in 1997 to prevent subsidiaries of Plcs from evading the safeguards on purchasing shares in their holding company.[33]

---

[27]   1963 Act, s.32.
[28]   1990 Act, s.225.
[29]   2001 Act, s.111.
[30]   1990 Act, s.224.
[31]   1990 Act, s.224.
[32]   See para.8–103 *et seq.*
[33]   European Communities (Public Limited Companies Subsidiaries) Regulations 1997 (SI 1997/67).

14–13 A subsidiary may not vote any shares it has in its parent company.[34] There is no restriction on dividends being paid to the subsidiary. When shares in a parent company are purchased, a form of capitalised reserve in the subsidiary is then created, in that any profits it possesses for distribution must be reduced by an amount equal to the purchase price for so long as the subsidiary holds those shares.[35] Those shares must not be shown in the consolidated accounts as an asset but disclosure must be made in the notes to the accounts of the shares' par value and the cost of acquiring them. A special return must be made to the Registrar of Companies within 28 days of the purchase.[36]

MINORITY PROTECTION

14–14 A dilemma that often confronts holding or parent companies is how to deal with a subsidiary in which independent shareholders have a stake. Especially when the subsidiary is an integral part of the parent's general business, the natural tendency is for the parent to make use of the subsidiary for the benefit of the entire enterprise and not just for the subsidiary alone. This practice raises the threshold question about directors' duties.[37] Do a subsidiary's directors, who are appointed by its parent and who put the advantage of the group enterprise before any discrete benefit to the subsidiary, violate their fiduciary duties? It would appear that they do,[38] although the question does not appear to have received exhaustive judicial consideration in this context.[39] If a breach of fiduciary duty of this nature occurs, when is it ratifiable by the majority shareholders or when does it amount to a fraud on the company or unfair discrimination against the minority? The standards discussed already apply in these circumstances, although application of them to parent–subsidiary relations might give rise to special difficulties. What often happens where conflicts of interest look likely is for the parent to buy out the minority shareholders at an attractive price in order to obtain a free hand in running the entire enterprise.

14–15 The leading early case on statutory oppression, *Scottish Co-op Wholesale Society v Meyer*,[40] is a textbook example of a parent unfairly exploiting its subsidiary to the detriment of the latter's minority shareholders. Having failed to buy out the minority at a relatively low price, the parent in effect ran down the subsidiary's business and removed the minority from their offices as the subsidiary's principal executives. The parent's main defence was that the circumstances—the parent refused to furnish the subsidiary with raw materials

---

[34] 1990 Act, s.224.

[35] 1990 Act, s.224(2)(b).

[36] 1990 Act, s.226.

[37] See generally, H. Yeung, "Corporate Groups: Legal Aspects of the Management Dilemma" [1997] *Lloyds Maritime and Commercial Law Quarterly* 208 and Lee, "Serving Two Masters—The Dual Loyalties of the Nominee Director in Corporate Groups" [2003] *J. Bus. L.* 449.

[38] *Lonrho Ltd v Shell Petroleum Co. (No 2)* [1982] A.C. 173.

[39] cf. *Lindgren v L & P Estates Ltd* [196] 1 Ch. 572 for the converse question.

[40] [1959] A.C. 324.

for its product and the parent's nominee directors on the subsidiary's board never took steps to reverse the company's decline—did not satisfy even the objective requirements for oppression. The Law Lords' answer to this was that:

> "all the evidence [shows no] trace that the [nominees] regarded themselves as owing any duty to the company of which they were directors. They were nominees of the [parent] and, if the [parent] doomed the company to destruction, it was not for them to put out a saving hand. Rather, they were to join in that work ... That is how they conducted the affairs of the company and it is impossible to suppose that that was not part of the deliberate policy of the [parent] ... It is not possible to separate the transactions of the [parent] from those of the company. Every step taken by the latter was determined by the policy of the former ... It is just because the [parent] could not only use the ordinary and legitimate weapons of commercial warfare but could also control from within the operations of the company that it is illegitimate to regard the conduct of the company's affairs as a matter for which the [parent] had no responsibility."[41]

14–16 Parent companies, therefore, must not take unfair advantage of subsidiaries in their business dealings with them. As it was put in the *Scottish Co-op* case:

> "whenever a subsidiary is formed as in this case with an independent minority of shareholders, the parent company must if it is engaged in the same class of business, accept as a result of having formed such a subsidiary an obligation so to conduct what are in a sense its own affairs as to deal fairly with its subsidiary. [In other words,] conducting what are in a sense its own affairs may amount to misconducting the affairs of the subsidiary."[42]

14–17 It was held by the Ontario courts in *Ford Motor Co. v Ontario Municipal Employees Retirement Board*[43] that the minority shareholder (a pension fund) in Ford's Canadian subsidiary had suffered oppression due to the manner in which the subsidiary's relations with its Detroit-based parent had been managed. That was because the transfer pricing arrangements imposed by the parent company were unfair to the subsidiary; had the subsidiary been independent, it would have been able to negotiate more favourable prices. On the evidence, the minority had a "reasonable expectation" that intra-corporate prices would be determined at arm's length, which had been unfairly disregarded. In contrast, in *Nicholas v Soundcraft Electronics Ltd*,[44] the petitioner and another established a company, of which they held 25 per cent of the issued shares and the remainder was held by the respondent, which was its parent company. The latter had assured financial support for the subsidiary but, at a time the parent was experiencing severe financial difficulties, it did not provide that support. Because the reason for the parent not doing so was to

---

[41] *ibid.* at 341.
[42] *ibid.* at 362.
[43] 263 D.L.R. (4th) 450 (2006).
[44] [1993] B.C.L.C. 360.

keep the entire group financially viable, its inaction in this regard was held not to constitute oppression.

14–18   Where the aggrieved minority only hold shares in the parent company and the mismanagement that constitutes oppression takes place in the subsidiary, that can amount to oppression of those shareholders where the parent's directors also represent a majority of the subsidiary's directors. In those circumstances, the affairs of the subsidiary are deemed to be part of the affairs of the holding company.[45]

PIERCING THE VEIL AND CREDITOR PROTECTION

14–19   On the question of disregarding the fact of incorporation—of what is often referred to as piercing the corporate veil—there is no hard and fast rule for groups.[46] It is only in very exceptional circumstances that a company that arranges its affairs in a group structure will be permitted to treat rights accruing to one of its subsidiaries or associates as being the parent company's entitlement. In *State (McInerney) Ltd v Dublin County Council*,[47] concerning a planning application, Carroll J. stressed that "the corporate veil is not a device to be raised or lowered at the option of the parent company or group."[48] Nor do the courts readily hold parent companies accountable for engagements entered into by their subsidiaries.

Separate Personality

14–20   The distinct legal personality of a holding company and of each of its subsidiaries, even wholly-owned subsidiaries, was emphasised in *Re Frederick Inns Ltd.*[49] Several of the companies in a group were heavily indebted to the Revenue. Before they all were wound up, they made a group settlement; several of them would sell property and pay the proceeds to the Revenue, which then credited that money towards the tax liabilities of the group. Payment by some of the companies, not indebted to the Revenue, of the tax liabilities of their related companies was held in the circumstances to be unlawful and that the money must be returned to the liquidator. This was because the Revenue received that money in the full knowledge of the entire circumstances and, furthermore, it is a fundamental principle that companies which are insolvent should not in effect make presents of their own assets. That the payments were

---

[45]   *Rackind v Gross* [2005] 1 W.L.R. 3505.

[46]   See generally, Rixon, "Lifting the Veil Between Holding and Subsidiary Companies" 102 *L.Q.R.* 415 (1986); Landers, "A Unified Approach to Parent, Subsidiary and Affiliate Questions in Bankruptcy" 42 *U. Chicago L. Rev.* 589 (1975); Posner, "The Legal Rights of Creditors of Affiliated Corporations: An Economic Approach" 43 *U. Chicago L. Rev.* 449 (1976) and Landers, "Another Word on Parents, Subsidiaries and Affiliates in Bankruptcy" 43 *U. Chicago L. Rev.* 527 (1976).

[47]   [1985] I.R. 1.

[48]   *ibid.* at 7. Also *Lac Minerals Ltd v Chevron Minerals Corp.* [1995] 1 I.L.R.M. 161 and *National Dock Labour Board v Pinn & Wheeler Ltd* [1989] B.C.L.C. 647.

[49]   [1994] I.L.R.M. 582.

in respect of the liabilities of other companies in the group did not alter that position. According to Lardner J.:

> "this principle [of separate legal personality] and the statutory rules of company law in which the principle is implicit apply to the relationship between holding companies and subsidiaries and to transactions between them and third parties. The assets of such companies are treated as owned by them legally and beneficially as distinct legal entitles. And except were circumstances enable a court to discover an agency or trustee relationship between them, a holding company is not treated as the owner of its subsidiaries' assets. And the liabilities of companies which are members of the same group are those of the individual companies which incur them. There is no common group liability for the obligations of individual members of the group imposed by law. The principle is reflected in many aspects of company law ... Taxing statutes also recognise the principle that each company is a separate legal entity, to the extent that they do not tax a holding company and its subsidiaries as if it were one."[50]

Asserting Rights

14–21 Ordinarily, a parent company has no right of action in damages or other entitlements in respect of a loss suffered by or right accruing to its subsidiary; it is for the latter alone to prosecute such claim as it may have.[51] However, where the parent company contracts with a third party to render some service to its subsidiary or to otherwise deal with it, and that party breaches that contract, the parent is entitled to damages for such foreseeable loss as it has suffered in consequence of the breach. In the *George Fischer* case,[52] there was a holding company and several operating subsidiaries, one of which carried out the sales function. The holding company contracted with the defendant to install equipment at the sales subsidiary, but that equipment was defective, leading to losses in group sales and increased operating costs. The parent company was held entitled to recover substantial damages for the losses that it had incurred.

14–22 Circumstances even can arise where a parent company has a right of action in negligence for what a third party has done in respect of its subsidiary. This was held to be the case in *Barings Plc v Coopers & Lybrand*,[53] where it was held that auditors of the since-defunct-plaintiff bank's Singapore subsidiary, who failed to detect the defalcations occurring there, owed a duty of care to the parent in London as well as to the subsidiary. On the facts, there was sufficient "proximity" between the parent and that auditors to found a duty of care. There is "no legal principle that a holding company is unable to recover damages for loss in the value of its subsidiaries, resulting directly from a

---

[50] *ibid.* at 587–588.
[51] *State (McInerney)* case [1983] I.R. 1, *Woolfson v Strathclyde Regional Council* 38 P. & C.R. 521 (1979) and *Stewart's Supermarkets Ltd v Secretary of State* [1982] N.I. 286.
[52] *George Fischer (Great Britain) Ltd v Multi Construction Ltd* [1995] 1 B.C.L.C. 260.
[53] [1997] 1 B.C.L.C. 427.

breach of duty to it, as distinct from a duty owed (or not owed as the case may be) to the subsidiaries."[54]

Incurring Liability

14–23   There is no reported major instance of a parent being held liable for its insolvent limited subsidiary's debts on the grounds that it controlled that subsidiary. In the absence of fraud or wholly exceptional circumstances, the principle in *Salomon & Co.*[55] would insulate the parent from liability. It could be argued that the justifications for limited liability do not obtain in these circumstances[56]; for instance, that limited liability was designed to insulate individual investors and not organisations that already possess limited liability. It also could be contended that, when the subsidiary is being run as an arm of the group enterprise, then loans advanced to it by the parent or by another subsidiary should not be treated as debts that must be preferred over outside unsecured creditors, on the grounds that those advances are more akin to equity investment. This is because funds placed by a parent in its subsidiary are paid over in the expectation of enhancing the entire group's profit and, accordingly, are more in the nature of equity than debt. The fact that the subsidiary was left seriously under-capitalised and was never given the opportunity to grow into an independently-profitable unit might give credence to such arguments in an appropriate case.

14–24   In one instance where an aspect of this matter was examined thoroughly, *Adams v Cape Industries Plc*,[57] the issue was whether a judgment obtained in Texas should be enforced in England against a company registered in England and which was never physically present in Texas. It was argued that the company should be deemed to have been present there because it had a wholly-owned marketing subsidiary which carried on the American side of its business there. Because, in the circumstances, the group was a highly-integrated economic unit, it was contended that the subsidiary's presence was the equivalent of the parent's presence there. That view was rejected. Even if economically they were the one entity, the court was concerned not with economics but with law. Most of the authorities tending to favour the one-unit contention can be explained by reference to particular terms of the Act relevant to the disputes or the contract under consideration at the time. Slade L.J. there summed up the law as follows:

> "There is no general principle that all companies in a group of companies are to be regarded as one. On the contrary, the fundamental principle is that each company in a group of companies (a relatively modern concept) is a separate legal entity possessed of separate legal rights and liabilities ... [S]ave in cases which turn on the wording of particular statutes or contracts, the court is not free to disregard [that] principle merely because it considers that justice so requires ... If a company chooses to

---

[54]   *ibid.* at 435.
[55]   [1897] A.C. 22.
[56]   See Landers, at fn.46.
[57]   [1990] 1 Ch. 433.

arrange the affairs of its group in such a way that the business carried on in a particular foreign country is the business of its subsidiary and not of its own, it is ... entitled to do so ... [T]he court is [not] entitled to lift the corporate veil as against a [holding] company which is the member of a corporate group merely because the corporate structure has been used so as to ensure that the legal liability (if any) in respect of particular future activities of the group (and correspondingly the risk of enforcement of that liability) will fall on another member of the group rather than the [parent] company."[58]

14–25 The Supreme Court came to a similar conclusion in an application to join a Plc to proceedings that had been brought against its subsidiary, for the purposes of rendering the Plc liable in the event of success on the main claim. In *Allied Irish Coal Suppliers Ltd v Powell Diffryn Int'l Fuels Ltd*,[59] Murphy J. accepted that there could be a most exceptional instance where a parent could be held so accountable, notwithstanding "the corner stone of company law", *Salomon & Co.* Even in such a case, it was said that the creditors with conflicting claims against the assets of the several companies involved would be entitled to a hearing. Ordinarily, it would be unjust to the parent's own creditors and to others interested in its assets and activities, to expose it to liability for its insolvent subsidiary's debts.

Exceptions

14–26 There are exceptions to the separate personality principle, however, either by virtue of statutory provision or where an agency relationship is established, or in certain instances of fraud. The extent to which there is an open-ended exception to do "justice" is questionable.

Statute

14–27 For a variety of purposes, modern tax laws treat parent and subsidiary companies as a single group, with consolidated entitlements and liabilities.[60] Several of the older tax cases which appear to disregard separate incorporation can be explained by reference to the statutory provisions in question there.[61] Arguments for treating companies in a group as one unit were accepted in some provisions to the 1990 Act dealing with winding up insolvent companies. Thus misfeasance proceedings may be brought not only against various officers of the insolvent company but also against any director of its holding company who is guilty of misfeasance in relation to it.[62] Where a parent or other

---

[58] *ibid.* at 532, 536–537 and 544.
[59] [1998] 2 I.R. 519.
[60] See fn.2.
[61] e.g. *Apthorpe v Peter Schoenhofen Brewing Co.*, 4 T.C. 41 (1899) and *Saint Louis Breweries v Apthorpe*, 4 T.C. 111 (1899), both holding that the English parent company "carried on business" in the USA through its subsidiaries there. Similarly, *Canada Rice Mills Ltd v R.* [1939] 3 All E.R. 991 and *Firestone Tyre & Rubber Co. v Llewellin* [1957] 1 W.L.R. 464.
[62] 1963 Act, s.298.

"related" company was closely involved in managing the insolvent company or led its creditors to believe that its liabilities would be covered, the court may order payment by that company of a contribution towards the liabilities of the insolvent company.[63] In *Re Bray Travel Ltd*,[64] where a number of inextricably-connected companies were being put into liquidation, the Supreme Court ordered that they all could be wound up as if they were a single entity. That decision was put on a firm statutory basis, enabling related companies' assets to be pooled and that they be wound up together where that is just and equitable to do so.[65]

14–28   In what circumstances group structures will be disregarded so as to impose statutory liability on the parent company for what strictly were the acts of a wholly-owned sub-subsidiary, arose in *Fyffes Plc v DCC Plc*.[66] It was held that, *inter alia*, the parent company of wholly-owned subsidiaries and a sub-subsidiary could all be deemed to be a single entity for the purpose of liability for insider trading. That was because, according to Laffoy J., the regime for supervising that type of market abuse could otherwise be avoided by way of astutely manipulating corporate structures. The judge upheld the contention that, notwithstanding that in the circumstances the parent company could not be held liable for those subsidiaries' unpaid debts, "against the factual background which existed in relation to the companies within the DCC group at the date of the [impugned] share sales,[67] Part V of the 1990 Act [on insider trading] should be applied so as to prevent the statutory remedy available under it being rendered ineffective."[68] For that reason, it was contended "because of the factual circumstances which prevailed, the act of Lotus Green (i.e. the foreign resident sub-subsidiary) in selling the shares and thereby making a profit was the act of DCC or, alternatively, should be treated as such. Further, the profit generated was DCC's or should be treated as such. If DCC was precluded [by law] from dealing, Lotus Green was similarly restricted."[69]

14–29   Following a review of the case law, Laffoy J. came to the following conclusions on the applicable principle:

  (i)   As a matter of law, Lotus Green may be regarded as having acted as the agent of DCC in relation to the holding and disposal of the shares in Fyffes, if to do otherwise would lead to an injustice. Whether it should be, depends on whether the inference is factually justified. This is to be determined having regard to all of the facts, including the nature of its interest in the shares, the relationship between Lotus

---

[63]   1990 Act, s.140.
[64]   Unreported, Supreme Court, July 13, 1981.
[65]   1990 Act, s.141; *cf. Re Dalhoff & King Holdings Ltd* [1991] 2 N.Z.L.R. 296.
[66]   [2005] I.E.H.C. 477, Laffoy J., unreported, December 21. This particular aspect of the case was not challenged in the appeal, which was decided against the defendants on the price-sensitivity question: [2007] I.E.S.C. 36, unreported, July 27, 2007.
[67]   Summarised at para.3–72.
[68]   At 89 of the judgment.
[69]   *ibid.*

Green and DCC. The views of the human agents of the companies are not in any way determinative of the question.

(ii) As a matter of law, Lotus Green and DCC may be treated as a single entity as regards the sale of the shares in Fyffes and the generation of the profit therefrom for the purpose of preventing the avoidance of the availability of an effective remedy under s. 109 and thus preventing an injustice to parties with a remedy under s. 109, if DCC is liable to account. It should be so treated if the plaintiff has established that:

(a) an evidential basis exists for finding that, as regards the holding and disposal of the shares, to borrow the terminology used by Murphy J. in the *Lac Minerals Limited* case, there was a factual identification of the acts of Lotus Green and DCC and

(b) not to so treat the companies would allow the DCC Group to evade its obligations under Part V.

In relation to the point at (a), the plaintiff argued that the companies in the DCC Group could have, but did not in fact, arrange their affairs so as to ensure that factual identification did not take place. In relation to the point at (b), the plaintiff did not and, on the evidence could not, assert that the purpose of the incorporation of Lotus Green and the hiving off of the shares to it was to avoid liability under Part V. The sole objective was to mitigate the tax liablity of the DCC Group. However, the reality of the situation is that by defending the plaintiff's statutory claim on the basis that DCC made no profit from the sale of the shares, if DCC was precluded from dealing by virtue of s. 108(6) and Lotus Green was not, the DCC Group would effectively evade liability under s. 109, if the profit generated by Lotus Green on the Share Sales were not treated as the profit of DCC To recognise this reality is to give a purposive meaning to Part V in light of the Directive.[70]

14–30 While rejecting the agency proposition, the judge concluded that the companies should be treated as a single entity. That was because, principally, Mr. Flavin was not a shadow director of Lotus Green and Lotus Green was not caught by s.108, while DCC Group was so caught but had made no profit. Therefore, not to treat the companies as one would have resulted in the unjust consequence of DCC Group avoiding any obligations under s.108.[71]

Fraud

14–31 To establish accountability or impose liability, the corporate veil, whether between individuals and their companies or between parent and subsidiary companies, will be lifted in instances of fraud.[72] One explanation for the *Re Bray Travel Ltd*[73] decision may be that the absence of any separate books or records, and other circumstances disclosed to the court there, strongly

---

[70] At 101–102.
[71] See para.3–72.
[72] See para.3–74 *et seq.* and 3–88.
[73] Unreported, Supreme Court, July 13, 1981.

suggested that there had been fraud in connection with those companies. Kenny J. referred to company property having been sold at a "gross under-value". Ordinarily, when deciding to disregard the separate corporate existence on the grounds of fraud, the motive for establishing the subsidiary calls for consideration. In the *Cape Industries* case,[74] it was held that the objective of minimising the parent's potential exposure to legal liability could not be a fraudulent motive for this purpose.

Agency

14–32   That the businesses and affairs of the parent and its subsidiary are closely integrated is not enough to establish an agency; the subsidiary has to have practically no independent commercial existence of its own for it to be considered an agent of its holding company. Although, in *Stewart's Supermarkets Ltd v Secretary of State*,[75] the parent had complete control of its wholly-owned subsidiary. Hutton J. held that the latter was not sufficiently inconsequential to be regarded as an agent or *alter ego* of its parent for the purpose of recovering statutory compensation for destruction of the subsidiary's premises.

14–33   One of the few instances where a parent was held entitled to a right ordinarily accruing to its subsidiary was *Munton Brothers Ltd v Secretary of State*[76] which involved a claim for compensation in respect of criminal damage to property and where the company that actually suffered the financial loss was the parent company of the one whose property was damaged. Because of the exceptionally close business relations between the two companies here, it was held that the subsidiary was the parent's "agent" or *alter ego* and, accordingly, damage done to the subsidiary was damage done to the parent. The subsidiary never really operated as an independent business entity; its function was to make up cloth supplied by the parent and then return the cloth to it, and the terms on which the subsidiary did this business were such that it never made a profit nor incurred a loss in any year. Gibson L.J. observed that, while the courts are extremely reluctant to hold that a company is its shareholders' agent or acts as a trustee for them, even for a sole proprietor-shareholder, "the same objections do not apply where it is sought to demonstrate that a subsidiary company is in fact agent of its parent company because the conception of incorporation is preserved intact".[77] The judge went on to hold that, even in the absence of an agency relationship, there are circumstances where justice demands that closely-integrated companies in a group situation should be treated as one. The reported cases do not provide clear guidance as to what those situations are—either regarding the relationship between the companies or the particular context in which the decision to pierce the veil arises. He concluded that the present instance was such a case because, otherwise, compensation would not be paid in respect of extensive consequential loss and

---

[74] [1990] 1 Ch. 433.
[75] [1982] N.I. 286, at para.3–76.
[76] [1983] N.I. 369.
[77] *ibid.* at 379.

the subsidiary was wholly owned, it had no separate business of its own and the parent company owned the property which it occupied.[78]

14–34　In the *Cape Industries* case,[79] the court examined carefully the internal arrangements of the group there and concluded that the subsidiary had a business of its own and was not simply its parent's *alter ego*, thereby insulating the parent from being accountable in any way for liabilities incurred by its subsidiary in Texas.[80]

Other Circumstances

14–35　On a number of occasions the courts have bypassed the separate corporate existence to enable a company obtain a benefit that otherwise it would have been denied. In *Smith, Stone & Knight Ltd v Birmingham Corp.*,[81] a company acquired a partnership, which it registered as a company, and then carried on the partnership business through that subsidiary. When the local authority compulsorily acquired the subsidiary's business premises, the parent sought compensation in respect of removal and disturbance. Its claim succeeded on the grounds that, because of the way the subsidiary was run, it ought to be treated as the parent's agent or *alter ego*. Criteria were set out there for determining when a subsidiary is its parent's agent, namely:

> "[W]ere the profits treated as profits of the ... parent company? Secondly, were the persons conducting the business appointed by the parent company? Thirdly, was the [parent] the head and brain of the trading venture? Fourthly, did the [parent] govern the adventure, decide what should be done and what capital should be embarked on the venture? Fifthly, did the [parent] make the profits by its skill and direction? Sixthly, was the [parent] in effectual and constant control?"[82]

14–36　In a later and somewhat similar case it was observed that there is "a general tendency to ignore the separate legal entities of various companies within a group, and to look instead at the economic entity of the whole group. This is especially the case when a parent company owns all the shares of the subsidiaries, so much that it can control every movement of the subsidiaries."[83] But these remarks exaggerate somewhat the legal position.

14–37　In the *Cape Industries* case, the court rejected the view that it is "free to disregard the principle of *Salomon v Salomon* merely because it considers

---

[78] Similarly, *DHN Food Distributors Ltd v London Borough of Tower Hamlets* [1976] 1 W.L.R. 852, which several commentators regard as either wrongly decided or else very specific to its own facts.

[79] [1990] 1 Ch. 433.

[80] Similarly, *Re Polly Peck Int'l Plc (No. 3)* [1996] 1 B.C.L.C. 428.

[81] [1939] 4 All E.R. 116.

[82] *ibid.* at 121.

[83] *DHN Food Distributors Ltd v London Borough of Tower Hamlets* [1976] 1 W.L.R. 852 at 860.

that justice so requires".[84] However, in *Re Bray Travel Ltd*,[85] the Supreme Court endorsed the view that "a court may, if the justice of the case so requires, treat two or more related companies as a single entity so that the business notionally carried on by one will be regarded as the business of the group, or another member of the group, if this conforms to the economic and commercial realities of the situation". Justice was invoked in the *Munton Bros* case[86] for reaching the conclusion that the holding company should receive compensation for the loss of its subsidiary's business. Justice also was the basis for treating the holding company and its several subsidiaries as one in *Fyffes Plc v DCC*,[87] in the context of the regime against insider trading.

14–38   The rationale for the holding in *Re Bray Travel Ltd* was that separate records were never kept for the different companies and, accordingly, it was practically impossible to carry out separate liquidations of them. A similar instance, although not involving liquidation, is *Power Supermarkets Ltd v Crumlin Investments Ltd*.[88] There the first defendant, a company that later was acquired by the Dunnes Stores group, had leased a unit in a shopping centre to the plaintiff. In the lease the first defendant covenanted not to allow any extra-large supermarket to be operated in the centre; not to "grant a lease for or to sell or permit or suffer the sale by any of its tenants or ... any sub or under tenants" of groceries in a unit greater than 3,000 square feet. Subsequently, the group decided to open a 3,000 square feet-plus supermarket in the unit. To that end, it incorporated a new company, the second defendant, and the first defendant conveyed to it the fee simple in the unit. All the evidence showed that the Dunnes companies involved were merely vehicles for carrying out the wishes of the controlling family and that their wishes prevailed in respect of each company in the group. The first defendant was the wholly-owned subsidiary of Cornelscourt Shopping Centre Ltd, which was a wholly-owned subsidiary of Dunnes Holding Co., which was an unlimited company whose shareholders were trustees of a discretionary trust for the Dunne family. Through another chain of subsidiaries, the second defendant's ownership could be traced back to Dunnes Holding Co. Since the time they were incorporated, there had been no meetings as such of either defendants' shareholders or board of directors. Instead, they were managed and controlled by members of the Dunne family meeting informally. Costello J. instanced the conveyance of the unit to highlight the reality of the relationship between the companies. The consideration was only £100, it contained none of the usual easements and it was not registered. In the light of all this, he said, it would be "very hard to find a clearer case ... for the application of [the] principle" that the corporate veil should be set aside "if the justice of the case so requires.[89]

---

[84] [1990] 1 Ch. 433 at 537.
[85] Unreported, Supreme Court, July 13, 1981.
[86] [1983] N.I. 369.
[87] [2005] I.E.H.C. 477, Laffoy J., unreported, December 21, 2005; that part of the judgment was not appealed: [2007] I.E.S.C. 36, unreported, July 27, 2007.
[88] [1981] I.E.H.C. 137; Costello J., unreported, June 22, 1981.
[89] At 8–9 of the judgment.

ACCOUNTS

14–39 Private holding companies are not obliged to prepare consolidated group accounts.[90] Where group accounts are not made up, every member of the company is entitled to be sent a copy of the latest balance sheet of each of its subsidiaries, along with every document that must be annexed to it and their directors' and auditors' annual reports.[91] Copies of these can be required for up to 10 years preceding the request. Exception is made for where the right to obtain these accounts is being abused. Where a private limited company makes up group accounts, it must comply with, *inter alia*, Pt V of the Schedule to the 1986 Act. If it is a non-profit company, the format is the Sixth Schedule to the 1963 Act.[92]

14–40 Most Plcs are required to make up group accounts,[93] in respect of which there are a variety of formats: the International Financial Reporting Standards (IFRS), in particular IAS27, which are obligatory for companies with securities listed on a stock exchange in the EC,[94] the Group Accounts Regulations of 1992,[95] which give effect to the EC's Seventh Directive,[96] Companies Acts accounts,[97] the Credit Institutions Accounts Regulations of 1992,[98] which give effect to EC Directives 86/635 and 89/117,[99] and the Insurance Undertakings Accounts Regulations of 1996,[100] which give effect to EC Directive 91/674.[101] There is an extended definition of what is a subsidiary for these purposes.[102] In certain circumstances, particular subsidiaries may be excluded from the accounts. Accounts in accordance with the 1992 Regulations are not required where the entire group falls below the financial and employee numbers thresholds for medium-sized companies.[103]

14–41 There are four categories of unlisted Plc that are exempted from having to prepare group accounts, on the basis that they themselves are wholly-owned or substantially-owned subsidiaries of other companies with satisfactory group accounts. The exemption for the latter three is from complying with the 1992 Regulations.

* One is where, at the end of the financial year, the company itself is a wholly-owned subsidiary of another company or other body corporate incorporated in the State.[104]

---

[90] 1963 Act, s.154.
[91] *ibid.*
[92] 1963 Act, s.152(3).
[93] 1963 Act, s.150 and see para.17–71 *et seq.*
[94] 1963 Act, s.150(2).
[95] European Communities (Companies: Group Accounts) Regulations, SI 1992/201.
[96] [1983] O.J. L493/1.
[97] 1963 Act ss.151–152.
[98] SI 1992/294.
[99] [1986] O.J. L372/1 and [1989] O.J. L44/40.
[100] SI 1996/23.
[101] [1991] O.J. L374/7.
[102] See para.14–05.
[103] Regulation 7(1) and see para.17–62.
[104] 1963 Act, s.151(2)(a).

- Another is where the company itself is either a wholly-owned or at least 90-per-cent-owned subsidiary of another company incorporated anywhere in the EEA.[105] If it is at least 90-per-cent-owned, its other shareholders must have approved the exemption. To qualify, its own parent's accounts must have been audited and its directors' report must have been drawn up in accordance with the law of where it is incorporated and also the Seventh Directive or the IFRS, and they must deal with all of its subsidiaries, including the exempted company. Additionally, the notes to the exempted company's accounts must disclose its parent's name and the location of its registered office, and the fact that it is exempted. Further, it must annex to its annual return copies of its parent's group accounts and directors' and auditors' reports.

- Another is where the company itself is a subsidiary of another company incorporated in the EEA, that satisfies the above requirements "to qualify", and 10 per cent or more of its own shareholders have not requested that group accounts be prepared in accordance with these Regulations.[106]

- Another still is where its own parent is incorporated outside the EEA and the parent either wholly owns the exempted company or the parent holds more than 50 per cent of its shares and a significant minority of members in the exempted company have not given notice requiring group accounts.[107] Its parent must satisfy requirements similar to those above "to qualify". Normally, having accounts prepared in accordance with the Canadian, Japanese or United States GAAP suffices for these purposes.

---

[105] 1992 Regulations, reg.8.
[106] 1992 Regulations, reg.9.
[107] 1992 Regulations, reg.9A.

CHAPTER 15

PUBLIC COMPANIES

15–01 By public companies here is meant companies with a widely dispersed ownership, in particular those whose securities are traded on a stock exchange or other public market for stocks and shares. All Irish companies that fall into this category are Plcs, although not every Plc has its securities quoted on an exchange. Many of the rules applicable to Plcs are contained in the 1983 Act or derive from other EC Directives. These are supplemented by regimes for companies with securities that are traded on or are about to obtain a quote on a stock exchange, regarding principally public securities offers/introductions, transfer of title to securities, insider trading and other market abuses and continuing disclosure. Many of the rules applicable to takeovers and mergers are not confined to quoted companies.

REGISTRATION

15–02 The form of the memorandum of association for Plcs, either limited by shares or limited by guarantee and with a share capital, must approximate to the Second Schedule in the 1983 Act.[1] But no new Plc may take the limited-by-guarantee form.[2] The company's name must describe it as a public limited company, or abbreviated as Plc, or the Irish equivalent. Before a Plc can commence doing business, it requires a certificate from the Registrar of Companies that all the prerequisites for its establishment have been met.[3] Procedures exist whereby a private company, an unlimited company and a joint stock company may re-register as a Plc.[4] A Plc may re-register as a private company.[5]

GOVERNANCE

15–03 Where companies have a recognised market for their securities, it is far easier for them to raise substantial additional funds because investors are assured of liquidity. Even though an investor's holding may be comparatively small, he can readily dispose of it on the market and does not have to accept a significant discount on the quoted price on account of his selling only a minority interest.

---

[1]   1983 Act, s.4(3).
[2]   1983 Act, s.7.
[3]   1983 Act, s.6 and Form 70.
[4]   1983 Act, ss.9–11 and 18.
[5]   1983 Act, ss.14 & 15.

One of the fundamental conditions imposed by most recognised securities markets is that the securities in question should be freely transferable.

15–04   A drawback on the other hand for many shareholders in such companies is that their proportionate stake in them is so small that it is virtually impossible for them to exercise any influence over the conduct of their affairs. Save in exceptional circumstances, for all practical purposes, governance as well as the management of the company is under the control of the board; general meetings are largely a formality, proposals emanating from the board almost invariably being passed and proposals the board dislikes almost invariably being rejected. Boards of directors tend to be dominated by professional managers, who have little or no financial stake in their companies other than their service contracts and remuneration packages. Ever since Berle and Means in 1932 published their analysis of this phenomenon, *The Modern Corporation and Private Property*,[6] numerous suggestions have been made to render boards of publicly-quoted companies more accountable and more responsive to the interests of their shareholders. Notwithstanding that these companies must publish substantial information concerning their affairs, many shareholders still lack sufficient information to fully evaluate management's performance. A huge obstacle is mobilising a large number of geographically and otherwise disparate number of shareholders to resist proposals coming from management. Whenever there is a major scandal involving such companies, for instance that in 2001 when energy company Enron collapsed in the US, calls are made to redress the imbalance between their directors and the generality of their shareholders. Issues of this kind, however, rarely become matters of public debate in Ireland.

Legislation

15–05   Apart from requiring the fullest disclosure of annual financial information, the Companies Acts contain no significant differences between the governance regimes for private companies and for Plcs, regarding convening and the conduct of general meeting, and how directors should be selected and conduct their business. The greater the number of shareholders there are, the more use will be made of the proxy machinery, but the statutory rules concerning proxies are the same for all types of companies. Plcs' annual accounts are subject to the full rigours of the 1986 Act and every Plc is required to have an audit committee. There is a more intensive statutory regulation of companies with securities that are listed on a stock exchange

---

[6]   A. Berle & G. Means (1932) (New Brunswick and London: Translation Publishers, 2006 reprint). The academic literature on the governance of major companies is enormous, especially in the US. Recent contributions to the debate include M. Roe, *Political Determination of Corporate Governance: Political Context, Corporate Impact* (New York: Oxford University Press, 2003); Bebchuk, "The Case for Increasing Shareholder Power" 118 *Harv. L. Rev.* 833 (2005), "Symposium: Management and Control of the Modern Business Corporation" 69 *U. Chicago L. Rev.* No. 3 (2002); "Symposium: Norms and Corporate Law" 149 *U. Penn. L. Rev. No.* 6 (2002); and "Symposium: Challenges to Corporate Governance" 62 *Law & Contemporary Problems* No. 3 (1999).

regarding how they raise finance from the public, undocumented securities, market abuses, annual accounts, and the disclosure of financial and other information concerning their affairs.

Listing Rules

15–06 Provisions in the Irish Stock Exchange's Listing Rules[7] directly relevant to questions of company governance include the following. A fundamental obligation of all listed companies is that of equal treatment of like securities holders: that a company "must ensure equality of treatment for all holders of all listed equity securities or listed preference shares who are in the same position". There also are six overarching "listing principles"[8] that a company must observe, namely:

- "take reasonable steps to enable its directors to understand their responsibilities and obligations as directors;

- take reasonable steps to establish and maintain adequate procedures, systems and controls to enable it to comply with its obligations;

- act with integrity towards holders and potential holders of its listed securities;

- communicate information to holders and potential holders of its listed equity securities in such a way as to avoid the creation or continuation of a false market in such equity securities;

- ensure that it treats all holders of the same class of its listed equity securities that are in the same position equally in respect of the rights attaching to such equity securities;

- deal with the Irish Stock Exchange in an open and co-operative manner."

15–07 All circulars issued on behalf of a listed company must be approved in advance by the Exchange and, in addition to any specific matters required by those rules, comply with their general requirements regarding format and contents.[9] Where a meeting is convened by the holders of listed shares, two-way proxy forms must be sent to all of them, enabling them to appoint a proxy of their own choice and stating that, unless the manner in which the proxy is to vote is indicated, he may vote at his discretion.[10] Where the number of retiring directors standing for re-election exceeds five, the proxy form must enable a vote to be cast against their re-election as a whole.[11] Not more than one third of the directors may be co-opted.[12]

---

[7] See para.15–49 *et seq.,* available at www.ise.ie.
[8] Listing Rules, Ch.5.
[9] Listing Rule 10.3.
[10] Listing Rule 6.3.6.
[11] Listing Rule 6.3.7.
[12] Listing Rule 6.10.

15–08   Whenever a company proposes to enter into what is described as a "class 1 transaction", a circular explaining what is involved must be sent to its shareholders and their consent to that course of conduct must be obtained.[13] These transactions are, principally, where their value exceeds 25 per cent of the company, measured by reference to the consideration involved and the company's gross capital, gross assets and profits. These transactions also include certain joint ventures, certain reverse takeovers, exceptional indemnities where the company's potential exposure exceeds 25 per cent of its average profits in the preceding financial year, break fees exceeding one per cent of the company's value (where it is being acquired) or else one per cent of its market capitalisation, and share issues by a major subsidiary which would result in the company's stake in it being very significantly diluted. Where a company is in severe financial difficulty and has to sell a substantial part of its business in so short a timeframe that an EGM cannot be convened, it may proceed with that disposal under such conditions as the Exchange may require.

15–09   Similar requirements of shareholder notification and prior approval exist for what are known as "related party transactions".[14] Additionally, that party may not vote on the relevant resolution and must take all reasonable steps to ensure that his associates do not do so. For these purposes, a related party includes:

i.   a substantial shareholder, i.e. a person who controls 10 per cent or more of the votes on substantially all matters at general meetings;

ii.   a director or shadow director of the company, or of its parent or any subsidiary company of it or of its parent;

iii. a person who would have been within category i. or ii. in the 12 months preceding the transaction;

iv.   a 50/50 joint venture partner;

v.   a person "exercising significant influence";

vi.   an "associate" of any of the above categories of that person, being his spouse or child, certain trustees and any company in respect of which that person or any members of his family control 30 per cent of the votes at general meetings or can appoint or remove a majority of the directors.

15–10   A related party transaction is one between the company and any such party, or an arrangement under which the company and that party invests in or provides finance to another undertaking or asset. It also includes certain purchases by a company of its own shares from that party, its directors or through intermediaries. But the above requirements do not apply to small transactions (less than 0.25 per cent of the company's value) and certain other such transactions that do not possess unusual features (such as issuing new securities, employee share schemes, credit on commercial terms, underwriting on commercial terms and insignificant transactions with a subsidiary or joint venturer).

---

[13]   Listing Rule 7.
[14]   Listing Rule 8.

Voting Rights Directive

15–10a In July 2007, an E.C. Directive on voting rights was adopted, which must be implemented by August 3, 2009.[15] Among its key provisions are:

- minimum notice period of 21 days for most general meetings (GMs), which can be reduced to 14 days where shareholders can vote by electronic means and the general meeting agrees to the shortened convocation period;

- internet publication of the convocation and of the documents to be submitted to the GM at least 21 days before the GM;

- abolition of share blocking and introduction of a record date in all Member States which may not be more than 30 days before the GM;

- abolition of obstacles on electronic participation to the GM, including electronic voting;

- right to ask questions and obligation on the part of the company to answer questions;

- abolition of existing constraints on the eligibility of people to act as proxy holder and of excessive formal requirements for the appointment of the proxy holder;

- disclosure of the voting results on the issuer's internet site.

ACQUISITIONS FROM FIRST MEMBERS

15–11 There are numerous instances in the law reports, especially around the start of the last century, of companies getting into financial difficulties because they paid excessive prices to buy property from their promoters.[16] While such transactions may be voidable, any right to rescind is lost when considerable time elapses or if third party rights would be prejudiced. And so long as the vendors retain control of the company, it is unlikely that they will institute a claim for negligence or breach of fiduciary duty against themselves.

15–12 To prevent one-sided transactions from occurring during a Plc's first two years' commercial existence, they are subject to valuing and reporting requirements, and they also must be approved by an ordinary resolution of the company.[17] These provisions apply to an agreement between a new Plc and any subscriber to its memorandum of association, or between a company that re-registered as a Plc and any of its members at the time of registration, whereby during the initial period that person is to transfer what may be called a costly asset to the company. It is hard to understand why this requirement was not extended to agreements with all promoters. The initial period is either two years from the time the new Plc became entitled to do business or two years from the date the company was re-registered. A costly asset in this context means any

---

[15] Directive 2007/36 on the Exercise of Certain Rights of Shareholders in Listed Companies [2007] O.J. L184/17.

[16] See para.8–62 *et seq.*

[17] 1983 Act, ss.32 and 33.

property or interest in property, other than cash, that is worth at least one tenth of the nominal value of the company's issued share capital.[18] These requirements do not apply to agreements made by the company in the ordinary course of its business or to arrangements made under the court's supervision.

15–13 The valuer's qualifications and powers are the same as those set down for valuations when issuing shares for a non-cash consideration.[19] His report must be given to the company during the six months immediately preceding the date of the acquisition agreement and must be circulated to all the company's members who are entitled to all notices of ordinary resolutions, and to the intended transferor. It must state the consideration to be received by and given by the company, specifying what cash amounts are involved and the method and date of valuation. It must contain or be accompanied by a note on the same matters as must be specified where shares are being allotted for a non-cash consideration, including a statement that the company is obtaining in exchange not less than what it is giving. A copy of the report and of the resolution approving the transfer must be delivered to the Registrar of Companies.[20]

15–14 Where a Plc agrees within this initial period to buy a costly asset from any of its first members, and the seller had not received the relevant report or knew or ought to have known that the statutory provisions were violated, the agreement, so far as it is not carried out, is void and the company may recover either the consideration it gave or its monetary equivalent.[21] Where the consideration for any such agreement is or includes an allotment of shares in the company, the allottee is liable to reimburse the company the same amount as must be paid by other persons to whom shares are allotted improperly for a non-cash consideration as must subsequent holders of shares unless they are protected by the defence of good faith purchasers for value without notice.[22]

SHARE CAPITAL

15–15 Many of the capital integrity requirements of the EC Second Directive 77/91 were implemented by the 1983 Act. Several of these apply to both private companies and Plcs but in some respects a more rigorous regime is imposed on Plcs.

Minimum Authorised Capital

15–16 To be registered as a Plc, the memorandum of association must stipulate that the authorised capital is at least €38,092.41.[23] The Minister is empowered to vary this amount and to require existing Plcs either to increase their

---

[18] 1983 Act, s.32(1).
[19] See para.15–23.
[20] 1983 Act, s.33(2).
[21] 1983 Act, s.32(7).
[22] 1983 Act, s.32(8).
[23] 1983 Act, s.19.

capital to the new minimum or else to apply for re-registration as another form of company.

Minimum Paid-Up Capital

15–17   A Plc may not allot shares unless the allottee has paid up at least one quarter of their nominal value, together with the full amount of any premium payable on them.[24] Employee share schemes are exempted from this.[25] Since one of the prerequisites of a Plc becoming entitled to do business or borrow is that it has allotted shares valued at least €38,092.41 nominally, no new Plc may act until it has at the very minimum €9,523 in paid-up capital. Where a Plc allots shares and less than one quarter of the nominal value and any premium on them is not paid up, the allotment is not invalid but the allottee is liable to the company for the outstanding differences.[26] As for transferees of those shares, previously the matter would be dealt with under the doctrine of estoppel, i.e. as a general rule, if the share certificate said that the shares were fully paid then the company would be estopped from denying this.[27] Now subsequent holders of the shares are made equally liable to the company, except where they satisfy what may be called the "bona fide purchaser for value defence", explained below.[28]

Consideration for Shares

15–18   When issuing shares for a consideration other than cash, companies should endeavour to obtain in exchange assets worth at least the nominal value of those shares.[29] When shares are issued for a non-cash consideration, a copy of the subscription contract and a return must be filed with the Registrar of Companies.[30] Plcs are subject to a number of additional obligations in this regard.

Cash Only

15–19   Shares taken by every subscriber to a Plc's memorandum of association, in pursuance of his undertaking in it to take shares, and any premium on them, must be paid for in cash.[31] Cash is defined to include a cheque the company receives in good faith and which the directors have no reason for suspecting will not be paid; it also includes the release of a liability for a liquidated sum and an undertaking to pay cash at a future date.[32]

Work or Service Contracts

15–20   A Plc may not accept in payment for its shares an "undertaking [to] do work or perform services", whether or not the person who is to work or to

---

[24]   1983 Act, s.28.
[25]   1983 Act, s.28(4).
[26]   1983 Act, s.28(2).
[27]   See para.9–94 *et seq.*
[28]   1983 Act, s.26(4).
[29]   See para.8–33 *et seq.*
[30]   1963 Act, s.58 and Form 52.
[31]   1983 Act, s.35.
[32]   1983 Act, s.2(3).

act is the allottee of the shares or another person, and whether the performance is to be done for the company or for another person.[33] That is to say, it may not accept service contracts and the like as consideration for its shares. Since the 1983 Act does not define the terms work or services, difficulties will arise about what exactly these terms mean. That the draftsman did not follow the formulation "undertaking to perform work or supply services" that is used in the Second Directive[34] may be significant. Remuneration packages for management that contain share incentive schemes will have to be designed with this prohibition in mind. Employee share schemes are not exempted.

Five Years Contracts

15–21   A Plc may not allot any of its shares in return, either wholly or partly, for an "undertaking which is to be or may be performed more than five years after the date of the allotment".[35] In other words, it may not allot shares where the *quid pro quo* is some contract that will be or can be performed more than five years after the allotment date. Any variation in a contract to be performed within five years that extends the time of due performance beyond that period is void. The company is entitled to claim the consideration plus interest where a contract to be performed within five years is not performed within that period.[36] But an undertaking simply to pay cash is not affected by the prohibition.

Independent Valuation

15–22   The discretion that companies possess in determining the worth of property and advantages being acquired in exchange for issuing their shares, as set out in *Re Wragg Ltd*,[37] is substantially constricted for Plcs by independent valuation and reporting requirements.[38] These ensure that the company will have an objective assessment of what the consideration is worth, and it can be assumed that shares will not be issued for substantially less than that amount unless there are very good reasons for doing so. These provisions also apply where the company both allots shares and at the same time transfers some other asset or benefit in return for some non-cash consideration. But they do not apply to allotments made in connection with an arrangement or merger as defined there.[39] Nor would it seem do they apply where the company resorts to two separate cash contracts and then operates a set-off. That is to say, the company allots shares for cash, the allottee separately agrees to sell the company assets for cash and the reciprocal debts are then set-off against each other. There is a definition of what is "cash" for these purposes[40] but it does not expressly reject the long-established principle that set-off is the equivalent of

---

[33]   1983 Act, s.26(2).
[34]   Article 7.
[35]   1983 Act, s.29.
[36]   1983 Act, s.29(5).
[37]   [1897] 1 Ch. 796.
[38]   1983 Act, ss.30 and 31.
[39]   1983 Act, s.30(2)–(4).
[40]   1983 Act, s.2(3).

a cash payment.[41] An assignment of a debt, on the other hand, is not deemed to be a cash payment for these purposes.[42]

15–23 Where a Plc proposes to allot shares in exchange wholly or partly for something other than cash, the consideration must be valued by someone who would be eligible to be the company's auditor.[43] Where it is reasonable to do so, he may delegate all or some of the task to such person as he believes is competent to do that job and who is neither an officer nor servant of the company, nor of an affiliate (but may be its auditor). The valuer is entitled to demand from the company's officers such information and explanations as are needed. The report must be made to the company within six months prior to the allotment taking place and a copy of it must be sent to the intended allottee. It must state the nominal value of the shares in question; the amount of any premium payable on them; a description of the non-cash consideration, the method used for valuing it and the date of valuation; the extent to which the shares are being paid for in cash and in other consideration; and limited details about any delegate who valued some or all of the assets.[44] It must contain or be accompanied by a note stating that the method of valuation used was reasonable in the circumstances; that there appears to have been no material change in value since the valuation was made; if a person other than one eligible to be the company's auditor was used to do some valuation, that it was reasonable to have him do it and to accept his assessment.[45] Perhaps most importantly of all, it must contain a note that the assets valued, together with any cash that is being paid, are worth not less than the nominal value of the shares to be allotted plus any premium on them. There is no requirement to disclose the valuer's report to the shareholders generally, but a copy of it must be delivered to the Registrar of Companies along with the return of the allotments.[46]

Enforcement

15–24 Where a Plc's shares are "watered" by being allotted for an undertaking to do work or provide services, or for an undertaking capable of being performed in more than five years, or the shares were allotted for some non-cash consideration and the allottee either did not receive a copy of the requisite valuer's report or was aware of some other breach of the requirements in this regard, the company has a claim for reimbursement by the allottee.[47] Subsequent holders in the extended sense of the shares are equally liable unless they satisfy the defence of bona fide purchasers for value without notice.[48] However, the court is given a discretion to exonerate persons who otherwise would be liable in this regard.[49] On application to it, the court may exempt such

---

[41] *North Sydney Investment Co. v Higgins* [1899] A.C. 203.
[42] *Re Ossary Estates Plc* [1988] B.C.L.C. 213.
[43] 1983 Act, s.30(5).
[44] 1983 Act, s.30(6).
[45] 1983 Act, s.30(8).
[46] 1983 Act, s.31(2).
[47] 1983 Act, ss.26(3), 29(2) and 30(10).
[48] 1983 Act, s.26(4).
[49] 1983 Act, s.34.

persons from liability, either wholly or partly, where it is "just and equitable" to do so and provided certain other criteria are met.[50]

10 Per Cent Margin

15–25   In the case of companies listed on the Irish Stock Exchange, the offer or placing price must not be less than 10 per cent of their middle market price at the time that the offer or placing terms were agreed.[51] A greater discount from that price is permitted where the issuer's shareholders have so agreed or the transaction is done under pre-existing authority to disapply the statutory pre-emption requirement.

Under Subscription

15–26   Whenever a Plc offers its shares for subscription but the offer is under-subscribed, the company is forbidden to allot those shares that were subscribed for unless the offer stated that allotments would be made in such circumstances and those circumstances occurred.[52] Where in breach of this shares have been allotted, if he acts expeditiously the allottee can avoid the allotment and have whatever he paid to the company refunded, even if the company is being wound up.[53] Any director responsible can be held liable for the amount that has to be repaid unless he can show that he was not negligent in this regard.[54]

Distributions

15–27   The prohibition against companies paying dividends or making other equivalent distributions from capital[55] is subject to an additional refinement in the case of Plcs, being a rigorous solvency standard. A Plc may make a distribution only when "the amount of its net assets is not less than the aggregate of [its] called-up share capital and its undistributable reserves" and that distribution will not have the effect of reducing net assets below this aggregate figure.[56] That is to say, the value of the company's assets, less its liabilities, must exceed its called-up share capital together with any undistributable reserves. Uncalled share capital may not be treated as an asset for this purpose. Called-up share capital is defined as to include calls made but not yet paid up, and capital the company will become entitled to but it has not yet received.[57] Undistributable reserves are defined as the share premium account, the capital redemption reserve fund, any reserve the company is not allowed either by statute or by its memorandum or articles to distribute and the excess of any accumulated unrealised profits that have not been capitalised over any accumulated unrealised losses that have not been duly written off.[58] The expansive

---

[50]   See para.8–52.
[51]   Listing Rule 6.5.10.
[52]   1983 Act, s.22.
[53]   1983 Act, s.22(2).
[54]   1963 Act, s.53(4).
[55]   See para.8–86 *et seq.*
[56]   1983 Act, s.46.
[57]   1983 Act, s.2(1).
[58]   1983 Act, s.46(2).

concept of called-up share capital and the inclusion of unrealised profits in undistributable reserves enhances the protection afforded to creditors.

Share Buy-Backs

15–28 Where a Plc intends to purchase its own shares, Pt XI (ss.206–234) of the 1990 Act imposes additional requirements, which are supplemented where the shares are listed on a stock exchange. These were further supplemented by the European Communities (Public Limited Companies Subsidiaries) Regulations 1997[59] giving effect to the Directive 92/101,[60] to prevent the Part XI requirements being circumvented by using subsidiary companies. These also apply to any foreign-registered company, that would not be a private company, if it has a principal place of business in the State.

15–29 The same basic requirements apply as apply for private companies[61]: the purchase should not result in more then one tenth of the company's issued capital being redeemable shares.[62] For Plcs, the authority given by the resolution shall not exceed 18 months, although a purchase can be made outside that period if the contract was concluded within it.[63] Where the purchase is to take place on a stock market, an ordinary resolution of the company suffices, which must specify the maximum number of shares that may be acquired, and the maximum and minimum prices to be paid for them, and may even determine those prices.[64] In such circumstances, the general meeting does not have to approve any individual purchase contract. Within 15 days of being passed, a copy of this resolution must be sent to the Registrar of Companies. In the return that must be sent to the CRO following any share purchases, a Plc must additionally state the aggregate amount paid for those shares and the maximum and minimum prices paid in respect of each class of share involved.[65] Within a day of the shares being purchased on a stock market, the Exchange's authorities must be notified of the fact, who may publish that information.[66] If they are not so notified or they find that resolutions made for share buy backs have been contravened, they must forthwith report the matter to the DCE.[67]

15–30 For the purpose of the regime that permits a company wherever registered to purchase shares in its holding company, the definition of subsidiary has been extended by regulation for Plcs if, but only if, the Plc is a shareholder or member of the company and, under agreement with the other members, entirely controls a majority of the voting rights in the company; or the Plc indirectly does so through another subsidiary.[68] Foreign-registered companies are

---

[59] SI 1997/67.
[60] [1992] OJ L347/64.
[61] See para.8–102 *et seq.*
[62] 1990 Act, s.211.
[63] 1990 Act, s.216.
[64] 1990 Act, s.215.
[65] 1990 Act, s.226(2).
[66] 1990 Act, s.229.
[67] 1990 Act, s.230.
[68] 1990 Act, s.224 and European Communities (Public Limited Company Subsidiaries) Regulations 1997 (SI 1997/67).

subsidiaries for these purposes. If the company is not a subsidiary solely by virtue of more than half its equity being held by a Plc or one of its subsidiaries, it may not subscribe for shares in its parent Plc or purchase shares in it that are not fully paid up, or otherwise provide the financial assistance to subscribe for or purchase those shares. If the company holds shares in its parent Plc that are not fully paid up, or the requisite advance authorisations have not been obtained, or the shares are held as treasury shares in excess of the prescribed limit, or the shares were acquired in contravention of the above prohibition, the shares must be cancelled and the company's share capital be thereby reduced. But this does not apply where the shares were previously disposed of. Certain transactions are excluded from those restrictions.

15–31   Except where publishing the relevant information would not significantly affect the share price or the shares are being redeemed under pre-agreed conditions as to date, number and price, any purchase on a stock exchange must be under a "buy-back programme".[69] Unless that programme is managed by an independent third party, which is not influenced by the company with regard to any purchasing decisions, the dates and number of shares to be traded must have been duly notified to the Exchange. Except where there is a tender offer to all shareholders in the relevant class or there is a market purchase under the shareholders' general authority, without any prior arrangement between the company and a related party, a purchase directly or indirectly from a related party must be notified to the Exchange and approved by the shareholders, with that party not voting.

Own Shares as Security

15–32   A lien or other charge taken by a Plc over its own shares is void, other than the following.[70] One is where its shares are not fully paid and the security is for the unpaid amount on them, as in Table A.[71] The other is where the company's ordinary business is lending money or otherwise providing credit and the transaction is entered into in the ordinary course of its business. There are two further exceptions where the company has re-registered as a Plc.

Own Shares Held by Nominee

15–33   Where a company issues its own shares or they are acquired by its nominee, they are deemed to belong beneficially to that nominee and not to the company.[72] This is not the case where they are shares in a Plc, their acquisition was in one way or another financed by it and a beneficial interest would ordinarily exist. These shares or such interest as the company has in them must not be shown in the balance sheet as an asset but any cost of acquiring them and their nominal value must be shown in notes to the profit and loss account.[73]

---

[69] Listing Rule 9.
[70] 1983 Act, s.44.
[71] Articles 11–14.
[72] 1983 Act, s.42.
[73] 1983 Act, s.42A.

15–34 Where a Plc acquires its own shares by way of forfeiture or surrender in lieu, or a nominee or other person acquires them in circumstances where the company has a beneficial interest, then within one or within three years, the company must cancel these shares and reduce its issued share capital accordingly.[74] In the meantime, the voting rights in respect of these shares may not be exercised.[75] Where the effect of cancelling the shares would reduce the authorised share capital below the €38,092.41 minimum, the company must take the requisite steps to re-register and cease being a Plc.

Financing Purchase of Own Shares

15–35 The procedure whereby, by making a statutory declaration and passing a special resolution a company is permitted to finance the purchase of its own shares,[76] cannot be availed of by Plcs. Nor may it be availed of by a Plc's subsidiary, of the kind described above. But a Plc may financially assist the purchase of its own shares, either by way of lending money in the ordinary course of its business or through an employees' share scheme, if its net assets are not reduced; or, if those are reduced, the assistance comes from profits that are available for distribution as dividends.[77]

15–36 Several arrangements connected principally with attracting subscriptions for and making a market for their own shares, and also connected with takeovers, are exempted from the prohibition against a company financing the purchase of its own shares.[78]

SECURITIES REGULATION

15–37 For many years markets in which shares and other securities, such as transferable debentures and public sector bonds, were traded were largely unregulated by the State. Instead, considerable reliance was placed on self-regulation, whereby stock exchanges and other professional bodies whose members were involved in securities trading policed their own and their members' conduct. A major exception to this pattern was the requirement since 1845 that, when companies are raising capital from the general public, they must publish and register a prospectus which discloses extensive details about the company's finances and management, its history and prospects.[79] Because a company issuing its securities or an issuing intermediary acting on its behalf knows, or at least ought to know, practically everything that has a bearing on what those securities are truly worth, it was felt that there should be full disclosure to prospective investors, coupled with enhanced standards of liability for all those involved in offering those securities for application or sale.

---

[74] 1983 Act, s.42.
[75] 1983 Act, s.43(4).
[76] 1963 Act, ss.60(2)–(11).
[77] 1963 Act, s.60(13).
[78] 1963 Act, s.60(12)(g)–(m).
[79] Companies Act 1845, 8 & 9 Vic. c.16, s.4.

15–38   What is known as the secondary market in securities was left largely unregulated, i.e. the circumstances in which existing securities holders sell stocks, shares or debentures on to others. There the fundamental rule of *caveat emptor* prevailed.[80] In contrast with private sales, generally those selling securities through stock exchanges have no direct dealings with their buyers as would trigger liability for misrepresentation or non-disclosure; the securities are quoted on the market at a price and, generally, the intending buyer has no notion as to who is selling them, nor generally does the intending seller have any indication as to who his buyer might be. All that an intending buyer of securities is entitled to know about the company is the contents of its published accounts and such information as is held by the Registrar of Companies, including any prospectus that may have been published at some time regarding those securities. Investors had to rely on self-regulation for maintaining discipline in the secondary markets.

15–39   Because the position as summarised here did not adequately protect investors from sharp practices and incompetence, in the 1930s in the US a comprehensive regime for regulating securities markets was introduced, presided over by the Securities Exchange Commission. This agency is reputed to have "transformed Wall Street" and "tamed the giant corporation".[81] In 1989 a similar body was established in Australia, now known as the Australian Securities and Investments Commission. Similar bodies exist in the Canadian provinces. As a result of EC Directives, the Irish stock market and market operators became subject to state regulation, under the Stock Exchange Act 1995, the Investment Intermediaries Act 1995, and the Investor Compensation Act 1998.[82] Functions comparable to those regulatory agencies are discharged by the "competent authority" in each Member State, which in Ireland has been designated as the Central Bank and Financial Services Authority of Ireland (the "Bank"); entirely different functions are discharged by the Director of Corporate Affairs, who in practice is mostly concerned with private companies.

The Directives

15–40   The Admissions Directive 79/279[83] laid down conditions for admitting shares and other securities to official listings on stock exchanges, obligations of companies that obtain a quotation for their securities, and required designating a "competent authority" to monitor compliance with its

---

[80]   *Seddon v North Eastern Salt Co.* [1905] 1 Ch. 326 and *Chase Manhattan Equities Ltd v Goodman* [1991] B.C.L.C. 897.

[81]   See generally, L. Loss & J. Seligman, *Fundamentals of Securities Regulation*, 5th edn (Maryland: Aspen Publishers, 2004) and J. Seligman, *The Transformation of Wall Street: A History of the SEC and Modern Corporate Finance*, 3rd edn (Maryland: Aspen Publishers, 2003).

[82]   See generally, A. Foy, *The Capital Markets, Irish and International Laws Regulations* (Dublin: Round Hall Sweet & Maxwell, 1998); N. Moloney, *EC Securities Regulations* (Oxford: Oxford University Press, 2002); E. Ferran, *Building an EU Securities Market* (Cambridge: Cambridge University Press, 2004); J. Fisher & J. Bewsey, *The Law of Investor Protection*, 2nd edn (London: Sweet & Maxwell, 2003).

[83]   [1979] O.J. L66/21.

requirements. It was implemented by the European Communities (Stock Exchange) Regulations 1984 (First Schedule).[84] The Listing Particulars Directive 80/390 and the Interim Reports Directive 82/121,[85] implemented at the same time, were replaced by the Directives on prospectuses and on transparency, and the remainder of the 1984 Regulations was repealed in 2007. The principal EC measures here are as follows.

15–41   *Listing Particulars Directive 2001/34*[86]: This replaced the 1979 Directive on the conditions for admission to a stock exchange listing. It was implemented by the European Communities (Admissions to Listing and Miscellaneous Provisions) Regulations 2007,[87] which simply gives legal effect to the 2001 Directive.

15–42   *Prospectus Directive 2003/71*[88]: This imposes requirements for companies seeking to raise funds from the investing public to publish a prospectus containing all relevant information concerning the company and the securities in question, and gives extensive powers to the "competent authority" to secure compliance with its requirements. It was implemented by Pt V (ss.38–55) of the 2005 Act and the Prospectus (Directive 2003/71/EC) Regulations 2005.[89] These also replaced an earlier Prospectus Directive (implemented in 1992), and also several provisions in the 1963 Act concerning prospectuses.

15–43   *Market Abuse Directive 2003/6*[90]: This imposes a regime for outlawing insider trading and other forms of market manipulation on stock exchanges, and misleading information being provided in respect of shares traded on them. It was implemented by Pt 4 (ss.29–37) of the 2005 Act and by the Market Abuse (Directive 2003/6/EC) Regulations 2005, which, *inter alia,* repealed Pt V (ss.107–121) of the 1990 Act that governed insider trading for most purposes.

15–44   *The Transparency Directive 2004/109*[91]: This deals with what accounts, reports and additional information should be published regarding the activities of listed companies. It was implemented by Pt 3 (ss.19–24) of the 2006 Act and by the Transparency (Directive 2004/109/EC) Regulations 2007.[92] As well as replacing the Interim Reports Directive, it also replaced the Major Shareholdings Directive 88/627, requiring disclosure to the company and to the stock exchange of whenever specified percentages in a company's

---

[84] SI 1984/282.
[85] [1980] O.J. L100/1 and [1982] OJ L48/26.
[86] [1980] O.J. L100/1 and [1982] OJ L48/26.
[87] SI 2007/286.
[88] [2003] O.J. L345/64 and also Commission Regulation 809/2004, [2004] OJ L149/1, implementing this Directive.
[89] SI 2005/324.
[90] [2003] O.J. L96/16.
[91] [2004] O.J. L 390/38.
[92] SI 2007/277.

shares have been acquired or disposed of. This part too was implemented by the 2007 Regulations.

15–45 *Regulation 1606/2002*[93]: This requires the annual audited accounts of listed companies to be prepared in accordance with International Financial Reporting Standards (IFRS). It has direct effect and also has been implemented by the European Communities (International Financial Reporting Standards and Miscellaneous Amendments) Regulations 2005.[94]

The Stock Exchange

15–46 A stock exchange is a public market where securities are traded; it usually has a physical location but, with the advent of the internet, that is no longer necessary. Shares and debentures of most of the major Irish companies are quoted on the Irish Stock Exchange, which is based at 28 Anglesea St, Dublin 2.[95] Some of those companies' securities are also traded on foreign stock exchanges, most notably the London exchange, Wall Street and the NASDAQ. In 2007, the Irish market in shares had a market capitalisation of €93.5 billion and was dominated by five companies, which accounted for a total of 55 per cent of the total capitalisation; of that, the two major banks accounted for 31 per cent.[96] In 2007, the Exchange introduced a new free-float weighting system for stocks included in its indices, whereby only shares available for actual trading are counted and shares tied up by interested parties and long-term shareholdings are excluded.

15–47 While many companies aspire to a quotation on the Exchange, exceptionally a quoted company decides to "go private", as when a takeover bidder acquires most of its shares and then seeks to have them de-listed. Where this happens, the acquirer often re-structures the company's management and finances—which may involve substantial redundancies in the workforce and the company incurring significant indebtedness—and then may re-float it on the Exchange.

15–48 At one time there were independent stock exchanges in Dublin and in Cork, and in the major cities of Britain. The Cork Exchange amalgamated with the Dublin Exchange in 1971 and, along with the Exchanges of Belfast, Glasgow, Birmingham and Manchester, in 1973 they merged with the London Exchange. All of those were subject to the same regulations and administrative procedures. In 1995 the formal links with London were ended and the exchange in Anglesea Street became known as the Irish Stock Exchange. Under the Stock Exchange Act 1995, the Central Bank and the Minister for Finance were given extensive regulatory powers over the Irish Exchange and any other such exchange as may be established in the State, as well as over all

---

[93] [2002] O.J. L 243/1.

[94] SI 2005/116.

[95] See www.ise.ie.

[96] See P. Egan, *Irish Corporate Procedures: A Guide to the Organisation and Regulation of Business in Ireland*, 3rd edn (Bristol: Jordans, 2007).

member firms of approved exchanges. The Irish Exchange is a registered company, with a memorandum and articles of association, membership, management and capitalisation as prescribed in this Act.[97] It was repealed by the Markets in Financial Instruments and Miscellaneous Provisions Act, 2007,[98] being replaced by Pt 6 of the European Communities (Markets in Financial Instruments) Regulations 2007.[99] Under these, the Exchange is a "market operator" that manages a "regulated market", and its authorised members are described as "authorised investment firms."

The Listing Rules

15–49 For a company's shares or debentures to obtain a quotation and be traded on the Irish Stock Exchange, it must not be a private company and it must comply with the Exchange's Listing Rules. If a company is in doubt about the application of any particular rule or if, on account of difficulties, it wishes to have a rule modified or waived, it should promptly consult the Exchange's authorities.[100] By virtue of the European Communities (Admissions to Listing and Miscellaneous Provisions) Regulations 2007,[101] these Rules are subject to the EC's Listing Particulars Directive 2001/34.[102]

15–50 Applicants for a listing must have a sponsor who is chosen from the Exchange's own list of approved sponsors.[103] Among the main conditions to be satisfied for acceptance by the Exchange[104] are that the equity securities have an aggregate market capitalisation in excess of €1 million, the company's business has a sound track record, there are independently-audited accounts for at least the three preceding years, and the company has sufficient working capital for the ensuing 12 months' activities. At least 25 per cent of the shares issued must be in public hands. The company's directors and senior management must have appropriate expertise and experience in the business. They must be free from conflicts of interests or there must be appropriate arrangements to prevent detriment to the company from such conflicts as may exist. The company must not be dominated by a controlling shareholder with more than 30 per cent of voting rights. Its securities must be fully paid, free from liens and freely transferable by way of electronic settlements. All securities of any particular class must be listed. The company must satisfy detailed requirements regarding audited accounts and reports, the contents of circulars, continuous notification and reporting to the Exchange (e.g. all resolutions passed by the members other than relating to ordinary business passed at AGMs, major interests in the company's shares, a variety of details relating to its capital and its directors, interests of directors and

---

[97] Stock Exchange Act 1995, s.9.
[98] Section 8 of this Act, which repeals the 1995 Act, is not yet in force (Jan. 2008).
[99] SI 2007/60, amended by SI 2007/63.
[100] Listing Rules, Ch.1.
[101] SI 2007/286.
[102] [2001] O.J.L 184/1.
[103] Listing Rules, Ch.2.
[104] Listing Rules, Ch.3.

connected persons in transactions with the company, lock-up arrangements and change of name or of accounting date) rights issues, pre-emption rights, proxy forms, title documents and dealing in the company's own securities. Several types of "significant transactions" must obtain shareholder approval and there are safeguards against transactions with "related parties". There is a "model code" designed to prevent managers and insider employees from abusing confidential information by dealing in the company's securities.

15–51 To effectively monitor compliance with its rules, quoted companies are required to supply the Exchange with such information as it considers appropriate to protect investors or to ensure the smooth operation of the market, and any other information reasonably required for ensuring that the rules are being complied with. Where the Exchange finds that the rules have been breached, it may censure the company or suspend its listing; it may cancel its listing entirely if "satisfied that there are special circumstances that preclude normal regular dealings in" the securities.[105] A listing may also be cancelled where less than 25 per cent in aggregate of the securities are in public hands. Provision exists for cancellation at the company's request. The Exchange retains a broad discretion to modify its rules or to dispense with compliance with any of their requirements.

Governance Code

15–52 In 2003 a voluntary Combined Code on Corporate Governance was published by the UK-based Financial Reporting Council,[106] which sets out numerous main principles and related supporting principles regarding several sensitive aspects of corporate governance, along with related guidance and good practice suggestions. It acknowledges, however, that circumstances may arise that can justify departing from its prescriptions: that "while it is expected that listed companies will comply ... most of the time ... departing from the provision ... may be justified in particular circumstances." Companies are exhorted in the preamble to review each provision in the Code carefully and to give a considered explanation whenever they depart from those provisions. However, in a survey published in March 2007,[107] it was said that only one third of listed companies on the Irish Exchange comply fully with it, the main areas where there was non-compliance being board balance, splitting the roles of chair and chief executive, directors' pay, internal controls and risk management systems.

The Central Bank and Irish Financial Services Regulatory Authority

15–53 When the (since repealed) Listing Particulars Directive was implemented in 1984 and the (since repealed) First Prospectus Directive was implemented in 1992, the Irish Stock Exchange was designated as the "competent authority" to oversee their application. On revoking those Regulations and

---

[105] Listing Rule 1.6.
[106] See www.frc.org.uk/combined.cfm.
[107] See "Most listed firms not adhering to code" *Irish Times*, March 26, 2007, p.16.

replacing them in 2005 with the regime for public securities offers and for market abuse, the Bank's Financial Services Authority became the market regulator. In discharging these functions, it is required to be "independent". It may delegate several of its functions to the Stock Exchange, subject to such conditions as it specifies but, notwithstanding, it has the "final responsibility" for overseeing application of these Directives. For the purpose of these regimes, the 2005 Act gives the Bank extensive authority to make rules, to issue written guidelines, to make a variety of directives and to impose administrative sanctions. Particular directions that are given or sanctions that are imposed may be appealed to the High Court.

The Takeover Panel

15–54   Formerly, takeovers of quoted Irish companies were subject to what is known as the City Code on Takeovers and Mergers. Compliance with it was supervised by a Panel on Takeovers and Mergers, the decisions of which could be appealed to an Appeal Committee.[108] Those were in effect United Kingdom administrative agencies, based in London, and the extent of their authority over events occurring in Ireland and whether their activities could be made subject to judicial review in this country raised questions of the conflict of laws and of constitutional law. Enactment of the Irish Takeover Panel Act 1997 has rendered these interesting issues academic because it establishes an indigenous regulatory agency, the principal function of which is to monitor bids for quoted companies, to ensure that competitions for corporate control are carried out fairly and that shareholders' interests are not prejudiced.[109]

15–55   The Panel is a company limited by guarantee, with a memorandum and articles of association, membership and management as prescribed by this Act.[110] Its principal function is to "monitor and supervise takeovers and other relevant transactions" so as to ensure that the statutory provisions and any rules adopted are complied with, and to make rules to this end.[111]

15–56   It has published an extensive set of rules regarding how takeovers should and should not be carried out.[112] It is empowered to apply to the High Court for orders securing compliance with those rules. Decisions of and directions given by the Panel can be challenged in the courts through the judicial review procedure and persons disciplined by the Panel have a right of appeal to the High Court.

PUBLIC SECURITIES OFFERS/INTRODUCTIONS

15–57   It is almost unheard of for a company immediately after its incorporation to go straight to the investing public to raise capital. As a general rule, a company will have been doing business for some time and, if it is proving to

---

[108] See generally, Johnston, "Takeover Regulation: Historical and Theoretical Perspectives on the City Code" 66 *Cam.L.J.* 422 (2007).
[109] See www.irishtakeoverpanel.ie.
[110] Ss.3–6.
[111] ss.5(1) & 7(1).
[112] See para.15–127 *et seq.*

be a commercial success and wishes to expand further, it may choose to raise additional funds by appealing to the public to put money into it.[113] At times, the major shareholders may wish to divest themselves of all or part of their stake in the company for cash and, to that end, may offer their securities for sale to the public. An offer to the public of a large block of securities is called a flotation. Where a company either directly or through an intermediary offers its shares or debentures to the public for subscription, a prospectus that complies with Pt V (ss.38–54) of the 2005 Act's requirements must be issued and that Act's and the 1983 Act's rules regarding allotments must be satisfied. To protect investors who have just acquired securities following a public offer, from potential drastic decline in the value of those securities, the Companies (Amendment) Act 1999 permits certain dealings in those securities in accordance with prescribed "stabilisation rules". Transactions within these rules are deemed not to constitute insider trading.

Modes of Issuing Securities to the Public

15–58   There are a number of different ways in which securities can be issued to the public, which in law includes any part of the public, and does not always entail having those securities listed on a stock exchange or traded on an unlisted market.

Direct Offer

15–59   One method is for the company itself to draw up a prospectus and offer its securities directly to the public. A prospectus is a detailed statement of the company's history, present financial situation and other matters regarding the company that would concern investors. If investors conclude that the company has good prospects and its shares are going at a reasonable price, they will apply to the company for the shares they wish to acquire. Usually, the offer will be made at a fixed price, so that the applications received may exceed the quantity of securities being offered. Where there has been an over-subscription in this sense, the company will have to decide on what basis the securities should be allocated among the various applicants. Sometimes the company and its advisers may misjudge the market and not attract sufficient applications for the quantity being offered; the offer is said to be under-subscribed. A company, however, will usually insure itself against this eventuality by having what is called an underwriting arrangement with a bank or other financial intermediary that agrees to acquire any surplus shares.

15–60   Occasionally, the securities will be offered not at a fixed price but by tender, which is a form of auction. In this way the company avoids disposing of its securities at what transpires to be an unduly low price (resulting in over-subscription) or an excessively high price (causing under-subscription).

---

[113] See generally, T. Power et al, *Financial Management*, 2nd edn (Dublin: Gill & Macmillan, 2005), Ch.11 and G. Arnold, *Handbook of Corporate Finance* (London: Financial Times Prentice Hall, 2004), Ch.17.

Instead, it obtains a price that approximates to their true market value. The most common tendering technique is to fix a minimum price and to announce that the securities will be allotted at the highest price above that at which all the securities are applied for.

Offer for Sale

15–61 An alternative method is the offer for sale, which involves the company initially allotting its securities to some financial intermediary, which then offers them to the public.[114] Therefore, instead of the investor subscribing for the securities and the company allotting them to him, he makes an application to the intermediary and, if it is accepted, buys the securities. Many companies prefer this method to the direct offer because it throws the entire risk of the offer on the intermediary, which also assumes most of the accompanying administrative burdens. The offer for sale may be at a fixed price or by way of tender. Offers for sale to the public must comply with the prospectus rules. Where the company is listed on the Irish Stock Exchange, the letters of allotment or of acceptance must be issued simultaneously and numbered serially; letters of regret must be posted at the same time or not later than three business days after the letters of allotment or acceptance; and a notice to that effect must be inserted in a national newspaper.[115]

Placing

15–62 Another method, that is availed of especially by relatively small companies, is placing.[116] This usually involves a financial intermediary acquiring the securities and then selling on blocks of them to a small number of financial institutions—banks, insurance companies, pension funds and the like. Alternatively, the intermediary may simply arrange with the financial institutions that they will take blocks of securities directly from the company. At the time the securities are placed in one or other of these ways, there is no intention that shortly afterwards they will be offered for sale to the public. However, those institutions may on occasion sell on all or part of their holdings to other institutions or to select groups of private investors. Sometimes a placing is accompanied by the securities being introduced on a stock exchange—either by obtaining an official listing or by being traded on an unlisted securities market. Where such an introduction is being sought, an adequate number of securities must be available for dealing so that a market can be maintained in them. Where the company is listed on the Irish Stock Exchange, in a vendor-consideration placing, it must ensure that all vendors have an equal opportunity to participate in the placing.[117]

Prospectus

15–63 Where securities are being offered to the public for the first time by a company or by persons acting on its behalf, since 1845 the law has required the publication and filing of a prospectus. That innovation was inspired by the

---

[114] See *Practical Commercial Precedents* Vol.1 part C1.
[115] Listing Rule 6.5.11.
[116] See *Practical Commercial Precedents* Vol.1 part C5.
[117] Listing Rule 6.5.9.

very first of the many committees in Britain that examined aspects of company law, the Gladstone Committee of 1841,[118] which was established to consider measures to "ensure the greater security of the public" from fraud and sharp practices in the market. The solution, it was concluded, was disclosure: "[p]ublicity is all that is necessary. Show up the roguery and it is harmless", declared the eminent future Prime Minister, who at the time presided over the Board of Trade. "So long as investors have been given all material information, it is for them to decide how to act on it and face the consequences of doing so". How this was achieved was to require, *inter alia,* a copy of every prospectus or circular addressed to the public to be filed.[119] But there were no requirements for pre-publication vetting of their contents, or remedies for non-compliance. These deficiencies were gradually remedied over the last 160 years; by 1990, an extensive range of matters were required to be disclosed and increased liabilities were imposed on directors and promoters.

15–64   Under the 1963 Act,[120] where securities were offered to the public by or on behalf of a company, it had to publish and file a prospectus. A topic that engendered considerable litigation in other jurisdictions was what exactly constitutes an offer to the public. A prescribed form and contents of a prospectus was set out in the 1963 Act's Third schedule, requiring considerable detail about the company, its finances and management, and any "material contracts" with the company. A range of securities offers to the public were excluded, in particular, genuine secondary market offers. Where a prospectus contained a material misstatement or omission, responsible directors and promoters were made liable in damages in circumstances where liability for breach of contract or in tort could not attach.

Offer to Public/Introduction

15–65   This regime has been replaced by Pt 5 (ss.38–55) of the 2005 Act, and the Prospectus (Directive 2003/71/EC) Regulations 2005[121] and such rules and guidelines as the Bank may issue to give effect to these.[122] Subject to exceptions, securities may not be offered to the public nor admitted to trading on a regulated market without their being the subject of a published prospectus that has been approved by the Bank, and which complies with the format and contents set out in those regulations.[123] A prospectus is defined as "a document or documents in such form and containing such information as may be [so] required" but not any advertisement in newspapers or journals that derives from a prospectus.[124]

---

[118] See generally, B. Hunt, *The Development of the Business Corporation in England 1800– 1867* (Cambridge, Mass.: Harvard University Press, 1936), Ch.5.

[119] 75 Hansard 277 (1844).

[120] Ss.43–52.

[121] SI 2005/324.

[122] See generally, Blair & Walker, (eds) *Financial Markets and Exchanges Law* (Oxford: OUP, 2007) Ch.16.

[123] Regulations 12–17.

[124] Regulation 2(1).

15–66 For these purposes, an offer to the public is expansively defined, as "a communication to persons in any form and by any means presenting sufficient information on the terms ... and the securities ... so as to enable an investor to decide to purchase or subscribe for th[em]" and includes placing them through financial intermediaries.[125] But it does not include trading in them on a stock exchange. Accordingly it does not matter that the form of communication is written, oral or electronic, or that it is not headed or prefaced with words such as "prospectus", "marvellous share offer", "fantastic investment opportunity" and the like. The test is whether, taking the communication in its totality, did it contain sufficient information as would enable one to make a positive investment decision. Most advertisements would not have sufficient detail to fall within this category and, further, are required to be "clearly recognisable as" advertisements only. However, offers to a variety of target parties and offers with regard to several categories of security are exempted from these prospectus requirements.

Ambit

15–67 As well as shares and debentures in companies, these requirements apply to an extensive category of securities, as defined by the Investment Services Directive of 1993.[126] But excepted from them entirely are, *inter alia,* where the offer has a total consideration less than €2.5 million, shares the main purpose of which is to enable their holder to occupy an apartment or other immovable property (e.g. a condominium) and certain non-equity securities of banks and other credit institutions.[127]

15–68 Additionally, the obligation to publish a prospectus that complies with this regime does not apply, *inter alia,* to: comparatively small offers; offers to sophisticated investors; bonus shares offers; offers made in the context of a takeover; or merger provided that a document equivalent to a prospectus has been furnished to the Bank, offers in connection with a directors' or employees' approved share scheme, and where the shares are being issued in substitution for shares of the same class already issued and that do not involve increasing the capital.[128] For these purposes, a small offer is where it is addressed to fewer than 100 people (other than "sophisticates"), or where the minimum consideration for a share or its unit denomination is at least €50,000, or it is limited to a total consideration of less than €100,000.[129] The concept "qualified investor" connotes persons deemed to be sophisticated in the market[130] and, accordingly, who do not have the same need for protection as consumer investors. These are, *inter alia*: authorised banks, investment firms and other comparable firms; entities whose sole purpose is to invest in securities; and entities with a securities portfolio exceeding €5 million which have traded regularly and substantially in the securities market in the proceeding 12 months. This category of

---

[125] Regulation 2(1).
[126] Directive 93/22, [1993] O.J. L141/27.
[127] Regulation 8
[128] Regulation 9.
[129] Regulation 10.
[130] Regulation 2(1).

"sophisticates" also include individuals and entities that have registered with the Bank as being "qualified", who satisfy either two of the above criteria or, instead, who satisfy one of them and also have worked for over a year in the financial markets in a position requiring knowledge of investment.[131] Such parties must be resident in the State. A register of these is kept with the Bank, which is made available to those intending to issue or offer securities.

15–69 Where securities are being admitted to trading on the Stock Exchange, there is no exception for small offers and an exception for sophisticated investors could not be applicable. There are similar exceptions to the publication requirement where they are bonus shares; or they are securities existing in context of a takeover or merger and an equivalent document has been furnished to the Bank; or they are securities existing in the context of an employees' or a directors' approved share scheme; or they are shares substituted for those of the same class already admitted to trading and that does not involve increasing the capital. Also excepted are shares of a class already admitted to trading where, over 12 months, less than 10 per cent of those are being admitted. A further exception exists for shares that already have been admitted to another regulated market but this is subject to several conditions being satisfied.

15–70 An exception exists for what is described as a "local offer", meaning where the total consideration is expressly limited to €2.5 million, apart from certain specified securities.[132]

Contents

15–71 What a prospectus in these circumstances must contain is subject to an overriding criterion of accuracy and relevance, similar to the "true and fair view" that company accounts are required to give. Every prospectus must set out all such information as, in the circumstances,

> "is necessary to enable investors to make an informed assessment of:
>
> (a) the assets and liabilities, financial position, profit and loss, and prospects of the issuer and of any guarantor, and
>
> (b) the rights attaching to [the] securities."[133]

This includes the minimum information required by the EC's Prospectus Regulation.[134] This information must be consistent and be presented in an easily accessible and comprehensive form. It must be accompanied by a summary in non-technical language that addresses the "essential characteristics and risks associated with" what is being offered.[135] A prospectus may comprise separate documents.[136] Certain information may be omitted with the consent of the

---

[131] Regulations 3–6.
[132] 2005 Act, s.38(1).
[133] Regulation 19(1).
[134] Regulation 809/2004, [2004] O.J. L149/1.
[135] Regulation 21.
[136] Regulations 22 & 29.

Bank.[137] Where a statement by an expert is included in a prospectus, he must have consented to it being there and not have withdrawn his consent.

15–72 In the case of "local offers" where the Prospectus Regulation would otherwise have applied, every document offering shares or debentures to the public must stipulate, on its front or prominently, that it has not been prepared in accordance with the EC prospectus regime, nor has it been reviewed by the Bank and, consequently, it may not contain all the information that the regime would require.[138] Additionally, it must stipulate certain prescribed caveats, for instance "past performance may not be a reliable guide to future performance" and so on. Before being issued, a copy of this document must be lodged with the Registrar of Companies.

Vetting

15–73 Perhaps the principal innovation of this regime is that, before being published, a draft of every prospectus must be submitted to the Bank for its approval.[139] Once it is so approved, a copy must be filed with the Bank forthwith and with the Registrar of Companies within 14 days.

Publication

15–74 On being so approved, the prospectus must be published in any of a variety of ways.[140] Most often this is done by making it available to the public, free of charge, at the offices of either the company, of the financial intermediary handling the offer or of the Exchange. It also can be done by inserting the prospectus in newspapers widely circulated in the State or on specified websites. Where the prospectus relates to equity securities, a notice must be published stating where it was made available and can be obtained.

15–75 If the securities are of a class that are being offered to the public for the first time and have not been admitted to trading, the prospectus must be published at least six working days before the offer closes. In other cases, it must be published as soon as practicable and, at the latest, the beginning of the offer or of the securities being admitted to trading. If, subsequent to the Bank's approval being obtained, some significant new factor arises that would affect any assessment of the securities, or some material mistake or inaccuracy in the information provided is found, a supplement dealing with these matters must be included in the prospectus.[141] Persons who have applied for or accepted securities on offer may withdraw from the transaction within two days of any such supplement being published.[142]

---

[137] Regulation 25.
[138] 2005 Act, s.49.
[139] Regulations 33–43.
[140] Regulations 44–50.
[141] Regulation 51.
[142] Regulation 52.

Enforcement and Liability

15–76 In addition to the penal sanctions and civil remedies that have existed for over 100 years, the prospectus regime is rendered effective by administrative oversight and quite punitive administrative sanctions that can be imposed by the Bank.[143]

15–77 *The Bank:* Requiring Bank approval for a draft prospectus is a major factor in ensuring compliance, especially as the Bank has extensive information-gathering powers, for instance to require relevant information and documents to be furnished to it and, if necessary, to have premises searched. Additionally, the Bank can, *inter alia*, require particular information to be disclosed, prohibit or suspend a public offer or admission to trading, and prohibit or suspend trading in the securities. However, Bank approval is no absolute guarantee of what the documents state being correct.[144]

15–78 There is a process whereby the Bank can impose administrative sanctions, being a caution or a reprimand, either in private or public; a penalty of up to €2.5 million; a direction disqualifying a person from being involved in the financial services sector and ordering the contravention to cease.[145] A judicial-type hearing takes place before an assessor, appointed by the Bank, and there is a right of appeal to the High Court against any sanction that was imposed. Directions given by the Bank and any adverse assessment can be enforced by it applying for a High Court order.

15–79 *Prosecution:* Breach of several of the major requirements in the prospectus regime is a criminal offence that can attract penalties up to €1 million and/or five years' imprisonment.[146] It is a defence to any such charge to show that the contravention arose from an honest mistake of fact; where a matter ought to have been disclosed, that the accused did not know of it; or that, in all the circumstances, the contravention was immaterial or that the accused should otherwise be excused. Similar defences exist for the specific offence of authorising the issue of a prospectus that includes an untrue statement or that omits something that should have been included in it.[147] Summary proceedings may be brought by the Bank, where the maximum penalty is €5,000 and/or 12 months' imprisonment.

15–80 *Civil Claim:* The law reports of the late nineteenth century are replete with instances of shareholders seeking redress because they were duped into buying shares or debentures that, in the event, proved to be largely or entirely worthless. Notable instances in the Irish Reports include *Aaron's Reefs Ltd v*

---

[143] Regulations 78–106.
[144] Regulation 43.
[145] Regulation 99. The first such action was taken by the Regulator in 2006: see "IFSRA bars Broadstone chiefs from sector for 18 months". *Irish Times*, July 8, 2006.
[146] 2005 Act, s.47.
[147] 2005 Act, s.48.

Twiss[148] and *Components Tube Co. v Naylor*,[149] in both of which investors had subscribed for shares on foot of defective prospectuses and were seeking rescission of their contracts to pay calls in respect of those shares. But the equitable remedy of rescission is lost where there has been, *inter alia,* an undue lapse of time or a significant change of circumstances.

15–81   It was held in *Houldsworth v City of Glasgow Bank*[150] that, in these instances, damages cannot be recovered from the company. Such compensatory remedies as there were consisted of claims for damages or equitable compensation against directors of the company and other promoters who caused the misleading prospectus to be published. In *Jury v Stoker*,[151] for instance, the plaintiff acquired shares in the newly formed Cork Milling Co., on foot of a prospectus which stated, wrongly, that the vendor from whom the company purchased its mills would be investing £7,500 in the company. Subsequently, the company was wound up and the plaintiff lost his entire investment. It was held that, in the circumstances, the directors responsible for the prospectus were liable for his loss, as they had deliberately misled the investors.

15–82   As the common law and equitable systems of remedies often were inadequate to protect the investing public, the Directors Liability Act 1890[152] was enacted, giving a statutory right to damages against those responsible for issuing a false or misleading prospectus. In an amended form, it became s.49 of the 1963 Act, which in turn has been replaced by ss.41–43 of the 2005 Act, imposing liability for not alone untrue statements but also for omitting any information that should have been included in the prospectus. The core stipulation is that, subject to exceptions and exemptions, the company itself and a variety of persons involved in a prospectus:

> "shall be liable to pay compensation to all persons who acquire any securities on the faith of a prospectus for the loss or damage that they may have sustained by reason of:
>
> (a) any untrue statement included thereon, or
> (b) any omission of information required by E.U. prospectus law to be contained in the prospectus."[153]

An expert who has consented to a statement made by him being included in the prospectus may be held liable for any loss or damage resulting from his statement being untrue.[154] In the case of a summary of a prospectus, liability only arises if it is misleading, inaccurate or inconsistent when read together with other parts or the prospectus.

---

[148] [1895] 2 I.R. 207; aff'd [1896] A.C. 294.
[149] [1900] 2 I.R. 1.
[150] (1880) 5 App. Cas. 317.
[151] (1882) 9 L.R. Ir. 385.
[152] 53 & 54 Vict., c. 64.
[153] 2005 Act, s.41(1).
[154] 2005 Act, s.41(2).

15–83   Those who may be made liable in respect of equity securities are the company itself, every director and person as having agreed to be named as one, every promoter of the prospectus, any other party who offered the securities or who sought their admission to trading, anyone who guaranteed the issue and anyone else who authorised the issuing of the prospectus. For these purposes, a promoter does not include a professional adviser to any of the above parties, or underwriter to the issue or professional adviser to him. The category of defendants where non-equity securities are involved is narrower, being the person who sought admission for them in the market or who offered them to the public, or who guaranteed them.[155]

15–84   To be rendered liable, causation and ensuing loss or damages must be established. It is not clear whether it must be shown that it was the particular untrue statement or omission that influenced the decision to acquire the securities in question. Liability is not strict; several defences are provided for.[156] One category is where, on becoming aware of the deficiency, the party withdrew his consent to the prospectus and gave public notice of that fact, along with the reasons. Another is belief, on reasonable grounds, that the statement was true or the matter in question was properly omitted. A third relates to statements made on the authority of an expert or made by some public official or in official document; it suffices if what is published "fair[ly] represented" what has been stated. In the case of an expert's statement or report, the defendant also must have had reasonable grounds for believing and did believe that the expert had the requisite competence and had consented to that statement being made in the prospectus. For these purposes, an expert includes an "engineer, valuer, accountant and any other individual or body [whose] profession … gives authority to [the] statement."

15–85   A statement of an expert shall not be contained in a prospectus unless, as required by EU prospectus law, he has consented to it being put there in the form and context, and has not withdrawn that consent.[157] An expert may not be made liable for having authorised a statement being included in a prospectus, except for an untrue statement he made in that capacity, not if he believed it was true and had reasonable grounds for so believing. Insofar as he may be liable for having authorised a prospectus to be issued, it is a defence that he withdrew that consent before publication or, if he did so subsequently and before the plaintiff acquired the securities, he gave public notice of withdrawing his consent and the reasons therefor. Where, notwithstanding his not giving or withdrawing consent, a person is named in a prospectus as being or agreeing to become a director, or an expert having consented to certain statements being in it, the company's directors and anyone else who authorised the prospectus to be issued, or the expert who authorised inclusion of the statement, must indemnify the person for any loss or damage that in consequence ensues to him, by having to defend legal proceedings.[158] Exempted from this liability is

---

[155] 2005 Act, s.43.
[156] 2005 Act, s.42.
[157] 2005 Act, s.45.
[158] 2005 Act, s.44.

any director who did not know about or who did not consent to the prospectus being issued.

TRANSFER OF SHARES

15–86 Until 10 years ago shares in Plcs were transferable in the same manner as shares in private companies: by furnishing the company with a duly-completed share transfer form, along with the certificate representing the shares.[159] Although bearer shares were permissible, they were rarely used. Today, most shares in listed companies are traded electronically. Definitive and also temporary (including renounceable) title documents must contain prescribed information.[160]

Undocumented Securities

15–87 Instead of share certificates, share transfer forms and the certification of transfers pending new share certificates being issued, a system of transferring title to shares and debentures electronically was authorised by the Companies Act 1990 (Uncertified Securities) Regulations 1996[161]—often referred to as the "dematerialisation" of share transfers. The system currently in use in Ireland and in the UK is known as CREST, which is owned by CrestCo, a wholly owned subsidiary of a bank, Euroclear SA/NV. There is an agreement between CrestCo and the Irish Stock Exchange, whereby CrestCo provides settlement services to the Exchange and the companies that have securities listed on it. CrestCo also provides settlement and asset recording services for Jersey, Guernsey, Manx, Dutch, German, Swedish, Swiss and US S&P equities and corporate stocks, as well as Eurotop 300 securities and other UK financial instruments.

15–88 The purpose of securities being transferable in this manner is not only to eliminate the costs incurred in exchanging documents and other paper, but also to reduce the risk of title problems arising in the course of agreed transfers being completed.[162] Ordinarily, risks of this nature rarely arise in direct face-to-face transactions where, on obtaining a signed share transfer form, the transferee immediately gives it to the company for registration. But under the former settlement regime for stock exchange transactions, the time between an agreement to sell/buy securities being made and the transferee's name being placed on the register could last several days and at times weeks. In October 1987, when stock markets crashed, trading volumes soared, resulting in severe delays in processing settlements. Some investors sought to take advantage of the hold-ups by attempting to avoid completion. The London Exchange's initial response was to attempt dematerialisation with a system having the acronym TAURUS, but it was not a success.

---

[159] See para.9–87 *et seq.*
[160] Listing Rules 6.5.15 & 6.6.
[161] SI 1996/68.
[162] See generally, Micheler, "English and German Securities Law: A Thesis in Doctrinal Path Dependence" 123 *L.Q.R.* 251 (2007), Micheler, "Foreword Quasi Negotiability? Legal Title and Transfer of Shares in a Paperless World" [2002] *J. Bus. L.* 358 and Blair & Walker (eds), *Financial Markets and Exchanges Law* (Oxford: OUP, 2007), Ch.7.

15–89 Securities may be "evidenced and transferred without a written instrument", provided that everything is done in accordance with the 1996 Regulations.[163] To that end, any requirements that transfers be executed under hand or by seal do not apply.[164] An operator of the requisite electronic system must be approved by the Minister. Additionally, before transfers may be effected under any such system, agreement must be reached with the Revenue with regard to paying the stamp duty chargeable on transfers.[165] Where a company's regulations do not provide for electronic registration and transfer of title (e.g. Table A), the directors may resolve to disapply its articles in this regard, in favour of uncertified securities.[166] But that decision can be overridden by an ordinary resolution of the members. One of the conditions for obtaining a listing on the Irish Stock Exchange is that the securities are eligible for settlement through the CrestCo system.[167]

Transfer Process

15–90 How the system works, briefly, is that any intending buyer or seller of securities approaches a "system participant", who is a person or body authorised by CrestCo to operate the system, usually a stock broker or a bank. There are eight Irish broker participants. Through CrestCo, the broker will be able to verify the validly of instructions given electronically, that the shares in question are in the seller's name and the buyer's ability to pay for them. If all is well, the transaction instruction will then be sent by CrestCo, resulting in the shares being put into the buyer's account with it and payment being credited to the seller's account with it, and the company will be instructed to amend its securities' register accordingly.

The Share Register

15–91 Once a company has chosen the uncertified title system, any member can request to have his shares dealt with in this manner by so applying in writing and delivering up the certificate he holds for his shares.[168] Thereafter, the company may not register any transfer of title to those securities unless required to do so by instruction through CrestCo, a High Court order, where there has been a statutory "takeout", or by some other legislation.[169] But it may change the name of a holder where title has transmitted by operation of law. If ever it refuses to register a transfer, within two months it must notify the transferee.

15–92 Where a company is instructed through CrestCo to transfer a specified number of its securities, it must do so unless it is prohibited from doing so by other legislation or the transfer has been voided under it, or the transfer is to a deceased person. It also may not do so if it is prohibited by court order, provided that both it and CrestCo had actual notice of that order before the

---

[163] Regulation 4(1).
[164] Regulation 5.
[165] Regulation 4(3).
[166] Regulation 8.
[167] Listing Rule 3.3.23.
[168] Regulation 24.
[169] Regulation 17.

instruction was sent. In certain circumstances it may not do so where there are linked transfers. The company may refuse to enter a transfer to a minor or to some entity that is not a natural person or that lacks legal personality. Provided the transaction has been carried out in accordance with the 1996 Regulations, entry of the transferee's name on the uncertified members' register is *prima facie* "evidence of" his title to those securities.[170] No notice of any trust is receivable by the registrar or may be entered on the securities' register.[171] Except with the consent of CrestCo or by order of the High Court, a company may not rectify this register.[172] CrestCo's consent is required before a company may close its register.[173]

Title Disputes

15–93 Disputes about the ownership of shares or debentures arise where either a purported transfer takes place that has not been authorised by their owner or, although he has authorised the transfer, they get put into the name of someone other than the intended transferee. Except where the company has issued a certificate that incorrectly states who owns the securities in question or their number, it is not directly prejudiced by any dispute between competing claimants to their ownership. Where that certificate is inaccurate, the company may be liable to the transferee (who does not get good title) through estoppel.[174] But this doctrine can have no application to uncertified securities.

15–94 Instead, once the company receives instructions to record a transfer, in accordance with the 1996 Regulations, it is obliged to carry them out unless it has actual notice that they were not properly authorised or the information with them was not correct, or the transaction is prohibited by court order or otherwise by law, or the transferee is deceased.[175] It is the owner of those securities who in the first place bears the loss because neither he nor his broker may deny that the transaction was authorised or the correctness of the information supplied.[176] However, he may have a remedy against the innocent broker or other party to the fraud, and even against CrestCo if it were at fault.[177] CrestCo is not bound by or compelled to recognise any form of trust or other interest in the securities, even if it has actual or constructive notice of it.[178]

Bearer Warrants

15–95 Exceptionally, in place of share certificates, fully paid-up shareholders in Plcs may be issued with share warrants to bearer.[179] Ownership of debentures

---

[170] Regulation 11.
[171] Regulation 10(6).
[172] Regulation 12.
[173] Regulation 13.
[174] See para.9–94 *et seq.*
[175] Regulation 25(4)–(7).
[176] Regulation 35(1)– (3).
[177] Regulation 35(8) and (9).
[178] Regulation 22.
[179] 1963 Act, s.88.

may be similarly evidenced. Title to securities represented by such instruments may be transferred by delivery. Provision is usually made for detaching coupons from the warrants so as to claim future dividends or interest. There is no provision for warrants in Table A. For exchange control purposes, Central Bank permission was required before an Irish company could issue such instruments. Where these are issued for shares, the register of members must record the date of issue and a statement of the shares included in them, distinguishing each by number where the shares have numbers.[180] Where or to such extent the company's articles so provide, the bearer of a share warrant is deemed to be a member of the company.

INSIDER TRADING

15–96 Insider trading differs from common law fraud and market manipulation in that the person who profits from the transaction neither does nor says anything in particular to influence the securities' price, or their purchaser's or seller's conduct. Instead, on account of information that he possesses concerning the company's affairs, that is not publicly available, he is in a far better position to assess the true value of those securities than are most investors. He resembles the player holding marked cards. The classic instance is the US case, *Texas Gulf Sulphur Co.*,[181] where geophysical surveys had been conducted in Canada on behalf of a mining company, which produced quite remarkable results. Thereupon, several of its directors purchased stock in the company and also purchased calls on its stock. Shortly afterwards, the company gave favourable stock options to its senior officers and employees. When drilling resumed at the end of winter, rumours began spreading of an imminent major ore strike for the company. Shortly afterwards, the company issued a press statement, which played down its prospects. But within a few days, a report was published in the *Northern Miner*, indicating the real extent of the discovery. Between the time the earlier results had been obtained and then, the company's share price had appreciated steadily, from $18 to $31. Proceedings were brought successfully against the directors and others, focusing on the profits they had made through this period from buying stock and options with the advantage of inside information.

15–97 Several rationales exist for outlawing the practice. Ordinarily, it does no direct harm to the company whose securities are being traded in, as it cannot suffer any immediate financial loss because those were sold at either above or below their true market value, as the case may be. But those who bought or sold the securities above or below that value are plainly prejudiced. In practice, it can be difficult to differentiate between those who were prompted to buy or sell because of the then-distorted price and those who would have bought or sold at the time in any event. In the case of insider trading by company officers, the practice flies in the face of fundamental fiduciary principles, that they should not make secret profits by virtue of their

---

[180] 1963 Act, s.118.
[181] *SEC v Texas Gulf Sulphur Co.* 401 F 2d 833 (2 Cir. 1968).

position. A form of abuse of insider information that is less amenable to regulation is where, relying on such information, the insider declines to deal in the relevant securities.[182]

15–98   Insider trading has been considered above with reference to directors' fiduciary duties.[183] As it is the directors who determine who the company may sue, there are significant practical difficulties in enforcing that obligation against a director who profited from insider trading. However, those who profit from this practice are not only officers of the companies whose securities are involved but also at times other company personnel, members of their families, persons working in the securities industry who have access to inside knowledge and those who are "tipped off" about the true value of a traded security. Because the losing parties in such trades on securities markets usually will not have any direct dealings with their buyer or seller, contract and tort liability are of little or no assistance to them. The existence of any potential common law liability on these grounds does not significantly deter the practice. For these reasons, as far back as 1942 rules were introduced in the US to outlaw the practice, it was outlawed in Britain in 1980 and Pt V (ss.107–121) of the 1990 Act imposed extensive criminal and civil liability on parties who profited from dealing with a company's securities, when they were "in possession of information that is not generally available but, if it were, would be likely to materially affect the price of those securities." This gave effect to an EC Directive of 1989[184] and to a Council of Europe Convention of 1989.[185] It was replaced in 2005. Additionally, directors and persons acting at their instigation may not deal in certain options in their company's or any related companies' securities.[186] The statutory regime is supplemented by the "Model Code" in the Stock Exchange's Listing Rules[187] and by provision in the Takeover Panel's Rules.[188]

15–99   A way of diminishing the opportunities for insider profiteering, addressed in the 2005 Market Abuse Regulations, is to require prompt disclosure of all material company information, thereby ensuring a degree of equality in the securities market. Outlawing insider trading creates an incentive against withholding such information; since it cannot be used to garner secret profits, there is no great advantage in not publishing it.

15–100   Part 4 (ss.29–37) of the 2005 Act, headed "market abuse", and the Market Abuse (Directive 2003/6/EC) Regulations 2005[189] give effect to the

---

[182] *cf.* Fried, "Insider Abstention" 113 *Yale L.J.* 455 (2003).

[183] See para.7–45 *et seq.*

[184] Directive 89/592, [1989] OJ L 334/30. See generally, Hopt, "The European Insider Dealing Directive" 27 *C.M.L.R.* 51 (1990), and N. Moloney, *EC Securities Regulations* (Oxford: Oxford University Press, 2002), p.775 *et seq.*

[185] Convention on Insider Trading 1989, *European Treaty Series* (No.130).

[186] 1990 Act, s.30.

[187] Appendix 1; *cf. Chase Manhattan Equities Ltd v Goodman* [1991] B.C.L.C. 897.

[188] Rule 4.1.

[189] SI 2005/342.

EC's Market Abuse Directive of 2003.[190] These deal with a variety of ways in which securities' markets can be improperly affected, one of which is insider trading. The core stipulation is that an insider "who possesses inside information shall not use that information by acquiring or disposing if, by trying to acquire or dispose of, for the person's own account or for the account of a third party, directly or indirectly, financial instruments to which that information relates".[191] An extensive range of securities come within this prohibition, including shares and debentures in companies which have been admitted to trading on a stock market in any EC state, or in respect of which a request for admission to the market has been made. But the transaction in question does not have to occur in that market. Transactions in accordance with "stabilisation rules", conducted shortly after a public share issue, are excluded from the prohibition.[192]

Insiders

15–101   For these purposes, those who are insiders may be divided between primary and secondary insiders. The former are those who, on account of their position vis-à-vis the company or the market, have ready access to the information; the latter are "tippees" and others who obtain the information from the former. Primary insiders are those who obtained the information by virtue of their position as directors or major shareholders of the company, or having access to the information through their employment, profession or duties (e.g. the company's auditors, lawyers and stock-brokers). Also included are those who obtained the information by virtue of their criminal activities, such as by corrupting the company's management or employees, or otherwise stealing the information. The secondary category of insiders is defined as those possessing the information who "know or ought to have known that it is insider information", regardless of where the information has come from or how it was obtained.

Inside Information

15–102   A regime that entirely prohibited directors and other insiders from trading in their company's shares, relying on some information about its affairs that is not available to the general public, would probably be unworkable, as they could rarely if ever buy or sell those shares. Any prohibition would have to be more narrowly focused. The key concept of inside information is defined principally as "information of a precise nature relating directly or indirectly to one or more issuers of [securities] or to one or more [securities] which has not been made public and which, if it were made public, would be likely to have a significant effect on the price of those [securities] or on the price of related derivative [securities]".[193]

---

[190] Directive 2003/6 [2003] O.J. L96/16. See generally, Blair & Walker, Ch.7 and Ferrarini, "The European Market Abuse Directive" 41 *C.M.L.R.* 711 (2004).

[191] Regulation 5(1).

[192] Companies (Amendment) Act, 1999.

[193] Regulation 2(1).

15–103   There are four major components to this definition. The information must be information of a precise nature, as contrasted with rumours and general talk of questionable accuracy. It is information that:

"(a) indicates

    (i) a set of circumstances which exists or may reasonably be expected to come into existence, or

    (ii) an event which has occurred or which may reasonably occur, and

(b) is specific enough to enable a conclusion to be drawn as to possible effect if that set of circumstances or event ... on the prices of [securities] or related derivative[s]."[194]

15–104   It further must be information that is not available to the public. What is meant by the public here and by information being non-public is not defined, but it would appear that reasonably extensive disclosure to the securities markets is the test.

15–105   Next, the information must relate either to the issuer of the securities, i.e. the company, or to the securities themselves. It may come from within the company itself (e.g. a dividend increase) or from the market (e.g. a pending takeover) and can relate to circumstances that will affect the company's assets or liabilities, its general business operations, including impacts of broader political, economic or environmental events.

15–106   Finally and critically, the information must be price-sensitive, in that if disclosed generally it is "likely to have a significant effect on the price" of the securities being traded. Whether or not the information is price-sensitive is to be determined from an *ex ante* perspective, meaning whether a significant movement in the price would probably occur if that information were published. In making this assessment, all variables in the market that affect the security should be considered, such as volume, supply, liquidity, volatility, etc. Even though the information in question is not accessible to the general public, where all the parties to the relevant transactions possess that information at the time, it was held by the E.C.J. that the Directive's prohibition on insider trading was not contravened.[195] In *Fyffes Plc v DCC Plc*,[196] where a large stake in the plaintiff company was disposed of by subsidiaries of the defendant company at a substantial profit to that group, at the trial the action for damages was dismissed because Laffoy J. concluded that the defendants' chief executive (who also was a defendant) did not have the requisite price-sensitive information. He had also been a director of the plaintiff and, in that capacity, had access to that company's internal trading reports for November and December 1999. The shares were sold in the following February. Although those reports indicated a dramatic decline in profitability for those periods, it was concluded that there

---

[194] Regulation 2(1).
[195] *Ipourgos Ikonomikon v Georgakis* (Case 391/04) [2007] 2 B.C.L.C. 692.
[196] [2005] I.E.H.C. 477, unreported, Laffoy J., December 21, 2005.

was substantial other material information in the public arena about other aspects of the company's affairs to deprive those reports of major significance in indicating how the company's share price was likely to perform. The judge found that, had those reports been available at the time to the "reasonable investor", he would have concluded that it was too early in the financial year to base on them a judgment about the company's prospects for the remaining half year. At the relevant time, the main focus of attention for potential investors in the company was the prospects of a merger or a major acquisition, and also an internet trading venture being developed, which would have dwarfed those two reports' bearing on price expectations.

15–107   These conclusions were rejected on appeal by the Supreme Court.[197] In determining whether particular information is price-sensitive for these purposes, one does not endeavour to ascertain how the "reasonable investor" would treat that information. Neither the statutory provision nor the EC Directive contained such a qualification. The test is whether in fact the information "would be likely materially to affect" the share price. Accordingly, the court must evaluate the state of the market at the relevant time and then, with such evidence as is available to it, make a call as to whether the share price would be materially affected if the information had been generally available. Here, the earlier two trading reports contained "bad news"; they were such as to cast serious doubts about the company's prospects for the first half of the year 2000 and possibly for the full year. In March 2000, when a "profit warning" sent by the company to the Stock Exchange was published, there was a rapid decline in the share price—almost immediately a drop of 15 per cent and thereafter a constant slide for the rest of the year. Fruit was the company's main business and the two late 1999 trading reports were in substance a quite detailed profit warning, far more informative than the more general sentiments contained in the March 2000 announcement. That the cause of the share price peaking around the time DCC sold the shares was due to the "dot.com mania" did not take away from the effect that disclosure of the information in the two reports would have had on the share price, especially as they related to the company's principal activities. That at the time the plaintiff may not have regarded the information as relevant was somewhat incongruous but did not take from the fact that the information was price-sensitive.

15–108   Denham J. summarised the appropriate test as follows:

> "The test ... is an objective test. Was there information? Was it generally available? If it was made generally available, would it be likely to materially affect the price of the shares on the market? The answer is equally clear. There was information. It was not generally available. It was bad news, it was information of a risk, it would concern the market. It was information likely to affect the price of the shares on the market. In considering the information it is not appropriate to offset that with information already in the market. The use of comparators is helpful. In this case there

---

[197] [2007] I.E.S.C. 36, unreported, July 27, 2007.

was a comparator in the 20th March, 2000 Announcement, which contained similar information. [It] being a useful comparator, illustrated the effect on the market of similar information – which was price-sensitive, there was a significant drop in the same price."[198]

The Prohibition

15–109　There is a significant difference in how the prohibition is formulated in the 2005 Regulations and in their 1990 predecessor. What those possessors of inside information are now forbidden to do is to "use [it] by acquiring or disposing of" the company's securities, or trying to do so, either "directly or indirectly" and either on their own account or for some third party.[199] Thus, the scope of what is proscribed is most extensive. It applies even where the insider makes use of nominees or fiduciaries, or he executes the transaction for the benefit of a third party. Even attempts to execute it are caught. There is no requirement that he makes a profit from the transaction. Under the 1990 Act, however, the scope was even more extensive, the prohibition being against simply "deal[ing]" in the securities while in possession of the relevant information.[200] Whether there is any distinction here in substance is debatable because it is reasonable to assume that the dealer will take account of and thereby "use" that information.

15–110　What also is prohibited is disclosing inside information, other than in the normal course of the person's professional activities; additionally, recommending or inducing another person to acquire or dispose of securities on the basis of that information.

15–111　These prohibitions do not apply to transactions that are completed on foot of agreements entered into before the party became aware of the information. Nor do they apply to where the information is used in the context of a public takeover of or merger with a company, in conformity with the Irish Takeover Panel Act 1997. Nor do they apply to trading in the company's own shares in an authorised buy-back programme or to secure their stabilisation.[201]

Enforcement and Liability

15–112　To deter breaches of the above requirements, companies are required to publicly disclose without delay inside information, subject to several qualifications and safeguards.[202] Companies with securities that are subject to this regime and those acting for them must draw up a list of persons working for them who have access to inside information concerning them, and must regularly update that list.[203] Directors and certain senior executives of such companies, as well as members of their families and other specified parties

---

[198] [2007] I.E.S.C. 36 at 96 (para 31 of Denham J.'s judgment).
[199] Regulation 5.
[200] 1990 Act, s.108.
[201] Regulation 9 and 1990 Act, s.223.
[202] Regulation 10.
[203] Regulation 11.

closely associated with them, must notify the Central Bank of transactions on their own account conducted in the company's securities or its derivatives.[204]

The Bank

15–113 The Central Bank has extensive supervisory and enforcement powers,[205] including to impose administrative sanctions up to a penalty of €2.5 million, similar to those it has for the Prospectus Regulations.[206] It can request sight of lists drawn up of persons with inside knowledge.[207] Transactions by directors, certain senior executives and others in the company's securities, for their own account, must be notified to the Bank.[208] Persons professionally involved in arranging securities transactions are required promptly to notify it of transactions that they suspect constitute insider trading.[209]

Prosecution

15–114 Insider trading is an offence, which may be prosecuted summarily by the Bank, with a maximum penalty of €5,000 and/or 12 months' imprisonment.[210] In a prosecution on indictment, the maximum penalty is €10 million and/or 10 years' imprisonment.[211]

Civil Claim

15–115 Insider trading is an actionable wrong involving potential dual liabilities. The unsuccessful defendant must compensate any other party to the impugned transaction who did not possess the same information.[212] The measure of this liability is the difference between the price at which the securities changed hands and the price at which they were likely to have changed hands if the information in question had been generally available. Often, however, it may not be possible to link up a defendant and the "other party" to his trade. In the US, insider trading damages claims often take the form of class actions. Additionally, the unsuccessful defendant is liable to the company for any profit earned from the transaction.[213]

15–116 It would appear that *scienter*, in the sense of intending to deceive or defraud, is not a prerequisite of civil liability; that liability is strict. In *Fyffes Plc v DCC Plc*,[214] which concerned an earlier version of the prohibition and

---

[204] Regulation 12.
[205] Regulations 27–54.
[206] Regulation 41.
[207] Regulation 11.
[208] Regulation 12.
[209] Regulation 13.
[210] Regulations 44–53.
[211] 2005 Act, s.32.
[212] 2005 Act, s.33(1)(a).
[213] 2005 Act, s.33(1)(b).
[214] [2005] I.E.H.C. 477, unreported, Laffoy J., December 21, 2005; [2007] I.E.S.C. 36, unreported, July 27, 2007.

liability rule, Laffoy J. concluded that liability was strict in that sense and, further, assuming the information involved was price sensitive, that it was not necessary to show that a defendant or his agent was aware of that fact.

MARKET MANIPULATION

15–117   It was not until 2005 that a comprehensive regime was adopted to regulate secondary market securities transactions (ss.29–37 of the 2005 Act and the Market Abuse (Directive 2003/6/EC) Regulations 2005),[215] giving effect to an EC Directive on Market Abuse.[216] Prior to then, particularly egregious forms of deceptive conduct in securities markets could fall foul of the criminal law. In 1814, Lord Cochrane and others were convicted of conspiracy to defraud investors, by spreading false rumours that caused the price of government bonds to jump, *viz.* that soldiers had returned from France with news of Napoleon's death (before his defeat at Waterloo).[217] Some scams involving securities are caught by the offence of making a gain or causing a loss by deception, contrary to s.6 of the Criminal Justice (Theft and Fraud Offences) Act 2001.

15–118   As stock markets are impersonal, it is very rare that a buyer or seller would have a remedy against the other party for breach of contract or in tort involving fraud or deception. Even in face-to-face share sales, the basic rule is *caveat emptor*; liability arises only where there has been breach of a particular term of the contract or there has been a fraudulent misrepresentation, or exceptionally where the party (generally the vendor) has a duty of care to make extensive disclosure to the other. To establish civil liability at common law, it generally is necessary to prove fraud, which involves four key components. These are that the defendant (or via his agent) made a statement to the plaintiff of a material fact that was false; the defendant knew it was false or was reckless as to whether or not it was false; the defendant intended the plaintiff to rely on what was said; and finally, the plaintiff was justified in relying on it in the circumstances.

15–119   Under the rubric of "market manipulation",[218] an extensive range of activities that distort securities prices in one form or another are outlawed by the 2005 Regulations; they are criminalised, made the subject of administrative penalties and are actionable wrongs. These apply to securities that have been admitted to trading on a regulated market in an EC Member State and to

---

[215] SI 2005/342.

[216] Directive 2003/6 [2003] O.J.L 96/16. See generally Ferrarini, "The European Market Abuse Directive" 41 *C.M.L.R.* 711 (2004), Haynes, "Market Abuse: an Analysis of its Nature and Regulation", 11 *Co.Law* 323 (2007) and Blair & Walker, Ch. 6.

[217] *R v De Begenger* (1814) 3 M. & S. 67, recounted in B. Vale, *The Audacious Admiral Cochrane* (London: Conway Maritime Press, 2004), Ch.7. See too *Scott v Brown, Doering, McNab & Co.* [1892] 2 Q.B. 724, concerning a conspiracy to artificially inflate share prices.

[218] Regulation 6.

securities in respect of which a request for admission has been made. These apply extraterritorially, in that they extend to actions carried out abroad. At least for the purpose of civil liability, it appears that there is no overriding requirement of *scienter*, i.e. knowledge or recklessness with regard to the falsity of any representations made, or intent to defraud.

Manipulation

15–120   What constitutes market manipulation covers four broad categories of activity.[219] One is trading or ordering trades in a manner that "give[s] or are likely to give false or misleading signals as to the supply of, demand for or price of" securities. These include, for example, arranging fictitious transactions, as where there is no genuine change of ownership of the securities, and also where colluding parties enter both buy and sell orders at the same time. Another is price-rigging: trading or ordering trades in a manner that "secure[s], by a person or persons acting in collaboration, the price of one or several [securities] at an abnormal or artificial level". It is a defence to these to show that there were "legitimate reasons" for so acting and that there was "conformity with accepted market practices". Another still is arranging transactions or orders to trade that "employ fictitious devices or any other form of deception or contrivance". Finally, there is spreading false rumours and the like: the "dissemination of information ... which gives or is likely to give false or misleading signals as to [securities] ... where the person who made the dissemination knew, or ought to have known, that the information was false or misleading". Some examples of manipulation and additional criteria amplifying the main strands of the definition are contained in the 2005 Regulations and the Annex to them. These include securing a dominant position over the demand for or supply of a security, which results in fixing prices or in creating other unfair trading conditions; dealing in securities at the close of the market, resulting in investors being misled by the closing prices; voicing an opinion in the media about the price of securities, while having previously taken a position in them, and thereby profiting from dealings in them without having sufficiently disclosed the conflict of interest.

15–121   Additionally, those who issue research or other information recommending or suggesting investment strategy for publicly traded securities must ensure that their recommendations are fairly presented and, if they have any conflict of interest, that must be disclosed.[220] To this end, the person must take reasonable care to ensure that facts are clearly distinguished from non-factual matter, that all sources are reliable (if not, that must be clearly disclosed), all projections and price targets are clearly labelled as such, and that the assumptions made in producing such forecasts are stated. Where the person is subject to some self-regulatory code or standards, reference to those must be clearly stated in the recommendations. All relationships and circumstances that may reasonably be expected to cause a conflict of interest must be

---

[219] Regulation 2(1).
[220] Regulations 16–26.

disclosed. Specific disclosure requirements exist for credit institutions and investment firms, for independent analysts, and where the recommendation was produced by some third party. In November 2007, in the first case of its kind, the Bank's Financial Regulator came to a settlement with *Phoenix Magazine* over inadvertent breaches by that publication of the disclosure requirements, through recommendations as to financial instruments in articles with no bylines. The magazine admitted the breaches, agreed to introduce measures (but not bylines) to support compliance with the Market Abuse Regulations in the future, and paid a fine of €5,000.

Enforcement and Liability

15–122   The system of administrative oversight, criminal responsibility and civil liability here is virtually the same as for insider trading.

The Bank

15–123   The Central Bank exercises numerous supervisory functions regarding market manipulation and can impose administrative sanctions up to a penalty of €2.5 million.[221]

Prosecution

15–124   The Bank can prosecute summarily for the offence, with a maximum penalty of €5,000 and/or 12 months' imprisonment.[222] In a prosecution on indictment, the maximum penalty is €10 million and/or 10 years' imprisonment.[223]

Civil Claim

15–125   Market manipulation also is an actionable wrong, involving potential dual liability, with a two-year limitation period. The unsuccessful defendant must "compensate" any other party who, "by reason" of the breach, acquired or disposed of the security in question.[224] This gives rise to difficult questions of reliance and causation: that the breach caused the transaction in question and the loss arose from it. It remains to be seen how these will be resolved but guidance most likely will be found in the US case law and literature on equivalent provisions there. This too applies to the question of how the compensation is to be calculated.

15–126   Additionally, the company whose securities were involved is entitled to recover "any profit" made from the transaction.[225] One of the issues that will now arise in the *Fyffes Plc v DCC Plc*[226] case, concerning insider trading, is how such profit is to be calculated.

---

[221] Regulation 41.
[222] Regulations 49–53.
[223] 2005 Act, s.32.
[224] 2005 Act, s.33(2)(a).
[225] 2005 Act, s.33(3)(b).
[226] [2005] I.E.H.C. 477, unreported, Laffoy J., December 21, 2005; [2007] I.E.S.C. 36, unreported, July 27, 2007.

TAKEOVERS AND MERGERS

15–127 Listed companies are always at risk of being the subject of a takeover bid,[227] which sometimes may be resisted by the directors or by significant shareholders. The general common law rules, equitable principles and provisions of the Companies Acts, that apply to takeovers and mergers,[228] are as applicable as much to Plcs and to such transactions involving listed companies, as to private companies.[229] Requirements for listed companies were adopted in the European Communities (Takeover Bids Directive 2004/25/EC) Regulations 2006[230], principally regarding action taken by a target company to frustrate a bid, including a novel optional "break-through" mechanism, and replacing the 1963 Act's "take-out" regime. These are supplemented by "general principles" contained in those Regulations[231] and in the schedule to the Irish Takeover Panel Act 1997, as well as the extensive Takeover Rules (hereinafter "the Rules") promulgated and administered by the Takeover Panel. These Rules also apply to takeovers structured as "arrangements" under s.201 of the 1963 Act.[232] A mechanism for effecting a type of takeover that is not used in Ireland is subject to regulations adopted in 1987,[233] to give effect to an EC Directive. It took 15 years for the EC's draft proposal for takeovers generally to be adopted as a Directive,[234] which is implemented by the 2006 Regulations. In 2005 a Directive on Cross-Border Mergers was adopted,[235] which was required to have been implemented by December 15, 2007. Takeovers involving an "undertaking" of any size or nature are also subject to the Competition Acts 2002–2006, designed to prevent monopoly and restrictive practices. At EC level, they may fall foul of Regulation 139/2004 on the control of concentrations between undertakings.[236]

15–128 The Takeover Bids Regulations 2006 apply to public offers made to the holders of securities that are listed on the Irish, the London, the New York or the NASDAQ Exchanges, to acquire all or some of those securities with a view to acquiring control of the company. What constitutes control for these purposes is not defined there but, under the 1997 Act, it means holding securities that control at least 30 per cent of the voting rights in the company, whether directly or indirectly.[237] The Panel's Rules also apply to dealings in securities that were listed sometime in the preceding five years and, whenever the Minister so prescribes, to any other Plc's securities.

---

[227] See *Practical Commercial Precedents* part C2.

[228] See Ch.12 and N. Moloney, *EC Securities Regulation* (Oxford: Oxford University Press, 2002), Ch.14.

[229] Except 1963 Act, s.204 in the case of listed securities.

[230] SI 2006/255.

[231] Regulation 7.

[232] Rule 41.

[233] European Communities (Mergers and Divisions of Companies) Regulations 1987 (SI 1987/137).

[234] Directive 2004/25 [2004] O.J. L142/12.

[235] Directive 2005/56 [2005] O.J. L310/1.

[236] [2004] O.J. L24/22.

[237] Section 1(1).

Principles

15–129   Certain general principles applicable to takeovers are laid down in the 2006 Regulations:

(a) All holders of the securities of an offeree of the same class must be afforded equivalent treatment; moreover, if a person acquires control of a company, the other holders of securities must be protected.

(b) The holders of the securities of an offeree must have sufficient time and information to enable them to reach a properly informed decision on an offer; where it advises the holders of securities, the board of the offeree must give its views on the effects of implementation of the offer on employment, conditions of employment and the locations of the offeree's places of business.

(c) The board of an offeree must act in the interests of the company as a whole and must not deny the holders of securities the opportunity to decide on the merits of an offer.

(d) False markets must not be created in the securities of the offeree, of the offeror or of any other company concerned by the offer in such a way that the rise or fall of the prices of the securities becomes artificial and the normal functioning of the markets is distorted.

(e) An offeror must announce an offer only after ensuring that he or she can fulfil in full any cash consideration, if such is offered, and after taking all reasonable measures to secure the implementation of any other type of consideration.

(f) An offeree must not be hindered in the conduct of its affairs for longer than is reasonable by an offer for its securities.

15–130   Some of these principles are expanded on in the amended schedule to the 1997 Act:

"1. All holders of the securities of an offeree of the same class must be afforded equivalent treatment; moreover, if a person acquires control of a company, the other holders of securities must be protected.

  2. The holders of the securities of an offeree must have sufficient time and information to enable them to reach a properly informed decision on the offer; where it advises the holders of securities, the board of the offeree must give its views on the effects of implementation of the offer on employment, conditions of employment and the locations of the offeree's places of business.

  3. The board of an offeree must act in the interests of the company as a whole and must not deny the holders of securities the opportunity to decide on the merits of the offer.

  4. False markets must not be created in the securities of the offeree, of the offeror or of any other company concerned by the bid in such a way that the rise or fall of the prices of the securities becomes artificial and the normal functioning of the markets is distorted.

  5. An offeror must announce an offer only after ensuring that he or she can fulfil in full any cash consideration, if such is offered, and after

taking all reasonable measures to secure the implementation of any other type of consideration.

6. An offeree must not be hindered in the conduct of its affairs for longer than is reasonable by an offer for its securities.
7. A substantial acquisition of securities (whether such acquisition is to be effected by one transaction or a series of transactions) shall take place only at an acceptable speed and shall be subject to adequate and timely disclosure."

Authority and Disclosure

15–131 Where the value of the transaction exceeds 25 per cent of the acquiring company's value, its shareholders should be sent a circular explaining it fully and their prior consent is required for the proposed bid to become effective.[238] An open offer that is subject to shareholder approval must state that this is the case.[239]

Financing

15–132 An exception is made to the prohibition against companies financing the purchase of their own shares where that involves the company incurring expenses to ensure compliance with the regulatory regime for takeovers.[240] Another exception is where the company it is being sought to take over has agreed to reimburse expenses incurred by the bidder and those terms were approved by the Panel.[241] Except where Panel approval has been obtained, the Takeover Rules prohibit the offeree or any associate of it to make any arrangement for compensating the bidder for the expenses incurred in a proposed takeover, in the event of it lapsing or not being made.[242]

Defences

15–133 There is far less scope for defensive measures in listed companies than in private companies or in unlisted Plcs.[243] Under the Takeover Rules, directors of the target company are required to obtain competent independent advice on every offer that is made for its shares.[244] Any director who has a conflict of interest may not make any statement or announcement concerning a bid unless the full nature of his conflict is adequately disclosed. A circular setting out the substance of the advice that the board obtained, along with the directors' considered views, must be sent to the shareholders. If the directors cannot

---

[238] Listing Rule 7.2.
[239] Listing Rule 5.8.
[240] 1963 Act, s.60(12)(k).
[241] 1963 Act, s.60(12)(k).
[242] R.21(2).
[243] See generally, Ogowewo "Tactical Litigation in Takeover Contests", (2007) *J. Bus. L.* 589, Kershaw, "The Illusion of Importance: Reconsidering the UK's Takeover Defence Prohibition" 56 *I. & C.L.Q.* 267 (2007) and Clarke, "Articles 9 and 11 of the Takeover Directive (2004/25) and the Market for Corporate Control" [2006] *J. Bus. L.* 355.
[244] Rule 3(1).

express a view or there are divergent views, the arguments for and against accepting the bid should be set out fully.

15–134 The 2006 Regulations strike at measures adopted that tend to prevent bids succeeding in two ways. Because directors of the company it is being sought to take over may be conflicted in their response to a bid, they are required to obtain their shareholders' consent for certain decisions they take that could prejudice the outcome of a bid.[245] If the directors' decision is other than in the "normal course" of the company's business and, if implemented, it may result in "frustrating[ing]" the bid, it requires shareholder approval before it may be implemented entirely or in part.

15–135 This is amplified in the Takeover Rules, which prohibit a variety of "frustrating action[s]" where a bid is imminent or has been made, unless the shareholders have approved of the measure or the Panel's consent has been obtained. These actions are allotting or issuing shares; granting an option on unissued shares; creating or issuing a security convertible into shares; disposing of or acquiring a substantial asset or profitable line of business, or agreeing to do so; entering into any contract other than in the ordinary course of business; or taking any other action that may result in an offer being frustrated or in the shareholders being deprived the opportunity to decide on the merits of an offer.[246] Accordingly, once the directors have reason to believe an offer is about to be made, they may not take the kind of action that was the subject of, *inter alia,* the *Ampol Petroleum* case,[247] the *Dawson International* case[248] and the *Criterion Properties* case.[249]

15–136 Perhaps the most innovative feature of these Regulations is their optional "break-through" provisions that, where adopted, override all agreements that significantly hinder a takeover bid being accepted by a majority of a company's shareholders,[250] subject however to compensating a party who has suffered loss in consequence of the agreement not being complied with. For these provisions to be applicable, the company's shares must be traded on a regulated market, its articles of association must not contain restrictions on the transfer of securities or on voting,[251] no securities conferring special rights in the company can be held by a government minister or his nominee, and it must have adopted a special resolution "opting in" to this regime and specifying when it is to become effective. This resolution may be revoked by way of another special resolution. Notice of any such resolution must be given to the Panel and, if the company has securities admitted or about to be admitted to any other stock market, to the regulatory authorities there.

---

[245] Regulation 15.
[246] Regulation 21(1).
[247] *Howard Smith Ltd v Ampol Petroleum Ltd* [1974] A.C. 821.
[248] *Dawson Int'l Ltd v Coats Patons Plc* [1989] B.C.L.C. 233.
[249] *Criterion Properties Plc v Stratford UK Properties LLC* [2004] 1 W.L.R. 846.
[250] Regulations 16–20.
[251] Article 11 of the Directive.

15–137 For so long as the company has "opted in", the provisions of any agreement between a person holding the company's securities and the company, or (after April 21, 2004) between a securities' holder and another such person, is rendered "invalid" insofar as it restricts freedom to accept a bid in any of the following ways. These are by restricting any transfer of the securities to the bidder during the offer period; by restricting any transfer of securities to any person, during the offer period, when the bidder holds at least 75 per cent in nominal value of them; by restricting the right to vote at a general meeting decision to take action that might "frustrate" the bid; or by restricting the right to vote at a general meeting held after the offer period ends, when the bidder holds at least 75 per cent in nominal value of all the company's securities. If the bidder holds that 75 per cent and requisitions the directors to convene an EGM,[252] and within 21 days it is not convened, the bidder can convene an EGM to be held within three months from the date of their requisition. Additionally, if the bidder holds that 75 per cent, at the first EGM held after the offer period, a proposed special resolution requires 14 (not 21) days' notice. The reference to the "offer period" and to "frustrat[ing]" actions here are to those indicated in the Panel's Takeover Rules. Although an agreement between the specified parties is not permitted to restrict transferring securities or entitlements to vote in the circumstances described above, a party to any such agreement who suffers loss by virtue of it being rendered so ineffective is entitled to be compensated. The amount to be awarded is such sum as the court considers "just and equitable" against the party who otherwise would have been liable for breach of agreement.

Profiteering

15–138 The Takeover Rules strike at several circumstances in which some shareholders and others may make unfair profits in the course of a takeover. To prevent insider trading, there is a requirement of strict confidentiality in respect of an offer or contemplated offer, applicable to the companies concerned, their associates and advisers.[253] Anyone who possesses confidential price-sensitive information may not deal in the relevant securities during the takeover period, other than the bidding company, and its dealings must be carried on within the constraints of these rules.[254] All dealings in those securities at those times, by the companies or their associates, must be disclosed.[255]

15–139 It is not permitted to make an arrangement with one or some of the shareholders under which they will obtain better terms for their shares than will be given to other shareholders.[256] This prohibition applies from the time that the offer is in reasonable contemplation. Compliance can be waived by the Panel. Where some shareholders have obtained better terms, the Panel can

---

[252] 1963 Act, s.132.
[253] Rule 2.1.
[254] Rules 4–7.
[255] Rule 8.
[256] Rule 16.

direct the bidder or person acting in concert with it to furnish more favourable consideration to the other shareholders.

15–140 Where the company has separate classes of shares, separate offers must be made for each class.[257] Where an offer is being made for shares that confer voting rights, a "comparable offer" must be made for every other class of shares, whether or not those shares have voting rights.[258] A similar requirement exists in the case of convertible securities, options and subscription rights.[259]

"Removing Dissidents"

15–141 The 1963 Act's provision that enables a successful bidder to "take out" the minority of shareholders who refused to accept the bid,[260] or that enables them to compel the successful bidder to buy their shares,[261] is modified for takeovers within the 2006 Regulations.[262] The principal difference is that the size of the majority stake the bidder has to acquire, before a "take-out" or "buy out" can be activated, is increased to 90 per cent of the shares' nominal value and also of the voting rights attached to them. In determining this ratio, for the purpose of "take-out", shares already in the beneficial ownership of the bidder or a subsidiary are not included. Where the bidder has the requisite number of shares, it can notify those who have the remaining shares of its intention to acquire them and, once three months then expires, the bidder is entitled to have those shares transferred to it on the very same terms as it acquired its stake in the company. Where it acquired its shares under alternative terms, the remaining shareholders may stipulate which of those alternatives they would prefer to be bought out for. A bidder will then send a transfer instrument to the target, accompanied by the consideration, and the shares will be registered in its name, the consideration being paid into a separate bank account for or being held in trust for those shareholders. If any of these are of the view that the rules applicable here were not complied with or is not satisfied with the terms, he may apply to the court for a declaration accordingly.

15–142 If the bidder does not move to acquire the dissenters' shares, they may require it to buy them out on the same terms as it gave for the others' shares. On being so notified, it is bound to acquire them on those terms. If any such shareholder disputes the terms, he may apply to the court for a declaration accordingly.

Employees

15–143 The offer document that is sent to the target's shareholders must state, *inter alia,* the bidder's intentions regarding safeguarding the target's and its subsidiaries' management and employees, including any material change in

---

[257] Rule 14(2).
[258] Rule 14(1).
[259] Rule 15.
[260] Section 204.
[261] See para.12–43 *et seq.*
[262] Regulations 22–28.

their conditions of employment.[263] When the target's board sends the circular to its shareholders stating its attitude to the bid, that must include views on how the bid would impact on its employees, including the likely repercussions for them of the bidder's strategic plans.[264] Where the offer has been revised, the revised offer document must be made available to the target's employees and, when sending the circular to the shareholders setting out the directors' views on this bid, there should be appended to it a separate opinion by the employees' representatives of the bid's effect on employment.[265]

The 1987 Regulations

15–144   The European Communities (Merger and Divisions) of Companies Regulations 1987[266] gave effect to the EC's Third and Sixth Directives. Their requirements apply only to Plcs and to certain unregistered companies.Their provisions apply to the commonest form of takeover. One is a merger by acquisition, where the bidder acquires all the target's assets and liabilities in return for shares in the bidder, with or without a cash payment, and it is envisaged that the target will shortly afterwards be wound up; for instance, a takeover using s.260 of the 1963 Act. The other is an essentially similar operation except that the bidder forms a new company which acquires the target and the latter is then wound up; again, the procedure under s.260 of the 1963 Act. Briefly, in either of these circumstances where a merger is proposed, the directors of both companies must draw up draft terms for a merger, setting out various relevant matters and they must draw up separate written reports on those draft terms, which explain them and discuss their implications for the company and its shareholders. A report on the draft terms must also be made by an independent person, who must give an opinion on, *inter alia,* whether the proposed terms are fair and reasonable. If either or both companies' last annual accounts are more than six months out of date, an accounting statement in the format of the balance sheet must be drawn up for the company. Copies of these documents must be sent to the Registrar of Companies and also be made available for inspection by shareholders at both companies' own registered offices. Before the merger can take place, the proposed terms must be approved by special resolutions of both companies' shareholders. Provision is made for acquiring the shares owned by dissenting shareholders and for protecting the interests of any creditors who object to the merger. Ultimately, the merger must be confirmed by order of the court, which is empowered to make various ancillary orders.

CONTINUING DISCLOSURE

15–145   Companies with securities listed on the Irish Stock Exchange and, at times, companies that have applied for a quotation there, are obliged to make

---

[263] Rule 24(1)(e) of the Takeover Rules 2001 as amended.

[264] Rule 25.2 of the Takeover Rules 2001 as amended.

[265] Rule 32.5/6 of the Takeover Rules 2001 as amended.

[266] SI 1987/137.

certain disclosures concerning their affairs over and above what is required of private companies and also of unquoted Plcs. Under the Market Abuse Regulations, quoted companies are obliged to publicly disclose inside information that directly concerns them, without delay and in a manner that enables fast access to it and its timely assessment by the public.[267] However, disclosure may be delayed where certain "legitimate interests" of the company may be prejudiced, provided however that the company can keep that information confidential and also that non-disclosure is not likely to mislead the public. Except in the case of confidential information being imparted, where a company or those acting for it discloses any inside information to a third party, there must be complete and effective disclosure to the public simultaneously. If that disclosure was unintentional, public disclosure must take place without delay.

15–146 Disclosures are required by the Exchange's Listing Rules which, *inter alia*, supplement what must be contained in the company's annual report and accounts, and in its auditors' report.[268] Self-regulation regarding continuous disclosure is now reinforced by Pt 3 (ss.19–24) of the 2006 Act and by the Transparency (Directive 2004/109/EC) Regulations 2007[269] which gives effect to the Transparency (Regulated Markets) Directive of 2004.[270] These require furnishing annual and half-yearly financial statements, management reports and responsibility statements, and provide for liability to persons who suffer loss in consequence of misleading statements or omissions contained in them. Liability can arise here if a person "discharging managerial responsibility" knew or was reckless as to whether the statement was untrue or misleading, or knew that the omission was a dishonest concealment of a material fact. These Regulations also require that the company and the Exchange authorities be notified of transactions in the company's shares that cross prescribed percentage thresholds. Additionally, any changes to rights attaching to its securities, and information about meetings, the issue of new shares and the payment of dividends must be disclosed to the public. Proxy forms must be made available electronically and the above information may be conveyed to securities-holders electronically. Where information is being disclosed to the public, that must be done as widely and as simultaneously as possible.

---

[267] SI 2005/342, Reg.10.
[268] Listing Rule 6.8.
[269] SI 2007/277.
[270] Directive 2004/109 [2004] O.J.L. 390/38. See generally, Chiu, "Examining the Justifications for Mandatory Ongoing Securities Regulation" 26 *Co. Law* 67 (2005) and Omoyele, "Continuing Obligations of Listed Public Companies" 26 *Co. Law.* 355 (2005).

CHAPTER 16

DISTINCTIVE COMPANIES

16–01   There are certain distinctive types of company, the principal features of which call for some consideration, namely non-profit companies, unlimited companies, financial companies, state-owned companies and unregistered companies.

NON-PROFIT COMPANIES

16–02   There are numerous organisations that are formed for purposes other than engaging in business, to the ultimate financial benefit of their members, which are registered under the Companies Acts.[1] While many sporting, charitable, political, social, cultural, professional and analogous organisations take some other legal form (such as mere associations or unincorporated companies and friendly societies), quite a number of these non-profit bodies are registered companies. Examples from the reported cases include the Cyclists' Touring Club,[2] the Dublin Gas Co. Employees' Social and Sports Club,[3] the Liverpool and District Hospital for Diseases of the Heart,[4] the New Zealand Netherlands Society "Oranje",[5] the Royal Automobile Club,[6] the Secular Society,[7] and the Ulster Society for the Prevention of Cruelty to Animals.[8]

16–03   These companies fall into four major categories, although there can be significant overlapping between them. The majority of them are donative bodies, i.e. most of their income is in the form of grants or donations; often they have charitable objects. But others are commercial, i.e. their main income is from selling goods or (usually) services. Many of these are mutual, i.e. they are controlled by those persons who purchase whatever product or service they provide. But others are entrepreneurial in the sense that they, either by law or

---

[1]   See generally, H. Hansmann, "The Role of Non-profit Enterprise" 89 *Yale L.J.* 835 (1980), "Developments in the Law: Non-profit Corporations" 105 *Harv. L. Rev.* 1579 (1992), and Warburton, "Charitable Companies" [1984] *Conv.* 112 .

[2]   *Cyclists' Touring Club v Hopkinson* [1910] 1 Ch. 179.

[3]   *Roper v Ward* [1981] I.L.R.M. 408.

[4]   *Liverpool & District Hospital for Diseases of the Heart v Attorney-General* [1981] 1 Ch. 193.

[5]   *New Zealand Netherlands Soc. "Oranje" Inc. v Kuys* [1973] 2 All E.R. 1222.

[6]   *Re RAC Motoring Services Ltd* [2000] 1 B.C.L.C. 307.

[7]   *Bowman v Secular Society Ltd* [1917] A.C. 406.

[8]   *Re Ulster Society for Prevention of Cruelty to Animals* [1936] N.I. 97.

in fact, are controlled by a self-perpetuating directorate. One form of non-profit company that has become prevalent is the condominium. It is a housing estate or block of flats, where titles to all the units are vested in the company and each unit owner possesses a transferable share in the company that represents his interest in the unit.[9] A category of non-profit company that is referred to in the 1963 Act is one without a share capital, with charitable objects and "under the control of a religion recognised by the State under Article 44 of the Constitution, and which exercises its functions in accordance with the laws, canons and ordinances of the religion concerned".[10]

16–04 What are commonly referred to as cooperatives are a variant of non-profit institutions. As a rule, cooperatives are commercial. But they tend to do business principally with their members, they try to limit the price they charge for whatever they sell to them and, even if they distribute some of their earned surplus to their members, their principal objective is not to earn high profits so that big dividends can be paid. Cooperatives in this sense are usually registered under either the Industrial and Provident Societies Acts 1893–1978, or the Companies Acts. Special legislation exists for two kinds of cooperatives, namely building societies and credit unions. One major building society, the ICS, was a registered company and its shares were listed on the Stock Exchange until it was taken over in 1984 by the Bank of Ireland.

16–05 Some provisions in the Companies Acts were designed specifically with non-profit and cooperative companies in mind. These also get special treatment in the tax laws[11] and, until 1982, were excluded from the reach of the Trade Disputes Act 1906.[12] Leaving aside questions of statutory construction, these companies occasionally pose special problems in the case law. In *Gaiman v National Association for Mental Health*,[13] for example, consideration was given to the extent to which the administrative law principles of natural justice obtain in guarantee companies, in particular as regards expulsions from membership.[14] Matters that call for further clarification include remuneration paid to the directors of these companies,[15] directors' fiduciary duties[16] and de-mutualisation.[17] In the US the vast non-profit sector has been subjected to increasing regulation in recent years.

---

9   *cf.* "Draft Guidance on the Governance of Apartment Owners' Management Companies" from the Office of the Director of Corporate Enforcement, December 2006, available at www.odce.ie.

10   1963 Act, s.128(4)(c).

11   See generally, M. Feeney, *The Taxation of Companies* (Haywards Heath: Tottel Publishing, 2006), paras 12.4 and 12.10.

12   *Smith v Beirne* 89 I.L.T.R. 24 (1955).

13   [1971] 1 Ch. 317.

14   *cf. Coleg Elidyn (Camphill Communities Wales) Ltd v Koeller* [2005] 2 B.C.L.C. 379.

15   *cf. Cyclists Touring Club v Hopkinson* [1910] 1 Ch. 179.

16   *cf. New Zealand Netherlands Soc. "Oranje" Inc. v Kuys* [1973] 2 All E.R. 1222.

17   *cf. Peskin v Anderson* [2001] 1 B.C.L.C. 372.

Guarantee Companies

16–06   Since 1862, companies could be limited by guarantee. At end-2006, there were 13,694 guarantee companies, comprising eight per cent of companies on the register. Non-profit companies are usually registered as limited by guarantee.[18] That is to say, in a winding up the members will be held liable for the company's unpaid debts to the extent that they undertook, or guaranteed, to be so liable.[19] A guarantee company's articles of association must state the number of members with which it proposes to be registered.[20] The company cannot use the sum guaranteed as security for current expenses.[21] Guarantee companies generally do not possess a share capital, although companies the membership of which is based on shareholdings and which also are limited by guarantee do exist.[22] Table C of the 1963 Act's First Schedule sets out a model memorandum of association and articles of association for guarantee companies without a share capital; Table D sets out model regulations for such companies with a share capital. Plcs may not adopt the latter hybrid form.[23]

Omitting "Limited" from Name

16–07   Before 2001 the Minister by licence could permit limited liability non-profit companies to omit the term "limited" from their names, subject to stipulated conditions. Today, to obtain that exemption from the Registrar of Companies,[24] he must be furnished with a statutory declaration by a director or secretary of the company as follows: that its objects are to promote "commerce, art, science, education, religion, charity" or an other prescribed object; further that, under its memorandum or articles of association, all profits and income must be devoted to those objects; payment of dividends to its members is prohibited and, if wound up, its assets are to be transferred to another company established to achieve any of the above objects. While it is so exempted, the company may not alter its own regulations in a manner inconsistent with that provided for above. If the Registrar discovers that any such company is acting in a manner incompatible with those objects or is paying a dividend to its members, he may direct that it shall inserted "limited" into its name. Paying a retirement gratuity to a company's salaried officer who also is one of its members does not contravene the proscription against paying dividends to members.[25]

16–08   In *Hennessy v National Agricultural etc. Association*,[26] a company that held a Minister's licence purported to merge with another company that possessed very different objects and that did not hold such a licence. Although

---

[18]   See generally, Rice, "Companies Limited by Guarantee—A New Look" 28 *Conv.* 214 (1964).
[19]   1963 Act, s.207(1)(e).
[20]   1963 Act, s.12(2).
[21]   *Re Irish Industrial & Agricultural Fair, Cork* 67 I.L.T.R. 175 (1933).
[22]   e.g. *Re Performing Right Soc. Ltd* [1978] 1 W.L.R. 1197.
[23]   1983 Act, s.7.
[24]   1963 Act, s.24.
[25]   *Cyclists Touring Club v Hopkinson* [1910] 1 Ch. 179.
[26]   [1947] I.R. 159.

its governing body was advised that the scheme for amalgamation was unlawful, the company nevertheless sought Ministerial consent to make the necessary changes in its regulations. They were informed that the Minister "as at present advised ... will be prepared to sanction the proposed alterations ..." It was held that the amendments made in pursuance of this authority were nonetheless wholly invalid. According to Overend J., "until the Minister had given his definite and final approval, the company's power to alter its articles did not come into existence ... Any amendments purporting to have been made without such previous approval were null and void. Being nullities, they are incapable of being made effective or binding ex post facto, by sanction of the Minister, by ratification by the [company], or in any other way."[27]

Annual Accounts and Return

16–09   The 1986 Act, which gives effect to the EC's Fourth Directive, does not apply to non-profit companies. These are any company "not trading for the acquisition of gain by the members"; a company with no share capital and which was formed with a charitable object, is controlled by any of several religious organisations and exercises it functions in accordance with the rules of that religion; and a charitable company without share capital in respect of which an order has been made by the Commissioners of Charitable Donations and Bequests.[28] These companies need not annex to their annual return a profit and loss account or balance sheet, nor any report of their auditors or directors.[29] But there must be annexed to it an auditors' report confirming that there has been an annual audit and that the accounts are satisfactory.

Altering Members' Liability

16–10   The basis on which cooperatives do business with their members is often set out in their articles of association, which can give rise to various related questions. The statutory right of companies to amend their own regulations cannot be surrendered or waived by contract with the members or even with outsiders. Subject to what is said below, therefore, a cooperative can alter those provisions in its regulations concerning how it is to do business and in, effect, unilaterally alter its trading arrangements with its members. But the courts will enjoin it from acting on the basis of its new arrangements where they are inconsistent with separate contractual stipulations.[30] Moreover, no member can be bound by an alteration to the company's regulations made after becoming a member that requires taking any additional shares, or "in any way increases his liability" to the company, "or otherwise to pay money to [it]".[31] Thus, for instance, where a dairy co-op's regulations required each member to hold three shares for every 250 pounds of butterfat they supplied, the court enjoined an otherwise proper alteration of this to a requirement of holding one share for every

---

[27]   *ibid.* at 191; *cf. Re Ulster Soc. for Prevention of Cruelty to Animals* [1936] N.I. 97.
[28]   1983 Act, s.2(1).
[29]   1963 Act, s.128(4), (5).
[30]   *British Murac Syndicate Ltd v Alperton Rubber Co.* [1915] 2 Ch. 186.
[31]   1963 Act, s.27.

60 pounds of butterfat supplied.[32] In another instance,[33] under a dairy co-op's regulations any member who did not supply the co-op with the entirety of their milk output could be fined £1 for every cow he owned. It was held that this was an unreasonable restraint of trade and also contravened the rule, which forbids a company by its regulations to "impose upon its members any pecuniary obligation over and above their statutory obligation to pay up the amount of their shares [, and n]o distinction can be made ... between an obligation to provide the company with money and an obligation to provide it with money's worth".[34]

16–11 However, members can agree in writing to increase their pecuniary obligations to the company, and that the terms of any such agreement may be incorporated in the company's regulations.[35] In those circumstances, the company's right to exact additional sums from members arises out of their separate contracts. That contract can take the form of agreeing that the company may change its regulations to exact contributions from the members; the scope of this levying power depends on the construction of that contract.[36]

16–12 In *Hennessy v National Agricultural etc. Assocation*,[37] one feature of a purported merger between two non-profit guarantee companies was that one of them should alter its memorandum of association to exclude some of its members and, in consequence, vary the liability of its guarantors. Overend J. held that this was unlawful. In his words, "[I]f, in a company limited by guarantee, the guarantors are discharged from liability to any appreciable extent, is not the effect upon the creditors of the company precisely the same as the effect of paying back capital to the shareholders ... ? Furthermore, is not the effect on the guarantors who remain to increase their liability?"[38] Other arrangements between non-profit limited companies and their members that at first sight look unexceptional can fall foul of the rule against distributions from capital, as the arrangements for granting long leases to the condominium owners in *Jenkins v Harbour View Courts Ltd*[39] demonstrates. McCarthy J.'s reasoning there was that:

> "[t]he prohibition against a return of capital blocks any return whatever the form, whether it be by a payment of money, by a transfer of assets in specie, or in any other way, unless [sections 72–76 of the 1963 Act] have been observed ... [It] can [not] really be contested that a grant of a leasehold interest in favour of shareholders for no consideration other than the payment of moneys subscribed for shares, or for a consideration so inadequate that it is plain that the substance of the transaction is a return of part of the capital of the company to shareholders, amounts to a prohibited return of capital."[40]

---

[32] *Macdonald v Normandy Co-Op* [1923] N.Z.L.R. 122.
[33] *Shalfoon v Cheddar Valley Co-Op* [1924] N.Z.L.R. 561.
[34] *ibid.* at 577.
[35] 1963 Act, s.27(2).
[36] *Black, White & Grey Cabs Ltd v Reid* [1980] 1 N.Z.L.R. 40.
[37] [1947] I.R. 159.
[38] *ibid.* at 191.
[39] [1966] N.Z.L.R. 1.
[40] *ibid.* at 27 and 28.

UNLIMITED COMPANIES

16–13 An unlimited company is one whose memorandum of association does not stipulate that it is a limited company.[41] At end-2006, there were 3, 145 unlimited companies, comprising 1.8 per cent of the register. In the event of its insolvency, each of its members are liable without limit for its unpaid debts. Even with a limited company, there are several circumstances where one or more of its members—more often, one or more of its directors or members—can be rendered liable for its debts, without any limit on their liability. Partnerships are unlimited companies that are outside the Companies Acts but, where all of the partners are bodies with limited liability (e.g. are limited companies) they are subject to the Companies Acts' auditing and accounts regime. In the past some public companies were incorporated with unlimited liability, principally in the banking sector. But there are no public companies presently registered in the State with unlimited liability. By definition, a Plc is not unlimited.[42]

16–14 Some provisions of the Companies Acts do not apply to unlimited companies. They are exempted from the 1986 Act's requirements regarding accounting principles, the contents and format of annual accounts, and having to annex a copy of their annual balance sheet and profit and loss account to the annual return that must be submitted to the CRO.[43] But this exemption does not apply where all of the company's own members enjoy limited liability, either under the 1963 Act or under the law of any other EC Member State. If the type of company has one or more subsidiaries, it must comply with the Group Accounts Regulations 1992.[44]

16–15 Although they are subject to the basic rules on capital integrity—that allotted shares and any premium on them must be paid for in money or money's worth, that shares shall not be allotted at a discount, that dividends must be paid from available profits, and the prohibition against companies financing the purchase of their own shares—unlimited companies may reduce their capital "in any way" without having to obtain formal court confirmation.[45] They are not subject to the regime in Pt XI (ss.206–234) of the 1990 Act for companies acquiring their own shares or shares in their holding company.[46]

16–16 The European Communities (Companies) Regulations 1973,[47] which, *inter alia*, largely replicate s.8(1) of the 1963 Act on *ultra vires* and *Turquand's* "excusing rule", as well as requiring certain information to be put on a company's letterhead and order forms, and that the delivery of various documents to the CRO to be published in the *Gazette*, do not apply to unlimited

---

[41] 1963 Act, s.6(2).
[42] 1983 Act, s.2(1).
[43] 1986 Act, s.1(1).
[44] SI 1992/201.
[45] 1963 Act, s.72(1).
[46] 1990 Act, ss.206 & 207(1).
[47] SI 1973/163.

companies. Nor do the European Communities (Branch Disclosures) Regulations 1993[48] apply to them. However, foreign unlimited companies with an
"establishment" in the State are required to register with the CRO under Pt XI
(ss.351–360) of the 1963 Act.

FINANCIAL COMPANIES

16–17   By financial companies is meant companies whose principal business
is performing financial services of one kind or another, for instance banks, insurance companies and investment companies. Because the financial services sector is a highly regulated industry, many of the activities of these companies are
subject to special rules which do not apply to companies generally. The main
objective of regulation here is to ensure that these companies do not become
insolvent, which could easily trigger off a series of business collapses and indeed
a slump in the entire economy. To that end the Central Bank is given extensive
authority over many financial companies. An enumeration of these companies
for certain purposes is contained in the 1999 No. 2 Act's 2nd Schedule.

16–18   Several provisions of the Companies Acts do not apply to them. They
are not entitled to avail of the exemption from having their accounts audited.[49]
Their directors are exempt from the 25-companies ceiling on the number of
directorships they may hold.[50] Where their business involves lending money
and the transaction is carried out in the ordinary course of its business, they are
partly exempted from the prohibition against companies financing the purchase of their own shares.[51] Where shares are taken as security, they do not
count for determining whether the company that issued them is a subsidiary of
the lender.[52] Where the company is acting as a professional dealer in securities
and is quoted on a stock exchange, those restrictions against it purchasing or
acquiring shares in its holding company or on financing their purchase do not
apply.[53] To the extent that these requirements involve matters of strict
company law, they include the following.

Banks

16–19   Banks are regulated under the Central Bank Acts 1942–2004.[54] The
Joint Stock Banking Companies Act 1857,[55] facilitated banks becoming registered companies and in 1858 they were permitted to have limited liability.[56]

---

[48]   SI 1993/395.
[49]   1990 Act, s.31(3)(IV).
[50]   1999 (No. 2) Act, s.45(3)(b).
[51]   1963 Act, s.60(12)(d).
[52]   1963 Act, s.155(3)(d).
[53]   2001 Act, s.111.
[54]   See generally, J. Breslin (with K. Smith), *Banking Law*, 2nd edn (Dublin: Thomson
      Round Hall, 2007), Ch.1, W. Johnston *et al, Arthur Cox Banking Law Handbook* (Hay-
      wards Heath: Tottel Publishing, 2007), and W. Blair (ed.), *Banking and Financial Ser-
      vices Regulation*, 3rd edn (Haywards Heath: Tottel Publishing, 2002).
[55]   20 & 21 Vic. c.49.
[56]   21 & 22 Vic. c.91.

Trustee savings banks are established under special legislation.[57] There also is a special legislative framework for credit unions[58] and for building societies.[59] The main banks in the State are registered companies.

16–20   The Bank of Ireland, which is a chartered corporation established in 1782 under an Act of Parliament of that year,[60] has registered under Pt IX of the 1963 Act. On several occasions the bank's charter has been amended by legislation. In 1935 limited liability was extended to it.[61] In 1966 legislation was enacted to facilitate its takeover of the Irish business of the old National Bank.[62] In 1971 general authorisation was given for the bank to alter its objects and to make such changes as it deems fit for the management and conduct of its business.[63] Any such proposed amendment can be challenged in court by the holders of at least 15 per cent of the bank's issued capital. In 1989 its statutory immunity from being taken over[64] was repealed.

16–21   Partnerships or other associations with more than ten members may not carry on a banking business unless they register as a company or are formed under other legislation.[65]

16–22   Before a company the objects of which include banking will even be registered, the Central Bank must have indicated to the Registrar of Companies its willingness to grant that body a banking licence.[66] By virtue of Bank guidelines, applicants must have a very substantial minimum capital before they will be issued with a licence and the Bank has very wide powers to intervene in their affairs should doubts arise about their solvency. The Bank can veto the appointment of an auditor of a licensed bank and bank auditors are obliged to supply the Bank with information regarding their company.

16–23   Acquiring a substantial interest in a bank's shares is subject to Ch. VI (ss.74–88) of the Central Bank Act 1989, and the EC (Licensing and Supervision of Credit Institutions) Regulations 1992.[67] The Central Bank's approval is required where more than 20 per cent of a bank's shares are being acquired, or where the acquisition would entitle the party to appoint or remove a director, or would otherwise entitle it to exercise significant influence over that bank. Refusal of consent by the Bank or conditions it may place on an intending acquirer may be appealed to the High Court. Where if the acquisition went ahead, the party would control more than 20 per cent of the total banking assets

---

[57]   Trustee Savings Banks Acts 1863–2001.
[58]   Credit Union Act 1997.
[59]   Building Societies Acts 1989–2006.
[60]   Bank of Ireland Act [1781–82], 21 & 22 Geo.III c.16.
[61]   Bank of Ireland Act 1935, s.2.
[62]   National Bank Transfer Act 1966.
[63]   Central Bank Act 1971, s.51.
[64]   Central Bank Act 1989, s.4.
[65]   1963 Act, s.372.
[66]   Central Bank Act 1971, s.15.
[67]   SI 1992/395.

in the State, the Minister's consent is required. There are restrictions on banks spending more than 15 per cent of their own funds on acquiring a non-financial business and also on spending more than 60 per cent of their own funds on acquiring a financial business.

16–24   Implementing an agreed takeover of all or part of a banking business is facilitated by Pt III (ss.32–42) of the Central Bank Act 1971. Where the transaction has obtained the Minister's approval and subject to such conditions as he may prescribe, the accounts and securities involved and any related legal proceedings vest in the acquiring party. These transactions are exempt from stamp duty. Approvals for these purposes are published as statutory instruments.[68]

16–25   Several provisions of the 1986 Act on the format and contents of annual accounts do not apply to banks and equivalent institutions. Those bodies excluded from these requirements are licensed banks; certified trustee savings banks; companies engaging solely in the business of hire purchase or credit sale with goods which the company owns; companies engaged in the business of accepting deposits or other repayable funds or granting credit for their own account.[69] But requirements concerning annexing documents to the annual return and information to be included in directors' reports, consistency of those reports with audited accounts and information regarding subsidiary and associate companies, apply to these otherwise exempted companies. Bank accounts must comply with a separate regime on accounts, the European Communities (Credit Institutions: Accounts) Regulations 1992.[70] Banks must file annual returns which include copies of the audited profit and loss account and balance sheet, and the directors' and auditors' reports.[71] In the case of banks which were registered since August 15, 1879, the accounts must be signed by the secretary and by at least three directors.[72] Where a bank or any of its subsidiary companies enters into a loan or other regulated credit transaction or arrangement with one of the bank's directors or a "connected party", information relating to the transaction must be disclosed.[73] The winding up of banks is governed by Ch. IV (ss.48–52) of the Central Bank Act 1989.

Insurers

16–26   Insurance companies—be they insurers or reinsurers—are regulated principally under the Insurance Acts 1909–2000, as well as numerous EC Regulations, and by several regulations implementing EC Directives on that topic.[74] Previously the Minister was the regulatory authority but that function

---

[68]   e.g. Central Bank Act 1971 (Approval of Scheme of National Irish Bank Ltd and Danske Bank A/S) Order 2007 (SI 2007/29).
[69]   1986 Act, s.2(1).
[70]   SI 1992/294, as amended.
[71]   1986 Act, s.7(1)(a)(iii).
[72]   1963 Act, s.156(2).
[73]   1990 Act, ss.44 and 45.
[74]   See generally, A. Buckley *Insurance Law*, 2nd edn (Dublin: Thomson Round Hall, 2006) and Blair and Walker (eds), *Financial Services Law* (Oxford: OUP, 2006), Ch.14.

is now discharged by the Central Bank. A minimum capital is prescribed before a company will be authorised to transact insurance business. The Bank may veto the appointment of any director, chief executive or authorised agent of an insurer if he is not suitably qualified. Insurers' auditors must disclose specific information about the company to the Bank, along the same lines as the disclosure requirement for bank auditors. Several provisions of the 1986 Act regarding companies' accounts do not apply to authorised insurance companies.[75] Instead, their accounts must comply with the European Communities (Insurance Undertakings: Accounts) Regulations 1996.[76] Certain other exceptions are made to the Companies Acts in respect of insurers. For instance, in determining what are realised profits for the purposes of ascertaining whether or how much a dividend may be paid, a special rule exists for assurance companies.[77] Many of the applications for court-approved schemes of arrangements concern reorganisation of liabilities incurred by insurers—very recently, arising from asbestos and other pollution claims.[78] Somewhat unusually, *Re Colonia Insurance (Ireland) Ltd*[79] involved a solvent scheme of arrangement for an insurance company in respect of run-off liabilities for reinsurance of non-life insurance business.

16–27   Provision is made in the Assurance Companies Act 1909, and in the Insurance Act 1989, for amalgamations and transfers of insurance businesses. Before two or more insurers merge or one acquires any class of insurance business from another, they must obtain High Court approval. Where such approval is given, the transfer of assets and liabilities is facilitated. In *Re Irish Life Assurance Plc*,[80] Kearns J. approved a proposed transfer of industrial insurance business by the Irish Life companies to the UK-based Royal Liver Assurance, which also had a substantial insurance business in the State. Objections had been made by Irish Life employees, but it was held that all the prerequisites for a valid transfer had been met and such concerns as those employees had were adequately met by the EC (Safeguarding of Employees Rights on Transfer of Undertakings) Regulations.[81] Administration, examination and liquidation of insurers are also subject to the European Communities (Reorganisation and Winding up of Insurance Undertakings) Regulations 2003.[82]

16–28   Provision is made in the Insurance (No. 2) Act 1983, for the High Court, on the Minister's application, to appoint an administrator to take control of and manage the affairs of non-life insurers which are insolvent or in comparable

---

[75]   1983 Act, s.2(3).
[76]   SI 1996/23, as amended.
[77]   1983 Act, s.48.
[78]   e.g. *Re British Aviation Insurance Co.* [2006] B.C.L.C. 665.
[79]   [2005] 1 I.R. 497.
[80]   [2002] 2 I.R. 9.
[81]   SI 1980/306. See too *Re Allied Dunbar Assurance Plc* [2005] 2 B.C.L.C. 220 and *Re Eagle Star Insurance Co.* [2007] 1 B.C.L.C. 27.
[82]   SI 2003/168.

difficulties. The winding up of insurers is governed by Pt IV (ss.44–47) of the Insurance Act 1936, and ss.30–32 of the Insurance Act 1989.

Investment Companies

16–29   An investment company is a company which simply holds investments in other companies on behalf of its members; the composition of these investments may change from time to time but the company does not engage in any other activities. They are to be contrasted with "investment firms" which are subject to the European Communities (Markets in Financial Instruments) Regulations 2007,[83] which cover a broad category of actors in the financial services sector. Part XIII (ss.252–262) of the 1990 Act treats investment companies, as defined there, differently in some respects from other companies. What the Oireachtas had in mind is an incorporated form of unit trust. To come within this Part, the company must possess two main characteristics. Its sole and exclusive object must be stated as "the collective investment of its funds in properties—meaning real or personal property of any kind, (including securities)—with the aim of spreading investment risk and giving members of the company the benefit of the results of the management of its funds."[84] Additionally, under its own regulations, the actual value of its paid up share capital must be equal to its net assets, and the company must always be authorised to purchase its members' shares on request by them. These provisions do not apply to what are known as "undertakings for collective investment in transferable securities" (UCITS) as provided for in Regulations of 1989,[85] or to what are known as unincorporated common contractual funds, which are within Pt II (ss.6–21) of the 2005 Act. There is a different definition of an investment company for the purposes of the 1983 Act's rules regarding dividends and distributions.[86]

16–30   These Part XIII companies cannot commence business without being so authorised by the Central Bank, which has extensive powers to regulate their affairs, for instance, regarding minimum paid up capital, investment policy and information dissemination. Numerous provisions of the Companies Acts do not apply to them, most notably some regarding allotting shares; the prohibitions against acquiring or financing the purchase of their own shares; the general prohibition against reducing share capital; the general entitlement to inspect the members' register; the requirement to submit annual returns to the Registrar of Companies; the rule regarding pre-emption for shares being issued; several provisions of the 1983 Act regarding maintenance of share capital; provisions of the 1990 Act regarding individual and group acquisitions, and ascertaining beneficial ownership of shares; their directors not holding more than 25 such offices; the obligation to contribute to the debts of a related insolvent company. These companies may opt to have their accounts audited

---

[83] SI 2007/60 and 663.

[84] 1990 Act, s.253(2).

[85] European Communities (Undertakings for Collective Investment in Transferable Securities) Regulations 1989 (SI 1989/78).

[86] Section 47(3) and (4).

in accordance with the generally accepted accounting standards of the US, Canada, Japan or other prescribed non-EC states. Their share capital need not possess a nominal value and the amount of their authorised capital can vary with their issued share capital. They can purchase their own fully paid up shares in accordance with their articles of association, without creating any corresponding reserve fund.

16–31 The definition of an investment company, for the purposes of what dividends and distributions are permissible, is not as restrictive. It is defined as a Plc, the business of which "consists of investing its funds mainly in securities, with the aim of spreading investment risk and giving members of the company the benefit of the results of the management of its funds."[87] Additionally, none of its holdings of securities should exceed 15 per cent of the value of its entire investments, its own regulations must forbid it from distributing any capital profits, most of its investment income must be distributed every year in dividends and it must have notified the Registrar of Companies of its intention to carry on business as an investment company. These companies' accounts must comply with Pt VI of the Schedule to the 1986 Act.

Investment Intermediaries

16–32 Those involved in the business of providing investment services or investment advice to third parties were governed by the Investment Intermediaries Act 1995, until it was repealed by the European Communities (Markets in Financial Instruments) Regulations 2007,[88] often referred to as "MiFi". Known as "investment firms", they are regulated by the Central Bank and are subject to special provisions regarding audits, inspections and takeovers. Those companies are exempted from several provisions of the 1963 Act, most notably regarding returns as to allotments; financing the purchase of own shares; notifying alterations in share capital; the general prohibition against reducing share capital; the general entitlement to inspect the members' register; the requirement to submit annual returns to the Registrar of Companies. Provision is made for their winding up on the petition of the Central Bank.

16–33 The Irish Stock Exchange, any other stock exchange that may be established in the State, and its member firms, are governed by the "MiFi" Regulations and regulated by the Central Bank. These contain special provisions regarding audits, inspections and takeovers, and for winding up on the petition of the Central Bank.

STATE COMPANIES

16–34 By state companies is meant registered companies that are owned either entirely or substantially by the State. Some of these perform a predominantly administrative function, others run an economic enterprise. Many public functions

---

[87] 1983 Act, s.47.
[88] SI 2007/60 and 663.

are performed by statutory corporations, for instance every Government Minister (a corporation sole), local government entities and numerous public bodies and agencies. The rights and obligations of these various entities are governed largely by their individual constitutive statute. For instance, what the Competition Authority is entitled to do or ought to do, or cannot do, is laid down in Pt 4 (ss.29–47) of the Competition Acts 2002–2006. The authority and functions of, for instance, the Electricity Supply Board, Radio Telefis Eireann and the Voluntary Health Insurance Board are laid down in each of those bodies' constitutive Acts. Legislation establishing these and equivalent bodies invariably stipulate that they are "bod[ies] corporate with perpetual succession and a seal and power to sue and be sued in its corporate name and … to acquire, hold and dispose of land or any interest in land and to acquire, hold and dispose of any other property", or words to this general effect.

16–35   Often, however, particular State functions are carried out by registered companies formed for that very purpose. Usually the Act under which the function in question is to be carried out will provide for a company to be registered for that very purpose and will prescribe various features that the company must possess. For instance, under the Irish Takeover Panel Act 1997, the Panel is a public company limited by guarantee and registered under the Companies Acts with the objects specified in that Act, with a memorandum and articles of association consistent with the Act, and the membership of which are several bodies and parties designated in the Act. Several provisions of the 1963 Act are declared not applicable to the Panel, being that it shall have seven or more members,[89] that its memorandum of association must state its objects,[90] that its remaining members shall be subject to unlimited liability if its membership falls below seven[91] and that any or all of its directors can be removed by way of an ordinary resolution.[92] Other State companies, that carry on a predominantly regulatory function, include the Irish Auditing and Accountancy Supervisory Authority, CERT Ltd (the State's national tourism training agency), Housing Finance Agency Plc, National Building Agency Ltd and Shannon Free Airport Development Co. Ltd.

16–36   Originally the Post Office (and also Telecom Éireann, until it was privatised in 1999) was part of a Government Department. Under the Postal and Telecommunications Act 1983, it became vested in a limited company with objects, obligations, functions and structures prescribed by that Act. *Inter alia*, the principal shareholder is to be the Minister for Enterprise; any other member holds his shares in trust for the Minister, and may not alienate them without the Minister's consent; funds for capital works, current expenditure and working capital are to be provided by the Minister for Finance, who may guarantee borrowings; "proper and usual accounts" must be kept, which must be audited annually; a proportion of the directors shall be company employees; special

---

[89]   Section 5(1).
[90]   Section 6(1)(b).
[91]   Section 36.
[92]   Section 182.

provision is made for disclosing a director's interests in a contract and not voting on the proposal, replacing that in the 1963 Act[93]; the company is exempted from having the word "limited" in its name.

16–37 Originally, major harbours in the country were owned and managed by trustees. Under the Harbours Acts, 1996–2000, most harbours became vested in private companies with the objects specified in s.11 of that Act, with a memorandum and articles of association to be approved by the Minister for the Marine, with the consent of the Minister for Finance, and which may not be amended without the consent of both Ministers. One share is to be issued to the Minister for Finance and the remaining shares are to be issued to the Minister for the Marine; the former's shares are not transferable but the latter may transfer one of his shares; however, that transferee must hold them in trust and cannot transfer or otherwise alienate them. There are detailed provisions regarding audits. The chief executive is a director and a proportion of the directors shall be company employees; at the directors' discretion, the harbourmaster may attend and participate at board meetings; again, special provision is made for disclosing a director's interest in a contract and not voting on the proposal, replacing that in the 1963 Act.[94]

16–38 Several of the major state-owned and managed manufacturing, trading and commercial bodies were privatised over the last 15 years and some others, most notably the ESB, have been prepared for privatisation insofar as their legal structures are concerned. Apart from the Post Office and the harbour companies, the principal State companies involved in predominantly commercial activities are Aer Rianta cpt, Coillte Teo and the subsidiaries of Coras Iompair Eireann.

Unregistered Companies

16–39 There are a handful of corporate bodies which carry on some trade or business but which were never registered under the Companies Acts. They instead were established principally by a royal charter or by letters patent. In December 2007 the following bodies were registered in this manner: the Bank of Ireland, the Dublin Corn Exchange Building Company, the Waterford City Gas Company and the Dundalk Gas Company. For these purposes, an unregistered company is as a "body corporate incorporated in and having a principal place of business in the State", other than four categories of corporation.[95] Those excluded are any body corporate incorporated by or registered under a public general statute, for instance many of the state-owned commercial bodies; any body exempted for the time being by the Minister; any non-profit body, in the sense that it was not formed to carry on business with a view to making gain or it is prohibited from distributing its assets among its members in any event. Application of the prescribed provisions to unregistered bodies does not affect their charter or other constituting instrument except insofar as those are not consistent with the legislation thereby applied.

---

[93] Section 194.
[94] Section 194.
[95] 1963 Act, s.377.

16–40 Within three months of being incorporated, every unregistered company must deliver to the Registrar of Companies a copy of its charter or other constituting instrument.[96] If this is a memorandum and articles of association, it must be so delivered within one month of that time and a notice that this was done must be published in the *Gazette*.[97]

16–41 Several provisions of the Companies Acts have been made applicable to these companies; most of these are set out in the schedule to the 1990 Act and almost all of that Act is so applicable. Some provisions have been adopted and made applicable to these companies.[98] Should any of them choose to register under the Companies Acts, the procedure for doing so is laid down in Pt IX (ss.328–343) of the 1963 Act. Part X (ss.344–350) of the 1963 Act empowers the court to wind up unregistered companies.

---

[96] 1963 Act, s.377(3).
[97] European Communities (Companies) Regulations 1973 (SI 1973/163), reg.7.
[98] Companies Act 1963 (Section 377(1)) Order 1999 (SI 1999/64).

CHAPTER 17

ACCOUNTS, DISCLOSURES AND INVESTIGATIONS

17–01   The interests of investors and of others who deal with companies are safeguarded by a variety of record-keeping, accounting and disclosure requirements. These are based on the premise that, if persons have relevant information about a company's affairs, they are sufficiently protected in their dealings with it. Armed with that knowledge, they can decide on what terms, if at all, they should put their funds or other assets into a company, or extend credit to it, or otherwise deal with it. Companies are required to have proper books of account, often audited by professionals, and to disclose annual financial information and other details about their activities to their members. In their annual returns to the Registrar of Companies, companies must disclose up-to-date details about their capital, management and ownership, and many companies must annex to those returns copies of their annual accounts (sometimes abridged) and reports. Generally, the only financial information about private limited companies and unlisted Plcs that is readily available to the public is what is disclosed with their annual returns. Companies with securities listed on the Irish Stock Exchange must make extensive disclosure about their members, management and activities, not alone to their shareholders but also to the Exchange authorities and to the general public. Where concerns arise about the beneficial ownership of a company's securities, several procedures exist to assist in ascertaining who those persons are. These concerns and other aspects of the conduct of a company's affairs can be investigated by way of, *inter alia*, appointing inspectors.

ACCOUNTS

17–02   To have a reasonable understanding of the nature of a company's business and how it is faring, one would need to see its up-to-date accounts: principally, its profit and loss account, balance sheet and cash flow statement.[1] Often decisions to invest in a company will be predicated on having access to

---

[1]   See generally, T. Power *et al*, *Financial Management*, 2nd edn (Dublin: Gill & Macmillan, 2005), Chs 2 and 3, N. Brennan & A Pierce, *Irish Company Accounts* (Dublin: Oak Tree Press, 1996) (hereinafter *"Brennan & Pierce"*), C. Connolly, *International Financial Accounting and Reporting* (Dublin: Institute of Chartered Accountants in Ireland, 2006) (hereinafter *"Connolly"*) and Freedman & Power, "Law and Accounting: Transition and Transformation" 54 *Mod. L. Rev.* 759 (1991).

those accounts. Generally, when a body is asked to extend substantial credit to a company, it will require sight of them. Where a company's securities are being offered for subscription or sale to the investing public, generally the prospectus accompanying the offer must contain extensive details from those accounts.[2] Ever since 1879 in the case of banks[3] and since 1900 in the case of all other companies,[4] their accounts have had to be audited by a person independent of the company; some exceptions to this were made in 1999. Since 1907,[5] annual accounts have had to be filed at the CRO along with the company's annual return; since 1986 most private limited companies have had to file at least abridged accounts.

The Legal Regime

17–03 The 1963 Act's requirements regarding accounts and audits (ss.147–164) have been substantially extended in the last 20 years. The Companies (Amendment) Act 1986, which gave effect to the EC Fourth Directive,[6] deals almost entirely with limited for-profit companies' annual accounts, and with their directors' and auditors' annual reports. Its central purpose is to ensure that the shareholders and, to an extent, the general public get a better picture of those companies' overall financial situation. The EC Seventh Directive concerning group consolidated accounts[7] was implemented by way of statutory instrument.[8] Additional significant changes to the regime were adopted in the European Communities (International Financial Reporting Standards and Miscellaneous Amendments) Regulations 2005,[9] amending the 1963 Act and implementing the EC's IAS Regulation,[10] which made obligatory the International Financial Reporting Standards (IFRS) for group companies with a listing on any stock exchange in the EC. Some of these do not apply to banks and other financial institutions, and insurance companies, for which there are separate prescribed regimes.[11] Under the Transparency (Directive 2004/109/EC) Regulations 2007,[12] which gave effect to the Transparency Directive,[13] listed companies are required to publish annual and half-yearly financial statements, management reports and responsibility statements, as well as being subject to other obligations regarding continuous disclosure.

---

[2] See para.15–71 *et seq.*

[3] Companies Act 1879, 42 & 43 Vic. c.76.

[4] Companies Act 1900, ss.2–23.

[5] Companies Act 1907, s.21. The history is summarised in *Caparo Industries Plc v Dickman* [1990] 2 A.C. 605 at 630–631.

[6] Directive 78/660, [1978] O.J. L222/11. See generally J. Dine, *E.C. Company Law* (Bristol: Jordans – loose leaf) Ch.20 on the 4th, 7th and 11th Directives.

[7] Directive 83/349, [1983] O.J. L493/1.

[8] European Communities (Companies: Group Accounts) Regulations 1992 (SI 1992/201).

[9] SI 2005/116.

[10] Regulation 1606/2002, [2002] O.J. L243/1.

[11] European Communities (Credit Institutions: Accounts) Regulations 1992 (SI 1992/294) and European Communities (Insurance Undertakings: Accounts) Regulations 1996 (SI 1996/23); also the European Communities (Credit Institutions) (Fair Value Accounting) Regulations 2004 (SI 2004/720).

[12] SI 2007/277.

[13] Directive 2004/109, [2004] O.J. L390/38.

17–04 On account of the burdens that full compliance places on small private businesses, a variety of exemptions have been made for them.[14] Small private companies may dispense with having their accounts audited, unless more than one tenth of their voting members object. Requirements regarding the formats and contents of annual accounts, and the notes to them, and group accounts, are lessened for medium-sized private companies/groups and are further reduced for small private companies. Large private companies are encouraged to have audit committees but their directors may decide against having them. The amount of information that small and medium-sized private companies must disclose in their annual returns is significantly less than what is required of large private companies and Plcs. To determine whether a private company is small, medium-sized or large for these purposes, the main criteria are their balance sheet total assets and their profit for the existing and the preceding financial years; for some purposes, the average number of people employed in those years is a factor.

17–05 In addition to the law, in the sense of legislation and regulations, stock exchange requirements and the conventions of the accountancy profession play a significant role in this area. Accounts of companies listed on the Irish Stock Exchange must comply with its Listing Rules.[15] A joint accounting bodies' Accounting Standards Board has been in existence since 1970. It is comprised of representatives from the three Chartered Institutes of Accountants (the Irish, the English and the Scottish Institutes), the Institute of Certified Accountants, the Institute of Cost and Management Accounts and the Institute of Public Finance and Accountancy. This Committee's function is to promulgate conventions (called statements of standard accounting practice, or "SSAPs", and financial reporting standards, or "FRSs"), which cover practically every aspect of assessing value that can arise in the course of an audit.[16] These conventions are known collectively as the generally accepted accounting principles, or the UK/Irish "GAAP".

17–06 Listed companies must comply with international accounting standards/international financial reporting standards, known as the IAS/IFRS.[17] These are issued by the International Accounting Standards Board and require formal adoption by the EC, and are then published in the EC's Official Journal. EC Regulation 1606/2002[18] applies directly to listed companies that prepare group accounts and requires them to follow the IFRS regime. Since 2005, all limited companies are encouraged, albeit not required, to cross over to the IFRS system.[19]

---

[14] See generally, B.Cheffins, *Company Law: Theory, Structure and Operation* (Oxford: Clarendon, 1997), p.508 et seq.
[15] Listing Rule 6.7–9.
[16] See generally, *Brennan & Pierce*, pp.10 and 17 et seq.
[17] See generally, *Connolly* and I.A.S.B., *International Financial Reporting Standards* (London: Lexis Nexis, 2006, annually updated).
[18] See fn.10.
[19] 1963 Act, s.149.

Keeping Accounts

17–07 Companies and their directors must keep proper basic accounts and records, without which audits would be unreliable if not impossible. Every company, large or small, limited or unlimited,

> "shall cause to be kept proper books of account, whether in the form of documents or otherwise, that:
>
> (a) correctly record and explain the transactions of the company,
> (b) will at any time enable the financial position of the company to be determined with reasonable accuracy,
> (c) will enable the directors to ensure that any annual accounts of the company comply with the requirements of the Companies Acts and, where applicable, Article 4 of the IAS Regulations;
> (d) will enable the annual accounts of the company to be readily and properly audited."[20]

These books must be kept in a "timely manner" and on a "continuous and consistent basis", and must give "a true and fair view of the state of affairs of the company ..."[21] Table A requires directors to keep "proper books of account" which shall be available at times for inspection by members.[22] But courts will not readily entertain proceedings brought by individual shareholders alleging breach of these articles.[23] Among the matters for which accounts must be kept are assets and liabilities, day-to-day receipts and expenditures, purchases and sales, services provided (where the company's business involves providing services) and stock held, together with records of stocktaking. Any director who does not take reasonable steps to secure compliance with these requirements commits an offence.[24] A duty to keep books and records is also contained in the Taxes (Consolidation) Act 1997.[25]

17–08 These books must be kept by the company for at least six years after any event to which they relate occurred.[26] They are normally kept at the company's registered office but may be kept somewhere else as the directors deem fit.[27] At all reasonable times, these must be available for inspection by the company's officers and by such other persons as the 1963–2006 Acts entitle to inspect them.[28]

17–09 If the company is wound up and is found to be insolvent, and inadequate bookkeeping either contributed towards its insolvency or otherwise impeded its orderly winding-up, every company officer who did not take

---

[20] 1990 Act, s.202(1).
[21] 1990 Act. s.202(2) and (4).
[22] Articles 125–127.
[23] *Devlin v Slough Estates Ltd* [1983] B.C.L.C. 497.
[24] 1990 Act, s.202(10).
[25] Section 886. *cf. Quigley v Burke* [1995] I.T.R. 265.
[26] 1990 Act, s.202(9).
[27] 1990 Act, s.202(5) and (6).
[28] 1990 Act, s. 202(8).

reasonable steps to ensure compliance with the above requirements can be convicted of a serious offence.[29] Additionally, the court may impose unlimited liability for all or part of the company's debts on any company officer or former officer who was in default in this regard.[30] That was done in *Meighan v Duignan*,[31] where a director of a comparatively small company was made liable for in excess of £90,000 on account of defective bookkeeping. Shanley J. held that the duty imposed here was not merely to be a passive custodian of records but was a positive and continuing obligation to create books and records in a particular form and with specified contents. Defective accounts-keeping is frequently a basis for having directors restricted or even disqualified.

Accounting Date

17–10 Companies are required to prepare yearly profit and loss accounts (or income statements) and balance sheets. A company's financial year is the period for which the profit and loss account is made up, whether or not it is an actual year. A company's first financial year starts once it is incorporated and each subsequent financial year starts at the end of the previous one.[32]

AUDIT

17–11 Most companies must have an auditor or auditors,[33] whose principal task is to examine the company's accounts and make a report on them annually to the shareholders. A professional and independent audit lends credibility to a company's accounts. Because the entire auditing process can be quite demanding of and expensive for small companies, provision was made in 1999 whereby they can be exempted from having their accounts audited in any particular year. Many companies conducting business on a substantial scale have an audit committee to supervise the whole process of monitoring their accounts and records. Since 2003 these committees have been made compulsory for some companies.

17–12 Part X (ss.182–205) of the 1990 Act, which gives effect to the EC Eighth Directive,[34] deals principally with auditors—their qualifications, appointment, functions, removal and responsibilities—as well as introducing an overriding obligation on company officers to keep proper accounts and imposing potential unlimited liability for failure to do so. A revised Eight Directive[35] on statutory audits of annual accounts and consolidated accounts has to be implemented by June 29, 2008. Part 8 (ss.72–79) of the 2001 Act, *inter alia*, makes auditors accountable to the DCE and obliges them to notify the DCE if they encounter inadequate book keeping or evidence suggesting that an indictable offence has been committed. Part 2 (ss.4–33) of the 2003 Act

---

[29] 1990 Act, s.203.
[30] 1990 Act, s.204.
[31] [1997] 1 I.R. 340.
[32] 1963 Act, s.2(1A).
[33] 1963 Act, s.160.
[34] Directive 84/253, [1984] O.J. L126/20.
[35] Directive 2006/43, [2006] O.J. L157/87.

replaced the system of self-regulation of auditors, by introducing the Irish Auditing and Accounting Supervisory Authority (the IAASA) to discharge that function, in much the same way as several other professions are regulated. Part III (ss.34–47) of this Act reinforces the regulatory regime in several important respects, as well as, *inter alia*, authorising the IAASA to monitor the accounts of Plcs and large private companies, requiring fuller disclosure of auditors' remuneration and obliging large companies to have audit committees (and also directors' compliance statements).[36]

Auditors' Status

17–13   For many purposes, a company's auditor is deemed by the Companies Acts to be one of its "officers". It is common to appoint a firm of accountants as the auditors; where this is done, the firm's partners who are qualified to be its auditors are deemed to have been appointed to the office.[37]

Appointment

17–14   Auditors are appointed annually, by a resolution of the AGM.[38] Requiring that they be appointed by the members ensures that they give primary consideration to the shareholders' interests and are not unduly subject to the directors' influence. They cannot be appointed for a duration longer than between one AGM and the next. But they are deemed to be reappointed at each subsequent AGM unless they become ineligible to hold the office or resign, or they are removed from office, or somebody else was duly appointed to the office. A function of the audit committee (where one exists) is to advise the board as to who it should recommend to be appointed as auditors, and to monitor the auditors' independence and the quality of their work.[39] The directors themselves are permitted to appoint the first auditors pending the first AGM being convened. A casual vacancy may be filled either by the directors or by the general meeting. Where the members fail to appoint, the Minister must be promptly notified of the fact and he is empowered to fill the vacancy.[40]

Qualifications

17–15   To ensue that the auditor is independent of the company, is competent to do the job and is honest, the law sets down rigorous qualifications.[41] It is a strict liability offence for an unqualified person to act as a company auditor.[42]

---

[36] Sections 205E and 205F of the 1990 Act (s.45 of the 2003 Act) have not been implemented to date and have been the subject of some criticism: *cf* Ahern, "Directors' Compliance Statements under the Microscope" 13(5) *C.L.P.* 137 (2006).

[37] 1963 Act, s.160(9).

[38] 1963 Act, s.160.

[39] 1990 Act, s.204B(2).

[40] 1963 Act, s.160(4).

[41] 1990 Act, ss.187–192.

[42] *Director of Corporate Enforcement v Gannon* [2002] 4 I.R. 439.

17–16 *Independence:* Auditors are required to be independent of the company and its officers, so that they can give an objective assessment of its accounts. What constitutes complete independence can be hard to define and occasionally difficult to achieve, especially within the comparatively small Irish economy. For instance, it is often contended that auditors' firms should not provide management consultancy services to the company, lest a conflict of interests arises which threatens their independence. The following are disqualified from being appointed as auditors[43]:

i   Any former officer or employee of the company during any part of the period to which the accounts being audited relate.
ii. Any partner of or employee of a present officer of the company.
iii. Any immediate member of the family of any of the company's officers, being a parent, spouse, brother, sister or child.
iv. A person falling within any of the above categories, who would be disqualified from being an auditor of certain connected companies—these are any of the company's subsidiaries, its holding company or another subsidiary of the holding company.
v.   A person in whose name a share in the company is registered, whether or not he is its beneficial owner.

17–17 *Professional Competence:* To be appointed as auditor, the principal competence requirement is practising membership of a recognised professional accounting body or holding professional qualifications which are recognised by the Minister for these purposes.[44] A firm is qualified if at least one of its members holds a valid practising certificate or is otherwise qualified, as described below, and specified particulars have been forwarded to the Registrar of Companies by his accountancy body.[45]

17–18 A person is qualified where "he is a member of a body of accountants for the time being recognised by the Supervisory Authority for th[is] purpose ... and holds a valid practising certificate from [it]".[46] The principal conditions on which IAASA recognition is granted to a body are that its standards for awarding practising certificates, relating to training, qualifications and repute, are up to the level laid down in the EC Eighth Directive; also, there are adequate standards regarding ethics, codes of conduct and practice, independence, professional integrity, technical standards and disciplinary procedures.[47] Any recognised body may be required to draw up a code of professional ethics for its members. Those accountancy bodies recognised in 2007 are the Institutes of Chartered Accountants in Ireland, in England and Wales and in Scotland; also the Association of Chartered and Certified Accountants, the Association of Certified Public Accountants and the Institute of Incorporated Public Accountants.[48] Any

---

[43] 1990 Act, s.187(2).
[44] 1990 Act, s. 187(1).
[45] 1990 Act, s.187(1A)–(1B).
[46] 1990 Act, s.186(1)(a)(i).
[47] 1990 Act, s.191.
[48] *cf.* 2003 Act, s.32.

person who was a member of any of these bodies on December 31, 1990 is also qualified, provided he holds a valid practising certificate. So too is any person who, on February 3, 1983, was authorised by the Minister to be a company auditor and that authorisation has not ceased.[49] A person undergoing training on January 1, 1990 who became a member of a recognised body before 1996 and who later obtained practising certificates from that body is rendered eligible.[50]

17–19   A person is also qualified to be an auditor where "he holds an accountancy qualification that is, in the opinion of the Supervisory Authority, of a standard which is not less than that required for membership [of any recognised professional body] and which would entitle him to be granted a practising certificate by that body if he were a member of it".[51] In other words, he holds qualifications which the IAASA regards as up to the standard required for membership of any of the above recognised accountancy bodies and for obtaining a practising certificate from that body. Those who benefit principally from this provision are persons with accountancy degrees from universities in Ireland or abroad, and those who qualified under some foreign accountancy body.

17–20   Apart entirely from this, the IAASA is empowered to declare that holding specified foreign accountancy or auditing qualifications shall be sufficient to act as a company auditor in this country.[52] This is designed to facilitate, in particular, the mobility of auditors within the EC. Before any foreign qualification is so recognised, the Authority must be satisfied that it is at least up to the standard required by the recognised professional bodies. Certain additional educational qualifications may be insisted on before any particular foreign qualification will be accepted.

17–21   *Honesty:* Requiring auditors to be honest is satisfied principally by reference to the disqualification regime under Pt VII of the 1990 Act. Anyone against whom a disqualification order was made cannot act as a company auditor for such period as the court directs.[53] Further, any such person may not become a partner in a firm of auditors, or give directions or instructions regarding any audit, or work in any capacity in the conduct of an audit.

17–22   *Registration:* The Registrar of Companies keeps a register of everyone who is qualified to be a company auditor.[54] A person's name and address must be registered in it before he can audit a company's books and records, or describe himself or hold himself out as a company auditor. All recognised accountancy bodies must supply the CRO with details of its members who are duly qualified and of any changes in the particulars that it has provided.

---

49   1990 Act, s.187(1)(a)(iv), (14) and (15).
50   1990 Act, s.188.
51   1990 Act, s.187(1)(a)(ii).
52   1990 Act, s.189.
53   1990 Act, s.195.
54   1990 Act, ss.198–200.

Removal

Auditors can be replaced relatively easily, without prejudice to any rights they may have for breach of contract or otherwise.[55] An ordinary resolution of the company is sufficient for this purpose, either removing them from office or not reappointing them at the end of their term.[56] Extended notice[57] must be given of the proposed removal resolution and a copy of it must be sent to them.[58] They may wish to contest any such proposal, either to protect their own reputation or in the wider interests of the company. To that end, they are entitled to submit written representations to the company concerning the situation and to have copies of those forwarded to the members for consideration. Auditors facing a resolution for their removal are entitled to speak in their defence at the meeting which is considering the proposal as such. Where auditors have been removed, the Registrar of Companies must be notified.[59]

17–24 Auditors who are removed from office are entitled to attend and be heard at the meeting which considers filling the vacancy and at the next AGM when their office would have expired unless it was renewed.[60] Giving auditors, threatened with removal, what in effect is a right of reply might protect them and, through them, the company from efforts to get rid of them because they were doing their job perhaps too well. Auditors are thereby encouraged to rebut pretexts to have them replaced and to disclose to the shareholders matters that arouse their concern. It is possible that, where auditors were improperly removed in suspicious circumstances but they chose not to avail of this right, they might later be held liable in negligence to the shareholders for not disclosing significant information they obtained during their audit, which would have prompted an investigation into the company's affairs. In any event, there are specific obligations to make appropriate disclosures at this juncture.

Resignation

17–25 Where auditors were not happy with the state of affairs in a company, often in the past they would simply resign without indicating their reason for doing so. Where auditors either intend to resign or do not wish to be re-appointed, they must first notify the company and state whether there are circumstances connected with their decision which should be drawn to the notice of the members of the company or its creditors.[61] If circumstances of that nature exist, those must be disclosed in the notice of resignation, and copies of it must be forwarded by the auditors to all the members and debenture-holders. But if the notice contains "needless publicity or defamatory matter", application may be made to the court to prevent it being

---

[55] See *Smith's Precedents*, Pt 36.
[56] 1963 Act, s.160(5).
[57] 1963 Act, s.142.
[58] 1963 Act, s.161.
[59] Form H3.
[60] 1963 Act, s.161(2A).
[61] 1990 Act, s.185.

sent to them.[62] A copy of every notice of resignation should be sent by the auditors to the Registrar of Companies, within 14 days.

17–26   Where the notice refers to circumstances which would concern the members or the creditors, the auditors may require that an EGM be convened to consider the matter. Exercise of this power may be restrained where it is being abused to obtain needless publicity for defamatory matter. That meeting must then be convened by the directors and, if so requested by the auditors, the directors must circulate any further statement made by the auditors concerning the circumstances of their resignation. An auditor who has resigned has the same right as a dismissed auditor to attend and speak at the next AGM or at the meeting at which his vacancy is proposed to be filled.

Remuneration

17–27   How much the auditors should be paid for their services is controlled by the shareholders. Auditors' remuneration, including expenses, must be fixed either by the AGM or in such manner as that meeting determined.[63] Where the directors filled a temporary vacancy or the appointment was made by the Minister, the appointers also determine the remuneration and expenses to be paid. In appropriate circumstances, the auditor may have a lien on the company's books in his possession in respect of the audit fee.[64] Without prejudice to any such lien, however, all books and other papers relating to the company can be demanded by an examiner appointed to the company or by its liquidator, and must be delivered up to that person.[65]

17–28   How much was paid to the auditors and to any affiliate firm of theirs must be disclosed in the notes to the annual accounts, with a break-down for audit work, audit-related work and non-audit work, provided the aggregate for all work in each category exceeds €1,000.[66] A function of the audit committee (where one exists) is to recommend whether or not the company should engage the auditors or an affiliate of theirs to do non-audit work. Where what is being paid for non-audit work exceeds that for audit and audit-related work, that must be addressed in the audit committee's yearly report, who must be satisfied that the non-audit work is being carried on by the auditors and that doing that work has not affected their independence.

Auditors' Powers

17–29   To carry out their task, auditors are given extensive powers to obtain books and records, and to demand information. They "have a right of access at all reasonable times to the books, accounts and vouchers of the company and

---

[62]   *cf. Jarvis Plc v Pricewaterhouse Coopers* [2000] 2 B.C.L.C. 368 and *P & P Design Plc v Pricewaterhouse Coopers* [2002] 2 B.C.L.C. 648.

[63]   1963 Act, s.160(8).

[64]   *cf. Kelly v Scales* [1994] 1 I.R. 42.

[65]   1963 Act, s.244(a).

[66]   1990 Act, s.205D.

shall be entitled to require from the officers [and employees] of the company such information and explanations that are within their knowledge or can be procured by them as he thinks necessary for the performance of the duties of the auditors".[67] The extent to which this power can be enforced by civil proceedings is not stated. But failure to provide, within two days of the request, any information or explanation being sought is an offence, except where it was not reasonably possible to comply.[68] Giving false or misleading information to the auditors is an offence where that is done knowingly or recklessly, and it is information to which they are entitled.[69]

17–30 Additionally, auditors are entitled to attend any general meeting of the company, to speak and be heard at the meeting on any matter which concerns their function as auditors.[70] All notices and other communications regarding general meetings must be sent to them. Where the company is a holding company with one or more subsidiaries in the State, the subsidiaries and their auditors are obliged to give the holding company's auditors such information and explanations as they need to carry out their audit.[71] Where the subsidiary is incorporated abroad and information concerning it is required by the holding company's auditors, that company is required to take such steps as are reasonably necessary to obtain that information.

Auditors' Duties

17–31 Being appointed by the company, the auditors' primary duty is to it, and is to make their report to the shareholders, as described below.[72] In auditing the books and records, they are "under a general duty to carry out such audit with professional integrity".[73] The very extent and nature of the audit may be stipulated in the "letter of engagement" entered into between them and the company. When making their report to the shareholders, they must consider whether the information contained in the directors' annual report is consistent with the information in the company's accounts for that year.[74] Auditors of listed companies must approve any preliminary statement of annual results and dividends.[75]

17–32 Where proper books of account are not kept, the auditors must notify the company promptly of that fact.[76] They also must notify the Registrar of Companies to that effect[77] unless, within seven days, the matter has been rectified. If the directors fail to take appropriate steps and the company is later wound up and found to be insolvent, the consequences can be very serious for

---

[67] 1990 Act, s.193(3).
[68] 1990 Act, s.197(3).
[69] 1990 Act, s.197(1).
[70] 1990 Act, s.193(5).
[71] 1990 Act, s.196.
[72] 1990 Act, s.193.
[73] 1990 Act, s.193(6).
[74] 1986 Act, s.15.
[75] Listing Rule 6.7.2(1).
[76] 1990 Act, s.194.
[77] Form 114.

them. If the inadequate bookkeeping contributed to the insolvency or caused substantial uncertainty about the company's worth, or substantially impeded the orderly liquidation, the auditors can suffer severe penal sanctions and even be made liable without limit for all or part of the company's liabilities if they are "officers" for this purpose.[78]

17–33 If, in their capacity as auditors, they find reasonable grounds for believing that either that company or one of its officers or agents have committed an indictable offence under the Companies Acts, they must forthwith notify the DCE and supply him with relevant details, allow him access to books and documents, and facilitate him in copying them.[79] In cases where a directors' compliance statement is required[80] but they have not caused one to be prepared or to be included in their annual report, or it does not contain the required statements, the auditors must report the relevant omission to the DCE.[81]

Auditors' Liability

17–34 The question of auditors' liability for inaccuracies in accounts they have audited is an aspect of the much broader issue of professionals' legal responsibility for exclusively financial loss.[82] If auditors negligently certify that the accounts presented to the shareholders give a true and fair view of the company's affairs, the company is entitled to be compensated for any ensuing loss to it. In what circumstances auditors have a duty of care to persons other than the company is a vexed question.

A Duty to Whom?

17–35 Whether a duty owed by the auditors to individual shareholders, to individual creditors, or to persons who acquired the company or a majority of the shares in it, has been the subject of extensive litigation.[83] The position may be summarised as follows. There is a contractual duty of care to the company and also a statutory duty to its shareholders as a *body* but not to any individual member or members, no matter how large their stake in the company may be. However, in those somewhat exceptional instances where there is sufficient "proximity" between the auditors and the plaintiff, and no special considerations of public policy arise warranting exoneration, there is a duty of care. Most of the cases on point turn on their own particular facts and, in those instances where in principle a duty of care exists, liability may still be avoided on account of some contractual stipulation or other representation that was made. In determining who is owed a duty of care, the overall approach remains

---

[78] 1990 Act, ss.203 and 204.

[79] 1990 Act, s.194(3A) and (3B).

[80] This is not yet in force.

[81] 1990 Act, s.205F(3), not yet (and perhaps never) in force.

[82] See generally, Jackson & Powell, *Professional Negligence*, 5th edn (London: Sweet & Maxwell, 2002), Ch.15.

[83] The only modern reported Irish case is *Kelly v Haughey Boland & Co.* [1989] I.L.R.M. 373. See generally, B. McMahon & W. Binchy, *Law of Torts*, 2nd edn (Dublin: Butterworths, 2000) on professional negligence (Ch.14).

that laid down in *Caparo Industries Plc v Dickman*,[84] where relying on audited accounts, the plaintiff purchased a substantial stake in a quoted company and followed this up by making a successful takeover bid for it. The plaintiff then contended that the company's stock had been substantially overvalued in the annual accounts, and sued the auditors for negligently certifying the value of the stock. According to the Law Lords, the question was whether, in the circumstances, it was "fair and reasonable" to impose non-contractual liability on the auditors, concluding that it was not. Their statutory duty was not owed to any individual shareholder, nor was there a sufficiently close relationship between the plaintiff and the auditors to conclude that they had assumed responsibility to the plaintiff for any auditing errors. The test is whether, in all the circumstances, the auditors could be regarded as having assumed responsibility to the particular plaintiff.[85]

17–36 There was held to be such a duty owed by the auditors of the wholly-owned Singapore subsidiary of the failed Barings Bank to its English holding company, where the auditors were acting on the latter's instructions.[86] Ordinarily, there is no duty of care to potential purchasers of shares in the company.[87] But circumstances can exist where such a duty will arise, notably to a bidder for control who the auditors *know* will rely on the accounts for that purpose.[88] Ordinarily, there is no duty of care owed to those who lend to the company.[89] But such a duty has been held to exist in favour of trustees for depositors of an investment company,[90] although not in favour of trustees for investors in a company,[91] but arguably in favour of the trustees of a regulatory agency's insolvency fund.[92]

17–37 The only comparatively modern reported Irish case to discuss the question of principle to any extent is *Kelly v Haughey, Boland & Co.*[93] where the plaintiffs acquired a small private crystal manufacturing company from the widow of its recently deceased owner. They alleged that the company's accounts had been negligently audited, in particular, that the figure disclosed for stock in trade was wrong. Assuming they were correct, the question remained whether the auditors owed them a duty of care. Lardner J., citing Woolf J., said that the answer depends on:

---

[84] [1990] 2 A.C. 605.

[85] See generally, Hemaj, "Taking Stock of Caparo", 27 *Co. Law* 82 (2006).

[86] *Barings Plc v Coopers & Lybrand* [1997] 1 B.C.L.C. 427.

[87] *James McNaughton Paper Group Ltd v Hicks Anderson & Co.* [1991] 2 Q.B. 113.

[88] *Morgan Crucible Co. v Hill Samuel & Co.* [1991] Ch. 295 and *Killick v PricewaterhouseCooper* [2001] 1 B.C.L.C. 65.

[89] *Al Saudi Banque v Clarke Pixley* [1900] 1 Ch. 313. *Cf. Electra Private Equity Partners v KPMG* [2001] 1 B.C.L.C. 589.

[90] *Deloitte Heskin & Sells v National Mutual Life Nominees Ltd* [1993] B.C.L.C. 1174.

[91] *Anthony v Wright* [1995] 1 B.C.L.C. 238.

[92] *Andrew v Kounnis Freeman* [1999] 2 B.C.L.C. 641.

[93] [1989] I.L.R.M. 373. See also *Golden Vale Coop Creameries Ltd v Arthur Anderson & Co*, High Court, O'Hanlon J., unreported, March 16, 1987 and *John Sisk and Son Ltd v Flynn*, High Court, Finlay P., unreported, July 18, 1984.

"whether the defendants knew or should have reasonably foreseen at the time the accounts were audited that a person might rely on those accounts for the purpose of deciding whether or not to take over the company and therefore could suffer loss if the accounts were inaccurate. Such an approach does place a limitation on those entitled to contend that there has been a breach of duty owed to them. First of all, they must have relied on the accounts and, secondly, they must have done so in circumstances where the auditors either knew that they would or ought to have known that they might. If the situation is one where it would not be reasonable for the accounts to be relied on, then, in the absence of express knowledge, the auditor would be under no duty. This places a limit on the circumstances in which and the period for which they can be relied on. The longer the period which elapses prior to the accounts being relied on, from the date on which the auditor gave his certificate, the more difficult it will be to establish that the auditor ought to have foreseen that his certificate would, in those circumstances, be relied on."[94]

The Standard of Care

17–38   Auditors are judged by the same general standards governing professional negligence as the law applies to medical practitioners, solicitors, architects, surveyors and the like. Many of the leading decisions in this area were given before the accountancy and auditing professions had even begun to aspire to their present level of expertise and sophistication, and perhaps should be treated in the light of this. It has been held that "the quality of the auditor's duty has [not] changed in any relevant respect since 1896. Basically that duty has always been to [act] with reasonable care and skill. [Nevertheless] the standards of reasonable care and skill are, upon expert evidence, more exacting today than those which prevailed [then]".[95] Auditing guidelines published by the professional bodies assist in determining the scope of the duty in a variety of circumstances. Auditors must pursue their activities in a manner one would reasonably expect of them. It remains to be established whether, for example, compliance with the auditing standards set down by the professional bodies is in itself sufficient performance of the legal duty, or whether any breach of those standards is tantamount to violating that duty.

17–39   Machinery for investigating allegations of bad auditing has been established by the several accountancy bodies. Information provided or answers given by a member at a disciplinary hearing may be used as evidence in any civil proceedings. A question that, therefore, arises is whether censure or criticism of an auditor by a disciplinary body is sufficient to establish that he has been negligent in the legal sense. While one reads occasionally in the newspapers of some of the largest accounting firms reaching seven-figure settlements of claims made against them, suits on this scale rarely go to trial.

17–40   A much-cited summary of the standard of care is that:

"It is the duty of an auditor to bring to bear on the work he has to perform that skill, care, and caution which a reasonably competent, careful and

---

[94]   [1989] I.L.R.M. 373 at 383.
[95]   *Re Thomas Gerrard & Son Ltd* [1968] Ch. 455 at 475.

cautious auditor would use. What is reasonable skill, care and caution must depend on the particular circumstances of each case. An auditor is not bound to be a detective, or, as was said, to approach his work with suspicion or with a foregone conclusion that there is something wrong. He is a watchdog, but not a bloodhound. He is justified in believing tried servants of the company in whom confidence is placed by the company. He is entitled to assume that they are honest, and to rely upon their representations, provided he takes reasonable care. If there is anything calculated to excite suspicion he should probe it to the bottom; but in the absence of anything of that kind he is only bound to be reasonably cautious and careful."[96]

With regard to the standard of care to be observed when conducting an audit, Lardner J. in the *Haughey Boland* case[97] was guided by expert evidence of the current practice in the profession and by the SSAPs which are promulgated by the accounting bodies. In *Lloyd Cheeham Ltd v Littlejohn & Co.*[98] Woolf J. observed that SSAPs are not rigid rules but they are strong evidence of what is the proper standard to be adopted and, unless there is some justification for doing so, a departure from them will be regarded as a breach of duty. The relevant SSAP in the *Haughey Boland* case was the one concerning stocktaking and in the *Littlejohn* case that concerning depreciation.

17–41 The auditors' function is not that of management consultants; they cannot be held responsible for not attempting to ensure that the company is properly managed. But they must take due care to ensure that the books and accounts are properly kept, and present a true and fair view. To this end, auditors may rely on representations made by company employees. For instance, they do not have to physically check all the stocks or to value independently all the major fixed assets. Pronouncements in many of the older cases about particular practices may very well no longer reflect today's accepted standards in the auditing profession.

17–42 If auditors discover material that arouses their suspicion or that in the circumstances should demand inquiry, they must investigate it further. In *Re Thomas Gerrard & Son Ltd*,[99] the managing director had for some time been secretly falsifying the accounts and defrauding the company by, *inter alia*, constantly attributing the prices of stock bought in one accounting period to the following period. The auditor came across some altered purchase invoices but did not follow up the matter. It was held that he was liable in negligence because, in those circumstances:

"he should have examined the suppliers' statements and where necessary have communicated with the suppliers. Having ascertained the precise facts so far as it was possible for him to do so, he should then have informed the board. It may be that the board would then have taken some action. But whatever the board did he should in each subsequent audit have made such

---

[96] *Re Kingston Cotton Mills Co. (No.2)* [1896] 2 Ch. 279 at 288–289.
[97] [1989] I.L.R.M. 373.
[98] [1989] B.C.L.C. 303.
[99] [1968] Ch. 455.

checks and such inquiries as would have insured that any mis-attribution in the cut-off procedure was detected. He did not take any of these steps ... [The court concluded] that he failed in his duty. It is important in this connection to remember that this is not a case of some isolated failure in detection. The fraud was repeated half-yearly on a large scale for many years."[100]

Where auditors discovered frauds by senior management, who controlled the company, in one instance it was contended that no particularly useful purpose would be served in reporting the matter to them and the question was left open whether they ought to have approached a regulatory agency or the police.[101] If the directors are involved in or condoning the fraud, it had been held that the auditors are obliged to report the matter to relevant third parties.[102] They now have a statutory duty to report suspected wrongdoing to the DCE.[103]

17–43 In a case decided at the turn of the twentieth century, *Irish Woollen Co. v Tyson*,[104] it was held that even minor irregularities in the books can be enough to call for thorough investigation. It was sought to hold the auditor responsible for approving accounts that had been falsified, thereby causing the company to pay dividends from capital. Three breaches of duty were alleged, namely, 1) that he failed to discover that the stock had been overvalued; 2) that he failed to discover that the book debts had been overvalued; 3) that he failed to discover that the trade liabilities had been understated. Holmes L.J. found in favour of the auditor in respect of 1) and 2). With respect to 3), he said that he did "not understand how the carrying over of the invoices (thus understating the trade liabilities) could have escaped detection by the auditor, who should have used due care and skill and who was not a mere machine. The invoices carried over were ultimately posted to the ledger. If they were posted to their true dates it would have been at once apparent that they were not entered in at the proper time. If they were posted under false dates, why was this not detected when the ledger accounts were checked with the invoices?"

Exemption from Audit

17–44 Small private limited companies may dispense with having their accounts audited, provided their directors so decide and not more than one tenth of their members with voting rights object.[105] This exemption may be availed of in respect of any financial year when the following conditions obtain, *viz*.:

• the company is subject to the 1986 Act;

• in both the previous and current financial years, its annual turnover was less than €7.3 million;

---

[100] *ibid.* at 476.
[101] *Sasea Finance Ltd v KPMG* [2000] 1 B.C.L.C. 236.
[102] *ibid.*
[103] 1990 Act, s.194. *Cf.* ODCE Decision Notice D/2006/2, "Auditor Reporting to the ODCE".
[104] 26 *Accountant L.R.* 13 (1900).
[105] 1999 No. 2 Act, Pt III (ss.32–39).

- its balance sheet assets were less then €3.65 million;

- it had less than 50 employees on average;

- its annual return was filed on time and the accounts and reports annexed to the return meet the statutory requirements;

- more than 10 per cent of the voting members have *not* served a notice, as described below.

The directors must record in their minutes that they are satisfied that the company falls below these thresholds in the current financial year.

17–45 This exemption cannot be availed of by parent or subsidiary companies subject to the EC's group accounts regulations, by licensed banks or bodies exempted from holding a banking license, by insurers or by any company in the financial services sector that is in a category set out in the 1999 (No. 2) Act's 2nd schedule. Where one or more members with at least 10 per cent of the total voting rights so request, by notice given during the immediately preceding financial year or during that year, the company may not avail of the exemption in that year.[106] For these purposes, total voting rights means the right either to cast or to control the casting of votes at general meetings, other than a right exercisable only in special circumstances.

17–46 Where in any financial year the company avails itself of this exemption, the balance sheet for that year must record that "the exemption provided for by Part II of the Companies (Amendment) (No. 2) Act, 1999" is being availed of because the company meets the above requirements, that no request has been made by more than 10 per cent of the shareholders with votes not to avail of it, and that the directors acknowledge the company's obligation to keep proper accounts that give the requisite "true and fair view" of its affairs, and of its profit or loss for the year, and to otherwise comply with the requirements regarding accounts. For so long as a company avails of this exemption, provisions empowering the auditors to require anything to be done, or requiring anything to be done on the basis of an auditors' report, do not apply.[107]

Audit Committee

17–47 All Plcs, other than wholly-owned subsidiaries of other Plcs, are required to have a committee of their directors to oversee the accounting and auditing function in a variety of ways.[108] The directors of what are known as "large" private limited companies are obliged to decide whether they should have an audit committee. To come within this category, in both the most recent and the preceding financial years, balance sheet total of assets must exceed €25 million and annual turnover must exceed €50 million; or the company and all its subsidiaries must have met these criteria in those years. This category also includes unlimited companies (and partnerships) where all

---

[106] 1999 No. 2 Act, s.32B.
[107] 1999 No. 2 Act, 1st schedule.
[108] 1990 Act, s.205B.

their members have limited liability or, if one or more of those members have unlimited liability, all of its own members have limited liability.[109] If the directors of these companies decide against establishing an audit committee, in their annual report they must state their reason for so deciding. Those ceilings may be altered by regulation[110] and regulations may exempt companies from the obligation here.[111]

17–48   Audit committees must comprise at least two board members, none of whom is the current board chair or, in the preceding three years, was employed by the company or any of its subsidiaries. If only one of the directors meets these requirements, he may be appointed as the committee, provided that any further conditions laid out in regulations are met and the fact is stated in the directors' annual report, along with the reasons. Audit committees must have written terms of reference that are approved by the board and reviewed by them each year, and submitted to the shareholders at the AGM. These terms must specify, *inter alia*, how the committee will discharge its responsibilities, and must provide for separate and joint meetings between it and the management, internal auditor and auditors.

17–49   Audit committees exercise an extensive supervisory function over the company's financial affairs, involving, *inter alia*, determining whether it is keeping the requisite basic accounts; reviewing the annual accounts and any group accounts before they are presented for the directors' approval; determining whether they present the requisite "true and fair" view of the company's affairs and of its profit or loss; recommending whether the board should approve the accounts; advising on the auditors' appointment, and monitoring their work and independence; recommending whether non-audit work should be given to the auditors or to any of their affiliates; being satisfied that there are adequate arrangements and resources to discharge the internal audit function reviewing any directors' compliance statement (when in force). Part of the directors' annual report must deal with how the committee monitored the auditors' work and independence. In 2006 the DCE published detailed guidelines as to how these committees should conduct their activities.[112]

ANNUAL ACCOUNTS AND REPORTS

17–50   Every year, a company must have prepared accounts which, along with prescribed reports, must be circulated among its members and debenture-holders. An annual return, containing all or part of these accounts must be filed with the Registrar of Companies by most companies.

---

[109] European Communities (Accounts) Regulations 1993 (SI 1993/396).

[110] 2003 Act, s.48(1)(i).

[111] 2003 Act, s.48.

[112] "ODCE Guidance on Audit Committees", Decision Notice D/2006/1.

Duty to Present Accounts

17–51 Once in every calendar year, the directors of every company not in a group are required to draw up and present to the AGM an individual profit and loss account (or income statement) and an individual balance sheet.[113] Where there is a group enterprise, group accounts must be drawn up and presented by the parent company to the AGM once a year in most cases.[114] Notwithstanding their importance in showing the financial position of a business,[115] there is no legal obligation to furnish cash flow statements. Any director who fails to take all reasonable steps to ensure compliance with these requirements commits a summary offence; it is a defence if he reasonably relied on another person to do so.[116]

17–52 A company's very first set of accounts must be presented not later than 18 months from when it was incorporated.[117] After that, the accounts must be presented to the AGM within nine months of the date the balance sheet was made up to, with a limited exception for group profit and loss accounts.[118] Before a company's annual accounts or group accounts are presented to the directors for approval, the audit committee (if one exists) must review them, determine whether they comply with the prescribed accounting standards and present a "true and fair" view of the company's financial position, and recommend whether or not they should be approved by the board.[119] After the board has approved them, two directors must sign the profit and loss account and the balance sheet on behalf of all of the directors.[120] At least 21 days before the AGM, copies of the following documents must be sent to the company's members and debenture-holders, and to anyone else entitled to receive them: the balance sheet, the profit and loss account (or income statement), group accounts insofar as they are not incorporated into these two accounts, the auditors' report on those accounts and the directors' annual report.[121] Every member of the company and debenture-holder is entitled, on demand, to be furnished with copies of these.

17–53 Listed companies must approve and publish their annual report and accounts, and responsibility statement, within four months of their financial year ending.[122] They also must publish half-yearly accounts, report and statement,[123] and must publish a preliminary statement of their annual results within 120 days of the relevant period ending.[124]

---

[113] 1963 Act, ss.148–149A.
[114] 1963 Act, ss.150–155.
[115] See generally, *Connolly*, Ch.21 and T. Power *et al*, *Financial Management*, 2nd edn (Dublin: Gill & Macmillan, 2005), p.22 *et seq.* and Ch.13.
[116] 1963 Act, s.148(11).
[117] 1963 Act, s.148(1).
[118] 1963 Act, s.148(7)–(9).
[119] 1990 Act, s.205B(2).
[120] 1963 Act, ss.156 and 157.
[121] 1963 Act, s.159.
[122] Transparency (Directive 2004/109/EC) Regulations 2007 (SI 2007/277), reg.4.
[123] *ibid.* reg.6.
[124] Listing Rules 6.9 and 7.

Accounting Principles and Rules

17–54   For companies within the 1986 Act, there are two alternative regimes governing their annual accounts. One is that contained in that Act and, where applicable, the 1992 Group Accounts Regulations. The other is the IFRS regime, which is compulsory for accounts of companies with securities listed on a stock exchange in the EC.[125] Most non-listed companies have the option of complying with IFRS requirements.[126] The legislation therefore distinguishes between Companies Acts accounts and IFRS accounts (either individual or group accounts). Once a company adopts the IFRS approach, it cannot readily revert to Acts accounts.[127] Unlimited companies' and non-profit companies' accounts must comply with the 6th Schedule to the 1963 Act.

Over-Arching Principles

17–55   Certain elementary and widely accepted "accounting principles" are stated in the 1986 Act,[128] which are complemented by "historical cost rules" and "alternative cost rules" set out in that Act's schedule. The "company is presumed to be carrying on business as a going concern." Accordingly, assets will be valued on a going-concern basis rather than on the assumption that the business has ended and they are being disposed of piecemeal. However, circumstances can arise which warrant dealing with the company's affairs other than as a going concern. Consistency from one year to the next is required in accounting policies. Prudence is required in determining the amount or value of any item; over-optimism is not allowed. In particular, only profits which were realised, i.e. in fact earned, at the balance-sheet date can be included in the profit and loss account. Where there is a distinct likelihood of a liability or loss having arisen in the year in question or in the previous year, full account should be taken of that matter. This also applies to liabilities and losses which only became apparent after the accounts were made up and before they were signed by the directors. Once an item of income or expense relates to the financial year, it should be dealt with in that year's accounts regardless of the actual date of receipt or payment. Departure from any of these principles must be stated in a note to the accounts.[129]

Historic v Current Costs

17–56   A controversy in accounting is the basis on which items should be costed; in particular, should items be included in accounts on a historic cost basis. The main argument against this is that, given the nature of inflation over the past 40 years or so, that approach exaggerates the amount of profits earned. In *Carroll Industries Plc v O'Culachain*,[130] where the company returned profits

---

[125] 1963 Act, s.150(2).

[126] 1963 Act, ss.148(2) and 150(3).

[127] 1963 Act, s.148(4)–(6) and 150(5)–(7).

[128] 1986 Act, s.5 and see M. Feeney, *The Taxation of Companies 2006* (Haywards Heath: Tottel Publishing, 2006), Ch. 3.3 on accounting principles with reference to taxation.

[129] 1986 Act, s.6.

[130] [1988] I.R. 705.

ascertained on a current cost basis, the Revenue sought to tax them computed in accordance with historic cost. Dealing with the general debate, Carroll J. concluded that no single approach was obligatory for all companies. The very nature of a company's business would determine which approach was the most appropriate for it. But for the purpose of computing income tax, the legislation presupposed use of historic cost. For the purpose of companies' accounts generally, the 1986 Act does not take sides in this debate. Instead, companies can choose which method is most appropriate for them. If they opt for historic cost, Pt II of that Act's schedule lays down several rules to be followed in making the computation. If instead they follow current cost, appropriate computation rules are set out in Pt III of that schedule.

True and Fair View

17–57 As well as stating the above broad guidelines, 1986 Act sets out formats which balance sheets and profit and loss accounts should take. The objective of these is to ensure that the accounts provide an accurate representation of the company's position. However, in several places the Act emphasises that these are subject to the overriding requirement that the accounts shall give a "true and fair view"[131] and, where it is necessary to do so for that purpose, the accounts should depart from the statutory formats and guidelines. Regarding formats:

> "every ... balance sheet of a company shall give a true and fair view of the state of affairs of the company as at the end of its financial year and every ... profit and loss account of a company shall give a true and fair view of the profit and loss of the company for the financial year. [This obligation] overrides [most] requirements of ... the Companies Acts ... as to the matters to be included in the accounts of a company or in notes to those accounts; and accordingly where a balance sheet or profit and loss account of a company drawn up in accordance with [the format] requirements would not provide sufficient information to [give a true and fair view], any necessary additional information shall be provided in that balance sheet or profit and loss account or in a note to the accounts".[132]

Similarly with the general "accounting principles",

> "if it appears to the directors ... that there are special reasons for departing from any of the[se] principles ... they may so depart, but particulars of the departure, the reasons for it and the effect on the balance sheet and profit and loss account of the company shall be stated in a note to the accounts ...".[133]

17–58 What exactly is meant by a "true and fair view" is not defined anywhere in the legislation, nor has it been the subject of judicial elaboration. It means that the accounts in question properly reflect the actual financial situation of the company. There are numerous accounting rules and conventions which, if rigidly applied in certain circumstances, would produce a somewhat distorted picture of the company's position. The overriding "true and fair"

---

[131] 1963 Act, ss.149(2), 150A(2) and 152(1).

[132] 1986 Act, s.3(1) and (4).

[133] 1986 Act. s.6.

requirement demands that those standards should not be used in that particular case. In 1983 the British Accounting Standards Committee obtained counsels' opinion on the meaning of the concept and its relationship with the many SSAPs promulgated by that body. Among the observations made there are that true and fair:

> "is an abstract or philosophical concept expressed in simple English …
> representing a very high level of abstraction which has to be applied to
> an infinite variety of concrete facts … Accounts will not be true and fair
> unless the information they contain is sufficient in quantity and quality
> to satisfy the reasonable expectations of the readers to whom they are
> addressed. On this question, accountants can express an informed profes-
> sional opinion on what, in current circumstances, it is thought that
> accounts should reasonably contain. But they can do more than that. The
> readership of accounts will consist of businessmen, investors, bankers
> and so forth, as well as professional accountants. But the expectations of
> the readers will have been moulded by the practices of accountants
> because by and large they will expect to get what they ordinarily get and
> that in turn will depend upon the normal practices of accountants."[134]

Contents and Formats of Accounts

17–59   For most limited companies, the layout and contents of their individual annual accounts must meet the requirements of the 1986 Act or the IFRS Regulations. Where a company has adopted the IFRS approach, it cannot ordinarily revert to the Act's method.[135] Small and medium-sized companies within the 1986 Act are subject to a less exacting regime. Certain additional information must be furnished by listed companies. Unless exempted by ministerial regulations, every company's annual accounts and any group accounts must state that they were prepared in accordance with recognised accounting standards.[136] Any material departure from those must be noted and explained. Notes to the accounts must disclose the accounting policies adopted with reference to, *inter alia*, depreciation and diminution in the value of the company's assets.[137]

Exemptions

17–60   Small- and medium-sized private limited companies enjoy partial exemptions, in that they need not comply with certain of the formats and may exclude certain details from their individual accounts.[138] Additionally, they may annex abridged accounts with their annual returns.[139] A company falls into either of these categories if, in the financial year in question and the

---

[134] L. Hoffman QC and M. Arden BL, 13 Sept. 1983. See generally, M. Gee, "The True and Fair View Debate: A Study in the Legal Regulation of Accounting", 54 *Mod. L. Rev* 874 (1991).

[135] 1963 Act, ss.148(4)–(6) and 150(5)–(7).

[136] 1990 Act, s.205A.

[137] 1990 Act, s.205C.

[138] 1986 Act, ss.10–12; credit institutions cannot avail of these.

[139] 1986 Act, ss.10–11.

preceding financial year, it is less than a specified size.[140] Private companies are not obliged to present group accounts.[141]

17–61   To qualify for the individual accounts exemption, the company must satisfy at least two of the following. A *small private* company is one which has a balance sheet total assets less than £1,904,607, an annual turnover of less than £3,809,214 and had less than 50 persons on average employed in the year.[142] A *medium-sized private* company is one with a balance sheet total assets less than £7,618,428, an annual turnover less than £15,236,856 and less than 250 persons on average employed in the year.[143] Where the financial year is not an actual year, these figures are proportionately adjusted. Where in two successive financial years a company ceases to satisfy two of the three prerequisites for its partly exempted status, it is no longer qualified for that status.[144] Where in two successive financial years a medium-sized company meets two of these prerequisites for a small company, it shall be treated as such.

17–62   Medium-sized private companies need not comply with the European Communities (Companies: Group Accounts) Regulations 1992.[145] To qualify for this exemption, the group most satisfy similar thresholds as just described.[146] Instead, they must follow the format in the 1963 Act's Sixth Schedule or give the same or equivalent information. Certain wholly-owned or 90 per cent- or 50 per cent-owned companies, which are holding companies with their own subsidiaries, are also exempted from them.[147]

Profit and Loss Account/Income Statement

17–63   A profit and loss account or income statement shows an overall trading record for the period in question: what were the outgoings and any liabilities assumed, what was earned, and the firm's ultimate profit or loss. Other than for IFRS accounts, the requisite formats and accounting rules are contained in the 1986 Act's Schedule.[148] Certain items can be abridged in small and medium-sized private companies' accounts.[149] There are some special provisions for investment companies.[150]

17–64   Four alternative formats exist for the profit and loss account, subject to the overriding "true and fair" requirement. While these differ in their order of presentation and in some details, there is considerable identity in what they should contain. Format 1 requires that the following be shown, namely: turnover,

---

[140] 1986 Act, s.8.
[141] 1963 Act, s.154.
[142] 1986 Act, s.8(2).
[143] 1986 Act, s.8(3).
[144] 1986 Act, s.9.
[145] SI 1992/201.
[146] Regulation 7.
[147] Regulations 8 and 9A.
[148] See generally, *Brennan & Pierce*, Chs 11 and 12.
[149] 1986 Act, s.11(1).
[150] Part VI (regs 56–59) of 1986 Act's schedule.

cost of sales, gross profit or loss, distribution costs, administrative expenses, other operating income, income from shares in group companies, income from shares in related companies, income from other financial assets, other interest receivable and similar income, amounts written off, financial assets and investments held as current assets, interest payable and similar charges, tax on profit or loss on ordinary activities, after-tax profit or loss on ordinary activities, extraordinary income, extraordinary charges, extraordinary profit or loss, tax on extraordinary profit or loss, other taxes not shown under any of the above items: profit or loss for the financial year. Formats 2 and 4 require, in addition to most of the above items: entries for raw materials, depreciation and staff costs. Abridged accounts can combine as one item turnover, cost of sales, other operating income and gross profit or loss (Format 1). The corresponding amounts for the previous financial year must always be given. Information and particulars which must supplement these accounts, in particular with regard to directors' remuneration and golden handshakes, auditors' remuneration, interest and similar charges, tax, turnover, staff and their remuneration, details of any extraordinary or exceptional items, and expenditure on research and development.

17–65   The amount of pre-tax profit or loss on ordinary activities must always be shown. Amounts representing income must not be set off against amounts representing expenditure. The following must always be shown: the aggregate amount of dividends paid and proposed to be paid; any transfers to and from reserves; the increase or reduction in the balance from the previous year; any profit or loss brought forward and any carried forward. The "accounting principles" relative to the profit and loss account are as follows: only profits which were realised at the balance sheet date should be stated; the liabilities and losses which must be stated are all those which have arisen or are likely to arise in respect of the accounting year and also the previous financial year, together with any liabilities and losses which arose between the balance sheet date and the date on which the accounts were signed; and account should be taken of all income and charges relating to the accounting year regardless of when the money was received or paid.[151]

Balance Sheet

A balance sheet shows an overall financial position at a particular time: what a firm's capital is, its reserves, its assets and liabilities. From a perusal of its balance sheet, it should be possible to judge what a company is in fact worth overall. Other than for IFRS accounts, the requisite formats and accounting rules are contained in the 1986 Act's schedule.[152] Small and medium-sized companies can have abridged balanced sheets. There are some special rules for investment companies,[153] for banks and other credit institutions,[154] and for insurers.[155]

---

[151] 1986 Act, s.5.
[152] See generally, *Brennan & Pierce*, Chs 14–22.
[153] See fn.150.
[154] European Communities (Credit Institutions: Accounts) Regulations 1992 (SI 1992/201).
[155] European Communities (Insurance Undertakings: Amounts) Regulations 1996 (SI 1996/23).

17–67 Two alternative, although substantially similar, formats exist for the balance sheet, subject to the overriding "true and fair" requirement. The corresponding amounts for the previous financial year must always be given. Information must be given in or in notes supplementing the balance sheet regarding, for example: share capital and debentures (e.g. authorised capital, aggregate of each class of shares allotted, redeemable shares, details of shares allotments made and of debentures issued during the financial year), fixed assets (e.g. acquisitions, disposals and transfers during the year, cumulative amount of provisions and provisions and adjustments made during the year), financial assets and investments held as current assets, reserves and provisions, provision for taxation, details of indebtedness, guarantees and other financial commitments.

17–68 Amounts representing assets and liabilities must not be set off against each other or vice versa. Research costs, preliminary expenses and the expenses of and commission on any issue of shares or of debentures may not be treated as an asset. The "accounting principles" relative to the balance sheet are that the company shall be presumed to be carrying on business as a going concern and, in determining the aggregate amount of any item, the amount of each individual asset or liability that falls to be taken into account should be taken separately (s.5). The proper approach to depreciation is dealt with in some detail in Pts II and III of the Act's schedule.

17–69 Small private companies[156] may have an abridged balance sheet which must contain details of the following: fixed assets (stating intangible, tangible and financial assets,) current assets (stating stock, debtors, investments and cash), creditors (stating amounts falling due within one year and amounts falling due later than that), profit and loss account provisions for liabilities and charges, reserves (revaluation and other) and capital, including called-up share capital and share premium accounts. These companies are also exempted from including in their balance sheet most of the notes required by the Act's schedule; they are the notes regarding debentures issued during the year, reserves and provisions, guarantees and other financial commitments, aggregate amount of loans made to assist persons to buy the company's own shares and the aggregate amount recommended for distribution by way of dividend.

17–70 Medium-sized private companies[157] must provide far more informative balance sheets but need not put in separate figures for the following items: goodwill, land and buildings, plant and machinery, fixtures, fittings, tools and equipment and payments on account and assets in course of construction, shares in group companies, loans to group companies, shares in related companies, loans to related companies, own shares, amounts owed by group companies, amounts owed by related companies, prepayments and accrued income, debenture loans, bank loans and overdrafts, amounts owed to group companies, amounts owed to related companies, other creditors including tax and social welfare, and accruals and deferred income.

---

[156] See para.17–61.
[157] *ibid.*

Group Accounts

17–71 Consolidated financial statements emerged with the rise of holding/
subsidiary companies as a significant form of business organisation, and are
the subject of the EC Seventh Directive.[158] Unless the company is exempted,
if it has one or more subsidiaries it must prepare consolidated group accounts
in accordance with the IFRS standards, in particular IAS27,[159] or the European
Communities (Companies: Group Accounts) Regulations 1992.[160] For the purpose of these Regulations and also of the 1986 Act, there is an extended definition of a "subsidiary".[161] As well as not applying to credit institutions and
insurers, both of which have their own regimes, a group that is below the financial and employee numbers thresholds for being medium-sized companies is
outside these Regulations.[162] They also do not apply where the company itself
is a substantial subsidiary of another company that has satisfactory group
accounts.[163] Where these do not apply and group accounts are made up, they
must be prepared in accordance with the 1963 Act.[164] But a private holding
company is not required to prepare such accounts.[165]

17–72 Relevant details of all foreign subsidiaries and also of any subsidiary
in liquidation must be included in the accounts. Interests in and the profit or
loss attributable to any "associated undertakings" also must be shown. But
there are some exceptional circumstances where a subsidiary does not have to
be included. An explanation must be given by way of a note to the group
accounts why the accounts of any subsidiary have not been incorporated into
them.[166] Where group accounts do not deal with a subsidiary, every member of
the parent company is entitled to be given a copy of its individual accounts, on
request.[167]

17–73 Unless there is good reason otherwise, a parent's and its subsidiaries'
individual accounts should use the same financial reporting framework. The
balance sheet and the profit and loss account must be consolidated in a consistent manner from year to year. Assets, liabilities, the net year end position, and
the annual profit or loss of all the entities must be dealt with as if they were a
single undertaking. There are provisions on valuations, on acquisition and
merger accounting and on changes to the group's composition. Subject to any
necessary modifications for groups, the 1986 Act's provisions on the format of

---

[158] Directive 83/349, [1983] O.J.L493/1 and see generally, P. Muchlinski, *Multinational
Enterprises and the Law*, 2nd edn (Oxford: O.U.P. 2006) at 359 *et seq.*

[159] 1963 Act s.150B and see generally *Connolly* Chs 30 and 31.

[160] 1963 Act s.150A and SI 1992/201, implementing the Seventh Directive and see generally *Brennan & Pierce* part 6.

[161] Regulation 4 and 1986 Act, s.1(3), and see para.19–05.

[162] Regulation 7 and see para.17–61.

[163] Regulations 8–9A.

[164] 1963 Act, ss.150A and 151–155 and 6th schedule.

[165] 1963 Act, s.154.

[166] 1986 Act, schedule, para.54(2)(a).

[167] 1963 Act, ss.150(10) and 154.

accounts applies, including its schedule. A range of information must be disclosed in notes to these accounts.

17–74 Where group accounts are made up, unless there are "good reasons against it", holding companies must ensure that their financial year coincides with that of their subsidiaries.[168] Where these years do not coincide, an explanation must be given by way of a note to the company's or to the group accounts.[169] The Minister is empowered to grant certain extensions of time to facilitate synchronisation of group companies' accounts.[170]

Required Disclosures

17–75 Various other matters must be disclosed in the annual accounts of all types of company. Some aspects of these are dealt with more extensively in the discussion of the subject matters to which they refer. Where Companies Acts accounts are prepared, Part V of the 1986 Act's schedule sets out the matters that must be contained either in the accounts or in notes to them. In the case of unlimited and non-profit companies, paras. 11 and 14 of the 1963 Act's 6th schedule details the matters that must be noted if they are not in the accounts.

17–76 Where IFRS accounts are prepared, the notes to them must contain the requisite information in respect of[171]:

- directors' remuneration[172];
- transactions with directors[173];
- directors' interests in shares or debentures (unless disclosed in the directors' report)[174];
- auditors' remuneration[175];
- certain details of share capital and debentures[176];
- restrictions on the distributability of profits[177];
- financial assistance for the purchase of the company's shares or shares in its holding company or in another subsidiary[178];
- details of staff numbers and remuneration[179];
- certain guarantees and other financial committments[180];

---

[168] 1963 Act s.150C, 1963 Act s.153.
[169] 1986 Act schedule, para.55.
[170] 1963 Act, s.153.
[171] 1963 Act, s.149A.
[172] 1963 Act, s.191.
[173] 1990 Act, ss.41–45.
[174] 1990 Act, s.63.
[175] 1986 Act, schedule, para.46, and 1990 Act, s.205D.
[176] 1986 Act, schedule, paras 26–28.
[177] 1986 Act, schedule, para.32A.
[178] 1986 Act, schedule, para.37(2).
[179] 1986 Act, schedule, para.42.
[180] 1986 Act, schedule, para.36.

- where a group, details of group undertakings and of securities held by subsidiaries.[181]

Additional information must be published in the annual report and accounts of listed companies.[182]

Directors' Remuneration

17–77 Information regarding directors' remuneration that must be disclosed is their aggregate emoluments, including pensions and "golden hand-shakes".[183] Emoluments here are principally directors' fees and salaries; they are defined to include percentages, contributions by the company to a pension scheme for directors, expense allowances that are charged to income tax, and an estimate of the value of any taxable fringe benefits. The pensions that must be recorded include pensions in respect of present and past services as a director, and paid to or receivable by a director or his nominee, or dependant or other person connected with him. But no separate entry need be made for a pension where the contribution by the company under it is substantially adequate to maintain the scheme. Compensation for loss of office in this context includes sums paid as consideration for or in connection with retirement from office.

17–78 What must be shown is the aggregate amounts paid under each of these three headings, including sums paid by the company's subsidiaries and by any other person. It is the amounts receivable in respect of the financial year in question that must be shown, whenever paid. In the case of sums not so receivable, the sums paid during the financial year must be shown; expenses charged to tax after the end of the relevant year must be shown in the first set of accounts in which it is practicable to do so. The accounts must distinguish between payments made in respect of services rendered or holding office as a director and in respect of other services and offices. The entry for "golden handshakes" must distinguish between those paid by the company and its subsidiaries, and those paid by any other person.

Directors' Contracts, Loans, Transactions, etc.

17–79 All loans made to any of the directors and equivalent arrangements with them, or with a connected person, must be disclosed, as must an extensive range of transactions with the company in which any director, including any shadow director, had a material interest.[184] Particulars regarding the principal terms of these various arrangements, as well as the aggregate amounts outstanding, must be contained either in the accounts or in notes to them. Where this information is not so disclosed, the auditors' report on the company's accounts is required to state that information, so far as that is reasonably possible.[185] Arrangements and transactions with the company of comparatively

---

[181] 1986 Act, ss.16 and 16A, and schedule, para.46.
[182] See para.15–146.
[183] 1963 Act, s.191.
[184] 1990 Act, ss.41–43, and see para.7–72 *et seq.*
[185] 1990 Act, s.46.

modest value need not be so disclosed.[186] Special provisions are made for licensed banks disclosing information about these matters.[187]

Directors' and Secretary's Interests in Securities

17–80 Whenever a director acquires or disposes of a beneficial interest in his company's shares or debentures or in those of a connected company, he is required to notify the company of that fact.[188] A notifiable interest for this purpose is defined very widely and includes any such interest held by his spouse or any minor child of the director. Details of those interests must be disclosed in notes to the annual accounts or in the directors' annual report, and similar details of interests held by the company's secretary.[189]

Directors' Report

17–81 Every company's directors are required to make an annual report "on the state of the company's affairs" and those of any subsidiaries, which must be laid before the company's AGM and circulated to every member and debenture-holder.[190] This must state what dividend is being recommended and how much it is proposed to carry to reserves, as well as such measures as were taken to keep proper books of account and the exact location of those books. Where it is necessary to understand fully the company's affairs, the report must deal with any changes during the financial year in the nature of the business or in the classes of business it does. It must also contain a list, stating the name, place of incorporation and nature of the business of all the subsidiaries and affiliates. The following additional information must be provided, regarding the company and any of its subsidiaries[191]: namely, a fair review of how the business developed over the year; particulars of any important events occurring since the end of the year which affect the company or its subsidiaries; an indication of likely future developments in the business; an indication of activities in the field of research and development; an indication of any branches the company has outside the State and where they are located. Large private limited companies' and Plcs' directors must also furnish analysis of certain financial and other indicators regarding the business, including information concerning employees and environmental questions. Additionally, where material, they must provide information regarding risk management, hedging and the exposure of the company to price, credit liquidity and cash flow risks.[192] For companies outside the 1986 Act, 1963 Act, s.158(4–6) applies regarding information about subsidiaries and associated companies. Where during the year the company was involved in various kinds of transactions in its own shares, relevant details must be given.[193] Where directors of a large

---

[186] 1990 Act, s.45.
[187] 1990 Act, ss.43(5) and (6), and 44.
[188] 1990 Act, s.53 and see para.17–101 *et seq.*
[189] 1990 Act, s.63.
[190] 1963 Act, ss.158–159.
[191] 1986 Act, s.13.
[192] 1986 Act, s.13(1)(a)(ii) and (f).
[193] 1986 Act, s.14.

private company decide to dispense with an audit committee or to have one with restricted functions, their report should contain an explanation.[194] If or when requiring a directors' compliance statement comes into force, the report of directors affected by it must contain that statement, which must stipulate certain matters.[195]

17–82 Additional information must be contained in what is called the "management report" to the shareholders of companies with securities listed on the Irish Stock Exchange.[196] In particular, there must be disclosed information concerning the rights and obligations attaching to shares or classes of shares; the holders of significant interests in the company's securities and especially securities carrying special rights in the company's regarding control of the company; employees' share schemes; restriction on voting rights; any inter-shareholder agreement that restrict the transfer of securities; rules in force concerning appointing and replacing directors and amending the articles of association; powers of the directors to issue and buy back company shares; significant events that will take effect or end or change in the event of the company being taken over; and agreements concerning compensation for directors or employees losing office or their jobs in consequence of a successful takeover bid.[197] If the company has opted for the IFRS approach to the accounts, this too has to be disclosed.[198] Listed companies must also provide a "responsibility statement", in which the officer[s] who sign it state that, to the best of their knowledge, the accounts were properly prepared and gave a true and fair view, as does the management reports.[199]

Auditors' Report

17–83 Most companies' accounts must be audited every year by a qualified auditor, who then makes a report on them. The auditors' primary obligation is to "make a report to the members on the individual accounts examined by them; and an every balance sheet, profit and loss account or income statement, and all group accounts, laid before the company in general meeting during their tenure of office".[200] They also must ensure that the information given in the directors' report is consistent with the accounts for that year.[201] Where the company's balance sheet does not have to be annexed to its annual return, the auditors must prepare a separate report to the directors confirming that they audited the accounts for the relevant year and that includes a copy of their report to the members.[202]

---

[194] 1990 Act, s.205B.

[195] 1990 Act, s.205E.

[196] Listing Rule 6.8.

[197] European Communities (Takeover Bids: Directive 2004/25/EC) Regulations 2006 (SI 2006/255), reg.21.

[198] European Communities (International Financial Reporting Standards and Miscellaneous Amendments) Regulations 2005 (SI 2005/116).

[199] Transparency (Directive 2004/109/EC) Regulations 2007 (SI 2007/277), reg.4(4).

[200] 1990 Act, s.193(1).

[201] 1986 Act, s.15.

[202] 1963 Act, s.128(6).

17–84 The auditors' report must be signed and dated by them and, in regard to most of the contents, state whether their opinion is qualified or unqualified. Where there has been disagreement about or a limit on the scope of their work, a qualification can be an adverse opinion or a disclaimer of opinion. They also may draw attention to some matter by way of emphasis, without qualifying their report. It must be read at the AGM and be open to inspection by any of the company's members. It must contain the following information[203]:

i.   an introduction identifying the relevant accounts and the financial reporting framework that was applied in framing them;

ii.   a description of the audit's scope and the auditing standards applied in framing them;

iii. whether, in the auditors' opinion, the accounts were properly prepared in accordance with the Companies Acts or the International Financial Reporting Standards[204];

iv.   whether the auditors have obtained all the information and explanations which, to the best of their knowledge and belief, are necessary for the purposes of their audit;

v.   whether, in their opinion, proper books of account have been kept by the company;

vi.   whether, in their opinion, proper returns adequate for their audit have been received from branches of the company not visited by them;

vii. whether the company's balance sheet and (unless it is framed as a consolidated profit and loss account) profit and loss account are in agreement will the company's books of account and returns;

viii. whether the accounts give a true and fair view in accordance with the relevant financial reporting framework;

ix.   whether, in the auditors' opinion, the contents of the directors' report to the members are consistent with its accounts for the period;

x.   whether, in their opinion, there existed at the balance sheet date what is described as a "capital haemorrhage" situation, which required that an EGM be convened[205];

xi.   where the accounts do not contain the required details of loans and comparable transactions with any of the directors, secretary and connected partners, details of those matters;

xii   set out conclusions on their review carried out on the director's compliance statement, where such statements are required,[206] including a copy of the report made to the directors when the auditors were of the view that the statement was not fair or reasonable.

Additional information must be contained in the report to shareholders of companies with securities listed on the Irish Stock Exchange.[207]

---

[203] 1990 Act, s.193(4)–(4F).

[204] Banks, discount companies and assurance companies may instead avail of Part III of the 6th schedule to the 1963 Act.

[205] See para.8–137.

[206] 1990 Act s.205E, not yet in force.

[207] Listing Rule 6.8.8–11.

Half-Yearly Reports

17–85   Listed companies also must send half-yearly reports to their members, being a condensed financial statement, an interim management report and a responsibility statement.[208]

Oversight by IAASA

17–86   In the case of Plcs and very large private limited companies, where the Supervisory Authority has a concern whether they comply with the statutory accounting requirements, it may notify the directors of the fact.[209] This notice may specify the matters of concern to the IAASA and call for explanations. That gives them some time to prepare fully compliant accounts. Where that is not done, the IAASA may apply to the court for a declaration of non-compliance. The court may give certain directions regarding revising the accounts and notifying persons who are likely to rely on them. To come within this category, a private limited company must have a balance sheet total in excess of £25 million and an annual turnover in excess of £50 million; a higher or lower amount may be specified by the Minister.

DISCLOSURES TO THE PUBLIC

17–87   Every company's name must be displayed legibly and conspicuously outside of its registered office and every other place it carries on business, and its name must be mentioned in a legible manner on all its business letters, notices, cheques, bills, notes, invoices, receipts and the like.[210] Every limited company's "letters and order forms" must state the following[211]: where it is registered and its registration number; the address of its registered office; details regarding its directors; that it is being wound up, if that is the case; that it has been exempted from having the words "ltd" or "teo" in its name, if that is the case. Any reference made there to its share capital must be to its paid-up share capital. Any website maintained by the company must display this information in a prominent and easily accessible place. An extensive range of information must be notified to the Registrar of Companies from time to time, and every year a company must submit an annual return to the CRO. Notice of the delivery of some of this information must be published by the company in the *Gazette*. Every company must maintain several registers, some of which members of the public are entitled to inspect.

---

[208] Listing Rule 6.9 and Transparency (Directive 2004/109/EC) Regulations 2007 (SI 2007/277) regs 6–9.

[209] 2003 Act, s.26.

[210] 1963 Act, s.114.

[211] European Communities (Companies) Regulations 1973 (SI 1973/163), amended by SI 2007/49.

Annual Return

17–88   Every company must make an annual return to the CRO.[212] Companies often designate filing agents for these purposes[213] and the process may
now be done electronically.[214] Companies that do not file these returns risk
being struck off the register,[215] their defaulting officers risk being prosecuted
and, if the company is wound up as insolvent, they also risk being subjected to
a restriction or a disqualification order for non-compliance. Where there has
been default in submitting a return, the Registrar can so notify the company
and may specify a sum that must be paid, along with filing the return, before a
specified date; failure to comply can result in a prosecution.[216] These returns
are admissible in evidence as to the truth of their contents, being documents
executed under a statutory duty and to be shown to members of the public.[217]

Return Date

17–89   This return must be made within 28 days of the annual return date,
which ordinarily is the anniversary of the previous return being delivered.[218]
Newly incorporated companies must submit their return within six months of
their date of incorporation. Application can be made to the court to extend the
time for submitting a return. Provision is made whereby, on notifying the Registrar,[219] a company can have a new annual return date, but it cannot again
change that date for another five years.

Contents

17–90   This return must contain the following information[220]: the company's
name, the date to which the return is made up; the financial year; the registered
office and other addresses; the secretary's name and address; details of who
will address any queries concerning the return; the authorised and issued share
capital; consideration for shares issued, specifying the cash and the non-cash
consideration; other details about shares or debentures; past and present members; details concerning the directors, being their names, dates of birth, nationality, occupations, residential addresses and other directorships; political
donations.

17–91   Subject to exceptions, companies must annex to their annual return
certified copies of their relevant balance sheet, profit and loss account, and
directors' and auditors' reports.[221] "Small" private companies[222] are exempted

---

[212] 1963 Act, s.125.
[213] Form J1 and J3.
[214] Form J2 and J4.
[215] 1982 Act, s.12.
[216] 2001 Act, s.66. European Communities (Companies) Regulations 1973 (SI 1973/163),
amended by SI 2007/49.
[217] *R. v Halpin* [1975] Q.B. 907.
[218] 1963 Act, s.127.
[219] Form B73.
[220] Form B1.
[221] 1986 Act, s.7.
[222] See para.17–61.

from annexing a profit and loss account and directors' report.[223] "Medium-sized" private companies[224] are permitted to file a profit and loss account that consolidates certain items under "gross profit or loss" and a balance sheet that is somewhat abridged.[225] Private unlimited companies and non-profit companies do not have to annex their balance sheet or any document or report relating to them but must annex to their return a copy of the auditors' report to the directors confirming that the accounts were audited.[226] Each of these documents must be certified by a director and the secretary as a copy of the document laid or to be laid before the AGM.[227]

17–92   These accounts and reports must cover the period since the previous annual return and must not have been made up more than nine months before that return was made up. If any of these do not comply with the 1986 Act's requirements regarding format and contents, additional material must be annexed to ensure such compliance. A translation must be supplied of any document that is not in English or Irish.

17–93   There is no particular mechanism whereby, should some error be found in a company's accounts, as filed, it can be corrected. It is possible that the High Court has an inherent jurisdiction to make such orders as may be necessary to ensure that any proper amendment is made, although such a jurisdiction has been rejected in England.[228]

The *Gazette*

17–94   Information published in the Companies Registration Office *Gazette* previously had to be published in the *Iris Oifigiúil*, the official Government periodical. Notification in the *Iris* became prominent in consequence of the EC Directives on company law,[229] although it already existed in respect of appointing a receiver and commencement of a winding-up. The civil sanction for non-publication in the *Gazette* of any of the requisite notice is that the document in question may not be relied upon by the company as against any other person unless the company "proves that such person had knowledge of [it]".[230]

17–95   Within six weeks of the relevant issue by the CRO or delivery to it, notice of the following must be published in the *Gazette*[231]:

(a)   the issue of its certificate of incorporation;
(b)   delivery of its memorandum and articles of association or other constitutive document;

---

[223] 1986 Act, s.10.
[224] See para.17–61.
[225] 1986 Act, s.11.
[226] 1963 Act, s.128.
[227] 1986 Act, s.7.
[228] In *Re A Company* (0077466 of 2003) [2004] 1 W.L.R. 1357.
[229] European Communities (Companies) Regulations 1973 (SI 1973/163).
[230] *ibid.* reg.10.
[231] *ibid.* reg.4. Time can be extended by the court: *ibid.* reg.11.

(c)	any amendment to the memorandum or articles and the amended text;

(d)	notice of any charge of directors or of prescribed information relating to any director;

(e)	details of any person other than the directors who are authorised to bind the company;

(f)	the annual return and accompanying accounting documents;

(g)	the location of the registered office and any change of address;

(h)	if there is a winding-up, a copy of any winding-up order, the liquidator's return for the company's final meeting and any order made for the company's dissolution.

17–96 If the company is being voluntarily wound up, the liquidator must publish a notice of that fact in the *Gazette* within 14 days of his appointment.[232] Where a company has been wound up by court order, within 21 days the liquidator must publish notice of that fact in the *Gazette*.[233] Where an examiner is appointed he must publish in the *Gazette* (as well as in two daily newspapers) notice of and the date of his appointment.[234]

Notifications to the CRO

17–97 As well as the annual return and notices itemised above, notice of a variety of decisions and acts affecting a company must be furnished to the Registrar of Companies. General regulations have been adopted regarding the form and content of these documents.[235] What must be notified are:[236]

(a)	special resolutions;

(b)	resolutions agreed by all the members equivalent to special resolutions;

(c)	resolutions or agreements made by all members of a particular class of shareholders, or that effectively bind them;

(d)	resolutions increasing the share capital;

(e)	resolutions attaching rights or restrictions to shares, or varying any such rights or restrictions;

(f)	resolutions classifying any unclassified shares;

(g)	resolutions converting shares from one class to another;

(h)	resolutions by Plcs to make market purchases of their own shares;

(i)	resolutions of the directors to re-register as a Plc;

(j)	resolutions of the directors to cancel shares or to reduce the authorised share capital after a Plc has acquired its own shares;

(k)	resolutions of the directors to allot additional shares in the company;

(l)	resolutions to voluntarily wind up the company on grounds of insolvency, or because either the period or the event for which it was incorporated has expired or has occurred, respectively;

---

[232] 1963 Act, s.252.

[233] 1963 Act, s.227.

[234] 1990 Amend. Act, s.12(2).

[235] Companies Act 1990 (Form and Contents of Documents Delivered to Registrar) Regulations 2002 (SI 2002/39).

[236] 1963 Act, s.143, 1990 Act, s.215 and 1983 Act, s.20.

A printed copy of every such resolution must be forwarded to the CRO within 15 days of it being passed. Where shares are allotted with rights not recorded in any of the above resolutions, relevant details must be sent to the CRO within one month.[237]

Accessible Registers

17–98 Several of the registers that companies are obliged to keep are open to public inspection, namely the registers of members and of debenture-holders, the register of directors and of their interests in securities in the company, the register of company charges.

Listed Companies

17–99 The legal disclosure obligations of listed companies were significantly expanded by the Transparency (Directive 2004/109/EC) Regulations 2004,[238] which deal with their annual and half-yearly financial reports, management statements and responsibility statements, liability for false or misleading information furnished, ongoing disclosure about major shareholdings[239] and other continuing obligations, and access to information. Extensive powers are conferred on the Central Bank and Financial Services Authority of Ireland to secure compliance with these requirements. Additional documentation and information must be supplied to the Stock Exchange.[240] Notification of specified "significant" transactions and "related party" transactions must be given to it.[241] It must be notified promptly about various developments regarding companies' capital, of significant changes in the ownership of their shares, of any changes in the board membership, accounting date, name of the company, of any variation in a "lock-up" arrangement or disposal of shares in any exemption to such arrangement, and of all resolutions passed other than in the ordinary course of the business.[242]

ASCERTAINING BENEFICIAL INTERESTS IN SECURITIES

17–100 Frequently the registered owner of shares is not their beneficial owner. For a variety of reasons, their real owner will choose to have them registered in some other person's name—be it a member of his family, some company which he controls or a nominee company which is in the business of holding shares on behalf of others. Many of the major banks have nominee companies for this very purpose. His reason may be to hide from the company the extent of his interest in it or to hide from others—be they his family, the Revenue or regulatory authorities—what his assets are. However, the public authorities, the company and its other members often have a distinct interest in

---

[237] 1983 Act, s.39.
[238] SI 2007/277 and see para.15–146.
[239] *cf.* SI 2007/277, reg.81, disapplying Pt IV, Ch.2 (ss.67–96) of the 1990 Act.
[240] Listing Rule 4.
[241] Listing Rules 7 and 8.
[242] Listing Rule 6.6.

ascertaining who the true beneficial owner of shares is; for instance, to monitor insider trading, fraud, tax evasion or building up by stealth a controlling interest in the company. Before 1990 the legislature hardly addressed the question of the anonymity of share-holdings—apart from restricting the use of bearer shares,[243] which are common in many continental European countries and are the reason why public companies there are referred to as *sociétés anonymes*. Table A, dealing with notice of shares held in trust, adds that "this shall not preclude the company from requiring the members or a transferee of shares to furnish the company with information as to the beneficial ownership of any share where such information is reasonably required by the company".[244] There does not appear to be any case law on this part of the clause. One of the objectives of the inspection system, as described next below, is to ascertain the identity of the individuals who actually own or control a company.

Disclosing Officers' Interests

17–101   Shareholders have a particular interest in knowing the extent, if any, of their directors' holdings of shares in or debentures of their company, and of those officers' dealings in those securities. In the case of listed companies, the financial press regularly reports on directors' transactions in their companies' shares. Whenever a director, shadow director or secretary of any company, or their spouse or minor child, acquires or disposes of an "interest" in their company's securities, the officer in question must notify the company of that fact within the following five days, or within five days of becoming aware of the transaction.[245] In the case of listed companies, they in turn must notify the Irish Stock Exchange of the fact.[246] All officers' securities transactions so notified must be recorded by the company in a register kept for this purpose and be disclosed in the directors' annual report.[247] This register may be inspected by members of the public,[248] who thereby can ascertain the full extent, if any, of the officers' stake in the company. Where the company has securities listed on the Irish Stock Exchange, various details concerning these transactions must be notified to the Exchange authorities.[249]

"Interest"

17–102   For these purposes, there are two central concepts, that of a relevant "interest" and of a transaction affecting that interest that must be notified. An "interest" here "include[s] any interest of any kind whatsoever" in shares or debentures, but any restriction on exercising any right attached to the interest should be disregarded.[250] A number of specific interests are then identified, being contractual rights to the securities or to options on them, interests via a

---

[243] Under the since-repealed Exchange Control Acts.
[244] Article 7.
[245] 1990 Act, ss.53–58.
[246] 1990 Act, s.65.
[247] 1990 Act, ss.59–63.
[248] 1990 Act, s.60(5).
[249] Listing Rule 6.11.
[250] 1990 Act, s.54(2).

stake in another company and interests under a trust. But certain interests that may fall broadly within one of these categories are excluded. A relevant interest exists notwithstanding that the shares cannot be identified.

17–103   An interest by way of contractual entitlement is where the officer, his spouse or minor child contracts to purchase the securities, or is otherwise entitled to exercise any right exercisable by their registered holder or to control the exercise of that right.[251] But holding a proxy vote or being appointed to represent some corporate body at the company's meeting is not a relevant interest. Additionally, the person has an interest if he holds an option to call for delivery of the securities to himself on his order, or has a right to acquire an interest in them, or is under an obligation to take an interest in them, whether absolute or conditional.[252] But rights or obligations to subscribe for shares do not come within this category, other than a right to subscribe granted by the company to the officer's spouse or minor child.[253]

17–104   An interest exists under a trust if the person is a beneficiary of the trust and the trust property includes an interest in the securities, as described above.[254] But for these purposes shall be disregarded, *inter alia*, an interest as a bare trustee, as a discretionary beneficiary, or in reversion or remainder.[255] Also disregarded is a life interest under a irrevocable settlement of the company's securities, where the settlor has no interest in the settlement income or property.[256] Also disregarded are where a stockbroker holds the securities as security, in the ordinary course of his business, and interests by virtue of holding units in a unit trust or equivalent financial arrangement, or under a charitable scheme.

17–105   An interest via a company arises if a company has an interest in the securities, as described above, and that company or its directors generally act in accordance with the officer's or connected person's instructions, or he can exercise or control at least one third of the votes cast at that company's general meetings. If the person controls those one third votes and that company in turn controls one third of the votes in another company, the relevant interest is deemed to also exist.[257]

Transactions

17–106   What the director or secretary involved must notify to the company are relevant transactions involving an interest in securities, as just described. These transactions are broadly defined as "any event in consequence of" which he, or his spouse or minor child becomes or ceases to be interested in the securities, or in any securities of the company's subsidiary, holding company

---

[251] 1990 Act, s.54(4), (8) and (9).
[252] 1990 Act, s.54(7) and (10).
[253] 1990 Act, s.64(3).
[254] 1990 Act, s.54(3).
[255] 1990 Act, s.55(1)(a).
[256] 1990 Act, s.55(1)(c) and (3).
[257] 1990 Act, s.54(5)–(6).

or sister subsidiary.[258] These also includes contracting to sell any of those securities.[259] In both of these instances, notification to the company must include the price when the securities are being purchased or sold.[260] This also includes his assigning a right to subscribe for the securities or obtaining from another company a right to subscribe for the company's or any of its group's securities, as well as exercising or assigning any such right to subscribe.[261] In these instances, notice to the company must include specific details of the transaction, *inter alia*, the consideration given for any assignment or obtaining a right to subscribe for shares.[262] In all instances, the notice must state the number or amount and the class of securities involved. None of these requirements apply to transactions in the shares of a wholly-owned subsidiary.[263]

Disclosing Stakes in Public Companies

17–107   Whenever anyone, their spouse, minor child or company they virtually control, or persons acting in concert, acquire an interest in more than 5 per cent of the voting shares in a Plc, they must notify the company of that fact within 5 days of the relevant transaction.[264] All transactions so notified must be recorded by the company in a register kept for this purpose,[265] which may be inspected by members of the public, who may require a copy to be made of it or any part of it.[266] Whenever any person acquires or ceases to have an interest in a notifiable percentage of the shares in a listed company, he must notify that fact to the Irish Stock Exchange.[267] If it appears to the Exchange that this requirement has not been satisfied, it must notify the DCE. For these purposes, the relevant percentages are 5 per cent, 10 per cent, 15 per cent, 20 per cent, 30 per cent, 50 per cent and 75 per cent.[268]

Private Company Disclosure Orders

17–108   To ascertain who is the beneficial owner of the voting shares in or debentures of a private company, other than a non-profit company, a variety of persons with a "financial interest" in the company can apply to the High Court for a "disclosure order", requiring a party to furnish information about such interest as he may have in the securities.[269] Those who may apply for such orders are any member, creditor, employee, co-adventurer, examiner, lessor, lessee, licensor, licensee, liquidator or receiver of the company or of a related company. The company and the person against whom the order is being sought must be given

---

[258] 1990 Act, s.53(2)(a).
[259] 1990 Act, s.53(2)(b).
[260] 1990 Act, s. 57(1).
[261] 1990 Act, s.53(2)(c) and (d).
[262] 1990 Act, s.57(2)–(4).
[263] 1990 Act, s.53(10).
[264] 1990 Act, ss.67–79.
[265] 1990 Act, s.80.
[266] 1990 Act, s.88.
[267] Transparency (Directive 2004/109/EC) Regulations 2007, regs 13–24, SI 2007/286.
[268] *ibid.* s.89–96 of the 1990 Act were repealed by these regulations.
[269] 1990 Act, ss.97–104.

at least 10 days' notice of an intention to so apply.[270] Before it so orders, the court must believe that the person against whom it is being sought has or can get information about who is or was interested in the securities, or who acts or has acted for such person, or anyone it believes is or was interested in those securities who may be able to confirm relevant facts or furnish such additional information as may be required.[271] A disclosure order will then be granted where the court is of the view that non-disclosure would prejudice the applicant's interest and it is just and equitable to so order; security for costs may be required.[272] It must identify the person to whom it is addressed and give his current address. For a specified period it may impose a restriction on rights and obligations attaching to the securities in question.[273] Within seven days of such order being made, notice of it must be given to the company, the Registrar of Companies, any registered holder of the securities who appears not to be resident in the State, and such other person as the court directs. Additionally, notice of the order must be advertised in at least two newspapers that circulate in the district where the company's registered office is located.[274] Where a restriction was imposed on incidents of the shares, when making the order, a person affected by it may apply for relief.[275]

17–109 A person to whom a disclosure order is addressed must give the court particulars of his present or past interest in the securities and of any other interest held in them, that he is aware of, and the identity of whoever may have immediately acquired any interest that he held in them.[276] What constitutes an "interest" for these purposes is not the interest envisaged by the provisions on disclosing officers' interests but those for disclosing stakes held in Plcs.[277] It includes a right to acquire a right to subscribe for securities which, if issued, would be voting shares. Unless the court otherwise directs, information obtained by it in this manner will be furnished to the company and to the applicant.

17–110 Disobedience of or failure to fulfil obligations imposed by a disclosure order, or where a party furnishes information that he knows is false or reckless about its veracity, results in the securities automatically becoming sterilised, without any need for a court order to that effect. In such circumstances, the party cannot "enforce ... whether directly or indirectly, by action or legal proceedings [any] right or interest of any kind in respect of" those securities.[278] But application can be made to the court for relief from all or some of these consequences.[279]

---

[270] 1990 Act, s.99.

[271] 1990 Act, s.98.

[272] e.g. *Re FH Lloyd Holdings Plc* [1985] B.C.L.C. 293 and *Re Lonrho Plc*, [1987] B.C.L.C. 53. *No. 3* [1989] B.C.L.C. 480 and *No. 4* [1988] B.C.L.C. 480 and [1990] B.C.L.C. 151.

[273] 1990 Act, s.101(4).

[274] 1990 Act, s.102.

[275] 1990 Act, s.101(5).

[276] 1990 Act, s.100.

[277] 1990 Act, ss.68 and 72–78.

[278] 1990 Act, s.104.

[279] e.g. *Re Geers Gross Plc* [1987] 1 W.L.R. 1649 and *Re Ricardo Group Plc No. 2* [1989] B.C.L.C. 766.

Public Company Investigation

17–111   A somewhat analogous process exists where a Plc seeks to ascertain who has an interest in any of its securities.[280] On the company's own initiative or on the requisition of those holding at least 10 per cent of its voting shares, it may require any person it believes has or had an interest in its shares, in the three proceeding years, to furnish relevant details of that interest. Any information so disclosed must be separately recorded in a publicly-accessible register. If any person who is or was interested in those shares fails to give that information, the company can apply to the court for an order that effectively sterilises those shares.[281] In their own regulations, listed companies can impose additional sanctions.[282]

INVESTIGATIONS

17–112   Since 1862[283] it has been possible to have inspectors appointed to investigate the affairs of companies on specified grounds.[284] These powers were regarded as an essential device for protecting shareholders, creditors and the general public interest, in that conventional criminal sanctions and civil law remedies were not always adequate. Unless a case can be proved beyond reasonable doubt, ordinarily convictions cannot be obtained. For many aggrieved shareholders or creditors, the cost of bringing civil proceedings in the High Court can be prohibitive, especially when generally they would have to pay the other side's costs if they lost their action. Following the establishment of the DCE and also following giving extensive investigative powers to numerous regulatory agencies, especially in the financial services sector, it is likely that there will be less resort to these general powers. Under these, often without any advance warning, a company or companies and any person involved in them, can be made subject to a virtual inquisition, being obliged to furnish extensive information about their affairs. Initially, it was the Minister who would appoint inspectors for this purpose. Because the very fact of such an appointment being made could considerably damage a company's reputation, in 1990 provision was made for officials (now the DCE), by way of enquiry, to order records to be produced to investigate the matter in question, in a manner that would not give rise to any or to at least the same publicity. One objective of these investigations is to ascertain whether matters of concern are sufficiently serious as to warrant a full-blown inspection of a company's affairs. Also in 1990, jurisdiction was conferred on the High Court to appoint inspectors. Powers given to inspectors to compel disclosure of confidential information have withstood challenges maintaining that they contravene the constitutional guarantees of private property and of privacy, and the privilege against self-incrimination.

---

[280] 1990 Act, ss.81–88.
[281] 1990 Act, ss.85 and 16.
[282] Listing Rules 6.3.9.
[283] Companies Act 1862, 25 & 26 Vic. c.89, ss.56 and 57.
[284] 1990 Act, Pt III (ss.7–24).

17–113 Since 1990, the following companies have been investigated by authorised officers or by inspectors:

Company	Section of 1990 Act	Appointee	Year
Ansbacher (Cayman) Limited	s.8	Ms Noreen Mackey B.L., Mr Paul Rowan FCA; Mr Justice Declan Costello was replaced by Judge Sean O'Leary and Mr Michael Cush, SC	2000
College Trustees Limited	s.19	Gerard Ryan CSA	1999
Faxhill Homes Limited	s.19	George Maloney FCCA	1998
Dunnes Stores ILAC Company Limited	s.19	Gerard Ryan FCA	1998
Kentford Securities Ltd	s.19	Gerard Ryan FCA	1998
National Irish Bank Ltd NIB Financial Services Ltd	s.8	John Blayney SC; Tom Grace FCA	1998
Ansbacher (Cayman) Ltd	s.19	Gerard Ryan FCA	1998
Guinness & Mahon (Ireland) Ltd	s.19	Gerard Ryan FCA	1998
Irish Intercontinental Bank Ltd	s.19	Gerard Ryan FCA	1998
Hamilton Ross Co Ltd	s.19	Gerard Ryan FCA	1998
Bula Resources (Holdings) Plc	s.14	Lyndon MacCann BL	1997
Celtic Helicopters Ltd	s.19	Gerard Ryan FCA	1997
Garuda Ltd	s.19	Peter Fisher CIMA	1997
Clonmannon Retirement Village Rayhill Properties Co. Ltd	s.19	Martin Cosgrove FCA	1997
Hilltop Catering Ltd Retirement			
Home Affairs			
CountyGlen Plc	s.8	Frank Clarke SC	1994
CountyGlen Plc	s.19	Peter Fisher CIMA	1993
Chestvale Properties Ltd & Hoddle Investments Ltd (Telecom)	s.14	John Glackin, Solicitor	1991
Siúcre Éireann cpt and others	s.8	Ciaran Foley SC; Aidan Barry FCA	1991
Siúcre Éireann cpt and others (Greencore)	s.14	Maurice Curran, Solicitor	1991

Production Orders

17–114 Even before the question of appointing an inspector arises, the DCE has extensive powers to investigate the affairs of a company. One is where the focus is on who owns any shares or debentures in it, where knowing that appears to him to be necessary either for the effective administration of Company Law, the effective discharge of his statutory functions or is in the public interest.[285] Any person who he believes has relevant information concerning any present or past "interest" in those securities can be obliged to provide that information to the DCE.

17–115   What constitutes an interest for these purposes is broadly defined, as a right to acquire or to dispose of the security or any interest in it, or to exercise any vote attached to it, or having a veto over others exercising any right in respect of the security, or where those persons can be required to act or are accustomed to act in according with the person's directions. While such an enquiry is being conducted, the DCE has extensive power to virtually sterilise the shares in question.[286]

17–116   Where the DCE has a variety of concerns about a company or aspects of its affairs, he can require that there be produced to him such books and documents as may relate to them and he can copy those records and require any present or past officer of the company, or employee, to explain their contents.[287] These concerns are where he is "of the opinion that there are circumstances suggesting that" it is necessary to decide if there should be a full inspection; the company's affairs are being or were conducted to defraud members, creditors or other persons, or otherwise fraudulently or unlawfully; or they were being conducted in a manner unfairly prejudicial to its members or creditors; or the company possesses any records relating to any of the above matters. It was held by the Supreme Court in *Dunnes Stores Ireland Co. v Ryan*[288] that, before an investigation can be commenced, there must be reasonable grounds for the DCE's decision, which must not be arbitrary or disproportionate. Where the company seeks reasons for the decision, those must be furnished. A reason given there, general concern about standards of corporate governance, was held not to be a sufficient ground. Because, however, aspects of the intended investigation had already been the subject of adverse comment by two judges, who had conducted separate inquiries into allegations of wrongdoing (the McCracken and the Buchanan reports), in the circumstances those were reasonable grounds. Reference there to some of the basis for production orders not being applicable to previous events was addressed by amendment in 2001. But the holding that defrauding the creditors of "any other person" did not include defrauding the Revenue was not directly addressed in those amendments.

17–117   In earlier proceedings concerning those same companies, Laffoy J. held that it is not necessary to give advance notice to a company before a production order is made to it.[289] Where an order is made, there is nothing to prevent the company from making representations to the DCE regarding it. But

---

[285] 1990 Act, s.15.
[286] 1990 Act, s.16.
[287] 1990 Act, s.19.
[288] [2002] 2 I.R. 60.
[289] *Dunnes Stores Ireland Co. v Ryan* [1999] 3 I.R. 542.

where the reason or reasons for making the order are requested, these should be furnished. In that instance, the Minister flatly refused to give any reason for his order. It was held that, in view of the very extensive range of documents being sought and the short time span allowed to comply with the order, it was excessive and unreasonable; some of the categories were of such a general nature as to give "the demand as a whole the hallmark of a trawl."[290]

17–118 Records protected by legal professional privilege are exempt from production.[291] In the case of records held by banks, their production should be required only where they relate to a person against whom a production order was made, whether a customer or otherwise, or the bank's own affairs are being investigated.[292]

17–119 Records relating to the company, falling within any of the above categories but held by any third party, can be the subject of a production order. But where those records are not the company's own books or documents, or copies of them, there are safeguards to protect the interests of those parties. Except where the DCE believes that the records are likely to be concealed, falsified or destroyed, he must notify the party of his intention to make the order, stating reasons why he believes the records in question relate to the company and fall within one or more of the above categories, and give the party 21 days to make submissions as to why the DCE is in error. Additionally, any document that would be privileged on any ground is exempt from being produced.

17–120 Every present or past officer or employee of the company is obliged to give the DCE all reasonable assistance, including explaining any of the records and, where records are not produced, indicating where they are.[293] Any such statement or explanation may be used in evidence against that person in any civil proceedings, and in a prosecution for giving false or misleading information, or for concealing, falsifying or destroying a document. The High Court may direct that the company in question shall bear all or part of the expenses incurred by the DCE in conducting his investigation of the company's records and related documentation.[294] Concealing, falsifying, destroying or otherwise disposing of a record that a person knows or suspects would be relevant to any such investigation, is an offence.[295]

17–121 Records or any other information obtained by way of a production order must not be published or disclosed, without the consent of the company in question.[296] But they may be disclosed to a variety of competent authorities, where the DCE is of the view that disclosure to them is appropriate in the circumstances, *inter alia*, for the purposes of an investigation or prosecution

---

[290] *ibid.* at 564.
[291] 1990 Act, s.23(1).
[292] 1990 Act, s.23(2).
[293] 1990 Act, s.19(5).
[294] 1990 Act, s.19(10).
[295] 1990 Act, s.19A.
[296] 1990 Act, s.21.

under the Companies Acts, the Insurance Acts or the Taxes Acts; for the purpose of assessing liability to a tax or duties, or other payment to a public authority; to assist any Minister in performing his functions; to assist the Takeover Panel, Stock Exchange, Competition Authority, a Tribunal of Inquiry, an Oireachtas Committee or a professional disciplinary body; winding-up proceedings commenced by the DCE against any body which has been ordered to produce records or any person named in a report made in connection with that procedure.

Search and Seizure

17–122   Where there are reasonable grounds for suspecting that "material information" exists in a place, on application by or on behalf of the DCE, a District Judge may issue a warrant authorising the place to be searched and that documents relating to that information be seized and retained, including computer equipment.[297] The information envisaged here is what could be required by the DCE, as described above, or by an inspector, as described below, or information that may provide evidence of company law offences, or relating to such offences. The maximum duration for warrants issued under this power is one month.

Inspections

17–123   One or more inspectors can be appointed by the DCE or by the High Court, as the case may be.

Appointment

17–124   An appointment can be made by the DCE, without reference to the court, to ascertain the individuals who beneficially own or control a company, or are financially interested in its success or failure, where he is of the opinion that there are circumstances requiring inspection for the effective administration of company law, the effective discharge of his statutory functions or in the public interest.[298] He also may appoint an inspector where he believes that there are circumstances suggesting that dealings in a company's shares by any of its officers or member of their families have not been notified to the company, or that a director has been dealing in options in his company's securities.[299]

17–125   Alternatively, the DCE may request a court appointment where he can demonstrate that a company's affairs are being conducted fraudulently or unlawfully, or in a manner that unfairly prejudices some of its members, or that those members have not been given all the information that they might reasonably expect.[300]

---

[297] 1990 Act, s.20.
[298] 1990 Act, s.14 and *Lyons v Curran* [1993] I.L.R.M. 375.
[299] 1990 Act, s.66.
[300] 1990 Act, s.8.

17–126   An application for a court appointment may also be made by the company itself, by any one of its directors or creditors, or by either at least 100 of its members or those members who hold at least one tenth of its paid-up shares (or one fifth in number, if a guarantee company).[301] No grounds whatsoever are stipulated here, leaving the court with a wide discretion. All that is required is that the application must be supported by such evidence as the court may require, including such evidence as may be prescribed. The court may require a sum of money to be lodged to cover security for costs, not exceeding €317,434. From time to time, the court may give the inspector such directions as it deems fit.

Conduct of Inspection

17–127   Comparatively little is prescribed about how inspections should be carried out, generally leaving it to the court to lay down such ground rules as the overriding requirement of fair procedures demands. While the inspection is under way, application can be made to the court for such directions as would ensure that it is conducted speedily and economically. In one of the *National Irish Bank* cases,[302] where inspectors had been appointed to investigate, *inter alia*, evasion of deposit interest retention tax (DIRT) by customers of the bank, it sought to restrict the scope of the enquiry after an Oireachtas Committee had been established to investigate DIRT evasion across the banking sector.[303] Although there was some overlap, Kelly J. refused the application on the grounds that the purpose and object of the two processes were dissimilar and distinct, and there was no duplication of process

17–128   The inspection established in 1991 into the sale to Board Telecom of a former bakery site at Ballsbridge in 1990, for IR£9.4 million, it having been purchased a year earlier for £4 million, attracted a barrage of resistance on a variety of grounds from several of the individuals and companies involved. In one instance, Murphy J. rejected the contention that material subject to a bank's duty of confidentiality could not be demanded by the inspector.[304] In another, the Supreme Court rejected the contention that the scope of questions being put about one of the protagonists' personal financial affairs went too far.[305] In another, where a protagonist had made a statutory declaration denying any involvement in the transaction, the Supreme Court held that this did not prevent the inspector from investigating whether any such connection existed and that he did not have to show a *prima facie* case for disbelieving the contents of that declaration.[306] But the mechanism for enforcing compliance with the inspectors' demands for information, which was equivalent to contempt of court, was held to be unconstitutional.[307] Additionally, it was held that

---

[301] 1990 Act, s.7.
[302] *Re National Irish Bank (No. 2)* [1999] 3 I.R. 190.
[303] See *Report into D.I.R.T.* (Pn 7963, 1999).
[304] *Glackin v Trustee Savings Bank* [1993] 3 I.R. 55.
[305] *Desmond v Glackin (No. 2)* [1993] 3 I.R. 67.
[306] *Probets v Glackin* [1993] 3 I.R. 134.
[307] *Desmond v Glackin (No. 2)* [1993] 3 I.R. 67.

the warrant appointing an inspector should set out such public interest considerations, if any, as warranted the appointment.[308]

17–129   Where he regards it as necessary for the purpose of the investigation, a court-appointed inspector may investigate the affairs of any other body that is related to a company, including where that is a purely commercial relationship.[309] Every officer or agent of any company being investigated, including its auditors, bankers and solicitors, is obliged to produce any book or document he has relating to the company, to meet the inspector when so requested and to furnish him with all reasonable assistance.[310] But records subject to legal professional privilege are exempt and any banking records sought must relate to the company being investigated.[311]

17–130   A similar obligation rests on any other person the inspector considers has information concerning the company's affairs. Details of any bank account maintained by any of the directors, whether alone or jointly and whether in the State or elsewhere, can be required, provided money linked with the company specified has gone through that account.[312] In this context, a director includes any past director, any person "connected with" a director, and any present or past "shadow director".

17–131   An inspector may interrogate on oath any officer or agent of the company, including its auditors, bankers and solicitors, and any other person he regards as having information concerning its affairs.[313] These enquiries are always conducted in private and information furnished to inspectors is not made public, other than in the interim or the final report made to the DCE or to the court. Usually, a signed transcript is kept of such examinations. Questioning witnesses should not be done in an oppressive manner. It has been held that a witness cannot be required to sign a confidentiality undertaking before certain factual matters are put to him.[314] In a series of cases principally arising from an inspection into the events behind Board Telecom's purchase of a site at Ballsbridge, unsuccessful attempts were made to restrict the extent of documentation being sought and the range of questions being put.[315] Where allegations of wrongdoing by named individuals are being investigated, it is possible that those persons should be given an opportunity to cross-examine their principal accusers who give evidence. In the National Irish Bank inspection of 1999, such an opportunity was furnished by the inspectors when court proceedings on this very question were imminent.

---

[308] *Probets v Glackin* [1993] 3 I.R. 134.

[309] 1990 Act, s.9.

[310] 1990 Act, s.10.

[311] 1990 Act, s.23.

[312] 1990 Act, s.10(3).

[313] 1990 Act, s.10(4).

[314] *Re Mirror Group Newspapers Plc* [1999] 1 B.C.L.C. 690.

[315] See fn.304–308 above and *Chestvale Properties Ltd & Hoddle Investment Ltd v Glackin* [1993] 3 I.R. 35.

17–132   Answers given by an individual to questions put to him by an inspector may be used in evidence against that person, in any civil or other non-criminal proceedings, and also in a prosecution for perjury relating to an answer given.[316] In *Re National Irish Bank Ltd*,[317] the Supreme Court held that the privilege against self-incrimination could not be invoked to justify refusing to answer questions. This was because the public interest in combating fraud, especially in uncovering possible malpractice and illegality in the banking system, was held sufficient to justify displacing it; the need to have these matters thoroughly investigated was a sufficiently proportionate justification to override that privilege. It is not clear whether this too is the case where the focus of the investigation is not of enormous general public interest. The extent to which answers given to coercive questioning can be used as evidence in subsequent prosecutions was held to be a matter for determination by the trial judge at that stage.

17–133   In proceedings in Canada involving Lord Conrad Black and the manner in which he managed the Hollinger companies (which owned, *inter alia*, the *Daily Telegraph*), he unsuccessfully claimed the privilege, where he was facing a prosecution in the US for how he managed those companies.[318] If a predominant purpose of the investigation was to get the witness to incriminate himself, the court may conclude that the privilege should obtain. But the purpose of the investigation there was to provide information to a public company's shareholders as to how its directors discharged their fiduciary duty to it. Because it was almost inevitable that, under the US–Canada mutual assistance treaty, the US authorities would seek access to the transcripts of his evidence, the court indicated that the judge who would deal with the application under that treaty would have to take account of the privilege then.

17–134   Confidentiality of information obtained by an inspector on foot of a production order or search warrant is protected by penal sanctions.[319] Where a company's employees have given evidence to an inspector, that company has no entitlement vis-à-vis the inspector to be furnished with a transcript of what they said.[320] But in appropriate circumstances, the court will grant persons access to those transcripts.[321] For instance, in the *Countyglen* proceedings,[322] some of the defendants got discovery orders permitting them to inspect the transcripts. In *Re Ansbacher (Caymen) Ltd*,[323] where the inspector unearthed evidence of a large scale and extremely sophisticated tax fraud, the court permitted the Revenue Commissioners to see transcripts but subject to certain conditions. The inspectors resisted the application because information and

---

[316] 1990 Act, s.18(1).
[317] [1999] 3 I.R. 145.
[318] *Catalyst Fund General Partners Inc. v Hollinger Inc.*, 261 D.L.R. (4th) 591 (2005).
[319] 1990 Act, s.21.
[320] *Re National Irish Bank (No. 4)* [2005] 3 I.R. 90.
[321] *British and Commonwealth Holdings Plc v Barclays de Zoete Wedd Ltd* [1999] 1 B.C.L.C. 86.
[322] *Countyglen Plc v Carway* [1998] 2 I.R. 540.
[323] [2004] 3 I.R. 193.

documents were supplied to them on the understanding that they were confidential and, if the information sought were then disclosed, that might jeopardise future investigations. Disclosure was confined to information about clients of the bank that was being investigated and persons who had failed to cooperate with the inspector's inquiries. In another *National Irish Bank* case,[324] in their report the inspectors were severely critical of members of the bank's audit committee but did not name them. An application by the DCE to have their names disclosed was rejected by Kelly J. on the grounds, *inter alia*, that the DCE already knew who those persons were and, further, no substantial benefit could be achieved by disclosing their identities, other than setting the DCE's mind at rest about the matter.

17–135　Where persons are likely to be criticised in a report, they are entitled to be given copies of the intended contents, so that they can comment on them before it is published.[325] This arises only at a comparatively late stage in the process and not at the earlier information-gathering phase.

The Report

17–136　The process concludes with the inspector delivering his report. The only stipulation about what it should contain is that it may recommend who should be required to pay for the inspection[326] and it must do so where the court so directs.

17–137　In the case of a DCE appointee, no special provision is made for reporting. In the case of a court appointee, he must make his final report to the court. He may be required by the court to make one or more interim reports to it before concluding his investigation. In coming to a conclusion or forming an opinion in the report, the inspector is not bound by the rules of evidence admissible in court proceedings. Where he is reaching a conclusion particularly adverse to a person or body, he very likely will endeavour to base it on evidence that is so admissible. Even if he cannot reach a definite conclusion about a matter he is charged to investigate but can form an opinion about it, ordinarily he has a duty to express that opinion.[327]

17–138　A copy of all reports to it must be delivered by the court to the DCE and there are a variety of persons and bodies to whom it may be furnish copies, namely: the persons who sought the inspection; any person whose conduct is referred to in the report; the company's auditors; any member of the company; any other person whose financial interests seem to be affected by the report's contents; the Central Bank; the Revenue Commissioners; the Irish Financial Services Regulatory Authority and the Minister.

---

[324] *Re National Irish Bank (No. 3)* [2004] 4 I.R. 186.
[325] *Maxwell v Dept of Trade and Industry* [1974] Q.B. 523.
[326] 1990 Act, s.13(3).
[327] *Lyons v Curran* [1993] I.L.R.M. 375.

17–139　Almost invariably the court will direct that the report should be published. Where it is to be disseminated among any of the above-mentioned parties or to be published, the court may order that certain sensitive matters be omitted. On being so published, the report's contents are privileged.[328]

Aftermath

17–140　In the light of the contents, the court is given a broad discretion about what should be done about a report to it: it "may make such orders as it deems fit".[329] One such order is that the company be wound up. Another is to "remedy any disability suffered by any person whose interests were adversely affected by the conduct of the affairs of the company, provided that ... the court shall have regard to the interests of any other persons who may be adversely affected by the order".[330] This was the basis in the *Ansbacher* case[331] for Finnegan P. allowing the Revenue limited access to the transcripts of evidence taken. In contrast, in one of the *National Irish Bank* cases,[332] Kelly J. expressed the view that there was no jurisdiction to make an order that would involve the inspectors, in one manner or another, revisiting issues that were in their final report, as to do so would be incompatible with its finality. The judge declined to order that the identities of persons referred to but not named in the report be revealed to the DCE. Arising from the contents of a report or any information obtained by the DCE under the above procedures, he may petition to have the company wound up on just and equitable grounds.[333]

17–141　Expenses of conducting an inspection are borne in the first instance by the Minister.[334] But the court has a broad discretion to direct that all or part of those expenses be borne by either a company that is the subject of the report or by the person who applied for the investigation; the latter's liability in this regard cannot exceed €317,435. Often an inspector's report will recommend who shall be required to pay those expenses. In the *Siucre Éireann cpt* case,[335] Lynch J. held that generally the Minister should be reimbursed by the company or companies under investigation or dealt with in the report; they in turn may be able to recoup all or some of that sum, as described below. But it was held that in the circumstances there, the companies should not be required to pay the Minister because the alleged wrongdoings that gave rise to the investigation had all take place at a time when 70 per cent of the shares in those companies were owned by the Minister. Although he was not aware of those transactions then, it was felt unfair that in substance those who had acquired those shares from him, in the companies' privatisation, should be required to foot the bill for what had occurred when he controlled the companies.

---

[328] 1990 Act, s.23(3).

[329] 1990 Act, s.12(1).

[330] 1990 Act, s.12(1)(b).

[331] [2004] 3 I.R. 193.

[332] *Re National Irish Bank (No. 4)* [2005] 3 I.R. 90.

[333] 1990 Act, s.12(2).

[334] 1990 Act, s.13.

[335] *Minister for Industry & Commerce v Siucre Eireann cpt* [1992] 2 I.R. 215.

Substantial unpaid tax liabilities had been unearthed by the inspectors but, since the companies had been privatised on the basis that such liabilities did not exist, the State had thereby gained on the price it got for the Minister's shares, and the wholly innocent present shareholders were not to be penalised for the benefit of the State. Additionally, the companies had incurred very substantial expenses themselves in the entire investigative process.

17–142 One of the companies whose affairs were considered in the report was registered in Jersey, for the purpose of acquiring shares in one of the holding company's subsidiaries. Because it did not carry on any business in the State,[336] nor was it a company the subject of the investigation, there was no jurisdiction to require it to pay any of the expenses, even though it had been "dealt with" in the report.[337]

17–143 Where as a result of the investigation, a person is convicted on indictment of an offence, or is ordered to pay damages or to restore property, or he obtains damages or property is returned to him, he can be required to repay all or part of the expenses incurred, either to the Minister or to such other person as he is ordered to repay those expenses. Where the basis of a repayment order is that the person was awarded damages or received property, he cannot be required to pay more than one tenth of the value of what he recovered and, further, any obligation to repay does not become effective until he has actually recovered.

17–144 It appears that the contents of a report can be relied on as evidence in any civil action; inspectors' reports are stated to be "admissible in any civil proceedings as evidence of the facts set out therein without further proof unless the contrary is shown".[338] In *Countyglen Plc v Carway*,[339] it was held by Laffoy J. that what is being rendered admissible are findings of primary facts that are clearly expressed as such, not deductions from any facts found. The analogy is with how factual matters under appeal are treated by the Supreme Court, where the distinction is between the very basic facts that are found and secondary or inferred facts. It is any of those findings that are rendered admissible, regardless of whether or not they were permitted to be circulated or published. No indication was given as to what weight should be given to those findings. It was contended that to give such evidential status to these reports would be unconstitutional but, in the event, those proceedings settled and the constitutional issue was never determined.

---

[336] 1990 Act, s.17.
[337] [1992] 2 I.R. 215 at 230–232.
[338] 1990 Act, s.22.
[339] [1998] 2 I.R. 540.

CHAPTER 18

CONTRACTS AND LIABILITY

18–01   Apart from their obligations to their members under their memoranda and articles of association, such as to pay dividends when duly declared, companies incur legal liability by being bound by contracts and by certain other consensual acts. Additionally, liability can be imposed on companies extra-contractually and for crimes committed in connection with their activities, and also for contempt of court. Because companies are pure legal constructs and depend on activity by individuals to function, the circumstances in which they can incur legal liability are based principally on the common law rules of agency and vicarious liability, and also statutory attribution, which are supplemented by provisions specific to company law.

18–02   With regard to contractual liability,[1] it must first be established that the person who negotiated the transaction in question was authorised by the company to do so. The transaction may be *ultra vires* the company; or its own regulations may place other restrictions on that agent's power to act. Subject to what is said below, since companies' memoranda and articles of association are public documents, those dealing with companies are deemed to know their contents; they have "constructive notice" of companies' objects and any other restrictions that these documents impose on company agents' authority.[2] In the past, companies would not be bound by contracts made on their behalf but contrary to such restrictions. Nor would companies be held to contracts made for them before they were incorporated. Nor could companies ratify either *ultra vires* or pre-incorporation contracts. Doing business with companies, therefore, presented special risks, in that contracts and other undertakings entered into with them could transpire not to be legally binding on them.

18–03   These very questions were the subject of the EC's First Directive on Company Law.[3] According to the central part of its preamble, "[w]hereas the basic documents of the company should be disclosed in order that third parties may be able to ascertain their contents and other information concerning the company, especially particulars of the persons who are authorised to bind the company; Whereas the protection of third parties must be ensured by provisions which restrict to the greatest possible extent the grounds on which obligations entered into in the name of the company are not valid …" Most of the

---

[1]   See generally, A. Griffiths, *Contracting With Companies* (Oxford: Hart, 2005).
[2]   *Ernest v Nicholls* (1857) 6 H.L. Cas. 401.
[3]   [1968] O.J.L65/41 (1968) (repealed).

matters that this Directive and also the Second Directive call to be disclosed were covered by the 1963 Act's requirements. Two of the principal legal traps, into which persons doing business with companies could fall, were removed by that Act, that dealt with pre-incorporation agreements and *ultra vires* engagements, respectively. Statutory Instrument 163 of 1973[4] deals with another of these pitfalls.

18–04 Account ought to be taken of the terms and background of EC Directives in construing legislation enacted to implement their terms into national law. In one English case regarding pre-incorporation agreements, the Court of Appeal examined carefully the relevant parts of the First Directive and even its background in French law.[5] Sections 37 and 8(1) of the 1963 Act were enacted in anticipation of this First Directive, which was not cast in its final form until 1968. There are some differences in terminology between key phrases in the Directive and in these sections, notably in respect of the degree of knowledge a third party dealing with the company must possess in order to attract certain legal consequences. Section 37(2) uses the term "express agreement to the contrary"; s.8(1) talks of being "actually aware" that the company lacks the requisite capacity. The need for consistency in commercial law and practice would suggest that, where possible, account should be taken of the EC measure when interpreting these sections.

FORMALITIES

18–05 Being entirely artificial persons in law, formerly companies could not make written contracts otherwise than under seal; having a seal was one of Blackstone's attributes of corporate personality.[6] Under the heading "Contracts, Deeds and Powers of Attorney", the 1963 Act sets down rules as to the minimum formalities for companies making contracts, and issuing bills of exchange and promissory notes.[7] The contracts rule is simply that the same formalities are required as if the transaction in question was one between individuals; there are no peremptory special requirements for companies regarding seals, counter-signatures and the like. Thus a company must use a seal or writing, or provide evidence in writing, as the case may be, only where those forms are demanded by the general law.[8] There are special statutory provisions regarding executing deeds and transacting other business abroad.[9]

---

4 European Communities (Companies) Regulations 1973.
5 *Phonogram Ltd v Lane* [1982] 1 Q.B. 938.
6 See para.3–03.
7 Sections 38 and 39.
8 See generally, P. McDermott, *Contract Law* (Dublin: Butterworths, 2001), p.912 *et seq.* and H. Beale *et al*, *Chitty on Contracts*, 29th edn (London: Thomson Sweet & Maxwell, 2004), Ch. 9.
9 See para.21–15 and 16.

Company Seal

18–06 Every company is required to have a seal with its name engraved on it.[10] It is usual for the seal to be put under the control of the directors or a committee of them.[11] Transactions that still need a seal for their execution include conveyances of land,[12] granting a power of attorney[13] and issuing certificates of title to shares.[14] Although debentures are usually issued under seal, it is not necessary that they take this form;[15] all that is required is some written instrument which is capable of being registered as a company charge. In *Re A Debtor's Summons*,[16] it was held that a legal assignment by a company of debts must be sealed because that transaction was not a "contract". Kennedy C.J. there could "not (though Parliament might if it intended so to do) stretch the denotation of the ordinary word 'contract' to include within it 'an absolute assignment', nor of the expression 'party to be charged therewith' to include a simple assignor of a piece of property or right".[17] Perhaps the assignment of chattels or of choses in action by way of security might be treated differently but, in the light of this decision, the prudent course is to execute the debenture under seal.

18–07 Where inadvertently the company's seal did not have its registered name engraved on it but, instead, its trading name was engraved and affixed on the document, the question arose whether that document was a deed.[18] It was a bond given by insurers for the performance of certain obligations undertaken by the company. Although the strict requirements of the Companies Act 1985 had not been complied with, it was held that beneficiaries of the document were entitled to treat it as a deed, as to hold otherwise would unjustly enrich the insurers and would be a disproportionate burden on innocent parties who sought to rely on the document. In those circumstances, the officer or agent of the company who was responsible for affixing the seal could have been made personally liable to a small fine.

Bills of Exchange and Cheques

18–08 A bill of exchange, cheque or promissory note issued by a company does not have to be sealed.[19] Any person who is duly authorised to do so may make, accept or endorse a bill or note for or on behalf of a company.[20] When signing cheques, bills and the like, company officers should make sure that the

---

[10] 1963 Act, s.114(1)(b).
[11] e.g. art.115 of Table A.
[12] *Catley Farms Ltd v ANZ Banking Group* [1982] 1 N.Z.L.R. 430 at 437.
[13] 1963 Act, s.40.
[14] 1963 Act, s.87.
[15] *Re Fireproof Doors Ltd* [1916] 2 Ch. 142
[16] [1929] I.R. 129.
[17] *ibid.* at 145–146.
[18] *OTV Birwelco Ltd v Technical & General Guarantee Co.* [2002] 2 B.C.L.C. 723.
[19] Bills of Exchange Act 1882, s.91(2).
[20] 1963 Act, s.39. See generally, M. Hapgood ed., *Paget's Law of Banking*, 13th edn (London: Lexis Nexis Butterworths, 2007), at 180–182.

company's name is clearly and correctly stated, and that it is stipulated that they are signing on its behalf; otherwise, they can incur personal liability on the instrument.[21] However, misdescribing the company in a bill or even in a deed does not exonerate it from liability, as extrinsic evidence is admissible to prove the identity of the party. Unless there has been misdescription or there are other relevant indicia to the contrary, the authorised signatory to a company cheque is not personally liable on it.[22]

Related Party Transactions

18–09 A related party transaction is a contract between a company and one or more of its managers or shareholders. Because such transactions can involve a conflict of interest, at times resulting in the other party making an undue profit at the company's expense, they are subject to a variety of regulations that do not apply to contracts with corporate "outsiders". In the case of companies with securities that are listed on the Irish Stock Exchange, additional rules exist for related party transactions.[23]

Contracts with Directors and Associates

18–10 On account of the conflict that can arise when a director is concluding a contract with his company, equity, the articles of association and numerous statutory provisions impose safeguards, to ensure that unfair advantage is not taken of the company.[24] Where a director is in any way interested, directly or indirectly, in a contract that his company is about to conclude, he must disclose the nature of that interest to his fellow directors. Where a company proposes to acquire a substantial asset from a director or to dispose of such an asset to him, the transaction requires general meeting approval. Making loans to directors or granting them "quasi-loans" or entering other "credit transactions" with them is strictly regulated. Most of these restrictions also apply where the other party to the transaction is a "connected person".

Contracts with Members

18–11 There are four main categories of regulation for contracts between a company and one or more of its members. One relates to subscription contracts, where the company agrees to allot shares for a non-cash consideration. In the case of such contracts with Plcs, certain forms of consideration are not allowed and there are requirements for independent valuation of property acquired in exchange for shares.[25] Related to this is the valuation needed where property is acquired from a Plc's promoters in the first two years of its existence.[26] Where shares are being offered for subscription or for sale that are or are about to be listed on a recognised stock exchange, rigorous prospectus rules

---

[21] 1963 Act, s.114 and see para.7–156.
[22] *Bondina Ltd v Rollaway Shower Blinds Ltd* [1986] 1 W.L.R. 517.
[23] Listing Rule 8.
[24] See para.7–55 *et seq.*
[25] See para.15–18 *et seq.*
[26] See para.15–11 *et seq.*

apply. There are share buy-back contracts, whereby a company purchases its own shares or redeems them. These are subject to a regime that principally ensures that contributed capital is not unduly depleted.[27] There are contracts with controlling shareholders, where the main concern is to prevent unfair advantage being taken due to conflicts of interest. Almost invariably, the contracting party here will be either a director of the company or a person with whom he is connected.[28]

Finally, there are the provisions for where a one member company contracts with its sole member[29] who represents the company in the transaction. If the contract is not in the ordinary course of business and is not in writing, its terms should be reduced to writing and recorded in the minutes of the next directors' meeting, following the contract being made. But failure to so does not affect the contract's validity.

PRE-INCORPORATION ACTS

18–12   Before a company is incorporated, it is common for promoters to enter into various arrangements on its behalf, like hiring staff and purchasing stocks. In the *Salomon & Co.* case,[30] for instance, the plaintiff had made a preliminary agreement with a trustee for the future company setting out the generous terms on which the company, when incorporated, would acquire the plaintiff's business. It is a general principle of contract law that a contract cannot be made on behalf of a non-existent principal, and any such contract purported to have been made cannot subsequently be given legal effect by a principal coming into being and ratifying it.[31] Therefore, pre-incorporation contracts made on behalf of companies could not on their incorporation bind them,[32] nor could they be ratified by the company.[33] In the past, the way legal effect was given to those contracts was for the company, on becoming incorporated, to enter into new contracts similar to the pre-incorporation engagements.

18–13   Persons dealing with embryo and newly-formed companies used to fall into the trap of discovering that their only security was a pre-incorporation agreement that was not enforceable against the company. They nevertheless might have a claim against the person who purported to make the contract for the company. There were no hard and fast rules as to when the so-called agent could be held personally responsible or when he could enforce the contract in his own name.[34] In *Kelner v Baxter*,[35] it was suggested that, in the absence of

---

[27]   See para.8–103 *et seq* and 15–28 *et seq*.

[28]   See para.7–55 *et seq*.

[29]   European Communities (Single Member Private Limited Companies) Regulations 1994 (SI 1994/275), reg.13.

[30]   [1897] A.C. 22.

[31]   See generally, F.M.B. Reynolds *Bowstead and Reynolds on Agency*, 18th edn (London: Sweet & Maxwell, 2005).

[32]   *Kelner v Baxter* (1866) L.R. 2 C.P. 174.

[33]   *Re Empress Engineering Co.* [1880] 16 Ch D 126.

[34]   See generally, Gross, "Pre-Incorporation Contracts" 87 *L.Q.R.* 367 (1971).

[35]   (1866) L.R. 2 C.P. 174.

adequate indications by them to the contrary, the actual signatories are personally liable "where a contract is signed by one who professes to be signing 'as agent', but who has no principal existing at the time, and the contract would be altogether inoperative unless binding upon the person who signed it, he is bound thereby".[36] The defendants, who were to be directors of a company in the process of formation, agreed to purchase stock that was offered to them, "on behalf of the proposed ... company"; they signed the stock list with their names "on behalf of the" company. In the light of the above principle, it was held that they were personally liable on the contract and that the rider to their signature "operate[d] no more than if a person should contract for a quantity of corn 'on behalf of my horses'".[37] But in a later instance it was in effect held that the agent's right to sue on, and incur liability under, the contract could be excluded where the contract purports to be made by the (non-existent) company itself rather than by somebody on its behalf.[38] A New Zealand judge sought to explain the cases in this area by saying that "there is, or should be, a presumption of personal liability so long as a presently binding contract is intended", but that "the result of each case will depend on its particular facts".[39] It was held by Barron J. in *Inver Resources Ltd v Limerick Corp.*[40] that an application for planning permission by a company that was not in existence at the time is not an entire nullity and a decision to grant it permission was not invalid. The uncertain status of pre-incorporation contracts has been the subject of considerable criticism.

Binding the Company

18–14 The principle that pre-incorporation acts are incapable of being ratified by the company was reversed to implement the EC First Directive.[41] A company can ratify any contract or other transaction made on its behalf or purportedly by it prior to its incorporation.[42] The effect of the ratification is to subject the company to all the liabilities and confer on it all the rights arising from the transaction as if the company had existed at the time the transaction had been concluded.[43] It was held in the *HKN Invest* case[44] that a company, even in liquidation, can ratify a pre-incorporation contract, even though a breach of its terms has occurred. Ratification there meant that "as a matter of law the contracts will have existed from their date of execution—it will not affect the

---

[36] *ibid.* at 183.

[37] *ibid.* at 185.

[38] *Newborne v Sensolid (Great Britain) Ltd* [1954] 1 Q.B. 45.

[39] *Marblestone Industries Ltd v Fairchild* [1975] 1 N.Z.L.R. 529 at 542.

[40] [1987] I.R. 159.

[41] See generally, B. Markesenis, "The Law of Agency and Section 9(2) of the European Communities Act, 1972" 32 *Cam. L.J.* 112 (1976).

[42] 1963 Act, s.37(1), e.g. *Clark v Libra Developments Ltd* [2007] 2 N.Z.L.R. 709.

[43] *cf. State (Finglas Industrial Estates) Ltd v Dublin County Council* [1983] I.E.S.C. 32, unreported, February 17, 1983.

[44] *HK Invest OY v Incotrade PVT Ltd* [1993] 3 I.R. 152. For a discussion of the case, see N. Steen, "Constructive Trusts and Pre-Incorporation Contracts: A Reappraisal" 26 *D.U.L.J.* 260 (2004).

rights of either party arising from the manner in which the contract has or has not been performed since then".[45]

18–15 Ratification need not comply with any particular formalities. It was held in *Taylor v Todd*,[46] concerning a contract to purchase land, that it could not be ratified by a company as purchaser because the identity of the purchaser was not determined until three-and-a-half years after that agreement had been reached. It was not a pre-incorporation contract as envisaged by the statute.

The "Agent's" Position

18–16 Another objective of the EC First Directive was to cut through the uncertainty surrounding *Kelner v Baxter*[47] and later cases, and establish a clear principle that, where there is no agreement to the contrary, persons who contract on behalf of an unincorporated company are fully liable on the contract until the company becomes a party to it. Up to the time when the company ratifies the contract, the persons who purported to act for or behalf of the company are personally bound by it.[48] They also are entitled to enforce the contract.[49] But their personal liability and benefit can be excluded by "express agreement to the contrary". The understanding negating the so-called agent's personal liability or entitlement under the contract, therefore, cannot arise by implication from the circumstances. In *Phonogram Ltd v Lane*,[50] which concerned the similar provisions of the British law, it was said that any purported exclusion of the agent's personal liability must be clear and unambiguous; that "where a person purports to contract on behalf of a company not yet formed, then however he expresses his signature he himself is personally liable on the contract ... unless there is a clear exclusion of personal liability ...".[51]

Transitional Agreements

18–17 A person may have been dealing with a partnership which, unknown to him, is converted into a registered company with the same name as that used by the partners. Any contracts made for the company before it is actually registered are governed by the principles set out above. As for post-registration contracts, it depends on the intentions of the parties whether the company is liable or liability can be imposed on the former partners.[52] For instance, in *Smallman Ltd v O'Moore*,[53] the partners publicised to some extent the conversion of their business but the plaintiff continued supplying goods to the business without

---

[45] [1993] 3 I.R. 152 at 161.
[46] [2004] 3 N.Z.L.R. 76.
[47] (1866) L.R. 2 C.P. 174.
[48] 1963 Act, s.37(2).
[49] *cf. Braymist Ltd v Wise Finance Co.* [2002] 1 B.C.L.C. 415.
[50] [1982] 1 Q.B. 938.
[51] *ibid.* at 944. See generally, Green, "Security of Transactions After *Phonogram*" 47 *Mod. L. Rev.* 671 (1984).
[52] *Pitner Lighting Co. of Ireland v Geddis and Pickering* [1912] 2 I.R. 163.
[53] [1959] I.R. 220.

knowing about the change. It was held that the parties were not *ad idem*, the plaintiff believing he was dealing with partners but the defendants dealing on behalf of their new company. However, the company had to pay for whatever goods it had accepted and used. Neither fraud nor estoppel were pleaded here. In the case of contracts made by a company which is in the process of changing its name—made in the new name but before the certificate of incorporation in that name has been issued—the company is liable on those contracts. An individual acting for the company in such a case is not personally liable as in the case of pre-incorporation contracts.[54]

Pre-Trading Certificate Contracts

18–18   A public company that has issued a prospectus inviting subscriptions for its shares is not permitted to commence business or to borrow until certain formalities have been complied with. Any contracts made or ratified by a company before it becomes entitled to do business are "provisional only" and do not bind the company until it has satisfied the above formalities.[55] On the other hand, the prohibition against a Plc from doing business until it is issued with an appropriate certificate does not invalidate any contracts that the company has concluded, but the directors can be required to indemnify the other party for any loss that he suffered in consequence.[56]

CAPACITY AND *ULTRA VIRES*

18–19   A company acts *ultra vires* when it enters into some transaction that falls outside of its objects or is otherwise prohibited by the Companies Acts.[57] In the *Rolled Steel Products Ltd* case,[58] it was stressed that *ultra vires* should not be confused with excess of authority; the former concerns the very capacity of the company to enter into transactions, the latter concerns whether those who concluded the transaction were duly authorised to do so by the company. The fact that the directors entered into a transaction for an improper purpose does not *ipso facto* render it *ultra vires*.[59] A transaction may also be *ultra vires* because it contravenes some separate statutory provision, be it in the Companies Acts or elsewhere, or exceptionally by virtue of public policy. For instance, before a statutory regime specific to the question was enacted,[60] any agreement made by a company that involved it financing the purchase of its own shares was *ultra vires*, "illegal and wholly void."[61]

---

[54]   *Badgerhill Properties Ltd v Cottrell* [1991] B.C.L.C. 805.
[55]   1963 Act, s.115(4).
[56]   1983 Act, s.6(8).
[57]   See para.3–28 *et seq*.
[58]   *Rolled Steel Products (Holdings) Ltd v British Steel Corp.* [1986] 1 Ch. 246.
[59]   See generally, Baxter, "Ultra Vires and Agency Untwined" 28 *Cam. L.J.* 280 (1970).
[60]   1963 Act, s.60.
[61]   *Re MJ Cummins Ltd* [1939] I.R. 60 at 71.

18–20   It was held in the *Ashbury Railway Carriage Co.* case[62] that *ultra vires* transactions are void and cannot be ratified by the company on whose behalf they are entered into. But this principle often operated most unfairly against persons dealing with companies in the utmost good faith. Whether this bar on ratification remains the law today is debatable because, under the 1963 Act,[63] it became possible for the members to change their company's objects. There are numerous instances of company liquidators successfully invoking *ultra vires* to defeat claims by small traders against companies that were engaged in some business not referred to in the objects clause. For example, in *Re Jan Beauforte (London) Ltd*,[64] without changing its objects, a company that had been incorporated to make women's dresses, embarked on the business of household furnishing. This latter business proved to be a failure and the company was forced into liquidation. It was held that the debts it had incurred in the course of its furnishing business were *ultra vires* and that even its supplier of coke fuel, which could equally have been consumed in the original as in the latter business, could not recover sums owing to it. It is somewhat unrealistic to expect small traders to check a company's objects clause every time they intend to sell something to it. Indeed, persons who examine objects clauses at times come away with the mistaken impression that the transaction in question is not *ultra vires*. An intelligent individual seeing the objects clause in the *Ashbury Railway Carriage Co.* case could quite easily have come to the conclusion that the company there was authorised to engage in general contracting works like financing the construction of railways. Nor could the objects clause in *Northern Bank Finance Corp. v Quinn*[65] be described as unambiguous.

18–21   Another objective of the EC First Directive was to protect persons dealing with companies from being caught in the *ultra vires* trap. It stipulates that,

> "[a]cts done by the organs of a company shall be binding upon it even if those acts are not within the objects of the company ... However, Member States may provide that the company shall not be bound where such acts are outside the objects of the company, if it proves that the third party knew that the act was outside those objects or could not in view of the circumstances have been unaware of it; disclosure of the statutes shall not of itself be sufficient proof thereof".[66]

Section 8(1) of the 1963 Act is almost identically worded:

> "[a]ny act or thing done by a company which if the company had been empowered to do the same would have been lawfully and effectively done, shall, notwithstanding that the company had no power to do such act or thing, be effective in favour of any person relying on such act or thing who is not shown to have been actually aware, at the time when he so relied thereon, that such act or thing was not within the powers of the company ...".

---

[62]   *Ashbury Railway Carriage & Iron Co. v Riche* (1875) L.R. 7 HL 653.
[63]   Section 10.
[64]   [1953] 1 Ch. 131.
[65]   [1979] I.L.R.M. 221.
[66]   Article 9(1).

This section has been supplemented by reg.6 of the European Communities (Companies) Regulations 1973,[67] which may encapsule *ultra vires* transactions as well as transactions which otherwise are beyond an authority given in the memorandum or articles of association; reg.6 is widely accepted as applying to traditional *ultra vires* as well. But it does not give persons dealing with companies any greater protection than that arising from the 1963 Act.

Binding the Company

18–22   The following questions arise in considering the extent to which, by virtue of s.8(1), *ultra vires* contracts and transactions are made legally effective:

18–23   *Parties Affected:* It does not merely enable outsiders to sue companies on what heretofore were *ultra vires* acts. "Any person" is entitled to its benefit. Thus, even "insiders", such as the principal shareholders and directors, may be able to sue on such acts, out provided that the *scienter* requirement, explained below, is satisfied.

18–24   *Things Affected:* It does not speak of contracts or transactions but of "[a]ny act or thing done" by a company. Accordingly, even non-contractual engagements fall within its scope, like gifts and promises of gifts that are completely "sterile", and torts and other breaches of legal duties committed in the course of *ultra vires* activities.

18–25   *Scienter:* It renders legally effective the act or thing done by the company provided that the person in question "is not shown to have been actually aware, at the time when he so relied thereon", that it was *ultra vires*. That is to say, if it is proved that the person in fact knew that the contract or act in question was *ultra vires*, then s.8(1) will not render that transaction effective. The EC formulation of this requirement is phrased more flexibly; it speaks of a person who "could not in view of all the circumstances have been unaware of" the engagement falling outside the objects clause; reg.6 of the 1973 Regulations referred to above speaks of a person" dealing ... in good faith" with a company. The question therefore has arisen whether the term "actually aware" extends beyond proved knowledge of *ultra vires*, i.e. beyond unequivocal recognition that the company had no legal capacity to do what it was purporting to do.

18–26   In *Northern Bank Finance Corp. v Quinn*,[68] the bank loaned the defendant money, taking as security a guarantee given by his unlimited investment company. Since that guarantee transpired to be *ultra vires*, the bank sought to rely on s.8(1) to validate it. But it was argued that, in the circumstances, the bank should have known the guarantee was *ultra vires* and, consequently, it had no rights under the section. While there was no convincing proof that the bank's solicitor saw the company's objects, it was held that in the light of the normal

---

[67]   SI 1973/163.
[68]   [1979] I.L.R.M. 221.

practice "the probabilities are" that he did read the memorandum but mistakenly concluded that the guarantee was *intra vires*. Thus, he was aware of the contents of the objects clause".[69] But was he "actually aware" that the company was exceeding its powers? Keane J. held that he was, reasoning that

> "the section was designed to ensure that ... persons who had entered into transactions in good faith with the company without ever reading the memorandum and accordingly with no actual knowledge that the transaction was *ultra vires* were not to suffer. I can see no reason in logic or justice why the legislature should have intended to afford the same protection to persons who had actually read the memorandum and simply failed to appreciate the lack of vires.
>
> [W]here a party is shown to have been actually aware of the contents of the memorandum but failed to appreciate that the company were not empowered thereby to enter into the transaction in issue, section 8(1) has no application."[70]

18–27 Perhaps a more convincing way of coming to this conclusion might be to place emphasis on the Directive's "could not in view of all the circumstances have been unaware" formula.[71] Accordingly, knowledge of the actual contents of the memorandum is treated as knowing what the company's objects are. It remains to be seen whether this principle equally applies to the legally unsophisticated person who may have seen the memorandum and the objects clause but did not appreciate their full significance. Another matter to be resolved is the position of the party who deliberately refrains from reading the memorandum which has been made available for his perusal.

18–28 One would have hoped that the Supreme Court would have clarified the position in *Re Frederick Inns Ltd*[72] but, instead, its decision introduces considerable confusion. Under threat of being wound up by the Revenue, a group of companies made a settlement of outstanding tax liabilities. This involved some companies in the group, which were insolvent, making payments in respect of the liabilities of other group companies. Lardner J. held that those payments were *ultra vires* and would be so even if the companies were not insolvent. Because, from the information at the Revenue's disposal, it should have known that those paying companies were insolvent, the judge held that the Revenue was sufficiently aware that the payments it received were *ultra vires*; the Revenue knew of those companies' precarious financial circumstances and must be presumed to know the law, that one company in a group cannot gratuitously alienate its property for the benefit of another group company. On appeal, however, Blaney J. for the Court found that (subject to what is said below) the Revenue could rely on s.8(1) because the tax official there "seems generally to have been of the belief that he was dealing with a group of

---

[69] *ibid.* at 228.
[70] *ibid.* at 229.
[71] *cf. International Sales Agencies Ltd v Marcus* [1982] 3 All E.R. 551.
[72] [1991] I.L.R.M 582 (H.C.); [1994] I.L.R.M. 387 (S.C.).

companies and that the payment was being made by some of the companies within the group on behalf of the entire group".[73]

18–29 In principle, "insiders" can rely on s.8(1). But this is subject to the proviso that they are not "actually aware" that the act in question is *ultra vires*. If "actually aware" is interpreted in the light of the Directive, then it would be only in the most exceptional circumstances that insiders can avail of the section. The company itself would have to be treated as being "actually aware" of what its own objects are.

18–30 *Extent of Validation:* What is saved from invalidity are engagements and the like that in the past would be *ultra vires* because they fell outside the company's objects. Whether s.8(1) goes further and validates other company transactions, like arrangements that contravene provisions of the Companies Acts, is an open question; probably not. The First Directive envisages only *ultra vires* in the traditional sense of outside the objects; the parallel provisions in the British law have been said to give relief only against "the old *ultra vires* doctrine".[74]

18–31 The Supreme Court's decision in *Re Frederick Inns Ltd*[75] introduces further confusion here. Having held that the Revenue there did not have the requisite *scienter* ("actually aware") to have the transactions invalidated, the Court went on to find that, by paying the Revenue, the companies' directors had been in breach of their fiduciary duty to the general creditors. Accordingly, Blayney J. concluded, those payments were not "lawfully and effectively done", which took them outside s.8(1) entirely. This does not seem right, as the "lawfully and effectively done" caveat appears to mean no more than that s.8(1) "saving" a transaction does not mean that the company is automatically bound by it. Rather, this "saving" is without prejudice to any other defence the company may be entitled to raise. The view that company directors owe fiduciary duties to the general creditors is questionable and the cases relied on by Blayney J. do not support the proposition.[76] Even if there were such a duty and it was broken, that can have nothing to do with *ultra vires*, which concerns the intrinsic capacity of companies to conclude transactions, as opposed to whether directors are abusing their powers. Accepting that the gratuitous payments there were *ultra vires* (the companies making them were insolvent)[77] but that the Revenue were not "actually aware" of that infirmity, then it must follow that the Revenue was entitled to rely on s.8(1) regardless of what was deemed to be the directors' breaches of duties. Of course, it does not automatically follow that contracts made in such circumstances bind the company if, under the general law of agency, the other party (the Revenue here) has notice

---

[73] [1984] I.L.R.M 387 at 394.
[74] See fn.72 above at 559.
[75] [1994] 1 I.L.R.M. 387.
[76] See para.20–09. See generally, Fealy, "The Role of Equity in the Winding Up of a Company" (1995) *D.U.L.J.* 18.
[77] Compare *Re PMPA Garage (Longmile) Ltd* [1992] 1 I.R. 315.

of directors' breaches of duty that would render the payments voidable at the company's instigation.[78] In such a case, the company would be entitled to recover the money for the benefit of its general creditors, including the Revenue. According to the Court, directors of insolvent companies hold corporate assets in trust for the general creditors; accordingly, the Revenue held the money it got under a resulting trust for them and was not entitled to set off that money against its own legitimate Revenue claims.

Officer Liability

18–32   Any company that suffers loss in consequence of s.8(1) validating an *ultra vires* transaction is empowered to claim compensation against any director or officer who was "responsible" for actually concluding the transaction in question. It is not clear whether liability under this is founded on negligence principles or is strict or absolute. The court possesses a discretion to exonerate the officer from liability in appropriate circumstances.[79]

Restitution and *Ultra Vires* Transactions

18–33   Apart entirely from s.8(1), companies ordinarily will not be permitted to enforce contracts which are *ultra vires* their own objects. Although there are various *obiter dicta* to the contrary, the non-enforceability view was endorsed in *Cabaret Holdings Ltd v Meeanee Sports and Rodeo Club Inc.*[80] In pursuance of an agreement, the plaintiff paid expenses incurred by the defendant company and subsequently sued the defendant to recover those sums. The agreement and the payment made under it were *ultra vires* the defendant and, accordingly, the defence was that as a result the money could not be recovered. It was held that once the agreement is *ultra vires* it cannot be enforced by either party; that "[i]t is not possible for a company or incorporated society to sue upon a contract into which it has no power to enter. To say that a corporation is not barred from recovery because a transaction is *ultra vires* is one thing. To say that it may sue upon a contract which never came into existence is a wholly different thing. That conclusion may occasion some regret but we regard it in the present state of the law as inevitable".[81]

18–34   In recent years, however, there have been dramatic developments in the law of restitution that, in consequence, protects companies or their creditors from suffering undue loss where they were parties to *ultra vires* transactions.[82] Even prior to these developments, the courts were inclined to order restitution in certain discrete cases. Thus, in *Re Lough Neagh Ship Co., Ex p. Workman*,[83] a company that failed to raise the necessary capital to pay for a ship that was being built for it borrowed the funds from the plaintiff and paid the builder. Even though this

---

[78]   See para.18–51 *et seq.*
[79]   1963 Act, s.319.
[80]   [1982] 1 N.Z.L.R. 673.
[81]   *ibid.* at 676.
[82]   See generally, R. Goff & G. Jones *The Law of Restitution*, 7th edn (London: Sweet & Maxwell, 2007).
[83]   [1895] I.R. 533.

loan was outside the company's borrowing powers, it was said in the first place that "the fact that the [loan] was really an advance of capital not in existence seems … to distinguish the case from" other instances where *ultra vires* loans were held not be recoverable.[84] In any event, it was held, the plaintiff was entitled to be subrogated for the shipbuilder. According to Porter, M.R., this:

> "is the case of a person interested in the affairs of the company, discharging with the privity and consent of the company, a liability of the latter by payment. This has the effect of placing the person making the payment in the position in which the creditor stood before he was paid off. [Therefore] the claimants became equitable assignees of [the ship-builder's] rights, including the right to sue the company; and on that ground are … entitled to sustain [their] claim. There has in the result been no real borrowing by the company at all … It is simply a change of creditor, not a new debt".[85]

Where money borrowed can be traced, the lender would be entitled to a tracing order.[86] In *Flood v Irish Provident Assurance Co.*,[87] it was held that premiums paid to an insurance company on *ultra vires* policies were recoverable as money paid without consideration.

18–35 In the *Westdeutsche Landesbank* case[88] concerning controversial "interest swaps" in Britain, where many local authorities got money from banks under agreements which, it transpired, were beyond those bodies' legal capacities, it was held that those banks were entitled to reclaim the money along with simple interest. This claim was not based on there being some resulting trust or on some implied contract but was found to be a personal action for money had and received by virtue of there being a failure of consideration. The outcome there was anticipated in *Re PMPA Garage (Longmile) Ltd (No. 2)*,[89] where an industrial and provident society had lent money to several related companies but those loans were *ultra vires* the society, being contrary to the Industrial and Provident Societies Act 1893.[90] Following an extensive survey of the case law in several countries, Murphy J. concluded that the party who has obtained goods or money under an *ultra vires* transaction can be compelled to return the property. While accepting the general proposition that a body corporate cannot enforce a contract which it never had the capacity to make, the judge observed that no court would permit the manifest injustice of a party retaining money or goods he got under a contract which, inadvertently, was *ultra vires*. Of course, if the society there had been a registered company, the contract would not have been unenforcible by virtue of s.8(1) of the 1963 Act unless the other parties were "actually aware" of the infirmity.

---

[84] *ibid.* at 539.
[85] *ibid.* at 540.
[86] *Shanahan Stamp Auctions Ltd v Farrelly* [1962] I.R. 386.
[87] (1912) 46 I.L.T.R. 214, [1912] 2 Ch. 597.
[88] *Westdeutsche Landesbank Girozentrale v Islington LBC* [1996] A.C. 669.
[89] [1992] 1 I.R. 332.
[90] *Re PMPA (Longmile) Ltd* [1992] 1 I.R. 315.

AGENCY AND AUTHORITY

18–36 Pre-incorporation and *ultra vires* considerations aside, there remains the question of in what circumstances *intra vires* engagements purportedly assumed on behalf of companies bind them; in other words, when is a person empowered to act as a company's agent. Two related matters arise here. One concerns the existence of authority to act on behalf of a company and the scope or range of that authority. The other asks the same question from a negative perspective, namely, whether any restriction exists on the authority of a person *prima facie* empowered to bind the company. For instance, managing directors generally have very extensive authority but a particular company's own regulations may considerably constrict its managing director's powers, like, for example, requiring board or even general meeting approval before certain kinds of transactions can be entered into by him.

18–37 It is usual to analyse questions of authority to bind companies in terms of agency law: whether the company empowered the person in question to act for it, either actually authorised the controverted transaction or clothed the person in question with apparent authority to enter into it, and whether any apparent authority was cut down by the company's own regulations. In the most authoritative case in the entire area, *Mahony (Public Officer of National Bank of Ireland) v East Holyford Mining Co.*,[91] the House of Lords approached the issue from a comparative negligence perspective. A group of fraudsters formed a company ostensibly to work a mine in Co. Tipperary and, by issuing a prospectus, persuaded numerous members of the public to invest in it. But instead of spending investors' funds on mining equipment and the like, the fraudsters withdrew them from the company's bank account for their own use. They misled the bank into believing that they were authorised to draw cheques on behalf of the company. When what transpired was discovered, the question became who should bear the loss of the fraud: the investors or the bank that, without actual authority to do so, handed over the funds to the fraudsters? It was held that the party that had been the more careless must bear the loss, in this case, the unfortunate shareholders. According to Lord Hatherley:

> "A banker dealing with a company must be taken to be acquainted with the manner in which, under the articles of association, the moneys of the company may be drawn out of his bank for the purposes of the company …
>
> But, after that, when there are persons conducting the affairs of the company in a manner which appear to be perfectly consonant with the articles of association, then those so dealing with them, externally, are not to be affected by any irregularities which may take place in the internal management of the company …
>
> Now, if the question came to be which of two innocent parties (as it is said) was to suffer loss, I apprehend, my Lords, that in point of law what must be considered in cases of that kind is this: which of the two parties was bound to do, or to avoid, any act by which the loss has been sustained. I think there can be no doubt that in this case the shareholders

---

[91] (1875) L.R. 7 H.L. 869.

of the company were the persons who were bound to see that nobody usurped or assumed the office of director unduly.

On the other hand, on the part of the bankers, I see no possible mode by which they might have pursued their inquiries in the manner contended for at the Bar without requiring all the minute books of the company to be produced to them, and without conducting a detailed investigation into all the transactions of the company as to the appointment of directors and the like—a duty they were not called upon to perform."[92]

18–38 The same result could be reached using agency principles as follows. By their inaction, the investors led the bank to believe that the fraudsters had authority to draw funds from the company's account and the bank acted in good faith on the basis of that holding-out.

The Kinds of Authority

18–39 There are three major categories of agency.[93] An agent can be someone with "actual authority" to conclude the transaction question: he was in fact given full authority to do so, either expressly or by clear implication. Or he may have "usual" or "ostensible" authority, by which is meant the scope of authority persons holding certain positions ordinarily possess; this is very similar to implied actual authority. For instance, in the context of purchases and sales of property, solicitors, estate agents and auctioneers all have varying degrees of usual authority to act for their clients. In the absence of notice of any restrictions on an agent's powers, a principal is bound by everything an agent does within his usual authority, even if the agent is not authorised to act in certain ways. Usual authority is not nullified by actions that are fraudulent and/or in furtherance of the person's own interests or those of some third party.[94] Apparent authority or "holding-out", is where a principal leads someone to believe that a person has authority to enter into certain transactions although in fact that authority does not exist.

18–40 In the case of companies, the acts of a director are rendered valid "notwithstanding any defect which may afterwards be discovered in his appointment or qualification".[95] In *Morris v Kanssen*,[96] that section's scope was confined narrowly to mere slips and irregularities in appointments. Companies generally follow the Table A model, under which there is to be a board of directors empowered to "manage ... the business of the company", and which allows for the appointment of a managing director and the delegation of some board functions to management committees.

---

[92] *ibid.* at 894, 897 and 898.
[93] See generally, F.M.B. Reynolds *Bowstead and Reynolds on Agency*, 18th edn (London: Sweet & Maxwell, 2005).
[94] *Hopkins v TL Dallas Group Ltd* [2005] 1 B.C.L.C. 543.
[95] 1963 Act, s.178.
[96] [1946] A.C. 459.

Actual Authority

18–41   Whether a person has actual authority to act for a company in a certain way is primarily a question of fact. For instance, in *Freeman & Lockyer v Buckhurst Park Properties (Mangal) Ltd*,[97] one K, a director of a small property development company, instructed the plaintiffs to do certain work for it. In its defence to a claim for fees for that work, the company contended that K was not authorised to enter into such contracts and that he was not its managing director. It was not essential that there was a formal board resolution recorded in the minutes for him to have been authorised to act in that capacity, but there had to have been a communication to him of the directors' consent that he so act. In the event, it was held that there was insufficient evidence to support a conclusion of actual appointment to that office.[98] A leading case on the effectiveness of a "poison pill" agreement was remitted for a full trial because there was insufficient evidence to show whether or not the two directors, who had signed that agreement for the company, had been authorised by the board to do so.[99]

Usual Authority

18–42   Company boards have usual authority to enter into virtually all kinds of engagements on the company's behalf. So too have managing directors, although there is no modern case law which defines the extent of their usual authority. Executive directors have implied authority to do all such things as fall within the usual scope of their particular office.[100] But ordinary directors have practically no usual authority to bind the company. The extent or authority held by other agents of the company—for instance several directors acting together,[101] solicitors[102] and employees[103]—depends on the scope of the functions assigned to them.

18–43   In the past, company secretaries were deemed to have very limited usual authority, but in recent years the scope of their implied powers has been expanded. As one judge put it:

> "A company secretary is a much more important person nowadays. …
> He is an officer of the company with extensive duties and responsibilities. This appears not only in the modern Companies Acts, but also by the role which he plays in the day-to-day business of companies. He is no longer a mere clerk. He regularly makes representations on behalf of the company and enters contracts on its behalf which come within the

---

[97] [1964] 2 Q.B. 480.
[98] *ibid.* at 501–502. Compare *SMC Electronics Ltd v Akhter Computers Ltd* [2001] 1 B.C.L.C. 433 (actual authority found) with the *Hopkins* case [2005] 1 B.C.L.C. 543 (no such authority).
[99] *Criterion Properties Plc v Stratford UK Properties L.L.C.* [2006] 1 B.C.L.C. 729.
[100] *Hopkins v TL Dallas Group Ltd* [2005] 1 B.C.L.C. 543.
[101] *Criterion* case [2006] 1 B.C.L.C. 729.
[102] *Euroafrica Shipping Lines Co. v Zegula Polska SA* [2004] 2 B.C.L.C. 97.
[103] Compare *SMC Electronics* case [2001] 1 B.C.L.C. 433 with *MCI World Com Int'l Inc v Primus Telecommunications Inc* [2004] 1 B.C.L.C. 42.

day-to-day running of the company's business. So much so that he may be regarded as held out as having authority to do such things on behalf of the company. He is certainly entitled to sign contracts connected with the administrative side of a company's affairs, such as employing staff, and ordering cars and so forth. All such matters now come within the ostensible authority of a company secretary".[104]

18–44 In quite a number of cases the alleged agent was the company chairman.[105] The difficulty with the chair's usual authority is that there are contrasting perceptions of the chair's role. Generally, its occupants are regarded as having no special functions apart from presiding over directors' meetings. But there is a breed of company chairman that has far more in common with managing directors.

Apparent Authority

18–45 A person or persons may be held out as authorised to act for a principal in certain ways, in which case the principal is bound by whatever was done within the scope of that holding-out, provided the agent was held out by somebody duly authorised to do so. The requirements for an effective holding-out were put as follows by Diplock L.J. in the *Freeman & Lockyer* case:[106]

"[i]t must be shown: (1) that a representation that the agent had authority to enter on behalf of the company into a contract of the kind sought to be enforced was made to the contractor; (2) that such representation was made by a person or persons who had 'actual' authority to manage the business of the company either generally or in respect of those matters to which the contract relates; (3) that he (the contractor) was induced by such representation to enter into the contract, that is, that he in fact relied on it ..."[107]

The holding-out must have been by the principal or by someone who was duly authorised by him to do so[108]; a holding-out by the agent himself is meaningless.[109]

18–46 Most of the major authorities on company agency concern holding-out. The *Mahony* case[110] can be explained on the grounds that the duped investors, by their inaction, held the fraudsters out to the bank as possessing authority to withdraw company funds from its bank accounts; the fraudsters were a *de facto* board of directors. In the *Freeman & Lockyer* case, even though K may not have been appointed managing director, the evidence

---

[104] *Panorama Developments (Guildford) Ltd v Fidelis Furnishing Fabrics Ltd* [1971] 2 Q.B. 711 at 716–717.
[105] e.g. *Hely Hutchinson v Brayhead Ltd* [1968] 1 Q.B. 549.
[106] [1964] 2 Q.B. 480.
[107] *ibid.* at 506. Also *Egyptian International Foreign Trade Co. v Soplex Wholesale Suppliers Ltd* [1985] B.C.L.C. 404.
[108] *ING Re (UK) Ltd v R&V Versicherung AG* [2007] 1 B.C.L.C. 108.
[109] *Armagas Ltd v Mundogas SA (The "Ocean Frost")* [1986] A.C. 717.
[110] (1875) L.R. 7 H.L. 869.

showed that, with the board's approval, he used to act in that capacity and the articles of association allowed for one member of the board to be appointed to that office. It was held that he therefore had been held out to the plaintiffs as being authorised to act as managing director; the board by its conduct "represented that he had authority to enter into contracts of a kind which a managing director or an executive director responsible for finding a purchaser would in the normal course be authorised to enter into on behalf of the company".[111]

18–47   Instances of company chairmen being held out as having extensive authority to bind their companies include *Hely-Hutchinson v Brayhead Ltd.*[112] The defendant's chairman, R, was also its chief financial executive and, with its board's acquiescence, he used to act as *de facto* managing director. The defendant had a stake in another company, in which the plaintiff was a major shareholder. There had been some discussions about the defendant putting further funds into that company. Immediately following a board meeting and in an office adjacent to the defendant's board room, R and the plaintiff agreed that, if the plaintiff lent money to that other company, the defendant would guarantee the loan. But later when the guarantee was called upon, the defendant denied R's authority to agree to give it. It was held that in the circumstances R did have ostensible authority in this regard; the Court was prepared, if necessary, to accept that he had actual authority to so agree. This decision has been criticised for employing different concepts of agency from those used here, thereby engendering confusion. In particular, there is the belief that R had actual authority. Since the defendant's board never in fact empowered him to negotiate the guarantee, he did not have actual authority. Since he was not in fact a managing director, concluding transactions of that nature fell outside his usual authority. Therefore, if there was any authority it must have been based on a holding-out.[113]

The Positive Constructive Notice "Heresy"

18–48   Something must be said of a doctrine that had some popularity around the 1930s but which is wrong, it being a simplistic perversion of *Turquand's* "excusing" rule,[114] which is explained below. The doctrine's thrust, inherent potential for mischief and eventual partial discrediting is well demonstrated by reference to *Kreditbank Cassel GmbH v Schenkers.*[115] It was sought to make a company liable on a bill of exchange issued in its name by its branch manager, who had neither actual nor usual authority to do so. The company's articles of association contained a regulation empowering the board to delegate, *inter alia*, the authority to draw bills. It was contended that the articles therefore operated as a kind of holding-out; that because the power here could have been delegated to the branch manager, he therefore *might* have been authorised to the company. That is to say, the articles operate as a positive, or power-conferring,

---

[111] [1964] 2 Q.B. 480 at 509.

[112] [1968] 1 Q.B. 549.

[113] See too *Kilgobbin Mink & Stud Farms Ltd v National Credit Co. Ltd* [1980] I.R. 175 and *First Energy (UK) Ltd v Hungarian Int'l Bank Ltd* [1993] B.C.L.C. 1409.

[114] See para.18–55 *et seq.*

[115] [1926] 2 K.B. 450, reversed [1927] 1 K.B. 826.

constructive notice. Carried, one hesitates to say, to its logical extreme, this means that, where a company's regulations allow for certain corporate powers to be delegated, then virtually anybody is deemed to have been authorised to bind the company in respect of those powers.

18–49   This view did not find full acceptance in *Kreditbank*. In the first place, it was said, the doctrine could not clothe impostors with power to bind the company; where the purported agent answers the description "messenger or office boy", that of itself "would take the case out of the category of persons who would ordinarily be entrusted with the power ... and would further carry with it notice of irregularity according to business usage".[116] In other words, whatever power-conferring capacity a power of delegation in the articles had, it cannot clothe persons with authority in excess of their usual authority. Therefore, it was held, since the branch manager's usual authority had not been shown to include power to draw bills of exchange on the company's behalf, the company was not liable on the bills in question. In the later *Freeman & Lockyer* case it was stressed that "constructive notice is not a positive doctrine. ... It does not entitle [a contractor] to say that he relied on some unusual provision in the constitution of the corporation ..."[117]

The Forgery "Heresy"

18–50   *Kreditbank Cassell* lends some support to the view that a forgery uttered in a company's name can never bind it unless, in the circumstances, "the person setting up the forgery [is] estopped from doing so".[118] The authority cited for this proposition was *Ruben v Great Fingall Consolidated*.[119] But the basis for *Ruben* (that a company cannot be held liable for something done in its name by one of its servants to line his own pockets, because the servant was acting outside the scope of his employment) was subsequently rejected by the House of Lords in *Lloyd v Grace, Smith & Co*.[120] Moreover, the *Mahony* case[121] concerned forgeries on two levels; namely a letter to the bank stating, wholly incorrectly, that the fraudsters were authorised to withdraw sums from the company's account, and later fraudulently-uttered withdrawal demands. Nevertheless, the judges in *Kreditbank* declined to depart from *Ruben*. It is difficult to see any logical reason why, in principle, a forgery uttered by some company agent acting within his usual or held-out authority should not bind the company where the contracting party was acting in good faith and was not put "on inquiry" about possible irregularities. The Australian High Court has roundly rejected the thesis.[122]

---

[116] [1926] 2 K.B. 450 at 460.
[117] [1964] 2 Q.B. 480 at 504.
[118] [1927] 1 K.B. 826 at 835.
[119] [1906] A.C. 439.
[120] [1912] A.C. 716.
[121] (1875) L.R. 7 H.L. 869.
[122] *Northside Developments Pty Ltd v Registrar General* (1990) 64 A.L.J.L.R. 427 at 443.

Limitations on Agents' Powers

18–51 Ordinarily, a principal is bound by whatever its agent does within the agent's, usual or held-out authority. Sometimes, however, agents will be denied authority to bind a company in a manner that falls within their usual or held-out authority. This restriction on agents' powers may be based either on the Companies Acts or on the company's own regulations; in the latter case, however, the company may be bound by a contract made in breach of its own articles, depending on the circumstances.

Statutory Restrictions

18–52 Statutory restrictions on a company's contracting power tend to fall into three major categories. One is where the Act states that non-compliance with its provisions does not invalidate the contract in question.[123] Another is where the Act stipulates the sanction for non-compliance with the section in question.[124] The third is where the provision is silent as to what happens when its requirements are broken. A court will have to decide whether such a provision is mandatory or merely directory. And if it is mandatory, it must then be determined whether the impugned transaction is void or voidable, or *ultra vires*, or whatever. There are no major modern Irish or British authorities squarely on these questions in the company law context.

Negative Constructive Notice

18–53 A company agent's powers to bind it may be restricted by the terms of the company's memorandum or articles of association, the contents of which everyone is deemed to have knowledge of as public documents. If by its own regulations a company is flatly prohibited from entering into certain transactions, then (subject to SI 1973/163)[125] it is not bound by any such transaction concluded by an agent otherwise authorised to act for it. One fundamental condition of a company being bound by what is done on its behalf is that "under its memorandum or articles of association the company was not deprived of the capacity to either enter into a contract of the kind sought to be enforced or to delegate authority to enter into a contract of that kind to the agent".[126]

18–54 The same principle has been held to apply where the company is permitted to enter into the transaction in question provided the members approve of it by special resolution. In *Irvine v Union Bank of Australia*,[127] the company's regulations restricted the board's borrowing powers except where extended by a special resolution. It was held that the bank could not recover a loan that the company, in excess of these powers, had obtained from it. By way of explanation, the Privy Council said that, "the bank would have seen that by the articles of association, the directors were expressly restricted from borrowing beyond a

---

[123] e.g. 1983 Act, s.6(8) and 1963 Act, s.178.
[124] e.g. 1963 Act, s.115.
[125] See para.18–64 *et seq.*
[126] *Freeman & Lockyer* case [1964] 2 Q.B. 504 at 506.
[127] (1887) 2 App. Cas. 366.

certain amount, and they must have known that if the general powers vested in the directors ... had been extended or enlarged by a resolution of a general meeting of the shareholders ... a copy of that resolution ought, in regular course, to have been forwarded to the Registrar of Joint Stock Companies, ... and would have been found amongst his records".[128] In other words, special resolutions, like the memorandum and articles of association, are public documents. Persons have "constructive notice" of any restrictions on contracting capacity contained in companies' regulations. But it is unlikely that this doctrine applies to the contents of each and every company document that is public in the sense that it must be registered with the CRO.

Turquand's Case and the "Internal Management" Rule

18–55 The invalidating effect of restrictions in the company's own regulations, which has parallels with the old *ultra vires* rule, is subject to two major qualifications. One is referred to as the "internal management" rule or as the "excusing rule" in *Turquand's* case. According to this and subject to the exceptions to it set out below, if a company's regulations prohibit certain forms of transactions unless specified internal formalities (other than special resolutions) have been complied with, an outsider dealing with the company is not obliged to ensure that those formalities in fact were satisfied. Thus, in *Royal British Bank v Turquand*,[129] under the company's articles the directors were allowed to borrow on bond only if the general meeting by ordinary resolution approved. In an action to recover borrowings the company had made without that approval, it was held that the breach of the company's own regulations did not provide it with a defence. A distinction is drawn between what may be called a flat prohibition and a conditional prohibition. Where, for example, borrowings are simply forbidden or borrowings in excess of a certain amount are flatly proscribed, a company therefore did not possess the authority to borrow, or to borrow more than that sum; (excess) borrowings could not be recovered from it.[130] But it is different where the restriction is couched in terms of a prohibition unless certain formalities are first satisfied. Here, the outsider is entitled to assume that those formalities were met; he is under no duty to satisfy himself that every detail of the company's internal management was properly executed. As the judge in *Turquand* explained:

> "the parties dealing with [registered companies] are bound to read the [memorandum and articles of association]. But they are not bound to do more. The party here, on reading the [articles], would find, not a prohibition from borrowing but a permission to do so on certain conditions. Finding that the authority might be made complete by a resolution, he would have the right to infer the fact of a resolution authorising that which on the face of the document appeared to be legitimately done".[131]

---

[128] *ibid.* at 379–380.
[129] (1856) 6 E. & B. 327.
[130] Subject to rights of subrogation.
[131] (1856) 6 E. & B. 327 at 332.

18–56   An example of this excusing rule in operation is the *Rudry Merthyr Steam Co.* case.[132] The company's articles of association empowered the directors to determine the number of their quorum, which by a board resolution they fixed at three. At a board meeting that only two directors attended, it was decided to affix the company's seal to a mortgage, which was done by the secretary in the two directors' presence. In an action on the mortgage, it was held that the irregularity of its execution did not invalidate it against the company because:

> "If a person looked at the deed and looked at the articles he would not see anything irregular at all; he would be at liberty to infer, and anyone in the ordinary course of business would infer, that if the directors had appointed a quorum they appointed the two who signed that deed. But supposing that three were wanted, he is not bound to go and look at the directors' minutes; he has no right to look at them except as a matter of bargain. The directors' minutes, unless he knows what they are, do not affect him at all. There is nothing irregular on the face of the deed even taken with the articles – there is nothing illegal in it."[133]

18–57   *The "On Inquiry" Exception:* *Turquand*'s excusing rule is subject to its own qualifications and exceptions, however. One has already been mentioned: where passing a special resolution is required to permit the transaction, then outsiders are deemed to have notice that it was not passed.[134] Nor does the excusing rule operate where the person dealing with the company was put on inquiry about a probable irregularity. That is to say, if a person was in a situation where his suspicions should have been aroused, then he should have inquired further into the alleged agent's authority. As one judge explained, the excusing rule "proceeds on the assumption that certain acts have been regularly done" but "[i]f there are circumstances which debar [a] person from relying on the prima facie presumption. ... he cannot claim the benefit of the rule".[135] When these circumstances arise depends on the facts of the case.

18–58   There are countless instances of circumstances not putting the contracting party on inquiry. Thus in *Mahony's* case[136] it was concluded that the bank there had done everything that could reasonably have been expected of it and there was nothing unusual about what the self-styled directors were doing which should have put it on notice. In *UIB Ltd v Euro Estates Ltd*,[137] the quorum for the plaintiff's directors' meetings was fixed at one "A" and one "B" director. Twelve months before the resolution in question was voted on, the two directors present, two "B" directors, had been issued with all the "B"

---

[132] *County of Gloucester Bank v Rudry Merthyr Steam & House Coal Colliery Co.* [1895] 1 Ch. 629.

[133] *ibid.* at 636, applied in *Re Bank of Syria* [1900] 2 Ch. 272, *Cox v Dublin Distillery Co. (No. 2)* [1915] 1 I.R. 345 and *Ulster Investment Bank Ltd v Euro Estates Ltd* [1982] I.L.R.M. 57.

[134] *Irvine* case (1887) 2 App. Cas. 366.

[135] *B. Liggett (Liverpool) Ltd v Barclays Bank* (1926) 1 K.B. 48 at 57.

[136] (1875) L.R. 7 H.L. 869.

[137] [1982] I.L.R.M. 57.

shares; the defendant bank had been provided with information to this effect. Carroll J. held that this did not put the bank on inquiry: "because such an agreement was made in August 1973 does not fix some one in June 1974 with a notice that the shareholding had not changed. Alternatively, there was nothing to prevent the 'A' ordinary shareholders agreeing that either ['B' director] would become an 'A' Director. There was no particular shareholding qualification required for directors in the articles".[138]

18–59 In *AL Underwood Ltd v Bank of Liverpool*[139] the principal shareholder and sole director of a company endorsed in that capacity cheques payable to the company and then lodged them in his own personal bank account. The defendant bank knew that he had recently converted his own business into a company but did not know that the company's bank account was with another bank. It nevertheless was held that the circumstances of a company's agent paying company cheques into his own account were so exceptional as to put the bank on inquiry; what occurred there was something unusual which ought to have attracted the attention of bank employees.

18–60 Many of the cases of irregularity concern contracts made by an inquorate board of directors, for instance *Rolled Steel Products (Holdings) Ltd v British Steel Corp.*[140] One S controlled a company which owed a very substantial sum of money to British Steel's predecessor in title and which was secured by his personal guarantee. S. was also a director and major shareholder of Rolled Steel. British Steel doubted S's financial ability to honour his guarantee and persuaded him to have that guarantee substituted by one from Rolled Steel. A board meeting of Rolled Steel's two directors then took place, which gave the new guarantee. Because S. did not declare his financial interest in the agreement, under the company's articles, he could not be counted in the quorum or vote.[141] Accordingly, the guarantee was not granted in accordance with the articles and would not bind the company if the person to whom it was given knew of that irregularity or should have made full enquiries. It was held that since British Steel were sufficiently aware of the likely irregularity, they could not avail of the "indoor management" plea.[142]

18–61 A more recent example of the nature of the transaction in question putting a party on notice is *Northside Developments Pty Ltd v Registrar General*,[143] concerning a guarantee given by the company. The guarantee was to secure the liabilities of several companies not directly connected with Northside but which were controlled by a man who was one of Northside's three directors. When executing the guarantee certain formalities regarding affixing the company seal had not been scrupulously complied with. The court refused

---

[138] *ibid.* at 66.
[139] [1924] 1 K.B. 775.
[140] [1986] 1 Ch. 246.
[141] See para.7–60 *et seq.*
[142] [1986] 1 Ch. 246 at 282–286; *cf. Cowan de Groot Properties Ltd v Eagle Trust Plc* [1991] B.C.L.C. 1045 at 113–117.
[143] 64 A.L.J.L.R. 427 (1990).

to enforce the guarantee; to enforce it, said one judge, would be to "furnish a charter for dealings between the fraudulent officials of companies and supine financiers".[144] The implications of this case for cross-guarantees within a group of related companies will require consideration.

18–62 *"Insiders" and "On Inquiry"*: The exception to the excusing rule for "insiders" dealing with their companies is merely a special application of the "on inquiry" exception. Insiders, such as directors, are in a position to know and ought to know whether the necessary internal formalities were complied with. As was said in *Morris v Kanssen*,[145] a director or *de facto* director cannot presume in his own favour that things done are rightly done if an inquiry that he ought to make would tell him that they were wrongly done. It is "the duty of directors, and equally those who purport to act as directors to look after the affairs of the company, to see that it acts within its powers and that its transactions are regular and orderly. To admit in their favour a presumption that that is rightly done which they have themselves wrongly done is to encourage ignorance and condone dereliction from duty ... His duty as director is to know; his interest when he invokes the rule is to disclaim knowledge. Such a conflict can be resolved in only one way".[146] For instance, in *Cox v Dublin City Distillery Co. (No.2)*,[147] the company's regulations fixed the quorum of directors at two and provided that no director should vote on any matter in which he was individually interested. At a series of board meetings the directors resolved to issue debentures as security for advances made by themselves to the company. It was held that the resolutions were invalid and that the debentures were void. On the other hand, debentures issued at that same time to outsiders were held to be valid despite the irregularities in the board resolutions authorising them.

18–63 It depends on the circumstances whether non-directors, such as persons in senior managerial positions and majority shareholders, can be characterised as *de facto* directors to render them "insiders" for the purpose of these rules. In *Hely-Hutchinson v Brayhead Ltd*,[148] the background to which is summarised above, a duly-appointed director was held not to be an insider for these very purposes. The plaintiff there sought to recover on a guarantee given by the defendant company's chairman and *de facto* managing director on its behalf. At the relevant time the plaintiff had a seat on the defendant's board. His claim nevertheless was upheld by the Court of Appeal on the grounds that there was actual authority in this instance. The trial judge upheld his claim on the grounds that the insider exception applies only where the director deals with the company *qua* director. But this is a travesty of the underlying rationale propounded in *Morris v Kanssen*.[149] What the case therefore suggests is that

---

[144] *ibid.* at 445. More recently still, *Hopkins v TL Dallas Group Ltd* [2005] 1 B.C.L.C. 543.
[145] [1946] A.C. 459.
[146] *ibid.* at 475–476.
[147] [1916] 1 I.R. 345.
[148] [1968] 1 Q.B. 549.
[149] [1946] A.C. 459.

exceptional situations can arise where insiders will not be assumed to know that company agents acted without proper authority.

"Organs" and SI 1973/163

18–64   Article 9(2) of the EC First Directive calls for the repeal of the negative constructive notice rule, i.e. that a company is not bound where the person or body that concluded the transaction on its behalf was forbidden to do so by the company's memorandum or articles of association: "[t]he limits on the powers of the organs of the company, arising under the statute or from a decision of the competent organs, may never be relied on as against third parties, even if they have been disclosed".[150] This objective was already partly achieved by the excusing rule in *Turquand's* case. In response to this Directive, S.I. 1973/163 was adopted, reg.6 of which stipulates that:

> "(1) In favour of a person dealing with a company in good faith, any transaction entered into by any organ of the company, being its board of directors or any person registered under these regulations as a person authorised to bind the company, shall be deemed to be within the capacity of the company and any limitation of the powers of that board or person, whether imposed by the memorandum or articles of association or otherwise, may not be relied upon as against any person so dealing with the company.
>
> (2) Any such person shall be presumed to have acted in good faith unless the contrary is proved".

18–65   Companies can register persons as organs authorised to bind them by delivering to the Registrar of Companies a notice of who those persons are; it would appear that no Irish company has yet done this. For the vast majority of companies, therefore, this regulation only applies to transactions entered into by their boards of directors. Subject to the "good faith" caveat, described below, it does not matter that there was some irregularity in the board's proceedings. As stated in a case concerning the English equivalent, "the irreducible minimum ... is a genuine decision taken by a person or persons who can on substantial grounds claim to be the board of directors acting as such (even if the proceedings of the board are marred by procedural irregularities of a more or less serious character".[151] This regulation may also validate *ultra vires* transactions within its scope but s.8(1) of the 1963 Act is more extensive in that regard.

18–66   *Scope:* A company that wants to claim the benefit of a forbidden transaction made by its agent cannot invoke this regulation to render that transaction effective. Only a person "dealing with" a company can claim under reg.6.[152] Although transactions made with "insiders", like directors are not automatically excluded, the person may be so involved in the transaction at the

---

[150] Recital.

[151] *Smith v Henniker-Major & Co.* [2003] Ch. 182 at para.41.

[152] See generally, C. Twigg-Flesner "Sections 35A and 322A Revisited: Who is a "Person Dealing with a Company" 26 *Co. Law* 195 (2005).

company side of it as to be excluded. In *Smith v Henniker Major & Co,*[153] that was held to be the case with a chairman of a one-person board, which approved an assignment of company property to himself in the mistaken but bona fide belief that he was entitled to do so. In *EIC Services Ltd v Phipps,*[154] that also was held to be the case in a dispute with shareholders concerning the issue of bonus shares, on the grounds that what is envisaged is a bilateral transaction between the company and the person in question. But bonus share issues do not involve any alteration of a company's assets or liabilities, nor alternation in proportionate shareholdings. The question of whether a rights issue to share-holders is excluded was left open but the view was expressed that all transac-tions with shareholders in that capacity did not come within this regime.[155]

18–67 Two major questions arise concerning the types of arrangement that are made binding by the regulation. An argument could be made that use of the terms "dealing" and "transaction" means that only arrangements that are of some economic benefit to the company are covered by it; that "sterile" arrange-ments like gifts are not. Against this view stand the words of the Directive itself, which do not in terms confine its scope to enforceable contracts. The other question is what precisely is meant by "entered into by [the] board of direc-tors"? Undoubtedly, it embraces transactions that the board formally approved of in advance or by subsequent ratification. And it most likely extends to trans-actions that the board subsequently acquiesced in. But the terms "entered into by" would appear to exclude what is done by any officer, such as a managing director, within their usual authority, or what is done by a person held out by the board to have authority to act in a particular way. If, however, subsequent acqui-escence falls within these terms, it is hard to see why transactions within usual and held-out authority should then be excluded. In *Re Frederick Inns Ltd,*[156] the Supreme Court held that reg.6 did not apply to the substantial payments made to the Revenue by insolvent companies because there was nothing on affidavit before the court to show that the transactions had been entered into by the direc-tors.[157] It should be noted that the formulation used in the parallel British pro-vision was transaction "decided on by the directors".[158] Companies are also bound by the acts of persons they have registered as authorised to act for them, as envisaged by these regulations. It is common practice in Germany to spe-cially register who a company's "organs" are.

18–68 Unlike s.8(1) of the 1963 Act, the Statutory Instrument does not state in positive terms what effect it has on transactions that fall within its terms. All it says is that "any limitations on the powers of that board or person ... may not be relied upon" to upset the transaction.

---

[153] [2003] Ch. 182.
[154] [2005] 1 All E.R. 338.
[155] *ibid.* at 348.
[156] [1994] 1 I.L.R.M. 387.
[157] *ibid.* at 394–395.
[158] Companies Act 1985, s.35 (since repealed by the 2006 Act).

18–69 *The "Good Faith" Exception:* Whereas s.8(1) of the 1963 Act introduced a *scienter* requirement where the Directive did not insist on one, although one was made optional, the statutory instrument imposes a good faith standard where the Directive is silent about *scienter.* To come within Reg.6, the person dealing with the company must have been acting in "good faith". It remains to be seen whether this deviation is within the choice of form and methods of implementation allowed by Art.189 of the Rome Treaty. Presumably good faith in this context will be given the same meaning as "on inquiry" is in general agency law. In *International Factors Ltd v Steeve Construction Ltd,*[159] Gibson L.J. defined "good faith" in the parallel Northern Irish provision, as "actual knowledge" that the transaction was not duly authorised or "that the person dealing with the company could not have been unaware" of that, which "amounts to a deliberate closing of one's mind to circumstances which would have pointed towards the conclusion" of absence of authority.[160] It depends on all the circumstances whether the other party to the transaction lacked "good faith" in this sense.

18–70 A crucially important matter is that SI 1973/163 provides that a person "shall be presumed to have acted in good faith until the contrary is proved". If the *Rolled Steel Products Ltd* case[161] had to be decided under this provision, it is most likely that the defendants would be regarded as not possessing good faith; they were aware of the plaintiff's directors' substantial financial interest in the transaction in question and they had originally proposed that his own personal guarantee should be substituted by a guarantee from the plaintiff company. On the other hand, in the *International Factors Ltd* case[162] and in *TCB Ltd v Gray*[163] it was held that, in the circumstances, the plaintiffs there had acted in good faith. The presumption of good faith furthermore suggests that somebody who, *Northern Bank v Quinn*[164]-style, read the company's regulations but who reasonably and honestly failed to appreciate that they proscribed the kind of transaction in question, was acting in good faith.

Breach of Warranty of Authority

18–71 Where a person purports to act as another's agent but without authority to do so and the purported principal refuses to be bound by the transaction in question, that "agent" is liable to the other party for breach of warranty of authority.

OTHER COMPANY LIABILITY

18–72 Apart from contract, companies may incur liability on other grounds—in tort, in equity, for breach of statutory duty, criminal responsibility

---

[159] [1984] N.I. 245.
[160] *ibid.* at 249.
[161] [1986] 1 Ch. 246.
[162] [1984] N.I. 245.
[163] [1986] Ch. 621.
[164] [1979] I.L.R.M. 221.

and for contempt of court. Generally, companies are not in any different a position in these regards than adult individuals; the same general principles of vicarious liability and attribution apply. Notwithstanding, on account of companies being legal constructs, these principles are adapted to some extent in respect of them. As well as corporate accountability for a particular wrong, the officer or employee involved may also be personally liable or responsible.[165]

Tort and Equity

18–73 The law of tort is concerned principally with securing compensation for persons who have suffered loss, either physical, proprietary, reputational or financial, in particular ways. The *ultra vires* doctrine never enabled companies to avoid extra-contractual liability[166]; a company cannot plead, as a defence to an action for tort, or breach of some equitable obligation, that it had been acting *ultra vires.*[167] In the case of most torts, where it is not necessary to prove a particular mental element on the defendant's part, companies will be held vicariously liable where a wrong was done in the course of their employees' or other agents' activities, in the same way as non-corporate employers and principals would be vicariously liable.[168] In *Pearson & Son Ltd v Dublin Corp.,*[169] a statutory corporation was held liable for a fraud committed by one of its employees in the course of his work although there was no suggestion that the actual members of the corporation had authorised or consented to the fraud.

18–74 In the case of torts the commission of which requires a distinct mental element, such as malice (e.g. malicious prosecution), liability does not arise vicariously. Liability is primary; it must be shown that the company itself had that element, which is done by attributing to it the mental element of its principal relevant officers. This, it has been said, "results from the fact that a corporation is an abstraction. It has no mind of its own any more than it has a body of its own; its active and directing will must consequently be sought in the person of somebody who for some purposes may be called an agent, but who is really the directing mind and will of the corporation, the very ego and centre of the personality of the corporation".[170] It depends on all of the circumstances who will be regarded as principal agents for the purpose of attributing their state of knowledge and intentions to the company.

18–75 In *EL Ajou v Dollar Land Holdings Plc,*[171] proceedings against a company to recover money of which the plaintiff had been defrauded, on the

---

[165] See para.7–152 *et seq.*

[166] *Campbell v Paddington Corp.* [1911] 1 K.B. 869.

[167] 1963 Act, s.8(1).

[168] See generally, B. McMahon & W. Binchy, *Law of Torts*, 3rd edn (London: Butterworths, 2000), Ch.43 and pp.1037–1038.

[169] [1907] A.C. 351.

[170] *Lennard's Carrying Co. v Asiatic Petroleum Co.* [1915] A.C. 705 at 713–714. See observations in *Superwood Holdings Plc v Sun Alliance & London Assurance Plc* [1995] 3 I.R. 303 at 308–330.

[171] [1994] 2 All E.R. 685.

basis that the company had been in "knowing receipt" of those funds, it was held that knowledge of a non-executive director who had no responsibilities for running the business but whose function was to organize the paper work, was attributable to the company for these purposes. The sum involved was very large but there was no record of the board of directors having agreed to the transaction. In those circumstances, it was held that the director in question had the *de facto* management and control of the transactions, and he was the company's directing mind and will in respect of them. On the other hand, for the purpose of establishing company liability on the basis of agency, it was held that the information known to that person could not in the circumstances be imputed to the company.

Statute

18–76 Many statutory duties are delegable; others are non-delegable. Some statutory duties that affect companies envisage primary liability only; the fact that any company employee acted in a manner inconsistent with what is required does not invariably render the company responsible. As with torts that require a distinct mental element, those involved in the activity in question must be sufficiently senior in the company that what they do is attributed to it. Some Acts contain their own express rules of attribution. Thus, under the Competition Act, 2002 and the Consumer Protection 2007,[172] which provide for, *inter alia*, punitive damages, there is a presumption that the company consented to the prohibited action where it is shown that a director or senior employee had knowledge of it. In determining whether a company should be held liable for the fraudulent trading of another company, which can result in unlimited liability for the insolvent company's unpaid debts, it was held that the English equivalent of s.297 of the 1963 Act contained its own implied special rule of attribution for this purpose.[173] Key considerations included the importance or seniority of the individual in the company's hierarchy, his significance and freedom to act in the relevant context, and the degree to which the board was informed or at least put on inquiry about his activities.

18–77 In *The Lady Gwendolen*[174] where, under the legislation in question, ordinary vicarious liability would not suffice to render the company liable, it was held that it was responsible for breach of shipping safety rules by one of its ship's captains because the head of the company's traffic department was aware of those breaches. The ship, which was owned by the Guinness brewery and which regularly carried stout from Dublin to Liverpool, collided with another ship in a fog when it had been travelling too fast. The owners' liability would have been limited if they could prove that the loss did not result from their "actual fault or privity". Even though under the general principles of vicarious liability for negligence, the company was responsible, the damages

---

[172] Sections 14(8) and 74(5) respectively.
[173] *Re Bank of Credit and Commerce Int'l SA (No.15)* [2005] 2 B.C.L.C. 328.
[174] [1965] P. 294.

awarded against it would be significantly reduced unless it was privy to the captain's wrongs or was specially at fault for what he had done. In the circumstances, it was held that the company was so responsible because "where, as in the present case, a company has a separate traffic department, which assumes responsibility for running the company's ships, [there is] no good reason why the head of that department, even though not himself a director, should not be regarded as someone whose action is the very action of the company itself, so far as concerns any thing to do with the company's ships".[175]

18–78   In the *Meridian Global Funds* case,[176] two senior executives knew that the disclosure requirements about transactions in the securities markets in question had not been complied with but the board of directors were unaware of that. What had to be decided was whether those executives' actions and knowledge were attributable to the company. To answer this, two principal matters called for consideration. One was the company's own rules for allocating responsibility within itself, being mainly its articles of association, along with common law agency principles. The other was the Act in question and the policy underlying it, which should indicate at what level within the company responsibility is being laid. It was held that the object of the statutory provision there was, in the context of fast-moving stock markets, to compel immediate disclosure of the identity of purchasers of securities. Accordingly, the activities of those who were authorised to initiate buy and sell securities transactions were attributable to the company; otherwise, the policy of the section would be entirely defeated. That the executives there were acting corruptly did not exonerate the company from liability for the breach of statutory duty.

18–79   These principles were not disputed in *Fyffes Plc v DCC Plc*[177] but were held not to apply in the context of Pt V of the 1990 Act concerning insider trading.[178] That was because that Act contained its own internal rule for attribution, s.108(6) and an expanded definition of who is a company "officer". On a proper construction of s.108(3), the price-sensitive information had to come from an individual who was not a company officer. Since the source of the impugned information was the first defendant's chief executive, it could not be held liable as a tippee under the then statutory version of what was prohibited. Similarly, the core prohibition in s.108(1) was on individuals dealing as principals, not as agents. The extent to which companies could incur liability was comprehensively provided for in s.109.

Crime

18–80   It has never seriously been suggested that the *ultra vires* doctrine prevents companies from being convicted of criminal offences. But there are

---

[175] *ibid.* at 343–344.
[176] *Meridian Global Funds Management (Asia) Ltd v Securities Commission* [1995] 2 A.C. 500.
[177] [2005] I.E.H.C. 477, unreported, Laffoy J., December 21, 2005; this part of the judgment was not appealed: [2007] I.E.S.C. 36, unreported, July 27, 2007.
[178] At 52–61 of Laffoy J.'s judgment.

some types of offence that it has been held companies are incapable of committing, notwithstanding their possession of corporate personality.[179] Because companies are legal constructs, penalties such as imprisonment cannot be imposed on them; they are principally subject to financial sanctions. Accordingly, companies cannot be convicted of murder. The extent to which persons can be rendered vicariously liable for crimes is circumscribed by the Constitution.

18–81 Except where it is so provided in legislation, there is no vicarious criminal liability for serious offences,[180] so that a company cannot be held responsible merely because its agents, within the scope of their authority, committed the offence. It is not sufficient that the company would be liable in civil law. In the case of common law offences and also of statutory offences where the legislation in question does not require otherwise, both the *actus reus* and *mens rea* must be identified with the company's senior management. In *Tesco Supermarkets Ltd v Nattress*,[181] the House of Lords rejected the doctrine of "enterprise" criminal liability, i.e. that offences committed by a company's subordinate officials and employees in the course of its general business render the company itself criminally responsible. The proper approach in cases of corporate crimes that require *mens rea* was summed up as follows:

> "A corporation ... must act through living persons, though not always one or the same person. Then the person who acts is not speaking or acting for the company. He is acting as the company and his mind which directs his acts is the mind of the company. There is no question of the company being vicariously liable ... If it is a guilty mind then that guilt is the guilt of the company. It must be a question of law whether ... a person in doing particular things is to be regarded as the company or merely as the company's servant or agent ...
>
> Normally the board of directors, the managing director and perhaps other superior officers of the company carry out the functions of management and speak and act as the company. Their subordinates do not. They carry out orders from above and it can make no difference that they are given some measure of discretion. But the board of directors may delegate some part of their functions of management, giving to their delegate full discretion to act independently of instructions from them. [There is] no difficulty in holding that they have thereby put such a delegate in their place so that within the scope of the delegation he can act as the company. It may not always be easy to draw the line ...".[182]

---

[179] See para.3–25 *et seq.*

[180] See generally, F McAuley & JP McCutcheon, *Criminal Liability: A Grammar* (Dublin: Round Hall Sweet & Maxwell, 2000), p.379 *et seq.*: C. Wells, *Corporations and Criminal Liability*, 2nd edn (Oxford: OUP, 2001*)*; "Developments in the Law—Corporate Crime: Regulating Corporate Behavior Through Criminal Sanction" 92 *Harv. L. Rev.* 1227 (1979); *cf.* Law Reform Commission's *Report on Corporate Killing* (LRC 77–2005).

[181] [1972] A.C. 153.

[182] *ibid.* at 170–171.

This approach to corporate criminal liability was reiterated in 2000, where a company was accused of manslaughter by virtue of gross negligence, arising from a serious rail crash at Paddington, in London.[183] Numerous recent cases on criminal liability under statutory provisions were distinguished there because, either expressly or by implication, those enactments contained special rules of attribution.

18–82   It depends on the entire circumstances of the case and the nature of the offence whether the wrong of a particular company functionary will be attributed to the company.[184] In the *Tesco Supermarkets* case,[185] which concerned charges under consumer protection legislation, it was held that the manager of one of the defendant supermarket chain's shops would not be sufficiently close to the board of directors for the purpose of attributing guilt to the company. Similarly, companies have been held not to be responsible for what was done by their depot engineer[186] or their weighbridge operator.[187] By contrast, in a case involving charges of violating war-time fuel rationing, it was held that the accused company's transport manager was sufficiently senior for these purposes.[188] In a prosecution under health and safety legislation, it was held that the relevant acts and omissions of the person in effective control of the work site were attributable to the company.[189] That was the foreman and the fact that he was in dereliction of his duties and was personally liable under the legislation afforded the company no defence. In a prosecution for a road traffic offence, where the penalties included mandatory disqualification from driving, it was held that this was no bar to a company being convicted, as otherwise there would be a huge gap in the legislation.[190] The disqualification here applied only to natural persons. Attribution of responsibility is a matter of law, not of fact. But in jury trials the jury must be directed to consider whether sufficient facts were proved as would justify the judge in holding that the company should be made responsible for what was done.[191]

18–83   The legislature has created many offences whereby an employer or supplier or occupier is made criminally responsible for designated acts of its employees and other agents; what has been called "situational liability". Sections 6(6) and 7(3) of the Competition Act 2002 creates such liability for unlawful anti-competitive arrangements and abuse of dominant position. For the purpose of determining such liability "any act done by an officer or employee of an undertaking for the purpose of, or in connection with [its] business or affairs shall be regarded as an act done by the undertaking". If the

[183] *Attorney General's Reference No. 2 of 1999* [2000] Q.B. 796.
[184] See generally, Sullivan, "The Attribution of Culpability to Limited Companies" 55 *Cam. L.J.* 515 (1996).
[185] [1972] A.C. 152.
[186] *Magna Plant Ltd v Mitchell* [1966] Crim. L.R. 394.
[187] *John Henshall (Quarries) Ltd v Harvey* [1965] 2 Q.B. 233.
[188] *Moore v I. Bresler Ltd* [1944] 2 All E.R. 515.
[189] *Police v Purser Asphalts & Contractors Ltd* [1990] 1 N.Z.L.R. 693.
[190] *Linework Ltd v Dept of Labour* [2001] 2 N.Z.L.R. 639.
[191] *R. v Andrews Weatherfoil Ltd* [1972] 1 W.L.R. 119.

offence in question is one which, under the relevant statute, is attributed to individual parties when the prohibited acts are done by their employees or agents, a company will be held responsible *qua* employer or principal for what its subordinates have done. For instance, in the *Meridian Global Funds* case,[192] the chief investment officer and portfolio manager of an investment company used funds being managed by the company to buy shares but failed to comply with a statutory requirement that they should notify the regulatory authority. This occurred without the knowledge or acquiescence of the company's management at the highest level. It was held that, notwithstanding, the company were rightly convicted because implicit in the regulatory scheme was that its criminal responsibility could be engaged in such circumstances; otherwise, the very intention of the legislature would be defeated.

18–84 Sometimes the offence in question may be one of strict liability, in the sense that *mens rea* need not be established. Liability will attach even if the employer expressly forbade his employee to do the proscribed act, if that act was done in the general course of the business. Often the legislature provides a defence here where the accused can demonstrate that all that was reasonably possible was done to prevent the prohibited state of affairs from occurring, like issuing appropriate instructions, supervision, improving modes of operation etc. An example was s.22 of the Consumer Information Act 1978, where taking adequate precautions and exercising all due diligence was a defence. That was the net issue in the *Tesco Supermarkets* case,[193] which concerned offences for which an employer or principal, in the course of whose business the offences were committed, is criminally liable notwithstanding that they are due to acts or omissions of his servants or agents which were done without his knowledge or consent, or even were contrary to his orders. The question was whether the employer, who was *prima facie* guilty, had exercised the requisite "due diligence" to ensure that what was done should not occur. It was held that the company had not done so because it was not enough for it to delegate the task to such subordinate officers as its store managers; the company itself, through its principal officers, should have taken the necessary precautions.[194]

18–85 Companies may invoke the common law privilege against self-incrimination[195] but the extent to which that can be taken away by legislation remains to be determined.

Contempt

18–86 Contempt of court generally involves disobedience of a court order, such as an injunction, or breach of an undertaking given to the court. Normally, the wording of the order will restrain the company, its servants or agents but,

---

[192] [1995] 2 A.C. 500.

[193] [1972] A.C. 152.

[194] *cf. Tesco Stores Ltd v Brent LBC* [1993] 1 W.L.R. 1037 and *Seaboard Offshore Ltd v Secretary of State* [1994] 1 W.L.R. 541.

[195] *New Zealand Apple & Pear Marketing Board v Master & Sons Ltd* [1986] 1 N.Z.L.R. 191.

even if those words are not used, often they will be implied. Corporate liability for a contempt of an order in these or these implied terms is vicarious; it is not essential that responsibility for the breach be traced to senior officers in the company.[196] Order 42, rule 32 of the Rules of the Superior Courts 1986 provides that "[a]ny judgment or order against a company wilfully disobeyed may, by leave of the Court, be enforced by sequestration against the corporate property, or by attachment against the directors or other officers thereof, or by order of sequestration against their property." However, while contempt involves a "wilful" breach, this word has been held to mean that it is established beyond reasonable doubt that the act in question was done deliberately and not casually or accidentally.[197] In *Re Supply of Ready Mixed Concrete (No. 2)*,[198] it was held that it was no answer to a contempt allegation that company employees were expressly ordered not to do the forbidden act and that senior management were not aware of its existence; this factor at most goes to mitigation. Once the proscribed act is done in the general course of their employment, the company is liable and is at risk of an order being made for the sequestration of its assets. Accordingly, the directors must take steps to ensure that the court's order or the undertaking is complied with. It is unclear the extent to which vicarious liability applies in cases of what is known as criminal contempt.[199]

Other

18–87 A judgment in favour of a party will be set aside where it has been obtained on the strength of that party's perjured evidence. Where a company has obtained a judgment, the same rule applies provided the witness had such standing in the company that his evidence should be attributed to it.[200]

18–88 The question of attribution also arises in the context of provisions exempting a party from liability, for instance in an insurance policy. In a recent instance, it was held that insurers were not liable under a policy in respect of serious sex abuse committed by the insured company's managing director.[201] But the policy was held to cover abuse committed by others who were only employees of the company.

---

[196] See generally, C.J. Millar, *Contempt of Court* (3rd edn., 2000), p.670 *et seq.*
[197] *Airscape Ltd v Powertech Logistics Ltd* [2007] I.E.H.C. 43, Laffoy J, unreported, February 5, 2007.
[198] [1995] 1 A.C. 456.
[199] *cf Re Hibernia National Review Ltd* [1976] I.R. 338, concerning criminal contempt on the letters page of the precursor of *Phoenix Magazine*.
[200] *Odyssey Re (London) Ltd v OIC Run-off Ltd* T.L.R. March 17, 2000.
[201] *K.R. v Royal & Sun Alliance Plc* [2007] 1 All E.R. (Comm) 161.

CHAPTER 19

EMPLOYEES

19–01 The main concern of company law is regulating relations between investors, and between investors and management. But the Companies Acts also contain provisions on dealings between companies and others who have interests in them, most notably creditors. In the past, relations between companies and their employees were regarded as mainly the concern of labour law. More recently, there has been a trend towards inserting into companies' legislation provisions that acknowledge employees' interest in and claims against their incorporated employer.[1] Two arguments can be made for granting employees rights against the company for which they work. If they are given a greater stake in the enterprise and a say in running the business, it is very likely that they will work more enthusiastically and be more sympathetic to management's dilemmas. Put simply, greater employee involvement in the company should improve productivity. Secondly, in the light of the extensive contribution that employees make to the commercial success of companies and because they can be so dependent economically on their enterprise, employees deserve greater rights vis-à-vis those companies.

19–02 At one time, the principal technique used to accommodate employee interests was to grant workers and their representatives greater negotiating power in their dealings with employers. To this end, the Industrial Relations Act 1990 makes strikes and peaceful picketing lawful, in the context of a trade dispute, and confers extensive immunities from suit on trade unions. Legislation granting employees directly-enforceable rights used to be confined to the most vulnerable classes of workers (e.g. children and women) and to particularly dangerous or outrageous work practices (e.g. the Factories Acts and the Truck Acts). Since the 1970s, however, numerous measures have been enacted that give extensive rights to most categories of workers, which also apply to company directors who have employment contracts. Over and above these, legislation dealing with companies as such rather than *qua* employers contain provisions specific to employee relations.

---

[1] See generally, R Kraakman et al, *The Anatomy of Corporate Law: A Comparative and Functional Approach* (Oxford: OUP, 2004), p.61 *et seq.*; B. Cheffins, *Company Law: Theory, Structure and Operation* (Oxford: Clarendon Press, 1997), Ch.12; and M. Blair & M. Roe (eds), *Employees and Corporate Governance* (Washington, D.C.: Brookings Institution, 1999).

DISCLOSURE AND CONSULTATION

19–03   Employers, whether or not incorporated, are required to disclose certain information about their activities to their employees' representatives and to consult with those representatives, notably where collective redundancies are envisaged, where it is proposed to transfer all or part of the business to some other company, and more generally under the Employees (Provision of Information and Consultation) Act 2006. Additionally, every company employee has *locus standi* to apply for a "disclosure order", to ascertain who really owns the shares in the company.[2] Employees also have *locus standi* to seek disqualification orders against company directors on certain grounds.[3] Until 2006, every directors' annual report to the shareholders had to contain an evaluation of the extent to which the policies set out in the company's "safety statement" have been fulfilled during the year covered by the report.[4]

19–04   Listed companies must include in their annual accounts details of staff costs (i.e. wages and salaries, pensions and social security costs), together with the average number of persons employed during the financial year broken down by categories of activity. Where a takeover bid is being made for a listed company, the bidder must inform the target's shareholders of, *inter alia*, the bidder's "strategic plans for the offeree and their likely repercussions on employment" and also of "its intentions with regard to safeguarding the employment of the employees … including any material change in the conditions of employment."[5] In its circular responding to the offer, the target must state the views of its board on, *inter alia*, effects of implementing the offer on employment and the likely repercussions of the bidder's strategic plans on employment.[6] A copy of this response must be made promptly available to employee representatives or, if there is no such person, to the employees themselves.[7] The same applies to any revised offer document that is sent to the target's shareholders.

ENTITLEMENT TO ACCOMMODATE EMPLOYEE INTERESTS

19–05   Without authority in the memorandum and articles of association to do so, or without all of the members being in agreement, formerly, major decisions within companies could not be made with the primary object of furthering employees' interests. The law identified companies almost exclusively with their shareholders. Directors must exercise their powers "bona fide in what they consider … is in the interests of the company"[8]; resolutions of shareholders, or any class of shareholders, are unlawful where they are not adopted "bona fide for the benefit of the company as a whole".[9] By the company as a whole was meant the

---

[2]   1990 Act, s.98(6).
[3]   1990 Act, s.160(2)(a)–(d).
[4]   Safety, Health & Welfare at Work Act 1989, s.12(6), since repealed by the Safety, Health & Welfare at Work Act 2005.
[5]   Irish Takeover Panel Act 1997, Takeover Rules, r.24.1(b) and (e).
[6]   Irish Takeover Panel Act 1997, Takeover Rules, r.25.2.
[7]   Irish Takeover Panel Act 1997, Takeover Rules, r.32.6.
[8]   See para.7–91 *et seq.*
[9]   See para.10–25 *et seq.*

shareholders in general or the hypothetical average shareholder. Ambiguous though these formulae may be, it was not permissible for directors or even a majority of the shareholders to place employees' interests before those of all of the shareholders. The classic instance is *Parke v Daily News Ltd*,[10] where a proposal by a newspaper company, that had sold off its assets, to distribute most of the proceeds among its employees as *ex gratia* redundancy pay, was challenged by a minority shareholder. That proposal was enjoined because such massive benevolence was *ultra vires*, although the case might more appropriately be regarded as one of fraud on a minority than *ultra vires* as presently understood because the proposal did not have unanimous shareholder support.

19–06 The position has been changed somewhat by the 1990 Act, according to which "the matters to which directors of a company are to have regard in the performance of their functions shall include the interests of the company's employees in general, as well as the interests of its members".[11] However, this does not entirely reverse the position under the *Daily News* case. It deals only with the directors and not alone allows them to take account of employees' interests but actually requires them to do so. This obligation is owed only to the company; employees do not have a right of action to enforce compliance with its requirements. Where the benevolence towards employees would be *ultra vires* or unfairly discriminates against minority shareholders, it is not validated; an objecting shareholder is entitled to have the proposed action blocked and, possibly, to recover extravagant payments that were made. The obligation here nevertheless is likely to have an indirect influence, as indicating a general legislative policy in favour of upholding measures adopted by companies for the benefit of their employees.

19–07 Even before 1990, devoting company resources to employees was permissible where that was incidental to and within the general scope of the company's business. As Bowen L.J. put it in *Hutton v West Cork Railway Co.*,[12] which also involved a minority shareholder challenge to company benevolence:

> "Most businesses require liberal dealings. The test … is … whether [the transaction is] done bona fide [and] is done within the ordinary scope of the company's business and whether it is reasonably incidental to the carrying on of the company's business for the company's benefit. Take this sort of instance. A railway company, or the directors of the company, might send down all the porters at a railway station to have tea in the country at the expense of the company. Why should they not? It is for the directors to judge, provided it is a matter which is reasonably incidental to the carrying on of the business of the company, and a company which always treated its employees with Draconian severity, and never allowed them a single inch more that the strict letter of the bond, would soon find itself deserted—at all events unless labour was very much more easy to obtain in the market than it often is. The law does not say that there are

---

[10] [1962] 1 Ch. 927.
[11] Section 52.
[12] (1883) 23 Ch D 645.

to be no cakes and ale, but there are to be no cakes and ale except such as are required for the benefit of the company."[13]

FINANCIAL PARTICIPATION—EMPLOYEE/SHAREHOLDERS

19–08   Some companies encourage and even help their employees to acquire shares in them. The view is that, by having a financial stake in the firm and being entitled to participate in its distributed profits, employees will more readily identify with the company and indeed become participants in a form of economic democracy. On the other hand, there is a danger that workers who invest most of their savings in their employer's business will lose everything if it fails; Marxists would tend to condemn schemes to distribute shares to employees as the carrots of class collaboration! Substantial stakes in State-owned companies that were recently privatised are held by employee share ownership trusts or ESOTs, notably in Eircom Plc and in Aer Lingus Plc.

19–09   It is for companies themselves to decide whether and on what terms their shares should be offered to employees[14]; there is no legal obligation on companies to allot shares to them. Part 17 (ss.509–519D) of the Taxes Consolidation Act 1997 provides a variety of tax incentives for schemes facilitating employees to purchase shares in their company.[15] One of the matters that the Pensions Board regulates is "self-investment" by occupational pension schemes, i.e. the fund investing heavily in the employing enterprise.

19–10   The prohibition against companies financing the purchase of their own shares[16] does not apply in three related circumstances. One is where a company loans money to any of its or its subsidiary's employees or former employees to enable them to acquire for themselves shares in it or in its holding company.[17] Another is where a company lends money whereby its or its subsidiary's shares are to be held beneficially by its employees or employees of its subsidiaries.[18] Loans under the former cannot be made to salaried directors; the scheme under the latter cannot. A third category, added in 2005, is any financial assistance by a company or its subsidiary in connection with either of them acquiring shares in the holding company, either on behalf of present or former employees, or of an employees' share scheme, or of an employees share ownership trust as designated in the tax legislation.[19]

19–11   Exception is made to the 1983 Act's authority and pre-emption requirements[20] in respect of employee share schemes. These are defined as

---

[13] *ibid.* at 672–673.
[14] See *BCM's Precedents*, E39.
[15] See generally M. Feeney *The Taxation of Companies* (Haywards Heath: Tottel Publishing, 2006) at 124 *et seq.*
[16] 1963, s.60.
[17] 1963, s.60(12)(f).
[18] 1963, s.60(12)(e).
[19] 1963, s.60(12)(n).
[20] Sections 20 and 23.

"any scheme for the time being in force, in accordance with which a company encourages or facilitates the holding of shares or debentures in the company or its holding company by or for the benefit of employees or former employees of the company or of any subsidiary", including salaried directors.[21] The requirement of shareholders' prior authority does not apply to shares being allotted in pursuance of such a scheme.[22] Shares being allotted in connection with a scheme need not be offered on a pre-emptive basis and employees offered shares under a scheme are not prevented from renouncing or assigning the offer, even to persons who are outside of the scheme.[23]

19–12 Public limited companies can give financial assistance for the above purposes, provided the funds come out of profits available for distribution or the company's net assets are not thereby reduced.[24] Plcs are forbidden to allot shares under employee share schemes where less than one quarter of the shares' nominal value has been paid up on them.[25] Nor may they allot shares in exchange for any service contract.[26]

19–13 At times a company's articles of association will stipulate that an employee shareholder shall cease to hold his shares on him ceasing to be employed by the company. For instance, in *Feighery v Feighery*,[27] the company's articles provided that whenever any member employed by the company in any capacity, other than as director, is dismissed or otherwise ceases to be employed by it, the directors could resolve that his shares shall be transferred to any other member of the company at fair value. The petitioner sought an interlocutory injunction to restrain the holding of a directors' meeting, at which he feared a decision would be made to dismiss him, thereby putting his shareholding in jeopardy, but without success.[28] A shareholder-employee in such circumstances who is unlawfully dismissed would be entitled to damages in respect of whatever loss he suffered by virtue of being deprived of his shares. But it has been held that where the relevant article (or clause in a shareholders' agreement) states that the employee may or shall lose his shares if he ceases to be employed "for whatever reason", that provision is effective even if he is unlawfully dismissed.[29]

19–14 Most share option schemes provide that the options shall cease once the individual ceases to be an employee of the company or of a company in the group, as the case may be. Sometimes they go so far as providing that shares acquired under the scheme shall revert to the company or one of its nominees.

---

[21] *ibid.* 1983 Act, s.2(1).
[22] *ibid.* s.20(10)(a).
[23] *ibid.* s.23(13)(b) and (6).
[24] 1963 Act, s.60(13).
[25] 1983 Act, s.28(4).
[26] 1983 Act, s.26(2).
[27] [1999] 1 I.R. 321.
[28] See also, *Avoca Capital Holdings* (2005) I.E.H.C. 302; Clarke J., unreported, *extempore*, July 29, 2005.
[29] *Holt v Faulks* [2000] 2 B.C.L.C. 816.

For instance, in *Walsh v Cassidy & Co.*[30] the plaintiff acquired shares in the company under a provision in its articles whereby shares were to be allotted to all company employees. But another of these regulations authorised the directors to expropriate the shares of any member who ceased to be "employed by [it]". It is implicit in Kingsmill Moore J.'s judgment that such a power should be construed as narrowly as is reasonably possible. He suggested that the clause there might not authorise expelling a member who acquires shares for full value and who subsequently took up some employment in the company. But he emphasised that any expulsion falling four square within the clause's terms would not be set aside merely because it would result in considerable hardship. On the other hand, "fraudulent" exercises of the expulsion power would be restrained.

19–15 Similar issues arise with share option schemes where the employee-company relationship is ended. In *Micklefield v SAC Technology Ltd,*[31] the employee shareholder was most unfortunate but it was not argued that he had been treated fraudulently. He was a company director and, under his contract, was entitled to six months' notice in writing of dismissal. He was entitled under a share option scheme to subscribe for shares at the end of a three-year period. When that period had almost expired, there was a very substantial difference between the option price and the price of the shares in the market, so that he stood to make a large profit. But he was peremptorily dismissed and given six months' salary in lieu of notice. He sought to exercise his options a few days later, when they fell due, but the company refused to allot him the shares on the grounds that he was no longer its employee. It was held that, once he was dismissed with salary in lieu of notice, he had ceased to be an employee of the company; accordingly, he was ineligible under the very terms of the scheme to exercise the options. Although certain aspects of the employment contract may survive termination of that contract, the status or relationship of employer/employee comes to an end. The doctrine that a person would not be permitted to take advantage of his wrongs was held not applicable there because the dismissal was not unlawful. Nor would the court imply a term that no dismissal could take effect until the notice period had expired.

19–16 In *Levett v Biotrace International Plc,*[32] under the company's scheme, if an option holder became subject to company disciplinary procedures and in consequence his employment was ended, his options lapsed. This was clarified by an accompanying letter, stating that the options would lapse where the relationship was ended "through breach of contract, gross misconduct or voluntary resignation". The plaintiff managing director was called to a disciplinary hearing and, at its conclusion, was summarily dismissed, without receiving any payment in lieu of notice. Because he had been unlawfully dismissed it was held that, under the terms of the scheme, he had not lost his options. On account of the principle that, generally, a person will not be permitted to take advantage of his own

---

[30]　[1951] Ir. Jur. Rep. 47.
[31]　[1991] 1 All E.R. 275.
[32]　[1999] I.C.R. 818 (Court of Appeal).

wrong, the provision in the scheme about options lapsing was construed as meaning where the employee is lawfully dismissed. However, either in so many words or indirectly, a scheme could provide that options shall lapse regardless of the legality of the dismissal; as for instance by providing that an option holder would not be entitled to any compensation for the loss of his options if he ceases to be employed by the company for any reason whatsoever.

19–17   In *Thompson v ASDA-MFI Plc*,[33] to exercise options under the company's scheme, the person had to be employed by the company or its subsidiary and, on ceasing to be so employed, options lapsed. The company sold its entire stake in its subsidiary to a third party and then claimed that the options held by those who were employed in its former subsidiary had lapsed. That was upheld, on the grounds that there was no basis for implying a term into the scheme whereby the company was precluded from disposing of its subsidiary. But the outcome there could be different today, by virtue of the regulations governing transfers of undertakings.

EXECUTIVE DIRECTORS

19–18   Employment law and company law significantly overlap in the case of executive directors, i.e. directors who are remunerated under service contracts with their companies. For most purposes, neither the Companies Acts nor the general common law/equitable principles concerning directors differentiate between executives and non-executive directors. They are subject to the same regime concerning, for example, disqualification, removal from office, remuneration, loans and equivalent transactions, fiduciary obligations and the various duties imposed by legislation on directors. Under their service contracts,[34] whether written or oral, they may have certain rights against the company or additional obligations to it. It would appear that a stipulation in a company's own regulations purporting to confer rights on, or impose obligations on, a particular director are not legally enforceable against it, as s.25 of the 1963 Act envisages only the position of persons so named *qua* shareholders. Depending on the circumstances, however, a stipulation to that effect in the articles of association may be the basis for implying a term into the service agreement.

Remuneration

19–19   The Companies Acts do not regulate how executive directors' remuneration is to be determined or on what basis it should be calculated, other than that any agreement regarding remuneration should not provide for it to be paid tax free.[35] Under Table A, it is for the general meeting to determine the amount and manner in which their remuneration shall be paid,[36] but many companies' own regulations confer that authority on the directors themselves or on a directors'

---

[33]   [1988] 1 Ch. 241.
[34]   See *BCM's Precedents*, part E.
[35]   1963 Act, s.185.
[36]   Article 76.

remuneration committee. Share options, contributions towards contingency and life insurance, and pensions often form part of the remuneration package. At times, under option schemes, entitlement to enforce options will lapse once the employment ends.

19–20 Ordinarily, an executive director's remuneration arrangement will be set out in a written agreement or in some other document incorporated into the parties' agreement. In those exceptional instances where that is not done, the question arises as to whether the person is entitled to be paid and, if so, how much. In *Craven-Ellis v Canons Ltd,*[37] the plaintiff had been appointed managing director but at that time he was not a director of the company, which was held to have rendered his appointment void. He claimed payment for work he had done for the company both before and after his purported appointment. His claim was upheld on the basis of "the implied obligation to pay ... imposed by law ... arising from the performance and acceptance of services".[38]

19-21 Ordinarily, an executive director's right against the company will be based on contract; where no contract exists, he may be entitled to a reasonable sum on a *quantum meruit* basis. In one instance, however, a director was found to have fallen between two stools and, in consequence, obtained no payment for his services. In *Re Richmond Gate Property Co.,*[39] the plaintiff was a validly-appointed managing director and the company's articles stipulated that the holder of that office should be paid "such remuneration ... as the directors may determine". But the board never decided how much he should be paid. It was held that he was not entitled to any remuneration because his contract left him "at the mercy of the board"; he "gets what they determine to pay him and, if they do not determine to pay him anything, he does not get anything".[40] Furthermore, the existence of the contract excluded any claim founded on *quantum meruit.* Some emphasis was placed on the fact that the articles there designated the plaintiff by name as managing director and the plaintiff was also a member of the company, so that the above reasoning may not be applied to officers who do not find themselves in that very situation. Remuneration on the basis of *quantum meruit* or an equitable allowance was refused in *Guinness Plc v Saunders*[41] for several reasons. Unlike the plaintiff in *Craven-Ellis,* the director there was a validly-elected director at the relevant time. A very substantial conflict existed between his own personal interests and the company's interests and there was no question of the Guinness directors and shareholders having actually approved the payment of the large "success fee".

---

[37] [1936] 2 K.B. 403.
[38] *ibid.* at 411.
[39] [1965] 1 W.L.R. 335.
[40] *ibid.* at 337.
[41] [1990] 2 A.C. 664.

Dismissal

19–22   Although the statutory entitlement to remove a director from office by ordinary resolution cannot be contracted out of, the company remains liable to that person in damages if it removes him in breach of contract.[42] Whether his removal was lawful depends on the express or implied terms of the service agreement. In *Harold Holdsworth & Co. (Wakefield) Ltd v Caddies*,[43] the plaintiff was appointed director of a company for a five-year period, his function being defined as running the company and its associated companies in such manner as may from time to time be assigned to or vested in him by the board. Following differences that arose between them, the board resolved that the plaintiff should confine his attentions to just one company in the group. It was held that this was not a breach of the service agreement because, under its terms, the board reserved the power to limit his responsibilities as it saw fit.

19–23   In *Glover v BLN Ltd*,[44] the plaintiff's contract as managing director provided that he could be removed without compensation for serious misconduct, serious neglect of duties, wilful disobedience of reasonable orders and the like. One issue before the court was whether, when dismissing him, the defendant's board possessed sufficient evidence of serious misconduct and neglect on his part. It was held that only one of the many allegations made against him would provide grounds for summary dismissal. At times the required standard of performance must be implied from the surrounding circumstances. A director whose conduct repudiates the service agreement can be removed almost instantaneously. In *Carvill v Irish Industrial Bank Ltd*,[45] what, to use a neutral term, was unwise conduct on the part of a small bank's managing director was held by Kenny J. to warrant immediate dismissal. But the Supreme Court concluded that, in the circumstances, his indiscretion was not sufficiently repudiatory for that purpose.

19–24   Unless the contract provides for a fixed term of service or for dismissal only on stated grounds, a director may lawfully be removed for any reason whatsoever if given proper notice. Proper notice means the period stipulated in the contract or, where the contract is silent, a reasonable period. In *Carvill*, for example, it was found that 12 months was a reasonable period.

19–25   Requirements similar to natural justice or fair procedures, involving extended notice, must be complied with before the members can pass a resolution to remove a director. The proposed resolution must follow the extended notice procedure and a copy of it must be forwarded by the company to the director in advance.[46] Ordinarily, he is entitled to have written representations circulated to the shareholders and to speak at the general meeting on the resolution. It was held in the *Glover* case[47] that, additionally, it is an implied term

---

[42]   1963 Act, s.182(7).
[43]   [1955] 1 W.L.R. 352.
[44]   [1973] I.R. 388.
[45]   [1968] I.R. 325.
[46]   1963 Act, s.142.
[47]   [1973] I.R. 388.

of a director's service contract, especially one that lays down grounds for removal from the board, that the removal procedures be fair. If, for example, the grounds stated for dismissal are misconduct or neglect of duty, then the director must be "told of the charges against him [and be] allow[ed] to meet the charges … and afford[ed] an adequate opportunity of answering them …"[48] It is of no relevance to this that the director is an employee and not an office-holder. Refusal to accord these procedural rights is a breach of contract regardless of how guilty the director may have been. The court in *Glover* did not consider whether or to what extent these rights could be excluded or waived by contract.

19–26   Many of the cases involving "oppression" in "quasi-partnerships" concern minority shareholders who were removed from their positions as executive directors or who have had their other salaried positions in the company ended while remaining on as directors—as in the leading cases of *Re Murph's Restaurants Ltd*[49] and *O'Neill v Phillips*.[50] It often is a defence to proceedings of this nature if a reasonable offer was made to buy the petitioner's shares.

CO-DETERMINATION—WORKER/DIRECTORS

19–27   The laws of some western European states oblige companies to place representatives of their workers on their boards of directors, of which the German *Mitbestimmung* system is perhaps the best known.[51] There is considerable variety among the different national schemes in respect of, for instance, the degree of compulsion to have workers' directors, the level in the company at which such directors act, the methods of selecting them and the weight and scope of their power to make decisions. The Worker Participation (State Enterprises) Act 1977 inaugurated a system of employee directors in the principal state-owned industrial and commercial enterprises.

19–28   Impetus for worker directors has come from the EC, in particular from the draft Fifth Directive on companies' structures,[52] which calls for worker participation on company boards. As originally envisaged, the scheme was somewhat like that pertaining in Germany, where representatives of the employees are entitled to membership of supervisory boards. Although these proposals have failed to secure support, a variant of them is provided for in the regime for the European company, or *Societas Europaea,* which can be incorporated in any EC Member State.[53] Minimum requirements for such representation are contained in the European Communities (European Public Liability Company) (Employee Involvement) Regulations 2006.[54]

---

[48] *ibid.* at 425.
[49] [1979] 1 I.L.R.M. 141.
[50] [1999] 1 W.L.R. 1092.
[51] See generally, Vagts, "Reforming the 'Modern' Corporation: Perspectives from the German" 80 *Harv. L. Rev.* 23 (1966).
[52] See generally, J. du Plessis & J. de Dine, "The Fate of the Draft Fifth Directive on Company Law: Accommodation Instead of Harmonisation" [1997] *J. Bus. L.* 23.
[53] See para.21–55.
[54] SI 2006/623.

CHAPTER 20

CREDITORS AND SECURITY

20–01 If a company is involved in commercial, trading or financial activities, nearly always it will have creditors.[1] Those liabilities may take the form of trade creditors (i.e. suppliers of goods and services who have not yet been paid), bank borrowing by way of overdraft and/or term loan, bills of exchange and acceptance credits. Many large companies raise credit in the capital markets, such as through syndicated loans, issuing bonds, sale and lease back arrangements. At times a company's major or significant creditor may be one or more of its shareholders. To enhance profitability from invested capital, a company may seek to obtain the advantages of significant leverage. The nature and extent of a company's liabilities to most creditors depend on the express and implied terms of the contracts it has with them, which can vary from comparatively simple agreements with suppliers to very detailed debentures. At times the creditors will include parties to whom the company is liable in tort. Often creditors will include employees in respect of unpaid remuneration and also the Revenue, social welfare and other public authorities to whom indebtedness arises by virtue of statute. A variety of post-judgment remedies are available to creditors that are no different whether the debtor is a corporate body, an individual or a partnership.

20–02 Although shareholders' entitlements and protection are the predominant concern of company law, a major secondary theme is protecting those who give credit to companies.[2] As the debtor is the corporation itself and not its shareholders, and since the vast majority of companies possess limited liability, companies' creditors are more exposed to risk than are individuals' creditors. Before addressing those rules specific to company creditors (other than the insolvency regime) there calls for brief consideration some of the major principles of company law that protect creditors' interests.

20–03 The various requirements to disclose information—be it to their auditors, to the Director of Corporate Enforcement, to the Registrar of Companies, in the *Gazette*, in newspapers and otherwise—assist those extending credit to

---

[1] See generally, T. Power *et al*, *Financial Management: An Irish Text*, 2nd edn (Dublin: Gill & Macmillan, 2005), Chs 15 and 21; and G. Arnold, *Handbook of Corporate Finance* (London: Financial Times Prentice Hall, 2004), Chs 15, 16 and 18.

[2] See generally, R Kraakman *et al*, *The Anatomy of Corporate Law: A Comparative and Functional Approach* (Oxford: OUP, 2004), Ch.4 and B. Cheffins, *Company Law: Theory, Structure and Operation* (Oxford: Clarendon Press, 1997), Ch.11.

a company to assess its credit worthiness. Additionally, every creditor is entitled to examine the company's book of registrable charges[3]; every debenture-holder must be sent a copy of the annual profit and loss account, balance sheet and group accounts, and the directors' and auditors' reports[4]; where an insolvent company is being wound up and a meeting of its creditors is being convened, a notice of the meeting must be inserted in at least two local daily newspapers[5]; the appointment of a receiver over the company's assets and of an examiner into the company's affairs must also be notified in that manner.[6]

20–04　The principles of capital integrity—of minimum amounts, anti-watering and maintenance of capital—are designed primarily to protect creditors. As the preamble to the EC Second Directive puts it, "provisions should be adopted for maintaining the capital, which constitutes the creditors' security …" In special circumstances and express statutory authority aside, a court might "pierce the veil" of an undercapitalised company; under-capitalisation is a significant feature in most actions against company officers and managers for fraudulent trading and even more so for reckless trading, as well as for restriction and disqualification.

20–05　Not alone must creditors give their consent to fundamental changes in the company's capital structure that directly affect their rights, but they have power to veto some other major changes that concern them indirectly. Every debenture-holder may apply to restrain a company from acting *ultra vires*.[7]

20–06　There are a number of statutory provisions that deal with discrimination between creditors, i.e. giving one creditor or one class of creditors advantage over others. Certain categories of creditors are entitled to be paid off in a winding-up before other unsecured creditors: principally, the State in a number of its manifestations, and company employees. On the other hand, paying some unsecured creditors before others might amount to a fraudulent preference. A floating charge granted within 12 months of an insolvent company being wound up may be invalid.

UNSECURED CREDITORS

20–07　Creditors may be either secured or unsecured. If the company becomes insolvent, generally unsecured creditors will not be paid all, or possibly any, of the amount that is owed to them. Secured creditors can look to their security granted by the company or otherwise to them, to ensure repayment, and they are unsecured only in respect of the difference between the value of their security and the amount of their debt. Most trade creditors tend to be unsecured; financial institutions that extend credit to companies almost

---

[3]　1963 Act, s.109.
[4]　1963 Act, s.159.
[5]　1963 Act, s.266(2); for voluntary winding-ups, 1963 Act, s.263.
[6]　1963 Act, s.107 and Companies (Amendment) Act 1990, s.12(2).
[7]　1963 Act, s.8(2).

invariably insist on having security. There is a special category of creditor who is preferred by law, meaning that in the event of insolvency that category is entitled to be paid before the generality of the unsecured creditors are paid. Occasionally some unsecured creditors will have agreed to be subordinated to others, in that those others are entitled to be paid first in an insolvency before the subordinated creditors can be paid. Finally, shareholders not alone may be creditors of their company, in their capacity as lenders or as suppliers to it, but also in their capacity as members as such; most notably, in respect of dividends that have been declared but remain to be paid. In a liquidation, these claims rank behind all other creditors' claims.

Involvement in Management

20–08   Apart from and often in addition to obtaining security, loan agreements with some financial institutions may contain a covenant that enables the lender to have a say in the company's management and even to alter its composition. This may involve authorising the lender to appoint one or more of the directors. Intervention may be triggered not just when financial catastrophe is imminent but when the company has not met stipulated guidelines, such as goals set out in a business plan regarding, *inter alia*, cash flow projections, finding a specified number of customers by a particular date, producing a working prototype. If these are not met, effective control of running the business may pass to those creditors. At times these covenants require major shareholders to pass resolutions at the behest of the lender, thereby in practical terms blurring the line between debt and equity.

Directors' Liability

20–09   Being agents of the company, its directors and other officers are not personally responsible for its unpaid debts. However, unless the court decides otherwise, every director of a company that is wound up and is insolvent will be subject to restrictions on the capitalisation of any other company they become involved with.[8] Directors who culpably disregarded the interests of their company's creditors run the risk of becoming disqualified from managing any company's business.[9] Additionally, in a winding-up there are several potential basis for holding directors liable for some if not all of their insolvent company's unpaid debts—most notably, for not keeping proper accounts, for fraudulent or wrongful trading, and for misfeasance.[10] Numerous transactions entered into when a company may be insolvent or is heading towards insolvency can be avoided at the instigation of a liquidator, and there is a summary remedy for recovering company property that was wrongfully disposed of.[11] It is a matter of some debate whether, in addition to these provisions, directors owe common law or fiduciary duties to safeguard creditors' interests. Much of this discussion does not address what would appear to be a central issue, *viz.*

---

[8]   1990 Act, s.150.
[9]   1990 Act, s.160.
[10]   See para.24–97 *et seq.*
[11]   See para.24–83 *et seq.*

whether the remedies summarised here are so inadequate that some overarching supplemental duty is called for.[12]

20–10   Since directors' duties are owed to the company itself and not to its shareholders, it would seem to follow that directors owe no general duty of care or fiduciary duty to their company's creditors. As Lord Lowry observed in the *Kuwait Asia Bank* case,[13] as a general principle "a director does not by reason only of his position as director owe any duty to creditors or to trustees for creditors of the company".[14] This point was emphasised more recently in the *Yukong Line* case,[15] where it was stated that: "where a director or a person having the management of an insolvent company acts in breach of his duty to the company by causing assets of the company to be transferred in disregard of the interests of its creditor or creditors ... he is answerable through the scheme which Parliament has provided ... [H]e does not owe a direct fiduciary duty towards an individual creditor, nor is an individual creditor entitled to sue for breach of the fiduciary duty owed by the director to the company".[16] Any legal obligations directors themselves may have to those creditors would seem to arise either from specific contracts with them, such as personal guarantees, and from specific provisions in the Companies Acts. An extra-contractual duty may arise in very exceptional circumstances. Lord Lowry qualified the above statement by observing that "although directors are not liable as such to the creditors of the company, a director may by agreement or representation assume a special duty to a creditor of the company. A director [for instance] may accept or assume a duty, of care in supplying information to a creditor analogous to [that] described ... in *Hedley Byrne* ...".[17]

20–11   However, where the company is or is most likely to be insolvent, then in exercising their powers the directors must give due regard to the interests of its creditors and, in particular, not subordinate those interests to their own or to the shareholders' interests. Failure to do so constitutes a breach of fiduciary duty, not to the creditors as such but to the company.[18] If the company was insolvent at the time, this breach of duty is one that cannot be ratified by the shareholders. For instance, in the *Colin Gwyer* case,[19] where the company was insolvent, its

---

[12]   See generally, Keay, "Formulating a Framework for Directors' Duties to Creditors: An Entity Maximisation Approach" 64 *Cam. L.J.* 614 (2005), Keay, "Directors' Duties to Creditors: Contractarian Concerns relating to Efficiency and Over-Protection of Creditors" 66 *Mod. L. Rev.* 665 (2003), Keay, The Directors' Duty to Take Into Account The Interests of Company Creditors: When is it Triggered?" 25 *Melbourne L.J.* 315 (2001), Milman, "Strategies for Regulating Managerial Performance in the 'Twilight Zone' ..." [2004] *J. Bus L.* 493. and Hu & Westbrook, "Abolition of the Corporate Duty to Creditors", 107 *Columbia L. Rev.* 1321 (2007).

[13]   *Kuwait Asia Bank v National Mutual Nominees* [1991] 1 A.C. 187.

[14]   *ibid.* at 217. See generally, Prentice, "Creditors' Interests and Director's Duties" 10 *Oxf. J.L.S.* 265 (1990) and Riley, "Directors' Duties and the Interests of Creditors" 10 *Co. Law* 87 (1990).

[15]   *Yukong Line Ltd v Rendsburg Investment Corp. of Liberia* [1998] 1 W.L.R. 294.

[16]   *ibid.* at 312.

[17]   [1991] 1 A.C. 187 at 219.

[18]   *Re Frederick Inns Ltd* [1994] I.L.R.M. 387. *cf.* Linnane, "Company Law Directors Duties to Creditors – The Story So Far" 2(9) *C.L.P.* 191 (1995).

[19]   *Colin Gwyer & Associates Ltd v London Wharf (Limehouse) Ltd* [2003] 2 B.C.L.C. 153.

directors resolved to settle proceedings it had brought against a party entitled to nominate one of their number, on terms that were excessively generous to that party. In declaratory proceedings brought by that party it was held that the resolution was invalid because, in the circumstances, the directors should have taken due account of the creditors' interests, which they did not. The principle is that "[w]here a company is insolvent or of doubtful solvency or on the verge of insolvency and it is the creditors' money which is at risk the directors when carrying out their duty to the company, must consider the interests of the creditors as paramount and take those into account when exercising their discretion."[20] The judge was of the view that no reasonable board of directors would have settled on those terms and, given the nature of the dispute there and that voluntary liquidation was very likely, the directors should have left the matter to be resolved by a liquidator and not "rushed ahead with such a far reaching decision ...".[21] There do not appear to be any clear guidelines as to at what stage of the company's financial difficulties does this duty arise and on how this duty is to be weighted against the directors' fiduciary duty to the company as a whole and their statutory duty to give due consideration to employee interests.[22]

20–12 Had the company there been wound up, the liquidator would have been able to successfully challenge that resolution and how it was implemented, by way of a claim for misfeasance.[23] Indeed, virtually all of the cases where courts pronounce on the fiduciary duty to consider creditors' interests, where a company either is or may very well be insolvent, are misfeasance proceedings[24]—including the Australian case that appears to have first discovered this principle, *Walker v Winborne*.[25] But neither there nor in the other common law jurisdictions do the courts grant a direct remedy against the errant directors on broad equitable grounds, without a winding-up or an examinership first commencing.

20–13 It is not entirely clear whether this orthodox view remains the law in Ireland, or whether directors of insolvent companies owe some general fiduciary duty or duty of care directly to the creditors. For the Supreme Court's decision in *Re Frederick Inns Ltd*[26] suggests that there is such a duty, although the court there did not so hold. The somewhat unclear judgment given by Blayney J. has been the subject of compelling critical commentary, particularly its assertion that the assets of an insolvent company are held by the directors in some form of trust for its creditors.[27] In *Jones v Gunn*,[28] McGuinness J. felt bound by that analysis to hold that, entirely separate from the statutory

---

[20] *ibid.* at 178.
[21] *ibid.* at 181.
[22] 1990 Act, s.52.
[23] 1963 Act, s.298.
[24] e.g. *Re MOA Investment Management Ltd* [2004] 1 B.C.L.C. 217 and *Re Pantone 485 Ltd* [2002] 1 B.C.L.C. 266. *Sojourner v Robb* [2006] N.Z.L.R. 808 may be explicable on a specific statutory duty to consider creditors' interests.
[25] 50 A.L.J.L.R. 466 (1976).
[26] [1994] I.L.R.M. 387.
[27] Fealy, "The Role of Equity in the Winding Up of a Company" 17 *D.U.L.J.* 18 (1995).
[28] [1997] 3 I.R. 1.

framework for winding up companies, directors of insolvent companies owe a direct duty to their creditors, which can be enforced by an individual creditor without having to wind up the company, and take his place with all other comparable creditors. A firm of architects were owed £35,660 by a company that had assets which were used to discharge practically all of a debt it owed to a related company. The firm obtained judgment against the company but, since it no longer had assets, did not seek to have it liquidated. Instead, the firm sued the company's directors and the related company for that sum, contending that there were "remedies available ... which arise from the fiduciary duty of the directors of the [company] and from general equitable principles."[29] The two English authorities relied on, to support this proposition, simply do not do so[30] and no reference was made to what was said in *Kuwait Asia*. In the 10 years since this case was decided, it does not appear to have been followed and it is doubtful if its thesis would be upheld on appeal. For the underlying basis of the statutory scheme for dealing with insolvent companies is that there should be an orderly liquidation of the corporate assets by a professional, who can be held to account in the courts, and that the interests of the various unsecured creditors are best advanced by measures taken by the liquidator, rather than having a scramble by individual creditors "going it alone." Granted, in US law there is a duty on directors along these lines but the Companies Acts in many of the major states there do not provide for remedies equivalent to the liquidator's misfeasance claim.

20–14   On the particular facts in *Jones v Gunn*, the defendant director may have owed a duty of care to the plaintiff firm under ordinary negligence principles, especially if that firm was the company's only creditor or only creditor of any substance. The requisite proximity would appear to have existed and the duty would be not to apply all of the company's remaining assets to pay a debt due to a related company, with the consequence that there are no funds to make any payment to the firm.

20–15   Had they been in force at the time, amendments to the liquidation regime in the 1990 Act would have provided adequate redress for the firm in *Jones v Gunn*, had it proceeded to wind up the company. Additionally, several of the major remedies available in liquidations may now be invoked by creditors where the principal reason why an insolvent company is not being wound up is lack of funds to pay for that process.[31] Further, on the application of, *inter alia*, any creditor, the court may direct any director or other officer of the company not to reduce his assets below a specified amount.[32] It also may direct any shareholder, director or other officer who is about to abscond or who is

---

[29] *ibid.* at 17.
[30] *Winkworth v Edward Baron Development Co.* [1986] 1 W.L.R. 1512 and *West Mercia Safewear v Dodd* [1988] B.C.L.C. 250. *cf. Peoples Department Stores Inc. v Wise*; 244 D.L.R. 4th 564 (2004).
[31] 1990 Act, s.251.
[32] 1990 Act, s.55.

improperly concealing property to be arrested and detained, and all his books, papers and moveable property seized.[33]

DCE's Proceedings

20–16 These *Mareva*-type orders, and arrest and seizure orders, may also be sought by the Director of Corporate Enforcement. Additionally, where the reason that an insolvent company has not been wound up is lack of assets to fund the liquidation, the DCE may invoke a variety of remedies that ordinarily require a winding up to have commenced.[34] These are:

1963 Act	
s.243	Inspection of books by creditors and members.
s.245	Examination of persons on oath.
s.245A	Order against person examined under s.245.
s.247	Arrest absconding contributory.
s.295	Frauds by company officers.
s.297	Offences of fraudulent trading.
s.297A	Liability for fraudulent or reckless trading.
s.298	Liability for misfeasance.
1990 Act	
s.139	Ordering return of assets wrongly taken.
s.140	Contribution to debts of related companies.
s.149	Duty to keep proper accounts.
s.205	Offence of not keeping proper accounts.
s.204	Liability for not keeping proper accounts.

20–17 These provisions operate outside the winding up context "with the necessary modifications".[35] In particular, if he has *locus standi*, where the aggrieved creditor obtains damages or recovers property in a claim for misfeasance, how is it to be shared with such other non-secured creditors as the company may have?[36] This provision is capable of a construction that only the DCE has *locus standi* to bring proceedings of this nature and that the only remedy for creditors is to invoke his support in this manner. Where in any such proceedings the DCE secures damages or property, a person with a claim against the company can apply for an order for a share of that money or property. No order may be made against the DCE in proceedings of this nature, other than in respect of his costs. In *Airscape Ltd v Powertech Logistics Ltd*,[37] an application by a creditor to have company officers examined under s.245 of the 1963 Act was refused by Laffoy J. The judge accepted that there was a public interest in such an enquiry taking place but observed that there was in existence a public body, the DCE, to perform that very function.

---

[33] 1963 Act, s.247.
[34] 1990 Act, s.251.
[35] 1990 Act, s.251(2).
[36] *cf. Re Prestige Grinding Ltd* [2006] 1 B.C.L.C. 440, concerning a claim by a liquidator against disqualified directors in respect of their liability to the creditors.
[37] [2007] I.E.H.C. 43, unreported, Laffoy J., February 5, 2007.

Shareholders' Liability

20–18   Where, as generally is the case, a company has limited liability, its creditors have no redress against its shareholders, other than indirectly to have any unpaid amounts on their shares called in by the company's liquidator. Provision exists since 1990 whereby, in exceptional circumstances, holding companies and closely associated companies can be made liable for the debts of their insolvent subsidiary or associate company, or requiring that their assets be pooled.[38] Exceptionally, a creditor may succeed in piercing the corporate veil and recovering all or part of his debt from one or more of the shareholders.

DEBENTURES

20–19   A company's principal indebtedness maybe provided for in one or more formal loan agreements.[39] Contracts for company indebtedness are frequently described with reference to debentures[40]; for instance that a company has issued a debenture or a creditor holds a debenture from a company. Legislation frequently refers to debentures. Part III (ss.43–98) of the 1963 Act is headed "Share Capital and Debentures"; ss.91–98 of that Act are headed "Special Provisions as to Debentures"; subject to exceptions, a private company may not offer debentures to the public.[41] Many of the statutory provisions which define the term "securities" define it as including debentures and debenture stock.

20–20   At common law a debenture is an instrument or document creating or acknowledging indebtedness of some permanence; for instance, a typical loan agreement with a financial institution, which sets out the terms of the loan and such security as is being provided. In the past when banks were reluctant to lend substantial sums to finance business ventures, companies often borrowed from the investing public by issuing debentures possessing several of the following characteristics: they are one of a series and are transferable, they provide for repayment of a principal sum on a named date or on a specified event occurring, and for payment of interest on the debt, and they contain a charge on the company's property securing the debt.

Nature of Debentures

20–21   The relationship between debenture or debenture stock-holders and the company is one of creditor and debtor. Until such time as the requisite funds have been lent to the company, that relationship does not exist. Questions of whether an instrument is a debenture arise in several different contexts; for

---

[38]   1990 Act, ss.140 and 141.

[39]   See *BCM's Precedents,* part D.

[40]   A comprehensive if somewhat dated account of the law is A. Topham (ed.), *Palmer's Company Precedents*, Pt III, Debentures and Debenture Stock, 12th edn (London: Stevens, 1921).

[41]   1963 Act, s.33 and 1983 Act, s.8.

instance, whether it is exempt from registration under the Bills of Sales Acts 1879–1883,[42] whether it must be registered as a charge in the CRO,[43] whether a register of the holders of the instruments must be left open to inspection,[44] whether the instrument represents an equity interest or indebtedness for stamp duty or for other taxation purposes.[45]

20–22 The term debenture is not a technical one; there is no precise received legal definition. Lindley L.J. once observed that:

> "What the correct meaning of 'debenture' is I do not know. I do not find anywhere any precise definition of it. We know that there are various kinds of instruments commonly called debentures. You may have mortgage debentures, which are charges of some kind on property. You may have debentures which are bonds; … You may have a debenture which is nothing more than an acknowledgement of indebtedness. And you may have a thing like this, which is something more; it is a statement by two directors that the company will pay a certain sum of money on a given day, and will also pay interest half-yearly at certain times and at a certain place, upon production of certain coupons by the holder of the instrument."[46]

The 1963 Act provides a partial definition for the term: "debenture includes debenture stock, bonds and any other securities of a company whether constituting a charge on the assets of the company or not".[47] An abundance of judicial *dicta* exists affirming the impossibility of giving a comprehensive definition. According to Chitty J., "it has no legal definition (but) the term itself imports a debt—an acknowledgement of a debt—and speaking of the numerous and various forms of instruments which have been called debentures without anyone being able to say the term is incorrectly used … generally, if not always, the instrument imports an obligation or covenant to pay".[48] According to Pollock M.R., "whatever the characteristics which you would expect to find or may find in the debentures, the root meaning of the word is "indebtedness"; that it does record an indebtedness".[49] Sometimes the term debenture is used colloquially to refer to the security given for the debt evidenced by the debenture. Although the term has an extensive meaning, it does not encompass instruments like bills of exchange or promissory notes,[50] deeds of covenant or several other types of documents in which a company undertakes to pay a sum of money.

---

[42] *Edmonds v Blaina Furnaces Co.* (1887) 26 Ch D 215.
[43] *Automobile Ass'n (Canterbury) Inc v Australia Secured Deposits Ltd* [1973] N.Z.L.R. 417.
[44] *Lemon v Austin Friars Investments Trust* [1926] 1 Ch. 1.
[45] *IRC v Pullman Car Co.* [1954] 2 W.L.R. 1029.
[46] *British India Steam Navigation Co. v IRC* (1881) 7 Q.B.D. 165 at 172–173.
[47] S.2(1).
[48] *Edmonds* case (1887) 36 Ch D 215 at 219.
[49] *Lemon* case [1926] 1 Ch. 1 at 13.
[50] *ibid.* at 20.

20-23 Debenture stock means a series of debentures that are transferable. Instruments that describe themselves as bonds can be debentures; historically, debentures grew out of bonds. The term "securities" ordinarily includes shares as well as other instruments but, in the context of the 1963 Act, debentures cannot include shares. As used in some parts of the Companies Acts, the term debenture has a more limited meaning; for instance, ss.91–98 of the 1963 Act deal only with debentures that are issued in a series and are registered. That an instrument describes itself as a debenture, or does not do so, is not conclusive; what matters is the substance of the instrument itself. As Chitty J. observed: "[i]n determining what is or is not a debenture ... I am not bound to hold that the instrument is a debenture because it is called a debenture by the company issuing it, not to hold it is not a debenture because it is not so called by the company. I must look at the substance of the instrument itself, and, without the assistance of any precise legal definition, form the best opinion I can whether the instrument (is a debenture)".[51]

Some Types of Debenture

22-24 There are a great variety of debentures. For instance, a debenture may be a single one or may form part of a series; it may be secured or unsecured; it may be convertible into the company's shares; it may be irredeemable. Exceptionally, a debenture may give its holder rights equivalent to some of those enjoyed by shareholders; for instance to attend and vote at general meetings, and/or to appoint or veto the appointment of directors.

Debenture Stock

20-25 Debentures can be issued in a series of stock that are transferable in much the same way as shares. Public companies occasionally make prospectus offers to apply for debenture stock, although, like public issues of preference shares, new issues of debentures to the investing public rarely occur these days. A debenture is almost always for a definite or ascertainable sum and can only be transferred in its entirety. Debenture stock is a portion of some large debenture, which can be transferred in fractional amounts and which can be consolidated into larger holdings. With debenture stock, sums are advanced to the company by numerous persons, but those sums comprise a single loan fund, the lenders being issued with stock certificates evidencing the amount of that fund which is theirs. Ordinarily, the company's own regulations or the terms of issue will stipulate the basic unit of which the debenture stock may be transferred—units of 1 or of 5, or whatever. Debenture stock is usually constituted by a trust deed, which provides for the security and for appointing a trustee to act on the stockholders' behalf, whose principal function is to ensure that the terms of the loan agreement are adhered to by the company and to otherwise safeguard the security.

20-26 Where debentures are issued in a series ranking *pari passu*, every company is required to keep a register of debenture-holders containing their

---

[51] *Edmonds* case (1887) 36 Ch D 215 at 220.

names and addresses, and stating the amounts held by each of them.[52] This must be open to inspection by any person. Every charge given by a company over its property to secure any issue of debentures must be registered with the Registrar of Companies.[53]

20–27   Issuing debentures or stock to the investing public is governed by broadly the same regime as for public share issues: principally, Pt 5 (ss.38–55) of the 2005 Act and the Prospectus (Directive 2003/71/EC) Regulations 2005.[54] Where they are listed on the Irish Stock Exchange and the requisite authority within the company exists, title to the debentures or stock can be transferred by way of the CREST system for uncertified securities.[55] The conditions under which "debt securities" obtain and retain a listing on the Exchange are set out in its Listing Rules.[56]

Redeemable Debentures

20–28   Generally, debentures are redeemable—as the case may be, at the option of the company or of the lender, at a fixed date or at a time determined by ballot, or on some other specified contingency. If they are redeemable on a fixed date, the company is not entitled to redeem them before then.[57] But if there is a market for them, the company may in substance redeem them by purchasing them. Occasionally, debentures are made redeemable at a premium in excess of the principal sum repayable. Where permissible under the articles of association, debentures that have been redeemed may be re-issued. Where the company has issued two or more series of debentures, difficulties can arise with regard to the respective priorities of the different series that have been reissued. Rights attached to a series may not be waived on a reissue, as that constitutes the issue of a new debenture.[58]

Perpetual Debentures

20–29   It has been customary to issue instruments described as perpetual or irredeemable debentures, which are redeemable only in the event of the company being wound up or on some other very grave default by the company. Doubts arose whether prolonged postponement of the right of redemption was a "clog on the equity" of redemption, which thereby rendered those instruments ineffective and void. To put an end to such doubts, it is provided that "debentures are thereby made irredeemable or redeemable only on the happening of a contingency, however remote, or on the expiration of a period, however long" shall not invalidate them.[59]

---

[52]   1963 Act, s.91.
[53]   1963 Act, s.99(2)(a).
[54]   See para.15–63 *et seq.*
[55]   See para.15–87 *et seq.*
[56]   Ch.15.
[57]   *Knightsbridge Estates Trust Ltd v Byrne* [1940] A.C. 613.
[58]   *Antofagasta (Chile) and Bolivia Railway Co. v Schroder* [1939] Ch. 732.
[59]   1963 Act, s.94.

20–30 In *Knightsbridge Estates Trust Ltd v Byrne*,[60] a company that had mortgaged its land to a single mortgagee, with the redemption date postponed to a distant period, sought a declaration that, on account of the "clog" doctrine, it should be permitted to redeem the loan at an earlier date. But it was held that the mortgage fell within the statutory definition of a debenture and, accordingly, its redemption date would not be cut down by a court of equity. A debenture is not validated where its terms, other than those relating to the date of maturity, constitute a clog on the equity of redemption.[61]

Convertible Debentures

20–31 A convertible debenture is one that entitles its owner, on or after a certain date or on some contingency occurring, to convert it into shares in the company. Conversion may be mandatory, at the company's election, or it may be at the holder's option. Where conversion occurs, the debenture-holder ceases to be a creditor of the company and, instead, becomes one of its members. Convertible debentures tend to be issued where the company is seeking to raise funds but either cannot or does not wish to issue shares at that particular time. Frequently, the business will be somewhat risky and investors will be reluctant to acquire an equity stake in it until it proves successful, but they may be prepared to lend funds with the option to convert the loan into equity at a later stage. At times, convertible debentures may carry entitlements similar to some of those enjoyed by shareholders, to make them a more attractive investment. Although debentures may be issued at a discount,[62] convertible debentures must ensure that their conversion into shares is not at a rate less than the shares' par value.[63]

Bonds

20–32 Debentures that are given in the form of a sealed instrument are bonds. Unless the company's articles of association require a seal to be used, it has been held that sealing is not necessary.[64] But there is a later decision of the Supreme Court[65] holding that assignments of debts must be sealed because they are not "ordinary contracts", from which it could be argued that debentures, especially creating a charge on land, must be sealed. A sealed debenture can be either a deed *inter partes* or a deed poll. If it is in the form of a deed poll, ordinarily the creditor must be described in some identifiable manner.

Bearer Debentures

20–33 Usually, where they are issued in a series, the principal outstanding and the interest accruing on debentures are payable to the registered holders

---

[60] [1940] A.C. 613.

[61] *Samuel v Jarrah Timber etc. Co.* [1904] A.C. 323.

[62] *Re Regent's Canal Ironworks Co.* (1876) 3 Ch D 43.

[63] *Mosely v Koffyfontein Mines Ltd* [1904] 2 Ch. 108; *Famatina Development Corp. v Bury* [1910] A.C. 439.

[64] *Re Fireproof Doors Ltd* [1916] 2 Ch. 142.

[65] *Re A Debtor's Summons* [1929] I.R. 139.

thereof. But debentures that are payable to bearer can exist,[66] as can debentures with interest coupons that are payable to their bearers. Unless the instrument otherwise provides, a bearer debenture is a negotiable instrument.[67] Those nevertheless are rare because, by virtue of since-repealed exchange control, they could only be issued with the Central Bank's permission.

Interest Payable from Profits

20–34 Usually the interest to be paid to debenture-holders is payable every year as a fixed percentage of the capital sum. But a loan made to a company, the interest which is payable out of profits when earned, has been held to be a debenture. *Lemon v Austin Friars Investment Trust Ltd*[68] concerned a document in which the company acknowledged that it owed a sum of money to the registered holder, described itself as an "income stock certificate", bore a number and was one of a series. That it did not in plain words provide for repayment of the entire loan in specified circumstances did not prevent it from being a debenture; it most likely was an implied term that the money became repayable in the event of the company being wound up. The instrument merely said that the loan was to be repaid from three quarters of the company's profits as and when profits were earned, which entitled the holder to an enforceable charge on a fractional proportion of the profits when ascertained. It was held that the instrument satisfied: "the primary qualification of a debenture ... namely, that it is an acknowledgement of indebtedness, and the fact that the possibility of payment is limited to three-fourths of the net profits may make the expectation of repayment less than it would otherwise be, but it does not prevent the fact of there being a source from which this recorded indebtedness may be resolved".[69]

Liability of Unspecified Amount

20–35 Although debentures usually are issued in respect of a fixed principal sum, at times instruments describing themselves as debentures are issued in respect of unspecified sums, for instance the common "all moneys" debenture taken by banks to secure sums advanced by way of overdraft.[70] In *Re White & Shannon Ltd*,[71] the question was raised whether an agreement to secure an unspecified amount can be a debenture. But McVeigh J. would venture no further than observing that "indebtedness in a principal sum is the significant and primary characteristic of a debenture".[72] This question was subsequently answered in the affirmative in England,[73] on the grounds that there were no authorities to the effect that those instruments were not debentures.

---

[66] e.g. *Re Dublin Drapery Co.* (1884) 13 L.R. Ir. 174.
[67] *Edelstein v Schuler & Co.* [1902] 2 K.B. 144.
[68] [1926] 1 Ch. 1.
[69] *ibid.* at 15.
[70] e.g. *Re Quest Cae Ltd* [1985] B.C.L.C. 266.
[71] [1965] N.I. 15.
[72] *ibid.* at 20.
[73] *NV Slavenburg's Bank v International Resources Ltd* [1980] 1 W.L.R. 1076.

Agreement to Issue Debentures

20–36   As equity looks on that as done which ought to be done, an agreement to issue a debenture is a debenture.[74] As one judge put it, "[a]ssuming that there is a clear definite contract to have debentures issued to them in respect of the loan ... they have as good a claim as any debentures could give them, except that their claim is equitable and not legal".[75] Where such an agreement constitutes a charge securing debentures, particulars of it must be registered at the CRO within 21 days of the charge being created[76]; depending on the circumstances, the court may permit an extension of the time for registration.

Trust Deeds

20–37   Where debentures or debenture stock are issued in a series, they are usually secured by a trust deed. The advantages of having trustees is that they can take a specific mortgage or charge on the company's land, as security, and they can monitor compliance by the company with the several provisions in the loan agreement. Where matters of concern arise, the trustees can make due enquiry of the company or elsewhere, convey relevant information to the holders and, if necessary, convene meetings of the holders to determine whether particular steps should be taken. One such step can be enforcing the debt against the company and realising such security as exists. Almost invariably where the debentures were issued to the public, the trustee will be a professional trust corporation.

20–38   Under these deeds between the company and trustees, a small sum will comprise the trust property, to which will be added the indebtedness and any security given. Usually, only guarantors will also be parties to the deed, which will contain conditions like covenanting to repay the capital sum and pay the interest; provide for keeping a register of the stock holders, for issuing them with stock certificates, for meetings of the stockholders; requiring the company to insure and properly maintain the charged property; specifying the circumstances in which the security will become enforceable, e.g. default, breach of other conditions, winding up, etc.; in such circumstances empowering the trustees to appoint a receiver and manager over that property, authorising the trustee to sell it and to pay off the loan and any outstanding interest with the proceeds.

Remuneration

20–39   Provision is usually made in trust deeds for remunerating the trustees. Whether or not trustees are entitled to be paid if a receiver has been appointed depends on the terms of the remuneration clause. In *Re British Consolidation Oil Corp*,[77] it was held that the remuneration clause there was "not one which gives the trustees remuneration only if they can prove that they

---

[74] *Levy v Abercorris Slate & Slab Co.* (1887) 37 Ch D 260.
[75] *Re Queensland Land & Coal Co.* [1894] 3 Ch. 181 at 183–184.
[76] 1963 Act, s.99(2)(a).
[77] [1919] 2 Ch. 81.

have done substantial or any work in each year" but was one that, "whether their duties are onerous or light, they are to be entitled to have the stipulated remuneration until the security comes to an end".[78]

Indemnity

20–40 Where trustees generally take action that involves expense or risk, they are entitled to be indemnified from the trust assets. Most debentures expressly provide the trustees with an indemnity. Where, however, under the trust deed they are required to take a certain step that involves minimal risk, the only indemnity they may be entitled to at that juncture is against the costs of defending legal proceedings arising from their action. For instance, where under the terms of the deed, they were required to serve a notice of default, where it had already been found that a default event had occurred, it was held unreasonable for the trustees to insist on a more extensive indemnity before serving the notice.[79]

20–41 In the past, it was common practice for trust deeds to contain extravagant indemnity clauses. Such provisions may not now exempt liability for misconduct or negligence. Any provision "in so far as it would have the effect of exempting a trustee thereof from or indemnifying him against liability for breach of trust where he failed to show the degree of care and diligence required of him as trustee" is invalid.[80] But trustees may be exonerated from liability for breach of their duties in at least two or possibly three circumstances. A release may be given in respect of a breach that has occurred. A provision in the deed may enable a majority of at least three quarters in value of the debenture-holders to give a release in respect of some prior specific breach, or on the trustee dying or ceasing to act.[81] The third case is where the clause was in force on April 1, 1964, and the trustee concerned has remained a trustee of the deed.[82] The benefit of such a clause can be extended to other trustees if a majority of not less than three quarters in value of the debenture-holders vote to do so.[83]

Majority Clauses

20–42 Trust deeds frequently contain majority clauses, i.e. clauses providing that the terms of the trust may be varied or abrogated with the consent of a stipulated majority of the debenture or stock-holders, as the case may be. These give the company and the trustees some flexibility to deal with unforeseen events. However, the court will not permit the stipulated majority to abuse their power to modify the trust deed's terms. As it was put in *Goodfellow v Nelson Line (Liverpool) Ltd*[84]:

> "The powers conferred by the trust deed on a majority of the debenture-holders must, of course be exercised bona fide, and the court can no

---

[78] [1919] 2 Ch. 81 at 92.
[79] *Concord Trust v Law Debenture Trust Corp.* [2006] 1 B.C.L.C. 616.
[80] 1963 Act, s.93.
[81] 1963 Act, s.93(2).
[82] 1963 Act, s.93(3).
[83] 1963 Act, s.93(4).
[84] [1912] 2 Ch. 324.

doubt interfere to prevent unfairness or oppression, but, subject to this, each debenture-holder may vote with regard to his individual interests, though these interests may be peculiar to himself and not shared by the other debenture-holders .... [W]here ... there is, as between different holders, a diversity of interest, it may be necessary or advisable as a matter of business fairness to make special provision for special interests, and ... there is [no] equity precluding a debenture-holder voting for or against a scheme containing such special provision merely because he is interested thereunder.... [H]owever, ... where there are diverse interests, and none the less where those interests are specially provided for, the court ought to consider carefully the fairness of any scheme by which a majority of debenture-holders seeks to bind a minority."[85]

20–43 Although the position here resembles that where a special resolution alters a company's articles of association, at least where there are different classes of lenders involved in the debenture,[86] an amendment to it will not be evaluated against a *Greenhalgh*-type "objective discrimination" criterion.[87] Something more in the nature of bad faith/abuse of power is required. This is because, under the principles for implying terms into contracts, it could not be said that across-the-board "non-discrimination" is either necessary to give the debenture business efficacy, or was manifestly envisaged by the parties, or is essential to give effect to their reasonable expectations. Had the parties intended that their discretions should be restricted in this manner, there would have been an express provision to that effect in the agreement between them and the company.

20–44 A secret bargain by one debenture-holder for special treatment might be considered as grounds for setting aside a majority vote to amend the deed.[88] A modification of the terms that substitutes shares and debentures, even shares and debentures of another company, for the existing debentures is permissible.[89] But a majority will never be permitted to sanction a sale by the company of all its assets in order that the proceeds be divided other than *pro rata* among the debenture-holders, such as among those holders who are willing to accept the lowest prices for their debentures.[90]

Transfers of Title

20–45 Being contractual rights against a company, the transfer of debentures is governed by the general principles regarding the assignment of contracts. Section 28(6) of the Supreme Court of Judicature (Ireland) Act 1877[91] authorises the transfer of debts and other choses in action by writing, provided that the debtor has been duly notified. Any such transfer is subject to existing

---

[85] [1912] 2 Ch. 324 at 333–334.
[86] *Redwood Master Fund Ltd v TD Bank Europe Ltd* [2006] 1 B.C.L.C. 149.
[87] See para.10–27.
[88] *British America Nickel Corp. v O'Brien* [1927] A.C. 369.
[89] *Re Hutchinson & Son Ltd*, 31 T.L.R. 324 (1915).
[90] *Re New York Taxi Cab Co.* [1913] 1 Ch. 1.
[91] 40 & 41 Vic. c. 57.

equities. Because debentures payable to bearer are negotiable instruments, their ownership changes hands by mere delivery of the document and is not encumbered by any existing equities. Debentures or debenture stock, the holders of which are registered with the company, are transferable in much the same way as shares.

Instrument

20–46 Except where ownership has changed by virtue of the operation of law, a company is not permitted to register the transfer of its debentures unless a properly executed instrument of transfer has been delivered to it.[92] Before 1963 it depended on the company's own regulations and the debentures' terms of issue what that instrument should contain. The Stock Transfer Act 1963 introduced a simplified transfer form for all registered securities, including debentures, debenture stock, loan stock and bonds. The form of the instrument of transfer is set out in that Act's first schedule; it must be executed by the transferor only and must specify who the transferee is, the consideration and the description and number of the amount of securities in question. Special provision is made for transfers by the CREST system of uncertified debentures quoted on the Irish Stock Exchange.[93]

Restriction

20–47 Unlike the position with shares, there is no statutory right to transfer debentures. Whether or to what extent debentures are freely transferable depends on the terms on which they were issued. Securities will not be listed on the Irish Stock Exchange unless they are freely transferable. Restrictions on transfer along the lines commonly imposed in respect of shares in private companies are most exceptional. Where a company refuses to register a transfer of debentures, it must notify the transferor of its refusal within two months of the transfer form being lodged.[94] Otherwise, within two months of then, the company must have ready for delivery the certificate of the debentures or the debenture stock, except where the terms of issue stipulate otherwise. Provision exists for the certification of transfers of debentures in the same manner as transfers of shares are certified.

Equities and Trusts

20–48 The power to transfer by way of assignment debts and other choses in action is "subject to all equities which formerly would have been entitled to priority over the right of the assignee".[95] That is to say, the transferee takes the debenture subject to any defects in the assignor's title and subject to certain claims which the company has against the assignor. A transferor cannot confer any greater title than he had himself; the company can rely against the transferee in respect of claims arising out of the debenture, whether they

---

[92] 1963 Act, s.81.
[93] See para.15–87 *et seq.*
[94] 1963 Act, s.84.
[95] Supreme Court of Judicature (Ireland) Act 1877, s.28(6).

arose before or after the notice of the transfer was given, and it may have a claim against the transferee arising out of some other transaction provided that the claim arose before notice of the assignment was given. Thus, the transferee's title to the debenture is subject to any equity, e.g. arising from an irregularity or fraud when the debenture was being issued, or some other claim of set-off or cross-claim, or other precise equity, available to the company against the original or any previous holder, arising before notice was given of the transfer.[96]

20–49 This greatly restricts transferability. However, debentures which are issued in a series usually expressly exclude equities and other personal claims and, accordingly, protect the transferee's interest from being defeated or devalued by some latent equity. For instance, in *Re Goy & Co. Ltd*,[97] one C, a director of the company and a holder of its debentures, was held guilty of misfeasance and was ordered to compensate the company. As security for a loan, he had transferred his debentures to R. It was contended that the company was entitled to deduct from what it then owed R the amount that C was obliged to pay it, on the grounds that it is "inequitable that a person entitled to a share of a fund should receive anything in respect of that share without paying what he may be bound to contribute to the same fund", and that "the transferee of a chose in action stands in no better position than his transferor".[98] But the debenture contained a condition excluding equities. It was held that "[t]here is nothing ... to prevent a debtor from contracting with his creditor that he will not avail himself against a transferee of any rights which he may possess against the creditor or any assignee of his".[99] Consequently, the company could not enforce against R the equities subsisting between it and C.[100] In one instance which concerned such a clause, it was observed that "any creditor would wish to agree with his debtor that the instruments securing the debt shall be as freely negotiable as possible. So far as the law permits, this debenture is drawn so as to approximate to an negotiable instrument".[101]

20–50 When someone other than the true or beneficial owner of debentures is registered as their holder, he holds them as trustee for their real owner. Most debentures contain a clause relieving the company, so far as is practicable, from the duty to accept notices of trusts or equities. In *Rearden v Provincial Bank*,[102] which concerned the similar article in Table A relieving the company of the duty to accept notice of trusts in its shares,[103] the purpose of those provisions was explained as "to spare the company of the responsibility of attending to any

---

[96] *Ithenaeum Life Assurance Soc. v Pooley* (1858) De G & J 294 and *Re Rhodesia Gold fields Ltd* [1910] 1 Ch. 239.
[97] [1900] 2 Ch. 149.
[98] *ibid.* at 153–154.
[99] *ibid.* at 154.
[100] *cf. Re Palmer's Decoration & Furnishing Co.* [1904] 2 Ch. 743.
[101] *Hilger Analytical Ltd v Rank Precision Industries Ltd* [1984] B.C.L.C. 301 at 305.
[102] [1896] 1 I.R. 532.
[103] Article 7.

trusts or equities whatever attached to their shares, so that they might safely and securely deal with the person who is the registered owner, and with him alone, recognising no other person and no different right; freeing them ... from all embarrassing enquiries into conflicting claims as to [securities], transfers, [interests] ... and the like ..."[104] But where a company's agents in fact have notice of some equitable interest held in the debentures, the clause does not relieve it from liability it otherwise would incur for ignoring those facts.[105]

<h2 style="text-align:center">SECURITY</h2>

20–51   To reduce risk, those who provide credit often require their debtor to furnish security. That may take the form of a guarantee by a person or body of substance.[106] Lenders of substantial sums to companies often require personal guarantees from the directors or the major shareholders; often companies in a group will be required to provide cross-guarantees for loans to associated companies. Or the security may take the form of a mortgage or other charge over property—either that of the company itself or of the guarantor's own property.[107] In this way, the creditor would expect to obtain priority over other creditors in an insolvency and, depending on the terms of the security, may give the creditor a degree of influence or control over events within the company. From the company's perspective, being able to furnish security gives it access to funds that might not be available to it otherwise.

Charges

20–52   There are four main kinds of consensual proprietary security: the pledge, the contractual lien, the mortgage and the equitable charge. Both the pledge and the lien are dependent on the creditor lawfully having possession of the goods or documents in question. In the case of a pledge, the owner delivers up possession as security, whereas in the case of a lien, the creditor retains possession of goods or documents delivered to him for some other purpose. A charge, in contrast, involves the debtor retaining possession of and making some use of the security in question. Provided the security is *intra vires* and was duly authorised by the company's management, the contract granting it binds the company.[108] For it to be an effective security, it must attach to the relevant property, which must be identifiable and in respect of which the company must be entitled to grant the interest in question. Any contractual or special statutory

---

[104] [1896] 1 I.R. 532 at 567.

[105] As occurred in the *Rearden* case.

[106] See generally, J. Breslin (with J. Smith), *Banking Law*, 2nd edn (Dublin: Thomson Round Hall, 2007), Chs 10 and 11, T. Parsons, *Lingard's Bank Security Documents*, 4th edn (London: Lexis Nexis, 2006), and R. Calnan, *Taking Security: Law and Practice* (Bristol: Jordans, 2006).

[107] See generally, W.J. Gough, *Company Charges*, 2nd edn (London: Butterworths, 1996); R. Goode, *Legal Problems of Credit and Security*, 3rd edn (London: Sweet & Maxwell, 2003); and *Breslin*, Chs 13–15.

[108] See Ch.18.

conditions for attachment must be satisfied. To obtain priority, usually certain registration conditions must also be complied with, which perfect the security.

20–53 A mortgage involves the debtor transferring legal or equitable owner-ship of property to the creditor but retaining possession of it. An equitable charge involves an agreement that the property should be available to the cred-itor as security, again with the debtor retaining possession of it. Both of these are commonly referred to as charges; there is no statutory definition for the term. The charged property can be land, chattels or choses in action.

20–54 Whether what the parties have agreed on in respect of that property con-stitutes creating a charge or otherwise depends on the true construction of their agreement—on whether those terms in their entirety point to it being a charge or to some other form of interest in the property, for instance an outright transfer of title in it,[109] or a mere contractual prohibition against taking certain steps.[110] In a sale, the owner of property transfers the title in it to another, who then is completely free to deal with the property in any way he wishes. A proper retention-of-title arrangement is not strictly a security by way of charge but is an outright sale of the goods, albeit subject to title in them remaining in the seller for the time being.[111] A pledge and a lien involves having possession of someone else's property coupled with the right to retain it until its owner discharges whatever obligation he owes the pledge- or lien-holder. But that holder acquires no proprietary interest in the prop-erty. How the parties themselves have characterised the transaction is of assistance in determining its nature but the label they put on it is not decisive.

20–55 According to Murphy J., in an instance where a purported reservation of title clause was held only to create a charge,[112] what matters is the very sub-stance of the transaction:

> "It would be wrong to infer that a particular transaction constituted a mortgage merely because the vendor [of property] structured it in such a way as to protect his commercial interests. On the other hand, parties cannot escape the inference that a transaction constitutes a mortgage … by applying particular labels to the transaction. The rights of the parties and the nature of the transaction in which they are engaged must be deter-mined from a consideration of the document as a whole and the obliga-tions and rights which it imposes on both parties … The description may be a material consideration but clearly it cannot be decisive … [I]t is the substance of the transaction as ascertained from the words used by the parties and the context in which the document is executed that deter-mines registrability under the Companies Acts."[113]

To constitute a charge in equity by deed or writing, it is not necessary that gen-eral words of charge should be used. It is sufficient that the court "can gather

---

[109] *Welsh Development Agency v Export Finance Co.* [1992] B.C.L.C. 148.

[110] *Re SSSL Realisations (2002) Ltd* [2007] 1 B.C.L.C. 29.

[111] See generally, *Breslin*, p.325 *et seq.*

[112] *Carroll Group Distributions Ltd v G & JF Bourke Ltd* [1990] 1 I.R. 481.

[113] *ibid.* at 486.

fairly from the instrument an intention by the parties that the property therein referred to should constitute a security".[114]

20–56 Most company charges are not outright mortgages, in that they do not involve the transfer of title in the security to the chargee, subject to an equity of redemption. Instead, the chargee obtains certain rights in respect of the charged assets, which may be pursued in the event of default. There are two categories of company charge, the fixed charge and the floating charge, neither of which have a statutory definition. The former is a charge on a specific identifiable item of property, like on land or buildings appropriately described, or on designated items of plant, machinery, motor vehicles, inventory, shares, insurance policies and items of industrial and intellectual property. Its "essence ... is that the charge is on a particular asset or class of assets which the chargeor cannot deal with free from the charge without the consent of the chargee".[115] If what is agreed is the creation of a charge that is not of the floating variety, then it is a fixed charge. While the possibility of an intermediate category has been mooted, for several purposes under the Companies Act it is critical to determine whether or not it is a floating charge. Apart from registration requirements, as described below, there are no significantly special company law rules governing fixed charges.

Floating Charge

20–57 A floating charge, by contrast, is a charge on a designated category or categories of assets but their actual constituent elements can change.[116] Its "essence ... is that it is a charge, not on any particular asset, but on a fluctuating body of assets which remain under the management and control of the chargeor, and which the chargeor has the right to withdraw from the security despite the existence of the charge".[117] For instance, a floating charge can be given over a company's stock in trade, raw materials and debtors, and, although these items constitute the security, the company is permitted to use and even dispose of them in the ordinary course of its business, and may replace them with new stock, materials and debts. The position is similar to that of a beneficiary in a trust, where the fund assets may change from time to time under the trustee's management. But for so long as those assets are under the trustee's control, the *cestui* has a beneficial interest in them; once the trustee disposes of them, that interest ceases.

20–58 The great advantage of the floating charge over a specific security is that the company remains relatively free to deal with the charged assets until it defaults and a receiver is appointed, or some other crystallising event occurs. Floating charges, therefore, are a convenient way of obtaining finance for companies with an appreciable portion of current assets, or inventory, in their

---

[114] e.g. *Kyrris v Oldham* [2004] 1 B.C.L.C. 305; compare *Re TXU Europe Group Plc* [2004] 1 B.C.L.C. 519 and *Flightline Ltd v Edwards* [2003] 1 B.C.L.C. 427.

[115] *Re Cosslett (Contractors) Ltd* [1998] Ch. 495 at 510.

[116] See generally, *Gough*, Pt II; *Goode*, Ch.IV; and *Breslin*, p.297 *et seq.*, Ferran, "Floating Charges—the Nature of the Security" 47 *Cam. L.J.* 213 (1988) and Pennington, "The Genesis of the Floating Charge" 23 *Mod. L. Rev.* 630 (1960).

[117] *Re Cosslett* case [1998] Ch. 495 at 510.

balance sheets. If the company has a sound business, it is in the interests of both parties that it remains largely free to use up or dispose of charged assets in the course of that business, because the profits thereby earned will be devoted to, *inter alia*, paying off the secured debt. Insofar as this capability gives ground for concern, a creditor may be able to address the matter through appropriate provisions in the security agreement.

20–59   Creditors, on the other hand, are not as enthusiastic about them because these charges rank in priority after any fixed charges, and after the State's and company employees' statutorily-preferred debts;[118] also because a company's most valuable current assets may be subject to retention of title clauses. Moreover, a floating charge given within twelve months of the company being wound up is invalid if the company was insolvent at the time the charge was created.[119] Especially in recessionary times, current assets may not obtain anything like their book value in a sale when the lender seeks to enforce the security. Another disadvantage of this charge was the "reputed ownership" rule in bankruptcy and the provisions of the Bills of Sale Acts, but these do not apply to charges given by registered companies.[120]

20–60   It is only in the past 150 years that it has been possible to grant a floating charge. Previously it was believed that charges on future property and charges on choses in action, like book debts, could not be given. But in 1862 it was held that a contract to grant a charge on future property, be it real or personal property, would be enforced in equity, and that the party who agreed to grant the charge held that property as trustee for the chargee.[121] Then in 1888 it was held that an assignment of future choses in action was enforceable in equity in the same manner.[122] These decisions enabled the Chancery Court in a series of leading cases to give full effect to floating charges. Most of these authorities are set out in *Re Dublin Drapery Co. Ltd*,[123] where a floating charge over the business of what was to become Clerys department store in O'Connell St, Dublin, was upheld. But the Scottish and the American courts never recognised the floating charge; it only became possible to grant such charges in Scotland and in the US following adoption of the Companies (Floating Charges) (Scotland) Act 1961, and art.9 of the Uniform Commercial Code, respectively.

20–61   While judges often describe the main attributes of these charges, there is no exhaustive judicial definition of the term. The lack of a comprehensive definition, like the lack of definitions for some other key legal concepts, was explained by Hoffman J. as resulting from the fact that:

> "a floating charge [is] not susceptible of being defined by the enumeration of an exhaustive set of necessary and sufficient conditions. All that can be

---

[118] See para.24–142.

[119] 1963 Act, s.288.

[120] *Re Royal Marine Hotel Co.* [1985] 1 I.R. 368.

[121] *Holroyd v Marshall* (1862) 10 H.L.C. 191.

[122] *Tailby v Official Receiver* (1888) 13 H.L.C. 523.

[123] (1884) 13 L.R. Ir. 174.

done is to enumerate its standard characteristics. It does not follow that the absence of one or more of those features or the presence of others will prevent the charge from being categorised as 'floating'; there are bound to be penumbral cases in which it may be difficult to say whether the degree of deviation from the standard case is enough to make it inappropriate to use such a term".[124]

20–62 Bearing these observations in mind, floating charges possess three basic features, namely:

1. Until it "crystallises", the charge does not fasten or attach to any specific property of the company but, instead, floats over whatever category of assets are charged.
2. Until crystallisation, the company is able to transfer the charged assets, whether by way of sale or as security, so as to confer on a third party a good title against the creditor who is secured by the charge; although complete freedom to transfer is not necessary.
3. In the event of the charge crystallising, as when the company defaults and a receiver is appointed, the charge then becomes converted into a specific charge over the category of assets in question, and in all respects takes on the attributes of a specific charge over those assets and any future assets of that category which the company acquires.

Whether the holder of a floating charge has a proprietary right or interest in the assets that comprise his security is a matter of debate; the answer lies in one's definition of exactly what is a proprietary entitlement.

20–63 Floating charges have been described on various occasions as follows and these descriptions are often analysed to determine if the agreed security is indeed a floating charge, and also to ascertain the precise incidents of these charges. According to Lord MacNaghten in *Government Stock etc. Co. Ltd v Manila Railway Co.*[125]:

> "A floating security is an equitable charge on the assets for the time being of a going concern. It attaches to the subject charged in the varying condition in which it happens to from time to time. It is of the essence of such a charge that it remains dormant until the undertaking charged ceases to be a going concern, or until the person in whose favour the charge is created intervenes. His right to intervene may of course be suspended by agreement. But if there is no agreement for suspension, he may exercise his right whenever he pleases after default."[126]

20–64 In *Illingworth v Houldsworth*,[127] the same judge said that:

> "I should have thought there was not much difficulty in defining what a floating charge is in contrast to what is called a specific charge. A specific

---

[124] *Re Brightlife Ltd* [1987] 2 W.L.R. 197 at 205.
[125] [1897] A.C. 81.
[126] *ibid.* at 86.
[127] [1904] A.C. 355.

charge, I think, is one that without more fastens on ascertained and definite property or property capable of being ascertained and defined; a floating charge, on the other hand, is ambulatory and shifting in its nature, hovering over and so to speak floating with the property which it is intended to affect until some event occurs or some act is done which causes it to settle and fasten on the subject of the charge within its reach and grasp."[128]

20–65   A particularly helpful description or test is that of Romer L.J. in *Re Yorkshire Woolcombers' Association*[129]:

"I certainly do not intend to attempt to give an exact definition of the term 'floating charge', nor am I prepared to say that there will not be a floating charge ... which does not contain all the three characteristics that I am about to mention, but I certainly think that if a charge has the[se] three characteristics, – it is a floating charge.

(1) If it is a charge on a class of assets of a company present and future;
(2) If that class is one which in the ordinary course of the business of the company, would be changing from time to time; and
(3) If you find that by the charge it is contemplated that, until some future step is taken by or on behalf of those interested in the charge, the company may carry on its business in the ordinary way as far as concerns the particular class of assets I am dealing with."[130]

20–66   Companies often give a floating charge over the entire assets of their business. At times the charge may only be on particular categories of property or on one category of property, for instance, all present and future book debts, all assets located abroad, all trading assets, etc. Charging instruments frequently confer a specific charge on certain designated property and at the same time give a floating charge over the remainder of the company's assets. As soon as a company gives a floating charge a present security comes into existence, but the chargee does not obtain equitable title in the assets which are charged until crystallisation occurs. Yet it would seem that the chargee possesses some kind of equitable interest in the assets prior to crystallisation, in that there are remedies available to him which cannot ordinarily be invoked by mere creditors.

Fixed or Floating?

20–67   A question that frequently arises is whether the charge in question is a specific or a floating security. The nature of the charged asset is rarely decisive on its own; while charges on current assets generally tend to be floating, the manner in which they may be used by the company may be so restricted by agreement as to take the charge out of this category. By the same token, a charge on fixed assets (e.g. land and buildings) that were never envisaged being disposed of in the business may nontheless be a floating charge. Often attempts are made to devise a specific security which nevertheless possesses

---

[128] *ibid.* at 358.
[129] [1903] 2 Ch.284.
[130] *ibid.* at 295.

some of the flexibility associated with floating charges, most notably the fixed charge on future book debts. Whether a charge is a fixed or a floating one depends, not on how it describes itself, but on its substance: does it possesses the characteristics of a floating charge set out above? This turns on the intention of the parties, not on the label that they used: was it intended that the company could comparatively freely deal with the charged assets until some crystallising event occurred?

20–68 Two steps are involved. First, the actual terms of the agreement must be ascertained. Then, in view of those terms, the nature of the charge is characterised, the determining factor being the circumstances and extent to which the company remains free to deal with the charged assets and remove them from the security. Unless the assets are identified with sufficient specificity to enable the chargee to exercise sufficient control over them, it cannot be a fixed security. If those assets are such that would never be disposed of in the course of the company's business, the presumption is that the security is fixed; for instance the shares in a management consultant's wholly-owned design subsidiary.[131] But if it is stipulated that any of those assets may be disposed of in the course of the company's business, at least without it being specified that any replacement assets are in substitution for them, it is a floating security.[132] On the other hand, where the debenture prohibits the company from charging, selling or otherwise disposing of or parting with the charged property in any way, it is a fixed charge.[133] Where the company is empowered to require that the chargee release some asset from the security, that does not render what otherwise would be a fixed charge a floating security.[134] Where the charging clause extends to assets that by the terms of the agreement could only be subject to a floating charge, the tendency is to categorise the entire security as floating. The extent to which post-contractual conduct may have a bearing on the nature of the security raises principally the question whether the parties have validly agreed to vary it or, alternatively, whether there has been an effective waiver by one of the parties.

Future Property

20–69 Charges can be given over future property because, once property as described in the charge is acquired, equity will compel the mortgagor to assign that property to the chargee. These are usually floating charges. But it is possible to have a fixed charge on future assets. In *Holroyd v Marshall*,[135] which was decided almost 10 years before floating charges obtained general judicial recognition, it was assumed that the charge on new machinery given there was a fixed charge. It is also possible to have a floating charge over a class of present assets only, although a charge so limited is most unusual. In each case it will depend on the parties' intentions, as evidenced by the terms of the

---

[131] *Arthur D Little Ltd v Ableco Finance LLC* [2002] 2 B.C.L.C. 799.

[132] *Ashborder BV v Green Gas Power Ltd* [2005] 1 B.C.L.C. 623.

[133] *Russel Cooke Trust Co. v Elliott* [2007] 2 B.C.L.C. 637.

[134] *Queens Moat Houses Plc v Capita IRG Trustees Ltd* [2005] 2 B.C.L.C. 199.

[135] (1862) 10 H.L.C. 191.

charging instrument and the surrounding circumstances, whether the security is indeed a fixed or a floating security.

The Undertaking

20–70   Where the charge is on all the company's property then the inference is that it is a floating charge. The charge in *Re Dublin Drapery Co Ltd*,[136] for instance, was on "the undertaking, stock in trade, land, premises, works, plant property and effects (both present and future) of the said company". As was explained in the *Florence Land Co.* case,[137] where the entire undertaking was charged, it is:

> "inconsistent to suppose that the moment you executed a bond or deben-ture you paralysed the entire company and prevented it carrying on its business, for if you read the words to mean a specific charge on the prop-erty of the company, then, of course, no practical use could be made of the money borrowed … [I]t would be an extravagant result … if the com-pany is formed to build and to let and mortgage its property, you can nei-ther lease nor mortgage without the assent of every individual bond or debenture holder … But if you read it as making a charge only to this extent, subject to the powers of directors whilst they are carrying on the business, then if they make default in payment of the principal or interest a creditor can apply … for a receiver and stop them from going on; but subject to that they carry on their business as usual … That appears … to be a rational view."[138]

A company was formed to invest in and to develop land, which issued a series of debentures that were secured by "all the [company's] estate, property and effects". In the absence of language indicating clearly an intention to give a fixed or a floating charge, it was reasonable to assume that the parties intended to have a floating charge, because a fixed charge on all the company's assets would prevent it from doing any business.

Chattels

20–71   Where the charge is over a category or categories of chattels—for instance plant and equipment, vehicles, raw materials and output—it depends on the extent to which the company is free to deal with them in the course of its business whether or not it is a floating security.[139] It is virtually if not actu-ally impossible to create a fixed charge over several types of chattel; other types are more amenable to being a fixed security. An excellent illustration of how at times finely balanced this issue can be is *Smith* (*Administrator of Coss-lett* (*Contractors*) *Ltd*) *v Bridgend CBC*,[140] concerning two coal-washing plants that were installed on a site, to process coal-bearing shale there. Under

---

[136] (1884) 13 L.R. Ir. 174.

[137] *Re Florence Land & Public Works Co.* (1878) 10 Ch. 530.

[138] *ibid.* at 537.

[139] See generally, Atherton & Makal, "Charges over Chattels: Issues in the Fixed/Floating Jurisprudence" 26 *Co Law* 10 (2005).

[140] [2002] 1 A.C. 336.

conditions in a standard-form building contract, the contractor on that site agreed with the employer, *inter alia*, that this plant "must be owned by the contractor"; that it should not be removed from the site without the engineer's consent; that if so removed, it "shall be deemed to revert in the contractor"; that if the contractor becomes insolvent and the engineer certifies that he has abandoned the contract, on giving notice the employer may expel the contractor from the site and take over completion of the work; in that event, the employer may use the equipment for that purpose and, also, he may at any time sell the equipment and apply the proceeds to satisfy any liabilities of the contractor. The contention that an outright transfer of title in the property rather than charge was created was rejected because the agreement did not say unambiguously that the plant "shall be and become" the employer's. "Deeming" it to be so was quite different and there were other features of the agreement incompatible with full ownership vesting in the employer; for instance, it could not be removed without the engineer's consent, the re-vesting clause, the power to sell the plant and apply the proceeds towards outstanding indebtedness.

20–72 In favour of it being a fixed charge, emphasis was placed on the agreement not permitting the contractor to remove the plant from the site without the engineer's consent. But the fact that the contractor's freedom to use the plant was subject to some restriction was held not to prevent the charge from being a floating one; it has always been accepted that property so charged may be subject to some constraints, for instance, a prohibition against creating further charges having priority. That restriction did not impair the company's ability to carry on its business and, further, was not imposed in order to protect the employer's security but simply to ensure that completion of the works there would be given priority. It was contended that, because the washing plant was large, was unlikely to be removed from the site during the currency of the four-year contract, and also received separate mention in the contract, it should be regarded as a specific security. But that was rejected because, as Lord Hoffman put it: "Although [it] was very large, it was not inconceivable that during the contract, just as it was found necessary to acquire a second plant, it might be found advantageous to replace one or both by a more efficient machine. In that case the contractor would have been entitled to withdraw the old machine from the site and the charge".[141]

Debts

20–73 The great advantage of obtaining debts by way of security is that, on default, the chargee does not have to incur the trouble and expense of taking possession of the charged property and arranging for its sale—often for far less than might be paid for it outside a distress sale. On default, the debtor is obliged thereafter to pay what is owing not to the company but directly to the chargee. Depending on the quality of the debtors, the security may be almost as good as cash.[142]

---

[141] [2002] 1 A.C. 336 at 353.

[142] See generally, McCormack, "The Nature of Security Over Receivables" 23 *Co. Law* 84 (2002) and the abundance of academic comment on the *Agnew* and the *Spectrum* cases discussed below, para.20–80.

20–74   In 1888 it was held that a charge could be given on future book debts.[143] By its very nature, such a charge is a floating charge because the company uses the funds it collects from its debtors to finance continued trading. In *Re Lakeglen Construction Ltd*,[144] Costello J. observed that "[w]hen a company charges all its book debts and when it is specifically permitted to continue trading, … such a charge should not be construed in a restrictive sense unless there is some other provision in the debenture or some fact in the surrounding circumstances which would call for a contrary interpretation".[145] There an "absolute charge" on book debts was held to be a floating charge.[146]

20–75   At times, creditors try to structure charges on book debts as fixed charges and, thereby, hope to get the enhanced priority of the specific security. In recent years the question of when is a charge on book debts fixed rather than floating has been the subject of extensive litigation and a vast body of academic comment. In the earliest of these cases, *Siebe Gorman & Co. v Barclays Bank*,[147] Slade J. held that it was possible, by appropriate drafting, to give a fixed charge on future book debts and that the charge there was a specific security. An even more restrictive agreement was considered in *Re Keenan Brothers Ltd*,[148] where the company gave its bankers a charge on all its book debts and other debts, present and future, which was described in the charging instrument as a "fixed charge". This went on to stipulate that the company would pay all money it received by way of book debts into a specified account with the bank; without the bank's written consent, the company could not make any withdrawal from that account or direct any payment from it; if called upon to do so by the bank, the company would execute a legal assignment of its debts to the bank. It was also provided that, at the company's request, the bank in its discretion could permit the transfer of funds from that special account to the company's trading account. Keane J. accepted that it is possible to create a fixed charge on book debts but held that, in the circumstances here, the charge was not a fixed one, principally because what the bank had sought to do was "to create a hybrid form of charge which incorporates all the advantages of a floating charge with none of the statutory limitations on its operation".[149] The parties' real intention was to enable the company to collect the book debts, lodge them to its bank account and use them in the business in the ordinary way. But this construction was overruled by the Supreme Court, which held that the parties had succeeded in creating a charge which possessed none of the typical characteristics of a floating charge.

20–76   As Henchy J. put it, because the book debts received were "relegated into a special account" and were then "virtually frozen and rendered unusable" by the company, save with the bank's written prior consent, this "restricted use

---

[143] *Tailby v Official Receiver* (1888) 13 H.L.C. 523.

[144] [1980] I.R. 347.

[145] *ibid.* at 355.

[146] Similarly, *Re Brightlife Ltd* [1987] Ch. 200 and *Buildlead Ltd (No. 2)* [2006] 1 B.C.L.C. 9.

[147] [1979] 2 Lloyd's Rep. 142.

[148] [1985] I.R. 401, also reported at [1985] B.C.L.C. 302 (H.C.); [1986] B.C.L.C. 242 (S.C.).

[149] [1985] I.R. 401 at 415.

permitted to the company of the assets charged was incompatible with the essence of a floating charge".[150] McCarthy J. concluded that "it is because it was described as a specific or fixed charge and was intended to be such, that the requirement of a special bank account was necessary: if it were a floating charge payment into such an account would be entirely inappropriate and, indeed, would conflict with the ambulatory nature of the floating charge ...".[151] Although it was "somewhat hybrid in form", it nevertheless was a specific charge on present and future book debts. Referring to what may be termed the policy objection to hybrid charges, McCarthy J. observed that "[i]f the borrower, the company, is driven to such financial straits that it is prepared to effect an immediate charge upon its book debts, the existence of which charge is [by registration], in effect, published to the commercial and financial world, I do not accept that an elaborate system set up to enable the company to benefit by the collection of such debts detracts from its qualifying as a specific or fixed charge".[152]

20–77 The reasoning there was dramatically extended in *Re Wogans (Drogheda) Ltd*,[153] which concerned a debenture that gave a most extensive range of securities to a non-clearing bank, including what purported to be a fixed charge on debts and other forms of income. It was stipulated that the company could get in those debts and realise them in the ordinary course of its business, but could not factor or similarly deal with them. It was further stipulated that the bank could designate a bank account at any time into which those debts must then be paid. But no such account had actually been designated in the intervening 12 months; all moneys received were paid into the company's account with its clearing bank, over which the secured creditor bank had no control other than via a general floating charge. At the trial, Denham J. held that, accordingly, for so long as the company was being permitted to use those debts in the ordinary course of its business, pending a special account being designated by the secured bank, the presumption was that it is a floating charge; this was fortified by the third requirement in the classic *Woolcombers* test[154] of a floating charge, namely is it contemplated that, until some future step is taken, the company could continue using the assets in question for its business. But that view was rejected on appeal.

20–78 According to Finlay C.J.:

"If a lender, having availed of a debenture in these terms as a concession delays the designation of a bank account or suspends for some period the operation of direct control over the bank account into which the proceeds of book debts is paid, thus permitting the company issuing the debenture to carry on trading in a more normal fashion than strict compliance with

---

[150] *ibid.* at 419.
[151] *ibid.* at 424.
[152] *ibid.* at 424. Followed in *Re AH Masser Ltd* [1986] I.R. 455 and *Jackson v Lombard & Ulster Banking Ltd* [1992] 1 I.R. 94.
[153] [1993] 1 I.R. 157.
[154] See para.20–65.

the terms of a fixed charge would permit, there does not appear to be any principle of law or of justice which would deprive such a lender of the rights agreed by the debtor company of a fixed charge over the assets, whereas, a lender with a more draconian approach to the rights which were granted to it by a debenture would be in a more advantageous position."[155]

20–79 It, therefore, would seem that in Ireland one can have a hermaphrodite security: a fixed charge over assets even though the company is permitted to use them up without restriction in the course of its business for a prolonged period. It is not explained in the judgment how this paradoxical state of affairs is reconciled with the *Woolcombers* test and the received view of floating charges. It seems that in Ireland a fixed charge exists once the creditor is legally in a position to bring about a state of affairs which will authorise him to control the use of the charged assets, even though he is presently not entitled to exercise that control. In other words, a charge which enables the creditor to crystallise it at any time and for any reason may be a fixed charge. In other common law jurisdictions that kind of arrangement would be regarded as a floating charge incorporating an automatic crystallisation clause. Under Irish law, apparently, it is a fixed charge, even it seems when the chargee's concession to deal with the property lasts for years. If this analysis is indeed correct, then the floating charge is practically defunct in Ireland.

20–80 It was held by a unanimous Privy Council in *Agnew v Commissioner of Inland Revenue*[156] and then by a unanimous House of Lords in *Re Spectrum Plus Ltd*[157] that a charge similar to that in the *Wogans* case was a floating charge because, under the very terms of the instrument, at all relevant times up to when those proceedings were commenced, the company was legally free to use its book debts in the ordinary course of its business. The position might very well change once the creditor required the company to pay the secured debts into a controlled bank account. But until that is done, there is no legal inhibition on the company making use of the debts, apart from the prohibition against factoring them. Following a careful analysis of the authorities in point (including *Keenan Bros*), it was held that a fixed charge exists where, under the agreement "the proceeds were not at the company's disposal. Such an arrangement is inconsistent with the charge being a floating charge, since the debts are not available to the company as a source of its cash flow. But ... it is not enough to provide in the debenture that the account is a blocked account if it is not operated as one in fact".[158] The *Wogans* case was not referred to either by counsel for the chargees nor by either court, presumably because it is founded on a fundamental misconception about the law on this topic; nor has the theory advanced in *Wogans* ever been seriously suggested to any other court in the common law world.

---

[155] [1993] 1 I.R. 157 at 170–171.

[156] [2001] 2 A.C. 710.

[157] [2005] 2 A.C. 680. See generally, J. Getzler & J. Payne (eds), *Company Charges: Spectrum and Beyond* (Oxford: OUP, 2006).

[158] [2001] 2 A.C. 710 at 730. See too, *Re Beam Tube Products Ltd* [2007] 2 B.C.L.C. 732.

20–81   The Supreme Court reconsidered the *Wogans* case in *Re Holidair Ltd*,[159] which concerned an almost identically-worded debenture. Blayney J. "distinguished" *Wogans* on grounds that are not easy to fathom.[160] If, as Costello P. had done at first instance, the court there had followed *Wogans*, a large construction company would have been forced into liquidation, leading to widespread job losses. Accordingly, it is far from clear whether the reasoning in *Wogans* would be followed today, i.e. that a fixed charge may, on sufferance, be permitted to operate temporarily as a floating charge and yet remain a fixed charge. Unless the very criteria for identifying a floating charge are different in Ireland from elsewhere, it would seem that *Wogans* was wrongly decided, a concession that the court in *Holidair* was unwilling to make. Instead, the court sought to make a factual distinction between the two cases with no real substance. The basis for the reasoning in *Wogans* is that where a charge describes itself as fixed and at some stage in its existence is capable of being operated only in a manner consistent with a fixed charge, then it was such a charge throughout. Why? Because when interpreting a contract, it is not admissible to have regard to parties' conduct after it was concluded (a doubtful enough proposition). But there was no dispute about the very interpretation of the debenture there; it was abundantly clear what the relevant words and sentences meant. The dispute was about something very different, i.e. the second stage: the characterisation of the instrument. Interpretation is concerned with ascertaining the parties' intentions from the words they used; characterisation is concerned with the actual legal effect of what those words are found to mean. Accordingly, the *Whitworth Street Estates*[161] line of authority on contractual interpretation was a complete red herring with regard to the issue really in dispute. We disagree with our colleague Dr Breslin's view that the analysis in *Wogans* "makes perfect sense".[162]

20–82   Although it was accepted as correct in *Keenan*, there remains the question whether the kind of charge held to be fixed in *Siebe Gorman* would still be regarded as fixed.[163] In *Spectrum Plus*, the House of Lords concluded that the reasoning in *Siebe* was fundamentally flawed because the debenture there did not entitle the bank to retain control over the proceeds of the book debts that were lodged to the company's account. Although the company was not free to "charge or assign [the funds] in favour of any other person", it was not prohibited from writing cheques against the account or otherwise withdrawing funds from it. In contrast, in *Keenan Bros.*, the debenture gave the bank total control over the disposition of funds in the company's account with it.

---

[159] [1994] 1 I.R. 416.

[160] The first-named author was junior counsel for the examiner, which may colour the views expressed here.

[161] *Whitworth Street Estates Ltd v Miller* [1970] A.C. 583, which was the cornerstone of the court's decision.

[162] *Breslin*, p.514.

[163] See generally, Smart, "Fixed or Floating?: *Siebe Gorman* past *Brumark*" 25 *Co. Law* 331 (2004) and Berg, "The Cuckoo in the Nest of Corporate Insolvency: Some Aspects of the *Spectrum* Case" [2006] *J. Bus L.* 22.

20–83   On this entire question, the Irish courts would seem now to have three options. One is to hold that *Wogans* and *Siebe* were wrongly decided, on the basis that for the security to be fixed, the charge must give the creditor full control over the charged funds. Another is to develop its own coherent set of principles for distinguishing these two types of charge. A third is to affirm *Wogan* and *Siebe* as representing the law notwithstanding the above criticisms.[164]

Composite Charges

20–84   Security documents frequently stipulate that they create both fixed charges and floating charges over various categories of assets; the question then arises of which kind of charge is a particular category of assets subject to. The answer lies in the parties' intentions with respect to the assets in question. Where those are of a kind that tend to get turned over in the course of the business the presumption is that they are subject to a floating charge. Where those are fixed in nature, the presumption is in favour of a specific charge. The parties' characterisation of the charge as falling into one category or another is an important indication of their real intentions but is not determinative. For instance, in *Re Armagh Shoes Ltd*,[165] the company had already given its bank a fixed charge over its land and buildings and a floating charge over the entire undertaking, when it executed a further charge in the bank's favour. This was expressed as a "fixed charge [on] all receivables, debts, plant, machinery, fixtures, fittings and ancillary equipment now or at any time hereinafter belonging to the mortgagor". Despite the express characterisation and the existence of the earlier floating charge on these items, Hutton J. held that the parties created a floating charge, because the parties must have intended that the company could continue dealing with the charged items in the course of its business.[166]

20–85   A more difficult case was *Welch v Bowmaker (Ireland) Ltd*,[167] which concerned the status of a charge over one parcel of land. The company gave an undesignated charge on its "undertaking and all its property and assets, present and future … for the time being"; at the same time it gave a specific charge over three identified properties it owned. But it also owned a fourth property and the question was whether, under the undesignated charge, that property was the subject of a fixed charge. Overruling Costello J., a divided Supreme Court held that it was a floating charge, on the basis of the principle of construction *generalia specialibus non derogant*; it was fair to infer from the express references to the other properties as being subject to a fixed charge that the fourth property was not to be so charged. Kenny J., dissenting, was persuaded by the fact that this property was owned by the company when the charge was given and it "certainly was not a class of asset which would be changing from time to time".[168]

---

[164] See comment in *Breslin*, p.520.
[165] [1982] N.I. 59.
[166] Similarly, *Ashborder BV v Green Gas Power Ltd* [2005] 1 B.C.L.C. 623.
[167] [1980] I.R. 251.
[168] *ibid.* at 258.

Restrictions on Dealing with the Charged Assets

20–86   A person who has given a specific charge over assets is not allowed to sell or otherwise to dispose of them without the chargee's consent; he may not deal with them as if the charge does not exist. A person who acquires assets that were disposed of in breach of this security does not acquire title to them unless he was a bona fide purchaser without notice or, if they are chattels, unless title can otherwise be acquired under the Sale of Goods Acts. But with a floating charge the security can continue to be used in the company's business. Although it is implicit that the company is not to do anything with the charged assets other than in the ordinary course of business, absent explicit restrictions on particular transactions, the courts take an expansive view of what constitutes dealings in the ordinary course of business. Because certain transactions with those assets could very well render the charge worthless, or at least take from their value, it is common for instruments creating charges to forbid certain kinds of prejudicial dealings with the assets, for instance, granting a fixed charge over some of them. Occasionally, the restrictions on use can be so extensive that the charge cannot truly be regarded as a floating charge.[169]

Ordinary Course of Business

20–87   In *Re Old Bushmills Distillery Co., Ex p. Brett*,[170] Lord Ashbourne C. observed that the courts are "anxious to uphold all reasonable bona fide transactions (in the charged property) that are entered into for the purpose of keeping up the business of a company and saving it from collapse or paralysis ..."[171] Curiously, most of the Irish cases on this question concern distillery companies dealing with stocks of whiskey that were subject to floating charges.[172] Dealing in the ordinary course of business includes selling some of the charged assets, leasing them on hire purchase,[173] a sale and leaseback of the assets[174] and giving a specific charge over the assets in priority to the floating charge.[175]

20–88   It depends on the circumstances whether a sale of the undertaking itself constitutes a transaction in the ordinary course of business. It undoubtedly is not so where the sale is with a view to ceasing doing business entirely.[176] But in *Re Borax Co.*,[177] where the company agreed to sell all its property and assets, except for certain investments, in return for securities in the purchaser company, it was held that the company there had not in fact stopped business or ceased to be a going concern. And in *Re HH Vivian & Co.*,[178] it was held that it is not inconsistent with the general terms of a floating

---

[169] *Re Buildlead Ltd (No. 2)* [2006] 1 B.C.L.C. 9.
[170] [1897] 1 I.R. 488.
[171] *ibid.* at 495.
[172] *ibid.* at 495. *Re Bushmills Distillery Co., Ex p. Brydon* [1896] 1 I.R. 301, *Cox v Dublin Distillery Co.* [1906] 1 I.R. 446 and *Coveney v Persse* [1910] 1 I.R. 194.
[173] *Dempsey v Traders Finance Corp.* [1933] N.Z.L.R. 1258.
[174] *Paintin & Nottingham Ltd v Miller* [1917] N.Z.L.R. 164.
[175] *Wheatly v Silkstone & Haigh Moor Colliery Co.* (1885) 29 Ch D 715.
[176] *Hubbuck v Helms* (1887) 56 L.J. Ch. 536.
[177] [1901] 1 Ch. 326.
[178] [1900] 2 Ch. 654.

charge for a company, with businesses being carried on at several branches, to dispose of all the assets of one of those branches. Presumably an *ultra vires* transaction or a fraudulent transaction would not be regarded as within the ordinary course of business.

Restrictive Clauses

20–89 A great variety of specific prohibitions on dealings with the charged property can be imagined; by far the most common restriction is on creating any mortgage or charge on the assets in question ranking in priority to or *pari passu* with the floating charge. The four major Irish cases on these clauses[179] concerned such restrictions and whether what the distillery companies had done there contravened those prohibitions. These clauses are strictly construed.[180] Prohibitions against creating any charge ranging in priority to or *pari passu* with the floating charge do not forbid persons from acquiring liens that rank in priority to the charge, like a solicitors' lien, a sub-contractors' statutory lien or, indeed, a general lien under contract.[181] As was explained in *Brunton v Electrical Engineering Corp.*,[182] where it was held that the charged assets could become subject to a solicitors' lien, these prohibitions do not apply to: "a mortgage or charge given by the general law, and arising through the company carrying on its business in the ordinary course. So long as the company are acting according to the ordinary course of business and not so as to give their [chargee] any advantage by their own direct act, but are merely allowing him, in the ordinary course of business, to acquire that lien which the law gives him … they are not creating a mortgage or charge in his favour".[183]

20–90   In one of the *Old Bushmills Distillery Co.* cases,[184] the company gave a charge on the undertaking, subject to a restrictive clause. But then, in order to raise additional funds, the company agreed that a syndicate, who comprised some of its creditors, should buy quantities of whiskey from it at specified prices and that, under the syndicate's direction, the money should be applied to satisfy the company's trade debts and other pressing liabilities. It was held that the transactions under this agreement were genuine sales of assets and were not charges forbidden by the restrictive clause. FitzGibbon L.J. observed there that "a financing motive, and even a financing disposal of the money received, will not deprive a transaction of its character as a dealing in the course of business".[185] Similarly in *Coveney v Persse Ltd*,[186] the company originally purported to sell whiskey together with an undertaking to repurchase it. But on taking legal advice that this arrangement could very well contravene the prohibition against granting other charges, the company amended the agreement. All references to pledges and to

---

[179] See fn.172 above.
[180] *Ex p. Brett* case [1897] 1 I.R. 88.
[181] *cf. George Barker (Transport) Ltd v Eynon* [1974] 1 W.L.R. 462.
[182] [1892] 1 Ch. 434.
[183] *ibid.* at 441.
[184] *Ex p. Brett* case [1897] 1 I.R. 488.
[185] *ibid.* at 504.
[186] [1910] 1 I.R. 194.

redemption were struck out, and it was made clear that the whiskey was to be the buyer's property but that the company had an option to repurchase the whiskey after four years. It was held that transactions under this agreement were sales, not mortgages or pledges that the debenture proscribed, and were made in the ordinary course of business. According to Palles C.B.:

> "I hold, not that the form only of the transaction was changed, its substance remaining the same—but that the substance was changed, that the real transaction was that which was represented by the documents ... The presence or absence of reciprocal rights is the determining element in ascertaining whether the document evidences a sale or a pledge. It is too much to ask us to hold that in a honest commercial transaction, in which the parties were at arms' length, the stipulation upon which, to their knowledge, the validity of the transaction depended is to be abrogated with the view of avoiding the transaction."[187]

20–91   In contrast, in another of the *Old Bushmills* cases,[188] the company applied to a financier to accept a bill against its whiskey and the transaction was carried out by what purported to be a sale of the whiskey to him, subject to the company's right to repurchase it. The bill was discounted at a bank and the whiskey was then transferred into the bank's name in the company's books and also at the bonded warehouse. It was held that the entire transaction there was a sham sale and that, accordingly, it contravened the express prohibition contained in the debenture. In FitzGibbon L.J.'s words, the bank:

> "was throughout a mortgagee and a mortgagee only and never bought any whiskey. The company transferred the whiskey and purported to sell it to people who [were] only trustees for the company, holding upon trust to mortgage to the bank ... but themselves standing in a fiduciary relation to the company, which made it impossible for them to claim to be out and out purchasers. The whole transaction was a colourable sale, and an evasion, for a real purpose of giving a security to the bank, leaving an equity of redemption still in the company".[189]

Similarly, in *Cox v Dublin City Distillery Co.*[190] it was held that pledging whiskey to the bank, by delivering to it the bonders' warrants for the whiskey along with the invoices, breached the prohibition in the debenture against granting other charges.

20–92   Persons who subsequently acquire an interest in the charged assets, who know that a restrictive clause in respect of them was breached by the company granting that interest, cannot have priority over the chargee.[191] What constitutes notice in this context is dealt with later.[192] Provided he has no knowledge of the

---

[187] *ibid.* at 214.
[188] *Ex p. Brydon* [1896] 1 I.R. 301.
[189] His account of the case as given in *Ex p. Brett* [1897] 1 I.R. at 505.
[190] [1906] 1 I.R. 446.
[191] See generally, *Goode*, Ch.V and Farrar, "Floating Charges and Priorities" 38 *Conv* 305 (1974).
[192] *Re Castell & Brown Ltd* [1898] 1 Ch. 315

restriction on granting other charges, that restriction does not operate against any subsequent equitable mortgagee who gets possession of the title documents to the property in question. Nor does the restriction stand in the way of creating a specific charge over property subsequently acquired when that charge arose out of the very acquisition. This is because the equitable rights arising from the contract of purchase make the charge attach to the property before the legal ownership vests in the company and, consequently, the charge has priority over the equity created by the restriction. Thus, the restriction does not override the charge that the vendor of after-acquired property gets to secure the purchase money, nor a charge to secure an advance by a third party of part of the purchase money.

Crystallisation of Floating Charges

20–93 By a floating charge crystallising is meant that the charge, so to speak, ceases to float over the assets in question and is converted into a fixed or specific security over those designated assets that the company then possessed or subsequently acquires. Until crystallisation occurs, the debenture-holder is not entitled to intervene unless the company jeopardises the security, does some act which is *ultra vires* its memorandum of association or has ceased to be a going concern. After crystallisation, the company is no longer free to deal with the assets in the course of its business and the holder of the charge becomes entitled to have them sold off to be reimbursed from their proceeds.[193] Where a floating charge crystallises before a receiver is appointed or before a winding-up commences, the chargee obtains priority over the statutorily preferred creditors (e.g. the Revenue and the employees) since his charge has become a fixed charge.[194] Due to the important consequences of crystallisation, it is vital to know what brings it about and precisely when it occurs.

Crystallising Events

20–94 Crystallisation occurs once a company goes into liquidation, even where it is being wound up merely to restructure its capital.[195] A compulsory winding-up is deemed to have commenced when the petition was presented and a voluntary winding-up begins once the members' resolution to wind up is passed.[196] Provision is made in the 1963 Act for notifying the Registrar of Companies and publicising the fact of a winding up having commenced.[197]

20–95 Crystallisation also occurs when a receiver is appointed under the charge.[198] But taking preliminary steps to have a receiver appointed does not of itself cause crystallisation. Appointment of a receiver is required to be publicised in several ways.

---

[193] e.g. *Re ELS Ltd* [1994] 1 B.C.L.C. 743.
[194] *Re Brightlife Ltd* [1987] 2 W.L.R. 197.
[195] *Re Crampton & Co.* [1914] 1 Ch. 594.
[196] 1963 Act, s.220.
[197] 1963 Act, ss.221, 227 & 252.
[198] *Taunton v Sheriff of Warwickshire* [1895] 2 Ch. 319.

20–96   Crystallisation occurs as well when, under a power in the charge, the debenture-holder intervenes and takes possession of the assets, at least where doing so causes the company to cease to carry on business as a going concern.[199]

20–97   As for whether the company itself ceasing to carry on business brings about crystallization, in *Halpin v Cremin*,[200] it was assumed that the business ceasing did not have a crystallising effect. But this matter does not appear to have been considered thoroughly there and most likely the case would not be followed today. There are several *dicta* that those circumstances constitute a crystallising event and it is settled that ceasing to do business is a ground for having a receiver appointed. One reason for not regarding ending the business as invariably a crystallising event is that trading can cease without the debenture-holder or third parties ever being aware of that fact; crystallisation in those circumstances could give rise to unfair consequences. However, in *Re Woodroffes (Musical Instruments) Ltd*[201] it was held that crystallisation occurs once the company ceases to carry on its business. According to Nourse J., that result:

> "is in accordance with the essential nature of a floating charge. The thinking behind the creation of such charges has always been a recognition that a fixed charge on the whole undertaking and assets of the company would paralyse it and prevent it from carrying on its business ... On the other hand, it is a mistake to think that the chargee has no remedy while the charge is still floating. He can always intervene and obtain an injunction to prevent the company from dealing with its assets otherwise than in the ordinary course of its business ... A cessation of the business necessarily puts an end to the company's dealings with its assets. That which kept the (floating) charge hovering has now been released and... causes it to settle and fasten on the subject of the charge."[202]

Automatic Crystallisation

20–98   An automatic crystallisation clause is a provision stipulating that, on any designated event occurring, a floating charge shall crystallise into a specific security.[203] For instance, the debenture in the *Re Woodroffes* case stated that the debenture-holders might at any time, by giving notice to the company, convert their floating charge into a fixed charge. Clauses of that nature are widely regarded as undesirable because they purport to bring about crystallisation, often without those doing business with the company being aware of what is happening and, indeed, some clauses could commence crystallisation without even the debtor company itself knowing that the charge had ceased to float over its assets. In Britain, the Cork Committee concluded that "[t]he practical consequences of automatic crystallisation of a floating charge without liquidation or

---

[199] *Biggerstaff v Rowatt's Wharf Ltd* [1896] 2 Ch. 93 at 105–106.

[200] [1954] I.R. 19.

[201] [1986] 1 Ch. 366.

[202] *ibid.* at 377–378.

[203] See generally, Boyle, "The Validity of Automatic Crystallisation Clauses", [1979] *J. Bus L.* 231.

receivership lead us to the conclusion that there is no place for it in a modern insolvency law. There are strong policy arguments against it; there is no need for it; the debenture-holder is sufficiently protected if he has the right to take steps to crystallise his security by appointing a receiver".[204]

20–99   But, it was held in *Re Brightlife Ltd*[205] that these clauses are permissible and effective, at least where the designated crystallising event involves delivering a notice to the debtor company. Hoffman J. rejected the arguments usually made against automatic crystallisation, while conceding that there were some persuasive practical commercial objections to those clauses. A floating charge is a purely contractual arrangement between debtor and creditor; "the rights and duties which the law may or may not categorise as a floating charge are wholly derived from the agreement of the parties, supplemented by the terms implied by law".[206] That charges crystallise when a winding-up commences, when a receiver is appointed and when the company ceases to do business is an implied term of security agreements. But there is no rule preventing the parties from stipulating that one or more of these events shall not cause crystallisation. The judge observed that "the commercial inconvenience of automatic crystallisation gives rise to a strong presumption that it was not intended by the parties. Very clear language will be required. But that does not mean that it is excluded by a rule of law".[207] According to the clause being considered in that case, crystallisation was to occur when the debenture-holder notified the company that the floating charge was to convert into a fixed charge as regards any of the assets specified in the notice and which the debenture-holder considered to be in jeopardy. In was held that delivering a notice in those terms crystallised the charge as regards the designated assets.

20–100   The New Zealand Supreme Court has upheld an automatic crystallisation clause that has another significant effect on priorities. In *Re Manurewa Transport Ltd*,[208] one clause in the debenture was that the charge shall crystallise "once the company mortgages, charges or encumbers or attempts to mortgage, charge or encumber" any of the charged assets. It was held that, once the company attempted to charge any of those assets, the charge consequently crystallised. This was because "a floating charge is not a word of art, it is a description for a type of security contained in a document which may provide a variety of circumstances whereupon crystallisation takes place".[209] In other words, a floating charge is not some special kind of proprietary interest but is merely a security all the incidents of which are stipulated by the parties; it is entirely for the company and the chargee to define their security's ambit and characteristics. On the basis of this reasoning, Hoffman J. in *Re Permanent Houses (Holdings)*

---

[204] *Report: Insolvency Law and Practice* Cmnd 8588 (1982), para.1579.
[205] [1987] 2 W.L.R. 197.
[206] *ibid.* at 205.
[207] *ibid.* at 204.
[208] [1971] N.Z.L.R. 909.
[209] *ibid.* at 917.

Ltd[210] held that designating default in payment of a loan can be made a crystallising event.

Effects of Crystallisation

20–101   Once a floating charge crystallises, beneficial ownership of the property in the assets covered by it immediately passes to the chargee.[211] In *Re Tullow Engineering Holdings Ltd,*[212] it was held that where the company had given a third party an option to purchase property and a floating charge over that property crystallises, the option then lapses. That option was to purchase certain shares held by the company. According to Blayney J.:

> "The effect of the crystallisation … was that there was an immediate equitable assignment of the shares to the debenture-holders so that in equity they became the owners of the shares. [The Company] was divested of its ownership in favour of the debenture-holders. Accordingly, it no longer had the capacity to enter into a contract to sell the shares in pursuance of the option which it granted. Its ownership had been terminated and its irrevocable offer to sell became a dead letter. No longer having the ownership of the shares, it could not contract to sell them. The only person who could do that was the receiver under the powers given in the debenture. And the purported exercise of the option did not alter the position."[213]

However, it does not seem to have been argued there that the principle stated in *Dempsey v Bank of Ireland*[214] should have applied, i.e. that a liquidator cannot take a better title to the assets than the company itself had. Accordingly, it could be contended, since the company's title to the shares was subject to an option, the receiver's title remained subject to that clause.[215]

20–102   It has never been decided whether a floating charge which has crystallised can afterwards lose its specific character and, so to speak, float again over what charged assets as remain. Decrystallisation in this sense is possible so long as the debenture-holder is in a position to deal directly with the company. If a winding-up has commenced, the liquidator takes control of the company and represents all the creditors, thereby rendering decrystallisation impossible. If a receiver is appointed, decrystallisation is possible provided the statutorily preferred creditors were paid off and either the receiver's task was completed or the receiver was removed under a power of removal contained in the instrument of appointment, thereby freeing the debenture-holder to bargain with the company. It would not be necessary again to register the charge under s.99 of the 1963 Act to render it effective against creditors.

---

[210] [1988] B.C.L.C. 563.
[211] e.g. *Re ELS Ltd* [1994] 1 B.C.L.C. 743.
[212] [1990] 1 I.R. 452.
[213] *ibid.* at 457.
[214] [1985] I.E.S.C. 181; unreported, December 6, 1985.
[215] *cf. Ash & Newman Ltd v Creative Devices Research Ltd* [1991] B.C.L.C. 403.

REGISTRATION OF CHARGES

20–103   To obtain priority for a security interest over other claims against the property charged, often certain steps must be taken to have that interest perfected.[216] Those steps do not always determine the order of priority but, unless they are taken, priority cannot be asserted against third parties who acquire an interest in the charged assets. Because those assets only beneficially belong to the secured creditor, any bona fide purchaser of them for value without notice obtains a better title to them. The objective of perfection is to ensure that third parties cannot get a better title. A common perfection requirement is that the security interest must be duly registered in a public register. For instance, charges on registered land should be recorded in the Land Registry, those on patents should be registered in the Register of Patents, those on trade marks should be registered with the Controller, those on Irish-registered ships in the ships' registery, agricultural chattel mortgages in the Circuit Court and individuals' bills of sale in the High Court.

20–104   Part IV (ss.99–112) of the 1963 Act establishes a system whereby, to be fully effective, most kinds of charges created by companies must be registered in the Registry of Companies.[217] Persons dealing with companies are deemed to have notice of the existence of all registered charges but not of the detailed contents of those securities. Registration does not to confer title or priority; it only protects an existing priority. Unregistered charges cannot take priority over other charges and can be disregarded by a liquidator.[218] But an unregistered charge is not an entire nullity; although it cannot establish rights against other creditors of the company or against a liquidator, it is not invalid and, accordingly, can give rise to certain rights and obligations against the company. For example, non-registration of a charge does not prevent the chargee from appointing a receiver under it.[219] As well as the duty to register charges at the CRO, companies are required to keep copies in their own registered office of every registrable charge, which can be inspected by any shareholder or creditor of the company.[220]

20–105   The system of registration was established in 1900, applying only to a limited category of charges, which was expanded in 1907 and again by the 1963 and the 1990 Acts. *Salomon v Salomon & Co. Ltd*[221] considerably influenced its establishment. The plaintiff owned a moderately successful business which he had incorporated into a limited company, of which he was the dominant shareholder. Part of the consideration the company gave him to acquire his business was an undertaking to pay him £10,000, which was secured by a floating charge. When the company was wound up and found to be insolvent, the question arose of whether in the circumstances he should be preferred to

---

[216] See generally, *Goode*, Chs II and III.

[217] See generally, *Gough*, Chs 17–32, *Breslin*, p.501 *et seq*, G. McCormack, *Registration of Company Charges*, 2nd edn (Bristol: Jordans, 2005) and de Lacy, "Company Charge Avoidance and Human Rights", [2004] *J. Bus. L.* 448.

[218] 1963 Act, s.99(1).

[219] *Alexander Hull & Co. v O'Carroll Kent & Co.* 89 I.L.T.R. 70 (1955).

[220] 1963 Act, s.109.

[221] [1897] A.C. 22.

the unsecured creditors; it was held that he should. But the view was then taken in the commercial world that persons dealing with companies should at least be given the protection of having the essential details of assets charged by companies under a floating charge recorded in the registry of companies and open for inspection by everybody, in much the same way as individuals' bills of sale are registered in the High Court.

Charges to be Registered

20–106   Perhaps the full details of each and every security interest given by a company over its assets should be registered. If that were so, persons dealing with any company could get a reasonably comprehensive picture of the extent to which its assets are subject to charges and analogous commitments. But the compulsory registration requirements are not that extensive; they apply only to "charges" which have been "created by the company" and which fall under one or more of the enumerated categories.[222] It is an offence for a company not to register charges which are so registrable.[223]

Charge

20–107   Registration applies only to charges. It does not apply to outright assignments of property rights,[224] nor to unambiguous retention of title clauses,[225] nor to pledges and most liens.[226] There is no definition of the term charge here other than that it includes a mortgage,[227] which may be legal or equitable. A charge other than a mortgage transfers neither the beneficial ownership in the property nor the right to possess the property; it exists independently of ownership and possession but confers an interest in the property which carries with it a right to resort to that property.

20–108   An agreement to create a present equitable interest in property as security is a charge and must be registered.[228] But an agreement to give a security at some future time, or in the event of some future event occurring, is not a charge.[229] A charge which is later executed in pursuance of that agreement is registrable; however, it could easily be invalidated as a "fraudulent preference" if the company was wound up and insolvent.[230] The deposit of title deeds with a lender raises a strong implication that a charge has been created over the property to which those deeds relate.[231] In *Re White & Shannon Ltd*,[232] it was held that a new charge was created when the benefit of a debenture was transferred

---

[222] 1963 Act, s.99(2).
[223] 1963 Act, s.100.
[224] *Re George Inglefield Ltd* [1933] Ch. 1.
[225] *Re WJ Hickey Ltd* [1988] I.R. 126.
[226] *Re Hamlet Int'l Plc* [1999] 2 B.C.L.C. 506.
[227] 1963 Act, s.99(10)(a).
[228] *Re Jackson & Bassford* [1906] 2 Ch. 467.
[229] *Re Gregory Love & Co.* [1916] 1 Ch. 203.
[230] *Re Eric Holmes Property Ltd* [1965] Ch. 1052.
[231] *Pryce v Bury* (1854) L.R. 16 Eq. 153 (Note).
[232] [1965] N.I. 15.

to another creditor and the security was extended to cover all money owing to that creditor as well as to the original debenture-holder.

20–109   A purely contractual lien, i.e. a stipulation in a contract giving someone a "lien" over chattels, documents or choses in action, may be a charge. It would seem that where the lien-holder's rights exist only so long as he has possession of the goods, it is not a charge, whether his rights arise under the general law or under contract.[233] What is known as the ship-owner's lien on sub-freights is a charge in this context[234]; that lien is a contractual right of the ship-owner to require payment of money owed by the shipper to the charterer and has no connection with actual possession of the goods. Banks have a general lien over documents they acquire in the course of banking business but, where title deeds are deposited with them as security for a loan, then the bank's rights are in the nature of a charge over the property to which those deeds relate and not merely a lien over those documents.[235] Although equitable liens are charges, they are not registrable because they are not created by the company.[236] A pledge is not a charge and, accordingly, is not registrable unless what is given to the creditor is the title documents to the property being pledged.[237] A right of set-off is not a charge for these purposes, although contractual rights to retain funds are not invariably rights of set-off and accordingly can be charges.

Created by the Company

20–110   Registration applies only to charges "created by" the company. If the charge arises other than by the company's own act, i.e. all security interests arising under the general law, it escapes registration. For example, legal and equitable liens, the unpaid landlord's common law remedy of distress and creditors' execution rights like *fieri facias*, attachment of debts and appointing a receiver. It would seem that registration of a judgment mortgage on company property need not be registered in this manner. So it was held in England with regard to charging orders on land.[238] Because companies do not always know that their property has been made the subject of such orders, it would be most impracticable and unjust if companies nevertheless were required to register charging orders within 21 days of their being made. If this method of registration were intended to apply to judgment mortgages, it can hardly be doubted that an express provision would have been made to that effect. However, the judgment creditor must give the company a copy of the affidavit registered against the company's land and, within three days of receiving it, the company must file a copy at the CRO.[239]

20–111   An equitable lien is a right arising from the general law that is based on a certain relationship between the parties but where, unlike in the legal lien,

---

[233] *Waitomo Wools (NZ) Ltd v Nelsons (NZ) Ltd* [1974] 1 N.Z.L.R. 484.
[234] *Re Welsh Irish Ferries Ltd* [1986] Ch. 471.
[235] *Re Farm Fresh Frozen Foods Ltd* [1980] I.L.R.M. 131.
[236] *Bank of Ireland Finance Ltd v Daly Ltd* [1978] I.R. 79.
[237] *Dublin City Distillery Ltd v Doherty* [1914] A.C. 823.
[238] *Re Overseas Aviation Engineering (GB) Ltd* [1963] 1 Ch. 24 at 47–52.
[239] 1963 Act, s.102.

the creditor does not possess the property secured; the most common example being the lien held by unpaid vendors of land in respect of the purchase price of what was their property. In *Bank of Ireland Finance Ltd v Daly Ltd,*[240] McMahon J. held that the unpaid vendor of land's lien need not be registered, following the reasoning of Brightman J. in an earlier case:

> "If such a lien is registrable, the time for registration would expire 21 days after the exchange of contracts for sale, because it is at that date that the lien is created; it is not created on completion because the purchase price is unpaid, but is discharged on completion to the extent that the purchase money is paid ... In most cases, the 21 day period would expire well before completion, because contracts for sale of land are not usually completed in three weeks. It would be a profound inconvenience, therefore, if every vendor to a company were compelled as a matter of course to register an unpaid vendor's lien on the exchange of contracts, on the off chance that circumstances might arise in the future which would render it desirable for the vendor to be able to rely on an unpaid vendor's lien ... [A]n unpaid vendor's lien is the creature of the law; and it does not depend upon contract, but upon the fact that the vendor has a right to specific performance of his contract."[241]

20–112 By contrast, where title deeds are deposited as security for a loan, an equitable charge is created. In *Re Farm Fresh Frozen Foods Ltd,*[242] Keane J. held that such charges must be registered because they arise from the act of the person depositing the deeds and not merely by operation of law. According to Templeman J. in a similar case:

> "As a general rule a deposit of title deeds to secure a debt creates a charge on the land; it does not make any difference whether the debt is owed by the debtor or whether it is owed by someone else, and the person who deposited the title deeds is in some way acting as a surety ... [The deposit of deeds] is a contractual lien [but] is also a contractual charge; true it is that the charge arises by presumption, but it does not arise by operation of law. What the court does is to say: we shall not compel the parties to write down in so many words what the effect of the deposit of title deeds is; we shall simply assume that when parties contract, and although they probably do not know the consequences, the person who takes the title deeds contracts not only to retain them but also to have an equitable charge on the land. The presumption reads into the contract the charge which is implied. If that is right, the charge was created by the company and is therefore registrable under [section 99]. No such shorthand appears to be employed in the case of an unpaid vendor's lien, where the parties are directing their minds to something entirely different; but where, as here, there is a security for a loan and unless something is said and done the security consists of a lien and also the charge, then it seems to me that the charge, at any rate for the purposes of [section 99], is created by the company and is therefore registrable. If I may turn round the 'inconvenient' argument given

---

[240] [1978] I.R. 79.
[241] *London & Cheshire Ins. Co. v Laplagrene Pty Co. Ltd* [1971] Ch. 499 at 514.
[242] [1980] I.R. 79.

[above], far from its being a profound inconvenience if the charge in the present case were registrable, it would be profoundly inconvenient if it were not, because the object of the section is to give information of incumbrances affecting the property of the company, and if the company could deposit title deeds and create a charge without registration the mischief at which the section is aimed could be largely and easily avoided."[243]

The Catalogue of Registrable Charges

20–113 Not every charge created by a company should be registered in this manner. There is a catalogue of the kinds of charges which ought to be registered.[244] In the original 1900 version, only four of these were listed, namely charges for securing an issue of debentures, charges on uncalled capital, company bills of sale and floating charges; two others were added in 1907 and several more in 1963, and the list was completed in 1990 with the addition of aircraft. Under an earlier version of the 1990 Act, practically every kind of company charge was to become registrable.[245] That, however, was not implemented. Instead, the Minister, by regulation, may add additional categories of charge to these enumerated; he also may delete any of the heads of charge from the list.[246]

20–114 Except for those charges that are expressly mentioned, specific charges over chattels, over choses in action and over other intangibles need not be registered. On the other hand, a particular charge may be registrable under more than one of the heads; for instance, a charge on book debts is most likely also a floating charge. It is not necessary that the company owned the property in question at the time it agreed to give the charge; a charge immediately executed or created over future company property is registrable.[247] Such an agreement must be distinguished from an agreement that at some time in the future the company will grant a charge, which is not a creation of a charge. Where the company acquires property which is subject to a charge which is registrable, the charge most be registered within 21 days of completion.[248]

20–115 *Land Charge:* The requirement that companies separately register every charge they give "on land, wherever situate, or on any interest therein" was adopted in 1907. Even though most land charges will be registered in either the Registry of Deeds or in the Land Registry,[249] it was felt that they should also be registered in the companies' registry so that persons can obtain a more comprehensive view of the company's obligations. An agreement to create a mortgage or a charge over land is an equitable mortgage and is registrable.[250] A mortgage or charge subsequently created on foot of such an agreement is also so registrable;

---

[243] *Re Wallace & Simmonds (Builders) Ltd* [1974] 1 All E.R. 561 at 573.

[244] 1963 Act, s.99(2).

[245] Companies (Amendment) Bill 1987, s.94, s.99(5).

[246] 1990 Act, s.122(b).

[247] *Independent Automatic Sales Ltd v Knowles & Foster* [1962] 1 W.L.R. 974.

[248] 1963 Act, s.101.

[249] See generally, J.C.W. Wylie, *Irish Land Law*, 3rd edn (Dublin: Butterworths, 1997), Chs 21 & 22.

[250] *Re Jackson & Bassford* [1906] 2 Ch. 467.

its validity is not affected by that agreement not having been registered.[251] The deposit of title deeds creates an equitable charge and is so registrable.[252] But an unpaid vendor's lien is not registrable.[253] Where an equitable charge is registered and, under a term of that charge, a legal mortgage is later executed, the latter need not be registered.[254] A land charge does not include "a charge for any rent or other periodical sum issuing out of land" or holding debentures which entitle the holder to a charge on land shall not be deemed to be an interest in land.[255]

20–116 Where the property in question is located abroad and the charge is made in this country, the charge must still be registered, even though further measures may be necessary to make the charge fully effective under the *lex situs*.[256] Where the property is located abroad and the *lex situs* requires that the charge be registered in that country, to make the charge fully effective there, a certificate saying that the charge was presented for registration there must be lodged with the registry of companies here.[257] There is no express provision about the consequences of contravening either of these requirements.

20–117 *Charge on Ship or Aircraft:* In addition to the Mercantile Marine Act 1955's registration requirements, a company charge on a "ship or any share in a ship" should be registered in the CRO.[258] The question of what exactly is a ship for these purposes arose in *Re South Coast Boatyard Ltd,*[259] where it was held that charges on ocean-going yachts are not registrable because the term "ship" here envisages vessels of burden as opposed to vessels whose primary function is to go as fast as possible. In 1990 charges on an aircraft or on any share in an aircraft were added to the catalogue.

20–118 *Floating Charge:* As has been explained above, a floating charge is a charge which is not specific. Because a company can continue carrying on its business in the ordinary way even though some or its entire assets may be the subject of a floating charge that can quite easily crystallise, it was essential to protect persons dealing with companies that these be registered. The duty to register every "floating charge on the undertaking or property of the company" includes floating charges over any part of the company's property.[260]

20–119 *Company Bills of Sale:* For over a hundred years a special statutory scheme has existed under which bills of sale must be registered but such instruments given by companies are exempt from that scheme.[261] Nevertheless, every

---

[251] *Re Columbian Fireproofing Co.* [1910] 2 Ch. 120.
[252] *Re Farm Fresh Frozen Foods Ltd* [1980] I.L.R.M. 131.
[253] *Bank of Ireland Finance Ltd v Daly Ltd* [1978] I.R. 79.
[254] *Cunard SS Co. v Hopwood* [1908] 2 Ch. 564.
[255] 1963 Act, s.99(2)(d) and (7).
[256] 1963 Act, s.99(4).
[257] 1963 Act, s.99(5).
[258] 1963 Act, s.99(2)(h).
[259] [1980] I.L.R.M. 186.
[260] *Mercantile Bank of India Ltd v Chartered Bank of India* [1937] 1 All E.R. 231.
[261] *Re Royal Marine Hotel Co.* [1895] 1 I.R. 368.

charge created by or evidenced by "an instrument which, if executed by an individual, would require registration as a bill of sale" must be registered in the CRO.[262] A bill of sale is not a transaction but is a written document that evidences a particular transaction, namely an assurance of a legal or an equitable interest in chattels.[263] In *Dublin City Distillery Ltd v Doherty*,[264] the company had sought to pledge stocks of whiskey which it had stored in a bonded warehouse as security for a loan, the purported pledge being by way of signed warrants and invoices representing different quantities of whiskey. It was held that these were not effective pledges. Even if they were pledges, it was held that, since they took a documentary form, they were bills of sale and, consequently, they should have been registered.

20–120   A pledge, a contractual lien and a mortgage where the security-holder takes delivery of the goods are not registrable as bills of sale because title to the goods passed when possession of them passed to the security-holder. It has been held that a trust receipt is not registrable[265], nor are what are known as letters of lien, or of hypothecation.[266]

20–121   Section 4 of the Bills of Sale (Ireland) Act 1879[267] exempts certain kinds of instruments from its registration requirement and, consequently, these need not be registered in the CRO either. Most of these exceptions are routine dealings with stock, whether of a mercantile or of a funding nature; in particular, transfers of goods in the ordinary course of business, bills of sale for goods located abroad or at sea, bills of lading, warehouse-keepers' certificates, warrants or orders for the delivery of goods and other documents which are used in the ordinary course of business to prove possession or control of goods, or authorising the possessor to transfer or to receive the goods therein mentioned either by indorsement or by delivery. An instrument that should be registered by an individual as a bill of sale is not registrable in the CRO where it does not create a charge on the company's assets.

20–122   *Charge Securing Series of Debentures:* Any form of charge given by a company "for the purpose of securing any issue of debentures" should be registered.[268] An issue of debentures is to be distinguished from a single debenture. The former is where several debentures are issued at one time; they are usually issued as part of a series, secured by a trust deed and are transferable as stock. In *Automobile Assn. (Canterbury) Inc. v Australian Secured Deposits Ltd,*[269] it was held that a single debenture does not fall within this category and, accordingly, is not registrable unless it is caught by any of the other heads. The company gave a charge over local government stock that it owned.

---

[262] 1963 Act, s.99(2)(c).
[263] See generally, M. Forde, *Commercial Law,* 3rd edn (Haywards Heath: Tottel, 2005), p.211 *et seq.*
[264] [1914] A.C. 823.
[265] *Re David Allister Ltd* [1922] 2 Ch. 211.
[266] *Re Hamilton Young & Co.* [1905] 2 K.B. 772.
[267] 42 & 43 Vic., c. 50.
[268] 1963 Act, s.99(2)(a).
[269] [1973] N.Z.L.R. 417.

Although that was a debenture, it was not a charge to secure an issue of debentures because the term "issue" in this context "must be construed as referring in a collective sense to the aggregate of a number of individual debentures issued by a company".[270] It would seem that the relevant series of debentures, for these purposes, need not be the company's own debentures.

20–123 *Charge on Industrial and Intellectual Property:* Charges on "any patent or a licence under a patent, on a trademark or on a copyright or a licence under a copyright" should be registered.[271] A charge given on a patent should also be registered in the Patents Office in accordance with the Patents Act 1992, in that no document which is unregistered will be admitted into evidence to show that the charge exists.

20–124 *Charge on Uncalled Capital and on Unpaid Calls:* Charges given on "un-called share capital" and also on "calls made but not paid" are registrable.[272]

20–125 *Charge on Goodwill:* Goodwill is a somewhat peculiar asset and its actual value as a security is questionable. In any event, company charges on "goodwill" should be registered.[273]

20–126 *Charge on Book Debts:* Charges on "book debts" must be registered.[274] These were held to mean "all such debts accruing in the ordinary course of a man's trade as are usually entered in trade books but to constitute a book debt it is not necessary that the debt should be entered in a book".[275] Money due to a company otherwise than in the ordinary course of its trade is not a book debt and, accordingly, is not registrable unless that fund is caught by a floating charge or by a charge securing an issue of debentures. This is the principal gap in the registration scheme, along with specific charges on stocks and shares. For instance, in *Re Brian Tucker Ltd*[276] a charge given over the proceeds of an insurance policy was held not to be registrable, since that was not a book debt.[277] In *Byrne v Allied Irish Banks Ltd,*[278] a charge over the actual proceeds of the sale of the company's premises was held not to be registrable for the same reason. In *Re Greenport Ltd,*[279] as security for a ten-year lease, the company agreed to place a sum in a deposit account and to give the lessor a charge over it, which the company agreed it would register in the CRO. But the company paid the money into its ordinary current account and never registered the charge. It was held that the security was not a charge on the company's book debts. In *Re SSSL Realisations (2002) Ltd,*[280]

---

[270] *ibid.* at 425.
[271] 1963 Act, s.99(2)(i).
[272] 1963 Act, s.99(2)(b)
[273] 1963 Act, s.99(2)(l).
[274] 1963 Act, s.99(2)(e).
[275] *Re Brian Tucker Ltd* [1990] 2 I.R. 549 at 553, citing *Halsbury's Laws of England.*
[276] *ibid.*
[277] Following *Paul & Frank Ltd v Discount Bank (Overseas) Ltd* [1967] Ch. 348.
[278] [1978] I.R. 446.
[279] [2004] 1 B.C.L.C. 555.
[280] [2005] 1 B.C.L.C. 1.

which concerned an intra-group debt subordination agreement, a clause that prohibited the companies from collecting debts due to them was held not to be in the nature of a charge at all, even though it may in some respects be as effective as a charge if the clause were complied with. In *Re Charge Card Services Ltd,*[281] where the company entered into a security arrangement regarding its own trading indebtedness, although those sums were book debts, the arrangement was not registrable for the simple reason that a charge in favour of a debtor of his own indebtedness to the chargor is conceptually impossible. This reasoning has since met the disapproval of the House of Lords as, while perhaps logically compelling, being out of line with commercial practice.[282] The original draft of what became s.122 of the 1990 Act proposed that this category be expanded to "a charge on any debts or other liabilities owing or incurred to the company".[283]

20–127 The deposit of a negotiable instrument, given to secure payment of book debts, for the purpose of securing an advance, is not be treated as a charge on those debts.[284] Where goods are supplied to a company subject to reservation of title and the supply contract designates the company the supplier's fiduciary agent in respect of the proceeds of sub-sales until the price of the goods is paid, the contract is not registrable under this heading[285] unless all it does is create a charge over these sums.[286]

20–128 *Extending the Catalogue:* The original proposals for the 1990 Act would have extended the above catalogue to all charges on funds accruing to the company; they also would have brought within the net any charge "on the company's interests in any stocks, shares or marketable securities".[287] However, a different approach was eventually adopted; enabling the Minister, by order, to add new heads of charge to those already enumerated.[288] Extending the net to all debts and liabilities due to the company might give rise to certain practical difficulties in transactions between financial institutions, so it was thought better to leave the precise delineation of any extension to a statutory instrument.

Mechanics of Registration

20–129 Registration is effected by sending in the requisite information in time to the CRO.

Who Should Register?

20–130 Within 21 days of the charge being created or the series of debentures being issued, the company should send the requisite particulars and

---

[281] [1987] Ch. 150.
[282] *Re Bank of Credit & Commerce Int'l (No. 8)* [1998] A.C. 214.
[283] Companies (Amendment) Bill 1987, s.94(5)(e).
[284] 1963 Act, s.99(6).
[285] *Re WJ Hickey Ltd* [1988] I.R. 126.
[286] *Carroll Group Distributors Ltd v G & JF Bourke Ltd* [1990] 1 I.R. 481.
[287] Companies (Amendment) Bill 1987, s.94 (and s.99(5)).
[288] 1963 Act, s.99(2A)–(2C).

documents to the Registrar of Companies.[289] Where a charge has not been duly registered, the company and every officer in default can be prosecuted by the Registrar. Because failure to register renders a charge virtually worthless, any other person "interested therein" may apply to have the charge registered. An interested person, for these purposes, includes the chargee and anybody else with a security interest in the charge; there are no reported authorities on the scope of the term. Where the registration is done by such a person, he is entitled to recover from the company the registration fee.

Time for Registration

20–131   The charge must be duly registered "within 21 days after the date of its creation".[290] Thus the relevant details and documents must be presented within three weeks of the charge being given. The court has a discretion to extend that time.

20–132   For the purposes of timely registration, the crucial concept is the date of the charge's "creation".[291] It depends on the parties' intentions and is a question of fact when the charge was actually created. A charge arising under a deed is created at the time the executed deed is delivered.[292] Where the company has agreed to give a charge on the occurrence of a particular contingency, the charge is not created until at least that contingency occurred.[293] A simple agreement to give a legal security can constitute creating a charge because the agreement operates immediately in equity as an equitable security; no further steps need be taken to give an effective security. It depends on the circumstances and the parties' intentions whether an agreement to give security in the future creates an equitable charge or whether it was intended that a formal document must be executed at the time envisaged. However, where the agreement created an equitable charge and a formal charge was executed subsequently, the former merges in the latter, and the date of creation then becomes the time the formal charge was given.[294] Where an existing charge is cancelled and it is substituted with a new charge, the latter is created at the time it was given—and not as of the date the initial charge was given.[295] Instead of applying to the court for late registration of an unregistered charge, the parties may choose to "re-create" the security in this manner and then register the new charge.

20–133   In the case of a charge securing a series of debentures that are issued to several debenture-holders, there is sufficient registration for the entire series if the required particulars are registered within 21 days after the covering trust deed was executed or, in the absence of such a deed, after the first debenture

---

[289] 1963 Act, s.100.
[290] 1963 Act, s.99(1).
[291] This concept also applies to invalidating floating charges under s.288 of the 1963 Act.
[292] *Esberger & Sons Ltd v Capital & Counties Bank* [1913] 2 Ch. 366.
[293] *Re Gregory Love & Co.* [1916] 1 Ch. 203.
[294] *Re Olderfleet Shipbuilding Co.* [1922] 1 I.R. 26.
[295] *Re Cardiff Working Men's Cottage Co.* [1906] 2 Ch. 627.

of the series has been executed.[296] In the case of a charge created abroad over property that is located outside the State, the 21 days runs from the time when, in due course of post and if dispatched with due diligence, the particulars would have arrived in this country.[297]

Particulars to be Registered

20–134   What must be given to the CRO are the "prescribed particulars of the charge ... verified in the prescribed manner".[298] While the Act does not specify in terms what these are, nor the method of verification, they can be ascertained from the "following particulars" which must be entered on the register of charges[299]: namely the date the charge was created by the company,[300] the amount secured by the charge, "short particulars" of the property charged and the persons entitled to the charge. It was proposed in 1987 that the particulars of the amount secured should include "a monetary limit of a fixed and definite sum" on that amount; this was omitted from the 1990 Act. In the case of a charge securing a series of debentures the holders of which rank *pari passu*, what must be provided are particulars of the total amounts secured by the whole series, the dates of the authorising resolutions and of the covering deed, if there is one, a "general description" of the property charged and the names of the trustees, if any. For these purposes, the company's registration number is not an essential particular.[301]

20–135   The CRO has issued forms which set out the particulars to be regis-tered, notably Form No. 47. In the case of single mortgages and charges, this form is divided into five columns, which are headed as follows:

–   date and description of the instrument creating or evidencing the charge;
–   amount secured by the charge;
–   names, addresses and occupations of the person entitled to the charge,
–   Short particulars of the property charged;
–   amount and rate per cent of the commission.

The parallel provisions in Britain contain no express obligation to furnish the CRO with the instrument, if any, creating or evidencing the charge. But the form of verification required there is either being shown the original instru-ment, getting a certified copy of the instrument or a statement of the particulars verified by the company's seal. Form No.47 would seem to preclude registra-tion of all charges that are not evidenced in writing.[302] The registration scheme applies to charges over property which is located in the State and is owned by foreign-registered companies.[303]

---

[296] 1963 Act, s.92(8).
[297] 1963 Act, s.99(3).
[298] 1963 Act, s.99(1).
[299] 1963 Act, s.103.
[300] *cf.* s.103(1)(b)(ii) and (iii) on where property is acquired and on where a judgment mort-gage is created.
[301] *Grove v Advantage Healthcare (T10) Ltd* [2000] 1 B.C.L.C. 661.
[302] *cf. Re CL Nye Ltd* [1971] Ch. 442.
[303] 1963 Act, s.111.

20–136 Where a debt has been satisfied, in whole or in part, or some of the property or undertaking has been released from the charge or no longer belongs to the company, the Registrar can record the fact.[304] He must be duly satisfied of these circumstances before recording a memorandum of satisfaction and must have notified the chargee or the judgment creditor, as the case may be. But there is no obligation on either companies or chargees to notify the CRO that a debt has been satisfied or that the property was released. Consequently, many companies' files give a distorted picture of outstanding charges. No provision exists for rectifying the details of charges that are registered.

Extending Time for Registration

20–137 Often creditors overlook the fact that their charge should have been registered until it becomes too late to do so. In much the same way as bills of sale which were not registered in time can be registered out of time, the late registration of company charges is possible where the court so directs.[305] Before doing so, the court must be satisfied that the delay "was accidental, or due to inadvertence or to some other sufficient cause, or is not of a nature to prejudice the position of creditors or shareholders of the company ..." Even where these cannot be established, the direction may be given where "on other grounds it is just and equitable to grant relief ..." Where the court allows late registration, almost always it will give appropriate directions so that any intervening charge-holders will not thereby be prejudiced. For instance, in *Re O'Carroll Kent Ltd*[306] the company agreed to issue a mortgage debenture but, when they presented it to the companies' office, an official there said that it could not be registered; that what was needed was the actual debenture itself. It was ascertained later that this advice was wrong. The company then applied for late registration and was allowed to so do "without prejudice to rights of any parties acquired prior to the actual date the registration was affected".

20–138 When making an application of this nature, the court must be told the reason for the delay; it is not enough simply to say that the applicant acted inadvertently.[307] The court is given a wide discretion here. Generally, an application will be refused when the company is in liquidation[308] or where an insolvent liquidation is imminent and manifestly cannot be avoided.[309] Nevertheless, special circumstances may warrant allowing registration in those cases. That happened in *Re O'Carroll Kent Ltd*,[310] where in an earlier proceeding[311] the applicant for the extension got the court to appoint a receiver

---

[304] 1963 Act, s.105.

[305] 1963 Act, s.106.

[306] 89 I.L.T.R. 72 (1955).

[307] *Re Kris Cruisers Ltd* [1949] 1 Ch. 138.

[308] *Re Ashpurton Estates Ltd* [1983] Ch. 110 and *Re Farm Fresh Frozen Foods Ltd* [1980] I.L.R.M. 131.

[309] *Re Barrow Borough Transport Ltd* [1990] 1 Ch. 227 and *Re Telomatic Ltd* [1994] 1 B.C.L.C. 90.

[310] 89 I.L.T.R. 72 (1955); also in *Re Braemar Investments Ltd* [1989] 1 Ch. 54.

[311] 89 I.L.T.R. 70 (1955).

and manager to protect the assets charged under the debenture. However, Dixon J. added, when granting the extension of time, that if the company were indeed wound up, if the liquidator felt that the creditors' interests had been prejudiced by the court's order, he could take appropriate proceedings.[312]

20–139   If late registration were permitted without any proviso, intervening chargees would be seriously prejudiced. For the charge is always a valid charge, except that it is rendered unenforceable for not being registered. Once it becomes registered, without qualification, its priority position is based on the date it was granted. It would rank before subsequent charges which were obtained by persons who were unaware of its existence; even if they searched the CRO register, no evidence of that charge would be disclosed. Accordingly, where an application for late registration is granted, it almost always is without prejudice to the rights of any parties acquired during the period between when the charge was created by the company and the date of its actual registration.[313] Certain transactions may be excluded from the formula.[314] It is not regarded as protecting unsecured creditors.[315] However, the actual words used do not expressly or by necessary implication confine its scope to secured creditors and an Irish court, in an appropriate case, might interpret it more generously. An obviously deserving case would be an unsecured creditor who gave the company substantial advances because he had consulted its file in the companies' office and learned that there was no charge over its assets. The practice in Australia is for the court to stipulate that unsecured creditors too should not be prejudiced where the circumstances so require.[316]

Conclusiveness of Registrar's Certificate

20–140   When a charge is registered, the Registrar issues a certificate to that effect, which shall be "conclusive evidence" that the requirements regarding registration were complied with.[317] Once they have this certificate, secured creditors can be confident that their charge cannot be challenged for not being duly registered in time, as required. A vexed question concerns details in the charge which are incorrect, most notably, the date the charge was given. Say the charge was created on January 1 but it was not until February 2 that the chargee addressed his mind to registration. Say that, rather than apply to the court for an extension of time, the chargee substituted January 22 for the creation date and then registers the charge. Does conclusivity prevent, say, an intervening chargee or a liquidator from contesting that registration?

---

[312] Similarly, *Barclays Bank v Stuart Landon Ltd* [2001] 2 B.C.L.C. 316.

[313] e.g. *Confiance Ltd v Timespan Images Ltd* [2005] 2 B.C.L.C. 693 at 701.

[314] e.g. *Re Fablehill Ltd* [1991] B.C.L.C. 830.

[315] *Watson v Duff, Morgan & Vermont Holdings Ltd* [1974] 1 W.L.R. 450.

[316] *Re Flinders Trading Co. Pty Ltd* 3 A.C.L.R. 218 (1978).

[317] 1963 Act, s.104.

20–141 This matter has not yet been dealt with in the Irish courts, but it and related questions have given rise to litigation in Britain.[318] The position adopted there is that the courts are bound by the statutory presumption of conclusiveness[319] and proceedings will not be entertained even to have the certificate rectified in an application for judicial review.[320] However, a party who suffers loss on account of the statutory presumption of compliance may have redress in proceedings for negligence. Because of the Constitution, an Irish court might not look so lightly on an "irrebuttable presumption".[321] If the alteration was made deliberately, a creditor who was thereby prejudiced would have a case in fraud. If the alteration was purely accidental, that creditor might have a good case in negligence.

---

[318] See generally, McCormack, "Conclusiveness in the Registration of Company Charges Procedure" 10 *Co. Law* 175 (1989).
[319] *Re CL Nye Ltd* [1971] 1 Ch. 442.
[320] *R. v Registrar of Companies, Ex p. Central Bank of India* [1986] 1 Q.B. 1114.
[321] *State (McEldowney) v Kelleher* [1983] I.R. 289.

CHAPTER 21

INTERNATIONAL AND EUROPEAN ASPECTS

21–01 With numerous companies carrying on business or conducting some activities in countries other than where they are incorporated, conflicts of laws questions arise regarding principally what courts have jurisdiction to determine disputes arising from foreign-related acts and what legal regime governs those actions, and the often related issue of the extraterritorial application of regulatory regimes. In recent years foreign companies have been playing a major role in the Irish economy, especially in the chemicals, information technology and financial services sectors. At the same time, some Irish companies have established their presence abroad, especially within the European Communities. Activities of Irish-registered companies outside the State are governed by the Companies Acts, and the activities of foreign companies with some presence or impacts in the State are subject to regulation by these Acts also.[1]

JURISDICTION

21–02 Adjudicative jurisdiction is concerned with what court or courts, or arbitrator, are legally competent to determine a particular dispute. Generally, companies can be sued in the courts of the country where they are registered or have a business establishment, and also in the courts where they have agreed to be sued, either under a prorogation clause in a contract or simply by submitting to jurisdiction. For certain types of dispute, some other courts may also exercise jurisdiction (e.g. the courts of the country where the breach of contract or the tort occurred). But there are some categories of dispute in respect of which one particular court only has jurisdiction. Where more then one court can take jurisdiction, provision usually exists for determining which of those courts should hear the case—usually, either the court which is first seised of it or the more "convenient" forum.

21–03 There are three principal sets of rules that govern this complex area of the law. EC Regulation 44/2001 on Jurisdiction and on Judgments[2] applies to most "civil and commercial disputes" between parties in EC Member States

---

[1] See generally, P. Muchlinski, *Multinational Enterprises and the Law*, 2nd edn (Oxford: OUP, 2006) and C. Wallace, *The Multinational Enterprise and Legal Control*, 2nd edn (The Hague: Martinus Nijhoff, 2002).

[2] [2001] O.J. L12/1.

except Denmark. Similar to it is the Lugano Convention[3] that applies to disputes with parties in Iceland, Norway and Switzerland. Where the dispute does not fall within this Regulation or Convention, jurisdiction of the Irish courts is determined principally with reference to Order 11 of the Rules of the Superior Courts. Within the EC, insolvency proceedings are governed by Regulation 1346/2000.[4] Where a court has jurisdiction to deal with the category of dispute in question (subject matter jurisdiction), that company must be properly served with the proceedings (to establish personal jurisdiction) before that court will try the case.

Brussels/Lugano

21–04 An extensive range of company law disputes come within the ambit of Regulation 44/2001 or the Lugano Convention.[5] There are certain kinds of dispute that may only be determined by the courts of one of the affected states. As regards other types of dispute, there is a limited choice of *fori*.

21–05 Exclusive jurisdiction exists in the courts of the state where a company has its "seat" over all "proceedings which have as their object the validity of the constitution, the nullity or dissolution of companies ... or the validity of decisions of their organs ...".[6] For these purposes, a company has its "seat" in the State if it is an Irish-registered company. The reason for overriding the general approach (that parties may be sued where they have a permanent establishment and also where they agreed to be sued) and conferring exclusive jurisdiction here, is to avoid the prospect of conflicting judgments being given as regards the very existence of a company and the validity of decisions taken by its shareholders or directors. What comes within this zone of exclusivity may be summarised as the capacity of the company, the composition and powers of its various organs, the formalities and procedures laid down for them, the extent of an individual member's liability for the debts and liabilities of the company, and other matters of that kind. In *Papamicolaou v Thielen*,[7] a Luxembourg court appointed an administrator of a company, which held 95 per cent of the shares in several Irish subsidiaries. A dispute arose as to whether he was entitled to convene meetings to remove a director of those subsidiaries. It was held by Keane J. that, since he purported to act as an organ of the parent Luxembourg company and the dispute concerned the validity of his decision, exclusive jurisdiction lay with the courts there.

21–06 Although a shareholders' agreement is not technically the constitution of a company, it was held in the *Formula One* case[8] that a dispute about

---

3   Convention opened for signature on September 16, 1988, [1998] O.J. L319/9.
4   [2002] O.J. L160/1.
5   See generally, H. Delany & D. McGrath, *Civil Procedure in the Superior Courts*, 2nd edn (Dublin: Thomson Round Hall, 2005), p.28 *et seq.*; L. Collins, *Dicey et al on the Conflict of Laws*, 14th edn (London: Sweet & Maxwell, 2006), Vol I, Ch.11 and A. Briggs & P. Rees, *Civil Jurisdiction and Judgments*, 4th edn (London: LLP, 2005).
6   Arts 22(2) and 16(2) and Collins, see fn.5 at 448–451.
7   [1998] 2 I.R. 42.
8   *Speed Investments Ltd v Formula One Holdings Ltd (No. 2)* [2005] 1 W.L.R. 1936.

whether certain directors were appointed in accordance with the terms of such an agreement came within this exclusive jurisdiction, the core issue in the dispute there being the composition of the company's board.

21–07   For disputes outside of this zone of exclusivity, companies can be sued, *inter alia*, at their domicile.[9] This is where they are registered; in the case of many continental European companies, it is where they have their principal base of operations.[10]

21–08   Where a dispute relates to the activities of a branch, agency or other establishment that a company has, the courts where that representative entity is located have jurisdiction.[11] This ancillary unit must be "a place of business which has the appearance of permanency such as the extension of a parent body, has a management and is equipped to negotiate business with third parties so that the latter, although knowing that there will if necessary be a legal link with the parent body, whose seat is [elsewhere], do not have to deal directly with such parent body."[12] Additionally, the dispute must relate to the activities of that external unit. Where the claim is one for breach of contract, ordinarily the negotiations would have had to be conducted through that unit. But the existence of an external unit or even the registration of a wholly-owned subsidiary in the state does not confer jurisdiction on the courts there over all kinds of disputes with the parent company,[13] except perhaps where the subsidiary has no real existence and was nothing more than the parent's agent.[14]

Common Law

21–09   Where neither the Brussels Regulation nor the Lugano Convention apply, jurisdiction over most disputes is governed by common law principles that are incorporated in RSC Ord.11,[15] which does not contain any rules specific to companies or their branches. Although the Irish courts' jurisdiction is far more extensive under these than under the Regulation or the Convention, there is a countervailing discretion not to accept jurisdiction where the case is more appropriately triable elsewhere.

21–10   Relying on the *forum non conveniens* doctrine,[16] the courts will decline to accept jurisdiction where the dispute concerns the internal affairs of a company and there is no good reason why the case cannot be tried in the state where it carries out its activities or it is registered. Thus, in *Re Harrods (Buenos Aires) Ltd*,[17] which concerned oppression proceedings involving an

---

9   Art.2(1).
10   *cf. The Deichland* [1990] 1 Q.B. 361.
11   Art.5(5) and Collins, see fn.5 at 420–423.
12   *Anton Durbeck GmbH v Den Norske Bank ASA* [2003] Q.B. 1160 at 1168.
13   *Adams v Cape Industries Plc* [1990] 1 Ch. 433 and *Multinational Gas & Petrochemical Co. v Multinational Gas and Petrochemical Services Ltd* [1983] Ch. 258.
14   *cf. Apthorpe v Peter Schoenhofen Brewing Co.* (1899) 4 T.C. 41, a tax case.
15   See generally, Delany & McGrath, fn.5 at 3 *et seq.*
16   See generally, Collins, fn.5, Ch.12.
17   [1991] B.C.L.C. 666.

English-registered company that carried on all its business in Argentina, the Court of Appeal declined to hear the matter. That was because, in addition to conducting its business there, the acts complained of were done there, the witnesses in the action were there and most of them spoke Spanish only, and the documents were there, most of them also in Spanish. The company was registered there too. Its incorporation in England appeared to be a historical accident and its presence there was largely a formal one. This was a case brought under the predecessor of Brussels/Lugano and is now regarded as having been wrongly decided, as the *forum non conveniens* doctrine has been held inapplicable to proceedings under Regulation 44/2001.

21–11   A more recent example of the court declining to accept jurisdiction is *Konamaneni v Rolls Royce Industrial Power (India) Ltd*,[18] which was a derivative action by minority shareholders in an Indian-registered company, which was joined as a defendant, brought against two English companies alleging that they bribed the plaintiffs' company's managing director. It was contended that he and his co-directors exercised such control in the company as to prevent it from suing the alleged wrongdoers; that accordingly, the plaintiffs could sue on the company's behalf under the "fraud on a minority" exception to the general rule. The main issues were whether the action had been brought for some ulterior purpose; whether the appropriate organ for determining whether there was the requisite wrongdoer control was the board or the general meeting; if it is the board, was it capable of taking independent decisions and, if yes, how should they be taken; the extent of the managing director's involvement in the alleged bribing. Notwithstanding that the defendant companies were registered in England, it was held that the case should be heard in India, where one of the defendants had registered under the external registry and had appointed an agent to accept service of proceedings, where two of the four plaintiffs lived (the other two living in the US and in Mauritius, respectively), where there was extensive litigation taking place that related closely to the issues arising in this case, and which was the country whose law was applicable.[19]

21–12   In *Pergamon Press Ltd v Maxwell*,[20] a dispute about whether a person who had been appointed a director of the New York subsidiary of an English company had since been lawfully removed, the English court refused to order that an EGM of the subsidiary be convened so that there could be a formal removal of the purported officer. But the observation made there, that "the court of New York is the only proper tribunal in which the [subsidiary's] members could seek to control the exercise of this discretionary power"[21] (i.e. to convene an EGM) probably goes too far, as suggesting that there never can be circumstances where the court where the parent company is incorporated may make an order of this nature. As Collins J. later pointed out, "it may be wholly unjust to require recourse to an offshore haven to pursue fraudulent directors

---

[18]   [2002] 1 W.L.R. 1269.
[19]   Similarly, *Reeves v Sprecher* [2007] 2 B.C.L.C. 614.
[20]   [1970] 1 W.L.R. 1167.
[21]   *ibid.* at 1171–1172.

in a case which has no connection with th[at] jurisdiction other than that it is the place of incorporation".[22]

21–13   As the statutory jurisdiction to approve a scheme of arrangement includes companies that can be wound up under the 1963 Act,[23] in appropriate circumstances, a scheme involving a foreign-registered company can be approved by the court.[24] The statutory "oppression" remedy[25] applies to Irish-registered companies only but can apply to a foreign company if the redress sought includes having it wound up.[26]

APPLICABLE LAW

21–14   The applicable law is concerned with what country's law or countries' laws govern a particular event, transaction or subject matter. To date, there is no EC-wide standard regime for what laws apply to non-contractual civil and commercial disputes. In countries of the common law tradition, and also in the Netherlands and the Scandinavian countries, in general the law that governs the affairs of companies is that of their place of incorporation. In contrast, in most continental European countries, the applicable law is that of where the company has its "real seat", or *siège réel*, meaning where its principal management is located, which resembles the concept of "residence" for tax and other purposes. The rationale for this latter approach is that it ensures that businesses being managed in the state in question are subject to its company law rules and not the perhaps lax laws of where they happen to be incorporated—be it Panama, Liechtenstein, Guernsey, the Bahamas, the Cayman Islands or wherever. How this objective is achieved to an extent in the common law counties is to require foreign companies doing business in them to register there as well, such as under the Branch Disclosures Regulations or under Pt XII (ss.351–360) of the 1963 Act.[27]

Specific Provisions

21–15   There are several external aspects of the affairs of Irish-registered companies that are the subject of specific statutory provision. For the purpose of consolidated group accounts, a subsidiary company includes a foreign-registered subsidiary.[28] AGMs may be held outside the State where the company's own regulations so provide and either at the previous AGM it was resolved to meet abroad or all of the members are agreeable to doing so.[29] The prohibition on bankrupts becoming directors includes persons who were declared bankrupt by a competent foreign court and have not obtained a

---

[22]   *Konamaneni* case [2002] 1 W.L.R. 1269 at 1288.
[23]   Section 201(7).
[24]   See para.21–41.
[25]   1963 Act, s.205.
[26]   See para.21–41.
[27]   See para.21–46 *et seq.*
[28]   See para.17–71 *et seq.*
[29]   1963 Act, s.140.

discharge there.[30] Foreign-resident directors of Irish-registered companies can be the subject of restriction or disqualification orders.[31] Except where the requisite bond has been provided, at least one director must be resident in the State.[32] If duly authorised under the company's seal, a person may execute deeds on its behalf in any foreign country.[33] If a company's objects envisage it transacting business abroad, and its articles so provide, it may have a fac-simile of its official seal for use there.[34] Any document annexed to the annual return that is not in the Irish or the English language must be accompanied by a certified translation in one of those languages.[35] For the purposes of allot-ting shares for cash in the context of the 1983 Act, cash includes any foreign currency.[36]

21–16 Where a company creates a charge that is registrable but the property affected is situated outside the State, the requisite 21 days for registering it in the CRO means 21 days after notice would have been received in the State if it had been sent with diligence from the country in question.[37] This is so even if further steps must be taken there to render the charge entirely valid and effec-tive.[38] Where registration there is necessary for that purpose, a certificate to that effect should be sent to the CRO.[39] Where a company acquires property outside the State that is subject to a charge that should be registered if it had been created by the company, the requisite 21 days for registration at the CRO is extended as described above.[40]

21–17 There also are some provisions that are equally applicable to Irish and to foreign-registered companies. Where for any purpose of the Companies Acts a statutory declaration is made outside the State, it may be made before a person who is entitled to practice as a solicitor in the State or before a person authorised by law to administer oaths there and certain additional requirements are com-plied with.[41] Where Pt III (ss.25–52) of the 1990 Act concerning transactions involving directors would otherwise apply, it is irrelevant that the transaction in question is governed by the law of some other State.[42] Trading conducted on a securities market regulated by the State is governed by Irish law.[43]

21–18 In cases where the EC Regulation on Insolvency Proceedings applies, it is the law of the Member State where "such proceedings are opened" that

---

[30] 1963 Act, s.183.
[31] *Re Euroking Miracle (Ireland) Ltd* [2003] 3 I.R. 80.
[32] 1999 (No. 2) Act, ss.43 and 44.
[33] 1963 Act, s.40.
[34] 1963 Act, s.41.
[35] 1986 Act, s.7(1)(b).
[36] 1983 Act, s.2(3).
[37] 1963 Act, s.99(3).
[38] 1963 Act, s.99(4).
[39] 1963 Act, s.99(5) and Form 47C.
[40] 1963 Act, s.101.
[41] 2006 Act, s.6.
[42] Section 25(8).
[43] European Communities (Market in Financial Instruments) Regulations 2007 (SI 2007/60).

governs the process, subject to several exceptions.[44] By opening proceedings is meant commencing them in a court with competent jurisdiction under Art.3. It was held by Kelly J. in *Re Eurofoods IFSC Ltd*[45] that, in a compulsory winding up, this is when a winding up petition is presented in the High Court and a provisional liquidator is appointed.[46] In the case of a voluntary winding up, the relevant time would seem to be when the resolution to wind up is passed by the company's members.

Internal Affairs

21–19 Where the dispute in question concerns the constitution or internal affairs of a foreign company, generally it must be determined by reference to the law of the State where it is incorporated.[47] That law governs, for example, the composition and powers of the company's various organs, whether its directors have been validly appointed, the nature and extent of the duties that its directors owe to the company, what company officials have authority to act on its behalf, the extent of its members' liability for the company's unpaid debts, the company's ability to pay dividends or make other distributions to its members, the validity of a transfer of assets and liabilities where companies have amalgamated. Thus in *Base Metal Trading Ltd v Shamurin*,[48] where directors of a Guernsey-registered company were sued for breach of fiduciary duty to it arising from speculative transactions conducted from its place of business in Moscow, it was held that the applicable law was that of Guernsey. Further in the *Konamaneni* case,[49] concerning alleged bribery of officers of an Indian company, it was held that the law applicable to the plaintiff's derivative action was the law of India; additionally, that the action should be determined in India and not in England. In *Kutchera v Buckingham Int'l Holdings Ltd*,[50] where a South African resident lent money to a Canadian public company, their contract stipulated that it was subject to Irish law and that the Irish courts had jurisdiction to try disputes arising from it. Holding that Irish law governed the dispute, the Supreme Court accepted that Canadian law may have some bearing on the outcome "because under the conflict of laws rules matters concerning the constitution of a corporation are governed by the laws of the place of incorporation of the company."[51]

21–20 This stance is reflected in the Rome Convention on the Law Applicable to Contractual Obligations,[52] which exempts from its scope "questions governed by the law of companies ... such as the creation, by registration or

---

[44] Article 4.

[45] [2004] 4 I.R. 370.

[46] See para 24–150 *et seq.*

[47] See generally, W. Binchy, *Irish Conflicts of Laws* (Dublin: Butterworth (Ireland), 1988), Ch.26 and L. Collins, *Dicey, Morris & Collins on the Conflict of Laws*, 14th edn (London: Sweet & Maxwell, 2006), Vol.2, p.1345 *et seq.*

[48] [2005] 1 W.L.R. 1157.

[49] *Konamaneni v Rolls Royce Industrial Power (India) Ltd* [2002] 1 W.L.R. 1269.

[50] [1988] I.R. 61.

[51] *ibid.* at 68.

[52] [1980] O.J. C282/1.

otherwise, legal capacity, internal organisation or winding up … and the personal liability of officers and members as such for the obligations of the company …".[53] Commenting on this,[54] it was said that the exclusion here "affects all the complex acts (contractual, administrative, registration) which are necessary to the creation of a company or firm and to the regulation of its internal organisation and winding-up, i.e. acts which fall within the scope of company law. Internal organisation includes the calling of meetings, the right to vote, the necessary quorum and appointment of officers of the company or firm, etc. Winding-up covers either the termination of the company as provided by its constitution or by operation of law, or its disappearance by merger or similar process. Although mergers and groupings are not specifically excluded, it is thought that the wording of the provision is apt to exclude them. The exclusion of legal capacity concerns limitations, for example, in respect of acquiring immovable property, but does not concern *ultra vires* acts by organs of the company or firm which fall under." Art. 1(2)(f) of the Convention excludes the question, *inter alia*, of whether an organ may bind a company contractually to a third party. Provisions in a shareholders' agreement dealing with these questions also would appear to fall outside the Convention.

21–21 At common law, a company may decide that some aspects of its internal affairs shall be subject to some other legal system. For instance, in *Adelaide Electric Supply Co. v Prudential Assurance Co*,[55] the company was registered in England but all of its business was carried on in Australia, where many of its shareholders resided and where it kept a branch register of members. To avoid double taxation of its dividends, in 1921 it resolved that thenceforth dividends should be declared and paid only in Australia. When later the value of the Australian pound fell below that of the English pound sterling, the question arose of whether dividends payable on its 5 per cent and 6.5 per cent preference shares were payable in English or in Australian currency. Because of where it was registered, any repayment of capital or distribution in a winding up would have to be made in English currency. But it is an established rule in the conflict of laws that, whatever law governs a contract as a whole, the performance of any particular obligation in it is subject to the law of the place where it is to be performed; as regards paying money, a stipulation to pay a sum in a designated place means to pay in the currency of that place. Accordingly, it was held, the effect of the resolution was to authorise payment of the dividends in Australian currency. And because the preference shareholders did not object in 1921 to the proposed change, which was made to benefit the entire company and which would have been most advantageous to those shareholders if exchange rates had moved in the other direction, the resolution could not be regarded as unlawfully discriminatory or oppressive, or as violating their class rights.

---

[53] Article 1(2)(e).
[54] Collins, fn.47, at 1350.
[55] [1934] A.C. 122.

Lifting the Veil

21–22   What law governs the circumstances in which courts will disregard
the distinct incorporation of a foreign company and "lift the veil" to render
its shareholders personally liable for its obligations, or to make it accountable for acts of its shareholders, does not appear to have attracted significant
judicial analysis. A recent academic account of this question concluded that
"there is no room for a single choice of law rule to govern the issue of corporate veil-piercing. Large parts of it can be readily understood in terms of
other legal doctrines, and what remains is of doubtful coherence. So, as to
the former, there can be no single choice of law rule because different issues
with diverse connecting factors are involved. As to the latter, you cannot
have a choice of law rule for that you cannot characterise."[56] In the insider-
trading case, *Fyffes Plc v DCC Plc*,[57] where it was accepted that the applicable law was the Irish regulatory regime, Laffoy J. concluded that the board
of the listed Plc defendant's Dutch sub-subsidiary did not function independently of its parent. Accordingly, for the purpose of incurring statutory liability for insider trading, the companies would be treated as a single entity.[58] In
contrast, in *Lonrho Ltd v Shell Petroleum Co. Ltd*,[59] where the question was
whether, for the purpose of discovering documents, they were in the "power"
of the defendants' wholly-owned Rhodesian subsidiaries; it was held that
they were not. That was because, on legal advice, those subsidiaries' directors flatly refused to comply with the parent companies' request to disclose
the material. Similarly, in another instance involving a question of procedure
rather than substantive rights/duties, *Adams v Cape Industries Plc*,[60] it was
held that a dafault judgement obtained in Texas against the English parent of
a US subsidiary was not enforceable in England. That was because the parent
never had a presence in the US and, accordingly, the courts there had no
jurisdiction over it. The presence of its wholly-owned marketing subsidiary
there was not sufficient for this purpose. In both instances it was accepted
that the position would be otherwise if the foreign subsidiary was the mere
alter ego of the English parent.

Interests in Securities

21–23   Although an enormous number and variety of transactions occur every
day in corporate securities, where more than one national legal system is potentially affected, very few disputes involving conflicts of laws aspects of these
have reached the courts.[61] The question of the law applicable in disputes about

---

[56] C.H. Tham, "Piercing the Corporate Veil: Searching for Appropriate Choice of Law
       Rules" [2007] 1 *Lloyd's Maritime and Commercial Law Quarterly 22* at 42–43. See too,
       Muchlinski, fn.1 above.
[57] [2005] I.E.H.C. 477; unreported, Laffoy J., December 21, 2005; this part of the judgment
       was not appealed: [2007] I.E.S.C. 36, July 27, 2007.
[58] See paras 14–28 and 29.
[59] [1990] 1 Ch.433.
[60] [1980] 1 W.L.R 627.
[61] See generally, M. Ooi, *Shares and Other Securities in the Conflict of Laws* (Oxford:
       OUP, 2003).

share ownership was considered in detail in *Macmillan Inc v Bishopsgate Investment Trust (No. 3)*,[62] which concerned a dispute about security interests in shares in a New York registered company controlled by the late Robert Maxwell. There was a series of transactions that took place mainly in London, in which those shares were given as security to several different banks, and the dispute was about which of those banks had the prior security interest. That depended on whether English or New York law applied. It was held that, for these purposes, the applicable law is that of the *lex situs*, i.e. where the shares are situated. In the case of non-negotiable securities, it is where the company is incorporated. This may not be the case for bearer securities or possibly where the share register is kept elsewhere. Additionally, contractual rights and obligations in respect of shares are governed by the proper law of the contract.[63]

MUTUAL ASSISTANCE

21–24 In recent years there has been a significant expansion in the categories of instance where the regulatory authorities in one state assist foreign regulatory authorities in carrying out their functions. The traditional conflict of laws rule was that the courts of one country will not, directly or indirectly, assist in enforcing the penal or revenue laws of another country. But this is now subject to extensive statutory exceptions in the criminal law and other fields. Regulations giving effect to EC Directives on prospectuses, on insider trading and other forms of market abuse, and on transparency, provide for cooperation with the regulatory authorities in other EC Member States.

21–25 Powers exercisable by the DCE under Pt II (ss.7–24) of the 1990 Act, concerning making production orders and appointing inspectors, can be exercised by him where an equivalent foreign regulatory authority requests his assistance in carrying out their enquiries.[64] For the purpose of monitoring acquiring or disposing of major shareholdings in listed companies, the Irish Stock Exchange authorities are required to cooperate with comparable authorities in other EC Member States.[65]

21–26 Subject to a given country being recognised for this purpose, an order made by a court there for a foreign company's "reorganisation or reconstruction" may be enforced by the High Court as it was the court's own order.[66] The High Court can enforce any order connected with winding up a company that is made by a court in any country recognised for these purposes by the Minister.[67] A certificate by a person purporting to be a Registrar of

---

[62] [1996] 1 W.L.R. 387.

[63] *cf. Pattni* v. *Ali* [2007] 2 W.L.R. 102.

[64] Section 23A.

[65] 1990 Act, ss.96 and 116. Also part 9 of the European Communities (Markets in Financial Instruments) Regulations 2007 (SI 2007/60).

[66] 1990 (Amendment) Act, s.36. No order recognising any country for these purposes has yet been made by the Minister.

[67] 1963 Act, s.250, applied to the United Kingdom by the Companies (Recognition of Countries) Order 1964 (SI 1964/42).

Companies in a foreign country recognised for these purposes by the Minister is *prima facie* evidence of incorporation there.[68]

REGULATING FOREIGN COMPANIES

21–27   The regulation of foreign registered companies gives rise to broad issues such as the State's jurisdiction under international law to prescribe standards applicable to such companies, as well as the courts' jurisdiction to make orders that affect them, for instance assuming adjudicative jurisdiction to determine disputes relating to them and ordering discovery of records held abroad by them.[69] Companies registered outside the State may do business in, or have some other presence in or involvement with persons in, the State—be it through having a subsidiary or else some branch or other establishment in the State, or through a local agent or otherwise. Several of those companies are subsidiaries of major multinational enterprises that have been attracted to Ireland by, *inter alia*, favourable corporation tax and other fiscal regimes, and by investment incentives given by Enterprise Ireland. Within the EC, Art.43 of the EC Treaty on freedom of establishment entitles companies registered in any EC Member State to set up agencies, branches or subsidiaries in any other such State. Under the Treaty on Friendship, Commerce and Navigation with the USA, of 1950,[70] somewhat comparable rights are given to US companies.

21–28   There are several connecting concepts applicable to a foreign companies' activities in a state. One is residence, meaning where the company's central management and control is located. Another is having a branch or having established a place of business. Under many company law regimes, where a company has located activities in this manner, it is required to register under an external companies' register. Another still is where the company carries on some activities but has no business location there. Parts of the Companies Acts apply to companies subject to the external registry regime. Some of those provisions apply to foreign companies that are connected in some other manner with the State.

Nationality

21–29   Strictly speaking, companies do not possess citizenship and, accordingly, do not have a nationality. For some purposes, however, they are treated as having a nationality, most notably in the context of diplomatic protection in public international law.[71] Where, as in EC law, rules draw distinctions between nationals of particular states and non-nationals, it often is necessary to attribute a nationality to a company for those rules to operate in a commercial context. Many international agreements treat companies as nationals for the purpose of the treaty in question, and go on to define how their nationality

---

[68]   1963 Act, s.389.
[69]   See generally, Muchlinski and Wallace, above fn.1.
[70]   Treaty of January 21, 1950 and Protocol of June 24, 1992.
[71]   See generally, I. Brownlie, *Principles of Public International Law*, 5th edn (Oxford: OUP, 1998), pp.426–427 and 428 *et seq.*

is to be determined, e.g. state where company is registered, state where its head office or *siège réel* is located. In the *Barcelona Traction* case,[72] which was brought by Belgium against Spain on behalf of the majority Belgian shareholders in a Canadian-registered company, the International Court of Justice held that Belgium lacked the requisite *locus standi* to prosecute those proceedings, suggesting that in the circumstances the company should be deemed a Canadian national. It had its head office, maintained its accounts and share registers, and held its board meetings in Canada, and had been listed with the Canadian tax authorities.

Residence

21–30   Where a company is resident is a vital consideration for several purposes. Foreign companies that are resident in the State are subject to the Irish courts' jurisdiction. They also are subject to corporation tax in respect of their worldwide (not just their Irish) profits, although the severity of this is mitigated where a double taxation agreement is applicable.[73] Additionally, where a close company is resident in the State, its distributions are subject to income tax under Schedule F, and are not generally subject to corporation tax or taken into account in computing income for that purpose. Only Irish-resident companies can be close companies for tax purposes and only such companies are entitled to the patent income exception. A plaintiff company's residence is also relevant for the purposes of giving security for a defendant's costs.[74] What constitutes a company's residence is the subject of a substantial body of case law and, for tax purposes, is amplified by s.23A of the Taxes Consolidation Act 1997 and also by provisions in double tax treaties.

21–31   For the purpose of adjudicative jurisdiction, a company is resident in a State if it or its agent is carrying on business there at a fixed place of business and for a sufficiently substantial period of time.[75] The classic test for residence for tax purposes is where the company's real business is carried on, being wherever its central management and control is actually located.[76] As Gibson J. pointed out in *Hood & Co. v Magee*,[77] "it is essential to keep steadily in mind that residence, as a question of fact depends on the particular evidence before the court; the danger must be avoided of extending a principle applied to such evidence to control dissimilar facts."[78] What in substance was a "one man" company had a sole director and manager who resided in the US, where a substantial part of its business as a linen merchant was conducted.

---

72 *Belgium v Spain,* 2nd phase [1970] I.C.J.R. 3.
73 See generally M. Feeney *The Taxation of Companies* (Haywards Heath: Tottel Publishing, 2006), Ch.14 and D. Davies, *Booth: Residence, Domicile and UK Taxation*, 11th edn (Haywards Heath: Tottel Publishing, 2007).
74 e.g. *Re Little Olympian Each Ways Ltd* [1995] 1 W.L.R. 560.
75 *Adams v Cape Industries Plc* [1990] 1 Ch. 433.
76 See generally, Collins, fn.47 at 1335 *et seq.* and R. Bramwell *et al., Taxation of Companies and Company Reconstructions*, 8th edn (London: Sweet & Maxwell, 2002), paras C2.2 and C2.14.
77 [1918] 2 I.R. 34.
78 *ibid.* at 43.

Notwithstanding, it was held to be resident in Belfast, where it bought and folded the linen for export, had an office and warehouse, and where its general meetings were held and minute books were kept. In the *De Beers* case,[79] which concerned the renowned diamond producer which was incorporated in South Africa, where its head office and mines were located, where its general meetings were always held and where several of its directors resided, it was held that, notwithstanding, the company resided in London. That was because the majority of its directors lived there, their meetings generally occurred there and, apart from the actual mining operations, real control was exercised from there; for instance, negotiations on contracts with the various diamond syndicates were directed from there.[80]

21–32   Subsidiary companies have their own residence, entirely separate from that of their parent.[81] But if the parent virtually usurps the powers of the subsidiary's board of directors, it will be treated as having the same residence as its parent.[82]

Doing Business

21–33   Where a non-resident company carries on a business is significant for several purposes. If it "carries on a trade in the State through a branch or an agency" then generally it is liable to corporation tax.[83] But a company can conduct business in the State without it ever having established a place of business here.[84]

21–34   Whether a company has carried on a business in the State is predominantly a question of fact. In *Cripps Warburg Ltd v Cologne Investment Co,*[85] one issue was whether a loan made by the plaintiff was caught by the Moneylenders Act 1900, which applied to those "whose business is that of moneylending", other than authorised banks and various other bodies. As the loan was one of only two transactions that the English-registered plaintiff had engaged in in Ireland, D'Arcy J. held that it did not conduct a moneylending business here. Similarly, in *Siucre Eireann,*[86] a Jersey-registered company did not do business here because its only activity in Ireland was to acquire 2425 shares in an Irish company and, in the following year, to sell them to another Irish company for IR£2 million, payment being made in the form of a loan note.

Applicable Provisions

21–35   Unless the contrary is stated, regulatory legislation is presumed not to apply to persons and bodies who are not in the State, nor to activities outside

---

[79]   *De Beers Consolidated Mines Ltd v Howe* [1906] A.C. 455.
[80]   cf. *Wood v Holden* [2006] 1 W.L.R. 1393.
[81]   *Adams v Cape Industries Plc* [1990] 1 Ch. 433.
[82]   *Unit Construction Co. v Bullock* [1960] A.C. 351.
[83]   Taxes Consolidation Act 1997, s.25.
[84]   *Rakusens Ltd v Baser Ambalaj Plastik Sanayi Ticaret AS* [2001] 1 B.C.L.C. 104.
[85]   [1980] I.R. 32.
[86]   *Minister for Industry and Commerce v Siucre Eireann cpt* [1992] 2 I.R. 215.

the State.[87] Where under the terms of the statutory provision in question it is not clear whether it was intended to apply extraterritorially, the courts endeavour to find some basis for it not having universal application. Sometimes, this is not possible.

21–36 Except where it is otherwise so provided, the word "company" in the Companies Acts means a company registered in the State.[88] This accords with the conflict of laws principle, that the law of the country of incorporation governs questions such as the capacity of companies, their internal affairs, their capital, and the protection of shareholders and creditors. Provisions of these Acts do not apply to the affairs of foreign-registered companies unless they are stated to be so applicable. Accordingly, in *Arab Bank Plc v Mercantile Holdings Ltd*,[89] it was held that the prohibition against subsidiary companies financing the purchase of their parent companies' shares[90] did not apply to a foreign-registered subsidiary. If the legislature intended to prohibit and indeed criminalise the actions of foreign companies that may very well be lawful in their state of incorporation, unequivocal language would be called for. In *Re Tuskar Resources Plc*,[91] where an application to appoint an examiner to an Irish-registered company whose only assets were shares in a Nigerian operating subsidiary was rejected, it was held that this subsidiary could not be a "related company" for those purposes under the law as it then stood.[92] Because it was registered in Guernsey, a company was not able to rely on s.37 of the 1963 Act that facilitates the enforcement of pre-incorporation contracts.[93]

21–37 Under the Stock Transfer Act 1963, a company includes a foreign-registered company. Reference in the Companies Acts to a "body corporate" or a "corporation" includes a foreign-registered company.[94] Although there is no equivalent definition in the State Property Act 1954, it was held by Finlay Geoghegan J. in *Re Clarke's of Ranelagh Ltd*[95] that property in the State belonging to dissolved foreign companies vests in the State under s.28 of that Act. This follows from the general conflicts of law rule that title to property is determined principally by the law of the State where that property is located, including choses in action such as debts. For the purpose of the definitions of a subsidiary of another company, a company includes any body corporate.[96] Companies Act group accounts are not required where, at the end of the financial year a company is the wholly-owned subsidiary of any body corporate that has been incorporated in the State.[97]

---

[87] *Pergamon Press Ltd v Maxwell* [1970] 2 All E.R. 809.
[88] 1963 Act, s.2(1).
[89] [1994] Ch. 71.
[90] 1963 Act, s.60(1).
[91] [2001] 1 I.R. 668.
[92] 1990 Act, s.4(5).
[93] *Rover International Ltd v Cannon Film Sales Ltd* [1987] B.C.L.C. 540.
[94] 1963 Act, s.2(3).
[95] [2004] 3 I.R. 264.
[96] 1963 Act, s.155(5).
[97] 1963 Act, s.151(2)(a).

21–38   Procedures for prosecuting company officers on indictment apply as much to foreign companies with a place of business established here as they apply to Irish-registered companies.[98] Power to compel production of a company's books and records, where it is suspected that one of its officers has committed an offence in connection with its affairs, applies also to foreign companies with a place of business in the State.[99] The safeguards for where there is a substantial property transaction between a company and any of its directors apply to foreign companies that have registered under Pt XI of the 1963 Act and also where the company is a wholly-owned subsidiary of an Irish-registered company, wherever it may have been incorporated.[100] In the case of Plcs, the regimes governing issuing a prospectus for securities that are or are about to be listed on a stock exchange, and on insider trading and other types of securities market abuses, apply regardless of where the company is registered.

21–39   The requirement for registering company charges applies to charges made by any foreign company on property that they have in the State, as well as to judgment mortgages affecting such property and receivers of that property.[101] It was held that this applies even where the company in question had not been duly registered under the special register kept for foreign companies operating in the State and where the Registrar of Companies declined to accept notification of the existence of the charge.[102] To obtain priority, the chargee must deliver prescribed details of the charge to the CRO within the requisite 21 days. Once that is done, priority is safeguarded notwithstanding that the existence of the charge is not recorded in any CRO register.

21–40   Production orders may be made by the DCE against, and inspectors may be appointed by the DCE into the affairs of, foreign companies provided they are carrying on business in the State or have done so.[103] In the *Siucre Éireann* case,[104] because one of the companies involved was registered in Jersey and carried on no business activities in the State, no order could be made against it in respect of the inspection into activities in which it had an involvement.

21–41   Subject to the EC Regulation on Insolvency Proceedings, the High Court's winding up jurisdiction[105] and its power to sanction schemes of arrangement[106] apply to, *inter alia*, unregistered companies, which includes foreign-registered companies[107]; in appropriate circumstances such companies

---

[98] 1963 Act, s382(7).
[99] 1963 Act, s.384.
[100] 1990 Act, ss.28(6) and 29(6).
[101] 1963 Act, s.111.
[102] *NV Slavenburg's Bank v Intercontinental Natural Resources Ltd* [1980] 1 All E.R. 955.
[103] 1990 Act, s.17.
[104] *Minister for Industry and Commerce v Siucre Eireann cpt* [1992] 2 I.R. 215.
[105] 1963 Act, s.212.
[106] 1963 Act, s.201.
[107] 1963 Act, s.345.

will be subjected to an Irish liquidation or sanctioned scheme. But unless the company is sufficiently connected with the State, neither of these jurisdictions will be exercised. In *Re Drax Holdings Ltd*,[108] concerning companies incorporated in the Cayman Islands and in Jersey that were established to raise finance for the acquisition of a major power station in England, it was held that they had a sufficient connection with England for the courts there to approve a scheme of arrangement. Their Eurobond trust deed and security agreements were subject to English law, their bank facility agreement was subject to the exclusive jurisdiction of the English courts and their principal asset was bonds held by their London bank. Additionally, arrangements had been made that, if the scheme obtained court approval, simultaneous orders would be made in their states of incorporation.[109]

21–42 Foreign companies' officers can be subjected to the disqualification order regime.[110] However, the restriction order regime applies only to officers of foreign companies which have established a place of business in the State.[111]

Branch/Establishment in the State

21–43 Several company law requirements apply to companies that have an actual place of business in the State. In the case of limited companies which "establish a branch" in the State, they must register with the Registrar of Companies and provide him with the information specified in the European Communities (Branch Disclosures) Regulations 1993.[112] Part II of these apply where the company is incorporated in the EC and Pt III applies where it is registered elsewhere. In the case of unlimited companies that possess an "establishment" in the State, the registration and reporting requirements are in Pt XI (ss.351–360) of the 1963 Act. Possessing a "permanent establishment" in a State is a key concept under double taxation arrangements.

Branch

21–44 What constitutes a branch in this context is not defined. For the purposes of EC Regulation 44/2001 on Jurisdiction and Judgments, a branch has been held to mean a location with the appearance of permanence and is equipped physically to transact business directly with third parties.[113] If a company's presence in the State is a branch, the 1993 Regulations apply.

Establishment

21–45 Establishing a place of business means more than just carrying on business; it connotes having a specified or identifiable place from which the

---

[108] [2004] 1 W.L.R. 1049.
[109] See too, *Re Sovereign Marine & General Ins. Co.* [2007] 1 B.C.L.C. 228.
[110] 1990 Act, s.159.
[111] 1990 Act, s.149(4).
[112] SI 1973/395.
[113] See L. Collins, *Dicey et al on the Conflict of Laws*, 14th edn (London: Sweet & Maxwell: 2006), Vol I, pp.421–423.

company does business with some regularity. It is not sufficient that the company carries on a business in the State if that is not being done from an identifiable location here. For instance, in *Re Oriel Ltd*,[114] an Isle of Man registered company acquired several garage sites in England, by way of a loan from an oil supplier, and charged those sites to the supplier. Although it had been carrying on a business in England of holding and mortgaging property, until it started trading in its own name from those sites, it was held not to have had an established place of business there. The test is whether the company has "some more or less permanent location, not necessarily owned or leased by [it], but at least associated with [it] and from which habitually or with some degree of regularity business is conducted."[115] The business does not have to form any significant part of the company's overall business or even be incidental to the company's main objects.[116] But it is not sufficient that the company acts through some local agent, or through a subsidiary or affiliate company.[117]

Disclosure to CRO

21–46 Where the company has a "branch" in the State, the following matters must be notified to the CRO[118] and, within 21 days of their notification, a notice of that fact must be placed in the *Gazette*. If they are not in Irish or in English, certified translations must be provided. Within 21 days of the company setting up its branch, it must deliver a certified copy of its memorandum and articles of association, or other constitutive documents. At the same time, it must notify the CRO of the following: its certificate of incorporation; its place of registration and the number with which it is registered; its name and legal form; the name of the branch, if different; the persons who are authorised to bind the company and specified personal details about them, along with the extent of their authority, with reference to the branch[119]; the name and address of a person resident in the State authorised to ensure compliance with the Branch Disclosure Regulations, along with his consent to so act[120]; the name and address of a person resident in the State who is authorised to accept service of any legal process against the company or any notices that are to be served on it. There also must be delivered to the CRO at this time copies of the latest yearly accounting documents in respect of the branch that were published in accordance with the law in the State where the company was incorporated. Notice sent by companies incorporated outside the EC must also include the State where they are incorporated, their objects and their principal place of business.

---

[114] [1986] 1 W.L.R. 180.
[115] *ibid.* at 188; *cf.* R. Bramwell *et al.*, *Taxation of Companies and Company Reconstructions*, 8th edn (London: Sweet & Maxwell, 2002) Ch.C2.3.
[116] *Rakusens Ltd v Baser Ambalaj Plastik Sanayi Ticaret AS* [2001] 1 B.C.L.C. 104.
[117] *Matchnet Plc v William Blair & Co LLC* [2003] 2 B.C.L.C. 195.
[118] Forms F 12 or 13.
[119] Form F 3.
[120] Form F 4.

21–47 Within 14 days of the following occurring, the relevant documents must be delivered to the CRO: any alteration to the memorandum or articles of association, along with the amended text; notice of any change in the persons notified as above; notice of any change in the branch's address and its new address; closure of the branch; notice of the company being wound up and certain particulars regarding the liquidator.[121] For these purposes, the same requirements apply as in the general regime on the register of details concerning a company's directors and secretary.

21–48 Except for financial companies, within 11 months of the end of its financial year every company with a branch must deliver to the CRO a copy of its annual accounts that were audited in accordance with the law in its state of registration, including any directors' report and the auditors' report.[122] For non-EC registered companies, even if there is no requirement under their law to have accounts, such accounts must be delivered and shall be consistent with the EC accounting regime. If it does not appear from the accounts of a non-EC-registered company, its called-up share capital must be notified.

21–49 Broadly similar requirements exist for companies that have an "establishment" in the State but do not have a branch here.[123] Details also must be given about the company secretary. Having to furnish copies of accounts does not apply if the company would be a private company if it had registered in the State.[124] Notice also must be given if the company ceases to have a place of business in the State.[125]

Letters and Forms

21–50 Where the company has a "branch" in the State, every letter and order form it uses must state the company's place of registration and its registered number, the company's legal form, the place of its registered office, the place where the branch is registered and its registration number, and the fact that it is being wound up if that is the case. For non-EC-registered companies, only the branch's place of registration and number need be stated; if required by the law where it is incorporated, the company's place of registration and number.[126] Equivalent provisions apply to branch websites and electronic communications.[127] Any reference to capital in the document shall be to called up capital. Where the company only has an "establishment" in the State, the fact that its members have limited liability must be stated.

---

[121] Forms F 2, 3, 4 and 14.

[122] Form F 7.

[123] 1963 Act, ss.352–355 and Form F 1.

[124] 1963 Act, s.354.

[125] 1963 Act, s.357.

[126] Regulation 8.

[127] European Communities (Companies) (Amendment) Regulations 2007 (SI 2007/49).

Service

21–51   The Companies Acts and other legislation require notices of various kinds to be served on a company. To commence legal proceedings against a company, ordinarily it has to be duly served with notice of them, at its registered office address. If the intended defendant does not have the requisite presence in the State, it will have to be duly served abroad.[128] Ordinarily, service on a subsidiary does not constitute service on the parent, nor does service on the latter amount to service on the former.

21–52   Foreign companies with a "branch" in the State are required to notify the CRO of a person resident in the State who is authorised to accept service of any such notice or process.[129] Posting it to or leaving it at this person's address is sufficient service.[130] Where such a person has not been notified to the CRO, or he has ceased to reside in the State or has died, or for any other reason he cannot be served, posting the document to or leaving it at the branch address suffices.

21–53   There are similar requirements for companies that do not have a branch but are "established" in the State. But the proceedings need not relate to the kind of business being carried on there.[131] These service requirements lapse two years after the company has notified the CRO that it has ceased to have a place of business here.[132] In an appropriate case, however, the court may put a stay on the action on the grounds that some foreign court is a more appropriate forum to hear the claim.[133]

EUROPEAN ECONOMIC INTEREST GROUPING

21–54   A mechanism for joint ventures between persons in two or more EC Member States is the European economic interest grouping, or EEIG. It was provided for by Regulation 2137/1985,[134] which was implemented by the European Communities (European Economic Interest Groupings) Regulations 1989.[135] An EEIG is established by concluding a contract of formation and then having it registered in the Registry of Companies. On being duly registered, it is a body corporate with legal personality. But its members do not enjoy limited liability; they have unlimited joint and several liability for their EEIG's debts, but cannot be proceeded against until the EEIG has been liquidated. An EEIG must not have more than 20 members, may not employ more than 500 persons and is prohibited from seeking investment from the public.

---

[128] See generally, H. Delany & D. McGrath, *Civil Procedure in the Superior Courts*, 2nd edn (Dublin: Thomson Round Hall, 2005), p.98 *et seq.*

[129] Regulations 4(2)(g) and 7(2)(h).

[130] Regulation 17.

[131] *Saab v Saudi American Bank* [1999] 2 B.C.L.C. 462.

[132] 1963 Act, s.356.

[133] *cf. Rome v Punjab National Bank (No. 2)* [1989] 1 W.L.R. 1211.

[134] [1985] O.J. L199/1.

[135] SI 1989/191.

EUROPEAN COMPANY

21–55 Since 2007, it has become possible to incorporate a new form of corporate entity, which for practically all purposes has a uniform status across the EC, the European Company or *Societas Europaea* ("SE"). Following 40 years of negotiations, Regulation 2157/2001[136] was adopted, providing for this legal entity. A mechanism for forming and recognising such entities in the State was provided for in the European Companies (European Public Limited Liability Company) Regulations 2007.[137] These "SE" companies must register in the Member State where their head office is located, and they must be treated in every other Member State as if they were a Plc formed in accordance with the laws of those states. In many respects, their governance, management and accounting requirements are those of the law of the state where they are registered (their "national law"). These companies are quite different from the virtually supranational entities first envisaged, being more in the nature of national companies of a European type.

21–56 An SE may be formed as a holding company or as a subsidiary, and that may be done, *inter alia*, by way of a company converting from a Plc or of two or more companies merging. Subject to Revenue approval, a company with a head office outside the EC may participate in forming an SE. The registered office may be transferred to another Member State, subject to certain safeguards. On being registered, an annual return date will be assigned by the Registrar of Companies but the SE may request another date that is most suitable or to alter the date so assigned.

21–57 SEs must have a minimum subscribed capital of €120,000, which is subject to the national law's rules regarding maintaining and changing capital, and transfer of title to securities. They may have either a two-tier (supervisory board and management board) or a single-tier (administrative board) management system. Provision must exist for employee involvement in their management.[138] Where their statutes so permit, a company or other legal entity may be a member of either board. No board member may serve for more than six years unless reappointed. A board member must be designated to discharge the function of company secretary.

21–58 An SE's statute may be amended by at least a two-thirds majority of the members voting, except in circumstances where the national law has a more onerous requirement. A simple majority suffices for other decisions, again unless the national law is more onerous. Winding up, liquidation and insolvency is governed by the national law.

---

[136] [2001] O.J. L294/1.
[137] SI 2007/21.
[138] See para.19–28

EC TREATY

21–59 EC measures on company law fall into five major categories. Directives specific to the subject apply either to all companies or to Plcs only. Adopted under Art.44(2)(g) of the EC Treaty, these are known by their numbers, beginning with the First Council Directive of 1968 and ending with the Fourteenth Directive of 2007.[139] In that year, the Tenth Directive on cross-border mergers was adopted, which remains to be implemented. There is no Fifth or Ninth Directive. There then are the Directives regulating public markets in securities, beginning with that on admission to stock exchange listings in 1979, followed by those an on company accounts, on disclosing share ownership, on market abuse and publishing prospectuses, and on transparency.[140] Next there is the regime for capital markets generally, particularly, banking and insurance, that in some respects directly involves company law. Fourthly, there is the regulation for establishing a European company. Finally, the very provisions in the EC Treaty on free movement of capital and on freedom of establishment from time to time impact on the subject.[141]

21–60 One consequence of Art.56(1) of the EC Treaty, which prohibits "restrictions on the movement of capital between Member States", has been restrictions on the system of "golden shares" retained by governments in recently-privatised enterprises. It was held by the European Court of Justice in *Commission v Portugal*[142] that this is a form of discrimination against nationals of other Member States. Notwithstanding that particular national rules do "not give rise to unequal treatment, they are liable to impede the acquisitions of shares in the undertaking concerned and to dissuade investors in other Member States from investing in the capital of those undertakings. They are therefore liable, as a result, to render the free movement of capital illusory"[143] But the Court has acknowledged that special circumstances can justify a golden share: that certain concerns could permit the retention by Member States of a degree of influence within undertakings that were initially public and subsequently privatised, where those undertakings are active in fields involving the provision of services in the public interest or strategic services (variously in the banking, insurance, energy, and transport sectors). Therefore a prior authorisation requirement could be justified provided it was proportionate, based on objective and non-discriminatory criteria which were known in advance to the undertakings concerned, and all persons affected by a restrictive measure had a legal remedy available to them. Since this was not made out on the facts, it was held that the Portuguese law there breached Art.56(1).

---

[139] See para.2–20 *et seq.*
[140] See para.15–40 *et seq.*
[141] See generally, C. Barnard, *The Substantive Law of the EU*, 2nd edn (Oxford: OUP, 2007), p.330 *et seq.*
[142] Case C 367/98 [2002] E.C.R. 4731.
[143] *ibid.* at 4774.

21–61 In *Commission v Spain*,[144] another of the golden share cases, the Spanish Government attempted to justify its prior authorisation requirement on the grounds of "overriding requirements of the general interest linked to strategic imperatives and the need to ensure continuity in public services". The Court rejected this because the companies concerned (a group of banks and a company producing tobacco) had no public service objectives.

21–62 Article 43 of the EC Treaty prohibits "restrictions on the freedom of establishment of nationals of a Member State in the territory of another", including restrictions on "the setting up of agencies, branches or subsidiaries by [those] nationals in the territory of any Member State." This includes the right to "set up and manage undertakings, in particular companies and firms … under the conditions laid down for its own nationals by the law of the country where such establishment is effected …". Article 48 adds that "[c]ompanies or firms formed in accordance with the law of a Member State and having their registered office, central administration or principal place of business within the Community shall … be treated in the some way as national persons who are nationals of Member States." In the present context, two main sets of issues arise under these provisions, *viz.* the extent to which a Member State where a company is incorporated may inhibit its activities in other Member States and, secondly, the extent to which a Member State may inhibit the activities of companies that are incorporated in another such State.[145] A Fourteenth Company Law Directive[146] has been proposed to address these and related issues, *inter alia*, what in the US is known as the "Delaware effect" or the "race to the bottom", i.e. companies seeking to evade the rules of the state where they conduct most of their business, by registering in another state where the regulatory regime is most indulgent to management and controlling shareholders, and where fees and taxes are lowest.

21–63 As a tax avoidance measure, in the *Daily Mail* case,[147] an English company sought to transfer its central management (or *siège réel*) to the Netherlands, but was refused consent to do so by the UK Treasury. It was held by the ECJ that, in those circumstances, the company's freedom of establishment rights were not infringed; that the questions of what connecting factor a company should have with its country of incorporation and the extent to which a company's "real head office" may be moved between Member States was a matter that required specific legislation to regulate. Of course, the company could have wound itself up in the UK and its members could have registered a new company in the Netherlands, but that would hardly alter the location of its *siège réel*. Nor could the company have been prohibited from setting up a subsidiary or a branch there.

---

[144] Case 463/00 [2003] E.C.R. 4581.

[145] See generally, Armour, "Who Should Make Corporate Law? EC Legislation versus Regulatory Competition" [2005] 58 *Current Legal Problems* 369 and Lowry, "Eliminating Obstacles to Freedom of Establishment: The Competitive Edge of UK Company Law" 63 *Cam. L.J.* 331 (2004).

[146] Comm. Doc. XV/6002/97EN. No draft of this has been formally introduced and the delay appears to be due to cases pending in the ECJ for decision, that relate to some fundamental questions involved here.

[147] *R (Ex p. Daily Mail & General Trust) v Treasury* Case 81/87 [1988] E.C.R. 5483.

21–64 The *Centros* case[148] concerned restrictions placed on a company incorporated in one Member State from registering a branch in another. The company was incorporated in the UK by two Danish citizens but never traded there. With a view to trading in Denmark, it applied to register a branch there under a regime similar to that in the EC (Branch Disclosures) Regulations, 1993. Its application was rejected on the grounds that what in substance was being sought was to register the company in Denmark and not just a branch. That was because its owners would have avoided the more onerous minimum capital requirements in Denmark (€25,000 approx.) by registering the company in a state where those amounts were much lower. It was held by the ECJ that this refusal was not justified and it was "immaterial" that the owners formed the company in the UK simply so that they could register a branch in Denmark, where its principal business would be carried on. Under the very terms of Art.43, any company incorporated in one Member State is entitled to set up a secondary establishment in another. A restriction could be placed on this freedom where it is shown that the members are seeking to defraud the company's creditors but that was not the case here. Similarly, in *Inspire Art*,[149] the ECJ held that the Netherlands authorities could not refuse to register a branch of a company registered in the UK, where the minimum capital requirements and also the rules on directors' liability were not as demanding.

21–65 Of these decisions, one observer has commented that they may induce more continental-European-based enterprises to incorporate in Ireland or in the UK, where the regulatory regime is not as rigorous in some respects. Referring in particular to the German private company, the GmbH, it was said that:

> "these decisions could be setting the stage for competition among Member States by their undermining of the real seat doctrine. As far as competition and harmonisation are concerned … the original legislative approach to harmonise company laws in Europe in order to avoid unhealthy competition between Member States has been supplemented by a judicial approach explicitly allowing for competition between the company laws of Member States. The important consequence of these decisions for the future of the GmbH should not be underestimated. …
> Since the end of 2002 nearly 20,000 English private companies with central administration in Germany have been incorporated. Thus the GmbH not only has to compete with home-grown challenges but is increasingly faced with foreign competitors. The possibility exists that the English and Irish company forms may become the most desirable in the European market. The consequential "race to the bottom" may result in the United Kingdom and Ireland as a kind of a European Delaware."[150]

---

[148] *Centros Ltd v Erhvervs-og Selskabsstyrelsen* Case 212/97 [1999] E.C.R. 1459.

[149] *Kamer van Koophandel v Inspire Art Ltd* Case 167/01 [2003] E.C.R. I–10155.

[150] Comment in 28 *Co. Law* 33 (2007) by Jaehne and Henning. This has led to proposals to amend the GmbH law in Germany: "Proposed Reform of the German GmbH", 28 *Co. Law*. 381 (2007).

21–66   Although direct taxation is exclusively within the competence of the individual Member States,[151] tax regimes must not impede free movement of capital and freedom of establishment to such extent that they fall foul of Arts 56 and 43. That tax obligations for persons differ in purely internal situations and in cross-border circumstances does not of itself contravene these provisions.[152] Nor does EC law lay down any general criteria for attributing competences in eliminating double taxation within the EC, apart from two measures regarding company groups.[153] How parent-subsidiary company arrangements should be treated for tax purposes when they are incorporated in different Member States has been considered on several occasions with reference to freedom of establishment.

21–67   In *Cadbury Schweppes Plc v Revenue Commissioners*,[154] a UK-registered company established a subsidiary in the International Financial Services Centre in Dublin, to avail of the advantageous tax conditions there. Under UK tax law, ordinarily companies are not taxed on the profits of their subsidiaries as they arise; instead, they are taxed when those profits are remitted by the subsidiary. But this does not apply in the case of what are called controlled foreign companies that are established in another country with lower taxation; in such cases, the subsidiary's profits are attributed to the parent as they arise, with credit given for any tax paid locally. The objective of this exception was to counter tax avoidance through the location of transactions in low tax countries. It was held by the ECJ that a measure that discouraged companies from having subsidiaries in lower-tax Member States was a restriction on freedom of establishment that requires justification. One such justification would be where the subsidiary's activities were entirely artificial arrangements intended to escape tax that would normally be payable. However, that was not so in the instant case, as the subsidiary carried on genuine economic activities in Dublin and was not simply a "front" or "letter box" company.

---

[151] See generally, L.W. Gormley, *EU Taxation Law* (Richmond: Richmond Law & Tax, 2005), in particular Ch.5 on company taxation, and J. Dine, *EC Company Law* (Bristol: Jordans – loose leaf) Chs 18 and 19.

[152] *Kerckhaert v Belgium* Case 513/04 [2007] 1 W.L.R. 1685. See generally, R. Bramwell *et al.*, *Taxation of Companies and Company Reconstructions*, 8th edn (London: Sweet & Maxwell, 2002), Ch.C6.

[153] Directive 90/435 on the common system of taxation for group companies, [1990] O.J., L255/6 and Convention on elimination of double taxation in association enterprises, [1990] O.J. L225/10. There also is a Directive on interest on savings, [2003] O.J. L157/38.

[154] Case C 196/04, [2007] Ch. 30.

CHAPTER 22

LITIGATION

22–01 Where companies are involved in legal proceedings, some special considerations arise that either are unique to corporate parties or where there must be some deviation from normal requirements on account of the party or the subject of the dispute being a registered company. Additionally, there are several provisions in the Companies Acts regarding procedural matters, such as when claims by or against companies may be stayed, limitation of actions and hearing proceedings *in camera*. In recent years, a variety of procedural issues have arisen in proceedings for restricting or disqualifying company directors and other corporate officers.

AVAILABLE FORA

22–02 Most company law litigation takes place in the High Court, although the Circuit Court has some jurisdiction in such proceedings. Disputes between shareholders or with officers are often submitted to arbitration. Summary prosecutions are brought in the District Court.[1]

High Court

22–03 Except where the context otherwise requires, any references to "the court" in the Companies Acts 1963–2006 means the High Court.[2] Virtually all proceedings under these Acts must be brought there. But where the claim does not arise directly from these Acts, it may be brought elsewhere: a claim, for instance, for due payment of a dividend that has been declared.

22–04 Many of the procedural requirements for claims under these Acts are provided for in the Rules of the Superior Court (RSC)—in Ord.75 for most proceedings, in Ord.75B for proceedings under the 1990 Act, in Ord.75A for proceedings relating to examinerships, and in Ord.74 for winding-up proceedings. Ord.75 rr.4–20 itemise the various categories of proceedings that must be commenced by way of petition and lays down how such actions are to be processed. Ord.75B rr.3–6 itemise the various categories of proceedings to be commenced by way of originating notice of motion, on notice or *ex parte* as the case may be.

---

[1]   1990 Act, s.240A.
[2]   1990 Act, s.235.

22–05 Most of these cases are listed for hearing in what is known as the Chancery list. In 2004 another listing system was introduced for what may be described as high-value cases of a commercial nature—the commercial list—designed to ensure that cases so listed are dealt with in an expeditious manner.[3] There is no automatic entitlement to admission to this list; application for a listing must be made to the Commercial Court, which must be satisfied that the prescribed criteria have been met.[4]

Circuit Court

22–06 Where a company has been struck off the register of companies for failure to make its annual return or a return required by the Revenue Commissioners, application by a creditor or by the Registrar of Companies to have it restored to the register may also be made to the Circuit Court.[5] Where an examiner has been appointed to a company whose total liabilities do not appear to exceed €317,435.52, the High Court may remit supervision of the examination to the judge of the Circuit Court where the company has its registered office or principal place of business.[6] Before 1936, the Circuit Court had a winding-up jurisdiction.[7]

Arbitration

22–07 Before a dispute can be determined by way of arbitration, the parties must have agreed in writing to having their differences resolved in this manner.[8] Whether certain categories of company law disputes are inherently non-arbitrable is an open question. But there are some kinds of relief that cannot be obtained in this manner—for instance, appointment of an examiner or of a liquidator. Where the subject matter of the dispute is within the terms of an arbitration clause, an application to the High Court, those proceedings will be stayed and the parties must then resort to their agreed arbitration arrangements.[9]

COMPANY PLAINTIFF/APPLICANT

22–08 Where a company is plaintiff, the main issues arising relate to authority to institute the proceedings and costs.

Authority to Sue

22–09 In companies that have adopted Table A, authority to authorise the bringing of proceedings lies with the directors.[10] But this power may be

---

[3] See generally, S. Dowling, *The Commercial Court* (Dublin: Thomson Round Hall, 2007).

[4] RSC Ord.63A.

[5] 1982 Act, s.12B(9)–(11); *cf. Re Deauville Communications Worldwide Ltd* [2002] 2 I.R. 32.

[6] 1990 Amendment Act, s.3(3).

[7] Courts of Justice Act 1936, s.18

[8] Arbitration Act 1954, s.2(1).

[9] *Re Via Net Works (Ireland) Ltd* [2002] 2 I.R. 47 at 57–58.

[10] See para.5–15.

delegated to the managing director or to individual directors.[11] Proceedings that have not been duly authorised by a company may be ratified by it. Where some of the directors have a conflict of interest in proceedings being considered by the company against a defendant, any endeavour by them to block the proceedings is a breach of their fiduciary duty.[12]

22–10　Where the company is in receivership, examinership or liquidation, authority to sue generally vests in the relevant insolvency officer. Where a receiver has been appointed over the assets of the company, almost invariably he has authority to commence proceedings that in any way affect the creditor's interest in those assets.[13] An examiner appointed over a company may obtain authority from the High Court to commence proceedings on its behalf.[14] A liquidator is authorised to "bring ... any action or other legal proceedings in the name or on behalf of the company".[15]

22–11　If at the commencement of a trial or during its course it comes to light that the company has been struck off the register of companies or has been dissolved, the proper course generally is to stay the proceedings so that application may be made to have it restored to the register.[16] Only very exceptional circumstances would warrant dismissing the entire proceedings.

Locus Standi

22–12　The question of *locus standi* arises principally in public law proceedings where a decision or act of some agency or official is being challenged. Where the company's very assets or activities are or are potentially prejudiced by the impugned decision or act, *locus standi* almost invariably exists. On the other hand, where the immediate detriment is to its members or the officers personally, depending on what exactly is in dispute the company may not possess *locus standi*. At times, the threshold for *locus standi* is heightened somewhat by statute; for instance, objectors to planning, compulsory purchase and related decisions are required to have a "substantial interest" in the matter in dispute.[17]

22–13　In *Ballintubber Heights Ltd v Cork Corporation*,[18] the applicant company sought to challenge a grant of planning permission, which at the same time had been appealed to An Bord Pleanála by one of its shareholders and directors. He and his wife lived on and owned a neighbouring property, and the only interest that the company had in these lands was an option to purchase them as

---

[11] *Mitchell & Hobbs (UK) Ltd v Mill* [1996] 2 B.C.L.C. 102.

[12] *Fusion Interactive Communication Solutions Ltd v Venture Investment Placement Ltd (No. 2)* [2005] 2 B.C.L.C. 571.

[13] *M. Wheeler & Co. v Warren* [1928] 1 Ch. 840.

[14] 1990 Amendment Act, s.9.

[15] 1963 Act, s.231(1)(a).

[16] *Steans Fashions Ltd v Legal & General Assurance Society* [1995] 1 B.C.L.C. 332.

[17] See generally, G. Simons, *Planning and Development Law*, 2nd edn (Dublin: Thomson Round Hall, 2007) at 582 *et seq.*

[18] [2002] I.E.H.C. 19; unreported, O'Caoimh J., June 21, 2002.

obtained immediately before the planning decision was challenged. Because the company's interest in the lands appeared to have been created simply to institute the proceedings, O Caoimh J. held that it did not have the requisite *locus*. On the other hand, where persons who have a broader interest in planning and environmental decisions seek to challenge them by way of judicial review, a company that they establish as the vehicle for prosecuting those proceedings generally will possess *locus standi*.[19] But *locus* may be conditional on the company furnishing security for the intended respondent's costs.

Security for Costs

22–14 Where a plaintiff, either individual or corporate, is not resident in the State, in an appropriate case the court may order that he furnishes security for the defendant's costs of the action before those proceedings may be further prosecuted.[20] It is only in exceptional circumstances that an order for security will be made against an EU national plaintiff who is resident in an EC Member State. Generally, the sum required is one third of the estimated costs. If the only basis for requiring security is non-residence and it is not shown that the plaintiff may not be able to satisfy a costs order, the amount of security that may be required is the costs of recovering those costs in the state where the plaintiff resides.[21] In a case involving a corporate plaintiff, security of £100,000 was ordered, representing the estimated costs in enforcing a costs order in Hong Kong, coupled with the risk of enforcement becoming more difficult if the plaintiff moved it assets to another country.[22]

22–15 In the case of any corporate plaintiff, if the evidence indicates that the company will not be able to pay the defendant's costs in the event of the company losing its action, the court may require that security for costs be furnished by it before the proceedings may be further prosecuted.[23] Although the power here is discretionary, generally security will be required where the defendant has a *prima facie* defence to the claim and the company does not appear to have the resources to satisfy a costs order that may be made against it, unless it comes within one of the accepted exceptions to the principle which would make it unjust to require security.[24] Unlike with personal litigants, the amount of security required is the entirety of the estimated costs.[25] Although the UK Act in this regard is worded identically, there are significant differences in the approach taken under it and that taken by the Irish courts. There and in other comparable jurisdictions, in exercising their discretion, the courts endeavour to make some assessment of the strength of the plaintiff's case,[26] and

---

[19] *Lancefort Ltd v An Bord Pleanala (No.2)* [1999] 2 I.R. 270.
[20] See generally, H. Delany & D. McGrath, *Civil Procedure in the Superior Courts*, 2nd edn (Dublin: Thomson Round Hall, 2005), Ch.12.
[21] *Nasser v United Bank of Kuwait* [2002] 1 W.L.R. 1868.
[22] *Textuna International Ltd v Cairn Energy Plc* [2005] 1 B.C.L.C. 579.
[23] 1963 Act, s.390. See generally H. Delany & D. McGrath, *Civil Procedure in the Superior Courts*, 2nd edn (Dublin: Thomson Round Hall, 2005), p.358 *et seq.*
[24] *Hidden Ireland Heritage Holidays Ltd v Indigo Services Ltd* [2005] 2 I.R. 115 at 121.
[25] *Lismore Homes Ltd v Bank of Ireland Finance Ltd* [2001] 3 I.R. 536.
[26] e.g. *Classic Catering Ltd v Donnington Park Leisure Ltd* [2001] 1 B.C.L.C. 537.

ordinarily they do not require that the entire amount of the estimated costs be furnished. Whether the more exacting (on plaintiffs) approach taken by the Irish courts accords with Art.6(1) of the European Convention on Human Rights remains to be determined.

22–16	Generally, to obtain a security for costs order, the defendant (whether personal or corporate) must establish two things, by way of affidavit. One is that he has a *prima facie* defence to the claim; if there is no realistic prospect of the company's claim being rejected, it would be unjust to deny it a hearing because it happens to be impecunious. It was held by the Supreme Court in the *Hidden Ireland* case[27] that the first of the defendants there had produced sufficient material to meet this requirement but the second defendant had not, as his response to a central allegation in the pleadings was incomplete and equivocal.

22–17	The other is that "it appears by credible testimony that there is reason to believe that the company will be unable to pay the costs of the defendant if successful in his defence".[28] To show this, it is not necessary to conduct a detailed analysis to the company's assets and liabilities; all that is required is establishing a "reason to believe" that the costs will not be met.[29] That the company's accounts show a net asset balance is not always determinative on this question; account also has to be had of the nature of its assets and their liquidity.[30] In the *Bula No. 3* proceedings,[31] where the plaintiff company relied on the valuable ore body it owned as showing solvency, Murphy J. observed that if indeed its assets exceeded its liabilities, it ought to be able to raise any requisite security by way of a loan secured on that asset.

22–18	Security will not be ordered in certain circumstances, the categories of which do not appear to be closed. One is where the company's impecuniosity is shown to have probably been caused by the alleged wrong that is the subject of the proceedings. The cases on this appear to proceed on the basis that it will be presumed that the defendant did act unlawfully, as alleged, and that it is for the plaintiff to demonstrate that its impecuniosity resulted from those alleged actions. Mere assertion that the impecuniosity was so caused does not suffice[32]; a "more rounded or complete analysis of" the company's financial affairs is called for.[33]

22–19	Even in the very exceptional case where it can be demonstrated conclusively that the company is insolvent in consequence of the defendant's wrongs, security may still be required. For in the *Superwood* litigation, where the Supreme Court had already held that the defendant insurers had unlawfully

[27]	*Hidden Ireland Heritage Holidays Ltd v Indigo Services Ltd* [2005] 2 I.R. 115.
[28]	1963 Act, s.390.
[29]	*Bula Ltd v Tara Mines Ltd (No. 3)* [1987] I.R. 494.
[30]	*Thistle Hotels Ltd v Orb Estates Plc* [2004] 2 B.C.L.C. 174.
[31]	[1987] I.R. 494.
[32]	*Jack O'Toole Ltd v McEoin Kelly* [1986] I.R. 277.
[33]	*Framus Ltd v CRH Plc* [2004] 2 I.R. 20 at 62.

refused to pay a claim for compensation made by the plaintiff companies, and had ordered an assessment of what consequential damages those companies would be entitled to get,[34] the court subsequently directed that the companies should lodge full security for the costs of an appeal from that assessment hearing.[35] Unlike almost all other cases on this issue, it was not a question of the companies' impecuniosity having been caused by the defendant's *alleged* wrongdoings: the defendants had already been held to have acted unlawfully. All but one of the companies had been in receivership for years; the only assets of the one not in receivership was its interest in those other companies. Had the court given consideration to the companies' prospect of success in that appeal, it would appear to have been overwhelming on the central net legal issue arising.[36] Insofar as the reason for requiring security can be gleaned from the unreported judgment given by Denham J., it would seem to have been the companies' refusal to settle their claim by accepting the lodgment made by the insurers; that, instead, the companies decided to fight their compensation claim, eventually resulting in an unsatisfactory award in the High Court. Security of €1.6 million approximately was ordered.[37] Several other aspects of this litigation have been reported.[38] Perhaps the case establishes that s.390 of the 1963 Act confers an extremely wide discretion, in respect of which there are no indicia about how it is to be exercised or, if such indicia exist, there are no criteria as to when they should be departed from.

22–20 Security may be refused where there has been undue delay in the defendant seeking it. In *Superwood*,[39] where there had been a delay of about 6 months, the Supreme Court held that this did not disentitle the defendants to their order, given the complexity of the proceedings. In *Hidden Ireland*[40] that court held that a delay of 12 months was so excessive in the circumstances that the application for security should be rejected.

22–21 Security may be refused where there are one or more co-plaintiffs who is an individual and who could not be required to furnish security. That appears to have been what was decisive in *Bula (No. 3)*,[41] in having the application rejected.

---

[34] *Superwood Holdings Plc v Sun Alliance and London Insurance Plc* [1995] 3 I.R. 303.

[35] [2002] I.E.S.C. 22; unreported, Supreme Court, April 12, 2002.

[36] ie. where in breach of contract a party refused to pay money in circumstances where he was obliged to do so, is the other party entitled to be compensated for his losses arising from being kept out of pocket to that extent? *Sempra Metals Ltd v Inland Revenue* [2007] 3 W.L.R. 354 holds unequivocally yes. M.F. represented the companies at a later stage in these procedings, which may colour the views expressed here.

[37] Unreported, October 17, 2003; per Murray J.

[38] Including the subsequent strike out of the appeal for failure to furnish the €1.6 million security: *Superwood Holdings Plc v Sun Alliance & London Insurance Plc* [2004] 2 I.R. 407. This decision has been challenged in the European Court of Human Rights, Application No.7812/04; *cf. McAteer & Beechfinch Ltd v Lismore (No. 2)* [2000] N.I. 477.

[39] [2002] I.E.S.C. 22; unreported, April 12, 2002.

[40] [2005] 2 I.R. 115.

[41] [1987] I.R. 494.

22–22 It remains to be determined whether the point of law involved in the proceedings being one of "exceptional public importance" warrants refusing an application for security.

22–23 Defendants are never required to give security for the costs of defending claims. But where a company defendant puts up a substantial counterclaim that goes significantly beyond what in substance is a defence to the claim being made against it, security may be required if the other considerations also obtain.[42]

Officer or Shareholder Liability for Costs

22–24 Whether and if so in what circumstances a successful defendant can recover his costs against an officer or shareholder in the plaintiff company does not appear to have been determined by the Irish courts. In one instance, the question was raised whether costs could be ordered against insurers who had full control of the defence in a personal injuries action but, in the event, it was not decided.[43] There is specific statutory jurisdiction in England to award costs against non-parties.[44]

Legal Aid

22–25 It is questionable whether a company is a "person" for the purposes of the Civil Legal Aid Act 1995. In England it was held that companies would never get legal aid for proceedings being brought on their own behalf. But a company there may get legal aid where it is a nominal plaintiff or is suing in a representative, fiduciary or official capacity on behalf of an individual.[45] Under the 1995 Act, a person will be refused legal aid for proceedings being brought in a representative, fiduciary or official capacity if he would be likely to be indemnified for his costs by those who are likely to benefit from his success in the action.

As Prosecutor

22–26 The scope for bringing a private prosecution generally is far more confined in Ireland than in the UK. Whether a registered company can ever be a common informer for the purpose of commencing a private prosecution remains to be determined here. Where the subject matter of the prosecution relates directly to the company's activities and interests, the view in England is that it has the requisite *locus standi*.[46] But it was held by the Supreme Court in *Cumann Luthcleas Gael Teo v Windle*[47] that Dublin Corporation could not institute such a prosecution for breach of the Fire Services Act 1981 because,

---

[42] *Thistle Hotels Ltd v Orb Estates Plc* [2004] 2 B.C.L.C. 174.

[43] *Curran v Finn (No. 2)* [2002] 4 I.R. 1. See, too, *Byrne v John S. O'Connor & Co.* [2006] 3 I.R. 379.

[44] e.g. *Landare Investments Ltd v Welsh Development Agency* [2006] 1 B.C.L.C. 451.

[45] *R. v Chester Legal Aid Office Ex p. Floods of Queensferry Ltd* [1998] 1 W.L.R. 1496.

[46] *R. (Gladstone Plc) v Manchester City Magistrates* [2005] 1 W.L.R. 1987.

[47] [1994] 1 I.R. 525.

inter alia, there was express power in that Act for a particular body corporate to prosecute, *viz.* the fire authority. Finlay C.J. went on to say that, notwithstanding the broad definition of the word "person" in the Interpretation Act, 1937 "a body corporate cannot be seen as a member of the public and that ... where a liability to criminal prosecution is involved, there are no grounds for implying a right in a body corporate to institute proceedings for an indictable offence by way of common informer."[48] This would suggest that even if the offence in question is not of the modern statutory variety and it directly affects a registered company, a private prosecution may only be instituted by some individual on behalf of the company rather than by the company itself.

COMPANY DEFENDANT/RESPONDENT

22–27 Where proceedings are being brought against a company, it may be neccessary to obtain court approval for prosecuting them in certain circumstances and, exceptionally, it may be neccessary to have it restored to the register of companies. It is only in very exceptional circumstances that a company officer will be permitted to represent it in court.

Staying/Authorising Proceedings

22–28 In several circumstances, proceedings against a company may not be instituted or may be stayed, either automatically or by way of court order. Where an application is made to summon meetings for the purpose of considering a "compromise or arrangement" with a company, its members or its creditors, the court may order that all proceedings against the company shall be stayed and it may restrain any further proceedings against it.[49] Where a company is in examinership, the examiner may apply to have any proceedings in existence against it stayed.[50] Fresh proceedings may not be commenced against it without the court's consent.[51] Where a provisional liquidator has been appointed over or a winding-up order has been made against a company, no action may be continued against it or commenced without leave of the court.[52] As soon as a winding up petition is presented, any creditor or contributory of the company may apply to have any proceeding against it stayed.[53] Where a company is being wound up voluntarily, the liquidator may apply to have proceedings against it stayed.[54]

Service

22–29 Service on Irish-registered companies is effected by leaving the document in question at the registered office or by posting it to that

---

[48] *ibid.* at 544.
[49] 1963 Act, s.201(2).
[50] 1990 Amendment Act, s.5(3).
[51] 1990 Amendment Act, s.5(3).
[52] 1963 Act, s.222.
[53] 1963 Act, s.217.
[54] 1963 Act, s.280.

address.[55] Special provision is made for serving foreign companies with a place of business in the State.[56]

Authority to Defend

22–30 The same principles govern authority to defend proceedings served on a company as apply to authority to commerce proceedings.

Nominal Defendant

22–31 At times, although a company is an essential defendant in proceedings, it strictly is a nominal defendant only and may have no independent position in the dispute between the other parties. Thus, for the purpose of derivative proceedings, the company is usually named as a defendant so that one or more of the reliefs being claimed may be made in its favour. Almost invariably, the company is not an active participant in proceedings for oppression.[57] This often is the case too in applications to rectify the register of members.

Dissolved Company

22–32 Where the company has been struck off the register of companies, application may be made to have it re-registered, which can be done within 20 years of the strike-off notice being published in the *Gazette*.[58] If it is re-registered, it is deemed to have been in existence throughout the intervening period and the court is given a wide discretion to make such orders as would put parties in nearly the same position as they were when the company was struck off.[59]

22–33 Intending plaintiffs are far more disadvantaged where the company has been wound up and dissolved. If the company's affairs had not in fact been fully wound up, the dissolution of the company can cause considerable hardship. Some time after the dissolution took place a person may discover that he has a claim against the company, for instance, for a disease or other damage that had not actually manifested itself previously.[60] Occasionally suggestions were made that a dissolution might be set aside where it was caused by fraud or possibly where no reasonable liquidator would have concluded that the company's affairs had been fully wound up. In 1907 a procedure was introduced for in effect resuscitating dissolved companies.[61] The court may declare a dissolution void in an appropriate case.[62]

---

[55] 1963 Act, s.379 and H. Delany & D. McGrath, *Civil Procedure in the Superior Courts*, 2nd edn (Dublin: Thomson Round Hall, 2005), pp.92–93.

[56] See para.21–51 *et seq.*

[57] e.g. *Arrow Trading & Investments v Edwardian Group Ltd* [2005] 1 B.C.L.C. 696.

[58] See para.23–104 *et seq.*

[59] See generally, Keay, "The Pursuit of Legal Proceedings Against Dissolved Companies" [2000] *J. Bus. L.* 405.

[60] e.g. *Bradley v Eagle Star Insurance Co.* [1989] A.C. 957.

[61] Companies Act 1907, s.31.

[62] 1963 Act, s.310 and see para.23–100 *et seq.*

Costs

22–34 No provision exists whereby a company (or any other type of defendant) can be required to furnish security for a plaintiff's costs in the event of his succeeding and the defendant not being able to pay his costs. Nor is there any provision authorising awarding costs against an officer or shareholder, or other third party, implicated in the defence of an action.[63] What is said above about legal aid equally applies to corporate defendants.

Criminal Proceedings

22–35 Because a company can only act through its designated agents, provision is made for it appearing at all stages of a trial on a charge of an indictable offence.[64] A company may so appear by a representative who has been duly appointed for that purpose. A statement in writing purported to having been signed by the managing director or other person managing the company's affairs is sufficient proof of authority. That person may answer any questions that may be put to an accused, may exercise a right of objection or election that would be open to an accused, and may enter a plea on behalf of the company. Once it is shown that the company was involved in activities as a corporate entity, it is not necessary to prove its existence by producing its certificate of incorporation.[65]

LIMITATION OF ACTIONS

22–36 In addition to general provisions for limiting the time within which legal proceedings may be commenced in the Statute of Limitations 1957–2006 and in the discrete statutory limitation regimes, several remedies given by the Companies Acts 1963–2006 have their own limitation periods, all of which begin to run once the cause of action accrues.

22–37 For limitations purposes, proceedings against directors and other officers for breach of fiduciary duty are characterised as claims against trustees for breach of trust, the relevant limitation period being six years from when the cause of action accrued.[66] But where the claim is for fraud or for fraudulent breach of trust, there is no fixed limitation period.[67] Nor is there such a period where the claim is to recover company property or the proceeds of company property if the officer in breach either still retains that property or he has converted it to his own use. Thus, in *Re Pantone 485 Ltd*,[68] where the defendant director had arranged for the company to lend money to other companies in which he had an interest but those loans were never repaid, on account of the borrowers' insolvency, it was held that the claim against him and those

---

[63] Compare *CIBC Mellon Trust Co. v Stolzenberg* [2005] 2 B.C.L.C. 618 and *Latimer Management Consultants Ltd v Ellinghan Investments Ltd* [2007] 1 W.L.R. 2569.
[64] 1963 Act, s.382.
[65] *Attorney General v Smith* [1947] I.R. 332.
[66] Statute of Limitations Act 1957, s.43 and *cf. Cateley v Pollard* [2007] 3 W.L.R. 317.
[67] Statute of Limitations Act 1957, s.44(2).
[68] [2002] 1 B.C.L.C. 266.

companies was not statute barred. Because, however, the director honestly and reasonably at the time believed that the borrowers would be able to repay the money, the claim failed on the facts.

22–38 Proceedings against directors to recover compensation for wrongful trading or for fraudulent trading are actions to "recover any sum recoverable by virtue of any enactment",[69] with a six-year limitation period.[70] Proceedings against directors seeking to declare them liable for failure to keep proper accounting records were held to fall into this category too.[71] Because the predominant purpose of this remedy was to compensate the company and through it its members and creditors, these proceedings were held not to constitute an action for a civil penalty, for which the limitation period is two years.[72] Whether proceedings to restrict or disqualify directors would come within this latter category is debatable; in Australia, for several purposes such proceedings are characterised as for a civil penalty.[73] Whether proceedings to impose some financial penalty are being brought by a regulatory agency are predominantly punitive or compensatory can depend on whether the cause of action is that of the company, its shareholders or its creditors.[74]

22–39 An application by a creditor to wind up a company for failure to pay a judgment debt has been held not to be an "action on a judgment" for limitations purposes, even though the petitioner's objective was to secure payment insofar as that remained possible.[75] This category of claim is confined to suing for judgment on an existing judgment, and does not apply to any other method of enforcing judgments, such as garnishee or attachment-of-assets proceedings. As characterised in *Ridgeway Motors (Isleworth) Ltd v ALTS Ltd*,[76] for these purposes, winding up applications are "*sui generis*, being in the nature of a wider legal proceeding available for the collective enforcement of the admitted or proved debts of the company for the benefit of the general body of creditors on a *pari passu* basis."[77]

22–40 Where proceedings under the Companies Acts do not reasonably fit any of the descriptions in the general limitations regime, it appears that they will not be forced or "shoehorned" into any of them. But if the proceedings broadly resemble one of those provided for in the general regime, the question arises whether the courts will apply that category by way of analogy to bar prosecution of the action. The status of "oppression" proceedings for these purposes does not appear to have received judicial consideration[78] although if

---

[69] *Re Farmizer (Products) Ltd* [1997] 1 B.C.L.C. 589.

[70] Statute of Limitations 1957, s.11(1)(e).

[71] *Re Network Agencies International Ltd* [1992] 2 N.Z.L.R. 325.

[72] Statute of Limitations 1957, s.11(7)(b).

[73] *Doyle v Australian Securities and Investments Commission* 80 A.L.J.L.R. 405 (2006).

[74] *Securities Comm v Midavia Rail Investments BVBA* [2006] 2 N.Z.L.R. 207.

[75] *Lowsley v Forbes* [1999] 1 A.C. 369.

[76] [2005] 2 B.C.L.C. 61.

[77] *ibid.* at 69.

[78] cf. *Ford Motor Co. v Ontario Municipal Employees Retirement Board* 263 D.L.R. (4th) 450 (2006) at 501–507.

a petitioner under s.205 of the 1963 Act waited for more than six years to commence his proceedings, it must be questionable whether indeed he was oppressed.

IN CAMERA PROCEEDINGS

22–41   Under Art.34.1 of the Constitution, legal proceedings must be heard in open court except where the law otherwise provides. The principal *in camera* provision in the Companies Acts is for "oppression" proceedings where, in the court's opinion a public hearing "would involve the disclosure of information, the publication of which would be seriously prejudicial to the legitimate interests of the company ...".[79] All or any part of proceedings involving a company examinership may be heard *in camera* if the court "in the interests of justice considers that the interests of the company concerned or if its creditors as a whole so require".[80]

22–42   In the two leading decisions on the former, directions of the High Court for *in camera* oppression hearings were set aside on appeal. In *Re R Ltd*,[81] where a chief executive who had been dismissed was the petitioner, his affidavit contained sensitive commercial information, *inter alia*, detailed accounts of the company, its four-year business plan and the terms of an incomplete commercial transaction. It was held that, to justify a hearing *in camera*, not alone must the evidence fit the statutory description of seriously prejudicial to the company if disclosed but "it must also be shown that a public hearing of the whole or that part of the proceedings ... would fall short of doing justice".[82] In other words, the sensitivity for the company of what would emerge at the hearing is not enough to warrant excluding the press and the public. Because a company is no more than a juristic person, the need to protect its privacy interests does not suffice. As Walsh J. explained, contrasting a family dispute, a "company is a creature of the law and by its very nature and by the provisions of the law under which it is created, it is open to public scrutiny".[83] Accepting that disclosure of the material at the trial would be inconvenient and possibly troublesome for the company, there was insufficient evidence to hold that such disclosure would very likely render the trial a "failure to do justice". Even if the *in camera* prerequisites are met, it was held that judgment should still be given in public.

22–43   To get over this hurdle, it was held in the *Irish Press (No. 1)* case[84] that the petitioner would have to show that the disclosures would be so damaging to the value of his shareholding that, in the event of his succeeding, the court could not grant him a just remedy. Alternatively, the respondent would have to show that such disclosures would be so damaging to the

---

[79]   1963 Act, s.205(7).
[80]   1990 Amendment Act, s.3.
[81]   [1989] 3 I.R. 126.
[82]   *ibid.* at 137.
[83]   *ibid.* at 138.
[84]   [1994] 1 I.R. 176.

company that a simple dismissal of the petition with costs would not be a just remedy. Alternatively still, either party would have to show that, in order to protect the value of his shareholding, he would be constrained from tendering evidence on a material aspect of the dispute. The company there sought an *in camera* hearing on the grounds that, if its serious financial position and its future plans were made public, that would prejudice revenues and staff morale, and would very likely deter an outside investor who might save the company. But it was held that this was not sufficient reason and, in any event, much of the prejudicial material was already in the public domain.

22–44 There also are certain kinds of applications in the courts that have been held not to constitute the administration of justice and, accordingly, need not be heard in public. Examinations by company liquidators of creditors and others connected with (often insolvent) companies, were held by the Supreme Court to fall into this category.[85] Applications to the High Court for directions by inspectors appointed under Pt II of the Companies Act 1990, were held by Murphy J. to fall into this category too.[86] On the other hand, Laffoy J. held that an application by a liquidator for leave to continue proceedings that had been commenced by the company, which could involve an *inter partes* contest, fell outside this category and consequently had to be made in open court.[87]

REPRESENTATION

22–45 It was held by the Supreme Court in *Battle v Irish Art Promotion Centre Ltd*,[88] that in legal proceedings a company cannot be represented by any of its directors but has to be represented by a qualified legal practitioner. As explained by O Dalaigh C.J.:

> "in the absence of statutory exception, a limited company cannot be represented in court proceedings by its managing director or other officer or servant. This is an infirmity of the company which derives from its own very nature. The creation of the company is the act of its subscribers; the subscribers, in discarding their own *personae* for the *persona* of the company, doubtless did so for the advantages which incorporation offers to traders. In seeking incorporation they thereby lose the right of audience which they would have as individuals; but the choice has been their own."[89]

22–46 It has been acknowledged that, in exceptional circumstances and in the interests of justice, this principle should be departed from and that someone could speak for a company other than a solicitor or counsel instructed by the company.[90]

---

[85] *Red Breast Preserving Co.* [1958] I.R. 234.
[86] *Re Countyglen Plc* [1995] 1 I.R. 220.
[87] *Re Greendale Developments Ltd (No. 1)* [1997] 3 I.R. 540.
[88] [1968] I.R. 252.
[89] *ibid.* at 254.
[90] *Arbuthnot Leasing Int'l Ltd* v *Havelet Leasing Ltd* [1990] B.C.L.C. 802. *cf. Jonathan Alexander Ltd v Proctor* [1996] 2 B.C.L.C. 91 on some costs ramifications of such representation.

In *All Finance Ltd v Havelet Leasing Ltd*,[91] where a *Mareva* injunction was obtained against a company, Scott J. permitted one of its directors and the beneficial owner of its shares to become a defendant and then apply to have the restraining order varied or lifted. Referring to the very high cost of commercial litigation, the judge rejected the suggestion that the director should finance the company's representation from his personal resources. However, the fact that a company lacks the funds to pay for its legal representation is not regarded on its own as a sufficiently exceptional circumstance to justify not applying the general principle.[92]

REFLECTIVE LOSS

22–47 Reflective loss is where the loss caused by some unlawful action falls directly on one party but, in consequence, another party related to him also suffers loss. In the case of actions involving fatal injuries, provision exists in the Civil Liability Act 1961, whereby the "dependants" of the deceased may recover damages from the wrongdoer who caused his death. Reflective loss in the company law context concerns where some wrong has been done to the company, thereby diminishing its net worth and, consequently, reducing the value of its shareholders' investment in it. In such circumstances, generally the aggrieved shareholder has no right of action against the wrongdoer; because the company has a separate legal personality and is perfectly capable of suing if it chooses to do so, only it is the appropriate plaintiff. Since the shareholders do not even have an insurable interest in their company's assets,[93] it would be strange that they would be entitled to sue for wrongs done to the company that, in consequence, caused them loss.

Statute

22–48 Special statutory provisions could give shareholders *locus standi* in such circumstances. It was held in England that the existence of reflective loss is not always a bar to "oppression" proceedings.[94] This question was adverted in *Re Via Net Works (Ireland) Ltd*,[95] where the Supreme Court suggested that the position in Ireland is different, but without deciding the issue or discussing the matter fully.

22–49 Another possible statutory grant of *locus standi* is s.14 of the Competition Act 2002, which confers a right of action on "any person who is aggrieved in consequence of" a breach of that Act, without defining who comes within this "aggrieved" category. It could be argued that s.14 does not throw that net so widely because, in *O'Neill v Ryan*,[96] the Supreme Court held

---

[91] [1992] 1 W.L.R. 455.

[92] *Radford v Freeway Clinic Ltd* [1994] 1 B.C.L.C. 445 and *RH Tomlinson (Trowbridge) Ltd v Secretary of State* [1999] 2 B.C.L.C. 760.

[93] *Macaura v Northern Assurance Co.* [1925] A.C. 619.

[94] *Clarke v Cutland* [2004] 1 W.L.R. 783.

[95] [2002] 2 I.R. 47.

[96] [1990] 2 I.R. 200.

that a shareholder in what now is Ryanair Plc could not sue companies that competed with it, to claim contravention of the EC's competition rules (now Arts 81 and 82 of the EC Treaty); that if the intention was to confer *locus standi* on persons in similar circumstances, express provision to that effect would have been made. The counter-argument would be that the words "person who is aggrieved" should be given its ordinary meaning; that where the immediate victim of the alleged wrongdoing is the company, once he can show that he has a genuine grievance, a shareholder or an individual director is not precluded from bringing proceedings for breach of the Competition Acts, which contain a civil punitive element in addition to a right to compensation.

Double Recovery

22–50   On account of the risk of "double recovery", even where the shareholder has an undoubted right of action against a wrongdoer and the company also has a right of action against it in respect of substantially the same wrong, ordinarily the shareholder will not be permitted to sue.[97] The rationale is that, if he were to sue and succeed, and the company were then to do likewise, the shareholder-plaintiff would recover twice—the damages awarded to him in his action and, indirectly, by virtue of the damages awarded to the company in its own action, which would enhance the value of his shareholding.

22–51   The leading case is *Johnson v Gore Wood & Co.*,[98] where the defendant firm of solicitors failed to serve efficaciously a notice to exercise an option to buy land. The company which had the option sued them and obtained substantial compensation in a settlement with the firm. Then the plaintiff, who owned most of the shares in the company, notified the firm that he would be suing them, on the basis that they had separately contracted with him in respect of exercising the option, by way of a direct undertaking to him. Because there would be inevitable double recovery if he were allowed to prosecute his action, it was held by the House of Lords that it should be stayed. As explained by Lord Millett:

> "where the company suffers loss caused by the breach of a duty owed both to the company and to the shareholder ... the shareholder's loss, in so far as this is measured by the diminution in value of his shareholding or the loss of dividends, merely reflects the loss suffered by the company in respect of which the company has its own cause of action. If the shareholder is allowed to recover in respect of such loss, then either there will be double recovery at the expense of the defendant or the shareholder will recover at the expense of the company and its creditors and other shareholders. Neither course can be permitted. This is a matter of principle; there is no discretion involved. Justice to the defendant requires the exclusion of one claim or the other; protection of the interests of the company's creditors requires that it is the company which is allowed to recover to the exclusion of the shareholder. These principles have been

---

[97] See generally, Mitchell, "Shareholders' Claims for Reflective Loss" 120 *L.Q.R.* 457 (2004) and Lin, "Barring Recovery for Diminution in Value of Shares on the Reflective Loss Principle" [2007] *Cam. L. J.* 537.

[98] [2002] 2 A.C. 1.

established in a number of cases, though they have not always been faithfully observed."[99]

Accordingly, the company's claim "trumps" that of the shareholder. It was since held in England that the "rule against reflective loss" also applies where the shareholder sues in his capacity as a creditor of the company or as one of its employees.[100]

22–52 The "number of cases" referred to by Lord Millett are where minority shareholders seek to sue those who control their company, alleging that they were causing loss to it, including *Foss v Harbottle*[101] and its principal modern embodiment, *Prudential Assurance Co. v Newman Industries Ltd (No 2)*.[102] *Johnson* is the first major instance where it was held that the doctrine in those cases also applies to actions against entire outsiders where the shareholder would appear to have a sound claim against them. In *O'Neill v Ryan*,[103] not alone had the plaintiff disposed of his shares before bringing that action but it does not appear to have been argued that the EC's competition rules gave him a good cause of action. *Johnson* has had its share of criticism. One commentator observed that the Lords "gave several policy reasons for preventing a shareholder from recovering reflective loss where the shareholder and the company both have causes of action against the defendant. Some of these reasons do not stand up to close analysis; others are of limited application."[104] That *Johnson* does not lay down a universal rule has since been acknowledged in several instances. Where exemplary damages can be recovered, under the Competition Act 2002, there seems to be no compelling reason why a person aggrieved should be prevented from suing because he held shares in the immediate victim of unlawful anti-competitive practices.

22–53 The analysis in *Johnson* was adopted unreservedly by the Supreme Court in *Madden v Anglo Irish Bank Corp.*,[105] where the plaintiff, a shareholder and creditor of the company, contended that the defendant caused it and him loss and damage in the manner in which it dealt with secured loans it had made to the company. He contended that it had caused the company to act *ultra vires* and to breach the prohibition against companies financing the purchase of their own shares. Because his entire loss was reflective of the company's loss, his claim was not allowed to proceed. This was a far easier case than *Johnson* because there was no independent contractual right between the plaintiff and the bank.[106]

---

[99] *ibid.* at 62.
[100] *Gardner v Parker* [2004] 2 B.C.L.C. 554.
[101] (1843) 2 Hare 461.
[102] [1982] 1 Ch. 204 (C.A.)
[103] [1990] 2 I.R. 200.
[104] Watts, note in 117 *L.Q.R.* 388 (2001).
[105] [2005] 1 I.L.R.M. 294.
[106] See too, *Horgan v Murray*, unreported, High Court, O'Sullivan J., December 17, 1999 and *Heaphy v Heaphy*, unreported, High Court, Peart J., January 15, 2004.

22–54   A more difficult case however was *Flanagan v Kelly*,[107] where the plaintiff shareholder had retained the defendant accountant to prepare a declaration of solvency in connection with the company's liquidation. He claimed personal loss on account of that declaration being prepared negligently. It was argued that, in a strict sense, no damage is inflicted on a company by winding it up; such loss as may ensure from that act falls directly on the shareholders and is not really derivative from some discrete loss that the company has suffered. Relying on *O'Neill v Ryan*, however, that contention was rejected by the Supreme Court (*per* Keane C.J.). But this case would seem to fall within one of the "exceptions" (if it can be so called) acknowledged in *Johnson* and endorsed in *Madden*, *viz.* where the company itself has no cause of action. It is difficult to envisage what cause of action the company would have against an accountant, whose negligence resulted in it being wound up in a creditors' rather than a members' voluntary liquidation.

The Derivative Claim

22–55   As is explained in the discussion above of minority shareholder protection,[108] where those who effectively control a company cause it damage and they prevent or are in a position to prevent it seeking redress against them, a shareholder may bring what is referred to a derivative claim against them. It strictly is the company's claim and, so that any damages or other recoveries ordered against the defendant go directly to the company, it is added as a defendant. Those circumstances in which claims of this nature may be brought are often referred to under the rubric "fraud on a minority". Unlike in several jurisdictions,[109] no special procedural rules have been adopted for these claims.

Pre-Trial Consideration

22–56   Because having to defend actions of this nature may actually cause the company more loss than the potential benefit of a successful outcome, courts often seek to ascertain whether there is a sufficient prospect of them succeeding before allowing them to proceed. This may arise where the defendants or the company apply to have the action struck out. Should the court accept as correct the plaintiff's allegation of the requisite "fraud" on the company and "control" by the defendants, and permit the matter to go to a full trial, which could result in those allegations (and thereby the plaintiff's very *locus standi*) being rejected? Or should it conduct a trial of these issues, which in substance could amount to hearing the full action? In England, the practice has been to deal with these as preliminary issues, on affidavit, where the court may permit limited discovery and some cross-examination.[110] As explained, this approach

---

[107] Unreported appeal decided *ex tempore* on January 15, 2001 from [1999] I.E.H.C. 116; unreported, O'Sullivan J., February 26, 1999. Compare *Pearce v European Reinsurance Consultants & Run Off Ltd* [2005] 2 B.C.L.C. 366.

[108] See para.10–47 *et seq.*

[109] e.g. Companies Act 2006, s.260 (UK), Australia (2001) and New Zealand (1993), and Comment, "A Statutory Derivative Action" 28 *Co. Law* 225 (2007).

[110] See paras 10–63 *et seq.*

is "concerned with avoiding the Scylla and Charybidis, on the one hand, of having a preliminary issue where the rule [in *Foss v Harbottle*] serves no useful purpose and, on the other side of the strait, of assuming that everything that the plaintiffs allege is necessarily correct as a matter of fact ...".[111]

22–57 A step that the court may take is to adjourn the case, so that it can be considered by the shareholders at an EGM, which may indicate whether it really is in the interests of the company as a whole for the action to proceed. If a substantial number of independent shareholders (i.e. those not connected with the plaintiffs or the alleged controlling fraudsters) are against the action, it will not be allowed to proceed.[112]

Costs

22–58 Because the plaintiff in such proceedings will not directly benefit from any recovery obtained, it going instead to the company, generally he must be indemnified by the company for legal costs he incurs in taking the claim. In *Smith v Croft*,[113] the indemnity in this context was described as a mechanism for ensuring that the minority shareholder "should not be prevented from pursuing an obviously just cause through lack of funds, for fear that he may, for some reason, fail at the end of the day and be at risk as to costs which he cannot possibly pay.[114] On the other hand, giving the indemnity could result in injustice if the plaintiff's case ultimately fails because the company and other defendants, who prove to be completely blameless, nevertheless are burdened with the plaintiff's costs. The test of whether a plaintiff should get an indemnity is whether "an independent board of directors exercising the standard of care which prudent businessmen would exercise in their own affairs [would] consider that [the company] ought to bring the action".[115] In answering this question, particular weight will be given to the views of any major independent shareholder, i.e. a shareholder who is neither in the plaintiff's nor in the defendant's camp. In *Smith*, there was such a shareholder, who opposed the plaintiff's action on the grounds that pursuing it would cause the company to lose its extremely valuable directors, who had built up a highly profitable business for the company. In the light of the allegations made against them and the independent shareholder's view, Walton J. refused to give the indemnity being sought.

Other Exceptions

22–59 The *Johnson* principle cannot apply where the defendant was in breach of a duty to the shareholder but owed no duty of any kind to the

---

[111] *Smith v Croft (No. 2)* [1988] 1 Ch. 114 at 138–134.

[112] As occurrred in *Smith v Croft (No. 2)* [1988] 1 Ch. 114. See *Airey v Cordell* [2007] Bus.L.R. 391 for another way of dealing with the dilemma.

[113] [1986] 1 W.L.R. 580.

[114] *ibid.* at 597.

[115] *ibid.* at 590. See too *Jaybird Group Ltd v Greenwood* [1986] B.C.L.C. 319; *Re A Company (No. 005136 of 1986)* [1987] B.C.L.C. 82; and *Wallersteiner v Moir (No.2)* [1975] Q.B. 373.

company in respect of the wrong. Where the defendant negligently drove into a director/shareholder in a car crash, seriously injuring him with the result that the company's profits fell significantly, the loss to it did not bar the personal damages claim.[116] In *George Fischer (Great Britain) Ltd v Multi Construction Ltd*,[117] a holding company contracted with the defendant to design and build a warehouse for one of its subsidiaries, for the latter to use as a distribution depot for its output. Cranes installed by the contractor were defective. In breach-of-contract proceedings by the parent, it recovered, *inter alia*, the loss it suffered by the defective equipment causing the subsidiary to lose sales and to incur greater operating costs. Whether a subsidiary in comparable circumstances would have a right of action in tort is debatable; if it did, then *Johnson* may be a bar to prosecuting it.

22–60 Another exception is where the company's claim is stultified by the defendant's actions preventing it from bringing proceedings. This occurred in *Giles v Rhind*,[118] where the plaintiff and defendant shareholders were parties to a confidentiality agreement, to which the company also was a party. The reason why the company could not sue was that it had been impoverished by the defendant's wrongdoing: he diverted the company's business from it and, consequently, it was not able to furnish the requisite security for costs. But it has been held that a company's impecuniosity due to some other cause does not entitle the shareholder to prosecute his action.[119]

22–61 An exception may also exist where the defendant has a good defence to any action that the company may bring. But the English courts have held *Johnson* to apply in such instances.[120] They also have held it to apply where a shareholder is suing in his capacity as an employee of the company.[121]

RESTRICTING AND DISQUALIFYING OFFICERS

22–62 In recent years there has been a veritable explosion in litigation brought by the DCE or by company liquidators aimed at disqualifying persons from acting as company directors or auditors, or at restricting the type of company in respect of which they may act in that capacity (1990 Part VII, ss. 149–168). By the end of 2007, there were about 700 restricted and over 1,800 disqualified directors on the CRO's registers. The circumstances warranting the making of such orders have been summarised above.[122] In general, the procedure for disqualification mirrors that for restriction.

---

[116] *Lee v Sheard* [1956] 1 Q.B. 192.
[117] [1995] 1 B.C.L.C. 260. See too *Gerber Garment Technology Inc. v Lectra Systems Ltd* [1997] R.P.C. 443.
[118] [2003] Ch. 618.
[119] *Gardner v Parker* [2004] 2 B.C.L.C. 554.
[120] *Day v Cook* [2002] 1 B.C.L.C. 1.
[121] *John v Price Waterhouse* [2001] E.W.H.C. 438, T.L.R., August 22, 2001.
[122] See para.6–44 *et seq.*

Restriction Proceedings

22–63 Ireland is the only jurisdiction in the common-law world that provides for the restriction, and not just the disqualification, of company directors. Applications to have the directors or shadow directors of insolvent companies restricted may be made by the company's liquidator or receiver, or by the DCE. Initially, there was no procedure provided for bringing these applications, and no burden on anyone to bring them. This led to a High Court Practice Direction in 1994, pursuant to which liquidators of companies being wound up under the supervision of the courts were compelled to apply for restriction.[123] However, there was still no mechanism compelling liquidators of companies in voluntary liquidation to do so. Now, the liquidator of any company is obliged to bring an application in the following circumstances,[124] unless relieved of that duty by the DCE. The person against whom the application is brought was a director of the company being wound up at the commencement of the winding-up or within 12 months prior to its commencement. Secondly, at the date of its commencement, it is proved or at any time during the course of its winding up the liquidator certifies, or it is otherwise proved, that the company is unable to pay its debts.[125] All references in this part to liquidators includes receivers.[126]

Commencement of proceedings

22–64 Applications for a declaration that a director of a company in voluntary liquidation be restricted are commenced by originating Notice of Motion and grounded on the affidavit of the applicant.[127] Applications in respect of several directors of one company are made on one Notice of Motion, except where the circumstances otherwise require. In court-ordered windings-up, restriction proceedings are commenced by Notice of Motion.[128] Where an application is opposed, the respondent director must file and serve an affidavit setting out the facts upon which it is opposed not less than four clear days before the return date of the motion for restriction. Although applications for the restriction of multiple directors of the same company are normally brought on the same motion, to save costs, each application may be dealt with separately by the court if appropriate.

Service

22–65 Questions of service have arisen with restriction applications brought against non-Irish-resident directors of Irish companies. In *Re Euroking Miracle (Ireland) Ltd,*[129] the four respondent directors all had English addresses. The

---

[123] See the comments of Murphy J. in *Business Communications v Baxter & Parsons* [1995] I.E.H.C. 133.

[124] 1990 Act, s.149.

[125] Within the meaning of s.214 of the 1963 Act.

[126] 1990 Act, s.154.

[127] HC28 – Companies Acts–Applications under s.150(1) Companies Act 1990, March 24, 2003, available at www.courts.ie.

[128] Rules of the Superior Courts 1986, Order 74, Rule 136, analysed by Finlay Geoghegan J. in *Re Euroking Miracle (Ireland) Ltd* [2003] 3 I.R. 80.

[129] [2003] 3 I.R. 80.

liquidator purported to serve an originating notice of motion on each, by registered post, at their English addresses. Although the court noted that the Rules of the Superior Courts 1986 do not make express provision for the service out of the jurisdiction of these applications, Finlay Geoghegan J. noted that Ord.9 r.16, dealing with the service of summonses in the jurisdiction, applies "insofar as practicable" to proceedings commenced by an originating notice of motion. The judge held that sending an originating notice of motion by registered post was sufficient discharge of the court's obligation to ensure that restriction applications were heard and determined in accordance with the principles of constitutional justice. However, she cautioned that:

> "[I]t would be a matter for each individual applicant liquidator to satisfy the court that, insofar as practicable, he has attempted to give actual notice of the application to a non-resident director by sending same, by registered post, to an address where he believes the director for stated reasons to be residing or having a place of business. Furthermore, that he has allowed sufficient time to elapse during which the registered letter would, as a matter of probability, either have been delivered or returned. The affidavit of service sworn should cover the several elements to satisfy the court that, as a matter of probability, the non-resident director has received actual notice of the application"[130]

With court-ordered windings-up, the notice of motion seeking restriction does not have to be served personally on the respondent directors, as there is no originating process. The originating notice of motion and the accompanying grounding affidavit must be issued out of the Central Office of the High Court and made returnable for a date not less than 28 days from the date of issue;[131] the notice of motion, affidavit and a copy of the Practice Direction must be served on the respondent directors not less than 21 days prior to the return date for the hearing of the motion.

Discovery

22–66 Liquidators of insolvent companies must file a report with the DCE in the prescribed form,[132] within 6 months of their appointment. The DCE has declared that these reports generally must be handled under strict conditions of confidentiality,[133] and has also indicated publicly his belief that disclosure of these reports is precluded under the Freedom of Information Act 1997. However, in *Re Silken Construction Ltd*,[134] the respondent directors brought an application for discovery of a report compiled by the applicant liquidator for the DCE. The DCE applied to be and was joined as a notice party. The liquidator and the DCE argued that if the report was held to be discoverable, this would inhibit liquidators from giving frank and candid information to the

---

[130] *ibid.* at 90.
[131] HC28 – Companies Acts – Applications under s.150(1) Companies Act 1990, March 24, 2003, available at www.courts.ie.
[132] Company Law Enforcement Act 2001 (Section 56) Regulations 2002 (SI 2002/324).
[133] Para. 5.3 of the DCE's 2002 Decision Notice D/2002/3, available at www.odce.ie
[134] [2003] 4 I.R. 443.

DCE, and prevent the effective discharge of his functions. Finlay Geoghegan J. held that the reasons furnished by the liquidator to support a conclusion as to whether a respondent director acted honestly and responsibly were matters which might "lead to a train of inquiry which may enable the respondent directors to advance their own case." She ordered discovery of certain specified answers in the report to be furnished by the liquidator to the directors. More generally, the judge held that restriction applications are matters to which the ordinary principles for discovery applies, to be determined by the usual criteria of relevance and necessity.

Time limits

22–67 A liquidator must bring applications for restriction against the directors not earlier than three months nor not later than five months after the date on which he has provided the report to the DCE, unless relieved of this obligation by the DCE. The court may extend this period, on notice to the DCE. In *Re E Host Europe Ltd*,[135] the liquidator failed to bring his application within the prescribed period, being late by three days. In considering, as a preliminary issue, whether to extend time to file and serve an affidavit supporting his application, Finlay Geoghegan J. noted that the time limit was a regulatory one, and that a breach of that provision could lead to the commission of an offence by the liquidator. However, the failure to bring an application within the specified time limit did not preclude a liquidator from bringing the application to restrict and, if the court granted an extension, the only consequence would be to relieve him from being considered guilty of an offence. The judge held that the position of the respondent directors was not material to the court's determination on the issue, and that the court would instead have regard whether fairness and justice demanded that the liquidator be relieved of the statutory consequences of failing to act within the specified time. She further held that inaction by the liquidator was not a justification for an extension of time, although in this instance she granted an extension.

22–68 A liquidator must wait for at least three months after the submission of his report before initiating a restriction application; during this time the DCE evaluates the report. In practical terms, this means that a liquidator has at most a two-month window within which to initiate proceedings. Although there is no rule in existence to ensure that the DCE makes his determination before the expiration of the five-month period, it would seem logical that if the DCE fails to do so, the liquidator cannot be faulted for failing to bring his restriction application timeously.

Delay

22–69 The general approach taken to complaints of delay by the courts is found in the Supreme Court decision in *Primor Plc v Stokes Kennedy Crowley*[136]: the court must first consider whether a delay in bringing civil proceedings is

---

[135] [2003] 2 I.R. 627.
[136] [1996] 2 I.R. 459.

inordinate, then whether that delay is inexcusable, before going on to decide whether it is in the interests of justice for the application to proceed regardless. In *Re Verit Hotel and Leisure (Ireland) Ltd*,[137] the Supreme Court ruled that a six-year delay from the commencement of a liquidation to the bringing of restriction proceedings – through inordinate and inexcusable – should not lead to their being struck out, since much of the delay complained of was explained by two sets of proceedings between the parties in the intervening period, and no prejudice to the respondents had been shown by them. Two more recent decisions of Finlay Geoghegan J suggest that a delay of a decade or more will be sufficient in itself to have restriction proceedings struck out. Firstly, in *Re Knocklofty House Hotel Ltd*,[138] she struck out two sets of restriction proceedings in respect of liquidations that had commenced 11 years and 12½ years before the issue of proceedings, respectively, on the basis of the length of delay alone, stating that no additional prejudice needed to be shown by the respondent directors. Then, in *Re Supreme Oil Company Ltd*,[139] she struck out proceedings solely on the basis of a 12-year delay. Delays of similar magnitude are unlikely to occur in windings-ups commenced since the 2001 Act, as it is an offence for a liquidator to fail to apply within a three- to five-month period from the delivery of his report to the DCE.

Burden of Proof

22–70   The applicant in restriction proceedings bears the burden of proving that the person against whom they are brought was a director of the company being wound up at the commencement of the winding-up or within the period of 12 months prior to its commencement, and that at the date of its commencement or at any time during the course of the winding up the liquidator certifies, or it is otherwise proved, that the company is unable to pay its debts. The applicant must also place before the court a grounding affidavit that contains sufficient information which he considers should be brought to the attention of the court for the purpose of making a determination on the question of restriction.[140] After this, the onus may be said to shift to the respondent director, to prove that he has acted honestly and responsibly in relation to the conduct of the affairs of the company and that there is no other reason why it would be just and equitable that he should be restricted. The standard of proof on him is on the balance of probability.[141] Ultimately, however, it is a matter for the court to be satisfied that the respondent has not acted honestly or responsibly, or that there is any other reason for restriction. In *Re Usit World Plc and Usit Ltd*,[142] the court refused to restrict, despite the respondent directors not having participated in the hearing of the application nor offered any exculpatory evidence to counter the case put the liquidator. Peart J. held that:

---

[137] [2001] 4 I.R. 550.
[138] [2005] 4 I.R. 497.
[139] [2005] 1 I.R. 571.
[140] Practice Direction HC28 – Companies Acts – Applications under s.150(1) Companies Act 1990, March 24, 2003, available at www.courts.ie
[141] [2005] I.E.H.C. 285; unreported, Peart J., August 10, 2005.
[142] *ibid.*

"there will inevitably be cases where the court can be satisfied, even in the absence of justification of conduct by a particular director, that he or she has acted honestly and responsibly. [S.150] cannot be fairly interpreted, in the absence of express wording to such effect, as meaning that a presumption of dishonesty and irresponsibility is to be inferred where a director takes no step to participate in the application. Such a presumption could fly in the face of matters glaring from the application itself from which the Court is satisfied as to honesty and responsibility. The task of the court is to be satisfied. [S.150] does not confine the Court as to the source of that satisfaction."[143]

A question that has arisen from time to time is whether the liquidator and the court may take into account the acts and omissions of a director in relation to other companies when considering restriction for his role played in the company the subject matter of the application. In that instance[144] there was a close interrelationship between the companies concerned, and two directors of one company were also directors of another. These facts, allied with the clear intermingling of issues relating to the various companies, led to the relevant restriction applications being heard together by the same court.

Format of application

22–71 Restriction applications normally proceed on the basis of affidavit evidence only, in the interests of expedition and costs. The option of cross-examination is available to the parties.[145] Notwithstanding the compulsion upon liquidators to bring these applications at the behest of the DCE or the court, the manner in which the liquidator runs his application is a matter for him alone. He is required to put before the court "all the facts the applicant considers should be brought to the attention of the court for the purpose of determining" whether circumstances warranting restriction exist.[146] In *Re Taylor Asset Managers Ltd*,[147] the liquidator was obliged to bring restriction applications in respect of four directors, including the celebrity Eddie Hobbs. The liquidator indicated in his grounding affidavit that he found no fault with the actions of Mr. Hobbs and two other directors. The remaining director, Mr. Taylor, swore a replying affidavit and attempted to compel the liquidator to employ this affidavit in the applications against Mr. Hobbs and the other two directors. Finlay Geoghegan J. refused to so direct, ruling that although the liquidator must pursue his restriction application "in a proper manner having regard to his role and position as liquidator" and as an officer of the court, "the judge hearing the application has no supervisory role" in relation to the running of the application.[148]

---

[143] *ibid.* at p.87 of the judgment.
[144] *ibid.*
[145] *Re GMT Engineering Services Ltd* [2003] 4 I.R. 133.
[146] Practice Direction HC28.
[147] Unreported, High Court, Finlay Geoghegan J., January 26, 2007. See also *Re Document Imaging Systems Ltd* [2005] 3 I.R. 103.
[148] See also, *Duignan v Carway (No. 2)* [2002] I.E.H.C. 1; unreported, McCracken J., January 23, 2002.

Costs

22–72   In successful restriction proceedings, the court may order that the applicant is entitled to the costs of the application, as well as to the whole or part of the costs and expenses incurred by the liquidator in investigating the matter and in collecting evidence.[149] In recent times, a practice has developed whereby the court measures the costs to be paid by restricted directors, in terms of a "contribution" towards the costs of the successful applicant.

22–73   A more vexed question is the issue of costs where the applicant is unsuccessful.[150] In a number of cases,[151] it has been held that the general rule, that costs follow the event,[152] is the basis upon which the court must exercise its discretion, and that the 1990 Act does not alter this for unsuccessful applications. But in *Re Doherty Advertising Ltd*,[153] where the court had refused to order that the second to fifth respondents be restricted, they were refused their costs as against the liquidator. O'Leary J. held that the rule that "costs follow the event" did not apply, and that costs "should not be normally awarded to a director who satisfies the court that he/she should not be the subject of a restriction order under s.150". The application had been brought on the instructions of the DCE and the liquidator faced possible criminal sanctions for not bringing it. In such circumstances, the judge found that the application itself was the "event" in question, rather than the adjudication of the court on the application. Such an application could not properly be called a claim or counterclaim, but was more analogous to the prosecution in a criminal case, where costs are very rarely awarded to an acquitted accused, usually only where the prosecution has misbehaved. O'Leary J. found some fault with the manner in which the liquidator had made his application, but held that such did not justify the awarding of costs against him. The correctness of this decision is questionable, and it is capable of giving rise to considerable injustice and indeed may deter legitimate risk-taking by directors. Proceedings for extradition and under European Arrest Warrants are comparable, but it never has seriously been suggested that successful respondents ordinarily should be refused their costs.

Settling proceedings

22–74   A liquidator cannot settle a restriction application on the grounds that "section 150 raises an issue between the directors and the courts".[154] In UK disqualification proceedings, facility exists whereby directors of insolvent companies may give an undertaking to the Secretary of State that they will not act as a directors without leave of the court for a specified period.[155]

---

[149] 1990 Act, s.150(4B), as inserted by s.11(1) of the 2006 Act.
[150] *cf.* G. Callanan, "The Costs of Restriction" 13(7) C.L.P. 175 (2006); R. White, "Restriction of Directors and the Applicant Liquidator's Costs" 10(10) C.L.P. 283 (2003).
[151] *Re Visual Impact and Displays Ltd* [2003] 4 I.R. 451; *Re Usit World Plc and Usit Ltd* [2005] I.E.H.C. 285, Peart J., unreported, August 10, 2005.
[152] Rules of the Superior Courts 1986, Order 99, Rule 1.
[153] [2006] I.E.H.C. 258; unreported, O'Leary J., July 14, 2006.
[154] *Duignan v Carway (No. 2)* [2002] I.E.H.C. 1; unreported, McCracken J., January 23, 2002.
[155] Company Directors Disqualification Act 1986, s.1A.

Disqualification Proceedings

22–75   Proceedings to have them entirely disqualified from being involved in the management of any company may be brought against any "officer" of a company, "including" its director, shadow director or secretary.[156] In certain circumstances, application for disqualification may be made by the prosecutor following a person's conviction on indictment for fraud or dishonesty.[157] In a variety of other circumstances, application may be made by any member, contributory, officer, employee, receiver, examiner, liquidator or creditor of the company, the DCE, the Registrar of Companies or the Director of Public Prosecutions.[158] In any of these instances, the court may of its own motion order disqualification. It was held by the European Court of Human Rights that the Convention's guarantee of a fair hearing applies to such proceedings, which must be prosecuted to conclusion within a reasonable time.[159] Ten days notice of any of these applications must be furnished. Unlike in restriction proceedings, the onus of proof throughout is on the applicant.[160] The general rule that costs follow the event applies to them. In successful applications, by either a liquidator, receiver, examiner, the DCE or the DPP, those costs will include that of investigating the matters that were the subject of the application and of collecting the requisite evidence, including any remuneration and expense applicable to those processes.[161]

---

[156] 1990 Act, s.159.

[157] *ibid.* s.160 (1).

[158] *ibid.* s.160 (2).

[159] *Davies v United Kingdom* 35 E.H.R.R. 720 (2002) and *Eastaway v United Kingdom* 40 E.H.R.R. 17 (2005).

[160] *Re Newcastle Timber Ltd* [2001] 4 I.R. 586.

[161] 1990 Act, s.160 (9B).

CHAPTER 23

WINDING UP AND STRIKING OFF

23–01 Companies go out of existence through the formal process of winding up or liquidation; the two expressions are coterminous. Companies also go out of existence by being struck off the register of companies. Unless it is duly wound up or else de-registered, a company continues in existence for year after year, while all of its shareholders or members may die. One of the characteristics of corporate personality is perpetual succession, until the corporate entity is extinguished through the statutory procedures. As Blackstone observed of corporations, they "have perpetual succession until they are formally dissolved. They are ... a person that never dies; in like manner as the River Thames is still the same river, though the parts which compose it are changing every instant."[1]

WINDING UP/LIQUIDATION

23–02 Winding up or liquidation is by far the most important and common of the procedures for achieving dissolution, which takes place some time after the liquidation has concluded.[2]

23–03 Originally, companies could be wound up for insolvency only. The Winding Up (Ireland) Act 1845,[3] provided that certain circumstances were deemed to constitute acts of bankruptcy by a company and, on their happening, the company was wound up by order of the High Court of Chancery; many of the then rules and practices regarding bankruptcy were applied to companies in liquidation. In 1848 provision was made whereby a company's members could petition the court for a winding-up order on grounds other than insolvency.[4] In 1856 the voluntary winding-up mechanism was adopted,[5] which did not require any court proceedings; the members could simply pass a special resolution for a winding-up and the liquidation commenced from that time. In his excellent treatise on the subject, Judge McPherson describes liquidation or winding up as a process whereby the assets of a company are collected and realised, the resulting proceeds are applied in discharging all its debts and liabilities, and any

---

[1] W. Blackstone, *Commentaries on the Law of England* (1765) Vol.1, Ch.18.
[2] See generally, M. Forde, *The Law of Company Insolvency* (Dublin: Round Hall, 1993) Part III and A.R. Keay, *McPherson's Law of Company Liquidation* (London: Sweet & Maxwell, 2001).
[3] 8 & 9 Vic. c. 98.
[4] 11 & 12 Vic. c. 45.
[5] 19 & 20 Vic. c. 47.

balance which remains after paying the costs and expenses of winding up is distributed among the members according to their rights and interests, or otherwise dealt with as the constitution of the company directs.[6]

23–04   The essential features of a winding-up, both voluntary and compulsory (i.e. by order of the court), were summarised by Lord Diplock as follows:

> "the making of a winding up order brings into operation a statutory scheme for dealing with the assets of the company that is ordered to be wound up. The scheme is now contained in Part V of the Companies Act [1948] and extends to voluntary as well as to compulsory winding up; but in so far as it deals with compulsory winding up its essential characteristics have remained the same since it was first enacted by the Companies Act 1862. The procedure to be followed when a company is being wound up varies in detail according to whether this is done compulsorily under an order of the court or voluntarily pursuant to a resolution of the company in general meeting, and, in the latter case, whether it is a members' voluntary winding up or a creditors' voluntary winding up; but the essential characteristics of the scheme for dealing with the assets of the company do not differ whichever of these procedures is applicable. They remain the same as those of the original statutory scheme in the Companies Act 1862 ...".[7]

23–05   Upon the making of a winding-up order:

> "(1) The custody and control of all the property and choses in action of the company are transferred from those persons who were entitled under the memorandum and articles to manage its affairs on its behalf to a liquidator charged with the statutory duty of dealing with the company's assets in accordance with the statutory scheme. Any disposition of the property of the company otherwise than by the liquidator is void.
> (2) The statutory duty of the liquidator is to collect the assets of the company and to apply them in discharge of its liabilities. If there is any surplus he must distribute it among the members of the company in accordance with their respective rights under the memorandum and articles of association. In performing these duties in a compulsory winding up the liquidator acts as an officer of the court, and if the company is insolvent the rules applicable in the law of bankruptcy must be followed.
> (3) All powers of dealing with the company's assets, including the power to carry on its business so far as may be necessary for its beneficial winding up, are exercisable by the liquidator for the benefit of those persons only who are entitled to share in the proceeds of realisation of the assets under the statutory scheme. The company itself as a legal person, distinct from its members, can never be entitled to any part of the proceeds. Upon completion of the winding up, it is dissolved."[8]

---

[6]   A.R. Keay, *McPherson's Law of Company Liquidation* (London: Sweet & Maxwell, 2001), p.1.
[7]   *Ayerst (Inspector of Taxes) v C & K Construction Ltd* [1976] A.C. 167 at 176–177.
[8]   *ibid.* at 176–177.

The Modes of Winding Up

23–06   There are three main methods of winding up companies—the members' voluntary winding-up, the creditors' voluntary winding-up and winding up by order of the court, otherwise known as an official liquidation. The main distinction between them is that the latter is carried out entirely within the court system whereas the two types of voluntary windings up in principle take place away from the court. Nevertheless, provision is made to facilitate court involvement in the voluntary processes in several ways; a voluntary liquidator may obtain court sanction for several kinds of transactions[9] and he may apply to the court to determine any question arising out of the liquidation or for him exercise any of the powers available in a compulsory liquidation.[10] Except where the Companies Acts provide otherwise, their winding-up provisions apply to all modes of liquidations.[11]

23–07   A fundamental distinction exists between the winding up of companies which are solvent and which are insolvent. The members' voluntary winding-up is designed for solvent companies. Although the great majority of compulsory liquidations involve insolvent companies, that mode is also used to wind up companies which are solvent, especially the petition to wind up on "just and equitable" grounds, which at times is used to seek redress against the oppression of minority shareholders. If the company being wound up is insolvent, then certain bankruptcy law rules apply to the process.[12] Not all of these rules are rendered thereby applicable, although several other provisions of the 1963–2006 Acts apply rules to insolvent liquidations which have parallels in bankruptcy.

Members' Voluntary Winding-Up

23–08   Members can take steps to voluntarily wind up their company, provided the company is registered under the 1963–2006 Acts, or one of the previous Companies Acts. The members' voluntary winding-up is a predominantly extra-curial process to enable a company's members or shareholders to bring its existence to an end. There are numerous reasons why they may want to wind up their company. For instance, they may be dissatisfied with the way in which it is being run; they may be unable to raise the additional funds it needs to stay in business; they may want to liquidate their investment but there is no ready market for their shares.

23–09   *Resolutions:* Members may wind up their company:

(i)   by passing a *special* resolution for a winding-up; or
(ii)   where the company was formed for a fixed duration and that period has expired, by passing an *ordinary* resolution for a winding-up; or

---

[9]   Enumerated in 1963 Act, s.231(1)(d)–(f).
[10]   *cf. Re Campbell Coverings Ltd* [1953] Ch. 488.
[11]   1963 Act, s.206(2).
[12]   See para.24–79.

(iii) if the company is insolvent, by passing an *ordinary* resolution for a winding-up. On account of the insolvency, this must be a creditors' voluntary winding-up.[13]

23–10 A special resolution is one which was passed by a majority of at least three quarters of the votes cast, at a meeting of which at least 21 days' notice was given.[14] If the holders of more than 90 per cent in value of the voting shares so agree, a special resolution may be passed by a three-quarters majority notwithstanding shorter notice. Notices of the intended resolution must sufficiently describe what is being proposed, so that all the company's members can form a reasoned judgment on it.[15] An ordinary resolution, which is all that is needed if the company is insolvent, means a simple majority of the votes cast.

23–11 The meeting to consider the proposal must have been properly convened, either by the directors or else under default powers, or be a court-ordered meeting. In one instance, where the meeting was convened by the company's secretary purportedly for the board, but without their clear authority to do so, the meeting and ensuing winding-up resolution were held to be invalid[16]; that departure from proper procedures would not be considered a "mere irregularity". By analogy with the position in official liquidations, it has been held that the court has jurisdiction to annul a winding-up resolution in an appropriate case.[17]

23–12 Within 14 days of the resolution being passed a notice thereof must be published in the *Gazette*.[18] A copy of that resolution and of the statutory declaration of solvency must be delivered to the Registrar of Companies.[19]

23–13 *Declaration of Solvency:* For the members themselves voluntarily to wind up their company, a majority of the directors must make a statutory declaration that, upon having made full inquiry, they are of the opinion that the company will be able to pay its debts in full within at most 12 months from when the winding-up commences.[20] This declaration must have been made not more than 28 days before the time the winding-up resolution was passed. It must contain a statement of the company's assets and liabilities as of not more than three months before that declaration was made. It must be accompanied by a report by an "independent person" stating that the directors' opinion regarding the company's solvency and the statement of affairs they drew up are reasonable. Formerly, directors often made unduly optimistic declarations of solvency but the requirement of independent verification has curbed that practice. To be independent for this purpose, the person verifying the declaration must

---

[13] 1963 Act, s.251.
[14] 1963 Act, s.141.
[15] See para.5–25 *et seq.*
[16] *Re State of Wyoming Syndicate* [1901] 2 Ch. 431.
[17] *Re Oakthorpe Holdings Ltd* [1987] I.R. 632.
[18] 1963 Act, s.256.
[19] 1963 Act, ss.143(4)(e) and 256(6).
[20] 1963 Act, s.256.

be qualified to be the company's auditor.[21] If it later transpires that the company was insolvent, the directors who made the declaration risk being held personally liable for all of the company's unpaid debts unless they can show that there were reasonable grounds for the view which they held.[22] It is questionable whether a director can be held liable in negligence for having signed a declaration of solvency.[23]

23–14 *Appointing Liquidator*: A duly-qualified liquidator must be appointed by the shareholders, who may fix his remuneration.[24] His function is "winding up the affairs and distributing the assets of the company …"[25] This appointment puts an end to the directors' powers. But the shareholders or the liquidator may permit them to continue exercising some or all of those powers.[26] Where the liquidator's office becomes vacant, it may be filled by the members in general meeting.[27] If for any reason they do not select a liquidator, he can be appointed by the court.[28] He also may be removed by the court for "cause shown" and be replaced.[29] A person who acts as a company's liquidator, without being qualified to do so, can be made the subject of a disqualification order; this jurisdiction extends to *de facto* liquidators.[30]

23–15 *Conduct of Liquidation*: A voluntary winding-up commences from the time the resolution to wind up is passed.[31] The company must then cease to carry on business except in so far as is necessary to facilitate the liquidation.[32] Although this mode of winding-up is entirely controlled by the company's members, any creditor may apply to the court to determine any matter.[33] In determining questions, the court shall have regard, *inter alia*, to the creditors' wishes.[34]

23–16 If at any time the liquidator forms the opinion that, contrary to the directors' declaration, the company will not be able to pay its debts in full, he must publicly advertise and call a meeting of the company's creditors, and provide them with a statement of the company's assets and liabilities and such further information as they may reasonably require.[35] A general meeting of the company must be summoned by the liquidator every year following the decision to wind up[36]; those attending should be given a statement of what the

---

[21] See para.17–15.
[22] Section 256(8).
[23] *Fay v Tegral Pipes Ltd* [2005] 2 I.R. 261.
[24] 1963 Act, s.258(1).
[25] *ibid.*
[26] 1963 Act, s.258(2).
[27] 1963 Act, s.259.
[28] 1963 Act, s.277(1).
[29] 1963 Act, s.277(2).
[30] *Cahill v Grimes* [2002] 1 I.R. 372.
[31] 1963 Act, s. 253.
[32] 1963 Act, s.254.
[33] 1963 Act, s.280.
[34] 1963 Act, s.309.
[35] 1963 Act, s.261.
[36] 1963 Act, s.262.

liquidator has done. A copy of this statement should be sent to the Registrar of Companies.[37]

23–17 When the company's assets have been collected and its creditors and shareholders are paid off, the liquidator must call a publicly-advertised general meeting and provide it with an account of the winding-up.[38] A copy of this account, together with a return of the holding of the terminal meeting, must be sent to the Registrar of Companies.[39] The company is deemed to be dissolved three months following the Registrar receiving these documents, although the court has power to defer the date of dissolution.[40]

Creditors' Voluntary Winding-Up

23–18 One form of winding up under the Companies Act 1862[41] was a hybrid of voluntary and official liquidation: winding-up subject to the supervision of the court. This was mainly designed to protect creditors' rights where the liquidation was strictly outside of the court; it also facilitated access to the court by contributories. It fell into disuse and was not continued by the 1963 Act; a similar procedure was abolished in Britain more recently.[42]

23–19 The policy underlying this mode of liquidation is that control over the winding-up should rest with those who are most affected by it. When the company is insolvent, those are its creditors. Accordingly, it is their wishes which are consulted when important questions arise. Thus, they appoint the liquidator and fix his remuneration,[43] they appoint a committee of inspection to advise and assist him in carrying out his functions,[44] they sanction certain exercises of his powers.[45] At any time a creditor may apply to the court for directions[46] and the court must take due account of their wishes and have regard to the value of each creditor's debt.[47] By contrast, the members are virtually excluded from any say in the liquidation, although they too can apply to the court for directions.[48]

23–20 If the company is insolvent, the position under a voluntary liquidation is practically no different from that in a compulsory liquidation; for instance, the normal bankruptcy rules govern the proof of debts, the assets available for division among the creditors and priorities between creditors.[49]

---

[37]   1963 Act, s.262.
[38]   1963 Act, s.263.
[39]   1963 Act, s.263(3).
[40]   1963 Act, s.263(4) and (5).
[41]   25 & 26 Vic., c.89.
[42]   Insolvency Act 1986.
[43]   1963 Act, s.267.
[44]   1963 Act, s.268.
[45]   1963 Act, s.276(1)(a).
[46]   1963 Act, s.280.
[47]   1963 Act, s.309.
[48]   1963 Act, s.280.
[49]   1963 Act, s.284(1).

23–21   *Resolution to Wind Up:* Although a creditors' voluntary winding-up is almost entirely under the control of the company's creditors, they cannot commence the process; the initiative is with the members and the creditors' entitlements only take effect once the members' resolution has been passed. A company may be wound up by ordinary resolution on the grounds that "it cannot by reason of its liabilities continue on its business".[50] Previously a special or extraordinary resolution was needed for this purpose. Once a winding-up resolution has been passed, the members cannot change their minds and revoke it. Because the Companies Acts deem the liquidation to have commenced once that resolution is passed, with several important immediate effects on the company and persons dealing with it, the passing of the resolution "immediately confers the irrevocable status of being in liquidation, with all the legal incidents thereof."[51] In exceptional circumstances, the court may annul that resolution.[52]

23–22   Where a special resolution to wind up was passed with the intention of having a members' voluntary winding-up, but no statutory declaration of solvency has been made, this cannot then be a members' winding-up; it must proceed as a creditors' winding-up. In *Re Oakthorpe Holdings Ltd*,[53] it was held that the court does not have jurisdiction to extend the period of time laid down for making this declaration, so that there could be a members' winding-up. According to Carroll J, a "time limit was provided by statute and no discretion was given to the court to extend it."[54]

23–23   Although generally seven days' notice of an EGM suffices for companies with Pt II of Table A,[55] because creditors must be given at least 10 days' notice, in effect the members' meeting cannot take place before that period expires. The notices must specify the place, the day and the hour of the meeting; also the general nature of the business to be transacted.[56] Because of the exceptional significance of what is being proposed, there should be no room for ambiguity in the notices sent out. It has been said that it is "of great importance that the steps taken in a matter of such consequence as the resolving to wind up a company should be perfectly regular."[57] For instance, in *Re Haycroft Gold Reduction & Mining Co.*,[58] the members' meeting was convened by the company secretary without the directors having first met and decided that a meeting should be held to wind up the company. The court refused to regard that departure from the normal lines of authority as a mere irregularity; the meeting was not properly called and the resolution was

---

[50] 1963 Act, s.251(1)(c).
[51] *Ross v PH Heeringa Ltd* [1970] N.Z.L.R. 170 at 172.
[52] *Re Oakthorpe Holdings Ltd* [1987] I.R. 632.
[53] [1987] I.R. 632.
[54] *ibid.* at 636.
[55] Part II, art.4.
[56] Article 51.
[57] *Re Bridport Old Brewery Co.* (1867) L.R. 2 Ch. App. 191 at 194.
[58] [1900] 2 Ch. 230.

invalid. In a later similar instance, it was again stressed that "proceedings of this kind ought to be conducted with substantial propriety."[59]

23–24 Within 14 days of its being passed, a notice of the resolution to wind up must be published in the *Gazette*[60]; if that is not done, any officer of the company responsible for the default and also the liquidator can be prosecuted. Within 15 days of it being passed, a copy of the resolution must be given to the Registrar of Companies.[61]

23–25 *Creditors' Meeting*: Either for the day of the members' meeting or the following day, a meeting of the company's creditors must be duly convened and held.[62] This meeting must be summoned by the company, meaning its directors. At least 10 days before the date of the members' meeting, notices convening the creditors' meeting must be posted to the creditors[63] and also those notices must be advertised in two daily newspapers circulating in the district where the company's registered office or its principal place of business is located.[64] Accordingly, many persons who are owed or who believe they are owed money by the company have reasonable notice of what the company proposes to do and have opportunity to make preparations for selecting a liquidator and otherwise. Prosecutions can be brought against either the company, the directors or a director for failure to give proper notice of the meeting.

23–26 Where no creditors' meeting has been convened or that meeting was not properly convened, it is debatable what the consequences are for the liquidation or for what is purported to have happened at any creditors' meeting. In 1981 the comparable British legislation was amended to provide that failure to send out notice of the meeting shall not invalidate any resolution passed or other thing done at whatever meeting did occur.[65]

23–27 The directors must choose one of their number to preside at this meeting.[66] They also must arrange to provide the meeting with "a full statement of the position of the company's affairs, together with a list of [its] creditors ... and the estimated amount of their claims ...".[67] It is preferable if the statement of affairs is in the form contained in Form No.13 of the High Court Rules for official liquidations.[68]

23–28 Often these meetings are attended by creditors' solicitors or financial advisers. The High Court rules regarding official liquidations permit

---

[59] *Re State of Wyoming Syndicate* [1900] 2 Ch. 431 at 436.
[60] 1963 Act, s.252.
[61] 1963 Act, s.143.
[62] 1963 Act, s.266.
[63] 1963 Act, s.266(1).
[64] 1963 Act, s.266(2).
[65] *cf. Re EV Saxton & Sons Ltd v R Miles (Confectioners) Ltd* [1983] 1 W.L.R. 952.
[66] 1963 Act, s.266(4); *cf. Re Salcombe Hotel Developments Co.* [1991] B.C.L.C. 44.
[67] 1963 Act, s.266(3).
[68] RSC, Appendix M, No. 13.

representation of creditors by proxy[69] and it seems that those provisions would apply by analogy to these meetings. Usually the chairman will explain to those assembled why the company finds itself in the predicament it is in and how the various categories of creditors stand to fare in the winding-up. The High Court Rules probably will also be applied by analogy to determine who is entitled to vote at the meeting.[70] However, the requirement that, for the purposes of voting, a secured creditor must either surrender his security or give particulars of it to the liquidator does not apply to these meetings.[71] Exactly how this exemption affects Ord.74 r.69, which states that a creditor who votes in respect of his entire debt is deemed to have surrendered his security, remains to be clarified.

23–29 *Appointing Liquidator and Committee of Inspection*: The main business transacted at these meetings is appointing a duly-qualified liquidator and a committee of inspection. Often the members will have chosen the same person as the creditors select. Where both meetings nominate different persons, precedence is given to the creditors' choice.[72] Resolutions of the creditors require a majority in value only for this purpose,[73] so that there is no realistic prospect of them being deadlocked on this question. Where the members and the creditors nominate different liquidators, any member, director or creditor may apply to the court, within 14 days, seeking either to have both nominees or some third party appointed to the office.[74] Either the creditors or the committee of inspection fix the liquidator's remuneration.[75]

23–30 At that meeting or later on, the creditors may decide to appoint a committee of inspection,[76] consisting of not more than five of their nominees. Ordinarily, the company can appoint three additional names to this committee; but the creditors can veto individual company nominees unless the court otherwise directs.

23–31 The powers of any liquidator who was appointed prior to the holding of the creditors' meeting are greatly circumscribed.[77] Except for taking custody of company property, disposing of perishable goods and goods of diminishing value, and taking such steps as are necessary to protect the company's assets, he may not exercise any of the normal liquidators' powers without obtaining the sanction of the court. Furthermore, he is required to attend the creditors' meeting and report to it on how he has exercised any of his powers.

23–32 *Creditor's Application*: Where a resolution for a members' voluntary liquidation is passed, a creditor is not precluded from petitioning the High

---

[69] RSC 1986, Ord.74 rr.74–83.
[70] *ibid.* rr.67–71.
[71] *ibid.* r.72.
[72] 1963 Act, s.267(3).
[73] 1963 Act, s267(3).
[74] 1963 Act, s.267(2).
[75] 1963 Act, s.269.
[76] 1963 Act, s.268.
[77] 1990 Act, s.131.

Court for a compulsory liquidation. Alternatively, if a creditor believes that the company is indeed insolvent, notwithstanding the directors' statutory declaration, the liquidation can be converted into a creditors' voluntary winding-up.[78] To do this, the aggrieved creditor and those supporting him must represent at least one fifth in number *or* in value of the company's creditors, they can apply within 28 days and must provide the court with evidence which indicates that the company will not be able to pay its debts in full within the time stated in the directors' declaration. The court may then order that the liquidation shall take the form of a creditors' voluntary winding-up. A copy of that order must be delivered to the Registrar of Companies.[79] The liquidator must then convene a meeting of the company's creditors.

Winding up by the Court

23–33 Winding up by order of the High Court—compulsory or official liquidation—is a more formal process which can be slower and more expensive than the voluntary modes. Instead of the dissolution machinery being administered by the members or the creditors, as the case may be, the conduct of the process is by the court; the liquidator carries out his duties under its direct supervision and the Companies Acts provide for a greater degree of court control. That a company is already in voluntary liquidation does not prevent the court from ordering that it be wound up. Most official liquidations are initiated by creditors who have not been paid what is owing to them.[80] The position regarding court winding-ups initiated by other parties may be summarised as follows, although many of the points made apply just as much to creditors' petitions.

23–34 *"Any Company"*: The High Court's power to order a winding-up applies to "any company".[81] This does not mean every conceivable kind of association and corporation. What are companies for the purpose of the Companies Acts 1963–2006, are companies which have been registered under those Acts or under any of the earlier Companies Acts—those of 1908, of 1862 and of 1844.

23–35 *Unregistered Companies*: Part X of the 1963 Act (ss.344–350) establishes a procedure for winding-up certain unregistered companies, including indigenous partnerships with at least eight members. The High Court has an inherent power to dissolve partnerships.[82] It can hardly be doubted that a deed of settlement company, if any still exist, is an unregistered company for the purposes of Pt X of the 1963 Act. The winding-up jurisdiction has been held to apply to friendly societies[83] and to industrial and provident societies.[84] That

---

[78] 1963 Act, s.256(5).

[79] 1963 Act, s.221.

[80] See para.24–76.

[81] 1963 Act, s. 213.

[82] R.C. L'Anson Banks (ed.), *Lindley and Banks on Partnership*, 18th edn (London: Sweet & Maxwell, 2002) at 712 *et seq.*

[83] *Re Independent Protestant Loan Fund Society* [1895] 1 I.R. 1.

[84] *Re Belfast Tailors Co. Partnership* [1907] 1 I.R. 49.

jurisdiction was given to the court in the case of building societies[85] and credit unions,[86] and also certified trustee savings banks.[87] In *Re Commercial Buildings Company of Dublin*,[88] it was held that the court could order the winding-up of a company incorporated by royal charter.

23–36 This jurisdiction may not invariably apply to companies established by statute either directly or, indirectly, by way of royal charter or an order in council or instrument issued under statutory authority. In *Re Portstewart Tramway Co.*,[89] the court acceded to a judgment creditor's petition to wind up a company that was established by order pursuant to the Tramways (Ireland) Acts. It was held that the winding-up jurisdiction was not precluded because these Acts authorised the appointment of a receiver over the company's assets. There is conflicting authority regarding whether a public utility company established by a private Act of Parliament could be dissolved in this fashion.[90] It is unlikely that the court's winding-up jurisdiction applies to companies established by a public act of the Oireachtas or of its predecessors.

23–37 *Grounds for Ordering a Winding-Up:* The principal grounds on which the court may order that a company be wound up are:[91]

• where by a special resolution the company resolves to be wound up in this way;

• where the company is unable to pay its debts;

• where there is "oppression" that would justify making an order under s.205 of the 1963 Act;

• where it is "just and equitable" to order a winding-up;[92]

• where the company does not commence business within a year of being incorporated or suspends its business for a year; and

• where the membership falls below the statutory minimum of two or seven, as the case may be.

23–38 Some of these grounds are self-explanatory. Oppression and the like under s.205 has been dealt with above in considering minority shareholder protection[93] and some of the principal applications of the "just and equitable" heading are also treated there.[94] Other examples include where the main object

---

85 Building Societies Act 1989, s.109.
86 Credit Union Act 1997, ss.133–135.
87 1963 Act, s.344.
88 [1938] I.R. 477.
89 [1896] 1 I.R. 265.
90 See cases considered in the *Commercial Buildings Co.* case [1938] I.R. 477.
91 1963 Act, s.213.
92 Section 213(ea) and (fa) apply this criterion to SEs and to investment companies.
93 See para.10–71 *et seq.*
94 See para.10–109 *et seq.*

for which the company was formed has become impracticable,[95] where its internal decision-making procedures are deadlocked[96] and where the majority have committed a significant fraud on the company.[97] By far the commonest ground on which orders for a winding-up are sought is under s.213(e), that the company is "unable to pay its debts".[98] Frequent petitioners under this head are the Revenue Commissioners.

23–39 At the hearing of the petition, or even earlier, the company or any creditor or contributory may apply to the court to stay the proceedings or to have further proceedings restrained; the court may grant that application on such terms as it thinks fit. If the court is satisfied that the applicant is a qualified petitioner and that the alleged grounds exist, it may order that the company be wound up and appoint a liquidator. Since, however, it has a discretion in the matter, the court may refuse to make that order where there are good reasons for doing so.[99] Or the court may adjourn the hearing, make an interim order or make such other order as it thinks fit. A provisional liquidator may be appointed by the court pending appointment of the liquidator proper.[100]

23–40 Whenever a winding-up order is made, a copy must be delivered to the Registrar of Companies.[101] On being appointed, the liquidator must publish that fact in the *Gazette* and deliver to the Registrar a copy of the court's appointing order.[102]

23–41 *Company's own petition*: The company itself can petition for a winding-up under any of the above grounds. However, petitions of that nature are extremely rare because, ordinarily, the company will elect for a voluntary liquidation. Exceptionally, where the requisite majority for a special resolution cannot be obtained, the company might then petition the court. But if it is insolvent, a simple majority of the members' votes will commence a creditors' voluntary winding-up.

23–42 Whatever the grounds being invoked, the company's decision to seek a winding-up cannot be made by the directors without reference to the members, who are entitled to be properly consulted before their company can be brought to an end. In *Re Galway & Salthill Tramways Co.*,[103] the directors of a transport undertaking petitioned to have it wound up on "just and equitable" grounds because it was losing money, its net assets were steadily diminishing

---

[95] Also called "failure of substratum", e.g. *Re Dublin & Eastern Regional Tourism Organisation Ltd* [1990] 1 I.R. 579. No failure of substratum was found in *Garvey v Metafile Ltd* [2006] I.E.H.C. 407; unreported, Laffoy J., December 20, 2006.

[96] e.g. *Re Vehicle Buildings & Insulations Ltd* [1986] I.L.R.M. 239.

[97] e.g. *Re Newbridge Steam Laundry Ltd* [1917] 1 I.R. 167.

[98] See para.24–76.

[99] *Re Bula Ltd* [1990] 1 I.R. 440.

[100] 1963 Act, s.226.

[101] 1963 Act, s.221.

[102] 1963 Act, s.227.

[103] [1918] 1 I.R. 62.

and it could not pay its debts as they were falling due. The argument that the equivalent of art.80 of Table A empowered the directors to make this application was rejected by O'Connor M.R., who observed that "the object of management is the working of the company's undertaking, while the object of a winding-up is its stoppage."[104] The petition was adjourned so that the members could meet and decide if they would support it.

23–43   Neither a receiver ordinarily nor an examiner, under the Companies (Amendment) Act 1990, are empowered to petition for a winding-up. However, in his report to the court, an examiner can recommend liquidation.[105] Circumstances can arise where a receiver and manager appointed over a company's assets is entitled to petition for a winding-up, on the company's behalf. That happened in *Re Emmadart Ltd*,[106] where a receiver had been appointed over a company with one asset remaining, an unoccupied shop held under a 25-year lease. A rate demand was presented by the local authority. There was an exemption from rates for companies being wound up. To gain the benefit of that exemption, a petition was presented by the receiver and the court ordered that the company be wound up. Because of the insolvency and the effect of a winding-up order would be to protect the company's remaining assets, it was held that the receiver was entitled to petition on its behalf.

23–44   *Contributory's/Member's Petition*: A contributory is someone who is obliged to contribute to a company's assets when it is being wound up, most notably a member with partly paid up shares. But for the purpose of presenting a winding-up petition, a fully paid up member or shareholder is also deemed to be a contributory.[107] In principle the contributory's petition can be based on any of the above grounds but usually his application will be based on alleged "oppression" or "just and equitable" grounds. It is most unusual for a contributory to seek a winding-up for insolvency; if his shares are fully paid he would be in effect throwing away his investment, and, if they are partly paid, he would be triggering his liability to pay what remains due on them. Moreover, it is far more convenient and cheaper to seek to have a members' meeting convened to consider a winding-up resolution.

23–45   There is some doubt about whether an order would ever be made, on a contributory's petition, winding up his company for being insolvent, because insolvency is a matter which primarily concerns creditors. If they are content to do nothing about the company, a contributory on his own is unlikely to be successful in the application. In *Re Chesterfield Catering Co.*,[108] the court confirmed the 100-year-old principle that "where a fully paid shareholder petitions for a compulsory winding-up he must show, on the face of his petition, a prima facie probability that there will be assets available for distribution among the

---

[104] *ibid.* at 65. Compare with *Re Equiticorp. Int'l Plc* [1989] B.C.L.C. 597.
[105] 1990 Amendment Act, s.19.
[106] [1979] 2 W.L.R. 868.
[107] 1963 Act, s.207.
[108] [1977] Ch. 373.

shareholders"[109] or some other "tangible interest" for the petitioner.[110] An example of such other tangible interest would be in an unlimited company; the shareholder may desire liquidation to put some cap on his liability for the company's debts. But that tangible interest must arise by virtue of the petitioner's membership of the company; he must show that the liquidation will deliver to him some advantage or minimise a disadvantage *qua* member. In *Re Instrumentation Electrical Services Ltd*,[111] it was held that two contributories lacked standing to seek a winding-up of their insolvent company because their petition disclosed neither any advantage they might obtain from a liquidation nor any disadvantage they might suffer if the company continued in being. The judge gave the petitioners opportunity to amend their petition so that they could show some benefit or detriment but no amendment was made.

23–46   An exception of sorts is made where the petition is based on the failure of the company to supply accounts and information. If as a result the petitioner is not able to demonstrate that he will be able to share in a surplus, he will not be deprived of *locus standi*.[112]

23–47   *Creditor's Petition*: Where the company is insolvent, in most cases it is a creditor who petitions to have it liquidated. Often the threat of liquidation is made to exact payment of a debt owed by the company. For if the statutory demand for payment is made and the money due is not received within three weeks,[113] the creditor can proceed with a winding-up petition—usually on the grounds of insolvency and exceptionally on "just and equitable" grounds.

23–48   Bowen L.J. once compared winding up as a form of equitable execution—a process through which the liquidator takes control of the company's assets and realises them for the benefit of its creditors.[114] Before a liquidation commences, the normal creditors' remedies are available to them. But once the winding-up order is made, those modes of redress virtually lapse,[115] and the unsecured creditor is then left to prove in the winding-up and receive his proportionate share from such assets as are realised. *Prima facie*, a creditor is entitled to have a company which does not pay its debt wound up,[116] although the court occasionally rejects petitions where insolvency has been established. Creditors are not expected to exhaust alternative remedies before seeking a winding-up order; once the stipulated sum is due or owing, the creditor can present his petition even where that is done mainly as a means of exerting pressure to obtain payment. Even the presence of a collateral motive, like the desire to eliminate a competitor, does not disentitle an unpaid creditor to a winding-up order.[117]

---

[109] *Re Othery Construction Ltd* [1996] 1 W.L.R. 69 at 72.
[110] *Re Costa Rica Gold Washing Co.* (1879) 11 Ch D 36.
[111] [1988] B.C.L.C. 550.
[112] *Re Newman & Howard Ltd* [1962] Ch. 257.
[113] 1963 Act, s.214(a) and see para.24–76.
[114] *Re Chapel House Colliery Co.* (1883) 24 Ch D 259 at 269.
[115] See para.23–63 *et seq.*
[116] *Bowes v Hope Life Insurance Co.* (1865) 11 H.L. Cas. 389.
[117] *Bryanston Finance Ltd v de Vries (No. 2)* [1976] Ch. 63.

But if many of the unsecured creditors are against liquidation, the court may stay its hand.

23–49   *Director's Petition*: Following an investigation by inspectors into a company's affairs under Part II of the 1990 Act, the DCE may petition that the company be wound up on "just and equitable" grounds.[118]

23–50   *Regulatory Authority Petition*: Among the powers given to several regulatory agencies is to petition for the winding-up of a company that is not complying with the regulatory regime. For instance, the Central Bank may petition to have a licensed bank wound up because it is insolvent, that it has contravened directions from the Bank, that its licence has been revoked and it has ceased doing business, or that the Bank considers it to be in the interests of the company's depositors that it be wound up.

23–51   *Attorney-General's Petition*: There is no express authority in the Companies Acts for the Attorney-General to seek the winding-up of a company. But it would seem that he has some inherent authority to apply to the court to have a company dissolved because it was formed for an unlawful purpose and perhaps otherwise than in the public interest.[119] It is possible that he has a more extensive power to seek the dissolution of charitable companies.[120]

23–52   *Discretion to Refuse Winding-Up*: The court is not obliged to order a winding-up where any of above grounds have been established. Instead, a company "*may* be wound up" in any of these circumstances. Thus, even if insolvency has been proved, the court nevertheless can decline to make the order. But it does not have a complete discretion where the petitioner demonstrates insolvency. Generally, that petitioner is entitled to the winding-up order; an unpaid creditor "is entitled *ex debito justitiae*" to an order.[121] Nevertheless, there are several well-established circumstances in which that order will not be made and there may be other special circumstances about a particular case which justify the court in declining to make the order, or adjourning the matter for some time and subject to appropriate conditions. The court does not lean in favour of adjournments because they prevent other petitions being presented.

23–53   In *Re Bula Ltd*,[122] following consideration of many of the reported cases on this point, McCarthy J. summed up the position as follows:

> "The section ... gives to the court a true discretion which should be exercised in a principled manner that is fair and just ... A creditor is

---

[118] 1990 Act, s.12. *cf. Re Golden Chemical Products Ltd* [1976] Ch. 300.

[119] *R. v Registrar of Companies, Ex p. Attorney-General* [1991] B.C.L.C. 476.

[120] See generally, H. Delany, *Equity and the Law of Truits in Ireland*, 4th edn (Thomson Round Hall: Dublin, 2007) at 316 *et seq.*

[121] *Re Western Canada Oil etc Co.* (1873) L.R. 17 Eq. 1 at 7.

[122] [1990] 1 I.R. 440.

prima facie entitled to his order so as to shift the initial burden to those who oppose the winding up; the petitioner does not have to demonstrate positively that an order for winding up is for the benefit of the class of creditors to which he belongs, but, if issue is joined on the matter, and the case made that the petition is not for that purpose but for an ulterior, though not in itself improper object, then the burden shifts back to the petitioner."[123]

23–54 In the past, a petitioning creditor at any time could withdraw his petition, for instance where the company paid his debt prior to the date of the hearing. Since 1910 if that person drops out of the proceedings, the court has had a discretion to substitute him with another willing petitioner. On account of this power, it would seem that payment or tender to the petitioner gives the court only a discretion to decide what should happen to his application; it may dismiss the application, adjourn it or allow another creditor to take it up. An important consideration is the financial state of the company. There is some risk for the petitioner accepting the company's offer of payment at this stage because, if another creditor proceeds with the application and the company is wound up, that payment is strictly an invalid disposition[124]; unless the court sanctions that payment, it must be refunded.[125]

Effects of a Winding-Up

23–55 Commencement of a winding-up freezes various transactions that concern the company. As one judge explained "[I]t is a basic concept of our law governing the liquidation of insolvent estates, whether in bankruptcy or under the Companies Acts, that the free assets of the insolvent at the commencement of the liquidation shall be distributed rateably amongst the insolvent's unsecured creditors as at that date".[126] A voluntary winding-up commences once the appropriate resolution was passed. A compulsory liquidation is deemed to have commenced, not when the winding-up order is made, but when the petition for a winding-up was presented in the Central Office of the High Court.[127]

Shareholders

23–56 From the time a winding-up commences, any transfer of shares in the company or alteration in the status of any member is void unless the court orders otherwise.[128] Even where a shareholder was defrauded by the company into subscribing for shares in it, rescission is no longer available after the winding-up commenced. However, in a voluntary winding-up the liquidator may permit shares to be transferred.

---

[123] [1990] 1 I.R. 440, at 448.
[124] See para.23–61.
[125] *Re Webb Electrical Ltd* [1988] B.C.L.C. 382.
[126] *Re Gray's Inn Construction Co.* [1980] 1 W.L.R. 711 at 717.
[127] 1963 Act, s.220.
[128] 1963 Act, ss.218 and 255.

Directors

23–57   In a voluntary winding-up, once the liquidator is appointed the directors' powers cease except where either the members or the liquidator authorised those directors to continue acting for the company.[129] There is no corresponding provision for a compulsory winding-up. But it seems to be universally accepted that, once an official liquidator is appointed, the directors' powers come to an end, although it is possible that they continue in office for certain limited purposes.

Contracts

23–58   In general, the advent of liquidation has no immediate effect on contracts persons have with the company. However, there are contracts with express and even implied terms that liquidation either lawfully terminates them or constitutes a repudiatory breach of them. Provisions to that effect are often contained in leases. Commencement of an official liquidation operates as a notice of immediate termination of employment contracts but those contracts are not immediately terminated by the commencement of a voluntary liquidation. There is a procedure whereby the liquidator may apply to disclaim onerous contracts.[130]

Litigation

23–59   Once the court appoints a provisional liquidator or orders that a company be wound up, all actions against the company are stayed.[131] But the court may allow proceedings to be brought or be continued on such terms as it deems fit. Once a petition to wind up a company has been presented, either the company or any creditor or contributory may apply to the court to stay or restrain any action or proceeding against the company.[132] If the company loses the action, the costs payable to the plaintiff have priority over the general costs of the liquidation.[133] In the case of a voluntary winding-up, the liquidator may apply to the court to have proceedings being brought against the company stayed[134]; it is for him to show why a stay should be ordered in any particular instance.

Company Property

23–60   Unlike the position in bankruptcies, the company's property does not automatically vest in the liquidator. But he may apply to the court to have title to all or part of that property vested in him.[135]

23–61   Any disposition of the company's property following commencement of a compulsory winding-up is void unless the court orders otherwise.[136] Payments out of a company's bank account in these circumstances have been

---

129 1963 Act, s.258(2).
130 1963 Act, s.290; see para.24–119 *et seq.*
131 1963 Act, s.222.
132 1963 Act, s.217.
133 *Re C.H.A. Ltd* [1999] 1 I.R. 437.
134 1963 Act, s.217.
135 1963 Act, s.230.
136 1963 Act, s.218.

held to be a disposition in favour of the bank. The principle governing decisions by the court to refuse to uphold any such disposition is that "[s]ince the policy of the law is to procure so far as practicable rateable payments of the unsecured creditors' claims ... the court should not validate any transaction or series of transactions which might result in one or more pre-liquidation creditors being paid in full at the expense of other creditors, who will receive only a dividend, in the absence of special circumstances making such a course desirable in the interests of the unsecured creditors as a body".[137]

23–62 In *Re Pat Ruth Ltd*,[138] the court refused to validate payments made into the company's overdrawn bank account between the time the petition was presented and the winding up order was made, on the grounds to do so would have preferred the bank over other unsecured creditors. In *Re Industrial Co. Ltd*,[139] Kearns J. refused to follow recent English case law to the effect that lodging funds to a company's bank account is not a disposition for these purposes.[140] Exercising discretion, however, as the bank had not been aware of the winding up and also the transactions in the account were in respect of current business debts which the liquidator would probably have had to repay anyway, it subsequently was held by McCracken J. in *Re Industrial Services Co. Ltd (No. 2)*[141] that some of the payments and the lodgements to the account that funded them should be validated.[142]

Creditors' Remedies

23–63 A creditor who has issued execution against a company's property or has attached a debt due to the company is not permitted to retain the benefit of these processes unless enforcement was completed before the winding-up commenced or the date the creditor received notice of the proposal to wind up.[143] Furthermore, before goods taken in execution are sold or the execution is completed, the liquidator may demand that the sheriff return those goods.[144] Rights arising under these two powers may be set aside by the court and a purchaser in good faith, under a sale by the sheriff, acquires a good title against the liquidator. Where the company is being wound up compulsorily, any execution, attachment, sequestration or distress put into force against company property after the winding-up commences is absolutely void.[145]

---

[137] *Re Gray's Inn Construction Co.* [1980] 1 W.L.R. at 718.

[138] [1981] I.L.R.M. 51.

[139] [2001] 2 I.R. 119.

[140] *Hollicourt (Contracts) Ltd v Bank of Ireland* [2001] Ch. 55 (where the CA disapproved of various dicta in *Re Gray's Inn Construction Co. Ltd* [1980] 1 All E.R. 814). See generally, J. Armour & H. Bennett, *Vulnerable Transactions in Corporate Insolvency* (Oxford: Hart, 2003), Ch.8.

[141] [2004] 4 I.R. 394.

[142] See *Re Worldport Ireland Ltd* [2005] I.E.H.C. 189, where Clarke J. followed the decision of Kearns J. *cf.* A. Keirse, "Post-Commencement Dispositions—An Analysis of Recent Case Law" 12(11) *C.L.P.* 317 (2005).

[143] 1963 Act, s.291.

[144] 1963 Act, s.292.

[145] 1963 Act, s.219.

23–64   Any judgment mortgage which is registered against the company's land within three months before the winding-up commences obtains no "priority or preference over simple contract creditors".[146] Whether a judgment mortgage registered within that period takes priority over tort creditors is debatable; at the time this rule was adopted in bankruptcy law, claims in tort could not be proved against an insolvent's estate.

23–65   Commencement of a winding-up is a crystallising event which converts any floating charge on all or part of the company's property into a fixed charge. A winding-up does not prevent the appointment of a receiver under a debenture, nor does it affect the receiver's entitlement to dispose of the charged assets. But it puts an end to the receiver's express authority to manage the business and to enter into contracts binding on the company for that purpose.

23–66   A lien or charge over any company records or documents is not effective against a liquidator. But this does not prejudice the effectiveness of any underlying transaction created or evidenced by the document.[147]

The Liquidator

23–67   Depending on what kind of winding-up it is, the members, the creditors or the court will appoint one or more liquidators, whose principal function is to dispose of the company's assets, pay or settle its debts and distribute to the members whatever capital and surplus that may remain. Having a capable liquidator makes a big difference to creditors and even more so to shareholders, in that they stand to benefit from the price the liquidator obtains for the assets.

23–68   Former officers and employees of the company, during the preceding 12 months, any of their partners and any close member of their family, may not act as its liquidator.[148] Disqualification orders under s.160 of the 1990 Act can be made against liquidators, including persons who *de facto* acted in that capacity. Any purported appointment is not effective until the liquidator has signified his written consent.[149] A committee of inspection, comprised of creditors' and contributories' representatives, is usually appointed in creditors' voluntary winding-ups and in compulsory winding-ups to monitor the conduct of the liquidation.

Voluntary Winding-Up

23–69   Although a liquidator in a voluntary winding-up owes certain statutory duties to the creditors and shareholders, he is not strictly speaking a trustee for either of those groups and is best regarded as simply an agent of the company. Numerous specific powers are conferred on liquidators, such as to sell

---

[146] 1963 Act, s.284(2).
[147] 1963 Act, s.244A.
[148] 1963 Act, s.300A.
[149] 1963 Act, s.276A.

company property and to "carry on the business of the company so far as may be necessary for [its] beneficial winding up"; also the power to "do all such other things as may be necessary for winding up the affairs of the company and distributing its assets". But the powers to pay any classes of creditors in full and to make compromises with company creditors and debtors, and with members owing outstanding calls, must be exercised with the consent of the members, or with the consent of the creditors or committee of inspection in the case of a creditors' voluntary winding-up. Liquidators act on behalf of the company and are not normally personally liable on contracts made in that capacity. Liquidators frequently apply to the court for directions as to what they are entitled to do. Where cause is shown, the court may remove a liquidator and appoint a replacement.[150]

Official Liquidator

23–70 A liquidator appointed by the court is described as the official liquidator. One consequence of making a winding-up order is to terminate the employment contracts of the company's employees[151] and to remove the directors and deprive them of their powers to act for the company. An official liquidator's powers include the power to "do such … things as may be necessary for winding up the affairs of the company and distributing its assets".[152] Some of these powers may be exercised only with the court's or the committee of inspection's consent: namely to bring or defend any action involving the company, to carry on the business for the time being, to appoint a solicitor, to pay any class of creditors and to make compromises with debtors or with members holding not-fully-paid shares. Any creditor or contributory may apply to the court in respect of the exercise of the liquidator's powers. Official liquidators often apply to the court for directions as to what they should do or for approval for what they have done. Although official liquidators have a right to resign,[153] the act of resignation does not of itself release them from their obligations.

23–71 A matter that can give rise to controversy is which of competing bids for company property being offered for sale should be accepted. The liquidator's and the court's primary duty is to get the maximum price obtainable. Although an official liquidator is not obliged to seek the court's consent to the terms of a sale, either prior approval or subsequent confirmation by the court is usually sought for disposals of major properties. In *Van Hool McArdle Ltd v Rohan Industrial Estate Ltd*,[154] it was held that, if the sale is subject to the court's prior approval, then the liquidator must accept the highest offer made— even if that offer was made subsequent to the liquidator having agreed with another party to sell him the property, subject to the court's consent. By contrast,

---

[150] 1963 Act, s.277(2).
[151] *Measures Bros Ltd v Measures* [1910] 2 Ch. 248.
[152] 1963 Act, s.231.
[153] 1963 Act, s.228(c).
[154] [1980] I.R. 237.

in *Re Hibernian Transport Co.*,[155] acting under the court's direction the liquidator accepted one offer but, before the court confirmed the sale, a higher offer was made. It was held that it would be a breach of faith for the court to go back on the earlier bargain. Where the liquidator went about the matter without any prior reference to the court, then if his action is subsequently questioned, the court "would only have been concerned to see whether he acted bona fide and in due discharge of his duties as liquidator".[156]

Provisional Liquidator

23–72　In an appropriate case before ordering a winding up, the court may appoint a provisional liquidator.[157] An application of this nature may be made *ex parte* unless the court otherwise directs. Where a provisional liquidator is appointed the court will stipulate what his powers and functions shall be and the property over which he is given control. The grounds normally relied upon for seeking such an appointment are that there is a significant danger of the company's assets being dissipated by the present directors and shareholders prior to the actual hearing of the petition. An application of this nature may be made at any time up to the date of the hearing and, indeed, also if the court's decision on the petition is being appealed. Once one is appointed, the directors become displaced and control of the company's affairs vests in the provisional liquidator; the practical effect being that the company's business becomes virtually paralysed. However, in special circumstances, the provisional liquidator may be authorised to manage the business for the time being.

23–73　The principal duty of the provisional liquidator is to take into his custody or under his control all the property and things in action to which the company is or appears to be entitled.[158] This is done with a view to protecting and preserving these assets for the benefit of all who will share in the ultimate realisation of them. His primary function therefore is to maintain the *status quo* pending determination of the winding-up proceedings. It has been observed that the term "provisional" here implies a qualification of the tenure of a liquidator's office and not of his powers. Nevertheless, he is confined to the powers which have actually been conferred on him and, even if there are no express restrictions on them, he must not proceed with a *de facto* winding-up. In exercising whatever powers were conferred on him, he is always under the control of the court.

The Director

23–74　Part 5 (ss.43–58) of the 2001 Act confers a variety of functions and powers on the DCE in the context of liquidations. On being notified of a liquidator's appointment, the Registrar of Companies must send a copy of the notice to the DCE. If the company is insolvent, the liquidator must also make a report to him on, *inter alia*, the conduct of the directors. The DCE is entitled

---

[155] [1972] I.R. 190.
[156] *Van Hool* case [1980] I.R. 234 at 240.
[157] 1963 Act, s.226.
[158] 1963 Act, s.229(1).

to require the liquidator to produce the company's books and records to him for examination, and further can apply for a court order that he may inspect them. He can apply to have absconding company officers arrested and detained, and their papers and personal property seized, and also to prevent them from removing their assets from the State or otherwise reducing them. He is authorised to be involved in court examinations of company officers and of others connected with the company, and to institute misfeasance proceedings against officers. He may apply to have directors restricted or disqualified from acting as such. He will be joined as a notice party to applications for relief from restriction or disqualification.[159] Where in the course of the liquidation the court encounters evidence of a criminal offence and refers the matter to the DCE, the liquidator must assist him by affording access to documents and other information, and to furnish all other assistance in the prosecution.

Conduct of the Liquidation

23–75 Where a compulsory liquidation is ordered, it is deemed to have commenced not as of the date of the court's order but from the time the winding-up petition was filed in the Central Office.[160] Accordingly, several kinds of transaction which took place between those dates may be void or voidable and may require to be sanctioned by the court.[161] A statement of the company's affairs which is verified by one or more of the company's officers must be filed by them in the court.[162] It must show the particulars of the company's assets, debts and liabilities; the names, addresses and occupations of its creditors; the securities held by its creditors and the dates when those securities were given; and any additional information that the court may stipulate. Every creditor or contributory is entitled to inspect the company's books and papers.[163]

23–76 Conduct of the winding-up is then left in the hands of the liquidator.[164] Usually the court will direct him to call a meeting of the creditors, or meetings of the creditors and contributories, to appoint a committee of inspection whose function it is to act with the liquidator.[165] Where at any time it is proved to the court's satisfaction that the winding-up should be stayed or the winding-up order should be annulled, the court may direct a stay or an annulment on such terms as it thinks fit.[166]

23–77 As soon as may be after the winding-up order is made, the liquidator must settle a list of contributories with a view to making calls, where shares are not fully paid up, and to adjusting rights between contributories.[167] At the

---

[159] *Re CMC (Ireland) Ltd* (2005) I.E.H.C. 340; unreported, Finlay Geoghegan J., October 24, 2005
[160] 1963 Act, s.220(2).
[161] 1963 Act, s.218.
[162] 1963 Act, s.224.
[163] 1963 Act, s.243.
[164] 1963 Act, s.231. See generally, Forde and Keay/McPherson, fn.1 above.
[165] 1963 Act, ss.232 and 233.
[166] 1963 Act, s.234.
[167] 1963 Act, ss.235, 237 and 238.

same time the liquidator must "cause the assets of the company to be collected and applied in discharge of its liabilities."[168] To this end, the court may, *inter alia*, order that any money, property or papers to which the company is *prima facie* entitled to be transferred to the liquidator and order that any money owing to the company be paid into a designated bank account.[169] The court may fix a time or times within which creditors must prove their debts or claims against the company[170]; those not proven in time are excluded from the benefit of any distribution. The court is empowered to order that any officer of the company attend a meeting of the creditors, contributories or committee of inspection in order to give them such information about the company as they need.[171] It moreover may summon before it and examine on oath any company officer or debtor, or person it believes is capable of providing information regarding the company[172]; what may be referred to as the liquidation *inquisitionsprozess*. And where it suspects that any contributory is about to abscond or to remove or conceal property, so as to evade paying calls or avoid being examined about the company, the court may order that he be arrested and detained, and that his property, books and papers be seized.[173]

23–78   Those creditors who have proved their debts or claims must be paid off in accordance with the priorities that are explained below.[174] Any rights between the contributories must then be adjusted and, if there is a surplus, it must be distributed among those members who are entitled to it.

Informal Liquidation

23–79   Companies short-circuit the statutory procedures by seeking to in effect wind themselves up without going through the requisite formalities. In *Davidson v King*,[175] the company had not traded for several years but was never wound up. The shareholders then decided to dispose of its entire assets and, from the proceeds, to pay themselves a dividend of 330 per cent. All that remained in the company thereafter was an amount equivalent to its issued share capital. Dealing with the question whether that large dividend should be treated as income or capital coming into a settlement, it was held that it was capital. This was because "the whole operations of this company … were realisation and liquidation and not trading or carrying on of the business of the company authorised by their memorandum of association."[176] According to Wilson J, he could "find no case where a limited company has been held entitled to realise its entire assets and after setting aside its nominal capital and paying its liabilities, to divide the surplus as income or profits under the guise

---

[168] 1963 Act, s.235(1).
[169] 1963 Act, s.239.
[170] 1963 Act, s.241.
[171] 1963 Act, s.246.
[172] 1963 Act, s.245.
[173] 1963 Act, s.247.
[174] See para.24–128 *et seq.*
[175] [1927] N.I. 1.
[176] *ibid.* at 11.

of declaring a dividend."[177] Taking such steps, it was said, "would be a fraud on the winding up provisions of the Companies Act."[178]

23–80 Notwithstanding these remarks, the practice is quite common of shareholders leaving behind their companies as defunct shells with hardly any assets in them and not liquidating them. Usually, they do not want to incur the cost of having a liquidator appointed. And if the company has creditors, usually it has so few assets that there seems little point in them petitioning the court to have it wound up. Eventually the company will be struck off the companies' register for failure to file returns.[179] Usually that will be the end of the matter for all practical purposes, although companies which have been struck off in this manner can be restored to the register in an appropriate case within twenty years of the strike off date.[180] Directors of companies struck off for failure to file annual returns may be disqualified for five years, unless they can show the Company had no liabilities at the time of dissolution.[181]

23–81 That practice is now discouraged by applying several of the main liquidation rules to companies which have been practically abandoned in this manner.[182] This applies if the company is insolvent or an attempt to execute a judgment against its property was unsuccessful and the reason, or main reason, why it is not being wound up is the insufficiency of its assets. Where it appears to the court that a company meets this description, several provisions of the Companies Acts, which normally apply only in liquidations, are made applicable to the company, its officers and property.[183]

Termination of Liquidation

23–82 In appropriate circumstances it is possible to have a liquidation annulled by the court or to have its progress stayed. Otherwise the liquidator is required to conclude the process, which leads to the company's dissolution. Within two years of the date of dissolution, it is possible to have the company resuscitated.

Annulling

23–83 The court may annul an official liquidation on such terms as the court deems fit.[184] Either the liquidator, any creditor or a contributory may apply for an annulment and the order will be made "on proof to the satisfaction of the court" that the winding-up should be terminated in this manner. There are no reported cases which deal with the circumstances in which an order will be

---

[177] *ibid.* at 12.
[178] *ibid.* at 12 Similarly, *MacPherson v European Strategic Bureau Ltd* [2000] 2 B.C.L.C. 683; *cf. Neville v Wilson* [1996] 2 B.C.L.C. 310.
[179] See para.23–96 *et seq.*
[180] See para.23–104 *et seq.*
[181] 1990 Act, s.160(h). For example, *DCE v McDonnell* [2005] 1 I.R. 503.
[182] 1990 Act, s. 251.
[183] See para.20–16 *et seq.*
[184] 1963 Act, s. 234(1).

made or the terms such an order might include. It was held by Carroll J in *Re Oakthorpe Holdings Ltd*[185] that the court has a jurisdiction to annul a voluntary winding-up. There an annulment was granted because the company's directors had not filed the statutory declaration of solvency in accordance with the requirements laid down.

Staying

23–84   The court may stay an official liquidation on such terms as it deems fit.[186] On several occasions this power has been applied to voluntary winding-ups.[187] It would seem that a voluntary winding-up cannot be stayed by the members of the company passing a resolution to that effect—or by such a resolution from the members and the creditors.

23–85   Applications for a stay are usually made to give effect to some scheme of arrangement with the creditors or agreed plan for reconstruction of the company; also where the company has succeeded in paying off all of its debts in full. A stay will be granted "on proof to the satisfaction to the court" that an order should be made. In exercising its jurisdiction, the court is guided by the criteria it follows when ordering that a bankruptcy sequestration should be annulled. This order will not be made merely because that is what all the creditors want or support. As explained in *Re Telescriptor Syndicate Ltd*,[188] before it would grant a stay the court must consider "not only whether what is proposed is for the benefit of the creditors, but also whether it is conducive or detrimental to commercial morality and to the interests of the public at large."[189] For instance, if the company's affairs are or ought to be under investigation, or misfeasance proceedings ought to be commenced, a stay will not be ordered. In Australia it has been held that a stay will never be granted if there is a substantial deficiency between the company's assets and liabilities, even where a scheme of arrangement has been put together which would render the company no longer insolvent.[190] However, these cases may have turned on the fact that the objective of the reorganisation schemes there was to obtain a substantial tax windfall.

Concluding

23–86   When all the assets have been realised and the creditors have been paid whatever dividend was due to them, in full if they were that fortunate, and any surplus is appropriately distributed, the liquidator will take steps to bring the liquidation to an end. In the case of official liquidations, there is no express requirement to hold final meetings of the company's creditors or members. Of course the liquidator could always convene such meetings. Usually what happens is that, having passed his final account, the official liquidator applies to the court

---

[185] [1987] I.R. 632.

[186] 1963 Act, s.234(2).

[187] Via 1963 Act, s.280.

[188] [1903] 1 Ch. 174.

[189] *ibid.* at 180; *cf. Re Calgary & Edmonton Land Co.* [1975] 1 W.L.R. 355.

[190] *Re Data Homes Pty Ltd* [1972] 2 N.S.W.L.R. 23.

for directions regarding how the balance should be disposed of. Then, once the Examiner has certified that the balance was dealt with in the manner so directed, the liquidator will then apply to the court for an order dissolving the company.

23–87 In creditors' voluntary liquidations, final meetings of the members and of the creditors must be convened.[191] Details of those meetings must be advertised in two daily newspapers circulating in the district where the company's registered office is located. An account of the liquidation must be given at those meetings and questions about it must be answered by the liquidator. Within a week of those meetings, a return must be made to the Registrar of Companies, stating that they were held, which should be accompanied by the liquidator's account presented at them.

23–88 A compulsory liquidation is deemed to have ended when the court's order dissolving the company has been notified to the Registrar of Companies.[192] A voluntary winding-up ordinarily ends at the date of dissolution. However, it continues if the liquidator retains funds which remain to be claimed or distributed, until they are either distributed or are paid into the Companies Liquidation Account.[193]

Dissolution of the Company

23–89 Dissolution of the company is the final step in the liquidation; from that time onwards, the company has ceased to exist, unless is subsequently resuscitated.

Procedure

23–90 The procedure for dissolving a company varies depending whether the liquidation is compulsory or is voluntary. Where the company is being wound up by the court and its affairs have been "completely wound up, the liquidator may apply to the court for the company's dissolution." An order may then be made that it be dissolved as from that date.

23–91 In the case of voluntary liquidations, dissolution occurs three months from the time the Registrar of Companies has received the liquidator's return and account. This applies even if in fact the company's affairs had not been fully wound up if, so far as the liquidator was aware, they had been wound up. Once "the liquidator has done all that he can to wind up the company, when he has disposed of the assets as far as he can realise them, got in the calls as far as he can enforce them, paid the debts as far as he is aware of them, and has done all that he can do in winding-up the affairs, so that he has completed his business so far as he can, and is *functus officio*",[194] the prerequisites have been fully met.

---

[191] 1963 Act, s.273.
[192] 1963 Act, s.307.
[193] 1963 Act, s.273(4).
[194] *Re London & Caledonian Ins. Co.* (1878) 11 Ch D 140 at 144. See too *Re Cornish Manures Ltd* [1967] 1 W.L.R. 807.

Effects of dissolution

23–92 Dissolution destroys the company's very existence. According to Blackstone,[195] the debts either to or by the corporation are entirely extinguished by its dissolution. Actions cannot any longer be brought by the company or against it. An application made in the course of a winding-up cannot be dealt with by the court, which no longer has any jurisdiction to wind it up. Formerly, the company's remaining real property devolved to the Crown by way of escheat and its personal property by way of *bona vacantia*. Under the State Property Act 1954, the property now vests in the State.[196] An exception to this principle is property which the company was holding in trust[197] or had given as security.

Unclaimed Amounts

23–93 It occasionally happens where a company is being wound up that, after paying off the creditors and distributing the surplus, it still has funds because all the liabilities that were admitted to proof have not been claimed or some of the surplus has not been claimed. Where that occurs in the case of a company that is being wound up voluntarily, the unclaimed sums must be lodged to the Companies Liquidation Account which is kept at the Bank of Ireland, and which is under the court's control.[198] The Winding Up Rules sets out the procedure for lodging funds to that account and how claims made in respect of such sums are dealt with.[199] Where a sum is not claimed within seven years of its being lodged, it must be paid into the Exchequer. However, if later the court is satisfied that an applicant is entitled to money paid over in this manner, it will order the Minister for Finance to pay that money to the applicant.

Disposing of Company Records

23–94 Where the company is being wound up compulsorily,[200] the court will direct how the liquidator shall dispose of the company's records. In the case of a voluntary winding-up,[201] the ultimate disposal of the records is determined by a special resolution of the company if it is a members' voluntary winding-up. In a creditors' voluntary winding-up, the determination is by the committee of inspection or by the creditors, if there is no committee; in the absence of any such determination the decision is the liquidator's, who can dispose of the records "as he thinks fit". However, during the three years immediately following the company's dissolution the records must be kept by the liquidator, who has absolute control over them.

---

[195] *Commentaries on the Law of England* (1765), Vol.1, Ch.18.
[196] Section 28; *cf. Re Clarke's of Ranelagh Ltd* [2004] 3 I.R. 264.
[197] *Re Heidelstone Co. Ltd* [2006] I.E.H.C. 408; unreported, Laffoy J., November 24, 2006.
[198] 1963 Act, s.307.
[199] RSC Ord.74, r.131.
[200] 1963 Act, s.305(1)(a).
[201] 1963 Act, s.305(1)(b).

STRIKING COMPANIES OFF THE REGISTER

23–95   An alternative process whereby the existence of a company comes to an end is where, on several specified statutory grounds, it is struck off the Register of Companies. Where a company had little or no assets, in the past it was common for the directors to allow it become defunct, until eventually it was struck off by the Registrar of Companies. That practice is now strongly discouraged, and allowing their company to be struck off can be a basis for imposing disqualification on directors who have persistently failed to make returns.

23–96   The Registrar may dissolve a company by striking it off on the grounds that it is defunct or that it has failed to make annual returns for one or more years.[202] If a company fails to make a return for one or more years, he may write to it to state that, unless all outstanding returns are made within one month, a notice will be published in the *Gazette* with a view to striking the name of the company off the register. If he is told that the company is not carrying on business, or does not receive all annual returns which are outstanding, he may publish in the *Gazette* a notice stating that, after one month, the name of the company will be struck off, and the company will be dissolved. Thereafter, unless cause to the contrary is previously shown by the company, he may strike its name off the register and shall publish notice thereof in the *Gazette*. On the publication of this notice, the company stands dissolved.

23–97   Another ground is where the Registrar has reasonable cause to believe that the company is being wound up but no liquidator appears to be acting, or that the company has been fully wound up and the returns required to be made by a liquidator have not been made for six consecutive months.[203] Still another ground is where a company does not send to the Revenue a statement of particulars concerning its affairs and business, required for corporation tax purposes, the Revenue may give notice of same to the Registrar.[204] Should the company fail to deliver this statement within one month of a follow-up warning letter from the Registrar, the process of strike off and dissolution will follow. The Registrar may also strike off a company for having no recorded directors,[205] or for not having at least one Irish-resident director.[206] Where a Plc was not, within a year of its incorporation, issued with a certificate from the Registrar entitling it to do business, on following certain procedures he may strike it from the register unless it gets that certificate.[207]

23–98   That the name of a company has been struck off does not affect the power of the court to wind it up.[208] The striking off of a company does not

---

[202] 1963 Act, s.311 and 1982 Act, s.12.
[203] 1963 Act, s.311(3).
[204] 1963 Act, s.311(7).
[205] 1999 (No.2) Act, s.48.
[206] 1999 (No.2) Act, s.43.
[207] 1983 Act, s.8.
[208] 1963 Act, s.311(7).

affect the liability of its directors, officers or members, which continues and may be enforced as if the company had not been dissolved in this manner.[209] Under s.28 of the State Property Act 1954, all property of a dissolved company automatically vests in the State and is held by the Minister for Finance.

RESUSCITATING DISSOLVED COMPANIES

23–99 For a comparatively short period after a company has been liquidated and then dissolved, it can be restored by court order to the register of companies. Where the company has been struck off, it may be returned either by way of administrative procedure or court order.

Set Aside Dissolution

23–100 If the liquidated company's affairs had not in fact been fully wound up, its dissolution and the drastic ensuing effects sometimes can cause considerable hardship. After the dissolution takes place, a person may discover that he has a claim against the company; for instance, for personal injury or other damage that has not manifested itself previously. Over the years, suggestions were made that a dissolution might be set aside where it was caused by fraud or possibly where no reasonable liquidator would have concluded that the company's affairs had been fully wound up. In 1907 a procedure was introduced for in effect resuscitating dissolved companies.[210] Today, the High Court is empowered to set aside a dissolution within two years of the company having been dissolved.[211] But there is no provision for resuscitation once that period has elapsed, which can lead to anomalous results.[212] This procedure can also be employed where companies have been dissolved for other reasons, as an alternative to s.12B of the 1982 Act.[213]

23–101 The court's resuscitation power is entirely discretionary. Its primary function is to revive the company so as to complete the winding up of its affairs by getting in any outstanding assets and, discharging so far as is possible any remaining liabilities. It was held in *Re Servers of the Blind League*[214] that this power would not be exercised where, as a result, persons would be deprived of a vested interest in an asset acquired otherwise than through the medium of the dissolved company. An application can be made by the liquidator and by any other person "who appears to the court to be interested". Thus a wide category of persons are given *locus standi*, including members and creditors,[215] and even contingent and prospective creditors.[216] For these purposes, the Revenue

---

[209] 1963 Act, s.311(6) and 1982 Act, s.12B(1).

[210] Companies Act 1907, s.31.

[211] 1963 Act, s.310.

[212] For example, *Butler v Broadhead* [1975] 1 Ch. 97 and *Bradley v Eagle Star Insurance Co.* [1989] A.C. 957.

[213] *Re Townreach Ltd* [1995] Ch. 28.

[214] [1960] 1 W.L.R. 564.

[215] *Re Thompson & Riches Ltd* [1981] 1 W.L.R. 682.

[216] *Re Deauville Communications Worldwide Ltd* [2002] 2 I.R. 32.

Commissioners will be regarded as a creditor only where and to the extent that they raised assessments on the company before its date of dissolution.[217] Especially now that tort claims can be proved in a liquidation and the limitation period for undiscovered personal injury torts has been extended appreciably, this period may be far too short.[218]

23–102   Once a company's dissolution is set aside, proceedings may be brought as if it had never been dissolved.[219] But restoration here does not operate to retrospectively validate transactions that took place in the intervening period, purportedly binding the company.[220] Nor will proceedings already taken against the company be retrospectively validated.[221] And in determining whether a claim against the company is statute-barred, the period during which it was dissolved will be taken into account.[222] But company property which had vested in the state by operation of s.24 of the State Property Act 1954, is deemed to never have so vested, and it seems that no order for the re-vesting of such property in the company is necessary.[223]

23–103   After two years from the dissolution date, it would seem that persons with claims against the company cannot obtains any redress, not even if the winding up yielded a large surplus for the shareholders. In *Butler v Broadhead*,[224] the company conveyed land to the plaintiffs and, some time later, it went into a members' voluntary liquidation. Several years later, the plaintiffs discovered that the company never had good title to the land. They sought to sue the shareholders, claiming restitution out of the substantial distributions to them that were made by the liquidator. It was held that the claim should be struck out because statute lays down a procedure for enforcing a company's debts. It would be inconsistent with the rule that all proofs must be lodged in time if redress could be given in an instance like this. The outcome might be different, however, if fraud is involved.

Restoring Struck Off Company

23–104   Even though it has been struck off the Register of Companies and, in one sense, has been dissolved, for the ensuing 20 years the company maintains a contingent existence, in that it (along with others) may apply to have it restored to the Register. Within 12 months of a company being struck off for being in default or for not making returns, application can be made to the Registrar of Companies to have it restored. Provided he has received all annual

---

[217] *Re Nelson Car Hire Ltd* 107 I.L.T.R. 97 (1973) and *Re Supatone (Eire) Ltd* 107 I.L.T.R. 105 (1973).

[218] See generally, Note "Recognising Product Liability Claims at Dissolution", 87 *Columbia L. Rev.* 1048 (1987).

[219] See generally, Keay, "The Pursuit of Legal Proceedings Against Dissolved Companies", [2001] *J. Bus. L.* 405.

[220] [1927] A.C. 252 at 269. See *Framus Plc v CRH Plc* [2000] 2 I.L.R.M. 177.

[221] *Smith v White Knight Laundry Ltd* [2002] 1 W.L.R 616.

[222] *Re C.W. Dixon Ltd* [1947] Ch. 251.

[223] 1963 Act, s.311A and 1982 Act, s.12C.

[224] [1975] Ch. 97.

returns or other particulars outstanding, if any, from the company, he may restore the name to the register.[225] Only the company itself can apply to the Registrar under s.311A, and only members or officers of the company may apply to the Registrar under s.12C; creditors have no standing to apply under either procedure. If more than 12 months have passed since the publication in the *Gazette* of the striking off notice, any application to restore the company must be made to the court.[226]

23–105   At any time within 20 years of the strike-off notice being published in the *Gazette,* application may be made to the High Court to have the company's name restored.[227] Application may be made by the company, by any member or creditor aggrieved, including a contingent or prospective creditor.[228] Any creditor and also the Registrar of Companies may so apply to the Circuit Court.[229] Most often, applications are made by a creditor, to pursue a legal claim against the company. Other instances include to enable the company to pursue a legal claim against a third party or to prove in another company's liquidation. *Re New Ad Advertising Co Ltd.*[230] was an application to enable the applicant to bring proceedings for "oppression". At times, as occurred in *Re Amantiss Enterprises Ltd,*[231] the company was wound up voluntarily, in ignorance of it already having been struck off.

23–106   Third parties may apply to intervene, to resist the application, on the grounds that acceding to it will directly prejudice their rights. Intervention will not be permitted if their case is simply that such claim as the company may assert against them would not succeed. What must be shown, to intervene, is that restoration would prejudice the party's rights irrespective of whether the applicant for restoration had a good claim against the company or the company has some claim against that party.[232] Where a notice party to such application succeeds in having it refused, in appropriate circumstances he will be awarded his costs.[233]

23–107   In exercising the discretion here relevant matters include: (i) will a real advantage accrue to creditors or, if the company is solvent, members if there is restoration, (ii) will some other good purpose be achieved by restoration, (iii) will any prejudice, and if so what, be caused to any person or persons by reason of the restoration, (iv) has the applicant applied with due expedition, (v) do the Registrar of Companies, the Chief State Solicitor and the Revenue

---

[225] 1963 Act, s.311A and 1982 Act, s.12C.
[226] *cf.* E Greir, "Companies Arising from the Dead" 13(5) C.L.P. 129 (2006).
[227] 1963 Act, s.311(8) and 1982 Act, s.12B(3).
[228] *Re Deauville Communications Worldwide Ltd* [2002] 2 I.R. 32.
[229] 1982 Act. s.12B(9)–(11). Circuit Court applications are subject to 1982 Act. s.12B(9) and the Circuit Court Rules (No. 4) (Restoration of Companies to the Register etc.) SI 2003/615. *cf. Re Deauville Communications Worldwide Ltd* [2002] 2 I.R. 32.
[230] [2006] I.E.H.C. 19; unreported, Laffoy J., November 14, 2005.
[231] [2000] 2 I.L.R.M. 177. *cf. Re Townreach Ltd* [1995] Ch. 28.
[232] *Re Jayham Ltd* [1995] 2 B.C.L.C. 455.
[233] *Re Bloomberg Developments Ltd* [2002] 2 I.R. 613.

agree to the restoration, (vi) have the defaults of the company which caused it to be struck off been rectified, and (vii) has the applicant's conduct been such as to make it just to restore? In all such applications, the presumption is in favour of restoration.[234] It was stated in *Re Priceland Ltd* that "the court would be very wary of refusing restoration so as to penalise a particular applicant or in a possibly futile attempt to safeguard the special interests of a single or limited class of affected persons".[235] Because restoration there would have operated to validate a rent review notice, thereby leaving the third party's tenant very substantially worse off, was held not to be a sufficient ground to refuse re-registration. That was because the financial loss that the party would suffer "is not caused by the striking off followed by restoration. It is simply a result of the terms of the lease it entered into. It is not unfair prejudice to keep the tenant to the terms of his lease."[236]

23–108 On so ordering, the court may "give such directions and make such provisions as seem just for placing the company and all other persons in the same position as nearly they may be"[237] as if the company had never been struck off. But the court cannot stipulate that the retrospective operation of its order should be restricted in some way, for instance in ease of some third party objector who stood to be prejudiced to an extent. In *Re Amantiss Enterprises Ltd*,[238] athough the company had been struck off in 1993 and put into voluntary liquidation in 1994, in 1996 it brought proceedings against third parties for breach of the Competition Acts. In 1999, the company applied to be restored to the register. While not opposing registration *per se*, the third parties contended that the order should not operate to validate the liquidation and subsequent institution of proceedings. But O'Neill J. held that there was no jurisdiction to qualify his order in that manner because the only directions that may be given are ones that support or complement the statutory fiction that the company's existence continued throughout.[239]

23–109 The order restoring the company must be lodged with the Registrar of Companies "forthwith" and, at the very outside, within three months of the date it was pronounced. Unless that is done in time, the order automatically lapses.[240]

23–110 Restoration to the register operates retrospectively.[241] Without qualification, it even can have the effect of relieving directors of personal liability. For instance, in *Re Richmond Building Products Ltd*,[242] a party

---

[234] *Re Priceland Ltd* [1997] 1 B.C.L.C. 467.
[235] *ibid.* at 477.
[236] *ibid.* Similarly *Re Amantiss Enterprises Ltd* [2005] 2 I.L.R.M. 177 and *Re Blue Note Enterprises Ltd* [2001] 2 B.C.L.C. 427.
[237] 1963 Act, s.311(8) and 1982 Act, s.12B(3).
[238] [2000] 2 I.L.R.M. 177.
[239] Similarly *Re Priceland Ltd* [1997] 1 B.C.L.C. 467.
[240] *Re Barrowland Ltd* [2004] 3 I.R. 27.
[241] *Tymans Ltd v Craven* [1952] 2 Q.B. 100 and *Clark v Libra Developments Ltd* [1007] 2 N.Z.L.R. 709.
[242] [2005] 3 I.R. 321.

purportedly sold goods to a company at a time when, unknown to him, it had been struck off. In those circumstances, the "directors" who dealt with him were personally liable. But when subsequently the company had been restored, Finnegan P. held that the effect of the court's order was to relieve them entirely of their liability and that the party's only avenue of redress was directly against the company. However, when ordering restoration, the court is now empowered to order that, in respect of a debt or liability incurred by the company during the period in which it was struck off, one or more officers of the company shall be liable for it, in whole or in part.[243]

23–111   Where, not knowing that it was struck off, a company commences proceedings, and the defence is that the action cannot be maintained, ordinarily they should be adjourned to enable the company to apply for restoration to the register, should it be indicated that this was its intention. That the company may be impecunious and later may not satisfy an order for security for costs is no reason for refusing the adjournment.[244]

---

[243] 1963 Act, s.311(8A).
[244] *Top Creative Ltd v St. Albans District Council* [2000] 2 B.C.L.C. 379.

CHAPTER 24

INSOLVENCY

24–01 Where a company is insolvent or is at risk of becoming insolvent, three legal regimes principally are potentially applicable, being receivership, examination and winding up.[1] Receivership, which strictly is not contingent on a company being or about to become insolvent, is a predominantly non-statutory mechanism, whereas the other two are governed almost entirely by the Companies (Amendment) Act 1990 and by Pt VI (ss.206–313) of the 1963 Act, respectively. The principal features of the insolvency regime are summarised here, and the several specialist works on insolvency and liquidations, and the ranking of creditors, should be consulted for a fuller account.

RECEIVERS

24–02 One way in which creditors may be able to enforce their security is by having a receiver or receivers of the charged assets appointed.[2] Debentures given by companies, especially where they grant a floating charge, often authorise the debenture-holder to appoint a receiver and manager in the event of default and the like. At times receivership is used not simply as a means of reimbursing creditors but more as a device for re-organising insolvent companies, so as to salvage their viable parts for the benefit of those involved. But the legal position of receivers somewhat restricts their effectiveness as company doctors. In recent years investor interests have expressed concern at the undue haste with which some creditors resort to receivership, thereby virtually wrecking inherently sound businesses that are temporarily short of funds; criticism has also been levelled at the way some receivers actually go about their task. Not too long ago the prevailing judicial response to those concerns was summed up by saying that "the moral of the matter is this, if you depend exclusively on borrowed money for the business you propose to carry on, you must at all costs retain the confidence of your lender".[3]

---

[1] See generally, M. Forde, *The Law of Company Insolvency* (Dublin: Round Hall, 1993) and R. Goode, *Principles of Corporate Insolvency Law*, 3rd edn (London: Thomson Sweet & Maxwell, 2005).

[2] See generally, M. Forde, *ibid.*, Part I, J. Breslin (with K. Smith) *Banking Law*, 2nd edn (Dublin: Thomson Round Hall) Ch.17, G. Lightman and G. Moss, *The Law of Administrators and Receivers of Companies*, 4th edn (London: Thomson Sweet & Maxwell, 2007) and H. Picarda, *The Law Relating to Receivers, Managers and Administrators*, 4th edn (Haywards Heath: Tottel Publishing, 2002).

[3] *Re B. Johnson & Co (Builders) Ltd* [1955] Ch. 634 at 651.

24–03   Part VII (ss.314–323) of the 1963 Act, as amended in 1990, regulates the position of receivers to some extent. However, their status, powers and duties are based primarily on non statutory sources; those rules have mainly been devised by the courts, applying general contract law and equitable principles to this context.

Receivers' Appointment and Tenure

24–04   The High Court possesses an inherent power to appoint a receiver over charged assets and will do so, for instance, where a winding-up of the company commences or where the creditor's security is put in jeopardy. By jeopardy is meant a risk of the assets in question being seized or taken to pay claims that are not truly prior to the security-holder's. But the fact that the company at the time is insolvent, or that the security if then realised would not cover the amount of the debt, does not of itself justify appointing a receiver.

24–05   Usually the debenture itself will authorise the creditor to appoint a receiver; then the creditor can designate someone as receiver once the conditions for exercising that power are satisfied, without ever resorting to the court. The vast majority of company receiverships take this form and the designated grounds for making an appointment are almost identical in most debentures. An appointment cannot be made for a reason outside of those grounds. For instance, unless the debenture authorises an appointment because the security is in jeopardy, the creditor cannot appoint a receiver for that reason; instead, he should apply to the court to have one appointed. The person who obtained the court order or who under the debenture made the appointment must publish the fact in the *Gazette* and in at least one daily newspaper circulating in the district, and also must notify the Registrar of Companies.[4] Where the Registrar becomes aware of a receiver being appointed, he must notify the DCE.[5]

24–06   A body corporate cannot be a receiver of company property, nor may an "undischarged bankrupt" act as one.[6] Persons who were closely connected with the company's management are disqualified from being its receiver; these are anyone who, within 12 months prior to the appointment, was an officer, servant or auditor of the company, or of any of its closely-associated companies—including any partner, employee, parent, spouse, brother, sister or child of such person.[7] A person who acted as a receiver can be the subject of a disqualification order.

24–07   The court determines the court-appointed receiver's remuneration. A company's liquidator, or any of its members or creditors, may apply to the court to fix the remuneration of a receiver appointed under any instrument, notwithstanding that the instrument purports to fix the remuneration.[8] The court may require reimbursal of any excess that was paid over the amount that it fixes.

---

[4]   1963 Act, s.107(1) and Form 53.
[5]   1963 Act, s.319(7).
[6]   1963 Act, ss.314 and 315(1)(a).
[7]   1963 Act, s.315(1).
[8]   1963 Act, s.318.

24–08   A receiver may be removed by the court for "cause shown".[9] Provided he gives one month's notice to the debenture-holder and the company, a receiver appointed under a debenture may resign.[10] A court-appointed receiver may only resign on such terms as the court fixes. On his ceasing to act, the receiver should notify the CRO, submitting an abstract and also his opinion as to whether or not the company is solvent.[11] A copy of this statement must be sent by the Registrar to the DCE.

Consequences of Appointment

24–09   Once a receiver is appointed, floating charges crystallise and become fixed. This prevents the company from dealing with the charged assets without the receiver's consent. Appointment of a receiver operates to suspend the company's powers and the directors' authority in relation to the assets covered by the receivership. As one judge put it:

> "appointment of a receiver and manager over the assets and business of a company does not dissolve or annihilate the company ... but it entirely supersedes the directors in the conduct of its business, deprives it of all power to enter into contracts in relation to that business, or to sell, pledge, or otherwise dispose of the property put into the possession or under the control of the receiver and manager. Its powers in these respects are entirely in abeyance".[12]

However, receivership does not wholly disable the company or the directors from acting. They retain power, for example, to sue in the company's name provided the receiver is indemnified against the costs. A receiver and manager cannot prevent the directors from authorising proceedings against a creditor for breach of contract, in wrongfully putting the company into receivership or for otherwise wrongfully causing it to become insolvent.

24–10   Appointment of a receiver by the court operates to dismiss the company's existing employees, although they may become employed by him. Appointment of a receiver out of court does not of itself automatically terminate employment contracts with the company. There are three qualifications to this principle: employment contracts are terminated where appointment of a receiver is accompanied by a sale of the business, where the receiver enters a new agreement with a particular employee that is inconsistent with the old contract, and where continuation in employment of a particular employee would be inconsistent with the receiver and the manager's very function. The strict contract law position is modified by the European Communities (Safeguarding Employees' Rights on Transfer of Undertakings) Regulations 2003.[13]

---

[9]   1963 Act, s.329.
[10]   1963 Act, s.319(2A).
[11]   1963 Act, s.322C and Form 57.
[12]   *Moss Steamship Co. v Whinney* [1912] A.C. 254 at 263; cited in *Kilgobbin Mink and Stud Farms Ltd v National Credit Company Ltd* [1980] I.R. 175.
[13]   SI 2003/131.

Receivers' Powers

24–11　It is common for debentures, authorising the appointment of receivers, to stipulate that they shall be agents of the company and not simply agents of the secured creditor. But because they have obligations to the latter, it has been held that receivers are in a "unique and exceptional position" in this regard. As stated by Denham J. in *Bula Ltd v Crowley (No. 3)*,[14] they are in "a position unlike that of the ordinary agent in commercial transactions. Thus the receiver is treated, while in the possession of the company's assets, as an agent of the company so that he may deal effectively with third parties. But the receiver is concerned for the benefit of the mortgagee bank to realise the security, which is usually ... by the sale of the assets".[15] For this reason, it was held that possession of assets by a receiver does not constitute "adverse possession" against his appointing creditors, for the purpose of the Statute of Limitations.

24–12　A receiver's function is to do everything necessary to realise the security. Particular powers to this end may be set out in the order of the court, or in the debenture and the instrument under which he was appointed; for instance, to sue in the company's name or otherwise to get in the property charged, to carry on the business and to raise money for that purpose, to realise charged property and execute conveyances in the company's name, and to make such arrangements and compromises as are appropriate. A receiver may bring proceedings to recover assets which were wrongfully taken from the company. Receivers may apply to the court for directions about any aspect of their functions; a similar application may be made by any of the company's officers or members or employees, or by creditors owed more than €1269.70.[16]

24–13　Appointment of a receiver suspends the directors' powers over the assets in question in so far as is necessary for discharging the receiver's functions. Because the authority of a receiver appointed over the entire undertaking is not coterminous with that of the directors, his powers are only as extensive as those provided for in the company's own regulations regarding giving security and the terms of the appointment. Thus, unless the power is expressly granted, a receiver may not use the company's seal. Nor may a receiver petition in the company's name for it to be wound up. If, however, the company is insolvent and a winding-up order would protect its assets, a receiver is empowered, by virtue of his duty to protect the security, to petition for a winding-up.

24–14　A receiver has authority to dispose of the assets that were charged. In *Industrial Development Authority v Moran*,[17] it was held that, although there was no express power given in the debenture there to use the company's seal, nevertheless by virtue of the Conveyancing Act 1881,[18] the receiver could execute an effective conveyance of the company's property. Kenny J. observed

---

[14]　[2003] 1 I.R. 396.
[15]　*ibid.* at 425.
[16]　1990 Act, s.178.
[17]　[1978] I.R. 159.
[18]　44 & 45 Vic. c.41.

that, where the receiver is empowered to carry any such sale into effect by deed in the name of and on behalf of the company, the "more usual and better practice is for him to execute the deed of transfer by writing the name of the company and underneath this to write words that indicate that the name of the company has been written by the receiver as attorney of the company under the power of attorney given by the debenture. In addition, he should execute the deed in his own name. In that way he has the best of both worlds".[19]

24–15 A receiver has one quite remarkable power to, in a sense, frustrate contracts with the company in circumstances where the company itself could not do so. Existing contracts remain binding on the company after a receiver or receiver-manager is appointed. But he is not bound by them and, to an extent, can disregard entirely the company's contractual obligations. This power is particularly useful for what has become known as "hiving down"— which is a method of salvaging the viable parts of the business and disposing of them unencumbered by crippling liabilities. *Airlines Airspares Ltd v Handley Page Ltd* [20] provides an excellent example. An aircraft manufacturer ran into financial difficulties and was put into receivership. It had one aircraft design that, most likely, would be very lucrative. The receiver caused the company to form a subsidiary that would acquire that design; he would then try to sell off the shares in the "clean" subsidiary with the valuable asset, thereby completing the hiving down. The company had entered an agreement under which the plaintiff was to be paid a commission on the sales of the aircraft in question; the plaintiff accordingly sought an injunction to prevent the receiver from selling the shares in the subsidiary. It was held that the receiver was not bound by this commission agreement and could not be prevented from completing his scheme for disposing of the company's viable parts.

24–16 The extent to which receivers in this way can avoid contracts with the company was stated as follows:

> "[T]he receiver, within limit[s] … is in a better position than the company, qua current contracts … [O]therwise almost any unsecured creditor would be able to improve his position and prevent the receiver from carrying out, or at any rate carrying out as sensibly and as equitably as possible, the purpose for which he was appointed … It would not be equitable for the receiver to prefer [one contractor] to other unsecured creditors, and it is in the best interests of all such creditors that he should be able to sell that part of [the company's] business which will constitute a viable unit in the way which will secure the highest price. If, in so doing, he does decline to take over [one] contract, he may, of course, render the [company] liable in damages and may also, to some extent, at any rate, damage their reputation as a trustworthy company which can be expected to honour its contracts. This, however … he is entitled to do, so long as the realisation of the net assets of the company … to the best advantage is not impaired."[21]

---

[19] [1978] I.R. 159 at 166.
[20] [1970] 1 Ch. 193.
[21] *ibid.* at 198–199.

But the fact that the company is in receivership provides it with no defence to an action against it for specific performance of a contract.

Receivers' Duties and Liabilities

24–17 A receiver appointed under a floating charge must be given a statement of the company's affairs and, within two months of obtaining it, he must send a copy to the Registrar of Companies, to the company and to debenture holders or their trustee.[22] And at six-monthly intervals, he must submit to the Registrar of Companies an abstract setting out certain financial information concerning his activities.[23] Where his appointment ceases, that abstract must contain a statement as to whether the company is insolvent, which on receiving it the Registrar must forward to the DCE.[24] On request from the DCE, a receiver must produce for examination his books and records concerning the receivership.[25]

24–18 There are certain "preferential" creditors (the State and company employees) who, in a winding-up, must be paid off before the holder of any floating charge can get paid.[26] A receiver, appointed by the holder of a floating charge, is obliged to pay those creditors from whatever assets are covered by the security in priority to any sums due to the chargee.[27] A receiver who does not ensure that these creditors are satisfied will be held responsible to them in damages for breach of statutory duty.

24–19 Receivers cannot be held liable on contracts existing with the company at the time of their appointment. For instance, in *Ardmore Studios (Ireland) Ltd v Lynch*,[28] it was held that a collective agreement that existed between the company and a trade union did not bind the receiver-manager appointed over the company's assets. Contracts made by receivers in the course of their duties bind them personally unless the contract provides otherwise.[29] But a receiver is entitled to an indemnity out of the company's assets in respect of that liability.

24–20 Receivers are fiduciaries for those who appointed them and owe those persons duties of good faith and to exercise their powers for proper purposes, and also a general duty of care. Receivers appointed out of court also owe a duty of care to the company and to whoever guaranteed the debt that gave rise to the receivership, in respect of exercising their powers of sale. Additionally, there are restrictions on receivers selling valuable assets to persons who were officers of the company within the preceding three years.[30]

---

[22] 1963 Act, s.319(1) and Form No. 17.
[23] 1963 Act, s.319(2) and Form No. 57.
[24] 1963 Act, s.391(2A).
[25] 1963 Act, s.323A.
[26] 1963 Act, s.285.
[27] 1963 Act, s.98.
[28] [1965] I.R. 1.
[29] 1963 Act, s.316(2).
[30] 1963 Act, s.316(2).

In *Standard Chartered Bank Ltd v Walker*,[31] the position at common law was summarised as follows:

> "The receiver is the agent of the company [and] owes [it] a duty to use reasonable care to obtain the best possible price which the circumstances of the case permit. He owes this duty not only to the company ... to clear off as much of its indebtedness to the bank as possible, but he also owes a duty to the guarantor because the guarantor is liable only to the same extent as the company. The more the overdraft is reduced, the better for the guarantor. It may be that the receiver can choose the time of sale within a considerable margin, but he should ... exercise a reasonable degree of care about it ...

> "If it should appear that the ... receiver [has] not used reasonable care to realise the assets to the best advantage, then the mortgagor, the company, and the guarantor are entitled in equity to an allowance. They should be given credit for the amount which the sale should have realised if reasonable care had been used. Their indebtedness is to be reduced accordingly."[32]

24–21 This analysis, which no longer represents the law in England,[33] is complemented by a statutory duty of care, which requires a receiver to exercise all reasonable care to obtain the best price reasonably obtainable as at the time of sale.[34] In determining whether due care was taken, it was emphasised by the Supreme Court in *Re Edenfell Holdings Ltd*[35] that the court should look at the matter from the point of view of the receiver at the time a sale was agreed and in the light of such expert evidence as was available to him then. That it can subsequently be shown that a better price could have been got is not sufficient. Account has to be taken of the fact that, if an offer is rejected by a receiver, the company could incur such additional interest charges and professional fees that would warrant accepting what objectively and with hindsight may have been an under value.[36]

24–22 As regards running the company's business, most debentures provide that receivers appointed under them are empowered, should they choose, to manage the business until such time as the assets are disposed of. But a receiver and manager is under no obligation to carry on the business at the expense of the debenture-holders, even though discontinuance of the business would be detrimental from the company's point of view. It was held previously that a receiver and manager, even when designated as the company's agent, was not an "officer" of the company for the purposes of a misfeasance suit. But this is no longer the case.[37]

---

[31] [1982] 3 All E.R. 938.
[32] *ibid.* at 942.
[33] A thorough survey is provided in *Silven Properties Ltd v Royal Bank of Scotland Plc* [2004] 4 All E.R. 484.
[34] 1963 Act, s.316A.
[35] [1996] 1 I.R. 443.
[36] See too, *Bula Ltd v Crowley (No. 4)* [2003] 2 I.R. 430.
[37] 1990 Act, s.142.

24–23 A receiver is not obliged to provide information to the guarantor of the secured debt or to the other creditors about the proposed selling price of the company's assets. But by being the company's designated agent, circumstances can arise where a receiver has an equitable obligation to render it accounts during the receivership. Receivers who encounter evidence of fraud or other criminal offences are required to disclose that evidence to the Director of Public Prosecutions and to cooperate with him in any resulting prosecution he may bring.[38] A receiver may seek the restriction or disqualification of company directors under certain circumstances.[39] Equally, a receiver may be the subject of disqualification proceedings.

EXAMINERS

24–24 The system of temporary protection, investigation and administration of companies' affairs by court-appointed examiners was introduced by the Companies (Amendment) Act 1990. This was part of the more extensive reform of Company Law which had been before the Oireachtas for several years. But the crisis in Iraq in August 1990 and the impact of those events on the Goodman group of companies caused the Oireachtas to be reconvened and the measure to be enacted within a few days. Significant amendments were made to this Act in 1999.[40]

24–25 What this procedure seeks to achieve is to save all or part of the undertaking and to prevent the company from being wound up. It extends to companies the kind of protection from creditors which individuals enjoy under Pt IV (ss.87–109) of the Bankruptcy Act 1988. It resembles the court administration procedure which has existed in Britain since 1986 and Chapter 11 of the United States Bankruptcy Act, which are aimed at rescuing ailing companies by encouraging a compromise between the claims of the creditors and of the company's owners. It involves an examiner being appointed by the High Court to look into the company's affairs, to see if there is any real prospect of rescuing the business. Among the effects of such an appointment are to freeze all new litigation involving the company and to prevent creditors, secured as well as unsecured, from levying execution against its assets. If there is a reasonable prospect of the company's survival, the examiner reports back to the court and he then seeks to negotiate a compromise between the creditors, the shareholders and the company. When this is voted on by all the parties affected, the arrangement is brought before the court, which will sanction it if it secured a reasonable degree of support, is "fair and equitable" to the parties and is not "unfairly prejudicial" to any creditor or shareholder.

Obtaining Protection

24–26 The procedure for having an examiner appointed is by way of a petition for protection to the High Court.[41] All or any part of these proceedings can be heard

---

[38] 1990 Act, s.179.
[39] 1990 Act, s.150(4A) and s.160(4).
[40] 1999 (No. 2) Act, ss.4–30.
[41] 1990 Amendment Act, s.3 and Rules of the Superior Courts, Ord.75A.

in camera.[42] Creditors' rights are impaired from the very moment the petition is presented. Either the company itself, its directors, any of its creditors or at least one tenth of its members may make the application. It must be accompanied by a report made by an independent accountant into the company's affairs, containing *inter alia* a statement of its affairs, expressing an opinion as to the company's prospects of survival as a going concern, and expressing a view as to whether its continuance would be more advantageous to the members and creditors as a whole than having the company wound up. It is not essential that this report sets out in detail the evidence which led the accountant to his opinion.[43] The applicant must nominate a proposed examiner, who must be someone who would be qualified to be the company's liquidator,[44] and be accompanied by his written consent to so act and also a copy of any proposed compromise that has already been considered. In exceptional circumstances where the independent report cannot be made available in time, the court may make an interim protection order.[45] If a winding-up has already commenced or if a receiver has been appointed to the company for more than three days, the application will not be considered.[46]

24–27   There are two prerequisites for appointing an examiner and thereby giving the company protection.[47] The company must be unable to pay its debts or be likely not to be able to do so. Secondly, the court must be satisfied that "there is a reasonable prospect of the survival of the company and the whole or any part of its undertaking as a going concern". At this juncture, the onus is on the applicant to show that the company has a reasonable prospect of surviving as a going concern. Subject to that, the court has a general discretion. In any such application, every creditor who wishes to be heard is entitled to be heard.[48] An application for protection will not be considered or not be further considered if it appears that the applicant or the independent accountant failed to disclose material information or they otherwise failed to exercise utmost good faith.[49] Nor will an application be acceded to where the proposed rescue package is not one for the survival of the existing business, as for instance in *Re Tuskar Resources Plc*,[50] where what was envisaged was in substance a reverse takeover of the applicant.

Effects of Protection

24–28   Once the petition has been presented, the company comes under the court's protection for the prescribed period. The immediate objective and consequence of protection is to provide the company or companies in question with extensive immunity against its creditors and against claims being made against it or them.

---

42   1990 Amendment Act, s.31.
43   *Re Tuskar Resources Plc* [2001] 1 I.R. 668.
44   1990 Amendment Act, s.28.
45   1990 Amendment Act, s.3A.
46   1990 Amendment Act, ss.2(1) and 3(6).
47   1990 Amendment Act, s.2.
48   1990 Amendment Act, s.3B.
49   1990 Amendment Act, s.4A.
50   [2001] 1 I.R. 668.

Shareholders

24–29   Unless the court gives directions otherwise, protection has no immediate effect on the company's members or shareholders. They can continue
participating in general meetings and may transfer their shares as if nothing
had happened. But no order may be made against it for relief under s.205 of
the 1963 Act against "oppression".[51]

Directors

24–30   The same principle applies to the company's directors; subject to the
court directing otherwise, during the protection they can continue to manage
its business and its affairs. The court may order that all or any of the directors'
powers be exercisable only by the examiner.[52] Moreover, the examiner is
authorised to convene, set the agenda for and to attend board and shareholders'
meetings.[53]

Contracts

24–31   Similarly, the advent of protection ordinarily does not affect subsisting contracts with the company, But goods held by the company under retention of title, a hire purchase agreement, a conditional sale or some other form
of bailment cannot be repossessed.[54] The company may apply to the court
either to affirm or to repudiate outstanding performance of contracts, other
than payment obligations.[55]

Litigation

24–32   Protection insulates the company from fresh litigation unless the court
directs otherwise. No proceedings "in relation to" the company may be commenced without the leave of the court and subject to such terms as the court
fixes.[56] The court readily grants leave to being proceedings, when sought,
although usually putting a stay on any steps following delivery of the statement
of claim. As for proceedings already in being relating to the company, the
examiner is authorised to apply to the court to have them stayed or for any
other order regarding the action.[57]

Company Property

24–33   Unless the court gave directions to the contrary, protection does not
affect the title to the company's property. There is no express provision
whereby title vests in the examiner, although he may be authorised by the court
to engage in transactions with that property, even property which is subject to

---

[51] 1990 Amendment Act, s.5(2)(g).
[52] 1990 Amendment Act, s.9.
[53] 1990 Amendment Act, s.7(2) and (3).
[54] 1990 Amendment Act, s.5(2)(e).
[55] 1990 Amendment Act, s.20.
[56] 1990 Amendment Act, s.5(3).
[57] 1990 Amendment Act, s.5(3).

a charge or is held under a hire purchase agreement.[58] But once the company comes under protection, its property cannot be affected at the behost of its creditors in any of the ways described below.

Creditors' Property

24–34   Where property belonging to a creditor is in the company's possession, he may not be able to recover it while the company is under protection. It was observed that the equivalent English Act "does not ... extinguish any entitlement whether of proprietary or contractual rights. It merely restricts to a substantial extent the enforcement of that entitlement while the [protection] remains in force".[59] Where, during the course of the protection, the company makes use of another's property in one way or another, the value of that use becomes an expense of the entire process which, eventually, must be defrayed from the company's own assets.[60]

Creditors' Remedies

24–35   Most of the remedies which the law affords creditors against their debtors' property are drastically curtailed where that debtor is a company and a petition for its protection has been presented.[61] A creditor who resorts to any of these remedies, while a company enjoys protection, commits contempt of court. If he does so deliberately and conscious of the legal implications, he risks a substantial fine and even imprisonment. Some of these restrictions can be waived by the examiner. Before being repealed in 1999, the right of set-off between bank accounts was restricted.

24–36   *Repossession*: Goods held under retention of title, a hire purchase or a credit sale agreement, or some other form of bailment, do not belong to the company until they have been paid for. But once protection commences, no steps may be taken to repossess such goods if they are in the company's possession, except with the examiner's consent.

24–37   *Enforcing Security*: Unless the examiner consents, no mortgage, lien or other encumbrance over all or part of the company's property can be enforced, in the sense of taking action to realise all or part of the security. Security affected includes those over the company's effects or income.

24–38   *Execution, Attachment, Sequestration and Distress*: The traditional creditors' remedies of execution by the sheriff (or *fieri facias*), attachment, sequestration and distress cannot be "put into force". This term in this context has a precise connotation. In the case of *fieri facias*, execution is enforced only when the sheriff has seized the goods. For all modes of execution, the test is whether proceedings have reached such a stage as the creditor has obtained a

---

[58]   1990 Amendment Act, s.11.
[59]   *Re Atlantic Computers Systems Plc (No. 1 & 2)* [1990] B.C.L.C. 729 at 741.
[60]   1990 Amendment Act, s.11.
[61]   1990 Amendment Act, s.5.

charge over the property. However, it would seem to follow from the previously mentioned restriction that, even when a charge has been so obtained, it cannot be realised—unless the two subsections are mutually exclusive.

24–39   *Judgment Mortgage*: There is no express reference in the 1990 Act to registering a judgment mortgage against the company's land. Such a measure hardly constitutes "action to realise" the security which is prohibited without the examiner's consent.

24–40   *Receiver*: A receiver may not be appointed over the property or undertaking of a company which enjoys protection. As for a receiver who already has been appointed during the preceding three days to all or to any part of the company's property, the court may make such order as it deems fit regarding what he may or should do.[62] In particular, the court may direct that he shall cease to act; that he may act only in respect of certain assets; that he delivers all books and papers and other records regarding the company to the examiner; that he gives the examiner all particulars of his dealings with the company's property or undertaking. In deciding whether to restrict the receiver's activities, the court must be satisfied that there is a reasonable prospect of the company, and all or part of its undertaking, surviving as a going concern.

24–41   *Winding-up*: Once protection commences, no winding-up resolution can be passed nor proceedings for a winding-up be commenced. Where a winding-up petition has already been presented, both petitions should be heard at the one time, except where a provisional liquidator has already been appointed.[63] If there is a provisional liquidator, the court may make such orders as it deems fit regarding what he should or should not do; in particular, that he shall be the examiner as well, that he shall cease to act, that he shall deliver papers concerning the company to the examiner and provide particulars regarding his dealings with the company's property.[64] A direction that he shall cease to act may not be made unless the court is satisfied that there is a reasonable prospect of the company, and all or part of its undertaking, surviving as a going concern.

24–42   *Sureties, Indemnors and the Like*: So long as the company is under protection, persons who have guaranteed or given indemnities for obligations to be performed by it are protected against proceedings concerning the company's liabilities and also against modes of enforcing execution against their property in connection with those obligations.[65] The category of persons who are so protected is defined as those who "under any enactment, rule of law or otherwise [are] liable to pay all or any part of the debts of the company".

---

[62] 1990 Amendment Act, s.6(1).
[63] 1990 Amendment Act, s.6(5).
[64] 1990 Amendment Act, s.6(2).
[65] 1990 Amendment Act, s.25A.

Examiner's Powers and Functions

24–43 The examiner's principal functions are twofold. One is to investigate the affairs of the company and report thereon to the court. Secondly, he must seek to put together some scheme or compromise, which will result in the company's survival, and report thereon to the court. To facilitate carrying out these tasks, the 1990 Act gives him a wide range of powers. Every business letter sent on behalf of the company and every invoice and order for goods must add, after the company's name, the words "in examination, under the Companies (Amendment) Act 1990."[66]

Directors' and Shareholders' Meetings

24–44 An examiner is entitled to reasonable notice of all meetings of the company's directors and of its shareholders, including a description of the business to be transacted.[67] He may convene any such meeting, set the agenda, preside at it, be heard at it, give reports and propose motions.

Powers of Auditors

24–45 All of the rights and powers of the company's auditors are conferred on its examiner.[68]

Production of Documents and Evidence

24–46 The examiner is empowered to get documents and evidence concerning the company's affairs.[69] Obligations to this end are imposed on all officers and agents of the company, and certain other persons. Officers and agents for these purposes include those of any "related company", former officers and agents, and present and past auditors, bankers and solicitors of the company. Regarding former officers and agents, as thus defined, they must produce to the examiner all books and documents concerning the company in their custody or over which they have power. They must attend before the examiner when required to do so, must give him all reasonable assistance in connection with his functions and they may be examined on oath by the examiner, either orally or on written interrogatories.[70] These same obligations apply to any other person who is in possession of any information concerning the company's affairs or who has such information. Any information covered by legal professional privilege does not have to be disclosed. Provision is made for obtaining details of transactions where any director of the company or "connected person" either has or had a bank account, either in his own name or jointly, either in the State or abroad.

---

[66] 1990 Amendment Act, s.12(4).
[67] 1990 Amendment Act, s.7(2) and (3).
[68] 1990 Amendment Act, s.7(1).
[69] 1990 Amendment Act, s.8(1).
[70] 1990 Amendment Act, s.8(4).

Certifying Liabilities

24–47 When a company obtains protection, its suppliers, bankers and others may be reluctant to continue dealing with it, and to extend credit to it, unless their position is duly safeguarded. If they cease dealing with the company, its business may very well collapse rapidly and there may no longer be any viable trading arrangements to be salvaged through a scheme with the creditors. Where the examiner is of the view that, unless particular transactions are entered into, the company's survival as a going concern would be seriously prejudiced, he may certify liabilities the company undertakes in respect of those transactions.[71] This applies only to liabilities incurred during the period when he is the examiner and the certification must be made at the time those liabilities were incurred or were to be incurred. The effect of any such certification is that the liability must be paid in full before any other claim against the company may be paid.[72] Those who extend credit to the company undergoing examination, whose entitlements are duly certified, are thereby virtually guaranteed payment.

Exercising Directors' Powers

24–48 When an examiner is appointed, the court may direct that the directors' powers shall be restricted.[73] Additionally, he may apply to the court to take over all or any of their functions and powers, for instance, to borrow money, to manage all or part of the company's business, and to bring and defend actions involving the company. Before it can make an order of this nature, the court must have regard to the following matters, although what weight or significance is given to them is not indicated, other than that they must show that it is "just and equitable" to confer on the examiner the powers being sought. Those matters are whether the conduct of the company's affairs are calculated to prejudice the interests of either the company, its employees or its creditors as a whole, or whether the interests of those parties would otherwise be safeguarded. Use of the term "interests" here and not just "rights", enables the court to consider a wide range of matters. Others which the court should take into account include whether a transfer of power to the examiner is expedient for preserving the company's assets, whether the company or its directors support a transfer of their powers, and "any other matter in relation to the company the court thinks relevant". When due account is taken of all of these, the question then is whether it is just and equitable to order a divesting of the directors' powers. Conditions may be imposed on any such order and ancillary orders may be made by the court.

Exercising Liquidators' Powers

24–49 Where the court orders that the examiner may exercise all or part of the directors' powers, it may also confer on him all or part of the powers which

---

[71] 1990 Amendment Act, s.10.
[72] 1990 Amendment Act, s.29.
[73] 1990 Amendment Act, s.9.

can be exercised by a liquidator.[74] Examples include disclaiming onerous property and contracts, suing to recover property fraudulently disposed of, and bringing wrongful trading and misfeasance claims.

24–50   The company, not the examiner as such, is empowered to repudiate certain contracts,[75] which resembles the power of disclaimer enjoyed by liquidators. Where the examiner is not a party to the company's application, he must be notified of the fact and may appear and be heard on the matter. It is only contracts the performance of which do not involve paying money that can be repudiated; a payment obligation cannot be ended in this manner. This power is exercisable only when proposals for a scheme or arrangement "are to be formulated"; the Act does not indicate how far advanced these proposals must be. Where the power is exercised, the other contracting party then stands as an unsecured creditor for the damages which ensue from this notional breach of contract. Where, to facilitate acceptance of proposals for a compromise, it is necessary to quantify the damages which would result from repudiating a contract, the court may hear the matter and determine how much the amount of those damages shall be.

Agreeing Claims

24–51   If he is empowered to do so by the court, either directly or by virtue of obtaining the powers of a liquidator, the examiner can ascertain and agree claims against the company.[76]

Disposing of Charged Property

24–52   Not alone are secured creditors prevented from enforcing their security while a company is under protection, but the examiner may dispose of or deal with their security in accordance with prescribed conditions.[77] The criterion for when an examiner is to be permitted by the court to dispose of or to otherwise deal with that property is whether doing so "would be likely to facilitate the survival of the whole or any part of the company as a going concern"; the court must be satisfied that this is indeed the case. When considering such applications, "the court has to make a balancing exercise between the prejudice that would be felt if the order is made by the secured creditor, against the prejudice that would be felt by those interested in the promotion of" this criterion.

24–53   The examiner cannot thereby interfere with the secured creditors' priority or substantially diminish the value of their security. Where that property is sold, the net proceeds of disposal must be applied towards discharging the sum secured. By the sum secured here is meant not alone the capital sum and outstanding interest but any cost which the security-holder is entitled to

---

[74]   1990 Amendment Act, s.9(4).
[75]   1990 Amendment Act, s.20.
[76]   1990 Amendment Act, ss.7(7) and 9(4).
[77]   1990 Amendment Act, s.11.

add in accordance with the general law and the security instrument. If that sum falls below what would have been realised in a free sale in an open market, the difference between the two prices must be applied by the examiner in discharging the secured debt. If the property is replaced by other property, for instance in a floating charge, any replacement is subject to the same order of priority.

Preventing "Detriment" to the Company, a Creditor or Member

24–54 The examiner has an extensive power to take appropriate action to protect the company, any creditor or member from suffering detriment:

> "Where an examiner becomes aware of any actual or proposed act, omission, course of conduct, decision or contract, by or on behalf of the company to which he has been appointed, its officers, employees, members or creditors or by any other person in relation to the income, assets or liabilities of that company which, in his opinion, is or is likely to be to the detriment of the company, or any interested party, he shall, subject to the rights of parties acquiring an interest in good faith and for value in such income, assets or liabilities, have full power to take whatever steps are necessary to halt, prevent or rectify the effects of such act, omission, course of conduct, decision or contract."[78]

Examiners have standing to bring disqualification proceedings in certain circumstances.[79] They may themselves be the subject of a disqualification declaration.

Contracting

24–55 Except where the contract provides otherwise, examiners are personally liable on any contract they enter into in the performance of their functions—whether the contract be in their own name, in the name of the company or otherwise.[80] This is one of the occupational risks of examiners. It is a question of fact whether any particular contract excludes their personal liability. However, an examiner is entitled to an indemnity out of the company's assets in respect of contracts properly entered into by him. That indemnity must be paid, along with his remuneration and expenses, before any other debt of the company can be paid.

Proposals for a Rescue Package

24–56 As soon as is practicable, the examiner must formulate proposals for rescuing the company, then convene and preside over meetings to consider them and report on those to the court.[81] If all of this cannot be done within the 70-day protection period, the court may extend that period for a further 30 days and may thereafter extend it for such further period as is necessary to vote on the proposals and seek confirmation of them.

---

[78] 1990 Amendment Act, s.7(5).
[79] 1990 Act, s.160(4)·
[80] 1990 Amendment Act, s.13(6).
[81] 1990 Amendment Act, s.18.

Contents of Proposals

24–57 Among the matters to be dealt with in those proposals are the following[82]:

- each class of members and of creditors must be specified;

- those classes whose interests will be "impaired" and those classes whose interest will not be impaired must be specified;

- whatever changes should be made in the management and direction of the company, where the examiner considers such changes would facilitate its survival as a going concern;

- whatever changes should be made in the company's memorandum and articles which the examiner considers would facilitate its survival;

- provisions for implementing the proposals;

- a full account of each class meeting and a copy of the proposals put to that meeting.

The only requirement regarding the proposals' intrinsic merits are their equality within classes, i.e. except where the class members agree otherwise, all members of the same class must be treated equally.

24–58 A statement of affairs, as of the date of the proposals, must be attached to them. There must be also be attached to them an estimate of how each class of creditor and member would fare in the event of a liquidation. Additional matters must be included where the court so directs, and the examiner may include such other matters as he deems appropriate.

Consideration of Proposals

24–59 The examiner must then convene meetings of such classes of members and of creditors as he deems appropriate to consider these proposals. There is no express requirement to include with the notices of these meetings copies of the actual proposals and of statements of affairs and estimate of the creditors' position in a liquidation. But the notices must be accompanied by a statement setting out the general effects that the proposals may have on any "material interest" of the company's directors, whether those interests are as directors of the company or as its creditors or otherwise. Where the proposals affect debenture-holders whose affairs are in the hands of trustees, the notices must explain the proposals' effects on those trustees and on any "material interest" they may have.

24–60 Having duly considered them, the various classes[83] must then vote on the proposals. Votes can be cast either in person or by proxy. Even the Revenue Commissioners and other State and local authorities, which generally are not permitted by law to compromise obligations due to them, are authorised to

---

[82] 1990 Amendment Act, s.22.
[83] See paras 11–62 and 11–69.

vote for and accept proposals they otherwise could not accept.[84] This is one of the main differences between rescue schemes under the 1990 Act and schemes of arrangement under s. 201 of the 1963 Act; under the latter, the Revenue are not free to accept bonds, securities and other forms of property in lieu of tax which is due and payable. For the creditors or any class of them to accept the proposals, a majority in both value and number of them is required.[85] If proposals are agreed and some classes of creditors and members accept them, they are then put before the court to be confirmed and made binding on all classes. If agreement cannot be reached on the proposals, the matter goes back to the court, which may direct that the company be wound up.

Confirmation of Proposals

24–61   The last stage in the process is the proposals being set down for consideration by the court.[86] At this hearing, the company and the examiner may appear and be heard; so also may any creditor or member whose interests are impaired. A creditor's interests are impaired if, under the proposals, he is to obtain less than the full amount which was due to him when the protection commenced.[87] A shareholder's interests are impaired if, under the proposals, either the nominal value of his shares is reduced; a fixed dividend to which he is entitled is reduced; his proportionate interest in the entire fixed capital is diminished; he is otherwise to be deprived of all or part of his rights as a shareholder, like voting rights; or he is to lose his entire shareholding.[88] Proposals can be made and confirmed which do not involve impairing any party's interests in the company. In deciding whether to accept the proposals, with or without modification, the following separate hurdles must be crossed. To use the parlance of American corporate reorganisation law, these are the standards against which any "cram down" of the dissenting creditors and members is to be judged.

24–62   *Class Acceptance*: The proposals must have secured acceptance by at least one class of creditors whose interests would be impaired. Acceptance requires a majority in value and in number.

24–63   *Material Irregularity*: One ground of objection which may be raised at the hearing is that there was a "material irregularity" at or in relation to any of the meetings at which the proposals were considered.[89] What deviations from proper procedure would amount to a material irregularity in this context depends on all the circumstances of the case.

24–64   *Improper Means and Improper Purpose*: Two other grounds of objection are that acceptance of the proposals was obtained by improper means

---

[84] 1990 Amendment Act, s.23(5).
[85] 1990 Amendment Act, s.23(4).
[86] 1990 Amendment Act, ss.24 and 25.
[87] 1990 Amendment Act, s.22(5).
[88] 1990 Amendment Act, s.22(6).
[89] 1990 Amendment Act, s.25(1)(a).

or that the proposals were made for an improper purpose.[90] Again, what methods and what objectives would be regarded as improper for these purposes depend on the circumstances of the case.

24–65   *Tax Avoidance*: Where the sole or primary purpose of the scheme is to avoid paying tax, it cannot be confirmed by the court.[91] This gives statutory form to several Australian cases where schemes of arrangement, designed primarily to make substantial gains from the tax losses of insolvent companies, were rejected by the courts. But the mere fact that the proposals, when implemented, will or may give rise to fiscal windfall should not thereby defeat them.

24–66   *Not Unfairly Prejudicial*: The position of individual creditors and shareholders within the various classes will be considered. A party may object on the grounds that the proposals would "unfairly prejudice" his interest and, if that complaint is sustained, the court may not give its sanction to the scheme.[92] By unfair prejudice here presumably is meant that, while a party's class in general may be getting fair and equitable treatment, his special individual circumstances may render that treatment unacceptably harsh. For instance, that person may stand to incur some unique tax penalty, with which fellow class members are not confronted. If this is indeed the case, the only way in which the proposals can be salvaged is for the court to permit departure from the equality-within-the-class principle in respect of that person.

24–67   *Fair and Equitable to Each Class*: Within each class, the members must be treated equally, save where the members agree or the court directs otherwise.[93] That the proposals are unfair and inequitable to a class of members or of creditors is not enumerated as one of the grounds of objection which can be raised at the confirmation hearing.[94] It is possible, however, that the basis for complaint on these grounds can also be used to demonstrate that the proposals "unfairly prejudice" the objector. When it comes to comparing each class, whose interests are impaired, with other classes also being impaired, the burdens which the different classes will bear must be "fair and equitable" in relation to each other. In other words, some classes must not be expected to bear far too great a reduction in their rights while others will be sacrificing very little. It depends on all the circumstances whether any particular class is being treated unfairly and inequitably for these purposes.

24–68   *Guarantees*: Often the scheme will make express provision concerning debts of the company which have been secured by guarantees—usually personal guarantees given by directors and major shareholders. Except where the creditor and the guarantor agrees, liability under a guarantee (or indemnity)

---

[90]   1990 Amendment Act, s.25(1)(b) and (c).
[91]   1990 Amendment Act, s.24(4)(b).
[92]   1990 Amendment Act, s.25(1)(b) and (c).
[93]   1990 Amendment Act, s.22(1)(d).
[94]   1990 Amendment Act, s.24(4)(c)(i).

is not affected by the compromise. But to be entitled to enforce the guarantee after the protection is ended, prior to the consideration meeting, the creditor must notify in writing the guarantor and offer to transfer to him such voting rights as the creditor has in respect of the scheme.[95] If the guarantor accepts that offer, he may so vote on the proposals. Failure to notify the guarantor to this effect prevents the creditor from enforcing the guarantee. Whenever the guarantor makes a payment to the creditor, the guarantor then in effect stands in the creditor's shoes for that amount in respect of the scheme.

24–69 *Leases***:** There also are restrictions on the extent to which a scheme may affect leases of land or of other property having "substantial value".[96] Except where the lessor or owner has agreed in writing, the rent or other periodic payment due may not be reduced, nor may any right of entry, possession, forfeiture or claim in damages for non-payment or breach of covenant be impaired.

Effects of Confirmation

24–70 Court confirmation of the proposals operates to bind the various parties affected by them. Regarding the creditors, on confirmation "the proposals shall … be binding on all the creditors or the classes of creditor, as the case may be, affected by the proposals in respect of any claim or claims against the company".[97] Unlike the position with bankruptcy schemes of arrangement, it is not stipulated that the confirmation binds only those creditors who had notice of the confirmation hearing. All creditors of the affected class, without qualification, are bound by the scheme. If a party who was completely unaware of the proposed scheme can show that the examiner knew of his existence but failed to take reasonable steps to appraise him of the situation, he may possibly have a right of action against the examiner for damages. Court protection comes to an end once the scheme as confirmed comes into effect, or on such earlier date as the court may direct.[98]

Contesting the Confirmation

24–71 The mere fact that a party has not been informed of the examination and thereby was prevented from participating in the decisions is not grounds for setting aside the confirmation. However, if any creditor or member can show that the confirmation was procured by fraud, they can apply to the court within 180 days of the decision to have it revoked.[99] If the court is satisfied that there was fraud, it may revoke its confirmation on such terms as it deems fit. But it is required to have regard for the interests of any bona fide purchaser for value of property without notice who relied on the confirmation. Even if there was no fraud or if the 180 days' period has expired, a confirmation may always

---

[95]   1990 Amendment Act, s.25A.
[96]   1990 Amendment Act, s.25B.
[97]   1990 Amendment Act, s.24(6).
[98]   1990 Amendment Act, s.26.
[99]   1990 Amendment Act, s.27.

be challenged by an application to have the company wound up on just and equitable grounds. For instance, if the proposals envisaged a certain course of action being taken in respect of the company but, without any suggestion of fraud, that action was not taken, the circumstances may very well warrant the company being wound up on just and equitable grounds.

Priority Status of Examiner's Expenses and Certified Liabilities

24–72 Where a scheme of arrangement is approved by the court, ordinarily it will make adequate provision for paying the examiner's remuneration and expenses, and also any liabilities duly certified as necessary to ensure the company's survival at the time. Where, however, no scheme is approved or one is approved but the company nevertheless goes into liquidation, the question arises of the priority ranking of what is owing to the examiner and to creditors with his certificates.

24–73 What is being claimed by the examiner and by certified creditors must first be sanctioned by the court, which may want to satisfy itself that the debts were reasonably incurred and there was no extravagance or waste.[100] For this purpose, examiners are required to make optimum use of the company's own staff and facilities. The sums so approved must be paid either from the company's revenue or from its assets, when realised, including investments. Examiners' remuneration costs and expenses must be paid in full, before any other claim against the company, whether secured or otherwise. Approved certified expenses have a similar priority, but they rank behind claims of creditors who have fixed (as opposed to floating) security. If the company is wound up, both categories of claim have priority over the costs, charges and expenses of the liquidation.

WINDING UP—LIQUIDATION

24–74 Unless a viable rescue scheme is put together by an examiner and obtains the requisite approval, or unless a company's creditors otherwise agree to allow it continue in business, the almost inevitable outcome of a company (not struck off the Register) becoming insolvent is that it will be wound up and a liquidator appointed to administer its affairs. That can be done by way of a creditors' voluntary winding-up or a winding-up by order of the court.[101] Where the company has no substantial assets to fund a liquidation, it may remain dormant until eventually being struck off by the Registrar of Companies. But the DCE can exercise a variety of powers in such circumstances.[102]

---

[100] 1990 Amendment Act, s.29.

[101] See generally, M. Forde, *The Law of Company Insolvency* (Dublin: Round Hall, 1993) Part III and A.R. Keay, *McPherson's Law of Company Liquidation* (London: Sweet & Maxwell, 2001).

[102] See para.20–16 *et seq.*

Commencing Winding Up

24–75 In a creditors' voluntary winding-up,[103] the initiative to wind up is always with the shareholders or members. The process commences where the members resolve to wind up their company but the statutory declaration of solvency has not been made. An ordinary resolution suffices where the grounds are the company's insolvency. Alternatively, the declaration of solvency has been made but creditors apply to the High Court and convince it that the company is unlikely to pay its debts within the 12-month period. Or the liquidator appointed by the members may form the view that the company is insolvent and, in consequence, convenes a creditors' meeting to consider the situation.

24–76 Alternatively the company can be wound up by order of the High Court.[104] Where an examiner cannot obtain agreement on some scheme to rescue a company or such scheme as is adopted does not secure court approval, the court may order that the company be wound up.[105] Occasionally, the company itself and exceptionally one or more of its members may petition to have it wound up on the grounds that it is "unable to pay its debts."[106] More often than not it is one or more of the creditors who seek a windingup on this basis. What constitutes insolvency here is mainly inability to meet current demands, i.e. cannot pay the day to day liabilities arising in the ordinary course of the business. That at the time the company possesses no liquid assets whatsoever, or that its liabilities exceed its assets, is not always treated as insolvency. Account will be taken by the court of contingent or prospective liabilities. Two states of affairs are deemed to constitute inability to pay debts, thereby making it much easier to establish that the company is insolvent.[107] One is where execution of a judgment or similar order against the company (notably *fieri facias*) is returned unsatisfied wholly or partly. The other is where a creditor, who is owed at least €1,269.74 by the company, demands in writing to be paid a liquidated sum and the company fails to pay or to satisfactorily secure or compound that debt within three weeks of that demand being made.

24–77 An order to wind up will not be made on these grounds where there is a bona fide dispute about the existence of the debt or the company has a substantial counterclaim.[108] According to one judge, "the winding up jurisdiction is not for the purpose of deciding a disputed debt (*i.e.*, disputed on substantial and not insubstantial grounds) since, until a creditor is established as a creditor he is not entitled to present the petition …".[109] Where it has been presented for some collateral purpose, the court will dismiss the pettition.[110]

---

[103] See paras 23–18 *et seq.*

[104] See paras 23–33 *et seq.*

[105] 1990 Amendment Act, s.24(11).

[106] 1963 Act, s.213(3).

[107] 1963 Act, s.214.

[108] *Re WMG (Toughening) Ltd* [2003] 1 I.R. 389. *cf.* A. Kierse, "Winding-up Petitions: Practical Application of the Stonegate Test" 12(4) *C.L.P.* 91.

[109] *Stonegate Securities Ltd v Gregory* [1980] 1 Ch. 576 at 580.

[110] *Re Bula Ltd* [1990] 1 I.R.440.

Where a creditors' voluntary winding up is in progress, courts hesitate to order a compulsory liquidation.[111] An order will be refused if winding up would be to the detriment of the creditors generally.[112]

The Liquidator

24–78 The nature of a creditors' voluntary winding up, the effects on the company and on those involved with it of the commencement of a winding up, and the functions of liquidators are summarised in the previous chapter. Where the company is insolvent, the liquidator must make a report in the specified format to the DCE within six months of being appointed and also at such other intervals as the DCE shall direct.[113] Between three and five months after submitting this report, the liquidator must apply to have the company's directors restricted.[114] This period may be extended by the court. The DCE may also relieve the liquidator of his obligation to make the application.

Asset-Swelling Measures

24–79 The main purpose of winding up an insolvent company is to pay off its creditors, according to their priorities. In a solvent liquidation, it also is to distribute what remains among the investors, according to their rights to repayment of capital and to participation in any surplus. To these ends, the Companies Acts contain several rules that protect creditors and investors against unfair advantage being taken of the company. There also are rules designed to prevent unfair discrimination between creditors. Although the general law of bankruptcy applies to some aspects of winding up insolvent companies, in *Re Irish Attested Sales Ltd*,[115] it was held that those bankruptcy rules that have the effect of increasing the insolvent's assets available for the creditors are not directly imported. Nevertheless, various provisions either apply or adapt some of those "asset-swelling" rules to company liquidations. Curiously, the Companies Acts do not contain an equivalent of s.58 of the Bankruptcy Act 1988, that strikes at what are termed "transactions at an undervalue".[116]

Arrest/Freeze Orders

24–80 Application can be made to the court for an order to arrest and detain any officer of the company or any contributory, who is about to leave the State or otherwise abscond, or to remove or conceal property, where his purpose is to avoid examination about the company's affairs or evade having to pay calls on his shares.[117] That order may direct that any books, records and moveable property he

---

[111] *Re Zirceram* [2000] 1 B.C.L.C. 751.
[112] *Re Genport Ltd* [1996] I.E.H.C. 34, unreported, McCracken J., November 21, 1996 and [2001] I.E.H.C. 156; unreported, McCracken J., November 6, 2001.
[113] 2001 Act, s.56.
[114] *ibid.* and 1990 Act, s.150.
[115] [1962] I.R. 70.
[116] *cf.* ss.238 and 423 of the UK Insolvency Act 1986 in similar vein. See generally, M. Forde, *Bankruptcy Law in Ireland* (Cork: Mercier Press, 1990), p.135.
[117] 1963 Act, ss.247 and 282D.

has be seized and detained. Additionally, a *Mareva*-type order can be obtained, prohibiting any officer of the company from removing his assets from the State or reducing them below a specified amount, where the applicant has a civil claim and there are grounds for believing that the officer will deal with those assets in a manner that would frustrate enforcement of any court order made in the proceedings.[118]

Examination

24–81   A inquisition on oath into the affairs of the company may be conducted by the court summoning before it any person known or suspected to possesses company property, or who is indebted to the company, and any person it deems capable of giving information about the company's formation, promotion, trade, property, dealings or affairs.[119] Application for an examination can be made, *inter alia*, by the DCE and also by any creditor who can show that the process should accrue some benefit for him.[120] Those persons may be required to produce any documents related to the company that they possess. They also may be required to set out in a written statement an account of transactions between themselves and the company. They moreover may be examined on oath.[121] They may not refuse to answer any question on the grounds of incriminating themselves.[122] But any such answer is not admissible against them in any criminal proceedings,[123] apart from a prosecution for perjury. Information gained from these examinations frequently provides the foundation for misfeasance actions and for proceedings for fraudulent or reckless trading.[124]

24–82   If in the course of an examination of this nature it appears that any person being questioned owes the company money or holds property belonging to it, the court may direct that the money be paid or the property be delivered up to the liquidator.[125] To this end, the court may order that premises be entered, forcibly if necessary, and searched, and that any records there or other property be seized.

Restitution of Assets Fraudulently Disposed Of

24–83   There is a procedure for recovering company property which had been disposed of in any way that defrauded the company, its creditors or its members.[126] Any creditor or contributory of the company, or the liquidator, can apply and, if they satisfy the court that the property was disposed of in that manner, the court is empowered to order its repayment or recovery. That order can

---

[118] 2001 Act, s.55.

[119] 1963 Act, ss.245 and 282B.

[120] *Re Comet Food Machinery Co.* [1999] 1 I.R. 485.

[121] *cf. Re PFTZM Ltd* [1995] 2 B.C.L.C. 354 on the oppressive resort to this power.

[122] *Re National Irish Bank Limited (under investigation) (No. 1)* [1999] 3 I.R. 145.

[123] Section 245(6); *cf. Re Jeffrey S Levitt Ltd* [1992] Ch. 457 and *Bishopsgate Investment Management Ltd v Maxwell* [1993] Ch. 1, holding there is no such principle under a comparable section of the British Act, which does not expressly deal with the point.

[124] e.g. *Re Aluminium Fabricators Ltd* [1984] I.L.R.M. 399.

[125] 1963 Act, ss.245A and 282C.

[126] 1990 Act, s.139.

be made against any person who appears to have the use, control or possession of such property or of the proceeds from its sale, or any development of the property. In deciding to make any order of this nature, account must be taken of the interests of any bona fide purchaser for value of the property.

Fraudulent Conveyance

24–84 Although the Companies Acts do not contain a broad restriction on disposals of an insolvent company's property an under-value, s.10 of the Fraudulent Conveyances Act 1634[127] declares void a wide category of transfers of property by a debtor done with the intention to defraud his creditors. The power to set aside transfers of property on these grounds is not exclusively a bankruptcy jurisdiction. In *Re Kill Inn Motel Ltd*,[128] Murphy J. confirmed that this power applies just as much to property transfers made by companies as by individuals.

Fraudulent Preference

24–85 For centuries it has been acknowledged that it is "unjust to permit a party, on the eve of bankruptcy, to make a voluntary disposition of his property in favour of a particular creditor, leaving the mere husk to the rest, and therefore, that a transfer made at such a period, and under such circumstances, as evidently showed that it was made in contemplation of bankruptcy and in order to favour a particular creditor, should be void".[129] Every transfer and the like by a company of its property, occurring within six months of its being wound up, is rendered void if it was made "in favour of any creditor ... with a view to giving such creditor, or any surety or guarantor for the debt due to such creditor, a preference over the other creditors ...".[130]

24–86 For the transfer or payment to be caught by this, the company must have been insolvent at the time the transfer was made, meaning that it was unable to pay its debts as they fell due. It matters not that the directors believed that the company was solvent, or that its financial position would shortly improve and it would not have to be wound up. Although most preferences involve cash payments, transfers of any kind of property and, it would seem, set-offs, made with the prohibited intention, are caught. A person taking title in good faith and for valuable consideration, through or under a creditor, to property that was fraudulently conveyed is not affected by this rule.

24–87 *Intention to Prefer:* While fraud in this context does not import moral blame, the courts have narrowly construed the *scienter* requirement. It must be

---

[127] 10 Car. 1 sess. 2, c.3. See generally, M. Forde, *Bankruptcy Law in Ireland* (Cork: Mercier Press, 1990) at 115 *et seq*. On the modern version of this in Britain, see J. Armour & H. Bennett eds, *Vulnerable Transactions in Corporate Insolvency* (Oxford: Hart, 2003) Ch.37.

[128] *Ex tempore* judgment of September 16, 1987 (available on www.justis.com).

[129] *Ex p. De Tastet v Carroll* (1813) 1 Stark 88 at 89.

[130] 1963 Act, s.286. See generally, M. Forde, *The Law of Company Insolvency*, at 235 *et seq*; H. Bennett & J. Armour, Ch. 4.

proved that the company's dominant intention was to prefer the transferee over other creditors. The mere fact of preference does not demonstrate this intent; the transaction will be upheld if it was entered into, for example, to withstand pressure being exercised against the company or its directors, or to obtain some advantage for the company. There are certain standard situations where the courts readily infer an improper intention, notably where the company's directors had given personal guarantees for the company's debts and, shortly before the winding-up commenced, they arranged to have those debts paid off and the guarantee cancelled. Another is where the company had agreed to give its creditor a charge once called upon to do so. But there are no hard and fast rules which determine what is improper here; in the end, it depends on all the circumstances of the case whether the company deliberately put one particular creditor at an advantage over all the others for no good business reason in connection with the company's interests.

24–88   In *Re John Daly & Co.*,[131] Porter M.R. said of the *scienter* requirement:

> "A 'view to prefer' is produced in one man's mind by the fact that the creditor is his brother or near relation; in another's because the creditor has been kind to him in the past; in that of a third, because he expects that after his bankruptcy the creditor (if now preferred) will aid him in business once again; in that of a fourth, because it is a first transaction with the creditor, and he thinks his a specially hard case; in that of a fifth, because he thinks his other creditors have treated him harshly. There is always some motive behind the 'view to prefer'. Yet, in cases where there is no trust, no pressure, and no obligation other than contract, neither natural love and affection, gratitude, expectation of benefit, sympathy, vindictiveness, or any other mental condition, can in such cases eliminate the view to prefer, which is the statutory condition of liability, however strongly the debtor may be convinced that he has done what is fair and right in according the preference".[132]

24–89   An improper intention was established in that case where the company, which was in serious financial difficulties, borrowed a substantial sum from its auditor. It was understood that the company would then raise funds, from which the auditor would be repaid. In the event, when the shareholders refused to permit the issue of debentures and following remonstrations by the auditor, he was repaid his loan. Shortly afterwards the company was wound up. It was held that the payment to the auditor was unlawful because no actual pressure was exerted on the company to pay him before the other creditors, and the reasonable inference, therefore, was to benefit him especially.

24–90   *Payments to Connected Person:* In many of the instances where payments were challenged on these grounds, the company had discharged a debt owing to one of its officers or to some other person or body which was closely connected with them. Even where the circumstances would warrant drawing the

---

[131] (1886) 19 L.R. Ir. 83.
[132] *ibid.* at 97.

inference of an improper intention, if the payment was made more than six months before the winding-up had commenced, it could not be challenged on these grounds; the only possibility then would be an attack based on the 1634 Act. This situation was addressed in 1990.[133] Where a payment was made to a "connected person" then the relevant period is extended to two years prior to the liquidation and, additionally, the payment is deemed to be improper unless the contrary is shown. Thus, it is for the connected payee to demonstrate a genuine commercial justification for the company preferring him over all the other creditors. A connected person for these purposes is a director or a shadow director of the company, a person "connected with" a director,[134] a "related company"[135] and also a trustee or surety or guarantor for the debt to any of those parties.

24–91 *Preferring Secured Creditor:* Some protection is afforded, principally to banks that extend credit to a company by an overdraft, that is guaranteed by a director, from unfairly suffering loss in consequence of the fraudulent preference rule. If the company in those circumstances reduced the overdraft, it may very well thereby prefer the bank; the guarantor and the bank would then be obliged to repay those sums to the liquidator. The bank has a statutory right of action against the guarantor as if he had undertaken to be personally liable to the extent of the interest in the security given.

Late Floating Charge

24–92 Invalidating late floating charges is an extension of the general principle underlying fraudulent preferences to a particular situation. There is always a danger that, when a company is getting into financial difficulties, one or more unsecured creditors who are in a strong bargaining position, like the company's bankers, may be able to obtain a charge over its assets and thereby improve their position if the company proves to be insolvent. A floating charge created by a company within 12 months of its being wound up is invalid unless it is proved that the company was solvent immediately after the charge was given.[136] Where the floating charge is given to a "connected person" (for instance, Mr Salomon in the *Salomon & Co.* case),[137] the relevant period for invalidation is extended to two years.

24–93 In *Crowley v Northern Bank Finance Corp.*,[138] it was held that, once the charge was created within the specified period, it is for the chargee to demonstrate that the company was solvent at the time. Solvency in this context means that the company was able to pay its debts as they fell due—not whether a business person would have regarded the company as solvent. To ascertain solvency, an examination of its financial history, both before and after the

---

[133] 1963 Act, s.286 as amended.
[134] 1990 Act, s.26.
[135] 1990 Act, s.140.
[136] 1963 Act ss.288 and 289. See generally, M. Forde, *The Law of Company Insolvency*, at 247 and, Bennett & Armour, *Vulnerable Transactions in Corporate Insolvency*, Ch.5.
[137] [1897] A.C. 22 (H.L.).
[138] [1981] I.R. 353.

charge was given, may be required. Where at that time the directors had intended to carry on the company's business, the company's fixed and movable assets must not be taken into account in determining solvency. But against that, account may be taken of the company's capacity to raise additional funds by borrowing after the charge was given.

24–94   An exception is made for a charge that is given in consideration for cash that was paid to the company either when the charge was created or later. In other words, a charge is not invalid where it was given, not to secure existing debts, but to raise additional funds. It was held in *Re Daniel Murphy Ltd*[139] that the critical time here is not the date the security was actually executed but when the company agreed to create the charge, provided that any delay in executing it was not intended to deceive creditors and was not unreasonably culpable. However, the 1990 amended version of the rule would seem to reverse the position as stated there, subject to a *de minimus* delay between getting the money and granting the charge. It was also held there that the rule in *Clayton's Case*[140] applies in this context. For an ordinary overdraft, this means that all subsequent lodgements first pay off the debit balance, and all subsequent withdrawals are fresh payments by the bank. Accordingly, if enough funds are turned over in the bank account during the 12-month or two-year period, the bank will have obtained a valid charge in respect of substantially what the company owed it at the outset.

24–95   If the chargee moves sufficiently quickly and enforces his security before the company goes into liquidation, he can retain the proceeds of realisation. In *Mace Builders (Glasgow) Ltd v Lunn*,[141] a company gave the defendant a floating charge and, within 12 months of that time, it went into liquidation. In the meantime, however, the chargee had demanded repayment of the sum owing to him, which was not done. He then appointed a receiver, who realised the security and paid off the debt. It was held that the prohibition does not operate retrospectively to invalidate what was done under the charge. In this case the chargee was a related company and, being a "connected person", the relevant period would now be two years before the liquidation. But that circumstance would not have affected the outcome in the case.

24–96   Where a floating charge is created in favour of an "officer" of the company, the exception for cash paid on or after the security being given does not apply. This is designed to prevent evasion by directors and the like, to whom the company was indebted, arranging to have their debt discharged and then obtaining a floating charge to secure fresh advances that the officer would make to the company.

---

[139] [1964] I.R. 1.
[140] (1816) 1 Mer. 572. See M. Forde, *The Law of Company Insolvency*, at 251 *et seq.*
[141] [1986] Ch. 459.

Fraudulent Trading

24–97   Liability for fraudulent trading can arise whether or not the company is insolvent. This wrong involves "knowingly [being] a party to the carrying on of any business of the company with intent to defraud creditors of the company, or creditors of any other person or for any fraudulent purpose".[142] Put briefly, if it is shown that the company was being managed with the intention of defrauding one or more of its creditors, or others, then those who were then running the business can be made responsible. Fraudulent trading is an offence, with a maximum penalty of a €63,487 fine or seven years' imprisonment, or both, where there is a conviction on indictment. It also is a civil wrong and proceedings can be instituted by either any creditor or contributory of the company, or by its liquidator, receiver or examiner. The civil wrong is remedied by imposing unlimited liability for all or part of the company's debts. The contention that the civil liability here was in substance criminal and accordingly was unconstitutional, because the usual procedures for criminal trials did not apply, was rejected by the Supreme Court.[143] Excessive and inexcusable delay in instituting or prosecuting proceedings will result in their being dismissed.[144]

24–98   *Ambit*: *In Re Aluminium Fabricators Ltd (No. 2)*[145], it was discovered that all cash payments made to the company were not recorded in the accounts made available to the auditors, but instead were recorded in a secret register which ultimately disappeared unaccountably from the company's premises. The cash was siphoned off by the two directors to their bank accounts in the Isle of Man, rendering the company hopelessly insolvent. O'Hanlon J. had no hesitation in concluding that the directors should be personally liable without limit for all the company's debts and liabilities. He observed that "[t]he privilege of limitation of liability which is afforded by the Companies Act ... cannot be afforded to those who use a limited company as a cloak or shield beneath which they seek to operate a fraudulent system of carrying on business for their own personal enrichment and advantage".[146]

24–99   In *R. v Grantham*,[147] an appeal against a conviction for fraudulent trading, the requirement of actual dishonesty was stressed:

> "there is nothing wrong in the fact that directors incur credit at a time when, to their knowledge, the company is not able to meet all its liabilities as they fall due. What is manifestly wrong is if directors allow a company to incur credit at a time when the business is being carried on in such circumstances that it is clear that the company will never be able to satisfy its creditors. However, there is nothing to say that directors who genuinely

---

[142] 1963 Act. ss.296 and 297A. See generally, M. Forde, *The Law of Company Insolvency*, at 258 *et seq.*
[143] *O'Keeffe v Ferris* [1997] 3 I.R. 463.
[144] *Southern Mineral Oil Ltd v Cooney* [1997] 3 I.R. 549.
[145] [1984] I.L.R.M. 399; No. 2, unreported, O'Hanlon J., May 13, 1983.
[146] At 17 of judgement of May 13, 1983.
[147] [1984] Q.B. 675.

believe that the clouds will roll away and the sunshine of prosperity will shine upon them again and disperse the fog of their depression are not entitled to incur credit to help them to get over the bad time."[148]

24–100   Although it was said in *Re WC Leitch Bros Ltd (No. 1)*[149] that "if a company continues to carry on business and incur debts at a time when there is to the knowledge of the directors no reasonable prospect of the creditors ever receiving payment of those debts, it is, in general, a proper inference that the company is carrying on business with intent to defraud",[150] the court was dealing with what constitutes evidence of fraud. Since usually it is extremely difficult to prove an actual fraudulent intent, a court often can only draw inferences from facts which do not unambiguously constitute fraud. It remains to be seen how s.40 of the 1983 Act on capital haemorrhages will affect establishing liability under this heading. Simply to prefer one creditor of an insolvent company over another is not fraudulent, not even when the creditor who is preferred is the company's dominant shareholder or its parent company, provided of course that the indebtedness is genuine. The tendency to construe the *scienter* and *mens rea* requirements narrowly is often criticised because, as a result, it is only in the most blatant instances that individuals are held responsible under this heading.

24–101   As for the other ingredients of this wrong, what amounts to carrying on business has been given an extensive meaning. It includes, for example, engaging in one significant commercial transaction, and collecting the assets acquired in the course of the business and distributing the proceeds among the company's debtors.

24–102   Because the civil wrong is also a crime, it was suggested in *Re Kelly's Carpetdrome Ltd*[151] that the burden of proof on plaintiffs is the criminal standard, beyond all reasonable doubt, and not the usual civil standard of the balance of probabilities. It is mainly for this reason and also because of the narrow concept of *scienter* in these cases that few claims for fraudulent trading are brought and even fewer succeed. Where a defendant can show any reasonably plausible explanation for his actions, the claim would usually fail.

24–103   Liability for fraudulent trading is not confined to officers of the company. Those who can be held responsible are any person who at the time was involved in carrying on its business and was knowingly a party to the fraud. A company's creditors—even its bankers—can conceivably be caught. In *Re Gerald Cooper Chemicals Ltd*,[152] it was held that "a creditor is party to the carrying on of a business with intent to defraud creditors if he accepts money which he knows full well has in fact been procured by carrying on the business with intent to defraud creditors for the very purpose of making the payment".[153]

---

[148] *ibid.* at 682, citing an earlier dictum of Buckley J.
[149] [1932] 2 Ch. 71.
[150] *ibid.* at 77.
[151] Unreported, Costello J., July 1, 1983.
[152] [1978] Ch. 262.
[153] *ibid.* at 268. *cf. Re Bank of Credit & Commerce Int'l SA (No.15)* [2005] 2 B.C.L.C. 328.

24–104 *Unlimited Liability:* One of the few instances where a claim succeeded in this country is *Re Hunting Lodges Ltd* [154] Directors and the secretary of a company that was insolvent and that owed large sums to the Revenue Commissioners arranged for the sale of the company's principal undertaking, a public house near Limerick called "Durty Nellies". But the full consideration was not paid to the company; part was diverted into the directors' and the secretary's own bank accounts. Carroll J. held that disposing of the undertaking constituted carrying on business for these purposes and that, in the circumstances, the defendants had the requisite fraudulent intent. However, the extent to which they should be rendered liable for the company's debts was held to depend on their particular circumstances. Two of them were directed to be liable without limit for the entire debts, but two others were made jointly liable only for £12,000, which was the amount diverted to their own benefit. So far, criteria have not been laid down for determining how extensive a personal liability should be imposed on those who have committed fraudulent trading.

Reckless Trading

24–105 The 1990 Act introduced the concept of "reckless trading", which was intended to answer criticisms of the narrow scope of fraudulent trading.[155] When creditors or others are seeking to render persons who managed a company personally responsible for its unpaid debts, applications ordinarily are brought under this heading rather than for fraudulent trading. No declaration of personal liability will be made unless the company is insolvent. Where the alleged wrongdoer was not an "officer" of the company, he can only be pursued for fraudulent trading; an officer for these purposes is defined as including "any auditor, liquidator, receiver or shadow director". Mere employees and agents of the company, and third parties, therefore, cannot be held accountable for reckless trading.

24–106 An application to hold a person accountable for reckless trading may be made by any creditor or contributory of the company, or by the liquidator, receiver or examiner. The applicant must have suffered loss or damage in consequence of the alleged reckless conduct, or he must be representing someone who has so suffered. Because of this requirement, it will be exceptional, if ever at all, that an examiner will make an application. That the action being complained of was performed outside the State or that the respondent may be held criminally responsible for what he has done is no bar to a claim.

24–107 *Ambit:* The kind of conduct which constitutes reckless trading is defined by s.297A as:

> "any person was, while an officer of the company, knowingly a party to the carrying on of any business of the company in a reckless manner ... Without prejudice to the generality of [this definition] an officer of the

---

[154] [1985] I.L.R.M. 75.

[155] 1963 Act, s.297A. See generally, M. Forde, *The Law of Company Insolvency* and Keay, "Wrongful Trading and the Liability of Company Directors: A Theoretical Perspective", [2005] 25 *Legal Studies* 431.

company shall be deemed to have been knowingly a party to the carrying on of any business of the company in a reckless manner if

(a) he was a party to the carrying on of such business and, having regard to the general knowledge, skill and experience that may reasonably be expected of a person in his position, he ought to have known that his actions or those of the company would cause loss to the creditors or the company or any of them, or

(b) he was a party to the contracting of a debt by the company and did not honestly believe on reasonable grounds that the company would be able to pay the debt when in fell due for payment as well as all its other debts (taking into account the contingent and prospective liabilities)."

24–108   Three categories of situation arise. One ((b) above) is where the officer was directly involved in contracting a debt on behalf of the company; for instance, by ordering supplies. If it can be shown that, at that time, he did not honestly believe on reasonable grounds that the company could repay that debt when in fell due, then he was trading recklessly. The exact significance of the phrase "honestly believe" here is not clear; does it mean that the person did not really believe that the debt could be paid, or is it necessary to go further and establish that he had some dishonest intention at the time? It is questionable whether a belief can be either honest or dishonest; whether a belief is held is a pure question of fact on which the good or evil intentions of the believer do not have any bearing.

24–109   Secondly ((a) above), is where the officer was directly involved in carrying on the business in circumstances where either his very actions or those of the company damaged the creditors or any one of them. For instance, he may have contracted a large debt which was repaid but at the expense of one or several of the creditors. Here, to be made liable, it must be shown that, at the time, he ought to have known that his or the company's actions would damage those creditors. Account will be taken of what general knowledge, skill and experience may reasonably be expected of him in determining whether he should have anticipated that damage. In *Re Continental Assurance Co of London Plc*,[156] concerning a small general insurer that went into liquidation in the early 1990s and was found to be heavily insolvent, it was held that in all the circumstances its directors had not been reckless. Much of the liquidator's case against them was based on hindsight and was criticised for wholly ignoring the realities of the position in which they found themselves at the time.

24–110   Thirdly, there are other situations which do not fall within (a) or (b) which amount to acting recklessly. A possible example may be not keeping proper records or having proper accounts. Indeed, there is express provision for unlimited liability for officers who do not ensure that proper accounts are kept, which contributed to the company's inability to pay its debts.[157]

---

[156] [2007] 2 B.C.L.C. 287.
[157] 1990 Act, s.204.

24–111 *Unlimited Liability:* If the court finds that the respondent had traded recklessly, it may declare him personally responsible, in whole or in part, for the company's debts. In most cases the court will not impose personal liability beyond the amount which was lost as a result of the impugned activities. No doubt, in time criteria will be adopted for determining the extent to which personal liability should be imposed. If in all the circumstances the respondent acted honestly and responsibly in relation to the actions being complained of, the court may relieve him, either wholly or in part, from personal liability.[158] When declaring someone liable under this heading, the court may make various ancillary orders.

Misfeasance

24–112 Liability for misfeasance can arise whether or not the company is insolvent. This is a summary procedure for ensuring that companies being wound up are compensated for losses arising from most wrongs done to them by their directors and other officers. Wrongs for this purpose are where any officer of the company "has misapplied or retained or become liable or accountable for any money or property of the company, or has been guilty of any misfeasance or other breach of trust in relation to the company".[159] Who is a company "officer" in this context is not defined, so that in principle shadow directors would seem to fall outside, but not *de facto* directors. Misfeasance can also be committed by any person who took part in forming or promoting the company, and also its receiver, liquidator or examiner, as well as a director of a subsidiary's holding company. On the application of the liquidator, or of a creditor or contributory, the court may investigate the matter and order restitution and/or compensation. It would appear that a fully paid up shareholder cannot initiate proceedings.

24–113 *Ambit:* Liability here has no application where the damage inflicted was not suffered by the company as such. This procedure provides no remedy for losses caused directly to creditors or to shareholders, either individually or collectively. Nor does it enlarge on the existing substantive law regarding officers' wrongs to the company; it merely is a special procedure for remedying the more serious of those wrongs when the company is being wound up.[160] Misfeasance in this context is "misfeasance in the nature of a breach of trust, that is to say, it refers to something which the officer … has done wrongly by misapplying or retaining in his own hands any moneys of the company, or by which the company's property has been wasted or the company's credit improperly pledged".[161] In *Re George Newman & Co.*,[162] for example, it was held to be misfeasance for directors of a company that was heavily insolvent to permit one of their number, without charge, to use company property for his own private ends.

---

[158] *cf. Re Hefferon Kearns Ltd* (No.2) [1993] 3 I.R. 181.
[159] 1963 Act, s.298. See generally, M. Forde, *The Law of Company Insolvency* at 253 *et seq.*
[160] *Re Eurocruit Europe Ltd* [2007] 2 B.C.L.C. 598.
[161] *Walker v Wimborne* (1976) 50 A.L.J. R. 446 at 450.
[162] [1895] 1 Ch. 674.

24–114 Misfeasance does not extend to mere negligence. In *Mont Clare Hotels Ltd*,[163] Costello J. reiterated the view that "it is not every error of judgment that amounts to misfeasance in law and it is not every act of negligence that amounts to misfeasance in law ... [S]omething more than mere carelessness is required, some act that, perhaps, may amount to gross negligence in failing to carry out a duty owed by the director to his company".[164] A director had arranged for the company to make a substantial loan to another company, of which he also was a director, but there was nothing in writing about that loan and no security was given. In the event, the borrower failed and, largely because it could not recover the loan, the company got into financial difficulties and eventually had to be wound up. In the light of all the circumstances, it was held that the director was not guilty of misfeasance for not ensuring that the loan was repaid. The claim against him for having actually made the loan and not getting any security was barred by the Statute of Limitations.

24–115 Failure to perform a duty that leads to the company's property being misapplied can constitute misfeasance. In *Re John Fulton & Co.*,[165] the company's auditor who certified erroneous accounts, on the strength of which the company improperly paid dividends, was ordered to compensate it for those amounts. The directors were made jointly responsible. And it was held that a paid director there could not plead in his defence that he was entirely ignorant of his duties, that he only saw what reports were submitted to the AGM and that he relied entirely on the auditor to look after the company's financial affairs.

24–116 *Exempting Liability:* It was held in *Re SM Barker Ltd*,[166] that, where the ex-directors accused of misfeasance were also the company's sole shareholders, who had in effect given themselves presents of its property, this did not constitute officer misfeasance. The directors-owners of a then-solvent company had agreed to sell their shares in it and, at the same time, resolved in general meeting that they should be released from a substantial debt they owed the company. That resolution was described as improvident and as regrettable, in that it did not observe various formalities. Gavan Duffy J. nevertheless concluded that they could not be held liable for misfeasance "because they were the owners, they were the complete masters of the company's situation; it is as such that they were in a position to profit and did profit, and not as directors or trustees for the shareholders. [Their release], whether valid in law or void or voidable, was the act of the company in general meeting ... . There was ... no concealment by the directors-owners, no trickery and no fraud".[167]

---

[163] Unreported, Costello J., December 2, 1986.
[164] *ibid.* at p.4 of the judgement. Similarly, *Re Continental Assur. Co. of London Plc (No.4)* [2007] 2 B.C.L.C. 287.
[165] [1932] N.I. 35.
[166] [1950] I.R. 123.
[167] *ibid.* at 138.

24–117   The outcome would have been different if at the time of the resolution the company had been insolvent. In *Re George Newman & Co.*,[168] it was said that "[t]he shareholders at a meeting duly convened for the purpose, can, if they think proper ... make presents to directors out of assets properly divisible amongst the shareholders themselves. But to make presents out of profits is one thing and to make them out of capital or out of money borrowed by the company is a very different matter. Such money cannot be lawfully divided amongst the shareholders themselves, nor can it be given away by them for nothing to their directors as to bind the company in its corporate capacity".[169] It was held by the Supreme Court in *Re Greendale Developments Ltd (No. 2)*[170] that the position is also different, even in the case of a solvent company, where the assent of all the shareholders is given informally rather than by way of a formal resolution. Why the lack of formality should make so significant a difference, rendering what was irregular *ultra vires*, was not explained.[171]

Related Company's Contribution

24–118   Where a company's wholly-owned subsidiary or a closely-related company becomes insolvent, a strong economic and moral argument can be made for requiring the holding company or otherwise connected company to pay at least part of the insolvent's debts. This would particularly be so where the insolvent was in fact doing the other company's more risky business and where there were good reasons for believing that the other company would rescue the insolvent if the need ever arose. Provision to this effect is made for "related companies". Before a contribution to their unpaid debts can be ordered, the court must be satisfied that "the circumstances that gave rise to the winding-up of the company are attributable to the actions or omissions of the related company"[172]; in other words, the related company had some decisive role in the events that triggered the winding-up. Additionally, the court is required to have regard to certain aspects of the relationship between both companies; notably, involvement of one in the other's management, the conduct of one towards the other's creditors, as well as the effect of a contribution order on the related company's own creditors.

Disclaiming Onerous Obligations

24–119   The somewhat anomalous bankruptcy rule about disclaiming onerous obligations applies to companies in liquidation.[173] Within 12 months of the winding-up commencing and with the court's consent, the liquidator may in a sense discriminate against particular creditors by disclaiming the company's obligations to them, on the grounds that performance would be unduly burdensome for the company. This power is often invoked to terminate leases. In one instance, the liquidator was permitted to disclaim freehold land constituting a

---

[168] [1895] 1 Ch. 674.
[169] *ibid.* at 686.
[170] [1998] 1 I.R. 8.
[171] See para.13–18.
[172] 1990 Act, s.140.
[173] 1963 Act, s.290. See generally, M. Forde, *The Law of Company Insolvency*, at 224.

cemetery and contracts relating to maintenance of the graves in it.[174] It was held by Carroll J. in *Minister for Environment v Irish Ispat Ltd*,[175] that a pollution licence under the Waste Management Act 1996 constituted property for this purpose, and the owners of the former Irish Steel plant at Haulbowline, Co. Cork, were permitted to disclaim it, without having to carry out expensive work in restoring a badly-polluted portion of those premises.

24–120   The court is empowered to make appropriate orders to give effect to any disclaimer. But those persons to whom the company owed the disclaimed obligations must not shoulder the entire cost of thereby benefiting the general creditors; any person damaged by the disclaimer is deemed to be a creditor for the amount of his loss and may prove it as a debt in the winding-up. In the circumstances in *Irish Ispat*, however, the court would not order the liquidator to spend money in mitigating or remedying the pollution. For the licence had been obtained by the company after it had ceased production, the company had no assets and was insolvent. Accordingly, the "polluter pays" principle could not be implemented.[176]

24–121   In *Tempany v Royal Liver Trustees Ltd*,[177] the position of guarantees of covenants in leases called for consideration when the liquidator sought to disclaim the lease. Keane J. conducted an exhaustive analysis of many authorities on this section and on its analogue in general bankruptcy law, and reached the following conclusions:

"1. The exclusive concern of the court in an application for leave to disclaim must be the interests of all persons interested in the liquidation …
2. In considering the extent, if any, to which the interests of those interested in the liquidation will be affected by the operation of a disclaimer it is necessary to consider whether the release of third parties such as (in the case of leasehold property) original lessees and sureties, is necessary 'for the purpose of releasing the company and the property of the company from liability'.
3. In the case of leasehold property which has been assigned by the original lessee to a company in liquidation, the release of the original lessee is not necessary for the purpose of releasing the company and the property of the company from liability. The position of a surety for the payment of the rent and performance of the covenants by a company holding property under a lease which goes into liquidation is no different; the release of the surety is not necessary for the purpose of releasing the company and the property of the company from liability.
4. The release of the surety in [such a] case not being necessary … the liability of the surety is not affected by the disclaimer by the liquidator of the interest of the company in the property".[178]

---

[174] *Re Nottingham General Cemetery Co.* [1955] Ch. 683.
[175] [2005] 2 I.R. 338.
[176] *cf. Environment Agency v Hillridge Ltd* [2004] 2 B.C.L.C. 358.
[177] [1984] I.L.R.M. 273.
[178] *ibid.* at 289–290. *cf. Hindcastle Ltd v Barbara Attenborough Associates Ltd* [1997] A.C. 70.

24–122 *Re Ranks (Ireland) Ltd*,[179] concerned the measure of damages payable to a party whose contract was being disclaimed. The contracts there were equipment leases and one of their terms was that, in the event of their being repudiated, a stipulated sum would become payable as damages. But Murphy J. held that this was not the proper measure of compensation in these circumstances. That measure was the difference between the rent which the company would have paid the lessor and the rent that the lessor is likely to earn during the unexpired residue of the leases.

Paying Off Creditors

24–123 Before any distribution can be made to the shareholders, the liquidator must first pay off the creditors or settle any claims they may have against the company. The intrinsic nature of a winding-up, insofar as it concerns company creditors, has been described graphically as follows:

> "liquidation is a form of collective enforcement of liabilities under [the] law … . Liquidation affects the contractual relationship between debtor and creditor. When the liquidation starts, no further liabilities under contract become payable until such time as it is clear that the pre-liquidation liabilities have been satisfied in full … . The beneficial interest in the company's assets is transferred to the liquidator … . [T]he making of a winding-up order brings into operation a statutory scheme for dealing with the assets of a company which is being wound up. It matters not whether the winding-up is by order or pursuant to a resolution. The assets of the company when realised provide a fund which the liquidator administers in many respects, but not in all, as if he were managing a trust fund. Creditors' contractual rights to be paid by the company become under the statutory scheme a statutory right to a share in the trust fund".[180]

24–124 When the company's liabilities exceed its assets, those creditors with various prior and preferential claims must be satisfied first. In that event, "the same rules shall prevail and be observed relating to the respective rights of secured and unsecured creditors and to debts provable and to the valuation of annuities and future and contingent liabilities as are in force … under the law of bankruptcy …".[181] This means that if the company is insolvent the bankruptcy rules govern the three matters mentioned there.

Proving Debts

24–125 By proof of debts is meant establishing the sums due to creditors so that they can be paid off in full or be given their proper share of the realised assets. What debts can be proved in a winding-up are defined as "all debts payable on a contingency, and all claims against the company, present or future, certain or contingent, ascertained or sounding only in damages … a just estimate being made, so far as possible, of the value of such debts or claims which

---

[179] [1989] I.R. 1.
[180] *Re Lines Bros Ltd* [1983] 1 Ch. 1 at 14.
[181] 1963 Act, s.284.

may be subject to any contingency or which sound only in damages, or for some other reason do not bear a certain value".[182] A detailed set of rules concerning proof of debts is contained in the 1st schedule of the Bankruptcy Act, 1988.[183] Every kind of legal claim, be it in contract or tort or otherwise, including future, contingent and unascertained claims, are admissible to proof. All debts are to be computed as of the date the winding-up commenced, from which time ceases to run against all creditors for statute of limitations purposes. Foreign currency claims are valued as of that date. Where two or more persons are seeking to prove in respect of what is in substance the same debt, it is the circumstances at the time the dividend is being paid that determine which one will be admitted to proof. The court is empowered to fix a time within which debts must be proved.

Compromises and Arrangements

24–126   The liquidator may make a compromise or arrangement with any creditors of the company and with persons claiming to be creditors or alleging that they have a claim against the company.[184] In a compulsory winding-up, any such settlement must have the court's approval; in a voluntary winding-up, it must be approved by the members or the creditors, respectively.

Liability of Contributories

24–127   Where there are insufficient funds to pay all the company's debts and the expenses incurred in the winding-up, the liquidator will claim against the contributories in respect of the deficiency, and also where it is necessary to adjust the rights of contributories between themselves. Contributories for these purposes in limited companies are, principally, members with amounts remaining unpaid on their shares.[185] Where a company's own regulations do not restrict the transferability of its shares, any shareholder with partly paid shares may transfer them up to the last moment before liquidation, even if the objective is simply to avoid liability as a contributory and the transferee happens to be a pauper.[186] It is at this stage in a company's existence that questions about title to shares frequently arise.

PRIORITIES AMONG CREDITORS

24–128   There are some categories of creditor whose claims against the company must be satisfied before those of others can be met. Except where legislation otherwise provides, if the company is insolvent the ordinary bankruptcy rules govern the rights of secured as against unsecured creditors, and the rights of both of these groups as between themselves.[187]

---

[182] 1963 Act, s.283(1). See generally, M. Forde, *The Law of Company Insolvency* at 278 *et seq.*

[183] See generally, M. Forde, *Bankruptcy Law in Ireland* (Cork: Mercier Press, 1990), Ch.8.

[184] 1963 Act, ss.231(1)(3) and 267(1)(a).

[185] 1963 Act, s.207(1)(d).

[186] *Re Discoverers Finance Corp.* [1910] 1 Ch. 312.

[187] See generally M. Forde, *The Law of Company Insolvency* at 309 *et seq.*

Retention of Title

24–129   Since they were first highlighted here in the 1970s, retention of title clauses have become a feature of Irish commercial life.[188] These arise where one firm sells goods to another but stipulates that, until those goods are paid for, the seller retains ownership of them. Often it is added that, if the buyer sells those goods before they are paid for, the original seller shall become entitled to the proceeds of that sale. Thus, in *Re Interview Ltd*,[189] where an Irish company agreed to import goods from Germany, the contract stipulated that the ownership and property in the goods was to remain in the seller until they were paid for. It was held that in this kind of arrangement the original buyer of the goods does not acquire ownership of them, but merely gets possession of them in the same way as a hirer under a hire purchase agreement, until the goods have been paid for. Retention of title stipulations, therefore, provide trade creditors with considerable security, in that suppliers of goods to companies in financial difficulties can retain the right to re-capture the goods that are not paid for, and perhaps can follow the proceeds of re-sale if those goods are sold.

24–130   The actual wording of the clause in question is crucial. Thus if the interest reserved by the original seller is not ownership of the goods but is some claim over them, then the goods may only be subject to a charge which, to be effective, must be duly registered. If the property is reserved not in the original contract but in a later supplementary contract, this may possibly be impeached as an unlawful attempt to contract out of the principle that in a liquidation creditors are entitled to be paid off *pari passu* or equally with each other according to the debts due to them. Difficulties can arise where the goods are altered physically or are mixed with other goods. In recent years the English courts have tended to read retention of title clauses as narrowly as is reasonably possible.

24–131   The extent to which these clauses can capture the proceeds of sub-sales has been substantially diminished by *Carroll Group Distributors Ltd v G. & JF Bourke Ltd*[190] The clause there applied to tobacco products purchased by a retailer over a period, and it provided that the proceeds from all sub-sales should be held in trust for the supplier in a separate bank account, with the details of that account to be provided to the seller. Murphy J. pointed out that it was very likely that the aggregate amount of those proceeds at various times would exceed the sums actually owing to the supplier, because those proceeds would include the retailer's mark-up on the goods and sums in respect of goods which already had been paid for. Accordingly, it was held, the "substance of the transaction as ascertained from the words used by the parties and the context in which the document [was] executed was to confer a charge on those proceeds in substitution for the property rights the supplier had retained in the goods".[191] It is not entirely clear

---

[188] See generally, M. Forde, *Commercial Law*, 3rd edn (Haywards Heath: Tottel Publishing, 2005) at 228 *et seq.*

[189] [1975] I.R. 382.

[190] [1990] 1 I.R. 481.

[191] *ibid.* at 486.

from the judgment whether it was this feature of the clause alone or whether it also was several other aspects of the clause that proved decisive.

Property Held in Trust

24–132   Property that the company holds in trust for others must be separated from the company's general assets. The existence of a trust depends on whether the "three certainties" are satisfied.[192] A particular source of difficulty is where money is set aside for some reason.[193] In *Re Kayford Ltd*,[194] a mail order firm that held considerable sums paid by customers, either as a deposit on or as the purchase price for goods ordered, got into financial difficulties. Being concerned about those customers, it instructed its bank to open a separate trust account for them and the money those customers had advanced was lodged in it. In liquidation proceedings, it was held that this money was held in trust for those customers.[195] Where creditors with retention of title have been held entitled to recover the proceeds of sub-sales of the goods affected, it has been because that money was being held in trust for them.

Property Subject to Equities

24–133   It is a principle of bankruptcy law that, when the bankrupt's property vests in the Official Assignee, his title is "subject to equities", meaning all equitable claims against that property continue, despite the change in ownership. An extension of this principle is that where certain contractual rights exist with reference to some of the insolvent's assets, those rights may still be exercisable following commencement of the bankruptcy or winding-up. In that event, the person with those rights may gain a distinct advantage over all the other creditors. In *Dempsey v Bank of Ireland*,[196] it was held by the Supreme Court that contractual rights to apportion a company's funds can be exercised even after the company has gone into liquidation because exercising those rights is not the same as proving a debt. The case concerned bonding arrangements sponsored by the Irish Travel Agents' Association, and the issue was whether a bank, which made payments under one travel agency's bond, could reimburse itself from that agency's bank account even though that agency had by then gone into liquidation. Under the arrangement, the bank entered into a guarantee to pay £75,000 towards the costs of catering for travellers who were stranded because the agency in question had insufficient funds. At the same time, the agency agreed to indemnify the bank against its liability under this guarantee and also agreed that the bank could debit its bank account with whatever was owing to the bank under that

---

[192] See generally, Ulph, "Equitable Proprietary Rights in Insolvency: The Ebbing Tide?" [1996] *J. Bus. L.* 482.

[193] See generally, W. Swadling ed., *The Quistclose Trust: Critical Essays* (Oxford: Hart 2004).

[194] [1975] 1 All E.R. 604.

[195] Contrast *Re Farepak Food & Gifts Ltd* [2007] 2 B.C.L.C. 1.

[196] Unreported, Supreme Court, December 6, 1985; sub nom *Re Eurotravel Ltd,* unreported, High Court, May 28, 1984.

indemnity. The agency had gone into liquidation before the bank sought to debit the account with £75,000, having paid the amount under the guarantee.

24–134   Giving judgment for the Court, Henchy J. held that this debit could be made because what was being claimed was not a right to prove a debt in the winding up but an entitlement to enforce a contractual right notwithstanding a winding up. For this reason, several leading cases on set-offs claimed by guarantors, which were applied in the court below, were distinguished. Applying first principles, the bank's claim succeeded because an insolvent company's assets are subject to the same burdens and equities as existed immediately prior to the winding up. Speaking of the situation where the assets vested in the liquidator (under s. 230 of the 1963 Act), Henchy J. said:

> "The general rule is that he acquires only such title to the assets as the company had – no more, no less. He cannot take any better title to any part of the assets than the company had. This means that he takes the assets subject to any pre-existing enforceable right of a third party in or over them. If that were not so, equities, liabilities and contractual rights validly and enforceably created while the assets were in the hands of the company would be unfairly swept aside and unjust distribution of the assets would result".[197]

When the agency's winding up commenced the bank had paid the £75,000 on the guarantee and, consequently, the agency's account was subject to the bank's contingent right to debit that sum, which it did shortly afterwards. If, immediately before the winding up, the bank had debited that sum, the debit could not have been questioned because "it would have been done under the terms of a guarantee which was entered into in good faith and which in no way offended the statutory provisions applicable in a winding up".[198] It therefore does not matter for these purposes that the bank exercised its contractual right to debit the account after the winding up had commenced.

Third Party Insurance

24–135   Formerly, a most unjust situation could arise where the company, that had been responsible for unlawfully injuring someone or his property, became insolvent. Where the company was insured for that particular liability, the proceeds of the insurance policy was not payable to the injured party. Instead, those proceeds would form part of the company's general assets and would be distributed in accordance with the general priorities and preferences among its creditors. Accordingly, if the company was heavily insolvent, the injured party would receive next to nothing from those proceeds. That state of affairs was rectified by s.62 of the Civil Liability Act 1961, which provides that money paid under the insurance policy must be used to discharge the injured party's claim and none of that money shall form part of the company's assets for the purpose of distribution among its other creditors. But this form

---

[197] At p.8. See also, *Glow Heating Ltd v Eastern Health Board* [1988] I.R. 110.
[198] At p.9.

of priority does not apply where the injured party commenced his claim *after* the company had actually been dissolved.

Set-Off

24–136   The right of set-off in insolvency arises by virtue of bankruptcy law, according to which, "[w]here there are mutual credits or debts as between the [insolvent] and any person claiming as a creditor, one debt or demand may be set-off against the other and only the balance found owing shall be recoverable on one side or the other".[199] Thus where there are "mutual debts" between the company and a creditor, one debt may be set off against the other. Set-off in this context is not confined to debts arising out of contract but extends, for example, to sums a company is entitled to claim as a tax deduction and as tax relief on litigation costs incurred. Set-off does not apply to secured debts unless the creditor waives his security and elects to prove in the liquidation instead. In *National Westminster Bank v Halesowen Presswork & Assemblies Ltd*,[200] a divided House of Lords held that the rule whereby mutual debts should be set off and only the balance claimed was enacted to protect the general public interest and, accordingly, was peremptory and could not be contracted out of.

24–137   Disputes concerning set-offs frequently involve different bank accounts. For instance, in *Re Tailtean Freight Services Ltd*,[201] when the bank heard that the company was about to be wound up, it opened a suspense account in the company's name, which is a temporary account in which entries of credits or charges are made until their proper disposition can be determined. The bank debited to it various cheques drawn by the company and also the amount of the cheques that had been lodged to the company's current account but were returned unpaid. This current account was in credit to a substantial amount and, when the liquidator was appointed, the credit balance was transferred to a new current account and later to a deposit account, each of which were denoted as the company "in voluntary liquidation". It was held that the bank was entitled to set off against the amount in this account the sums owing to it on the suspense account. There is no mutuality, and accordingly there can be no set-off, between money borrowed by a company for a particular purpose, which is held by a bank, and debts owed by the company to the bank, where the special purpose was known to the bank.

24–138   That a company's debtors are the subject of a floating charge does not prevent them from setting-off against mutual debts incurred by the company to them, for the company is entitled to carry on its business as if the charge did not exist. But when crystallisation occurs, such as by the chargee appointing a receiver and a manager, they then have no right of set-off against new debts that thereafter are incurred with them on the company's behalf. On crystallisation, the floating security becomes converted into a specific charge,

---

[199] Bankruptcy Act 1988, First Schedule, r.17(1). See generally, R. Derham, *The Law of Set-off*, 3rd edn (Oxford: OUP, 2003).
[200] [1972] A.C. 785.
[201] [1975] I.R. 376.

which causes the title in future debts, as they arise, to vest in the chargee. Moreover, the requisite mutuality would not exist where the pre-crystallisation debt was owed to the company alone but the post-crystallisation credit was granted by the receiver-manager, who in reality does not act simply on the company's behalf.

Specifically Secured Debts

24–139 A creditor has specific or fixed security if he possesses a mortgage, charge or lien on the company's property other than a floating charge.[202] Several options are open to the secured creditor, *viz.* rest on the security and not prove for the debt; realise the security and prove for the deficiency; value the security and prove for the deficiency; surrender the security and prove for the entire debt. Charges that were duly registered take priority from their date of creation; except that a later legal charge ranks before an equitable charge where there was neither actual nor constructive notice of the equity or the legal chargee has a better equity. A charge that is not duly registered is void against any creditor of the company and against the liquidator.[203] Accordingly, any subsequently created charge will take priority over an unregistered one; this is so even where the owner of the registered charge knew, at the time that charge was given or later, of the other charge's existence. A charge that is registered under an extension of time given will almost invariably be made subject to the rights arising from other charges that were given and duly registered in the intervening period.

Execution Creditors

24–140 Judgment creditors who have taken no active steps to enforce their security are not entitled to be paid in priority to the secured or even the ordinary creditors. A creditor who has issued execution against a company's property or attached a debt due to it is not entitled to retain the benefit of that process unless it was completed before the winding up commenced or, if earlier, the date the creditor received notice of the meeting at which it was proposed to have the company wound up.[204] But the court may override this rule and make such order in favour of the creditor as it thinks fit.

Insolvency Process Expenses

24–141 In a voluntary winding-up, the liquidator's remuneration, together with all costs, charges and expenses incurred in the winding-up, must be paid before the other preferred debts.[205] In *Re Red Breast Preserving Co.*,[206] it was held that ordinarily the same rule should apply in a compulsory winding up.

---

[202] See generally, R. Goode, *Legal Problems of Credit and Security*, 3rd edn (London: Sweet & Maxwell, 2003) and J. Breslin (with K. Smith) *Banking Law*, 2nd edn (Dublin: Thomson Round Hall) Chs 13–16.

[203] 1963 Act s.99(1) and see paras 20–103 *et seq.*

[204] 1963 Act ss.219, 291 and 292; see para.23–63 *et seq.*

[205] 1963 Act s.281.

[206] [1958] I.R. 234.

A source of dispute in several major cases has been whether various kinds of taxes which become payable during a winding up should be regarded as costs of the liquidation. Before costs and charges can be paid in an official liquidation, they must have been approved by the Examiner or by the Taxing Master of the High Court, as the case may be.

Preferred Debts

24–142 Legislative provisions give certain categories of creditors the right to be paid off before unsecured creditors and even before those who hold floating charges on the company's assets. There are three main categories of preferential creditor today, namely the Revenue Commissioners, company employees and the local rating authority.[207] Claims for preferential payment must be made to the liquidator not later than six months after he advertised for claims in at least two daily newspapers.[208] In the absence of express statutory authority, a debt cannot acquire preferential status, either by subrogation or otherwise.[209]

Floating Charges

24–143 Before a floating charge crystallises, mutual debts arising can be set off; the sheriff may seize and sell property subject to the charge; a garnishee order may be made against accounts owing to the company.[210] Charges arising out of the general law, like unpaid vendors' liens and solicitors' liens, property held in trust and, subject to what is said below about notice, specific charges and liens, all take priority over a floating charge. Although preference over the company's floating charge is given to certain debts owing to the State and to company employees and the rating authorities,[211] those may be defeated by the operation of an "automatic crystallisation" clause that converts the floating security into a fixed charge before winding-up commences. As between registered floating charges over the entire undertaking, the first in time prevails. But a subsequent registered floating charge over part of the undertaking gets priority if it was made under a power reserved in the general charge to give such security.

24–144 Subsequent legal and equitable specific charges lose their priority where the floating charge prohibited the company from making the charge in question only where the person in whose favour the later charge was given knew or had notice of that prohibition. What constitutes that notice is a complicated matter. But recording in the registry of companies a prohibition against subsequent charges does not of itself amount to notice of that proscription. The doctrine of constructive notice of public documents in the company law context has hitherto been confined to questions of the company's capacity to be bound by transactions, as opposed to priorities between outsiders claiming the benefit of transactions entered into by the

---

[207] Principally, 1963 Act, s.285 and Taxes Consolidation Act 1997, ss.995, 1000 and 1001.
[208] 1963 Act, s.285(14).
[209] *Re Bell Lines Ltd* [2006] I.E.H.C. 188, unreported, Dunne J., April 28, 2006.
[210] See generally, Goode, *Legal Problems of Credit and Security*, Ch.5.
[211] 1963 Act, s.285.

company. In *Welch v Bowmaker (Ireland) Ltd*,[212] where the company gave a bank an equitable charge by deposit of title deeds over property that was the subject of an earlier floating charge, and the floating charge forbade creating any additional charges, it was held that the specific charge had priority. According to Henchy J., "it is settled law that there is no duty on the bank in a situation such as this to seek out the precise terms of the debenture [and] actual or express notice of the prohibition must be shown before the subsequent mortgagee can be said to be deprived of priority".[213]

Ordinary and Deferred Creditors

24–145 By ordinary creditors here is meant creditors who neither fall into any of the above-mentioned categories, nor are members of the company to whom the amount is owed in their "character of ... member[s] by way of dividends, profits or otherwise".[214] This latter category are known as deferred creditors. They include members who are owed dividends that have been declared and capital that is being repaid but not, for example, shareholder-directors who are voted directors' remuneration by the shareholders in general meeting, nor members who were deceived by the company into purchasing its shares and in consequence are entitled to damages.

24–146 Ordinary creditors must be paid off before the deferred creditors and before making any payment to the contributories. If the company is insolvent, the ordinary creditors must be paid equally or *pari passu*, i.e. the same amount per euro owed to them.[215] This is not a peremptory rule, since these creditors are permitted to agree that any particular liability may be postponed in favour of, or subordinated to, other claims against the company.

EC CROSS-BORDER INSOLVENCY PROCEEDINGS

24–147 Cross-border insolvency proceedings in EC Member States (other than receiverships and also proceedings involving Denmark) are governed by Regulation 134/2000 (the Insolvency Regulation).[216] Prior to May 2002, procedures to administer insolvent companies and to realise their assets were left to be determined by the domestic laws of the respective Member States. In *Re Tuskar Resources Plc*,[217] McCracken J. acknowledged that, while he had jurisdiction to appoint an examiner to an Irish-incorporated company despite all of its activities being located abroad, he recognised the practical inability of the Irish Court to have its orders enforced abroad was a fact which he could take

---

[212] [1980] I.R. 251.
[213] *ibid.* at 256.
[214] 1963 Act, s.207(1).
[215] 1963 Act, s.275.
[216] [2006] O.J. L160/1, implemented by the European Communities (Corporate Insolvency) Regulations (SI 2002/333). See generally, R. Goode, *Principles of Corporate Insolvency Law*, 3rd edn (London: Thomson Sweet & Maxwell, 2005) Ch.13 and J. Israel, *European Cross Border Insolvency Regulation* (Mortsel: Intersentia Publishers, 2005).
[217] [2001] 1 I.R. 668.

into account in determining whether or not there was a reasonable prospect of survival of the whole or part of the company as a going concern, and thus in determining, whether or not an examiner should be appointed in the first place. There is a separate EC transnational insolvency regime for banks and other credit institutions, and for insurers.[218]

24–148 The fundamental goal of the EC Insolvency Regulation is that, as regards the various types of insolvency proceedings set out in the Annex, and irrespective of the place of incorporation of the company, there should be a uniform set of rules as to the Member State or States in which such proceedings may be opened; the extent of the assets of the company in respect of which they may be opened; the automatic recognition throughout the EC of insolvency proceedings properly commenced in a Member State; the enforceability throughout the EC of the orders of a court of a Member State in the same way as if they were governed by the Brussels I Regulation. Not all Irish insolvency proceedings fall under this Regulation; while it applies to compulsory winding-up by the court, creditors' voluntary winding up (with confirmation of the court) and examinership, it does not apply to receiverships, schemes of arrangement or members' voluntary windings up.

24–149 The Regulation splits insolvency proceedings into two categories, main proceedings and secondary proceedings. Main insolvency proceedings may only be opened in the Member State in which the company has its "centre of main interests". These proceedings in essence apply to the entire of the company's assets and affairs irrespective of where they are actually situate. Secondary insolvency proceedings are restricted to the assets of the company situated in the territory of the Member State of which such proceedings are opened, and can only be opened where the company possesses an "establishment".

24–150 In *Re Eurofood IFSC Ltd*,[219] Eurofood was a wholly-owned subsidiary of an Italian company, Parmalat SpA. It was incorporated in Ireland and had its registered office here, operating in the IFSC pursuant to a certificate issued by the Minister for Finance. Its day-to-day administration was conducted on its behalf in Ireland by Bank of America pursuant an agreement governed by Irish law and containing an Irish jurisdiction clause. It prepared annual accounts which it filed in the CRO and it paid Irish tax. It maintained books of account in Dublin, and its auditors and solicitors were Irish. It had four directors, two of whom were Irish and two Italian. With one exception, all board meetings were held in Dublin. An extraordinary administrator was appointed to Parmalat SpA in Italy following the collapse of the group business. A creditor of Eurofood then presented a petition in the High Court to wind up that company. A provisional liquidator was appointed. Shortly afterwards, an Italian court purported to appoint an extraordinary administrator to Eurofood, being the same individual who had also been

---

[218] EC Directives 2001/24 and 2001/17, [2001] O.J. L125/15 and L110/28.
[219] ECJ Case C–341/04, [2006] Ch. 508.

appointed as extraordinary administrator of Parmalat SpA and of other companies in the group.

24–151   When the petition came on for hearing, the extraordinary administrator objected to the making of any winding-up order on the basis that main insolvency proceedings had already been opened in Italy. However, Kelly J. held[220] that the appointment of the Irish provisional liquidator constituted a judgment opening insolvency proceedings in Ireland. He held that, since the Irish proceedings were first in time, the Italian court should have recognised the Irish order and should have declined to make any order appointing an extraordinary administrator. In addition, he found, as a fact, that the centre of main interests of Eurofood was in Ireland. The matter was appealed to the Supreme Court, which in turn referred the issue to the European Court of Justice. The ECJ rejected the arguments that the centre of main interest should be determined as Italy.

24–152   Thus, as a general principle, once main insolvency proceedings have been opened in one Member State, they must be automatically recognised and will be deemed to have effect throughout the EC unless and until secondary insolvency proceedings are opened in some other Member State. As stated by the ECJ in *Eurofood*

> "If an interested party, taking the view that the centre of the debtor's main interest is situated in a Member State other than that in which the main insolvency proceedings were opened, wishes to challenge the jurisdiction assumed by the Court which opened those proceedings, it may use, before the Courts of the Member State in which they were opened, the remedies prescribed by the national law of that Member State against the opening decision."[221]

24–153   Another consequence of the Insolvency Regulation relates to the enforceability of foreign revenue debts. At common law, it was well established that the Revenue claims of foreign states could not be enforced, directly or indirectly, in Ireland.[222] However, in *Re Cedarlease Ltd*,[223] a contrary position was held to now prevail. In a winding-up petition presented by Her Majesty's Customs and Excise, Laffoy J. found that in circumstances where foreign revenue authorities could now prove in an Irish windingup, it necessarily followed that they also have *locus standi* to petition for the winding up of the company, and a winding up order was made.

---

[220] [2004] 4 I.R. 370.
[221] [2006] Ch. 508 at 543 and see *Re Eurofood IFSC Ltd (No. 2)* [2006] 4 I.R. 307.
[222] *Buchanan Ltd v McVey* [1954] I.R. 89.
[223] [2005] 1 I.R. 470.

INDEX